Oxford Latin Desk Dictionary

Edited by
James Morwood

OXFORD
UNIVERSITY PRESS

OXFORD
UNIVERSITY PRESS

Great Clarendon Street, Oxford OX2 6DP

Oxford University Press is a department of the University of Oxford.
It furthers the University's objective of excellence in research, scholarship,
and education by publishing worldwide in

Oxford New York

Auckland Cape Town Dar es Salaam Hong Kong Karachi
Kuala Lumpur Madrid Melbourne Mexico City Nairobi
New Delhi Shanghai Taipei Toronto

With offices in

Argentina Austria Brazil Chile Czech Republic France Greece
Guatemala Hungary Italy Japan South Korea Poland Portugal
Singapore Switzerland Thailand Turkey Ukraine Vietnam

Oxford is a registered trade mark of Oxford University Press
in the UK and in certain other countries

Published in the United States
by Oxford University Press Inc., New York

British Library Cataloguing in Publication Data

Data available

Library of Congress Cataloging in Publication Data

Data available

ISBN 978-0-19-861005-2
ISBN 978-0-19-861070-0 (US edition)

7

Typeset in Nimrod, Arial and Meta
by Alliance Phototypesetters, Pondicherry, India
Printed in Great Britain by
Clays Ltd, St Ives plc

Contents

Preface

When it first appeared in 1994, this dictionary was in part a response to the completion in 1982 of the monumental *Oxford Latin Dictionary*. There was clearly a need for a shorter, more accessible and considerably less expensive dictionary to take account of the important philological advances which that work had made. Within its modest compass, the *Pocket Oxford Latin Dictionary* presented a Latin language cleansed of suspect accretions and an English language cleansed of Victorian usage. Now, ten years later, it appears in a new, improved edition.

POLD was based on S.C. Woodhouse's Latin Dictionary, first published by Routledge and Kegan Paul in 1913 and subsequently reprinted many times. In the English into Latin section, the spirit of Woodhouse has been allowed some free play, even though the pruning knife, if not the axe, had to be much at work on his inventive and lively luxuriance. Save for the tidying up of typographical conventions, this section is unchanged from the first edition.

In a modern dictionary, the Latin into English section is of the greater importance. It is in this section of this dictionary that the *Oxford Latin Dictionary* makes itself especially felt. In the first edition, the section was centred on the Latin of the so-called Golden Age (from 100 BC to the death of Livy). In the new edition many words have been added, thus broadening the scope of the dictionary to include Plautus and Terence (third and second centuries BC) and Pliny the Younger and Tacitus (late first and second centuries AD). Furthermore, many words from late and medieval Latin have been included, together with an appendix by Richard Ashdowne summarizing the more significant of the differences between classical Latin and later forms of the language. A notable new feature of the Latin–English section is the inclusion of well over a hundred boxed notes which provide further cultural or grammatical information. These many additions should considerably enhance the volume's usefulness, not only to classicists but to historians and others too.

A number of new sections have been added, and the old appendices have been improved. In particular, the grammar section has been greatly extended and completely redesigned. The maps, three of which appeared only in the original hardback volume, are an integral part of the revised edition.

In redesigning the grammar section we have taken a conscious decision to employ the order of cases that Latin learners in the UK are generally taught; this order may surprise readers outside the UK who have been brought up on the traditional ordering of the cases of nouns, adjectives, and pronouns. The accusative case thus appears in our tables immediately below the nominative (the overall order being nom., acc., gen., dat., and abl.). The traditional ordering, where the genitive directly follows the nominative, dates back to classical times, and it was indeed used in the British Isles until the advent of Kennedy's *Latin Primer* in 1866. The fact that this order is no longer the norm in the UK is due almost entirely to the overwhelming use of Kennedy's primer in Latin teaching in British schools since the late 19th century. There are sound pedagogical reasons for Kennedy's ordering—most notably, it emphasises the fact that all neuters have identical nom. and acc.—, and since a dictionary should provide only a handy reference summary of word inflections, we feel justified in our choice of the UK order for this Oxford volume.

Not for the first time, I am considerably indebted to Richard Ashdowne of New College for his invaluable assistance and support. His role has gone far beyond that of an amanuensis, and he has made a substantial contribution to both the content and the design of this revision.

JAMES MORWOOD
Wadham College,
Oxford

The Pronunciation of Classical Latin

The English sounds referred to are those of standard southern British English.

Consonants

Consonants are pronounced as in modern English, but note the following:

c is always hard, as in cat (never soft as in nice).

g is always hard, as in God (except when it is followed by **n**: **gn** is sounded 'ngn' as in hangnail, so **magnus** is pronounced 'mangnus').

h is always sounded, as in hope.

i is used as a consonant as well as a vowel; as a consonant it sounds like English 'y', so Latin **iam** is pronounced 'yam'.

q occurs, as in English, only before **u**; **qu** is sounded as in English quick.

r is rolled as in Scots English, and is always sounded; so in Latin **sors** both r and s are sounded.

s is always soft, as in sit (never like 'z', as in rose).

v in Classical Latin was pronounced like English 'w'; so **vīdī** sounds 'weedee'. This sound is often written **u** (and thus not distinguished in print from the vowel **u**), and indeed the Romans themselves made no distinction in writing. There was no 'v' sound in Classical Latin.

Where double consonants occur, as in English 'sitting', both consonants are pronounced; so **ille** is pronounced 'ille' (the l is sounded long as in English 'hall-light').

☑ Note that in words containing consonantal **i** between two vowels, this **i** was pronounced as a double consonant (though written single); so the first syllable of **maior** is heavy although the a is short, because the consonantal **i** is double.

Vowels

Latin had five different simple vowel sounds, each of which could be short or long:

a short, as in English cup (*not* as in cap).

ā long, as in English father.

e short, as in English pet.

ē long, as in English aim (or, more accurately, French gai).

i short, as in English dip.

ī long, as in English deep.

o short, as in English pot.

ō long, as in English mobile (or, more accurately, French beau).

u short, as in English put.

ū long, as in English cool.

☑ Throughout this dictionary, except in the English–Latin section and in words marked as **LM** (i.e. Late/Medieval), all naturally long vowels are marked with a macron: all vowels not so marked are short.

Latin also had six diphthongs. A diphthong can be defined as a vowel (**a**, **e**, or **o**) followed by a glide (**i**, **e**, or **u**).

ae as in English h<u>igh</u>.

au as in English h<u>ow</u>.

ei as in English <u>eigh</u>t.

eu e-u (as in Cockney English t<u>ell</u>, *not* as in English y<u>ew</u>).

oe as in English b<u>oy</u> (only shorter).

ui u-i (as in French <u>oui</u>).

☑ In 'Church Latin' (the Latin used in the Roman Catholic Church), it is conventional to pronounce sounds in an 'Italian' way; e.g. **c** and **g** are pronounced as 'ch' and 'j'/'dg' (as in '<u>ch</u>urch' and '<u>j</u>udge') before **e**, **i** and **ae**, **gn** is pronounced 'ny' (as in 'vi<u>ney</u>ard'), **v** is pronounced like English 'v' (as in 'le<u>v</u>el'), and **ae** is pronounced 'ay' (as in 'd<u>ay</u>').

Number of syllables and stress

1 Except in obvious diphthongs (**ae**, **au**, **oe**, and often **eu**), every single vowel signals a separate syllable, as in English 'recipe' (three syllables). Thus Latin **dēsine** is three syllables and **diem** is two.

2 The stress in words with two syllables almost always falls on the first syllable.

3 The stress in words of more than two syllables falls on the penultimate syllable if this is metrically 'heavy' (i.e. contains a long vowel, a diphthong, or a vowel followed by two consonants), e.g. **festīna**, **agénda**. It falls on the antepenultimate (third from last) syllable when the penultimate is metrically 'light' (i.e. contains a short vowel before either another vowel or a single consonant), e.g. **dóminus**. This pair of rules is natural for English speakers.

4 For the purposes of syllable weight, **x** always counts as two consonants ('ks') while **qu** always counts as a single consonant ('kʷ'). Strictly speaking, a syllable can be light even where it contains a short vowel that is followed by two consonants, provided that those two consonants are one of the following pairs (so-called 'mute plus liquid' combinations): br, bl, cr, cl, dr, gr, gl, pr, pl, tr.

☑ The distinction observed here between syllable *weight* and vowel *length*, i.e. between metrically heavy and light syllables and naturally long and short vowels, is relatively recent. Older books use 'long' and 'short' indifferently for both syllables and vowels, thereby encouraging mispronunciation. See also the section on Some Common Metres of Latin Verse.

Abbreviations

abl.	ablative	ir.	irregular
acc.	accusative	LM	Late/Medieval Latin
act.	active	m(asc).	masculine
a(dj).	adjective	med.	medical
ad(v).	adverb	mil.	military
c.	with nouns common (i.e. m. or f.) with dates *circa* ('around')	mus.	musical
		n.	noun
cf.	*cōnfer* ('compare')	NB	*notā bene* ('note well')
CL	Classical Latin	neg.	negative
comp.	comparative	nom.	nominative
conj.	conjunction	n(t).	neuter
dat.	dative	num.	numeral
decl.	declension	pass.	passive
dep.	deponent	perf.	perfect
e.g.	*exemplī grātiā* ('for example')	pl.	plural
etc.	*et cētera* ('and so on')	plpf.	pluperfect
f(em).	feminine	pple.	participle
fig.	figurative	prep.	preposition
fl.	*flōruit* ('flourished, was in his prime')	pres.	present
fut.	future	pron.	pronoun
gen.	genitive	rel.	relative
i.e	*id est* ('that is')	sing., sg.	singular
impers.	impersonal	subj.	subjunctive
impf.	imperfect	sup.	superlative
impv.	imperative	usu.	usually
indecl.	indeclinable	v. (i./t.)	verb (intransitive/transitive)
ind(ic).	indicative	viz.	*vidēlicet* ('namely')
infin.	infinitive	voc.	vocative
int.	interjection		

Using the Dictionary

1 In the Latin–English section, if words inflect (i.e. change their endings), they are followed immediately by their inflectional information. Nouns are followed by their gen., adjectives by their nom. sg. endings for the feminine (if different from the masc.) and neuter, verbs by their principal parts (where not predictable).

2 The remaining forms of words can be predicted from the inflectional information given, and the Summary of Grammar in the centre of this volume provides tables of declension for nouns, adjectives, and pronouns, notes on the formation of adverbs, and tables of conjugation for verbs.

3 The numerals ①, ②, ③, and ④ after verbs refer to their conjugation (see the Summary of Grammar). In the Latin–English section we also print those principal parts of verbs which cannot be predicted from their conjugation. We assume the following (underlined forms) to be the regular patterns:

[1] parō, **par-āre**, **par-āvī**, **par-ātum**

[2] moneō, **mon-ēre**, **mon-uī**, **mon-itum**

[3] regō, **reg-ere**, rēxī, rēctum
[NB we take **-itum** to be the regular 3rd conjugation supine.]

[4] audiō, **aud-īre**, **aud-īvī** *or* **aud-iī**, **aud-ītum**

Mixed conjugation verbs are not marked as such, since they are primarily part of the 3rd conjugation, but can be identified as being all (and only) those verbs marked ③ which have a 1 sg. pres. ind. act. in **-iō**.

4 Verbs marked *ir.* are given in the Summary of Grammar.

5 In the English–Latin section, the first gender given in the case of nouns and the first conjugation given in the case of verbs apply to any unmarked words which precede them. For example, in the entry

aptness, *n*. convenientia, congruentia;
(tendency, propensity) proclivitas, *f*.

all the nouns are feminine.

ā, **ab** (also **abs**) *prep with abl* from; by (of the agent); away from; since, starting with; at
□ ~ **tergō** from behind

abacus, **ī** *m* counting-board; sideboard; square stone on the top of columns

abaliēnātiō, **ōnis** *f* legal transfer of property

abaliēnō ① *v* transfer by sale or contract; remove

abavus, **ī** *m* great-great-grandfather, ancestor

abbas, **atis** *m* LM abbot

abbatia, **ae** *f* LM monastery, abbey

abbatissa, **ae** *f* LM abbess

abdicātiō, **ōnis** *f* renunciation; disowning (of a son)

abdicō ① *v* resign; abolish; disinherit

abdō, **didī**, **ditum** ③ *v* hide, conceal; plunge; remove

abdōmen, **inis** *nt* lower part of the belly, paunch; gluttony

abdūcō, **ūxī**, **uctum** ③ *v* lead away, carry off; abduct, seduce

abeō, **īre**, **iī/īvī**, **itum** *v ir* go away, depart; vanish; escape; be changed
□ **ē mediō** ~ **die**

aberrātiō, **ōnis** *f* diversion, relief

aberrō ① *v* go astray, deviate (from); disagree (with)

abhinc *adv* from this time, since, ago; from this place

abhorreō ② *v usu with* ab *and* abl be averse (to), shudder at; be inconsistent (with)

abiciō, **iēcī**, **iectum** ③ *v* throw away; slight, give up; humble, debase

> ❗ The first syllable of this verb scans as heavy in the present stem even though the 'a' is short; this is because the 'i' represents 'ii' pronounced as consonant + vowel 'yi'.

abiectē *adv* in a spiritless manner; in humble circumstances; negligently

abiectus, **a**, **um** *adj* downcast, mean, abject, base

abiēgnus, **a**, **um** *adj* made of fir

abiēs, **etis** *f* white fir; ship; spear

abigō, **ēgī**, **āctum** ③ *v* drive *or* send away

abitus, **ūs** *m* going away; departure; way out, exit

abiūdicō ① *v* deprive by judicial verdict

abiungō, **ūnxī**, **ūnctum** ③ *v* unyoke, remove, separate

abiūrō ① *v* deny on oath, repudiate

ablēgātiō, **ōnis** *f* sending away, dispatch

ablēgō ① *v* send away, remove

abluō, **uī**, **ūtum** ③ *v* wash away, blot out, purify; quench, remove

abnegō ① *v* deny, refuse; keep back

abnuō, **uī**, **ūtum** ③ *v* deny, refuse, reject

aboleō, **ēvī** ② *v* abolish, destroy

abolēscō, **ēvī** ③ *v* cease, be extinct, fall into disuse

abolitiō, **ōnis** *f* abolition, cancellation, annulment

abōminor ① *v dep* (seek to) avert (by prayer); detest

aborior, **abortus sum** ④ *v dep pass* away, disappear; miscarry

abortiō, **ōnis** *f* abortion, miscarriage

abortīvus, **a**, **um** *adj* abortive; addled

abortus, **ūs** *m* miscarriage

abrādō, **āsī**, **āsum** ③ *v* scratch off, shave; 'knock off', rob

abripiō, **ripuī**, **reptum** ③ *v* drag away by force; abduct, kidnap

abrogātiō, **ōnis** *f* repeal of a law

abrogō ① *v* repeal wholly, abolish

abrumpō, **ūpī**, **uptum** ③ *v* break off, tear asunder, cut through

abruptiō, **ōnis** *f* breaking, breaking off

abruptus, **a**, **um** *adj* precipitous, steep; hasty, rash

abs ▶ **ā**

abscēdō, **essī**, **essum** ③ *v* go away, depart; desist

a

abscessus, **ūs** *m* going away, absence

abscīdō, **īdī**, **īsum** ③ *v* cut off, remove

abscindō, **idī**, **issum** ③ *v* cut off, tear away; put an end to

abscīsus, **a**, **um** *adj* steep, abrupt

abscondō, **(di)dī** ③ *v* hide; keep secret

absēns, **ntis** *adj* absent

absentia, **ae** *f* absence

absiliō, **liī/luī** ④ *v* leap away; fly apart

absimilis, **e** *adj* unlike

absistō, **stitī** ③ *v* stand off, go away; desist from, leave off

absolūtē *adv* completely, perfectly

absolūtiō, **ōnis** *f* finishing, acquittal, perfection

absolūtus, **a**, **um** *adj* free, complete, unconditional

absolvō, **lvī**, **lūtum** ③ *v* absolve (from), discharge, dismiss, release; finish; pay, satisfy

absonus, **a**, **um** *adj* out of tune, discordant, incongruous

absorbeō, **buī/psī**, **ptum** ② *v* absorb, suck in

absque *prep with abl* without, except

abstēmius, **a**, **um** *adj* sober, temperate; fasting

abstergeō, **rsī**, **rsum** ② *v* wipe off *or* dry *or* clean; remove

absterreō ② *v* frighten away

abstinēns, **ntis** *adj* abstinent, temperate

abstinenter *adv* abstinently

abstinentia, **ae** *f* abstinence; fasting; moderation

abstineō, **tentum** ② *v* restrain, keep away; abstain, forbear

abstō, **stitī**, **stitum** ① *v* stand at a distance

abstrahō, **āxī**, **actum** ③ *v* drag away from; separate

abstrūdō, **ūsī**, **ūsum** ③ *v* thrust away, conceal

abstrūsus, **a**, **um** *adj* secret, reserved

abstulī *pf of* ▸ **auferō**

absum, **abesse**, **āfuī** *v ir* be absent *or* away (from) *or* distant; be wanting

absūmō, **mpsī**, **mptum** ③ *v* spend, use up, waste, squander, ruin

absurdus, **a**, **um** *adj* of a harsh sound; absurd, nonsensical

abundanter *adv* abundantly, copiously

abundantia, **ae** *f* abundance, plenty, riches

abundē *adv* abundantly

abundō ① *v* abound (in), be rich

abusque *prep with abl* all the way from

abūsus, **ūs** *m* misuse, wasting

abūtor, **abūsus sum** ③ *v dep* use up, waste; misuse

ac *conj* and, and besides; than

> **!** ac is usu. found before words beginning with consonants, rarely before vowels; cf. **atque**.

acadēmīa, **ae** *f* academy, university

acadēmicus, **a**, **um** *adj* academic

acalanthis, **idis** *f* a small song-bird

acanthus, **ī** *m* bear's-foot; the gum arabic tree

accēdō, **essī**, **essum** ③ *v* go *or* come to *or* near, approach; attack; fall to one's share, be added, come over to; be like, enter upon

accelerō ① *v* accelerate, hasten; make haste

accendō, **ndī**, **ēnsum** ③ *v* set on fire, light, illuminate; inflame

accēnseō, **ēnsum** ② *v* attach as an attendant to

accēnsus, **ī** *m* supernumerary soldier; attendant, orderly

accentus, **ūs** *m* accent, intonation

acceptiō, **ōnis** *f* taking, accepting; meaning, sense

acceptum, **ī** *nt* (financial) credit

acceptus, **a**, **um** *adj* welcome, well-liked; (of money) received

accersō ▸ **arcessō**

accessiō, **ōnis** *f* approach; increase, addition; (med) fit

accessus, **ūs** *m* approach, admittance, attack

accidentia, **ium** *npl* [LM] accidents (Aristotelian qualities)

accīdō, **īdī**, **īsum** ③ *v* cut short, weaken

accidō, **idī** ③ *v* fall at *or* near; happen

accingō, **īnxī**, **īnctum** ③ *v* gird on *or* about; provide (with), prepare (for)

acciō ④ *v* send for, summon

accipiō, cēpī, ceptum ③ *v* accept, collect, take, receive; undertake; hear, learn, find; get; sustain; obey; treat □ **sat** ∼ take *or* exact security

accipiter, tris *m* hawk

accītus, ūs *m* summons, call

acclāmātiō, ōnis *f* acclamation, shout; crying against

acclāmō ① *v* shout (at), cry out against

acclārō ① *v* make clear, reveal

acclīnis, e *adj* leaning (on), sloping; inclined, disposed (to)

acclīnō ① *v* lay down, rest (on), lean against, incline (to)

acclīvis, e *adj*, **acclīvus, a, um** *adj* sloping upwards

accola, ae *m/f* neighbour

accolō, luī, ultum ③ *v* dwell near

accommodātiō, ōnis *f* adjustment, willingness to oblige

accommodātus, a, um *adj* fit, suitable

accommodō ① *v* adjust, fit, suit; apply; synchronize

accommodus, a, um *adj* fit, convenient

accrēdō, didī ③ *v with dat* give credence to, believe

accrēscō, ēvī, ētum ③ *v* grow on, increase, swell, be annexed to

accrētiō, ōnis *f* increasing, increment

accubitiō, ōnis *f* reclining (at meals)

accubō, buī, itum ① *v* lie near *or* by; recline at table; sit down

accumbō, buī ③ *v* lie down, recline at table

accumulātor, ōris *m* heaper up

accumulō ① *v* accumulate, heap up

accūrātiō, ōnis *f* carefulness, painstakingness

accūrātus, a, um *adj* accurate, with care, meticulous

accūrō ① *v* take care of, attend to; do carefully

accurrō, (cu)currī, ursum ③ *v* run *or* hasten to

accursus, ūs *m* rushing up; attack

accūsābilis, e *adj* blameable, reprehensible

accūsātiō, ōnis *f* accusation

accūsātor, ōris *m* accuser, plaintiff; informer

accūsātōrius, a, um *adj* accusatory

accūsitō ① *v with acc of person and crime* accuse repeatedly

accūsō ① *v* accuse, blame, reprimand

acer, eris *nt* maple-tree

ācer, cris, cre *adj* sharp, sour, pungent, piercing; violent; keen, furious, swift, active, ardent, courageous; drastic, critical; bracing, of keen intellect

acerbitās, ātis *f* acerbity, sourness; severity, bitterness; anguish, hardship

acerbō ① *v* embitter; aggravate

acerbus, a, um *adj* unripe, sour, bitter; crude; shrill, rough, violent; severe; grievous

acernus, a, um *adj* of maple

acerra, ae *f* box *or* casket for incense

acervātim *adv* in heaps, summarily, without any order

acervō ① *v* heap up

acervus, ī *m* heap

acēscō, cuī ③ *v* turn sour

acētāria, ōrum *ntpl* salad prepared with vinegar

acētum, ī *nt* vinegar; sourness of disposition; sharpness of wit

acidus, a, um *adj* acid, sour

aciēs, iēī *f* edge, point; battle-array, line of battle; the sight of the eyes; pupil of the eye; quickness of apprehension

acinācēs, ācis *m* scimitar

acinum, ī *nt*, **acinus, ī** *m* grape, ivy-berry; pip, seed

acipēnser, eris *m* sturgeon

aclys, ydis *f* javelin

aconītum, ī *nt* wolf's-bane, aconite

acquiēscō, ēvī, ētum ③ *v* lie down to rest; acquiesce (in), assent; subside

acquīrō, īsīvī, īsītum ③ *v* acquire, get, obtain

acquīsītiō, ōnis *f* acquisition

ācriculus, a, um *adj* shrewd, acute

ācrimōnia, ae *f* acrimony, sharpness, briskness

ācriter *adv* sharply, vehemently; severely, steadfastly

acroāma, atis *nt* item in an entertainment, act, 'turn'

acroāsis, **is** *f* lecture

ācta, **ōrum** *ntpl* acts, exploits; chronicles, record

acta, **ae** *f* sea-shore

āctiō, **ōnis** *f* action; plot (of a play); legal process

āctitō ① *v* act or plead frequently

āctīvus, **a**, **um** *adj* active

āctor, **ōris** *m* plaintiff, advocate; agent; player, actor; herdsman

āctuārius[1], **(i)ī** *m* short-hand writer, clerk, book-keeper, secretary

āctuārius[2], **a**, **um** *adj* swift, nimble, light

āctum, **ī** *nt* deed, exploit

āctuōsus, **a**, **um** *adj* active, busy

āctus, **ūs** *m* act, performance, action; delivery

actūtum *adv* forthwith, instantly, in no time at all

aculeātus, **a**, **um** *adj* prickly; stinging, sharp, subtle

aculeus, **ī** *m* sting, prickle, point; sarcasm

acūmen, **inis** *nt* sharpened point, sting, sharpness, cunning, fraud

acuō, **uī**, **ūtum** ③ *v* whet, sharpen; spur on, provoke

acus, **ūs** *f* needle, pin

acūtē *adv* acutely

acūtulus, **a**, **um** *adj* subtle, clever

acūtus, **a**, **um** *adj* sharp, pointed; violent, severe; glaring; acute, quick-witted; high-pitched

ad *prep with acc* to, towards, near by, at, before, up to, until, about; in comparison with, according to; in addition to, after, concerning; *with gerund(ive)* in order to

adaequē *adv* equally, so much; in like manner, so also

adaequō ① *v* equalize, level, compare (to); be equal

adamantēus, **a**, **um** *adj* adamantine

adamantinus, **a**, **um** *adj* hard as the hardest iron

adamās, **ntis** *m* the hardest iron; diamond

adamō ① *v* love passionately

adaperiō, **ruī**, **rtum** ④ *v* throw open, uncover

adapertilis, **e** *adj* that may be opened

adaptō ① *v* adjust, fit

adaquō ① *v* water

adauctus, **ūs** *m* increase, growth

adaugeō, **xī**, **ctum** ② *v* increase, intensify

adbibō, **bibī** ③ *v* drink, drink in

addecet ② *v impers* it is fitting

addēnseō ② *v* make more dense, close up (the ranks)

addīcō, **īxī**, **ictum** ③ *v* be propitious; adjudge; confiscate; knock down to, award; consecrate; sacrifice

addictiō, **ōnis** *f* adjudication, assignment

addictus, **ī** *m* a person enslaved for debt *or* theft

addiscō, **didicī** ③ *v* learn besides

additāmentum, **ī** *nt* addition

addō, **didī** ③ *v* add, give, bring to, say in addition; attach, annex
▫ ~ **gradum** gather pace, speed up

addubitō ① *v* doubt, hesitate

addūcō, **ūxī**, **uctum** ③ *v* bring *or* lead to *or* along; lead on, induce, contract, tighten

adedō, **ēsse**, **ēdī**, **ēsum** *v ir* eat up, eat into, squander

adēmptiō, **ōnis** *f* taking away

adeō[1] *adv* so much, to such a degree, so, so far, just, even, much more, much less, 'you know'

adeō[2], **īre**, **iī/īvī**, **itum** *v ir* go to *or* approach, address, accost, visit; attack; undergo, take a part in; enter on (an inheritance)

adeps, **ipis** *m/f* fat, lard, grease; corpulence; bombast

adeptiō, **ōnis** *f* obtaining, attainment

adeptus ▶ *pple* from **adipīscor**

adequitō ① *v* ride up to

adf- ▶ **aff-**

adg- ▶ **agg-**

adhaereō, **haesī**, **haesum** ② *v*, **adhaerēscō** ③ *v* adhere, stick, cling to

adhaesiō, **ōnis** *f* adhesion, linkage

adhibeō ② *v* apply, hold (to), use; invite, admit

adhinniō ④ *v* whinny (to)

adhortātiō, **ōnis** *f* exhortation

adhortātor, **ōris** *m* encourager

adhortor ① *v dep* exhort, encourage

adhūc *adv* to this point, until now; yet, still; besides

adiaceō ② *v with dat* lie beside *or* near to

adiciō, **iēcī**, **iectum** ③ *v* throw to, add to

> ❗ The first syllable of this verb scans as heavy in the present stem even though the 'a' is short; this is because the 'i' represents 'ii' pronounced as consonant + vowel 'yi'.

adiectiō, **ōnis** *f* addition

adigō, **ēgī**, **āctum** ③ *v* drive, bring, drive in, bind by oath

adimō, **ēmī**, **emptum** ③ *v* take away, rescue, deprive

adipīscor, **adeptus sum** ③ *v dep* reach, get, obtain, arrive (at), overtake

aditus, **ūs** *m* access, way, means, opportunity

adiūdicō ① *v* adjudge, impute

adiūmentum, **ī** *nt* help, assistance

adiūnctiō, **ōnis** *f* union, addition

adiūnctum, **ī** *nt* quality, characteristic

adiungō, **ūnxī**, **ūnctum** ③ *v* join to, yoke, add to

adiūrō ① *v* swear solemnly, confirm by oath

adiūtō ① *v* help

adiūtor, **ōris** *m* assistant, helper, supporter

adiūtōrium, **(i)ī** *nt* help, assistance

adiūtrīx, **īcis** *f* female assistant, helper

adiuvō, **iūvī**, **iūtum** ① *v* assist, help, cherish, favour, mitigate

adl- ▶ all-

admētior, **mēnsus sum** ④ *v dep* measure out

adminiculum, **ī** *nt* prop, support, stay, means, aid, assistance

administer, **trī** *m* servant, assistant, supporter

administrātiō, **ōnis** *f* administration; aid, assistance; execution, management, care of affairs

administrātor, **ōris** *m* director, manager

administrō ① *v* administer, manage, serve

admīrābilis, **e** *adj* admirable, wonderful, strange

admīrābilitās, **ātis** *f* wonderful character, remarkableness

admīrābiliter *adv* admirably, astonishingly

admīrātiō, **ōnis** *f* admiration, wondering

admīrātor, **ōris** *m* admirer

admīror ① *v dep* admire, wonder at

admisceō, **ixtum** ② *v* mix, mingle with; mix up with, involve

admissārius, **(i)ī** *m* stallion; sodomite

admissiō, **ōnis** *f* letting in, admission

admissum, **ī** *nt* crime, offence

admittō, **īsī**, **issum** ③ *v* let in, admit, grant, permit, commit, let go, give rein to

admixtiō, **ōnis** *f* (ad)mixture

admodum *adv* quite, very, excessively; altogether, entirely; just so; certainly

admōlior ④ *v dep* make an effort

admoneō ② *v* admonish, warn; remind; persuade

admonitiō, **ōnis** *f* reminding; warning, advice; rebuke

admonitor, **ōris** *m* one who reminds

admonitus, **ūs** *m* admonition, warning

admoveō, **mōvī**, **mōtum** ② *v* move *or* bring to, apply, use, direct; lay on

admurmurō ① *v* murmur in protest *or* approval

adnatō ① *v* swim toward

adnectō, **exum** ③ *v* tie on, annex

adnexus, **ūs** *m* tie, connection

adnītor, **nīxus/nīsus sum** ③ *v dep* lean upon, strive

adnō ① *v* swim to, sail to *or* towards

adnotō ① *v* note down, notice

adnumerō ① *v* count out, pay, count (in)

adnūntiō ① *v* announce

adnuō, **uī**, **ūtum** ③ *v* nod at *or* to, assent, promise, grant, indicate by a nod

adoleō, **ultum** ② *v* burn; honour by burnt offering

adolēscō, **ēvī**, **ultum** ③ *v* grow up, increase

adopertus, **a**, **um** *adj* covered

adoptīvus, **a**, **um** *adj* adoptive

adoptō ① *v* select, adopt

ador, **ōris** *nt* coarse grain

adorior, **ortus sum** ④ *v dep* attack, undertake, try

adornō ① *v* equip, set off, prepare, adorn

adōrō ① *v* adore, worship; beg

adp- ▸ **app-**

adpōtus, **a**, **um** *adj* intoxicated, drunk

adprīmē *adv* to the highest degree, extremely

adr- ▸ **arr-**

adrādō, **āsī**, **āsum** ③ *v* scrape, shave, prune

ads- ▸ **ass-**

adscēnsus ▸ **ascēnsus**

adsum, **esse**, **fuī** *v ir* be near, be present, arrive; *with dat* aid

adūlātiō, **ōnis** *f* fawning, flattery

adūlātor, **ōris** *m* flatterer

adūlātōrius, **a**, **um** *adj* flattering, adulatory

adulēscēns, **ntis** *m/f* young man *or* girl

adulēscentia, **ae** *f* youth (time of life)

adulēscentula, **ae** *f* young woman

adulēscentulus, **ī** *m* young man, mere youth

adūlor ① *v dep* fawn upon (as a dog); flatter

adulter¹, **erī** *m*, **adultera**, **ae** *f* adulterer

adulter², **era**, **erum** *adj* adulterous; counterfeit

adulterīnus, **a**, **um** *adj* counterfeit, false

adulterium, **(i)ī** *nt* adultery

adulterō ① *v* commit adultery (with); falsify, corrupt

adultus, **a**, **um** *adj* full grown, adult

adumbrātiō, **ōnis** *f* sketch

adumbrō ① *v* shadow out, sketch in outline; represent

aduncitās, **ātis** *f* hookedness, curvature

aduncus, **a**, **um** *adj* crooked, hooked

adurgeō, **ursī** ② *v* press hard, pursue

adūrō, **ussī**, **ustum** ③ *v* burn, scorch; consume

adusque *prep with acc* right up to, as far as; *adv* wholly

advectīcius, **a**, **um** *adj* imported, foreign

advectus, **a**, **um** *adj* imported; immigrant

advehō, **ēxī**, **ectum** ③ *v* carry, bring, convey (to)
  □ **advehor** arrive by travel, ride to

advena, **ae** *m/f* foreigner, stranger, interloper; *adj* alien, foreign

adveniō, **vēnī**, **ventum** ④ *v* come to, arrive at; develop

adventīcius, **a**, **um** *adj* coming from abroad, foreign, unusual

adventō ① *v* approach, arrive

adventor, **ōris** *m* visitor, customer

adventus, **ūs** *m* arrival, approach, attack; LM Advent

adversārius, **a**, **um** *adj* opposite
  ■ **adversārius**, **(i)ī** *m* opponent, enemy
  ■ **adversāria**, **ōrum** *ntpl* memorandum-book

adversātor, **ōris** *m* antagonist

adversātrīx, **īcis** *f* female antagonist

adversor ① *v dep with dat* be against, oppose, withstand

adversum, **adversus** *adv* opposite, against; *prep with acc* towards, opposite to, against

adversus, **a**, **um** *adj* opposite, directly facing; adverse, evil, hostile; unfavourable
  ■ **rēs adversae** *fpl* adverse circumstances
  □ **adversō flūmine** against the stream

advertō, **rtī**, **rsum** ③ *v* turn *or* direct to, apply
  □ **animum advertō** notice,
  ▸ **animadvertō**

advesperāscit, **āvit** ③ *v impers* evening approaches

advigilō ① *v* watch by, take care

advocātiō, **ōnis** *f* legal support; delay; pleading in the law courts

advocātus, **ī** *m* counsellor, advocate, witness

advocō ① *v* call for, summon, call in as counsel

advolō ① *v* fly to, hasten towards

advolvō, lvī, lūtum ③ *v* roll to *or* towards
- □ **genibus advolvor** fall at the knees (of anyone)

advor- ▶ **adver-**

adytum, ī *nt* innermost part of a temple, sanctuary

aedēs, dis *f* (also **aedis**) *sg* temple; *pl* house, room

aedicula, ae *f* small house, chapel, niche, closet

aedificātiō, ōnis *f* house-building; building; ⌊LM⌋ instruction, education

aedificātor, ōris *m* builder, architect

aedificium, (i)ī *nt* building

aedificō ① *v* build, make, create

aedīlicius, a, um *adj* of an aedile

aedīlis, is *m* aedile

❗ In the early Roman republic, the two **aedīlēs** were magistrates elected annually by the plebeians, were effectively the deputies of the **tribūnī plēbis**, and oversaw the temple and cults of the plebeians. After 367 BC there were, as well as these **aedīlēs plēbēiī**, also two **aedīlēs curūlēs**, originally elected by the patricians but later by them in alternation with the **plēbs**. They held joint responsibility for care of the fabric and people of the city, its corn supply and its public games; the office was a common step on the **cursus honōrum**.

---

aedīlitās, ātis *f* aedileship

aeditu(m)us, ī *m* one who has charge of a temple, sacristan

aeger, gra, grum *adj* sick, infirm, sad, sorrowful, painful, grievous

aegis, idis *f* the aegis (Minerva's shield); shield, defence

aegrē *adv* uncomfortably, reluctantly, with difficulty, scarcely
- □ **∼ est** *with dat* be disagreeable *or* displeasing to

aegrēscō ③ *v* become sick, grow worse, grieve

aegrimōnia, ae *f* sorrow, anxiety, melancholy

aegritūdō, inis *f* sickness, disease, grief, sorrow

aegrōtātiō, ōnis *f* sickness, disease, morbid desire

aegrōtō ① *v* be sick, be mentally ill

aegrōtus, a, um *adj* sick, diseased

aemulātiō, ōnis *f* emulation, rivalry

aemulātor, ōris *m* imitator, rival

aemulātus, ūs *m* emulation, envy

aemulor ① *v dep* emulate; be envious, jealous of

aemulus, a, um *adj* emulous; envious, grudging; (of things) comparable (with); *m/f* rival

aenigma, atis *nt* enigma, riddle, obscure saying

aequābilis, e *adj* equal, alike, uniform, steady, equable

aequābilitās, ātis *f* equality, fairness, uniformity

aequābiliter *adv* uniformly, equally

aequaevus, a, um *adj* of the same age

aequālis, e *adj* even, equal, of the same age, coeval; *m/f* contemporary

aequālitās, ātis *f* evenness; equality

aequāliter *adv* equally, evenly

aequanimitās, ātis *f* evenness of mind, patience, calmness

aequātiō, ōnis *f* equal distribution

aequē *adv* equally, in the same manner as, justly

aequinoctiālis, e *adj* equinoctial

aequinoctium, (i)ī *nt* equinox

aequiperō ① *v* compare, liken; *with dat* become equal (with)

aequitās, ātis *f* evenness, conformity, symmetry, equanimity, fairness, impartiality

aequō ① *v* level; equal; compare; reach as high *or* deep as

aequor, oris *nt* level surface, plain, surface of the sea, sea

aequoreus, a, um *adj* of the sea, bordering on the sea

aequus, a, um *adj* level, even, equal, like, just, kind, favourable, impartial, fair, patient, contented
- □ **aequō animō** calmly
- ■ **aequum, ī** *nt* plain, flat ground
- □ **ex aequō** from the same level

āēr, eris *m* air, atmosphere; cloud, mist

aerārium, (i)ī *nt* treasury

aerārius, a, um *adj* pertaining to copper, brass, *etc.*; *m/f* a citizen of the lowest class

aerātus, a, um *adj* covered with *or* made of copper *or* brass

aereus, a, um *adj* made of copper, bronze *or* brass

aeripēs, edis *adj* brazen-footed

āerius, a, um *adj* aerial, towering, airy

aerūgō, inis *f* rust of copper, verdigris; canker of the mind, envy, ill-will, avarice

aerumna, ae *f* toil, hardship, calamity

aerumnōsus, a, um *adj* full of trouble, wretched, calamitous

aes, aeris *nt* copper ore, copper; bronze; money, pay, wages, bronze statue, *etc.*
▫ ~ **aliēnum** debt

aesculus, ī *f* a variety of oak tree, perhaps either durmast or Hungarian oak

aestās, ātis *f* summer; a year

aestifer, era, erum *adj* producing heat, sultry

aestimābilis, e *adj* having worth *or* value

aestimātiō, ōnis *f* valuation, value, price

aestimātor, ōris *m* valuer, appraiser; judge

aestimō ① *v* value; estimate; consider

aestīva, ōrum *ntpl* summer-quarters; the campaigning season

aestīvō ① *v* pass the summer

aestīvus, a, um *adj* summer-like, summer…

aestuārium, (i)ī *nt* estuary, inlet, tidal opening

aestuō ① *v* boil, foam, billow, seethe; rage, waver, be undecided

aestuōsus, a, um *adj* hot, sultry, billowy

aestus, ūs *m* heat, fire, tide, swell of the sea; passion; hesitation, anxiety

aetās, ātis *f* life-time, age, period; generation

aetātula, ae *f* the tender age of childhood

aeternitās, ātis *f* eternity, immortality

aeternō ① *v* immortalize

aeternus, a, um *adj* eternal, everlasting, imperishable
■ **aeternum** *adv* for ever

aethēr, eris *m* upper air, heaven, sky

aetherius, a, um *adj* ethereal, heavenly

aethra, ae *f* brightness, splendour; clear sky

aevum, ī *nt* time, life, time of life, age, old age, generation

affābilis, e *adj* easy of access, affable, friendly

affatim *adv* sufficiently, amply

affātus, ūs *m* address, speech, converse

affectātiō, ōnis *f* seeking after; affectation

affectiō, ōnis *f* mental condition, feeling, disposition, affection, love

affectō ① *v* try to accomplish, aim at, desire, aspire, lay claim to, pretend

affectus¹, ūs *m* disposition, state (of body and mind), affection, passion, love

affectus², a, um *adj* endowed with; disposed; impaired, sick

afferō, afferre, attulī, allātum *v ir* bring to, deliver, bring word, allege, produce, contribute, cause

afficiō, fēcī, fectum ③ *v* affect, move, influence

affīgō, īxī, īxum ③ *v with dat* fasten to, fix on; impress on

affingō, īnxī, ictum ③ *v* add (to), embellish, counterfeit, attribute (wrongly)

affīnis, e *adj* neighbouring, adjacent, related by marriage, connected (with)

affīnitās, ātis *f* neighbourhood; relationship (by marriage)

affirmātiō, ōnis *f* affirmation, assertion

affirmō ① *v* affirm, assert, confirm

afflātus, ūs *m* breathing on, breeze, blast, breath; inspiration

afflictātiō, ōnis *f* grievous suffering, torment, affliction

afflictō ① *v* strike repeatedly, damage, vex

afflīgō, īxī, īctum ③ *v* afflict, throw down, crush, grieve, humble, weaken, damage

afflō ① *v* blow *or* breathe on; inspire

affluenter *adv* abundantly, copiously, lavishly

affluentia, ae *f* abundance, profusion, superfluity

affluō, **ūxī**, **ūxum** ③ *v* flow on; flock together, abound

affor ① *v dep* speak to, address

affulgeō, **lsī** ② *v with dat* shine on; smile upon

affundō, **ūdī**, **ūsum** ③ *v* pour upon (into)
□ **affundor** prostrate oneself

agāsō, **ōnis** *m* driver, groom, stable-boy; lackey

age *int* [fossilized imperative from **agō**] come! well! all right!

agedum *int* [fossilized imperative from **agō** and **dum**] come! well! all right!

agellus, **ī** *m* little field, farm

ager, **grī** *m* field, ground, territory, country, farm

agger, **eris** *m* heap, mound, dam; mudwall; rampart; causeway

aggerō¹, **essī**, **estum** ③ *v* carry to, bring, add, heap up, on *or* into

aggerō² ① *v* heap up, fill up, increase

aggestus, **ūs** *m* piling up

agglomerō ① *v* gather into a body

agglūtinō ① *v* glue to, fasten to

aggravō ① *v* aggravate, weigh down, oppress

aggredior, **gressus sum** ③ *v dep* approach, attack, undertake

aggregō ① *v* join together, attach
□ **sē aggregāre** ally oneself to

agilis, **e** *adj* agile, nimble, quick, busy

agilitās, **ātis** *f* activity, quickness

agitātiō, **ōnis** *f* agitation, exercise; violent motion

agitātor, **ōris** *m* driver, charioteer

agitō ① *v* agitate, drive *or* shake *or* move about, revolve; consider, pursue, exercise, manage; keep, celebrate, disturb, distress

agmen, **inis** *nt* herd, flock, troop, swarm, army (on the march)
□ **prīmum** ∼ the vanguard
□ **novissimum** ∼ the rear(guard)

agna, **ae** *f* female lamb

agnātus, **ī** *m* relation on the father's side; one born after a father has made his will

agnīna, **ae** *f* flesh of a lamb

agnōmen, **inis** *nt* an additional name denoting an achievement, a nickname

agnōscō, **nōvī**, **nitum** ③ *v* recognize, acknowledge

agnus, **ī** *m* lamb

agō, **ēgī**, **āctum** ③ *v* drive, act, do, transact, carry off, steal, apply, rouse, cause to bring forth, urge, deal, think, manage, exercise, accuse, deliver (a speech), play (as an actor), behave (as), pass, spend, disturb
□ **grātiās** ∼ *with dat* thank
□ ∼ **dē** *with abl* discuss
□ **āctum est dē** *with abl* it's all up with …!

agrārius, **a**, **um** *adj* agrarian

agrestis, **e** *adj* rustic, rude, wild, savage
■ **agrestis**, **is** *m* countryman, peasant

agricola, **ae** *m* farmer, cultivator

ai *int* ah! alas!

aiō *v ir* say; say yes, assent, affirm

> ❗ **aiō** has only forms only in the pres. (aiō, ais, ait, —, —, aiunt; subj. only aiat, aiant; pple. aiēns) and impf. (all persons, aiēbam, aiēbās etc., indic. only).

āla, **ae** *f* wing; upper arm, arm-pit; an army's wing

> ❗ The cavalry of a Roman **legiō** were usu. formed into wings on the flanks of the overall formation. They were divided into **turmae**.

alacer, **cris**, **cre** *adj* cheerful, brisk, active, courageous, eager, ready

alacritās, **ātis** *f* cheerfulness, eagerness, liveliness

ālāris, **e** *adj*, **ālārius**, **a**, **um** *adj* pertaining to an army's wing, of the auxiliary cavalry

ālātus, **a**, **um** *adj* winged

alauda, **ae** *f* lark

albātus, **a**, **um** *adj* clothed in white

albeō ② *v* be *or* grow white

albēscō ③ *v* become white

albicō ① *v* be white

albidus, **a**, **um** *adj* whitish, pale

albulus, **a**, **um** *adj* white, pale

album, **ī** *nt* white (the colour); white tablet, list of names, register

albus, **a**, **um** *adj* white, pale, hoary, bright, clear, favourable, fortunate

alcēdō, **inis** *f*, **alcyōn**, **onis** *f* kingfisher

alcēdonia, **ōrum** *ntpl* halcyon days

ālea, **ae** *f* die, dice-play, gambling, chance, venture, risk

āleātor, **ōris** *m* dice-player, gambler

āleātōrius, **a**, **um** *adj* of dice
□ **āleātōria damna** losses at gambling

āleō, **ōnis** *m* gambler

āles, **itis** *m/f* bird, fowl; augury; *adj* winged, swift

alga, **ae** *f* sea-weed; rubbish

algeō, **lsī** ② *v* be cold, feel chilly, endure cold

algor, **ōris** *m*, **algus**, **ūs** *m* coldness

aliā *adv* by another way

āliātum, **ī** *nt* food seasoned with garlic

aliās *adv* at another time, elsewhere, otherwise

alibī *adv* elsewhere, in another place

alicubī *adv* somewhere, anywhere

alicunde *adv* from some place, from some source or other

aliēnātiō, **ōnis** *f* transference, aversion, dislike

aliēnigena, **ae** *m* stranger, foreigner

aliēnō ① *v* alienate, transfer by sale, estrange; *in passive* avoid (with antipathy); be insane

aliēnus, **a**, **um** *adj* another's, foreign; contrary, averse, hostile; unfavourable, insane
□ **aes aliēnum** debt

āliger, **era**, **erum** *adj* winged

alimentum, **ī** *nt* nourishment, food

aliō *adv* to another place; to another subject; to another purpose

ālipēs, **edis** *adj* wing-footed, swift

aliptēs, **ae** *m* one who anoints (athletes), trainer of gymnasts

aliquā *adv* somehow

aliquamdiū *adv* for some time

aliquandō *adv* sometimes, at length, formerly, hereafter

aliquantō, **aliquantum** *adv* somewhat, to some (considerable) extent

aliquantus, **a**, **um** *adj* a certain quantity *or* amount *or* number of

aliquī, **aliquae**, **aliquod** *adj* some, any

aliquis, **quid** *pn* someone, somewhat, something

> **❗** **aliquis** usu. refers to a non-specific 'someone' unknown (i.e. contrasting with 'no one'), e.g. **aliquō diē moriar** 'I shall die (on) some (unknown) day'; cf. **quīdam**.

aliquō *adv* to some place *or* other

aliquot *adj indec* some, a number of

aliter *adv* otherwise, else; in a different way

ālium, **(i)ī** *nt* garlic

aliunde *adv* from another person *or* place

alius, **alia**, **aliud** *adj* another, different, changed
□ **alius ... alius** one ... another

> **❗** Used with another **ali-** 'other' word, **alius** makes a double statement, e.g. **aliī aliud dīcunt** 'some people say one thing, others another' or 'different people say different things'.

allābor, **lāpsus sum** ③ *v dep* glide towards, move forwards

allabōrō ① *v* make a special effort

allāpsus, **ūs** *m* gliding approach; flowing towards *or* near

allātrō ① *v* bark at; rail at

allectō ① *v* allure, entice

allēgātiō, **ōnis** *f* intercession; allegation

allegō, **ēgī**, **ēctum** ③ *v* choose, admit

allēgō ① *v* depute, commission

allevō ① *v* lift up, raise; alleviate, diminish, weaken, console

alli- ▶ **āli-**

alliciō, **xī**, **ectum** ③ *v* draw gently to, entice, attract

allīdō, **īsī**, **īsum** ③ *v* dash against; shipwreck

alligō ① *v* bind to, bind, impede, entangle; bind by an obligation

allinō, **lēvī**, **litum** ③ *v* smear over

allocūtiō, **ōnis** *f* address, consolation, harangue

alloquium, **(i)ī** *nt* address, encouragement

alloquor, **locūtus sum** ③ *v dep* speak to, address, harangue

allūdō, **ūsī**, **ūsum** ③ *v* frolic around, play with, jest

alluō, **uī** ③ *v* wash against, bathe

alluviēs, **iēī** *f* flood-land by a river

almus, **a**, **um** *adj* nourishing, kind, propitious

alnus, **ī** *f* alder; plank, bridge, boat

alō, **aluī**, **al(i)tum** ③ *v* nurse, nourish, maintain; promote; cherish

Alpīnus, **a**, **um** *adj* of the Alps

alsius, **a**, **um** *adj* liable to injury from cold

alsus, **a**, **um** *adj* cool

altāria, **ium** *ntpl* altar

altē *adv* on high, highly, deeply, far back

alter, **era**, **erum** *adj* another, the other, any other, the former, the latter
□ **unus et** ∼ one or two, a few

alterās ▶ **aliās**

altercātiō, **ōnis** *f* contention, dispute, debate

altercor ① *v dep* bicker, dispute, quarrel; dispute in the law-courts

alternō ① *v* do by turns, vary; alternate, waver

alternus, **a**, **um** *adj* alternate, one after the other, by turns, mutual
□ **alternīs vicibus** alternately, by turns

alteruter, **tra**, **trum** *adj* either, one of two

altisonus, **a**, **um** *adj* high-sounding, lofty; sublime

altitonāns, **ntis** *adj* thundering from on high

altitūdō, **inis** *f* height, depth; (fig) loftiness, profundity, noblemindedness, secrecy

altivolāns, **ntis** *adj* high-flying

altor, **ōris** *m* nourisher, foster-father

altrīnsecus *adv* on the other side

altrīx, **īcis** *f* female nourisher, wet-nurse

altum, **ī** *nt* the deep, the sea; a height

altus, **a**, **um** *adj* high, deep, shrill, lofty, noble; deeply rooted; far-fetched

ālūcinor ① *v dep* wander in mind, talk idly, dream

alumnus, **a**, **um** *adj* nourished, brought up; *m* nursling, foster-child, disciple

alūta, **ae** *f* a piece of soft leather; a beauty patch

alveus, **ī** *m* cavity; tub; tray; hold of a ship, boat; gaming-board; bee-hive; bathing-tub; river-bed

alvus, **ī** *f* belly, paunch, womb, stomach; bee-hive

ama ▶ **hama**

amābilis, **e** *adj* amiable, pleasant

amābiliter *adv* lovingly, amicably, pleasantly

āmandō ① *v* send away, dismiss

amāns, **ntis** *m/f* lover, sweetheart, mistress

amanter *adv* lovingly, affectionately

amāracus, **ī** *m/f*, **amāracum**, **ī** *nt* marjoram

amāritiēs, **iēī** *f* bitterness, harshness

amāritūdō, **inis** *f* bitterness; sharpness, disagreeableness

amārus, **a**, **um** *adj* bitter, harsh, shrill, sad, calamitous; ill-natured

amātiō, **ōnis** *f* love-making, petting

amātor, **ōris** *m* lover, devotee

amātōrius, **a**, **um** *adj* loving, amorous, procuring love

amātrīx, **īcis** *f* sweetheart, mistress

ambāgēs, **gis** *f*, **ambāgēs**, **gum** *fpl* round-about way, shifting, shuffling, prevarication; long-winded story; obscurity, ambiguity

ambedō, **ēsse**, **ēdī**, **ēsum** *v ir* gnaw round the edge, consume

ambigō ③ *v* hesitate, be in doubt, argue, wrangle

ambiguitās, **ātis** *f* ambiguity

ambiguus, **a**, **um** *adj* changeable, varying, doubtful, dark, ambiguous, wavering, fickle

ambiō ④ *v* surround, solicit, ask, aspire to; canvass

ambitiō, **ōnis** *f* ambition; currying favour, vain display; effort, canvassing

ambitiōsus, **a**, **um** *adj* ambitious, eager to please; importunate; showy

ambitus, **ūs** *m* circuit; canvass, bribery; circumlocution; ostentation

ambō, **ae**, **ō** *adj* both (two together)

ambrosia, **ae** *f* food of the gods

ambrosius, **a**, **um** *adj* immortal, divine

ambulācrum, **ī** *nt* walkway planted with trees, promenade, park

ambulātiō, **ōnis** *f* walking about; place for promenading

ambulātiuncula, **ae** *f* little walk; small place for walking

ambulō ① *v* go about, take a walk, travel

ambūrō, **ussī**, **ustum** ③ *v* burn around, scorch, burn wholly up; make frost-bitten

ambustulātus, **a**, **um** *adj* scorched, toasted

amen *int* [Hebrew 'truth'] LM truly; so be it, amen

āmēns, **ntis** *adj* mad, frantic

āmentia, **ae** *f* madness, stupidity

ames, **itis** *m* pole for supporting bird-nets

amethystus, **ī** *f* amethyst

amīca, **ae** *f* female friend, sweetheart, mistress, courtesan

amiciō, **cuī/xī**, **ctum** ④ *v* clothe, wrap about; veil

amīcitia, **ae** *f* friendship, alliance, affinity

amictus, **ūs** *m* upper garment, cloak, dress, clothing

amīcula, **ae** *f* mistress, lady-friend

amiculum, **ī** *nt* mantle, cloak

amīculus, **ī** *m* little friend, dear friend, humble friend

amīcus, **ī** *m* friend, ally, lover, patron; counsellor, courtier
■ ~, **a**, **um** *adj* friendly, fond of

āmissiō, **ōnis** *f* loss

amita, **ae** *f* father's sister, aunt

āmittō, **īsī**, **issum** ③ *v* lose, dismiss, let fall, let slip

ammirālius, **(i)i** *m* LM emir, governor

amnis, **is** *m* stream, river

amō ① *v* love, like, be fond of, make love; have a tendency to
□ **amābō (tē)** *used as int* please

amoenitās, **ātis** *f* pleasantness, delight, charm

amoenus, **a**, **um** *adj* pleasant, agreeable, charming

āmōlior ④ *v dep* remove, obliterate; avert, refute

amōmum, **ī** *nt* Eastern spice-plant; spice from this plant

amor, **ōris** *m* love; the beloved; Cupid; eager desire
■ **amōrēs**, **um** *mpl* girlfriend

āmoveō, **mōvī**, **mōtum** ② *v* remove, move away, steal; banish

amphisbaena, **ae** *f* a species of serpent supposed to have a head at both ends of its body

amphitheātrum, **ī** *nt* amphitheatre

amphora, **ae** *f* large earthenware jar, usually two-handled

amplectō ③ *u*, **amplector**, **amplexus sum** ③ *v dep* embrace, lay hold of; surround, contain; cherish; understand

amplexor ① *v dep* love, esteem

amplexus, **ūs** *m* embracing, embrace, surrounding

amplificātiō, **ōnis** *f* enlargement, amplification

amplificē *adv* magnificently, splendidly

amplificō ① *v* amplify, enlarge, praise loudly

ampliō ① *v* make wider, enlarge, adjourn

amplitūdō, **inis** *f* width, breadth, size, bulk; importance; fulness of expression

amplius *adv* more, further

ampliusculē *adv* rather more

amplus, **a**, **um** *adj* ample, large, wide; distinguished

ampulla, **ae** *f* bottle *or* flask for holding liquids; *pl* inflated expressions, bombast

amputātiō, **ōnis** *f* pruning, lopping off

amputō ① *v* lop off, prune, shorten

amulētum, **ī** *nt* charm

amygdalum, **ī** *nt* almond tree

an *conj* whether? or, either

> **!** Usu. introducing the second part of a double question, **an** may introduce a single emphatic question (as if the first part of a double question has been omitted), e.g. **an timēs?** 'Or is it the case that you are afraid?'

anadēma, **atis** *nt* band for the hair

anapaestus, **ī** *m* anapaest, metrical foot, two shorts followed by a long

anas, **atis** *f* duck

anathema, **atis** *nt* LM cursing, anathema

anaticula, **ae** *f* duckling

anatocismus, **ī** *m* compound interest

anceps, **itis** *adj* two-edged, two-headed; dangerous, doubtful; double, undecided

ancīle, **is** *nt* small figure-of-eight shield

ancilla, **ae** *f* maid-servant, female slave

ancillula, **ae** *f* little serving-maid, young female slave

ancora, **ae** *f* anchor

ancorāle, **is** *nt* anchor cable

andabata, **ae** *m* a gladiator who fought blindfolded

androgynus, **ī** *m* hermaphrodite

andrōn, **nis** *m* the men's apartment in a house

anē(t)um, **ī** *nt* dill, anise

anetīnus, **a**, **um** *adj* of a duck, duck's

ānfrāctus, **ūs** *m* curving, bending, circuit, windings; circumlocution

angelus, **i** *m* LM angel, messenger

angina, **ae** *f* a suffocating obstruction, quinsy

angiportus, **ūs** *m*, **angiportum**, **ī** *nt* narrow street *or* alley

angō, **ānxī**, **ānctum** ③ *v* press tight, throttle; cause pain, vex, trouble

angor, **ōris** *m* suffocation, choking, anguish, vexation

anguicomus, **a**, **um** *adj* with snaky hair

anguifer, **era**, **erum** *adj* snake-bearing

anguilla, **ae** *f* eel

anguīnus, **a**, **um** *adj* of a snake, snaky

anguis, **is** *m/f* snake, serpent; (constellation) the Dragon

angulus, **ī** *m* angle, corner, nook, out-of-the-way spot

angustiae, **ārum** *fpl* strait, defile, narrowness; want, perplexity, trouble; narrow-mindedness

angustō ① *v* make narrow, constrict, crowd together

angustus, **a**, **um** *adj* narrow, confined; scanty, poor, needy, low, mean; narrow-minded

> **❗** See note at **clāvus**.

anhēlitus, **ūs** *m* panting, puffing, breathing, breath, exhalation

anhēlō ① *v* pant, gasp, breathe out

anhēlus, **a**, **um** *adj* panting, puffing

anicula, **ae** *f* little old woman

anīlis, **e** *adj* old-womanish

anīlitās, **ātis** *f* old age (in women)

anima, **ae** *f* air, breeze, breath, soul, life

animadversiō, **ōnis** *f* observation, attention, reproach, punishment

animadvertō, **rtī**, **rsum** ③ *v* observe, attend to, remark, notice, understand, perceive; avenge, punish, blame

animal, **ālis** *nt* animal

animālis, **e** *adj* made of air, animal

animāns, **ntis** *adj* living; *m/f/nt* being, animal

animō ① *v* animate, encourage, give life to, revive

animōsus, **a**, **um** *adj* courageous, bold, strong, ardent, energetic, stormy

animula, **ae** *f* little life

animus, **ī** *m* (rational) soul, mind, will, purpose, desire, character; courage; anger; pride; pleasure, inclination; memory, judgment, consciousness, opinion; vital power, life

    ▢ **bonō animō esse** be of good heart

    ▢ **ex animō** from the heart, with sincerity

    ▢ **aequō animō** with equanimity, calmly

ann- ▸ **adn-**

annālēs, **ium** *mpl* annals, year-books

annālis, **e** *adj* relating to the year, chronicle, history

annatō ① *v* swim towards

anniversārius, **a**, **um** *adj* annual, yearly

annōn *conj* or not?

> **❗** In indirect questions, **annōn** is usu. replaced with **necne**.

annōna, **ae** *f* year's produce, provision, victuals, price of grain *or* other food

annōsus, **a**, **um** *adj* aged, old

annōtinus, **a**, **um** *adj* of last year

annus, **ī** *m* year, season, year's produce; age

annuus, **a**, **um** *adj* yearly, lasting a year

anquīrō, **sīvī**, **sītum** ③ *v* search diligently after, inquire into, examine judicially

ānsa, **ae** *f* handle; opportunity

ānser, **eris** *m/f* goose

ante *prep with acc* before, in front of; *adv* in front, before (of time), forwards

> ❗ ante is usu. only a prep. and governs the acc.; the corresponding adv. is **anteā**. However, ante may be used adverbially with the abl. expressing time at which, e.g. **paucīs ante diēbus** 'a few days earlier'.

anteā *adv* before this, formerly.

antecapiō, **cēpī**, **ceptum** ③ *v* take beforehand, anticipate

antecēdēns, **ntis** *adj* previously existent

antecēdō, **essī**, **essum** ③ *v* go before, precede; excel, surpass

antecellō ③ *v* surpass, excel

antecessiō, **ōnis** *f* going before; antecedent cause

antecursor, **ōris** *m usu in pl* leading troops, vanguard

anteeō, **īre**, **iī/īvī** *v ir* go before; surpass; anticipate; prevent

anteferō, **ferre**, **tulī**, **lātum** *v ir* carry before; prefer

antegredior, **gressus sum** ③ *v dep* go before, precede

antehāc *adv* before this time; earlier

antelūcānus, **a**, **um** *adj* before daybreak

antemerīdiānus, **a**, **um** *adj* before noon

antenna, **ae** *f* sail-yard; sail

antepīlānī, **ōrum** *mpl* men who fought in the first *or* second line

antepōnō, **posuī**, **positum** ③ *v* place before; prefer

antequam *conj* before

antēs, **ium** *mpl* rows (of plants)

antesignānus, **ī** *m* leader; *pl* troops who fought in the front rank of a legion

antestō, **stitī** ① *v with dat* surpass

antestor ① *v dep* call as a witness

anteveniō, **vēnī**, **ventum** ④ *v* come before; anticipate, forestall

antevertō, **tī**, **ersum** ③ *v* act first, precede; give priority to

anticipātiō, **ōnis** *f* preconception

anticipō ① *v* occupy beforehand; anticipate

antidotum, **ī** *nt* antidote, remedy

antiphona, **ae** *f* 🄻🄼 antiphon, psalm (sung responsively/alternately)

antīquārius, **(i)ī** *m* antiquarian, student of the past

antīquē *adv* in the old way, in an old-fashioned manner

antīquitās, **ātis** *f* antiquity, the ancients; virtue of olden time

antīquitus *adv* in former times

antīquō ① *v* reject (a bill)

antīquus, **a**, **um** *adj* old, ancient; aged; of the old stamp, simple, honest, venerable

antistes, **itis** *m/f* high-priest; chief priestess; *with gen* master (in); 🄻🄼 bishop

antistita, **ae** *f* chief priestess

antlia, **ae** *f* a mechanism for raising water, treadmill

antrum, **ī** *nt* cave, cavern

ānulārius, **(i)ī** *m* ring-maker

ānulus, **ī** *m* ring; signet-ring

ānus, **ī** *m* ring, anus

anus, **ūs** *f* old woman; sibyl; *f adj* aged, old

ānxietās, **ātis** *f* anxiety; carefulness

ānxius, **a**, **um** *adj* anxious, uneasy; disturbed; concerned; careful

apage *int* be off! get away with (you)!

aper, **prī** *m* wild boar

aperiō, **ruī**, **rtum** ④ *v* open; discover; show, explain

apertus, **a**, **um** *adj* open; public; exposed; wide, extended; cloudless; clear; frank

apex, **icis** *m* point, top, summit; cap, crown; conical cap of a priest; highest honour; 🄻🄼 *pl* letters

aphractum, **ī** *nt*, **aphractus**, **ī** *f* undecked boat

apis, **is** *f* bee

apīscor, **aptus sum** ③ *v dep* reach, obtain

apium, **(i)ī** *nt* wild celery *or* parsley

aplustre, **is** *nt* ornamented stern-port of a ship

apodȳtērium, **(i)ī** *nt* undressing-room in a bathing-house

apologus, ī *m* narrative; fable

apostolicus, **a**, **um** *adj* ⎣ᴸᴹ⎦ apostolic
■ **apostolicus**, **i** *m* pope

apostolus, **i** *m* ⎣ᴸᴹ⎦ apostle

apothēca, **ae** *f* store-house, store-room, wine-cellar

apparātus[1], **ūs** *m* preparation; provision; equipment; splendour, pomp

apparātus[2], **a**, **um** *adj* prepared, ready; splendid, sumptuous

appāreō ② *v* appear; be evident; *with dat* attend *or* serve
□ **appāret** it is clear

appāritiō, **ōnis** *f* service, attendance; servants

appāritor, **ōris** *m* (public) servant; lictor, clerk

apparō ① *v* prepare, fit out, provide; attempt

appellātiō, **ōnis** *f* appeal; calling by name; name, title; pronunciation

appellātor, **ōris** *m* appellant

appellitō ① *v* call *or* name frequently

appellō[1] ① *v* call upon; address; dun; appeal (to); bring into court; accuse; name, entitle, pronounce

appellō[2], **pulī**, **pulsum** ③ *v* drive to; bring to land; come ashore

appendix, **cis** *f* appendage; supplement

appendō, **ndī**, **ēnsum** ③ *v* weigh out

appetēns, **ntis** *adj with gen* eager for; avaricious

appetentia, **ae** *f* longing after, appetite

appetītiō, **ōnis** *f* desire; grasping (at)

appetītus, **ūs** *m* desire, appetite

appetō, **īvī/iī**, **ītum** ③ *v* seek *or* grasp after; assail; strive eagerly after, long for; approach

appingō ③ *v* paint upon; add in writing

applaudō, **sī**, **sum** ③ *v* strike together; clap; applaud

applicātiō, **ōnis** *f* application, inclination

applicātus, **a**, **um** *adj* situated close (to); devoted (to)

applicō, **cāvī/cuī**, **cātum/citum** ① *v* join to, place near; apply (to); devote (to); connect

appōnō, **posuī**, **positum** ③ *v* put *or* lay to; apply to; add to; serve up

apportō ① *v* carry, convey, bring to; cause

appositus, **a**, **um** *adj* adjacent, near; fit, appropriate

apprehendō, **ndī**, **ēnsum** ③ *v* seize, lay hold of

approbātiō, **ōnis** *f* approbation; proof; decision

approbō ① *v* approve; prove; confirm; justify; allow; make good

approperō ① *v* hasten, hurry

appropinquātiō, **ōnis** *f* approach, drawing near

appropinquō ① *v* approach, draw near

appugnō ① *v* attack, assault

appulsus, **ūs** *m* driving to; landing; approach; influence

aprīcātiō, **ōnis** *f* a basking in the sun

aprīcor ① *v dep* sun oneself

aprīcus, **a**, **um** *adj* exposed to the sun; sunny

Aprīlis, **is** *m* April

aps- ▶ abs-

aptē *adv* closely, snugly; fitly, suitably

aptō ① *v* fit, apply, put on; adjust; prepare, furnish

aptus, **a**, **um** *adj* attached to; connected, suitable, adapted; *with ex and abl* dependent (upon)

apud *prep with acc* at the house of, at, by, near, with; among; in; before; in the time of; in the works of

aput ▶ apud

aqua, **ae** *f* water; rain; sea; lake; river

aquaeductus, **ūs** *m* aqueduct

aquārius, **a**, **um** *adj* relating to water
■ **~**, **(i)ī** *m* water-carrier; overseer of the public water supply; Water-bearer (as a constellation)

aquāticus, **a**, **um** *adj* aquatic; watery, rainy

aquātiō, **ōnis** *f* fetching of water

aquātor, **ōris** *m* water-carrier

aquila, **ae** *f* eagle; standard of a Roman legion

aquilifer, **erī** *m* standard-bearer

aquilō, **ōnis** *m* north wind; north

aquilōnius, **a**, **um** *adj* northern

aquor ① *v dep* fetch water

aquōsus, **a**, **um** *adj* abounding in water, humid, rainy

āra, ae *f* altar; sanctuary; home; refuge, shelter

arabarchēs, ae *m* Egyptian tax-gatherer

arānea, ae *f* spider; cobweb

arāneōsus, a, um *adj* covered with spiders' webs

arāneus, ī *m* spider

arātiō, ōnis *f* ploughing; tilled ground

arātor, ōris *m* ploughman, farmer

arātrum, ī *nt* plough

arbiter, trī *m* eye-witness; umpire, arbiter, lord, master, governor

arbitrātus, ūs *m* arbitration; choice; pleasure, will

arbitrium, (i)ī *nt* judgment of an arbitrator; sentence; will, mastery, authority

arbitror ① *v dep* observe, perceive, pass sentence; believe, think, be of an opinion

arbor, oris *f* tree; mast; oar; ship

arboreus, a, um *adj* of *or* belonging to trees

arbuscula, ae *f* shrub; sapling

arbustum, ī *nt* copse, plantation, grove of trees; shrub

arbuteus, a, um *adj* of the strawberry tree

arbutum, ī *nt* wild strawberry; wild strawberry tree

arbutus, ī *f* wild strawberry tree

arca, ae *f* chest, strong-box, coffer; purse; coffin; prison-cell, ark

arcānum, ī *nt* secret, mystery

arcānus, a, um *adj* secret, hidden, mysterious

arceō, ī ② *v* keep off, prevent; protect

accessō, īvī/iī, ītum ③ *v* send for, call; procure; summon, accuse

archiepiscopus, i *m* [LM] archbishop

architēctōn, nis *m* architect, builder

architectūra, ae *f* architecture

architectus, ī *m* architect; inventor, designer

arcitenēns, ntis *adj* holding a bow (epithet of Apollo); (constellation) the Archer

arct- ▶ **art-**

Arctos, ī *f* the Great Bear *or* the Little Bear; the north

Arctōus, a, um *adj* northern

Arctūrus, ī *m* brightest star in the constellation Bo

arcula, ae *f* small box, casket

arcus, ūs *m* arch; bow; rainbow; anything arched *or* curved

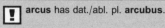

> **!** arcus has dat./abl. pl. **arcubus**.

ardaliō, ōnis *m* busybody, fusspot

ardea, ae *f* heron

ardēns, ntis *adj* burning; glowing, fiery; eager, ardent, passionate

ardeō, arsī, (arsum) ② *v* burn, blaze; flash; glow, sparkle; be inflamed; be in a turmoil

ardēscō, arsī ③ *v* take fire, kindle; be inflamed

ardor, ōris *m* fire, flame, heat; brightness; ardour, love, intensity

arduus, a, um *adj* steep, high; difficult, arduous

ārea, ae *f* open space; building site; threshing-floor; granary; courtyard; field of action

ārefaciō, fēcī, factum ③ *v* dry up

arēna, ae *f* sand; sandy land *or* desert; seashore; place of contest, amphitheatre

arēnāria, ae *f* sand-pit

arēnōsus, a, um *adj* sandy

āreō ② *v* be dry; be thirsty

ārēscō ③ *v* become dry

argentāria, ae *f* banking-house, banking business; silver-mine

argentārius, (i)ī *m* banker, financial agent

■ ~**, a, um** *adj* pertaining to silver *or* money

argentātus, a, um *adj* silvered

argenteus, a, um *adj*, **argenteolus, a, um** *adj* of silver; silvery

argentum, ī *nt* silver; silver plate; money

argilla, ae *f* white clay, potter's earth

argūmentātiō, ōnis *f* argumentation; proof

argūmentor ① *v dep* support *or* prove by argument, reason

argūmentum, ī *nt* argument, proof; subject, plot (of a play)

arguō, uī, ūtum ③ *v* prove, assert, accuse; convict; condemn

argūtātiō, **ōnis** f creaking

argūtiae, **ārum** fpl clever use of words; verbal trickery; wit

argūtus, **a**, **um** adj melodious; distinct, clear; sagacious, witty; cunning, sly; talkative, rustling, rattling

āridulus, **a**, **um** adj dry, parched

āridum, **ī** nt dry land

āridus, **a**, **um** adj dry, parched; barren; thirsty; poor; shrivelled

ariēs, **etis** m ram; battering-ram; the Ram (in the zodiac)

arietō ① v butt like a ram; strike violently

arista, **ae** f beard of an ear of grain; ear of corn; grain crop

arithmētica, **ōrum** ntpl arithmetic

āritūdō, **inis** f dryness, drought

arma, **ōrum** ntpl arms, weapons; tools; tackling; shield; soldiers, army; war; battle
   □ **vī et armīs** by force of arms

armāmenta, **ōrum** ntpl tackle of a ship

armāmentārium, **(i)ī** nt arsenal, armoury

armārium, **(i)ī** nt cabinet, cupboard; book-case

armātūra, **ae** f armour, harness; armed soldiers

armentālis, **e** adj of cattle

armentum, **ī** nt herd (of large cattle); a head of cattle

armifer, **armiger**, **era**, **erum** adj armed, warlike
   ■ ~, **erī** m armour-bearer, squire

armilla, **ae** f bracelet

armipotēns, **ntis** adj powerful in arms, valiant, warlike

armisonus, **a**, **um** adj sounding with the clash of arms

armō ① v equip; arm; kindle; incite to war; rig (a ship)

armus, **ī** m forequarter (of an animal), shoulder

arō ① v plough, till; furrow, wrinkle; produce by ploughing

arrabō, **ōnis** m down-payment, deposit, pledge

arrēpō, **psī**, **ptum** ③ v creep towards

arrīdeō, **rīsī**, **rīsum** ② v smile upon; please

arrigō, **ēxī**, **ēctum** ③ v set upright, raise; animate, rouse

arripiō, **uī**, **eptum** ③ v snatch away; take hold of; pick up (knowledge); appropriate; arrest; assail

arrōdō, **ōsī**, **ōsum** ③ v gnaw or nibble at

arrogāns, **ntis** adj arrogant

arrogantia, **ae** f arrogance, conceit

arrogō ① v ask, question; arrogate to one's self, claim; confer (upon)

ars, **tis** f skill; art; work of art; profession; theory; manner of acting; cunning, artifice

artē adv closely, tightly, briefly, in a confined space
   □ ~ **dormiō** sleep soundly

artēria, **ae** f windpipe; artery

arthrīticus, **a**, **um** adj affected with rheumatism

articulus, **ī** m joint; part; moment of time, critical moment

artifex, **icis** m artist, artificer; maker, author; adj skilful; artful

artificiōsus, **a**, **um** adj skilful; ingenious; artificial, unnatural

artificium, **(i)ī** nt handicraft, art, trade; skill; theory, system; cunning

artō ① v compress, contract; abridge, limit

artus¹, **ūs** mpl joints; limbs

artus², **a**, **um** adj close, thick, narrow; short; strict; scanty, brief

ārula, **ae** f small altar

arundineus, **a**, **um** adj of reeds; reedy

arundō, **inis** f reed; fishing rod; arrow-shaft; arrow; pen; shepherd's pipe

arvīna, **ae** f fat, lard

arvum, **ī** nt arable field; country; dry land; stretch of plain

arvus, **a**, **um** adj arable

arx, **cis** f stronghold, citadel; the Capitoline hill at Rome; defence, refuge

ās, **assis** m a copper coin of small value

ascendō, **ndī**, **ēnsum** ③ v mount up, ascend

ascēnsiō, **ōnis** f ascent; progress, advancement

ascēnsus, **ūs** m ascending, ascent; approach; a stage in advancement

asciō ④ v take to, associate, admit, take on as staff

ascīscō, scīvī, scītum ③ *v* receive, admit, approve of, associate; appropriate, adopt

ascrībō, psī, ptum ③ *v* add in writing; ascribe, impute; appoint; enrol; reckon, number

asella, ae *f* she-ass

asellus, ī *m* ass, donkey

asīlus, ī *m* gadfly

asinus, ī *m* ass; blockhead

asōtus, ī *m* debauchee

aspectō ① *v* look *or* gaze at; observe; (of places) look towards

aspectus, ūs *m* looking at, glance, view; sight; horizon; appearance; aspect, mien

asper, era, erum *adj* rough; uneven; harsh, sour; bitter; rude, violent, unkind, savage; wayward; austere; wild, fierce; critical, adverse

aspergō¹, rsī, rsum ③ *v* besprinkle; defile, stain

aspergō², inis *f* besprinkling; spray

asperitās, ātis *f* roughness; severity; harshness; tartness; shrillness; fierceness

aspernor ① *v dep* despise

asperō ① *v* make rough; sharpen; make fierce, violent

aspersiō, ōnis *f* sprinkling

aspiciō, xī, ectum ③ *v* look at, behold; (of places) look towards; consider, contemplate

aspīrātiō, ōnis *f* exhalation; aspiration; sounding an 'h'

aspīrō ① *v* breathe *or* blow upon; infuse; be favourable to; assist; aspire to

aspis, idis *f* asp

asportātiō, ōnis *f* carrying away

asportō ① *v* carry away, remove

asprētum, ī *nt* rough ground

assa, ōrum *ntpl* sweating bath

assecla ▸ assecula

assectātiō, ōnis *f* waiting on, attendance

assectātor, ōris *m* follower, companion; disciple

assector ① *v dep* accompany, attend; support

assec(u)la, ae *m* attendant, servant; hanger-on, sycophant

assēnsiō, ōnis *f* assent, applause

assēnsor, ōris *m* one who agrees or approves

assēnsus, ūs *m* assent, approbation, applause

assentātiō, ōnis *f* flattering agreement, toadyism

assentātor, ōris *m* flatterer, 'yes-man'

assentātrīx, īcis *f* female flatterer

assentior, sēnsus sum ④ *v dep* assent to, approve, comply with

assentor ① *v dep* agree completely with; flatter

assequor, secūtus sum ③ *v dep* follow on, pursue; overtake; gain, attain to; equal, rival; understand

asser, eris *m* pole, post, stake

asserō, ruī, rtum ③ *v* assert; free; claim

assertor, ōris *m* restorer of liberty; protector, advocate; champion

asservō ① *v* keep, preserve, watch, observe

assessor, ōris *m* assessor, counsellor

assevēranter *adv* earnestly, emphatically

assevērātiō, ōnis *f* affirmation, asseveration; seriousness

assevērō ① *v* act with earnestness; assert strongly

assideō, sēdī, sessum ② *v* sit by; be an assessor; besiege; *with dat* resemble

assīdō, sēdī ③ *v* sit down

assiduē *adv* continually, constantly

assiduitās, ātis *f* attendance; assiduity, care; recurrence, repetition

assiduō ▸ assiduē

assiduus, a, um *adj* assiduous; continual, unremitting

assignātiō, ōnis *f* distribution *or* allotment of land; plot of land

assignō ① *v* assign; impute

assiliō, siluī, sultum ④ *v* leap up, rush (at)

assimilis, e *adj* similar, like

assimulō ① *v* make like; compare; counterfeit, pretend, feign

assistō, stitī ③ *v* stand at *or* by, attend, be present at; make a stand

assoleō ② *v* be accustomed *or* in the habit of

assuēfaciō, fēcī, factum ③ *v* accustom (to)

assuēscō, ēvī, ētum ③ *v* accustom (to); become accustomed

assuētūdō, inis *f* custom, habit; intimacy

assuētus, a, um *adj* accustomed, customary, usual

assula, ae *f* splinter, chip (of wood *or* stone)

assultō ① *v* jump at; attack

assultus, ūs *m* attack, assault

assūmō, mpsī, mptum ③ *v* take up, adopt, receive; add to; usurp, arrogate

assūmptiō, ōnis *f* adoption; minor premiss

assuō ③ *v* sew *or* patch on

assurgō, surrēxī, surrēctum ③ *v* claim, rise *or* stand up; rise, soar

assus, a, um *adj* roasted; dry

ast ▸ **at**

asternō ③ *v* prostrate oneself, lie prone (on)

astō, stitī ① *v* stand at *or* by; assist; stand upright

astrepō, puī ③ *v* make a noise at, shout in support

astrictus, a, um *adj* bound by rules; terse, brief; parsimonious

astringō, īnxī, ictum ③ *v* tighten, bind, fasten; oblige, contract

astrologia, ae *f* astronomy, astrology

astrologus, ī *m* astronomer, astrologer

astrum, ī *nt* star, constellation; sky

astruō, ūxī, ūctum ③ *v* build on; add to; ⌊LM⌋ affirm, declare

astupeō ② *v* be stunned *or* astonished (at)

āstus, ūs *m* craft, cunning, trick

āstūtia, ae *f* cunning, slyness, trick

āstūtus, a, um *adj* clever, expert; sly, cunning

asylum, ī *nt* place of refuge, sanctuary

asymbolus, a, um *adj* making no contribution; scot-free

at *conj* (also **ast**) but, yet; but then; on the contrary; at least

atat *int* ah!

atavus, ī *m* great-great-great-grandfather; ancestor

āter, tra, trum *adj* black; gloomy, dismal, unlucky

āthlēta, ae *m* wrestler, athlete

atomus, ī *f* atom

atque *conj* and, and also, and even, and too; yet, nevertheless; *after words expressing comparison* as, than

> **!** atque, a variant form of ac, is usu. found before words beginning with a vowel or 'h', rarely before consonants.

atquī *conj* but, yet, notwithstanding, however, rather; but now; and yet; well now

ātrāmentum, ī *nt* writing-ink; blacking

ātrātus, a, um *adj* darkened; wearing mourning

ātriēnsis, is *m* steward

ātriolum, ī *nt* small ante-room

ātrium, (i)ī *nt* hall in a Roman house; palace; ⌊LM⌋ graveyard

atrōcitās, ātis *f* fierceness; savageness, cruelty; severity

atrōciter *adv* savagely, cruelly, fiercely, severely

atrōx, ōcis *adj* savage, cruel, fierce, severe

attāctus, ūs *m* touch

attamen *adv* but yet, but however, nevertheless

attat ▸ **atat**

attendō, ndī, ntum ③ *v* turn towards; apply; attend to, listen carefully

attentē *adv* diligently, carefully

attentiō, ōnis *f* attention

attentō ① *v* try, attempt; assail, attack

attentus, a, um *adj* attentive; careful

attenuō ① *v* thin, weaken, lessen, diminish

atterō, trīvī, trītum ③ *v* rub against; wear out, impair

Atticē *adv* in the Attic manner; elegantly

Atticus, a, um *adj* Attic, Athenian; classic, elegant

attineō, tentum ② *v* hold on *or* fast; delay; belong (to), concern, relate to

attingō, tigī, tāctum ③ *v* touch; arrive at; border upon; affect; mention in passing; achieve, win; relate to; treat in hostile manner

attollō ③ *v* lift up; erect, build; exalt; extol

attondeō, **ndī**, **ōnsum** ② *v* clip, prune

attonitus, **a**, **um** *adj* thunder-struck; stupefied, amazed; inspired, frenzied

attonō, **nuī**, **nitum** ① *v* strike with lightning; drive crazy

attorqueō ② *v* whirl at

attrahō, **āxī**, **actum** ③ *v* attract; drag on

attrectō ① *v* touch, handle; deal with

attribuō, **uī**, **ūtum** ③ *v* assign; attribute *or* impute to

attribūtiō, **ōnis** *f* assignment of a debt; attribution of a quality

au *int* oh! ow! oh dear!

auceps, **cupis** *m* bird-catcher; bird-seller

auctificus, **a**, **um** *adj* giving increase

auctiō, **ōnis** *f* public sale, auction

auctiōnārius, **a**, **um** *adj* pertaining to an auction

auctiōnor ① *v dep* put up to public sale

auctō ① *v* increase

auctor, **ōris** *m/f* creator, maker, inventor; father; teacher; leader; founder, author; promoter; adviser; protector; witness; vendor; bail; guardian, champion

auctōrāmentum, **ī** *nt* wages, pay; reward

auctōritās, **ātis** *f* authority, power; reputation, credit; opinion, judgment; command; influence, importance; credibility

auctōror ① *v dep* bind oneself, hire oneself

auctus, **ūs** *m* growth, increase, bulk

aucupium, **(i)ī** *nt* bird-catching; game birds

aucupor ① *v dep* go bird-catching; lie in wait for

audācia, **ae** *f* boldness; courage, valour; audacity

audāc(i)ter *adv* boldly, courageously

audāx, **ācis** *adj* bold, courageous, audacious; foolhardy, rash; desperate

audēns, **ntis** *adj* daring, bold

audentia, **ae** *f* boldness, courage

audeō, **audēre**, **ausus sum** ② *v semi-dep* dare, venture

audientia, **ae** *f* hearing; audience, attention

audiō ④ *v* hear; listen, hearken; regard; grant; obey

audītiō, **ōnis** *f* hearing; report, hearsay

audītor, **ōris** *m* hearer, auditor; disciple

audītōrium, **(i)ī** *nt* lecture-room, audience

audītus, **ūs** *m* hearing; listening; sense of hearing; hearsay

auferō, **auferre**, **abstulī**, **ablātum** *v ir* bear away; snatch away; carry off; obtain; destroy

aufugiō, **fūgī** ③ *v* flee away *or* from

augeō, **auxī**, **auctum** ② *v* increase, augment; make a lot of

augēscō ③ *v* grow, become greater

augmen, **inis** *nt* growth, increase, bulk

augur, **uris** *m/f* augur; soothsayer

! **augurēs** formed one of the four great Roman colleges of priests. They were responsible for the observation and application of the auspices (**auspicium**).

---

augurālis, **e** *adj* pertaining to augurs, relating to soothsaying
■ **augurāle**, **is** *nt* place of augury, commander's hut

augurātiō, **ōnis** *f* prediction by means of augury

augurātō *adv* after taking the auguries

augurātus, **ūs** *m* office of an augur; augury

augurium, **(i)ī** *nt* profession of an augur, soothsaying, prediction

auguror ① *v dep* act as augur; foretell; conjecture, speculate

Augustus[1], **ī** *m* August (month)

augustus[2], **a**, **um** *adj* sacred, venerable; majestic, august

aula, **ae** *f* inner court of a house; hall; palace; royal court; courtiers

aulaeum, **ī** *nt* curtain of a theatre; canopy; tapestry

aura, **ae** *f* air, gentle breeze; breath; wind; gleam, glittering; odour, exhalation
◻ ~ **populāris** the breath of popular favour

aurātus, **a**, **um** *adj* gilt, golden

aureolus, **a**, **um** *adj* golden, splendid

aureus, **a**, **um** *adj* golden; gilded; shining like gold; beautiful
◻ **mīliārium aureum** golden milestone erected by Augustus at the head of the forum in Rome, from which all distances were reckoned

auricomus, **a**, **um** *adj* golden-haired

auricula, **ae** *f* ear

aurifer, **era**, **erum** *adj* gold-bearing

aurifex, **icis** *m* goldsmith

aurīga, **ae** *m* charioteer; helmsman; (constellation) the Wagoner; groom

auris, **is** *f* ear; hearing

aurītus, **a**, **um** *adj* hearing well; long-eared

aurōra, **ae** *f* dawn, daybreak

aurum, **ī** *nt* gold

auscultō ① *v* listen to; overhear; obey

ausim *subj* from ▶ **audeō**

auspex, **icis** *m* diviner by birds; soothsayer; patron, supporter

auspicātō *adv* after taking the auspices; auspiciously

auspicātus, **a**, **um** *adj* consecrated by auguries; favourable, auspicious

auspicium, **(i)ī** *nt* auspices; the right of taking auspices; leadership, authority; sign, omen

❗ The auspices refer to the consultation of the gods by the **augurēs** through such signs as thunder and lightning, the flight and general behaviour of birds, including the sacred chickens, and from unusual behaviour of quadrupeds.

auspicor ① *v dep* take the auspices

auster, **trī** *m* south wind; south

austēritās, **ātis** *f* harshness; gloominess; severity

austērus, **a**, **um** *adj* austere; harsh; sour; sharp; rough, dark, stern; unornamented

austrālis, **e** *adj* southern

austrīnus, **a**, **um** *adj* southern

ausum, **ī** *nt* daring attempt, enterprise; crime, outrage

ausus *pple* from ▶ **audeō**

aut *conj* or; or else, either

❗ **aut** ... **aut** is used where one alternative excludes the other(s), i.e. 'X or Y but not both'; cf. **vel**.

autem *conj* but; however; indeed; on the contrary

autumnālis, **e** *adj* autumnal

autumnus, **ī** *m* autumn

autumō ① *v* say yes, affirm; say, mention

auxiliāris, **e** *adj* help-bringing, auxiliary

auxiliārius, **a**, **um** *adj* helping, auxiliary

auxilior ① *v dep* give aid; *with dat* assist

auxilium, **(i)ī** *nt* help, aid, assistance
■ **auxilia**, **ōrum** *ntpl* auxiliary contingents

avāritia, **ae** *f* avarice, rapacity, miserliness

avārus, **a**, **um** *adj* avaricious, covetous, stingy

avē *int* greetings!

āvehō, **ēxī**, **ectum** ③ *v* carry away
◻ **avehor** ride away, go away

āvellō, **vellī/vulsī**, **vulsum** ③ *v* pluck away, tear off; separate by force

avēna, **ae** *f* oats; wild oats; stem, stalk, straw; oaten pipe, pan pipes

aveō ② *v* be eager *or* anxious; desire

āverruncō ① *v* avert (something bad)

āversor¹ ① *v dep* turn oneself away in disgust *or* horror; avoid, refuse; reject

āversor², **ōris** *m* embezzler

āversus, **a**, **um** *adj* turned away; averse; hostile

āvertō, **rtī**, **rsum** ③ *v* turn away from *or* aside; steal, misappropriate; divert, estrange

avia, **ae** *f* grandmother

aviārium, **(i)ī** *nt* haunt of wild birds; aviary

aviditās, **ātis** *f* covetousness, greed; ardent desire, lust

avidus, **a**, **um** *adj* eager, greedy; avaricious; lustful

avis, **is** *f* bird; omen, portent

avītus, **a**, **um** *adj* ancestral; of a grandfather

āvius, **a**, **um** *adj* out of the way; pathless; straying
■ **āvia**, **ōrum** *ntpl* remote places

āvocō ① *v* call away; remove; divert the mind

āvolō ① *v* fly away; hasten away

avunculus, **ī** *m* (maternal) uncle *or* great-uncle

avus, **ī** *m* grandfather; ancestor

axis, **is** *m* axle; chariot; axis (of the earth); north pole; heaven; sky; region, clime; board, plank

axulus, **ī** *m* plank, board

Bb

babae *int* hey!

bāca, **ae** *f* (also **bacca**) berry; olive-berry; pearl

bācātus, **a**, **um** *adj* set with pearls

baccar, **aris** *nt* an aromatic root

Baccha, **ae** *f* (also **Bacchē**) a votary of Bacchus

Bacchānālia, **ium** *ntpl* Bacchanalian orgies, feast of Bacchus

Bacchantēs, **ntum** *fpl* votaries of Bacchus

Bacchēus, **a**, **um** *adj*, **Bacchicus**, **a**, **um** *adj* Bacchic

bacchor ① *v dep* celebrate the rites of Bacchus; revel, rave; riot, run wild

bācifer, **era**, **erum** *adj* berry-bearing

bacillum, **ī** *nt* little staff; lictor's staff

baculum, **ī** *nt* stick, walking-stick, lictor's staff

bāiulus, **ī** *m* porter, carrier

bālaena, **ae** *f* whale

balanus, **ī** *f* acorn; balsam; shell-fish

balatrō, **ōnis** *m* buffoon, joker

bālātus, **ūs** *m* bleating of sheep

balbus, **a**, **um** *adj* stammering, stuttering

balbūtiō ④ *v* stammer, stutter; speak obscurely, babble

ballaena ▶ **bālaena**

bal(i)neārius, **a**, **um** *adj* pertaining to baths

bal(i)neātor, **ōris** *m* bath-attendant

bālō ① *v* bleat, baa

balsamum, **ī** *nt* balsam-tree, balm

balteus, **ī** *m* belt, sword-belt, baldric; woman's girdle

baptisma, **atis** *nt* LM baptism

barathrum, **ī** *nt* abyss, chasm; the infernal region

barba, **ae** *f* beard

barbaria, **ae** *f*, **barbariēs**, **iēī** *f* foreign country; barbarousness; barbarism (in language); brutality

barbaricus, **a**, **um** *adj* outlandish; barbarous

barbarus, **a**, **um** *adj* foreign, barbarous; uncivilized; cruel, savage
■ ~, **ī** *m* foreigner, barbarian

barbātulus, **a**, **um** *adj* having a small beard

barbātus, **a**, **um** *adj* bearded; adult
■ ~, **ī** *m* ancient Roman, philosopher

barbitos, **ī** (*acc* **ton**, *voc* **te**) *m/f* lyre

barbula, **ae** *f* little beard

bārō, **ōnis** *m* block-head, lout

barrus, **ī** *m* elephant

bāsiātiō, **ōnis** *f* a kiss

basilica, **ae** *f* oblong hall with double colonnade used for a law-court and as an exchange; LM church

basiliscus, **ī** *m* basilisk

bāsiō ① *v* kiss

basis, **is** *f* pedestal; base; foundation

bāsium, **(i)ī** *nt* a kiss

beātitās, **ātis** *f*, **beātitūdō**, **inis** *f* supreme happiness, blessedness

beātus, **a**, **um** *adj* happy, blessed; wealthy; abundant

bellātor, **ōris** *m* warrior; *adj* warlike

bellātrīx, **īcis** *f* female warrior

belliātus, **a**, **um** *adj* pretty, beautiful

bellicōsus, **a**, **um** *adj* fond of war, warlike

bellicus, **a**, **um** *adj* of *or* belonging to war, military; warlike

belliger, **era**, **erum** *adj* waging war, martial

belligerō ① *v* wage *or* carry on war

bellipotēns, **ntis** *adj* powerful in war

bellō ① *v*, **bellor** ① *v dep* wage war, fight

bellum, **ī** *nt* war; combat, fight
□ **bellī** *loc used as adv* at the wars

bellus, **a**, **um** *adj* handsome, pretty, neat, agreeable, polite

bēlua, **ae** *f* beast; monster; brute; fool, idiot

bēluōsus, **a**, **um** *adj* abounding in beasts *or* monsters

bene *adv* well, rightly, beautifully, pleasantly; opportunely

benedīcō, **īxī**, **ictum** ③ *v with dat* speak well of; speak kindly to; ⅬⅯ *with acc or dat* bless

benedictio, **onis** *f* ⅬⅯ blessing, benediction

benedictum, **ī** *nt* kind word

benefactum, **ī** *nt* good deed

beneficentia, **ae** *f* beneficence, kindness

beneficiāriī, **ōrum** *mpl* soldiers exempted from certain military services

beneficium, **(i)ī** *nt* benefit, kindness; favour, help; ⅬⅯ benefice

beneficus, **a**, **um** *adj* beneficent, kind

benevolēns, **ntis** *adj* benevolent, well-wishing, kind-hearted

benevolentia, **ae** *f* benevolence, goodwill, kindness, favour

benevolus, **a**, **um** *adj* well-wishing, kind, friendly, devoted

benignitās, **ātis** *f* good-heartedness, kindness, liberality, bounty

benignus, **a**, **um** *adj* kind-hearted, mild, affable; liberal, bounteous; fruitful

beō ① *v* make happy, bless

bēs, **bessis** *m* two-thirds of any whole

bēstia, **ae** *f* beast; wild beast

bēstiārius, **(i)ī** *m* fighter with wild beasts at public shows

bēstiola, **ae** *f* little creature, insect

bēta, **ae** *f* beet; beetroot

betulla, **ae** *f* birch tree

bibliothēca, **ae** *f* library

biblus, **i** *m* ⅬⅯ book

bibō, **bibī**, **—** ③ *v* drink; imbibe; absorb, suck up; drink in; get drunk

bibulus, **a**, **um** *adj* fond of drinking, ever thirsty; soaking, spongy

biceps, **itis** *adj* two-headed; with two summits

bicolor, **ōris** *adj* of two colours

bicorniger, **ī** *adj* the two-horned (god), epithet of Bacchus

bicornis, **e** *adj* two-horned; two-pronged

bidēns¹, **ntis** *adj* two-pronged

bidēns², **ntis** *m/f* sheep; two-pronged hoe

bīduum, **ī** *nt* period of two days

biennium, **(i)ī** *nt* period of two years

bifāriam *adv* in two parts; in two ways

bifer, **era**, **erum** *adj* bearing fruit or flowers twice a year

bifidus, **a**, **um** *adj* cloven, forked

biforis, **e** *adj* having two leaves *or* casements; from a double pipe

biförmis, **e** *adj* two-shaped

bifrōns, **ntis** *adj* with two faces

bifurcus, **a**, **um** *adj* two-forked

bīga, **ae** *f* often pl in form two-horsed chariot; pair of horses

bīgātus, **ī** *m* a piece of money stamped with a representation of the bigae

biiugis, **e** *adj*, **biiugus**, **a**, **um** *adj* two-horsed

bilībris, **bre** *adj* weighing two pounds

bilinguis, **e** *adj* two-tongued; speaking two languages; double-tongued, treacherous

bīlis, **is** *f* gall, bile; wrath, anger; madness, folly

bilūstris, **tre** *adj* lasting two lustres, lasting ten years

bimaris, **e** *adj* situated between two seas

bimembris, **bre** *adj* having limbs of two kinds, part man part beast

bimestris, **tre** *adj* two months old; lasting two months

bīmus, **a**, **um** *adj* two years old; for two years

bīnī, **ae**, **a** *adj* two by two; two each

bipatēns, **ntis** *adj* opening two ways; wide open

bipedālis, **e** *adj* two feet long, wide *or* thick

bipennifer, **era**, **erum** *adj* bearing a two-edged axe

bipennis, **e** *adj* two-edged
■ ~, **is** *f* two-edged axe

bipertītō *adv* in two parts *or* divisions

bipēs, **edis** *adj* two-footed

birēmis, **is** *f* ship with two banks of oars

bis *adv* twice

bisanteus, **ei** *m* ⃞LM bezant, gold coin

bisulcus, **a**, **um** *adj* forked; cloven-footed

bitūmen, **inis** *nt* bitumen, pitch, asphalt

bivium, **(i)ī** *nt* a meeting-place of two roads

bivius, **a**, **um** *adj* traversable both ways

blaesus, **a**, **um** *adj* mispronouncing one's words through a speech defect, drunkenness, *etc.*, stammering

blandīmentum, **ī** *nt* blandishment, flattery, charms

blandior ④ *v dep* flatter, coax; allure; please

blanditia, **ae** *f* flattering, compliment; *pl* flatteries, courtship, blandishment

blandus, **a**, **um** *adj* flattering; pleasant, alluring, charming, gentle

blatta, **ae** *f* cockroach; moth

boārius, **a**, **um** *adj* of oxen
□ **forum boārium** the cattle market at Rome

bōlētus, **ī** *m* mushroom

bolus, **ī** *m* a throw at dice; what is caught in a fishing net, a haul; profit, gain

bombus, **ī** *m* buzzing, booming

bonitās, **ātis** *f* goodness; kindness, benevolence

bonum, **ī** *nt* good; wealth, goods; benefit; advantage; profit; endowment, virtue
□ **summum** ~ the supreme good (philosophical term)

bonus, **a**, **um** *adj* good; kind; beautiful; pleasant; right; useful; considerable; rich; virtuous; promising, happy; favourable; high, honourable

boō ① *v* cry aloud, roar; call loudly upon

boreās, **ae** *m* north wind

borēus, **a**, **um** *adj* northern

bōs, **bovis** *m*/*f* ox, bull; cow

bovārius ▶ **boārius**

brācae, **ārum** *fpl* trousers, breeches

brācātus, **a**, **um** *adj* breeched

bracchium, **brāchium**, **(i)ī** *nt* arm; fore-arm; claw; branch, shoot; earthwork connecting fortified points; yard-arm

bracchiolum, **brāchiolum**, **ī** *nt* a little arm

bractea, **brattea**, **ae** *f* thin sheet of gold metal

bravium, **(i)i** *nt* ⃞LM prize

brevi *adv* briefly, in a few words

breviloquentia, **ae** *f* brevity of speech

brevis, **e** *adj* short, little, brief; small; concise; shallow
□ **(in) brevi** soon

brevitās, **ātis** *f* shortness; smallness; brevity

breviter *adv* shortly, briefly

brūma, **ae** *f* winter solstice; winter

brūmālis, **e** *adj* wintry

brūtus, **a**, **um** *adj* heavy, unwieldy; dull, stupid

būbō, **ōnis** *m* horned *or* eagle owl

bubulcitō ① *v*, **bubulcitor** ① *v dep* take care of *or* drive cattle; be a farm labourer

bubulcus, **ī** *m* ploughman, farm-labourer

būbulus, **a**, **um** *adj* of cattle *or* oxen; rawhide, oxhide

būbus *dat*/*abl pl* of ▶ **bōs**

būcaeda, **ae** *m* ox-slaughterer; one beaten with oxhide whips

bucca, **ae** *f* cheek

buccula, **ae** *f* little cheek; cheek-piece of a helmet

būcerus, **a**, **um** *adj* ox-horned

būcina, **ae** *f* trumpet; war-trumpet; watch-horn

būcinātor, **ōris** *m* trumpeter; proclaimer

būcolicus, **a**, **um** *adj* pastoral, bucolic

būcula, **ae** *f* heifer

būfō, **ōnis** *m* toad

bulbus, **ī** *m* bulb; onion

bulla, **ae** *f* bubble; boss, knob, stud; locket hung round the necks of children

burgenses, **ium** *mpl* LM townspeople

bustum, **ī** *nt* pyre, tomb

būteō, **ōnis** *m* a species of hawk

būtŷrum, **ī** *nt* butter

buxifer, **era**, **erum** *adj* bearing box-trees

buxum, **ī** *nt* box-wood; top; flute

buxus, **ī** *f* evergreen box-tree; box-wood; (poet) flute

Cc

caballus, **ī** *m* horse, riding horse, pack-horse

cacabus, **ī** *m* cooking-pot

cacātus, **a**, **um** *nt* voided as excrement

cac(c)hin(n)ātiō, **ōnis** *f* immoderate *or* boisterous laughter, guffawing

cac(c)hin(n)ō ① *v* laugh loudly *or* boisterously, guffaw; laugh loudly at

cac(c)hin(n)us, **ī** laugh, guffaw

cacūmen, **inis** *nt* tip, end; peak, summit

cacūminō ① *v* make pointed *or* tapered

cadāver, **eris** *nt* dead body, corpse

cadō, **cecidī**, **cāsum** ③ *v* fall (down, from); be slain; abate, decay; happen; end, close; fall through, fail

cādūceum, **ī** *nt*, **cādūceus**, **ī** *m* herald's staff; wand of Mercury

cādūcifer, **era**, **erum** *adj* staff-bearer ■ ~, **erī** *m* Mercury

cadūcus, **a**, **um** *adj* ready to fall; tottering, falling, fallen; frail, perishable, vain

cadus, **ī** *m* large jar for wine, jar; funeral urn

caecitās, **ātis** *f* blindness

caecō ① *v* blind; obscure; make morally blind

caecus, **a**, **um** *adj* blind; obscure; hidden, secret; confused; rash; vain, uncertain; dark, gloomy

caedēs, **dis** *f* felling; slaughter; murder; persons slain; blood, gore

caedō, **cecīdī**, **caesum** ③ *v* fell, hew; cut; slaughter; murder

caelātor, **ōrls** *m* engraver, worker in bas-relief

caelātūra, **ae** *f* engraving

caelebs, **ibis** *adj* unmarried, single, widowed

caeles, **itis** *adj* heavenly ■ ~, **itis** *m* a god

caelestis, **e** *adj* heavenly; divine; god-like ■ **caelestēs**, **um** *m*/*fpl* the gods

caelicola, **ae** *m*/*f* inhabitant of heaven

caelifer, **era**, **erum** *adj* supporting the sky

caelō ① *v* engrave, chase

caelum[1], **ī** *nt* heaven; sky; climate, weather

caelum[2], **ī** *nt* graving-tool, chisel

caementarius, **(i)i** *m* LM mason

caementum, **ī** *nt* small stones, rubble (used in concrete)

caenum, **ī** *nt* mud, filth; (of persons) scum

caepa, **ae** *f*, **caepe**, **is** *nt* onion

caerimōnia, **ae** *f* ritual; reverence, worship; sanctity

caesariēs, **iēī** *f* long, flowing *or* luxuriant hair

caesim *adv* by cutting; with the edge of the sword; in short clauses

caesiō, **ōnis** *f* hewing *or* cutting down of trees

caespes, **itis** *m* turf, sod, grassy ground; altar

caestus, **ūs** *m* boxing-glove

calamister, **trī** *m* curling-tongs

calamistrātus, **a**, **um** *adj* curled with the curling-iron

calamitās, **ātis** *f* disaster, ruin, misfortune; defeat

calamitōsus, **a**, **um** *adj* calamitous; miserable; ruinous; damaged

C

calamus, **ī** *m* reed, cane; reed-pen; reed-pipe; arrow; angling-rod; stalk

calathus, **ī** *m* wicker basket, flower basket; wine-cup; vessel for cheese *or* curdled milk

calātor, **ōris** *m* servant, attendant

calcar, **āris** *nt* spur

calceō [1] *v* put shoes on

calceus, **ī** *m* shoe

calciō ▶ **calceō**

calcitrātus, **ūs** *m* kicking with the heels

calcitrō [1] *v* kick with the heels; be refractory

calcō [1] *v* tread under foot; trample upon, spurn, despise

calculus, **ī** *m* pebble, stone used for reckoning; reckoning, calculation

caldārium, **(i)ī** *nt* hot-bath

calefaciō, **fēcī**, **factum** [3] *v* warm, heat; excite

caleō [2] *v* be warm *or* hot, be flushed; be in love; be excited

calēscō [3] *v* grow warm *or* hot; become inflamed

caliga, **ae** *f* soldier's boot

cālīginōsus, **a**, **um** *adj* foggy, misty

cālīgō¹ [1] *v* be dark

cālīgō², **inis** *f* mist; darkness, gloom; moral *or* intellectual darkness

calix, **cis** *m* cup, goblet; [LM] chalice

calleō [2] *v* have experience *or* skill in, know; know how to

calliditās, **ātis** *f* shrewdness, skilfulness; slyness

callidus, **a**, **um** *adj* expert, skilful; crafty, sly

callis, **is** *m* rough track, path; pasturage

callum, **ī** *nt* hardened skin, hide; callousness; lack of feeling

cālō, **ōnis** *m* soldier's servant

calor, **ōris** *m* warmth, heat; passion, zeal, ardour; love

calt(h)a, **ae** *f* marigold

calumnia, **ae** *f* sophistry; false accusation, false claim

calumniātor, **ōris** *m* false accuser, pettifogger

calumnior [1] *v dep* contrive false accusations; depreciate, find fault with

calvitium, **(i)ī** *nt* baldness

calvus, **a**, **um** *adj* bald

calx¹, **cis** *f* heel

calx², **cis** *f* chalk, limestone, goal (because the goal-line was marked with chalk)

camēlus, **ī** *m* camel, dromedary

Camēna, **ae** *f* Muse; poetry

camera, **ae** *f* [LM] room, chamber

camīnus, **ī** *m* smelting furnace, forge; domestic stove

campanum, **i** *nt* [LM] bell

campester, **tris**, **tre** *adj* flat, level, open; of the Campus Martius

campestre, **is** *nt* loin-cloth worn by athletes

campus, **ī** *m* plain, field; field of battle; level surface; place for games, exercise, *etc.*; field of action; expanse of water, sea

□ **Campus Martius** an open space by the side of the Tiber at Rome

canālis, **is** *m/f* channel, conduit, canal

cancellarius, **(i)ī** *m* [LM] chancellor

cancellī, **ōrum** *mpl* railing, lattice; barrier; boundaries, limits

cancer, **crī** *m* crab; Cancer, the sign of the zodiac; cancer

candefaciō, **fēcī**, **factum** [3] *v* make white; make hot

candēla, **ae** *f* candle; waxed cord

candēlābrum, **ī** *nt* stand for candles, candelabrum

candeō [2] *v* be of brilliant whiteness, shine; become *or* be hot

candēscō, **duī** [3] *v* grow light; grow white; become hot

candidātus, **ī** *m* candidate; aspirant

candidus, **a**, **um** *adj* dazzling white, clear, bright; clean, spotless; candid, frank; lucky; fair-skinned

candor, **ōris** *m* dazzling whiteness, brightness; beauty; candour; kindness, moral purity

cāneō [2] *v* be hoary, be white

cānēscō [3] *v* grow hoary; grow old, be white

canīcula, **ae** *f* bitch; dog-star, dog-days

canīnus, **a**, **um** *adj* canine; abusive, snarling

canis, is *m/f* dog; hound; subordinate, 'jackal'; dog-star; the lowest throw at dice

canistrum, ī *nt* wicker basket

cānitiēs, iēī *f* white or grey colouring; grey hair; old age

canna, ae *f* reed, cane; reed-pipe

canō, **cecinī**, **cantum** ③ *v* sing; crow; sound, play (an instrument); recite; celebrate in song *or* poetry; prophesy; blow (signals); sound (for a retreat)

canor, ōris *m* song, music, tune

canōrus, a, **um** *adj* melodious, harmonious

cantharis, idis *f* blister-beetle; Spanish fly (used in medicine and as a poison)

cantharus, ī *m* large drinking vessel with handles

cant(h)ērius, (i)ī *m* poor-quality horse, gelding

canticum, ī *nt* song; passage in a comedy chanted or sung; ⎣ᴍ⎦ canticle

cantilēna, ae *f* refrain; little song; ditty

cantiō, ōnis *f* incantation, spell

cantitō ① *v* sing over and over

cantō ① *v* sing; play, recite; praise; forewarn; enchant; bewitch

cantor, ōris *m* singer; poet; eulogist

cantus, ūs *m* song, poem; singing; melody; prophecy; incantation

cānus, a, **um** *adj* white, hoary, grey; foamy; old, aged

capācitās, ātis *f* capacity, largeness

capāx, ācis *adj* spacious, roomy; capable

capella, ae *f* she-goat; kid

caper, prī *m* he-goat

capessō, īvī/iī, ītum ③ *v* seize eagerly; manage; undertake; pursue with zeal

capillātus, a, **um** *adj* having long hair

capillus, ī *m* hair of the head; hair

capiō, **cēpī**, **captum** ③ *v* take, seize; capture, occupy; get, obtain; captivate, win over; make choice of; find out; understand; choose, select; undertake

◻ **cōnsilium** ∼ decide, resolve, have an idea; deliberate, take counsel

capistrum, ī *nt* halter

capitāl, is *nt* (also **capitāle**) capital crime *or* the punishment due to it

capitālis, e *adj* belonging to the head *or* life; deadly, mortal; dangerous; excellent, first-rate

Capitōlium, (i)ī *nt* the Capitoline hill at Rome

capitulare, is *nt* ⎣ᴍ⎦ order, rescript

capra, ae *f* she-goat

caprea, ae *f* roe-deer

capreolus, ī *m* a young roebuck; rafter

caprigenus, a, **um** *adj* of goats

caprimulgus, ī *m* country bumpkin; nightjar

capripēs, edis *adj* goat-footed

capsa, ae *f* cylindrical case (for books)

capsula, ae *f* small box for books; chest

captātor, ōris *m* legacy hunter; one who strives to obtain

captiō, ōnis *f* deception, fraud; disadvantage; a piece of sophistry

captiōsus, a, **um** *adj* harmful, disadvantageous, captious

captīvitās, ātis *f* captivity; capture

captīvus, a, **um** *adj* taken prisoner (in war, as booty); of captives
■ ∼, ī *m* prisoner, captive

captō ① *v* snatch, endeavour to catch; strive after; hunt legacies; ensnare

captus, ūs *m* capacity, ability, potentiality

capulus, ī *m* handle; sword-hilt

caput, itis *nt* head; top; end; source; beginning; principal point; mouth (of a river); article, chapter; life; person; civil rights; intelligence; author, leader, chief; capital city; capital as opposed to interest

carbasus, ī *f*, (in pl **carbasa**, ōrum *nt*) linen; sail; linen garment; awning

carbaseus, a, **um** *adj* made of linen

carbō, ōnis *m* charcoal; glowing coal

carbunculus, ī *m* (live) coal

carcer, eris *m* prison, jail; barriers at the beginning of a race-course; starting-point; beginning

carchēsium, (i)ī *nt* drinking-cup

cardiacus, a, **um** *adj* of the heart or stomach; suffering in the stomach

cardō, inis *m* door-hinge; pole, axis; chief point *or* circumstance

carduus, **ī** *m* thistle

cārectum, **ī** *nt* bed of sedge

careō ② *v with abl* be without, want; be absent from; miss, lose, be free from

cārex, **icis** *f* reed-grass; sedge

carīna, **ae** *f* bottom of a ship, keel; ship

cariōsus, **a**, **um** *adj* rotten

cāritās, **ātis** *f* dearness; high price; love

carmen, **inis** *nt* song, strain; poem; oracle, prophecy; magic formula; instrumental music

carnifex, **icis** *m* executioner, murderer, butcher, torturer; scoundrel

carnificīna, **ae** *f* work *or* trade of an executioner; torture

carnificius, **a**, **um** *adj* of a hangman

carnificō ① *v* execute, butcher

carnuf- ▸ **carnif-**

carō, **carnis** *f* flesh; meat

carpatinus, **a**, **um** *adj* made of hide

carpentarius, **(i)i** *m* ⓁⓂ carpenter

carpentum, **ī** *nt* two-wheeled carriage

carpō, **rpsī**, **ptum** ③ *v* pick, pluck (off); gather; browse; tear off; rob, plunder; enjoy, use; slander; weaken; consume; harass
□ ~ **viam**/**iter** proceed on a journey

carptim *adv* in detached parts

carrus, **ī** *m* Gallic wagon

cārus, **a**, **um** *adj* dear, costly; precious, loved

casa, **ae** *f* hut, cottage; shop, booth

cāseus, **ī** *m* cheese

casia, **ae** *f* cinnamon

cassida, **ae** *f*, **cassis**, **idis** *f* helmet (usu. of metal)

cassis, **is** *m often in pl* hunting-net

cassus, **a**, **um** *adj* empty; lacking, deprived of; vain, fruitless
□ **in cassum** in vain

castanea, **ae** *f* chestnut-tree; chestnut

castellānī, **ōrum** *mpl* garrison of a fort

castellum, **ī** *nt* fortified settlement, garrison; refuge, stronghold

castīgātiō, **ōnis** *f* punishment, reprimanding

castīgātor, **ōris** *m* corrector, reprover

castīgō ① *v* chastise, punish; correct, mend

castimōnia, **ae** *f* chastity, abstinence; purity of morals

castitās, **ātis** *f* chastity

castoreum, **ī** *nt* aromatic secretion obtained from the beaver

castrēnsis, **e** *adj* of *or* connected with the camp *or* active military service

castrō ① *v* castrate; impair, weaken

castrum, **ī** *nt* fortified post, settlement
■ **castra**, **ōrum** *ntpl* military camp; war-service; day's march; field of activity
□ **pōnō** ~ pitch camp
□ **moveō** ~ break camp

castus, **a**, **um** *adj* pure; spotless; chaste; pious; sacred

casula, **ae** *f* ⓁⓂ chasuble (vestment of a priest)

cāsus, **ūs** *m* fall, overthrow; error; accident, chance, event; occasion; misfortune; danger, risk; death; (grammar) case
□ **cāsū** by chance, by accident

catafracta, **ae** *m*, **catafractēs**, **ae** *m* coat of mail

catafractus, **ī** *m* soldier armed in mail

catagraphus, **a**, **um** *adj* (of material) figured

catapulta, **ae** *f* machine for discharging bolts or other missiles, catapult

catasta, **ae** *f* platform where slaves were exhibited for sale

catella, **ae** *f* little chain

catellus, **ī** *m* little dog, puppy

catēna, **ae** *f* chain; fetter; bond, restraint

catēnātus, **a**, **um** *adj* chained, fettered

caterva, **ae** *f* crowd; troop, company; flock

catervātim *adv* in troops; in disordered masses

cathedra, **ae** *f* arm-chair, easy chair; chair of a teacher; ⓁⓂ bishop's chair

catulus, **ī** *m* young dog, puppy, whelp

catus, **a**, **um** *adj* knowing, shrewd, wise, prudent

cauda, **ae** *f* tail

caudex ▶ **cōdex**

caulae, **ārum** *fpl* railing, lattice barrier; holes, pores

caulis, **is** *m* stalk; cabbage

caupō, **ōnis** *m* shopkeeper; innkeeper

caupōna, **ae** *f* inn, tavern, lodging-house

caurus ▶ **cōrus**

causa, **ae** *f* (formerly **caussa**) cause, reason, motive; occasion; pretence; excuse; matter, subject; affair, business; process, suit; (political) party; blame, fault; connection, friendship; condition, state
   □ **causā** *with gen* on account of, because of
   □ **causam dīcō** plead a case

causidicus, **ī** *m* advocate, barrister

causor ① *v dep* allege as an excuse; plead a cause, bring an action

causula, **ae** *f* speech in a petty lawsuit

cautēs, **tis** *f* rough pointed rock; cliff, reef

cautiō, **ōnis** *f* caution, heedfulness; stipulation; pledge

cautus, **a**, **um** *adj* cautious, heedful; made safe, secured

cavaedium *nt* [from **cavum** and **aedium**] inner court in a house

cavea, **ae** *f* enclosure, cage, coop; audience's part of a theatre; theatre

caveō, **cāvī**, **cautum** ② *v* be on one's guard, take care; beware of; give security; get security; order *or* stipulate (by will, in writing)
   □ **cavē** *with* (**ne**/**ut** *and*) *subj* (mind that you) don't ... !

caverna, **ae** *f* cavern, grotto, cave, hole; vault of the sky

cavillātiō, **ōnis** *f* quibbling; banter, jeering

cavillātor, **ōris** *m* jester, banterer, captious critic

cavillor ① *v dep* cavil at; scoff, jeer, satirize

cavō ① *v* hollow out; pierce through; make by hollowing out

cavum, **ī** *nt*, **cavus**, **ī** *m* hole, cavity; cave, burrow

cavus, **a**, **um** *adj* hollow, concave; deep-channelled

cecidī ▶ **cadō**

cecīdī ▶ **caedō**

cecinī ▶ **canō**

cēdō, **cessī**, **cessum** ③ *v* go, walk; turn out, come to pass; fall to, devolve; yield, give way; withdraw; go off; succeed; allow, grant; give up

cedo (*pl* **cette**) *impv* give here! pray! let us hear, tell! suppose, what if?

cedrus, **ī** *f* cedar; cedar-oil

celeber, **bris**, **bre** *adj* much frequented, populous; renowned, famous

celebrātiō, **ōnis** *f* throng; celebrating of a festival

celebrātus, **a**, **um** *adj* crowded; festive; current, popular

celebritās, **ātis** *f* crowded conditions; crowding; renown

celebrō ① *v* frequent, crowd; inhabit; practise, perform; celebrate; make known

celer, **eris**, **ere** *adj* swift, quick; lively; hurried; rash, hasty

celerēs, **um** *mpl* bodyguard of the Roman kings

celeritās, **ātis** *f* swiftness, quickness

celeriter *adv* quickly

celerō ① *v* quicken, accelerate; make haste

celēs, **ētis** *m* small fast boat

celeuma, **atis** *nt* call of the boatswain giving the time to rowers

cella, **ae** *f* cell; cellar; storehouse; larder; principal *or* subsidiary chamber in a temple; slave's room, 'garret'

cellarium, **(i)i** *nt* LM pantry

cellārius, **(i)ī** *m* butler, storekeeper

cellula, **ae** *f* little room

cēlō ① *v* hide, conceal; keep in ignorance; keep dark

celōx, **ōcis** *f* cutter, yacht

celsus, **a**, **um** *adj* high, lofty; great, sublime; haughty

cementarius, **(i)i** *m* LM mason

cēna, **ae** *f* dinner, supper, course for dinner

cēnāculum, **ī** *nt* upper-room, attic

cēnātiō, **ōnis** *f* dining-room

cēnitō ① *v* dine often

cēnō ① *v* dine, sup, dine on

cēnseō, **cēnsum** ② *v* count, reckon; tax, assess; estimate, value; think, be of the opinion; decree; vote to

cēnsitor, ōris *m* census-taker, registration official

cēnsor, ōris *m* censor; censurer, critic

> ❗ The **cēnsōrēs** were two Roman magistrates originally elected every 4-5 years for 18 months to take responsibility for maintaining the list of Roman citizens; later they had much wider powers and influence and were always ex-consuls.

cēnsōrius, a, um *adj* of *or* belonging to a censor; austere, moral

cēnsūra, ae *f* censorship; judgment, control

cēnsus, ūs *m* valuation of every Roman citizen's estate; registering of a man (his age, family, profession, *etc.*); sum assessed; property

centaurēum, ēī *nt* centaury (a herb)

centēnī, ae, a *adj* a hundred each; a hundred

centē(n)sima, ae *f* hundredth part

centē(n)simus, a, um *adj* the hundredth

centiceps, itis *adj* hundred-headed

centimanus, a, um *adj* hundred-handed

centō, ōnis *m* patched quilt, blanket *or* curtain

centum *adj indec* a hundred

centumvirī, ōrum *mpl* a panel of judges chosen annually to decide civil suits

centuria, ae *f* century

> ❗ In the Roman army, the century (commanded by a **centuriō**) was the smallest normal division of a **legiō** and comprised 100 men.

□ ~ **comitiāta** a political unit for voting

> ❗ The oldest of the three elective assemblies of the people, the **centuria comitiāta** enacted laws, elected senior magistrates, declared war and peace, and could inflict the death penalty

centuriātim *adv* by centuries

centuriō¹ ① *v* arrange (recruits, *etc.*) in military centuries

□ **comitia centuriāta** the assembly in which the Romans voted by centuries

centuriō², ōnis *m* commander of a century, captain, centurion

cēpī ▶ **capiō**

cēra, ae *f* wax; wax-covered writing-tablet; letter; seal of wax; waxen image

cerasus, ī *f* cherry-tree; cherry

cērātus, a, um *adj* provided, coated, fastened *or* caulked with wax

Cereālis, e *adj* of Ceres, of corn
■ **Cereālia, ium** *ntpl* the festival of Ceres

cerebrum, ī *nt* brain; understanding, anger

cēreus, a, um *adj* waxen; wax-coloured; pliant, soft
■ ~, **ī** *m* wax taper

cernō, crēvī, crētum ③ *v* sift; discern, perceive; decide; determine; make formal acceptance of an inheritance

cernuus, a, um *adj* head foremost

cerrītus, a, um *adj* possessed by Ceres, frantic, mad

certāmen, inis *nt* contest, struggle; battle, rivalry, combat; point of contention

certātim *adv* with rivalry, in competition; eagerly

certātiō, ōnis *f* striving, contention

certē *adv* certainly, surely; really; yet indeed, at least

certō¹ *adv* certainly, surely; in fact

certō² ① *v* fight, contend; strive; contend at law

certus, a, um *adj* certain; sure, safe; distinct; fixed, agreed upon; steady, resolute; constant, faithful; unerring
□ **certiōrem faciō** inform
□ **prō certō sciō/habeō** know for certain

cērula, ae *f* red pencil

cērussa, ae *f* white powder used as a cosmetic; white lead

cerva, ae *f* hind, doe; deer

cervīcal, ālis *nt* pillow

cervīnus, a, um *adj* pertaining to a deer *or* stag

cervīx, īcis *f* neck

cervus, ī *m* hart, stag
■ **cervī** *pl* defensive palisade, stakes stuck into the ground, chevaux-de-frise

cessātiō, ōnis *f* relaxation, respite; idleness

cessātor, ōris *m* idler, sluggard

cessō ① *v* hold back, leave off, delay, loiter; cease (from); idle; be wanting; go wrong

cētārium, (i)ī *nt* fish-pond

cētārius, (i)ī *m* fishmonger

cēterōquī *adv* in other respects, otherwise

cēterum *adv* for the rest; but; besides

cēterus, a, um *adj* the other
■ **cēterī** *pl* the others, the rest

cette *pl* from ▶ **cedo**

cētus, ī *m* whale; porpoise; dolphin; sea-monster

ceu *adv* as, just as; as if

chalybēius, a, um *adj* of steel

chalybs, bis *m* steel, iron

Chaos *nt* formless state of primordial matter; pit of the Lower World

charta, ae *f* (leaf of) paper; writing

Chēlae, ārum *fpl* the claws of Scorpio which extended into the sign Libra

chelydrus, ī *m* venomous water-snake

chelys, *acc* **yn** *f* lyre

chīrographum, ī *nt* handwriting; manuscript; bond

chīrūrgia, ae *f* surgery

chīrūrgus, ī *m* surgeon

chlamydatus, a, um *adj* wearing a chlamys

chlamys, ydis *f* a Greek cloak *or* cape frequently for military use

chorda, ae *f* string of a musical instrument

chorēa, ae *f* dance

chorus, ī *m* dance with singing; chorus, choir; band, group

chrisma, atis *nt* [LM] consecrated oil, chrism

chrȳsolithos, ī *m/f* topaz

cibus, ī *m* food; fare

cicāda, ae *f* cricket, cicada

cicātrīx, īcis *f* scar, cicatrice

ciccum, ī *nt* a proverbially worthless object

cicer, eris *nt* chick-pea

cicindēla, ae *f* firefly; candle

cicōnia, ae *f* stork

cicūta, ae *f* hemlock; shepherd's pipe

cieō, cīvī, citum ② *v* move; shake; rouse; disturb; provoke; call on, invoke; produce

cimentarius [LM] ▶ **caementarius**

cīmex, icis *m* bed-bug

cinaedus, ī *m* catamite

cincinnātus, a, um *adj* with curled hair

cincinnus, ī *m* ringlet; (fig) rhetorical flourish

cīnctūtus, a, um *adj* wearing a girdle *or* loin-cloth

cinerārius, (i)ī *m* hair-curler, hairdresser

cingō, cīnxī, cīnctum ③ *v* gird; surround; beleaguer; crown

cingulum, ī *nt* band, belt; sword-belt

cinis, eris *m/f* ashes; ruins

cinnamum, ī *nt* the cinnamon shrub

circā *adv* (all) around; *prep with acc* about, near to; concerning

circēnsēs, ium *mpl* games and exercises of wrestling, running, fighting, *etc.*, in the circus

circiter *adv/prep with acc* about, near; towards

circueō, īre, īvī/iī, itum *v* *ir* go *or* march around; encompass; go about canvassing; circumvent

circuitiō, ōnis *f* a going round; patrol; circumlocution

circuitus, ūs *m* going round, circuit; way round; circumference; circumlocution

circulor ① *v* *dep* form groups round oneself

circulus, ī *m* circle; orbit; ring, hoop; company

circum *adv* (all) around, about; *prep with acc* around, about, among; at, near

circumagō, ēgī, āctum ③ *v* drive in a circle, turn round; wheel

circumcīdō, cīdī, cīsum ③ *v* cut around, clip; diminish; remove

circumclūdō, ūsī, ūsum ③ *v* enclose on all sides

circumcolō ③ *v* dwell round about

circumcursō ① *v* run about over; run around (a person)

circumdō, dedī, datum ① *v* put round; surround; enclose

circumdūcō, dūxī, ductum ③ *v* lead *or* draw around; lead out of the way; cheat; cancel

circumeō ▸ circueō

circumferō, ferre, tulī, lātum *v ir* carry about *or* round; spread round, divulge; purify; turn (eyes, face, hands, *etc.*) to a new direction

circumfluō, flūxī ③ *v* flow round; be rich in

circumfluus, a, um *adj* circumfluent, surrounding; surrounded with water

circumforāneus, a, um *adj* connected with (the business of) the forum; itinerant

circumfundō, ūdī, ūsum ③ *v* pour around
◻ **circumfundor** flow round; surround

circumgredior, gressus sum ③ *v dep* go round behind by a flanking movement

circumiaceō ② *v* lie round about

circumiciō, iēcī, iectum ③ *v* cast *or* place around; encompass with

circumiectus¹, ūs *m* encompassing, embrace

circumiectus², a, um *adj* surrounding

circumit- ▸ circuit-

circumligō ① *v* bind round *or* to; encircle

circumliniō ④ *v,* **circumlinō, lēvī, litum** ③ *v* smear *or* anoint round, decorate

circumluō ③ *v* wash *or* flow around

circummittō, mīsī, missum ③ *v* send around

circummūniō ④ *v* wall around, fortify

circummūnītiō, ōnis *f* circumvallation

circumplector, plexus sum ③ *v dep* embrace, surround, circumvallate

circumplicō ① *v* coil round

circumpōnō, posuī, positum ③ *v* put *or* place around

circumrētiō ④ *v* encircle with a net

circumrōdō, rōsī ③ *v* gnaw all round; slander

circumsaepiō, psī, ptum ④ *v* fence round, enclose

circumscrībō, psī, ptum ③ *v* draw a line around; circumscribe; hem in; cheat; circumvent

circumscrīptē *adv* concisely; in periodic style

circumscrīptiō, ōnis *f* encircling; circle; boundary; outline; deceiving; periodic sentence

circumscrīptor, ōris *m* cheat; defrauder

circumsedeō, sēdī, sessum ② *v* sit around; besiege

circumsīdō ③ *v* besiege, surround

circumsiliō ④ *v* leap around

circumsistō, stetī ③ *v* stand round

circumsonō ① *v* resound on every side, ring again with; echo round

circumspectiō, ōnis *f* careful consideration

circumspectō ① *v* look about searchingly

circumspectus, a, um *adj* circumspect, cautious; wary; carefully considered

circumspiciō, spexī, spectum ③ *v* look about; take heed; survey; seek for

circumstō, stetī ① *v* stand round; surround

circumstrepō ③ *v* make a noise around

circumvādō, vāsī ③ *v* form a ring round, surround

circumvagus, a, um *adj* moving round, encircling

circumvallō ① *v* surround with siege works

circumvectiō, ōnis *f* circular course; transport

circumvector ① *v dep* sail round, travel round

circumvehor, vectus sum ③ *v dep* make the round of; travel round; sail around

circumveniō, vēnī, ventum ④ *v* come round; surround; beat; oppress; circumvent

circumvinciō, vīnxī, vīnctum ④ *v* tie round

circumvolitō ① *v* fly around about

circumvolō ① *v* fly around

circumvolvō, volūtum ③ *v* roll round, twine around

circus, ī *m* circle; circus (at Rome)

cirrus, ī *m* lock of curly hair; tuft

cis *prep with acc* on this side (of); within

Cisalpīnus, **a**, **um** *adj* lying on the south side of the Alps

cisium, **(i)ī** *nt* two-wheeled carriage

cista, **ae** *f* chest, box

cisterna, **ae** *f* cistern

cistophorus, **ī** *m* an Asiatic coin

citātus, **a**, **um** *adj* quick, rapid
□ **equō citātō** at full gallop

citerior, **ius** *adj* on this side, hithermost; nearer

cithara, **ae** *f* lyre

citharista, **ae** *m* lyre-player

citharistria, **ae** *f* female lyre-player

citharoedus, **ī** *m* one who sings to the lyre

citimus, **a**, **um** *adj* nearest, next

cito, *comp* **citius**, *sup* **citissimē** *adv* soon; quickly

citō ① *v* cite; summon; excite; encourage

citrā *prep with acc* on this side; within, short of; without, apart from

citreus, **a**, **um** *adj* of citron

citrō *adv* to this side, hither
□ **ultrō citrōque** to and fro; in and out; on both sides

citrum, **ī** *nt* wood of the citron-tree; table made of citron-wood

citus, **a**, **um** *adj* quick, swift, rapid

cīvicus, **a**, **um** *adj* civic, civil; legal
□ **cīvica corōna** a crown of oak leaves presented to one who had saved a fellow-countryman in war

cīvīlis, **e** *adj* civic, civil; political, public, polite, courteous

cīvīliter *adv* in a civil sphere; in a manner suited to citizens

cīvis, **is** *m/f* citizen; countryman *or* woman

cīvitās, **ātis** *f* citizenship; citizens; city; state

clādēs, **dis** *f* defeat; destruction; ruin; plague; slaughter; calamity

clam *adv/prep with acc* secretly; unknown to

clāmātor, **ōris** *m* shouter

clāmitātiō, **ōnis** *f* shouting, bawling

clāmitō ① *v* shout repeatedly; proclaim

clāmō ① *v* shout; shout the name of

clāmor, **ōris** *m* shout, cry, clamour; applause; noise, din

clanculum *adv* secretly

clandestīnus, **a**, **um** *adj* secret, hidden, clandestine

clangor, **ōris** *m* clang, noise

clārē *adv* brightly; clearly; aloud; lucidly

clāreō ② *v* shine; be famous

clārēscō, **ruī** ③ *v* begin to shine; become clear *or* evident; become famous

clārisonus, **a**, **um** *adj* loud- *or* clear-sounding

clāritās, **ātis** *f* clearness, brightness; distinctness; celebrity, renown

clāritūdō, **inis** *f* clearness, brightness; distinctness; celebrity, renown

clārō ① *v* make visible, brighten, make illustrious

clārus, **a**, **um** *adj* clear, bright; loud, distinct; evident; illustrious, famous

classiārius, **(i)ī** *m* mariner; sailor, seaman; *pl* naval forces

classicum, **ī** *nt* military trumpet-call

classicus, **a**, **um** *adj* belonging to the fleet; belonging to the highest class of citizen

classis, **is** *f* class of the Roman people; army; fleet

claudeō ② *v*, **claudō**, **clausum** ③ *v* limp, halt; be weak, be imperfect

claudicō ① *v* limp, be lame; waver, be defective

claudō, **clausī**, **clausum** ③ *v* shut, close; conclude, finish; enclose; imprison; surround; besiege

claudus, **a**, **um** *adj* limping, lame; defective, wavering, uncertain

claustra, **ōrum** *ntpl* bolts, bars; enclosure; barrier; door, gate; bulwark; dam

claustrum, **i** *nt* LM cloister

clausula, **ae** *f* conclusion, end; close of a periodic sentence

clāva, **ae** *f* cudgel, club

clāviger, **erī** *m* club-bearer; key-bearer

clāvis, **is** *f* door-key

clāvus, **ī** *m* nail; tiller, helm, helm of the ship of state; rudder
□ **lātus** ~ a broad purple stripe

> ❗ Members of the equestrian and senatorial ranks bore one or possibly two upright purple stripes on their tunics. The **lātus clāvus** ('broad stripe') was worn by senators, and in the imperial period their sons, while the **angustus clāvus** ('narrow stripe') was worn by men of equestrian rank.

clēmēns, **ntis** *adj* merciful, gentle, mild; quiet, peaceable; courteous; moderate

clēmentia, **ae** *f* clemency, mercy; mildness; calmness

clepō, **psī**, **ptum** ③ *v* steal

clepsydra, **ae** *f* water-clock

clēricus, **i** *m*, **clerus**, **i** *m* [LM] cleric, clergy

cliēns, **ntis** *m* client; vassal; dependent

clientēla, **ae** *f* clientship; vassalage; patronage; clients; vassals

clima, **atis** *nt* [LM] region

clīmactēricus, **a**, **um** *adj* critical

clipeātus, **a**, **um** *adj* furnished with a shield

clipeus, **ī** *m* round, usually bronze shield; disc of the sun

clītellae, **ārum** *fpl* pack-saddle

clitellārius, **a**, **um** *adj* bearing a pack-saddle

clīvōsus, **a**, **um** *adj* hilly, steep

clīvus, **ī** *m* sloping ground, slope

cloāca, **ae** *f* sewer, drain

clueō ② *v* be called, be named, be reputed

clūnis, **is** *m/f* buttocks, haunches

coacervātiō, **ōnis** *f* heaping together *or* up

coacervō ① *v* heap together *or* up; amass

coacēscō, **ī** ③ *v* become sour

coāctor, **ōris** *m* collector (of money, taxes, *etc.*)

coāctū *adv* by force

coāctum ▶ **cōgō**

coaequō ① *v* make level, regard as equal

coāgmentō ① *v* join, connect; construct

coāgmentum, **ī** *nt* joint

coalēscō, **aluī**, **alitum** ③ *v* grow together; close; become unified *or* strong

coarguō, **uī** ③ *v* prove, make manifest; refute; convict

coccum, **ī** *nt* scarlet colour; scarlet cloth

cochlea, **ae** *f* snail; [LM] *pl* spiral staircase

coctilis, **e** *adj* (of bricks) baked; built of baked bricks

cocus ▶ **coquus**

cōdex, **icis** *m* trunk of a tree; piece of wood; (bound) book; account-book

cōdicillus, **ī** *m* rescript of the Emperor, petition to the Emperor; codicil; *pl* set of writing tablets

coēgī ▶ **cōgō**

coemō, **ēmī**, **ēmptum** ③ *v* buy up

coēmptiō, **ōnis** *f* legal (fictitious) sale of a woman to a man

coeō, **īre**, **īvī/iī**, **itum** *v ir* go *or* come together, meet, clash; assemble; conspire; curdle; heal; unite

coepī, **isse**, **coeptum** *v ir* begin

> ❗ In CL this verb has perfect stem forms and past meaning only; its pres. is sometimes supplied by **incipiō**. The action begun is usu. expressed by an infin.

coeptō ① *v* begin, attempt

coeptum, **ī** *nt* beginning, undertaking

coerceō ② *v* enclose; limit; correct, keep in order; punish; restrain

coercitiō, **ōnis** *f* coercion, restraint; punishment

coetus, **ūs** *m* meeting, assembly, company

cōgitābundus, **a**, **um** *adj* wrapped in thought, thoughtful, pensive

cōgitātiō, **ōnis** *f* thinking, meditation; thought; intention; plan; opinion; reasoning power

cōgitō ① *v* consider, ponder, think; meditate; intend; look forward to; imagine

cōgnātiō, **ōnis** *f* relationship by birth; relatives, family; affinity

cōgnātus, **a**, **um** *adj* related by birth; related; similar; having affinity with ■ **cognātus**, **ī** *m* relation, relative

cognitiō, **ōnis** *f* getting to know; idea, notion; examination, inquiry

cognitor, **ōris** *m* attorney; guarantor of identity

cognōmen, **inis** *nt* family name; sobriquet

cognōmentum, **ī** *nt* surname; name

cognōscō, **nōvī**, **nitum** ③ *v* learn, get to know; inform oneself of; understand; investigate; observe, perceive; identify

cōgō, **coēgī**, **coāctum** ③ *v* drive together; collect; curdle; force, compel; prove conclusively

cohaereō, **haesī**, **haesum** ② *v* adhere (to); stick together; be consistent

cohaerēscō, **haesī** ③ *v* cohere; stick, adhere

cohērēs, **ēdis** *m/f* co-heir, joint-heir

cohibeō ② *v* hold together; restrain; curb; hinder; confine

cohonestō ① *v* honour, grace; make respectable

cohorrēscō, **ruī** ③ *v* shudder

cohors, **rtis** *f* farmyard; cohort; bodyguard; attendants

> [!] A Roman **legiō** was divided into ten cohorts as its principal subdivision, and each cohort consisted of three **manipulī**.

cohortātiō, **ōnis** *f* exhortation, encouragement

cohortor ① *v dep* cheer up, encourage; exhort

coitiō, **ōnis** *f* meeting; conspiracy, combination

coitus, **ūs** *m* meeting; sexual intercourse

colaphus, **ī** *m* blow, buffet

collabefīō, **fierī**, **factus sum** *v ir semi-dep* collapse, break up; be overthrown politically

collābor, **lāpsus sum** ③ *v dep* collapse, fall in ruins; fall in a swoon *or* in death

collacrimō ① *v* weep together, weep over

collātiō, **ōnis** *f* placing together; payment of tribute; tax; comparison

collaudātiō, **ōnis** *f* high praise

collaudō ① *v* praise very much

collectiō, **ōnis** *f* collection; recapitulation

collēga, **ae** *m* colleague

collēgium, **(i)ī** *nt* college, corporation; brotherhood; colleagueship

collibet ② *v impers*, **collibuit**, **isse**, **libitum est** ② *v impers with dat* it pleases

collīdō, **īsī**, **īsum** ③ *v* strike *or* dash together; crush; bring into conflict with each other

colligō[1], **ēgī**, **ēctum** ③ *v* collect, assemble; acquire; pick up; infer; reckon; sum up
□ **sē/animum colligere** recover oneself *or* one's spirits

colligō[2] ① *v* bind together, connect; fetter

collinō, **lēvī**, **litum** ③ *v* besmear; pollute

collis, **is** *m* hill

collocātiō, **ōnis** *f* placing together; arrangement; marrying

collocō ① *v* put in a particular place together, arrange; bestow; employ; lay out; give in marriage

collocūtiō, **ōnis** *f* conversation, conference; discussion

colloquium, **(i)ī** *nt* conversation, discourse, interview

colloquor, **locūtus sum** ③ *v dep* talk together, converse

collubet ▶ collibet

collūceō ② *v* shine brightly

collūdō, **ūsī**, **ūsum** ③ *v* play together; act in collusion

collum, **ī** *nt* neck

colluō, **uī**, **ūtum** ③ *v* wash, rinse out

collūsiō, **ōnis** *f* secret understanding

collūsor, **ōris** *m* playmate, fellow gambler

collūstrō ① *v* lighten up; survey on all sides

colluviēs, **iēī** *f*, **colluviō**, **ōnis** *f* filth, offscouring; 'cesspool'; turmoil

collybus, **ī** *m* cost of exchange

collȳrium, **(i)ī** *nt* eye-salve

colō, **coluī**, **cultum** ③ *v* cultivate; take care of; dwell, inhabit; honour, pay

court to, revere; worship; adorn;
exercise; practise

colocāsia, **ae** *f* the Egyptian bean

colōnia, **ae** *f* colony

colōnus, **ī** *m* farmer

color, **ōris** *m* colour, complexion;
outward show; excuse

colōrātus, **a**, **um** *adj* variegated;
sunburnt

colōrō ① *v* colour, paint; dye; tan

colōs ▸ **color**

coluber, **brī** *m*, **colubra**, **ae** *f*
serpent, snake

colubrifer, **era**, **erum** *adj* snaky;
snake-haired

cōlum, **ī** *nt* strainer, filter, sieve

columba, **ae** *f* dove, pigeon

columbus, **ī** *m* male pigeon

columella, **ae** *f* small column, pillar

columen, **inis** *nt* height, peak; roof,
gable; summit, head, chief; the highest
embodiment *or* peak (of a quality)

columna, **ae** *f* column, pillar

columnārium, **(i)ī** *nt* a pillar-tax

colurnus, **a**, **um** *adj* made of hazel

colus, **ī** *m*, **colus**, **ūs** *f* distaff

coma, **ae** *f* hair of the head; wool;
foliage

comāns, **ntis** *adj* hairy; long-haired;
leafy

comātus, **a**, **um** *adj* long-haired; leafy
□ **Gallia Comāta** Transalpine Gaul

combibō, **bibī** ③ *v* drink up, absorb

combūrō, **ussī**, **ustum** ③ *v* burn,
burn up

comedō, **ēsse**, **ēdī**, **ēs(t)um** *v ir* eat
up, consume; waste, squander

comes, **itis** *m/f* companion, comrade,
partner; attendant; ⟨LM⟩ count

comētēs, **ae** *m* comet

cōmicus, **a**, **um** *adj* comic
■ ∼, **ī** *m* comic actor; writer of comedy

cōmis, **e** *adj* courteous, kind, friendly;
elegant

cōmitās, **ātis** *f* courteousness,
kindness, friendliness; good taste

comitātus, **ūs** *m* escort, train,
retinue; company; ⟨LM⟩ county

cōmiter *adv* courteously, kindly,
civilly, readily

comitiālis, **e** *adj* pertaining to the
comitia

comitium, **(i)ī** *nt* a place in the forum,
where the comitia were held
■ **comitia**, **ōrum** *ntpl* elections

comitō ① *v*, **comitor** ① *v dep*
accompany, attend

commaculō ① *v* stain deeply, pollute,
defile; sully

commeātus, **ūs** *m* passage; leave;
merchandise; convoy, provisions

commeminī, **isse** *v ir* recollect
thoroughly, remember

commemorātiō, **ōnis** *f* reminding,
recalling, citation

commemorō ① *v* recall; mention

commendābilis, **e** *adj* praiseworthy

commendātiō, **ōnis** *f* entrusting;
recommendation; excellence;
approval

commendō ① *v* commend to;
recommend; entrust

commentāriolum, **ī** *nt* notebook;
treatise

commentārius, **(i)ī** *m*,
commentārium, **(i)ī** *nt* note-book,
memorandum; commentary; notes,
jottings

commentātiō, **ōnis** *f* thinking out,
mental preparation

commentīcius, **a**, **um** *adj* invented,
devised; imaginary; forged, false

commentor ① *v dep* think about;
study beforehand; imagine

commentum, **ī** *nt* invention, fiction,
fabrication; scheme

commentus *pf pple* of
▸ **comminīscor**

commeō ① *v* go to and fro; pass; travel

commercium, **(i)ī** *nt* commercial
intercourse, trade, dealings;
relationship

commereō ② *v*, **commereor** ② *v dep*
merit fully, deserve; be guilty of

commētior, **mēnsus sum** ④ *v dep*
measure

commīlitium, **(i)ī** *nt* companionship
in military service; comradeship

commīlitō, **ōnis** *m* fellow-soldier

comminātiō, **ōnis** *f* threatening

comminīscor, **mentus sum** ③ *v dep*
devise, invent; forge; fabricate; state
falsely

comminuō, **uī**, **ūtum** ③ *v* break into
pieces; break up; crush

comminus *adv* hand to hand; at hand, near

commisceō, mixtum ② *v* mix together

commiseror ① *v dep* pity; excite compassion

commissum, ī *nt* enterprise, trust, secret; crime

commissūra, ae *f* joint, seam

committō, mīsī, missum ③ *v* join, unite; commit, entrust; match (one against another); compare; venture; begin; perpetrate; engage in
□ ~ **proelium** join battle

commoditās, ātis *f* fitness, convenience; advantage; obligingness

commodō ① *v* oblige, lend, provide, give

commodum, ī *nt* convenience; profit; wages; advantage

commodus, a, um *adj* suitable, convenient, fit; advantageous; lucky; obliging, pleasant
■ **commodē** *adv* properly, neatly

commonefaciō, fēcī, factum ③ *v* remind; impress upon

commoneō ② *v* remind

commōnstrō ① *v* point out

commorātiō, ōnis *f* stay (at a place); delay; (fig) dwelling on a point

commorior, morī, mortuus sum ③ *v dep* die together

commoror ① *v dep* sojourn, stay; stay long, be inactive; dwell upon

commōtiō, ōnis *f* agitation; the arousing of emotion

commoveō, mōvī, mōtum ② *v* move vigorously; stir up; excite; disturb; astonish; affect

commūnicātiō, ōnis *f* communication, an imparting

commūnicō ① *v* communicate; impart; share with; receive a share of; [LM] take communion

commūniō¹ ④ *v* fortify; strengthen, reinforce, entrench

commūniō², ōnis *f* mutual participation, association, sharing; [LM] company; Eucharist, communion

commūnis, e *adj* shared by, joint, common, general, ordinary; affable; public

commūnitās, ātis *f* joint possession, partnership; fellowship, kinship

commūniter *adv* in common, commonly, generally

commūtābilis, e *adj* changeable, variable

commūtātiō, ōnis *f* change; exchange

commūtō ① *v* change entirely, alter; exchange, barter

cōmō, mpsī, mptum ③ *v* arrange, 'do' (hair); dress, adorn

cōmoedia, ae *f* comedy

cōmoedus, ī *m* comedian, comic actor

compactus, a, um *adj* joined together, sturdy

compāgēs, gis *f*, **compāgō, inis** *f* the action of binding together; joint, structure, framework

compar, aris *adj* like, equal (to); equal, comrade; partner

comparābilis, e *adj* comparable

comparātiō, ōnis *f* preparation; acquirement

compāreō ② *v* appear, be visible; be present; be in existence

comparō ① *v* unite; compare; prepare; provide (for); acquire; raise (a force); appoint

compellō¹, pulī, pulsum ③ *v* drive together or along; collect; impel; force

compellō² ① *v* accost, address; chide, rebuke, tell off, call to account; abuse

compendium, (i)ī *nt* abridgement; a short cut; profit; savings
□ ~ **faciō** gain

compēnsō ① *v* balance, compensate

comperendinō ① *v* adjourn the trial of

comperiō, rī, rtum ④ *v* find out, learn, know for certain

compēs, edis *f* shackle (for the feet); fetter

compescō, ī ③ *v* confine, curb, restrain

competens, ntis *m/f* [LM] catechumen

competītor, ōris *m* rival, competitor

competō, īvī/iī, ītum ③ *v* meet; happen; coincide; suit, agree; correspond; be sound *or* capable

compīlātiō, ōnis *f* burglary

compīlō ① *v* rob, pillage

compingō, pēgī, pāctum ③ *v* join; fasten up; shut up

Compitālia, ium *ntpl* festival celebrated at cross-roads in honour of the rural gods

compitum, ī *nt* cross-roads

complaceō ② *v with dat* please

complector, plexus sum ③ *v dep* clasp around; encompass, embrace; lay hold of; contain; comprehend (mentally); comprise

complēmentum, ī *nt* something that fills out *or* completes

compleō, ēvī, ētum ② *v* fill up; fill; complete; fulfil; perfect; supply; recruit; make good

completorium, (i)ī *nt* ⟨LM⟩ compline

complex, icis *m* ⟨LM⟩ ally

complexiō, ōnis *f* combination, connection; summary; dilemma

complexus, ūs *m* embrace; sexual intercourse

complicō ① *v* fold up

complōrātiō, ōnis *f*, **complōrātus, ūs** *m* lamentation, (vocal) mourning

complōrō ① *v* bewail

complūrēs, a *adj* several, many

compluvium, (i)ī *nt* a quadrangular, inward-sloping, central portion of roof, designed to guide rain-water into the **impluvium**

compōnō, posuī, positum ③ *v* put *or* lay together; arrange, compose; adjust; compare; match; construct, build; compose (books, *etc.*); soothe, appease, settle; bury

comportō ① *v* carry, transport, collect

compos, ōtis *adj usu with gen* in possession of; participating, guilty of □ ∼ **mentis** in full possession of one's faculties

compositiō, ōnis *f* arrangement; matching

compositō *adv* by arrangement, concertedly

compositor, ōris *m* writer, composer

compositus, a, um *adj* well-arranged; calm

compotiō ④ *v* put someone (*acc*) in possession of something (*gen or abl*)

compōtor, ōris *m* drinking-companion

comprānsor, ōris *m* table-companion

comprecātiō, ōnis *f* public supplication *or* prayers

comprecor ① *v dep* supplicate, implore, pray that

comprehendō, ndī, ēnsum ③ *v* seize *or* grasp; comprise; include; attack; embrace; describe; express; arrest *or* lay hold of; understand

comprehēnsiō, ōnis *f* arrest; comprehension, idea; dilemma

comprimō, essī, essum ③ *v* press *or* squeeze together; keep *or* hold back *or* in; suppress; seduce

comprobātiō, ōnis *f* approval

comprobō ① *v* approve; attest, confirm

cōmptus, a, um *adj* adorned; elegant, neat, polished

compungō, ūnxī, ūnctum ③ *v* prick, puncture

computatio, onis *f* ⟨LM⟩ reckoning (esp. of the dates of religious festivals)

computō ① *v* calculate, count up, reckon, estimate

cōnāmen, inis *nt* attempt; effort, exertion

cōnātum, ī *nt* attempted action

cōnātus, ūs *m* attempt, undertaking; effort; impulse

concaedēs, ium *fpl* barricade

concalefaciō, fēcī, factum ③ *v* make warm, heat

concalēscō, luī ③ *v* become warm, warm up

concallēscō, luī ③ *v* become hard *or* callous; become insensible

concamerō ① *v* cover with an arch; vault over

concavus, a, um *adj* hollowed out, concave; hollow

concēdō, essī, essum ③ *v* go away, depart, withdraw; yield to, submit; allow, grant; forgive

concelebrō ① *v* go to a place often *or* in large numbers, haunt; celebrate; publish

concentus, ūs *m* singing together, harmony, melody; concord

concerpō, psī, ptum ③ *v* tear in pieces, tear up; pluck off; abuse

concertātiō, ōnis *f* dispute, controversy

concertō ① *v* dispute, fight, argue over

concessiō, **ōnis** *f* permission, grant, plea of excuse; the act of yielding

concessus, **ūs** *m* concession; permission

concha, **ae** *f* shell-fish, cockle; pearl; mussel-shell; oyster-shell; Triton's trumpet

□ ∼ **persica** mother of pearl

conchȳliātus, **a**, **um** *adj* purple-dyed

conchȳlium, **(i)ī** *nt* shell-fish; purple, purple dye

concidō, **cidī** ③ *v* fall down *or* into decay; fail; faint; be slain; die

concīdō, **cīdī**, **cīsum** ③ *v* cut to pieces; break up; beat, thrash; cut down, kill; weaken; destroy

conciō, **cīvī**, **citum** ② *v* move, stir up; excite, incite

conciliābulum, **ī** *nt* place of assembly

conciliātiō, **ōnis** *f* union; winning over

conciliātor, **ōris** *m* mediator, agent

conciliō ① *v* call together; unite, reconcile; mediate; procure; win over; obtain; recommend; bring about, cause

concilium, **(i)ī** *nt* assembly; council

concinnitās, **ātis** *f* neatness, elegance

concinnō ① *v* fix, put right

concinnus, **a**, **um** *adj* neat, pretty, elegant, pleasing

concinō, **cinuī** ③ *v* sing together; celebrate in song; sound together

concipiō, **cēpī**, **ceptum** ③ *v* take up; conceive; devise; understand; take in; produce, form

concitātiō, **ōnis** *f* rapid motion; passion; excitement, disturbance

concitātus, **a**, **um** *adj* rapid; passionate, energetic

concitō ① *v* rouse, spur, excite; disturb; pursue; cause

conclāmātiō, **ōnis** *f* shouting together; acclamation

conclāmō ① *v* cry (out) together; shout; bewail (the dead); proclaim

conclāve, **is** *nt* room; public lavatory

conclūdō, **ūsī**, **ūsum** ③ *v* enclose together; conclude, end; comprise; infer; stop; close

conclūsiō, **ōnis** *f* conclusion, end; siege; peroration; logical conclusion from premisses

concolor, **ōris** *adj* of the same colour

concoquō, **coxī**, **coctum** ③ *v* heat thoroughly; digest; mature; put up with; consider well; devise

concordia, **ae** *f* harmony, concord

concordō ① *v* harmonize, be in agreement

concors, **rdis** *adj* agreeing, harmonious

concrēdō, **didī**, **ditum** ③ *v* entrust for safe keeping, confide

concremō ① *v* burn up entirely

concrepō, **puī**, **pitum** ① *v* rattle, clash; snap (one's fingers)

concrēscō, **ēvī**, **ētum** ③ *v* grow together; curdle; congeal; clot

concrētiō, **ōnis** *f* formation into solid matter

concrētus, **a**, **um** *adj* clotted, stiff, frozen; constructed, formed

concubīna, **ae** *f* concubine

concubitus, **ūs** *m* lying together; sexual intercourse

concubius, **a**, **um** *adj*:

□ **concubiā nocte** in the early part of the night

conculcō ① *v* trample upon; oppress; despise

concumbō, **ubuī**, **ubitum** ③ *v* lie with

concupīscō, **īvī/iī**, **ītum** ③ *v* long much for, covet, desire ardently

concurrō, **(cu)currī**, **cursum** ③ *v* run *or* assemble together; join battle; be in conflict; meet; happen simultaneously

concursātiō, **ōnis** *f* running together; skirmish

concursātor, **ōris** *m* skirmisher

concursiō, **ōnis** *f* concourse, meeting; repetition

concursō ① *v* run hither and thither; run together, clash; run to visit

concursus, **ūs** *m* concourse, crowd; encounter; combination

concutiō, **ussī**, **ussum** ③ *v* shake violently, brandish; weaken; harass; rouse

condemnō ① *v* condemn, doom; convict; prosecute a law suit against

condēnseō ② *v* compress

condēnsus, **a**, **um** *adj* dense, thick; wedged together

condiciō, **ōnis** *f* condition, situation, rank; stipulation; term; agreement; marriage; married person
□ **condiciōnem ferō** reach terms

condīcō, **īxī**, **ictum** ③ *v* agree (upon), declare; promise; undertake; give notice, engage oneself

condīmentum, **ī** *nt* spice, seasoning

condiō ④ *v* preserve, pickle; embalm; spice; season, flavour; render pleasant

condiscipulus, **ī** *m* schoolfellow, fellow-pupil

condiscō, **didicī** ③ *v* learn thoroughly

conditor, **ōris** *m* builder, founder, author

conditōrium, **(i)ī** *nt* tomb

condītus, **a**, **um** *adj* seasoned, flavoured

condō, **didī**, **ditum** ③ *v* build, found; compose, write; make; hide; sheathe; lay *or* treasure up; preserve, pickle; bury; thrust (into)

condolēscō, **luī** ③ *v* be painful, ache; feel grief

condōnō ① *v* give as a present; forgive; remit; devote *or* sacrifice

condormiō ④ *v* sleep soundly

condormīscō, **īvī/iī** ③ *v* fall asleep

condūcō, **dūxī**, **ductum** ③ *v* lead together, assemble; hire; undertake; contract for; be of use; profit

conductor, **ōris** *m* hirer; contractor; lessee

conduplicō ① *v* double, make twofold

cōne- ▶ **conne-**

cōnfarreātiō, **ōnis** *f* marriage ceremony

> ❗ **cōnfarreātiō** was an ancient ceremonial form of Roman marriage involving the offering of an emmer-wheat cake in sacrifice before ten witnesses.

cōnfectiō, **ōnis** *f* making ready, preparation; compiling; mastication

cōnfector, **ōris** *m* finisher; slayer

cōnfectus, **a**, **um** *adj* exhausted

cōnferciō, **rsī**, **rtum** ④ *v* stuff together, press close together

cōnferō, **cōnferre**, **contulī**, **collātum** *v ir* bring *or* carry together, collect; contribute, add; join; bestow; lay out; apply; discourse *or* talk together; match; compare; put off; refer; transfer; impute; compress; betake oneself, go
□ **signa** ∼ join battle

cōnfertim *adv* in a compact body *or* bunch

cōnfertus, **a**, **um** *adj* close-packed, filled

cōnfessiō, **ōnis** *f* confession, acknowledgement; admission; admission of guilt

cōnfestim *adv* immediately, speedily

cōnficiō, **fēcī**, **fectum** ③ *v* do, accomplish; finish; effect; arrange; produce, cause; conquer; kill; use up; consume, weaken, overwhelm; spend

cōnfīdēns, **ntis** *adj* bold, daring; over-confident, presumptuous

cōnfīdentia, **ae** *f* confidence; boldness; impudence, audacity

cōnfīdō, **fidere**, **fīsus sum** ③ *v semi-dep with dat* trust to, have confidence in

cōnfīgō, **īxī**, **īxum** ③ *v* fasten together; pierce through, strike down

cōnfingō, **īnxī**, **ictum** ③ *v* fashion, fabricate, invent, feign

cōnfīnis, **e** *adj* adjoining, contiguous, allied, akin

cōnfīnium, **(i)ī** *nt* common boundary; border

cōnfirmātiō, **ōnis** *f* confirmation, encouragement

cōnfirmō ① *v* confirm; strengthen; encourage; prove; say boldly

cōnfiteor, **fessus sum** ② *v dep* confess, admit; reveal

cōnflagrō ① *v* be burnt down; be utterly destroyed

cōnflictō ① *v* harass, torment; strike frequently, buffet

cōnflīgō, **īxī**, **ictum** ③ *v* strike together, collide, clash; strive; fight; dispute

cōnflō ① *v* blow on, ignite; melt; inflame; raise, bring about; arouse

cōnfluō, **ūxī** ③ *v* flow together; flock together

cōnfodiō, **ōdī**, **ossum** ③ *v* dig up; wound fatally; pierce

cōnfōrmātiō, **ōnis** *f* shape, form; idea, notion; figure of speech

cōnfōrmō ① *v* shape, fashion; train, educate

cōnfragōsus, **a**, **um** *adj*, **confragus**, **a**, **um** *adj* rough, uneven; hard

cōnfremō, **muī** ③ *v* murmur, echo

cōnfricō ① *v* rub

cōnfringō, **ēgī**, **āctum** ③ *v* break in pieces; ruin, subvert

cōnfugiō, **fūgī** ③ *v* flee to, have recourse to

cōnfundō, **ūdī**, **ūsum** ③ *v* pour *or* mix together; upset, confuse; bewilder

cōnfūsiō, **ōnis** *f* mingling; confusion, disorder, trouble

cōnfūtō ① *v* check, repress; silence; disprove

cōnfutuō, **uī**, **ūtum** ③ *v* fuck violently

congelō ① *v* congeal; curdle; freeze; grow hard

congeminō ① *v* redouble

congemō, **muī** ③ *v* utter a cry of grief *or* pain; bewail

congeriēs, **iēī** *f* heap, pile, mass; accumulation

congerō, **essī**, **estum** ③ *v* heap up, get together; build; compile; confer

congerrō, **ōnis** *m* boon-companion

congestus, **ūs** *m* bringing together, assembling; heap, pile, mass

congiārium, **(i)ī** *nt* largess for soldiers; gift in corn, oil, wine, *etc.*

conglobō ① *v* make into a ball; crowd together

conglūtinō ① *v* glue together

congrātulor ① *v dep* congratulate

congredior, **gressus sum** ③ *v dep* meet; join battle

congregātiō, **ōnis** *f* society, association

congregō ① *v* collect (into a flock); unite

congressiō, **ōnis** *f* meeting, visit, interview; conflict, attack; sexual intercourse

congressus, **ūs** *m* conference, interview; encounter, fight; sexual intercourse

congruēns, **ntis** *adj* consistent; harmonious, fitting

congruō, **ruī** ③ *v* come together; agree, accord; suit

cōnī- ▷ **conni-**

coniciō, **iēcī**, **iectum** ③ *v* throw together; cast, fling; drive; direct; conjecture; interpret

> **!** The first syllable of this verb scans as heavy in the present stem even though the 'o' is short; this is because the 'i' represents 'ii' pronounced as consonant + vowel 'yi'.

coniectō ① *v* conjecture; interpret; think *or* imagine

coniectūra, **ae** *f* conjecture; inference; interpretation; prophecy

coniectus, **ūs** *m* throwing; directing; shot; glance; hail

cōnifer, **cōniger**, **era**, **erum** *adj* coniferous, cone-bearing

coniugālis, **e** *adj* conjugal, matrimonial

coniugātor, **ōris** *m* one who unites (in a pair)

coniugium, **(i)ī** *nt* marriage, wedlock; wife; husband

coniūnctim *adv* in combination, jointly

coniūnctiō, **ōnis** *f* union, conjunction; agreement; mutual love; familiarity; match; fellowship

coniungō, **ūnxī**, **ūnctum** ③ *v* yoke together; connect; couple; ally; associate

coniūnx, **ugis** *m/f* (also **coniux**) husband, wife, spouse, mate

coniūrātiō, **ōnis** *f* conspiracy, plot; band of conspirators; taking an oath

coniūrātus, **a**, **um** *adj* leagued ▪ **coniūrātī**, **ōrum** *mpl* conspirators

coniūrō ① *v* swear together; conjure, conspire

conl- ▷ **coll-**

conm- ▷ **comm-**

connectō, **exuī**, **exum** ③ *v* tie, fasten *or* join together, connect; implicate

connītor, **nīxus/nīsus sum** ③ *v dep* endeavour eagerly; struggle; strain, strive

connīveō, **nīvī/nīxī** ② *v* close the eyes; wink at, overlook, turn a blind eye

cōnōpēum, **ī** *nt* mosquito-net

cōnor 1 *v dep* try, venture, undertake

conp- ▸ **comp-**

conquassō 1 *v* shake violently; unsettle

conqueror, questus sum 3 *v dep* complain of, bewail

conquiēscō, ēvī, ētum 3 *v* repose, rest; be inactive; go to sleep; find rest

conquīrō, īsīvī/īsiī, īsītum 3 *v* search for diligently; rake up; hunt down

conquīsītiō, ōnis *f* levying

cōnsaepiō, psī, ptum 4 *v* enclose, fence

cōnsalūtātiō, ōnis *f* greeting, exchange of greetings

cōnsalūtō 1 *v* greet, hail; salute as

cōnsanguineus, a, um *adj* related by blood; brotherly, sisterly
■ **cōnsanguineī, ōrum** *mpl* relatives

cōnsanguinitās, ātis *f* blood-relationship, kinship

cōnscelerātus, a, um *adj* wicked, depraved; criminal

cōnscelerō 1 *v* stain with crime, pollute

cōnscendō, ndī, ēnsum 3 *v* mount, ascend; embark

cōnscientia, ae *f* conscience, consciousness; knowledge; remorse

cōnscindō, idī, issum 3 *v* rend to pieces; slaughter

cōnsciscō, īvī/iī, ītum 3 *v* decree
□ **mortem sibi cōnsciscere** commit suicide

cōnscius, a, um *adj* conscious; knowing; guilty; witnessing; self-conscious

cōnscrībillō 1 *v* scrawl over, cover with scribbling

cōnscrībō, psī, ptum 3 *v* enlist *or* enrol; compose, write
□ **patrēs cōnscrīptī** the title by which senators were addressed

cōnsecrātiō, ōnis *f* consecration; deification

cōnsecrō 1 *v* consecrate; dedicate; hallow; deify

cōnsector 1 *v dep* go towards; seek after; imitate; pursue, hunt down; attack

cōnsecūtiō, ōnis *f* consequence; order, sequence; logical consequence

cōnsenēscō, nuī 3 *v* grow old; become weak; lose consideration *or* respect; fall into disuse

cōnsēnsiō, ōnis *f* agreement, unanimity; conspiracy

cōnsēnsus, ūs *m* unanimity, concord

cōnsentāneus, a, um *adj* agreeable; consistent, fitting

cōnsentiō, ēnsī, ēnsum 4 *v* consent; agree; decree; conspire; be consistent with

cōnsequēns, ntis *adj* following; following as a logical consequence; consistent

cōnsequor, secūtus sum 3 *v dep* follow after; overtake; get *or* obtain; procure; imitate; reach, come up to; befall; bring about, achieve

cōnserō¹, ēvī, situm 3 *v* sow, plant

cōnserō², ruī, rtum 3 *v* join; link; engage
□ **manum** ∼ engage in hostilities

cōnserva, ae *f* fellow-slave (female)

cōnservātiō, ōnis *f* keeping, preservation

cōnservātor, ōris *m* keeper; defender; saviour

cōnservō 1 *v* preserve, keep from danger; maintain

cōnservus, ī *m* fellow-slave

cōnsessor, ōris *m* assessor

cōnsessus, ūs *m* assembly; audience; court

cōnsīderātus, a, um *adj* thought out, cautious, deliberate

cōnsīderō 1 *v* inspect; consider, contemplate

cōnsīdō, sēdī, sessum 3 *v* sit down; settle; sink down; encamp; take up one's residence; hold a session; abate; cease

cōnsignō 1 *v* seal up; attest

cōnsilior 1 *v dep* take counsel; advise

cōnsilium, (i)ī *nt* counsel, advice; reason; purpose, plan; stratagem; resolution, will; judgment; prudence
□ ∼ **capiō** decide, resolve, have an idea; deliberate, take counsel

cōnsimilis, e *adj* similar, like

cōnsistō, stitī, stitum 3 *v* stand (together *or* fast); be frozen; make a stand; be steadfast; be in existence; consist (of); halt; cease

cōnsitor, ōris *m* sower, planter

cōnsociātiō, **ōnis** *f* association, uniting

cōnsociō ① *v* associate, unite; share

cōnsōlātiō, **ōnis** *f* consolation, comfort; encouragement

cōnsōlātor, **ōris** *m* comforter

cōnsōlātōrius, **a**, **um** *adj* consolatory, consoling

cōnsōlor ① *v dep* console, solace; alleviate, allay

cōnsonō, **ī** ① *v* make a noise together, resound; agree; harmonize

cōnsonus, **a**, **um** *adj* sounding together; harmonious

cōnsōpiō ④ *v* lull to sleep, make unconscious

cōnsors, **rtis** *adj* partaking of; brotherly, sisterly; *m/f* colleague, partner; fellow

cōnsortiō, **ōnis** *f* fellowship; partnership; association

cōnsortium, **(i)ī** *nt* fellowship, participation

cōnspectus[1], **ūs** *m* look, sight, view; presence; contemplation; range of view

cōnspectus[2], **a**, **um** *adj* visible; remarkable

cōnspergō, **rsī**, **rsum** ③ *v* besprinkle, sprinkle

cōnspiciō, **spexī**, **spectum** ③ *v* catch sight of, see; observe; descry

cōnspicor ① *v dep* get a sight of, see

cōnspicuus, **a**, **um** *adj* in sight, visible; illustrious, remarkable

cōnspīrātiō, **ōnis** *f* concord, harmony; unanimity; conspiracy

cōnspīrō ① *v* harmonize, agree; conspire

cōnspurcō ① *v* befoul, pollute

cōnstāns, **ntis** *adj* steadfast, firm, immovable, constant; secure; consistent; sure, steady

cōnstantia, **ae** *f* steadfastness, firmness, constancy, perseverance; resolution; agreement

cōnsternātiō, **ōnis** *f* confusion, dismay; mutiny; sedition; disturbance, disorder

cōnsternō[1], **strāvī**, **strātum** ③ *v* bestrew; throw down; pave

cōnsternō[2] ① *v* terrify, confuse

cōnstīpō ① *v* crowd together

cōnstituō, **uī**, **ūtum** ③ *v* put, set, place; constitute, appoint; decree, decide, determine; fix, establish; range; build; establish; agree (upon); manage; dispose; intend; settle

cōnstitūtiō, **ōnis** *f* constitution, disposition; ordering; arrangement; ordinance

cōnstitūtum, **ī** *nt* institution, law; agreement, compact

cōnstō, **stetī** ① *v* stand still; last; be settled *or* certain *or* known; cost; agree (with); exist *or* be; consist (of); stand firm

□ **cōnstat** ① *v impers* it is agreed

cōnstringō, **īnxī**, **ictum** ③ *v* bind fast *or* tight; compress

cōnstrūctiō, **ōnis** *f* building, construction

cōnstruō, **ūxī**, **ūctum** ③ *v* heap up; make, build

cōnstuprō ① *v* ravish, rape

cōnsuēfaciō, **fēcī**, **factum** ③ *v* accustom

cōnsuēscō, **ēvī**, **ētum** ③ *v* accustom; become accustomed; be accustomed; have intercourse with

cōnsuētūdō, **inis** *f* custom, habit, use; manner; companionship, familiarity, conversation

cōnsul, **lis** *m* consul, one of the chief Roman magistrates

> **!** Elected annually, the two **cōnsulēs** were the chief magistrates of Rome during the republican period, exercising civil and military power. Each year was 'named' after the two consuls for that year. In inscriptions, **cōnsul** is often abbreviated as **COS** (pl. **COSS**).

cōnsulāris, **e** *adj* consular; of *or* proper to a consul; ex-consular

cōnsulātus, **ūs** *m* consulship

cōnsulō, **luī**, **ltum** ③ *v* take counsel; consider; consult (someone); take steps; *with dat* consult the interest of; take care of; provide for

cōnsultātiō, **ōnis** *f* consultation, deliberation

cōnsultē, **cōnsultō** *adv* deliberately, on purpose

cōnsultō ① *v* consult, to take counsel

cōnsultor, **ōris** *m* adviser; consulter; lawyer

cōnsultum, ī *nt* decision; decree

cōnsultus, a, um *adj* well-considered; knowing, experienced

cōnsummō 1 *v* add up, finish

cōnsūmō, mpsī, mptum 3 *v* use up; eat; consume; squander, destroy; employ

cōnsurgō, surrēxī, surrēctum 3 *v* rise, stand; arise

contabulō 1 *v* board over; cover

contāctus, ūs *m* touch, contact; contagion

contāgēs, gis *f* contact; infection

contāgiō, ōnis *f*, **contāgium**, (i)ī *nt* contagion, contact, touch; influence; infection

contāminō 1 *v* contaminate, pollute, debase, spoil

contegō, ēxī, ēctum 3 *v* cover (up); hide

contemerō 1 *v* defile, pollute

contemnō, mpsī, mptum 3 *v* scorn, contemn

contemplātiō, ōnis *f* view, survey, contemplation; meditation

contemplātus, ūs *m* contemplation

contemplor 1 *v dep*, **contemplō** 1 *v* survey, observe; contemplate

contemptim *adv* contemptuously; fearlessly

contemptiō, ōnis *f* contempt, scorn, disdain

contemptor, ōris *m* contemner, despiser

contemptus[1], ūs *m* contempt, scorn

contemptus[2], a, um *adj* contemptible, vile

contendō, ndī, ntum 3 *v* stretch, strain; hurl; contend; fight; dispute; strive, exert; labour; demand; urge; state emphatically; go, march; hasten; compare

contentē *adv* with great exertion

contentiō, ōnis *f* exertion; contest, fight; dispute; comparison; contrast; antithesis

contentus[1], a, um *adj* tense, tight; energetic, vigorous

contentus[2], a, um *adj* contented, satisfied

conterminus, a, um *adj* bordering upon

conterō, trīvī, trītum 3 *v* grind, bruise, crumble; waste; spend; exhaust

conterreō 2 *v* frighten thoroughly

contestor 1 *v dep* call to witness

contexō, xuī, xtum 3 *v* entwine, twist together; connect, compose

contextus, ūs *m* connection, coherence; series

conticēscō, cuī 3 *v* cease to talk, fall silent

contignātiō, ōnis *f* raftering; storey, floor

contignō 1 *v* rafter, floor

contiguus, a, um *adj* adjoining, bordering upon

continēns, ntis *adj* contiguous, adjacent; uninterrupted; temperate, restrained, self-disciplined
■ ~, ntis *f* mainland

continenter *adv* without interruption; temperately

continentia, ae *f* abstemiousness, continence, self-control

contineō, tentum 2 *v* hold together; bind; contain; retain; comprise; confine; keep secret; hinder, prevent; stop

contingō, tigī, tāctum 3 *v* touch; seize; border upon; reach; influence; affect; stain; befall; come to pass; be akin; be connected with

continuātiō, ōnis *f* continuation, prolongation

continuō[1] *adv* immediately, forthwith

continuō[2] 1 *v* put in a line; join; deal with successively, prolong

continuus, a, um *adj* continuous; successive

cōntiō, ōnis *f* assembly, meeting; oration

cōntiōnābundus, a, um *adj* delivering a public speech

cōntiōnālis, e *adj* belonging to a public assembly

cōntiōnātor, ōris *m* haranguer of the people; demagogue

cōntiōnor 1 *v dep* deliver an oration to a public assembly

cōntiuncula, ae *f* small *or* negligible meeting

contorqueō, rsī, rtum 2 *v* brandish; fling; twist round

contrā *prep with acc* against; opposite to; contrary to; face to face; *adv* against; opposite to; contrary to; on the contrary; otherwise; mutually; face to face

contractiō, **ōnis** *f* contraction; abridgement

contractus, **a**, **um** *adj* close; abridged; stinted

contrādīcō, **īxī**, **ictum** ③ *v* speak against, contradict, oppose

contrādictiō, **ōnis** *f* objection, contradiction

contrahō, **āxī**, **actum** ③ *v* draw together; gather; tighten; abridge; check; agree; incur; get; cause

contrārius, **a**, **um** *adj* opposite, contrary; inimical; harmful
□ **ex contrāriō** on the contrary

contrectō ① *v* touch repeatedly, handle

contremīscō, **muī** ③ *v* tremble all over; tremble at

contribuō, **buī**, **būtum** ③ *v* incorporate; contribute

contrīstō ① *v* make sad, afflict; darken

contritio, **onis** *f* [LM] grief, contrition

controversia, **ae** *f* controversy; dispute

controversiōsus, **a**, **um** *adj* much disputed, debatable

controvors- ▶ **controvers-**

contrucīdō ① *v* cut down, slaughter

contrūdō, **ūsī**, **ūsum** ③ *v* thrust, press in

contubernālis, **is** *m/f* tent-companion; comrade, mate

contubernium, **(i)ī** *nt* companionship in a tent; attendance on a superior; common war tent

contueor ② *v dep* look at, behold, see

contumācia, **ae** *f* stubbornness

contumāx, **ācis** *adj* stubborn, defiant

contumēlia, **ae** *f* insult, affront, ignominy; damage

contumēliōsus, **a**, **um** *adj* insolent, abusive

contumulō ① *v* bury

contundō, **udī**, **ūsum** ③ *v* bruise, crush; subdue utterly

conturbātiō, **ōnis** *f* confusion, panic

conturbātus, **a**, **um** *adj* disturbed, perplexed

conturbō ① *v* upset, throw into confusion; disquiet; go bankrupt

contus, **ī** *m* long pole, pike

cōnūbium, **(i)ī** *nt* intermarriage; marriage

cōnus, **ī** *m* cone; apex of a helmet

convalēscō, **luī** ③ *v* recover, get better, grow strong

convallis, **is** *f* a valley (much shut in)

convāsō ① *v* pack up (baggage)

convectō ① *v*, **convehō**, **ēxī**, **ectum** ③ *v* carry together, gather

convellō, **llī**, **ulsum** ③ *v* pull *or* pluck up; wrench; shatter; overthrow

convenae, **ārum** *mpl* refugees, immigrants

conveniēns, **ntis** *adj* fitting; appropriate

convenientia, **ae** *f* agreement, harmony; fitness

conveniō, **vēnī**, **ventum** ④ *v* come together, assemble; meet; agree; fit, suit; be due; visit, prosecute

conventiculum, **ī** *nt* small assemblage; place of assembly

conventiō, **ōnis** *f*, **conventum**, **ī** *nt* agreement, compact

conventus, **ūs** *m* meeting, assembly; provincial court; district

converrō ③ *v* sweep together, sweep up

conversō ① *v* turn, turn over in the mind
□ **conversor** ① *v dep* be a constant visitor (to)

convertō, **rtī**, **rsum** ③ *v* turn round; convert; change, transform; translate

convestiō ④ *v* clothe, dress, cover

convexus, **a**, **um** *adj* convex; arched, vaulted

convīcium, **(i)ī** *nt* cry, clamour; bawling; reproach, abuse

convīctiō, **ōnis** *f* companionship, intimacy

convīctor, **ōris** *m* messmate, friend

convīctus, **ūs** *m* living together, intimacy; banquet, feast

convincō, **īcī**, **ictum** ③ *v* convict, prove clearly

convīva, **ae** *m/f* table companion, guest

convīvālis, **e** *adj* convivial

convīvātor, **ōris** *m* host

convīvium, **(i)ī** *nt* feast, entertainment, banquet

convocō ① *v* call together, convoke, assemble

convolō ① *v* fly together; (fig) run together

convolvō, **lvī**, **lūtum** ③ *v* roll together *or* round, writhe

convorrō ▸ **converrō**

cooperiō, **ruī**, **rtum** ④ *v* cover wholly, overwhelm

cooptātiō, **ōnis** *f* co-option, adoption

cooptō ① *v* choose, elect, admit

coorior, **coortus sum** ④ *v dep* arise; break forth

cophinus, **ī** *m* large basket, hamper

cōpia, **ae** *f* abundance, plenty; riches; store; provisions; ability; power; opportunity, means; access to a person

cōpiae, **ārum** *fpl* (mil) forces

cōpiōsus, **a**, **um** *adj* plentiful, rich, wealthy; eloquent

cōpō ▸ **caupō**

cōpula, **ae** *f* bond, tie

cōpulātiō, **ōnis** *f* connecting, uniting

cōpulō ① *v* couple, bind *or* tie together, connect, unite

coquō, **coxī**, **coctum** ③ *v* cook; boil, fry, bake; burn; parch; ripen; digest; mature, cherish, stir up

coquus, **ī** *m* cook

cor, **rdis** *nt* heart; mind, judgment
□ **cordī esse** be pleasing

corallium, **(i)ī** *nt* coral

cōram *prep with abl* in the presence of, face to face; *adv* face to face; personally

corbis, **is** *m/f* basket

corcillum, **ī** *nt*, **corculum**, **ī** *nt* little heart

corium, **(i)ī** *nt* skin, leather, hide

corneus¹, **a**, **um** *adj* of horn, resembling horn

corneus², **a**, **um** *adj* of the cornel-tree

cornicen, **inis** *m* trumpeter, bugler

corniger, **era**, **erum** *adj* horn-bearing, horned

cornipēs, **edis** *adj* horn-footed, hoofed

cornīx, **īcis** *f* crow

cornū, **ūs** *nt* horn; hoof; bill of a bird; horn of the moon; end, tip; peak, cone

of a helmet; bow; trumpet; wing of an army; funnel

cornum, **ī** *nt* cornel-berry

cornus, **ī** *f* cornel-cherry-tree, cornel wood

corōlla, **ae** *f* small garland

corōna, **ae** *f* garland, wreath, crown; circle (of men); cordon of troops thrown round an enemy position

corōnō ① *v* crown, wreathe; surround

corporeus, **a**, **um** *adj* corporeal; fleshy

corpus, **oris** *nt* body; flesh; corpse; trunk; frame; corporation

corpusculum, **ī** *nt* little body, atom

corrēctiō, **ōnis** *f* improvement, correction

corrēctor, **ōris** *m* corrector, improver, reformer

corrēpō, **psī** ③ *v* creep, move stealthily

corrigō, **ēxī**, **ēctum** ③ *v* straighten, set right; correct

corripiō, **puī**, **eptum** ③ *v* snatch up, lay hold of; rebuke, chastise; shorten; hasten; seize unlawfully
□ ~ **viam** hasten on one's way

corrōborō ① *v* strengthen, corroborate

corrogō ① *v* collect money by begging

corrūgō ① *v* make wrinkled

corrumpō, **ūpī**, **uptum** ③ *v* spoil, destroy, deface; falsify; bribe; corrupt, seduce

corruō, **ruī** ③ *v* break down, fall to the ground

corruptēla, **ae** *f* corruption, enticement to sexual misconduct, bribery; corrupting influence

corruptiō, **ōnis** *f* corruption; bribery

corruptor, **ōris** *m* corrupter, seducer, briber

cortex, **icis** *m* bark, rind; cork

cortīna, **ae** *f* cauldron, cauldron on oracular tripod (at Delphi)

cōrus, **ī** *m* north-west wind

coruscō ① *v* brandish, shake; flash, coruscate

coruscus, **a**, **um** *adj* vibrating, tremulous; flashing

corvus, **ī** *m* raven; military engine

corylētum, **ī** *nt* copse of hazel-trees

corylus, **ī** *f* hazel-tree

corymbus, ī *m* cluster of ivy-berries *or* flowers *or* fruit

cōs, ōtis *f* flint-stone; whetstone ■ **cōtēs** *pl* rocks

costa, ae *f* rib; side

costos, ī *f*, **costum**, ī *nt* an aromatic plant *or* its powdered root

cothurnātus, a, um *adj* wearing the buskin; in lofty style

cothurnus, ī *m* high boot worn by Greek tragic actors; elevated style, tragic poetry

cōtīdiānus, a, um *adj* daily

cōtīdiē *adv* every day, daily

cott- ▷ **cōt-**

coturnīx, īcis *f* quail

covinnārius, (i)ī *m* charioteer

coxa, ae *f* hip

crābrō, ōnis *m* wasp, hornet
□ **irritō crābrōnēs** disturb a hornets' nest

crāpula, ae *f* drunkenness; next day's sickness

crās *adv* tomorrow; in the future

crassitūdō, inis *f* thickness, density

crassus, a, um *adj* thick, dense, fat, gross, stupid, crass

crastino ① *v* LM put off

crāstīnus, a, um *adj* of tomorrow

crātēr, ēris *m*, **crātēra**, ae *f* mixing-bowl; crater of a volcano, basin of fountain; Cup (constellation)

crātis, is *f* wicker-work; harrow; frame-work

creātor, ōris *m* creator, author, founder; father

creātrīx, īcis *f* creatress, mother

creatura, ae *f* LM creature

crēber, bra, brum *adj* thick, close, pressed together, frequent, numerous; abundant

crēb(r)ēscō, b(r)uī ③ *v* become frequent, increase

crēbritās, ātis *f* frequency, closeness in succession

crēbrō *adv* frequently; in many places

crēdibilis, e *adj* trustworthy, credible

crēditor, ōris *m* lender, creditor

crēditum, ī *nt* loan

crēdō, didī, ditum ③ *v with dat* believe, trust; entrust; think, be of the opinion

crēdulitās, ātis *f* credulity, trustfulness

crēdulus, a, um *adj* credulous

cremō ① *v* burn, consume by fire

creō ① *v* create, make, produce; choose; elect; cause; establish

crepida, ae *f* slipper, sandal

crepīdō, inis *f* pedestal; brink; pier, bank, sidewalk

crepitāculum, ī *nt* rattle

crepitō ① *v* rattle, clatter, rustle

crepitus, ūs *m* rattling, clashing, rustling; (of thunder) crash; (of the teeth) chattering; fart

crepō, puī, pitum ① *v* rattle, rustle, clatter; snap the fingers; jingle; harp on, grumble at the way that

crepundia, ōrum *ntpl* child's rattle; cymbals

crepusculum, ī *nt* twilight, dusk

crēscō, crēvī, crētum ③ *v* grow; arise, spring; appear; get advantage; increase; attain honour, be advanced, be strengthened

crēta, ae *f* chalk; clay; paint; clayey soil

crētātus, a, um *adj* marked with chalk; powdered

crētiō, ōnis *f* declaration respecting the acceptance of an inheritance

crētōsus, a, um *adj* abounding in chalk *or* clay

crēvī ▷ **crēscō**

crībrum, ī *nt* sieve

crīmen, inis *nt* crime, offence, fault; scandal; reproach; accusation

crīminātiō, ōnis *f* accusation, indictment

crīminor ① *v dep* accuse; charge (with)

crīminōsus, a, um *adj* accusatory; reproachful, vituperative

crīnālis, e *adj* worn in the hair; covered with hair-like filaments

crīnis, is *m* hair; tail of a comet

crīnītus, a, um *adj* hairy; having long locks
□ **stella crīnīta** comet

crispō ① *v* curl, crisp; shake, brandish

crispus, a, um *adj* curled; curly-headed; quivering

crista, ae *f* crest; cock's comb; plume (of a helmet)

cristātus, **a**, **um** *adj* tufted, crested; plumed

criticus, **ī** *m* literary critic

croceus, **a**, **um** *adj* of saffron; saffron-coloured; yellow

crocinum, **ī** *nt* saffron oil used as a perfume

crocinus, **a**, **um** *adj* of saffron, yellow

crocodīlus, **ī** *m* crocodile

crocum, **ī** *nt*, **crocus**, **ī** *m* crocus; saffron; saffron-colour

cruciāmentum, **ī** *nt* torture, torment

cruciātus, **ūs** *m* torture; severe physical *or* mental pain

cruciō ① *v* torture; grieve

crūdēlis, **e** *adj* cruel, bloodthirsty

crūdēlitās, **ātis** *f* cruelty, barbarity

crūdēscō, **duī** ③ *v* become fierce *or* savage

crūdus, **a**, **um** *adj* raw; bloody; undigested; unripe, sour; fresh; immature; vigorous; harsh; cruel

cruentō ① *v* stain with blood

cruentus, **a**, **um** *adj* gory, bloody; blood-thirsty; blood-red

crumēna, **ae** *f* purse; supply of money, resources

cruor, **ōris** *m* gore, blood; murder

crūs, **ris** *nt* leg, shank, shin

crusta, **ae** *f* rind, shell, crust, bark

crustulārius, **(i)ī** *m* seller of cakes

crustum, **ī** *nt* pastry, cake

crux, **cis** *f* cross; torture, trouble, misery, destruction; gallows, rack

cryptoporticus, **ūs** *f* covered portico

cubiculārius, **(i)ī** *m valet-de-chambre*

cubiculum, **ī** *nt* bedroom

cubīle, **is** *nt* couch, bed; marriage-bed; lair

cubitō ① *v* lie down

cubitum, **ī** *nt* elbow; forearm; cubit

cubō, **buī**, **bitum** ① *v* lie down; lie asleep; recline at table

cucumis, **eris** *m* cucumber

cucurbita, **ae** *f* gourd

cucurrī ▶ **currō**

cūdō ③ *v* strike, stamp; mint (coin)

cūiās, **ātis** *adj* of what country *or* town?

culcitula, **ae** *f* small mattress

culex, **icis** *m* gnat, midge

culīna, **ae** *f* kitchen; fare, victuals

culmen, **inis** *nt* top, summit; gable; acme, eminence

culmus, **ī** *m* stalk, stem; thatch

culpa, **ae** *f* fault, crime, blame; negligence

culpō ① *v* blame, find fault with; accuse, censure

culta, **ōrum** *ntpl* tilled land

culter, **trī** *m* knife

cultor, **ōris** *m* husbandman; cultivator, inhabitant; supporter; worshipper

cultrīx, **īcis** *f* female inhabitant

cultūra, **ae** *f* agriculture; care, culture, cultivation

cultus[1], **ūs** *m* worship, reverence; culture; refinement; adorning; splendour, smartness; livelihood

cultus[2], **a**, **um** *adj* cultivated, polished, elegant, civilized

culullus, **ī** *m* a drinking vessel *or* its contents

cūlus, **ī** *m* anus

cum[1] *prep with abl* with; along with; amid; *with words expressing strife, contention, etc.* against

> **!** When **cum** governs a personal pronoun, it is placed after it, forming a single word, i.e. **mēcum**, **tēcum**, **nōbīscum** etc.; note also **quīcum** and **quibuscum**.

cum[2] *conj* when; since; although; as soon as

> **!** **cum** is usu. followed by the subj. when the verb in its clause is in a past tense; otherwise it is followed by the indic. However, **cum** with a pf. or plpf. indic. may indicate repeated present or past action respectively ('whenever'). **cum** may also take an indic. where it introduces the main information of a sentence, in which case the **cum** clause must follow the main clause ('inverted **cum**'). Cf. also **quandō**.

cumba, **ae** *f* small boat, skiff

cumulātus, **a**, **um** *adj* heaped, abundant, great

cumulō ① *v* heap up; accumulate; fill full

cumulus, **ī** *m* heap, pile; surplus, increase; summit, crown

cūnābula, **ōrum** *ntpl* cradle; earliest dwelling-place; earliest childhood

cūnae, **ārum** *fpl* cradle; one's earliest years

cūnctābundus, **a**, **um** *adj* lingering, loitering

cūnctāns, **ntis** *adj* hesitant, clinging; stubborn

cūnctātiō, **ōnis** *f* delay, hesitation

cūnctātor, **ōris** *m* delayer

cūnctor ① *v dep* tarry, linger, hesitate

cūnctus, **a**, **um** *adj* all together, total, complete

cuneātim *adv* in a closely packed formation

cuneātus, **a**, **um** *adj* wedge-shaped

cuneus, **ī** *m* wedge; battalion, *etc.*, drawn up in the form of a wedge; rows of seats in a theatre

cunīculōsus, **a**, **um** *adj* abounding in rabbits

cunīculus, **ī** *m* rabbit; underground passage; mine; channel

cunnus, **ī** *m* the female pudenda

cupiditās, **ātis** *f* longing, desire; passion; avarice; ambition

cupīdō¹, **inis** *f* desire, greediness; appetite; love; desire of material gain

Cupīdō², **inis** *m* the god of love

cupidus, **a**, **um** *adj* longing for, desiring, eager; loving; greedy, passionate

cupiēns, **ntis** *adj* desirous, eager for, anxious

cupiō, **īvī/iī**, **ītum** ③ *v* long for, desire; covet

cupītor, **ōris** *m* one who seeks after

cuppēdia¹, **ae** *f* gourmandism

cuppēdia², **ōrum** *ntpl* delicacies

cupresseus, **a**, **um** *adj* of cypress

cupressifer, **era**, **erum** *adj* cypress-bearing

cupressus, **ī** *f* cypress-tree; spear of cypress-wood

cūr *adv* why?

cūra, **ae** *f* attention, care; administration; office; written work; task, responsibility; sorrow; anxiety, concern; trouble; love; object of love

cūrātiō, **ōnis** *f* administration, management; treatment, charge

cūrātor, **ōris** *m* manager, superintendent; guardian

curculiō, **ōnis** *m* corn-weevil

cūria, **ae** *f* division of the Roman people, senate-house, senate

cūriātus, **a**, **um** *adj* pertaining to cūriae

□ **comitia cūriāta** *ntpl* the assembly in which people voted according to cūriae

□ **lēx cūriāta** *f* law passed by the assembly of the thirty divisions of the Roman people

cūriō, **ōnis** *m* chief priest of a cūria

cūriōsus, **a**, **um** *adj* careful, diligent; curious, inquisitive

cūrō ① *v* take care of, mind; worry *or* care about; order; attend to; heal; cure

curriculum, **ī** *nt* race; race-track; chariot; course of action

■ **curriculō** *adv* at full speed

currō, **cucurrī**, **cursum** ③ *v* run, hasten

currus, **ūs** *m* chariot; triumphal chariot; triumph

cursim *adv* swiftly, hastily

cursitō ① *v,* **cursō** ① *v* run to and fro

cursor, **ōris** *m* runner; chariot-racer; courier

cursūra, **ae** *f* running

cursus, **ūs** *m* running; course, voyage, journey; race; direction; march; career

> **!** From the 2nd cent. BC there developed a standard **cursus honōrum** ('career path') followed by leading citizens of Rome. The first step was to be **quaestor** often followed by the aedileship; this was followed by the praetorship and then the consulship.

curtus, **a**, **um** *adj* mutilated; incomplete

curūlis, **e** *adj* of curule rank, *i.e.* of consuls, praetors or curule aediles

curvāmen, **inis** *nt* curvature; curved form, arc

curvō ① *v* make curved, bend; make (a person) stoop

curvus, **a**, **um** *adj* crooked, bent, curved, stooping

cuspis, **idis** *f* point, spike; spear; trident (of Neptune); scorpion's sting

custōdēla, ae f charge, custody (of a person or thing)

custōdia, ae f watch, guard, care; watch-house; guard-post; confinement; prison

custōdiō ④ v watch, guard; preserve; take heed; retain

custōs, ōdis m/f keeper; guardian; protector; watchman; jailer; container

cutis, is f skin

cyathus, ī m wine-ladle, wine-measure

cycnēus, a, um adj of a swan; swan-like

cycnus, cygnus, ī m swan

cylindrus, ī m cylinder; roller (for levelling the ground)

cymbalum, ī nt cymbal

cymbium, (i)ī nt small cup, especially for wine

Cynosūra, ae f (constellation) the Lesser Bear

cyparissus ▶ **cupressus**

cytisus, ī m/f a fodder plant, tree-medick

Dd

daedalus, a, um adj skilful; skilfully made

daemōn, nis m a supernatural being or spirit

dalmatica, ae f LM sleeved tunic, dalmatic (vestment of a deacon)

damma, ae f fallow-deer, doe, small member of deer family

damnātiō, ōnis f condemnation

damnō ① v condemn, sentence; discredit

damnōsus, a, um adj detrimental, injurious, destructive; prodigal

damnum, ī nt damage, injury, loss; hurt, fine

danīsta, ae m money-lender

danīsticus, a, um adj of money-lending, of usury

danunt = dant: ▶ **dō**

dapifer, eri m LM waiter

daps, pis f sacrificial feast; banquet

dapsilis, e adj abundant, plentiful

datiō, ōnis f giving, transfer, assigning

datō ① v make a practice of giving

dator, ōris m giver

dē prep with abl down from; from; away from, out of; about; (made) of; concerning; for; by reason of; after, from the time of, according to
□ ~ **imprōvīsō** unexpectedly

dea, ae f goddess

> ❗ The dat./abl. pl. of **dea** is **deābus**, distinguishing it from the dat./abl. pl. of **deus**.

dealbō ① v whitewash, whiten

dēbacchor ① v dep rage, rave

dēbellātor, ōris m conqueror

dēbellō ① v bring a battle or war to an end; vanquish

dēbeō ② v owe, be in debt; be obliged or bound or destined

dēbilis, e adj weak, feeble; crippled

dēbilitās, ātis f weakness, debility

dēbilitō ① v weaken; maim

dēbitor, ōris m debtor

dēbitum, ī nt debt; duty

dēcantō ① v reel off, chant; repeat

dēcēdō, essī, essum ③ v go away, depart; retire, yield; cease; die; disappear; decrease

decem adj indec ten

December, bris m December

decempeda, ae f ten-foot measuring rod

decemvirālis, e adj belonging to the decemviri

decemvirātus, ūs m office of decemvir

decemvirī, **ōrum** *mpl* commission of ten (magistrates at Rome)

decēns, **ntis** *adj* fitting; becoming, decent; symmetrical, well-proportioned

dēcernō, **crēvī**, **crētum** ③ *v* distinguish; judge; decide; settle; propose

dēcerpō, **psī**, **ptum** ③ *v* pluck *or* pull off; destroy; catch, snatch, reap

dēcertō ① *v* fight out; dispute

dēcessiō, **ōnis** *f* going away, departure; retirement; diminution; abatement

dēcessor, **ōris** *m* magistrate retiring from his post

dēcessus, **ūs** *m* departure; retirement; decrease; ebb; death

decet ② *v impers* it is becoming *or* right *or* proper

dēcidō, **idī** ③ *v* fall down; pass away; die

dēcīdō, **īdī**, **īsum** ③ *v* cut off; determine, put an end to

deciē(n)s *adv* ten times

decima, **ae** *f* tenth part; tithe

decimānus, **a**, **um** related to the tenth, belonging to the tenth legion *or* cohort
  □ **porta decimāna** the rear gate of a Roman camp

decimō ① *v* choose by lot every tenth man (for punishment)

decimus, **a**, **um** *adj* tenth

dēcipiō, **cēpī**, **ceptum** ③ *v* deceive, cheat

dēclāmātiō, **ōnis** *f* delivering of a set speech

dēclāmō ① *v* declaim, make speeches

dēclārō ① *v* declare; prove; mean

dēclīnō ① *v* turn aside; avoid; deviate

dēclīvis, **e** *adj* sloping downwards, declining
  ■ **declīve**, **is** *nt* slope, declivity

dēclīvitās, **ātis** *f* falling gradient

dēcoctor, **ōris** *m* insolvent person, defaulting debtor

dēcolor, **ōris** *adj* discoloured, faded; degenerate

dēcoquō, **coxī**, **coctum** ③ *v* boil down; waste away; become bankrupt

decor, **ōris** *m* beauty, grace; charm

decorō ① *v* adorn, grace; glorify

decōrus, **a**, **um** *adj* decorous; proper; suitable; graceful, handsome; noble

dēcrēscō, **ēvī**, **ētum** ③ *v* decrease; diminish; dwindle

dēcrētum, **ī** *nt* decree, decision; principle, doctrine

decum- ▸ **decim-**

dēcumbō, **ubuī** ③ *v* recline at the dinner table; lie ill

decuria, **ae** *f* group of ten, group

> ❗ The **decuria** was generally a division of cavalry.

decuriō[1] ① *v* divide into companies of ten

decuriō[2], **ōnis** *m* the head of a **decuria**

dēcurrō, **(cu)currī**, **ursum** ③ *v* run down; sail shorewards *or* downstream; have recourse to; drill

dēcursus, **ūs** *m* downward course; declivity; charge downhill

dēcurtātus, **a**, **um** *adj* mutilated, cut short

decus, **oris** *nt* grace, ornament; glory; beauty; virtue, decorum; honour, respectability, dignity

dēcutiō, **ussī**, **ussum** ③ *v* shake down *or* off

dēdecet ② *v impers* it is unsuitable for *or* unbecoming to

dēdecorō ① *v* disgrace

dēdecōrus, **a**, **um** *adj* dishonourable

dēdecus, **oris** *nt* disgrace, infamy; shame; dishonour

dedī ▸ **dō**

dēdicātiō, **ōnis** *f* dedication, consecration

dēdicō ① *v* dedicate, devote

dēdignor ① *v dep* disdain; refuse, reject with scorn

dēdiscō, **didicī** ③ *v* unlearn, forget

dēditīcius, **a**, **um** *adj* having surrendered

dēditiō, **ōnis** *f* surrender

dēditus, **a**, **um** *adj* devoted to, fond of

dēdō, **dēdidī**, **dēditum** ③ *v* surrender; abandon; yield

dēdoleō ② *v* cease to grieve

dēdūcō, **dūxī**, **ductum** ③ *v* lead *or* draw down; bring away *or* off; establish (a colony); launch; conduct;

escort; derive; compose; withdraw; subtract

dēductiō, ōnis *f* transportation, deduction

deerrō 1 *v* go astray

dēfaecō ⋗ **dēfīcō**

dēfatīgātiō, ōnis *f* weariness, fatigue

dēfatīgō 1 *v* tire, exhaust; lose heart

dēfectiō, ōnis *f* failure, deficiency; defection, revolt

dēfector, ōris *m* rebel, renegade

dēfectus, ūs *m* failure; eclipse

dēfendō, ndī, ēnsum 3 *v* defend, guard; preserve; keep off; affirm, maintain

dēfēnsiō, ōnis *f* defence

dēfēnsō 1 *v* protect

dēfēnsor, ōris *m* defender, guardian, protector

dēferō, ferre, tulī, lātum *v ir* bring *or* carry down *or* off; convey; bring word; bestow; present; tell; transfer; accuse, indict

dēfessus, a, um *adj* tired, worn out

dēfetīgō ⋗ **dēfatīgō**

dēfetīscor, fessus sum 3 *v dep* grow weary *or* faint

dēficiō, fēcī, fectum 3 *v* fail; cease; faint; be discouraged; sink under; be wanting *or* defective; decay; die; desert, forsake

dēfīcō 1 *v* cleanse, clean

dēfīgō, īxī, īxum 3 *v* fix down, fasten; thrust into; astound, bewitch

dēfīniō 4 *v* limit; define; determine; end

dēfīnītiō, ōnis *f* definition

dēfīnītus, a, um *adj* definite, precise, limited

dēfīō, fierī *v ir semi-dep* be lacking

dēfīxiō, ōnis *f* binding with a spell, putting a spell on

dēflagrō 1 *v* be burnt down; 'burn out'; burn down; destroy

dēflectō, xī, xum 3 *v* bend *or* turn aside *or* off; divert, modify

dēfleō, ēvī, ētum 2 *v* weep abundantly for, mourn the loss of

dēflōrēscō, ruī 3 *v* fade, wither

dēfluō, ūxī, ūxum 3 *v* flow down; glide down; fade; disappear; be ended

defluum, i *nt* LM downpour

dēfodiō, ōdī, ossum 3 *v* dig; bury

dēfōrmis, e *adj* ill-formed, ugly; shapeless; odious; base

dēformitās, ātis *f* deformity, ugliness, degradation; lack of good taste

dēfōrmō[1] 1 *v* shape, fashion; delineate, describe

dēfōrmō[2] 1 *v* disfigure; spoil, impair

dēfraudō 1 *v* cheat, defraud

dēfrēnātus, a, um *adj* unbridled

dēfricō, cuī, c(ā)tum 1 *v* rub hard

dēfringō, ēgī, āctum 3 *v* break off

dēfrūdō ⋗ **dēfraudō**

dēfrūstror 1 *v dep* foil *or* thwart completely

dēfugiō, ūgī 3 *v* avoid, run away (from), escape

dēfundō, ūdī, ūsum 3 *v* pour down *or* out

dēfungor, fūnctus sum 3 *v dep with abl* discharge, finish; have done with; have died

dēgener, eris *adj* degenerate; low-born; base

dēgenerō 1 *v* degenerate; deteriorate, decline

dēgō, gī 3 *v* spend, pass; live

dēgravō 1 *v* weigh down; overpower

dēgredior, gressus sum 3 *v dep* march down, descend; dismount

dēgustō 1 *v* taste, take a taste of; try; test

dehinc *adv* after this; hence; henceforth; next; since then

dehīscō 3 *v* gape, split open

dehonestāmentum, ī *nt* disfigurement, disgrace

dehonestō 1 *v* disgrace

dehortor 1 *v dep* dissuade

dēiciō, iēcī, iectum 3 *v* throw down; dislodge; fell; kill; rob of; dispossess

dēiectus, ūs *m* throwing down; fall; declivity, slope

dein, deinde *adv* afterward; then; next

deinceps *adv* in succession; in a series

dēlābor, lāpsus sum 3 *v dep* slip *or* fall down; descend; sink

dēlātiō, ōnis *f* accusation, denunciation

dēlātor, **ōris** *m* accuser, informer

dēlectābilis, **e** *adj* delightful, agreeable

dēlectātiō, **ōnis** *f* delight, pleasure, amusement

dēlectō ① *v* entice; delight; amuse; charm

dēlectus ▸ **dīlectus**

dēlēgō ① *v* assign; delegate, depute; transfer; attribute

dēlēnīmentum, **ī** *nt* charm, allurement

dēlēniō ④ *v* mitigate, smooth down; soften, bewitch; mollify

dēleō, **lēvī**, **lētum** ② *v* efface; suppress; destroy; kill; annul

dēlīberābundus, **a**, **um** *adj* deep in thought

dēlīberātiō, **ōnis** *f* deliberation, consideration

dēlīberō ① *v* consult, deliberate; resolve

dēlībō ① *v* taste (of), touch on (a subject) lightly; diminish, detract (from)

dēlibūtus, **a**, **um** *adj* smeared, covered; overflowing (with feeling)

dēlicātus, **a**, **um** *adj* charming, elegant; delicate, tender; voluptuous; luxurious; effeminate

dēliciae, **ārum** *fpl* delight, pleasures; dalliance; airs and graces; darling, sweetheart

dēlictum, **ī** *nt* fault, offence, crime

dēligō¹, **lēgī**, **lectum** ③ *v* choose out, select, cull, pick off

dēligō² ① *v* tie up, fasten

dēlinquō, **līquī**, **lictum** ③ *v* fail (in duty); offend, do wrong

dēliquēscō, **licuī** ③ *v* melt away; dissipate one's energy

dēlīrō ① *v* be crazy, speak deliriously

dēlīrus, **a**, **um** *adj* crazy, insane; senseless

dēlitēscō, **tuī** ③ *v* go into hiding; withdraw

delphīnus, **ī** *m*, **delphīn**, **nis** *m* dolphin

dēlūbrum, **ī** *nt* shrine, temple

dēlūdificor ① *v dep* make a complete fool of

dēlūdō, **ūsī**, **ūsum** ③ *v* deceive, dupe

dēmānō ① *v* run down, percolate

dēmēns, **ntis** *adj* senseless; mad, foolish

dēmentia, **ae** *f* madness, folly

dēmereō ② *v* oblige, win the favour of

dēmergō, **rsī**, **rsum** ③ *v* plunge (into), sink; conceal

dēmētior, **mēnsus sum** ④ *v dep* measure out

dēmetō, **essuī**, **essum** ③ *v* mow, reap, cut off

dēmigrō ① *v* go away

dēminuō, **uī**, **ūtum** ③ *v* lessen, diminish

dēminūtiō, **ōnis** *f* diminution, decrease

dēmīror ① *v dep* wonder, be amazed

dēmissiō, **ōnis** *f* letting down; low spirits, dejection

dēmissus, **a**, **um** *adj* low-lying; hanging down; downcast; humble; unassuming; (of the voice) low

dēmittō, **mīsī**, **missum** ③ *v* let sink, lower; send down; dismiss; thrust (into); plunge; sink; depose, demote

dēmō, **mpsī**, **mptum** ③ *v* take away; subtract

dēmōlior ④ *v dep* pull down, demolish; destroy

dēmōnstrātiō, **ōnis** *f* demonstration, clear proof

dēmōnstrō ① *v* point at; prove, demonstrate; describe; represent

dēmorior, **morī**, **mortuus sum** ③ *v dep* die off

dēmoror ① *v dep* keep back, delay; linger, stay

dēmorsicō ① *v* bite pieces off, nibble at

dēmoveō, **mōvī**, **mōtum** ② *v* move away, put away, remove

dēmulceō, **lsī**, **lctum** ② *v* stroke, entrance

dēmum *adv* at length, at last
□ **tum ~** only then

dēnārius, **a**, **um** *adj* containing ten
■ **~**, **(i)ī** *m* Roman silver coin originally worth ten **asses**

dēnārrō ① *v* relate fully

dēnegō ① *v* refuse, deny

dēnī, **ae**, **a** *adj* ten each, by tens

d

dēnique *adv* at last, finally, in fact; in short

dēnōminātus, **a**, **um** *adj* named

dēnotō ① *v* specify, point out; brand

dēns, **ntis** *m* tooth; tusk; ivory

dēnseō, **ētum** ② *v*, **dēnsō** ① *v* thicken; press close together

dēnsus, **a**, **um** *adj* thick, dense; thickly planted with; frequent; concise

dentāle, **is** *nt* the share-beam of a ploughshare

dentātus, **a**, **um** *adj* toothed; having prominent teeth

dēnūbō, **ūpsī**, **ūptum** ③ *v* marry (away from her paternal home)

dēnūdō ① *v* make naked, uncover; reveal; rob, despoil

dēnumerō ① *v* pay (money) in full, pay down

dēnūntiātiō, **ōnis** *f* denunciation, declaration; threat; summons

dēnūntiō ① *v* announce, declare; foretell; threaten; summon (a witness)

dēnuō *adv* anew, afresh, again

deonerō ① *v* unload

deorsum, **deorsus** *adv* downwards, beneath, below

dēpacīscor, **pactus sum** ③ *v dep* bargain for, agree upon

dēpāscō, **āvī**, **āstum** ③ *v* pasture; eat up, waste, consume

dēpecīscor ▶ **dēpacīscor**

dēpellō, **pulī**, **pulsum** ③ *v* expel; dislodge; avert

dēpendeō ② *v* hang down, from *or* on; depend upon

dēpendō, **ndī**, **ēnsum** ③ *v* pay, expend

dēperdō, **didī**, **ditum** ③ *v* ruin; lose

dēpereō, **īre**, **iī** *v ir* perish; be lost; be hopelessly in love with

dēpingō, **īnxī**, **ictum** ③ *v* paint, depict, portray; describe

dēplangō, **ānxī** ③ *v* mourn by beating the breast

dēplōrō ① *v* lament, mourn for; give up for lost

dēpōnō, **posuī**, **positum** ③ *v* lay down *or* aside; deposit; commit; entrust; resign; fix, set, plant

dēpopulō ① *v*, **dēpopulor** ① *v dep* lay waste, plunder

dēportō ① *v* carry, convey

dēposcō, **poposcī** ③ *v* ask for earnestly, require

dēpositum, **ī** *nt* deposit, trust

dēprāvō ① *v* distort; deprave, corrupt

dēprecābundus, **a**, **um** *adj* entreating earnestly

dēprecātor, **ōris** *m* intercessor; one who pleads for the removal (of)

dēprecor ① *v dep* pray against; beg off; beg pardon; avert by prayer

dēpre(he)ndō, **ndī**, **ēnsum** ③ *v* catch, find out; discern, perceive; reach, overtake; catch in the act; surprise

dēprimō, **essī**, **essum** ③ *v* depress; keep down; sink; humble

dēprōmō, **mpsī**, **mptum** ③ *v* bring out

dēpugnō ① *v* fight it out *or* hard

dēputō ① *v* reckon

derelicta, **ae** *f* ⓛⓜ widow

dērelinquō, **liquī**, **lictum** ③ *v* leave behind, abandon, neglect

dērepente *adv* suddenly

dērīdeō, **rīsī**, **rīsum** ② *v* laugh at, deride

dērīdiculum, **ī** *nt* laughing-stock, ridiculousness

dērigēscō, **guī** ③ *v* grow stiff *or* rigid

dēripiō, **puī**, **reptum** ③ *v* tear off, remove

dērīsor, **ōris** *m* mocker, scoffer

dērīsus, **ūs** *m* ridicule, scorn

dērīvātiō, **ōnis** *f* turning off (into another channel)

dērīvō ① *v* divert, turn *or* draw off

dērogō ① *v* make *or* propose (modifications to a law); take away, diminish

dēruptus, **a**, **um** *adj* craggy, steep, precipitous

dēsaeviō ④ *v* work off *or* vent one's rage

dēscendō, **ndī**, **ēnsum** ③ *v* descend; fall; alight; slope; penetrate; stoop, demean oneself

dēscēnsus, **ūs** *m* climbing down

dēscīscō, **īvī/iī**, **ītum** ③ *v* desert, defect

dēscrībō, **psī**, **ptum** ③ *v* copy; describe; establish

dēscrīptiō, **ōnis** *f* delineation; description

dēsecō, **cuī**, **ctum** ① *v* cut off

dēserō, **ruī**, **rtum** ③ *v* forsake; desert; give up; fail

dēserta, **ōrum** *ntpl* wilderness

dēsertor, **ōris** *m* abandoner; deserter; fugitive

dēsertus, **a**, **um** *adj* desert, lonely, waste

dēserviō ④ *v with dat* serve diligently, be devoted to

dēsīderābilis, **e** *adj* desirable; missed

dēsīderium, **(i)ī** *nt* desire, wishing, longing for; regret for what is absent; petition; request; favourite, darling

dēsīderō ① *v* wish for, desire; need, want; require; miss

dēsidia, **ae** *f* idleness, sloth

dēsidiōsus, **a**, **um** *adj* indolent, lazy

dēsīdō, **sēdī** ③ *v* sink, settle down

dēsignātiō, **ōnis** *f* appointment, designation

dēsignō ① *v* mark out, designate; denote; appoint; choose; perpetrate

dēsiliō, **siluī**, **sultum** ④ *v* leap down, alight

dēsinō, **sīvī/iī**, **situm** ③ *v* leave off, cease, desist

dēsipiō ③ *v* be out of one's mind, lose one's reason

dēsistō, **stitī**, **stitum** ③ *v* leave off, cease, desist from; stand apart, be away

dēsōlō ① *v* abandon, desert; empty

dēspectō ① *v* look down at; overlook; despise

dēspectus, **ūs** *m* prospect, panorama; contempt

dēspēranter *adv* despairingly

dēspērātiō, **ōnis** *f* despair

dēspērātus, **a**, **um** *adj* desperate, despaired of

dēspērō ① *v* despair (of)

dēspicientia, **ae** *f* contempt (for)

dēspiciō, **spexī**, **spectum** ③ *v* look down upon; despise

dēspoliō ① *v* rob, plunder

dēspondeō, **ndī**, **ōnsum** ② *v* promise (in marriage)
□ **animum** ∼ despair

dēspūmō ① *v* skim off

despuō ③ *v* spit (out), reject

dēstillō ▶ distillō

dēstinātiō, **ōnis** *f* designation; resolution, determination

dēstinō ① *v* fix, determine, design; destine

dēstituō, **uī**, **ūtum** ③ *v* leave, desert, abandon; give up; disappoint

dēstringō, **īnxī**, **ictum** ③ *v* strip off; draw (a sword); graze (gently); censure

dēstruō, **ūxī**, **ūctum** ③ *v* pull down; destroy, ruin

dēsubitō *adv* suddenly

dēsuētūdō, **inis** *f* discontinuance, disuse

dēsultor, **ōris** *m* a rider in the circus who jumped from one horse to another

dēsum, **esse**, **fuī** *v ir with dat* be wanting, fail

dēsūmō, **mpsī** ③ *v* pick out, choose

dēsuper *adv* from above

dētegō, **ēxī**, **ēctum** ③ *v* uncover, lay bare; reveal

dētendō, **ndī**, **ēnsum** ③ *v* strike (tents), let down

dētergeō, **rsī**, **rsum** ② *v* wipe off; strip off, rub clean

dēterior, **ius** *adj* inferior; worse, meaner

dēterminō ① *v* set bounds to, limit, determine

dēterō, **trīvī**, **trītum** ③ *v* wear away

dēterreō ② *v* deter, discourage

dētestābilis, **e** *adj* abominable, detestable

dētestātiō, **ōnis** *f* solemn curse

dētestor ① *v dep* call down a solemn curse on; detest; avert

dētexō, **xuī**, **xtum** ③ *v* finish weaving, complete

dētineō, **tentum** ② *v* hold down *or* off, detain; occupy; delay the end of

d

dētondeō, (to)tondī, tōnsum ② *v* shear off, strip off; LM give the tonsure

dētonō, tonuī ① *v* expend one's thunder

dētorqueō, rsī, rtum ② *v* turn *or* twist away; distort; divert

dētractor, ōris *m* detractor, defamer

dētrahō, āxī, actum ③ *v* draw off; remove; lessen; take away; detract from; impair

dētrectātiō, ōnis *f* refusal

dētrectō ① *v* refuse; disparage, belittle

dētrīmentum, ī *nt* detriment, loss, damage; defeat

dētrūdō, ūsī, ūsum ③ *v* thrust down *or* from; expel; dispossess; reduce; postpone

dētruncō ① *v* lop off; behead; mutilate

dēturbō ① *v* dislodge; pull down; upset; topple

deūrō, ussī, ustum ③ *v* burn down; (of cold) wither

deus, ī *m* god

> ❗ The (rare) voc. of **deus** is **deus**; in the pl. its nom./voc. is usu. **dī**, its gen. may be **deum** and its dat./abl. may be **dīs**.

dēvāstō ① *v* lay waste

dēvehō, ēxī, ectum ③ *v* carry away, convey
  □ **dēvehor** travel downstream

dēveniō, vēnī, ventum ④ *v* arrive (at); land, turn (to)

dēverberō ① *v* whip hard

dēversor ① *v dep* put up at an inn; lodge

dēversōrium, (i)ī *nt* inn, lodging-house

dēverticulum, ī *nt* by-road; digression; port of call

dēvertō, rtī, rsum ③ *v* turn aside; lodge; digress

dēvexitās, ātis *f* downward slope, incline

dēvexus, a, um *adj* sloping, shelving

dēvinciō, vīnxī, vīnctum ④ *v* bind fast, tie up; oblige

dēvincō, īcī, ictum ③ *v* conquer entirely, subdue

dēvītō ① *v* avoid

dēvius, a, um *adj* out-of-the-way, devious; straying

dēvocō ① *v* call down *or* away, summon

dēvolō ① *v* fly down *or* away; hasten down, hasten away

dēvolvō, lvī, lūtum ③ *v* roll down

dēvorō ① *v* devour; absorb; gulp down; check; drink in; use up

dēvōtiō, ōnis *f* devoting; vow; curse

dēvoveō, vōvī, vōtum ② *v* vow, devote; curse; bewitch

dexterē *adv* skilfully

dextrōvorsum *adv* to the right

diabolicus, a, um *adj* LM of the Devil

diabolus, i *m* LM the Devil

diaconus, i *m*, **diacon, nis** *m* LM deacon

diadēma, atis *nt* diadem, ornamental headband

diaeta, ae *f* course of medical treatment; room; cabin (on a ship)

dialectica, ae *f* LM logic

Diālis, e *adj* of Jupiter

dica, ae *f* lawsuit, legal action

dicācitās, ātis *f* mordant *or* caustic raillery

dicāx, ācis *adj* witty, smart, sarcastic

diciō, ōnis *f* sway; dominion; authority

dīcō¹, dīxī, dictum ③ *v* say, tell; order; call; declare; express; plead; designate

> ❗ **dīcō** does not mean 'tell' in the sense of 'tell a story' or 'tell someone to do something'. It very frequently introduces indirect statement; if the first clause of indirect statement to be introduced by **dīcō** is negated, **dīcō** … **nōn** is replaced with **negō** (so too **dīcō** … **nihil** by **negō quicquam** *etc.*). cf. **inquam**. The 2sg. impv. of **dīcō** is **dīc**.

dīcō² ① *v* dedicate, consecrate; set apart; devote (oneself); assign

dicrotum, ī *nt* a light galley, perhaps propelled by two banks of oars

dictamnum, ī *nt*, **dictamnus**, ī *f* dittany

dictāta, ōrum *ntpl* dictated lessons *or* exercises

dictātor, ōris *m* dictator; chief magistrate

> **!** In times of military or domestic crisis at Rome a single citizen was appointed **dictātor** by a magistrate authorised by the senate in order to carry out a single task or command the army; his deputy (the **magister equitum**) was the commander of cavalry. Existing magistrates became subordinate to him for the period of his office, which could not exceed six months, although in early times a **dictātor** would resign on completion of his task. The nature of the office changed radically when Julius Caesar was appointed **dictātor perpetuus**.

dictātōrius, a, um *adj* of a dictator

dictātūra, ae *f* dictatorship

dictiō, ōnis *f* saying, delivery; speech; oracular utterance

dictitō ① *v* say often; plead often

dictō ① *v* say often; dictate (for writing); compose

dictum, ī *nt* saying, word; maxim; *bon mot*, witticism; order

didicī ▸ **discō**

dīdō, dīdidī, dīditum ③ *v* distribute, spread

dīdūcō, dūxī, ductum ③ *v* draw *or* lead aside; separate; divide; scatter; open out

diērectus *int* go and be hanged! (the sense of this uncertain word is one of peremptory dismissal)

diēs, diēī *m* day; daylight; festival; red letter day; lifetime
□ **in diem** each day

> **!** **diēs** is generally masculine, especially when used as a measure of time, but is feminine in the sg. when referring to a particular or appointed day.

diffāmō ① *v* spread the news of; slander

differō, ferre, distulī, dīlātum *v ir* put off, delay; disperse; spread; publish; differ; disagree

differtus, a, **um** *adj* filled, crowded

difficilis, e *adj* difficult; obstinate, morose, intractable

difficultās, ātis *f* difficulty; trouble; intractability

diffīdentia, ae *f* mistrust, distrust

diffīdō, fīsus sum ③ *v semi-dep with dat* lack confidence (in); despair

diffindō, idī, issum ③ *v* split; put off

diffingō ③ *v* remodel

diffiteor ② *v dep* disavow, deny

diffluō, ūxī ③ *v* flow away in all directions; melt away; waste away

diffugiō, ūgī ③ *v* flee in different directions; scatter, disperse

diffundō, ūdī, ūsum ③ *v* pour forth; diffuse, spread; cheer

diffutuō, uī, ūtum ③ *v* indulge in promiscuous sexual intercourse

dīgerō, essī, estum ③ *v* distribute, spread over; arrange, dispose

digitus, ī *m* finger; toe; a finger's-breadth

dignātiō, ōnis *f* esteem; repute; rank

dignitās, ātis *f* worthiness, merit; dignity, authority; office; grace; value, honour

dignor ① *v dep* consider worthy

dignus, a, **um** *adj* worthy, deserving; deserved

dīgredior, gressus sum ③ *v dep* depart, go away; leave (a subject of discussion)

dīgressiō, ōnis *f* going away; digression

dīgressus, ūs *m* departure; digression

dīiūdicō ① *v* decide, judge, determine; distinguish

dīiungō, ūnxī, ūnctum ③ *v* unyoke; separate; disjoin

dīlābor, lāpsus sum ③ *v dep* fall apart *or* to pieces; disperse; melt away; decay

dīlacerō ① *v*, **dīlaniō** ① *v* tear to pieces

dīlapidō ① *v* bring into a state of partial ruin *or* collapse

dīlargior ④ *v dep* give away freely

dīlātiō, **ōnis** *f* delaying; interval of space

dīlātō ① *v* make wider, enlarge, extend, dilate

dilector, **oris** *m/f* LM worshipper

dīlectus, **ūs** *m* recruitment, levy; choice

dīligēns, **ntis** *adj* careful, diligent, frugal, thrifty

dīligentia, **ae** *f* carefulness, attentiveness; economy, frugality

dīligō, **ēxī**, **ēctum** ③ *v* esteem highly, hold dear

dīlūcēscō, **cuī** ③ *v* dawn, become light

dīlūcidus, **a**, **um** *adj* plain, distinct, lucid

dīluō, **uī**, **ūtum** ③ *v* wash (off); temper; dilute; dissolve; weaken; refute

dīluviēs, **iēī** *f*, **dīluvium**, **(i)ī** *nt* inundation, flood

dīmētior, **mēnsus sum** ④ *v dep* measure out

dīmicātiō, **ōnis** *f* fight, combat; struggle

dīmicō, **micāvī/micuī** ① *v* fight; struggle, strive

dīmidius, **a**, **um** *adj* half
  ■ **dīmidium**, **(i)ī** *nt* a half

dīmittō, **īsī**, **issum** ③ *v* send out *or* forth; dismiss; disband; release; divorce; break up; detach; let slip; give up, renounce

dimminu- ▶ **dēminu-**

dīmoveō, **mōvī**, **mōtum** ② *v* separate; put aside; remove

dīnumerō ① *v* count, enumerate

dio(e)cesis, **is** *f* LM diocese

diōta, **ae** *f* two-handled wine-jar

diplōma, **atis** *nt* letter of recommendation

dīrēctus, **a**, **um** *adj* straight, vertical; steep; direct, simple

dīreptiō, **ōnis** *f* plundering

dīreptor, **ōris** *m* plunderer

dīrigō, **ēxī**, **ēctum** ③ *v* direct, guide; steer; set in order

dirimō, **ēmī**, **ēmptum** ③ *v* pull apart; separate; break up, dissolve

dīripiō, **puī**, **eptum** ③ *v* snatch away; tear to pieces; rob, loot

dīrumpō, **ūpī**, **uptum** ③ *v* break apart, shatter, burst

dīruō, **ruī**, **rutum** ③ *v* demolish, destroy

dīrus, **a**, **um** *adj* fearful, awful; horrible

dīs, **ītis** *adj* [contracted form of **dīves**] rich

discēdō, **essī**, **essum** ③ *v* go off in different directions; march off; be divided; cease; die; depart from

disceptātiō, **ōnis** *f* debate

disceptātor, **ōris** *m* arbitrator

disceptō ① *v* dispute; debate; arbitrate

discernō, **crēvī**, **crētum** ③ *v* separate; distinguish

discerpō, **psī**, **ptum** ③ *v* pluck *or* tear in pieces; mangle

discessiō, **ōnis** *f* withdrawal, dispersal

discessus, **ūs** *m* going apart; separation; departure; marching off

discidium, **(i)ī** *nt* separation, divorce, discord

discīnctus, **a**, **um** *adj* wearing loose clothes; easy-going

discindō, **idī**, **issum** ③ *v* cut in two; divide

discingō, **īnxī**, **īnctum** ③ *v* ungird, strip

disciplīna, **ae** *f* instruction; knowledge; discipline; system; method

discipula, **ae** *f* female pupil

discipulus, **ī** *m* pupil, disciple, trainee

disclūdō, **ūsī**, **ūsum** ③ *v* separate; keep apart

discō, **didicī** ③ *v* learn, acquire knowledge of

discolor, **ōris** *adj* of another colour; of various colours; variegated

disconveniō ④ *v* be inconsistent, be different

discordia, **ae** *f* disagreement, discord

discordō ① *v* be at variance, quarrel; be different

discors, **rdis** *adj* discordant, disagreeing; different

discrepō, puī ① *v* be out of tune; disagree, differ

discrībō, īpsī, īptum ③ *v* divide, assign, distribute

discrīmen, inis *nt* separating line; division; distinction, difference; crisis, risk

discrīminō ① *v* divide up, separate

discrīptiō, ōnis *f* assignment, division

discruciō ① *v* torture

discumbō, cubuī, cubitum ③ *v* lie down; recline at table; go to bed

discurrō, (cu)currī, cursum ③ *v* run about

discursus, ūs *m* running about; separation, dispersal

discus, ī *m* discus, quoit

discutiō, ussī, ussum ③ *v* shatter, shake violently; dissipate; bring to nothing

disertus, a, um *adj* eloquent; skilfully expressed

disiciō, iēcī, iectum ③ *v* scatter; disperse; squander; frustrate

disiungō, ūnxī, ūnctum ③ *v* (also **dīiungō**) unyoke; separate; disjoin

dispār, aris *adj* unequal, unlike

disparō ① *v* separate, divide

dispellō, pulī, pulsum ③ *v* drive apart *or* away; disperse

dispendium, (i)ī *nt* expense, cost; loss

dispēnsātiō, ōnis *f* management; stewardship

dispēnsātor, ōris *m* steward; treasurer

dispēnsō ① *v* manage; dispense, distribute; pay out; arrange

disperdō, didī, ditum ③ *v* destroy *or* ruin utterly

dispereō, īre, iī *v ir* perish, be destroyed

dispergō, rsī, rsum ③ *v* scatter about, disperse

dispertiō ④ *v* distribute, divide; assign

dispiciō, spexī, spectum ③ *v* look about (for); discover; espy; consider

displiceō ② *v* displease

displōdō, ōsum ③ *v* burst apart

dispōnō, posuī, positum ③ *v* distribute, set in order; post, station; arrange

dispudet ② *v impers* be deeply ashamed

disputātiō, ōnis *f* discussion, argument, debate

disputō ① *v* argue, debate

disquīsītiō, ōnis *f* inquiry

disr- ▸ diss-, dīr-

dissecō, cuī, ctum ① *v* cut apart *or* in pieces

dissēminō ① *v* broadcast, disseminate

dissēnsiō, ōnis *f* dissension, disagreement

dissentiō, ēnsī, ēnsum ④ *v* dissent, disagree; differ

disserō¹, ruī, rtum ③ *v* discuss, set out in words

disserō², sēvī, situm ③ *v* sow

dissertō ① *v* discuss

dissideō, sēdī, sessum ② *v* be at variance; disagree; be separated

dissignō ▸ dēsignō

dissiliō, siluī ④ *v* leap *or* burst apart

dissimilis, e *adj* unlike, dissimilar

dissimilitūdō, inis *f* unlikeness, difference

dissimulanter *adv* dissemblingly

dissimulātiō, ōnis *f* dissimulation, dissembling

dissimulātor, ōris *m* dissembler

dissimulō ① *v* dissemble, disguise; hide; ignore

dissipātiō, ōnis *f* squandering; scattering

dissipō ① *v* disperse; squander; destroy completely; circulate

dissociābilis, e *adj* incompatible; discordant

dissociō ① *v* separate, part; set at variance

dissolūtiō, ōnis *f* disintegration, dissolution; destruction; disconnection; refutation

dissolūtus, a, um *adj* loose; lax; negligent; dissolute

dissolvō, lvī, lūtum ③ *v* unloose; dissolve, destroy; melt; pay; refute; annul

dissonus, a, um *adj* dissonant, discordant; different

dissuādeō, āsī, āsum ② *v* dissuade, advise against

d

dissuāsor, **ōris** *m* discourager, one who advises against

dissultō ① *v* fly *or* burst apart; bounce off

distaedet ② *v impers* it wearies, it is distasteful

distantia, **ae** *f* distance; difference

distendō, **ndī**, **ntum** ③ *v* stretch in different directions, stretch out, extend; swell out; fill

distillō ① *v* trickle down

distīnctiō, **ōnis** *f* distinction; difference

distīnctus, **a**, **um** *adj* separate, distinct; definite, lucid

distineō, **tentum** ② *v* keep apart; separate; prevent, distract; hold up

distinguō, **īnxī**, **īnctum** ③ *v* divide, part; distinguish; decorate

distō ① *v* stand apart, be distant; be different

distorqueō, **rsī**, **rtum** ② *v* twist this way and that

distrahō, **āxī**, **actum** ③ *v* pull *or* draw apart; wrench; separate; sell; distract; set at variance; estrange

distribuō, **uī**, **ūtum** ③ *v* divide, distribute

distribūtiō, **ōnis** *f* division, distribution

distringō, **īnxī**, **ictum** ③ *v* stretch out; detain; distract; pull in different directions

disturbō ① *v* disturb; demolish; upset

dītēscō ③ *v* grow rich

dithyrambus, **ī** *m* a form of verse used especially for choral singing

dītō ① *v* enrich

diū *adv* a long while; long since
- □ **diūtius** longer
- □ **diūtissimē** very long

diurnus, **a**, **um** *adj* daily

dīus, **a**, **um** *adj* daylit, divine

diūtinus, **a**, **um** *adj* lasting, long

diūturnitās, **ātis** *f* long duration

diūturnus, **a**, **um** *adj* lasting long

dīva, **ae** *f* goddess

dīvellō, **vellī**, **vulsum** ③ *v* tear to pieces; tear away; estrange, break up

dīvendō, **didī**, **ditum** ③ *v* sell in small lots; sell up

dīverberō ① *v* split; strike violently

dīversitās, **ātis** *f* difference

dīversus, **a**, **um** *adj* opposite; separate, apart; unlike, different; hostile; contrary; distant; distinct

dīves, **itis** *adj* rich; talented

> **!** Contracted forms from **dīves** are often found: in the sg., nom. **dīs**, acc. m./f. **dītem** n. **dīs**, gen. **dītis**, dat./abl. **dītī**; in the pl., nom./acc. m./f. **dītēs** n. **dītia**, gen. **dītium**, dat./abl. **dītibus**. Its comp. and sup. may be **dītior** and **dītissimus**.

dīvidō, **īsī**, **īsum** ③ *v* separate, divide; distribute; distinguish; break up

dīviduus, **a**, **um** *adj* divisible; divided; half; parted

dīvīnātiō, **ōnis** *f* prophecy, prognostication

dīvīnitus *adv* by divine agency *or* inspiration; divinely, excellently

dīvīnō ① *v* divine; prophesy; guess

dīvīnus, **a**, **um** *adj* divine; prophetic; blessed; excellent
- ∎ ∼, **ī** *m* prophet

dīvīsiō, **ōnis** *f* division; distribution

dīvīsor, **ōris** *m* distributor; a candidate's agent hired to distribute bribes

dīvīsus, **ūs** *m* division

dīvitiae, **ārum** *fpl* riches, wealth

dīvortium, **(i)ī** *nt* separation; divorce; point of separation; watershed; by-way, roundabout route

dīvulgō ① *v* publish, disseminate news of

dīvum, **ī** *nt* sky, open air
- □ **sub dīvō** in the open air

dīvus, **ī** *m* god

dō, **dare**, **dedī**, **datum** ① *v* give; ascribe; grant, permit; furnish, offer; lend; tell of; enable, cause

> **!** In the present stem forms of **dō** the vowel after the 'd' is always short if it is 'a', except in the 2sg. indic. and imperative (**dās** and **dā** respectively).

doceō, **doctum** ② *v* teach; tell; show

docilis, **e** *adj* teachable, responsive

doctor, **ōris** *m* teacher, instructor, trainer

doctrīna, ae f teaching, instruction; science, learning; system of rules

doctus, a, um adj learned, wise, expert

documentum, ī nt example; warning; instruction; proof

dōdrāns, ntis m three-quarters

dogma, atis nt doctrine, dogma, teaching

doleō ② v feel or suffer pain; grieve for

dōlium, (i)ī nt large earthenware vessel for storing liquids, grain, etc.

dolor, ōris m pain; grief; anguish; sorrow; resentment

dolōsus, a, um adj crafty, deceitful

dolus, ī m fraud, deceit; treachery, cunning

domābilis, e adj able to be tamed

domesticus, a, um adj domestic, familiar; native; private, personal

domicilium, (i)ī nt dwelling, abode, home

domina, ae f mistress of a family; lady; wife; lady-love

dominātiō, ōnis f dominion; despotism

dominātus, ūs m absolute rule, dominion

dominica, ae f 〔LM〕 Sunday

dominor ① v dep act as a despot, rule; be in control

dominus, ī m master of the house; owner; lord, ruler; host; lover

domitō ① v tame, break in

domitor, ōris m tamer; conqueror

domō, muī, mitum ① v tame; conquer

domus, ūs/ī f house; home; household; family; native country
□ **domī** at home

> ❗ In the sg., **domus** declines **domus, domum, domūs/domī, domuī/domō, domō**. It has a locative **domī**, and 'homewards' is expressed by the acc. without a preposition. Its plural endings are second declension, except that the acc. can be **domūs** as well as **domōs**.

dōnābilis, e adj worthy to be the recipient (of)

dōnārium, (i)ī nt part of temple where votive offerings were received and stored; treasure chamber

dōnātiō, ōnis f donation, gift

dōnātīvum, ī nt gratuity, bounty

dōnec conj as long as, until

> ❗ See note at **dum**.

d

dōnicum conj until

dōnō ① v present (with something (abl)), bestow; forgive; give up

dōnum, ī nt gift, present; offering

dormiō ④ v sleep; rest; go to bed (with)

dormītō ① v feel sleepy, drowsy; do nothing

dorsum, ī nt back; slope of a hill, ridge

dōs, ōtis f dowry; talent, quality

dōtālis, e adj forming part of a dowry, relating to a dowry

dōtātus, a, um adj provided with a (good) dowry

drachma, ae f a Greek silver coin

dracō, ōnis m snake

dromas, ados m dromedary

Druidae, ārum mpl, **Druidēs, um** mpl druids

dubitanter adv doubtingly; hesitatingly

dubitātiō, ōnis f doubt; hesitation; irresolution

dubitō ① v doubt; be uncertain or irresolute; hesitate over

> ❗ When **dubitō** means 'hesitate' it is followed by an infin. When it means 'doubt' and is not negated, it is followed by an indirect statement expressed by an acc. and infin.; where **dubitō** itself is negated the indirect statement is expressed by a clause introduced by **quīn** with a subj. verb.

dubium, (i)ī nt doubt

dubius, a, um adj doubtful; variable; uncertain; dangerous; critical

ducatus, **us** *m* LM duchy

ducēnī, **ae**, **a** *adj* two hundred each; two hundred

ducentēsimus, **a**, **um** *adj* two-hundredth

ducentī, **ae**, **a** *adj* two hundred

dūcō, **dūxī**, **ductum** ③ *v* lead, conduct, draw, bring; run (a wall, *etc.*); derive; guide; persuade; deceive; prolong; think, esteem; reckon; pass; spend
  □ **uxōrem** ~ marry (a woman), take as wife

! The 2sg. impv. of **dūcō** is **dūc.**

ductō ① *v* lead; deceive, beguile

ductor, **ōris** *m* leader, commander

ductus, **ūs** *m* conducting; generalship

dūdum *adv* a little while ago; formerly
  □ **iam** ~ long ago

duellum ▶ **bellum**

duim *old subj* of ▶ **dō**

dulcēdō, **inis** *f* sweetness; charm

dulcis, **e** *adj* sweet; pleasant, charming; dear, beloved

dum *conj* while, as long as; until; provided that

! **dum** meaning 'while' is followed in almost all circumstances by the pres. indic. regardless of the time referred to.
····> **dum** meaning 'for exactly as long as' is followed by any appropriate tense of the indic.
····> **dum** meaning 'until' followed by an indic. expresses factual 'up to the time at which' but followed by a subj. expresses a condition needing to be fulfilled 'until such time as'; from the latter sense **dum** (= **dum modo**) can also express 'provided, on condition that', cf. English 'as/so long as'.

dūmētum, **ī** *nt* thicket

dummodo *conj* provided that

dūmōsus, **a**, **um** *adj* overgrown with thorn, briar *or* the like

dumtaxat *adv* only, at least; so far

dūmus, **ī** *m* thorn *or* briar bush

duo, **duae**, **duo** *adj* two

duodecim *adj indec* twelve

duodecimus, **a**, **um** *adj* twelfth

duodēnī, **ae**, **a** *adj* twelve each, by twelves

duodēvīcēnī, **ae**, **a** *adj* eighteen each

duodēvīcēsimus, **a**, **um** *adj* eighteenth

duodēvīgintī *adj indec* eighteen

duovirī, **ōrum** *mpl* board of two men

duplex, **icis** *adj* twofold, double; divided; 'two-faced'

duplicō ① *v* double; enlarge; bend double

dūritia, **ae** *f*, **dūritiēs**, **iēī** *f* hardness; austerity; rigour

dūrō ① *v* make hard; dry; harden, 'steel'; become hard *or* stern, *etc.*; endure; last out; survive

dūrus, **a**, **um** *adj* hard; harsh; hardy, vigorous; stern; unfeeling; inflexible; burdensome, difficult

dux, **cis** *m/f* leader, guide; commander, general; LM duke

Ee

eā *adv* along that path, that way

eādem *adv* by the same route

eātenus *adv* so far, to such a degree; *int* well, that's that

ēbibō, bibī ③ *v* drink up, drain; absorb; squander

ēblandior ④ *v dep* obtain by flattery

ēbrietās, ātis *f* drunkenness

ēbriōsus, a, um *adj* addicted to drink

ēbrius, a, um *adj* drunk; intoxicated

ebulum, ī *nt*, **ebulus, ī** *m* danewort

ebur, oris *nt* ivory; ivory statue

ēcastor *int* interjection used by women by Castor!

ecce *int* look! see! behold! here!

eccerē *int* see there!

ecclēsia, ae *f* the assembly of the people; a meeting of the assembly; LM church

eccōs *int* here they (m.) are!

eccum *int* here he is!

ecf- ▶ **eff-**

ēchidna, ae *f* serpent, viper

echīnus, ī *m* sea-urchin

ēchō, ūs *f* echo

ecloga, ae *f* a short poem

ecqui, quae/qua, quod *pn* is there any?

ecquid *adv* is it true that … ? at all?

ecquis, quid *pn* is there anyone who?

eculeus, ī *m* young *or* small horse, pony

edāx, ācis *adj* voracious, gluttonous; devouring

ēdentō ① *v* knock the teeth from

ēdentulus, a, um *adj* toothless

edepol *int* by Pollux!

ēdīcō, īxī, ictum ③ *v* publish, declare

ēdictum, ī *nt* proclamation, edict

ēdiscō, didicī ③ *v* learn by heart; study; get to know

ēdisserō, ruī, rtum ③ *v*, **ēdissertō** ① *v* relate, expound

ēditiō, ōnis *f* publishing; edition; statement

ēditus, a, um *adj* high, lofty

edō, ēsse, ēdī, ēsum *v ir* eat; devour; spend (money) on food

ēdō, didī, ditum ③ *v* put forth, emit; publish; relate; bring forth; beget; proclaim; bring about; cause

ēdoceō, ctum ② *v* teach *or* inform thoroughly

ēdomō, muī, mitum ① *v* tame completely, conquer

ēdormiō ④ *v* sleep; sleep off

ēducātiō, ōnis *f* bringing up; rearing

ēducātor, ōris *m* bringer up, tutor; foster-father

ēducātrīx, īcis *f* nurse, foster-mother

ēdūcō, dūxī, ductum ③ *v* lead *or* draw out; bring away; rear; educate; raise, produce

ēducō ① *v* bring up, rear

edūlis, e *adj* eatable

ēdūrus, a, um *adj* very hard

effarciō ▶ **efferciō**

effectus, ūs *m* execution, performance; effect

effēminātus, a, um *adj* womanish, effeminate

effēminō ① *v* emasculate; unman, enervate

efferciō, rsī, rtum ④ *v* stuff, cram, fill out

efferō¹, ferre, extulī, ēlātum *v ir* bring *or* carry out; produce; utter; raise, advance; proclaim; carry out for burial

efferō² ① *v* make savage

efferus, era, erum *adj* savage, cruel, barbarous

effervēscō, vī ③ *v* boil up, seethe; become greatly excited

effētus, a, um *adj* exhausted, worn out

efficāx, ācis *adj* efficacious, effectual

efficiō, fēcī, fectum ③ *v* effect, execute, accomplish, make; produce; prove; make up

effigiēs, iēī *f*, **effigia, ae** *f* portrait, image, effigy, statue; ghost

e

effingō, **īnxī**, **ictum** ③ *v* form, mould; represent, portray; stroke

efflāgitātiō, **ōnis** *f* urgent demand

efflāgitō ① *v* demand *or* ask urgently

efflō ① *v* blow *or* breathe out; breathe one's last

effluō, **ūxī** ③ *v* flow out; escape; vanish; be forgotten

effodiō, **ōdī**, **ossum** ③ *v* dig out; gouge out

effor ① *v dep* utter; declare; speak

effrēnō ① *v* unbridle, let loose

effrēnus, **a**, **um** *adj* unbridled; unrestrained, unruly

effringō, **frēgī**, **frāctum** ③ *v* break open

effugiō, **fūgī** ③ *v* escape; flee from, avoid; be unnoticed; escape the knowledge of

effugium, **(i)ī** *nt* flight; way of escape

effulgeō, **lsī** ② *v* shine forth, glitter; be *or* become conspicuous

effultus, **a**, **um** *adj* propped up, supported (by)

effundō, **ūdī**, **ūsum** ③ *v* pour out, shed; send out; shoot in great numbers; discharge; let fall; give up; waste, squander; bring forth

effūsē *adv* over a wide area; in a disorderly manner; immoderately

effūsiō, **ōnis** *f* pouring forth; prodigality, excess

effūsus, **a**, **um** *adj* vast, wide; dishevelled; disorderly; extravagant

effūtiō ④ *v* blurt out

effutuō, **ūtum** ③ *v* wear out with sexual intercourse

ēgelidus, **a**, **um** *adj* lukewarm, tepid

egēns, **ntis** *adj* needy, very poor; destitute of

egēnus, **a**, **um** *adj* in want of, destitute of

egeō ② *v with gen or abl* want; need; require, be without

ēgerō, **essī**, **estum** ③ *v* carry *or* bear out; discharge; utter

egestās, **ātis** *f* extreme poverty, want

ēgī ▸ agō

ego *pn* I; I myself

egomet *pn* I myself; I for my part

ēgredior, **gressus sum** ③ *v dep* march *or* come out; set sail; land; go beyond; ascend; overstep

ēgregius, **a**, **um** *adj* excellent, eminent; illustrious

ēgressus, **ūs** *m* departure; flight; landing; place of egress, mouth (of a river); digression

ehem *int* hah! what! an exclamation expressing gratified surprise, recollection, *etc.*

ēheu *int* alas!

eho *int* here, you! hey! hi!

ei *int* exclamation expressing anguish or similar

eia *int* exclamation expressing deprecation, concession, astonishment, urgency

ēiaculor ① *v dep* shoot out; discharge

ēiciō, **iēcī**, **iectum** ③ *v* throw *or* cast out; thrust out; expel; banish; vomit; dislocate; cast ashore; reject

ēiectō ① *v* cast out

ēiulātus, **ūs** *m* wailing, shrieking

ēiūrō ① *v* abjure; resign; reject on oath (of a judge); forswear, disown

eiusmodī *gen used as adj* of the kind

ēlābor, **lāpsus sum** ③ *v dep* escape; slip away

ēlabōrō ① *v* take pains, exert oneself; bestow care on

ēlanguēscō, **guī** ③ *v* begin to lose one's vigour; slacken, relax

elatio, **onis** *f* LM pride

ēlēctilis, **e** *adj* choice, dainty

ēlēctiō, **ōnis** *f* choice, selection

ēlectrum, **ī** *nt* amber; alloy of gold and silver

ēlegāns, **ntis** *adj* elegant, fine, handsome; tasteful; fastidious, critical; discriminating, polite

ēlegantia, **ae** *f* elegance; niceness; taste; politeness

elegī, **ōrum** *mpl* elegiac verses, elegy

elegīa, **ae** *f*, **elegeia**, **ae** *f* elegy

elementa, **ōrum** *ntpl* elements; rudiments; beginnings

elephā(n)s, **ntis** *m*, **elephantus**, **ī** *m* elephant; ivory

ēlevō ① *v* lift up, raise; alleviate; lessen; make light of

ēlicēs, **um** *mpl* trench, drain

ēliciō, **cuī** ③ *v* entice, coax; call forth; draw forth

ēlīdō, īsī, īsum ③ *v* strike *or* dash out; expel; shatter; crush out; strangle; destroy

ēligō, lēgī, lēctum ③ *v* pick out, choose

ēlixus, a, um *adj* thoroughly boiled

elleborōsus, a, um *adj* in need of hellebore, out of one's mind

elleborum, ī *nt* one of several acrid and poisonous plans much used medicinally, especially as a cure for insanity

ēlluō ▸ hēlluō

ēloquēns, ntis *adj* eloquent, articulate

ēloquentia, ae *f*, **ēloquium, (i)ī** *nt* eloquence, articulateness; the art of public speaking

ēloquor, locūtus sum ③ *v dep* speak out, utter

ēlūceō, ūxī ② *v* shine forth; show itself; be manifest

ēluctor ① *v dep* force a way through; surmount a difficulty

ēlūcubrō ① *v*, **ēlūcubror** ① *v dep* compose at night; burn the midnight oil over

ēlūdificor ① *v dep* fool completely

ēlūdō, ūsī, ūsum ③ *v* elude, escape from; parry; baffle; cheat; frustrate; mock, make fun of

ēluō, uī, ūtum ③ *v* wash clean; wash away, clear oneself (of)

ēluviēs, iēī *f* overflow, flood; washing away (of dirt); scourings (of dirt)

em *int* there!

ēmancipō ① *v* emancipate (a son from his father's authority); alienate; make subservient

ēmānō ① *v* flow out; arise, emanate from; become known

emāx, ācis *adj* fond of buying

ēmendātiō, ōnis *f* correction

ēmendō ① *v* correct; repair

ēmentior ④ *v dep* falsify, invent; feign

ēmereō ② *v*, **ēmereor** ② *v dep* earn; serve out one's time

ēmergō, rsī, rsum ③ *v* rise up out of the water, emerge; escape; appear; arrive

ēmeritus, ī *m* veteran

ēmētior, mēnsus sum ④ *v dep* measure out; pass through

ēmicō, micuī ① *v* spring forth, shine forth, appear suddenly

ēmigrō ① *v* move, depart

ēminēns, ntis *adj* lofty; prominent; eminent

ēmineō ② *v* project; stand out; be pre-eminent; excel

ēminus *adv* at long range

ēmittō, mīsī, missum ③ *v* send out *or* forth; set free; fling; let fall; publish; empty; drain off

emō, ēmī, ēmptum ③ *v* buy; gain

ēmolliō ④ *v* soften; enervate, mellow

ēmolumentum, ī *nt* advantage; benefit

ēmorior, morī, mortuus sum ③ *v dep* die away; die; perish

ēmoveō, mōvī, mōtum ② *v* remove; dislodge

emporium, (i)ī *nt* centre of trade, mart

ēmptiō, ōnis *f* the act of buying, purchase

ēmptor, ōris *m* buyer, purchaser

ēmungō, ūnxī, ūnctum ③ *v* wipe the nose; trick, swindle

ēmūniō ④ *v* fortify; make roads through

ēn *int* behold! see!

ēnārrābilis, e *adj* that may be described *or* explained

ēnārrō ① *v* explain *or* relate in detail

ēnatō ① *v* escape by swimming

ēnecō, cuī, c(ā)tum ① *v* kill, deprive of life

ēnervō ① *v* weaken, enervate

ēnicō ▸ ēnecō

enim *conj* indeed, for, yes indeed; certainly

   ▫ ∼ **vērō** positively! well, of course; certainly

ēniteō ② *v* shine forth; be outstanding

ēnitēscō, tuī ③ *v* become bright; stand out

ēnītor, nīsus/nīxus sum ③ *v dep* force one's way up; strive; give birth to

ēnō ① *v* swim out

ēnōdis, e *adj* without knots; smooth

ēnormis, e *adj* irregular; immense, enormous

ens, entis *nt* LM thing, being

ēnsis, is *m* sword

e

ēnūbō, **psī** ③ *v* marry out of one's rank *or* outside one's community

ēnumerō ① *v* count up; pay out; specify, enumerate

ēnumquam *adv* at any time at all? ever?

ēnūntiō ① *v* speak out, say, express, declare; disclose

eō[1] *adv* to that place, thither; there, in that place; so far; therefore; so much (more *or* less)

eō[2], **īre**, **iī/īvī**, **itum** *v ir* go; walk, march; flow; come in; ride, sail; turn out
□ ~ **īnfitiās** deny

eōdem *adv* to the same place *or* purpose

Ēōus, **a**, **um** *adj* eastern; of the dawn

ephippium, **(i)ī** *nt* cloth on which the rider of a horse sits

epigramma, **atis** *nt* epigram; inscription

episcopus, **i** *m* 〔LM〕 bishop

epistula, **ae** *f*, **epistola**, **ae** *f* letter, dispatch

epos *nt* (*only in nom and acc sg*) epic poem

ēpōtō, **ōtum** ① *v* drink down; absorb; swallow up

epulae, **ārum** *fpl* food, dishes; banquet, feast

epulor ① *v dep* dine sumptuously, feast

epulum, **ī** *nt* banquet, feast

equa, **ae** *f* mare

eques, **itis** *m* horseman, rider; horse-soldier
■ **equitēs** *pl* cavalry; order of knights

equester, **tris**, **tre** *adj* equestrian; of, belonging to, or connected with cavalry; belonging to the order of knights

equidem *adv* I for my part; truly, indeed

equīnus, **a**, **um** *adj* concerning horses

equitātus, **ūs** *m* cavalry

equitō ① *v* ride

equus, **ī** *m* horse

era, **ae** *f* (also **hera**) mistress; lady of the house

ērādīcō ① *v* scrape away, scrape clean; root out; erase, delete

ergā *prep with acc* opposite to; against, towards

ergastulum, **ī** *nt* prison on large estate to which refractory slaves were sent for work in chain-gangs; *in pl* convicts

ergō *adv* therefore; then, now

ēricius, **(i)ī** *m* some kind of spiked barrier

erifuga, **ae** *m* one who runs away from his master

ērigō, **rēxī**, **rēctum** ③ *v* erect; raise; build; rouse, excite, stimulate

erīlis, **e** *adj* of a master or mistress

ērīnāceus, **ī** *m* hedgehog

ēripiō, **puī**, **reptum** ③ *v* snatch away, take by force; rescue

ērogātiō, **ōnis** *f* paying out, distribution

ērogō ① *v* pay out, expend

errābundus, **a**, **um** *adj* wandering

errāticus, **a**, **um** *adj* roving, erratic; wild

errātum, **ī** *nt* error, mistake; lapse

errō[1] ① *v* wander *or* stray about; go astray; err, mistake; vacillate

errō[2], **ōnis** *m* truant

error, **ōris** *m* straying about; winding; maze; uncertainty; error; deception; derangement of the mind

ērubēscō, **buī** ③ *v* redden; blush for shame

ēructō ① *v* bring up noisily; discharge violently

ērudiō ④ *v* educate, instruct, teach

ērudītiō, **ōnis** *f* learning

ērudītulus, **a**, **um** *adj* learned

ērudītus, **a**, **um** *adj* learned, skilled

ērumpō, **rūpī**, **ruptum** ③ *v* break out; sally forth, break out of

ēruō, **ruī**, **rutum** ③ *v* pluck *or* dig *or* root up; overthrow; destroy; elicit

ēruptiō, **ōnis** *f* sally, sudden rush of troops from a position

erus, **ī** *m* master; owner

ervum, **ī** *nt* vetch; fodder, feed

ēsca, **ae** *f* food; bait; dish, meal

ēscendō, **ndī**, **ēnsum** ③ *v* ascend, go up, mount

essedārius, **(i)ī** *m* fighter in a war-chariot

essedum, **ī** *nt*, **esseda**, **ae** *f* war-chariot; light travelling carriage

essentia, **ae** *f* LM essence

ēste *impv pl* of ▸ **edō**

ēsuriō 4 *v* be hungry; desire eagerly

ēsurītiō, **ōnis** *f* state of hunger

et *conj* and; also; even; moreover
□ **et ... et** both ... and

> ❗ **et** linking clauses rarely introduces a second clause containing a negative; instead **nec** (or **neque**) is used.

etenim *conj* and indeed, the fact is, for

etēsiae, **ārum** *mpl* etesian winds

ethnicus, **i** *m* LM pagan

etiam *conj* and also, too, besides; even now; yes indeed, yes
□ **~ atque ~** more and more

etiamnum, **etiamnunc** *conj* even now, still, yet

etiamsī *conj* even if, although

etiamtum *conj* even then; yet

etsī *conj* although, even if

eu *int* well done! bravo!

euge *int* oh, good! fine!

euhāns, **ntis** *adj* uttering the name Euhan (Bacchus)

Euhius, **(i)ī** *m* title given to Bacchus

euhoe *int* cry of joy used by the votaries of Bacchus

eunūchus, **ī** *m* eunuch

euouae LM abbreviation standing for and consisting of the final six vowels of the phrase **in saecula saeculorum, amen**

eurīpus, **ī** *m* narrow channel of the sea, strait; canal

eurōus, **a**, **um** *adj* eastern

eurus, **ī** *m* east (or south east) wind; the east

ēvādō, **āsī**, **āsum** 3 *v* go *or* come out; escape, avoid; turn out

ēvagor 1 *v dep* wander off; spread; overflow

ēvalēscō, **luī** 3 *v* increase in strength; prevail, have sufficient strength (to)

ēvānēscō, **nuī** 3 *v* pass away, disappear, die out

evangelia, **ae** *f*, **evangelium**, **(i)i** *nt* LM gospel

ēvānidus, **a**, **um** *adj* vanishing, passing away

ēvāstō 1 *v* devastate

ēvehō, **ēxī**, **ectum** 3 *v* carry away, convey out; carry up; exalt
□ **ēvehor** ride out

ēvellō, **vellī**, **vulsum** 3 *v* pluck *or* tear out; root out

ēveniō, **vēnī**, **ventum** 4 *v* come out; come about, happen

ēventum, **ī** *nt* occurrence, event; issue, outcome

ēventus, **ūs** *m* occurrence, event; result; success

ēverberō 1 *v* beat violently

ēversiō, **ōnis** *f* overthrowing; destruction

ēversor, **ōris** *m* one who destroys *or* overthrows

ēvertō, **tī**, **rsum** 3 *v* turn upside down; churn up; ruin, overthrow

ēvidēns, **ntis** *adj* apparent, evident

ēvigilō 1 *v* be wakeful; watch throughout the night; devise *or* study with careful attention

ēvinciō, **vīnxī**, **vīnctum** 4 *v* bind *or* wreathe round

ēvincō, **vīcī**, **victum** 3 *v* defeat utterly; prevail; persuade

ēviscerō 1 *v* disembowel; eviscerate

ēvītābilis, **e** *adj* avoidable

ēvītō 1 *v* shun, avoid

ēvocātī, **ōrum** *mpl* veterans again called to service

> ❗ Soldiers who had completed their service sometimes volunteered for recall and were accorded some privileges within the army if they did so.

ēvocātor, **ōris** *m* one who orders out troops

ēvocō 1 *v* call out; summon; lure *or* entice out

ēvolō 1 *v* fly out; rush forth

ēvolvō, **lvī**, **lūtum** 3 *v* unroll, unfold; extricate; peruse; explain; roll out *or* away; wrench out, eject

ēvomō, **muī** 3 *v* vomit out

ēvulgō 1 *v* make public, divulge

ex (**ē** used before consonants) *prep with abl* out of, from; down from, off; by; after; on account of; in accordance with
□ **~ aequō** from the same level

□ ∼ **imprōvīsō/īnspērātō** unexpectedly

□ ∼ **itinere** out of the way, away from the road

□ ∼ **pauxillō** little by little

□ ∼ **mediō abeō** die

ex- ▶ **exs-**

exāctiō, **ōnis** f method of levying taxes

exāctor, **ōris** m expeller; exactor; collector of taxes

exāctus, **a**, **um** adj exact, accurate

exacuō, **cuī**, **ūtum** ③ v make sharp or pointed; stimulate

exadvorsum adv opposite

exaedificō ① v complete the building of, construct

exaequō ① v equalize, make equal; regard as equal; be equal (to)

exaestuō ① v boil up; seethe, rage

exaggerō ① v heap up, accumulate; magnify

exagitō ① v drive out; stir up; disturb continually; attack, scold; discuss

exāmen, **inis** nt swarm (of bees); crowd; apparatus or process of weighing, balance

exāminō ① v weigh; consider, examine

examussim adv perfectly, exactly

exanimis, **e** adj, **exanimus**, **a**, **um** adj lifeless, dead

exanimō ① v deprive of life; kill; alarm greatly; exhaust

exardēscō, **arsī**, **arsum** ③ v catch fire; blaze, flare up

exārēscō, **ruī** ③ v dry up

exarō ① v plough or dig up; plough; note down (by scratching the wax on the tablets)

exasperō ① v roughen; irritate

exauctōrō ① v release or dismiss from military service

exaudiō ④ v hear; comply with, heed

excēdō, **essī**, **essum** ③ v go out or away; withdraw; digress; go beyond; die; leave; surpass; exceed

excellēns, **ntis** adj distinguished, excellent

excellentia, **ae** f superiority, excellence

excellō, **luī**, **lsum** ③ v be pre-eminent, excel

excelsus, **a**, **um** adj lofty, high; sublime

exceptiō, **ōnis** f exception, qualification

exceptō ① v take out, take up; inhale, take (to oneself)

excerpō, **psī**, **ptum** ③ v pick out; select

excessus, **ūs** m departure; death; digression

excidium, **(i)ī** nt military destruction

excidō, **dī** ③ v fall out; escape; be deprived of; lose control of one's senses; fall away, disappear

excīdō, **īdī**, **īsum** ③ v cut out or off, cut down; raze; destroy

excieō, **cīvī**, **cītum** ② v, **exciō** ④ v rouse; call out, send for; summon; evoke

excipiō, **cēpī**, **ceptum** ③ v exempt; take out; except; catch; receive; listen to; follow after

excitō ① v rouse up, wake up; raise, erect; arouse

exclāmātiō, **ōnis** f exclamation, saying

exclāmō ① v call or cry out; exclaim

exclūdō, **ūsī**, **ūsum** ③ v shut out, exclude; hatch; prevent

excōgitō ① v think out, devise

excolō, **luī**, **ultum** ③ v improve; develop; honour

excommunicatio, **onis** f [LM] excommunication

excoquō, **coxī**, **coctum** ③ v boil; temper (by heat); boil away; dry up, parch

excors, **rdis** adj silly, stupid

excrēmentum, **ī** nt excrement; spittle, mucus

excrēscō, **ēvī**, **ētum** ③ v grow out or up; grow

excruciō ① v torture; torment

excubiae, **ārum** fpl watching; watch, guard

excubitor, **ōris** m watchman, sentinel

excubō, **buī**, **bitum** ① v sleep in the open; keep watch; be attentive

excūdō, **ūdī**, **ūsum** ③ v strike out; forge; fashion

excurrō, (cu)currī, cursum ③ *v* run out; make an excursion; sally; extend; project

excursiō, ōnis *f* running forth; sally

excursus, ūs *m* running out; excursion; sally, sudden raid

excūsābilis, e *adj* excusable

excūsātiō, ōnis *f* excuse

excūsō ① *v* excuse; plead as an excuse; absolve

excutiō, ussī, ussum ③ *v* shake out *or* off; cast out; search, examine

exedō, ēsse, ēdī, ēsum *v ir* eat up, consume; hollow

exemplar, āris *nt* model, pattern, example; copy

exemplum, ī *nt* sample; example; precedent; warning; punishment; portrait; copy

exenterō ① *v* disembowel

exeō, īre, iī, itum *v ir* go out *or* away; march out; escape; die; perish; rise; exceed

exerceō ② *v* drill, exercise, train; employ; practise; administer; cultivate; harass

exercitātiō, ōnis *f* exercise, practice

exercitātus, a, um *adj* practised, skilled; troubled

exercitium, (i)ī *nt* exercise

exercitō ① *v* practise

exercitus, ūs *m* army; swarm, flock

exēsus, a, um *adj* porous

exhālō ① *v* breathe out; evaporate; die

exhauriō, hausī, haustum ④ *v* drain; empty; drink up; exhaust; see through to the end

exhērēs, ēdis *adj* disinherited

exhibeō ② *v* present; furnish; exhibit; produce

exhorrēscō, ruī ③ *v* be terrified; tremble at

exhortor ① *v dep* exhort, encourage, incite

exigō, ēgī, āctum ③ *v* drive out; thrust; exact; finish; examine, weigh; make to conform with

exiguitās, ātis *f* scarcity, smallness of size

exiguus, a, um *adj* scanty, small, petty, short, poor

exīlis, e *adj* small, thin; poor

eximius, a, um *adj* select, extraordinary, excellent, fine

eximō, ēmī, ēmptum ③ *v* take out, remove; free, release

exinde, exim, exin *adv* thence; after that; then

exīstimātiō, ōnis *f* judgment; opinion; reputation; credit

exīstimō, exīstumō ① *v* judge, value, esteem, think

exitiābilis, exitiālis, e *adj* destructive, deadly

exitiōsus, a, um *adj* destructive, pernicious, deadly

exitium, (i)ī *nt* ruin, mischief; death

exitus, ūs *m* egress, departure; end; outlet; result; death

exoculō ① *v* knock the eyes out from

exolēscō, ēvī, ētum ③ *v* grow up; grow out of use; die out

exonerō ① *v* unload, disburden, discharge

exoptō ① *v* long for

exōrābilis, e *adj* capable of being moved by entreaty

exōrdior, ōrsus sum ④ *v dep* begin, commence

exordium, (i)ī *nt* beginning; introduction, preface

exorior, ortus sum ④ *v dep* arise; begin; spring up; cheer up

exōrnō ① *v* furnish with, adorn, embellish; dress up

exōrō ① *v* obtain by entreaty; win over by entreaty

exōsculor ① *v dep* kiss fondly

exōsus, a, um *adj* hating

exōticus, a, um *adj* foreign, exotic

expallēscō, luī ③ *v* turn very pale

expandō, ndī, passum/pānsum ③ *v* spread out, expand; expound

expatrō ① *v* waste in dissoluteness, squander

expavēscō, ī ③ *v* become frightened

expediō ④ *v* extricate; make ready; free

  □ **expedit** ④ *v impers* it is profitable *or* expedient

expedītiō, ōnis *f* expedition, campaign

expedītus, a, um *adj* free, easy; ready; ready for action; without baggage; unencumbered; dealt with, cleared up

expellō, **pulī**, **pulsum** ③ *v* expel; banish; reject

expendō, **ndī**, **ēnsum** ③ *v* pay; pay out; weigh, judge; pay a penalty

expergēfaciō, **fēcī**, **factum** ③ *v* arouse, awake

expergīscor, **rrēctus sum** ③ *v dep* awake; bestir oneself

experiēns, **ntis** *adj* active, enterprising

experientia, **ae** *f*, **experīmentum**, **ī** *nt* trial, experiment; experience

experior, **pertus sum** ④ *v dep* make trial of, put to the test, experience, find; attempt

expers, **rtis** *adj with gen* destitute of, without; lacking experience; immune (from)

expertus, **a**, **um** *adj* well-proved, tested

expetō, **īvī/iī**, **ītum** ③ *v* ask for; desire; aspire to; demand; happen; fall on (a person)

expiātiō, **ōnis** *f* atonement, expiation, purification

expīlō ① *v* plunder, rob, despoil

expiō ① *v* atone for, expiate; make amends for; avert by expiatory rites

expiscor ① *v dep* try to fish out (information)

explānō ① *v* explain

expleō, **ēvī**, **ētum** ② *v* fill out *or* up, complete; finish; satisfy; satiate; fulfil, discharge

explicō, **cāvī/cuī**, **cātum/citum** ① *v* unfold; display; disentangle; exhibit; spread out

explōdō, **ōsī**, **ōsum** ③ *v* drive (an actor) off the stage; reject

explōrātor, **ōris** *m* spy, scout

explōrō ① *v* reconnoitre; test, try out; investigate

expoliō ④ *v* polish; refine

expōnō, **posuī**, **positum** ③ *v* set out; expose; disembark; publish; exhibit, explain

exportō ① *v* export, carry out

exposcō, **poposcī** ③ *v* ask for, demand, request; demand the surrender of

expostulātiō, **ōnis** *f* complaint, protest

expostulō ① *v* demand, call for; remonstrate, complain about

exprimō, **pressī**, **pressum** ③ *v* squeeze, squeeze out; copy, portray; express; extort

exprobrātiō, **ōnis** *f* reproaching, reproach

exprobrō ① *v* bring up as a reproach

exprōmō, **mpsī**, **mptum** ③ *v* bring out; disclose, reveal

expugnābilis, **e** *adj* open to assault

expugnātiō, **ōnis** *f* taking by storm

expugnātor, **ōris** *m* conqueror

expugnāx, **ācis** *adj* effectual in overcoming resistance

expugnō ① *v* take by assault, storm; conquer; plunder; achieve; persuade

expurgō ① *v* cleanse, purify; exculpate

exquīrō, **īsīvī**, **īsītum** ③ *v* inquire into; look for

exquīsītus, **a**, **um** *adj* meticulous; recherché, choice, special

exrādīcitus *adv* from the very roots, utterly and completely

exs- ▸ **ex-** without the 's'

exsanguis, **e** *adj* bloodless; pale, wan; feeble

exsatiō ① *v* satisfy, satiate; glut

exsaturābilis, **e** *adj* capable of being satiated

exsaturō ① *v* satisfy, sate, glut

exscindō, **idī**, **issum** ③ *v* demolish, destroy

exscrībō, **psī**, **ptum** ③ *v* copy, write out

exsecō, **secuī**, **sectum** ① *v* cut out *or* away; castrate

exsecrābilis, **e** *adj* accursed, detestable

exsecrātiō, **ōnis** *f* imprecation, curse

exsecror ① *v dep* curse; detest

exsequiae, **ārum** *fpl* funeral procession

exsequor, **secūtus sum** ③ *v dep* follow (to the grave); pursue; accomplish; relate; pursue with vengeance *or* punishment

exserō, ruī, rtum ③ *v* stretch forth; thrust out, lay bare

exsiccō ① *v* dry up; empty (a vessel)

exsiliō, luī ④ *v* spring forth, leap up

exsilium, (i)ī *nt* exile

exsistō, stitī, stitum ③ *v* step forth, appear; arise; become; prove to be

exsolvō, lvī, lūtum ③ *v* set free; pay; throw off; release; perform

exsomnis, e *adj* wakeful, vigilant

exsors, rtis *adj* without share in, exempt from lottery

exspatior ① *v dep* wander from the course; spread out

exspectātiō, ōnis *f* expectation, expectancy

exspectō ① *v* await, expect; anticipate; hope for

exspēs *adj* (*nom sg only*) hopeless

exspīrō ① *v* breathe out; exhale; expire; die; cease

exspoliō ① *v* plunder

exspuō, puī, ūtum ③ *v* spit out; eject; rid oneself of

externō ① *v* terrify, madden

exstillō ① *v* trickle away, dissolve; let fall in drops

exstimulō ① *v* goad; stimulate

exstīnctiō, ōnis *f* extinction

exstinguō, īnxī, īnctum ③ *v* quench, extinguish; kill; destroy

exstō ① *v* stand out *or* forth; project; be visible; exist, be on record

exstruō, ūxī, ūctum ③ *v* pile up; build up, raise

exsūdō ① *v* exude; sweat out

exsul, lis *m/f* exile

exsulō ① *v* be an exile

exsultātiō, ōnis *f* exultation, joy

exsultō ① *v* jump about; let oneself go; exult

exsuperābilis, e *adj* able to be overcome

exsuperō ① *v* excel; overtop; surpass; overpower

exsurgō, surrēxī ③ *v* rise, stand up; take action

exsuscitō ① *v* awaken; kindle; (fig) stir up, excite

exta, ōrum *ntpl* bowels, entrails

extemplō *adv* immediately, forthwith

extendō, ndī, entum/ēnsum ③ *v* stretch out, extend; enlarge; prolong; continue

extenuō ① *v* make thin; diminish

extergeō, rsī, rsum ② *v* wipe clean

exterminō ① *v* banish, expel; dismiss

externus, a, um *adj* external; foreign, strange

exterreō ② *v* strike with terror, scare

exter(us), era, erum *adj* outer, external, foreign
- **exterior** *comp*
- **extrēmus, extimus** *sup*

extimēscō, muī ③ *v* take fright, be alarmed; dread

extimus, a, um *adj* [sup of **exter**] uttermost, utmost, extreme, last

extollō ③ *v* raise; lift up; extol, praise, advance

extorqueō, rsī, rtum ② *v* twist *or* wrench out; extort

extorris, e *adj* exiled

extortor, ōris *m* robber

extrā *prep with acc* outside, without; out of, beyond; except; *adv* outside, without; out of, beyond; except

extrahō, āxī, actum ③ *v* draw out, extract; prolong

extrāneus, a, um *adj* external, extraneous, foreign; not belonging to one's family *or* household

extraordinārius, a, um *adj* supplementary; special; immoderate

extrārius, a, um *adj* situated outside; extraneous; not belonging to one's household, strange

extrēmum, ī *nt* limit, outside; end

extrēmus, a, um *adj* [sup of **exter**] uttermost, utmost, extreme, last

extrīcō ① *v* disentangle, extricate, free

extrīnsecus *adv* from without; on the outside

extrūdō, ūsī, ūsum ③ *v* thrust out; drive out

extundō, udī, ūsum ③ *v* beat *or* strike out; produce with effort; extort

exturbō ① *v* thrust out; divorce; disturb

exūberō ① *v* surge *or* gush up; be abundant, be fruitful

exulcerō ① *v* make sore *or* raw; exasperate, aggravate

exululō ① *v* invoke with howls

exundātiō, **ōnis** *f* overflowing

exundō ① *v* gush forth; overflow with

exuō, **uī**, **ūtum** ③ *v* put off; doff; strip; deprive of; lay aside; cast off

exurgeō, **rsī** ② *v* squeeze out

exūrō, **ussī**, **ustum** ③ *v* burn up; destroy; parch, dry up

exuviae, **ārum** *fpl* things stripped off; spoils, booty; something belonging to a person, serving as a memento

Ff

faba, **ae** *f* bean

fābella, **ae** *f* story, fable; play

faber¹, **brī** *m* artisan, workman; smith; carpenter

faber², **bra**, **brum** *adj* of the craftsman *or* his work

fabrica, **ae** *f* art, craft

fabricātor, **ōris** *m* maker, fashioner

fabricō ① *v*, **fabricor** ① *v dep* fashion, forge, shape; build, construct

fabrīlis, **e** *adj* of *or* belonging to a workman; of a metal-worker, carpenter *or* builder

fābula, **ae** *f* story; tale; fable; drama, play talk
  □ **fābulae!** rubbish!

fābulor ① *v dep* talk, converse, chat; invent a story

fābulōsus, **a**, **um** *adj* storied, fabulous; celebrated in story

facessō, **s(īv)ī/sīī**, **ītum** ③ *v* do; perpetrate; go away

facētiae, **ārum** *fpl* wit, joke

facētus, **a**, **um** *adj* witty, humorous; clever, adept; elegant, fine

faciēs, **iēī** *f* face, look, pretence; appearance, beauty

facilis, **e** *adj* easy; pliable; gentle; courteous; good-natured, affable

facilitās, **ātis** *f* easiness, facility; readiness; good nature, courteousness, affability

facinorōsus, **a**, **um** *adj* doing wrong, criminal, wicked

facinus, **oris** *nt* deed, crime, outrage

faciō, **fēcī**, **factum** ③ *v* make; do; fashion; cause; compose; practise; commit; render; value
  □ ~ **lucrī** make a profit
  □ ~ **minoris** consider of less importance
  □ **fac ut** *with subj* see to it that ... ! please ... !

> ❗ In CL, **faciō** had no passive forms from its pres. stem: in their place appeared the corresponding tenses of **fīō**, **fierī**. The 2sg. impv. of **faciō** is **fac**.

factiō, **ōnis** *f* faction, party

factiōsus, **a**, **um** *adj* factious, seditious, turbulent

factitō ① *v* do frequently; practise

factum, **ī** *nt* deed, exploit

facultās, **ātis** *f* capability; possibility; means; opportunity; skill; quantity available; means

fācundia, **ae** *f* eloquence

fācundus, **a**, **um** *adj* eloquent

faecula, **ae** *f* lees of wine (used as a condiment or medicine)

faenebris, **bre** *adj* pertaining to usury; lent at interest

faenerātiō, **ōnis** *f* usury, money-lending

faenerātor, **ōris** *m* usurer, money-lender

faeniculum, **ī** *nt* fennel, especially used as a condiment or medicament

faenīlia, **ium** *ntpl* place for storing hay, barn

faenisex, **cis** *m* man who cuts hay, mower

faenum, **ī** *nt* hay

faenus, eris/oris *nt* interest; profit; gain
□ **faenore** on loan, at interest

faex, cis *f* sediment, dregs; dregs of the people

fāgus, ī *f* beech-tree

fala, ae *f* wooden siege-tower

falārica, ae *f* a heavy missile (thrown generally by a catapult)

falcārius, (i)ī *m* scythe-maker

falcātus, a, um *adj* armed with scythes; sickle-shaped, curved

falcifer, era, erum *adj* carrying a scythe; scythed

Falernum, ī *nt* Falernian wine

fallācia, ae *f* deceit, trick, stratagem

fallāx, ācis *adj* deceitful, fallacious; spurious

fallō, fefellī, falsum ③ *v* cheat, deceive; disappoint; escape notice

falsiparēns, ntis *adj* having a pretended father

falsus, a, um *adj* false; deceiving; deceived; spurious
□ **falsō** wrongly, mistakenly; lyingly

falx, cis *f* sickle; scythe; curved blade

fāma, ae *f* rumour; fame; renown; ill repute; news

famēlicus, a, um *adj* starved, famished, hungry

famēs, mis *f* hunger; famine; craving

familia, ae *f* household, all persons under the control of one man, whether relations, freedmen, or slaves; family; servants *or* slaves belonging to one master; estate

familiāris, e *adj* of the household; familiar; intimate; very friendly; *as noun m/f* acquaintance, friend

familiāritās, ātis *f* familiarity, intimacy, close friendship

fāmōsus, a, um *adj* famed, renowned; infamous, notorious; slanderous, libellous

famulāris, e *adj* of slaves, servile

famulātus, ūs *m* state of being a slave, servitude

famulor ① *v dep* be a servant, attend

famulus, a, um *adj* servile, subject
■ **famula, ae** *f* female slave; maid-servant
■ **famulus, ī** *m* slave, servant; attendant

fānāticus, a, um *adj* fanatic, frantic; belonging to a temple

fandus, a, um *adj* that may be spoken; proper, lawful

fānum, ī *nt* sanctuary, temple

fār, farris *nt* husked wheat, grain

farciō, rsī, rtum ④ *v* stuff, cram

farctum, ī *nt* stuffing, filling, insides

farrāgō, inis *f* mixed fodder; a hotch-potch

farreus, a, um *adj* made from grain
■ **farreum, ī** *nt* cake made from grain

fars, tis *f* stuffing, filling, insides

fās *nt indec* divine law; right; obligation

fascia, ae *f* band; puttees

fasciculus, ī *m* bundle, packet; bunch (of flowers)

fascinō ① *v* cast a spell on, bewitch

fascis, is *m* bundle, parcel
■ **fascēs** *pl* bundles of rods, carried before the highest magistrates of Rome, usually with an axe bound up in the middle of them; the power *or* office of a magistrate

> ❗ The **fascēs** were bundles of wooden rods around 5 ft. long bound together with red thongs; outside of the city of Rome an axe was also bound in among the rods. They were carried by **lictōrēs** and symbolised a magistrate's authority and power.

fāstī, ōrum *mpl* list of festivals; calendar; list of consuls who gave their names to the year

fastīdiō ④ *v* disdain; be scornful; feel aversion to, be squeaming

fastīdiōsus, a, um *adj* squeamish; exacting, fussy; disdainful; nauseating

fastīdium, (i)ī *nt* squeamishness, loathing; scornful contempt; pride; fastidiousness

fastīgium, (i)ī *nt* slope, declivity; gable, roof; sharp point, tip; summit; height; depth; highest rank, dignity

fastus, ūs *m* contempt; haughtiness

fāstus, a, um *adj*
□ **diēs** ∼ day on which the courts could sit

fātālis, e *adj* destined, fated; fatal
■ **fātāliter** *adv* by destiny *or* fate

fateor, fassus sum ② *v dep* confess; acknowledge

fātidicus, a, um *adj* prophetic

fātifer, era, erum *adj* deadly; fatal

fatīgō ① *v* weary, tire, fatigue; harass; importune; overcome

fātiloquus, a, um *adj* prophetic

fatīscō ③ *v*, **fatīscor** ③ *v dep* gape, crack; grow weak *or* exhausted

fātum, ī *nt* fate, destiny; doom; ill-fate; death

fatuus, a, um *adj* foolish, silly; idiotic

faucēs, ium *fpl* throat; narrow entrance; defile; gulf, abyss

Faunus, ī *m* a rustic god

faustus, a, um *adj* favourable; auspicious; lucky, prosperous

fautor, ōris *m* patron; admirer; supporter

faveō, fāvī, fautum ② *v with dat* favour, befriend; back up

favīlla, ae *f* ashes, embers

Favōnius, (i)ī *m* west wind

favor, ōris *m* favour, good-will; bias, applause

favus, ī *m* honey-comb

fax, facis *f* torch; firebrand; love-flame; fire, torment

faxim *old pf subj* of ▶ **faciō**

faxō *old fut pf* of ▶ **faciō**

febrīculōsus, a, um *adj* prone to fever, fever-ridden

febris, is *f* fever, attack of fever

Februārius, (i)ī *m* February

fēcī ▶ **faciō**

fēcunditās, ātis *f* fertility, fecundity

fēcundus, a, um *adj* fruitful, fertile; abundant

fel, fellis *nt* gall, bile; poison; bitterness, venom

fēlēs, is *m/f* cat

fēlīcitās, ātis *f* good fortune, felicity

fēlīx, īcis *adj* fruitful; lucky, happy, fortunate; successful

fellō ① *v* suck

fēmella, ae *f* woman, girl

fēmina, ae *f* female, woman

fēmineus, a, um *adj* womanly, feminine, womanish, effeminate

femur, feminis/femoris *nt* thigh

fēn- ▶ **faen-**

fenestra, ae *f* window; loop-hole

fera, ae *f* wild beast

fērālis, e *adj* funereal; deadly, fatal
  ■ **Fērālia, ium** *ntpl* festival of the dead

ferāx, ācis *adj* fruitful, fertile

ferculum, ī *nt* frame *or* stretcher for carrying things; dish; course (at dinner)

ferē *adv* nearly, almost; about; in general; *with negatives* hardly

ferentārius, (i)ī *m* light-armed soldier, skirmisher

feretrum, ī *nt* bier

fēriae, ārum *fpl* holiday

fēriātus, a, um *adj* keeping holiday, at leisure

ferīna, ae *f* game, flesh of wild animals

ferīnus, a, um *adj* of wild beasts

feriō ④ *v* strike, knock; hit; slay, kill; strike (a bargain); enter into *or* conclude (a treaty)

feritās, ātis *f* wildness, savageness

fermē ▶ **ferē**

ferō, ferre, tulī, lātum *v ir* carry; bring; bear away; plunder; bear with; lead; produce, bring forth; endure; receive; propose; exhibit
  □ **ferunt** they say
  □ **fertur** it is said

ferōcia, ae *f* fierceness, ferocity; insolence

ferōcitās, ātis *f* fierceness, savageness; excessive spirits; aggressiveness

ferōx, ōcis *adj* wild, bold; warlike; cruel; defiant, arrogant

ferrāmentum, ī *nt* iron tool

ferrāria, ae *f* iron mine

ferrātilis, e *adj* clad in chains

ferrātus, a, um *adj* bound *or* covered with iron; with iron points *or* studs

ferreus, a, um *adj* of iron, iron; hard, cruel; firm

ferriterium, (i)ī *nt* place of those put in irons

ferritrībāx, ācis *adj* wearing out fetters

ferrūgineus, a, um *adj* of the colour of iron-rust, sombre

ferrūgō, inis *f* iron-rust; colour of iron-rust; dusky colour

ferrum, **ī** *nt* iron; sword; any tool of iron; weapon

fertilis, **e** *adj* fruitful, fertile; abundant

fertilitās, **ātis** *f* fruitfulness, fertility

ferus, **a**, **um** *adj* wild, savage; cruel
■ ~, **ī** *m* wild beast

fervefaciō, **fēcī**, **factum** ③ *v* make intensely hot, heat, boil

fervēns, **ntis** *adj* boiling hot, burning; inflamed, impetuous

ferveō, **rbuī** ② *v* be intensely hot; boil; seethe, be roused

fervēscō ③ *v* grow hot

fervidus, **a**, **um** *adj* boiling hot, fiery; torrid; roused; hot-blooded

fervor, **ōris** *m* heat; ardour, passion

fessus, **a**, **um** *adj* wearied, tired; feeble

festīnātiō, **ōnis** *f* haste, speed, hurry

fēstīnō ① *v* hasten; hurry

festīvus, **a**, **um** *adj* lively, festive

fēstum, **ī** *nt* holiday, festival; feast-day

fēstus, **a**, **um** *adj* festal; solemn, merry

fētiālēs, **ium** *mpl* Roman college of priests who represented the Roman people in their dealings with other nations

fētidus, **a**, **um** *adj* foul-smelling, stinking

fētūra, **ae** *f* bearing, breeding; young off-spring, brood

fētus[1], **ūs** *m* birth; offspring; produce

fētus[2], **a**, **um** *adj* pregnant with; fertile; full (of); having newly brought forth

fibra, **ae** *f* fibre, filament; entrails; leaf, blade (of grasses, *etc.*)

fībula, **ae** *f* clasp, buckle, brooch

fictilis, **e** *adj* made of earthenware
■ **fictile**, **is** *nt* earthenware vessel *or* statue

fictor, **ōris** *m* one who devises *or* makes

fictus, **a**, **um** *adj* feigned, false; counterfeit

ficulneus, **a**, **um** *f* of a fig-tree
■ **ficulnea**, **ae** *f* LM fig-tree

fīcus, **ī/ūs** *f* fig-tree

fidēlis, **e** *adj* faithful; loyal; trustworthy; dependable

fidēlitās, **ātis** *f* faithfulness, fidelity

fīdēns, **ntis** *adj* confident; bold

fidēs[1], **ēī** *f* faith, trust, confidence; belief, credence; loyalty; honesty; allegiance; promise; security; protection

fidēs[2], **dis** *f* (*usu pl* **fidēs**, **ium**) lyre

fidicen, **inis** *m* lyre-player

fidicina, **ae** *f* female lyre-player

fīdō, **fīsus sum** ③ *v semi-dep with dat or abl* trust (in), have confidence (in)

fīdūcia, **ae** *f* trust, confidence; boldness, courage
□ **fīdūciā** on the responsibility (of); trusting in

fīdūciārius, **a**, **um** *adj* holding on trust; held on trust

fīdus, **a**, **um** *adj* trusty, faithful, loyal

figlīnae, **ārum** *fpl* potter's workshop, pottery

figlīnum, **ī** *nt* earthenware pottery

fīgō, **īxī**, **īxum** ③ *v* fix, fasten; transfix; establish

figulus, **ī** *m* potter

figūra, **ae** *f* shape, figure, form; image

figūrō ① *v* form, fashion, shape

fīlia, **ae** *f* daughter

> ❗ The dat./abl. pl. of **fīlia** is **fīliābus**, distinguishing it from the dat./abl. pl. of **fīlius**.

fīliola, **ae** *f* little daughter

fīliolus, **ī** *m* little son

fīlius, **(i)ī** *m* son

filix, **cis** *f* fern, bracken

fīlum, **ī** *nt* thread; cord; string; texture

fimum, **ī** *nt*, **fimus**, **ī** *m* dung, excrement

findō, **fidī**, **fissum** ③ *v* cleave, split; divide

fingō, **fīnxī**, **fictum** ③ *v* shape, form, fashion, make; contrive; invent; make a pretence of; deceive

fīniō ④ *v* limit; define; end, finish; mark out the boundaries of

fīnis, **is** m/f boundary, limit; end; purpose; death
  ■ **fīnēs**, **ium** pl country, territory

fīnitimus, **a**, **um** adj bordering on, adjoining, neighbouring

fīō, **fierī**, **factus sum** v ir semi-dep be made or done; happen; become; take place

> **!** This verb supplies the equivalents used in place of the non-existent pres. stem passives of **faciō** and its compounds; thus **fīō** is both 'I become' and 'I am made'. Compounds in **-ficiō** usu. have regular pres. stem passive forms.

firmāmen, **inis** nt (poet), **firmāmentum**, **ī** nt support, prop, mainstay

firmitās, **ātis** f firmness, strength

firmiter adv firmly, strongly; steadfastly

firmitūdō, **inis** f stability; strength

firmō ① v make firm or steady; strengthen; harden; confirm; establish; encourage

firmus, **a**, **um** adj firm; strong; steady; valid; bold

fiscella, **ae** f, **fiscina**, **ae** f small wicker-basket

fiscus, **ī** m money-bag, purse; imperial exchequer

fissilis, **e** adj easily split; split

fistula, **ae** f pipe, tube; shepherd's pipe

fīsus pple from ▶ **fīdō**

fīxus, **a**, **um** adj fixed fast, immovable; fitted with

flābra, **ōrum** ntpl gusts or blasts of wind

flaccidus, **a**, **um** adj flaccid, flabby

flagellum, **ī** nt whip, scourge; thong; vine-shoot

flāgitātiō, **ōnis** f importunate request, demand

flāgitātor, **oris** m one who makes pestering demands, demander

flāgitiōsus, **a**, **um** adj disgraceful, scandalous; infamous

flāgitium, **(i)ī** nt shameful or base action; crime; scandal, disgrace

flāgitō ① v demand importunely; ask repeatedly (for)

flagrāns, **ntis** adj blazing, glowing; ardent, passionate

flagrantia, **ae** f blaze

flagrō ① v blaze, flame, burn; be inflamed; be excited

flāmen[1], **inis** m priest of one particular deity

flāmen[2], **inis** nt blast; gale, wind

flamma, **ae** f blaze, flame; ardour; fire of love; object of love

flammeus, **a**, **um** adj flaming, fiery; fiery red
  ■ **flammeum**, **ī** nt flame-coloured bridal veil

flammō ① v inflame, set on fire; excite

flātus, **ūs** m blowing; snorting; breath; breeze

flāveō ② v be yellow or gold-coloured

flāvēscō ③ v turn yellow or gold

flāvus, **a**, **um** adj yellow, flaxen, gold-coloured, blonde

flēbilis, **e** adj lamentable; doleful; tearful

flectō, **xī**, **xum** ③ v bend, bow, curve, turn; prevail on, soften

fleō, **ēvī**, **ētum** ② v weep, cry; weep for

flētus, **ūs** m weeping; tears

flexanimus, **a**, **um** adj persuasive

flexibilis, **e** adj flexible, pliant

flexilis, **e** adj pliant, pliable, supple

flexus, **ūs** m turning, winding; swerve; bend; turning point

flō ① v blow; sound; cast (by blowing)

floccus, **ī** m tuft of wool
  □ **nōn floccī faciō** consider of no importance

flōreō ② v blossom; flourish; be in one's prime

flōrēscō ③ v (begin to) blossom; increase in physical vigour or renown

flōreus, **a**, **um** adj flowery

flōridulus, **a**, **um** adj flowery, bright

flōridus, **a**, **um** adj blooming; flowery; florid

flōrifer, **era**, **erum** adj flowery

flōs, **ōris** m blossom, flower; youthful prime

flōsculus, **ī** m little flower, floweret; the best of anything, the 'flower'

fluctuō ① *v*, **fluctuor** ① *v dep* rise in waves, surge; float; be in a state of agitation; waver

fluctus, **ūs** *m* flood; wave, billow

fluentisonus, **a**, **um** *adj* resounding with the noise of the waves

fluentum, **ī** *nt* stream; river

fluidus, **a**, **um** *adj* liquid; soft, feeble

fluitō ① *v* float; flow; waver

flūmen, **inis** *nt* stream, river
□ **adversō flūmine** against the current
□ **secundō flūmine** with the current

fluō, **ūxī**, **ūxum** ③ *v* flow; stream; emanate; proceed (from); fall gradually; hang loosely

fluviālis, **e** *adj* river...

fluvius, **(i)ī** *m* river; running water

fluxus, **a**, **um** *adj* flowing; fluid; loose; transient; frail; dissolute

focilō ① *v* revive

focus, **ī** *m* fireplace, hearth; family, household

fodiō, **fōdī**, **fossum** ③ *v* dig, dig up; stab

foederātus, **a**, **um** *adj* allied (to Rome)

foeditās, **ātis** *f* foulness; ugliness; shame

foedō ① *v* defile; pollute; disfigure, disgrace, sully

foedus[1], **eris** *nt* league, treaty; agreement
□ ~ **feriō** enter into *or* conclude a treaty

foedus[2], **a**, **um** *adj* foul, filthy; ugly; base, vile; abominable

foen- ▶ **faen-**

folium, **(i)ī** *nt* leaf

folliculus, **ī** *m* bag *or* sack; pod; shell

follis, **is** *m* pair of bellows; bag; scrotum

fōmentum, **ī** *nt* poultice; alleviation, consolation

fōmes, **itis** *m* chips of wood, *etc.* for kindling a fire

fōns, **ntis** *m* spring, fountain; (fig) source; principal cause

fontānus, **a**, **um** *adj* of a spring

for ① *v dep* speak, talk; say

forāmen, **inis** *nt* aperture, hole

forās *adv* out of doors, abroad, forth, out

forceps, **ipis** *f* pair of tongs, pincers

fore *infin* be about to be

> ❗ **fore** is an alternative form of the fut. infin. from **sum**. It commonly appears in indirect speech to form part of a phrase expressing a fut. pass. meaning, e.g. **dīcō fore ut urbs dēleātur** 'I say that the city will be destroyed'.

---

forēnsis, **e** *adj* public; pertaining to the courts

forfex, **icis** *f* pair of shears; tongs, pincers

forīs *adv* out of doors; abroad

foris, **is** *f* (*often pl* **forēs**, **um**) door, gate; opening, entrance

fōrma, **ae** *f* form, figure, shape; mould; pattern; sort; beauty

formīca, **ae** *f* ant

formīcātiō, **ōnis** *f* sensation of ants crawling over the skin

formīdābilis, **e** *adj* terrifying

formīdō[1], **inis** *f* fear, terror, dread; a thing which frightens, bogey

formīdō[2] ① *v* dread; be afraid of

formīdolōsus, **formīdulōsus**, **a**, **um** *adj* fearful; terrible

fōrmō ① *v* shape, fashion, form; model

fōrmōsus, **a**, **um** *adj* beautiful, handsome

fōrmula, **ae** *f* set form of words, formula; principle, rule, legal process

fornāx, **ācis** *f* furnace, oven

fornicātus, **a**, **um** *adj* arched, vaulted

fornix, **cis** *m* arch, vault; brothel

forō ① *v* bore, pierce

fors, **rtis** *f* fortune, chance; accident

forsan, **forsit**, **forsitan**, **fortasse** *adv* perhaps

forte *adv* by chance; as luck would have it

fortis, **e** *adj* strong, powerful; hardy; courageous; valiant; manful

fortitūdō, **inis** *f* strength; firmness; courage; valour; manfulness

fortuītus, **a**, **um** *adj* casual; accidental

fortūna, **ae** f fortune; chance; luck; prosperity; condition; fate, destiny
∎ **fortūnae**, **ārum** pl possessions

fortūnātus, **a**, **um** adj lucky, happy, fortunate; rich

forulī, **ōrum** mpl bookcase

forum, **ī** nt market; court of justice; forum (at Rome)

forus, **ī** m gangway in a ship; row of benches erected for spectators at games

fossa, **ae** f ditch, trench

fossor, **ōris** m one who digs the ground

fovea, **ae** f pit; pitfall

foveō, **fōvī**, **fōtum** ② v keep warm; favour; cherish; maintain, foster

frāga, **ōrum** ntpl wild strawberries

fragilis, **e** adj brittle, frail; impermanent

fragilitās, **ātis** f brittleness; frailty

fragmen, **inis** nt fragment
∎ **fragmina**, **um** pl fragments, ruins; chips

fragmentum, **ī** nt fragment

fragor, **ōris** m crash; noise

fragōsus, **a**, **um** adj brittle; ragged

frāgrō ① v smell strongly

frangō, **ēgī**, **āctum** ③ v break, dash to pieces, smash; crush; weaken; wear out; vanquish; break in

frāter, **tris** m brother; cousin; [LM] monk, religious brother

frāternus, **a**, **um** adj brotherly, fraternal; friendly

fraudō ① v cheat; defraud; steal

fraudulentus, **a**, **um** adj swindling

fraus, **dis** f deceit; fraud; crime; responsibility for an action

fraxinus, **ī** f ash-tree; spear or javelin of ash

frēgī ▶ **frangō**

fremitus, **ūs** m roaring; shouting; clashing; muttering; loud murmur or buzz of applause, etc.

fremō, **muī** ③ v roar; growl; rage; murmur; clamour for

fremor, **ōris** m low, confused noise, murmur

frendeō, **frēsum** ② v, **frendō** ③ v gnash the teeth, grind up small

frēnō ① v bridle; curb

frēnum, **ī** nt bridle, bit; check

frequēns, **ntis** adj frequent; usual, general; crowded; populous

frequenter adv often, frequently; in crowds

frequentia, **ae** f frequency; crowd; abundance of persons or things

frequentō ① v frequent; repeat often; haunt; throng; crowd; celebrate

fretum, **ī** nt, **fretus**, **ūs** m strait, narrow sea; sea

frētus, **a**, **um** adj with abl relying upon, trusting to

fricō, **fricuī**, **frictum** ① v rub, chafe

frīgeō ② v be cold; lack vigour; have a cold reception

frīgēscō, **īxī** ③ v become cold

frīgidārium, **(i)ī** nt cooling room (in baths)

frīgidulus, **a**, **um** adj chilly, cold

frīgidus, **a**, **um** adj cold, cool, chilly; dull; torpid
∎ **frīgida**, **ae** f cold water, cold bath

frīgus, **oris** nt cold, coldness; frost, winter

fringilla, **ae** f a songbird, perhaps the chaffinch

frit nt indec a tiny particle, perhaps the grain at the top of an ear of corn

fritillus, **ī** m dice-box

fritinniō ④ v chirp, twitter

frīvolus, **a**, **um** adj frivolous, trifling; silly; worthless; trashy

frondātor, **ōris** m pruner

frondeō ② v be in leaf, become leavy

frondēscō, **duī** ③ v become leafy, shoot

frondeus, **a**, **um** adj leafy

frondōsus, **a**, **um** adj leafy, abounding in foliage

frōns[1], **ndis** f leafy branches; foliage, leaves

frōns[2], **ntis** f forehead; brow; foremost part of anything

frūctuōsus, **a**, **um** adj fruitful; profitable

frūctus[1] pple from ▶ **fruor**

frūctus[2], **ūs** m fruit, crops; profit

frūgālitās, **ātis** f thrift, sober habits, self-restraint

frūgī adj indec honest, worthy; virtuous; thrifty

◻ **~ sum** do one's duty, do the right thing

> ! **frūgī** was originally the dat. sg. of **frūgēs** and is thus indeclinable as an adj.; it has comp. **frūgālior** and sup. **frūgālissimus.**

frūgifer, era, erum *adj* fruit-bearing, fertile

frūmentārius, a, um *adj* of *or* concerned with corn
◻ **rēs frūmentāria** corn supply

frūmentātiō, ōnis *f* the collecting of corn; foraging

frūmentātor, ōris *m* forager

frūmentor ① *v dep* forage

frūmentum, ī *nt* corn, grain

frūnīscor, frūnītus sum ③ *v dep* enjoy, have the pleasure of

fruor, frūctus/fruitus sum ③ *v dep with abl* enjoy, profit by

frūstrā *adv* in vain, to no purpose

frūstrātiō, ōnis *f* deceiving, disappointment

frūstror ① *v dep* disappoint, frustrate; deceive

frustum, ī *nt* morsel, scrap of food

frutex, icis *m* shrub, bush; blockhead

fruticōsus, a, um *adj* bushy

frūx, ūgis *f* (*usu pl* **frūgēs, um**) fruits, crops

fūcō ① *v* colour; paint; dye

fūcōsus, a, um *adj* sham, bogus

fūcus, ī *m* dye; bee-glue; drone; pretence, sham

fuga, ae *f* flight; fleeing; avoidance; exile

fugāx, ācis *adj* flying swiftly; swift; avoiding; transitory

fugiō, fūgī ③ *v* flee *or* fly, run away; go into exile; shun, avoid

fugitāns, ntis *adj* inclined to avoid

fugitīvus, a, um *adj* fugitive
■ **~, ī** *m* runaway

fugō ① *v* put to flight, chase away; rout; drive into exile

fuī ▸ sum

fulciō, lsī, ltum ④ *v* prop up, support; stop

fulcrum, ī *nt* head- *or* back-support of a couch

fulgeō, lsī ② *v* gleam; glitter, shine forth, be bright

fulgor, ōris *m* lightning; flash; glittering, brightness; glory

fulgur, uris *nt* lightning

fulgurat ① *v impers* there is lightning

fulica, ae *f* a water-fowl, probably the coot

fūlīgō, inis *f* soot; lamp-black

fulmen, inis *nt* lightning, thunderbolt; crushing blow

fulmineus, a, um *adj* of lightning; destructive

fulminō ① *v* lighten; cause lightning to strike; strike like lightning

fultūra, ae *f* prop

fulvus, a, um *adj* reddish yellow, tawny

fūmeus, fūmidus, a, um *adj,* **fūmifer, era, erum** *adj* full of smoke, smoky

fūmō ① *v* smoke, steam

fūmōsus, a, um *adj* full of smoke, smoky; smoked

fūmus, ī *m* smoke, steam, vapour

fūnāle, is *nt* torch of wax- or tallow-soaked rope; chandelier

fūnambulus, ī *m* tightrope walker

funda, ae *f* sling; casting-net

fundāmen, inis *nt* foundation

fundāmentum, ī *nt* foundation, groundwork, basis

fundātor, ōris *m* founder

funditor, ōris *m* slinger

funditus *adv* from the very bottom; utterly, totally

fundō¹, ūdī, ūsum ③ *v* pour out, shed; cast (metals); rout; scatter; produce; give birth to; utter freely

fundō² ① *v* found; establish; give a firm base to

fundus, ī *m* bottom; land; farm; estate

fūnebris, bre *adj* funereal; deadly, fatal

fūnereus, a, um *adj* funereal; deadly; fatal

fūnerō ① *v* bury; kill

fūnestō ① *v* pollute by murder

fūnestus, a, um *adj* fatal, deadly; destructive

fungor, fūnctus sum ③ *v dep with acc or abl* perform; discharge (a duty)

f

fungus, ī *m* fungus, mushroom

fūnis, is *m* rope, cable

fūnus, eris *nt* burial, funeral; funeral rites; corpse; death

fūr, ris *m/f* thief

furca, ae *f* (two-pronged) fork; prop

furcifer, erī *m* scoundrel, gallows bird

furcilla, ae *f* wood pitchfork; prop

furfur, ris *m* bran

furiae, ārum *fpl* frenzy; mad craving for; Furies, avenging spirits

furiālis, e *adj* frenzied, mad; avenging

furibundus, a, um *adj* raging, mad, furious; inspired

furiō ① *v* madden, enrage

furiōsus, a, um *adj* furious, mad, frantic, wild

furnus, ī *m* oven

furō, ruī ③ *v* rage, be mad *or* furious; be wild

furor, ōris *m* fury, rage, madness

fūror ① *v dep* steal, plunder

fūrtim *adv* by stealth, secretly; imperceptibly

fūrtīvus, a, um *adj* stolen; secret, furtive

fūrtum, ī *nt* theft; stolen article; trick, deception

fuscus, a, um *adj* dark, swarthy, dusky; husky; hoarse

fūsilis, e *adj* molten

fūstis, is *m* staff; club; stick

fūstuārium, (i)ī *nt* death by beating (a punishment meted out to soldiers)

fūsus, ī *m* spindle

fūtilis, futtilis, e *adj* vain; worthless

futuō, tuī, tūtum ③ *v* have sexual relations with (a woman)

futūrus, a, um *adj* future; about to be *fut pple* from ▶ **sum**

futūtiō, ōnis *f* copulation

Gg

gaesum, ī *nt* Gallic javelin

galea, ae *f* helmet

galērum, ī *nt*, **galērus, ī** *m* cap *or* hat made of skin

gallīna, ae *f* hen

gallus, ī *m* cock

gānea, ae *f*, **gāneum, ī** *nt* common eating house (the resort of undesirable characters); gluttonous eating

gāneō, ōnis *m* glutton, debauchee

ganniō ④ *v* whimper, snarl

garcifer, eri *m* ⟨LM⟩ boy

garriō ④ *v* chatter, jabber; talk nonsense

garrulus, a, um *adj* chattering, garrulous; blabbing

gaudeō, gāvīsus sum ② *v semi-dep* rejoice, be glad, be pleased with

gaudium, (i)ī *nt* joy, gladness; delight

gausapa, ae *f*, **gausape, is** *nt* cloth of woollen frieze; cloak of this material

gāvīsus *pple* from ▶ **gaudeō**

gāza, ae *f* (royal) treasure

gelidus, a, um *adj* icy, cold; frozen

gelō ① *v* freeze

gelū, ūs *nt* frost; ice, snow; cold, chilliness

gemellus, a, um *adj* twin-born ∎ ~, **ī** *m* twin

geminō ① *v* double; repeat; double the force of; pair (with)

geminus, a, um *adj* twin-born; double; both

gemitus, ūs *m* sigh, groan; roaring

gemma, ae *f* bud; jewel; cup; seal, signet

gemmātus, a, um *adj* jewelled

gemmeus, a, um *adj* set with precious stones

gemō, muī ③ *v* moan, groan; lament (over); grieve that

gena, ae *f* cheek, eyes

gener, erī *m* son-in-law

generātim *adv* by kinds, by tribes; generally

generātor, ōris *m* begetter, father, sire

generō ① *v* beget, father, produce

generōsus, a, um *adj* of noble birth; noble; of good stock

genesta ▶ genista

genetīvus, a, um *adj* acquired at birth

genetrīx, īcis *f* mother

geniālis, e *adj* connected with marriage; merry, genial; festive

genista, ae *f* Spanish broom, greenweed and similar shrubs

genitālis, e *adj* generative; fruitful

genitor, ōris *m* begetter, father; creator; originator

genius, (i)ī *m* tutelary deity *or* genius; talent

gēns, ntis *f* clan; tribe; family; race; nation

gentiles, ium *mpl* Ⓛ️Ⓜ️ pagans, heathens

gentīlicius, a, um *adj* of *or* belonging to a particular Roman **gens**

gentīlis, e *adj* of the same **gens**

genū, ūs *nt* knee

genuīnus, ī *m* back-tooth, molar

genus, eris *nt* birth, descent, origin; offspring; race; kind; family; nation; gender

geōmetrēs, ae *m* geometrician, surveyor

geōmetria, ae *f* geometry

germānitās, ātis *f* brotherhood, sisterhood; affinity between things deriving from the same source

germānus, a, um *adj* (of brothers and sisters) full; genuine, true
■ **germāna, ae** *f* sister
■ **germānus, ī** *m* brother

germen, inis *nt* sprout, bud; shoot

gerō, essī, estum ③ *v* bear, carry; wear; have; carry on, perform, do; govern, administer; achieve; carry in the womb
□ ~ **mōrem** gratify, accommodate oneself to
□ **sē gerere** behave

gestāmen, inis *nt* something worn *or* carried on the body; load, burden; means of conveyance

gestātor, ōris *m* bearer, traveller

gestiō ④ *v* exult; desire eagerly

gestō ① *v* carry (about); wear

gestus¹, a, um *adj pple* from ▶ **gerō**
■ **rēs gestae** *fpl* exploits

gestus², ūs *m* movement of the limbs; bodily action, gesture; gesticulation

gibber, era, erum *adj* hump-backed

gignō ③ *v* beget, bear, bring forth, produce

gilvus, a, um *adj* dun-coloured

gingīva, ae *f* gum (in which the teeth are set)

glaber, bra, brum *adj* hairless, smooth

glaciālis, e *adj* icy, frozen

glaciēs, iēī *f* ice

gladiātor, ōris *m* gladiator

gladiātōrius, a, um *adj* gladiatorial

gladius, (i)ī *m* sword

glaeba, ae *f* clod; cultivated soil; lump, mass

glāns, ndis *f* acorn, beach-nut; missile discharged from a sling

glārea, ae *f* gravel

glāreōsus, a, um *adj* gravelly

glaucus, a, um *adj* bluish grey

glēba ▶ glaeba

glīs, īris *m* dormouse

glīscō ③ *v* swell; increase in power *or* violence

globōsus, a, um *adj* round, spherical

globus, ī *m* sphere; dense mass; closely packed throng

glomerō ① *v* form into a ball; assemble, mass together

glomus, eris *nt* ball-shaped mass

glōria, ae *f* glory, fame, renown; vainglory, boasting

glōrior ① *v dep* boast; glory in

glōriōsus, a, um *adj* glorious, famous; vainglorious, boasting

glubō ③ *v* strip the bark from, peel

glūten, inis *nt* glue

gnāruris, e *adj* acquainted with, knowing

gnārus, a, um *adj* having knowledge *or* experience of; known

gnāv- ▶ nāv-

g

grabātus, ī *m* low couch *or* bed; camp-bed

gracilis, **e** *adj* thin, slender; meagre, lean; scanty, poor; simple, plain

grāculus, ī *m* jackdaw

gradātim *adv* step by step, by degrees

gradior, **gressus sum** ③ *v dep* step, walk

gradus, **ūs** *m* step, pace; position; rank; degree; rung (of ladder); stair
 □ **suspēnsō gradū** on tiptoe
 □ **addō gradum** gather pace, speed up

Graeculus, **a**, **um** *adj* Grecian, Greek (mostly in a contemptuous sense)

grallae, **ārum** *fpl* stilts

grāmen, **inis** *nt* grass; herb, plant

grāmineus, **a**, **um** *adj* of grass, grassy; made of grass *or* turf

grammaticus, **a**, **um** *adj* grammatical
 ■ ~, ī *m* grammarian, scholar, expert on linguistic and literary questions

> **!** A **grammaticus** would teach children between the ages of roughly 12 to 15; he taught the correct use of language and the study of poetry.

grandaevus, **a**, **um** *adj* of great age, old

grandēscō ③ *v* grow, increase in size *or* quantity

grandis, **e** *adj* old; grown up; great; grand; tall; lofty; powerful

grandō, **inis** *f* hail, hail-storm

grānum, ī *nt* grain, seed

graphium, **(i)ī** *nt* sharp-pointed writing implement; stylus

grassor ① *v dep* march on, advance; roam in search of victims, prowl; proceed; run riot

grātēs, **ium** *fpl* thanks
 □ **grātēs agō** thank

grātia, **ae** *f* grace; gracefulness; good-will; kindness; favour; obligation
 □ **referō grātiam** render thanks
 □ **grātiās agō/habeō** thank, be thankful to
 □ **grātiam faciō dē** politely decline an invitation
 □ **gratiā** *with gen* for the sake of, for the purpose of

grātificor ① *v dep* gratify; bestow

grātiōsus, **a**, **um** *adj* agreeable, enjoying favour; kind

grātīs *adv* without payment, for nothing

grātor ① *v dep with dat* congratulate; rejoice with

grātuītus, **a**, **um** *adj* free of charge; unremunerative

grātulābundus, **a**, **um** *adj* congratulating

grātulātiō, **ōnis** *f* congratulation; rejoicing, joy

grātulor ① *v dep* congratulate; rejoice

grātum, ī *nt* favour

grātus, **a**, **um** *adj* agreeable; pleasing, popular; thankful

gravātē *adv* grudgingly; reluctantly

gravēdō, **inis** *f* cold in the head, catarrh

gravidus, **a**, **um** *adj* pregnant; laden, weighed down with

gravis, **e** *adj* heavy; weighty, burdensome; burdened; important; solemn; serious; grievous; difficult; deep (of sound); strong (of smell)

gravitās, **ātis** *f* weight, heaviness; severity; authority

graviter *adv* heavily, severely; grievously; with reluctance

gravō ① *v* load, burden; oppress, aggravate
 □ **gravor** regard as a burden, show reluctance *or* annoyance

gregālis, **e** *adj* common; living in a flock *or* herd; belonging to the same flock *or* herd

gregārius, **a**, **um** *adj* belonging to the rank and file
 □ **mīles** ~ common soldier

gregātim *adv* in flocks

gremium, **(i)ī** *nt* lap, bosom; female genital parts; interior

gressus, **ūs** *m* going; step; *pl* the feet

grex, **gis** *m* flock, herd; company; crew

grūs, **gruis** *m/f* crane

grȳps, **grȳphis** *m* griffin

gubernāculum, ī *nt* helm, rudder; helm of 'ship of state'

gubernātiō, **ōnis** *f* steering; direction, control

gubernātor, **ōris** *m* helmsman, pilot; one who directs *or* controls

gubernō ① *v* steer (a ship); govern

gula, **ae** *f* gullet, throat; appetite

gulōsus, **a**, **um** *adj* fond of choice food

gurges, **itis** *m* whirlpool, eddy; 'flood', 'stream'

gustō ① *v* taste; sip; have some experience of

gutta, **ae** *f* drop; spot; speck

guttur, **uris** *nt* gullet, throat; appetite

gymnasium, **(i)ī** *nt* sports centre

gymn(ast)icus, **a**, **um** *adj* gymnastic, athletic

gynaecēum, **ī** *nt* women's apartments in a Greek house

gȳrus, **ī** *m* circle; circuit; course

Hh

habēna, **ae** *f* rein; thong; whip

habeō ② *v* have, hold, possess; contain; handle, use; manage; esteem; regard, treat (as); marry
  □ ~ **male** bother, annoy
  □ **prō certō** ~ know for certain

habilis, **e** *adj* handy, manageable; apt, fit

habitābilis, **e** *adj* habitable

habitātiō, **ōnis** *f* lodging, residence

habitātor, **ōris** *m* dweller, inhabitant

habitō ① *v* inhabit, dwell; live (in a place)

habitus, **ūs** *m* condition, state, dress, 'get-up'; expression, demeanour; character

hāc *adv* by this way; on this side

hāctenus *adv* hitherto; thus far; thus much

haedus, **ī** *m* kid

haereō, **haesī**, **(haesum)** ② *v* stick, cling, adhere, be fixed; be in difficulties; doubt; linger

haeresis, **is** *f* LM heresy

haereticus, **i** *m* LM heretic

haesitō ① *v* stick hesitate, be undecided; be stuck

hālitus, **ūs** *m* breath; steam, vapour

hālō ① *v* emit (vapour, *etc.*); be fragrant

(h)ama, **ae** *f* water-bucket

Hamadryas, **ados** *f* wood-nymph, hamadryad

hāmātus, **a**, **um** *adj* hooked

hāmus, **ī** *m* hook; fish-hook; barb of arrow

hara, **ae** *f* coop, pigsty

harenga, **ae** *f* herring

hariola, **ae** *f* female fortune-teller

hariolor ① *v dep* tell fortunes

hariolus, **ī** *m* prophet, seer

harmonia, **ae** *f* harmony; coupling

harpagō, **ōnis** *m* grappling-hook

harund- ▸ **arund-**

haruspex, **icis** *m* soothsayer

hasta, **ae** *f* spear, lance, pike; spear stuck in the ground at public auctions

hastātus, **a**, **um** *adj* armed with a spear
  ■ **hastātī**, **ōrum** *mpl* first line of a Roman army

hastīle, **is** *nt* shaft of a spear; spear; cane

hau, **haud** *adv* not, by no means

> ❗ **haud** negates individual words in a clause, never the whole clause.

haudquāquam *adv* by no means, in no way

hauriō, **hausī**, **haustum** ④ *v* draw (up *or* out); drink; drain; swallow; derive; have one's fill of; experience to the full

haustus, **ūs** *m* drinking; drink, draught; the drawing (of water)

hebdomas, **ados** *f* week, terminal point of a seven-day period

hebenus, **ī** *m/f* ebony

hebeō ② *v* be blunt; be sluggish

hebes, **etis** *adj* blunt, dull; languid; stupid

hebēscō ③ *v* grow blunt *or* feeble

hebetō ① *v* blunt, make dull; weaken

hedera, ae *f* ivy

hederiger, era, erum *adj* ivy-bearing

hei *int* exclamation expressing anguish or similar

heia *int* exclamation expressing deprecation, concession, astonishment or urgency

helciārius, (i)ī *m* one who tows boats

hĕlluō, ōnis *m* glutton, squanderer

hĕlluor ① *v dep* be a glutton; squander; spend immoderately

hem *int* what's that? ah! alas!

hendecasyllabī, ōrum *mpl* verses consisting of eleven syllables

hera ▶ era

herba, ae *f* grass; herb

herbidus, a, um *adj* grassy

herbifer, era, erum *adj* full of grass *or* herbs; bearing magical *or* medicinal plants

herbōsus, a, um *adj* grassy

herc(u)le *int* by Hercules!

hērēditās, ātis *f* heirship; inheritance

hērēs, ēdis *m/f* heir, heiress

herī *adv* yesterday

hērōicus, a, um *adj* heroic, epic

hērois, idis *f* heroine

hērōs, ōos/ōis *m* hero

hērōus, a, um *adj* heroic

Hesperia, ae *f* the western land, Italy

hesperius, a, um *adj* western

Hesperus, erī *m* evening-star

hesternus, a, um *adj* of yesterday

hetaeria, ae *f* religious brotherhood, fraternity

heu *int* oh! alas!

heus *int* ho! ho there! listen!

hiātus, ūs *m* opening, cleft; wide-opened jaw

hīberna, ōrum *ntpl*, **hībernāculum, ī** *nt* winter-quarters

hībernō ① *v* spend the winter; be in winter-quarters

hībernus, a, um *adj* of winter; wintry

hibiscum, ī *nt* marsh mallow

hīc *adv* here; in the present circumstances

hic, haec, hoc *pn* this

> **!** Inverse, the masc. and neut. nom. forms **hic** and **hoc** commonly scan as heavy before words beginning with vowels (the single 'c' representing a double 'cc', e.g. *hocc from *hod-ce).
> ····> In legal speeches, **hic** often refers to the speaker's own client.

hicine, haecine, hocine *pn* this?

hiemālis, e *adj* of *or* belonging to winter, wintry

hiemō ① *v* pass the winter; be stormy

hiem(p)s, mis *f* winter; stormy weather

hilaris, e *adj* cheerful, lively, light-hearted

hilaritās, ātis *f* cheerfulness, light-heartedness

hilaritūdō, inis *f* merriment

hilarō ① *v* gladden

hilarus, a, um *adj* cheerful, lively, light-hearted

hinc *adv* from this place; henceforth; from this cause

hinniō ④ *v* neigh

hinnītus, ūs *m* neighing

hiō ① *v* be wide open, gape; be greedy for; be open-mouthed (with astonishment, *etc.*)

hircus, ī *m* he-goat

hirsūtus, a, um *adj* rough, hairy, shaggy, bristly, prickly; rude

hirūdō, inis *f* leech

hirundinīnus, a, um *adj* of swallows

hirundō, inis *f* swallow

hīscō ③ *v* (begin to) open, gape; open the mouth to speak

hispidus, a, um *adj* rough, shaggy, hairy; bristly; dirty

historia, ae *f* history; story

historicus, a, um *adj* historical

histriō, ōnis *m* actor; performer in pantomime

histriōnālis, e *adj* concerning an actor; theatrical

hiulcō ① *v* cause to crack, crack open

hiulcus, a, um *adj* gaping, cracked

hodiē *adv* today; at the present time

hodiernus, a, um *adj* of this day; present

holus ▸ olus

homicīda, ae *m/f* murderer; killer of men

homō, inis *m* human being, person; man, woman; fellow

□ **novus** ∼ nouveau riche, upstart

> ❗ **homō** refers to man in the sense of mankind, in contrast to gods and animals; cf. **vir**.

homunculus, ī *m* little man; worthless *or* puny person

honestās, ātis *f* honourableness, honour; integrity

honestō ① *v* honour (with); adorn, grace

honestus, a, um *adj* worthy; decent; of high rank; honourable; handsome

honor, ōris *m* honour; regard; office, dignity; grace

honōrārius, a, um *adj* complimentary, supplied voluntarily

honōrificus, a, um *adj* conferring honour

honōrō ① *v* honour

honōrus, a, um *adj* conferring honour

hōra, ae *f* hour; season (of the year); time

■ **Hōrae, ārum** *fpl* the Seasons (personified)

hordeum, ī *nt* barley

hōria, ae *f* fishing boat

hornō *adv* this year

hornus, a, um *adj* this year's

horrendus, a, um *adj* dreadful, terrible, horrible

horreō ② *v* stand on end, bristle; have a rough appearance; shiver, tremble; shudder at

horrēscō, ruī ③ *v* bristle up, grow rough; begin to shake; tremble, shudder (at)

horreum, ī *nt* storehouse; barn

horribilis, e *adj* rough; terrible, horrible; monstrous

horridus, a, um *adj* rough, bristly; horrible; unkempt; grim

horrifer, era, erum *adj*, **horrificus, a, um** *adj* dreadful, frightening; chilling

horrisonus, a, um *adj* sounding dreadfully

horror, ōris *m* shivering; dread, awe; rigidity (from cold, *etc.*)

horsum *adv* in this direction

hortāmen, inis *nt* encouragement

hortātiō, ōnis *m* encouragement; exhortation

hortātor, ōris *m* encourager; exhorter

hortātus, ūs *m* exhortation

hortor ① *v dep* exhort; encourage

hortulus, ī *m* small garden; *pl* pleasure-grounds

hortus, ī *m* garden; *pl* pleasure-grounds

hospes, itls *m* guest; visitor; host; stranger

hospita, ae *f* female guest, hostess; landlady

hospitālis, e *adj* of *or* for a guest; hospitable

hospitāliter *adv* in a hospitable manner

hospitium, (i)ī *nt* hospitality; entertainment; guest accommodation; lodgings

hostia, ae *f* sacrificial animal

hosticus, a, um *adj* of *or* belonging to an enemy, hostile

hostīlis, e *adj* of an enemy, hostile

hostis, is *m/f* stranger, foreigner; enemy

hūc *adv* hither; to this place; so far

huiusmodī *gen used as adj indec* of this kind

hūm- ▸ **ūm-**

hūmānitās, ātis *f* human nature; civilization, culture; humane character

hūmāniter *adv* moderately; in a friendly manner

hūmānus, a, um *adj* human; humane; civilized; considerate

humī *adv* on the ground

humilis, e *adj* low; low-lying; mean; humble, lowly

humilitās, ātis *f* lowness; meanness; insignificance

humō ① *v* inter, bury

humus, ī *f* earth, soil, ground

> ❗ **humus** has a locative **humī**, and 'to the ground' is expressed by the acc. without a preposition.

hyacinthinus, a, um *adj* belonging to the hyacinth

hyacinthus, ī *m* hyacinth; sapphire

Hyadēs, **um** *fpl* group of five stars in the constellation of Taurus associated with rainy weather

hyalus, ī *m* glass

hydra, **ae** *f* water-serpent; snake

hydrōps, **ōpis** *m* dropsy

hydrus, ī *m* water-snake

Hymen, **nis** *m* god of marriage; marriage; wedding-refrain

Hymenaeus, ī *m* god of marriage; marriage; wedding-refrain

Hyperboreus, **a**, **um** *adj* northern

hypocauston, ī *nt* system of hot-air channels for heating baths

hypogēum, ī *nt* underground room *or* chamber

Ii

---

iaceō ② *v* lie; be situated; be still; lie still; lie dead; lie in ruins

iaciō, **iēcī**, **iactum** ③ *v* throw, cast, hurl; throw away; utter; pile up (structures)

iactanter *adv* arrogantly

iactantia, **ae** *f* boasting, ostentation

iactātiō, **ōnis** *f* shaking; boasting; showing off

iactō ① *v* throw, hurl; toss; utter with force; boast (of); torment
□ **sē iactāre** glory (in)

iactūra, **ae** *f* throwing (away, overboard); loss; cost

iactus, **ūs** *m* throwing, throw, cast

iaculātor, **ōris** *m* javelin-thrower

iaculor ① *v dep* throw a javelin; hurl; shoot at

iaculum, ī *nt* dart, javelin

iam *adv* now, already

iambus, ī *m* iambus (a metrical foot consisting of one light syllable followed by one heavy syllable), a line of verse made up of iambī

iamdūdum *adv* just now; already for a long time; long ago

iamprīdem *adv* a long time ago; for a long time now

iānitor, **ōris** *m* door-keeper, porter

iānua, **ae** *f* door, house-door; entrance

Iānuārius, **(i)ī** *m* January

Iānus, ī *m* Janus (a Roman god of gates and doorways)

iaspis, **idis** *f* jasper

ibī *adv* there

ibidem *adv* in that very place; at that very instant

ībis, **idis**/**is** *f* ibis (Egyptian bird)

ictus, **ūs** *m* blow, stroke; musical *or* metrical beat

idcircō *adv* therefore, for that reason

īdem, **eadem**, **idem** *pn* the same

identidem *adv* continually; repeatedly; again and again

ideō *adv* for the reason (that); for that reason, therefore

īdōlon, ī *nt* spectre, apparition

idōneus, **a**, **um** *adj* fit, suitable; able

Īdus, **ūs** *fpl* Ides (the 15th day of March, May, July, October, the 13th day of the other months)

iēcī ▶ **iaciō**

iecur, **iecinoris**/**iecoris** *nt* liver

iēiūnus, **a**, **um** *adj* fasting; hungry; barren; insignificant; poor; uninteresting

igitur *adv* therefore

ignārus, **a**, **um** *adj* ignorant (of), having no experience of; unknown

ignāvia, **ae** *f* laziness; faint-heartedness

ignāvus, **a**, **um** *adj* idle, sluggish; cowardly

ignēscō ③ *v* take fire, kindle; become inflamed (with passion)

igneus, **a**, **um** *adj* of fire; fiery; ardent

ignifer, **era**, **erum** *adj* bearing *or* containing fire

ignipotēns, **ntis** *adj* god of fire

ignis, **is** *m* fire; brightness; glow of passion

ignōbilis, **e** *adj* unknown; ignoble; obscure; of low birth

ignōbilitās, **ātis** *f* obscurity

ignōminia, **ae** *f* ignominy, dishonour

ignōminiōsus, **a**, **um** *adj* disgraced; disgraceful

ignōrantia, **ae** *f* ignorance

ignōrātiō, **ōnis** *f* ignorance

ignōrō ① *v* be ignorant of; fail to recognize

ignōscō, **ōvī**, **ōtum** ③ *v with dat* forgive, pardon

ignōtus, **a**, **um** *adj* unknown; ignorant (of)

īlex, **icis** *f* holm-oak

īlia, **ium** *ntpl* side part of the body extending from the hips down to the groin; private parts; inwards

īlicet *adv* at once, immediately; *int* it's all up! off with you!

īlicētum, **ī** *nt* oak coppice

īlicō *adv* just here, just there; directly, immediately

īlignus, **a**, **um** *adj* of the holm-oak

illābor, **lāpsus sum** ③ *v dep* slide *or* flow (into); fall *or* sink (onto)

illāc *adv* that way, on that side

illacessītus, **a**, **um** *adj* unattacked, free from invasion

illacrimābilis, **e** *adj* unlamented; inexorable

illacrimō ① *v*, **illacrimor** ① *v dep* bewail, lament

illaesus, **a**, **um** *adj* uninjured; inviolate

illaetābilis, **e** *adj* joyless

illaqueō ① *v* ensnare, entangle

ille, **a**, **illud**, **ius** *pn* he, she; it; that; the well-known; the former

illecebra, **ae** *f* allurement, enticement

illepidus, **a**, **um** *adj* lacking grace *or* refinement

illī *adv* there

illīberālis, **e** *adj* ungentlemanly, unladylike; not having the qualities of a free man

illīc *adv* there, over there

illiciō, **lexī**, **lectum** ③ *v* allure, entice

illicita, **ōrum** *ntpl* forbidden things; disloyalty

illicitus, **a**, **um** *adj* forbidden, unlawful, illicit

illīdō, **īsī**, **īsum** ③ *v* strike *or* dash against

illigō ① *v* bind *or* tie up; bind

illinc *adv* thence; on that side

illinō, **lēvī**, **litum** ③ *v* smear over; anoint

illō *adv* thither; to that point

illūc *adv* thither

illūcēscō, **lūxī** ③ *v* begin to dawn

illūdō, **ūsī**, **ūsum** ③ *v* speak mockingly of; trick out; use for sexual pleasure

illūminō ① *v* light up; brighten

illūnis, **e** *adj* moonless

illūstris, **tre** *adj* clear, bright; famous

illūstrō ① *v* illuminate; make famous *or* illustrious; make clear

illuviēs, **iēī** *f* dirt, filth; filthy condition

imāginātiō, **ōnis** *f* fancy, thought

imāginor ① *v* picture, imagine

imāgō, **inis** *f* image, likeness; idea; appearance; echo; ghost, phantom

imbēcillitās, **ātis** *f* weakness, feebleness; moral *or* intellectual weakness

imbēcillus, **a**, **um** *adj* weak, feeble

imbellis, **e** *adj* unwarlike; not suited *or* ready for war

imber, **bris** *m* (shower of) rain; (any) liquid; shower of missiles

imberbis, **e** *adj* beardless

imbibō, **bibī** ③ *v* imbibe, absorb into one's mind

imbrex, **icis** *f* (sometimes *m*) tile

imbrifer, **era**, **erum** *adj* rain-bringing, rainy

imbuō, **uī**, **ūtum** ③ *v* wet, soak; give initial instruction (in)

imitābilis, **e** *adj* that may be imitated

imitāmen, **inis** *nt* imitation; copy

imitātiō, **ōnis** *f* imitation; mimicking; copy

imitātor, **ōris** *m* one who imitates *or* copies

imitātrīx, **īcis** *f* female imitator

imitor ① *v dep* imitate; simulate; copy; resemble

immadēscō, **duī** ③ *v* become wet *or* moist

immānis, **e** *adj* huge, vast, immense, monstrous; inhuman, savage

immānitās, **ātis** f hugeness, vastness; brutality; barbarity

immānsuētus, **a**, **um** adj savage

immātūrus, **a**, **um** adj unripe, immature, untimely

immedicābilis, **e** adj incurable

immemor, **oris** adj forgetful; heedless

immēnsus, **a**, **um** adj endless, vast, immense
■ **(per) immēnsum** adv to an enormous extent or degree

immerēns, **ntis** adj undeserving (of ill-treatment), blameless

immergō, **rsī**, **rsum** ③ v plunge into, immerse

immeritus, **a**, **um** adj undeserving; undeserved; **immeritō** adv unjustly; without cause

immētātus, **a**, **um** adj unmeasured

immigrō ① v move (into)

immineō ② v overhang; threaten, be imminent; be a threat (to)

imminuō, **uī**, **ūtum** ③ v diminish; impair

immīsceō, **īxtum** ② v mix in, mingle; confuse

immītis, **e** adj harsh, sour; merciless

immittō, **mīsī**, **missum** ③ v send (to); admit; throw (into); put in; give the rein to

immō adv rather, more correctly

immōbilis, **e** adj immovable; unalterable

immoderātus, **a**, **um** adj unlimited; immoderate; disorderly

immodestia, **ae** f lack of self-control, licentiousness

immodicus, **a**, **um** adj excessive, immoderate

immolō ① v offer (a victim) in sacrifice

immorior, **morī**, **mortuus sum** ③ v dep with dat die (in a particular place, position, etc.)

immortālis, **e** adj immortal; eternal

immortālitās, **ātis** f immortality

immōtus, **a**, **um** adj unmoved, immovable; unchanged; inflexible

immūgiō ④ v bellow

immundus, **a**, **um** adj unclean, impure, filthy

immūnis, **e** adj exempt from tribute or taxation; free or exempt from

immūnitās, **ātis** f freedom, immunity

immūnītus, **a**, **um** adj unfortified

immurmurō ① v murmur, mutter (at or to)

immūtābilis, **e** adj unchangeable

immūtō ① v change, alter

impācātus, **a**, **um** adj not pacified

impār, **aris** adj uneven, unequal; inferior

imparātus, **a**, **um** adj not prepared; unready

impatiēns, **ntis** adj impatient (of)

impatientia, **ae** f impatience

impavidus, **a**, **um** adj fearless, intrepid

impedīmentum, **ī** nt hindrance, impediment; pl baggage of an army

impediō ④ v entangle; hamper; hinder

impedītus, **a**, **um** adj obstructed; not easily passable; difficult

impellō, **pulī**, **pulsum** ③ v push or thrust against; impel; urge on

impendeō ② v hang over; impend; threaten

impendium, **(i)ī** nt expense, expenditure, payment

impendō, **ndī**, **ēnsum** ③ v expend, spend; devote (to)

impēnsa, **ae** f outlay, cost, expense

impensē adv without stint; lavishly

impēnsus, **a**, **um** adj immoderate, excessive

imperātor, **ōris** m commander-in-chief; person in charge, ruler

> **❗** **imperātor** (tr. 'commander') was originally a title of honour for a (victorious) general in charge of an army (comprising two or more legions), and he was either one of the consuls or the proconsul or propraetor in command of a province. The title came to denote supreme military power and Julius Caesar was first to assume it for life. Augustus adopted it as part of his name, and this model was followed by Otho, Vespasian and subsequent emperors; it is the derivation of the word 'emperor'.

imperātōrius, **a**, **um** adj of or belonging to a commanding officer; imperial

imperātum, **ī** nt command, order

imperfectus, **a**, **um** *adj* unfinished, imperfect; not complete in every respect

imperiōsus, **a**, **um** *adj* masterful; domineering; dictatorial

imperītia, **ae** *f* inexperience, ignorance

imperitō ① *v* command, govern

imperītus, **a**, **um** *adj* inexperienced (in), unskilled, ignorant (of)

imperium, **(i)ī** *nt* command; rule; empire; supreme power

impermissus, **a**, **um** *adj* not permitted, illicit

imperō ① *v with dat* command, rule (over)

imperterritus, **a**, **um** *adj* fearless

impertiō ④ *v* impart; give a share of

impervius, **a**, **um** *adj* impassable

impetrābilis, **e** *adj* easy to achieve *or* obtain; effective, successful

impetrō ① *v* get, obtain by request

impetus, **ūs** *m* assault, attack; vigour; violent mental urge

impexus, **a**, **um** *adj* uncombed

impietās, **ātis** *f* failure in duty *or* respect, *etc.*

impiger, **gra**, **grum** *adj* active, energetic

impingō, **pēgī**, **pāctum** ③ *v* thrust, strike *or* dash against

impiō ① *v* stain by an act of impiety

impius, **a**, **um** *adj* irreverent; wicked; impious

implācābilis, **e** *adj* relentless, irreconcilable

implācātus, **a**, **um** *adj* not appeased, insatiable

implacidus, **a**, **um** *adj* restless, unquiet

impleō, **ēvī**, **ētum** ② *v* fill; fulfil

implicō, **cāvī/cuī**, **cātum/citum** ① *v* enfold; involve; encumber; entangle
□ **implicor** be intimately connected with

implōrō ① *v* invoke, entreat, appeal to; ask for (help, protection, favours, *etc.*)

implūmis, **e** *adj* unfledged

impluō, **ūvī/uī** ③ *v* rain (upon)

impluvium, **(i)ī** *nt* quadrangular basin in the floor of an atrium which receives the rain-water from the roof

impōnō, **posuī**, **positum** ③ *v* put upon *or* in; impose; assign; place in command *or* control (of)

importō ① *v* bring *or* convey in, import; bring about, cause

importūnitās, **ātis** *f* persistent lack of consideration for others; relentlessness

importūnus, **a**, **um** *adj* inconvenient; troublesome

importuōsus, **a**, **um** *adj* having no harbours

impotēns, **ntis** *adj* powerless, impotent, wild, headstrong; having no control (over), incapable (of)

impotentia, **ae** *f* weakness; immoderate behaviour, violence

imprānsus, **a**, **um** *adj* without having had one's morning meal

imprecor ① *v dep* call down upon, pray for; utter curses

impressiō, **ōnis** *f* push, thrust, assault

imprīmīs *adv* especially, above all; firstly

imprimō, **pressī**, **pressum** ③ *v* impress, imprint; press upon; stamp

improbitās, **ātis** *f* want of principle, shamelessness

improbō ① *v* express disapproval of, condemn

improbus, **a**, **um** *adj* morally unsound; disloyal; ill-disposed, shameless; excessive; presumptuous

imprōvidus, **a**, **um** *adj* improvident; thoughtless, unwary

imprōvīsus, **a**, **um** *adj* unforeseen, unexpected
□ **dē/ex imprōvīsō** unexpectedly

imprūdēns, **ntis** *adj* ignorant; foolish; unwarned

imprūdentia, **ae** *f* imprudence; ignorance

impūbēs, **beris/bis** *adj* below the age of puberty; beardless

impudēns, **ntis** *adj* shameless, impudent

impudentia, **ae** *f* shamelessness, effrontery

impudīcitia, **ae** *f* sexual impurity (often of homosexuality)

impudīcus, **a**, **um** *adj* unchaste, flouting the accepted sexual code

i

impugnō ① *v* fight against, attack, assail

impulsor, **ōris** *m* instigator

impulsus, **ūs** *m* shock, impact; incitement

impūne *adv* safely, with impunity; scot-free

impūnitās, **ātis** *f* impunity

impūnītus, **a**, **um** *adj* unpunished

impūrus, **a**, **um** *adj* unclean, filthy, foul; impure; morally foul

imputō ① *v* impute, charge; ascribe

īmulus, **a**, **um** *adj* lowest in position, bottommost

īmus, **a**, **um** *adj* inmost, deepest, bottommost

> ❗ Facing the dinner table at an upper-class Roman dinner, the couch to the right and the place to the right on each couch was described as **īmus**. The family usually reclined on this couch, with the head of the family on the left (**summus in īmō**); the most important guest sat to his left on the right of the middle couch (**īmus in mediō**). See also **medius**.

in *prep with acc* to; into; against; for; towards; until; *with abl* at; in; on; within; among
  □ ~ **diēs** day by day, every day
  □ ~ **perpetuum** for ever
  □ ~ **rem** to the point
  □ ~ **prīmīs** especially
  □ ~ **mediō** open to all

> ❗ In titles of speeches, **in** (lit. 'against') indicates a speech for the prosecution.

inaccessus, **a**, **um** *adj* inaccessible

inaedificō ① *v* build (in a place); wall up

inaequālis, **e** *adj* uneven; unequal

inaestimābilis, **e** *adj* beyond all price

inamābilis, **e** *adj* disagreeable, unattractive

inambulātiō, **ōnis** *f* the action of walking up and down; walk, promenade

inambulō ① *v* walk up and down

inamoenus, **a**, **um** *adj* unlovely, disagreeable

inanimus, **a**, **um** *adj* lifeless, inanimate

ināniō ④ *v* empty

inānis, **e** *adj* empty, void; foolish
  ■ **ināne**, **is** *nt* the void

inarātus, **a**, **um** *adj* unploughed, untilled

inardēscō, **arsī** ③ *v* kindle, take fire; become glowing

inassuētus, **a**, **um** *adj* unaccustomed

inaudāx, **ācis** *adj* not daring, timid

inaudiō ④ *v* get an inkling of, hear mention of

inaudītus, **a**, **um** *adj* unheard (of), novel, new

inaugurātō *adv* with the taking of omens by augury

inaugurō ① *v* take omens by the flight of birds; consecrate by angury

inaurō ① *v* gild, make rich

inausus, **a**, **um** *adj* undared

inb- ▶ **imb-**

incaeduus, **a**, **um** *adj* not felled

incalēscō, **luī** ③ *v* grow hot; become heated

incallidus, **a**, **um** *adj* not shrewd, simple

incandēscō, **duī** ③ *v* become red-hot

incānēscō, **nuī** ③ *v* turn grey *or* hoary

incānus, **a**, **um** *adj* quite grey, hoary

incarnatio, **onis** *f* LM incarnation

incassum *adv* without effect, to no purpose

incautus, **a**, **um** *adj* incautious, off one's guard; unprotected

incēdō, **essī**, **essum** ③ *v* step, walk, march along; advance; befall

incelebrātus, **a**, **um** *adj* unrecorded

incēnātus, **a**, **um** *adj* without having had dinner

incendiārius, **(i)ī** *m* incendiary, fire-raiser

incendium, **(i)ī** *nt* fire, conflagration; passion; fiery heat

incendō, **ndī**, **ēnsum** ③ *v* set fire to, kindle; inflame; aggravate

incēnsus, **a**, **um** *adj* not registered at a census

inceptō ① *v* begin

inceptum, **ī** *nt* beginning, undertaking

incertus, a, um *adj* uncertain; doubtful, inconstant; variable

incessō, ss(īv)ī ③ *v* assault, attack; reproach, abuse

incessus, ūs *m* walking; advance; gait; procession

incestō ① *v* pollute, defile

incestus, a, um *adj* unchaste; unholy

inchoō ▸ incohō

incidō, cidī, cāsum ③ *v* fall (into); meet (with); arise, occur

incīdō, īdī, īsum ③ *v* cut into; make an end to; engrave

incingō, īnxī, īnctum ③ *v* gird (with); wrap (tightly) round (with)

incipiō, cēpī, ceptum ③ *v* begin; undertake

incircumcisus, i *m* ⎣LM⎦ one who is uncircumcised, gentile

incitāmentum, ī *nt* incentive, stimulus

incitātus, a, um *adj* fast-moving, aroused, passionate
　□ **equō incitātō** at full gallop

incitō ① *v* incite; stir up, spur on; set in rapid motion

incitus, a, um *adj* rushing, headlong

inclāmō ① *v* cry out (to), call upon; abuse, revile

inclārēscō, ruī ③ *v* become famous

inclēmēns, ntis *adj* harsh

inclēmentia, ae *f* harshness

inclīnātiō, ōnis *f* the act of leaning; tendency, inclination

inclīnō ① *v* bend; lower; incline; decay; grow worse; set (of the sun); deject

inclitus, a, um *adj* renowned, famous, celebrated

inclūdō, ūsī, ūsum ③ *v* shut in *or* up; enclose

incōgitāns, ntis *adj* thoughtless

incognitus, a, um *adj* not known, untried; untested

incohō ① *v* start; set going

incola, ae *m/f* inhabitant; resident alien

incolō, luī ③ *v* dwell in, inhabit

incolumis, e *adj* uninjured, safe; unimpaired

incolumitās, ātis *f* safety

incomitātus, a, um *adj* unaccompanied

incommodus, a, um *adj* inconvenient, troublesome; disadvantageous, disagreeable
　■ **incommodum, ī** *nt* inconvenience; misfortune; set-back

incomparābilis, e *adj* beyond comparison, unequalled

incompertus, a, um *adj* not known

incompositus, a, um *adj* clumsy, disorganized

incōmptus, a, um *adj* dishevelled; untidy; unpolished

inconcessus, a, um *adj* forbidden

inconcinnus, a, um *adj* awkward; clumsy

inconditus, a, um *adj* rough, crude; uncivilized; disordered, not disciplined

incōnstāns, ntis *adj* changeable, fickle

incōnstantia, ae *f* changeableness; fickleness

incōnsultus, a, um *adj* rash, ill-advised

incontinēns, ntis *adj* intemperate

incoquō, coxī, coctum ③ *v* boil in *or* down; boil

incorruptus, a, um *adj* unspoilt, uncorrupted

incrēb(r)ēscō, b(r)uī ③ *v* become stronger *or* more intense; spread

incrēdibills, e *adj* incredible

incrēdulus, a, um *adj* disbelieving

incrēmentum, ī *nt* growth, increase

increpatio, onis *f* ⎣LM⎦ rebuke

increpitō ① *v* chide, utter (noisy) reproaches at

increpō, puī, pitum ① *v* make a sharp, loud noise; protest at; remark indignantly

incrēscō, ēvī ③ *v* grow (in *or* upon)

incruentus, a, um *adj* bloodless, without shedding of blood

incubō, buī, bitum ① *v* *with dat* lie in *or* on; sit upon; brood over; keep a jealous watch (over)

incūdō, ūdī, ūsum ③ *v* hammer out

inculcō ① *v* force upon, impress, drive home

incultus, a, um *adj* uncultivated; unkempt; rough, uncouth
　■ **incultus, ūs** *m* want of cultivation *or* refinement; uncouthness, disregard

i

incumbō, **cubuī**, **cubitum** ③ *v* lay oneself upon, lean *or* recline upon; apply oneself earnestly (to); press forward

incūnābula, **ōrum** *ntpl* the apparatus of the cradle; one's earliest years; birth-place

incūria, **ae** *f* carelessness, neglect

incūriōsus, **a**, **um** *adj* careless, negligent; indifferent

incurrō, **(cu)currī**, **cursum** ③ *v* run into *or* towards, attack, invade; meet (with); befall

incursiō, **ōnis** *f* attack; raid

incursō ① *v* run against, dash against, attack; make raids upon

incursus, **ūs** *m* attack, raid

incurvō ① *v* make crooked *or* bent; cause to bend down

incurvus, **a**, **um** *adj* crooked, curved

incūs, **ūdis** *f* anvil

incūsō ① *v* blame; criticize; condemn

incustōdītus, **a**, **um** *adj* not watched over; unsupervised

incutiō, **ussī**, **ussum** ③ *v* strike on *or* against; instil

indāgō, **inis** *f* ring of huntsmen *or* nets

inde *adv* thence, from that place; from that time; from that cause; thenceforwards; next

indēbitus, **a**, **um** *adj* that is not owed, not due

indecoris, **e** *adj* inglorious, shameful

indecorō ① *v* disgrace

indecōrus, **a**, **um** *adj* unbecoming, unseemly; ugly

indēfēnsus, **a**, **um** *adj* undefended; defenceless

indēfessus, **a**, **um** *adj* unwearied; indefatigable

indemnātus, **a**, **um** *adj* uncondemned

index, **icis** *m/f* informer, tale-bearer; sign, token

indicium, **(i)ī** *nt* information; token; disclosure; evidence (before a court)

indīcō, **dīxī**, **dictum** ③ *v* declare publicly; inflict (on) by one's pronouncement

indicō ① *v* betray; reveal; give information

indictus, **a**, **um** *adj* not said *or* mentioned

□ **indictā causā** without the case's being pleaded; unheard

indidem *adv* from the same place, source *or* origin

indigena, **ae** *m* native

indigēns, **ntis** *adj* needy, indigent

indigeō ② *v* need, require; lack

indīgestus, **a**, **um** *adj* chaotic; jumbled

Indigitēs, **um** *mpl* deified heroes, tutelary deities (local as opposed to foreign gods)

indignātiō, **ōnis** *f* indignation; anger; angry outburst

indignitās, **ātis** *f* unworthiness, shamelessness; baseness; humiliation

indignor ① *v dep* regard with indignation, resent; be indignant

indignus, **a**, **um** *adj* unworthy, undeserving; undeserved; shameful

indigus, **a**, **um** *adj* having need (of); lacking; needy

indīligēns, **ntis** *adj* careless, negligent

indīligentia, **ae** *f* negligence, want of care; want of concern (for)

indipīscor, **deptus sum** ③ *v dep* overtake; acquire

indiscrētus, **a**, **um** *adj* indistinguishable

indistīnctus, **a**, **um** *adj* not properly arranged, applied without distinction

indō, **didī**, **ditum** ③ *v* put in *or* on; introduce

indocilis, **e** *adj* unteachable, ignorant

indoctus, **a**, **um** *adj* untaught; unlearned; ignorant; untrained

indolēs, **lis** *f* innate character; inborn quality

indolēscō, **luī** ③ *v* feel pain of mind; grieve

indomitus, **a**, **um** *adj* untamed; untamable; fierce

indormiō ④ *v* sleep (in *or* over)

indōtātus, **a**, **um** *adj* not provided with a dowry

indubitō ① *v* have misgivings (about)

indūcō, **dūxī**, **ductum** ③ *v* lead *or* conduct into; bring in; bring (performers) into the arena, onto the stage, *etc.*; introduce; put on; persuade; spread (with)

inductiō, ōnis *f* leading *or* bringing in; application

indulgēns, ntis *adj* kind, mild

indulgentia, ae *f* kindness; gentleness

indulgeō, lsī, ltum ② *v with dat* be kind *or* lenient (to); grant; give way to; accede (to)

induō, uī, ūtum ③ *v* put on; dress oneself in; assume; fall *or* be impaled (upon)

indūrō ① *v* make hard

indusiātus, a, um *adj* wearing an indusium (a kind of tunic)

indusium, (i)ī *nt* outer tunic

industria, ae *f* diligence, assiduity, industry
□ **dē/ex industriā** on purpose

industrius, a, um *adj* diligent, assiduous, industrious

indūtiae, ārum *fpl* truce, armistice

inedia, ae *f* fasting, starvation

inēlegāns, ntis *adj* lacking in taste; clumsy, infelicitous

inēluctābilis, e *adj* from which there is no escape

inēmptus, a, um *adj* not bought

inēnarrābilis, e *adj* indescribable

ineō, īre, lī/īvī, itum *v ir* go into, enter (into *or* upon); commence; form a plan

ineptiae, ārum *fpl* foolery, absurdities

ineptus, a, um *adj* silly, foolish; having no sense of what is fitting

inermis, e *adj* unarmed, defenceless; (fig) unprepared

inerrō ① *v* wander in, on *or* among

iners, rtis *adj* unskilful; sluggish; unadventurous; feeble

inertia, ae *f* unskilfulness; idleness, sloth

inēvītābilis, e *adj* unavoidable

inexcūsābilis, e *adj* inexcusable

inexōrābilis, e *adj* inexorable, relentless, stubborn

inexpertus, a, um *adj* inexperienced (in); untried

inexpiābilis, e *adj* inexpiable; implacable

inexplēbilis, e *adj* insatiable

inexplōrātus, a, um *adj* unexplored; not investigated

inexpugnābilis, e *adj* impregnable; invincible

inex(s)pectātus, a, um *adj* unforeseen

inex(s)tīnctus, a, um *adj* that is never extinguished

inex(s)uperābilis, e *adj* insurmountable; invincible; unsurpassable

inextrīcābilis, e *adj* impossible to disentangle *or* sort out

īnfabrē *adv* without art, crudely

īnfacētus, a, um *adj* coarse, boorish

īnfācundus, a, um *adj* unable to express oneself fluently

īnfāmia, ae *f* ill-fame, dishonour

īnfāmis, e *adj* disreputable, infamous

īnfāmō ① *v* bring into disrepute; defame

īnfandus, a, um *adj* unutterable; abominable

īnfāns, ntis *adj* speechless; inarticulate; newly born, young
■ **īnfāns, ntis** *m/f* little child

īnfantia, ae *f* infancy; inability to speak

īnfaustus, a, um *adj* unlucky, unfortunate; inauspicious

īnfectus, a, um *adj* not done, unmade; unfinished, impossible

īnfēcunditās, ātis *f* barrenness

īnfēcundus, a, um *adj* unfruitful, infertile

īnfēlīcitās, ātis *f* misfortune

īnfēlīcō ① *v* bring bad luck on

īnfēlīx, īcis *adj* unfortunate, unhappy; unproductive

īnfēnsō ① *v* treat in a hostile manner

īnfēnsus, a, um *adj* hostile, bitterly hostile, enraged

īnferī, ōrum *mpl* the dead

īnferiae, ārum *fpl* offerings to the dead

īnferior, ius *adj* comp of
□ **īnferus** lower, later, inferior, worse; **īnferius** *adv* further down, at a lower level

īnfernus, a, um *adj* lower; infernal;
■ **infernum, i** *nt* ⟨LM⟩ Hell

īnferō, ferre, intulī, illātum *v ir* bring into *or* upon; bring forward (with hostile intention); produce, cause; inflict; bury

īnferus, era, erum *adj* below, underneath, lower
■ **īnferior, ius** *comp*
■ **īnfimus** *sup*

īnfestus, a, um *adj* hostile; dangerous; disturbed

īnficĕtiae, ārum *fpl* gaucheries

īnficiō, fēcī, fectum ③ *v* dye; stain; infect; imbue; corrupt

īnfidēlis, e *adj* treacherous, disloyal

īnfidēlitās, ātis *f* faithlessness; inconstancy

- **īnfīdus, a, um** *adj* faithless; treacherous

īnfīgō, īxī, īxum ③ *v* fix, thrust in; fasten on

īnfĭmus, a, um *sup adj* lowest, worst

īnfindō, idī, issum ③ *v* cleave; plough a path into

īnfīnītus, a, um *adj* boundless, endless, infinite in quantity *or* amount

īnfirmitās, ātis *f* weakness; sickness

īnfirmō ① *v* weaken; diminish; annul

īnfirmus, a, um *adj* weak, feeble; sickly; irresolute

īnfit *v ir* (s)he begins (to speak)

īnfitiās *adv*:
□ ~ **eō** refuse to acknowledge as true, deny

īnfitior ① *v dep* deny, disown

īnflammō ① *v* set on fire, kindle; excite; inflame

īnflātus, a, um *adj* puffed up; turgid, bombastic

īnflectō, exī, exum ③ *v* bend; curve; change

īnflexibilis, e *adj* inflexible, rigid

īnflīgō, īxī, īctum ③ *v* knock *or* dash (against); inflict, impose

īnflō ① *v* blow into *or* upon; puff out

īnfluō, ūxī, ūxum ③ *v* flow into

īnfodiō, ōdī, ossum ③ *v* bury, inter

īnfōrmis, e *adj* shapeless; deformed, ugly

īnfōrmō ① *v* shape, form; fashion; form an idea of

īnfortūnium, (i)ī *nt* misfortune, punishment

īnfrā *adv/prep with acc* below, underneath; under; later (than); less (than)

īnfrāctus, a, um *adj* broken; humble in tone

īnfremō, ī ③ *v* bellow, roar

īnfrendō ③ *v* gnash the teeth (usually in anger)

īnfrēnis, e *adj*, **īnfrēnus, a, um** *adj* not bridled; unrestrained

īnfrēnō ① *v* bridle

īnfrequēns, ntis *adj* not crowded; below strength; present only in small numbers

īnfrequentia, ae *f* insufficient numbers; depopulated condition (of a place)

īnfringō, frēgī, frāctum ③ *v* break, crush; weaken; diminish, dishearten; foil, invalidate

īnfula, ae *f* woollen headband knotted with ribands

īnfundō, ūdī, ūsum ③ *v* pour into *or* on; pour out

īnfuscō ① *v* darken; corrupt

ingeminō ① *v* redouble; increase in intensity

ingemō, muī ③ *v* groan (over)

ingenerō ① *v* implant

ingeniōsus, a, um *adj* clever, ingenious; naturally suited (to)

ingenium, (i)ī *nt* innate quality, nature; natural disposition; capacity; talent; gifted writer

ingēns, ntis *adj* vast, huge; great; momentous

ingenuus, a, um *adj* indigenous, natural; free-born; generous; frank

ingerō, essī, estum ③ *v* throw upon; heap on; obtrude; force *or* thrust on a person

inglōrius, a, um *adj* obscure, undistinguished

ingluviēs, iēī *f* gullet, jaws; gluttony

ingrātus, a, um *adj* unpleasant; unthankful

ingravēscō ③ *v* grow heavy; increase in force *or* intensity

ingravō ① *v* aggravate, make worse

ingredior, gressus sum ③ *v dep* step *or* go into, enter; begin; walk

ingruō, uī ③ *v* advance threateningly; make an onslaught (upon)

inguen, inis *nt* groin; the sexual organs

inhabilis, **e** *adj* difficult to handle; not fitted; awkward

inhaereō, haesī, haesum ② *v* stick in, cling (to); be firmly attached (to)

inhibeō ② *v* restrain, curb; prevent

inhiō ① *v* gape; be open-mouthed with astonishment; covet

inhonestō ① *v* disgrace

inhonestus, **a**, **um** *adj* shameful; of ill repute

inhonōrātus, **a**, **um** *adj* not honoured

inhorrēscō, ruī ③ *v* bristle up; quiver; tremble, shudder at

inhūmānitās, ātis *f* churlishness

inhūmānus, **a**, **um** *adj* inhuman; uncivilized, churlish

inhumātus, **a**, **um** *adj* unburied

iniciō, iēcī, iectum ③ *v* throw in *or* into; put on; instil (a feeling, *etc.*) in the mind

> ❗ The first syllable of this verb scans as heavy in the present stem even though the 'i' is short; this is because the second 'i' represents 'ii' pronounced as consonant + vowel 'yi'.

inimīcitia, ae *f* hostility, enmity

inimīcus, **a**, **um** *adj* hostile, inimical, harmful
■ **inimīcus, ī** *m* enemy, foe

inīquitās, ātis *f* inequality; unfairness; unevenness of terrain

inīquus, **a**, **um** *adj* unequal, uneven; disadvantageous; unjust; unkind; hostile

initiō ① *v* initiate (into); admit (to) with introductory rites

initium, (i)ī *nt* beginning
  □ **ab initiō** from the beginning

initus, ūs *m* entry, start

iniūcundus, **a**, **um** *adj* unpleasant

iniungō, ūnxī, ūnctum ③ *v* join *or* fasten (to); attach to; impose (upon)

iniūrātus, **a**, **um** *adj* unsworn

iniūria, ae *f* wrong, injury; abuse, insult; offence; sexual assault

iniūriōsus, **a**, **um** *adj* wrongful, insulting

iniūrius, **a**, **um** *adj* unjust, harsh

iniussū *adv with gen* without (the) orders (of)

iniussus, **a**, **um** *adj* unbidden

iniūstus, **a**, **um** *adj* unjust, wrongful; severe; excessive, unsuitable

inl- ▶ **ill-**

inm- ▶ **imm-**

innāscor, nātus sum ③ *v dep* be born (in *or* on)

innatō ① *v* swim (in *or* on); swim (into); float upon

innātus, **a**, **um** *adj* natural, inborn

innāvigābilis, **e** *adj* unnavigable

innectō, exuī, exum ③ *v* tie, fasten (to); devise, weave (plots)

innītor, nīxus/nīsus sum ③ *v dep* *with dat* lean *or* rest (upon)

innō ① *v* swim *or* float (in *or* on); sail (on)

innocēns, ntis *adj* harmless; innocent; virtuous

innocentia, ae *f* harmlessness; innocence; integrity

innocuus, **a**, **um** *adj* harmless; innocent

innōtēscō, tuī ③ *v* become known

innoxius, **a**, **um** *adj* harmless, innocuous; innocent; unhurt

innūbō, ūpsī ③ *v with dat* marry (into a family)

innumerābilis, **e** *adj* countless

innumerus, **a**, **um** *adj* numberless

innuō, uī, ūtum ③ *v* nod *or* beckon (to)

innūptus, **a**, **um** *adj* unmarried

innūtrītus, **a**, **um** *adj* nourished, brought up

inobservābilis, **e** *adj* difficult to trace

inobservātus, **a**, **um** *adj* unobserved

inoffēnsus, **a**, **um** *adj* free from hindrance; uninterrupted

inolēscō, ēvī, litum ③ *v with dat* grow in *or* on

inopia, ae *f* want, scarcity; destitution, dearth

inopīnāns, ntis *adj* not expecting, off one's guard

inopīnātus, **a**, **um** *adj* unexpected, unforeseen

inopīnus, **a**, **um** *adj* unexpected

inops, pis *adj* destitute (of), needy; helpless; poor, meagre

inōrnātus, **a**, **um** *adj* unadorned; uncelebrated

inp- ▶ imp-

inquam *v ir* say

> ⚠️ **inquam** is used to introduce direct speech, and is usu. inserted after the first word of that direct speech. Its pres. indic. is **inquam, inquis, inquit, inquimus, inquitis, inquiunt**; apart from pf. **inquit** and impf. **inquiēbat, inquiēbant**, other forms are rare or non-existent.

inquiēs, ētis *adj* restless, impatient; full of tumult

inquiētus, a, um *adj* restless; sleepless

inquinō ① *v* daub; stain, pollute; soil; 'smear'

inquīrō, īs(īv)ī, īsītum ③ *v* search out; inquire into

inquīsītiō, ōnis *f* search; inquiry

inquīsītor, ōris *m* investigator, examiner

inr- ▶ irr-

īnsānābilis, e *adj* incurable; irremediable

īnsānia, ae *f* madness, folly; mad extravagance

īnsāniō ④ *v* be mad, act crazily

īnsānus, a, um *adj* mad, insane; frenzied; wild
■ **īnsānum** *adv* outrageously, awfully

īnsatiābilis, e *adj* insatiable

īnscēnsiō, ōnis *f* going aboard, embarkation

īnsciēns, ntis *adj* not knowing, unaware

īnscientia, ae *f* ignorance

īnscītia, ae *f* ignorance

īnscītus, a, um *adj* ignorant, uninformed

īnscius, a, um *adj* not knowing, ignorant; unskilled

īnscrībō, psī, ptum ③ *v* write in *or* on, inscribe; brand; record as

īnscrīptiō, ōnis *f* inscription

īnsculpō, psī, ptum ③ *v* carve (in *or* on), engrave; engrave on the mind

īnsecō, secuī, sectum ① *v* cut; incise

īnsectātiō, ōnis *f* hostile pursuit; criticism

īnsectō ① *v*, **īnsector** ① *v dep* pursue with hostile intent; pursue with hostile speech, *etc.*

īnsenēscō, nuī ③ *v* grow old in; wane

īnsepultus, a, um *adj* unburied

īnsequor, īnsecūtus sum ③ *v dep* follow closely, pursue; persecute; come after in time

īnserō¹, ēvī, situm ③ *v* sow *or* plant in; graft on; implant

īnserō², ruī, rtum ③ *v* put in; insert

īnsertō ① *v* thrust in, introduce

īnserviō ④ *v with dat* serve the interests of; take care of

īnsideō, sēdī, sessum ② *v* sit (at *or* on); lie in ambush (in); be troublesome (to)

īnsidiae, ārum *fpl* ambush; plot, snare

īnsidiātor, ōris *m* one who lies in wait (to attack, rob, *etc.*)

īnsidior ① *v dep* lie in ambush

īnsidiōsus, a, um *adj* deceitful; insidious; hazardous

īnsīdō, sēdī, sessum ③ *v* sit down in *or* on, settle on; take possession of; be firmly implanted in

īnsigne, is *nt* distinctive mark, emblem; badge of honour
■ **īnsignia, um** *pl* dress, insignia

īnsigniō ④ *v* mark with a characteristic feature; distinguish

īnsignis, e *adj* notable; famous; remarkable; manifest

īnsiliō, luī/līvī ④ *v* leap into *or* on

īnsimulō ① *v* accuse, charge; allege

īnsincērus, a, um *adj* corrupt; not genuine

īnsinuō ① *v* work in; insinuate; creep into

īnsistō, stitī ③ *v* stand *or* tread on; set foot in, visit; stop; persevere (with); set about

īnsitus, a, um *adj* innate

īnsociābilis, e *adj* intractable, implacable

īnsolēns, ntis *adj* unaccustomed (to), arrogant; insolent; excessive

īnsolentia, ae *f* unfamiliarity; strangeness; haughtiness; extravagance

īnsolēscō ③ *v* grow proud

īnsolitus, a, um *adj* unaccustomed (to)

īnsomnis, e *adj* sleepless

īnsomnium, (i)ī *nt* wakefulness; vision, dream

īnsonō, nitum ① *v* make a loud noise; sound; resound

īnsōns, ntis *adj* guiltless; harmless

īnsōpītus, a, um *adj* unsleeping, wakeful

īnspectō ① *v* look at, observe; look on, watch

īnspērāns, ntis *adj* not expecting

īnspērātus, a, um *adj* unhoped for, unexpected; unforeseen
  □ **ex īnspērātō** unexpectedly

īnspiciō, spexī, spectum ③ *v* look into *or* at, inspect; examine; observe

īnspīrō ① *v* blow into *or* on; inspire; excite

īnstabilis, e *adj* shaky; unstable; inconstant

īnstāns, ntis *adj* present; urgent

īnstar *nt indec* counterpart, equal; moral worth; standard; to the extent, degree, *etc.* (of); image, likeness; manner

īnstaurātiō, ōnis *f* renewal, repetition

īnstaurō ① *v* renew, repeat; restore

īnsternō, strāvī, strātum ③ *v* spread *or* strew on; cover (with); lay over

īnstīgō ① *v* urge on; incite, rouse

īnstillō ① *v* pour in drop by drop, drop in

īnstimulō ① *v* goad on

īnstīnctor, ōris *m* instigator

īnstīnctus¹, ūs *m* inspiration; instigation, impulse

īnstīnctus², a, um *adj* roused, fired; infuriated

īnstipulor ① *v dep* make conditions, bargain

īnstita, ae *f* band on a dress

īnstitor, ōris *m* shopkeeper, pedlar

īnstituō, uī, ūtum ③ *v* set up; institute; found; build; make; establish; instruct, educate; start on

īnstitūtiō, ōnis *f* arrangement; instruction, education

īnstitūtum, ī *nt* plan; habit, custom; mode of life

īnstō, stitī ① *v* stand in *or* upon; threaten; press hard (on); press on (with)

īnstrēnuus, a, um *adj* sluggish, inactive, spiritless

īnstrepō, puī, pitum ③ *v* make a loud noise

īnstrūctus, a, um *adj* equipped, fitted out; learned, trained, skilled

īnstrūmentum, ī *nt* equipment, tools; an item of such equipment; means

īnstruō, ūxī, ūctum ③ *v* build, construct; draw up; set in order; instruct, teach; equip, furnish (with)

īnsuēscō, ēvī, ētum ③ *v* become accustomed (to); accustom

īnsuētus, a, um *adj* unaccustomed, unused, unusual

īnsula, ae *f* island; tenement-house; block of flats

īnsulsitās, ātis *f* dullness, stupidity

īnsulsus, a, um *adj* boring, stupid

īnsultō ① *v* leap, jump, dance *or* trample (upon *or* in); behave insultingly, mock (at)

īnsum, inesse, īnfuī *v ir with dat* be in *or* on; belong to; be involved in

īnsuō, uī, ūtum ③ *v* sew up (in); sew (on *or* in)

īnsuper *adv/prep with acc* above, on top; in addition (to); over

īnsuperābilis, e *adj* insurmountable; unconquerable

īnsurgō, surrēxī, surrēctum ③ *v* rise; rise up against

intābēscō, buī ③ *v* pine away; melt away

intāctus, a, um *adj* untouched, intact; untried; virgin

intāminātus, a, um *adj* undefiled, untainted

intectus, a, um *adj* uncovered; naked; open

integellus, a, um *adj* unharmed

integer, gra, grum *adj* whole, entire; safe; healthful; fresh; undecided, open-minded; heartwhole; innocent; pure; upright
  □ **ab/dē/ex integrō** afresh, anew

integō, ēxī, ēctum ③ *v* cover

integritās, ātis *f* soundness; chastity; integrity

integrō ① *v* renew; refresh

integumentum, ī *nt* covering, shield, guard

intellegēns, **ntis** *adj* intelligent; discerning

intellegentia, **ae** *f* intellect, understanding

intellegō, **intelligō**, **ēxī**, **ēctum** ③ *v* understand

intemerātus, **a**, **um** *adj* undefiled; chaste

intemperāns, **ntis** *adj* unrestrained; licentious

intemperiēs, **iēī** *f* lack of temperateness (of weather, *etc.*); outrageous behaviour

intempestīvus, **a**, **um** *adj* unseasonable, ill-timed; untimely

intempestus, **a**, **um** *adj* unseasonable; stormy, unhealthy □ **nox intempesta** the dead of night

intemptātus, **a**, **um** *adj* unattempted; not attacked, unassailed

intendō, **ndī**, **ēnsum** ③ *v* stretch; strain, exert; direct

intentō ① *v* point (at); point (weapons, *etc.*) in a threatening manner; threaten

intentus, **a**, **um** *adj* intent (upon); eager; strict

intepēscō, **puī** ③ *v* become warm

inter *prep with acc* between, among; during

> ! With a pl. acc. pn. **inter** expresses the reciprocal meaning 'each other', e.g. **inter sē amant** 'they love each other'.

interaestuō ① *v* be periodically inflamed

interbītō ③ *v* fail, come to nothing

intercalārius, **a**, **um** *adj* (of days or months) inserted in the calendar for the purposes of adjustment, intercalary

intercalō ① *v* insert (a day or month) into the calendar; postpone

intercēdō, **essī**, **essum** ③ *v* come between, intervene; put a veto on; interrupt; go bail (for); forbid; oppose; interfere

interceptor, **ōris** *m* usurper, embezzler

intercessiō, **ōnis** *f* intervention; veto (of a magistrate)

intercessor, **ōris** *m* mediator; one who vetoes

intercidō, **idī** ③ *v* happen; perish; fall from memory; cease to exist

intercīdō, **īdī**, **īsum** ③ *v* cut through, sever

intercipiō, **cēpī**, **ceptum** ③ *v* intercept; steal; interrupt

interclūdō, **ūsī**, **ūsum** ③ *v* cut off; hinder; blockade

intercursō ① *v* run in between

intercursus, **ūs** *m* interposition

interdīcō, **īxī**, **ictum** ③ *v* forbid; interdict; prohibit, debar (from)

interdictum, **ī** *nt* prohibition; provisional decree of a praetor

interdiū *adv* by day

interdius *adv* in the daytime

interdō, **dare**, **dedī**, **datum** ① *v* put between

interdum *adv* sometimes, now and then

intereā *adv* meanwhile

intereō, **īre**, **iī**, **itum** *v ir* perish, die; be ruined; cease

interequitō ① *v* ride among *or* between

interfector, **ōris** *m* murderer, assassin

interficiō, **fēcī**, **fectum** ③ *v* kill; destroy

interfluō, **ūxī** ③ *v* flow between *or* through

interfor ① *v dep* interrupt; break in upon a conversation

interfūsus, **a**, **um** *adj* poured *or* spread out between; suffused here and there

interiaceō ② *v* lie between

interibi *adv* meanwhile

intericiō, **iēcī**, **ectum** ③ *v* throw between; introduce, insert

> ! The second syllable of this verb scans as heavy in the present stem even though the 'e' is short; this is because the second 'i' represents 'ii' pronounced as consonant + vowel 'yi'.

interim *adv* meanwhile; at the same time

interimō, **ēmī**, **ēm(p)tum** ③ *v* do away with; kill; destroy

interior, **ius** *adj* inner, more inward; more remote; more intimate

interitus, ūs *m* violent *or* untimely death; extinction; dissolution

interluō, uī ③ *v* flow between

intermisceō, mixtum ② *v* intermingle, mix

intermissiō, ōnis *f* intermission; pause

intermittō, mīsī, missum ③ *v* leave off; leave off temporarily; leave a gap (between)

intermorior, morī, mortuus sum ③ *v dep* perish; pass out

internāscor, nātus sum ③ *v dep* grow between *or* among

interneciō, ōnis *f* massacre; extermination

internōdium, (i)ī *nt* space between two joints in the body

internōscō, ōvī, ōtum ③ *v* distinguish between; pick out

internūntius, (i)ī *m* intermediary, go-between

internus, a, um *adj* inward, internal; domestic

interō, trīvī, trītum ③ *v* powder *or* crumble (on *or* into); crumble up

interpellātiō, ōnis *f* interruption in speaking

interpellō ① *v* interrupt (in speaking); obstruct

interpolis, e *adj* having received a new appearance, refurbished; not genuine

interpolō ① *v* refurbish, touch up, improve

interpōnō, posuī, positum ③ *v* put, lay *or* set between; interpose; insert; introduce

interpres, etis *m/f* intermediary, go-between; interpreter; translator

interpretātiō, ōnis *f* interpretation; meaning

interpretor ① *v dep* interpret; explain; regard

interprimō, pressī, pressum ③ *v* interrupt by pressing, throttle

interrēgnum, ī *nt* space between two reigns, interregnum

interrēx, gis *m* one who holds office between the death of a supreme magistrate and the appointment of a successor

interritus, a, um *adj* fearless

interrogātiō, ōnis *f* question; inquiry; questioning

interrogō ① *v* ask, question; examine; indict

interrumpō, ūpī, uptum ③ *v* drive a gap in, break up; cut short, interrupt

intersaepiō, psī, ptum ④ *v* separate; block

interscindō, idī, issum ③ *v* cut through, sever

intersum, esse, fuī *v ir* be *or* lie between, be in the midst; be present; take part in; be different
  □ **interest** it makes a difference, it matters; it is of advantage *or* importance

> **!** The thing which is important may be expressed either by an indirect statement, indirect question or by a clause containing a subj. verb and introduced by *ut* (following the rules for result clauses). The person to whom the thing is important is in the gen. except that a personal pn. is replaced with the fem. abl. sg. of the corresponding possessive adj., e.g. **meā interest** 'it is important to me'.

intervāllum, ī *nt* space between two things, interval; distance; respite

interveniō, vēnī, ventum ④ *v* come between; intervene; occur, crop up; occur by way of a hindrance

interventus, ūs *m* intervention; occurrence of an event

intervertō, rtī, rsum ③ *v* embezzle; cheat

intestābilis, e *adj* detestable, infamous

intestīna, ōrum *ntpl* intestines, guts

intestīnus, a, um *adj* internal; domestic, civil

intexō, xuī, xtum ③ *v* weave (into), embroider (on); cover by twining; insert (into a book, *etc.*)

intimus, a, um *adj* inmost; most secret; most intimate

intolerābilis, e *adj*, **intolerandus, a, um** *adj* insupportable, insufferable

intolerāns, ntis *adj* unable to endure, impatient (of); insufferable

intolerantia, ae *f* impatience

intonō, tonuī ① *v* thunder; make a noise like thunder; thunder forth

intōnsus, **a**, **um** *adj* uncut;
unshaven, unshorn; not stripped of
foliage

intorqueō, **rsī**, **rtum** ② *v* twist *or* turn
round, sprain; hurl *or* launch a
missile at

intrā *prep with acc* within; within the
space of; under, fewer than; *adv*
within; under

intractābilis, **e** *adj* unmanageable,
intractable

intremō, **muī** ③ *v* tremble

intrepidus, **a**, **um** *adj* undaunted,
fearless, untroubled

intrīnsecus *adv* on the inside

intrō¹ *adv* within, inside, indoors

intrō² ① *v* go into; enter; penetrate

intrōdūcō, **dūxī**, **ductum** ③ *v* lead *or*
bring in; introduce

introeō, **īre**, **iī/īvī**, **itum** *v ir* go inside,
enter; invade

introitus, **ūs** *m* going in, entry;
invasion

intrōmittō, **mīsī**, **missum** ③ *v* send
in; admit

intrōrsum, **intrōrsus** *adv* to within,
inwards; internally

intrōspiciō, **spexī**, **spectum** ③ *v*
examine; inspect; look upon

intubum, **ī** *nt*, **intubus**, **ī** *m* endive *or*
chicory

intueor ② *v dep* look at *or* on;
consider; observe; consider; bear in
mind

intumēscō, **muī** ③ *v* swell up, rise;
become swollen

intumulātus, **a**, **um** *adj* unburied

intus *adv* inside, within; at home

intūtus, **a**, **um** *adj* defenceless;
unsafe

inultus, **a**, **um** *adj* punished; scot-
free

inumbrō ① *v* cast a shadow

inundō ① *v* overflow, inundate, flood;
swarm

inurbānus, **a**, **um** *adj* rustic, boorish,
dull

inūrō, **ussī**, **ustum** ③ *v* burn in (with a
hot iron); brand (on *or* with)

inūsitātus, **a**, **um** *adj* unusual

inustus, **a**, **um** *adj* branded into

inūtilis, **e** *adj* useless; unprofitable;
disadvantageous, inexpedient

invādō, **āsī**, **āsum** ③ *v* go into; invade;
rush into; take possession of, usurp;
seize; attack; rush on (in order to
embrace)

invalidus, **a**, **um** *adj* infirm, weak,
feeble; ineffectual

invehō, **ēxī**, **ectum** ③ *v* carry *or* bring
in; import
□ **invehor** ride, drive, sail, *etc.* in;
inveigh against

inveniō, **vēnī**, **ventum** ④ *v* invent;
contrive; find; discover; manage to get

inventor, **ōris** *m* inventor; author,
contriver; discoverer

inventrīx, **īcis** *f* inventress

inventum, **ī** *nt* invention, discovery

invenustus, **a**, **um** *adj* unlovely,
unattractive

inverēcundus, **a**, **um** *adj* shameless,
immoral

invergō ③ *v* tip (liquids) upon

invertō, **rtī**, **rsum** ③ *v* turn upside
down; pervert; change

investīgō ① *v* search out, track
down

investitura, **ae** *f* LM investiture

inveterāscō, **ī** ③ *v* grow old; become
established *or* customary

invicem *adv* by turns, in turn;
reciprocally, mutually

invictus, **a**, **um** *adj* unconquered;
invincible

invideō, **vīdī**, **vīsum** ② *v with dat* envy,
grudge; hate; refuse

invidia, **ae** *f* envy, jealousy; spite;
dislike

invidiōsus, **a**, **um** *adj* arousing
hatred, odium *or* envy; envious

invidus, **a**, **um** *adj* ill-disposed;
envious

invigilō ① *v with dat* stay awake (over);
watch (over) diligently

inviolābilis, **e** *adj* sacrosanct,
imperishable

inviolātus, **a**, **um** *adj* unhurt;
unviolated; inviolable

invīsitātus, **a**, **um** *adj* unvisited,
unseen

invīsō, **īsī**, **īsum** ③ *v* go to see, visit;
watch over

invīsus, **a**, **um** *adj* hateful, hated

invītāmentum, **ī** *nt* inducement

invītātiō, **ōnis** *f* invitation

invītō ① *v* invite; entertain; allure, entice; incite

invītus, **a**, **um** *adj* against one's will, reluctant

invius, **a**, **um** *adj* impassable; inaccessible

invocō ① *v* call upon; invoke; pray for

involō ① *v* fly into *or* at, rush upon; seize on

involvō, **lvī**, **lūtum** ③ *v* wrap (in), cover, envelop; roll along

iō *int* ritual exclamation uttered under strong emotion

iocor ① *v dep* jest, joke

iocōsus, **a**, **um** *adj* fond of jokes; full of fun; funny

ioculāris, **e** *adj* laughable

ioculor ① *v dep* jest; joke

ioculus, **ī** *m* little joke

iocus, **ī** *m* jest, joke; sport

ipse, **a**, **um** *pn* he, she, it; self, very, identical

īra, **ae** *f* anger, wrath, rage

īrācundia, **ae** *f* irascibility; passion

īrācundus, **a**, **um** *adj* irascible, angry

īrāscor, **īrātus sum** ③ *v dep* be angry, fly into a rage

īrātus, **a**, **um** *adj* angry; enraged

īre *infin* from ▶ **eō**

irpex, **icis** *m* a kind of harrow

irrāsus, **a**, **um** *adj* unshaven

irreligātus, **a**, **um** *adj* unbound, unmoored

irremeābilis, **e** *adj* along *or* across which one cannot return

irreparābilis, **e** *adj* irreparable, irrecoverable

irrepertus, **a**, **um** *adj* not found, undiscovered

irrēpō, **psī** ③ *v* creep in *or* into; steal into; insinuate oneself (into)

irreprehēnsus, **a**, **um** *adj* blameless

irrētiō ④ *v* entangle; catch in a net

irreverēns, **ntis** *adj* disrespectful

irreverentia, **ae** *f* disrespect

irrevocābilis, **e** *adj* irrevocable, unalterable

irrīdeō, **rīsī**, **rīsum** ② *v* laugh at, mock, make fun of

irrīdiculē *adv* without wit

irrigō ① *v* water, irrigate; inundate; wet, moisten; diffuse

irriguus, **a**, **um** *adj* watering; well-watered

irrīsor, **ōris** *m* mocker, scoffer

irrīsus, **ūs** *m* mockery; laughing-stock

irrītābilis, **e** *adj* easily provoked, sensitive

irrītāmen, **inis** *nt*, **irrītāmentum**, **ī** *nt* incentive, stimulus

irrītātiō, **ōnis** *f* incitement, provocation

irrītō ① *v* provoke, annoy; excite; stimulate; aggravate

irritus, **a**, **um** *adj* invalid, void; of no effect; vain, useless

irrōrō ① *v* wet with dew; besprinkle, water; rain on

irrumātiō, **ōnis** *f* being sucked off

irrumō ① *v* be sucked off

irrumpō, **ūpī**, **uptum** ③ *v* break *or* burst *or* rush into; interrupt; invade

irruō, **uī** ③ *v* rush *or* dash in; charge (at)

irruptiō, **ōnis** *f* violent *or* forcible entry; assault

is, **ea**, **id** *pn* he, she, it; this, that

> **!** In the cases apart from the nom., **is** is often confused in meaning with **sē**. To put it simply, **eum** *etc.* never refers to the same thing as the subject of its own clause, e.g. **māter eam lavat** 'the mother washes her (≠ herself)'; in purpose clauses, fear clauses and reported speech it cannot refer to the subject of the main clause either, e.g. **puer dīcit eum mortuum esse** 'the boy says that he (≠ the boy) has died'; cf. **sē**.

iste, **a**, **ud** *pn* this *or* that of yours; that which you refer to; the well-known

> **!** In legal speeches, **iste** often refers to the client of the opposing speaker.

isthmus, **ī** *m* isthmus; strait

istī, **istīc** *adv* there by you; over there; here

istic, **istaec**, **istoc/istuc** *pn* that of yours; that which you refer to

istinc *adv* from over there, from here; from *or* on your side

istō, **istōc** *adv* to the place where you are; to the point you have reached; to this place

istōrsum *adv* in that direction

istūc *adv* to the place where you are; to the point you have reached

ita *adv* so, thus; even so; yes

itaque *conj* and so; therefore, consequently

item *adv* similarly, likewise

iter, **itineris** *nt* journey; march; route; road, foot-way
□ **ex itinere** out of the way, away from the road

iterato *adv* ⃞ a second time

iterō ⃞ *v* do a second time, repeat; renew, revise

iterum *adv* again, for the second time

itidem *adv* in the same manner, likewise

itiō, **ōnis** *f* going

itus, **ūs** *m* going, gait; departure

iuba, **ae** *f* mane of a horse; crest (of a helmet)

iubar, **aris** *nt* radiance of the heavenly bodies, brightness; first light of day; source of light

iubeō, **iussī**, **iussum** ⃞ *v* order, command; decree
□ **salvēre iubeō** greet, welcome

> ⚠ Unlike other verbs of commanding, **iubeō** is followed by an acc. of the person ordered and an infin. of what the person is ordered to do. Just as **dīcō** … **nōn** (**nēmō** *etc.*) is replaced with **negō**, so **iubeō** … **nōn** is replaced with **vetō**.

iūcunditās, **ātis** *f* pleasantness, charm

iūcundus, **a**, **um** *adj* pleasant, agreeable; delightful

iūdex, **icis** *m/f* judge; arbitrator; umpire; juror; critic

iūdicium, **(i)ī** *nt* judicial investigation; judgment; verdict; opinion; discernment

iūdicō ⃞ *v* judge, give judgement; sentence; decide; appraise

iugālis, **e** *adj* yoked together; nuptial

iugerum, **ī** *nt* two-thirds of an acre of land

iūgis, **e** *adj* continual, constant; ever-flowing

iugō ⃞ *v* marry; join (to)

iugulō ⃞ *v* cut the throat, kill; butcher

iugulum, **ī** *nt*, **iugulus**, **ī** *m* collarbone; throat

iugum, **ī** *nt* yoke (for oxen), team; pair (of horses, *etc.*); ridge (of a mountain)

iūmentum, **ī** *nt* beast of burden

iūnctūra, **ae** *f* joint; association

iuncus, **ī** *m* rush

iungō, **iūnxī**, **iūnctum** ⃞ *v* yoke, harness; join; clasp (hands); unite

iūnior, **ōris** *adj* younger

iūniperus, **ī** *f* juniper

lūnius, **(i)ī** *m* June

iūre *adv* justly, rightly; deservedly

iūrgium, **(i)ī** *nt* quarrel, dispute; abuse

iūrgō ⃞ *v* quarrel, scold

iūriscōnsultus, **ī** *m* lawyer, jurist

iūrisdictiō, **ōnis** *f* jurisdiction, legal authority; administration of justice

iūrō ⃞ *v* swear, take an oath; conspire

iūs[1], **iūris** *nt* broth, soup, sauce

iūs[2], **iūris** *nt* law; right; authority; court of justice; code; (war) conventions

iūs iūrandum, **iūris iūrandī** *nt* oath

iussū *m abl* only with possessive adj or gen by order of

iussum, **ī** *nt* order, command

iūstitia, **ae** *f* justice; equity

iūstitium, **(i)ī** *nt* cessation of judicial and all public business, due to national calamity

iūstus, **a**, **um** *adj* just, equitable; lawful; legitimate; well grounded; proper; right; regular; impartial
■ **iūsta**, **ōrum** *ntpl* due observances; funeral offerings

iuvenālis, **e** *adj* youthful, young

iuvenca, **ae** *f* young cow, heifer

iuvencus, **ī** *m* young bull; young man

iuvenēscō, **nuī** ⃞ *v* grow up; grow young again

iuvenīlis, **e** *adj* youthful

iuvenis, is *adj* young, youthful
■ **iuvenis, is** *m/f* youth, young man
or woman

iuventa, ae *f* youth

iuventās, ātis *f*, **iuventūs, ūtis** *f*
youth

iuvō, iūvī, iūtum ① *v* help, assist;
delight; benefit
  □ **iuvat** ① *v impers* it pleases

iuxtā *prep with acc* near by, near to; *adv*
close; alike; equally
  □ ~ **ac** as much as

Kk

Kalendae, ārum *fpl* the first day of
the month

Kyrie *int/n indec* LM 'Lord', (the first
word of) part of the Mass

Ll

labāscō ③ *v* fall to pieces, break up;
waver

labefaciō, fēcī, factum ③ *v* loosen;
shake; cause to totter; undermine

labefactō ① *v* shake; cause to waver;
make unsteady, loosen; undermine

labellum, ī *nt* lip

lābēs, bis *f* land-slip; subsidence;
disaster, ruin; fault; stain, blemish,
dishonour

labō ① *v* totter, be ready to fall; waver

lābor, lāpsus sum ③ *v dep* slide *or*
glide down; fall down; drop; perish; go
wrong

labor, ōris *m* labour, toil, exertion;
hardship, distress

labōriōsus, a, um *adj* laborious,
painstaking

labōrō ① *v* labour, take pains; strive; be
sick; be oppressed *or* troubled; be in
danger; work (at)

lābrum, ī *nt* basin, vat; bathing-place

labrum, ī *nt* lip; edge (of a vessel, ditch,
river, *etc.*)

lābrusca, ae *f* wild vine

labyrinthēus, a, um *adj* of a
labyrinth

labyrinthus, ī *m* labyrinth, maze

lac, lactis *nt* milk; milky juice

lacer, era, erum *adj* mangled, torn;
rent

lacerātiō, ōnis *f* mangling; tearing

lacerna, ae *f* cloak

lacerō ① *v* tear, mangle; shatter,
torment, harass; 'lash'

lacerta, ae *f* lizard

lacertōsus, a, um *adj* muscular,
brawny

lacertus, ī *m* lizard; muscular part of
the arm; strength

lacessō, ssīvī/ssiī, ssītum ③ *v*
excite, provoke, challenge; harass;
assail

lacinia, ae *f* edge of garment, fringe,
hem

lacrima, ae *f* tear

lacrimābilis, e *adj* mournful; tearful

lacrimō ① *v*, **lacrimor** ① *v dep* shed
tears, weep

lacrimōsus, a, um *adj* tearful,
weeping; causing tears

lactēns, ntis *adj* unweaned, sucking;
juicy

lacteolus, a, um *adj* milk-white

lacteus, a, um *adj* milky; milk-white
  □ ~ **orbis** / **circulus** Milky Way

lactūca, ae *f* lettuce

lacūna, ae *f* pool; hollow, pit, cavity

lacūnar, **āris** *nt* panelled ceiling

lacus, **ūs** *m* lake; pond; tank, reservoir, trough

◻ ~ **Curtii** an area in the Roman forum

laedō, **laesī**, **laesum** ③ *v* hurt; injure; annoy

laena, **ae** *f* woollen double cloak

laetābilis, **e** *adj* joyful

laetitia, **ae** *f* joy; gladness

laetor ① *v dep* rejoice, be joyful

laetus, **a**, **um** *adj* joyful, cheerful, glad; fortunate; luxuriant, lush; pleasing, welcome, beautiful; rich

laevus, **a**, **um** *adj* left; unfavourable, harmful

■ **laeva**, **ae** *f* left hand

lagēna, **ae** *f* flask; bottle

lagōna, **ae** *f* bottle with a narrow neck

laguncula, **ae** *f* small flask

laicus, **a**, **um** *adj* Ⓛᴹ lay (i.e. not belonging to the clergy)

lambō, **ī** ③ *v* lick; wash

lāmenta, **ōrum** *ntpl* wailing, weeping, groans, laments

lāmentābilis, **e** *adj* doleful; lamentable

lāmentātiō, **ōnis** *f* lamentation, wailing

lāmentor ① *v dep* lament; bewail

lamia, **ae** *f* witch

lampas, **adis** *f* torch; lamp

lampyris, **idis** *f* glow-worm, fire-fly

lāna, **ae** *f* wool; soft hair; down

lānātus, **a**, **um** *adj* woolly

lancea, **ae** *f* light spear, lance

lancinō ① *v* tear in pieces, rend apart, mangle

lāneus, **a**, **um** *adj* woollen

langueō ② *v* be sluggish; be unwell; wilt; lack vigour

languēscō, **uī** ③ *v* become faint *or* languid *or* weak; wilt

languidulus, **a**, **um** *adj* drooping, wilting; drowsy

languidus, **a**, **um** *adj* languid, faint, weak; ill; sluggish; inert

languor, **ōris** *m* faintness, feebleness; languor; apathy

laniēna, **ae** *f* butcher's shop

lānificus, **a**, **um** *adj* wool-working, spinning, weaving

lāniger, **era**, **erum** *adj* wool-bearing, fleecy; woolly

laniō ① *v* tear, mutilate; pull to pieces

lanista, **ae** *m* manager of a troop of gladiators, trainer

lānūgō, **inis** *f* down, youth

lānx, **ancis** *f* plate, dish; pan of a pair of scales

lapathum, **ī** *nt*, **lapathus**, **ī** *m/f* sorrel

lapicīda, **ae** *m* stone-cutter

lapideus, **a**, **um** *adj* of stone; stony

lapidō ① *v* throw stones at; stone

■ **lapidat** *v impers* it rains stones

lapidōsus, **a**, **um** *adj* full of stones, stony; gritty

lapillus, **ī** *m* little stone, pebble; precious stone, gem

lapis, **idis** *m* stone; milestone; precious stone

lappa, **ae** *f* bur; plant bearing burs

lāpsō ① *v* slip, lose one's footing

lāpsus[1] *pple* from ▶ **lābor**

lāpsus[2], **ūs** *m* gliding, sliding; slipping and falling

laqueāre, **is** *nt* panelled ceiling

laqueātus, **a**, **um** *adj* panelled

laqueus, **ī** *m* noose, snare; trap

lār, **aris** *m* tutelary household god; home

lārdum, **ī** *nt* bacon

largior ④ *v dep* give bountifully; give presents corruptly; bestow, grant, permit; overlook, condone

largitās, **ātis** *f* abundance; munificence

largiter *adv* plentifully; liberally; greatly

largītiō, **ōnis** *f* distribution of doles, land, *etc.*, largess; bribery

largītor, **ōris** *m* liberal giver; briber

largus, **a**, **um** *adj* lavish; plentiful; bountiful

lāridum ▶ **lārdum**

lāsarpīcifer, **era**, **erum** *adj* silphium-bearing

lascīvia, **ae** *f* playfulness; wantonness, lasciviousness

lascīviō, **iī** ④ *v* frisk; sport; run riot

lascīvus, **a**, **um** *adj* wanton; frolicsome; sportive; mischievous; free from restraint in sexual matters

lassitūdō, **inis** *f* faintness, weariness

lassō ① *v* tire, weary; wear out

lassulus, **a**, **um** *adj* tired, weary

lassus, **a**, **um** *adj* languid, weary, tired

lātē *adv* widely, far and wide

latebra, **ae** *f* hiding-place, retreat; lair; subterfuge

latebrōsus, **a**, **um** *adj* full of lurking places; lurking in concealment

lateō ② *v* lie hid, lurk; escape notice

later, **eris** *m* brick; ingot

latericius, **a**, **um** *adj* made of bricks

latex, **icis** *m* water; (any) liquid; spring water; juice; wine; oil

latibulum, **ī** *nt* hiding-place, den

Latīnē *adv* in Latin

Latīnus, **a**, **um** *adj* Latin

latitō ① *v* remain in hiding; be hidden

lātitūdō, **inis** *f* breadth, width; extent

lātor, **ōris** *m* mover *or* proposer (of a law)

lātrātor, **ōris** *m* barker, one who barks

lātrātus, **ūs** *m* barking

latrō, **ōnis** *m* brigand, bandit; plunderer

lātrō ① *v* bark; bark at

latrōcinium, **(i)ī** *nt* robbery with violence; bandit raid; pillage; band of robbers

latrōcinor ① *v dep* engage in brigandage *or* piracy

latrunculus, **ī** *m* robber, brigand

latus, **eris** *nt* side; flank

lātus, **a**, **um** *adj* broad, wide; spacious; extensive

> **❗** See note at **clāvus**.

laudābilis, **e** *adj* praiseworthy

laudātiō, **ōnis** *f* praising; eulogy

laudātor, **ōris** *m* one who praises, eulogist

laudō ① *v* praise, extol; deliver a funerary eulogy of

laurea, **ae** *f* laurel-tree; laurel wreath *or* branch; triumph, victory

laureātus, **a**, **um** *adj* adorned with a laurel
  ☐ **laureātae litterae** a despatch reporting a victory

laureus, **a**, **um** *adj* of the laurel tree, laurel

lauriger, **era**, **erum** *adj* crowned with laurel

laurus, **ī** *f* bay-tree, laurel; laurel crown; triumph

laus, **dis** *f* praise; glory; excellence; merit
  ■ **laudes** *pl* LM lauds (part of the daily cycle of prayer)

lautumiae, **ārum** *fpl* stone-quarry, especially used as a prison

lautus, **a**, **um** *adj* clean; well-turned-out, fine; sumptuous

lavātiō, **ōnis** *f* the action of washing; facilities for washing

lavō, **lāvī**, **lautum/lavātum/lōtum** ① *v* wash; bathe, soak

laxāmentum, **ī** *nt* respite; opportunity

laxitās, **ātis** *f* roominess, largeness

laxō ① *v* expand, extend; open up; slacken; relax; weaken

laxus, **a**, **um** *adj* wide, loose; roomy; slack; open; lax

lea, **ae** *f* lioness

leaena, **ae** *f* lioness

lebēs, **ētis** *m* caldron

lectīca, **ae** *f* litter

lectīcārius, **(i)ī** *m* litter-bearer

lēctiō, **ōnis** *f* reading (aloud); perusal; choosing

lectisternium, **(i)ī** *nt* special feast of supplication at which a banquet was offered to the gods, couches being spread for them to recline upon

lēctitō ① *v* read repeatedly; be in the habit of reading

lēctor, **ōris** *m* reader

lectulus, **ī** *m* bed or couch

lectus, **ī** *m* couch, (bridal-)bed

lēgātiō, **ōnis** *f* embassy

lēgātum, **ī** *nt* bequest, legacy

lēgātus, **ī** *m* ambassador, legate; deputy; commander

> **❗** The governor of a province was permitted to nominate a number (which varied) of **lēgātī** or staff to assist him, usu. drawn from among the senatorial class.

lēgerupa, **ae** *m* law-breaker

lēgerupiō, **ōnis** *f* law-breaking

lēgifer, **era**, **erum** *adj* law-giving

legiō, **ōnis** *f* Roman legion; army

> ❗ The Roman legion varied in size through history: its establishment ranged from around 4000 to 6000 men in the infantry though its actual strength was often smaller. It would also include up to around 300 cavalry. Its chief division was into 10 **cohortēs**.

legiōnārius, **a**, **um** *adj* of a legion, legionary

lēgitimus, **a**, **um** *adj* lawful, right; legitimate; real, genuine; just; proper

legō, **lēgī**, **lēctum** ③ *v* gather; choose; furl; traverse; read

lēgō ① *v* send as an envoy; choose as deputy; bequeath

legūmen, **inis** *nt* pulse, leguminous plant

lembus, **ī** *m* small fast-sailing boat

lemurēs, **um** *mpl* malevolent ghosts of the dead, spectres, shades

lēna, **ae** *f* procuress; brothel-keeper

lēnīmen, **inis** *nt* alleviation, solace

lēniō ④ *v* mitigate; allay, ease; explain away

lēnis, **e** *adj* smooth, soft, mild, gentle, easy, calm

lēnitās, **ātis** *f* slowness; gentleness, mildness

lēnō, **ōnis** *m* brothel-keeper, bawd, procurer

lēnōcinium, **(i)ī** *nt* pandering; allurement, enticement; flattery

lēnōnius, **a**, **um** *adj* of a pimp

lēns, **ntis** *f* the lentil-plant

lentēscō ③ *v* become sticky; relax

lentitūdō, **inis** *f* slowness in action; apathy

lentō ① *v* bend under strain

lentus, **a**, **um** *adj* pliant; tough; clinging; slow; lazy; calm; procrastinating; phlegmatic

lēnunculus, **ī** *m* skiff

leō, **ōnis** *m* lion

leopardus, **ī** *m* leopard

lepidus, **a**, **um** *adj* agreeable, charming, delightful, amusing; witty

lepōs, **ōris** *m* charm, grace; wit; humour

leprae, **ārum** *fpl* leprosy

lepus, **oris** *m* hare

lētālis, **e** *adj* deadly, fatal, mortal

Lēthaeus, **a**, **um** *adj* of Lethe; causing forgetfulness; of the underworld

Lēthē, **ēs** *f* Lethe, the river of forgetfulness

lētifer, **era**, **erum** *adj* deadly; fatal

lētum, **ī** *nt* death; death and destruction

leuuga, **ae** *f* ⸤LM⸥ league (approx. 3 miles)

levāmen, **inis** *nt* alleviation, solace

levāmentum, **ī** *nt* alleviation, mitigation, consolation

levis, **e** *adj* light; nimble; trivial, trifling; gentle; capricious; fickle, inconstant

lēvis, **e** *adj* smooth; polished; free from coarse hair; smooth

levitās, **ātis** *f* lightness; restlessness; mildness; fickleness; shallowness

levō ① *v* lift; support; relieve, lessen; free from

lēvō ① *v* smooth; polish

lēx, **gis** *f* law; rule; principle; condition □ ~ **cūriāta** law passed by the assembly of the thirty divisions of the Roman people

lībāmen, **inis** *nt*, **lībāmentum**, **ī** *nt* drink-offering; first-fruits

lībella, **ae** *f* small silver coin; plumb-line, level

libellus, **ī** *m* little book; memorial; petition; pamphlet, defamatory publication; programme

libēns, **ntis** *adj* willing; cheerful

Līber, **erī** *m* Bacchus; wine

liber, **brī** *m* inner bark of a tree; book; volume

līber, **era**, **erum** *adj* free; unimpeded; void of; frank, free-spoken; licentious; outspoken

līberālis, **e** *adj* gentlemanly; well-bred; liberal; open-handed; generous; lavish

līberālitās, **ātis** *f* nobleness, kindness; frankness; liberality; gift

līberātor, **ōris** *m* deliverer, liberator

līberē *adv* freely; frankly; shamelessly

līberī, **ōrum** *mpl* children

līberō ① *v* release, free; acquit; absolve

līberta, **ae** *f* freedwoman

lībertās, ātis *f* freedom; liberty; frankness of speech, outspokenness

lībertīnus, a, um *adj* of a freedman
■ **lībertīna, ae** *f* freedwoman
■ **lībertīnus, ī** *m* freedman

lībertus, ī *m* freedman

libet, uit, libitum est ② *v impers* it pleases, is agreeable
□ **libet mihi** I feel like, I want

libīdinōsus, a, um *adj* lustful, wanton; capricious

libīdō, inis *f* desire; lust; passion

Libitīna, ae *f* goddess of funerals

lībō ① *v* nibble, sip; pour in offering; impair; graze, skim

lībra, ae *f* Roman pound (about three-quarters of a modern pound); level; balance; scales; one of the twelve signs of the zodiac

lībrāmentum, ī *nt* weight, counterpoise

lībrārius, a, um *adj* of books
■ **lībrārius, (i)ī** *m* copyist, secretary; bookseller

lībrō ① *v* weigh; level; balance, poise

lībum, ī *nt* cake; consecrated cake

liburna, ae *f* light, fast-sailing warship

liburnica, ae *f* a fast warship

licēns, ntis *adj* free, unrestrained

licentia, ae *f* liberty, licence; freedom; disorderliness; outspokenness

liceō ② *v* fetch (a price)
□ **liceor** bid at an auction

licet, uit, licitum est ② *v impers with dat of person permitted* it is lawful *or* permitted; one may *or* can; *int* yes, all right!; *conj with verb in subj* although

licitus, a, um *adj* lawful; permitted

līcium, (i)ī *nt* thread; leash *or* heddle (in weaving)

līctor, ōris *m* lictor

> **!** Each magistrate who held **imperium** was accompanied wherever he went by a set number of **līctōrēs**; they preceded him in single file, carrying the **fascēs** on their left shoulder, and would announce his arrival, clear his path and, when necessary, execute his powers of arrest. A consul had twelve **līctōrēs**, a praetor six.

ligāmen, inis *nt*, **ligāmentum, ī** *nt* bandage; string

lignārius, (i)ī *m* carpenter; timber-merchant

lignātiō, ōnis *f* collecting firewood

lignātor, ōris *m* one who collects firewood

ligneus, a, um *adj* of wood, wooden

lignor ① *v dep* collect firewood

lignum, ī *nt* wood; firewood; timber; 'stump'

ligō¹, ōnis *m* mattock, hoe

ligō² ① *v* bind, fasten; attach; tie up

ligustrum, ī *nt* privet, white-flowered shrub

līlium, (i)ī *nt* lily

līma, ae *f* file; polishing, revision

limbus, ī *m* ornamental border to a robe

līmen, inis *nt* lintel, threshold; entrance; house

līmes, itis *m* strip of uncultivated ground to mark the division of land; stone to mark a boundary; boundary; track; channel; route

līmō ① *v* file; polish; file down; detract gradually from

līmōsus, a, um *adj* miry, muddy

limpidus, a, um *adj* clear

līmus¹, ī *m* mud; slime

līmus², a, um *adj* oblique, sidelong

līnea, ae *f* string, cord; fishing-line; plumb-line; finishing-line

līneāmentum, ī *nt* line; *pl* outlines, features

līneus, a, um *adj* made of flax *or* linen

lingō, līnxī, līnctum ③ *v* lick

lingua, ae *f* tongue; speech, language; dialect

līniger, era, erum *adj* wearing linen

linō, lēvī, litum ③ *v* smear, plaster (with); erase; befoul

linquō, līquī ③ *v* leave, quit, forsake; abandon

linter, tris *f* small light boat; trough, vat

linteum, ī *nt* linen cloth; linen; sail; napkin; awning

linteus, a, um *adj* of linen

līnum, ī *nt* flax; linen, thread; rope; fishing-line; net

lippitūdō, inis *f* inflammation *or* watering of the eyes

lippus, a, um *adj* having watery *or* inflamed eyes

liquefaciō, fēcī, factum ③ *v* melt, dissolve

liqueō, licuī/liquī ② *v* be clear to a person; be evident

liquēscō ③ *v* become liquid, melt; decompose

liquidus, a, um *adj* liquid, fluid; clear; manifest; smooth; melodious; evident

liquō ① *v* melt; strain

līquor ③ *v dep* dissolve; waste away; flow

liquor, ōris *m* fluid, liquid

līs, lītis *f* quarrel; lawsuit

litania, ae *f* [LM] prayer, litany

lītigiōsus, a, um *adj* quarrelsome, contentions

lītigō ① *v* quarrel; go to law

litō ① *v* obtain *or* give favourable omens from a sacrifice; make an (acceptable) offering (to)

lītorālis, e *adj*, **lītoreus, a, um** *adj* of the seashore

littera, ae *f* letter of the alphabet
■ **litterae, ārum** *pl* letter, literature; writings; the elements of education

litterātus, a, um *adj* learned; cultured

litūra, ae *f* smearing; erasure; blot

lītus, oris *nt* seashore, coast

lituus, ī *m* curved staff carried by augurs; a kind of war-trumpet curved at one end

līveō ② *v* be livid *or* discoloured; be envious

līvidus, a, um *adj* livid, slate-coloured; discoloured by bruises; envious, spiteful

līvor, ōris *m* bluish discoloration (produced by bruising, *etc.*), envy, spite

lixa, ae *m* camp-follower

locātiō, ōnis *f* hiring out *or* letting (of property)

locō ① *v* place, station; contract (for); farm out (taxes) on contract

locuplēs, ētis *adj* rich, well-to-do; rich (in)

locus, ī *m* place, position

locusta, ae *f* locust; lobster

locūtus *pple* from ▶ **loquor**

logī *int* fairy-tales! rubbish!

lolium, (i)ī *nt* a grass found as a weed in corn, darnel

longaevus, a, um *adj* of great age, ancient

longē *adv* far off; far; a great while; very much; by a large margin
□ ∼ **lātēque** far and wide

longinquitās, ātis *f* length; distance; duration

longinquus, a, um *adj* far off, distant; of long duration
□ **ē longinquō** from a distance

longitūdō, inis *f* length

longus, a, um *adj* long, tall; lasting a long time, tedious

lopas, adis *f* limpet

loquācitās, ātis *f* talkativeness

loquāx, ācis *adj* talkative, loquacious

loquēla, loquella, ae *f* speech, utterance

loquor, locūtus sum ③ *v dep* speak, talk, say; mention

lōrārius, (i)ī *m* flogger

lōrīca, ae *f* cuirass; parapet, breast-work

lōrum, ī *nt* thong; *pl* rawhide whip; reins

lōtus, ī *f* lotus plant; nettle plant

lub- ▶ **lib-**

lūbricus, a, um *adj* slippery; sinuous; inconstant; hazardous; ticklish; deceitful

lūcar, āris *nt* sum of money allocated for public entertainments

lucellum, ī *nt* small *or* petty gain

lūceō, lūxī ② *v* shine; glitter; be conspicuous

lucerna, ae *f* oil lamp

lucernaris, e *adj* [LM] by candlelight

lūcēscō ③ *v* begin to shine, grow light

lūcidus, a, um *adj* bright, shining; clear

Lūcifer[1]**, erī** *m* morning star [LM] Lucifer, the Devil

lūcifer[2]**, era, erum** *adj* light-bringing

lūcifugus, a, um *adj* avoiding the light of day

Lūcīna, ae *f* goddess of childbirth; childbirth

lucripeta, ae *m* one who is avaricious *or* money-grubbing

lucror ⬚ *v dep* gain, win; make a profit (out of)

lucrōsus, **a**, **um** *adj* gainful, lucrative

lucrum, **ī** *nt* gain, profit; avarice
◻ **faciō lucrī** make a profit

luctāmen, **inis** *nt* struggling, exertion

luctātor, **ōris** *m* wrestler

lūctificus, **a**, **um** *adj* dire, calamitous

luctor ⬚ *v dep* wrestle; struggle; fight (against)

lūctuōsus, **a**, **um** *adj* mournful; grievous

lūctus, **ūs** *m* sorrow, lamentation; mourning; instance *or* cause of grief

lūcubrō ⬚ *v* work by lamp-light, 'burn the midnight oil'; make *or* produce at night

lūculentus, **a**, **um** *adj* excellent; fine; beautiful

lūcus, **ī** *m* grove

lūdibrium, **(i)ī** *nt* mockery; laughing-stock

lūdibundus, **a**, **um** *adj* having fun; carefree

lūdicer, **lūdicrus**, **cra**, **crum** *adj* connected with sport *or* the stage
■ **lūdicrum**, **ī** *nt* stage-play; show; source of fun, plaything

lūdificātiō, **ōnis** *f* mockery

lūdificātor, **ōris** *m* mocker

lūdificō ⬚ *v,* **lūdificor** ⬚ *v dep* make sport of, trifle with

lūdō, **ūsī**, **ūsum** ⬚ *v* play; sport; tease; trick

lūdus, **ī** *m* play, game, pastime; sport, entertainment, fun; school, elementary school

> ❗ Often with their origins in religious festivals, **lūdī** (games) were frequent in Rome, including the **lūdī circēnsēs** (chariot races), gladiatorial and hunting shows (**vēnātiōnēs**), and the staging of plays (the **lūdī scaenicī**). Schools for gladiators were also known as **lūdī**, as were elementary schools for children.

luēs, **uis** *f* plague, pestilence; scourge, affliction

lūgeō, **lūxī**, **lūctum** ⬚ *v* mourn, lament; be in mourning

lūgubris, **bre** *adj* mourning; mournful; grievous

lumbus, **ī** *m* the loins; the loins as the seat of sexual excitement

lūmen, **inis** *nt* light; daylight; day; lamp, torch; life; eye; (of a person) glory, cynosure

lūna, **ae** *f* moon; month

lūnāris, **e** *adj* lunar

lūnātus, **a**, **um** *adj* crescent-shaped

lūnō ⬚ *v* make crescent-shaped, curve

luō[1], **luī** ⬚ *v* wash

luō[2], **luī**, **lūtum/luitum** ⬚ *v* pay; atone for
◻ **poenam** ∼ suffer punishment

lupa, **ae** *f* she-wolf; prostitute

lupānar, **āris** *nt* brothel

lupātus, **a**, **um** *adj* furnished with jagged teeth
■ **lupātī**, **ōrum** *mpl* jagged toothed bit

Lupercālia, **ium** *ntpl* festival promoting fertility held on 15 February

Lupercus, **ī** *m* priest in the Lupercalia

lupīnus, **a**, **um** *adj* of *or* belonging to a wolf; made of wolf-skin

lupus, **ī** *m* wolf; grappling iron; sea-bass

lūridus, **a**, **um** *adj* sickly yellow; sallow, wan, ghastly

luscinia, **ae** *f* nightingale

luscus, **a**, **um** *adj* blind in one eye

lūsor, **ōris** *m* player; tease; one who treats (of a subject) lightly

lūstrālis, **e** *adj* relating to purification; serving to avert evil

lūstrō ⬚ *v* purify; illuminate; move round, over *or* through; go about; review, survey

lūstrum, **ī** *nt* purificatory ceremony; period of five years

lustrum, **ī** *nt* haunts of wild beasts; *pl* den of vice

lūsus, **ūs** *m* play, game; sport, amusement; amorous sport

lūteolus, **a**, **um** *adj* yellow

lūteus, **a**, **um** *adj* yellow; saffron

luteus, **a**, **um** *adj* of mud *or* clay; good for nothing

lutulentus, **a**, **um** *adj* muddy; turbid; dirty; morally polluted

lutum, **ī** *nt* mud, clay; dirt

lūtum, **ī** *nt* yellow dye; any yellow colour

lūx, **lūcis** *f* light (of the sun, stars, *etc.*); daylight, day; splendour; eyesight

luxuria, **ae** *f*, **luxuriēs**, **iēī** *f* luxury, extravagance, rankness, thriving condition

luxuriō ① *v*, **luxurior** ① *v dep* grow rank *or* luxuriant; frisk; indulge oneself

luxuriōsus, **a**, **um** *adj* luxuriant, exuberant; immoderate; wanton; luxurious; self-indulgent

luxus, **ūs** *m* luxury, soft living; sumptuousness

lychnus, **ī** *m* lamp

lympha, **ae** *f* water; water-nymph

lymphātus, **a**, **um** *adj* frenzied, frantic

lynx, **yncis** *m/f* lynx

lyra, **ae** *f* lyre; lyric poetry; Lyre (constellation)

lyricus, **a**, **um** *adj* lyric

lyristēs, **ae** *m* lyre-player

Mm

macellum, **ī** *nt* provision-market

macer, **cra**, **crum** *adj* lean, meagre, poor

māceria, **ae** *f* wall of brick *or* stone

mācerō ① *v* make soft, soak; worry, annoy

machaera, **a** *f* single-edged sword

māchina, **ae** *f* machine; siege-engine

māchināmentum, **ī** *nt* siege-engine

māchinātiō, **ōnis** *f* mechanism; engine of war

māchinātor, **ōris** *m* engineer; (fig) projector

māchinor ① *v dep* devise; plot

maciēs, **iēī** *f* leanness, meagreness; poverty

macrēscō, **ruī** ③ *v* become thin, waste away

macte *int* well done! bravo!

mactō ① *v* honour; sacrifice; slaughter

macula, **ae** *f* spot; stain, blemish; mesh in a net

maculō ① *v* spot; pollute; dishonour, taint

maculōsus, **a**, **um** *adj* spotted; disreputable

madefaciō, **fēcī**, **factum** ③ *v* make wet; soak
□ **madefīō, fierī** be moistened, be made wet

madeō ② *v* be wet *or* sodden; be wet with tears, perspiration, *etc.*

madēscō, **duī** ③ *v* become moist *or* wet

madidus, **a**, **um** *adj* moist, wet; drenched; drunk

maenas, **adis** *f* Bacchante, female votary of Bacchus; frenzied woman

maereō ② *v* be sad, grieve, lament; bewail

maeror, **ōris** *m* sadness, grief, mourning

maestitia, **ae** *f* sadness, grief

maestus, **a**, **um** *adj* sad, melancholy; gloomy; woeful; distressing

māgālia, **ium** *ntpl* huts

mage ▸ **magis**

magicus, **a**, **um** *adj* magical

magis *adv* more, rather

magister, **trī** *m* master, chief; expert, tutor, teacher; pilot of a ship
□ **magister equitum** dictator's lieutenant; master of the horse

> **!** The **lūdī magister** was an elementary teacher of children aged between approx. 7 and 12. He taught reading, writing and some mathematics.

magisterium, **(i)ī** *nt* office of a president; instruction

magistra, **ae** *f* instructress

magistrātus, ūs *m* magistracy; office; magistrate

magnanimus, a, um *adj* noble in spirit, brave, generous

magnēs, ētis *m* magnet

magnidicus, a, um *adj* boastful

magnificentia, ae *f* greatness, nobleness; grandeur; splendour

magnificus, a, um *adj* noble, eminent, stately; sumptuous, magnificent, boastful

magniloquentia, ae *f* exalted diction; braggadocio

magniloquus, a, um *adj* boastful

magnitūdō, inis *f* greatness, bulk; intensity; importance

magnopere *adv* much, greatly, especially, strongly

magnus, a, um *adj* great, large, tall; loud; much; noble, grand; mighty

magus, a, um *adj* magical
■ **magus, ī** *m* magician, sorcerer

maiestās, ātis *f* majesty; authority; grandeur; high treason

maior, ius *adj* greater
□ **nātū** ~ older
□ **maiōre opere** all the more

maiōrēs, ōrum *mpl* ancestors

Maius, (i)ī *m* May

māla, ae *f* cheeks, jaws

malacia, ae *f* dead calm

male *adv* badly, ill, wickedly, unfortunately; amiss
□ **habēre male** bother, annoy

> [!] **male** sometimes has the force of a negative, e.g. **male sanus** for **īnsānus**.

maledīcō, īxī, ictum ③ *v* speak ill of, abuse

maledictum, ī *nt* reproach, taunt

malefaciō, fēcī, factum ③ *v* do evil *or* wrong, injure

maleficium, (i)ī *nt* misdeed, crime; injury

maleficus, a, um *adj* wicked, criminal, harmful

malesuādus, a, um *adj* ill-advising

malevolus, a, um *adj* spiteful, malevolent

mālifer, era, erum *adj* apple-bearing

malignitās, ātis *f* ill-will, spite, malice; niggardliness

malignus, a, um *adj* spiteful; niggardly; narrow

malitia, ae *f* wickedness; vice, fault

malleolus, ī *m* fire-dart

malleus, ī *m* hammer, mallet

mālō, mālle, māluī *v ir* wish *or* choose rather, prefer

malum, ī *nt* evil, calamity, misfortune
■ ~ *int* the devil! the hell! for goodness' sake!

mālum, ī *nt* apple

mālus¹, ī *m* pole; mast of a ship

mālus², ī *f* apple-tree

malus, a, um *adj* bad, evil, wicked; unfortunate; weak

malva, ae *f* mallow-plant

mamma, ae *f* breast, udder

manceps, ipis *m* contractor, agent

mancipium, (i)ī *nt* formal mode of purchase; property; right of ownership; slave

mancipō ① *v* transfer, sell; surrender

mancus, a, um *adj* maimed, crippled; powerless

mandātum, ī *nt* order, commission

mandō¹, ndī, mānsum ③ *v* chew, champ

mandō² ① *v* commit to one's charge, commission; command; entrust (to)

māne *nt indec* morning
■ ~ *adv* in the morning; early next day

maneō, mānsī, mānsum ② *v* stay, remain; await; abide by; last; endure

mānēs, ium *mpl* gods of the Lower World; shades *or* ghosts of the dead; mortal remains; underworld; death

mangō, ōnis *m* slave-dealer

manica, ae *f* long sleeve; handcuff

manifestus, a, um *adj* clear, evident; plainly guilty; flagrant
■ **manifestō** *adv* in the act, openly

manipulāris, e *adj* belonging to the ranks, private
■ **manipulāris, āris** *m* common soldier; marine

manipulātim *adv* in handfuls; in companies

manipulus, ī *m* handful, bundle; company of soldiers

> ❗ The **manipulus** was a division of the Roman army comprising three *centuriae*.

mannus, ī *m* pony

mānō ① *v* flow, pour; be shed; be wet; spring

mānsiō, ōnis *f* stay, visit; stopping-place on a journey

mānsitō ① *v* spend the night, stay

mānsuēfaciō, **fēcī**, **factum** ③ *v* tame; civilize; make mild

mansuēscō, **ēvī**, **ētum** ③ *v* tame; become *or* grow tame

mānsuētūdō, inis *f* mildness, clemency

mānsuētus, a, um *adj* tame; mild, gentle

mantēle, is *nt*, **mantēlium**, (i)ī *nt* hand-towel; napkin

mantica, ae *f* travelling-bag, knapsack

mantō ① *v* remain, stay, wait for

manubiae, ārum *fpl* general's share of the booty; prize-money; profits

manūmittō, **īsī**, **issum** ③ *v* sometime as two words
□ **manū mittō** set at liberty, emancipate, free

manus, ūs *f* hand; fist; trunk (of an elephant); handwriting; band of soldiers; company; armed force of any size; workman; legal power of a husband
□ **cōnferō manum** join battle

mapālia, ium *ntpl* huts in which the Nomadic Africans lived

mappa, ae *f* table-napkin; cloth dropped as a signal to start a race in the circus

marceō ② *v* be enfeebled, weak *or* faint

marcēscō ③ *v* pine away; become weak, enfeebled *or* languid

marchia, ae *f* [LM] march, area governed by a marquis

marchio, onis *m* [LM] marquis

marcidus, a, um *adj* withered, rotten; exhausted

mare, ris *nt* sea; sea-water

margarītum, ī *nt* pearl

marginō ① *v* provide with borders

margō, inis *m/f* edge; rim; border

marīnus, a, um *adj* of *or* belonging to the sea, marine; sea-born
□ **rōs marīnus** rosemary

marisca, ae *f* fig; haemorrhoids, piles

maritimus, a, um *adj* sea…, maritime; (of people) used to the sea
■ **maritima**, ōrum *ntpl* sea-coast

marītō ① *v* marry, give in marriage

marītus, a, um *adj* married, united, 'wedded'
■ **marīta**, ae *f* wife
■ **marītus**, ī *m* husband; mate

marmor, **oris** *nt* marble; marble statue; sea

marmoreus, a, um *adj* made of marble; marble-like

Mars, **rtis** *m* (also **Māvors**) god of war; war, battle; warlike spirit; the advantage in war

marsuppium, (i)ī *nt* pouch, bag, purse

Martiālis, **e** *adj* of *or* belonging to Mars

Martius, a, um *adj* of *or* belonging to Mars; March

martyrium, (i)i *nt* [LM] martyrdom

mās, **maris** *adj* male; masculine; manly

māsculus, a, um *adj* male; manly; virile

massa, ae *f* lump, mass; bulk, size

Massicum, ī *nt* Massic wine

mastīgia, ae *m* one who deserves a whipping, rascal

matara, ae *f* Gallic throwing spear

māter, **tris** *f* mother; matron; origin, source; motherland, mother-city

mātercula, ae *f* affectionate term for mother

māterfamiliās, **mātrisfamiliās** *f* mistress of the house; respectable married woman

māteria, ae *f*, **māteriēs**, iēī *f* material; timber; subject-matter

māternus, a, um *adj* motherly, maternal

mātertera, ae *f* maternal aunt

mathēmaticus, ī *m* mathematician; astrologer

mātrimōnium, (i)ī *nt* marriage, matrimony

mātrimus, a, um *adj* having a mother living

mātrōna, ae *f* wife, matron

mātrōnālis, e *adj* of *or* befitting a married woman

matula, ae *f* jar; chamber-pot; blockhead, fool

mātūrēscō, ruī ③ *v* become ripe, ripen; mature

mātūritās, ātis *f* ripeness

mātūrō ① *v* make ripe; hasten; make haste to

mātūrus, a, um *adj* ripe; mellow; mature; seasonable, timely; early; speedy

mātūtīnus, a, um *adj* of *or* belonging to the early morning
■ **matutinae, arum** *fpl,* **matutinum, i** *nt* ⟦LM⟧ morning prayers, matins

Māvors, tis ▶ **Mars**

maximus, a, um *adj* [sup of **magnus**] greatest, etc.
□ **maximō opere** most urgently

mē *pn acc/abl* of ▶ **ego**

meātus, ūs *m* movement, course

medēns, ntis *m* physician, doctor

medeor ② *v dep* heal, cure; remedy

mēdica, ae *f* a kind of clover, lucerne

medicābilis, e *adj* curable

medicāmen, inis *nt* drug, remedy, medicine; dye

medicāmentum, i *nt* drug, remedy, medicine

medicīna, ae *f* medical art; medicine; treatment, remedy

medicīnus, a, um *adj* medical

medicō ① *v* heal, cure; medicate; dye

medicor ① *v dep* heal, cure

medicus, a, um *adj* healing, medical
■ **medicus, i** *m* physician, doctor

medimnum, i *nt,* **medimnus, i** *m* a dry measure, Greek 'bushel' (six modiī)

mediocris, cre *adj* middling, moderate, tolerable, mediocre

mediocritās, ātis *f* medium, moderateness; mediocrity

meditāmentum, i *nt* training exercise

meditātiō, ōnis *f* contemplation, meditation; practising

mediterrāneus, a, um *adj* remote from the coast, inland

meditor ① *v dep* think about constantly, ponder; intend; devise; reflect; practise; work over in performance

medium, (i)ī *nt* middle; public, publicity
□ **in mediō** open to all
□ **ē mediō abeō** die

medius, a, um *adj* mid, middle; neutral; ambiguous; middling, ordinary; moderate

> [!] The formal circular dinner table at the Roman upper-class **cēna** was surrounded on three sides by couches on which the diners reclined; on each couch there were three places. Both the middle couch and the middle place on each were described as **medius**. Guests were usually placed **in mediō**, and its rightmost place (**īmus in mediō**), adjacent to the host who reclined at the head of the neighbouring couch (**summus in īmō**), was the position of greatest honour, also known as the **locus cōnsulāris**. Note that **medius** is an adj. and agrees with the noun e.g. **in mediō fōrō** 'in the middle of the forum'; **summus** and **īmus** are used in a similar way.

medulla, ae *f* marrow, kernel; innermost part; quintessence

medullitus *adv* to the very marrow

medullula, ae *f* the marrow of one's bones; inmost part

megistānes, um *mpl* nobles of Parthia and other eastern countries, grandees

mehercle ▶ **hercle**

meiō, mī(n)xī, mī(n)ctum ③ *v* urinate

mel, mellis *nt* honey; sweetness; darling

melicus, a, um *adj* musical, lyrical
■ **melicus, i** *m* a lyric poet

mēlinum, i *nt* white pigment, Melian white

melior, ius *adj* [comp of **bonus**] better

mellifer, era, erum *adj* honey-producing

mellītus, a, um *adj* sweetened with honey; honey-sweet

melos, ī *nt* song

membrāna, **ae** *f* membrane; skin; parchment

membrātim *adv* limb by limb

membrum, **ī** *nt* limb; the genital member

meminī, **isse** *v ir* remember; retain in the mind; attend to; recall in writing, speech, *etc.*

memor, **oris** *adj* mindful (of), remembering, unforgetting; grateful; commemorative

memorābilis, **e** *adj* memorable, remarkable

memoria, **ae** *f* memory; recollection; time within remembrance; history

memoriter *adv* word for word, verbatim

memorō ① *v* remind of; mention; relate

menda, **ae** *f* blemish, fault; error

mendācium, **(i)ī** *nt* lie; counterfeit

mendāx, **ācis** *adj* lying, false; deceitful; counterfeit

mendīcitās, **ātis** *f* beggary

mendīcō ① *v* beg for; be a beggar

mendīcus, **ī** *m* beggar

mendōsus, **a**, **um** *adj* faulty, erroneous; prone to error

mendum, **ī** *nt* blemish, fault; error

mēns, **mentis** *f* mind, intellect; reason, judgement; frame of mind; disposition, intention

mēnsa, **ae** *f* table; meal; course (at a meal); banker's counter

mēnsārius, **(i)ī** *m* money-changer, banker; treasury official

mēnsis, **is** *m* month

mēnsor, **ōris** *m* land-surveyor; surveyor of building-works

mēnstruus, **a**, **um** *adj* monthly

mēnsula, **ae** *f* little table

mēnsūra, **ae** *f* measuring; length, area, capacity, *etc.*

mentiō, **ōnis** *f* mention

mentior ④ *v dep* lie, deceive; feign; speak falsely about; give a false impression; mimic

mentula, **ae** *f* the male sexual organ

mentum, **ī** *nt* chin

meō ① *v* go along, pass, travel

merācus, **a**, **um** *adj* undiluted, neat

mercātor, **ōris** *m* trader, merchant

mercātūra, **ae** *f* trade, commerce

mercātus, **ūs** *m* gathering for the purposes of commerce; market; fair

mercēnnārius, **a**, **um** *adj* hired, mercenary
■ ~, **(i)ī** *m* hired worker; mercenary

mercēs, **ēdis** *f* hire, pay, wages, salary; reward; rent, price

mercimōnium, **(i)ī** *nt* merchandise, purchase

mercor ① *v dep* trade; buy

merda, **ae** *f* dung, excrement

merenda, **ae** *f* afternoon meal

mereō ② *v*, **mereor** ② *v dep* earn, get; deserve; be rewarded
◻ ~ **stipendia** serve as soldier; draw pay as a soldier

meretrīcius, **a**, **um** *adj* of, belonging to, *or* typical of a courtesan

meretrīcula, **ae** *f* courtesan

meretrīx, **īcis** *f* courtesan, kept woman

merges, **itis** *f* sheaf of corn

mergō, **rsī**, **rsum** ③ *v* immerse; plunge; bury; hide; drown; overwhelm; plunge in ruin

mergus, **ī** *m* a sea-bird, probably a gull

merīdiānus, **a**, **um** *adj* pertaining to noon; southern

merīdiēs, **iēī** *m* midday, noon; south

merīdiō ① *v* take a siesta

meritum, **ī** *nt* desert; service, kindness; due reward

meritus, **a**, **um** *adj* deserved, due

mersō ① *v* dip (in), immerse; overwhelm, drown

merula, **ae** *f* blackbird; a dark-coloured fish, the wrasse

merus, **a**, **um** *adj* pure, unmixed; bare, only, mere; sheer
■ **merum**, **ī** *nt* wine unmixed with water

merx, **cis** *f* a commodity; *pl* goods, merchandise

messis, **is** *m/f* harvest, crop; harvest time

messor, **ōris** *m* reaper, harvester

mēta, **ae** *f* cone-shaped turning post at either end of a race-track; limit; end; conical shape; cone

metallum, ī *nt* metal; mine; quarry

mēticulōsus, a, um *adj* timorous; involving fear, awful

mētior, **mēnsus sum** ④ *v dep* measure; traverse; walk *or* sail through; estimate, gauge

metō, **messuī**, **messum** ③ *v* reap, mow, cut off

mētor ① *v dep* measure off, mark out

metuō, **uī**, **ūtum** ③ *v* be afraid of; be afraid to; fear

> ❗ **metuō** is followed by the same constructions as **timeō**.

metus, **ūs** *m* fear; anxiety; awe; object of dread

meus, a, um *adj* my, mine

> ❗ **meus** has voc. sg. m. **mī**.

mī *dat* of ⋗ **ego**

mīca, **ae** *f* particle, grain, crumb

micō, **micuī** ① *v* move quickly, quiver; dart; throb; flash, glitter

migrātiō, **ōnis** *f* change of abode; move

migrō ① *v* change one's residence *or* position; pass into a new condition; move, shift

mihǐ *pn dat* of ⋗ **ego**

mīles, **itis** *m* soldier; foot-soldier; soldiery

mīli- ⋗ **mīlli-**

mīlitāris, e *adj* military; warlike

mīlitia, **ae** *f* military service; campaign

mīlitō ① *v* serve as a soldier

milium, **(i)ī** *nt* millet

mīlle *adj indec* (*in pl* **mīlia** *or* **mīllia**) thousand; thousands; innumerable
□ **mīlle passūs** *mpl* a mile

> ❗ In its sg., **mīlle** is an indeclinable numeral adj. Its plural is either (a) indeclinable, formed with a numeral adv., e.g. [**cum**] **ter mīlle puerīs**, or (b) declined as a neuter i-stem qualified by a cardinal numeral and taking the noun being counted in the gen. (pl.), e.g. [**cum**] **tribus mīlibus puellārum**.

mīllē(n)simus, a, um *adj* a thousandth

mīlliārium, **(i)ī** *nt* milestone
□ ~ **aureum** golden milestone erected by Augustus at the head of the forum in Rome from which all distances were reckoned

mīlliē(n)s *adv* a thousand times

mīlvus, ī *m* kite

mīma, **ae** *f* actress performing in mimes

mīmus, ī *m* actor in mimes; mime; farce

mina, **ae** *f* silver (Greek) coin

mināclae, **ārum** *fpl* threats

minae, **ārum** *fpl* threats, menaces; warning signs

mināx, **ācis** *adj* threatening; boding ill

Minerva, **ae** *f* a person's natural capacity, intelligence, tastes, *etc.*; weaving; spinning

mingō ⋗ **meiō**

minimus, a, um *adj* [sup of **parvus**] least, smallest

minister, **trī** *m* attendant; servant; agent; accomplice

ministerium, **(i)ī** *nt* service; employment; commission; public works

ministra, **ae** *f* female servant; female religious official

ministrō ① *v with dat* attend (to), serve; furnish; supply

minitor ① *v dep with dat* threaten

minor[1] ① *v dep with dat* threaten

minor[2], **minus** *adj* [comp of **parvus**] smaller, lesser, younger, etc.
□ **nātū** ~ younger
□ **faciō minōris** consider of less importance
■ **minōrēs**, **um** *mpl* descendants

minuō, **uī**, **ūtum** ③ *v* lessen; impair; abate; make smaller; grow less

minus *adv* less; not so well; not quite

minūtātim *adv* bit by bit

minūtus, a, um *adj* small, insignificant, petty

mīrābilis, e *adj* wonderful, marvellous, extraordinary

mīrābundus, a, um *adj* wondering

mīrāculum, ī *nt* wonder, marvel; amazing event

mīrandus, a, um *adj* remarkable

mīrātor, **ōris** *m* admirer

mīrificus, **a**, **um** *adj* wonderful; amazing

mīror ① *v dep* wonder at, be amazed (at); admire

mīrus, **a**, **um** *adj* wonderful, astonishing

misceō, **mixtum/mistum** ② *v* mix, mingle; embroil; confound; stir up

misellus, **a**, **um** *adj* poor, wretched

miser, **era**, **erum** *adj* wretched, unfortunate, miserable; distressing

miserābilis, **e** *adj* pitiable; wretched

miserātiō, **ōnis** *f* pity, compassion

miserē *adv* wretchedly; desperately

misereor ② *v dep* pity
□ **mē miseret**, **miserētur** ② *v impers with gen* it distresses me (for); I pity

miserēscō ③ *v with gen* have compassion (on)

miseria, **ae** *f* wretchedness, misery; distress; woe

misericordia, **ae** *f* pity, compassion; pathos

misericors, **rdis** *adj* merciful, tender-hearted

miseror ① *v dep* feel sorry for

missa, **ae** *f* [LM] Mass, Eucharist; dismissal

missilis, **e** *adj* that may be thrown, missile

missiō, **ōnis** *f* sending (away); release; discharge (of soldiers); reprieve

missitō ① *v* send repeatedly

missus, **ūs** *m* sending (away); despatch; shooting, discharge of missiles

mītēscō ③ *v* become soft and mellow; ripen; grow mild; soften

mītigō ① *v* soften; lighten, alleviate; soothe; civilize

mītis, **e** *adj* mild; sweet and juicy, mellow; placid; soothing; clement

mitra, **ae** *f* an oriental head-dress

mittō, **mīsī**, **missum** ③ *v* send; cast, hurl; throw away; dismiss; disregard, say nothing of; subject (to)
□ **manū** ～ set free, manumit

mnēmosynum, **ī** *nt* souvenir

mōbilis, **e** *adj* quick, active; movable; changeable; inconstant

mōbilitās, **ātis** *f* agility, quickness of mind; mobility; inconstancy

moderābilis, **e** *adj* controllable

moderāmen, **inis** *nt* rudder; management, government

moderātiō, **ōnis** *f* moderation; guidance, government

moderātor, **ōris** *m* governor, master; user; one who restrains

moderātus, **a**, **um** *adj* moderate; restrained; sober; temperate

moderor ① *v dep* guide; control; regulate; govern

modestia, **ae** *f* restraint, temperateness; discipline; modesty

modestus, **a**, **um** *adj* restrained, mild; modest; reserved; disciplined

modicus, **a**, **um** *adj* moderate; temperate, restrained

modius, **(i)ī** *m* Roman dry measure, peck

modo *adv* only; just now; provided that; if only
□ **modo** ... **modo** at one time ... at another

modulor ① *v dep* sing; play; set to music

modus, **ī** *m* measure; size; rhythm; metre; mode; manner; bound, limit; end; moderation

moecha, **ae** *f* adulteress

moechor ① *v dep* commit adultery

moechus, **ī** *m* adulterer

moenia, **ium** *ntpl* town walls, fortified town

mola, **ae** *f* millstone; *pl* mill; cake of ground barley and salt (for sacrifices); sacrificial meal

molāris, **is** *m* rock as large as a millstone used as a missile; molar tooth

mōlēs, **lis** *f* huge, heavy mass, lump; monster; massive structure; danger; trouble; effort; vast undertaking

molestus, **a**, **um** *adj* troublesome, tiresome

mōlīmen, **inis** *nt* effort, vehemence; bulk; weight

mōlīmentum, **ī** *nt* exertion, labour

mōlior ④ *v dep* labour to bring about; strive; labour at, perform with effort; propel, set in motion; build

mollēscō ③ *v* become soft; become gentle *or* effeminate

molliculus, **a**, **um** *adj* soft, delicate; somewhat unmanly

molliō ④ *v* soften; mitigate; make easier; tame, enfeeble

mollis, e *adj* soft, tender, mild; mellow; pleasant; weak; effeminate; impressionable; sensitive

mollitia, ae *f*, **mollitiēs, iēī** *f* softness; tenderness; weakness; effeminacy

molō, luī ③ *v* grind

mōmen, inis *nt* movement; impulse; a trend

mōmentum, ī *nt* movement, impulse; effort; moment; importance; influence

momordī ▶ mordeō

monachus, i *m* ⬛ monk

monasterium, (i)i *nt* ⬛ monastery

monazon, ontis *m* ⬛ monk

monēdula, ae *f* jackdaw

moneō ② *v* warn; advise; presage

moneta, ae *m* ⬛ money

monial, lis *f* ⬛ nun

monīle, is *nt* necklace, collar; collar (for horses and other animals)

monimentum ▶ monumentum

monitiō, ōnis *f* advice; warning

monitor, ōris *m* counsellor, preceptor; prompter

monitus, ūs *m* warning, command; advice, counsel

mōns, ntis *m* mountain; towering heap; huge rock

mōnstrātor, ōris *m* guide, demonstrator

mōnstrō ① *v* show, point out; teach; reveal

mōnstrum, ī *nt* unnatural thing *or* event regarded as on omen, portent, sign; monstrous thing; monster; atrocity

mōnstruōsus, a, um *adj* strange, monstrous, ill-omened

montānus, a, um *adj* mountain...; mountainous
 ▪ **montānus, ī** *m* mountain- or hill-dweller

monticola, ae *m/f* mountain-dweller

montuōsus, a, um *adj* mountainous

monumentum, ī *nt* memorial, monument; tomb; record; a literary work, book; history

mora, ae *f* delay; hindrance, obstacle

morātor, ōris *m* delayer; loiterer

mōrātus, a, um *adj* endowed with character *or* manners of a specified kind; gentle, civilized

morbidus, a, um *adj* diseased; unhealthy

morbus, ī *m* sickness, disease, illness, distress; weakness, vice

mordāx, ācis *adj* biting, snappish; tart; cutting, sharp; caustic

mordeō, momordī, morsum ② *v* bite; sting; hurt, distress; vex; criticize, carp at

mordicus *adv* by biting, with the teeth; tenaciously

moribundus, a, um *adj* dying

mōrigerus, era, erum *adj* compliant, indulgent

morior, morī, mortuus sum ③ *v dep* die; fail; decay

moror ① *v dep* delay, stay behind; devote attention to

mōrōsus, a, um *adj* hard to please, pernickety

mors, mortis *f* death; corpse; annihilation

morsus, ūs *m* bite; sting; anguish, pain

mortālis, e *adj* mortal; transient; human; of human origin

mortālitās, ātis *f* mortality; death

mortārium, (i)ī *nt* mortar

mortifer, mortiferus, era, erum *adj* death-bringing, deadly

mortuus, a, um *adj* dead, deceased

mōrum, ī *nt* fruit of the black mulberry

mōrus, ī *f* black mulberry-tree

mōs, mōris *m* custom, usage; manner; style; civilization; law
 ▪ **mōrēs** *pl* character; behaviour; morals
 ▫ **gerō mōrem** *with dat* gratify, accommodate oneself to; behave

mōtō ① *v* set in motion, shake, stir, *etc.*

mōtus, ūs *m* moving, motion; commotion; disturbance; emotion; prompting; manoeuvre

moveō, mōvī, mōtum ② *v* move, stir; brandish; agitate; affect; provoke; set in motion; shift; influence

mox *adv* soon, next in position

mucrō, ōnis *m* sharp point; sword

mūcus, ī *m* mucus, snot

mūgil, mūgilis, lis *m* grey mullet

mūgiō ④ *v* low, bellow; make a loud deep noise

mūgītus, ūs *m* lowing, bellowing; roaring, rumble

mūla, ae *f* she-mule; mule

mulceō, lsī, lsum ② *v* stroke, touch lightly; soothe, appease; charm, beguile

Mulciber, eris/erī *m* Vulcan; fire

mulcō ① *v* beat up; worst

mulctra, ae *f*, **mulctrum, ī** *nt* milking-pail

mulgeō, lsī, lsum/lctum ② *v* milk

muliebris, bre *adj* womanly, female, feminine; womanish, effeminate
□ **muliebria patī** be used as a catamite

mulier, eris *f* woman; wife, mistress

muliercula, ae *f* (little, weak, foolish, *etc.*) woman

mūliō, ōnis *m* muleteer, mule-driver

mullus, ī *m* red mullet

mulsum, ī *nt* drink from honey and wine

multa, ae *f* fine; penalty

multicavus, a, um *adj* porous

multifāriam *adv* in many places

multifidus, a, um *adj* splintered

multigenus, a, um *adj* of many different sorts

multimodīs *adv* in many different ways

multiplex, icis *adj* having many windings; having many layers *or* thicknesses; multifarious; changeable

multiplicō ① *v* multiply; increase

multitūdō, inis *f* great number, multitude; crowd; mob

multivolus, a, um *adj* that lusts after many, amorous

multō¹ *adv* much, by far; long (before or after)

multō² ① *v* punish; fine

multum *adv* much, plenty

multus, a, um *adj* much, great; many a; large, intense; assiduous; tedious

mūlus, ī *m* mule

munditia, ae *f*, **munditiēs, iēī** *f* cleanness, elegance of appearance, manners *or* taste

mundus¹, ī *m* toilet, ornaments; world; universe

mundus², a, um *adj* clean, elegant; delicate, refined

mūnia, ōrum *ntpl* duties, functions

mūniceps, ipis *m* citizen of a municipium; native of the same municipium

mūnicipālis, e *adj* of, belonging to *or* typical of a **municipium**; (in contempt) provincial

mūnicipium, (i)ī *nt* town subject to Rome, but governed by its own laws; free town

mūnificentia, ae *f* bountifulness, munificence

mūnificus, a, um *adj* bountiful, liberal, munificent

mūnīmen, inis *nt* fortification; defence

mūnīmentum, ī *nt* fortification; bulwark; defence

mūniō ④ *v* fortify; build (a road); defend; safeguard

mūnītiō, ōnis *f* fortifying; fortification; repair

mūnītor, ōris *m* one who builds fortifications

mūnus, eris *nt* function, duty; gift; public show

mūnusculum, ī *nt* small present *or* favour

mūrālis, e *adj* of walls; of *or* connected with a (city) wall; turreted

mūrena, ae *f* kind of eel, the moray

mūrex, icis *m* purple dye; purple cloth

murmur, ris *nt* murmur, murmuring; humming; growling; whisper; rustling; roaring (of the sea, a lion *or* the thunder)

murmurō ① *v* hum, murmur, mutter; roar

murreus, a, um *adj* having the colour of myrrh, *i.e.* reddish-brown

mūrus, ī *m* wall; city wall

mūs, ris *m* mouse

Mūsa, ae *f* Muse; poetic composition
■ **Mūsae** *pl* sciences, poetry

musca, ae *f* fly

muscārium, (i)ī *nt* fly-swat

muscōsus, a, um *adj* mossy

mūsculus, ī *m* mouse; mussel

muscus, ī *m* moss

mūsicē *adv* musically; luxuriously

mūsicus, ī *m* musician

mussitō ① *v* mutter; keep quiet (about)

mussō ① *v* say in an undertone, mutter; keep quiet (about)

mustēla, **mustella**, **ae** *f* weasel

mustum, **ī** *nt* unfermented grape-juice, must

mūtābilis, **e** *adj* changeable; inconstant

mūtātiō, **ōnis** *f* changing; exchange

mutilō ① *v* maim, mutilate; lop off

mutilus, **a**, **um** *adj* mutilated; hornless, having stunted horns

mūtō ① *v* alter, change; exchange; shift; substitute (for)

muttiō ④ *v* mutter, murmur

mūtuātiō, **ōnis** *f* borrowing

mūtuor ① *v dep* borrow

mūtus, **a**, **um** *adj* silent, dumb, mute; speechless

mūtuus, **a**, **um** *adj* borrowed, lent; mutual, in return
■ **mūtuum**, **ī** *nt* loan

myoparōn, **nis** *m* light naval vessel

myrīcē, **ēs** *f* tamarisk (bush)

myrtētum, **ī** *nt* myrtle-grove

myrteus, **a**, **um** *adj* of myrtle

myrtum, **ī** *nt* myrtle-berry

myrtus, **ī** *f* myrtle, myrtle-tree

mystērium, **(i)ī** *nt* sacred mystery; secret

mysticus, **a**, **um** *adj* belonging to the sacred mysteries; mysterious

Nn

naevus, **ī** *m* mole (on the body); birth-mark

Nāias, **adis** *f*, **Nāis**, **idos** *f* water-nymph; nymph

nam *conj* for

namque *conj* certainly; for; now, well then

nancīscor, **nactus/nānctus sum** ③ *v dep* get, obtain, receive; meet with

nānus, **ī** *m* dwarf

narcissus, **ī** *m* the flower narcissus

nardum, **ī** *nt*, **nardus**, **ī** *f* nard; nard-oil

nāris, **is** *f* nose
■ **nārēs**, **ium** *pl* nostrils; nose

nārrābilis, **e** *adj* that can be narrated

nārrātiō, **ōnis** *f* narrative, story

nārrātus, **ūs** *m* narrative, story

nārrō ① *v* tell, narrate; describe, tell about

nāscor, **nātus sum** ③ *v dep* be born; proceed (from), rise; grow

nāsus, **ī** *m* nose; sense of smelling

nāsūtus, **a**, **um** *adj* having a long nose

nāta, **ae** *f* daughter

nātālēs, **ium** *mpl* parentage, origins

nātālis, **e** *adj* of *or* belonging to birth, natal; native
■ ∼, **is** *m* birthday
■ **natale**, **is** *nt* [LM] feastday, esp. Christmas

natātor, **ōris** *m* swimmer

natēs, **ium** *fpl* buttocks

nātiō, **ōnis** *f* race, nation, people; class, set

nativitas, **tatis** *f* [LM] Christmas

nātīvus, **a**, **um** *adj* innate; natural, native

natō ① *v* swim; float; be inundated; sway, lack firmness, waver

nātūra, **ae** *f* nature; character
□ **rērum** ∼ the way things happen

nātūrālis, **e** *adj* natural; innate

nātus, **a**, **um** *adj* born
■ ∼ *m/f* son, daughter; *pl* children, offspring

nātū *adv* by birth
□ ∼ **maior** older
□ ∼ **minor** younger

nauarchus, **ī** *m* commander of a warship

naucum, **ī** *nt* a thing of trifling value

naufragium, **(i)ī** *nt* shipwreck; ruin; wreckage

naufragus, **a**, **um** *adj* shipwrecked; causing shipwreck; ruined

naupēgus, **ī** *m* shipwright

m

n

nausea, **ae** *f* sea-sickness; nausea

nauseō ① *v* be sea-sick; feel sick

nauta, **ae** *m* sailor, seaman

nauticus, **a**, **um** *adj* nautical
■ **nauticī**, **ōrum** *mpl* seamen, sailors

nāvālis, **e** *adj* nautical, naval
■ **nāvāle**, **is** *nt* dock, slipway

nāvicula, **ae** *f* little ship, boat

nāviculārius, **(i)ī** *m* ship-owner

nāvifragus, **a**, **um** *adj* shipwrecking

nāvigābilis, **e** *adj* navigable, suitable for shipping

nāvigātiō, **ōnis** *f* sailing, sea-voyage

nāviger, **era**, **erum** *adj* ship-bearing, navigable

nāvigium, **(i)ī** *nt* vessel, ship

nāvigō ① *v* sail, navigate

nāvis, **is** *f* ship
□ ~ **longa** ship of war
□ ~ **onerāria** merchant ship
□ **nāvem solvō** set sail

nāvita ▶ **nauta**

nāviter *adv* diligently; wholly

nāvō ① *v* devote oneself to; accomplish
□ **operam** ~ devote energies to

nāvus, **a**, **um** *adj* active, industrious

nē *particle* (*usu only with* **ego**, **tu**, **ille**, **iste** *or* **hic**) (affirmative) verily; indeed

-ne *particle in direct questions* interrogative not implying anything about the answer expected e.g. **vidēsne** do you see? *in indirect questions* whether

> 🛈 Attached to the end of the first word of a sentence, which is usu. emphatic, **-ne** introduces a factual yes/no question, e.g. **mēne timēs?** 'do you fear me?' or, if one takes **mē** as emphatic because it is in first position, 'am I the one you fear?'. In double questions, **-ne** may be used instead of **utrum**.

nē *adv/conj* not; that not; in order that not; lest

> 🛈 The neg. conj. **nē** introduces several different types of clause, all of which contain a subj. verb.
> ⋯⟶ **nē** regularly introduces neg. purpose clauses and neg. indirect commands (prohibitions).

⋯⟶ In main clauses, **nē** with a 2sg. or pl. pf. subj. expresses a neg. direct command; **nē** with the pres. subj. (rarely 2sg. or pl.) expresses a neg. direct command.

⋯⟶ **nē** introduces positive fear clauses, e.g. **timeō nē Rōma dēleātur** 'I am afraid Rome may be destroyed'; in this construction **nē** may itself be negated with **nōn**.

⋯⟶ **nē** may replace **quōminus** after positive verbs meaning 'prevent, hinder'.

⋯⟶ After any use of **nē**, the words for 'some-, any-' are **quis** and its adj. **quī** *etc.*

□ ~ ... **quidem** not even

nebula, **ae** *f* mist, fog; cloud

nebulō, **ōnis** *m* rascal, scoundrel

nec *adv/conj* (also **neque**) neither; nor; and not
□ **nec nōn** and also
□ **nec** ... **nec** neither ... nor

> 🛈 **nec** replaces **et** before a clause containing a negative. If the negative is **nōn**, it is then omitted, while **nihil**, **nēmō**, **nūllus**, **nusquam** and **numquam** are replaced by **quicquam**, **quisquam**, **ūllus**, **usquam** and **umquam** respectively.

necdum *conj* and (but) not yet

necessārius, **a**, **um** *adj* necessary; indispensable; connected by close ties of friendship, relationship *or* obligation
■ ~, **(i)ī** *m* close relative; near friend

necesse *adv* essential; inevitable

necessitās, **ātis** *f* necessity; constraint; poverty

necessitūdō, **inis** *f* obligation, affinity; compulsion

necessum ▶ **necesse**

necne *conj* or not

> 🛈 Found almost exclusively in indirect questions, **necne** is the reported equivalent of the **annōn** normally used in direct questions.

necnōn *conj strong affirmative* (and) also, (and) furthermore

necō ① *v* kill

necopīnāns, ntis *adj* not expecting; unawares

necopīnātus, a, um *adj*, **necopīnus, a, um** *adj* unexpected, unforeseen

nectar, aris *nt* nectar, the drink of the gods; anything sweet, pleasant *or* delicious

nectareus, a, um *adj* sweet as nectar

nectō, nex(u)ī, nexum ③ *v* bind, tie *or* join together, link; contrive

nēcubi *adv* (so) that at no place, lest at any place; (so) that on no occasion, lest on any occasion

nēcunde *adv* (so) that from nowhere, lest from anywhere

nēdum *conj* still less; not to speak of; much more

nefandus, a, um *adj* impious, wicked; abominable

nefārius, a, um *adj* offending against moral law, wicked

nefās *nt indec* sin, crime (against divine law); wicked action; portent, horror
■ **nefās!** *int* oh horror!

nefāstus, a, um *adj* contrary to divine law
□ **diēs nefāstī** days unfit for public business

negitō ① *v* deny *or* refuse repeatedly

neglegēns, ntis *adj* heedless, neglectful

neglegentia, ae *f* heedlessness, neglect

neglegō, negligō, ēxī, ēctum ③ *v* not to heed, neglect; overlook; do without

negō ① *v* say no, deny; refuse, decline; say … not

> ❗ **negō** replaces **dīcō** in introducing a negated indirect statement. After **negō**, negatives like **nēmō, nūllus** etc. are replaced by words meaning 'any', e.g. **quisquam, ūllus** etc.

negōtiātor, ōris *m* wholesale trader *or* dealer

negōtior ① *v dep* do business, trade

negōtiōsus, a, um *adj* active, occupied

negōtium, (i)ī *nt* business; difficulty; trouble; situation

nēmō *m/f* no one, nobody
□ ~ **nōn** every(one)

> ❗ **nēmō** has irreg. declension: acc. **nēminem**, gen. **nūllĭus**, dat. **nēminī**, abl. **nūllō**.

nemorālis, e *adj* belonging to a wood *or* forest, sylvan

nemorivagus, a, um *adj* forest-roving

nemorōsus, a, um *adj* well-wooded

nempe *conj* without doubt; why, clearly; admittedly

nemus, oris *nt* wood, forest

nēnia, ae *f* funeral dirge sung; incantation, jingle

neō, nēvī, nētum ② *v* spin; weave; produce by spinning

nepōs, ōtis *m* grandson; descendant; spendthrift, playboy
■ **nepōtēs** *pl* descendants

neptis, is *f* granddaughter; female descendant

Neptūnus, ī *m* Neptune; sea

nēquam *adj indec* worthless; bad

> ❗ **nēquam** is indeclinable, but has comp. **nēquior** and sup. **nēquissimus** which decline regularly.

n

nēquāquam *adv* by no means, not at all

neque *adv/conj* neither; nor; and not
□ **neque … neque** neither … nor

> ❗ A variant of **nec**, often used for reasons of euphony, **neque** was supplanted by **nec** in more colloquial and/or later authors.

nequedum ▶ **necdum**

nequeō, īre, īvī *v ir* be unable (to)

nēquicquam, nēquīquam *adv* in vain

nēquiter *adv* badly; wickedly

nēquitia, ae *f*, **nēquitiēs, iēī** *f* (moral) badness, vice; villainy; naughtiness

Nērēis, idos *f* sea-nymph

Nēreus, ei/eos *m* Nereus; the sea

nervōsus, a, um *adj* sinewy; vigorous

nervus, **ī** *m* sinew; nerve; bow-string; string (of a lute, *etc.*); fetter; strength, vigour

nesciŏ ④ *v* not to know; be unfamiliar with

> ❗ The 'o' of the 1sg. pres. indic. act. is often short in this verb.

nescioquis, **quid** *pn* someone or other

nescius, **a**, **um** *adj* not knowing, ignorant

neu ▶ **nēve**

neuter, **tra**, **trum** *adj* neither (of two)

neutrō *adv* to neither side

nēve *adv* and not, nor, and that not
□ **nēve/neu** ... **nēve/neu** neither ... nor

nex, **cis** *f* violent death, murder

nexilis, **e** *adj* woven together, intertwined

nexum, **ī** *nt*, **nexus**, **ūs** *m* obligation between creditor and debtor

nexus, **ī** *m* one reduced to quasi-slavery for debt, bondman

nī *adv/conj* if ... not; unless
□ **quid** ∼? why not?

nictō ① *v* blink

nīdāmenta, **ōrum** *ntpl* materials for a nest

nīdor, **ōris** *m* rich, strong smell, fumes

nīdulus, **ī** *m* little nest

nīdus, **ī** *m* nest; set of nestlings; eyrie

niger, **gra**, **grum** *adj* black, dark; discoloured, sombre; ill-omened

nigrāns, **ntis** *adj* black, dark-coloured; shadowy; murky

nigrēscō, **ruī** ③ *v* become black, grow dark

nigrō ① *v* be black

nihil *nt indec* nothing; *adv* not at all

nihilōminus *adv* nevertheless, notwithstanding

nihilum¹ *adv* nothing as yet

nihilum², **ī** *nt* nothing
□ **dē nihilō** for nothing; for no reason

nīl *nt indec* [contraction of **nihil**] nothing

nimbōsus, **a**, **um** *adj* full of, *or* surrounded by, rain clouds

nimbus, **ī** *m* rain-cloud; cloud; cloud-burst; shower

nimiō *adv* by a very great degree, far

nīmīrum *adv* without doubt, evidently, forsooth

nimis *adv* too much; exceedingly

nimium *adv* too much, too, very much

nimius, **a**, **um** *adj* excessive, too great, too much; intemperate; over-confident

ningit, **nīnxit** ③ *v impers* it snows

nisi *conj* if not; unless

> ❗ **nisi** follows the same construction as **sī**.

nīsus, **ūs** *m* resting one's weight on the ground; endeavour; exertion; strong muscular effort; advance

niteō ② *v* shine, glitter; be sleek and plump

nitēscō ③ *v* begin to shine

nitidus, **a**, **um** *adj* shining, glittering, bright; polished; spruce; sleek

nītor, **nīsus/nīxus sum** ③ *v dep* lean *or* rest (on); endeavour; exert oneself; rely (on)

nitor, **ōris** *m* brightness, splendour; beauty; elegance, smartness

nivālis, **e** *adj* snowy, snow-covered; snow-like

niveus, **a**, **um** *adj* snowy; snow-white

nivōsus, **a**, **um** *adj* full of snow, snowy

nix, **nivis** *f* snow; white hair

nixus, **ūs** *m* straining; *pl* the efforts of childbirth, travail

nō ① *v* swim; float

nōbilis, **e** *adj* famous, celebrated; high-born; superior
■ ∼, **is** *m* nobleman

nōbilitās, **ātis** *f* renown, glory; high birth; excellence; nobleness

nōbilitō ① *v* make known; render famous; render notorious

noceō ② *v with dat* hurt, injure, impair

noctivagus, **a**, **um** *adj* night-wandering

noctū *adv* by night, at night

noctua, **ae** *f* the little owl

nocturnus, **a**, **um** *adj* nocturnal; under conditions of night

nōdō ① *v* tie in a knot *or* knots

nōdōsus, **a**, **um** *adj* tied into many knots, full of knots; knotty

nōdus, **ī** *m* knot; rope; difficulty; intricacy; bond

nōlo, **nōlle**, **nōluī** *v ir* not to wish; be unwilling; refuse

> **!** The imperatives of **nōlō** are used with infinitives to give direct neg. commands, e.g. **nōlīte venīre** 'don't come'.

nōmen, **inis** *nt* name; family; celebrity

nōmenc(u)lātor, **ōris** *m* slave whose duty it was to attend his master and inform him of the names of those he met; announcer

nōminātim *adv* by name, expressly

nōminātiō, **ōnis** *f* naming; nomination (to an office)

nōminitō ① *v* name, term

nōminō ① *v* name; nominate; accuse, mention, speak of, make famous

nōn *adv* not

nona, **ae** *f* [LM] none(s), afternoon prayers

Nōnae, **ārum** *fpl* the Nones; the fifth day of the month, except in March, May, July, and October, when the Nones fell on the seventh day

nōnāgintā *adj indec* ninety

nōnānus, **a**, **um** *adj* of the ninth legion

nōndum *adv* not yet

nōngentī, **ae**, **a** *adj* nine hundred

nōnne *particle* is it not the case that …?

> **!** **nōnne** introduces direct yes/no questions of the form 'isn't X the case?' or 'surely X is the case, isn't it?': these tend to expect the answer 'yes', e.g., **nōnne nōs amātis?** 'don't you love us?'. In indirect questions, **nōnne** is usu. reported by **num**.

nōnnēmō *m/f* some persons, a few

nōnnihil *nt indec* a certain amount *adv* in some measure

nōnnūllus, **a**, **um** *adj* not a little; some, several

nōnnunquam *adv* sometimes

nōnus, **a**, **um** *adj* the ninth

norma, **ae** *f* carpenter's square; standard, pattern

nōs *pn* we

nōscitō ① *v* recognize; be acquainted with

nōscō, **nōvī**, **nōtum** ③ *v* get a knowledge of, learn to know; know

noster, **tra**, **trum** *adj* our, our own, ours; one of us, our friend; favourable to us; dear, good

nota, **ae** *f* mark, sign; letter; word; writing; spot; brand, tattoo-mark

notābilis, **e** *adj* remarkable, notable

notārius, **(i)ī** *m* secretary, shorthand writer

notātiō, **ōnis** *f* marking

nōtēscō, **tuī** ③ *v* become known; become famous

nothus, **a**, **um** *adj* spurious; illegitimate; (of animals) cross-bred

nōtiō, **ōnis** *f* judicial examination *or* enquiry

nōtitia, **ae** *f*, **nōtitiēs**, **iēī** *f* celebrity; knowledge; conception; acquaintance; carnal knowledge

notō ① *v* mark; write down; observe; censure; brand, stain, scar

Notus, **Notos**, **ī** *m* south wind

nōtus, **a**, **um** *adj* known; notorious; familiar

novācula, **ae** *f* razor

novāle, **is** *nt*, **novālis**, **is** *f* fallow-land; enclosed land, field

novellus, **a**, **um** *adj* young, tender

novem *adj indec* nine

November, **Novembris**, **bris** *m* November

novendiālis, **e** *adj* lasting nine days; held on the ninth day after a person's death

novēnus, **a**, **um** *adj* nine each; nine at a time

noverca, **ae** *f* stepmother

novercālis, **e** *adj* of a stepmother

novīcius, **a**, **um** *adj* new, new kind of

noviē(n)s *adv* nine times

novissimus, **a**, **um** *adj* last, rear; most recent; utmost

novitās, **ātis** *f* newness, novelty; unfamiliarity, surprise

novō ① *v* make new, renew; alter

novus, **a**, **um** *adj* new; young, fresh, recent
   □ ∼ **homō** first in one's family to attain the consulate

nox, **noctis** *f* night; darkness; blindness
   □ **nocte/noctū** by night

noxa, **ae** *f* hurt, injury; crime; punishment; harm

noxia, **ae** *f* wrongdoing, injury

noxius, **a**, **um** *adj* harmful, noxious; guilty, criminal

nūbēs, **bis** *f* cloud; smoke; swarm; gloominess; threat (of war, calamity, *etc.*)

nūbifer, **era**, **erum** *adj* cloud-capped; that brings clouds

nūbigena, **ae** *m* cloud-born

nūbilis, **e** *adj* marriageable; nubile

nūbilus, **a**, **um** *adj* cloudy; lowering ■ **nūbilum**, **ī** *nt* cloudy sky *or* weather

nūbō, **psī**, **ptum** ③ *v with dat* marry (a husband)

nudius *adv* [from **nunc** and **diēs**]: □ ~ **tertius** (by Roman reckoning) the day before yesterday

nūdō ① *v* bare; strip, uncover; plunder; reveal, disclose

nūdus, **a**, **um** *adj* naked, bare; destitute; unarmed

nūgae, **ārum** *fpl* trifles, nonsense; trash; frivolities; bagatelle

nūgātor, **ōris** *m* one who plays the fool; teller of tall stories

nūgātōrius, **a**, **um** *adj* trifling, worthless, futile, paltry

nūgor ① *v dep* play the fool, talk nonsense; trifle

nullatenus *adv* [LM] by no means

nūllus, **a**, **um** *adj* not any, no

num *particle* is it the case that …?; *in indirect questions* whether

> ❗ **num** introduces direct yes/no questions of the form 'is X the case?' or 'surely X isn't the case, is it?': these tend to expect the answer 'no', e.g. **num tū timēs?** 'surely you aren't afraid, are you?'. In indirect questions, **num** may reflect either **num** or **nōnne** from the direct question actually asked, and implies no expected answer. Wherever **num** is used, the words for 'some-, any-' are **quis** and its adj. **quī** etc.

nūmen, **inis** *nt* nod; bias; divine will; divine presence; deity, god

numerābilis, **e** *adj* possible *or* easy to count

numerō ① *v* count, number

numerōsus, **a**, **um** *adj* numerous; harmonious

numerus, **erī** *m* number; rhythm; poetry, metre; class

nummātus, **a**, **um** *adj* moneyed

nummus, **ī** *m* coin, money

numquam *adv* at no time, never; not in any circumstances

nūmus ▶ **nummus**

nunc *adv* now, at present □ **nunc** … **nunc** one time … another time

nunciam *adv* here and now; now at last

nuncupō ① *v* call, name; express

nūndinae, **ārum** *fpl* market-day; (fig) traffic

nūndinor ① *v dep* buy *or* sell in the market; practise trade of a discreditable kind

nūndinum, **ī** *nt* the period from one market-day to the next

nunquam ▶ **numquam**

nūntiō ① *v* announce; relate, inform

nūntius, **a**, **um** *adj* bringing tidings, reporting ■ ~, **(i)ī** *m* messenger; message

nūper *adv* recently, not long ago; in modern times

nūpta, **ae** *f* wife, married woman

nūptiae, **ārum** *fpl* marriage

nūptiālis, **e** *adj* nuptial

nurus, **ūs** *f* daughter-in-law; young woman

nusquam *adv* nowhere, in no place; to no place; on no occasion □ **nusquam esse** not exist

nūtō ① *v* nod; sway to and fro; waver; waver in allegiance

nūtrīcius, **(i)ī** *m* tutor; foster-father

nūtrīcula, **ae** *f* nurse

nūtrīmen, **inis** *nt*, **nūtrīmentum**, **ī** *nt* nourishment, sustenance

nūtriō ④ *v* suckle, nourish, foster, bring up; tend; deal gently with

nūtrīx, **īcis** *f* wet-nurse, nurse

nūtus, **ūs** *m* nod; will, command

nux, **cis** *f* nut; thing of no value

nympha, **ae** *f*, **nymphē**, **ēs** *f* nymph, young wife, maiden

Oo

ō *int* o! oh!
□ ~ **sī** if only

ob *prep with acc* for; by reason of; on behalf of; in payment for

obaerātus, a, um *adj* involved in debt
■ ~, **ī** *m* debtor

obambulō 1 *v* walk up to, so as to meet; traverse

obarmō 1 *v* arm

obarō 1 *v* plough up

obc- ▶ **occ-**

obdō, didī, ditum 3 *v* put before *or* against; shut; expose to danger

obdormiō 4 *v*, **obdormīscō** 3 *v* fall asleep, sleep off

obdūcō, dūxī, uctum 3 *v* lead *or* draw before; cover *or* lay over; overspread; wrinkle; screen

obdūrēscō, ī 3 *v* be persistent, endure

obdūrō 1 *v* persist, endure

obeō, īre, iī/īvī, itum *v ir* meet with; visit; review; enclose; accept; die; set

obequitō 1 *v* ride up to

obēsus, a, um *adj* fat, stout, plump

obex, icis *m/f* bolt, bar; barrier; obstacle

obf- ▶ **off-**

obiaceō 2 *v* lie at hand

obiciō, iēcī, iectum 3 *v* throw before *or* towards; expose (to); interpose; lay to one's charge

> **!** The first syllable of this verb scans as heavy in the present stem even though the 'o' is short; this is because the 'i' represents 'ii' pronounced as consonant + vowel 'yi'.

obiectō 1 *v* expose (to); lay to one's charge

obiectus, ūs *m* placing something in the way of; barrier

obīrātus, a, um *adj with dat* angry with *or* at

obitus, ūs *m* approaching; approach, visit; setting (of the sun, *etc.*); death

obiurgō 1 *v* chide; rebuke

oblectāmen, inis *nt*, **oblectāmentum, ī** *nt* delight, pleasure, source of pleasure

oblectātiō, ōnis *f* delighting

oblectō 1 *v* delight, please, amuse

oblīdō, īsī, īsum 3 *v* squeeze; crush, stifle

obligō 1 *v* bind *or* tie around; swathe, render liable; place under a moral obligation; bind (by oath, *etc.*)

oblīmō 1 *v* cover with mud; silt up

oblinō, lēvī/līvī, litum 3 *v* smear, daub; sully, defame

oblīquus, a, um *adj* slanting, oblique; indirect; zigzag

oblitterō 1 *v* cause to be forgotten

oblīviō, ōnis *f* oblivion; forgetfulness

oblīviōsus, a, um *adj* forgetful, having a bad memory

oblīvīscor, oblītus sum 3 *v dep often with gen* forget

oblīvium, (i)ī *nt* forgetfulness, oblivion

oblongus, a, um *adj* of greater length than breadth, elongated

obloquor, locūtus sum 3 *v dep with dat* interpose remarks, interrupt

obluctor 1 *v dep with dat* struggle against

obmōlior 4 *v dep* put in the way as an obstruction; block up

obmurmurō 1 *v* murmur in protest (at)

obmūtēscō, tuī 3 *v* lose one's speech; become silent

obnītor, nīsus/nīxus sum 3 *v dep* thrust *or* press against; struggle against

obnoxius, a, um *adj* indebted, accountable, subservient (to); exposed to; submissive; vulnerable

obnūbō, psī, ptum 3 *v* veil, cover (the head)

obnūntiō 1 *v* announce adverse omens

o

oboediēns, **ntis** *adj* obedient, submissive

oboediō ④ *v with dat* obey; comply with

oboleō ② *v* smell, stink

oborior, **ortus sum** ④ *v dep* arise, appear *or* spring up before; well up (of tears)

obp- ▶ **opp-**

obrēpō, **psī**, **ptum** ③ *v* creep up to; approach unawares; sneak in

obruō, **ruī**, **rutum** ③ *v* overwhelm; bury; sink; drown; suppress; smother (in)

obsaepiō, **psī**, **ptum** ④ *v* enclose, seal up; block, obstruct

obscēnus, **a**, **um** *adj* inauspicious; repulsive; ill-boding; detestable; foul; obscene (applied to the sexual and excretory parts)

obscūritās, **ātis** *f* darkness; obscurity; unintelligibility

obscūrō ① *v* darken, obscure; conceal; make indistinct; cause to be forgotten

obscūrus, **a**, **um** *adj* dark, shady, obscure; gloomy; uncertain; incomprehensible

obsecrātiō, **ōnis** *f* supplication, entreaty; public act of prayer

obsecrō ① *v* implore; beg
■ **obsecrō (tē)** *int* please

obsequēns, **ntis** *adj with dat* compliant (with)

obsequenter *adv* compliantly; obediently; with deference

obsequium, **(i)ī** *nt* compliance (with), deference; servility; discipline

obsequor, **secūtus sum** ③ *v dep with dat* comply (with), gratify, submit (to)

obserō[1], **ēvī**, **itum** ③ *v* sow, plant; sow (with)

obserō[2] ① *v* bolt, fasten; obstruct

observātiō, **ōnis** *f* observation

observō ① *v* watch, observe; attend to; respect; pay court to

obses, **idis** *m/f* hostage; security, bail

obsessiō, **ōnis** *f* besieging, blockade

obsessor, **ōris** *m* besieger; frequenter

obsideō, **sēdī**, **sessum** ② *v* besiege, blockade; frequent; surround; occupy; throng

obsidiō, **ōnis** *f* siege, blockade

obsidium, **(i)ī** *nt* siege

obsīdō ③ *v* besiege; occupy

obsignō ① *v* seal up; stamp; impress

obsistō, **stitī**, **stitum** ③ *v with dat* stand in the way; resist, oppose; hinder

obsitus, **a**, **um** *adj* overgrown, covered (with)

obsolēscō, **ēvī**, **ētum** ③ *v* fall into disuse; be forgotten about

obsolētus, **a**, **um** *adj* worn-out, dilapidated; hackneyed

obsōnium, **(i)ī** *nt* purchasing of food, getting provisions, catering; dish of food; pension

obsōnō ① *v* buy provisions, furnish an entertainment; feast

obstetrīx, **īcis** *f* midwife

obstinātiō, **ōnis** *f* firmness; stubbornness

obstinātus, **a**, **um** *adj* steady; stubborn

obstinō ① *v* be determined on

obstīpus, **a**, **um** *adj* awry, crooked, bent sideways *or* at an angle

obstō, **stitī** ① *v with dat* stand in the way of; block the path of; withstand; hinder

obstrepō, **puī** ③ *v* roar against; make a loud noise

obstringō, **īnxī**, **ictum** ③ *v* bind, tie *or* fasten up; place under an obligation; involve *or* implicate in

obstruō, **ūxī**, **ūctum** ③ *v* pile before *or* against; block up; stop, stifle

obstupefaciō, **fēcī**, **factum** ③ *v* strike dumb with any powerful emotion, daze; paralyse
□ **obstupefīō**, **fierī** be astonished

obstupēscō, **puī** ③ *v* be stupefied; be struck dumb; be astounded

obsum, **esse**, **obfuī/offuī** *v ir with dat* hurt; be a nuisance to; tell against

obsuō, **uī**, **ūtum** ③ *v* sew up

obtegō, **ēxī**, **ēctum** ③ *v* cover over; conceal; protect

obtemperō ① *v with dat* comply with, obey

obtendō, **ndī**, **ntum** ③ *v* stretch *or* spread before; conceal; plead in excuse

obtentus, **ūs** *m* spreading before; cloaking, disguising, spreading out *or* over as a veil *or* covering; excuse, pretext

obterō, trīvī, trītum ③ *v* crush; destroy; trample on, speak of *or* treat with the utmost contempt

obtestātiō, ōnis *f* earnest entreaty, supplication

obtestor ① *v dep* call upon as a witness; invoke, entreat; aver

obtexō, xuī ③ *v* veil, cover

obticēscō, cuī ③ *v* meet a situation with silence

obtineō, tentum ② *v* hold; support; obtain; gain; prevail

obtingō, igī ③ *v with dat* fall to one's lot; occur to the benefit *or* disadvantage of

obtorpēscō, puī ③ *v* become numb; lose feeling

obtorqueō, rsī, rtum ② *v* bend back; twist *or* turn

obtrectātiō, ōnis *f* detraction, disparagement

obtrectātor, ōris *m* detractor, malicious critic

obtrectō ① *v* detract from; disparage, belittle

obtruncō ① *v* cut to pieces, mutilate, kill

obtueor ② *v dep* look *or* gaze at

obtundō, udī, ūsum ③ *v* strike, beat, batter; make blunt; deafen

obtūsus, a, um *adj* blunt; dull; obtuse

obtūtus, ūs *m* gaze; contemplation

obumbrō ① *v* overshadow; darken; conceal; defend

obuncus, a, um *adj* bent, hooked

obustus, a, um *adj* having the extremity burnt to form a point; scorched by burning

obveniō, vēnī, ventum ④ *v with dat* come to one by chance; happen; fall to the lot of; come up

obversor ① *v dep* appear before one; go to and fro publicly

obvertō, rtī, rsum ③ *v* turn *or* direct towards; direct against

obviam *adv with dat* in the way of; towards, against; at hand
□ ~ **eō** go to meet

obvius, a, um *adj* in the way, easy; hostile; exposed (to)

obvolvō, lvī, lūtum ③ *v* wrap round, muffle up, cover; cloak

occaecō ① *v* blind; darken; conceal

occallēscō, luī ③ *v* become callous; acquire a thick skin

occāsiō, ōnis *f* opportunity, right *or* appropriate time

occāsus, ūs *m* sun-setting, west; ruin, end, death

occidēns, ntis *m* quarter of the setting sun, the west

occīdiō, ōnis *f* massacre; wholesale slaughter

occidō, cidī, cāsum ③ *v* fall down; set (of the sun, *etc.*); die, perish; be ruined

occīdō, īdī, īsum ③ *v* kill, slay

occiduus, a, um *adj* going down, setting; western; declining

occinō, nuī ③ *v* break in with a song *or* call; interpose a call

occipiō, cēpī, ceptum ③ *v* begin

occlūdō, ūsī, ūsum ③ *v* shut up, close; lock

occō ① *v* harrow (ground)

occubō ① *v* lie dead

occulcō ① *v* trample down

occulō, luī, cultum ③ *v* cover up; conceal

occultātiō, ōnis *f* concealment

occultō ① *v* keep hidden, conceal; cover up

occultus, a, um *adj* hidden, concealed

occumbō, cubuī, cubitum ③ *v* meet with (death); meet one's death

occupātiō, ōnis *f* taking possession of; preoccupation with business, *etc.*, employment

occupō ① *v* occupy; seize; reach (a destination); engross

occurrō, (cu)currī, cursum ③ *v with dat* run towards *or* to meet; appear before; counteract; occur

occursō ① *v* run repeatedly *or* in large numbers; mob; obstruct

occursus, ūs *m* meeting

Ōceanus, ī *m* ocean

ocellus, ī *m* (little) eye; darling

ōcior, ius *adj* swifter, more speedy; sooner

ocrea, ae *f* greave, leg-covering

octāvus, a, um *adj* eighth
■ **octāva, ae** *f* 〖LM〗 period of celebration following the major Christian feasts, the eighth day following the feast (reckoned

inclusively), being the end of this period, octave

octingentī, **ae**, **a** *adj* eight hundred

octo *adj indec* eight

Octōber, **bris** *m* October

octōgēnī, **ae**, **a** *adj* eighty each

octōgintā *adj indec* eighty

octōnī, **ae**, **a** *adj* eight each

octuplus, **a**, **um** *adj* eightfold

octussis, **is** *m* eight **asses**

oculārius, **a**, **um** *adj* dealing with the eyes

oculus, **ī** *m* eye; eyesight; bud

ōdī, **isse** *v ir* hate; dislike

odiōsus, **a**, **um** *adj* disagreeable, offensive; tiresome, annoying

odium, **(i)ī** *nt* hatred, spite; unpopularity

odor, **ōris** *m* smell, scent, odour; perfume

odōrātus, **a**, **um** *adj* sweet-smelling, fragrant

odōrifer, **era**, **erum** *adj* fragrant

odōrō ① *v* perfume, make fragrant

odōror ① *v dep* smell out, scent; get a smattering (of)

odōrus, **a**, **um** *adj* odorous, fragrant; keen-scented

oestrus, **trī** *m* gad-fly; wild passion, desire, frenzy

offa, **ae** *f* lump of food, cake

offendō, **ndī**, **ēnsum** ③ *v* strike or dash against; light upon; stumble; offend, displease; upset; harm

offēnsa, **ae** *f* offence, displeasure; offence to a person's feelings; resentment

offēnsiō, **ōnis** *f* striking against, stumbling-block; offence

offēnsō ① *v* knock or strike against, bump into

offēnsus[1], **ūs** *m* collision, knock

offēnsus[2], **a**, **um** *adj* offended; offensive, odious

offerō, **ferre**, **obtulī**, **oblātum** *v ir* bring before; offer; exhibit; bring forwards; inflict; offer one's services

officīna, **ae** *f* workshop

officiō, **fēcī**, **fectum** ③ *v with dat* block the path (of); check; impede

officiōsus, **a**, **um** *adj* dutiful, attentive; officious

officium, **(i)ī** *nt* service; duty; courtesy

offīgō, **īxī**, **īxum** ③ *v* fasten, nail down

offirmō ① *v* secure; make inflexible

offūcia, **ae** *f* paint, wash; make-up

offula, **ae** *f* (small) piece of food (esp. meat)

offulgeō, **lsī** ② *v with dat* shine forth in the path of

offundō, **ūdī**, **ūsum** ③ *v* pour or spread over

ogganniō ④ *v* growl at, snarl

ōh *int* oh! ah!

ohē *int* hey! hey there!

olea, **ae** *f* olive; olive-tree

oleaster, **trī** *m* wild olive-tree

olēns, **ntis** *adj* fragrant; stinking

oleō, **ī** ② *v* smell; smell of; be fragrant; stink

oleum, **ī** *nt* olive-oil; oil

olfaciō, **fēcī**, **factum** ③ *v* smell

olidus, **a**, **um** *adj* stinking

ōlim *adv* formerly, in times past; at a future time, some day; sometimes

olitor, **ōris** *m* vegetable-grower

olitōrius, **a**, **um** *adj* pertaining to vegetables

olīva, **ae** *f* olive; olive-tree; olive-branch; staff of olive-wood

olīvētum, **ī** *nt* olive-yard

olīvifer, **era**, **erum** *adj* olive-bearing

olīvum, **ī** *nt* olive-oil; wrestling

ōlla, **ae** *f* pot, jar

olle, **a**, **ud** *pn* [archaic form of **ille**] he, she; it; that; the well-known; the former

olor, **ōris** *m* swan

olōrīnus, **a**, **um** *adj* belonging to a swan or swans

olus, **eris** *nt* vegetables

ōmen, **inis** *nt* augury, sign, token (of good or bad luck)

ōmentum, **ī** *nt* the fatty membrane covering the intestines

ōminor ① *v dep* forebode, presage

ōminōsus, **a**, **um** *adj* presaging ill; ill-omened

omittō, **mīsī**, **missum** ③ *v* let go; lay aside; give up; neglect; disregard; cease

omnigenus, **a**, **um** *adj* of every kind

omnimodīs *adv* in every way

omnīnō *adv* altogether, utterly; in all; in general

omniparēns, ntis *adj* parent *or* creator of all things

omnipotēns, ntis *adj* almighty

omnis, e *adj* all, every

omnivolus, a, um *adj* that desires all

onager, grī *m* wild ass

onerārius, a, um *adj* that carries loads, cargo, *etc.*
  □ **nāvis onerāria** merchant-ship

onerō ① *v* load, burden, freight; overload; overwhelm; oppress; aggravate

onerōsus, a, um *adj* burdensome, heavy; tiresome

onus, eris *nt* load, burden; affliction, trouble, responsibility

onustus, a, um *adj* laden, burdened, freighted; weighed down

onyx, ychis *m* yellow marble; onyx box

opācō ① *v* shade, overshadow

opācus, a, um *adj* shady; darkened, overshadowed; retired

opalus, ī *m* opal

opella, ae *f* little effort; trifling duties

opera, ae *f* pains, work, labour; task; care, attention, endeavour
  ■ **operam dō** *with dat* apply oneself to; be at the service of, help
  ■ **operae** *pl* labourers; hired rowdies

operīmentum, ī *nt* cover, lid, covering

operiō, ruī, rtum ④ *v* cover over; shut; conceal

operōsus, a, um *adj* painstaking; laborious; elaborate

opertus, a, um *adj* hidden; obscure, secret

opifer, era, erum *adj* bringing help

opifex, icis *m/f* craftsman, artificer; artisan; Ⓛ̲Ⓜ̲ creator

ōpiliō, ōnis *m* shepherd, herdsman

opīmus, a, um *adj* fruitful; rich; sumptuous; plentiful
  □ **spolia opīma** spoils taken by a victorious Roman general from the enemy leader he had killed in single combat

opīniō, ōnis *f* opinion, belief; report, imagination; reputation

opīnor ① *v dep* hold as an opinion, think, believe

opitulor ① *v dep with dat* bring aid to; help; bring relief to

oportet ② *v impers* it is necessary *or* proper (that); it is inevitable that

opperior, per(ī)tus sum ④ *v dep* wait (for); await

oppetō, īvī/iī, ītum ③ *v* meet, encounter; perish

oppidānus, a, um *adj* of *or* in a town (other than Rome); provincial, local
  ■ **oppidānī, ōrum** *mpl* townsmen, townsfolk

oppidō *adv* exceedingly, utterly, altogether

oppidulum, ī *nt* small town

oppidum, ī *nt* town

oppīlō ① *v* stop up, block

oppleō, ēvī, ētum ② *v* fill (completely); overspread

oppōnō, posuī, positum ③ *v* put against *or* before; oppose; pledge; wager; object, say in answer

opportūnitās, ātis *f* convenience, advantageousness; right time; opportuneness; opportunity

opportūnus, a, um *adj* convenient; opportune; advantageous; ready to hand; liable to

opprimō, essī, essum ③ *v* press on *or* against; crush; overpower; beat down; surprise; suppress; conceal, cover

opprobrium, (i)ī *nt* scandal, disgrace; reproach, taunt

opprobrō ① *v* reproach, criticize

oppugnātiō, ōnis *f* assault

oppugnātor, ōris *m* attacker

oppugnō ① *v* attack, assault; batter

ops- ▸ **obs-**

ops, pis *f* power, might, strength, ability, help
  ■ **opēs, opum** *fpl* wealth; resources; assistance

opt- ▸ **obt-**

optābilis, e *adj* desirable

optimās, ātis *m* aristocrat; *pl* the best class of citizens

optimus, a, um *adj* best

optiō¹, ōnis *f* choice

optiō², ōnis *m* junior officer

optō ① *v* choose; wish for, desire

opulentia, ae *f* riches, wealth; sumptuousness

opulentus, a, um *adj* wealthy; abounding with resources; well supplied (with); sumptuous

opus¹, eris *nt* work, effort; structure; *pl* siege-works
□ **maiōre opere** all the more
□ **maximō opere** most urgently

opus² *nt indec* need, necessity
□ **opus est** it is needful
□ **opus est mihi** *with abl of thing needed* I have need of

opusculum, ī *nt* little work, trifle

ōra, ae *f* border, edge; sea-coast, bank; region; climatic region

ōrāculum, ī *nt* oracle

ōrātiō, ōnis *f* speech; conversation; LM prayer

ōrātor, ōris *m* speaker, orator; ambassador; advocate

oratorium, (i)i *nt* LM place of prayer

orbis, is *m* disc, circle; orb; ring; wheel; circuit; the world
□ ~ **terrārum/terrae** the world

orbita, ae *f* wheel-track, rut; orbit

orbitās, ātis *f* bereavement; loss of a child; orphanhood; childlessness

orbō ① *v* bereave (of parents, children, *etc.*), deprive (of)

orbus, a, um *adj* bereaved; parentless, orphan; childless; deprived *or* destitute (of anything)

Orcus, ī *m* the god of the underworld, Dis; death; the underworld

ōrdinārius, a, um *adj* regular; usual

ōrdinātim *adv* in good order

ōrdinō ① *v* set in order, arrange, regulate

ōrdior, ōrsus sum ④ *v dep* begin; undertake; embark on

ōrdō, inis *m* row, regular series; order; class of citizens; arrangement; method; degree; rank; LM monastic order

Orēas, adis *f* mountain-nymph, Oread

orgia, ōrum *ntpl* secret rites (of Bacchus)

orichalcum, ī *nt* yellow copper ore, brass

ōricilla, ae *f* little ear

oriēns, ntis *m* east, orient; daybreak, dawn

orīgō, inis *f* beginning, source; birth, origin

orior, ortus sum ④ *v dep* rise; appear on the scene; arise; begin; be born

oriundus, a, um *adj* descended; originating from

ōrnāmentum, ī *nt* equipment; ornament, decoration, jewel; (mark of) distinction

ōrnātus, ūs *m* military equipment; armour; costume, garb, get-up; adornment

ornātus, a, um *adj* adorned, well-dressed; beautiful

ōrnō ① *v* adorn; honour; praise

ornus, ī *f* ash-tree

ōrō ① *v* plead; pray (to); beseech, supplicate

orsa, ōrum *ntpl* words, utterance

ōrsus *pple* from ▶ **ordior**

ortus¹ *pple* from ▶ **orior**

ortus², ūs *m* rising, sunrise; birth; beginnings, origin

ōs, ōris *nt* mouth; speech; face; assurance

os, ossis *nt* bone

oscen, inis *m* bird which gives omens by its cry; song-bird

ōscillum, ī *nt* a small mask hung on trees

ōscitō ① *v* gape; yawn

ōsculātiō, ōnis *f* kissing

ōsculor ① *v dep* kiss

ōsculum, ī *nt* mouth; kiss

ostendō, ndī, tentum/tēnsum ③ *v* hold out for inspection, show; exhibit; demonstrate; offer

ostentātiō, ōnis *f* exhibition, display; 'showing off'

ostentō ① *v* show off, display; offer

ostentum, ī *nt* prodigy; marvel

ostentus, ūs *m* display; demonstration, advertisement

ōstium, (i)ī *nt* mouth (of a river); entrance; exit; door

ostrea, ae *f* oyster; sea-snail

ostrifer, era, erum *adj* bearing oysters

ostrum, ī *nt* purple; anything dyed purple

ōtior ① *v dep* be at leisure, enjoy a holiday

ōtiōsus, a, um *adj* at leisure, unoccupied; free from public affairs; quiet; free, unemployed; undisturbed (by); superfluous; useless

ōtium, (i)ī *nt* leisure; rest; peace; ease; lull

ōvātus, a, um *adj* egg-shaped, oval

ovīle, is *nt* sheepfold

ovis, is *f* sheep

ovō ① *v* celebrate a minor triumph; exult, rejoice

ovum, ī *nt* egg; wooden balls set up in the Circus, and removed one by one at the completion of each lap
　□ **ab ovō usque ad māla** from the hors d'oeuvre to the dessert, *i.e.* from beginning to end

Pp

pābulātiō, ōnis *f* foraging

pābulātor, ōris *m* forager

pābulor ① *v dep* forage

pābulum, ī *nt* food, nourishment; fodder; food, sustenance

pācālis, e *adj* associated with peace

pācātus, a, um *adj* peaceful, calm

pācifer, era, erum *adj* bringing peace, peaceful

pācificātiō, ōnis *f* peace-making

pācificātor, ōris *m* peace-maker

pācificō ① *v* negotiate about peace, appease

pācificus, a, um *adj* making *or* tending to make peace

pacīscō, pactum ③ *v*, **pacīscor, pactus sum** ③ *v dep* make a bargain *or* agreement; agree, enter into a marriage contract; negotiate

pācō ① *v* impose a settlement on; bring under control

pactiō, ōnis *f* agreement, compact

pactum, ī *nt* agreement, compact; manner, way
　□ **quō pactō?** how?

paeān, nis *m* hymn, hymn usually of victory

paedagōgium, (i)ī *nt* training establishment for slave-boys

paedagōgus, ī *m* slave in charge of children

paedīcō ① *v* commit sodomy with

paedor, ōris *m* filth, dirt

paelex, icis *f* mistress

paene *adv* nearly, almost, practically

paenīnsula, ae *f* peninsula

paenitentia, ae *f* regret; change of mind

paenitet ② *v impers* it gives reason for regret
　□ **mē paenitet** *with gen of thing regretted* I repent (of)

paenula, ae *f* hooded weatherproof cloak

paenulātus, a, um *adj* wearing a paenula

paetus, a, um *adj* having a cast in the eye, squinting slightly

pāgānus, a, um *adj* rustic; civilian

pāgina, ae *f* column *or* page of writing; piece of writing

pāgus, ī *m* country district *or* community

pāla, ae *f* spade

palaestra, ae *f* wrestling-place; gymnastics

palaestricus, a, um *adj* of wrestling

palam *adv/prep with abl* openly, publicly; openly in the presence of

Palātīnus, a, um *adj* the name of one of the hills of Rome, the Palatine

Palātium, (i)ī *nt* the Palatine Hill

palātum, ī *nt* palate; sense of taste

palea, ae *f* chaff, husk

palear, āris *nt* dewlap

Palīlia, ium *ntpl* Feast of Pales (a tutelary deity of sheep and herds) on 21 April

palimpsestum, ī *nt* palimpsest

paliūrus, ī *m* the shrub, Christ's thorn

palla, **ae** *f* rectangular outdoor garment worn by women, mantle of a tragic actor

palleō ② *v* be *or* look pale; fade; become pale at

pallēscō, **luī** ③ *v* grow pale; blanch; fade

pallidulus, **a**, **um** *adj* pale, wan

pallidus, **a**, **um** *adj* pale

palliolum, **ī** *nt* small cloak

pallium, **(i)ī** *nt* rectangular outdoor garment worn by men; bed-cover

pallor, **ōris** *m* paleness, wanness

palma, **ae** *f* palm of the hand; hand; palm-tree; date; oar; victory, first place

palmātus, **a**, **um** *adj* having a palm-leaf pattern

palmes, **itis** *m* vine-branch or -shoot

palmētum, **ī** *nt* palm-grove

palmifer, **era**, **erum** *adj* palm-bearing

palmula, **ae** *f* oar

pālor ① *v dep* wander abroad, stray; scatter; wander aimlessly

palpātor, **ōris** *m* confidence trickster

palpebra, **ae** *f* eyelid

palpitō ① *v* throb, beat, pulsate

palpō ① *v* stroke, caress; act in a soothing manner

palūdāmentum, **ī** *nt* military cloak; general's cloak

palūdātus, **a**, **um** *adj* wearing a military cloak

palūdōsus, **a**, **um** *adj* fenny, boggy, marshy

palumbēs, **bis** *m/f* wood-pigeon, ring-dove

pālus, **ī** *m* stake, prop

palūs, **ūdis** *f* flood-water, fen, swamp

palūster, **tris**, **tre** *adj* marshy; of marshes

pampineus, **a**, **um** *adj* of *or* covered with vine-shoots *or* foliage

pampinus, **ī** *m/f* vine-shoot, vine foliage

pānārium, **(i)ī** *nt* bread basket

pandō, **ndī**, **pānsum/passum** ③ *v* spread out, extend; unfold; reveal

pandus, **a**, **um** *adj* spreading round in a wide curve; arched

pangō, **pepigī/pānxī**, **pāctum** ③ *v* fix; drive in; (fig) settle, stipulate for; conclude; compose

pānicum, **ī** *nt* Italian millet

pānis, **is** *m* bread, loaf; food

pannōsus, **a**, **um** *adj* dressed in rags, tattered

pannus, **ī** *m* cloth, garment; charioteer's coloured shirt; rags

panthēra, **ae** *f* leopard

panticēs, **um** *mpl* belly, paunch, guts

pantomīmus, **ī** *m* mime performer in a pantomime

papa, **ae** *m* [LM] Pope

papāver, **eris** *nt* poppy; poppy-seed

papāvereus, **a**, **um** *adj* of poppy, poppy-

pāpiliō, **ōnis** *m* butterfly, moth

papilla, **ae** *f* nipple, teat, dug (of mammals)

papula, **ae** *f* pimple, pustule

papȳrifer, **era**, **erum** *adj* papyrus-bearing

papȳrum, **ī** *nt*, **papȳrus**, **ī** *f* paper-reed; papyrus

pār, **aris** *adj* equal; fair; fit *m/f* equal; mate, partner *nt* pair; couple

parābilis, **e** *adj* procurable, easily obtainable

parabola, **ae** *f* explanatory illustration, comparison; parable

paramenta, **orum** *npl* [LM] vestments, altar hangings

parasceve, **es** *f* [LM] day of preparation (for the Passover), Good Friday

parasītus, **ī** *m* guest, parasite, sponger, hanger-on; [LM] deceiver

parātus[1], **ūs** *m* preparation; equipment, paraphernalia; attire

parātus[2], **a**, **um** *adj* prepared, ready; equipped

parcō, **pepercī/parsī** ③ *v with dat* act sparingly, be thrifty with; spare; pardon; forbear; refrain from

parcus, **a**, **um** *adj* sparing, economical; niggardly, parsimonious; moderate

parēns, **ntis** *m/f* father, mother, parent; ancestor; originator; producer, source

parentālis, **e** *adj* of *or* belonging to parents

parentō ① *v* perform the rites at the tombs of the dead; make an offering of appeasement (to the dead)

pāreō ② *v* be visible; *with dat* obey; comply with; be subject to; submit to

pariēs, etis *m* wall (of a house)

parilis, e *adj* like, equal

pariō, peperī, par(i)tum ③ *v* bring forth, bear; produce, create; procure, get

pariter *adv* equally, as well; together; in the same manner; simultaneously

parma, ae *f* small round shield

parō ① *v* get ready, prepare, furnish, provide; intend; plan; obtain; buy

parochus, ī *m* commissary

parricīda, ae *m/f* parricide (murderer); murderer of a near relative; traitor

parricīdium, (i)ī *nt* parricide (murder); murder of a near relation, treason, rebellion

pars, rtis *f* part, piece, portion, share; function, office; role; party, side
  ◻ **pars … pars** some … others
  ▪ **partēs, ium** *fpl* party; faction

parsimōnia, ae *f* frugality, thrift, parsimony; temperance

parthenicē, ēs *f* a flower, perhaps camomile

particeps, ipis *adj* sharing in *m/f* participant, sharer

participium, (i)ī *nt* participle

participō ① *v* inform of; share with others in; partake of; make a party to

particula, ae *f* small part, little bit, particle, atom

partim *adv* partly, in part

partiō ④ *v* share, divide up

partior ④ *v dep* share, distribute, divide up

partum, ī *nt* a thing acquired, acquisition

parturiō ④ *v* be in travail *or* labour; bring forth; produce; be pregnant with

partus, ūs *m* bringing forth, birth; foetus, embryo; offspring, progeny

parum *nt indec* used as *adv* too little, not enough; encore!

parumper *adv* for a short while

parvulus, a, um *adj* tiny, small, little, petty, slight

parvus, a, um *adj* little, small, petty, mean; young; cheap

pasceolus, ī *m* small leather purse

pascha, ae *f*, **pascha, atis** *nt* 🄻🄼 Easter

pāscō, pāstum ③ *v* feed, pasture; provide food for; nurture; feast

pascua, ae *f* 🄻🄼 pasture

pāscuum, ī *nt* pasture

passer, eris *m* sparrow; blue thrush

passim *adv* here and there, hither and thither; at random

passio, onis *f* 🄻🄼 suffering, passion

passum, ī *nt* raisin-wine

passus¹ *pple* from ▸ **patior**

passus², ūs *m* step, pace (five Roman feet); track, trace
  ▪ **mīlle passūs** *pl* a mile

passus³, a, um *adj* spread out; dried (of grapes, *etc.*)

pāstor, ōris *m* herdsman, shepherd; 🄻🄼 bishop

pāstōrālis, e *adj* pastoral; 🄻🄼 episcopal

pāstus, ūs *m* pasture, feeding ground; pasturage

patefaciō, fēcī, factum ③ *v* open, throw open; disclose, bring to light

patella, ae *f* small dish *or* plate; knee-cap

pateō ② *v* be open; be accessible; be visible; be exposed to; stretch out, extend; be evident; be available

pater, tris *m* father
  ◻ **pater familiās** head of a family
  ◻ **patrēs** forefathers
  ▪ **patrēs (cōnscrīptī)** *pl* senators

patera, ae *f* broad, shallow offering dish

paterfamiliās, patrisfamiliās *m* mistress of the house; respectable married woman

paternus, a, um *adj* fatherly, paternal

patēscō, tuī ③ *v* open; extend; become clear *or* known

pathicus, a, um *adj* submitting to sexual intercourse

patibulātus, a, um *adj* fastened to a yoke

patibulum, ī *nt* fork-shaped yoke; gibbet

patiēns, ntis *adj* patient; capable of enduring

patientia, ae *f* patience; forbearance; submissiveness

patina, ae f dish, pan, stew-pan, casserole

patior, passus sum ③ v dep bear, undergo; suffer; allow; leave, let be

patria, ae f fatherland, native country; home, source

patricīd- ▶ **parricīd-**

patricīda, ae m/f (also **parricīda**) parricide (murderer); murderer of a near relative; traitor

patricius, a, um adj patrician, noble

patrimōnium, (i)ī nt private possessions, estate, fortune

patrīmus, a, um adj having a father still living

patrissō ① v take after one's father

patrius, a, um adj belonging to a father, paternal; hereditary; of one's native land

patrō ① v accomplish, bring to completion

patrōcinium, (i)ī nt protection, defence, patronage, legal defence

patrōcinor ① v dep champion, defend

patrōna, ae f protectress, patroness

patrōnus, ī m protector, patron; pleader, advocate

patruēlis, is m/f of or belonging to a paternal uncle

patruus, ī m paternal uncle; type of harshness and censoriousness

patulus, a, um adj wide open, gaping; wide-spreading

paucitās, ātis f small number, fewness

pauculus, a, um adj very few, little

paucus, a, um adj few, little
  ■ **pauca** ntpl a few words

paulātim adv by degrees, gradually

paull- ▶ **paul-**

paulō adv by a little; somewhat

paulum adv a little, somewhat

paulus, a, um adj little, small
  ■ **paulum, ī** nt a little, a little bit

pauper, eris adj poor; meagre, unproductive

pauperiēs, iēī f, **paupertās, ātis** f poverty

pauxillātim adv little by little

pauxillum, ī nt a little
  □ **ex pauxillō** little by little

pavefaciō, fēcī, factum ③ v terrify

paveō, pāvī ② v be frightened or terrified at

pavēscō ③ v become alarmed

pavidus, a, um adj fearful, terrified, panic-struck

pavīmentum, ī nt paved surface or floor, pavement

pavitō ① v be in a state of fear or trepidation (at)

pāvō, ōnis m peacock

pavor, ōris m fear, dread, alarm, terror, anxiety

pāx, pācis f peace; tranquillity of mind; favour, grace; leave
  □ **pāce tuā** by your leave

paxillus, ī m wooden pin, peg

peccātum, ī nt error, sin

peccō ① v make a mistake; err; commit a fault; sin

pecten, inis m comb; quill with which the lyre is struck

pectō, pexī, pexum/pectitum ③ v comb, card (wool, etc.)

pectus, oris nt breast; soul; feeling; courage; understanding

pecuārius, (i)ī m cattle-breeder, grazier

peculātor, ōris m embezzler of public money

peculātus, ūs m embezzlement of public money or property

pecūliāris, e adj one's own

pecūlium, (i)ī nt private property of a son, daughter, or slave, held with the father's or master's consent

pecūnia, ae f property, wealth; money

pecus¹, oris nt cattle; herd, flock

pecus², udis f farm animal; animal; sheep

pedālis, e adj measuring a foot

pedes, itis m pedestrian, foot-soldier
  ■ **peditēs** pl infantry

pedester, tris, tre adj on foot, pedestrian

pedetem(p)tim adv step by step, slowly; cautiously

pedica, ae f shackle, fetter; snare

pēdīcō ▶ **paedīcō**

pēdis, is m/f louse

pedisequa, ae f waiting-woman

pedisequus, ī m male attendant, manservant

peditātus, **ūs** *m* infantry

pēditum, **ī** *nt* fart

pedum, **ī** *nt* shepherd's crook

peior, **ius** *adj* worse

peiūrium, **(i)ī** *nt* perjury, dishonesty

pelagus, **ī** *nt* open sea

pellāx, **ācis** *adj* seductive, glib

pēllex ▶ paelex

pelliciō, **lexī**, **lectum** ③ *v* attract; seduce; charm; inveigle

pellicula, **ae** *f* skin, hide

pellis, **is** *f* skin, hide; leather

pellītus, **a**, **um** *adj* covered with skins

pellō, **pepulī**, **pulsum** ③ *v* push, strike; drive out, banish; impel

pelōris, **idis** *f* mussel

pelta, **ae** *f* crescent-shaped shield

peltātus, **a**, **um** *adj* armed with the pelta

pēlvis, **is** *f* shallow bowl *or* basin

Penātēs, **ium** *mpl* the household gods; the gods of the state; one's home; dwelling

pendeō, **pependī** ② *v* hang (down), be suspended; hang loose; be unstable, movable; be uncertain; depend (on)

pendō, **pependī**, **pēnsum** ③ *v* weigh; pay, pay out; consider

pendulus, **a**, **um** *adj* hanging down; suspended

penes *prep with acc* in the possession *or* power of

penetrābilis, **e** *adj* that can be pierced; penetrable; piercing

penetrālis, **e** *adj* innermost; penetrating
  ■ **penetrāle**, **is** *nt* inner part of a place; inner shrine

penetrō ① *v* pierce, penetrate (into); gain entrance

pēnis, **is** *m* male sexual organ, penis

penitus *adv* inwardly; deep, deeply, far within; utterly, completely

penna, **ae** *f* feather; wing

pennātus, **a**, **um** *adj* winged

pēnsiō, **ōnis** *f* payment, instalment; rent

pēnsō ① *v* weigh, weigh out; pay *or* punish for; counterbalance, compensate; ponder, examine

pēnsum, **ī** *nt* quantity of wool given to be spun *or* woven; task, stint

pēnūria, **ae** *f* want, need, scarcity

penus, **ī** *m/f*, **penus**, **ūs** *m/f* provisions, food

pependī ▶ pendō

pepercī ▶ parcō

pepulī ▶ pellō

per *prep with acc* through, throughout, all over; during; by (means of); for the sake of; *in compounds* thoroughly, very; by (in oaths, *etc.*)

pēra, **ae** *f* satchel

perabsurdus, **a**, **um** *adj* highly ridiculous

perācer, **cris**, **cre** *adj* very sharp

peracūtus, **a**, **um** *adj* very penetrating; very sharp

peraequē *adv* equally

peragitō ① *v* harass with repeated attacks

peragō, **ēgī**, **āctum** ③ *v* execute, finish, accomplish; pierce through; pass through; relate

peragrō ① *v* travel over every part of, scour

perambulō ① *v* walk about in, tour; make the round of

perangustus, **a**, **um** *adj* very narrow

perantīquus, **a**, **um** *adj* very ancient

perarō ① *v* furrow; inscribe (scratch on a waxen tablet)

perbeātus, **a**, **um** *adj* very fortunate

perbene *adv* splendidly

perbibō, **bibī** ③ *v* drink deeply, drink in

perbītō ③ *v* perish

percallēscō, **luī** ③ *v* become callous

percārus, **a**, **um** *adj* very dear

percelebrō ① *v* make thoroughly known

percellō, **culī**, **culsum** ③ *v* strike down; strike; overpower; dismay, demoralize, upset

percieō ② *v*, **perciō**, **itum** ④ *v* excite; set in motion

percipiō, **cēpī**, **ceptum** ③ *v* take possession of; perceive, take in

percommodus, **a**, **um** *adj* very convenient

percontātiō, **ōnis** *f* question, interrogation

percontor ① *v dep* question; investigate

percoquō, **coxī**, **coctum** ③ *v* cook thoroughly; bake, heat

percrēb(r)ēscō, **b(r)uī** ③ *v* become very frequent, become very widespread

percūnctor ① *v* investigate

percurrō, **(cu)currī**, **cursum** ③ *v* run *or* hasten through *or* over; traverse; pass quickly over

percussor, **ōris** *m* assassin

percussus, **ūs** *m* buffeting; beating

percutiō, **ussī**, **ussum** ③ *v* strike forcibly; kill; shock, make a deep impression on

perdiscō, **didicī** ③ *v* learn thoroughly

perditor, **ōris** *m* destroyer

perditus, **a**, **um** *adj* ruined, lost, desperate, abandoned, morally depraved

perdiū *adv* for a long while

perdīx, **īcis** *m/f* partridge

perdō, **didī**, **ditum** ③ *v* lose; destroy; ruin; waste; spoil, impair

perdoceō, **doctum** ② *v* teach (thoroughly)

perdomō, **muī**, **mitum** ① *v* tame thoroughly, subjugate completely

perdūcō, **dūxī**, **ductum** ③ *v* lead *or* bring through, conduct; prolong; cover over, coat

perduelliō, **ōnis** *f* treason

perduellis, **is** *m* national enemy

peredō, **esse**, **ēdī**, **ēsum** *v ir* eat up, consume, waste

peregrē *adv* abroad; to, in, *or* from foreign parts

peregrīnātiō, **ōnis** *f* foreign travel

peregrīnor ① *v dep* travel about *or* abroad; reside abroad

peregrīnus, **a**, **um** *adj* outlandish, strange, foreign *m/f* foreigner, alien

perendinus, **a**, **um** *adj* after tomorrow

perennis, **e** *adj* continuing throughout the year; constant, uninterrupted; enduring

pereō, **īre**, **iī/īvī**, **itum** *v ir* pass from view, vanish, disappear; be destroyed, perish; be desperately in love (with) □ **periī** I am ruined

perequitō ① *v* ride (through *or* over), traverse; ride hither and thither, ride *or* drive about

pererrō ① *v* wander through, roam *or* ramble over

perexiguus, **a**, **um** *adj* very little *or* small

perfacilis, **e** *adj* very easy

perfectus, **a**, **um** *adj* finished, complete, perfect

perferō, **ferre**, **tulī**, **lātum** *v ir* bear *or* carry through; convey; report; tell; endure; undergo

perficiō, **fēcī**, **fectum** ③ *v* finish, complete; perform; accomplish

perfidia, **ae** *f* faithlessness, treachery

perfidiōsus, **a**, **um** *adj* treacherous

perfidus, **a**, **um** *adj* faithless, treacherous, false, deceitful; LM heretic(al)

perflō ① *v* blow through *or* over

perfluō, **ūxī** ③ *v* flow (through)

perfodiō, **ōdī**, **ossum** ③ *v* dig *or* pierce through

perforō ① *v* bore through; pierce

perfringō, **frēgī**, **frāctum** ③ *v* break through; break *or* dash in pieces; smash

perfruor, **frūctus sum** ③ *v dep with abl* have full enjoyment of, enjoy

perfuga, **ae** *m* deserter

perfugiō, **ūgī** ③ *v* take refuge, escape; go for refuge (to the enemy)

perfugium, **(i)ī** *nt* refuge; asylum; excuse

perfundō, **ūdī**, **ūsum** ③ *v* pour over, wet; overspread, imbue

perfungor, **fūnctus sum** ③ *v dep with abl* perform, discharge; have done with

perfurō ③ *v* rage, storm (throughout)

pergama, **orum** *npl* LM citadel(s)

pergō, **rrēxī**, **rrēctum** ③ *v* advance; continue, proceed, go on

pergrandis, **e** *adj* very large, of very advanced age

pergrātus, **a**, **um** *adj* very agreeable *or* pleasant

perhibeō ② *v* present, give, bestow; regard, hold; name

perhorrēscō, **ruī** ③ *v* tremble *or* shudder greatly; recoil in terror from

perīclitor ① *v dep* risk; try, test; be in danger; risk

perīculōsus, **a**, **um** *adj* dangerous, hazardous, perilous

p

perīc(u)lum, **ī** *nt* trial, proof; danger, peril; risk; liability

peridōneus, **a**, **um** *adj* very suitable, very well-fitted

perimō, **ēmī**, **emptum** ③ *v* destroy; kill; prevent

perinde *adv* just (as), equally □ ∼ **ac** just, as if

perītia, **ae** *f* practical knowledge, skill, expertise

perītus, **a**, **um** *adj* experienced, practised, skilful, expert

periūcundus, **a**, **um** *adj* very welcome, agreeable

periūrium, **(i)ī** *nt* false oath, perjury

periūrō ① *v* swear falsely

periūrus, **a**, **um** *adj* perjured; false, lying

perlābor, **lāpsus sum** ③ *v dep* glide along, over *or* through, skim

perlegō, **lēgī**, **lēctum** ③ *v* scan, survey; read through

perlīberālis, **e** *adj* very decent, ladylike

perlitō ① *v* make auspicious sacrifice

perlūceō ② *v* be transparent; shine through; shine out

perlūcidulus, **a**, **um** *adj* transparent, translucent

perlūcidus, **a**, **um** *adj* transparent, pellucid

perluō, **luī**, **ūtum** ③ *v* wash off *or* thoroughly; bathe

perlūstrō ① *v* go *or* wander all through; view all over, scan, scrutinize

permadefaciō, **fēcī**, **factum** ③ *v* drench thoroughly

permagnus, **a**, **um** *adj* very great

permaneō, **ānsī**, **ānsum** ② *v* continue *or* persist in staying; persist

permānō ① *v* flow through; leak through; permeate

permeō ① *v* go *or* pass through, cross, traverse; pervade

permētior, **mēnsus sum** ④ *v dep* measure exactly; travel over

permisceō, **mixtum** ② *v* mix *or* mingle together; confound; embroil; disturb thoroughly

permissus, **ūs** *m* permission, authorization

permittō, **mīsī**, **missum** ③ *v* let go through; allow full scope to, give rein to; allow, permit; leave (to another) to do *or* decide; grant

permoveō, **mōvī**, **mōtum** ② *v* move *or* stir up thoroughly; move deeply; excite

permulceō, **lsī**, **lsum/lctum** ② *v* rub gently, stroke, touch gently; charm, please, beguile; soothe, alleviate

permultus, **a**, **um** *adj* very much, very many

permūniō ④ *v* fortify thoroughly

permūtātiō, **ōnis** *f* change; exchange, barter

permūtō ① *v* exchange (for); swap

perniciēs, **iēī** *f* destruction, ruin; fatal injury

perniciōsus, **a**, **um** *adj* destructive, ruinous, fatal

pernīcitās, **ātis** *f* nimbleness

pernīx, **īcis** *adj* nimble, agile, travelling quickly

pernoctō ① *v* spend the night

pernōscō, **ōvī**, **ōtum** ③ *v* get a thorough knowledge of

pernōtēscō, **tuī** ③ *v* become known

pernox, **ctis** *adj* lasting all night

pernumerō ① *v* reckon up, count out (money) in full

pērō, **ōnis** *m* thick boot of raw hide

perobscūrus, **a**, **um** *adj* very obscure, very vague

perōdī, **isse**, **ōsus sum** *v ir* hate greatly, detest

peropportūnus, **a**, **um** *adj* very favourably situated, very convenient

perōrō ① *v* deliver the final part of a speech, conclude

perpācō ① *v* subdue completely

perparvus, **a**, **um** *adj* very little, very trifling

perpaucus, **a**, **um** *adj* very few

perpellō, **pulī**, **pulsum** ③ *v* compel, constrain, prevail upon; enforce

perpendiculum, **ī** *nt* plummet □ **ad** ∼ perpendicularly

perpendō, **ndī**, **ēnsum** ③ *v* weigh carefully; assess carefully

perperam *adv* wrongly, incorrectly

perpetior, **pessus sum** ③ *v dep* endure to the full

perpetrō ① *v* carry through, accomplish

perpetuitās, **ātis** *f* continuity; permanence

perpetuus, **a**, **um** *adj* uninterrupted; continuous; lasting; invariable
□ **in perpetuum** for ever

perplaceō ② *v with dat* please greatly

perplexus, **a**, **um** *adj* entangled, muddled; intricate, cryptic

perpluō ③ *v* let the rain through, leak; (of rain) come through

perpoliō ④ *v* polish thoroughly; put the finishing touches to

perpopulor ① *v dep* ravage, devastate completely

perpōtō ① *v* drink heavily; drink up

perquam *adv* extremely

perquīrō, **īsīvī/īsiī**, **īsītum** ③ *v* search everywhere for

perrārus, **a**, **um** *adj* very rare, exceptional

perreptō ① *v* creep through, crawl over

perrumpō, **rūpī**, **ruptum** ③ *v* break *or* rush through, force one's way through; cleave, sever; violate

persaepe *adv* very often

perscrībō, **psī**, **ptum** ③ *v* write in full *or* at length; give a full account *or* report of in writing

perscrūtor ① *v dep* search high and low; study carefully

persequor, **secūtus sum** ③ *v dep* follow perseveringly, pursue; pursue with hostile intent; strive after; go through with; catch up with

persevērantia, **ae** *f* steadfastness, persistence

persevērō ① *v* persist, persevere in

persicus, **a**, **um** *adj*
■ **concha persica** *f* mother of pearl

persimplex, **icis** *adj* very simple

persolvō, **lvī**, **lūtum** ③ *v* pay in full; pay off

persōna, **ae** *f* mask; personage, character, part

persōnātus, **a**, **um** *adj* masked

personō, **nuī**, **nitum** ① *v* resound, ring with; cause to resound; make loud music; shout out

perspectō ① *v* look all around; watch steadily

perspiciō, **exī**, **ectum** ③ *v* look *or* see through; look into; look at, examine, inspect; study, investigate

perspicuus, **a**, **um** *adj* transparent, clear; evident

perstō, **stitī** ① *v* stand firm; last, endure; persevere, persist in

perstringō, **īnxī**, **ictum** ③ *v* graze, graze against; make tight all over; offend, make unfavourable mention of; paralyse; travel round the edge of

persuādeō, **āsī**, **āsum** ② *v with dat* persuade, convince; prevail upon, persuade to do

persultō ① *v* leap *or* skip *or* prance about; range (over), scour

pertaedet, **pertaesum est** ② *v impers* be very wearied with

pertegō, **ēxī**, **ēctum** ③ *v* cover completely, thatch

pertemptō ① *v* test, try out; explore thoroughly; agitate thoroughly

pertendō, **ndī**, **ēnsum** ③ *v* persevere, persist; press on

perterreō ② *v* frighten *or* terrify thoroughly

pertica, **ae** *f* pole, long staff, measuring rod, perch

pertimēscō, **muī** ③ *v* become very scared (of)

pertinācia, **ae** *f* obstinacy, defiance

pertināx, **ācis** *adj* firm, constant, steadfast, obstinate

pertineō ② *v* continue *or* extend through *or* to, reach; belong *or* pertain to, be relevant to

pertrahō, **āxī**, **actum** ③ *v* draw *or* drag through *or* to, bring *or* conduct forcibly to; draw on, lure

pertundō, **tudī**, **tūsum** ③ *v* bore through, perforate

perturbātiō, **ōnis** *f* confusion, disturbance; mental disturbance, perturbation; passion

perturbō ① *v* disorder, confuse; disturb; frighten

perūrō, **ussī**, **ustum** ③ *v* burn up; fire; scorch; make sore

pervādō, **āsī**, **āsum** ③ *v* go *or* come through; spread through; penetrate; pervade

pervagor ① *v dep* wander *or* range through, rove about; pervade, spread widely; extend

pervastō ① *v* devastate completely

pervehō, **ēxī**, **ectum** ③ *v* bear, carry *or* convey through
□ **pervehor** sail to, ride to

perveniō, vēnī, ventum ④ *v* come through to, arrive at, reach

perversus, a, um *adj* askew, awry; perverse, evil, bad

pervertō, rtī, rsum ③ *v* overthrow; subvert; destroy, ruin, corrupt

pervestigō ① *v* make a thorough search of; explore fully

pervetus, eris *adj* very old

pervicācia, ae *f* stubbornness, obstinacy; firmness, steadiness

pervicāx, ācis *adj* stubborn, obstinate; firm, steadfast

pervideō, vīdī, vīsum ② *v* take in with the eyes *or* mind

pervigil, lis *adj* keeping watch *or* sleepless all night long

pervigilium, (i)ī *nt* vigil, watch

pervigilō ① *v* remain awake all night; keep watch all night

pervincō, vīcī, victum ③ *v* conquer completely; carry (a proposal), gain an objective; persuade

pervius, a, um *adj* passable, traversable; penetrable

pervolō ① *v* fly *or* flit through; wing one's way; move rapidly through the air

pervor- ▷ **perver-**

pervulgō ① *v* make publicly known, spread abroad

pēs, pedis *m* foot; metrical foot; foot (as a linear measure); sheet (of a sail)

pessimus, a, um *adj* worst

pessum *adv* to the lowest part, to the bottom
□ ∼ **dō** destroy, ruin

pestifer, era, erum *adj* pestilential; destructive

pestilēns, ntis *adj* pestilential, unhealthy, unwholesome; destructive

pestilentia, ae *f* pestilence, unhealthy atmosphere *or* region; plague

pestis, is *f* plague, pestilence; destruction, ruin, death

petauristārius, (i)ī *m* acrobat

petītiō, ōnis *f* attack, thrust; request, petition; candidature; lawsuit

petītor, ōris *m* seeker, striver after, applicant, candidate; claimant, plaintiff

petō, īvī/iī, ītum ③ *v* make for; seek; fetch; seek after; attack; ask for; desire; be a candidate for

petulāns, ntis *adj* pert, saucy, impudent, petulant; wanton, lascivious

petulantia, ae *f* impudent *or* boisterous aggressiveness; wantonness, immodesty

petulcus, a, um *adj* butting

phalānx, angis *f* body of soldiers drawn up in close order

phalerae, ārum *fpl* ornaments worn by men of arms and horses

phalerātus, a, um *adj* with fine trappings

phantasma, atis *nt* spectre, apparition

pharetra, ae *f* quiver

pharetrātus, a, um *adj* wearing a quiver

pharmacopōla, ae *m* medicine- *or* drug-seller; quack

phasēlus, ī *m/f* kidney-bean; light ship

Philippus, ī *m* two-drachma coin, minted by Philip II of Macedon

philomēla, ae *f* nightingale

philosophia, ae *f* philosophy

philosophor ① *v dep* philosophize

philosophus, ī *m* philosopher

philtrum, ī *nt* love-potion

philyra, ae *f* linden-tree, lime-tree

phōca, ae *f*, **phōcē, ēs** *f* seal

piāculāris, e *adj* atoning, expiatory

piāculum, ī *nt* expiatory offering *or* rite; sin

piāmen, inis *nt* atonement

pīca, ae *f* magpie; jay

picātus, a, um *adj* sealed with pitch

picea, ae *f* spruce

piceus, a, um *adj* made of pitch; pitchblack

pictor, ōris *m* painter

pictūra, ae *f* art of painting; picture; mental image

pictūrātus, a, um *adj* decorated with colour

pīcus, ī *m* woodpecker

pietās, ātis *f* piety; dutifulness; affection, love; loyalty; gratitude

piger, **gra**, **grum** *adj* slow, sluggish, inactive; inert

piget ② *v impers* it affects with revulsion *or* displeasure, it irks

pigmentum, **ī** *nt* colour, colouring, paint

pignerō ① *v* pledge, pawn; appropriate

pignus, **oris/eris** *nt* pledge, pawn, surety; token, proof; stake; Ⓜ child

pigritia, **ae** *f*, **pigritiēs**, **iēī** *f* sloth, sluggishness, laziness, indolence

pīla, **ae** *f* squared pillar; pier, pile

pila, **ae** *f* ball

pīlānus, **ī** *m* a soldier of the third rank

pīlentum, **ī** *nt* luxurious carriage used by women

pīleum, **ī** *nt*, **pīleus**, **ī** *m*, **pilleus**, **ī** *m* felt cap; freedom, liberty

pilleātus, **a**, **um** *adj* wearing the felt cap of manumission

pīlum, **ī** *nt* javelin

pilus, **ī** *m* hair; trifle

pīlus, **ī** *m* the first century of the first cohort of a legion
  □ **prīmum pīlum dūcō** command the first century of the first cohort of a legion

pinacothēca, **ae** *f* picture-gallery

pīnētum, **ī** *nt* pine-wood

pīneus, **a**, **um** *adj* of the pine, covered in pines

pingō, **pīnxī**, **pictum** ③ *v* paint; embroider; embellish; tattoo

pinguēscō ③ *v* grow fat; become strong *or* fertile

pinguis, **e** *adj* fat; plump; rich; dull, slow-witted; slothful

pīnifer, **pīniger**, **era**, **erum** *adj* pine-bearing

pinna, **ae** *f* feather; wing; raised part of an embattled parapet

pinniger, **era**, **erum** *adj* winged; finny

pinnipēs, **edis** *adj* having wings on the feet

pīnus, **ī** *f*, **pīnus**, **ūs** *f* pine-tree; ship; pine-wood torch

piō ① *v* appease, propitiate; cleanse, expiate

pīpiō ① *v* (of birds) cheep

pīrāta, **ae** *m* corsair, pirate

pīrāticus, **a**, **um** *adj* piratical

pirum, **ī** *nt* pear

pirus, **ī** *f* pear-tree

piscārius, **a**, **um** *adj* of *or* connected with fish

piscātor, **ōris** *m* fisherman

piscātōrius, **a**, **um** *adj* of *or* for fishing

piscātus, **ūs** *m* catch of fish, seafood

piscīna, **ae** *f* fish-pond; swimming-pool

piscis, **is** *m* fish

piscor ① *v dep* fish

piscōsus, **a**, **um** *adj* teeming with fish

pisculentus, **a**, **um** *adj* fishy, full of fish

pistor, **ōris** *m* miller, baker

pistrīnum, **ī** *nt* mill, bakery (also as a place of punishment *or* drudgery)

pistris, **is** *f* sea monster; whale

pītuīta, **ae** *f* mucus, phlegm

pius, **a**, **um** *adj* pious, religious, faithful, devout; dutiful

pix, **picis** *f* pitch

plācābilis, **e** *adj* easily appeased, placable; appeasing, pacifying

plācātus, **a**, **um** *adj* kindly disposed; peaceful, calm

placenta, **ae** *f* a kind of flat cake

placeō ② *v with dat* be pleasing (to), satisfy
  □ **placet** it seems good (to); it is resolved *or* agreed on (by)

placidus, **a**, **um** *adj* gentle, calm, mild, peaceful, placid

plācō ① *v* calm, assuage, placate, appease, reconcile (with)

plāga, **ae** *f* blow, stroke; wound

plaga, **ae** *f* open expanse (of land, sea or sky), tract; hunting-net

plāgigerulus, **a**, **um** *adj* bearing (the marks of) blows, much beaten

plāgipatidēs, **ae** *m* one who has suffered whipping

plāgōsus, **a**, **um** *adj* lavish with blows

plagūsia, **ae** *f* shellfish, scallop

plānē *adv* plainly, clearly; utterly, quite

planēta, **ae** *m* wandering star, planet

planeta, **ae** *f* Ⓜ chasuble

plangō, **ānxī**, **ānctum** ③ *v* strike, beat; beat the breast in mourning, mourn for

Ⓟ

plangor, **ōris** *m* beating, striking; lamentation

plānitiēs, **iēī** *f* flat *or* even surface, level ground, plain

planta, **ae** *f* sprout, shoot; sole of the foot

plantāria, **ium** *ntpl* slips, cuttings

plānus, **a**, **um** *adj* level, flat, plane, even; obvious

platanus, **ī** *f* plane-tree

platea, **platēa**, **ae** *f* street

plaudō, **plausī**, **plausum** ③ *v* clap, strike, beat; *with dat* applaud

plausor, **ōris** *m* applauder

plaustrum, **ī** *nt* wagon, cart; Charles's Wain

plausus, **ūs** *m* clapping; applause

plēbēcula, **ae** *f* mob, common people

plēbēius, **a**, **um** *adj* pertaining to the common people, plebeian; common, everyday

plēbicola, **ae** *m* one who courts the favour of the people

plēbiscītum, **ī** *nt* resolution of the people

plēbs, **bis**/**bī** *f*, **plēbēs**, **ēī** *f* common people, plebeians; mob, common herd, masses

> **!** Originally **plēbs** referred to the non-patrician population of Rome. Later it referred to the common people, with the implication of low status.

plectō¹, **exī**, **exum** ③ *v* plait, twine

plectō² ③ *v* buffet, beat; punish

plectrum, **ī** *nt* quill to strike the strings of a musical instrument

plēnus, **a**, **um** *adj* full, filled with; plump, stout; plenteous; entire; whole

plērumque *adv* generally, mostly, commonly, often

plērusque, **plēraque**, **plērumque** *adj* the greater part *or* number of, most of
  ■ **plērīque**, **plēraeque**, **plēraque** *pl* most (people), very many

plicō ① *v* fold, bend; twine, coil

plōrātus, **ūs** *m* wailing, crying

plōrō ① *v* wail, weep aloud, weep over

plūma, **ae** *f* feather, plumage; down

plumbeus, **a**, **um** *adj* leaden; blunt, dull; heavy; stupid

plumbum, **ī** *nt* lead

plūmeus, **a**, **um** *adj* feathery; composed of *or* filled with feathers

plūmiger, **era**, **erum** *adj* feathered

plūmipēs, **edis** *adj* having feathers on the feet, feather-footed

plūmōsus, **a**, **um** *adj* feathered

pluō, **pluī**/**plūvī** ③ *v* rain; fall like rain
  ■ **pluit** *impers* it rains, is raining

plūrēs, **a** *adj* more, a number of; very many

plūrimus, **a**, **um** *adj* very much *or* many, (the) most, very long *or* large *or* big

plūs *n*/*adj* more
  □ **plūris** of more value

> **!** In the sg. **plūs** is a neuter noun which is followed by a gen., e.g. nom. & acc. **plūs vīnī** 'more wine'; its only other cases are gen. **plūris** and abl. **plūre**. Its pl. is adjectival and agrees with the case (and gender) of the noun it qualifies; the gen. is **plūrium**.

pluteus, **ī** *m* movable screen of wood or wickerwork used for protection in siege warfare; upright board forming the back of a couch

pluvia, **ae** *f* rain

pluviālis, **e** *adj* rainy; consisting of rain; rain-swollen

pluvius, **a**, **um** *adj* rainy, causing *or* bringing rain

pōculum, **ī** *nt* drinking-vessel, cup; drink

podagra, **ae** *f* gout

poēma, **atis** *nt* poem

poena, **ae** *f* punishment, penalty
  □ **dō poenās** pay the penalty

poenitudo, **inis** *f* [LM] repentance

poēsis, **is** *f* poetry; poem

poēta, **ae** *m* poet

poēticus, **a**, **um** *adj* poetic

pol *int* by Pollux!

polenta, **ae** *f* barley-meal

poliō ④ *v* smooth, polish; refine, give finish to

polītus, **a**, **um** *adj* refined, polished

pollēns, ntis *adj* strong, potent, exerting power

pollentia, ae *f* power

polleō ② *v* exert power *or* influence; be strong

pollex, icis *m* thumb

polliceor ② *v dep* promise

pollicitātiō, ōnis *f* promise

pollicitor ① *v dep* promise (assiduously)

pollūcibilis, e *adj* sumptuous; ostentatious

polluō, luī, lūtum ③ *v* soil, defile, pollute; contaminate; violate; defile with illicit sexual conduct

polus, ī *m* pole; heaven, sky

polyandrium, (i)i *nt* ⟨LM⟩ cemetery

polypus, ī *m* octopus, nasal tumour

polyspaston, ī *nt* crane

pōmārium, (i)ī *nt* orchard

pōmerium, (i)ī *nt* space left free from buildings round the walls of a Roman *or* Etruscan town

pōmifer, era, erum *adj* fruit-bearing

pōmōsus, a, um *adj* rich in fruit

pompa, ae *f* ceremonial procession

pōmum, ī *nt*, **pōmus, ī** *f* fruit; fruit-tree

ponderō ① *v* weigh; weigh up

pondō *adv* in *or* by weight

pondus, eris *nt* weight; burden; value; importance, gravity; pound's weight

pōne *adv/prep with acc* behind

pōnō, posuī, positum ③ *v* put, place; lay; station; plant; lay aside; appoint

pōns, ntis *m* bridge; deck (of a ship); floor of a tower

ponticulus, ī *m* little bridge

pontifex, icis *m* Roman high priest; ⟨LM⟩ bishop, pontiff

> **!** The **pontifex maximus** was the chief priest of Rome. The Roman emperors assumed this priesthood and thus had control of all sacred and religious matters.

pontificalis, e *adj* pontifical, of *or* pertaining to a **pontifex**; ⟨LM⟩ of a bishop, episcopal; of the Pope, papal

pontificātus, ūs *m* pontificate, the office of **pontifex**; ⟨LM⟩ see, bishopric; papacy

pontificius, a, um *adj* pontifical, of *or* pertaining to a **pontifex**

pontus, ī *m* sea

popīna, ae *f* cook-shop, bistro, low-class eating house

poples, itis *m* knee

poposcī ▷ poscō

populābilis, e *adj* that may be ravaged *or* laid waste

populābundus, a, um *adj* intent on pillage *or* plunder

populāris, e *adj* popular; of the common people; of the same country □ ~ **aura** the breeze of popular favour ■ ~ *m* fellow-citizen, compatriot; member of the 'popular' party

populāritās, ātis *f* courting of popular favour

populāriter *adv* in everyday language; in a manner designed to win popular support

populātiō, ōnis *f* plundering, devastation

populātor, ōris *m* devastator, ravager, plunderer

pōpuleus, a, um *adj* of a poplar

populō ① *v*, **populor** ① *v dep* ravage, devastate; plunder; despoil

populus, ī *m* people, nation

pōpulus, ī *f* poplar-tree

porca, ae *f* female pig, sow

porculus, ī *m* piglet

porcus, ī *m* hog, pig

porrigō, rēxī, rēctum ③ *v* put forward, extend; stretch *or* spread (oneself) out; offer

porrīgō, inis *f* scaly condition, scurf, dandruff

porrō *adv* onward, further off; further; besides; again, moreover

porrum, ī *nt*, **porrus, ī** *m* leek

porta, ae *f* gate; entrance

portendō, ndī, ntum ③ *v* portend, presage; reveal by portents

portentum, ī *nt* omen, portent; something unnatural *or* extraordinary, monster, monstrosity; fantastic story

porticus, ūs *f* colonnade, portico

portiō, ōnis *f* part, portion, share; proportion □ **prō portiōne** proportionally

portitor, **ōris** *m* ferryman; Charon; toll-collector, customs-officer

portō ① *v* carry, bear, convey

portōrium, **(i)ī** *nt* duty, toll

portuōsus, **a**, **um** *adj* well provided with harbours

portus, **ūs** *m* harbour, haven, port; mouth of a river

poscō, **poposcī** ③ *v* ask for insistently, demand; demand for punishment, trial, *etc.*

positor, **ōris** *m* builder, founder

positus, **ūs** *m* situation, position; arrangement

possessiō, **ōnis** *f* possession; estate

possessor, **ōris** *m* owner, occupier

possibilis, **e** *adj* possible

possideō, **sēdī**, **sessum** ② *v* possess, have

possum, **posse**, **potuī** *v ir* be able; have power; can

post¹ *adv* behind, back; backwards; after

post² *prep with acc* behind; after; inferior to

> ❗ **post** is usu. only a prep. and governs the acc.; the corresponding adv. is **posteā**. However, **post** may be used adverbially with the abl. expressing time at which, e.g. **paucīs post diēbus** 'a few days later'.

posteā *adv* hereafter, thereafter, afterwards

posteāquam *adv* after, ever since

posterior, **ius** *adj* later in order; later, latter; inferior

posteritās, **ātis** *f* future time; posterity

posterus, **a**, **um** *adj* following, next, ensuing, future
  ■ **posterī**, **ōrum** *mpl* posterity, descendants

postgenitus, **a**, **um** *adj* born at a later time, yet to be born

posthabeō ② *v* esteem less, subordinate (to); postpone

posthāc *adv* hereafter, henceforth, in future

postīcum, **ī** *nt* back door

postīcus, **a**, **um** *adj* back, rear

postibi, **postid** *adv* aferwards

postillā *adv* after that, afterwards

postis, **is** *m* post, door-post; door

postmodo, **postmodum** *adv* afterwards, presently, later

postmoenium, **(i)ī** *nt* area *or* part behind a wall

postpōnō, **posuī**, **positum** ③ *v* esteem less than; postpone

postquam *conj* after, since

postrēmō *adv* at last

postrēmus, **a**, **um** *adj* last; worst

postrīdiē *adv* on the day after, on the following *or* next day

postulātiō, **ōnis** *f* petition, request

postulātum, **ī** *nt* demand, request

postulō ① *v* ask for, demand, require, request, desire; accuse, prosecute

postumus, **a**, **um** *adj* last; last-born; born after the death of the father

potēns, **ntis** *adj* able, mighty, powerful, potent, efficacious
  □ **suī** ~ one's own master

potentātus, **ūs** *m* dominion, command

potentia, **ae** *f* power; efficacy, virtue; ability

potestās, **ātis** *f* power, faculty, opportunity; authority; dominion; command

pōtiō, **ōnis** *f* drink, draught; potion, philtre

potior¹ ④ *v dep* take possession of, get, obtain, acquire, receive; possess

potior², **ius** *adj* more powerful; preferable

potis, **e** *adj* able (to), capable (of); possible

potissimus, **a**, **um** *adj* principal; most powerful, chief

potius *adv* rather, preferably; more (than)

pōtō, **pōt(āt)um** ① *v* drink; tipple; drink to excess

prae *prep with abl* before, in front of; in comparison with; in the face of, under the pressure of

praeacūtus, **a**, **um** *adj* sharpened at the end, very sharp

praealtus, **a**, **um** *adj* very high; very deep

praebeō ② *v* offer; present; show; give; expose

praecaveō, **cāvī**, **cautum** ② *v* guard (against), beware

praecēdō, **essī**, **essum** ③ *v* go before, precede; surpass

praecellō ③ *v* excel; surpass

praecelsus, **a**, **um** *adj* exceptionally high *or* tall

praeceps, **cipitis** *adj* headlong; impetuous, sheer; involving risk of sudden disaster
□ **in** ∼ headlong

praeceptor, **ōris** *m* teacher, instructor

praeceptum, **ī** *nt* rule, precept; order, instruction; teaching

praecerpō, **psī**, **ptum** ③ *v* pluck before time; pluck *or* cut off

praecīdō, **īdī**, **īsum** ③ *v* cut off in front; cut back, cut short

praecingō, **īnxī**, **īnctum** ③ *v* gird, surround, encircle; encompass

praecinō, **inuī**, **centum** ③ *v* sing before; predict

praecipēs ▶ **praeceps**

praecipiō, **cēpī**, **ceptum** ③ *v* take *or* obtain in advance, anticipate; teach, recommend, order

praecipitō ① *v* throw down headlong, precipitate; destroy; suffer ruin; drive headlong; fall headlong

praecipuus, **a**, **um** *adj* particular, peculiar, especial; special

praecīsus, **a**, **um** *adj* abrupt, precipitous; clipped, staccato

praeclārus, **a**, **um** *adj* very bright; beautiful; splendid, noble, excellent, brilliant; glorious

praeclūdō, **ūsī**, **ūsum** ③ *v* block up, bar; prevent; forbid access to

praecō, **ōnis** *m* crier; auctioneer

praecōnsūmō, **mpsī**, **mptum** ③ *v* use up prematurely

praecoquis, **e** *adj*, **praecox**, **ocis** *adj* ripened too soon; premature; unseasonable; precocious

praecordia, **ōrum** *ntpl* vitals, diaphragm; breast; chest as the seat of feelings

praecurrō, **(cu)currī**, **cursum** ③ *v* run before, hasten on before; precede; anticipate

praecursor, **ōris** *m* forerunner; member of advance-guard

praecursōrius, **a**, **um** *adj* travelling in advance, precursory

praeda, **ae** *f* booty, spoil, loot; prey, game

praedābundus, **a**, **um** *adj* pillaging

praedātor, **ōris** *m* plunderer, pillager; hunter

praedātōrius, **a**, **um** *adj* plundering, rapacious; piratical

praedicāmentum, **i** *nt* LM category (in Aristotelian philosophy)

praedicātiō, **ōnis** *f* proclamation, publication; commendation

praedicātor, **oris** *m* LM preacher

praedicō ① *v* publish; proclaim; cite; describe (as), call; praise; LM preach

praedīcō, **īxī**, **ictum** ③ *v* say *or* mention beforehand; foretell; warn; recommend

praedictum, **ī** *nt* prediction; forewarning; command

praediscō ③ *v* learn in advance

praeditus, **a**, **um** *adj* endowed (with)

praedium, **(i)ī** *nt* land, estate

praedīves, **itis** *adj* very rich; richly supplied

praedō, **ōnis** *m* brigand; pirate

praedor ① *v dep* plunder, loot, pillage, spoil; take as plunder

praedūcō, **dūxī**, **ductum** ③ *v* run (a ditch *or* a wall) in front

praedulcis, **e** *adj* very sweet

praedūrus, **a**, **um** *adj* very hard; very strong

praeeō, **īre**, **iī/īvī**, **itum** *v ir* go before, precede; dictate

praefectūra, **ae** *f* command; office of praefectus; district

praefectus, **ī** *m* director, president, chief; governor

praeferō, **ferre**, **tulī**, **lātum** *v ir* bear before; prefer; display, reveal; give precedence to

praeferōx, **ōcis** *adj* very high-spirited

praefestīnō ① *v* be in a hurry

praeficiō, **fēcī**, **fectum** ③ *v* put in charge (of); appoint to the command (of)

praefīgō, **īxī**, **īxum** ③ *v* fasten before; fix on the end *or* surface (of); obstruct

praefīniō ④ *v* fix the range of; determine

praefodiō, **ōdī** ③ *v* dig a trench in front of; bury beforehand

praefor ① *v dep* say *or* utter beforehand, mention first; recite (a preliminary formula); address with a preliminary prayer

praefrīgidus, **a**, **um** *adj* very cold

praefringō, **āctum** ③ *v* break off at the end, break off short

praefulgeō, **lsī**, **ltum** ② *v* shine with outstanding brightness; be outstanding

praegelidus, **a**, **um** *adj* outstandingly cold

praegestiō ④ *v* have an overpowering desire, be very eager (to)

praegnāns, **ntis** *adj*, **praegnās**, **ātis** *adj* with child, pregnant

praegravis, **e** *adj* very heavy; burdensome

praegravō ① *v* weigh down; burden

praegredior, **gressus sum** ③ *v dep* go ahead; go before, precede; surpass

praegustō ① *v* taste in advance

praeiūdicium, **(i)ī** *nt* precedent, example; prejudgement

praeiūdicō ① *v* prejudge

praelābor, **lāpsus sum** ③ *v dep* flow, glide ahead *or* past

praelegō, **lēgī**, **lēctum** ③ *v* select; sail along; read aloud

praelongus, **a**, **um** *adj* exceptionally long

praelūceō, **ūxī** ② *v* shine forth; outshine; light the way (for)

praemātūrē *adv* prematurely, very early *or* promptly

praemeditor ① *v dep* consider in advance

praemetuō ③ *v* fear beforehand

praemittō, **mīsī**, **missum** ③ *v* send in advance (of)

praemium, **(i)ī** *nt* booty, plunder, prize; reward; punishment; payment

praemoneō ② *v* forewarn

praemonitus, **ūs** *m* forewarning

praemorior, **morī**, **mortuus sum** ③ *v dep* die beforehand

praemūniō ④ *v* fortify, defend in advance; safeguard

praenatō ① *v* swim by; flow by

praenōmen, **inis** *nt* first name

praenōscō, **nōvī** ③ *v* foreknow

praenūntiō ① *v* announce in advance

praenūntius, **a**, **um** *adj* acting as harbinger; heralding

praeoccupō ① *v* seize upon beforehand; anticipate

praeoptō ① *v* choose in preference; prefer

praeparātiō, **ōnis** *f* preparation

praeparō ① *v* furnish beforehand; provide in readiness; plan in advance; prepare

praepediō ④ *v* shackle, fetter; hinder

praependeō ② *v* hang down in front

praepes, **etis** *adj* flying straight ahead; nimble, fleet; winged

praepinguis, **e** *adj* outstandingly rich

praepōnō, **posuī**, **positum** ③ *v* put before; prefer (to); put in charge (of)

praepositus, **i** *m* [LM] abbot; provost (deputy to an abbot)

praeposterus, **a**, **um** *adj* in the wrong order; wrong-headed; topsy-turvy

praepotēns, **ntis** *adj* very powerful

praeproperus, **a**, **um** *adj* very hurried, precipitate; too hasty

praeripiō, **ripuī**, **reptum** ③ *v* snatch away (before the proper time); seize first; forestall

praerogātīva, **ae** *f* tribe which voted first

praerumpō, **rūpī**, **ruptum** ③ *v* break off

praeruptus, **a**, **um** *adj* broken off; precipitous; hasty, rash

praes, **dis** *m* surety, bondsman

praesaepe, **is** *nt*, **praesaepēs**, **is** *f*, **praesaepium**, **(i)ī** *nt* stall; brothel

praesaepiō, **psī**, **ptum** ④ *v* fence in front

praesāgiō ④ *v* have a presentiment (of); portend

praesāgium, **(i)ī** *nt* sense of foreboding; prognostication

praesāgus, **a**, **um** *adj* having a foreboding; ominous

P

praescius, **a**, **um** *adj* foreknowing, prescient

praescrībō, **psī**, **ptum** ③ *v* write before; prescribe, appoint

praescrīptum, **ī** *nt* precept, rule; route

praesecō, **secuī**, **sec(ā)tum** ① *v* cut in front, cut

praesēns, **ntis** *adj* present, in person, at hand, ready; prompt; favourable; effectual; immediate; present, aiding
◻ **in** ~ for the present

praesentārius, **a**, **um** *adj* quick, ready; paid on the spot in cash, in ready money

praesentia, **ae** *f* presence; helpful presence

praesentiō, **nsī**, **ēnsum** ④ *v* feel *or* perceive beforehand; have a presentiment of

praesēp- ▸ **praesaep-**

praesertim *adv* especially, particularly

praeses, **idis** *m* guardian, warden, custodian

praesideō, **sēdī** ② *v with dat* preside (over); guard, protect, defend; superintend

praesidium, **(i)ī** *nt* help, assistance; defence, protection; convoy, escort; garrison; stronghold

praesignis, **e** *adj* pre-eminent, outstanding

praestābilis, **e** *adj* pre-eminent, distinguished, excellent

praestāns, **ntis** *adj* excellent; distinguished (for)

praestituō, **uī**, **ūtum** ③ *v* determine in advance

praestō¹ *adv* ready, at one's service

praestō², **stitī**, **stitum/stātum** ① *v* stand out; be superior (to); surpass; answer for; fulfil; maintain; show; furnish

praestōlor ① *v dep* expect; await

praestringō, **īnxī**, **ictum** ③ *v* bind *or* tie up; graze, weaken, blunt

praestruō, **ūxī**, **ūctum** ③ *v* block up, contrive beforehand

praesultō ① *v* dance before

praesum, **esse**, **fuī** *v ir with dat* be in charge (of), be in control (of); take the lead (in)

praesūmō, **m(p)sī**, **mptum** ③ *v* consume beforehand; perform beforehand; spend *or* employ beforehand; presuppose

praetendō, **ndī**, **ntum** ③ *v* stretch out; spread before; extend in front; allege in excuse; offer *or* show deceptively, make a pretence of

praeter *prep with acc/adv* past; except; excepting; along; beyond; unless, save; besides

praetereā *adv* besides; moreover

praetereō, **īre**, **iī/īvī**, **itum** *v ir* go by *or* past; pass by; escape the notice of; neglect; surpass

praeterfluō ③ *v* flow past

praetergredior, **gressus sum** ③ *v dep* march *or* go past

praeterhāc *adv* beyond this point; further

praeteritus, **a**, **um** *adj* past

praeterlābor, **lāpsus sum** ③ *v dep* glide *or* slip past

praetermittō, **mīsī**, **missum** ③ *v* let pass; omit; neglect; pass over, make no mention of

praeterquam *adv* beyond, besides; except, save

praetervehor, **vectus sum** ③ *v dep* drive, ride *or* sail by; pass by

praetervolō ① *v* fly past; slip by

praetexō, **xuī**, **xtum** ③ *v* weave in front, fringe; cloak (with); pretend

praetexta, **ae** *f* toga with a purple border worn by curule magistrates and children

praetextātus, **a**, **um** *adj* wearing the toga praetexta

praetextus, **ūs** *m* show; pretext

praetor, **ōris** *m* Roman magistrate

> ❗ In the republican period, subordinate only to the consuls, a **praetor** was a magistrate at Rome whose chief task was the administration of law; his power, however, permitted him to lead an army and govern a province, and he presided over the senate in the absence of the consuls. Until the middle of the 2nd cent. BC there was a single praetor, the office then being split first into two (the **praetor urbānus** and **praetor inter peregrīnōs**) and subsequently into four then six. Under Sulla the number

increased to eight and under Caesar to sixteen. In the imperial period, reduced to twelve in number, they retained their function of presiding over courts, games and occasionally the senate.

praetōriānus, **a**, **um** *adj* praetorian

praetōrium, **(i)ī** *nt* general's headquarters building *or* tent; imperial bodyguard

praetōrius¹, **(i)ī** *m* an ex-praetor

praetōrius², **a**, **um** *adj* of *or* belonging to a commander (of a Roman military force), praetorian

praetrepidō ① *v* tremble in anticipation

praetūra, **ae** *f* praetorship

praeūrō, **ussī**, **ustum** ③ *v* scorch at the extremity *or* on the surface

praevaleō ② *v* have greater power, influence *or* worth; prevail

praevalidus, **a**, **um** *adj* very *or* outstandingly strong; strong in growth

praevehor, **vectus sum** ③ *v dep* travel past *or* along

praeveniō, **vēnī**, **ventum** ④ *v* arrive first *or* beforehand; anticipate, forestall

praevertō, **rtī**, **rsum** ③ *v* anticipate; preoccupy; attend to first; outstrip, outrun

praevideō, **vīdī**, **vīsum** ② *v* foresee, see in advance

praevius, **a**, **um** *adj* going before, leading the way

prandeō, **ndī**, **pránsum** ② *v* eat one's morning *or* midday meal

prandium, **(i)ī** *nt* meal eaten about midday, luncheon

prātum, **ī** *nt* meadow

prāvitās, **ātis** *f* bad condition; viciousness, perverseness, depravity

prāvus, **a**, **um** *adj* crooked; misshapen, deformed; perverse, vicious, corrupt; faulty; bad

precārius, **a**, **um** *adj* obtained by prayer; doubtful, precarious

precātiō, **ōnis** *f* prayer, supplication

precēs, **um** *fpl* prayer, entreaty; good wishes

precor ① *v dep* pray to, beseech, entreat; ask for; invoke

prehendō, **ndī**, **ēnsum** ③ *v* take hold of, seize hold of; catch in the act

prelatus, **i** *m* LM prelate, bishop

prēlum, **ī** *nt* wine- *or* oil-press

premō, **essī**, **essum** ③ *v* press; squeeze; oppress; curb; thrust; overpower; keep in subjection; afflict; pursue; have intercourse with

prēnsō ① *v* grasp at; accost; canvass

pressō ① *v* press, squeeze

pressus, **a**, **um** *adj* firmly planted, deliberate

pretiōsus, **a**, **um** *adj* valuable, precious; costly

pretium, **(i)ī** *nt* price, worth, value; wages, reward; bribe
▫ **(operae)** ∼ **est** it is worth while

prīdem *adv* some time ago, previously

prīdiē *adv* on the day before

prima, **ae** *f* LM prime (part of the daily cycle of prayer)

prīmaevus, **a**, **um** *adj* youthful

prīmānus, **a**, **um** *adj* of the first legion

prīmārius, **a**, **um** *adj* of the first rank

prīmipīlus, **ī** *m* senior centurion of a legion

prīmitiae, **ārum** *fpl* first-fruits; beginnings

prīmordium, **(i)ī** *nt* beginnings, origin

prīmōris, **is** *adj* first; foremost, extreme
■ **prīmōrēs** *mpl* nobles, men of the first rank

prīmum *adv* first, in the first place, at the beginning; for the first time
▫ **quam** ∼ as soon as possible

prīmus, **a**, **um** *adj* first, foremost; most distinguished
▫ **prīma lux** early dawn
▫ **in prīmīs** especially
▫ **ad prīma signa** in the front line

prīnceps, **ipis** *adj* first; *m/f* chief; general; prime mover
▫ ∼ **senātūs** senator whose name stood first on the censors' list

prīncipālis, **e** *adj* first, original, principal; imperial, with the emperor

prīncipātus, **ūs** *m* pre-eminence; supremacy, post of commander-in-chief; rule; beginning

prīncipium, **(i)ī** *nt* beginning, origin, principle

prior, ius *adj* former, previous; in front; better
- **priōrēs, um** *mpl* ancestors
- **prior, is** *m* LM abbot

prīscus, a, um *adj* old, ancient; archaic

prīstinus, a, um *adj* former, antique, ancient

prius *adv* before, sooner

priusquam *conj* before

prīvātim *adv* in private, privately

prīvātus, a, um *adj* private

prīvigna, ae *f* stepdaughter

prīvignus, ī *m* stepson

privilegium, (i)i *nt* LM privilege, charter, bull

prīvō ① *v* deprive (of); free *or* release (from)

prīvus, a, um *adj* one's own, private; separate, single

prō¹ *prep with abl* before, in front of; from the front of; for, in favour of; instead of; in proportion to
□ ∼ **certō habeō** know for certain

> **!** In titles of speeches, **prō** indicates a speech on behalf of the defendant.

prō² *int with voc, acc or nom* good god! good heavens!

proavia, ae *f* great-grandmother

proavītus, a, um *adj* ancestral

proavus, ī *m* great-grandfather; remote ancestor

probābilis, e *adj* probable; commendable

probātor, ōris *m* one who approves

probitās, ātis *f* honesty, probity; virtue

probō ① *v* test; recommend; approve of; prove

probrōsus, a, um *adj* shameful; disreputable

probrum, ī *nt* disgrace; abuse, insult; disgrace, shame

probus, a, um *adj* good; clever; honest, virtuous

procāx, ācis *adj* pushing, impudent; undisciplined; frivolous

prōcēdō, essī, essum ③ *v* go forward *or* before, proceed; advance; get on; be successful; make progress

procella, ae *f* storm, gale; tumult, commotion

procellōsus, a, um *adj* stormy, boisterous

procer, eris *m* usu. in pl. great men, noblemen

prōcēritās, ātis *f* height; great length

prōcērus, a, um *adj* high, tall; long

prōcessus, ūs *m* advance, progress

prōcidō, idī ③ *v* fall prostrate, collapse

prōcinctus, ūs *m* readiness for battle

prōclāmō ① *v* call *or* cry out; appeal noisily

prōclīnō ① *v* tilt forward; cause to totter

prōclīvis, e *adj* sloping down; downward; prone (to); easy

Procnē, ēs *f* swallow

prōcōnsul, lis *m* ex-consul; governor of a province

prōcōnsulāris, e *adj* proconsular

prōcrāstinō ① *v* put off till the next day, postpone; delay

prōcreō ① *v* bring into existence, beget, procreate; produce, create

prōcrēscō ③ *v* grow on to maturity, grow larger

prōcubō ① *v* lie outstretched

prōcūdō, ūdī, ūsum ③ *v* forge, hammer out, beat out

procul *adv* far, some way off, far away

prōculcō ① *v* trample on

prōcumbō, ubuī, ubitum ③ *v* lean *or* bend forward; sink down, prostrate oneself

prōcūrātiō, ōnis *f* charge, management; superintendence

prōcūrātor, ōris *m* manager, overseer; agent; governor; LM proctor

prōcūrō ① *v* attend to; administer; expiate (by sacrifice)

prōcurrō, (cu)currī, cursum ③ *v* run *or* rush forwards; extend, project

prōcursātiō, ōnis *f* sudden charge, sally

prōcursō ① *v* run frequently forward, dash out

prōcursus, ūs *m* forward movement; outbreak

prōcurvus, a, um *adj* curved outwards *or* forwards

procus, ī *m* wooer, suitor

prōdeō, **īre**, **iī**, **itum** *v ir* go *or* come forward *or* forth; project; appear in public, appear on the stage; advance, proceed

prōdīcō, **īxī**, **ictum** ③ *v* give notice of *or* fix a day

prōdigiōsus, **a**, **um** *adj* prodigious, strange, wonderful, unnatural

prōdigium, **(i)ī** *nt* omen, portent, monster; marvel; monstrous creature

prōdigus, **a**, **um** *adj* wasteful, lavish, prodigal

prōditiō, **ōnis** *f* betrayal, treachery

prōditor, **ōris** *m* traitor; betrayer

prōdō, **didī**, **ditum** ③ *v* give birth to; nominate; publish; betray; hand down

prōdūcō, **dūxī**, **ductum** ③ *v* lead *or* bring forward; draw out; accompany to the tomb; lengthen; prolong; bring forth

proelior ① *v dep* join battle, fight; contend

proelium, **(i)ī** *nt* battle, combat; conflict, dispute

profānō ① *v* desecrate, profane

profānus, **a**, **um** *adj* secular, profane; not initiated; impious

profectiō, **ōnis** *f* setting out; departure

profectō *adv* without question, undoubtedly, assuredly

prōfectus, **ūs** *m* progress, success

profectus *pple* from ▸ **proficīscor**

prōferō, **ferre**, **tulī**, **lātum** *v ir* carry *or* bring out, bring forth; extend; prolong; defer; reveal; utter; produce; publish

profēstus, **a**, **um** *adj* not kept as a holiday, common, ordinary

prōficiō, **fēcī**, **fectum** ③ *v* make headway; advance; help; develop; be successful

proficīscor, **profectus sum** ③ *v dep* set out, depart; proceed, arise *or* spring from

profiteor, **professus sum** ② *v dep* declare publicly; promise, volunteer; profess (oneself) to be

prōflīgātus, **a**, **um** *adj* profligate, depraved

prōflīgō ① *v* defeat decisively, crush, overwhelm; ruin *or* destroy utterly

prōflō ① *v* blow out, exhale

prōfluō, **ūxī**, **ūxum** ③ *v* flow forth *or* along; emanate (from)

profor ① *v dep* speak out

profugiō, **ūgī** ③ *v* flee, run away (from)

profugus, **a**, **um** *adj* fugitive; runaway; refugee

profundō, **ūdī**, **ūsum** ③ *v* pour out; lavish, squander; break out

profundus, **a**, **um** *adj* deep, profound; boundless; insatiable
 ■ **profundum**, **ī** *nt* depths, abyss, chasm; boundless expanse

profūsus, **a**, **um** *adj* excessive; lavish; extravagant

prōgeniēs, **iēī** *f* race, family, progeny

prōgenitor, **ōris** *m* ancestor

prōgignō, **genuī**, **genitum** ③ *v* beget; produce

prōgnātus, **a**, **um** *adj* born (of), descended (from)

prōgredior, **gressus sum** ③ *v dep* march forwards, go on, proceed

prōgressus, **ūs** *m* advance, progress

prohibeō ② *v* keep off, hold at bay; prevent, restrain; stop, forbid; avert; defend

prōiciō, **iēcī**, **iectum** ③ *v* throw forth *or* before, fling down *or* away; expose; expel; renounce

prōiectus, **a**, **um** *adj* jutting out, projecting; precipitate; abject; grovelling

proinde *adv* accordingly, so then
 □ ~ **ac** just as if

prōlābor, **lāpsus sum** ③ *v dep* glide *or* slip forwards; fall into decay, go to ruin; collapse

prōlātiō, **ōnis** *f* postponement; enlargement

prōlātō ① *v* lengthen, enlarge; prolong; put off, defer

prōlectō ① *v* lure, entice

prōlēs, **lis** *f* offspring, progeny, descendants, race

prōliciō ③ *v* lure forward, lead on

prōlogus, **ī** *m* prologue

prōloquor, **locūtus sum** ③ *v dep* speak out, declare

prōlūdō, **ūsī**, **ūsum** ③ *v* carry out preliminary exercises before a fight; rehearse for

prōluō, **uī**, **ūtum** ③ *v* wash out; wash away; wash up; purify

prōluviēs, **iēī** *f* overflow, flood; bodily discharge

prōmereō ② *u*, **prōmereor** ② *v dep* deserve, merit; deserve well of; earn; gain

prōmineō ② *v* jut out, stick up

prōmīscam, **prōmīscē** *adv* without distinction, all at the same time *or* in the same place; commonly

prōmiscuus, **a**, **um** *adj* common, shared; general, indiscriminate

prōmissum, **ī** *nt* promise

prōmissus, **a**, **um** *adj* hanging down, long

prōmittō, **mīsī**, **missum** ③ *v* send *or* put forth, let hang down; promise, guarantee

prōmō, **prōm(p)sī**, **prōmptum** ③ *v* take *or* bring out *or* forth; bring into view; bring out *or* display on the stage; make known

prōmonturium, **(i)ī** *nt* promontory, headland; mountain spur

prōmoveō, **mōvī**, **mōtum** ② *v* move forwards; advance, push forward

prōmptuārium, **(i)ī** *nt* store-room, cupboard

prōmptus¹, **ūs** *m*:
  □ **in prōmptū sum** be in full view; be obvious; be within easy reach for use

prōmptus², **a**, **um** *adj* plainly visible, evident; at hand, ready, prompt, quick, glib, insincere

prōmulgō ① *v* make known by public proclamation; publish

prōmuntorium ▶ prōmontorium

prōmus, **ī** *m* butler; steward

pronepōs, **ōtis** *m* great-grandson

prōnuba, **ae** *f* a married woman who conducted the bride to the bridal chamber

prōnūntiātiō, **ōnis** *f* proclamation; delivery; verdict

prōnūntiō ① *v* proclaim, announce; recite, declaim; tell, report; promise publicly

prōnus, **a**, **um** *adj* stooping, bending down; inclined downwards; setting, sinking; disposed, prone to; easy

propāgātiō, **ōnis** *f* propagation; prolongation; the action of extending

propāgō¹ ① *v* propagate; extend, enlarge, increase

propāgō², **inis** *f* a layer *or* set by which a plant is propagated; offspring, children, race, breed

prōpalam *adv* openly

prope *adv*/*prep with acc* near, almost

propediem *adv* before long, shortly

prōpellō, **pulī**, **pulsum** ③ *v* drive *or* push forwards; propel; drive away; impel

propemodo, **propemodum** *adv* just about, pretty well

prōpēnsus, **a**, **um** *adj* ready, eager, willing; favourably disposed

properanter *adv* hurriedly, hastily

properipēs, **edis** *adj* swift-footed

properō ① *v* hasten; do with haste

properus, **a**, **um** *adj* quick, speedy

prōpexus, **a**, **um** *adj* combed so as to hang down

propheta, **ae** *m* 〖LM〗 prophet

propheto ① *v* 〖LM〗 prophesy

propinquitās, **ātis** *f* nearness, proximity; relationship, affinity; intimacy

propinquō ① *v* bring near; draw near

propinquus, **a**, **um** *adj* near, neighbouring
  ■ ~, **ī** *m* kinsman

propior, **ius** *adj* nearer; more like; closer

propitiō ① *v* win over, propitiate; soothe

propitius, **a**, **um** *adj* favourably inclined, well-disposed, propitious

prōpōnō, **posuī**, **positum** ③ *v* put out; set *or* post up; display; expose (to); report; propose, intend

prōpositum, **ī** *nt* intention, purpose; theme, point

prōpraetor, **ōris** *m* an ex-praetor; one sent to govern a province as **praetor**

proprietās, **ātis** *f* quality; special character; ownership

proprius, **a**, **um** *adj* one's own; personal; special; peculiar, proper
  ■ **proprior**, **ius** *comp* better suited

propter *adv*/*prep with acc* near, hard by, at hand; because of; on account of

proptereā *adv* therefore, on account of that

prōpugnāculum, **ī** *nt* bulwark, rampart; defence

prōpugnātor, **ōris** *m* defender; champion

prōpugnō ① *v* fight; fight in defence of

prōpulsō ① *v* drive off; ward off, repel

prōquaestor, **ōris** *m* deputy *or* treasurer; ex-quaestor

prōra, **ae** *f* prow; ship

prōrēpō, **psī**, **ptum** ③ *v* crawl *or* creep forth

prōrēta, **ae** *m* look-out (at the prow of a ship)

prōripiō, **ripuī**, **reptum** ③ *v* drag *or* snatch away; rush *or* burst forth

prōrogātiō, **ōnis** *f* extension of a term of office; postponement

prōrogō ① *v* prolong, keep going; put off, defer

prōrsus *adv* forward; straight ahead; absolutely

prōrumpō, **rūpī**, **ruptum** ③ *v* rush forth, break out

prōruō, **ruī**, **rutum** ③ *v* rush forward; tumble down; overthrow; hurl forward

prōsāpia, **ae** *f* family, lineage

proscaenium, **(i)ī** *nt* scaffold before the scene for the actors to play on; stage

proscindō, **idī**, **issum** ③ *v* cut, plough; castigate, lash

prōscrībō, **psī**, **ptum** ③ *v* announce publicly; post up, advertise (for sale); outlaw, proscribe

prōscrīptiō, **ōnis** *f* advertisement; proscription

prōscrīptus, **ī** *m* proscribed person, outlaw

prōsequor, **secūtus sum** ③ *v dep* follow up, pursue; accompany

prōsiliō, **luī** ④ *v* leap *or* spring forth; start out; gush

prōspectō ① *v* gaze out (at); look out on

prōspectus, **ūs** *m* view, prospect

prōspeculor ① *v dep* look out for

prosperō ① *v* cause to succeed, further

prosperus, **a**, **um** *adj* favourable, prosperous; successful; propitious

prōspiciō, **exī**, **ectum** ③ *v* see in front; foresee; take care (that); see to

prōsternō, **strāvī**, **strātum** ③ *v* throw to the ground, overthrow, prostrate; overthrow cause the downfall of

prōstituō, **tuī**, **tūtum** ③ *v* prostitute; dishonour

prōstō, **stitī** ① *v* prostitute oneself

prōsubigō, **ēgī**, **āctum** ③ *v* dig up in front of one

prōsum, **prōdesse**, **fuī** *v ir with dat* do good, benefit, profit

> ❗ Conjugated exactly like **sum**, in this verb **prō-** becomes **prōd-** before forms beginning with **e-** (as in, e.g., the infin.).

prōtegō, **ēxī**, **ēctum** ③ *v* cover; furnish with a projecting roof; protect; defend

prōtēlō ① *v* rout

prōtendō, **ndī**, **ntum** ③ *v* stretch out, extend; prolong

prōterō, **trīvī**, **trītum** ③ *v* crush, tread under foot; oppress

prōterreō ② *v* frighten off *or* away

protervus, **a**, **um** *adj* violent, reckless; impudent, shameless

prōtinam *adv* at once, forthwith; straight on

prōtinus *adv* forward, straight on; immediately

prōtrahō, **āxī**, **actum** ③ *v* drag forward; bring to light, reveal; prolong

prōtrūdō, **ūsī**, **ūsum** ③ *v* thrust forwards *or* out; put off

prōturbō ① *v* drive *or* push out of the way

prout *adv* according as, in proportion as; inasmuch as

prōvectus, **a**, **um** *adj* advanced, late; elderly

prōvehō, **ēxī**, **ectum** ③ *v* carry forward; convey out to sea

prōveniō, **vēnī**, **ventum** ④ *v* come forth; come into being; prosper

prōventus, **ūs** *m* growth; crop, produce; success; successful course

prōverbium, **(i)ī** *nt* proverb, saying

prōvidentia, **ae** *f* foresight, foreknowledge; providence

prōvideō, **vīdī**, **vīsum** ② *v* provide (for); foresee

prōvidus, **a**, **um** *adj* prophetic; provident; characterized by forethought

P

prōvincia, ae f command, government, administration, province

prōvinciālis, e adj provincial

prōvīsor, ōris m one who foresees; one who takes care (of)

prōvocātiō, ōnis f challenge; appeal; right of appeal

prōvocō ① v call forth, call out; challenge, excite

prōvolō ① v fly forth; rush out

prōvolvō, lvī, lūtum ③ v roll forward or along, bowl over
  □ **prōvolvor** prostrate oneself

proximitās, ātis f near relationship; resemblance; similarity

proximus, a, um adj nearest; next; immediately preceding, immediately following; next of kin

prūdēns, ntis adj foreseeing, aware (of); intelligent, prudent; skilled (in)

prūdentia, ae f practical understanding; intelligence, prudence; practical grasp; foreknowledge

pruīna, ae f hoar-frost, rime

pruīnōsus, a, um adj frosty

prūna, ae f glowing charcoal, a live coal

prūnum, ī nt plum

prūrīgō, inis f itching, irritation; sexual excitement

prūriō ④ v itch; be sexually excited

psallō, ī ③ v play on the cithara

psalmodia, ae f [LM] psalm-singing, psalmody

psalmus, i m [LM] psalm

psalterium, (i)i m [LM] psalter, book containing the Psalms

psaltria, ae f female player on the lute

psittacus, ī m parrot

-pte particle own

pūbēns, ntis adj full of sap, vigorous

pūbertās, ātis f puberty; virility

pūbēs¹, bis f manpower, adult population; private parts

pūbēs², eris adj adult, grown-up; full of sap

pūbēscō, buī ③ v reach physical maturity; ripen

pūblicānus, ī m contractor for public works, farmer of the Roman taxes

pūblicitus adv at public expense

pūblicō ① v confiscate; make public property

pūblicus, a, um adj public, common
  ▪ **pūblicē** adv publicly, at public expense, officially
  ▪ **pūblicum, ī** nt public purse; public property; public place, agora
  ▪ **pūblicus, ī** m public slave

pudendus, a, um adj disgraceful, scandalous

pudēns, ntis adj modest; bashful

pudeō ② v be ashamed; make ashamed
  □ **mē pudet** I am ashamed

pudibundus, a, um adj shamefaced, blushing

pudīcitia, ae f chastity, purity

pudīcus, a, um adj chaste, virtuous

pudor, ōris m shame, shyness, modesty; decency; dishonour

puella, ae f girl, maiden; sweetheart

puellāris, e adj girlish, maidenly

puellula, ae f young girl

puer, erī m boy, son, young male slave
  □ **ā puerō** from boyhood

puerīlis, e adj childish, boyish, youthful; immature

pueritia, ae f boyhood; callowness

puerpera, ae f a woman in labour

puerperium, (i)i nt childbirth

pugil, lis m boxer, pugilist

pugilātōrius, a, um adj for punching, for boxing

pugillārēs, ium mpl writing-tablets

pugiō, ōnis m dagger, poniard

pugna, ae f fight; battle, combat; conflict, dispute

pugnātor, ōris m fighter, combatant

pugnāx, ācis adj combative, pugnacious; quarrelsome

pugneus, a, um adj of fists, 'fisty'

pugnō ① v fight; contend, clash

pugnus, ī m fist

pulc(h)er, c(h)ra, c(h)rum adj beautiful, handsome; glorious; illustrious; noble

pulc(h)ritūdō, inis f beauty; attractiveness

pullārius, (i)ī m keeper of the sacred chickens

pullātī, ōrum *mpl* people in mourning-dress

pullitiēs, iēī *f* set of young birds, brood

pullulō 1 *v* sprout, send forth new growth; spring forth

pullus[1], ī *m* young animal; young chicken; darling, pet

pullus[2], a, um *adj* dingy, sombre

pulmō, ōnis *m* lungs; jellyfish

pulmōneus, a, um *adj* of the lungs

pulpitum, ī *nt* stage

puls, ltis *f* a dish made by boiling crushed spelt or other grain in water, a kind of porridge

pulsō 1 *v* push, strike, beat, batter; assail

pulsum ▸ pellō

pulsus, ūs *m* stroke; beat; pulse; impulse

pultiphagus, a, um *adj* eating porridge

pultō ▸ pulsō

pulvereus, a, um *adj*, **pulverulentus**, a, um *adj* dusty

pulvīnar, āris *nt*, **pulvīnus**, ī *m* cushioned couch on which images of the gods were placed

pulvis, eris *m* dust, powder, arena, battlefield

pūmex, icis *m* pumice

pūmiliō, ōnis *m* dwarf

pūn- ▸ poen-

pūnctim *adv* with the point

pūnctum, ī *nt* prick, small hole, puncture; spot; vote
□ ~ **temporis** a moment

pungō, **pupugī**, **pūnctum** 3 *v* prick, puncture; vex, trouble

pūniceus, a, um *adj* scarlet, crimson

pūniō 4 *v* punish; avenge

pupa, ae *f* doll

pūpillus, ī *m* ward

puppis, is *f* stern, poop; ship

pūpula, ae *f* pupil of the eye

pūpulus, ī *m* little boy

pūrgāmen, inis *nt* impurity; means of purification

pūrgāmentum, ī *nt* means of cleansing *or* purifying; rubbish, filth

pūrgātiō, ōnis *f* cleaning

pūrgō 1 *v* make clean, clean, cleanse, purify; justify, excuse, clear, exonerate

purificatio, onis *f* LM purification; Candlemas

purpura, ae *f* purple colour, purple; purple dye; purple-dyed cloth

purpurātus, a, um *adj* dressed in purple

purpureus, a, um *adj* purple-coloured, purple; radiant, glowing

purpurissum, ī *nt* dark red *or* purple cosmetic, rouge

pūrus, a, um *adj* clean, pure, undefiled; clear, chaste, naked, unadorned; without an iron point

pusillus, a, um *adj* very little, petty, insignificant

pustula, ae *f* inflamed sore, blister

putāmen, inis *nt* hard outer cover; nutshell

putātor, ōris *m* pruner

puteal, ālis *nt* structure surrounding the mouth of a well (in the Comitium at Rome)

puteālis, e *adj* derived from a well

pūteō 2 *v* stink

puter, **tris**, **tre** *adj* (also **putris**, **e**) rotten, decaying; stinking, putrid, crumbling

pūtēscō 3 *v* begin to rot, go off

puteus, ī *m* well

pūtidus, a, um *adj* rotten; stinking; unpleasant; offensive; tiresomely affected; pedantic

putō 1 *v* trim, prune; assess, estimate, regard (as); think, suppose, believe

putrefaciō, **fēcī**, **factum** 3 *v* cause to rot, putrefy

putrēscō 3 *v* rot, putrefy; crumble, moulder

pyra, ae *f* funeral pile, pyre

pȳramis, idis *f* pyramid

pyrōpus, ī *m* an alloy of gold and bronze; a red precious stone

pyxis, idis *f* small box *or* casket; LM pyx

Qq

quā *adv* in which direction; where; by what means, how; in so far as

quācumque *adv* wherever

quadra, **ae** *f* segment, slice

quadrāgēnī, **ae**, **a** *adj* forty each

quadragesimalis, **e** *adj* LM lenten

quadrāgēsimus, **a**, **um** *adj* fortieth
  ■ **quadragesima**, **ae** *f* LM Lent

quadrāgiē(n)s *adv* forty times

quadrāgintā *adj indec* forty

quadrāns, **ntis** *m* fourth part, quarter; coin worth a quarter of an **as**

quadrātus, **a**, **um** *adj* squared, square-set

quadrīduum, **ī** *nt* period of four days

quadriennium, **(i)ī** *nt* period of four years

quadrifāriam *adv* in four ways, into four parts

quadrifidus, **a**, **um** *adj* split into four

quadrīgae, **ārum** *fpl* chariot with four horses

quadriiugus, **a**, **um** *adj* yoked four abreast

quadrīmus, **a**, **um** *adj* four years old

quadringēnārius, **a**, **um** *adj* of four hundred each

quadringēnī, **ae**, **a** *adj* four hundred each

quadringentē(n)simus, **a**, **um** *adj* the four hundredth

quadringentī, **ae**, **a** *adj* four hundred

quadrirēmis, **mis** *f* galley with four rowers to every 'room'

quadrivium, **(i)i** *n* LM the four 'higher' subjects of the medieval university curriculum, viz. mathematics, geometry, astronomy and music

quadrō 1 *v* quadruple; form a rectangular pattern

quadrupedāns, **ntis** *adj* galloping

quadrupēs, **edis** *adj* four-footed
  ■ ~, **edis** *m/f* quadruped

quadruplex, **icis** *adj* fourfold; quadruple

quaeritō 1 *v* seek; search for

quaerō, **sīvī/siī**, **sītum** 3 *v* look *or* search for; get, procure; inquire into

quaesītiō, **ōnis** *f* inquisition

quaesītus, **a**, **um** *adj* elaborate, contrived

quaesō 3 *v* ask (for); pray; please

quaestiō, **ōnis** *f* inquiry, investigation, question; examination by torture

quaestor, **ōris** *m* quaestor

> **!** A **quaestor** was the staff officer to the governor of a province, principally responsible for financial matters. He sometimes acted as the commander's second-in command and/ or as commander of one of the governor's legions.

quaestōrius, **a**, **um** *adj* of a quaestor
  ■ ~, **(i)ī** *m* ex-quaestor

quaestuōsus, **a**, **um** *adj* profitable

quaestūra, **ae** *f* quaestorship; public money

quaestus, **ūs** *m* gaining, acquiring; gain, profit, income

quālibet *adv* wherever one likes; no matter how

quālis, **e** *adj* of what sort, kind *or* nature, of what kind

quāliscumque, **quālecumque** *adj* of whatever sort *or* quality; any kind of

quālum, **ī** *nt*, **quālus**, **ī** *m* wicker basket

quam *adv/conj* how; how much; in what way; than; *with sup* as ... as possible
  □ **tam** ... ~ as ... as

□ ~ **prīmum** as soon as possible
□ *with comp* ~ **ut**/**quī** [too ...] to ...

> ❗ When **quam** is used to mean 'than' the two things compared are in the same case; after this use of **quam** the words for 'some-, any-' are as after **nec**, i.e. **quisquam**, **ūllus** etc.

quamdiū *adv* as long as; how long

quamlibet *adv* however, however much

quamobrem *adv* why? for what reason? for which reason

quamprīmum *adv* as soon as possible

quamquam *conj* although; yet

> ❗ **quamquam** is only ever a conj. and is always followed by a clause with an indic. verb; cf. **quamvīs**.

quamvīs *adv*/*conj* to any degree you like; although; however

> ❗ **quamvīs** is both conj. and adv.; as the former it takes a clause with a subj. verb while as the latter it simply qualifies an adj., e.g. **quamvīs sapiēns, pauper est** 'although wise, he is poor'.

quandō *adv* at what time? when? *after* **si, nisi, num, nē** at any time

> ❗ **quandō** meaning 'when' is a question word; after Plautus it very rarely introduces a temporal clause.

quandōcumque *adv* whenever, as often as, as soon as

quandōque *adv* whenever; at some time *or* other

quandoquidem *conj* since, seeing that

quantillus, a, um *adj* how little?

quantō *adv* (by) how much

quantopere *adv* how greatly; in what degree

quantulus, a, um *adj* how little, how small, how trifling

quantuluscumque, **quantulacumque**, **quantulumcumque** *adj* however small *or* insignificant

quantus, a, um *adj* how great, as great as
□ **quantī** at what price?

quantuscumque, **quantacumque**, **quantumcumque** *adj* however great (or small); whatever

quantuslibet, **quantalibet**, **quantumlibet** *adj* no matter how great; however great

quantusvīs, **quantavīs**, **quantumvīs** *adj* however great

quāpropter *adv* wherefore; why

quārē *adv* in what way? how? whereby; wherefore, why

quārtus, a, um *adj* fourth

quasi *adv* as if, just as; as good as, practically

> ❗ See note at **tamquam**.

quassātiō, ōnis *f* violent shaking

quassō ① *v* shake repeatedly; wave, flourish; batter; weaken

quassus, a, um *adj* shaking, battered, bruised

quātenus *adv* how far; to what extent; how long, seeing that, since

quater *adv* four times

quaternī, ae, a *adj* four each, by fours; four together

quatiō, assum ③ *v* strike, shatter; shake; agitate, discompose; urge on

quattuor *adj indec* four

quattuordecim *adj indec* fourteen

quattuorvirī, ōrum *mpl* body of four men; board of chief magistrates

-que *conj* and
□ **-que** ... **et** both ... and

> ❗ **-que** attaches to the end of the first word of the second thing being joined, e.g. **canēs fēlēsque** 'cats and dogs'.

quemadmodum *adv* how, in what way

queō, īre, īvī *v ir dep* be able (to)

quercus, ūs *f* oak, oak-tree; garland of oak leaves

querēla, **querella**, **ae** *f* complaint; plaintive sound

querimōnia, ae *f* complaint; 'difference of opinion'

quernus, a, um *adj* of oak, made of oak-wood

q

queror, questus sum ③ *v dep* complain; protest that *or* at

querulus, a, um *adj* complaining, querulous; giving forth a mournful sound

questus, ūs *m* complaint

quī[1] *adv* why? by what means? how?

quī[2]**, quae, quod** *pn* who, which, that; which? any

quia *conj* because; ⓛⓜ that

quianam *adv* why ever?

quīcumque, quaecumque, quodcumque *pn* whoever, whatever

quid *adv* why? how? in what respect?

quīdam, quaedam, quoddam *pn* a certain

> ❗ **quīdam** usu. refers to a particular 'someone' or 'something' whom one could but does not name, e.g. **diē quōdam nātus** 'born on some (i.e. a certain but unnamed) day'; cf. **aliquis**.

quidem *adv* indeed, certainly, in fact □ **nē ... ~** not even

quidnam *adv* what? how?

quidnī *adv* why not?

quiēs, ētis *f* rest, quiet, repose, peace; sleep; death

quiēscō, ēvī, ētum ③ *v* rest, keep quiet; repose in sleep

quiētus, a, um *adj* calm, quiet; peaceful, sleeping; undisturbed

quīlibet, quaelibet, quidlibet/ quodlibet *pn* whoever *or* whatever you please

quīn *conj* that not; (but) that; indeed; why not? nay more

> ❗ **quīn** usu. introduces a subordinate clause dependent on a clause containing a negative. It is regular if the main clause contains a verb meaning 'doubt, hinder, prevent', although it is sometimes replaced with **quōminus**. It may also correspond to the English meaning 'without -ing', e.g. **numquam ēst quīn bibat** 'she never eats without drinking'.

Quīnctīlis, lis *m* July

quīncūnx, uncis *m* five-twelfths (of an as); a pattern in which trees were planted; interest at five per cent

quīndecim *adj indec* fifteen

quīndecimvirī, ōrum *mpl* college *or* board of fifteen; college of priests who had charge of the Sibylline books

quīngēnī, ae, a *adj* five hundred each

quīngentē(n)simus, a, um *adj* five-hundredth

quīngentī, ae, a *adj* five hundred

quīnī, ae, a *adj* five each; five apiece; five at a time

quīnquāgēnī, ae, a *adj* fifty each; fifty at a time

quīnquāgē(n)simus, a, um *adj* fiftieth

quīnquāgintā *adj indec* fifty

quīnquātria, ōrum *ntpl*, **quīnquātrūs, uum** *fpl* feast in honour of Minerva on 19-23 March

quīnque *adj indec* five

quīnquennālis, e *adj* quinquennial, occurring every five years

quīnquennis, e *adj* five years old; lasting for five years

quīnquennium, (i)ī *nt* (period of) five years

quinquerēmis, e *adj* (of a galley) with five rowers to each 'room'

quīnquevirī, ōrum *mpl* board of five

quīnquiē(n)s *adv* five times

quīntadecumānī, ōrum *mpl* soldiers of the fifteenth legion

quīntāna, ae *f* street *or* market in a Roman camp

quīntānī, ōrum *mpl* soldiers of the fifth legion

Quīntīlis ▸ Quīnctīlis

quīntō, quīntum *adv* for the fifth time

quīntus, a, um *adj* fifth

quippe *adv* the reason is that, for; of course, naturally; seeing that; inasmuch as; as being; indeed, namely

Quirīnālia, ium *ntpl* a festival in honour of Romulus, celebrated on 17 February

quiritātus, ūs *m* cry of protest

Quirītēs, ītum *mpl* citizens of Rome collectively in their peacetime functions

quis, quid *pn* who? which? what? anyone; anything; someone; something ∎ **quid** why?

quisnam, quaenam, quidnam *pn* who tell me? what, tell me?

q

quispiam, quaepiam, quodpiam/ quidpiam/quippiam *pn* anyone, anybody, anything, any; someone, something, some

quisquam, quicquam *pn* any, any one, anybody, anything

quisque, quaeque, quodque/ quicque/quidque *pn* each, every, everybody, everything
□ **optimus** ∼ all the best people

> ❗ **suus quisque** (with both words usu. agreeing with the same noun) means '(each) in respect of his own', e.g. **sua quaeque māla sub arbore iacent** 'each tree's apples lie beneath it', lit. 'the apples of each lie beneath their own tree'.

quisquiliae, ārum *fpl* waste materials, refuse, trash

quisquis, quodquod/quicquid/ quidquid *pn* whoever, whatever, everyone who

quīvīs, quaevīs, quodvīs/quidvīs *pn* who *or* what you please, anyone, anything

quō *adv* whither; whither? for what purpose? what for?; so that thereby
□ ∼ ... **eō** as ... so; *with comp* the more ... the more

quoad *adv* how soon? how far? till, until; as far as; for as long as

> ❗ See note at **dum**.

quōcircā *conj* on account of which; wherefore

quōcumque, quōcunque *adv* whithersoever, to wheresoever

quod *conj* that, in that, because; as to the fact that; although; since
□ ∼ **sī** but if

quoius, a, um *adj* whose?

quōlibet *adv* whithersoever *or* to wheresoever you please

quom ▸ **cum**

quōminus *conj* so as to prevent (something happening); so that ... not

> ❗ After verbs meaning 'hinder, prevent' the action impeded is expressed by a clause introduced by **quōminus** and having a subj. verb. However, **quōminus** may sometimes be replaced with **nē**, and if the verb of preventing is negated, **quōminus** is regularly replaced with **quīn**.

quōmodo *adv* in what manner, in what way, how

quōnam *adv* to whatever place

quondam *adv* formerly; some day; at times

quoniam *adv* seeing that, since, because

> ❗ **quoniam** often introduces clauses indicating the reason the speaker has for making the assertion, i.e. '... [and I say that] because ...'

quōpiam *adv* somewhere

quōquam *adv* to any place, anywhere

quoque *conj* also, too

quōquō *adv* whithersoever, to wheresoever

quōr ▸ **cūr**

quōrsum, quōrsus *adv* to what end? to what place?

quot *adj indec* how many? as many as; every

quotannīs *adv* every year

quōtīdiē, quottīdiē ▸ **cottīdiē**

quotiē(n)s *adv* how often? how many times? whenever

quotiē(n)scumque *adv* as often as

quotquot *adj indec* however many

quotus, a, um *adj* having what position in a numerical series? bearing what proportion to the total?

quōusque *adv* until what time? till when? how long?

q

Rr

rabidus, a, um *adj* mad, raging, frenzied, wild

rabiēs *f* savageness, ferocity; passion, frenzy

rabiōsus, a, um *adj* raving, rabid, mad

racēmifer, era, erum *adj* bearing clusters

racēmus, ī *m* bunch *or* cluster (of grapes *or* other fruit)

rādīcitus *adv* by the roots; utterly

radiō ① *v* beam, shine

radius, (i)ī *m* pointed rod used by teachers, *etc.*, for drawing diagrams, *etc.*; spoke (of a wheel); beam, ray

rādīx, īcis *f* root; radish; foot of a hill; origin; base

rādō, rāsī, rāsum ③ *v* scrape, scratch, shave (off); erase; skirt, graze; strip off; hurt, offend

raeda, ae *f* four-wheeled carriage

raedārius, (i)ī *m* coachman

rāmālia, ium *ntpl* brushwood, twigs

rāmenta, ae *f* scraping, scrap

rāmeus, a, um *adj* of a bough

rāmōsus, a, um *adj* having many branches, branching

rāmulus, ī *m* twig, little bough

rāmus, ī *m* branch, twig

rāna, ae *f* frog

rancidus, a, um *adj* rotten, putrid, nauseating

rapāx, ācis *adj* rapacious; inordinately greedy

raphanus, ī *m* radish

rapiditās, ātis *f* swiftness, rapidity

rapidus, a, um *adj* swift, rapid

rapīna, ae *f* plunder, booty; the carrying off of a person

rapiō, puī, ptum ③ *v* snatch, tear *or* drag away; carry off; plunder; ravish

raptim *adv* hastily, hurriedly

raptō ① *v* drag violently off; ravage

raptor, ōris *m* robber, ravisher

raptum, ī *nt* plunder; prey

raptus, ūs *m* violent snatching *or* dragging away; robbery, carrying off, abduction

rāpulum, ī *nt* little turnip

rāpum, ī *nt* turnip

rārēfaciō, fēcī, factum ③ *v* rarefy

rārēscō ③ *v* thin out, open out; become sparse

rārō *adv* seldom, rarely

rārus, a, um *adj* thin, loose in texture; scattered; rare; few; sporadic

rāsilis, e *adj* worn smooth, polished

rāstrum, ī *nt* drag-hoe

ratiō, ōnis *f* account; calculation, computation; sum, number; transaction, business; matter, affair; consideration of; judgement, reason; method, order; system, theory

ratis, is *f* raft; boat

ratiuncula, ae *f* small account; slight reason; petty argument

ratus, a, um *adj pple* from ▶ **reor**; established, authoritative; fixed, certain

raucisonus, a, um *adj* hoarse-sounding, raucous

raucus, a, um *adj* hoarse; husky; raucous

rāvus, a, um *adj* greyish, tawny

rea, ae *f* defendant; guilty party; debtor

rebellātrīx, īcis *f adj* rebellious

rebelliō, ōnis *f* revolt, rebellion

rebellis, e *adj* insurgent, rebellious

rebellō ① *v* revolt, rebel

reboō ① *v* resound

recaleō ② *v*, **recalēscō, luī** ③ *v* grow warm again

recalfaciō, fēcī ③ *v* make warm again

recalvus, a, um *adj* bald in front, balding

recandēscō, duī ③ *v* glow again with heat; become white

recantō ① *v* charm away; withdraw

recēdō, essī, essum ③ *v* retire, withdraw; depart; recede; vanish

recēns, **ntis** *adj* fresh, recent
□ ∼ **ā vulnere** fresh from a wound

recēnseō, **nsuī**, **ēnsum** ② *v* review, count; review the roll of

receptāculum, **ī** *nt* receptacle; place of refuge, shelter

receptō ① *v* recover; receive, admit (frequently)

receptus, **ūs** *m* withdrawal, retreat; refuge

recessus, **ūs** *m* retiring, retreat; recess; haunt, refuge

recidīvus, **a**, **um** *adj* recurring

recidō, **cidī**, **cāsum** ③ *v* fall back, lapse; rebound (on to its author)

recīdō, **cīdī**, **cīsum** ③ *v* cut away; curtail

recingō, **īnxī**, **īnctum** ③ *v* ungird, unfasten

recinō ③ *v* chant back, echo; call out

reciper- ▶ **recuper-**

recipiō, **cēpī**, **ceptum** ③ *v* get back; retake, regain, recover; withdraw; admit; accept; entertain; undertake
□ **sē recipere** retreat

reciprocus, **a**, **um** *adj* moving backwards and forwards, marked by alternations of fortune

recitātor, **ōris** *m* reciter

recitō ① *v* read out, recite

reclāmō ① *v* cry out in protest at

reclīnis, **e** *adj* leaning back, reclining

reclīnō ① *v* bend *or* lean back

reclūdō, **ūsī**, **ūsum** ③ *v* open; open up, lay open; disclose, reveal

recognōscō, **nōvī**, **nitum** ③ *v* recognize; recollect; examine; inspect

recolligō, **lēgī**, **lēctum** ③ *v* recover

recolō, **luī**, **cultum** ③ *v* cultivate afresh; go over in one's mind

reconciliātiō, **ōnis** *f* reconciliation; the restoration (of good relations, *etc.*)

reconciliātor, **ōris** *m* restorer

reconciliō ① *v* restore; reconcile

reconditus, **a**, **um** *adj* hidden, concealed; abstruse, recondite, obscure

recondō, **didī**, **ditum** ③ *v* shut up; hide, bury, store away; replace; close again

recoquō, **coxī**, **coctum** ③ *v* renew by cooking, rehash; reheat, melt down

recordātiō, **ōnis** *f* recollection

recordor ① *v dep* think over; call to mind, remember

recreō ① *v* make anew, restore; refresh, revive

recrepō, **puī** ① *v* sound in answer, resound

recrēscō, **crēvī**, **crētum** ③ *v* grow again

recrūdēscō, **duī** ③ *v* become raw again; break out again

rēctā *adv* directly, straight

rēctē *adv* vertically; rightly, correctly, properly, well

rēctor, **ōris** *m* guide, director, helmsman; horseman; driver; leader, ruler, governor; preceptor

rēctus, **a**, **um** *adj* straight, upright; direct; honest; proper; morally right

recubō ① *v* recline, lie at ease

recumbō, **buī** ③ *v* lie down; recline at table; sink down

recuperātor, **ōris** *m* recoverer, receiver; assessor

recuperō ① *v* get again; regain, recover

recūrō ① *v* cure

recurrō, **currī**, **cursum** ③ *v* run *or* hasten back; return; have recourse (to)

recursō ① *v* keep rebounding or recoiling; keep recurring to the mind

recursus, **ūs** *m* running back, retreat, return

recurvō ① *v* bend back

recurvus, **a**, **um** *adj* bent back on itself, bent round

recūsātiō, **ōnis** *f* refusal; objection; counterplea

recūsō ① *v* decline, reject, refuse

recutiō, **ussī**, **ussum** ③ *v* strike so as to cause to vibrate

redardēscō ③ *v* blaze up again

redarguō, **guī** ③ *v* refute; prove untrue

reddō, **didī**, **ditum** ③ *v* give back, return, restore; give up, resign; assign; render; utter in reply

redēmptiō, **ōnis** *f* ransoming; purchasing

redēmptor, **ōris** *m* contractor; [LM] redeemer

redeō, **īre**, **iī**, **itum** *v ir* go *or* come back; return

r

redhibeō ② *v* give back, cancel the sale of

redigō, **ēgī**, **āctum** ③ *v* drive back, return; restore; bring down (to); reduce

redimīculum, **ī** *nt* female headband

redimiō ④ *v* encircle with a garland; surround

redimō, **ēmī**, **ēmptum** ③ *v* buy back; ransom, redeem; buy off; rescue; buy; contract for

redintegrō ① *v* restore, renew, refresh

reditiō, **ōnis** *f* return, returning

reditus, **ūs** *m* return, returning; revenue

redivīvus, **a**, **um** *adj* re-used, second-hand

redoleō ② *v* emit a scent, be odorous

redōnō ① *v* give back again; forgive

redūcō, **dūxī**, **ductum** ③ *v* lead *or* bring back; escort home; withdraw; draw back; bring *or* reduce (to)

reductor, **ōris** *m* restorer

reductus, **a**, **um** *adj* receding deeply, set back

redundō ① *v* flow back; overflow; abound (in)

redux, **cis** *adj* coming back, returning

refectorium, **(i)i** *nt* 𝕃𝕄 refectory, dining-hall

refellō, **ī** ③ *v* refute, rebut

referciō, **rsī**, **rtum** ④ *v* stuff *or* cram full

referō, **ferre**, **rettulī**, **relātum** *v ir* carry, bring *or* put back; tell; propose; record; ascribe; restore; repay; render an account; answer
□ **pedem** ~ return, go back
□ ~ **grātiam** render thanks

rēfert, **ferre**, **rētulit** *v ir impers* it concerns, is of importance to
□ **meā rēfert** it matters to me

> ❗ **rēfert** follows the same construction as **interest**.

refertus, **a**, **um** *adj* crammed full to bursting with; crowded

reficiō, **fēcī**, **fectum** ③ *v* make again, restore, rebuild, repair; reappoint

refigō, **īxī**, **īxum** ③ *v* unfix, unfasten, detach

reflāgitō ① *v* demand repeatedly in a loud voice

reflectō, **exī**, **exum** ③ *v* bend back; turn back; turn round

reflō ① *v* blow back again

refluō ③ *v* flow back

refluus, **a**, **um** *adj* flowing back

reformīdō ① *v* dread, shun, shrink from

refōrmō ① *v* transform, remould; form (a new shape); restore

refoveō, **fōvī**, **fōtum** ② *v* refresh; revive; warm again

refrēnō ① *v* curb, check; restrain

refricō ① *v* gall; excite again

refrīgerō ① *v* make cool

refrīgēscō, **īxī** ③ *v* grow cold, cool down

refringō, **frēgī**, **frāctum** ③ *v* break open

refugiō, **ūgī** ③ *v* run away; flee to; shrink back; recoil from

refugium, **(i)ī** *nt* refuge

refugus, **a**, **um** *adj* fleeing back; receding, drawing back

refulgeō, **lsī** ② *v* radiate light; gleam

refundō, **ūdī**, **ūsum** ③ *v* pour back

refūtō ① *v* check; refute

rēgālis, **e** *adj* kingly, royal, regal

regerō, **essī**, **estum** ③ *v* carry back; throw back; throw back by way of retort

rēgia, **ae** *f* palace

rēgificus, **a**, **um** *adj* fit for a king

regimen, **inis** *nt* control, steering; direction

rēgīna, **ae** *f* queen

regiō, **ōnis** *f* line; district, locality, region; boundary-line

rēgius, **a**, **um** *adj* kingly, royal; splendid, princely

reglūtinō ① *v* unglue, unstick

rēgnātor, **ōris** *m* king, lord

rēgnō ① *v* have royal power, reign; hold sway, lord it

rēgnum, **ī** *nt* kingship, monarchy, tyranny; kingdom

regō, **rēxī**, **rēctum** ③ *v* guide, conduct, direct; govern, rule

regredior, **gressus sum** ③ *v dep* go *or* come back, return; retire, retreat

regressus, **ūs** *m* going back, return

rēgula, **ae** *f* ruler, rod, bar; basic principle, rule

regulāris, **e** *adj* [LM] under a (monastic) rule

rēgulus, **ī** *m* petty king

reiciō, **iēcī**, **iectum** ③ *v* reject; refuse; repulse; refer (a matter) for consideration, *etc.*; put off

> ❗ The first syllable of this verb scans as heavy even though the 'e' is short; this is because the 'i' represents 'ii' pronounced as consonant + vowel 'yi'.

relābor, **lāpsus sum** ③ *v dep* slide *or* glide back; recede, ebb

relanguēscō, **guī** ③ *v* become faint; abate; lose one's passion *or* ardour

relātiō, **ōnis** *f* motion, proposition

relaxō ① *v* loosen; open up

relēgātiō, **ōnis** *f* banishment

relēgō ① *v* banish; remove; remove from the scene

relegō, **lēgī**, **lēctum** ③ *v* pick up again; pick out; read over *or* out; recount

relevō ① *v* lift, raise; lighten; relieve; alleviate; refresh

relicus, **relicuos** ▶ **reliquus**

rēligiō, **ōnis** *f* supernatural feeling of constraint; scruple; sanction; religious awe; superstition; sanctity; ritual; conscientiousness

rēligiōsus, **a**, **um** *adj* pious, devout; religious; scrupulous

religō ① *v* tie out of the way; bind fast; moor

relinquō, **līquī**, **lictum** ③ *v* leave behind; leave; disregard

reliquiae, **ārum** *fpl* remains, relics, remnants

reliquum, **ī** *nt* remainder, residue; the future

reliquus, **a**, **um** *adj* remaining; future; remaining alive

relūceō, **ūxī** ② *v* shine out

relūcēscō, **ūxī** ③ *v* grow bright again

reluctor ① *v dep* struggle (against), resist

remaneō, **nsī** ② *v* stay behind; remain, continue to be; persist

remedium, **(i)ī** *nt* cure; remedy

remeō ① *v* go *or* come back, return

remētior, **mēnsus sum** ④ *v dep* go back over

rēmex, **igis** *m* rower, oarsman

rēmigium, **(i)ī** *nt* rowing; oarage; crew of rowers

rēmigō ① *v* row

remigrō ① *v* return

reminīscor ③ *v dep* recall to mind, recollect

remissiō, **ōnis** *f* sending back; relaxation

remissus, **a**, **um** *adj* mild, gentle; subdued

remittō, **mīsī**, **missum** ③ *v* send back; relax, slacken; grant, concede; remit

remōlior ④ *v dep* heave back

remollēscō ③ *v* become soft again; grow soft

remordeō, **morsum** ② *v* bite back; gnaw, nag

remoror ① *v dep* wait, linger; delay, hold up, check

remōtus, **a**, **um** *adj* distant, remote

removeō, **mōvī**, **mōtum** ② *v* move back; remove; withdraw

remūgiō ④ *v* bellow back, moo in reply; resound

remulceō, **lsī**, **lsum** ② *v* stroke back

remulcum, **ī** *nt* tow-rope

remūnerō ① *v*, **remūneror** ① *v dep* reward, recompense, remunerate

rēmus, **ī** *m* oar

renārrō ① *v* tell over again

renāscor, **nātus sum** ③ *v dep* be born again; be renewed, be revived

rēnēs, **(i)um** *mpl* kidneys

renīdeō ② *v* shine (back), gleam; smile back (at)

rēnō, **ōnis** *m* reindeer-skin

renovō ① *v* make new again; restore; refresh; resume

renūntiō ① *v* report, declare, announce; renounce, call off

renuō, **nuī** ③ *v* give a refusal, disapprove; refuse

reor, **ratus sum** ② *v dep* think, suppose, imagine, deem

repāgula, **ōrum** *ntpl* door-bars

repandus, **a**, **um** *adj* spread out, flattened back

reparābilis, **e** *adj* capable of being recovered *or* restored

r

reparcō, **persī** ③ *v* be sparing with, grudge

reparō ① *v* recover, restore, repair, renew; revive

repellō, **reppulī**, **repulsum** ③ *v* drive *or* push back; reject; repulse

rependō, **ndī**, **ēnsum** ③ *v* weigh *or* balance (against); weigh out in return; pay in return; purchase, compensate

repēns, **ntis** *adj* sudden, unexpected; completely new

repente, **repentīnō** *adv* suddenly, unexpectedly; all at once

repentīnus, **a**, **um** *adj* sudden, done to meet a sudden contingency

repercutiō, **ussī**, **ussum** ③ *v* cause to rebound; reflect; strike against

reperiō, **repperī**, **repertum** ④ *v* find, find out; discover; invent

repertor, **ōris** *m* discoverer, inventor, author

repertum, **ī** *nt* discovery

repetō, **īvī/iī**, **ītum** ③ *v* return to; get back; demand back; repeat; recall; attack again

repetundae, **ārum** *fpl* the recovery of extorted money

repleō, **ēvī**, **ētum** ② *v* fill again; fill up, replenish; restore to its full number

replētus, **a**, **um** *adj* full (of)

rēpō, **psī**, **eptum** ③ *v* creep, crawl

repōnō, **posuī**, **positum** ③ *v* put *or* lay back; replace; stage (a play) again; store away

reportō ① *v* carry *or* bring back; report; bring home from war

reposcō ③ *v* demand back; claim as one's due

repraesentō ① *v* exhibit, pay in ready money; revive

reprehendō, **ndī**, **ēnsum** ③ *v* catch hold of; censure, reprehend, rebuke

reprehēnsiō, **ōnis** *f* reproof, criticism

reprimō, **essī**, **essum** ③ *v* hold in check; check, restrain; repress

repudiō ① *v* divorce, repudiate; refuse

repudium, **ī** *nt* formal renouncement of marriage contract

repugnō ① *v* fight back, offer resistance (to); object (to); be inimical (to)

repulsa, **ae** *f* electoral defeat; rebuff

repulsō ① *v* drive back; reject

reputātiō, **ōnis** *f* consideration, reflection

reputō ① *v* think over, reflect on

requiēs, **ētis** *f* rest, relaxation, recreation

requiēscō, **ēvī**, **ētum** ③ *v* rest; take a holiday; quieten down; rest (upon)

requiētus, **a**, **um** *adj* rested; improved by lying fallow

requīritō ① *v* seek *or* demand repeatedly

requīrō, **īsīvī/īsiī**, **īsītum** ③ *v* seek; search for; need; ask about

rēs, **eī** *f* thing; matter; affair; fact; condition; property; profit, advantage; world, universe, case (in law), suit; power; valour; exploit
  □ ∼ **frūmentāria** corn supply
  ■ **rēs pūblica**, **rēī pūblicae** *fsg* republic, state
  ■ **rēs novae** *fpl* political changes, revolution
  ■ **rēs gestae** *fpl* exploits
  ■ **rēs adversae** *fpl* adverse circumstances
  ■ **rēs secundae** *fpl* prosperity
  □ **rē vērā** actually, really
  □ **in rem** to the point

resānēscō, **nuī** ③ *v* be healed

rescindō, **idī**, **issum** ③ *v* cut away; tear open; annul, rescind

rescīscō, **rescīvī/rescii**, **rescītum** ③ *v* find out

rescrībō, **psī**, **ptum** ③ *v* write in return *or* in answer; enrol in place of another

resecō, **cuī**, **ctum** ① *v* cut back, prune; cut at the base

resēminō ① *v* reproduce

resequor, **secūtus sum** ③ *v dep* reply to

reserō ① *v* unbar; open; disclose, uncover

reservō ① *v* keep back, hold in reserve; preserve; reserve (for)

reses, **idis** *adj* motionless, inactive, idle, sluggish

resideō, **sēdī** ② *v* sit, remain in a place; be left

resīdō, sēdī ③ *v* sit down; settle; abate; subside, quieten down

residuus, a, um *adj* remaining

resignō ① *v* unseal; open; resign

resiliō, luī ④ *v* leap *or* spring back; recoil; rebound; shrink (back again)

resīmus, a, um *adj* turned up, snub; turned back on itself

resipīscō, pīvī/piī/puī ③ *v* become reasonable again

resistō, stitī ③ *v* come to a standstill, stop; *with dat* resist, stand up (to)

resolvō, lvī, lūtum ③ *v* loosen, release, disperse, melt; relax; pay; enervate; pay back; break up; finish

resonō ① *v* resound, re-echo

resonus, a, um *adj* echoing

resorbeō ② *v* swallow down; *pass* ebb

respectō ① *v* keep on looking round *or* back; await; have regard for

respectus, ūs *m* looking back (at); refuge; regard, consideration (for)

respergō, ersī, ersum ③ *v* sprinkle, spatter

respiciō, spexī, spectum ③ *v* look round (for), look back (at); take notice of

respīrāmen, inis *nt* means *or* channel of breathing

respīrātiō, ōnis *f* taking of breath

respīrō ① *v* breathe out; take breath; enjoy a respite

resplendeō ② *v* shine brightly (with reflected light)

respondeō, ndī, ōnsum ② *v* reply; say (*or* write) in answer; say in refutation; answer a summons to appear

respōnsiō, ōnis *f* answer, refutation, defence

respōnsō ① *v* answer, reply (to); re-echo

respōnsor, ōris *m* answerer

respōnsum, ī *nt* answer, reply; answer given by an oracle; opinion of one learned in the law

rēspūblica, reīpūblicae *f* republic; state; the public good

respuō, uī ③ *v* spit out; refuse *or* reject (with abhorrence)

restāgnō ① *v* overflow; be covered with flood-water

restinguō, īnxī, īnctum ③ *v* quench, extinguish; slake; neutralize

restiō, ōnis *m* dealer in rope

restis, is *f* rope, cord

restituō, uī, ūtum ③ *v* replace, restore; rebuild; revive; give back, reverse; reinstate

restitūtiō, ōnis *f* rebuilding; reinstatement

restō, stitī ① *v* stay put; stand firm; resist; remain, be left

restringō, īnxī, ictum ③ *v* draw tight; fasten behind one; tie up

resultō ① *v* leap back, rebound; echo

resūmō, mpsī, mptum ③ *v* pick up again; resume; recover

resupīnō ① *v* cause to be flat on one's back; knock flat on one's back; pull back, bend back

resupīnus, a, um *adj* lying flat on; leaning back

resurgō, surrēxī, surrēctum ③ *v* rise (again); flare up again, revive

resurrectiō, onis *f* [LM] resurrection

resuscitō ① *v* rouse again, reawaken

retardō ① *v* delay, hold up

rēte, is *nt* net

retegō, ēxī, ēctum ③ *v* uncover, lay bare, reveal; disclose

retentō ① *v* hold fast; hold back

retexō, xuī, xtum ③ *v* unweave, unravel; destroy gradually

rētiārius, (i)ī *m* net fighter in the arena

reticeō ② *v* keep silent; leave unsaid

rēticulum, ī *nt*, **rēticulus, ī** *m* (little) net; mesh-work bag

retināculum, ī *nt* rope; hawser; rein; towing-rope; *pl* band

retineō, tentum ② *v* hold fast; hold back; detain; retain; maintain; restrain; cling to

retorqueō, rsī, rtum ② *v* twist back; cast back; fling back; turn aside

retractō ① *v* undertake anew; draw back, be reluctant; reconsider; withdraw

■ **retractātus, a, um** *adj* remote, distant; in a state of revision

retrahō, āxī, actum ③ *v* drag *or* pull backwards; summon back; win back; withdraw

r

retrō *adv* backwards, behind; back again, conversely

retrōrsum, **retrōrsus**, **retrōversus** *adv* back, backwards; in reverse order

retundō, **re(t)tudī**, **retū(n)sum** ③ *v* blunt; weaken; repress, quell

reus, **ī** *m* defendant; guilty party; debtor

revalēscō, **luī** ③ *v* grow well again

revehō, **ēxī**, **ectum** ③ *v* carry *or* bring back
  □ **revehor** ride *or* sail back

revellō, **vellī**, **vulsum** ③ *v* wrench off, tear down; tear out; remove

reveniō, **vēnī**, **ventum** ④ *v* come back, return

rēvērā *adv* (also **rē vērā**) in reality, in fact

reverentia, **ae** *f* respect, deference; awe, reverence

revereor ② *v dep* stand in awe of; venerate

revertō, **rtī** ③ *v*, **revertor**, **versus sum** ③ *v dep* turn back, come back, return

revinciō, **vīnxī**, **vīnctum** ④ *v* hold down *or* restrain with bonds; hold firmly in place

revincō, **vīcī**, **victum** ③ *v* conquer in one's turn; refute; convict

revirēscō, **ruī** ③ *v* grow green again; grow strong *or* young again

revīsō ③ *v* revisit, go back and see

revīvīscō, **īxī**, **īctum** ③ *v* come to life again, revive (in spirit)

revocābilis, **e** *adj* capable of being revoked *or* retracted

revocāmen, **inis** *nt* summons to return

revocō ① *v* call back, recall, summon back; restrain; reduce (to); refer (to); revoke

revolō ① *v* fly back

revolūbilis, **e** *adj* that may be rolled back to the beginning; rolling backward

revolvō, **lvī**, **lūtum** ③ *v* roll back; unroll; revolve; go back over in thought *or* speech

revomō, **muī** ③ *v* vomit up again, spew out

rēx, **gis** *m* king, tyrant, despot; master; leader, head; patron; great man

rhētor, **oris** *m* a teacher of public speaking, rhetorician

> **!** The final stage of Roman education was the study of rhetoric, as taught by **rhētorēs**, whose pupils usually began at around age 15. In the republic their skill was viewed with suspicion but they came to enjoy greater favour in the imperial period.

rhētoricus, **a**, **um** *adj* rhetorical

rhīnocerōs, **ōtis** *m* rhinoceros

rhombus, **ī** *m* instrument whirled on a string to produce a whirring noise; turbot

rhonchus, **ī** *m* snore, snort of disdain

rictus, **ūs** *m* the open mouth *or* jaws

rīdeō, **rīsī**, **rīsum** ② *v* laugh; smile; mock; laugh at *or* over

rīdiculum, **ī** *nt* joke, piece of humour

rīdiculus, **a**, **um** *adj* laughable, funny; silly
  ■ **~**, **ī** *m* buffoon, jester

rigeō ② *v* be stiff *or* numb; stand on end; be solidified

rigēscō, **guī** ③ *v* grow stiff *or* numb; stiffen, harden

rigidus, **a**, **um** *adj* stiff, hard, rigid; inflexible; stern

rigō ① *v* moisten, wet, water, irrigate

rigor, **ōris** *m* stiffness, rigidity, coldness, numbness, hardness; inflexibility; severity

riguus, **a**, **um** *adj* irrigating; well-watered

rīma, **ae** *f* narrow cleft, crack, chink, fissure; flash of lightning

rīmor ① *v dep* probe, search; rummage about for, examine, explore

rīmōsus, **a**, **um** *adj* full of cracks *or* fissures

ringor ③ *v dep* bare one's teeth

rīpa, **ae** *f* bank; shore of the sea

rīsor, **ōris** *m* one who laughs

rīsus, **ūs** *m* laughter

rīte *adv* with the proper rites; duly, correctly

rītus, **ūs** *m* religious observance *or* ceremony, rite
  □ **rītū** *with gen* in the manner of

rīvālis, **is** *m* rival

rīvus, **ī** *m* brook, stream; channel

r

rixa, **ae** *f* violent *or* noisy quarrel, brawl, dispute

rixor ① *v dep* quarrel violently, brawl, dispute

rōbīgō, **inis** *f* rust; mildew, blight; a foul deposit in the mouth

rōboreus, **a**, **um** *adj* made of oak

rōborō ① *v* give physical strength to; reinforce

rōbur, **oris** *nt* any hard wood; oak; oak-wood; trunk (of such wood); strength, power, might; man-power; courage; resolve

rōbustus, **a**, **um** *adj* made of oak; hard, firm, strong, hardy, robust; physically mature

rōdō, **rōsī**, **rōsum** ③ *v* gnaw; eat away, erode; backbite, carp at

rogālis, **e** *adj* of a funeral pyre

rogātiō, **ōnis** *f* proposed measure

rogātū *adv* by request

rogitō ① *v* ask frequently *or* insistently

rogō ① *v* ask, question; propose (a law, a magistrate); request, solicit for favours

rogus, **ī** *m* funeral-pyre; remains

rōrifer, **era**, **erum** *adj* bringing dew

rōrō ① *v* drop *or* distil dew; drip *or* run with moisture

rōs, **rōris** *m* dew
    □ **rōs marīnus** rosemary

rosa, **ae** *f* rose

rosārium, **(i)ī** *nt* rose-garden

rōscidus, **a**, **um** *adj* dewy; wet

rosētum, **ī** *nt* garden of roses

roseus, **a**, **um** *adj* of roses; rose-coloured

rōsiō, **ōnis** *f* erosion

rōstra, **ōrum** *ntpl* platform for speakers in the Roman forum

rōstrātus, **a**, **um** *adj* having a beaked prow

rōstrum, **ī** *nt* snout *or* muzzle (of an animal), beak, bill; ship's beak

rota, **ae** *f* wheel; chariot; ⓛⓜ court

rotō ① *v* whirl round; revolve, rotate

rotundō ① *v* make round, round off

rotundus, **a**, **um** *adj* round, circular; smooth and finished

rubefaciō, **fēcī**, **factum** ③ *v* redden

rubēns, **ntis** *adj* coloured *or* tinged with red

rubeō ② *v* be red, become red

ruber, **bra**, **brum** *adj* red (including shades of orange)

rubēscō, **buī** ③ *v* turn red, redden, become red

rubētum, **ī** *nt* bramble-thicket

rubeus, **a**, **um** *adj* of *or* produced from a bramble

rubia, **ae** *f* madder

rubicundus, **a**, **um** *adj* suffused with red, ruddy

rūbīgō ▶ **rōbīgō**

rubor, **ōris** *m* redness; blush; modesty, feeling of shame; cause for shame

rubrica, **ae** *f* ⓛⓜ rubric

rubus, **ī** *m* bramble, blackberry

rudēns, **ntis** *m* rope

rudīmentum, **ī** *nt* first lesson; early training; beginning

rudis¹, **is** *f* wooden sword used in practice fights *or* presented to a gladiator on his discharge

rudis², **e** *adj* rough, unwrought; raw; untrained; unbroken; ill-made, rudely finished, coarse; ignorant (of)

rudō, **dītum** ③ *v* bellow, roar, bray, creak loudly

rūga, **ae** *f* wrinkle; crease, small fold

rūgiō ④ *v* roar

rūgōsus, **a**, **um** *adj* full of wrinkles, folds *or* creases

ruīna, **ae** *f* tumbling down, downfall, ruin; ruins; debris, disaster; landslide

ruīnōsus, **a**, **um** *adj* ruinous; ruined

rūminō ① *v*, **rūminor** ① *v dep* chew over again; chew the cud

rūmor, **ōris** *m* hearsay, rumour; reputation; ill repute

rumpō, **rūpī**, **ruptum** ③ *v* burst, break down; force open; violate; rupture; break off

ruō, **ruī**, **rutum** ③ *v* collapse, fall, go to ruin; rush (headlong) (towards), hurry (on); sweep headlong; disturb violently; overthrow

rūpēs, **pis** *f* steep rocky cliff, crag

ruptor, **ōris** *m* one who breaks *or* violates

rūricola, **ae** *m/f* one who tills the land; country-dweller

rūrigena, **ae** *m* born in the country

r

rūrsum, **rūrsus** *adv* backwards; on the other hand; again; in one's turn

rūs, **ris** *nt* country; country estate

> ❗ rūs has a locative **rūrī** or **rūre**, and 'to the country' is expressed by the acc. without a preposition.

ruscum, **ī** *nt* butcher's broom

russus, **a**, **um** *adj* red

rūsticānus, **a**, **um** *adj* living in the country

rūsticitās, **ātis** *f* lack of sophistication

rūsticus, **a**, **um** *adj* rural, rustic; agricultural; coarse, boorish; crude, clumsy; simple
- **rūstica**, **ae** *f* countrywoman
- **rūsticus**, **ī** *m* countryman

rūsum ▶ **rūrsum**

rūta, **ae** *f* rue

rutābulum, **ī** *nt* long implement with a flattened end

rutilō ① *v* glow with a bright *or* golden red colour; colour bright *or* golden red

rutilus, **a**, **um** *adj* red, reddish; ruddy

rūtrum, **ī** *nt* shovel

Ss

sabbatum, **i** *nt* LM the Sabbath, Saturday

saburra, **ae** *f* gravel (for ballast)

saccipērium, **(i)ī** *nt* wallet

sacculus, **ī** *m* little bag

saccus, **ī** *m* large bag; sack

sacellum, **ī** *nt* shrine

sacer, **cra**, **crum** *adj* holy, sacred; divine

sacerdōs, **ōtis** *m/f* priest; priestess; LM bishop

sacerdōtium, **(i)ī** *nt* priesthood

sacrāmentum, **ī** *nt* oath taken by newly enlisted soldiers; oath, solemn obligation; LM sacrament, sacred power

sacrārium, **(i)ī** *nt* sanctuary, shrine

sacrātus, **a**, **um** *adj* hallowed, holy, sacred

sacrifer, **era**, **erum** *adj* carrying sacred objects

sacrificium, **(i)ī** *nt* sacrifice, offering to a deity; LM Eucharist

sacrificō ① *v* sacrifice, offer up as a sacrifice

sacrificulus, **ī** *m* sacrificing priest

sacrificus, **a**, **um** *adj* sacrificial

sacrilegium, **(i)ī** *nt* sacrilege; robbery of sacred property

sacrilegus, **a**, **um** *adj* sacrilegious; profane, impious
- **sacrilegus**, **ī** *m* temple-robber

sacrista, **ae** *m* LM sacristan

sacrō ① *v* consecrate; devote to destruction; doom; make subject to religious sanction; hallow, sanctify

sacrōsānctus, **a**, **um** *adj* sacrosanct, inviolable

sacrum, **ī** *nt* sacred object; consecrated place; temple

saeculāris, **e** *adj* of a generation; LM secular, not belonging to a religious order
  □ **lūdī saeculārēs** games celebrated at fixed intervals
  □ **carmen saeculāre** hymn sung at the ludī saeculārēs

saec(u)lum, **ī** *nt* generation, life-time; race; century; indefinitely long period; the times
  □ **in saecula saeculorum** LM for ever and ever

saepe *adv* often, oftentimes, frequently
  □ **saepenumerō** oftentimes, very often

saepēs, **pis** *f* hedge; fence

saepīmentum, **ī** *nt* fence; enclosure

saepiō, **psī**, **ptum** ④ *v* fence in; enclose; surround

saeptum, **ī** *nt* fold, paddock; enclosure; voting enclosure in the Campus Martius

saeta, ae *f* hair; bristle; fishing-line

saetiger, era, erum *adj* bristly

saetōsus, a, um *adj* bristly, shaggy

saevidicus, a, um *adj* spoken furiously

saeviō 4 *v* be fierce *or* furious, rage; be violent

saevitia, ae *f* rage, fierceness, ferocity; cruelty, barbarity, violence

saevus, a, um *adj* raging, furious, ferocious, barbarous, cruel; violent

sāga, ae *f* witch, sorceress, wise woman

sagāx, ācis *adj* keen-scented; acute, sharp, perceptive

sagīna, ae *f* stuffing, overstuffing; fatted animal; diet of gladiators and athletes

sagitta, ae *f* arrow

sagittārius, (i)ī *m* archer, bowman; Archer (constellation)

sagittifer, era, erum *adj* carrying arrows; archer

sagmen, inis *nt* bundle of grass torn up with its earth

sagulum, ī *nt* small military cloak

sagum, ī *nt* coarse woollen cloak; military cloak

sāl, salis *m* salt; sea-water; sea; shrewdness; a quality which gives 'life' to a person or thing
■ **salēs** *pl* jokes, witticisms

salapūtium, (i)ī *nt* short person, little squirt

salārium, (i)ī *nt* regular official payment to the holder of a civil *or* military post

salārius, a, um *adj* of, or relating to, salt

salāx, ācis *adj* highly sexed; aphrodisiac

salebra, ae *f* rut, irregularity; roughness (of style or speech)

salictum, ī *nt* collection of willows, osier-bed

saliēns, ntis *f* fountain, *jet d'eau*

salignus, a, um *adj* of willow

salillum, ī *nt* little salt-cellar

salīnae, ārum *fpl* salt-pans

salīnum, ī *nt* salt-cellar

saliō, saliī/saluī, saltum 4 *v* leap, jump; move suddenly; gush, spurt; (of male animals) mount, cover

salīva, ae *f* spittle; distinctive flavour

salix, icis *f* willow-tree, willow

salsus, a, um *adj* salted; salty, briny; salted with humour, witty, funny

saltātor, ōris *m* dancer

saltātrīx, īcis *f* female dancer, dancing girl

saltātus, ūs *m* dancing, a dance

saltem *adv* at least, at all events
□ **nōn/neque** ~ not *or* nor even, not so much as

saltō 1 *v* dance, jump; portray *or* represent in a dance

saltuōsus, a, um *adj* characterized by wooded valleys

saltus¹, ūs *m* leap, spring, jump

saltus², ūs *m* narrow passage through forest, mountainous country, defile, pass; woodland interspersed with glades, passes, *etc.*

salūber, salūbris, bris, bre *adj* healthy, salutary, beneficial

salūbritās, ātis *f* good health; wholesomeness

salum, ī *nt* sea in motion, swell, billow

salūs, ūtis *f* health, well-being, safety; greeting, salutation; ⓛⓜ eternal life, salvation

salūtāris, e *adj* healthful, salutary

salūtātiō, ōnis *f* greeting, salutation; formal morning call paid by a client on his patron

salūtifer, era, erum *adj* health-giving

salūtō 1 *v* greet, salute; call to pay one's respects to

salvē *int* hail! welcome! farewell! good-bye!
□ **salvēre iubeō** greet; bid good day

salvus, a, um *adj* safe, well, sound, undamaged, intact

sambūcistria, ae *f* female player on a small harp

sānābilis, e *adj* curable

sanciō, sānxī, sānctum 4 *v* ratify solemnly, confirm; enact

sānctitās, ātis *f* sacrosanctity; moral purity, virtue

sānctus, a, um *adj* sacred, inviolable; venerable; holy; upright, virtuous; ⓛⓜ *m/f* saint

sandapila, ae *f* pauper's bier

sandyx, ycis *f* red dye; scarlet cloth

sānē *adv* certainly; truly, 'and that's a fact'; admittedly

sanguineus, **a**, **um** *adj*, **sanguinolentus**, **a**, **um** *adj* bloody, blood-stained; blood-red

sanguis, **inis** *m* blood; race, family, consanguinity; life; vigour

saniēs *f* matter discharged from a wound, ulcer

sānitās, **ātis** *f* health; soundness of mind, good sense

sānō ① *v* heal, cure, restore to health

sānus, **a**, **um** *adj* healthy; sound in mind, rational

sapa, **ae** *f* new wine

sapiēns, **ntis** *adj* wise, sensible, understanding; *m/f* wise person

sapientia, **ae** *f* wisdom

sapiō, **īvī/iī** ③ *v* taste (of); be intelligent, show good sense

sapor, **ōris** *m* taste, flavour; sense of taste

sarcina, **ae** *f* bundle, burden, load, pack

sarcinārius, **a**, **um** *adj* employed in carrying packs

sarcinula, **ae** *f* (little) pack, bundle

sarciō, **rsī**, **rtum** ④ *v* make good; redeem; restore

sarculum, **ī** *nt* hoe

sarmentum, **ī** *nt* shoot; *pl* twigs, cut twigs, brushwood

sat, **satis** *adv* sufficient, enough; adequately, sufficiently
▢ ~ **accipiō** take *or* exact security
■ **satius** *comp* better, preferable

sata, **ōrum** *ntpl* crops, cultivated plants

Satanas, **ae** *m* LM Satan, the Devil

satelles, **itis** *m* attendant, bodyguard; *pl* retinue; accomplice, violent supporter

satiās, **ātis** *f* sufficiency, abundance; distaste caused by excess

satietās, **ātis** *f* satiety; the state of being sated

satin *int* [from **satis** and **-ne**] really?

satiō¹ ① *v* satisfy; satiate; fill to repletion

satiō², **ōnis** *f* planting, sowing

satisfaciō, **fēcī**, **factum** ③ *v with dat* give satisfaction (to), satisfy; make amends; give sufficient attention (to)

satisfactiō, **ōnis** *f* satisfaction for an offence, apology, indemnification

sator, **ōris** *m* sower, planter; founder, originator

satum ▸ **serō**

satur, **ura**, **urum** *adj* well-fed, replete; rich; saturated

satura, **ae** *f* stage medley, satire

saturitās, **ātis** *f* satiety, fullness, exhaustion

Sāturnālia, **ium** *ntpl* festival in honour of Saturn, beginning on 17 December

saturō ① *v* fill to repletion, sate, satisfy; drench, saturate

satus, **a**, **um** *adj* sprung (from); native

satyrus, **ī** *m* satyr; satyric play

sauciō ① *v* wound; gash

saucius, **a**, **um** *adj* wounded; physically distressed, afflicted; pierced; stricken

sāv- ▸ **suāv-**

sāviolum, **ī** *nt* tender kiss

sāvium, **(i)ī** *nt* kiss; sweetheart

saxātilis, **e** *adj* of rock, rocky; living among rocks

saxeus, **a**, **um** *adj* rocky, stony, made of stones

saxificus, **a**, **um** *adj* petrifying

saxōsus, **a**, **um** *adj* rocky, stony

saxum, **ī** *nt* rock, boulder; stone

scaber, **bra**, **brum** *adj* scurfy, scabbed, having a rough surface

scabiēs, **iēī** *f* scurf; scab, mange, itching

scabō, **ī** ③ *v* scratch

scaccarium, **(i)i** *nt* LM chess; chessboard; exchequer

scaena, **ae** *f* stage of a theatre; background; the drama; sphere in which actions, *etc.*, are on public display

scaenicus, **a**, **um** *adj* theatrical
■ **scaenicus**, **ī** *m* actor

scālae, **ārum** *fpl* ladder; flight of steps

scalprum, **ī** *nt* tool for scraping, paring *or* cutting away

scamnum, **ī** *nt* bench, stool

scandō ③ *v* climb, mount, ascend

scandula, **ae** *f* wooden slat used for roofing *etc.*; shingle

scapha, **ae** *f* light boat, skiff

scapulae, **ārum** *fpl* shoulder-blades; shoulders

scāpus, **ī** *m* stem, stalk; shaft of a column

scarabaeus, **ī** *m* beetle

scatebra, **ae** *f* gush of water from the ground, bubbling spring

scateō ② *v* gush out; swarm (with), be alive (with)

scatūrīgō, **inis** *f* bubbling spring

scelerātus, **a**, **um** *adj* accursed; heinously criminal; sinful

scelerō ① *v* defile

scelerōsus, **a**, **um** *adj* steeped in wickedness

scelestus, **a**, **um** *adj* wicked, villainous

scelus, **eris** *nt* crime

scēptrifer, **era**, **erum** *adj* bearing a sceptre

scēptrum, **ī** *nt* sceptre; phallus; kingship

schisma, **atis** *nt* LM schism

schoenobatēs, **ae** *m* tightrope-walker

schola, **ae** *f* lecture; school

scholasticus, **ī** *m* student, teacher

sciēns, **ntis** *adj* expert, knowledgeable

scientia, **ae** *f* knowledge; understanding, expert knowledge

scilicet *adv* one may be sure (that), it is clear (that); naturally; yes, but at the same time; evidently; to be sure, doubtless; I ask you!

scindō, **idī**, **issum** ③ *v* split, cleave, tear apart; separate

scintilla, **ae** *f* spark

scintillō ① *v* send out sparks

scio ④ *v* know; know of
□ **prō certō** ∼ know for certain

> ❗ The 'o' of the 1sg. pres. indic. act. is often short in this verb.

scīpiō, **ōnis** *m* ceremonial rod, baton

scirpea, **ae** *f* large basket made of bulrushes

scirpus, **ī** *m* bulrush

scīscitor ① *v dep* inquire (of)

scīscō, **īvī**, **ītum** ③ *v* ascertain; vote for *or* approve (a resolution)

scissūra, **ae** *f* cleft, fissure

scītor ① *v dep* seek to know; inquire (about); question

scītum, **ī** *nt* ordinance, statute

scītus, **a**, **um** *adj* having practical knowledge of, neat, ingenious; nice, excellent

scobis, **is** *f* sawdust

scomber, **brī** *m* mackerel

scōpārius, **(i)ī** *m* floor-sweeper

scopulus, **ī** *m* rock, boulder

scorpiō, **ōnis** *m* scorpion

scorteus, **a**, **um** *adj* of hide, leathern

scortillum, **ī** *nt* young prostitute

scortum, **ī** *nt* harlot, prostitute; male prostitute

scrība, **ae** *m* public clerk; secretary

scriblīta, **ae** *f* cheese tart

scrībō, **psī**, **ptum** ③ *v* write; compose; draft

scrīnium, **(i)ī** *nt* receptacle for holding letters *or* papers, writing-case

scrīptor, **ōris** *m* writer, scribe, copyist

scrīptum, **ī** *nt* something written; written communication; literary work

scrīptūra, **ae** *f* writing; literary work, composition; LM (holy) scripture

scrobis, **is** *m/f* pit

scrūpeus, **a**, **um** *adj* composed of sharp rocks

scrūpulus, **ī** *m* cause for uneasiness *or* misgiving

scrūta, **ōrum** *ntpl* trash, a job lot

scrūtor ① *v dep* search, examine; inquire into

sculpō, **psī**, **ptum** ③ *v* carve, engrave, chisel

sculptilis, **e** *adj* engraved

scurra, **ae** *m* loafer, city-bred clown

scurrīlis, **e** *adj* impudent, rude

scurror ① *v dep* play the 'man about town', *i.e.* dine off one's jokes

scūtātus, **a**, **um** *adj* armed with a long wooden shield

scutica, **ae** *f* strap

scutula, **ae** *f* small dish

scūtum, **ī** *nt* (oblong wooden) shield, buckler

S

scyphus, **ī** *m* two-handled drinking-vessel

sē, **sēsē** *acc*, **suī** (*gen*), **sibī** (*dat*), **sē** (*abl*) *pn* himself, herself, itself, themselves

> ❗ Often confused in meaning with **eum**, **sē** refers to the same thing as the subject of its own clause *except* in purpose clauses, fear clauses and reported speech (i.e. indirect statement, question and command) where it usu. refers to the subject of the main clause. For example, **māter sē lavat** 'the mother washes herself' but **puer dīcit sē aegrum esse** 'the boy says that he (= the boy) is ill'; cf. note at **is**.

sēbum, **ī** *nt* suet, tallow, hard animal fat

sēcēdō, **cessī**, **cessum** ③ *v* draw aside, withdraw; retire; secede

sēcernō, **crēvī**, **crētum** ③ *v* separate off; cut off; set aside; treat as distinct

sēcessiō, **ōnis** *f* withdrawal; secession; estrangement

sēcessus, **ūs** *m* withdrawal; secluded place; retirement

sēclūdō, **ūsī**, **ūsum** ③ *v* shut off, shut up

secō, **secuī**, **sectum** ① *v* cut, cut off; cut up; make an incision in; cleave a path through; form by cutting

sēcrētus, **a**, **um** *adj* separate, apart (from); private, secret; remote; hidden
■ **sēcrētum**, **ī** *nt* secret, mystic rite; retired haunt

sectilis, **e** *adj* capable of being cut into thin layers

sector ① *v dep* follow continually; pursue; pursue with punishment; hunt out; run after; attend

sectūrae, **ārum** *fpl* quarry

sēcubitus, **ūs** *m* sleeping apart from one's spouse *or* lover

sēcubō, **buī** ① *v* sleep apart from one's spouse *or* lover

secundānī, **ōrum** *mpl* soldiers of the second legion

secundō ① *v* (of winds) make (conditions) favourable for travel

secundum *prep with acc* after; along; next to; in favour of; in conformity with; according; *adv* after; along; next

secundus, **a**, **um** *adj* second; following; next; inferior, secondary; favourable
□ **rēs secundae** prosperity

secūrifer, **secūriger**, **era**, **erum** *adj* armed with an axe

secūris, **is** *f* axe, hatchet; authority

sēcūritās, **ātis** *f* freedom from care; carelessness; safety, security

sēcūrus, **a**, **um** *adj* unconcerned; careless; safe, secure; untroubled; nonchalant

secus *adv* otherwise; wrongly
□ **nōn ~** just so

secūtus *pple* from ▶ **sequor**

sed *conj* but; however; yet; but also
□ **~ enim** but in fact
□ **~ etiam** but also

sēdātus, **a**, **um** *adj* calm, untroubled

sēdecim *adj indec* sixteen

sedeō, **sēdī**, **sessum** ② *v* be seated, sit; remain; rest; be decided on

sēdēs, **dis** *f* seat; home, residence

sedīle, **is** *nt* seat, bench, chair

sēditiō, **ōnis** *f* violent political discord, mutiny, sedition

sēditiōsus, **a**, **um** *adj* factious, seditious; turbulent

sēdō ① *v* settle, allay; restrain; calm down

sēdūcō, **dūxī**, **ductum** ③ *v* lead aside; separate off

sēductus, **a**, **um** *adj* distant; retired, secluded

sēdulitās, **ātis** *f* assiduity, painstaking attention (to)

sēdulus, **a**, **um** *adj* attentive, painstaking, sedulous
■ **sēdulō** *adv* with all one's heart

seges, **etis** *f* corn-field; crop

sēgnis, **e** *adj* slow, sluggish, inactive, unenergetic

sēgnitia, **ae** *f*, **sēgnitiēs**, **iēī** *f* sloth, sluggishness

sēgregō ① *v* separate (into parts); break off

sēiungō, **ūnxī**, **ūnctum** ③ *v* separate; exclude

sēlibra, **ae** *f* half-pound

sēligō, **lēgī**, **lēctum** ③ *v* select, choose

sella, **ae** *f* seat, chair, stool
□ **~ curūlis** magistrate's chair

sellisternium, (i)ī *nt* formal religious banquet

sellula, ae *f* sedan-chair

semel *adv* once, a single time; once and for all; the first time; at any time, once, ever

◻ ~ **atque iterum** once and again

sēmen, inis *nt* seed; shoot; slip, cutting; parentage, descent; germ, spark

sēmentis, is *f* sowing; crop

sēmermis, e *adj* badly- *or* poorly-armed

sēmēsus, a, um *adj* half-eaten

sēmiadapertus, a, um *adj* half-open

sēmianimis, e *adj*, **sēmianimus, a, um** *adj* half-alive

sēmiapertus, a, um *adj* half-open

sēmibōs, bovis *m* half-bull, *i.e.* the Minotaur

sēmicaper, prī *m* half-goat (Pan)

sēmicremātus, a, um *adj*, **sēmicremus, a, um** *adj* half-burned

sēmiermis, e *adj*, **sēmiermus, a, um** *adj* half-armed

sēmifactus, a, um *adj* half-made, half-finished

sēmifer, era, erum *adj* half-wild; half-monster

sēmihiāns, ntis *adj* half-open

sēmihomō, inis *m* half-man, half-human

sēmilacer, era, erum *adj* half-mangled

sēmilautus, a, um *adj* half-washed

sēmimarīnus, a, um *adj* half belonging to the sea

sēmimās, aris *m* half-male

sēmimortuus, a, um *adj* half-dead

sēminex, cis *adj* half-dead

sēminō ▯ *v* plant, sow

sēminūdus, a, um *adj* half-naked

sēmiplēnus, a, um *adj* half-full; half-manned

sēmiputātus, a, um *adj* half-pruned

sēmireductus, a, um *adj* half bent back

sēmirefectus, a, um *adj* half-repaired

sēmirutus, a, um *adj* half-ruined *or* demolished

sēmis, issis *m* half an as; half; interest at six per cent per annum

sēmisepultus, a, um *adj* half-buried

sēmisomnus, a, um *adj* half-asleep, drowsy

sēmisupīnus, a, um *adj* half-lying on one's back

sēmita, ae *f* side-path, track, lane

sēmitārius, a, um *adj* of *or* associated with by-ways, alleys *etc.*

sēmivir, rī *m* half man; ~ *adj* effeminate

sēmivīvus, a, um *adj* half-alive, almost dead

sēmōtus, a, um *adj* distant, remote

semper *adv* always

sempiternus, a, um *adj* everlasting

sēmuncia, ae *f* twenty-fourth part (of a pound, *etc.*); a minimal amount

sēmustus, a, um *adj* half-burnt, singed

senātor, ōris *m* member of the senate, senator

❗ Members of the Roman senate were wealthy landowners: their status entitled them to wear a toga bearing the **lātus clāvus** and to have privileged seats at games and religious ceremonies. When sitting in the senate they were collectively addressed as **patrēs (et) cōnscriptī**.

senātōrius, a, um *adj* senatorial

senātus, ūs *m* senate

❗ The Roman senate, which usually met in the **cūria** ('senate-house'), was made up of a varying number of wealthy citizens, in the late republic numbering several hundred and including ex-magistrates, and was summoned and presided over by the principal Roman magistrates, whom it served to advise; right of membership, which was effectively for life though forfeited for disgrace, was determined by the **cēnsōrēs**. By the end of the republican period it came to have considerable power and authority in overseeing Roman policy and administration. In the imperial period

S

its number was for a long time fixed at 600, including only the very richest citizens; many former functions (including foreign, military and financial policy) then rested with the emperor, but because its decrees came to have full legal force (having been 'merely' advice in the republic) the senate retained considerable power especially in legitimating emperors.

····▶ **senātus populusque Rōmānus** was the formula denoting the senate and the Roman people, frequently abbreviated to SPQR.

senātūs cōnsultum *nt* decree *or* recommendation of the senate

> ❗ After a debate in the senate, a vote was taken and a decree issued.

senecta, ae *f*, **senectūs, ūtis** *f* old age; old men collectively

seneō ② *v* be old

senēscō, nuī ③ *v* grow old; grow weak, be in a decline; become exhausted

senex, senis *m* old man; ∼ *adj* old, aged

sēnī, ae, a *adj* six apiece; six

senīlis, e *adj* aged, senile

senior, ōris *adj* older

senium, (i)ī *nt* condition of old age; melancholy, gloom

sēnsim *adv* slowly, gradually, cautiously

sensualiter *adv* 🄻🄼 physically, corporeally

sēnsus, ūs *m* faculty of feeling, perception, sensation, sense; emotion; idea; epigrammatic notion; meaning

sententia, ae *f* opinion, sentiment; judgment; advice; vote; meaning; period; sentence
▢ **ex sententiā (meā)** to (my) liking, satisfactory

sentīna, ae *f* bilgewater; scum *or* dregs of society

sentiō, sēnsī, sēnsum ④ *v* discern by the senses; feel, hear, see; undergo; perceive, notice; think, deem; vote, declare; intend

sentis, is *m* any thorny bush *or* shrub, briar, bramble

sentus, a, um *adj* rough, rugged, uneven

seorsum, seorsus, sōrsum *adv* separately, apart from the rest

sēpar, aris *adj* separate

sēparātim *adv* separately, individually

sēparō ① *v* separate, divide; cut off, isolate

sepeliō, pultum ④ *v* bury, submerge, overcome; suppress

sēpia, ae *f* cuttle-fish; ink

sēpōnō, posuī, positum ③ *v* put away from one; disregard; isolate; reserve

septem *adj indec* seven

September, bris *adj* of September; seventh (later the ninth) month of the Roman year

septemfluus, a, um *adj* that flows in seven streams

septemgeminus, a, um *adj* sevenfold

septemplex, icis *adj* sevenfold; of seven layers

septendecim *adj indec* (also **septemdecim**) seventeen

septēnī, ae, a *adj* seven each; seven at a go; seven

septentriōnēs, um *mpl* (also **septemtriōnēs**) Great Bear; Little Bear; north, northern regions, north wind

septiē(n)s *adv* seven times

septimānus, a, um *adj* of *or* relating to the seventh; belonging to the seventh legion; concerning the nones of March, May, July *or* October (the nones falling on the seventh day of those months)

septimus, a, um *adj* seventh

septingentē(n)simus, a, um *adj* seven hundredth

septingentī, ae, a *adj* seven hundred

septuāgēnī, ae, a *adj* seventy each

septuāgintā *adj indec* seventy

sepulcrālis, e *adj* sepulchral, of the tomb

sepulcrētum, ī *nt* graveyard

sepulcrum, ī *nt* grave, sepulchre, tomb; *pl* the dead

sepultūra, ae *f* burial

sequāx, **ācis** *adj* that follows closely *or* eagerly; pliant, tractable

sequester, **tra**, **trum** *adj* intermediary;
■ **sequestra**, **ae** *f* female go-between, mediatress

sequor, **secūtus sum** ③ *v dep* follow, come *or* go after, attend; pursue; aim at; comply (with), conform (to); succeed

sera, **ae** *f* bar (for fastening doors)

serēnitās, **ātis** *f* fine weather; favourable conditions

serēnō ① *v* clear up, brighten; lighten

serēnus, **a**, **um** *adj* clear, fine, bright, cloudless; cheerful, glad, joyous, tranquil
■ **serēnum**, **ī** *nt* fair weather

serēscō ③ *v* grow dry

sēria, **ae** *f* large earthenware jar

sēricus, **a**, **um** *adj* silken

seriēs *f* row, succession, series; line of ancestors *or* descendants

sērius[1] *adv* later, too late
□ ~ **aut citius** sooner or later

sērius[2], **a**, **um** *adj* serious, weighty, important; sober, grave
□ **sēriō** in earnest
■ **sēria**, **ōrum** *ntpl* business

sermō, **ōnis** *m* speech, talk; conversation; gossip; subject of talk; language, dialect

sērō *adv* late, at a late hour; too late

serō[1], **—**, **sertum** ③ *v* string together; join, engage (in)

serō[2], **sēvī**, **satum** ③ *v* sow, plant; beget; broadcast; foment
□ ~ **negōtium** cause trouble

sērōtinus, **a**, **um** *adj* late, belated, deferred

serpēns, **ntis** *f* snake, serpent; the constellation Draco

serpō, **psī** ③ *v* crawl; move slowly on, glide; creep on

serpyllum, **ī** *nt* wild thyme

serra, **ae** *f* saw

serta[1], **ae** *f* garland

serta[2], **ōrum** *ntpl* chains of flowers, garlands, festoons

serum, **ī** *nt* whey

sērus, **a**, **um** *adj* late; too late; slow, tardy

serva, **ae** *f* female slave

servābilis, **e** *adj* capable of being saved

servātor, **ōris** *m* watcher, observer; preserver, saviour

servātrīx, **īcis** *f* female preserver, protectress

servīlis, **e** *adj* slavish, servile; of *or* belonging to slaves

serviō ④ *v with dat* be a slave, serve, wait on; be of use (to); be subject (to); labour for

servitium, **(i)ī** *nt* slavery, servitude; slaves; the slave class

servitūs, **ūtis** *f* slavery, servitude, bondage

servō ① *v* save, preserve; protect; keep, observe; look after; pay attention to

servulus, **servolus**, **ī** *m* young (worthless) slave

servus[1], **ī** *m* slave

servus[2], **a**, **um** *adj* having the status of a slave, servile

sescentī, **ae**, **a** *adj* six hundred; an indefinitely large number

sēsquipedālis, **e** *adj* of a foot and a half; (of words) a foot and a half long

sēsquiplāga, **ae** *f* 'a blow and a half'

sessilis, **e** *adj* fit for sitting upon

sēstertium, **(i)ī** *nt* [originally gen pl after **centēna mīlia**] a hundred thousand sesterces

 See note at **sēstertius**.

sēstertius[1], **(i)ī** *m* sesterce, two and a half **assēs**

> ! The **sēstertius** (from **sēmis tertius** 'third half') was a silver coin worth 2½ **assēs** and thus one quarter of a **dēnārius**; its symbol is HS. Its old gen. pl. **sēstertium** became a neuter noun representing a sum of 1000 **sēstertiī**; these were counted with distributive rather than cardinal numerals (e.g. **bīna sēstertia** '2000 sesterces'). With a numeral adv. **sēstertium** indicates 100,000 **sēstertiī** (**centēna mīlia** being understood, e.g. **octiēns sēstertium** '800,000 sesterces').

sēstertius[2], **a**, **um** *adj* two and a half

sētius *adv* the less

seu ▶ **sīve**

sevēritās, **ātis** *f* gravity, sternness, strictness, severity

sevērus, **a**, **um** *adj* grave, strict, austere, stern, severe; forbidding

sēvocō ① *v* call apart, draw aside; separate, appropriate

sex *adj indec* six

sexāgēnī, **ae**, **a** *adj* sixty each; sixty at a time

sexāgintā *adj indec* sixty

sexangulus, **a**, **um** *adj* six-cornered, hexagonal

sexcentī ▶ **sescentī**

sexta, **ae** *f* LM sext (part of the daily cycle of prayer)

sextādecimānī, **ōrum** *mpl* soldiers of the sixteenth legion

sextāns, **ntis** *m* one-sixth of any unit

Sextīlis, **e** *adj* of the sixth, later the eighth month of the Roman year
■ ~, **is** *m* (month) August

sextus, **a**, **um** *adj* sixth

sexus, **ūs** *m* sex

sī *conj* if
□ **sī minus** if not

> ❗ Followed by a clause with an indic. verb, **sī** expresses a factual condition; if the conditional clause contains a subj. verb, the condition is unfulfilled or hypothetical. After **sī** the words for 'someone, anyone' are **quis** and its adjective **quī**. **sī** does not usu. introduce an indirect question (cf. English 'they asked if …').

sibī *pn dat* of ▶ **sē**

sībilō ① *v* hiss; hiss at

sībilum, **ī** *nt*, **sībilus**, **ī** *m* hissing, whistling; hiss of contempt *or* disfavour

sībilus, **a**, **um** *adj* hissing

Sibylla, **ae** *f* prophetess, a sibyl

Sibyllīnus, **a**, **um** *adj* of *or* connected with a sibyl, sibylline

sīc *adv* in this *or* in such a manner, so, thus; to such an extent

sīca, **ae** *f* dagger

sīcārius, **(i)ī** *m* assassin, murderer

siccitās, **ātis** *f* dryness; drought; dried up condition

siccō ① *v* dry, staunch; dry up by evaporation; empty; suck dry

siccus, **a**, **um** *adj* dry; rainless, not carrying moisture; thirsty; abstemious
■ **siccum**, **ī** *nt* dry ground

sīcine *adv* so? thus?

siclus, **i** *m* LM shekel

sīcubi *adv* if anywhere, if at any place

sīcunde *adv* if from any place *or* source

sīcut, **sīcutī** *adv* just as, in the same way as; as it were; just as for instance; just as if; as indeed (is the case)

sīdereus, **a**, **um** *adj* relating to stars; starry; heavenly; star-like

sīdō, **ī** ③ *v* settle; sink down; sit down; run aground

sīdus, **eris** *nt* star, constellation; climate, weather; glory; *pl* star, the stars

sigillum, **ī** *nt* statuette; embossed figure, relief; figure woven in tapestry

signātor, **ōris** *m* witness (to a will, *etc.*)

signifer, **era**, **erum** *adj* holding the constellations
■ **signifer**, **erī** *m* standard-bearer

significātiō, **ōnis** *f* giving signs *or* signals; expression, indication, sign; suggestion, hint

significō ① *v* show, point out, indicate; intimate, signify; express

signō ① *v* mark; affix a seal to, seal up; coin, stamp; inscribe; indicate; LM make the sign of the cross

signum, **ī** *nt* mark, token, sign; standard, ensign; cohort; signal, password; image, picture, statue; seal, signet; constellation
□ **signa cōnferō** join battle
□ **ad prīma signa** in the front line

silēns, **ntis** *adj* silent
■ **silentēs**, **silentum/silentium** *mpl* the dead

silentium, **(i)ī** *nt* stillness, silence; repose, tranquillity; omission to speak *or* write of; neglect

sileō ② *v* be silent, not to speak (about); be quiet; not to function

silēscō, **luī** ③ *v* grow quiet

silex, **icis** *m/f* pebble-stone, flint; boulder, stone

siliqua, **ae** *f* pod

silva, **ae** *f* wood, forest; brushwood; thicket-like growth; branches and foliage of trees, bushes, *etc.*; trees

S

silvānī, **ōrum** *mpl* gods associated with forest and uncultivated land

silvestris, **tre** *adj* covered with woods, wooded; found in woodland; living in woodlands; wild, untamed, savage

silvicola, **ae** *adj* inhabiting woodlands

silvicultor, **ōris** *m*, **silvicultrīx**, **īcis** *f* one inhabiting woodlands, woodland-dweller

sīmia, **ae** *f* monkey, ape

similis, **e** *adj* like, resembling, similar

similitūdō, **inis** *f* likeness, resemblance, similarity; comparison, simile

simītū *adv* at the same time, together

simplex, **icis** *adj* simple, unmixed; artless, ingenuous, naive; harmless

simplicitās, **ātis** *f* simplicity; plainness, frankness, candour

simpliciter *adv* simply, just; candidly, frankly

simul *adv* together, at the same time, as well

simulac, **simulatque** *conj* as soon as, the moment that

simulācrum, **ī** *nt* likeness, image, statue; pictorial representation; ghost, phantom; shade; sham

simulāmen, **inis** *nt* imitation, simulation

simulātiō, **ōnis** *f* pretence, simulation; excuse, pretext

simulātor, **ōris** *m* one who copies or imitates; feigner

simulō ① *v* imitate, copy, represent; simulate, counterfeit, pretend; act the part of; cause to resemble

simultās, **ātis** *f* state of animosity, quarrel, feud

sīmulus, **a**, **um** *adj* flat-nosed, snub-nosed

sīmus, **a**, **um** *adj* flat-nosed, snub-nosed; flattened

sīn *conj* if however, but if; but if (despite what has been said)

sināpi, **is** *nt* mustard

sincērus, **a**, **um** *adj* sound, whole; genuine, pure; faithful, straightforward

sindōn, **nis** *f* woven material of a fine texture, muslin

sine *prep with abl* without

singillātim *adv* singly, one by one

singulāris, **e** *adj* single, singular; unusual, remarkable

singulī, **ae**, **a** *adj* one to each recipient; every single; individual; isolated

singultim *adv* sobbingly, with sobs

singultō ① *v* catch the breath, gasp; utter with sobs; gasp out (one's life)

singultus, **ūs** *m* sobbing; convulsive catching of breath

sinister, **tra**, **trum** *adj* left, on the left; unlucky, bad; auspicious, lucky, favourable; perverted
   ■ **sinistra**, **ae** *f* left hand or side;
   ■ **sinistrā** *adv* on the left

sinō, **sīvī/siī**, **situm** ③ *v* let, leave; allow, permit, leave alone, let be; grant

sīnum, **ī** *nt* bowl for serving wine, *etc.*

sinuō ① *v* bend into a curve; bend; billow out

sinuōsus, **a**, **um** *adj* characterized by the action of bending; winding, sinuous; full of folds or recesses

sīnus, **ī** *m* bowl for serving wine, *etc.*

sinus, **ūs** *m* curve; fold; hollow; bosom, lap; bay, gulf; pocket for money; asylum; inmost part; hiding-place; embrace

sīnus, **ī** *m* bowl

sīphō, **ōnis** *m* tube

sīquandō *adv* (also **sī quandō**) if ever, if at any time

sīquidem *conj* (also **sī quidem**) at any rate if, always assuming that; if it is really the case that; seeing that, inasmuch as

sīquis, **quae/qua**, **quid** *pn* (also **sī quis**) if any one, if any person

Sīrius, **(i)ī** *m* greater dog-star, Sirius
   ■ **~**, **a**, **um** *adj* of the dog-star

sirpe *nt* the plant *silphium*

sīs *int* [contracted from **sī** and **vīs**] please

sistō, **stetī/stitī**, **statum** ③ *v* set up, erect, place firmly, plant, station; stand still; stand firm

sistrum, **ī** *nt* metal rattle used in the worship of Isis

sitiēns, **ntis** *adj* thirsting, producing thirst, arid, dry, parched; thirsty (for)

sitiō ④ *v* be thirsty; long greatly for; be in need of water

sitis, **is** *f* thirst; aridity, dryness; violent craving (for)

situs[1], **ūs** *m* situation, position, site; structure; neglect, disuse, stagnation; rottenness, mould

situs[2], **a**, **um** *adj* laid up, stored; positioned, situated; centred (on)

sīve *conj* (also **seu**) or if
□ **sīve/seu** ... **sīve/seu** whether ... or

sixtus ▸ **xystus**

smaragdus, **ī** *m* emerald; beryl, jasper

smyrna, **ae** *f* myrrh

sobrīnus, **ī** *m* cousin on mother's side, child of mother's siblings

sōbrius, **a**, **um** *adj* sober; staid, sensible, temperate

soccus, **ī** *m* low-heeled, loose-fitting shoe *or* slipper, worn by Greeks; shoe worn by comic actors; comedy

socer, **erī** *m* father-in-law
□ **socerī**, **ōrum** parents-in-law

socia, **ae** *f* sharer, partner, companion, associate; spouse; ally, confederate

sociālis, **e** *adj* social; of *or* relating to allies; conjugal

societās, **ātis** *f* association; partnership; trading company; society; fellowship; connection; affinity

sociō ① *v* unite in partnership *or* an alliance; associate (one's resources, *etc.*) with those of a partner; share; combine

socius, **a**, **um** *adj* sharing, associated; allied, confederate
■ **~**, **(i)ī** *m* sharer, partner, companion, associate; spouse; ally, confederate

sōcordia, **ae** *f* sluggishness, torpor, inaction

sōcorditer *adv* negligently

sōcors, **rdis** *adj* sluggish, inactive

socrus, **ūs** *f* mother-in-law

sodālicium, **(i)ī** *nt* close association, partnership

sodālis, **is** *m* companion, comrade, crony

sodālitās, **ātis** *f* close association; religious fraternity; electioneering gang

sōdēs *adv* [contraction of **sī audēs**] if you do not mind, please

sōl, **sōlis** *m* sun; east; sunlight; heat of the sun; day

sōlāciolum, **ī** *nt* (little) comfort *or* solace

sōlācium, **(i)ī** *nt* solace, comfort, consolation

sōlāmen, **inis** *nt* source of comfort, solace

solea, **ae** *f* sole, sandal; sandal worn by a beast of burden

soleō, **solitus sum** ② *v semi-dep* be accustomed (to), be apt (to), be the common practise

solidō ① *v* make solid; strengthen, consolidate

solidus, **a**, **um** *adj* solid, firm, complete, entire; unwavering, strong; solid, lasting, real

sōlitūdō, **inis** *f* loneliness, solitariness; desert, waste; emptiness, solitude

solitus[1] *pple* from ▸ **soleō**

solitus[2], **a**, **um** *adj* accustomed, usual, customary, normal

solium, **(i)ī** *nt* throne; bath-tub

sollemnis, **e** *adj* solemn, ceremonial; traditional, customary

sollers, **rtis** *adj* clever, skilled, resourceful

sollertia, **ae** *f* skill, cleverness; resourcefulness

sollicitātiō, **ōnis** *f* incitement to disloyalty *or* crime

sollicitō ① *v* harass, molest; tug at, shake up; disturb, pester; torment; rouse, stimulate; strive to influence; incite to revolt; attempt to seduce

sollicitūdō, **inis** *f* anxiety, uneasiness

sollicitus, **a**, **um** *adj* restless; in a state of turmoil; uneasy, apprehensive; accompanied by anxiety *or* uneasiness

sōlor ① *v dep* comfort, console; relieve, mitigate

solstitiālis, **e** *adj* of *or* belonging to the summer solstice

solstitium, **(i)ī** *nt* solstice; summer-time, heat of the summer-solstice

sōlum *adv* only, merely
□ **nōn ~** ... **sed** not only ... but

solum, **ī** *nt* base, foundation; earth, ground, soil; sole of the foot *or* shoe

sōlus, **a**, **um** *adj* alone, sole; solitary; lonely; deserted

solūtiō, **ōnis** *f* payment

S

solūtus, a, um *adj* unbound; free; unrestrained, profligate; free to act as one pleases; lax, careless

solvō, lvī, lūtum ③ *v* loosen, unbind; separate, disengage; dissolve; melt; open; fulfil, perform; pay, deliver, release; acquit
□ **nāvem** ∼ set sail

somnifer, era, erum *adj*, **somnificus, a, um** *adj* inducing sleep

somniō ① *v* dream; dream of *or* see in a dream

somnium, (i)ī *nt* dream, vision; fantasy, day-dream

somnus, ī *m* sleep; sloth

sonābilis, e *adj* noisy, resonant

sonipēs, edis *m* horse, steed

sonitus, ūs *m* noise, loud sound

sonō, sonuī, sonitum ① *v* make a noise, sound, resound (with); utter; be heard

sonor, ōris *m* sound, noise, din

sonōrus, a, um *adj* noisy, loud, resounding, sonorous

sōns, ntis *adj* guilty, criminal; ∼ *m/f* criminal

sonus, ī *m* noise, sound

sophōs *int* well done! bravo!

sōpiō¹ ④ *v* cause to sleep; render insensible by a blow *or* sudden shock

sōplō², **ōnis** *f* penis

sopor, ōris *m* sleep

sopōrifer, era, erum *adj* bringing sleep *or* unconsciousness

sopōrō ① *v* rend to sleep, render unconscious, stupefy

sopōrus, a, um *adj* that induces sleep

sorbeō ② *v* suck up, drink up, absorb, soak up; engulf

sorbum, ī *nt* sorb, service-berry

sordeō ② *v* be dirty; seem mean, unworthy, not good enough, *etc.*

sordēs, dis *f* dirt, filth, nastiness, squalor; baseness, lowness; niggardliness

sordidātus, a, um *adj* shabbily dressed; wearing mourning clothes

sordidus, a, um *adj* dirty, foul, filthy; vulgar, low; poor; paltry, niggardly, sordid

soror, ōris *f* sister; Ⓛ︎Ⓜ︎ religious sister, nun
■ **sorōrēs** *pl* the Muses; the Fates

sorōrius, a, um *adj* of *or* concerning a sister

sors, rtis *f* lot, drawing of lots; decision by lot; response of an oracle; fate, destiny; part; share; investment, capital, principal

sōrsu- ▸ **seorsu-**

sortior ④ *v dep* cast *or* draw lots; obtain by lot; appoint by lot; choose

sortītus, ūs *m* process of lottery

sospes, itis *adj* safe and sound, unscathed

sospita, ae *f* female preserver (cult title of Juno at Lanuvium)

sospitō ① *v* preserve, defend

spadō, ōnis *m* eunuch

spargō, rsī, arsum ③ *v* strew, scatter; sprinkle; discharge in large numbers, shower; let stream out in all directions; place in scattered positions; spread about

sparus, ī *m* hunting-spear, javelin

spatior ① *v dep* walk about, range, stalk; spread out

spatiōsus, a, um *adj* roomy, ample, spacious, long; protracted

spatium, (i)ī *nt* room, space; place for walking, interval; period; length; time available for a purpose

speciēs, iēī *f* visual appearance; look; sight; outward appearance; semblance; pretence; display, splendour, beauty; vision; image, likeness; species; artistic representation

specimen, inis *nt* sign, evidence; token, symbol; Ⓛ︎Ⓜ︎ beauty

speciōsus, a, um *adj* showy, handsome, beautiful, splendid, brilliant; specious, plausible

spectābilis, e *adj* able to be seen *or* looked at; worth looking at

spectātor, ōris *m* witness, spectator; sightseer; critical observer

spectātrīx, īcis *f* female observer *or* watcher

spectō ① *v* look at; watch, observe; (geographically) lie, face; examine; test, prove; consider, pay regard to, regard (as)

specula, ae *f* raised look-out post

S

speculātor, **ōris** *m* spy, scout; look-out man

speculor ① *v dep* keep a close watch on, observe, spy out; look out, watch for

speculum, **ī** *nt* looking-glass, mirror

specus, **ūs** *adj* cave, abyss, chasm; hole, pit; hollow (of any kind)

spēlunca, **ae** *f* cave, grotto, cavern

spernō, **sprēvī**, **sprētum** ③ *v* reject with scorn, disdain; scorn; disregard

spērō ① *v* look forward to, hope for; hope; anticipate

> **!** **spērō** is usually followed by an acc. and fut. infin. denoting what one hopes will happen.

spēs, **eī** *f* hope; expectation; object of hope; joy

spīca, **ae** *f* ear of corn

spīceus, **a**, **um** *adj* consisting of ears of corn

spīculum, **ī** *nt* sting; javelin; arrow; sharp point of a weapon

spīna, **ae** *f* thorn; spine; backbone; thorn-bush

spīnētum, **ī** *nt* thicket (of thorn-bushes)

spīneus, **a**, **um** *adj* thorny, covered with thorns

spīnōsus, **a**, **um** *adj* thorny, prickly; crabbed, difficult

spīnus, **ī** *f* thorn-bush

spīra, **ae** *f* coil

spīrāculum, **ī** *nt* air-hole, vent

spīrāmentum, **ī** *nt* breathing-passage

spīritus, **ūs** *m* breath of air, breeze; breath, breathing; soul, mind; life

spīrō ① *v* breathe; blow; live; breathe out; exhale; breathe the spirit of

spissēscō ③ *v* become more compact, thicken

spissō ① *v* thicken, condense

spissus, **a**, **um** *adj* thick, dense; closely packed, crowded

splēn, **nis** *m* spleen

splendeō ② *v* shine, be bright; be brilliant *or* distinguished

splendēscō, **duī** ③ *v* become bright, begin to shine

splendidus, **a**, **um** *adj* bright, shining, glittering, brilliant; splendid, sumptuous; illustrious; showy, striking

splendor, **ōris** *m* brightness; brilliance, splendour; magnificence; personal distinction

spoliātiō, **ōnis** *f* robbing, plundering, spoliation

spoliātor, **ōris** *m* one who plunders *or* despoils

spoliō ① *v* strip *or* rob of clothing; plunder, rob, despoil

spolium, **(i)ī** *nt* skin, hide (of an animal, stripped off); booty, spoil
■ **spolia opīma** *ntpl* spoils taken by a general after a single combat with the opposing general

sponda, **ae** *f* bed, couch

spondeō, **spopondī**, **spōnsum** ② *v* give a pledge *or* undertaking; guarantee; act as surety for

spondēus, **ī** *m* spondee (metrical foot of two long syllables)

spōnsa, **ae** *f* woman promised in marriage, betrothed

spōnsālia, **ōrum** *ntpl* betrothal

spōnsiō, **ōnis** *f* solemn promise; wager at law

spōnsor, **ōris** *m* one who guarantees the good faith of another; surety

spōnsus, **ī** *m* affianced husband

sponte *adv* of one's own accord, freely, voluntarily, spontaneously; by oneself, alone

sporta, **ae** *f* basket, hamper

sportella, **ae** *f* little basket

sportula, **ae** *f* little basket; food *or* money given by patrons to clients

sprētor, **ōris** *m* one who despises *or* scorns

sprētum, **sprēvī** ▶ **spernō**

spūma, **ae** *f* foam, froth

spūmēscō ③ *v* become foamy

spūmeus, **a**, **um** *adj* foamy, frothy

spūmō ① *v* foam; be covered with foam

spūmōsus, **a**, **um** *adj* foaming, frothy

spuō, **uī**, **ūtum** ③ *v* spit, spit out

spurcō ① *v* soil, infect; deprave

spurcus, **a**, **um** *adj* dirty, foul; morally polluted

spurius, **a**, **um** *adj* ⓛⓜ illegitimate

spūtō ① *v* spit out

spūtum, ī *nt* spittle

squāleō ② *v* be covered with a rough *or* scaly layer; be dirty

squālidus, **a**, **um** *adj* having a rough surface; coated with dirt, filthy

squālor, **ōris** *m* dirtiness, filthiness, dirty *or* neglectful state as a sign of mourning

squāma, **ae** *f* scale; metal-plate used in the making of scale-armour

squāmeus, **squāmiger**, **squāmōsus**, **a**, **um** *adj* scaly

st *int* hush! sh!

stabiliō ④ *v* make firm *or* steady; hold still; fix *or* establish firmly

stabilis, **e** *adj* firm, steady, stable; lasting; immovable, constant

stabulō ① *v* house (domestic animals, poultry, *etc.*); be housed

stabulum, ī *nt* stall, shed, fold, stable; bee-hive; stabling

stacta, **ae** *f* myrrh oil

stadium, (i)ī *nt* running-track

stāgnō ① *v* form *or* lie in pools; be under water

stāgnum, ī *nt* pool, lagoon; water

stāmen, **inis** *nt* warp (in the loom); thread (on the distaff, to spin); thread of life spun by the Fates

stāmineus, **a**, **um** *adj* of *or* consisting of threads

stannum, ī *nt* alloy of silver and lead

statārius, **a**, **um** *adj* stationary

statim *adv* at once, immediately, instantly

statiō, **ōnis** *f* standing (still); halting-place; armed post; guard-duty; guard; station, place; anchorage

statīvus, **a**, **um** *adj* stationary, permanent

stator, **ōris** *m* one who establishes *or* upholds (cult-title of Jupiter)

statua, **ae** *f* statue

statūmen, **inis** *nt* support

statuō, **uī**, **ūtum** ③ *v* place, put up; set up, appoint; determine, resolve (to); decide; judge

statūra, **ae** *f* the height of the body in an upright position, stature

status[1], **ūs** *m* standing, position; posture; condition, circumstance, state; rank

status[2], **a**, **um** *adj* fixed, appointed; regular

stēlla, **ae** *f* star

stēllāns, **ntis** *adj* starry; having the appearance of stars

stellātus, **a**, **um** *adj* furnished with star-like points of light

sterculīnum, ī *nt* dung-hill, muck-heap

stercus, **oris** *nt* dung, excrement, muck

sterilis, **e** *adj* barren, sterile; fruitless; unprofitable, futile

sternāx, **ācis** *adj* liable to throw its rider (of a horse)

sternō, **strāvī**, **strātum** ③ *v* spread, strew; extend; level, knock down; cause to subside; lay low, defeat utterly

sternuō, **uī** ③ *v* sneeze

stertō, **tuī** ③ *v* snore

stetī ▸ **stō**

stillicidium, (i)ī *nt* fall (of a liquid) in successive drops

stillō ① *v* fall in drops; drip; cause to drip, pour in drops

stilus, ī *m* spike, stem; stylus, pen

stimulātrīx, **īcis** *f* female instigator, woman who goads on

stimulō ① *v* urge forward with a goad, torment, 'sting'; incite, rouse to frenzy

stimulus, ī *m* goad; spur; pointed stake; incitement

stinguō ③ *v* extinguish, put out; annihilate

stīpātor, **ōris** *m* one of the train surrounding a king; bodyguard, close attendant

stīpendiārius, **a**, **um** *adj* mercenary; paying tribute in the form of cash

stīpendium, (i)ī *nt* tax, contribution; pay; (a year of) military service; campaign
     ◻ **stīpendia mereor** complete (so many years of) military service

stīpes, **itis** *m* trunk (of a tree); stake

stīpō ① *v* crowd, press together, compress, surround closely

stips, **pis** *f* small offering

stipula, **ae** *f* stalk; stubble; straw; reed played on as a pipe

stīria, **ae** *f* icicle

S

stirps, pis *f* stock, stem, stalk; root; plant, shrub; family, ancestral race; offspring, posterity

stīva, ae *f* shaft of a plough-handle

stō, stetī, statum ① *v* stand; stand still; be fixed; stand erect; be *or* become upright, endure, persist; remain; adhere (to); be one's fault
□ **per tē stetit quōminus vincerem** it was due to you that I did not conquer

Stōicus, a, um *adj* Stoic

stola, ae *f* long upper garment

stolidus, a, um *adj* dull, stupid, brutish

stomachor ① *v dep* be angry, boil with rage

stomachōsus, a, um *adj* irritable, short-tempered

stomachus, ī *m* gullet; stomach; annoyance; ill-temper

storea, ae *f* matting of rushes

strāgēs, gis *f* overthrow; massacre, slaughter, cutting down; havoc; confused heap; destruction, devastation

strāmen, inis *nt* straw for bedding, *etc.*, litter

strāmentum, ī *nt* straw, litter; coverings

strāmineus, a, um *adj* made of straw

strangulō ① *v* choke; suffocate, smother

strātum¹, ī *nt* coverlet; bed, couch; horse-blanket

strātum², strāvī ▶ sternō

strēnuitās, ātis *f* strenuous behaviour, activity

strēnuus, a, um *adj* active, vigorous, energetic

strepitō ① *v* make a loud *or* harsh noise

strepitus, ūs *m* noise, din; crashing, rustling, clattering sound (of a musical instrument); noisy talk, uproar

strepō, itum ③ *v* make a loud noise; shout confusedly; resound

striātus, a, um *adj* striated, fluted

strictūra, ae *f* hardened mass of iron

strīdeō ② *v*, **strīdō, dī** ③ *v* creak, hiss, whistle, buzz, rattle; produce a high-pitched utterance; be filled with a shrill sound

strīdor, ōris *m* hissing, buzzing, rattling, whistling; high-pitched sound

strīdulus, a, um *adj* making a high-pitched *or* shrill sound

strigilis, is *f* instrument with a curved and channelled blade for scraping the skin

> ❗ The strigil was used during bathing to remove from the skin the olive oil poured on in order to loosen sweat and dirt.

strigōsus, a, um *adj* lean, scraggy

stringō, īnxī, ictum ③ *v* draw *or* tie tight; skin, brush; graze; pluck, strip off; prune; unsheathe

strix, gis *f* owl

strophium, (i)ī *nt* twisted breast-band; head-band

strūctūra, ae *f* building, construction; structure; masonry, concrete

struēs, uis *f* heap, pile; row of sacrificial cakes

strūma, ae *f* swelling of the lymphatic glands

struō, ūxī, ūctum ③ *v* build, construct; arrange; devise, contrive

studeō ② *v with dat* devote oneself to, concern oneself (with), strive after; concentrate on; support; study

studiōsus, a, um *adj* eager, zealous, studious, scholarly; affectionate, fond; devoted

studium, (i)ī *nt* zeal, eagerness (for), study, application; devotion, goodwill, support

stultitia, ae *f* stupidity, folly, fatuity

stultus, a, um *adj* foolish, silly; inept

stupefaciō, fēcī, factum ③ *v* stun with amazement, stupefy
■ **stupefīō, fierī, factus sum** *v ir semi-dep* be astonished

stupeō ② *v* be stunned *or* benumbed; be astonished *or* stupefied (at)

stupor, ōris *m* numbness, torpor; stupefaction; stupidity

stuppa, ae *f* tow, coarse flax

stuppeus, a, um *adj* of tow

S

stuprō ① *v* have illicit sexual intercourse with

stuprum, **ī** *nt* dishonour, shame; illicit sexual intercourse, rape

sturnus, **ī** *m* starling

stylus ▸ **stilus**

suādeō, **suāsī**, **suāsum** ② *v* advise, recommend, urge; advocate

suāsor, **ōris** *m* adviser, counsellor

suasus, **ūs** *m* persuasion

suāvidicus, **a**, **um** *adj* speaking pleasantly

suāviloquēns, **ntis** *adj* speaking agreeably

suāviolum, **ī** *nt* tender kiss

suāvior ① *v dep* kiss

suāvis, **e** *adj* sweet, pleasant, agreeable, delightful

suāvium, **(i)ī** *nt* kiss; sweetheart

sub *prep with abl* under, below, beneath; under the power of; *with acc* near to; about; a little before; to a position under; up to; directly after

subaquilus, **a**, **um** *adj* rather dark-skinned

subblandior ④ *v dep* fondle *or* caress a little

subc- ▸ **succ-**

subdō, **didī**, **ditum** ③ *v* place *or* insert below; place under; subject, expose (to); substitute fraudulently; supply

subdolus, **a**, **um** *adj* sly, deceitful, treacherous

subdūcō, **dūxī**, **ductum** ③ *v* draw from under *or* from below; withdraw (from); extricate; steal (away); reckon up, calculate

subductiō, **ōnis** *f* hauling up of a ship onto the beach

subedō, **ēsse**, **ēdī**, **ēsum** *v ir* eat away below

subeō, **īre**, **iī/īvī**, **itum** *v ir* go, move *or* pass underneath; come up to, approach; undergo, endure; come next; succeed to; steal in on, come over; suggest itself

sūber, **eris** *nt* cork-tree; its thick spongy outer bark, cork

subf- ▸ **suff-**

subfuscus, **a**, **um** *adj* rather dark in appearance

subg- ▸ **sugg-**

subiciō, **iēcī**, **ectum** ③ *v* throw up; place below; place under; lay before; put under the control of; expose; place next; interpose; suborn; introduce

> **!** The first syllable of this verb scans as heavy in the present stem even though the 'u' is short; this is because the 'i' represents 'ii' pronounced as consonant + vowel 'yi'.

subiectō ① *v* throw up from below; apply below

subiectus, **a**, **um** *adj with dat* situated under; open *or* exposed (to); subject (to)

subigō, **ēgī**, **āctum** ③ *v* conquer, subjugate; plough; force; drive under

subinde *adv* immediately after, thereupon; constantly, repeatedly

subitārius, **a**, **um** *adj* got together to meet an emergency, hastily enrolled

subitō *adv* suddenly, unexpectedly; at short notice; in no time at all

subitus, **a**, **um** *adj* sudden, unexpected

■ **subitum**, **ī** *nt* emergency, crisis

subiugalis, **is** *m* ⸤LM⸥ beast of burden

subiungō, **ūnxī**, **ūnctum** ③ *v* yoke; subjoin; add; bring under the control (of)

sublābor, **lāpsus sum** ③ *v dep* collapse; sink *or* ebb away; creep up

sublātum ▸ **tollō**

sublātus, **a**, **um** *adj* high-pitched; bold, self-assured

sublegō, **ēgī**, **ēctum** ③ *v* pick up from the ground, steal away

sublevō ① *v* lift, raise, support; lighten, alleviate; assist, encourage

sublica, **ae** *f* wooden stake *or* pile

subligō ① *v* fasten (to)

sublīmis, **e** *adj* high, lofty, exalted; imposingly tall; sublime; eminent

sublīmitās, **ātis** *f* height; loftiness

sublūceō ② *v* shine faintly, glimmer

subluō, **ūtum** ③ *v* wash; flow at the foot of

sublūstris, **tre** *adj* faintly lit, dim

submergō, **rsī**, **ersum** ③ *v* cause to sink, submerge

S

subministrō ① *v* supply, furnish, afford

submissus, **a**, **um** *adj* stooping; quiet

submittō, **īsī**, **issum** ③ *v* raise, rear; send up; send (reinforcements); drop; make subject (to)

submoveō, **mōvī**, **mōtum** ② *v* remove; drive off, dislodge; expel; ward off; keep at a distance

subnectō, **exuī**, **exum** ③ *v* bind under, add, subjoin, fasten up

subnīxus, **a**, **um** *adj with abl* relying on; elated by

subnūbilus, **a**, **um** *adj* somewhat cloudy, overcast

subolēs, **lis** *f* shoot, sucker; race; offspring; progeny

subolēscō ③ *v* grow up

subolet ② *v impers* there is an inkling

suborior, **ortus sum** ④ *v dep* come into being, be provided

subortus, **ūs** *m* the springing up (of a fresh supply)

subp- ▶ **supp-**

subr- ▶ **surr-**

subrēmigō ① *v* make rowing movements underneath

subrīdeō, **rīsī** ② *v* smile

subrubeō ② *v* be tinged with red *or* purple

subruō, **ruī**, **rutum** ③ *v* weaken at the base, undermine

subscrībō, **psī**, **ptum** ③ *v* write underneath; append; inscribe at the foot; give support (to)

subsecō, **secuī**, **sectum** ① *v* cut away below; pare (the nails)

subsellium, **(i)ī** *nt* bench, low seat; court, courts

subsequor, **secūtus sum** ③ *v dep* follow close behind, follow, succeed; follow the lead of

subsidiārius, **a**, **um** *adj* acting as a support to the front line
■ **subsidiāriī**, **ōrum** *mpl* the reserves

subsidium, **(i)ī** *nt* body of troops in reserve; aid; support; safeguard; means of assistance

subsīdō, **sēdī**, **essum** ③ *v* squat down; settle down; subside; lie in wait (for); fall to the ground

subsistō, **stitī** ③ *v* stop short; stand firm; stop short, cease from; remain, tarry, settle down

substernō, **strāvī**, **strātum** ③ *v* spread out (as an underlay)

substringō, **īnxī**, **ictum** ③ *v* draw in close, gather up; draw tight
◻ **aurem** ∼ strain to hear

substrūctiō, **ōnis** *f* (act of building) a foundation, substructure

substruō, **ūxī**, **ūctum** ③ *v* build up from the base; support by means of substructures

subsum, **esse** *v ir with dat* be underneath; be a basis for discussion; be close at hand as a reserve *or* refuge

subsūtus, **a**, **um** *adj* stitched at the bottom

subter *prep with abl* below, beneath, under, underneath; *with acc* to a position under; *adv* below, beneath, under, underneath; to a position underneath

subterfugiō, **ūgī** ③ *v* evade, avoid by a stratagem

subterlābor ③ *v dep* glide *or* flow beneath, slip away

subterrāneus, **a**, **um** *adj* underground

subtexō, **xuī**, **xtum** ③ *v* weave beneath; veil; subjoin, attach as a sequel (to)

subtīlis, **e** *adj* fine-spun, fine; slender, delicate, exact; minutely thorough

subtrahō, **āxī**, **actum** ③ *v* draw from under, undermine; withdraw (from); detach from the main body; rescue from the threat (of); remove

subūcula, **ae** *f* under-tunic worn by both sexes

subulcus, **ī** *m* swineherd

Subūra, **ae** *f* valley between the Esquiline and Viminal hills of Rome (a centre of night life)

suburbānī, **ōrum** *mpl* people dwelling near the city

suburbānus, **a**, **um** *adj* situated close to the city; growing or cultivated near the city

suburgeō ② *v* drive up close

subvectiō, **ōnis** *f* transporting (of supplies) to a centre

S

subvectō ① *v* convey (often *or* laboriously) upwards

subvehō, ēxī, ectum ③ *v* convey upwards; convey up
□ **subvehor** sail upstream

subveniō, vēnī, ventum ④ *v with dat* come to the help (of); relieve

subvertō, rtī, rsum ③ *v* overturn, cause to topple; overthrow, destroy, subvert

subvexus, a, um *adj* sloping up

subvolō ① *v* fly upwards

subvolvō ③ *v* roll uphill

succēdō, cessī, cessum ③ *v* go below *or* under; come to the foot (of), come up (to); move on upwards; move up into the position (of); take the place (of); succeed (to)

succendō, endī, ēnsum ③ *v* set alight, kindle from below; inflame

succēnseō, sum ② *v* be angry

succenturiātus, ī *m* reservist

successiō, ōnis *f* succession (of a person) to a position of authority, ownership

successor, ōris *m* successor

successus, ūs *m* the action of coming up close; success, good result

succidō, idī ③ *v* collapse through the lower parts giving way

succīdō, īdī, īsum ③ *v* cut from below, cut down

succiduus, a, um *adj* giving way under one

succingō, īnxī, īnctum ③ *v* gather up with a belt *or* girdle; prepare for action; surround

succlāmātiō, ōnis *f* answering shout

succlāmō ① *v* shout in response (to)

succrēscō ③ *v* grow up from below; grow up as a replacement *or* successor

succumbō, cubuī, cubitum ③ *v* sink to the ground; collapse; lie down (under); lower itself; give in (to)

succurrō, currī, cursum ③ *v with dat* run *or* move quickly to the rescue (of); come into one's mind

succutiō, ussī, ussum ③ *v* shake from below

sūcinum, ī *nt* amber

sūcinus, a, um *adj* made of amber, amber-coloured

sūcōsus, a, um *adj* full of sap, juicy

sūcula, ae *f* windlass

sūcus, ī *m* juice, sap; vital fluid in trees and plants

sūdārium, (i)ī *nt* handkerchief, napkin

sūdātor, ōris *m* one who sweats

sudis, dis *f* stake, pointed stick; spike

sūdō ① *v* sweat, perspire; become damp with surface moisture

sūdor, ōris *m* sweat, perspiration

sūdus, a, um *adj* clear and bright

suēscō, ēvī, ētum ③ *v* become accustomed (to)

suētus, a, um *adj* wont, accustomed; usual, familiar

sufferō, ferre, sustulī, sublātum *v ir* submit to, endure, to suffer

sufficiō, fēcī, fectum ③ *v* supply, provide; suffuse, imbue, steep; appoint in place of another; have sufficient strength (to), stand up (to); have sufficient wealth *or* resources for; be sufficient for; be available for

suffīgō, īxī, īxum ③ *v* fasten beneath as a support; crucify

suffīmen, inis *nt*, **suffīmentum, ī** *nt* a substance used to fumigate

suffiō ④ *v* fumigate

sufflō ① *v* puff up

suffodiō, ōdī, ossum ③ *v* undermine, dig under; pierce *or* prod below

suffrāgātiō, ōnis *f* public expression of support (for)

suffrāgium, (i)ī *nt* voting; vote; right of voting; recommendation

suffrāgor ① *v dep* express public support (for), canvass *or* vote for; lend support (to)

suffugium, (i)ī *nt* shelter

suffulciō, lsī, ltum ④ *v* underprop, keep from falling

suffundō, ūdī, ūsum ③ *v* pour in *or* on; cause to well up to the surface; cover *or* fill with a liquid that wells up from below

suggerō, essī, estum ③ *v* heap up; supply, feed; subjoin

suggestus, ūs *m* raised surface; platform, dais

suggillō, sūgillō ① *v* insult, humiliate

S

sūgō, sūxī, sūctum ③ *v* suck; (fig) take in

suillus, a, um *adj* of pigs

sulcō ① *v* furrow, plough; cleave

sulcus, ī *m* furrow; rut; trail of a meteor; track, wake

sulfur, sulp(h)ur, ris *nt* brimstone, sulphur

sultis *int* [contraction of **sī** and **vultis**] please

sum, esse, fuī *v ir* be, exist, live; happen; remain; be possible *or* allowable

> **!** With a common noun in the (so-called 'predicative') dative, **sum** means 'be a source of', e.g. **auxiliō esse** 'be a source of help'. With a proper noun or personal pn. in the dat., **sum** expresses possession, e.g. **est mihi canis** 'a dog belongs to me' or 'I have a dog'.

summ- ⋗ subm-

summa, ae *f* total number *or* amount; sum; sum-total; a whole; the whole of a thing; the overall matter in question; an activity's general purpose

summātim *adv* summarily, briefly

summē *adv* in the highest degree, intensely

summus, a, um *adj* highest, greatest, very great; chief, principal; the farthest, utmost, last, extreme; very deep
  ◻ ∼ **mōns** the top of the mountain

> **!** At the dinner table at an upper-class dinner party, the couch on the left and the left place on each couch were described as **summus**. Guests were often placed on the left couch (**in summō**); the head of the family (and thus the host) reclined on the left of the opposite couch (**summus in īmō**). See also **medius**.

sūmō, mpsī, mptum ③ *v* take, take up; take hold of; receive; spend; have recourse to; adopt as suitable; adopt; embrace; assume; take on

sūmptuārius, a, um *adj* concerned with the spending of money

sūmptuōsus, a, um *adj* expensive, costly, sumptuous

sūmptus, ūs *m* expense, lavish expenditure; expenses; charge

suō, suī, sūtum ③ *v* sew, stitch together

suovetaurīlia, ium *ntpl* purificatory sacrifice consisting of a boar, a ram, and a bull

supellex, lectilis *f* furniture, furnishings; outfit, paraphernalia

super *adv/prep with acc/abl* above, on, over; beyond; on top of; besides; about; concerning; in addition to

supera, ōrum *ntpl* heaven

superābilis, e *adj* that may be got over *or* surmounted; that may be conquered

superaddō, didī, ditum ③ *v* add *or* affix on the surface

superātor, ōris *m* conqueror

superbia, ae *f* pride, lofty self-esteem, disdain

superbiō ④ *v with abl* show pride *or* disdain on account (of), plume oneself (on)

superbus, a, um *adj* haughty, proud, arrogant; disdainful; glorying (in); that is a source of pride; grand, proud, sumptuous

supercilium, (i)ī *nt* eyebrow; gravity, haughtiness, stern looks, pride; overhanging edge, brow

superēmineō ② *v* overtop, stand out above the level of

superfluō, ūxī ③ *v* overflow; superabound; be superabundantly supplied with

superfundō, ūdī, ūsum ③ *v* pour over

supergredior, gressus sum ③ *v dep* pass over *or* beyond; exceed, surpass

superī, ōrum *mpl* gods above

superiaciō, iēcī, iactum ③ *v* throw *or* scatter on top *or* over the surface; shoot over the top of

superimmineō ② *v* stand above in a threatening position

superimpōnō, posuī, positum ③ *v* place on top *or* over

superincidēns, ntis *adj* falling on top

superincubāns, ntis *adj* lying on top

superincumbō, buī ③ *v* lean over

superiniciō, iēcī, iectum ③ *v* throw *or* scatter on over the surface

superīnsternō, strāvī, strātum ③ *v* lay on over the surface

superior, ius *adj* higher, upper, superior, better; past, previous; elder, stronger; victorious

supernē *adv* at *or* to a higher level, above; in the upper part; on top

supernus, a, um *adj* situated above

superō ① *v* climb over; overtop; rise to a higher level; get beyond; surpass; be superior; defeat, surmount; survive; be present in excess of one's needs; abound; remain; remain alive; be situated beyond; vanquish

superoccupō ① *v* take by surprise from above

superpendēns, ntis *adj* overhanging

superpōnō, posuī, positum ③ *v* place over *or* on top; put in charge

superscandō ③ *v* climb over

supersedeō, sēdī, sessum ② *v with abl* refrain (from), desist (from)

superstagnō ① *v* spread in flood, overflow

supersternō, strāvī, strātum ③ *v* spread *or* lay on top

superstes, itis *adj* outliving, surviving; standing over

superstitiō, ōnis *f* superstition; irrational religious awe

superstitiōsus, a, um *adj* superstitious, full of unreasoning religious awe

superstō ① *v* stand over *or* on top (of)

supersum, esse, fuī *v ir* have the strength (for); be superfluous (to); be left over; remain alive, survive; remain to be performed

superus, a, um *adj* upper; earthly; heavenly, celestial
  □ **superum mare** the Adriatic Sea
  ■ **superior** *comp*
  ■ **suprēmus** *sup*

supervacāneus, a, um *adj* redundant; unnecessary

supervacuus, a, um *adj* superfluous, redundant; unnecessary

supervādō ③ *v* surmount

supervehor, vectus sum ③ *v dep* ride, sail, *etc.*, over *or* past

superveniō, vēnī, ventum ④ *v* arrive on the scene; *with dat* come up (with a person, catching him in a given activity *or* situation)

supervolitō ① *v* fly to and fro over

supervolō ① *v* fly over

supīnō ① *v* lay on the back; turn up; tilt back

supīnus, a, um *adj* lying face upwards, flat on one's back; turned palm upwards; directed *or* flowing backwards; flat, low-lying; languid, passive

suppeditō ① *v* be available when required, supply the needs (of); make available as required; supply (with)

suppernātus, a, um *adj* having the leg cut from beneath, hamstrung

suppetiae, ārum *fpl* help, rescue

suppetō, īvī/iī, ītum ③ *v* turn up as a support, give backing (to); be available for one's needs; suggest itself

supplēmentum, ī *nt* supplement; reinforcement

suppleō, ēvī, ētum ② *v* complete, fill up; make (a whole)

supplex, icis *adj* suppliant, making humble entreaty; expressing *or* involving supplication

supplicātiō, ōnis *f* offering of propitiation to a deity

suppliciter *adv* suppliantly, in an attitude of humble entreaty

supplicium, (i)ī *nt* act performed to propitiate a deity; punishment; torment; penalty, punishment

supplicō ① *v with dat* make humble petition to; make propitiary offerings to, do worship

suppōnō, posuī, positum ③ *v* place under; substitute; introduce fraudulently into a situation

supportō ① *v* transport (supplies, *etc.*) to a centre

supprimō, pressī, pressum ③ *v* press down *or* under; suppress; keep back, contain; stop, check

suprā *prep with acc* above, over, on the upper side of; beyond; earlier than; more than

suprāscandō ③ *v* climb on top of

suprēma, ōrum *ntpl* funeral rites *or* offerings; last rites

suprēmus, a, um *adj* highest; topmost; last, latest, dying; greatest
  □ **manus suprēma** finishing touches

sūra, ae *f* calf of the leg

surculus, ī *m* twig; cutting, graft

S

surditās, **ātis** *f* deafness

surdus, **a**, **um** *adj* deaf; unresponsive to what is said; falling on deaf ears; muffled, muted

surgō, **surrēxī**, **surrēctum** ③ *v* rise, get up; rouse oneself to action; stand high; grow tall

surrēpō, **psī**, **ptum** ③ *v* creep, creep (up to); steal on, insinuate itself

surripiō, **puī**, **eptum** ③ *v* steal, kidnap, remove by stealth

surrupiō ▸ **surripiō**

sūrsum *adv* upwards; on high, above

sūs, **suis** *m*/*f* pig, sow

suscipiō, **cēpī**, **ceptum** ③ *v* take (up), catch from below; support; receive; take under one's protection; adopt; undertake, perform; venture upon; accept; acknowledge (a new-born child); get *or* have a child

suscitō ① *v* dislodge, cause to rise; restore to health; venture upon; enter on the performance of; face, accept; rouse

suspectus, **ūs** *m* looking up; high regard

suspendium, **(i)ī** *nt* the act of hanging oneself

suspendō, **ndī**, **nsum** ③ *v* hang (up); keep poised; keep in suspense

suspēnsus, **a**, **um** *adj* in a state of anxious uncertainty *or* suspense; light □ **suspēnsō gradū** on tiptoe

suspicāx, **ācis** *adj* mistrustful

suspiciō, **spexī**, **spectum** ③ *v* look upwards (to); look up at; esteem, admire; be suspicious of

suspīciō, **ōnis** *f* suspicion, mistrustful feeling; trace

suspicor ① *v dep* suspect; have an inkling of; infer

suspīrātus, **ūs** *m* sigh; deep breath

suspīritus, **ūs** *m* sigh

suspīrium, **(i)ī** *nt* sigh; heartthrob

suspīrō ① *v* sigh; utter with a sigh

sustentō ① *v* support, hold up; uphold, bear up against; delay

sustineō, **tentum** ② *v* hold up, support, sustain; stand up to, withstand; shoulder; have the necessary endurance (to); submit (to); endure; hold back

sustollō ③ *v* raise on high

sustulī ▸ **tollō**

susurrō ① *v* whisper; rustle

susurrus[1], **ī** *m* whisper, whispered report; soft rustling sound

susurrus[2], **a**, **um** *adj* whispering

sūtilis, **e** *adj* made by sewing, consisting of things stitched together

sūtor, **ōris** *m* shoemaker; cobbler

sūtrīnus, **a**, **um** *adj* of a shoe maker

sūtūra, **ae** *f* seam, stitch, piece of sewing

suus, **a**, **um** *adj* his own, her own, its own, their own; especially dear to him; belonging to him at birth; normal to him; due *or* allotted to him; convenient for him

 See note at **quisque**.

syllaba, **ae** *f* syllable

symphōnia, **ae** *f* harmony, group of singers *or* musicians

synodus, **i** *m* ⓁⓂ synod

Tt

tabānus, **ī** *m* gadfly

tabella, **ae** *f* tablet; voting-tablet; board for games; placard; board; *pl* wax-coated wooden tablets, threaded together to form a notebook

tabellārius, **(i)ī** *m* letter-carrier, courier

tābeō ② *v* rot away, decay

taberna, **ae** *f* hut, booth, inn; tavern; shop *or* stall

tabernāculum, **ī** *nt* tent

tabernārius, **(i)ī** *m* shopkeeper, tradesman

tābēs, **bis** *f* wasting away; decay; putrefaction; fluid resulting from corruption *or* decay

tābēscō, ī ③ *v* waste *or* dwindle away; melt away; decompose

tābidus, **a**, **um** *adj* wasting away, emaciated, putrefying, rotten; accompanied by wasting

tābificus, **a**, **um** *adj* causing decay *or* wasting

tābitūdō, **inis** *f* wasting away

tabula, **ae** *f* board, plank; votive-tablet; writing-tablet; letter, will; panel; picture; game board; tablet of stone *or* metal set up as a permanent record; *pl* account-books; document; will

tabulārium, **(i)ī** *nt* collection of (inscribed) tablets; record-office, registry

tabulātiō, **ōnis** *f* structure of boards, boarding

tabulātum, **ī** *nt* floor, storey, tier formed by the horizontal branches of a tree

tābum, **ī** *nt* viscous fluid consisting of putrid matter, gore

taceō ② *v* be silent; say nothing about

taciturnitās, **ātis** *f* maintaining silence

taciturnus, **a**, **um** *adj* saying nothing, making no noise

tacitus, **a**, **um** *adj* silent; quiet; secret, hidden; unmentioned; tacit

tāctilis, **e** *adj* able to be touched

tāctus, **ūs** *m* touch, sense of touch

taeda, **ae** *f* pine-wood, pine-torch; wedding; pine-tree

taedet, **uit**, **taesum est** ② *v impers with gen or with infin and acc of person affected* be tired *or* sick (of)

taedifer, **era**, **erum** *adj* torch-bearing

taedium, **(i)ī** *nt* weariness, ennui; an object of weariness

taenia, **ae** *f* ribbon

taeter, **tra**, **trum** *adj* foul, monstrous, vile, horrible

tālāria, **ium** *ntpl* skirts; winged sandals

tālāris, **e** *adj* reaching down to the ankles

tālea, **ae** *f* long, thin piece of wood, metal, *etc.*

talentum, **ī** *nt* talent of silver (currency)

tālis, **e** *adj* such, of such a kind; such (a)

talpa, **ae** *f sometimes m* mole (animal)

tālus, **ī** *m* ankle, ankle-bone; knuckle-bone of a sheep; *pl* the game played with such bones

tam *adv* so; so much (as)

tamen *conj* nevertheless, all the same; yet
□ ∼ **etsī** even though

tametsī *conj* even though

tamquam *adv* just as; just as if

> ❗ **tamquam** (like **quasi**) is often found in prose to change a metaphor into a simile, bold metaphors being felt by Latin prose writers to be too poetic.

tandem *adv* at length, at last, after some time; really, I ask you, after all

tangō, **tetigī**, **tāctum** ③ *v* touch; put one's hand on; reach; be next to, border on; arrive (at); affect, move; touch on, make a mention of

tantillus, **a**, **um** *adj* so small; so small a quantity

tantīsper *adv* for so long (as); for the present

tantopere *adv* so very, to such a great degree

tantulus, **a**, **um** *adj* so small, such a little

tantum *adv* so much, to such a degree, so; only, just, merely
□ ∼ **nōn** all but, almost
□ ∼ **abest ut ... ut ...** it is so far from being the case that ... (that the result is) that ...

tantummodo *adv* only, merely

tantus, **a**, **um** *adj* so great

tantusdem, **tantadem**, **tantundem** *adj* just as great
■ **tantundem**, **īdem** *nt* the same quantity, just as much

tapēs, **ētis** *m*, **tapēte**, **is** *nt*, **tapētum**, **ī** *nt* woollen cloth *or* rug used as a covering, hanging, *etc.*

tarandrus, **ī** *m* reindeer

tardēscō ③ *v* become slow

tardipēs, **edis** *adj* slow-footed, lame

tarditās, **ātis** *f* slowness of movement, action, *etc.*

tardō ① *v* delay, check

tardus, **a**, **um** *adj* slow; tardy, late; dull, stupid

t

tarmes, **itis** *m* woodworm

Tartara, **ōrum** *ntpl*, **Tartarus**, **ī** *m* the infernal regions, the underworld

Tartareus, **a**, **um** *adj* of *or* belonging to the underworld; Tartarean

taurea, **ae** *f* leather whip

taureus, **a**, **um** *adj* derived from a bull

taurifōrmis, **e** *adj* having the form of a bull

taurīnus, **a**, **um** *adj* of *or* derived from a bull; made of ox-hide

taurus, **ī** *m* bull; the constellation Taurus

taxus, **ī** *f* yew-tree

tē *acc/abl* of ▷ **tū**

techna, **ae** *f* trick, ruse

tēctum, **ī** *nt* roof; house, dwelling; (rough *or* improvised) shelter

tēgillum, **ī** *nt* piece of rush matting

tegimen, **inis** *nt* covering, cover

tegō, **tēxī**, **tēctum** ③ *v* cover; hide, conceal; roof over; shield, protect

tēgula, **ae** *f* roof-tile

tegumen, **inis** *nt*, **tegumentum**, **ī** *nt* ▷ **tegimen**

tēla, **ae** *f* cloth in the process of being woven on a loom; the upright threads in a loom; a loom

tellūs, **ris** *f* earth; ground

tēlum, **ī** *nt* missile, javelin; sword; (any offensive) weapon; sunbeam, thunderbolt

temerārius, **a**, **um** *adj* accidental; rash, foolhardy, thoughtless, reckless, hasty

temere *adv* blindly, heedlessly; without due thought *or* care; without reason; at random, casually; readily, easily

temeritās, **ātis** *f* recklessness, thoughtlessness, impetuosity

temerō ① *v* violate; defile, pollute; violate sexually

tēmētum, **ī** *nt* strong wine; intoxicating liquor

temnō ③ *v* scorn, despise

tēmō, **ōnis** *m* beam *or* pole of a cart, chariot, *etc.*; Charles's Wain

temperāns, **ntis** *adj* restrained, self-controlled

temperantia, **ae** *f* moderation, restraint, self-control

temperātus, **a**, **um** *adj* temperate, moderate

temperī *adv* at the right time, seasonably

temperiēs, **iēī** *f* mixture of substances, qualities, *etc.*, in due proportion; climate, temperateness; (moderate) temperature

temperō ① *v* exercise restraint, exercise moderation (in respect of); be moderate in one's conduct (towards); restrain oneself, refrain (from); temper; cause to moderate violence, *etc.*; modify; control physically; control, regulate

tempestās, **ātis** *f* portion of time, season; weather; storm; violent disturbance

tempestīvus, **a**, **um** *adj* seasonable; opportune, physically in one's prime, ripe (for marriage); timely

templum, **ī** *nt* temple, shrine; zone, space, region; plank

tempt- ▷ **tent-**

tempus, **oris** *nt* time, season; a sufficiency of time (for a particular purpose); opportunity; season (of the year); condition *pl* times; temples of the head

■ **temporī**, **temperī** *adv* at the right time

tēmulentus, **a**, **um** *adj* drunken

tenācitās, **ātis** *f* the quality of holding on to a thing

tenāx, **ācis** *adj* holding fast, tenacious; persistent, steadfast; stubborn, obstinate

tendō, **tetendī**, **tentum/tēnsum** ③ *v* stretch out, extend; pitch tents; encamp; string *or* draw (a bow, *etc.*); distend; direct one's course, proceed; reach; exert oneself; aim (at); aim (to do)

tenebrae, **ārum** *fpl* darkness, obscurity; night; dark corner; ignorance; concealment; gloomy state of affairs; LM vespers

tenebricōsus, **a**, **um** *adj* dark

tenellulus, **a**, **um** *adj* tender, delicate

tenellus, **a**, **um** *adj* tender

teneō, **tentum/tēnsum** ② *v* hold, keep, possess; occupy; retain; hold a position; include; reach in journeying;

maintain; detain, hold up; keep in
check; bind

tener, era, erum *adj* soft, delicate,
tender; immature, young; soft,
effeminate

tenor, ōris *m* a sustained and even
course of movement; course, tenor

tēnsa, ae *f* wagon on which the images
of the gods were carried to public
spectacles

tentābundus, a, um *adj* testing
every stop *or* move

tentāmen, inis *nt* attempt, effort

tentāmentum, ī *nt* trial, attempt,
experiment

tentō ① *v* handle, feel; attempt, try;
prove; test; try out; attack; brave; make
an attempt on

tentōrium, (i)ī *nt* tent

tenuis, e *adj* thin, slender; slight,
faint; fine; weak; trivial

tenuō ① *v* make thin; reduce, lessen;
wear down

tenus *prep with abl* reaching to, as far
as, up to

tepefaciō, fēcī, factum ③ *v* make
warm

tepefactō ① *v* be in the habit of
warming

tepeō ② *v* be (luke)warm; feel the
warmth of love, glow; be lukewarm in
one's feelings

tepēscō, puī ③ *v* become warm

tepidārium, (i)ī *nt* 'warm' room in
Roman baths

tepidus, a, um *adj* lukewarm, tepid;
mild, warm

tepor, ōris *m* warmth, mild heat

ter *adv* three times

terebinthus, ī *f* terebinth tree *or* its
wood

terebrō ① *v* bore through, drill a hole
in

teres, etis *adj* smooth and rounded

tergeminus, a, um *adj* threefold,
triple

tergeō ② *v*, **tergō, rsī, rsum** ③ *v* rub
clean, polish; press

tergiversor ① *v dep* turn one's back on
a task *or* challenge; hang back

tergum, ī *nt*, **tergus, oris** *nt* back;
hide, skin; surface
  □ **terga dō/vertō** to turn tail, flee
  □ **ā tergō** from behind

Terminālia, ium *ntpl* festival of the
god of boundaries (Terminus) on 23
February

terminātiō, ōnis *f* marking the
boundaries of a territory

terminō ① *v* mark the boundaries of,
form the boundaries of; restrict;
conclude

terminus, ī *m* boundary, limit; end;
post, stone, *etc.*, marking the boundary
of a property

ternī, ae, a *adj* three each; three

terō, trīvī, trītum ③ *v* rub, bruise,
grind; polish, rub smooth; wear out *or*
away; handle constantly; use up (time)

terra, ae *f* earth; land, ground, soil;
country; region

terrēnus, a, um *adj* belonging to the
ground, earthy, earthly; mortal

terreō ② *v* terrorize, overawe, terrify;
deter

terrestris, tre *adj* by *or* on land,
terrestrial

terreus, a, um *adj* one born of the
earth

terribilis, e *adj* frightening, terrible

terrificō ① *v* terrify

terrificus, a, um *adj* terrifying, awe-
inspiring

terrigena, ae *m* one born of the earth

terriloquus, a, um *adj* uttering
frightening words

territō ① *v* frighten, terrify; try to
scare

terror, ōris *m* dread, terror

tersus, a, um *adj* neat, spruce

tertia, ae *f* ⓁⓂ terce (part of the daily
cycle of prayer)

tertium *adv* for a third time

tertius, a, um *adj* third

tessera, ae *f* square tile; die; tablet
on which the password was
written; fragment of earthenware,
shard

testa, ae *f* object made from burnt
clay; earthenware jar; fragment of
earthenware, shard

testāmentum, ī *nt* will, testament
  □ **~ Vetus/Novum** ⓁⓂ Old/New
  Testament

testātiō, ōnis *f* action of testifying to a
fact

testātus, a, um *adj* known on good
evidence

testificor ① *v dep* assert solemnly, testify (to a fact); demonstrate; invoke as a witness

testimōnium, (i)ī *nt* testimony; proof

testis[1], **is** *m/f* witness; spectator

testis[2], **is** *m* testicle

testor ① *v dep* be a witness, testify (to); declare solemnly; invoke as a witness

testū *nt indec*, **testum, ī** *nt* earthenware pot

testūdineus, a, um *adj* made of tortoiseshell

testūdō, inis *f* tortoise; tortoise shell; lyre; roof; a covering formed of the shields of soldiers held over their heads; movable wooden screen for siege-engines *or* men engaged in siege operations

tetendī ▸ **tendō**

tetigī ▸ **tangō**

tetrarchēs, ae *m* tetrarch (a minor king under Roman protection)

tetricus, a, um *adj* austere

tetulī *old pf of* ▸ **ferō**

texō, texuī, textum ③ *v* weave; plait (together); construct with elaborate care

textilis, e *adj* woven

textor, ōris *m* weaver

textum, ī *nt* woven fabric, cloth; framework; web

textūra, ae *f* weaving, texture

thalamus, ī *m* an inner chamber; bedroom; marriage

theātrālis, e *adj* theatrical, of the stage

theātrum, ī *nt* theatre

thermae, ārum *fpl* hot baths

> ❗ The Roman baths were a social focal point for communities and over time became increasingly elaborate. They typically had an **apodȳtērium** ('changing-room') and rooms of increasing temperature (**frīgidārium**, **tepidārium** and **caldārium**) each often containing a pool. Many also had exercise grounds (**palaestrae**) and large pools for swimming (**piscīnae**).

thermopōlium, (i)ī *nt* hot-drink counter

thēsaurus, ī *m* treasure-chamber, vault; treasure

thiasus, ī *m* orgiastic Bacchic dance

tholus, ī *m* circular building with a domed roof, rotunda

thōrāx, ācis *m* breastplate, cuirass

Thrāx, ācis *m* Thracian; gladiator with sabre and short shield, gladiator

thronus, ī *m* throne

thymbra, ae *f* an aromatic plant, perhaps Cretan thyme

thymum, ī *nt* thyme

thynnus, ī *m* tunny-fish

thyrsus, ī *m* Bacchic wand tipped with a fir-cone, tuft of ivy *or* vine leaves

tiāra, ae *f*, **tiārās, ae** *m* ornamented felt head-dress

tibī *pn dat of* ▸ **tū**

tībia, ae *f* reed-pipe

tībīcen, inis *m* piper, prop

tībīcina, ae *f* female performer on the tibia

tigillum, ī *nt* small plank *or* beam

tīgnum, ī *nt* timber, beam, board

tigris, is/idis *m/f* tiger; tigress

tilia, ae *f* lime-tree

timeō ② *v* fear, be afraid (of); be afraid (to)

> ❗ Verbs of fearing are followed by one of three constructions: they may take a direct object in the acc., an infin. of what one is afraid to do (e.g., **timet loquī** 'he is afraid to speak'), or a fear clause with a subj. verb introduced by **nē** expressing what one fears may be the case (e.g. **timēmus nē fūrēs pecūniam auferant** 'we fear that thieves may steal the money'). In a negated fear clause ('I fear that something may not happen'), **nē nōn** can be replaced with **ut**.

timidus, a, um *adj* fearful, timid

timor, ōris *m* fear; object *or* source of fear

tīnctilis, e *adj* obtained by dipping

tīnctus, ūs *m* dyeing; dipping

tinea, ae *f* grub, maggot

tinnīmentum, ī *nt* ringing sound

tinnītus, ūs *m* ringing, clanging, jangling

tinnulus, a, um *adj* emitting a ringing *or* jangling sound

tintinnō, tintinō ① *v* make a ringing *or* jangling sound

tīnus, ī *m* laurustinus (kind of bay-tree)

tīrō, ōnis *m* recruit; beginner, novice

tīrōcinium, (i)ī *nt* inexperience in military service; first campaign; apprenticeship, youthful inexperience

tītillō ① *v* tickle, titillate; provoke; stimulate sensually

titubō ① *v* stagger, totter; falter

titulus, ī *m* placard, tablet, label; inscription; title; pretext; distinction, honour

tōfus, ī *m* tufa

toga, ae *f* the formal outer garment of a Roman citizen, toga; peace;
□ **toga candida** toga worn by candidates for office
□ **toga virīlis** toga worn by adults (without the purple border)

> **!** The **toga** was worn over the **tunica** by free Roman males on formal occasions. It was a large semicircle of undyed light woollen cloth (up to 5.5m in diameter) and worn wrapped over the left shoulder and (usually) under the right arm, the weight being supported by the left arm. Men in mourning wore a dark **toga pulla**, while high-born boys and holders of certain high offices word a **toga praetexta** (with a purple border along its edge). Candidates for election wore specially a whitened toga. A triumphing general would wear a **toga picta** dyed purple and decorated with gold thread.

togātus, a, um *adj* dressed in *or* wearing a toga; having a civilian occupation

tolerābilis, e *adj* bearable, tolerable, patient; able to be withstood

tolerō ① *v* bear, endure, tolerate; support; provide food for

tollō, sustulī, sublātum ③ *v* lift, raise; acknowledge (a new-born child); remove; eliminate; steal

tolūtim *adv* at a trot

tōmentum, ī *nt* stuffing

tondeō, totondī, tōnsum ② *v* shear, clip; prune back; browse on

tonitrus, ūs *m* thunder

tonō, nuī, nitum ① *v* thunder; speak in thunderous tones, utter thunderously; make *or* resound with a noise like thunder

tōnsa, ae *f* oar

tōnstrīna, ae *f* barber's shop

tōnsūra, ae *f* shearing, clipping

tormentum, ī *nt* twisted rope; machine for discharging missiles in war, catapult, ballista, *etc.*; torture; torment

tornus, ī *m* turner's lathe

torōsus, a, um *adj* muscular, brawny

torpeō ② *v* be numb *or* lethargic; be struck motionless from fear

torpēscō, puī ③ *v* grow numb, become slothful

torpidus, a, um *adj* numbed, paralysed

torpor, ōris *m* numbness, torpor, paralysis

torquātus, a, um *adj* wearing a collar *or* necklace

torqueō, torsī, tortum ② *v* turn, twist; hurl; torture; torment; bend, distort; spin, whirl; wind (round)

torquēs, torquis, quis *m/f* collar of twisted metal; wreath

torrēns¹, ntis *m* torrent, rushing stream

torrēns², ntis *adj* burning hot; rushing; torrential

torreō, tostum ② *v* parch, roast, scorch, burn; dry up

torrēscō ③ *v* be scorched

torridus, a, um *adj* parched, dried up; shrivelled, desiccated

torris, is *m* firebrand

tortilis, e *adj* twisted, coiled

tortor, ōris *m* torturer

tortuōsus, a, um *adj* winding; tortuous

tortus, a, um *adj* crooked, twisted

torus, ī *m* muscle; marriage-bed, marriage; bolster, cushion; couch

torvus, a, um *adj* pitiless, grim; savage

tot *adj indec* so many

totidem *adj indec* the same number as, as many

tōtus, a, um *adj* all, the whole of, entire

t

toxicum, ī *nt* poison

trabālis, e *adj* of *or* used for wooden beams

trabea, ae *f* short purple *or* partly purple garment

trabēs, **trabs**, **bis** *f* tree-trunk, beam, timber; ship

tractābilis, e *adj* manageable; tractable; easy to deal with

tractātiō, ōnis *f* management; treatment; discussion

tractim *adv* in a long-drawn-out manner

tractō ① *v* handle, manage; practise; manipulate; perform; examine, discuss, treat (a subject)

tractus, ūs *m* dragging *or* pulling along; drawing out; extent; tract, region; lengthening

trādō, **didī**, **ditum** ③ *v* hand *or* pass over; deliver; surrender; hand down, bequeath; entrust; introduce; relate, tell of

trādūcō, **dūxī**, **ductum** ③ *v* lead *or* bring across *or* over; lead along *or* parade; transfer; convert

tragicus, a, um *adj* tragic; suitable to tragedy
∎ **tragicus**, ī *m* tragic poet, tragic actor

tragoedia, ae *f* tragedy

tragoedus, ī *m* tragic actor

trāgula, ae *f* spear fitted with a throwing strap

trahea, ae *f* a drag used as a threshing implement

trahō, **āxī**, **actum** ③ *v* draw, drag, haul; drag along; trail; draw *or* stretch out; extend; contract; drink; breathe in; carry off as plunder; attract; protract, delay; spend *or* get through (time)

trāiciō, **iēcī**, **iectum** ③ *v* throw, cast *or* shoot over *or* across; convey across, transport; transfix, thrust through; transfer; cross over

trāiectus, ūs *m* crossing over; way *or* route across

trāma, ae *f* cloth

trāmes, **itis** *m* footpath; track; bed (of a stream)

trānō ① *v* swim across *or* through; fly across

tranquillitās, **ātis** *f* tranquillity; calmness, fair weather

tranquillus, a, um *adj* quiet, calm, still, peaceful
∎ **tranquillum**, ī *nt* calm weather; calm state of affairs

trāns *prep with acc* across, over, beyond, through

trānsabeō, **īre**, **iī** *v ir* go away beyond

trānsadigō, **ēgī**, **āctum** ③ *v* pierce through; thrust through

trānscendō, **ndī**, **ēnsum** ③ *v* climb *or* step over, transgress, overstep

trānscrībō, **psī**, **ptum** ③ *v* copy; transfer

trānscurrō, **(cu)currī**, **cursum** ③ *v* run across; run *or* hasten through

trānscursus, ūs *m* rapid movement across a space

trānsd- ▷ **trād-**

trānsenna, ae *f* snare (for birds)

trānseō, **īre**, **iī/īvī**, **itum** *v ir* go over *or* across, pass over; pass by; go through; go over (to a side, *etc.*); omit, say nothing of; pass away

trānsferō, **ferre**, **tulī**, **lātum** *v ir* carry *or* bring over; transport; transfer; bring over (to a new course of action)

trānsfigō, **īxī**, **īxum** ③ *v* pierce through; thrust (through)

trānsfodiō, **ōdī**, **ossum** ③ *v* dig through to the other side of; run through

trānsfōrmis, e *adj* that undergoes transformation

trānsfōrmō ① *v* change in shape, transform

trānsfuga, ae *m* deserter

trānsfugiō, ī ③ *v* go over to the enemy, desert

trānsfugium, **(i)ī** *nt* desertion

trānsgredior, **gressus sum** ③ *v dep* step over; change one's policy; surpass; omit

trānsgressus, ūs *m* crossing to the other side

trānsigō, **ēgī**, **āctum** ③ *v* thrust *or* run through, pierce through; come to terms about, settle; conclude, finish

trānsiliō, **siluī/silīvī** ④ *v* leap across *or* over; skip; overstep, exceed

trānsitiō, **ōnis** *f* passing over, passage; desertion; infection, contagion

trānsitus, **ūs** *m* passage; passage over; transition

trānslūceō ② *v* shine through *or* across; be transparent

trānslūcidus, **a**, **um** *adj* transparent

trānsmarīnus, **a**, **um** *adj* (from) over the sea

trānsmigrō ① *v* change one's residence from one place to another

trānsmissus, **ūs** *m* crossing

trānsmittō, **īsī**, **issum** ③ *v* send *or* pass over; go to the other side of; travel to the other side (of)

trānsmūtō ① *v* change about

trānsnō ① *v* swim across, sail across; swim to the other side

trānsportō ① *v* carry across; convey across

trānstrum, **ī** *nt* cross-beam; rower's seat

trānsultō ① *v* spring across

trānsuō, **suī**, **ūtum** ③ *v* pierce through

trānsvehō, **ēxī**, **ectum** ③ *v* carry across; carry past

□ **trānsvehor** sail, ride *or* travel to the other side

trānsverberō ① *v* transfix

trānsversus, **a**, **um** *adj* lying across, moving across

trānsvolitō ① *v* fly over *or* through

trānsvolō ① *v* fly across

trăvehō ▸ **trānsvehō**

trecēnī, **ae**, **a** *adj* three hundred each; three hundred; lots of three hundred (men)

trecentī, **ae**, **a** *adj* three hundred; (used to denote a large number)

tredecim *adj indec* thirteen

tremebundus, **a**, **um** *adj* trembling, quivering, vibrating

tremefaciō, **fēcī**, **factum** ③ *v* cause to tremble

tremendus, **a**, **um** *adj* terrible, awe-inspiring

tremēscō ③ *v* tremble, quiver, vibrate; tremble at

tremō, **muī** ③ *v* tremble, quake; tremble (at)

tremor, **ōris** *m* trembling, shuddering; quivering, quaking

tremulus, **a**, **um** *adj* shaking; moving tremulously; quivering

trepidanter *adv* tremblingly, anxiously

trepidātiō, **ōnis** *f* trepidation, perturbation

trepidō ① *v* be in a state of alarm *or* trepidation; scurry, bustle; tremble, quiver, shake; be nervous

trepidus, **a**, **um** *adj* alarmed, anxious; marked by apprehensiveness *or* alarm; behaving in an excited manner; quivering, trembling

trēs, **tria** *adj* three

trēsvirī, **ōrum** *mpl* board of three

triāriī, **ōrum** *mpl* the third line of the early Roman army; the reserves

tribūlis, **is** *m* fellow tribesman

tribūnal, **ālis** *nt* dais, platform

tribūnātus, **ūs** *m* the office of tribune

tribūnicius, **a**, **um** *adj* belonging to a tribune

■ **tribūnicius**, **(i)ī** *m* ex-tribune

tribūnus, **ī** *m* tribune; military tribune

> **!** Each **legiō** had a number of middle-ranking officers (usu. six) known as **tribūnī mīlitum**, who were often called upon to command detachments smaller than a legion.
> The **tribūnī plēbis** were officers of the common people (**plēbs**) who asserted the right of the people and could veto an act performed by a magistrate. The office was first created in c. 500-450 BC.

tribuō, **uī**, **ūtum** ③ *v* grant, bestow, award (to); allocate

tribus, **ūs** *f* (division of the people) tribe

> **!** The Roman people were divided into tribes (**tribūs**) which were used as voting units and were the basis of army recruitment, the census, and taxation.
> The dat./abl. pl. of **tribus** is **tribubus**.

tribūtim *adv* by tribes

tribūtum, **ī** *nt* tribute, tax

tribūtus, **a**, **um** *adj* organized by tribes

trīcae, **ārum** *fpl* tricks, nonsense, complications

trīclīnium, **(i)ī** *nt* dining-room

tricorpor, **oris** *adj* having three bodies

t

tricuspis, **idis** *adj* having three prongs

tridēns, **ntis** *adj* three-pronged
■ ~, **ntis** *m* trident

tridentifer, **tridentiger**, **erī** *m* carrying a trident

trīduum, **ī** *nt* space of three days; LM esp. the final three days of Holy Week (i.e. Maundy Thursday, Good Friday and Holy Saturday)

triennia, **ium** *ntpl* triennial festival

triennium, **(i)ī** *nt* period of three years

triēns, **ntis** *m* third part, third; third part of an **as**

trietēricus, **a**, **um** *adj* triennial
■ **trietērica**, **ōrum** *ntpl* triennial rites

trietēris, **idis** *f* period of three years

trifāriam *adv* in three ways, into three parts

trifaucis, **e** *adj* having three throats

trifidus, **a**, **um** *adj* divided to form three prongs

trifolium, **(i)ī** *nt* clover

trifōrmis, **e** *adj* of three forms, triple, threefold

trigeminus, **a**, **um** *adj* born as one of triplets

trigintā *adj indec* thirty

trilībris, **bre** *adj* of three pounds weight

trilinguis, **e** *adj* that has three tongues

trilīx, **īcis** *adj* having a triple thread

trīmus, **a**, **um** *adj* three years old

trīnī, **ae**, **a** *adj* three in each case, three at a time; three, triple

trinitas, **tatis** *f* LM the Trinity

trinōdis, **e** *adj* having three knots *or* bosses

triōbolum, **ī** *nt* three-obol piece (a trivial sum)

Triōnēs, **um** *mpl* the constellations Great and Little Bear

tripēs, **edis** *adj* three-legged

triplex, **icis** *adj* threefold, triple, tripartite

tripudiō ① *v* leap, jump, dance, caper

tripudium, **(i)ī** *nt* solemn religious dance; favourable omen (when the sacred chickens ate so greedily that the food dropped to the ground)

tripūs, **podis** *m often in pl* three-legged stand, tripod; the oracle at Delphi

triquetrus, **tra**, **trum** *adj* three-cornered, triangular

trirēmis, **e** *adj* having three oars to each bench
■ **trirēmis**, **is** *f* trireme

trīste *adv* sadly, sorrowfully; harshly, severely

trīstis, **e** *adj* depressed, gloomy, unhappy; bitter; ill-humoured; stern, austere; unhappy; grim, unpleasant; sour

trīstitia, **ae** *f* unhappiness, despondency, gloom; sourness

trisulcus, **a**, **um** *adj* divided into three forks *or* prongs

trīticeus, **a**, **um** *adj* of wheat

trīticum, **ī** *nt* wheat

trītūra, **ae** *f* rubbing, friction; threshing

trītus, **a**, **um** *adj* well-trodden, well-worn; worn; common; familiar

triumphālis, **e** *adj* of *or* associated with the celebration of a triumph; having triumphal status; triumphant
■ **triumphālia**, **ium** *ntpl* the insignia of a triumph

triumphō ① *v* triumph; celebrate a triumph; exult, triumph over

triumphus, **ī** *m* triumphal procession, triumph

> **!** A Roman general who had won a major victory ending a war with a foreign enemy was often awarded a triumphal procession by a vote of the senate and people. Dressed in a special costume and laurel wreath, and preceded by his lictors, he made his way on a four-horse chariot from the **porta triumphālis** to the temple of Jupiter on the Capitol, accompanied by the senate and the magistrates, his army, enemy captives, the spoils of war and animals for sacrifice.

triumvir, **rī** *m* one of the three **triumvirī**, who were the 'board of three' or triumvirate
□ **triumvirī capitālēs** superintendents of public prisons and executions

triumvirātus, **ūs** *m* triumvirate

trivium, **(i)ī** *nt* place where three roads meet; 'the gutter'; LM the three 'lower' subjects of the medieval university curriculum, viz. grammar, rhetoric and logic

trivius, **a**, **um** *adj* having a temple at a spot where three roads meet

troc(h)lea, **ae** *f* a block with pulleys, block-and-tackle equipment

trochus, **ī** *m* metal hoop (used for games or exercise)

troclea ▸ **trochlea**

Trōiugena, **ae** *adj* born of Trojan stock

tropa *adv* in a drinking game

tropaeum, **ī** *nt* trophy; monument, victory

tropice *adv* LM figuratively

trucīdātiō, **ōnis** *f* slaughtering, massacre

trucīdō ① *v* slaughter, butcher, massacre

truculentus, **a**, **um** *adj* ferocious, aggressive

trudis, **dis** *f* metal-tipped pole; barge-pole

trūdō, **ūsī**, **ūsum** ③ *v* thrust, push, shove; drive, force; drive on

trulla, **ae** *f* scoop, ladle

trulleus, **ī** *m* wash-basin

truncō ① *v* maim, mutilate; strip of branches, foliage; cut off

truncus¹, **ī** *m* trunk (of a tree); body of a man, trunk, torso

truncus², **a**, **um** *adj* maimed, mutilated, dismembered; trimmed of its branches; stunted in growth

trusō ① *v* keep pushing *or* thrusting

trux, **cis** *adj* harsh, savage, pitiless, cruel

tū *pn* you (*sg*)

tuba, **ae** *f* (straight) trumpet; war-trumpet

tūber, **eris** *nt* tumour, protuberance, excrescence

tubicen, **inis** *m* trumpeter

Tubilūstrium, **(i)ī** *nt* feast of trumpets (on 23 March and 23 May)

tueor ② *v dep* look at, scan, view; keep safe, protect, watch over; preserve from danger; defend; look after; uphold

□ **torva** ∼ look grim

tugurium, **(i)ī** *nt* primitive dwelling, hut, shack

tulī ▸ **ferō**

tum *adv* then; at that time; besides; afterwards; in that case; at that moment

□ **quid tum?** what then? what further?

□ **tum … tum** both … and; … as well as …; first … then; at this moment … at that moment

□ **cum … tum** both … and especially; not only … but also

□ **tum dēmum**, **tum dēnique** then and not till then

□ **tum prīmum** then for the first time

tumefaciō, **fēcī**, **factum** ③ *v* cause to swell; puff up

tumeō ② *v* swell, become inflated; be puffed up; be bombastic; be swollen with conceit, presumption, *etc.*

tumēscō, **muī** ③ *v* (begin to) swell; become inflamed with pride, passion, *etc.*

tumidus, **a**, **um** *adj* swollen, swelling, distended; puffed up with pride *or* self-confidence; bombastic

tumor, **ōris** *m* swollen *or* distended condition; swell (of the sea, waves); excitement, passion, conceit

tumulō ① *v* cover with a burial mound

tumulōsus, **a**, **um** *adj* full of hillocks

tumultuārius, **a**, **um** *adj* raised to deal with a sudden emergency; improvised; unplanned; haphazard

tumultuātiō, **ōnis** *f* confused uproar

tumultuō ① *v*, **tumultuor** ① *v dep* make a confused uproar; make an armed rising

tumultuōsus, **a**, **um** *adj* turbulent, full of commotion *or* uproar

tumultus, **ūs** *m* tumult, uproar, disturbance; turbulence; alarm; agitation (of the mind *or* feelings); sudden outbreak of violence *or* disorder; muddle

tumulus, **ī** *m* rounded hill, knoll; burial-mound, grave

tunc *adv* then, at the very time, at that

tundō, **tutudī**, **tū(n)sum** ③ *v* beat; bruise, pulp, crush

tunica, **ae** *f* tunic

tunicātus, **a**, **um** *adj* wearing a tunic

turba, **ae** *f* disorder; dense *or* disorderly mass of people, multitude, crowd; confusion, disturbance

turbāmentum, **ī** *nt* means of disturbing

turbātiō, **ōnis** *f* disturbance

turbātor, **ōris** *m* one who disturbs

turbidus, **a**, **um** *adj* wild, confused, disordered; muddy, turbid; foggy; troubled, turbulent; gloomy; unruly, mutinous

turbineus, **a**, **um** *adj* gyrating like a spinning-top

turbō[1] ① *v* disturb, confuse, trouble, disorder; make muddy *or* turbid

turbō[2], **inis** *m* whirlwind, tornado; whirlpool, eddy; spinning-top; whirling motion; whorl *or* fly-wheel of a spindle

turbulentus, **a**, **um** *adj* violently disturbed, stormy, turbulent; turbid; marked by turmoil *or* violent unrest; unruly, riotous

turdus, **ī** *m* thrush

tūreus, **a**, **um** *adj* of *or* connected with incense

turgeō, **tursī** ② *v* swell out, become swollen *or* tumid

turgēscō ③ *v* begin to swell

turgidulus, **a**, **um** *adj* (poor little) swollen

turgidus, **a**, **um** *adj* swollen, inflated

tūribulum, **ī** *nt* censer, thurible

tūricremus, **a**, **um** *adj* burning incense

tūrifer, **era**, **erum** *adj* yielding *or* producing incense

tūrilegus, **a**, **um** *adj* incense-gathering

turma, **ae** *f* small troop, squadron (of cavalry); company

turmālis, **e** *adj* belonging to a squadron of cavalry

turmātim *adv* in troops *or* squadrons of cavalry

turpiculus, **a**, **um** *adj* somewhat ugly

turpis, **e** *adj* ugly; foul; disgraceful, dishonourable, degrading; loathsome; guilty of disgraceful behaviour; indecent, obscene

turpō ① *v* make ugly; pollute, disfigure

turriger, **era**, **erum** *adj* bearing a tower; wearing a turreted crown

turris, **is** *f* tower; howdah

turrītus, **a**, **um** *adj* crowned with towers; tower-shaped

turtur, **uris** *m* turtle-dove

tūs, **ūris** *nt* frankincense

tussicula, **ae** *f* slight cough

tussis, **is** *f* cough

tūtāmen, **inis** *nt*, **tūtāmentum**, **ī** *nt* means of protection

tūte [= **tū + te**] you yourself

tūtēla, **ae** *f* protection, guardianship, tutelage, defence; charge

tūtō ① *v*, **tūtor** ① *v dep* guard, protect, defend; guard against, avert

tūtor, **oris** *m* protector; guardian

tūtus, **a**, **um** *adj* safe, secure; watchful; free from risk; that may safely be trusted
  ■ **tūtō** *adv* safely

tuus, **a**, **um** *adj* your (*sg*)

ty(m)panum, **ī** *nt* small drum; revolving cylinder

tȳphōn, **nis** *m* whirlwind, cyclone

tyrannis, **idis** *f* tyranny, position *or* rule of a tyrant

tyrannus, **ī** *m* despot, tyrant; monarch

Uu

ūber, **eris** *adj* plentiful, abundant, copious; rich, luxuriant, fertile
  ■ ~, **eris** *nt* teat, pap, udder; soil rich in nourishing quality; fertility

ūbertās, **ātis** *f* fruitfulness, fertility; abundance, plenty

ūbertim *adv* plentifully, copiously

ubī *adv* where; where? when

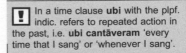

In a time clause **ubi** with the plpf. indic. refers to repeated action in the past, i.e. **ubi cantāveram** 'every time that I sang' or 'whenever I sang'.

ubīcumque *adv* wherever; in any place whatever

ubinam *adv* where in the world?

ubiquāque *adv* everywhere

ubīque *adv* everywhere, anywhere, wherever

ubivīs *adv* anywhere you like, no matter where

ūdus, a, um *adj* wet

ulcerō 1 *v* cause to fester

ulcerōsus, a, um *adj* full of sores

ulcīscor, ultus sum 3 *v dep* take vengeance (on) *or* revenge (for); avenge

ulcus, eris *nt* ulcer, sore

ūlīgō, inis *f* waterlogged ground, marsh

ūllus, a, um (*gen* **ūllīus**) *adj* any, any one

ulmeus, a, um *adj* of elm

ulmus, ī *f* elm-tree; elm-wood

ulna, ae *f* forearm; the span of the outstretched arms

ulterior, ius *adj* farther away, more distant; additional, further

ulterius *adv* farther away; to a further degree; any more

ultimus, a, um *adj* last; utmost; farthest; greatest; lowest, meanest; least; latest; earliest
□ **ultima ratiō** the last resort

ultiō, ōnis *f* revenge, vengeance, retribution

ultor, ōris *m* avenger, revenger

ultrā *adv* beyond, farther off, more, besides; *prep with acc* beyond, past; more than

ultrīx, īcis *f adj* avenging, vengeful

ultrō *adv* into the bargain; conversely; of one's own accord, on one's own initiative
■ ~ **tē** *int* away with you!
□ ~ **citrōque** to and fro

ulula, ae *f* the tawny owl

ululātus, ūs *m* howling, yelling

ululō 1 *v* howl, yell, shriek; celebrate *or* proclaim with howling

ulva, ae *f* sedge

ultus *pple* from ▶ **ulcīscor**

umbilīcus, ī *m* navel; centre of a country, region; ornamental end of the cylinder on which a book was rolled, middle, centre

umbō, ōnis *m* boss (of a shield)

umbra, ae *f* shade, shadow; ghost (of a dead person); sheltered conditions, privacy; darkness; empty form, phantom

umbrāculum, ī *nt* shelter, shade; parasol

umbrifer, era, erum *adj* providing shade, shady

umbrō 1 *v* cast a shadow on, shade

umbrōsus, a, um *adj* shady, shadowy

ūmectō 1 *v* moisten, make wet

ūmeō 2 *v* be wet; be moist

umerus, erī *m* shoulder

ūmēscō 3 *v* become moist *or* wet

ūmidulus, a, um *adj* somewhat moist

ūmidus, a, um *adj* moist, wet; full of sap

ūmor, ōris *m* moisture; liquid; bodily fluid *or* discharge

umquam *adv* at any time, ever; at some time

ūnā *adv* at the same time; in one company, together

ūnanimitās, ātis *f* unity of purpose, concord

ūnanimus, a, um *adj* acting in accord

uncia, ae *f* twelfth part, twelfth; ounce; inch

unciārius, a, um *adj* concerned with a twelfth part

unciātim *adv* ounce by ounce

ūnctitō 1 *v* smear often

ūnctus, a, um *adj* oily, greasy; anointed, oiled

uncus[1]**, ī** *m* hook; hook used to drag executed criminals, clamp

uncus[2]**, a, um** *adj* hooked, curved round at the extremity

unda, ae *f* wave, sea; sea-water; river, spring; water; advancing mass

unde *adv* from what place? where … from? whence? from whom; out of which; from what source, cause, *etc.*? from what stock, family, rank, *etc.*?

undecim *adj indec* eleven

undecimus, a, um *adj* eleventh

undēvīgintī *adj indec* nineteen

undique *adv* from all sides *or* directions, from every side *or* place; in all respects

undō ① *v* rise in waves; surge, seethe; well up; billow; undulate

undōsus, **a**, **um** *adj* abounding in waves, flowing water, *etc.*

ūnetvīcēsimānus, **a**, **um** *adj* of the 21st legion

ungō ▸ **unguō**

unguen, **inis** *nt* fat, grease

unguentārius, **(i)ī** *m* dealer in ointments, maker of ointments

unguentātus, **a**, **um** *adj* anointed *or* greased with ointments

unguentum, **ī** *nt* ointment, unguent

unguis, **is** *m* nail (of a human finger *or* toe), claw, talon, hoof
□ **ad/in unguem** to an exact measurement *or* standard

ungula, **ae** *f* hoof

unguō, **ūnxī**, **ūnctum** ③ *v* smear with oil, grease, *etc.*; anoint with oil, unguents, *etc.*

ūnicē *adv* to a singular degree; especially

ūnicus, **a**, **um** *adj* one and only, sole; unique, singular

ūnigena, **ae** *adj* one sharing a single parentage, *i.e.* brother or sister

unigenitus, **a**, **um** *adj* 🄻🄼 only-begotten

ūnimanus, **a**, **um** *adj* one-handed

ūniter *adv* so as to form a singular entity

ūniversus, **a**, **um** *adj* occurring all at once; the whole of, entire; whole; *pl* all without exception; taken all together

unquam ▸ **umquam**

ūnus, **a**, **um** *adj* one; a, an; only; a single, alone, sole; one and the same; the one and only; a certain
□ **in ūnum** so as to form a single mass
□ **ad ūnum** to a man; without exception

ūnusquisque, **ūnaquaeque**, **ūnumquodque/ūnumquidque** *pn* everyone

urbānitās, **ātis** *f* sophistication, polish, suavity

urbānus, **a**, **um** *adj* of *or* belonging to the city; elegant, sophisticated, witty; polished, refined

urbs, **bis** *f* city; (city of) Rome

urgeō, **ursī** ② *v* press, squeeze; push, thrust, shove; spur on; weigh down; be oppressive to; press hard in attack; follow hard on the heels of; crowd in; 'keep on at'; pursue with vigour

ūrīnātor, **ōris** *m* diver

urna, **ae** *f* water-jar; urn; cinerary urn; urn used in drawing lots; voting urn; (fig) urn of fate; a liquid measure (about thirteen litres)

ūrō, **ussī**, **ustum** ③ *v* burn; burn up; destroy by fire; scorch; make sore, cause to smart; corrode; inflame with desire; keep alight

ursa, **ae** *f* she-bear; Great Bear

ursus, **ī** *m* bear

urtīca, **ae** *f* stinging-nettle

ūrūca, **ae** *f* caterpillar

ūrus, **ī** *m* aurochs, the long-horned wild ox of primeval Europe

ūsitātus, **a**, **um** *adj* familiar, everyday

uspiam *adv* anywhere, somewhere

usquam *adv* at *or* in any place, anywhere; to any place; at any juncture

ūsque *adv* continuously, constantly; all along, all the way; all the while, as long *or* as far as, until
■ ~ **ad** *with acc* right up to

ūsquequāque *adv* in every conceivable situation; wholly, altogether

ustor, **ōris** *m* someone employed to burn dead bodies

ustulō ① *v* scorch, char, burn partially

ūsūcapiō, **cēpī**, **captum** ③ *v* acquire ownership of (a thing) by virtue of uninterrupted possession

ūsūrpō ① *v* make use of; employ; practise, perform; carry out; take possession of; take to oneself; assert one's possession of (a right *or* privilege) by exercising it; make frequent use of (a word, expression); call habitually (by a name); speak habitually of (as)

ūsus, **ūs** *m* use, employment; practical experience; practice; habitual dealings; value, utility; requirement, need

ut *adv/conj* (also **utī**) in what manner, how; in the manner that, as; however; such as; for, as being, inasmuch as; how much *or* greatly; when, as soon as
□ **ut ... ita** as well as ... no less; while ... while; *conj* so that; in order that; as

if; as if it were; to wit, namely; although; as is usual

> **!** **ut** is used in a number of very different constructions.
> ····▸ With an indic. verb, **ut** may introduce a clause of comparison.
> ····▸ **ut** may introduce a purpose clause; a neg. purpose clause is introduced by **nē**.
> ····▸ **ut** may introduce a result clause; a neg. result clause is introduced with **ut** … **nōn** (or **nēmō, nihil** etc.).
> ····▸ **ut** may introduce an indirect command; an indirect prohibition is introduced by **nē**.
> ····▸ After **vereor** (and sometimes **timeō**), **ut** corresponds to **nē nōn**.

utcumque, utcunque *adv* in whatever manner *or* degree; no matter how; whenever; in any event; as best one can

utēnsilia, ium *ntpl* necessaries

ūter, tris *m* leather bag for wine, oil, *etc.*; inflated bag to keep one afloat

uter, tra, trum *adj* whichever *or* which of the two, either one of the two

uterque, utraque, utrumque *pn* each of the two

uterus, erī *m* womb; belly, abdomen

utī ▸ ut

ūtibilis, e *adj* useful, serviceable

ūtilis, e *adj* useful, serviceable, advantageous, profitable, helpful

ūtilitās, ātis *f* the quality of being useful, usefulness, utility, advantage, expediency

utinam *adv* how I wish that! if only!

utīque *adv* in any case; certainly; at all costs

ūtor, ūsus sum ③ *v dep with abl* use, make use of, employ, apply, enjoy; practise, exercise; experience

utpote *adv* as one might expect, as is natural

ūtrārius, (i)ī *m* water-carrier

utrimque *adv* from *or* on both sides; at both ends

utrō *adv* to which side (of two)

utrobīque ▸ utrubīque

utrōque *adv* to both sides, in both directions

utrubīque *adv* in both places; in both cases

utrum *adv* whether; whether?

> **!** **utrum** may introduce both direct and indirect double questions. In direct questions it has no English equivalent, e.g. **utrum manēre vīs an abīre?** 'do you want to stay or to go?'; in indirect questions it translates 'whether, if', e.g. **rogāvit utrum manēre vellet an abīre** 'she asked whether he wanted to stay or to go'. cf. **an, -ne.**

utut *adv* however, in whatever manner

ūva, ae *f* grapes; bunch of grapes; cluster

ūvēscō ③ *v* become wet

ūvidulus, a, um *adj* wet, damp

ūvidus, a, um *adj* wet, soaked, dripping; moistened with drinking

uxor, ōris *f* wife
 □ **uxōrem dūcō** marry (a woman), take as wife

uxōrius, a, um *adj* of *or* belonging to a wife; excessively fond of one's wife

vacātiō, ōnis *f* exemption, immunity; vacation; exemption from military service

vacca, ae *f* cow

vaccīnium, (i)ī *nt* whortleberry

vacēfīō, fierī *v ir semi-dep* become empty

vacillō ① *v* stagger, totter; be in a weak condition

vacō ① *v* be empty *or* unfilled; be without occupants; be devoid (of), be

free (from); be available (for); have
leisure; be unemployed; have time for
□ **vacat** there is room, space *or*
opportunity (to)

vacuō ① *v* empty

vacuus, a, um *adj* empty, void;
insubstantial; destitute *or* devoid (of);
empty-handed; plain, bare;
unobstructed, clear; unoccupied,
deserted; ownerless; idle, having
leisure; fancy-free

vadimōnium, (i)ī *nt* bail, security,
surety

vādō ③ *v* go, advance, proceed

vador ① *v dep* accept sureties from (the
other party) for his appearance or
reappearance in court at an appointed
date

vadōsus, a, um *adj* full of shallows

vadum, ī *nt* shallow, ford; bottom of the
sea; shoal; *pl* waters

vae *int* ah! alas! woe!
□ ∼ **victīs** alas for the conquered!

vafer, fra, frum *adj* sly, cunning, crafty

vagē *adv* so as to move in different
directions over a wide area

vāgīna, ae *f* scabbard, sheath

vāgiō ④ *v* utter cries of distress, wail,
squall

vāgītus, ūs *m* cry of distress, wail,
howl, squalling

vagor ① *v dep* wander, roam, rove;
move freely to and fro; vary, fluctuate

vagus, a, um *adj* roving, wandering;
moving at random, shifting,
inconstant; scattered

valdē *adv* in a high degree, intensely,
strongly; exceedingly

valēns, ntis *adj* strong, stout,
vigorous; healthy; powerful; potent,
effective

valeō ② *v* be healthy, be well; be strong
or vigorous; have the ability *or* power
to; take effect; be powerful; have
influence; be worth
□ **valēre iubeō/dīcō** to bid farewell
or goodbye
□ **valē** goodbye!

valēscō ③ *v* become sound in health;
become powerful

valētūdō, inis *f* health, soundness;
good health; bad health, indisposition,
illness

validus, a, um *adj* strong, stout,
sturdy, powerful; healthy, sound, well;
fit, active; brisk; influential, telling

vāllāris, e *adj*
□ **corōna** ∼ crown *or* garland
awarded to the first soldier to cross the
vallum surrounding an enemy camp

vāllō ① *v* surround *or* fortify (a camp,
etc.) with a palisaded rampart; furnish
with a palisade

vallēs, vallis, is *f* valley

vāllum, ī *nt* a palisade of stakes on top
of an **agger**, a palisaded earthwork

vāllus, ī *m* stake; palisade, palisaded
earthwork

valvae, ārum *fpl* double *or* folding-
door

vānēscō ③ *v* melt into nothingness,
vanish; become useless

vāniloquentia, ae *f* idle talk, chatter;
boastful speech

vānitās, ātis *f* emptiness;
untruthfulness; futility, foolishness,
empty pride; fickleness

vannus, ī *f* winnowing basket

vānus, a, um *adj* empty, hollow,
illusory; vain, useless; foolish,
fatuous, trifling; silly; unreliable,
ineffectual; devoid (of)

vapor, ōris *m* steam, exhalation,
vapour; heat

vapōrō ① *v* cover *or* fill with vapour;
heat, warm; be hot

vappa, ae *f* flat wine
■ ∼, **ae** *m* a worthless person

vāpulō ① *v* be beaten *or* thrashed; be
battered

variantia, ae *f* diversity, variety

variātiō, ōnis *f* divergence of
behaviour

vāricus, a, um *adj* straddling

varietās, ātis *f* diversity, variety;
change, vicissitude

variō ① *v* mark with contrasting
colours, variegate; vary; cause
(opinions) to be divided; waver;
fluctuate, undergo changes

varius, a, um *adj* variegated; various;
changeable, inconstant; wavering;
multifarious; many-sided

vārus, a, um *adj* bent-outwards;
bandy; bow-legged; contrasting

vas, adis *m* surety

vās, sis *nt*, **vāsa, ōrum** *ntpl* vessel,
utensil; equipment, kit

vāsculum, ī *nt* cooking utensil

vastātiō, ōnis *f* laying waste, ravaging

vastātor, ōris *m* destroyer, ravager

vastitās, ātis *f* desolation; devastation

vastō ① *v* leave desolate; plunder, destroy, lay waste; ravage

vastus, a, um *adj* desolate; vast, huge, enormous; awe-inspiring; clumsy, ungainly

vātēs, ātis *m/f* prophet; poet, bard

vāticinātiō, ōnis *f* prophesying, predicting

vāticinātor, ōris *m* prophet

vāticinor ① *v dep* prophesy; rave, talk wildly

vāticinus, a, um *adj* prophetic

-ve *conj* or

vēcordia, ae *f* frenzy

vēcors, rdis *adj* mad; frenzied

vectīgal, ālis *nt* revenue derived from public property

vectīgālis, e *adj* yielding taxes, subject to taxation

vectis, is *m* crowbar, lever

vectō ① *v* carry, convey
□ **vector** ride, travel

vector, ōris *m* passenger; one that carries *or* transports

vectōrius, a, um *adj* used for transporting *or* conveying

vectūra, ae *f* transportation, carriage; charge for transportation

vegetus, a, um *adj* vigorous, active

vēgrandis, e *adj* far from large, puny

vehemēns, ntis *adj* violent, vehement; vigorous, powerful, strong

vehiculum, ī *nt* cart, wagon

vehō, ēxī, ectum ③ *v* carry, convey
□ **vehor** ride; sail; travel

vel *conj* or; even; for instance; or rather; even; *with sup* quite, altogether
□ **vel ... vel** either ... or

> ⚠ **vel ... vel** is used to express two or more possibilities which need not exclude each other, i.e. 'X or Y or possibly both'; cf. **aut**.

vēlāmen, inis *nt* covering, clothing

vēlāmentum, ī *nt* cover; olive-branch wrapped in wool carried by a suppliant

velatus, a, um *adj* ⓛⓜ veiled

vēles, itis *m* light-armed foot-soldier

vēlifer, era, erum *adj* carrying a sail

vēlitāris, e *adj* of *or* belonging to the velites

vēlivolus, a, um *adj* speeding along under sail; characterized by speeding sails

velle *infin* from ▶ **volō**

vellicō ① *v* pinch, nip; criticize carpingly

vellō, vellī/vulsī, ulsum ③ *v* pluck *or* pull out, tear *or* pull up; tug at, pluck

vellus, eris *nt* fleece; hide, fur; piece *or* lump of wool

vēlō ① *v* cover, clothe; conceal, cover up

vēlōcitās, ātis *f* swiftness, rapidity, speed

vēlōx, ōcis *adj* swift, rapid, speedy

vēlum, ī *nt* sail; curtain, awning; a woven cloth; ⓛⓜ veil
□ **vēla dō** expose the sails to the wind

velut, **velutī** *adv* just as, just like; as for example; as it were; as if, as though; as being

vēmēns ▶ **vehemēns**

vēna, ae *f* blood-vessel, vein; artery; pulse; fissure, pore, cavity, (underground) stream; vein of ore, *etc.*; supply *or* store (of talent)

vēnābulum, ī *nt* hunting-spear

vēnālīcius, (i)ī *m* slave-dealer

vēnālis, e *adj* for sale; on hire; open to the influence of bribes

vēnāticus, a, um *adj* for hunting

vēnātiō, ōnis *f* hunting, chase; beasts hunted, game; animal hunt in the arena

vēnātor, ōris *m* hunter

vēnātrīx, īcis *f* huntress

vēnātus, ūs *m* hunting, hunt

vēndibilis, e *adj* that can (easily) be sold, marketable

vēnditātor, ōris *m* one who puffs up the merits (of)

vēnditiō, ōnis *f* sale

vēnditō ① *v* offer for sale; cry up; pay court (to)

vēndō, didī, ditum ③ *v* sell, betray for money; promote the sale of

venēficium, **(i)ī** *nt* poisoning; magic, sorcery

venēficus, **a**, **um** *adj* of *or* connected with sorcery
■ **venēfica**, **ae** *f* female poisoner; sorceress
■ **venēficus**, **ī** *m* poisoner

venēnātus, **a**, **um** *adj* poisonous, venomous; poisoned

venēnifer, **era**, **erum** *adj* venomous

venēnō ① *v* imbue *or* infect with poison

venēnum, **ī** *nt* poison; potent herb used for medical *or* magical purposes

vēneō, **īre**, **iī/īvī**, **itum** *v ir* be sold (as a slave); be disposed of for financial gain

venerābilis, **e** *adj* venerable, august

venerābundus, **a**, **um** *adj* expressing religious awe (towards)

venerātiō, **ōnis** *f* reverence, veneration

venerātor, **ōris** *m* one who reveres

venerō ① *v*, **veneror** ① *v dep* worship, revere, venerate; honour; supplicate

venia, **ae** *f* pardon, forgiveness; leave, permission; favour, indulgence; relief, remission

veniō, **vēnī**, **ventum** ④ *v* come; go; arrive; arise, come to pass; proceed

vēnor ① *v dep* hunt

venter, **tris** *m* belly; paunch, abdomen; stomach; swelling; embryo

ventilō ① *v* expose to a draught; fan; brandish

ventitō ① *v* come frequently, resort

ventōsus, **a**, **um** *adj* windy; swift (as the wind); fickle, changeable; vain, puffed up

ventus, **ī** *m* wind; puff, breeze

vēnum *m* [only in acc **vēnum** and dat **vēnō**] sale:
□ **vēnum/vēnō dō** (**vēndō**) sell
□ **vēnum eō** (**vēneō**) be sold

vēnumdō, **dare**, **dedī**, **datum** ① *v* put up for sale

Venus, **eris** *f* goddess of love; beloved person; object of love; loveliness; beauty; charm; (planet) Venus; best throw at dice; sexual intercourse

venustās, **ātis** *f* attractiveness, charm, grace

venustus, **a**, **um** *adj* attractive, charming, graceful, pretty, neat

vēpallidus, **a**, **um** *adj* deathly pale

vepris, **is** *m* thorn-bush

vēr, **ris** *nt* spring; spring-time of life

vērāx, **ācis** *adj* speaking the truth, truthful

verbēna, **ae** *f* a leafy branch *or* twig from various aromatic trees *or* shrubs used in religious ceremonies *or* for medicinal purposes

verber, **eris** *nt* lash, thong of a sling; blow, stroke; *pl* an instrument for flogging

verberō[1] ① *v* lash, scourge, flog; batter, hammer; assail

verberō[2], **ōnis** *m* one worthy of a beating, scoundrel

verbōsus, **a**, **um** *adj* prolix, lengthy; long-winded

verbum, **ī** *nt* word; language; discourse, wording; talk
■ **verba dō** *with dat* deceive

vērē *adv* truly, really, indeed; correctly

verēcundia, **ae** *f* modesty; respect; uncertainty, diffidence; sense of shame

verēcundus, **a**, **um** *adj* modest

verendus, **a**, **um** *adj* that is to be regarded with awe *or* reverence
■ **verenda**, **ōrum** *ntpl* genitals

vereor ② *v dep* show reverence *or* respect; be afraid of, fear; be afraid (to do something); be afraid (that)

> ❗ **vereor** is followed by the same constructions as **timeō**.

vergō ③ *v* slope down (towards); look towards; sink (towards something); tilt down

vērīsimilis, **e** *adj* (also **vērī similis**) having the appearance of truth

vēritās, **ātis** *f* truth, truthfulness, frankness
□ **Veritas** LM Christ

vermiculus, **ī** *m* grub, larva

vermis, **is** *m* worm, maggot

verna, **ae** *m/f* slave born in the master's household

vernāculus, **a**, **um** *adj* domestic, home-grown; indigenous, native, belonging to the country; low-bred, proletarian

vernīlis, **e** *adj* servile, obsequious

vernīliter *adv* obsequiously, fawningly

vernō ① *v* carry on *or* undergo the process proper to spring

vernus, a, um *adj* of the spring, vernal

vērō *adv* in fact, certainly, to be sure, indeed; moreover; on the other hand; yet

verpa, ae *f* penis

verrēs, ris *m* boar

verrō, ersum ③ *v* sweep clean; sweep together; sweep (to the ground); skim, sweep; sweep along

verrūca, ae *f* wart

verruncō ① *v* turn out

versābundus, a, um *adj* revolving

versātilis, e *adj* revolving; versatile

versicolor, ōris *adj* having colours that change

versiculus, ī *m* brief line of verse

versipellis, is *m* werewolf

versō ① *v* keep turning round, spin, whirl; keep going round, keep turning over; turn over and over; stir; drive this way and that; turn this way and that; manoeuvre; sway, 'manipulate'; adapt; ponder; maintain
   □ **versor** come and go frequently; be in operation; be involved (in), concern oneself (in); dwell (upon); pass one's time (in)

versus, ūs *m* line; row; furrow; bench of rowers; line of writing; line of verse

versūtia, ae *f* cunning, craft

versūtus, a, um *adj* full of stratagems *or* shifts, wily, cunning, adroit

vertex, icis *m* whirlpool, eddy; crown of the head; peak, top, summit (of anything); pole

verticōsus, a, um *adj* full of whirlpools *or* eddies

vertīgō, inis *f* whirling *or* spinning movement, gyration, giddiness, dizziness

vertō, rtī, rsum ③ *v* turn, turn around *or* about; turn upside down; overthrow; alter, change; transform; turn out; cause to develop (into); pass into a new frame of mind; translate
   □ **tergum ∼** turn tail, flee

verū, ūs *nt*, **verum, ī** *nt* spit, point of javelin

vērum[1] *conj* but; but at the same time

vērum[2], **ī** *nt* truth

vērumtamen *conj* nevertheless, but even so

vērus, a, um *adj* true, real, genuine; just; right; proper

verūtum, ī *nt* short throwing spear

vervēx, cis *m* wether

vēsānia, ae *f* madness, frenzy

vēsāniēns, ntis *adj* raging, frenzied

vesāniō ④ *v* act in a frenzy, rage

vēsānus, a, um *adj* mad, frenzied; wild

vēscor ③ *v dep* take food, eat; enjoy, put to use; feed on, devour

vēscus, a, um *adj* thin, attenuated

vēsīca, ae *f* bladder; balloon

vēsīcŭla, ae *f* small bladder-like formation

vespa, ae *f* wasp

vesper, eris/erī *m* evening; evening-star; west
   □ **sub vesperum** towards evening
   □ **vespere/vesperī** in the evening

vespera, ae *f* evening; ⌊LM⌋ vespers

vesperāscō, ī ③ *v* grow towards evening

vespertiliō, ōnis *m* bat

vespertīnus, a, um *adj* evening…, of the evening; situated in the west

vespillō, ōnis *m* man of disreputable trade

vester, tra, trum *adj* your (*pl*)

vestiārius, a, um *adj* concerned with clothes

vestibulum, ī *nt* fore-court, entrance

vestīgium, (i)ī *nt* footprint, track; sole of the foot; trace, mark, imprint, vestige; instant
   □ **ē vestīgiō** at once, immediately

vestīgō ① *v* track down, search for; search out; try to find out by searching; investigate

vestīmentum, ī *nt* clothing; *pl* clothes

vestiō ④ *v* dress, clothe; cover

vestis, is *f* garments, clothing, clothes; cloth
   □ **mūtō vestem** change into mourning garments

vestītus, ūs *m* clothes, dress
   □ **redeō ad vestītum** resume (normal) dress (after mourning)

veterāmentārius, a, um *adj* dealing with old *or* worn articles

veterānus, a, um *adj* veteran, having experience of action

veternus, ī *m* morbid state of torpor

vetō, **vetuī**, **vetitum** ① v forbid; prohibit, be an obstacle to

❗ vetō usu. follows the same construction as **iubeō**, which it replaces where the indirect command is negated (i.e. is a prohibition).

vetulus, **a**, **um** adj elderly, ageing

vetus, **eris** adj aged, old; as he was in previous days
■ **veterēs**, **um** mpl 'old-timers'; old authors or writers

❗ vetus usu. has comp. **vetustior** but sup. **veterrimus**.

vetustās, **ātis** f old age; antiquity; long duration

vetustus, **a**, **um** adj ancient, old-established; long-established

vexāmen, **inis** nt, **vexātiō**, **ōnis** f shaking; disturbance, upheaval

vexillārius, **(i)ī** m standard-bearer
■ **vexillāriī** pl troops serving for the time being in a special detachment

vexillum, **ī** nt standard, banner; detachment of troops

vexō ① v agitate, buffet; harry, ravage; afflict, upset; persecute; disturb

via, **ae** f way; road, passage; channel; march, journey; manner, method, means

viāticum, **ī** nt provision for a journey, travelling allowance; money saved by soldiers from day to day

viātor, **ōris** m traveller

vībēx, **ēcis** f, **vībīx**, **īcis** f weal, mark from a blow

vibrō ① v brandish, wave; crimp, corrugate; rock; propel suddenly; flash; dart; glitter

vīburnum, **ī** nt guelder rose

vicārius, **(i)ī** m substitute, deputy; successor

vīcātim adv by (urban) districts, street by street; in or by villages

vīcēnī, **ae**, **a** adj twenty each

vīcēsimānus, **a**, **um** adj of the 20th legion

vīcī ▶ **vincō**

vicia, **ae** f vetch

vīcīnālis, **e** adj of or for the use of local inhabitants

vīcīnia, **ae** f neighbourhood; nearness; neighbours

vīcīnitās, **ātis** f neighbourhood; nearness; neighbours

vīcīnus, **a**, **um** adj neighbouring, in the neighbourhood, near; similar
■ **vīcīnum**, **ī** nt neighbourhood, neighbouring place, vicinity (of)
■ **vīcīnus**, **ī** m neighbour

vicis gen f no nom change; succession; place, turn; part; exchange, retaliation, return, interchange
▯ **in vicem** by turns; reciprocally; instead of
▯ **vicem** after the manner of, in the place of
▯ **meam vicem** in my place
▯ **vice** after the manner of

vicissim adv in turn; conversely

vicissitūdō, **inis** f change, alternation; vicissitude

victima, **ae** f an animal offered in sacrifice; a full-grown victim

vīctitō ① v live, subsist

victor, **ōris** m conqueror, victor

victōria, **ae** f victory

victrīx, **īcis** f female conqueror; f adj victorious

vīctus, **ūs** m livelihood, food; way of life

vīculus, **ī** m small village, hamlet

vīcus, **ī** m street; village; district of Rome

vidēlicet adv it is clear (that), evidently, plainly; namely; (expressing irony) of course, no doubt

videō, **vīdī**, **vīsum** ② v see; look at, behold, observe, perceive; understand; regard; take care; pay regard to; in passive appear, seem; be seen; be deemed
▯ **vidētur** it seems good

viduitās, **ātis** f widowhood

vīdulus, **ī** m bag for carrying one's belongings

viduō ① v widow; bereave of a husband

viduus, **a**, **um** adj bereft, deprived (of); widowed; divorced; not supporting a climbing plant, unsupported

viētus, **a**, **um** adj shrivelled, wrinkled

vigeō ② v be strong or vigorous; thrive, flourish, be active; be effective

vigēscō ③ v acquire strength

vigil, **lis** *adj* awake, on the watch, alert; wakeful
  ■ **~**, **is** *m/f* sentry, guard; member of fire brigade

vigilāns, **ntis** *adj* watchful, vigilant

vigilantia, **ae** *f* vigilance, alertness

vigilia, **ae** *f* wakefulness, lying awake; watch, guard; patrol; watchfulness, vigilance
  ■ **vigiliae nocturnae** *fpl* ⟨LM⟩ vigils, night prayer

vigilō ① *v* watch; be awake; stay awake; spend time (on a task) by remaining awake; spend (a night, *etc.*) awake; be watchful *or* alert

vīgintī *adj indec* twenty

vigor, **ōris** *m* vigour; physical *or* mental energy

vīlica, **ae** *f* wife of a farm overseer

vīlicus, **ī** *m* farm overseer, manager

vīlipendō ③ *v* despise, slight

vīlis, **e** *adj* cheap; worthless; contemptible; humble, mean, common

vīlitās, **ātis** *f* cheapness; worthlessness

vīlla, **ae** *f* rural dwelling with associated farm buildings

villōsus, **a**, **um** *adj* shaggy, hairy

vīllula, **ae** *f* small farmstead *or* country-house

villus, **ī** *m* shaggy hair, tuft of hair

vīmen, **inis** *nt* flexible branch, withy; basket

vīmineus, **a**, **um** *adj* of wickerwork

Vīnālia, **ium** *ntpl* wine-festivals (on 22 April and 19-20 August)

vīnārius, **(i)ī** *m* wine-merchant

vincibilis, **e** *adj* likely to win; that can be won

vinciō, **vīnxī**, **vīnctum** ④ *v* tie up; bind, encircle; bond; link; fetter

vincō, **vīcī**, **victum** ③ *v* conquer, overcome; defeat; subdue; win; surmount; exceed, excel; prevail

vinculum, **ī** *nt* band, bond, cord, rope, chain, fetter; band; prison; imprisonment; tether; mooring-rope; restraint, tie

vīndēmia, **ae** *f* grape-gathering; produce of a vineyard in any given year

vindex, **icis** *m/f* champion, defender; protector; avenger, revenger; one who punishes (an offence)

vindiciae, **ārum** *fpl* interim possession (of disputed property)

vindicō ① *v* vindicate, lay legal claim to; save, preserve; free; avenge, punish; defend, protect

vindicta, **ae** *f* the ceremonial act of claiming as free one who contends he is wrongly held in slavery; vengeance; punishment

vīnea, **ae** *f* vines; movable penthouse used to shelter siege-workers

vīnētum, **ī** *nt* vineyard

vīnitor, **ōrls** *m* vineyard worker

vīnōsus, **a**, **um** *adj* immoderately fond of wine; intoxicated with wine

vīnum, **ī** *nt* wine

viola, **ae** *f* violet stock, gillyvor; violet colour

violābilis, **e** *adj* that may be violated *or* suffer outrage

violāceus, **a**, **um** *adj* violet-coloured

violārium, **(i)ī** *nt* bed of violets

violātiō, **ōnis** *f* profanation, violation

violātor, **ōris** *m* profaner, violator

violēns, **ntis** *adj* vehement, violent

violentia, **ae** *f* violence, aggressiveness

violentus, **a**, **um** *adj* violent, aggressive

violō ① *v* profane; defile, pollute; dishonour, outrage; transgress against; pierce, wound; violate

vīpera, **ae** *f* viper

vīpereus, **a**, **um** *adj*, **vīperīnus**, **a**, **um** *adj* of vipers

vir, **rī** *m* man; male; husband, lover; a true man; soldier

> ❗ vir refers to man in contrast to woman, and hence often means 'husband'; cf. **homō**. **vir** may have a short gen. pl. **virum** as well as regular **virōrum**.

virāgō, **inis** *f* a warlike *or* heroic woman

virectum, **ī** *nt* area of greenery

vireō ② *v* be green *or* verdant; be lively *or* vigorous; be full of youthful vigour

vīrēs, **ium** *fpl* strength; control; resources, assets; value; meaning

virēscō ③ *v* turn green

virga, ae *f* twig, shoot, spray, rod, stick; magic wand

virgātus, a, um *adj* made of twigs; striped

virgeus, a, um *adj* consisting of twigs *or* shoots

virgineus, a, um *adj* of, belonging to *or* characteristic of a girl of marriageable age; virgin

virginitās, ātis *f* maidenhood, virginity

virgō, inis *f* a girl of marriageable age; virgin; Virgo (constellation); aqueduct at Rome noted for the coolness of its water

virgultum, ī *nt* shrub; *pl* low shrubby vegetation, brushwood

viridis, e *adj* green; fresh, blooming, sappy; marked by youthful vigour

viridō ☐ *v* make green; be green

virīlis, e *adj* male, masculine; of a man; manly; bold; firm; vigorous
  □ **prō virīlī parte** with the utmost effort; as far as a man may
  □ **toga** ∼ the plain white toga worn by a Roman on reaching puberty

virītim *adv* man by man, per man, individually

vīrōsus, a, um *adj* having an unpleasantly strong taste *or* smell, rank

virtūs, ūtis *f* manliness, manhood; goodness, virtue; excellence, worth; resolution, valour
  □ **tuā virtūte** thanks to you
  ■ **virtutes, um** *mpl* ⓁⓂ miracles

vīrus, ī *nt* venom; poisonous fluid; malignant quality; secretion with medicinal *or* magical potency

vīs *f* strength, force; vigour, power, energy; violence; meaning, signification; nature; efficacy, virtue (of drugs, *etc.*)
  ■ **vīrēs** *fpl* strength; power; military strength

> ❗ **vīs** in the sg. has only acc. **vim** and abl. **vī**; the plural **vīrēs** is regular, with gen. **vīrium**.

vīscātus, a, um *adj* smeared with bird-lime

vīscerātiō, ōnis *f* a communal sacrificial feast at which the flesh of the victim was shared among the guests

viscum, ī *nt*, **viscus, ī** *m* mistletoe; bird-lime

vīscus, eris *nt*, **vīscera, um** *ntpl* the soft fleshy parts of the body, internal organs; entrails, flesh; offspring; innermost part, heart (of)

vīsō, īsī, īsum ③ *v* go and look (at), look, view; visit

vīsum, ī *nt* vision

vīsus, ūs *m* the faculty of seeing; sight, vision; supernatural manifestation

vīta, ae *f* life; living, manner of life; the course of a life

vītābilis, e *adj* to be avoided

vītābundus, a, um *adj* taking evasive action

vītālis, e *adj* of life; vital; life-giving, alive

vītāliter *adv* so as to endow with life

vitellus, ī *m* little calf; yolk of an egg

vīteus, a, um *adj* belonging to a vine

vītigenus, a, um *adj* produced from the vine

vitiō ☐ *v* spoil, harm, impair; deflower; invalidate

vitiōsus, a, um *adj* faulty, defective; corrupt; wicked, vicious

vītis, is *f* vine; vine-branch; centurion's staff

vītisator, ōris *m* vine-planter

vitium, (i)ī *nt* fault, defect, blemish; error; shortcoming

vītō ☐ *v* avoid, shun, keep clear of

vitreārius, (i)ī *m* maker of glassware

vitreus, a, um *adj* of glass; resembling glass in its colour (greenish), translucency, *or* glitter

vītricus, ī *m* stepfather

vitrum, ī *nt* glass; woad

vitta, ae *f* linen headband; woollen band

vittātus, a, um *adj* wearing *or* carrying a ritual **vitta**

vitula, ae *f* calf, young cow

vitulīna, ae *f* veal

vitulus, ī *m* (bull-)calf

vituperō ☐ *v* find fault with, criticize adversely

vīvārium, (i)ī *nt* game enclosure *or* preserve

vīvāx, **ācis** *adj* long-lived, tenacious of life; vivifying; lively, vigorous

vīvēscō ③ *v* come to life

vīvidus, **a**, **um** *adj* lively, vigorous, spirited; lifelike

vivifico ① *v* [LM] restore to life

vīvō, **īxī**, **īctum** ③ *v* live, be alive; really live; live (on); live (by); pass one's life (in); survive

vīvus, **a**, **um** *adj* alive, living; lively

vix *adv* hardly, scarcely, not easily

vixdum *adv* scarcely yet, only just

vocābulum, **ī** *nt* word used to designate something, term, name

vōcālis, **e** *adj* able to speak; having a notable voice; tuneful

vocāmen, **inis** *nt* designation, name

vocātiō, **ōnis** *f* invitation

vocātus, **ūs** *m* peremptory *or* urgent call

vōciferātiō, **ōnis** *f* loud outcry, shout, roar

vōciferor ① *v dep* utter a loud cry, shout, yell, cry out, announce loudly

vocitō ① *v* call

vocō ① *v* call; call upon, summon; name; invite; challenge; demand

vol- ▸ **vul-**

volaemum, **ī** *nt* a large kind of pear

volantēs, **ium** *mpl* birds

volātilis, **e** *adj* equipped to fly, flying, fleeing; fleeting, transient

volātus, **ūs** *m* flying, flight

volēns, **ntis** *adj* willing, welcome

volitō ① *v* fly about; flutter, move swiftly through the air; go to and fro

volō[1] ① *v* fly; speed

volō[2], **velle**, **voluī** *v ir* be willing; wish, desire; want; mean, signify; maintain, claim

volō[3], **ōnis** *m* volunteer

volūbilis, **e** *adj* spinning, rotating; rolling; coiled; flowing, fluent

volūbilitās, **ātis** *f* rotundity

volucer, **cris**, **cre** *adj* flying, winged; swift; fleeting, transitory
  ∎ **volucris**, **is** *f* bird

volūmen, **inis** *nt* roll of papyrus, book; coil, twist

voluntārius, **a**, **um** *adj* of one's own free will, voluntarily undergone

voluntās, **ātis** *f* will, wish, choice, desire, inclination; good-will, sympathy; approval

volup *adv* agreeably, delightfully

voluptās, **ātis** *f* delight; pleasure; source of pleasure; sexual intercourse

volūtābrum, **ī** *nt* place where pigs wallow

volūtō ① *v* roll, wallow; turn over in one's mind; think *or* talk over

volvō, **lvī**, **lūtum** ③ *v* roll, roll over; cause to roll, wrap up; cause (the eyes) to travel restlessly; unroll; turn over in the mind; grovel; turn round

vōmer, **eris** *m* ploughshare

vomitus, **ūs** *m* throwing up, vomit

vomō, **muī** ③ *v* be sick, vomit; discharge, spew out; belch out

vorāgō, **inis** *f* deep hole, chasm, watery hollow

vorāx, **ācis** *adj* ravenous; insatiable; devouring

vorō ① *v* devour; engulf, eat away

vort- ▸ **vert-**

vōs *pn* you (*pl*)

voster ▸ **vester**

vōtīvus, **a**, **um** *adj* offered in fulfilment of a vow

votō ▸ **vetō**

vōtum, **ī** *nt* vow; votive offering; prayer; desire, hope

voveō, **vōvī**, **vōtum** ② *v* vow; pray *or* long for

vōx, **ōcis** *f* voice, sound, word, words; speech; language

Vulcānus, **ī** *m* Vulcan, the god of fire; fire

vulgāris, **e** *adj* usual, common, commonplace, everyday; of the common people; shared by all

vulgātor, **ōris** *m* divulger

vulgātus, **a**, **um** *adj* common, ordinary; conventional; well-known

vulgivagus, **a**, **um** *adj* widely ranging; promiscuous

vulgō[1] *adv* commonly, publicly; en masse; far and wide

vulgō[2] ① *v* make common to all; make public, publish; spread abroad; prostitute; publish the news (that)

vulgus, **ī** *nt* the common people, general public, crowd

v

vulnerō *v* wound, hurt, distress

vulnificus, **a**, **um** *adj* causing wounds

vulnus, **eris** *nt* wound; emotional hurt; injury

vulpēcula, **ae** *f* (little) fox

vulpēs, **pis** *f* fox

vultur, **uris** *m* vulture

vulturius, **(i)ī** *m* vulture

vultus, **ūs** *m* countenance, facial expression; face; looks, features

Xx

xiphiās, **ae** *m* swordfish

xystus, **ī** *m* open-air walk; LM cloisters

Zz

zea, **ae** *f* emmer wheat

zelus, **i** *m* LM zeal

Zephyrus, **ī** *m* a west wind

zizania, **orum** *npl* LM tares

zōna, **ae** *f* belt, girdle; celestial zone

zōnula, **ae** *f* (little) girdle

Summary of Grammar

This Summary of Grammar is intended to be a handy reference guide to the patterns of inflections (i.e. endings) found in the vast majority of Latin words. It thus concentrates on the regular patterns and the most important or frequent irregular exceptions. We do not, however, offer any guidance on the word order and constructions of Latin. For these, the reader is referred to the companion *Latin Grammar* (Oxford, 1999).

Nouns

The declension of a noun can be worked out from the its endings in the nom. and/or gen. sg., as given in the Latin–English section of the dictionary. For example, **nauta** has gen. sg. **nautae** and thus declines like **domina**; all nouns that have gen. sg. in **-is** are third declension, and they form all their cases (except sometimes the nom. sg.) from the same stem as the gen. sg.

	1st decl.	2nd decl.		3rd decl.	
	girl, f.	*master*, m.	*war*, n.	*king*, m.	*shore*, n.
singular					
nom.	puell-a	domin-us	bell-um	rēx	lītus
acc.	puell-am	domin-um	bell-um	rēg-em	lītus
gen.	puell-ae	domin-ī	bell-ī	rēg-is	lītor-is
dat.	puell-ae	domin-ō	bell-ō	rēg-ī	lītor-ī
abl.	puell-ā	domin-ō	bell-ō	rēg-e	lītor-e
plural					
nom.	puell-ae	domin-ī	bell-a	rēg-ēs	lītor-a
acc.	puell-ās	domin-ōs	bell-a	rēg-ēs	lītor-a
gen.	puell-ārum	domin-ōrum	bell-ōrum	rēg-um	lītor-um
dat.	puell-īs	domin-īs	bell-īs	rēg-ibus	lītor-ibus
abl.	puell-īs	domin-īs	bell-īs	rēg-ibus	lītor-ibus

	3rd decl. cont.			
	ship, f.	*sea*, n.	*city*, f.	*animal*, n.
singular				
nom.	nāv-is	mare	urb-s	animal
acc.	nāv-em	mare	urb-em	animal
gen.	nāv-is	mar-is	urb-is	animāl-is
dat.	nāv-ī	mar-ī	urb-ī	animāl-ī
abl.	nāv-e	mar-ī	urb-e	animāl-e
plural				
nom.	nāv-ēs	mar-ia	urb-ēs	animāl-ia
acc.	nāv-ēs (-īs)	mar-ia	urb-ēs (-īs)	animāl-ia
gen.	nāv-ium	mar-ium	urb-ium	animāl-ium
dat.	nāv-ibus	mar-ibus	urb-ibus	animāl-ibus
abl.	nāv-ibus	mar-ibus	urb-ibus	animāl-ibus

	4th decl.		5th decl.	
	step, m.	*horn*, n.	*thing*, f.	*day*, m./f.
singular				
nom.	grad-us	corn-ū	r-ēs	di-ēs
acc.	grad-um	corn-ū	r-em	di-em
gen.	grad-ūs	corn-ūs	r-eī	di-ēī
dat.	grad-uī	corn-ū	r-eī	di-ēī
abl.	grad-ū	corn-ū	r-ē	di-ē
plural				
nom.	grad-ūs	cornu-a	r-ēs	di-ēs
acc.	grad-ūs	cornu-a	r-ēs	di-ēs
gen.	grad-uum	corn-uum	r-ērum	di-ērum
dat.	grad-ibus	corn-ibus	r-ēbus	di-ēbus
abl.	grad-ibus	corn-ibus	r-ēbus	di-ēbus

Notes

1 Neuter nouns of all declensions (viz. 2nd, 3rd, and 4th) always have the acc. identical to the nom. In their plural, the nom./acc. always ends in **-a**.

2 The vocative case is the same as the nominative for all nouns of all declensions, except that 2nd declension nouns ending in **-us** form vocative sg. in **-e** (e.g. **domine**) unless they end in **-ius**, when the vocative sg. is in **-ī** (e.g. **fīlī** from **fīlius**).

3 Some 2nd declension nouns have nom. sg. in **-er** (e.g. **puer**, **ager**). Of these, some keep their **-e-** in the other cases while others drop it (e.g. gen. sg. **puer-ī**, **agr-ī**).

4 Nouns of the second declension with nom. sg. in **-ius** or **-ium** often form a 'contracted' gen. sg. in **-ī** rather than **-iī** (e.g. **fīlī**, **ingenī**).

5 The 3rd declension includes nouns with stems ending in consonants (e.g. **rēx** = **rēg-s**, **lītus**) and those ending in **-i** (e.g. **nāvis** etc.). The two groups differ in their gen. pl.: a basic practical rule is that nouns with one more syllable in the gen. sg. than in the nom. sg. form their gen. pl. in **-um**, while the remainder have gen. pl. **-ium**; however, note that most nouns with a monosyllabic nom. sg. ending in two consonants (**-ns**, **-rs**, **-bs**, **-ps**, **-rx**, and **-lx**), together with neuters with nom. sg. in **-ar** or **-al** have gen. pl. **-ium**, while **canis**, **iuvenis**, **senex**, **pater**, **māter**, and **frāter** have gen. pl. in **-um**.

6 The locative case (expressing 'place at which') for the first and second declensions is identical to the gen. for place names that are singular in form, and to the dat./abl. for names that are plural in form, e.g. **Rōma** → **Rōmae**, **Athēnae** → **Athēnīs**, **Corinthus** → **Corinthī**. For the third declension, the locative singular ends in **-ī** or **-e** while the plural again is identical to the dat./abl., e.g. **Carthāgō** → **Carthāginī**, **Gādēs** → **Gādibus**. Note also the locatives **domī**, **humī**, and **rūrī**.

7 The following very common nouns have some irregular forms: **dea**, **fīlia**, **deus**, **vir**, **vīs**, **domus**. These are detailed in their dictionary entries. **Iuppiter** ('Jupiter, Jove') declines **Iuppiter**, **Iovem**, **Iovis**, **Iovī**, **Iove**.

Adjectives

	2nd & 1st decl.		
	bonus *good*		
	m.	f.	n.
singular			
nom.	bon-us	bon-a	bon-um
acc.	bon-um	bon-am	bon-um
gen.	bon-ī	bon-ae	bon-ī
dat.	bon-ō	bon-ae	bon-ō
abl.	bon-ō	bon-ā	bon-ō
plural			
nom.	bon-ī	bon-ae	bon-a
acc.	bon-ōs	bon-ās	bon-a
gen.	bon-ōrum	bon-ārum	bon-ōrum
dat.	bon-īs	bon-īs	bon-īs
abl.	bon-īs	bon-īs	bon-īs

Note

Like **bonus** decline some adjectives in **-er** such as **miser, misera, miserum** (keeping the **-e-** like **puer**) and **pulcher, pulchra, pulchrum** (dropping the **-e-** like **ager**).

	3rd decl.				
	ācer *swift*			ingēns *huge*	
	m.	f.	n.	m. & f.	n.
singular					
nom.	ācer	ācr-is	ācr-e	ingēns	ingēns
acc.	ācr-em	ācr-em	ācr-e	ingent-em	ingēns
gen.	ācr-is	ācr-is	ācr-is	ingent-is	
dat.	ācr-ī	ācr-ī	ācr-ī	ingent-ī	
abl.	ācr-ī	ācr-ī	ācr-ī	ingent-ī	
plural					
nom.	ācr-ēs	ācr-ēs	ācr-ia	ingent-ēs	ingent-ia
acc.	ācr-ēs	ācr-ēs	ācr-ia	ingent-ēs (-īs)	ingent-ia
gen.	ācr-ium	ācr-ium	ācr-ium	ingent-ium	
dat.	ācr-ibus	ācr-ibus	ācr-ibus	ingent-ibus	
abl.	ācr-ibus	ācr-ibus	ācr-ibus	ingent-ibus	

	3rd decl.			
	pauper *poor*		laetior *happier*	
	m. & f.	n.	m. & f.	n.
singular				
nom.	pauper	pauper	laetior	laetius
acc.	pauper-em	pauper	laetiōr-em	laetius
gen.	pauper-is		laetiōr-is	
dat.	pauper-ī		laetiōr-ī	
abl.	pauper-e		laetiōr-e	
plural				
nom.	pauper-ēs	pauper-a	laetiōr-ēs	laetiōr-a
acc.	pauper-ēs	pauper-a	laetiōr-ēs	laetiōr-a
gen.	pauper-um		laetiōr-um	
dat.	pauper-ibus		laetiōr-ibus	
abl.	pauper-ibus		laetiōr-ibus	

Notes

1 Many 3rd declension adjectives (e.g. **trīstis**, **fortis**, **omnis**) have nom. sg. m. & f. in -**is**, declining like **ācer** in all other forms.

Like **ingēns** decline all present participles and all adjectives with nom. sg. in -**x** (e.g. **audāx**, **ferōx**). The latter have a stem in -**c**- (so gen. sg. **audācis** etc.). Note that present participles have their abl. sg. in -**e** when used as participles (e.g. in the ablative absolute construction) but in -**ī** when used simply as adjectives.

2 There are very few consonant stem adjectives declining like **pauper**, but note that comparative adjectives with nom. sg. in -**ior**, -**ius** follow essentially the same pattern, except in the nom./acc. sg. n.

Comparison of adjectives

Most adjectives form their comparative and superlative by adding -**ior** and -**issimus** to their stem respectively. For example, **laetus** forms comparative **laetior** and superlative **laetissimus**. All comparatives decline like **laetior** and all superlatives like **bonus**.

Adjectives ending in -**er** (like **miser**, **pulcher**, and **ācer**) form their comparatives regularly (**miserior**, **pulchrior**, **ācrior**), but have superlatives in -**errimus** (**miserrimus**, **pulcherrimus**, **ācerrimus**). Note also the six superlatives in -**illimus**, from **facilis**, **difficilis**, **gracilis**, **humilis**, **similis**, and **dissimilis** (e.g. **facillimus**).

Adjectives that end in -**eus**, -**ius**, or -**uus** usually stay the same in the comparative and superlative, making use of the Latin words for 'more' or 'most', as, for example, **dubius**, **magis dubius**, **maximē dubius**.

Some common adjectives have irregular comparison:

	comparative	superlative
bonus *good*	melior *better*	optimus *best*
malus *bad*	peior	pessimus
magnus *great*	maior	maximus
multus *much*	(plūs)	plūrimus
parvus *small*	minor	minimus
senex *old man*	nātū maior	nātū maximus
iuvenis *young man*	iūnior *or* nātū minor	nātū minimus

Adverbs

Adverbs can be regularly formed from adjectives. From adjectives of the **bonus** type (though not **bonus** itself), adverbs are usually formed by adding -ē to the stem, e.g. **lentus → lentē, miser → miserē**. Some add -ō, for example **tūtō** from **tūtus, subitō** from **subitus**. From 3rd declension adjectives, the adverb is generally formed by adding -**ter** to the stem, so **ācer → ācriter, fortis → fortiter**; some, however, simply use the acc. sg. n., for example **facilis → facile**.

Comparison of adverbs

Comparative adverbs are the same as the acc. sg. n. of the corresponding adjective (and therefore usually end in -**(i)us**), while the superlative is formed by changing the corresponding adjective's nom. sg. m. from -**us** to -**ē**; for example, **fortiter** has comparative **fortius** and superlative **fortissimē**, and **ācriter** has **ācrius** and **ācerrimē**.

Some common adverbs have irregular comparison:

	adverb	comparative	superlative
bonus	bene *well*	melius	optimē
malus	male *badly*	peius	pessimē
magnus	magnopere *greatly*	magis	maximē
multus	multum *much*	plūs	plūrimum
parvus	paul(l)um *little*	minus	minimē
—	diū *for a long time*	diūtius	diūtissimē
—	[post *later*]	posterius	postrēmō
—	[prope *near*]	propius	proximē

Numerals

		cardinal	ordinal	adverb
		one	*first*	*once*
1	I	ūnus	prīmus	semel
2	II	duo	secundus, alter	bis
3	III	trēs	tertius	ter
4	IV	quattuor	quārtus	quater
5	V	quīnque	quīntus	quīnquiēns
6	VI	sex	sextus	sexiēns
7	VII	septem	septimus	septiēns
8	VIII	octō	octāvus	octiēns
9	IX	novem	nōnus	noviēns
10	X	decem	decimus	deciēns
11	XI	ūndecim	ūndecimus	ūndeciēns
12	XII	duodecim	duodecimus	duodeciēns
13	XIII	tredecim	tertius decimus	terdeciēns
14	XIV	quattuordecim	quārtus decimus	quattuordeciēns
15	XV	quīndecim	quīntus decimus	quīndeciēns
16	XVI	sēdecim	sextus decimus	sēdeciēns
17	XVII	septendecim	septimus decimus	septiēnsdeciēns
18	XVIII	duodēvīgintī	duodēvīcēnsimus	duodēvīciēns
19	XIX	ūndēvīgintī	ūndēvīcēnsimus	ūndēvīciēns
20	XX	vīgintī	vīcēnsimus	vīciēns
30	XXX	trīgintā	trīcēnsimus	trīciēns
40	XL	quadrāgintā	quadrāgēnsimus	quadrāgiēns

50	L	quīnquāgintā	200	CC	ducentī
51	LI	ūnus et quīnquāgintā	300	CCC	trēcentī
60	LX	sexāgintā	400	CCCC	quadringentī
70	LXX	septuāgintā	500	D	quīngentī
80	LXXX	octāgintā	600	DC	sescentī
90	XC	nōnāgintā	700	DCC	septingentī
100	C	centum	800	DCCC	octingentī
101	CI	centum et ūnus	900	DCCCC	nōngentī
		1000	CD *or* M	mīlle	

Notes

1 The cardinal numbers 1 to 3 decline as follows:

	m.	f.	n.
nom.	ūnus	ūna	ūnum
acc.	ūnum	ūnam	ūnum
gen.	ūnĭus	ūnĭus	ūnĭus
dat.	ūnī	ūnī	ūnī
abl.	ūnō	ūnā	ūnō

	m.	f.	n.	m. & f.	n.
nom.	duo	duae	duo	trēs	tria
acc.	duōs, duo	duās	duo	trēs	tria
gen.	duōrum	duārum	duōrum	trium	
dat./abl.	duōbus	duābus	duōbus	tribus	

2 The cardinal numbers 4 to 100 are indeclinable (except that where **ūnus**, **duo** and **trēs** appear as part of the form, they are declined). The cardinal numbers for hundreds from 200 to 900 decline like the plural of **bonus**.

3 The ordinal numbers all decline like **bonus**.

4 The endings **-ēns** and **-ēnsimus** are often found as **-ēs** and **-ēsimus**.

5 To form cardinal numbers between 20 and 99, the order is either that of 'twenty-four' (**vīgintī quattuor**) or 'four-and-twenty' (**quattuor et vīgintī**), though the latter is more usual if the number includes **ūnus** (e.g. **ūnus et trīgintā**). For numbers greater than 100, the order is usually that of English: hence, 752 is **septingentī quīnquāgintā duo**.

6 Cardinal numbers involving thousands can be expressed in two ways, either with the noun **mīlia** in the relevant case itself modified by a cardinal number and followed by a genitive noun dependent on it, or with the indeclinable adjective **mīlle** qualified by a numeral adverb and followed by the noun in the relevant case. For example, 'with three thousand sailors' is either **cum tribus mīlibus nautārum** or **cum ter mīlle nautīs**. A 'mile' is **mīlle passūs** ('a thousand paces') and so 'two miles' is **duo mīlia passuum** (lit. 'two thousands of paces').

. . . .

Pronouns

Personal pronouns

| | *I, we* | *you* | *he, she, it, that* | | |
			m.	f.	n.
singular					
nom.	ego	tū	is	ea	id
acc.	mē	tū	eum	eam	id
gen.	meī	tuī	eius	eius	eius
dat.	mihĭ	tibĭ	eī	eī	eī
abl.	mē	tē	eō	eā	eō
plural					
nom.	nōs	vōs	iī (eī, ī)	eae	ea
acc.	nōs	vōs	eōs	eās	ea
gen.	nostrī (-um)	vestrī (-um)	eōrum	eārum	eōrum
dat.	nōbīs	vōbīs	eīs, iīs	eīs, iīs	eīs, iīs
abl.	nōbīs	vōbīs	eīs, iīs	eīs, iīs	eīs, iīs

Reflexive pronoun

	himself, herself, itself, themselves
acc.	sē, sēsē
gen.	suī
dat.	sibĭ
abl.	sē, sēsē

Notes

1 The possessive adjectives corresponding to **ego**, **tū**, **nōs**, **vōs**, and **sē** are respectively **meus**, **tuus**, **noster**, **vester**, and **suus**. Possessives in **-us** decline like **bonus** (**meus** has voc. sg. masc. **mī**); **noster** and **vester** decline like **pulcher**. There is no adjective corresponding to **is**, whose genitive is used instead.

2 The dative of **ego** is sometimes **mī**.

3 The gen. forms **nostrum** and **vestrum** are used in partitive constructions, e.g. **ūnus vestrum** 'one of you'. The alternative forms **nostrī** and **vestrī** are used where the genitive expresses the object of an action, esp. with the gerund(ive); regardless of number and gender, **nostrī** and **vestrī** (likewise **suī**) always take the masc. gen. sg. of the gerund(ive), e.g. **vestrī irrīdendī causā** 'for the sake of mocking you'.

Demonstrative pronouns

	this			that		
	m.	f.	n.	m.	f.	n.
singular						
nom.	hic	haec	hoc	ille	illa	illud
acc.	hunc	hanc	hoc	illum	illam	illud
gen.	huius	huius	huius	illĭus	illĭus	illĭus
dat.	huic	huic	huic	illī	illī	illī
abl.	hōc	hāc	hōc	illō	illā	illō
plural						
nom.	hī	hae	haec	illī	illae	illa
acc.	hōs	hās	haec	illōs	illās	illa
gen.	hōrum	hārum	hōrum	illōrum	illārum	illōrum
dat.	hīs	hīs	hīs	illīs	illīs	illīs
abl.	hīs	hīs	hīs	illīs	illīs	illīs

Like **ille** declines **iste** ('that'), as does **ipse** ('self') except its nom./acc. sg. n. **ipsum**.

Relative pronoun

	the same			who, which		
	m.	f.	n.	m.	f.	n.
singular						
nom.	īdem	eadem	idem	quī	quae	quod
acc.	eundem	eandem	idem	quem	quam	quod
gen.	eiusdem	eiusdem	eiusdem	cuius	cuius	cuius
dat.	eīdem	eīdem	eīdem	cui	cui	cui
abl.	eōdem	eādem	eōdem	quō	quā	quō
plural						
nom.	(e)īdem	eaedem	eadem	quī	quae	quae
acc.	eōsdem	eāsdem	eadem	quōs	quās	quae
gen.	eōrundem	eārundem	eōrundem	quōrum	quārum	quōrum
dat./abl.	eīsdem *or* īsdem			quibus *or* quīs		

The interrogative **quis** ('who?') declines exactly like **quī** except that the nom. sg. f. may be **quis** and the nom./acc. sg. n. is usually **quid**. The indefinite **quis** ('someone, anyone') declines in the same way as interrogative **quis** except that the nom./acc. pl. n. may be **qua**.

As well as being a relative pronoun, **quī** can also be interrogative or indefinite: distinguish **quis** and **quid** as (pro)nouns from **quī** and **quod** which can only be used as adjectives.

Pronominal adjectives

	the other (of two)		
	m.	f.	n.
singular			
nom.	alter	altera	alterum
acc.	alterum	alteram	alterum
gen.	alterĭus	alterĭus	alterĭus
dat.	alterī	alterī	alterī
abl.	alterō	alterā	alterō
plural			
nom.	alterī	alterae	altera
acc.	alterōs	alterās	altera
gen.	alterōrum	alterārum	alterōrum
dat./abl.	alterīs	alterīs	alterīs

Among the other pronominal adjectives, **ūllus**, **nūllus**, **sōlus**, and **tōtus** are declined like **ūnus**; **alius** declines like **ille** (except with nom. sg. m. **alius**). Like **alter** decline both **uter** and **neuter**, though with stems **utr-** and **neutr-** in all forms except the nom. sg. m.

Verbs

Latin verbs take different endings according to person, number, tense, voice, and mood. There are four regular sets of inflections for verbs, known as conjugations. In this dictionary the conjugation of a verb is shown by a number in square brackets following the verb. The citation (headword) form of a Latin verb is usually its 1 sg. pres. ind. act., often followed by its principal parts, from which one can predict the rest of its forms: they are, in order, the infinitive, the 1 sg. perf. ind. act., and the supine.

There is also a mixed conjugation containing a small number of (common) verbs. These follow the 3rd conjugation for most forms, but have the endings of the 4th conjugation where the latter have two successive vowels.

A number of Latin verbs (some in each conjugation) are passive in form but active in meaning. These are called deponent verbs and their forms are identical to verbs of their conjugations in the passive. A very small number of verbs are semi-deponent: they are active in form and meaning in the present, future and imperfect, but deponent in the perfect, pluperfect, and future perfect.

Latin also has a number of irregular verbs, some of which are very common indeed. We give the irregular forms in full.

Regular Verbs

Active—Indicative

	parō 1 *I prepare*	**moneō** 2 *I warn*	**regō** 3 *I rule*	**audiō** 4 *I hear*
present				
sg 1	parō	moneō	regō	audiō
2	parās	monēs	regis	audīs
3	parat	monet	regit	audit
pl 1	parāmus	monēmus	regimus	audīmus
2	parātis	monētis	regitis	audītis
3	parant	monent	regunt	audiunt
future				
sg 1	parābō	monēbō	regam	audiam
2	parābis	monēbis	regēs	audiēs
3	parābit	monēbit	reget	audiet
pl 1	parābimus	monēbimus	regēmus	audiēmus
2	parābitis	monēbitis	regētis	audiētis
3	parābunt	monēbunt	regent	audient
imperfect				
sg 1	parābam	monēbam	regēbam	audiēbam
2	parābās	monēbās	regēbās	audiēbās
3	parābat	monēbat	regēbat	audiēbat
pl 1	parābāmus	monēbāmus	regēbāmus	audiēbāmus
2	parābātis	monēbātis	regēbātis	audiēbātis
3	parābant	monēbant	regēbant	audiēbant

Imperative

sg 2	parā	monē	rege	audī
3	parātō	monētō	regitō	audītō
pl 2	parāte	monēte	regite	audīte
3	parantō	monentō	reguntō	audiuntō

Participle

pres.	parāns	monēns	regēns	audiēns
fut.	parātūrus	monitūrus	rēctūrus	audītūrus

Gerund

	parandum	monendum	regendum	audiendum

. . . .

Active—Indicative

	1st conj.	2nd conj.	3rd conj.	4th conj.
perfect				
sg 1	parāvī	monuī	rēxī	audīvī
2	parāvistī	monuistī	rēxistī	audīvistī
3	parāvit	monuit	rēxit	audīvit
pl 1	parāvimus	monuimus	rēximus	audīvimus
2	parāvistis	monuistis	rēxistis	audīvistis
3	parāvērunt	monuērunt	rēxērunt	audīvērunt
future perfect				
sg 1	parāverō	monuerō	rēxerō	audīverō
2	parāveris	monueris	rēxeris	audīveris
3	parāverit	monuerit	rēxerit	audīverit
pl 1	parāverimus	monuerimus	rēxerimus	audīverimus
2	parāveritis	monueritis	rēxeritis	audīveritis
3	parāverint	monuerint	rēxerint	audīverint
pluperfect				
sg 1	parāveram	monueram	rēxeram	audīveram
2	parāverās	monuerās	rēxerās	audīverās
3	parāverat	monuerat	rēxerat	audīverat
pl 1	parāverāmus	monuerāmus	rēxerāmus	audīverāmus
2	parāverātis	monuerātis	rēxerātis	audīverātis
3	parāverant	monuerant	rēxerant	audīverant

Infinitive

pres.	parāre	monēre	regere	audīre
fut.	parātūrus esse	monitūrus esse	rēctūrus esse	audītūrus esse
perf.	parāvisse	monuisse	rēxisse	audīvisse

Supine

	parātum	monitum	rēctum	audītum

The 3 pl. perf. ind. act., particularly in verse, may also end in **-ēre** or sometimes **-erunt**.

Mixed conjugation

Verbs such as **faciō** and **capiō** follow the pattern of **regō** for all forms based on the present stem, but they take the endings of the 4th conjugation where the latter have two successive vowels: so **capiō** and **capiunt** vs. **capis** and **capit**, and likewise **capiam**, **capiēbam**, **capiēns** etc.

Passive—Indicative

	1st conj.	2nd conj.	3rd conj.	4th conj.
present				
sg 1	paror	moneor	regor	audior
2	parāris	monēris	regeris	audīris
3	parātur	monētur	regitur	audītur
pl 1	parāmur	monēmur	regimur	audīmur
2	parāminī	monēminī	regiminī	audīminī
3	parantur	monentur	reguntur	audiuntur
future				
sg 1	parābor	monēbor	regar	audiar
2	parāberis	monēberis	regēris	audiēris
3	parābitur	monēbitur	regētur	audiētur
pl 1	parābimur	monēbimur	regēmur	audiēmur
2	parābiminī	monēbiminī	regēminī	audiēminī
3	parābuntur	monēbuntur	regentur	audientur
imperfect				
sg 1	parābar	monēbar	regēbar	audiēbar
2	parābāris	monēbāris	regēbāris	audiēbāris
3	parābātur	monēbātur	regēbātur	audiēbātur
pl 1	parābāmur	monēbāmur	regēbāmur	audiēbāmur
2	parābāminī	monēbāminī	regēbāminī	audiēbāminī
3	parābantur	monēbantur	regēbantur	audiēbantur

Imperative

	1st conj.	2nd conj.	3rd conj.	4th conj.
sg 2	parāre	monēre	regere	audīre
3	parātor	monētor	regitor	audītor
pl 2	parāminī	monēminī	regiminī	audīminī
3	parantor	monentor	reguntor	audiuntor

Gerundive

	1st conj.	2nd conj.	3rd conj.	4th conj.
	parandus	monendus	regendus	audiendus

Passive—Indicative

	1st conj.	2nd conj.	3rd conj.	4th conj.
perfect				
sg 1	parātus sum	monitus sum	rēctus sum	audītus sum
	... es *etc.*	... es *etc.*	... es *etc.*	... es *etc.*
future perfect				
sg 1	parātus erō	monitus erō	rēctus erō	audītus erō
	... eris *etc.*	... eris *etc.*	... eris *etc.*	... eris *etc.*
pluperfect				
sg 1	parātus eram	monitus eram	rēctus eram	audītus eram
	... erās *etc.*	... erās *etc.*	... erās *etc.*	... erās *etc.*

Infinitive

	1st conj.	2nd conj.	3rd conj.	4th conj.
pres.	parārī	monērī	regī	audīrī
fut.	parātum īrī	monitum īrī	rēctum īrī	audītum īrī
perf.	parātus esse	monitus esse	rēctus esse	audītus esse

Participle

	1st conj.	2nd conj.	3rd conj.	4th conj.
perf.	parātus	monitus	rēctus	audītus

Notes

1 In those passive forms that include the perfect participle, the participle is adjectival and agrees with its subject, e.g. **parātī erāmus**. The same applies to passive subjunctives containing the participle.

2 The future infinitive is made up of the supine (not the perfect participle) with **īrī**; the supine does not change in this form.

3 Except in the present indicative, any passive 2 sg. form ending in **-ris** may instead end in **-re**; this applies equally to the subjunctive forms on pp. 224–5.

4 For verbs like **capiō** the principle given at the foot of p. 221 applies to the passive as to the active, thus **capior** and **capiuntur** beside **caperis** and **capitur**, similarly **capiar** and **capiēbar**.

Active—Subjunctive

	1st conj.	2nd conj.	3rd conj.	4th conj.
present				
sg 1	parem	moneam	regam	audiam
2	parēs	moneās	regās	audiās
3	paret	moneat	regat	audiat
pl 1	parēmus	moneāmus	regāmus	audiāmus
2	parētis	moneātis	regātis	audiātis
3	parent	moneant	regant	audiant
imperfect				
sg 1	parārem	monērem	regerem	audīrem
2	parārēs	monērēs	regerēs	audīrēs
3	parāret	monēret	regeret	audīret
pl 1	parārēmus	monērēmus	regerēmus	audīrēmus
2	parārētis	monērētis	regerētis	audīrētis
3	parārent	monērent	regerent	audīrent
perfect				
sg 1	parāverim	monuerim	rēxerim	audīverim
2	parāverīs	monuerīs	rēxerīs	audīverīs
3	parāverit	monuerit	rēxerit	audīverit
pl 1	parāverīmus	monuerīmus	rēxerīmus	audīverīmus
2	parāverītis	monuerītis	rēxerītis	audīverītis
3	parāverint	monuerint	rēxerint	audīverint
pluperfect				
sg 1	parāvissem	monuissem	rēxissem	audīvissem
2	parāvissēs	monuissēs	rēxissēs	audīvissēs
3	parāvisset	monuisset	rēxisset	audīvisset
pl 1	parāvissēmus	monuissēmus	rēxissēmus	audīvissēmus
2	parāvissētis	monuissētis	rēxissētis	audīvissētis
3	parāvissent	monuissent	rēxissent	audīvissent

• •

Passive—Subjunctive

	1st conj.	2nd conj.	3rd conj.	4th conj.
present				
sg 1	parer	monear	regar	audiar
2	parēris	moneāris	regāris	audiāris
3	parētur	moneātur	regātur	audiātur
pl 1	parēmur	moneāmur	regāmur	audiāmur
2	parēminī	moneāminī	regāminī	audiāminī
3	parentur	moneantur	regantur	audiantur
imperfect				
sg 1	parārer	monērer	regerer	audīrer
2	parārēris	monērēris	regerēris	audīrēris
3	parārētur	monērētur	regerētur	audīrētur
pl 1	parārēmur	monērēmur	regerēmur	audīrēmur
2	parārēminī	monērēminī	regerēminī	audīrēminī
3	parārentur	monērentur	regerentur	audīrentur
perfect				
sg 1	parātus sim	monitus sim	rēctus sim	audītus sim
	... sīs *etc.*	... sīs *etc.*	... sīs *etc.*	... sīs *etc.*
pluperfect				
sg 1	parātus essem	monitus essem	rēctus essem	audītus essem
	... essēs *etc.*	... essēs *etc.*	... essēs *etc.*	... essēs *etc.*

Notes

1 As with the indicative, in those passive forms that include the perfect participle, the participle is adjectival and agrees with its subject, e.g. **parātī sīmus**.

2 There is no future subjunctive: in indirect questions, a future tense, if active, is reported with the future participle (agreeing with its subject) and **sim** or **essem** *etc.* according to sequence.

3 Any subjunctive passive 2 sg. form ending in **-ris** may instead end in **-re**.

4 For verbs like **capiō** the principle given at the foot of p. 221 applies to the subjunctive as to the indicative; thus the present subjunctive **capiam** and **capiar** has the **-i-** throughout like **audiam** and **audiar** while **caperem** and **caperer** do not.

Irregular Verbs

	sum, esse, fuī *I am, to be*		**possum, posse, potuī** *I can, to be able*	
	indicative	subjunctive	indicative	subjunctive
present				
sg 1	sum	sim	possum	possim
2	es	sīs	potes	possīs
3	est	sit	potest	possit
pl 1	sumus	sīmus	possumus	possīmus
2	estis	sītis	potestis	possītis
3	sunt	sint	possunt	possint
future				
sg 1	erō		poterō	
2	eris		poteris	
3	erit		poterit	
pl 1	erimus		poterimus	
2	eritis		poteritis	
3	erunt		poterunt	
imperfect				
sg 1	eram	essem	poteram	possem
2	erās	essēs	poterās	possēs
3	erat	esset	poterat	posset
pl 1	erāmus	essēmus	poterāmus	possēmus
2	erātis	essētis	poterātis	possētis
3	erant	essent	poterant	possent

For these verbs, the tenses formed from the perfect stem are formed regularly, from the stems **fu-** and **potu-** (thus **fuī** and **potuī** as, for example, **monuī**). Neither verb has a present or perfect participle; the future participle of **esse** is **futūrus**. The imperatives from **esse** are **es** and **estō** in the singular, and **este** and **suntō** in the plural. The present and perfect infinitives are formed regularly; **esse** has a future infinitive which is either **futūrus esse** or **fore**.

Summary of Grammar

	volō, velle, voluī *I want*		nōlō, nōlle, nōluī *I do not want*		mālō, mālle, māluī *I prefer*	
	indic.	subj.	indic.	subj.	indic.	subj.
present						
sg 1	volō	velim	nōlō	nōlim	mālō	mālim
2	vīs	velīs	nōn vīs	nōlīs	māvīs	mālīs
3	vult	velit	nōn vult	nōlit	māvult	mālit
pl 1	volumus	velīmus	nōlumus	nōlīmus	mālumus	mālīmus
2	vultis	velītis	nōn vultis	nōlītis	māvultis	mālītis
3	volunt	velint	nōlunt	nōlint	mālunt	malint
future						
sg 1	volam		nōlam		mālam	
2	volēs *etc.*		nōlēs *etc.*		mālēs *etc.*	
imperfect						
sg 1	volēbam	vellem	nōlēbam	nōllem	mālēbam	māllem
2	volēbās *etc.*	vellēs *etc.*	nōlēbās *etc.*	nōllēs *etc.*	mālēbās *etc.*	māllēs *etc.*

Tenses formed from the perfect stem are formed regularly for all three verbs, from the stems **volu-**, **nōlu-**, and **mālu-**. Present participles are **volēns** and **nōlēns**; **mālō** has no participle. The only imperatives are from **nōlō**: **nōlī** and **nōlītō** in the singular, and **nōlīte** and **nōluntō** in the plural. There are no supines.

	eō, īre, iī, itum *I go*		fīō, fierī *I become; I am made*	
	indicative	subjunctive	indicative	subjunctive
present				
sg 1	eō	eam	fīō	fīam
2	īs	eās	fīs	fīās
3	it	eat	fit	fīat
pl 1	īmus	eāmus	(fīmus)	fīāmus
2	ītis	eātis	(fītis)	fīātis
3	eunt	eant	fīunt	fīant
future				
sg 1	ībō		fīam	
2	ībis *etc.*		fīēs *etc.*	
imperfect				
sg 1	ībam	īrem	fīēbam	fierem
2	ībās *etc.*	īrēs *etc.*	fīēbās *etc.*	fierēs *etc.*

Tenses formed from the perfect stem are formed regularly for **eō**, from the stem **i-**, although **ii-** before **-s-** usually becomes **ī-**; thus **iī**, **īstī**, **iit** *etc.* A perfect stem **īv-** is occasionally found. The present participle is **iēns** (gen. sg. **euntis**) and the future participle **itūrus**. The imperatives from **eō** are **ī** and **ītō** in the singular, and **īte** and

euntō in the plural. The future and perfect infinitives are formed regularly; the gerund is **eundum**. The impersonal 3 sg. pres. indic. **ītur** is common.

fīō has no forms in tenses/moods other than those given. Note that **fīō** takes the place of the passive forms from the present stem of **faciō** and its compounds.

ferō, ferre, tulī, lātum *I bear, carry*

	active		passive	
	indicative	subjunctive	indicative	subjunctive
present				
sg 1	ferō	feram	feror	ferar
2	fers	ferās	ferris	ferāris
3	fert	ferat	fertur	ferātur
pl 1	ferimus	ferāmus	ferimur	ferāmur
2	fertis	ferātis	feriminī	ferāminī
3	ferunt	ferant	feruntur	ferantur
future				
sg 1	feram		ferar	
2	ferēs *etc.*		ferēris *etc.*	
imperfect				
sg 1	ferēbam	ferrem	ferēbam	ferrer
2	ferēbās *etc.*	ferrēs *etc.*	ferēbāris *etc.*	ferrēris *etc.*

Imperative

sg 2	fer	ferre	
3	fertō	fertor	
pl 2	ferte	feriminī	
3	feruntō	feruntor	

Infinitive

pres.	ferre	ferrī
fut.	lātūrus esse	lātum īrī
perf.	tulisse	lātus esse

The present participle, gerund, and gerundive are formed regularly (**ferēns**, **ferendum**, and **ferendus**). Forms from the perfect stem (**tul-**) are all regular.

Summary of Grammar

	edō, ēsse, ēdī, ēsum *I eat*	
	indicative	subjunctive
present		
sg 1	edō	edam *or* edim
2	ēs	edās *or* edīs
3	ēst	edat *or* edit
pl 1	edimus	edāmus
2	ēstis	edātis
3	edunt	edant *or* edint
imperfect		
sg 1	edēbam	ēssem
2	edēbās *etc.*	ēssēs *etc.*

Imperative	
sg 2	ēs
3	ēstō
pl 2	ēste
3	eduntō

All the other forms of this verb are regular, although note the common 3 sg. passive forms **ēstur** (pres. indic.) and **ēssētur** (impf. subj.).

Roman Dates and Times

Dates

From the early republic, a particular year was referred to by the names of the consuls for that year together with the word **cōnsulēs** (more usually in the *ablative*, e.g. **L. Pīsōne (et) A. Gabīniō cōnsulibus**). In later times, historians related all dates to the foundation of Rome (accepted as, in modern terms, 753 BC) and referred to dates AUC (**ab urbe conditā**). Thus 1 BC is AUC 753 while AD 1 is AUC 754.

The adjectives referring to the Roman months (**mēnsis, is** *m*.) are:

Iānuārius	January
Februārius	February
Martius	March
Aprīlis	April
Maius	May
Iūnius	June
Iūlius (Quīnctīlis)	July (named after Julius Caesar)
Augustus (Sextīlis)	August (named after Augustus Caesar)
September	September
Octōber	October
November	November
December	December

The words ending in **-us** decline like **bonus**, those ending in **-er** like **ācer** and those in **-is** like **trīstis**.

The Roman year originally began on 1st March. Hence the fact that September, October, November, and December mean the 7th, 8th, 9th, and 10th month respectively. The original names for July and August (given in brackets above) meant the 5th and 6th.

Julius Caesar's reform of 46 BC in effect invented the modern year. He at last established the figure of 365 days, missing only a quarter day per year—hence the leap year—, and the months with their modern number of days.

The three key days of the Roman month were:

Kalendae, ārum *f.pl*.	Kalends (on the 1st)
Nōnae, ārum *f.pl*.	Nones (9 days before the Ides, on the 5th, in some months the 7th)
Īdūs, uum *f.pl*.	Ides (on the 13th, in some months the 15th)

☑ The following memory rhyme may be helpful:

> In March, July, October, May,
> Nones is the 7th, Ides the 15th day.

Dates and Times

• •

The rules for forming Roman dates

The adjectives for the months always agree with the word for the key day of the month.

1 If the date falls on one of these days, the ablative is used:

Īdibus Martiīs
on the Ides of March, 15th March

2 If the date falls *on the day before* one of these days, **prīdiē** + *accusative* is used:

prīdiē Īdūs Martiās
the day before the Ides of March, 14th March

3 All other dates are counted back from the next key day (Kalends, Nones, or Ides). The counting is done inclusively, i.e. including both the key day and the date referred to.

The expression **ante diem** + the appropriate ordinal number (**secundus, tertius, quārtus** etc.) agreeing with **diem** (acc. m. sg.) is followed by the *accusative* of the key day and the adjective indicating the month agreeing with it (acc. f. pl.):

ante diem tertium Nōnās Iānuāriās
three days before the Nones of January

In our calendar the Nones of January are the 5th. Count three days back from 5th January (including that day) and it transpires that the Roman date referred to is 3rd January.

The Roman date is frequently abbreviated to, for example, **a.d. iii Nōn. Iān**.

4 For dates *after* the Ides in any month, the counting has to be done from the Kalends *of the next month*. Inclusive counting will lead to the inclusion of both the key day and the last day of the month in which the date actually falls. Thus **a.d. vii Kal. Apr.** is a date in *March*. In the **vii** are included both 1st April (the Kalends) and 31st March. Counting back we thus arrive at 26th March as the modern equivalent.

If you are converting an English date into Latin, the easiest way to proceed is to add two to the number of the days in the English month (e.g. for 26th March, add 2 to 31 = 33) and subtract the modern date (33–26th = 7).

5 In leap years, February had 29 days, the 24th and the 25th both being called **a.d. vi Kal. Mart.** of which the second was called **diēs bi(s)sextus**. Hence a leap year was an **annus bi(s)sextus**.

Times

The Roman day was generally divided into 12 equal hours (**hōrae**) during daylight (each hour varying in length according to the time of year and the latitude). The night was similarly divided into 12 equal hours; for military purposes, it was also divided into 4 equal watches (**vigiliae**) for purposes of guard duty, etc.

Roman Weights and Measures

Weights

The **lībra** (*f.*) or **ās** (*m.*), three quarters of a modern pound or 327 grams, was divided into 12 **ūnciae** (an **ūncia** was 27.3 grams, almost exactly the same weight as a modern ounce). The other units were a **sextāns** (a sixth of the **lībra**, 54.6 grams), **quadrāns** or **terūncius** (a quarter, 81.8 grams), **triēns** (109 grams—a quarter of a modern pound), **quīncūnx** (136 grams), **sēmis** (164 grams), **septūnx** (191 grams), **bēs** (218 grams—half a modern pound), **dōdrāns** (245 grams), **dēxtāns** (273 grams), and **deūnx** (300 grams).

Lengths and Areas

The **pēs** (*m.*) was very slightly less than a modern foot (30 cm, 0.971 feet). A **passus** (*m.*) was 5 Roman feet (1.48 metres, 4.85 feet). The mile (**mīlle passūs**) consisted of 1,000 Roman feet (1480 metres, 4850 feet, 9/10 of a modern mile).

A **iūgerum** (*nt.*) was a measure of land 240 ×120 Roman feet, 5/8 of an English acre (1.544 hectares).

Roman Money

The **sēstertius** (*m.*) was the unit in which Roman money was usually counted. It was a silver coin worth 2½ **assēs** (*m.*, singular **ās, assis**). That is how it got its name: 'half a third', *sēmis-tertius*, i.e. 2½. The **dēnārius** (*m.*), also a silver coin, was worth four **sēstertiī** ('sesterces' in English), i.e. 10 **assēs**. The **aureus**, a gold coin first minted by Julius Caesar, was originally worth 25 **dēnāriī**, but later its value declined. Coins below the value of the **sēstertius** were made of copper.

Sums up to 2,000 sesterces were given as one would expect: the cardinal number with the plural of **sēstertius**: **trecentī sēstertiī** = *three hundred sesterces*.

For sums from 2,000 to 1,000,000 sesterces, the word **sēstertia** (*nt.pl.*) was used to mean 'a thousand sesterces' with distributive numerals (e.g. for 1 to 10, **singulī, -ae, -a; bīnī; ternī; quaternī; quīnī; sēnī; septēnī; octōnī; novēnī; dēnī**): **terna sēstertia** = *three thousand sesterces*.

For sums of 1,000,000 sesterces and above, the word **sēstertium** (originally a *gen. pl.*) was used with adverbial numbers (**semel, bis, ter**, etc.). **sēstertium** has the meaning 'a hundred thousand sesterces'. Thus **ūndeciēs sēstertium** = *1,100,000 sesterces*.

Abbreviations

The word **sēstertius** is abbreviated to HS (the H is made up of II joined together, while the S stands for **sēmis** ('half'), i.e. 2½ (**assēs**)).

The word **sēstertia** is abbreviated to HS. A line is placed above the numeral: **HS $\overline{\text{XIV}}$** = *14,000 sesterces*.

sēstertium is abbreviated to HS with a line over the letters as well as the numeral: **$\overline{\text{HS}}$ $\overline{\text{XIV}}$** = *1,400,000 sesterces*. This can also be written **$\overline{\text{HS}}$ $\lfloor\overline{\text{XIV}}\rfloor$**.

Some Common Metres of Latin Verse

Quantity

The scansion of Latin verse of the classical period is quantitative, not accentual as in English. Syllables are either light or heavy, regardless of where the accent falls on any given word.

(a) All syllables are heavy which contain a long vowel or diphthong, e.g. **lāetī**, **sōlēs**, **Rōmānī**. For the purposes of scansion heavy syllables are marked with a macron –, light syllables with the symbol ˘. This convention sometimes results in a syllable containing a short vowel being marked with a macron; see below.

(b) If a short vowel is followed by two consonants, whether in the same or in different words, the syllable is heavy, e.g.

$$\bar{} \ \bar{} \mid \bar{} \ \bar{} \ \breve{} \mid \bar{} \ \text{Ro} \mid \text{ma} \ \bar{} \mid \breve{} \ \breve{} \mid \bar{} \ \bar{}$$

tan|tae | mo|lis e|rat Ro|ma|nam | con|de|re | gen|tem.

In this line the syllables underlined are heavy although in each case the vowel is short.

(c) Exceptions to rule (b): if a short vowel is followed by a combination of mute (**p, t, c, b, d, g**) and liquid (**r** and less commonly **l**), the syllable may be scanned either light or heavy, e.g. **pătris**, **volŭcris**, **latĕbrae**. This is really a question of pronunciation; such syllables can be pronounced either **pāt-ris** or **pă-tris** (**tr** making one sound).

Elision

A final open vowel followed by a vowel in the next word is elided, as in the French *c'est*, but in Latin the elision is not written, e.g.

cont[icu]|er(e) om|nes in|tentiqu(e) | ora te|nebant

The final **e** of **conticuēre** elides before the following **o** of **omnia** and the final **e** of **que** elides before the following **ō** of **ōra**.

huc se | provec|ti de|sert(o) in | litore | condunt

The final **ō** of **dēsertō** elides before the following **i** of **in**.

More surprisingly, a final syllable ending in **-m** elides before a following vowel, e.g.

pars stupet | innup|tae don(um) | exiti|ale Mi|nervae

The **-um** of **dōnum** elides before the **e** of **exitiāle**.

In reading Latin verse aloud the elided vowel or syllable should be lightly sounded.

The metres

Iambics

We start with iambics, because they are the simplest of the metres. An iambic metron (= unit of measurement) consists of two iambic feet:

˘ – ˘ –

• •

Catullus 4 is written in pure iambic trimeters, that is to say lines consisting of three iambic metra. The rhythm goes:

> te tum te tum te tum te tum te tum te tum

or more technically (counting in feet):

$$\overset{1}{\smallsmile\,-}\ \Big|\ \overset{2}{\smallsmile\,-}\ \Big|\ \overset{3}{\smallsmile_\wedge-}\ \Big|\ \overset{4}{\smallsmile_\wedge-}\ \Big|\ \overset{5}{\smallsmile\,-}\ \Big|\ \overset{6}{\smallsmile\,\smallsmile}\ \Big|$$

There is a rhythmical pause between words (called a caesura) half-way through the third or fourth foot. So the opening lines of Catullus 4 scan as follows:

> phase|lus il|le $_\wedge$ quem | vide|tis, hos|pites,
>
> ait | fuis|se $_\wedge$ na|vium | coler|rimus.

Note that the last syllable may be heavy or light.

(It is a very difficult feat to write in pure iambics, and poets usually allowed a spondee (– –) in the first, third, and fifth feet.)

Limping iambics

These scan exactly like iambic trimeters except that the last foot is a spondee (– –) or trochee (– ◡). This has a peculiar effect on the rhythm, making the line drag or limp at the end. Catullus 8 is written in this metre:

> miser | Catul|le, $_\wedge$ de|sinas | inep|tire
>
> et quod | vides | peris|se $_\wedge$ per|ditum | ducas.

Dactylic hexameters

The dactylic hexameter consists of five dactylic metra (– ◡ ◡) plus a sixth foot of two syllables. A spondee (– –) may be substituted for a dactyl in any of the first four feet; the fifth foot is nearly always a dactyl and the sixth is always a spondee or trochee (– ◡). There is usually a strong caesura (a break between words after the first long syllable of the foot) in the middle of the third foot:

> arma vi|rumque ca|no, $_\wedge$ Troi|ae qui | primus ab | oris
> *(3rd foot strong caesura)*

If there is a weak caesura (a break between words after – ◡) or no caesura in the third foot, there are usually strong caesuras in the second and fourth feet:

> quidve do|lens $_\wedge$ re|gina de|um $_\wedge$ tot | volvere | casus
> *(3rd foot weak caesura; strong caesuras in 2nd and 4th feet)*

> inde to|ro $_\wedge$ pater | Aene|as $_\wedge$ sic | orsus ab | alto
> *(no 3rd foot caesura; strong caesuras in 2nd and 4th feet)*

This is the metre used by Homer and all subsequent epic poets. Virgil uses it in his *Eclogues*, *Georgics* and *Aeneid*. Horace uses it in all the *Satires* and *Epistles*.

Elegiac couplets

These consist of a dactylic hexameter followed by the first half of the same (up to the third foot strong caesura) repeated.

$$-\ \smallsmile\smallsmile\ \Big|\ -\ \smallsmile\smallsmile\ \Big|\ -\ \smallsmile\smallsmile\ \Big|\ -\ \smallsmile\smallsmile\ \Big|\ -\ \smallsmile\smallsmile\ \Big|\ -\ \smallsmile$$

$$-\ \smallsmile\smallsmile\ \Big|\ -\ \smallsmile\smallsmile\ \Big|\ -\ \Big\|\ -\ \smallsmile\smallsmile\ \Big|\ -\ \smallsmile\smallsmile\ \Big|\ \smallsmile$$

Elegiac couplets were used for epigrams early in the Greek tradition and soon developed into longer poems; they were the first Greek metre to be used in Latin verse. Catullus was the first Roman poet to use them for longer poems (e.g. 76 and 68—the latter 160 lines long) besides epigram. They were Ovid's favourite metre; he uses them in the *Amores, Ars Amatoria, Tristia* etc.

Lyric metres

There is a wide variety of lyric metres which first appear in the Greek poems of Sappho and Alcaeus, who wrote in the Aeolic dialect about 600 BC. Horace claims to have been the first to adapt these metres to Latin poetry (*Odes* 3.30.13–14) but Catullus had in fact led the way in the previous generation.

In these metres, which are musical rhythms, we cannot speak of feet or metra; the unit is the line and many systems are constructed in four-line stanzas.

Hendecasyllables (i.e. lines of eleven syllables)

This is Catullus' favourite metre. Its rhythm goes:

> tum tum tum te te tum te tum te tum tum

or, more technically:

> $-\ \smile\ -\ \smile\ \smile\ -\ \smile\ -\ \smile\ -\ \smile$

The second syllable may be light or heavy (usually heavy). As usual the last syllable can be light or heavy.

> $-\ -\ -\ \smile\smile\ -\ \ \smile\ -\ \smile\smile\ -$
> cui dono lepidum novum libellum

> $-\smile\ -\ \ \smile\ \smile\ -\ \smile\ \ \ \smile\smile\ -\ -$
> arida modo pumic(e) expolitum?

> $-\ -\ -\smile\smile\ -\ \ \smile\ -\ \smile\smile\ -$
> Corneli, tibi: namque tu solebas ...

Sapphics

This was the favourite metre of the Greek lyric poetess Sappho, who lived in Lesbos in the sixth century BC. Catullus uses it in the first and last of his poems to Lesbia (51 and 11).

Unlike the other metres given here, it is composed in four-line stanzas. The first three lines follow the same pattern:

> tum te tum tum tum te te tum te tum tum

or more technically:

> $-\ \smile\ -\ -\ -\ \smile\smile\ -\ \smile\ -\ \smile$

The last line goes:

> tum te te tum tum

> $-\ \smile\ \smile\ -\ \smile$

The last syllable of any line as usual can be light or heavy.

> $-\smile\ -\ \ -\ \ -\ \smile\ \ \smile-\ \smile\ -\smile$
> ille mi par esse deo videtur

> $-\smile\ -\ -\ \ -\ \ \ \smile\ \ \smile-\ \smile\ \ -\ -$
> ille si fas est superare divos

> $-\ \ \smile\ -\ \ -\ \ -\ -\ \smile\ \ \smile-\smile\ \ \ -$
> qui sedens adversus identidem te

> $\quad-\ \ \smile\ \ \smile\ -\ -$
> spectat et audit.

a, **an** *indefinite article* (generally unexpressed in Latin); (one) unus, una, unum; (a certain) quidam

aback *adj*:
□ **taken** ∼ stupefactus, attonitus, consternatus

abandon *vt* relinquo, derelinquo, desero, destituo, abicio, omitto, neglego ③

abandoned *adj* derelictus; desertus; fig flagitiosus, perditus

abandonment *n* derelictio, destitutio *f*

abashed *adj* pudibundus

abbreviate *vt* imminuo, contraho ③

abbreviation *n* contractio *f*

abdicate *vt&i* me abdico ① + *abl*; depono ③

abdomen *n* abdomen *nt*

abduct *vt* rapio ③

abduction *n* raptus *m*

aberration *n* error *m*

abet *vt* adiuvo, instigo ①; faveo ② + *dat*

abetter *n* instigator, impulsor *m*

abhor *vt* abhorreo ②; detestor, aversor ①

abhorrence *n* odium *nt*

abhorrent *adj* perosus; odiosus; alienus

abide *vt* (endure) patior ③; tolero ①; subeo *ir*; exspecto ①
■ ∼ *vi* (dwell) habito ①; maneo ②
□ ∼ **by** sto ① + *abl*

ability *n* facultas; peritia *f*; ingenium *nt*
□ **to the best of one's** ∼ summa ope

abject *adj* abiectus, vilis; humilis

ablaze *adj* ardens, fervens

able *adj* potens; capax, peritus; ingeniosus
□ **be** ∼ **(to)** posse, quire *ir*; valere ②; sufficere ③

able-bodied *adj* validus, robustus, firmus

aboard *adv* in nave
□ **go** ∼ **a ship** navem conscendere ③

abode *n* domicilium *nt*; sedes *f*; (sojourn) commoratio; mansio *f*

abolish *vt* aboleo ②; exstinguo, tollo, rescindo ③

abolition *n* abolitio, dissolutio *f*

abominable *adj* detestabilis, exsecrabilis, infandus; odiosus

abomination *n* detestatio *f*; odium *nt*
□ ∼**s** (vile acts) nefaria *ntpl*

abortive *adj* abortivus; fig irritus

abound *vi* abundo, redundo ①; supersum *ir*; supero ①
□ ∼ **in** abundo ① + *abl*

abounding *adj* abundans; copiosus, largus; creber

about *prep* circa, circum, ad, apud; circiter; sub *all* + *acc*; de + *abl*
■ ∼ *adv* circiter; ferme; (more or less) quasi
□ **be** ∼ **to** … (e.g. write, etc.) scripturus, etc.
□ **go** ∼ aggredior, incipio ③
□ **bring** ∼ efficio ③

above *prep* (higher) super, supra; (beyond, more than) ante; praeter, ultra *all* + *acc*
■ ∼ *adv* supra; insuper; plus, magis; (upwards) sursum
□ **from** ∼ desuper, superne
□ **be** ∼ emineo ②; fig dedignor ①; fastidio ④
□ **over and** ∼ insuper
□ ∼ **all** super omnia

above-board *adv* aperte, candide

above-mentioned *adj* quod supra dictum est

abrasion *n* attritus *m*

abreast *adv* ex adverso

abridge *vt* contraho ③

abridgement *n* contractio *f*

abroad *adv* (out of doors) foris; (to the outside of a house) foras; (in foreign parts) peregre; (here and there) passim, undique
□ **from** ∼ extrinsecus; peregre
□ **be** *or* **live** ∼ peregrinor ①; patria careo ②

a

abrupt *adj* praeruptus; praeceps; fig subitus, repentinus; improvisus

abruptly *adv* raptim

abscess *n* ulcus *nt*

abscond *vi* me clam subduco, me abdo ③, lateo ②; latito ①

absence *n* absentia; peregrinatio *f*; fig (of mind) oblivio *f*

absent *adj* absens
□ be ∼ abesse *ir*, peregrinari ①

absentee *n* peregrinator *m*

absent-minded *adj* obliviosus

absolute *adj* absolutus; summus
■ ∼ly *adv* absolute; prorsus; (entirely) penitus

absolution *adj* absolutio; indulgentia *f*

absolve *vt* veniam do ①; absolvo ③; libero ①; dimitto ③

absorb *vt* absorbeo ②; haurio ④; combibo ③; fig teneo ②

absorbent *adj* bibulus

abstain *vi* abstineo ②

abstemious *adj* abstemius; sobrius

abstinence *n* abstinentia *f*, (fasting) ieiunium *nt*

abstinent *adj* abstinens
■ ∼ly *adv* abstinenter, continenter

abstraction *n* (concept) imago *f*

abstruse *adj* abstrusus; reconditus; obscurus, occultus
■ ∼ly *adv* abdite, occulte

absurd *adj* absurdus, insulsus; ineptus, ridiculus
■ ∼ly *adv* inepte, absurde

absurdity *n* ineptia; insulsitas; res inepta *f*

abundance *n* abundantia, copia, ubertas *f*

abundant *adj* abundans; amplus; copiosus, plenus; uber
□ be ∼ abundo ①

abundantly *adv* abunde, abundanter, copiose; effuse; (fruitfully) feliciter

abuse¹ *vt* (misuse) abutor ③ + *abl*; fig (insult, *etc*.) maledico ③ + *dat*; convicior, lacero ①

abuse² *n* (wrong use) abusus; perversus mos *m*; (insult) iniuria *f*, convicium *nt*; violatio *f*

abusive *adj* contumeliosus; maledicus
■ ∼ly *adv* contumeliose; maledice

abyss *n* profundum *nt*; (whirlpool) gurges *m*; fig vorago *f*

academic *adj* academicus
■ ∼ally *adv* ut solent academici

academy *n* Academia *f*; collegium *nt*

accede *vi* accedo, annuo ③; assentior ④

accelerate *vt* accelero, festino, appropero ①

acceleration *n* festinatio *f*

accent¹ *n* accentus; tenor; fig sonus *m*; lingua *f*

accent² *vt* (in speaking) acuo ③; (in writing) fastigo ①

accept *vt* accipio; recipio ③; (approve of) probo ①; (agree to) assentior ④ + *dat*

acceptable *adj* acceptus, gratus; iucundus

acceptance *n* acceptio; approbatio *f*

access *n* aditus; accessus *m*
□ gain ∼ admittor ③

accessible *adj* patens; fig affabilis, facilis

accession *n* (to the throne) regni principium *nt*

accessory *adj* adiunctus; (to crimes) conscius + *gen*
■ ∼ *n* particeps *m/f*, conscius *m*

accident *n* casus *m*
□ by ∼ casu, fortuito, temere

accidental *adj* fortuitus
■ ∼ly *adv* casu; fortuito

acclamation *n* acclamatio *f*, clamor, consensus, plausus *m*

acclimatize *vt* assuefacio ③

accommodate *vt* accommodo, apto ①; fig (have room for) capio ③

accommodation *n* (lodging) deversorium *nt*

accompany *vt* comitor ①; (escort) deduco ③; mus concino ③

accomplice *n* particeps, conscius + *gen*; (in crimes *or* vices) satelles *m*

accomplish *vt* exsequor, perficio; perago ③; impleo ②

accomplished *adj* eruditus; doctus

accomplishment *n* exsecutio, effectio; (skill) ars *f*

accord¹ *n* consensus *m*, concordia *f*
□ of one's own ∼ sponte; ultro
□ with one ∼ uno ore

accord² *vt* (grant) concedo ③
■ ~ *vi* (agree) congruo ③; concordo ①; convenio ④

accordance *n* ▶ accord *n*
□ **in ~ with** secundum + *acc*

according *prep*:
□ ~ **to** de, ex, pro *all* + *abl*; secundum + *acc*

accordingly *adv* itaque; ita; (therefore) igitur, ergo

account¹ *n* (reckoning, of money) ratio; (narrative) memoria; narratio; (esteem) reputatio *f*; (advantage) commodum *nt*
□ **on ~ of** ob, propter + *acc*
□ **on that ~** propterea; ideo
□ **call to ~** rationem posco ③
□ **of little** *or* **no ~** nullius pretii, vilis
□ **take into ~** rationem habeo ② + *gen*

account² *vt* (esteem) aestimo ①; habeo ②; pendo, pono ③
□ ~ **for** *vi* rationem reddo ③

accountable *adj* reus, rationem reddere debens

accountant *n* tabularius *m*

accrue *vi* orior; accresco ③; provenio ④

accumulate *vt* accumulo, coacervo ①; congero ③
■ ~ *vi* cresco; congeror ③

accumulation *n* (heap) cumulus; acervus; fig congestus *m*

accuracy *n* cura; subtilitas *f*

accurate *adj* accuratus; subtilis
■ ~**ly** *adv* accurate, subtiliter

accusation *n* accusatio *f*; crimen *nt*

accuse *vt* accuso; criminor ①; (blame) reprehendo ③

accuser *n* accusator; (informer) delator *m*

accustom *vt* assuefacio ③
□ ~ **oneself** assuefieri *ir*, consuescere ③
□ **be ~ed** soleo ②

accustomed *adj* assuetus, consuetus, solitus

ache¹ *vi* doleo ②
□ **my head ~s** caput mihi dolet

ache² *n* dolor *m*

achieve *vt* patro ①; consequor, conficio, perficio ③

achievement *n* res gesta *f*; facinus *nt*

aching *n* dolor *m*

acid *adj* acidus; acidulus

acidity *n* aciditas *f*

acknowledge *vt* agnosco, recognosco ③; fateor, confiteor ②

acknowledgement *n* agnitio; confessio *f*

acme *n* fastigium *nt*; (the acme of folly) summa dementia *f*

aconite *n* aconitum *nt*

acorn *n* glans *f*
■ ~**-bearing** *adj* glandifer

acquaint *vt* certiorem facio ③
□ ~ **oneself (with)** noscere, cognoscere ③

acquaintance *n* scientia; (friendship) familiaritas; notitia *f*; (person) familiaris *m/f*

acquainted *adj* (with) gnarus; prudens; peritus *all* + *gen*
□ **become ~** noscere, cognoscere ③

acquiesce *vi* acquiesco, inacquiesco ③; assentior ④; probo ①

acquiescence *n* assensus *m*; approbatio *f*

acquire *vt* comparo ①; nanciscor, consequor, pario, adipiscor ③; fig disco ③

acquisition *n* (acquiring) conciliatio, comparatio *f*; (thing acquired) quaesitum *nt*

acquit *vt* absolvo ③; libero, purgo ①
□ ~ **oneself** se gerere ③

acquittal *n* absolutio *f*

acre *n* iugerum *nt*

acrid *adj* acerbus, acer

acrimonious *adj* acerbus; fig asper, truculentus

acrimony *n* acrimonia; amaritudo *f*

acrobat *n* funambulus *m*

across *prep* trans + *acc*
■ ~ *adv* ex transverso, in transversum

act¹ *vi* ago, facio; gero ③; (behave) me gero ③; (exert force) vim habeo ②; (on the stage) in scaenam prodeo *ir*
■ ~ *vt* (as actor) (comoediam, primam partem) ago ③

act² *n* (deed, action) factum, gestum *nt*; (exploit) facinus *nt*; (decree) decretum *m*; (in a play) actus *m*
□ **be caught in the ~** deprehendor ③
■ ~**s** *pl* acta *ntpl*

action *n* actio *f*; actus *m*; (battle) pugna *f*; (gesture) gestus *m*; (law) actio *f*

a

□ **bring an ~ against someone** actionem alicui intendere ③

active *adj* agilis; impiger, industrius, operosus; strenuus; vividus
■ **~ly** *adv* impigre; strenue

activity *n* agilitas, mobilitas; industria, navitas *f*

actor *n* (in a play) comoedus, histrio; mimus; artifex scaenicus; (doer) auctor; qui agit *m*

actress *n* mima *f*

actual *adj* verus, ipse
■ **~ly** *adv* re vera, re ipsa

acumen *n* sagacitas *f*; ingenium *nt*

acute *adj* acutus; acer; (perspicacious) sagax, subtilis
■ **~ly** *adv* acute; acriter; (shrewdly) sagaciter

adamant *n* adamas *m*

adapt *vt* accommodo, apto ①

adaptable *adj* habilis

adaptation *n* accommodatio *f*

add *vt* addo; appono, adiungo, adicio ③; (in speaking) adicio ③; (in writing) subiungo ③
□ **~ up** computo ①
□ **be ~ed** accedo ③

adder *n* coluber *m*, vipera *f*

addicted *adj* deditus, studiosus
□ **be ~ (to)** deditus esse

addition *n* additamentum *nt*; adiectio; accessio *f*
■ **in ~** *adv* insuper

addle-headed *adj* inanis, vanus, fatuus, stultus

address[1] *vt* (direct to) inscribo ③; (speak to) alloquor, aggredior ③

address[2] *n* (speaking to) alloquium *nt*; allocutio; (direction) inscriptio *f*; (petition) libellus supplex *m*; (speech) oratio, contio *f*

adduce *vt* (witnesses) profero *ir*; (quote) cito ①; adduco ③

adept *adj* peritus

adequate *adj* sufficiens, par

adhere *vi* adhaereo; cohaereo ②; fig sto (in) ① + *abl*

adherent *n* assectator; fautor; particeps *m/f*; socius *m*; (dependant) cliens *m*

adhesive *adj* tenax, lentus

adieu *int* ave, salve, vale
□ **bid ~** valedico ③; valere iubeo ②

adjacent *adj* confinis, conterminus; vicinus

adjoining *adj* adiacens, confinis, vicinus

adjourn *vt* comperendino ①; differo, profero ③
■ **~** *vi* differror *ir*

adjournment *n* dilatio, prolatio *f*

adjudge *vt* adiudico ①

adjudicate *vt* addico, decerno ③

adjudication *n* addictio; (verdict) sententia *f*, arbitrium *nt*

adjust *vt* apto ①; dispono ③; (settle) compono ③; ordino ①

adjustment *n* accommodatio, compositio *f*

adjutant *n* optio *m*

administer *vt* (manage) administro, curo, procuro ①; (medicine) adhibeo ②; (an oath) adigo ③; (justice) exerceo ②; reddo ③

administration *n* administratio; cura; procuratio *f*; magistratus *m*; (of public affairs) summa rerum *f*

administrator *n* administrator; procurator *m*

admirable *adj* admirabilis; mirabilis, admirandus; insignis

admirably *adv* admirabiliter; praeclare, insigniter

admiral *n* praefectus classis *m*

admiration *n* admiratio *f*

admire *vt* admiror; amo ①

admirer *n* admirator; mirator; laudator; amans *m*

admission *n* admissio *f*; aditus, accessus *m*; (confession) confessio *f*

admit *vt* admitto; recipio, introduco; (adopt) ascisco ③; (confess) fateor, confiteor ②
□ **it is ~ted** constat ①

admittance *n* admissio *f*, aditus, accessus *m*

admonish *vt* moneo, commoneo ②

admonition *n* monitio, admonitio; adhortatio *f*; monitum *nt*

admonitory *adj* monitorius

ado *n* tumultus *m*
□ **with much ~** aegre, vix
□ **without more ~** statim

adolescence *n* adolescentia *f*

adolescent *adj* adolescens

adopt *vt* (a child) adopto, (an adult) arrogo ①; fig ascisco; assumo ③; (a policy) capio ③; ineo ④

adoption *n* adoptio, adoptatio; (of an adult) arrogatio; fig assumptio *f*

adoptive *adj* adoptivus

adorable *adj* adorandus, venerandus; (lovable) amandus

adoration *n* adoratio *f*; (love) amor *m*

adore *vt* adoro, veneror, fig admiror, amo ①

adorer *n* cultor *m*; (lover) amator *m*

adorn *vt* orno, decoro, illustro ①; excolo, como ③

adornment *n* exornatio *f*; ornatus *m*; ornamentum *nt*

adrift *adj* in salo fluctuans
■ **be** ~ *vi* fluctuor ①

adroit *adj* callidus, dexter, sollers, peritus, ingeniosus
■ ~**ly** *adv* callide, sollerter, perite, ingeniose

adroitness *n* dexteritas *f*

adulation *n* adulatio, assentatio *f*

adult *adj* adultus; pubes
■ ~ *n* adultus homo *m*

adulterate *vt* adultero, vitio ①; corrumpo ③

adulterer *n* adulter; moechus *m*

adulteress *n* adultera; moecha *f*

adulterous *adj* adulterinus
■ ~**ly** *adv* adulterio, per adulterium

adultery *n* adulterium; stuprum *nt*
□ **commit** ~ moechor ①

advance¹ *vt* promoveo ②; (lift up) tollo, attollo ③; exalto ①; (an opinion) exhibeo ②; profero *ir*; (lend) commodo ①; (accelerate) maturo ①
□ ~ **someone's interests** alicui consulo ③; rebus alicuius studeo ②
■ ~ *vi* procedo, progredior, incedo ③; mil gradum *or* pedem infero *ir*; fig proficio ③

advance² *n* progressus *m*; (attack) incursio *f*; (in rank) accessio dignitatis *f*; (increase, rise) incrementum *nt*

advanced *adj* provectus; (of age) grandis

advance-guard *n* antecursores *mpl*, primum agmen *nt*

advantage *n* lucrum, commodum, emolumentum *nt*; utilitas *f*; fructus; usus *m*; (blessings) bona *ntpl*
□ **have the** ~ **over** praesto ① + *dat*; superior sum *ir*
□ **make** *or* **take** ~ **of** utor ③ + *abl*
□ **be of** ~ **to** prosum *ir* + *dat*

advantageous *adj* fructuosus; utilis; commodus
■ ~**ly** *adv* utiliter; bene; commode

advent *n* adventus *m*

adventure *n* casus *m*; (as action) facinus *nt*

adventurous *adj* audax
■ ~**ly** *adv* audacter

adversary *n* adversarius *m*; inimicus *m*; inimica *f*

adverse *adj* adversus, infestus; fig asper
■ ~**ly** *adv* secus, infeliciter

adversity *n* res adversae *fpl*; calamitas *f*; res asperae *fpl*

advertise *vt* (publish) divulgo ①; (try to sell) vendito ①

advertisement *n* venditatio ①

advertiser *n* venditator *m*

advice *n* consilium *nt*; (information, intelligence) indicium *nt*
□ **ask** ~ consulo ③
□ **give** ~ moneo ②

advisable *adj* commodus, utilis
□ **it is** ~ expedit ④

advise *vt* moneo; (recommend) suadeo ② + *dat*; consulo ③; (counsel against) dissuadeo ②; (exhort) hortor ①; (inform) certiorem facio ③

adviser *n* consultor, monitor, suasor, auctor *m*

advocacy *n* patrocinium *nt*

advocate¹ *n* advocatus, causidicus; patronus; (one who recommends) suasor *m*; (defender) defensor *m*

advocate² *vt* suadeo ②

aedile *n* aedilis *m*

aegis *n* aegis *f*

afar *adv* procul, longe
□ **from** ~ e longinquo

affability *n* comitas, affabilitas, facilitas *f*

affable *adj* affabilis, comis, facilis

affably *adv* comiter

affair *n* res *f*; negotium *nt*

affect *vt* afficio ③; commoveo ②; percutio ③; (pretend) simulo ①

affection *n* (of mind *or* body) affectus *m*; affectio *f*; (love) amor *m*; gratia;

benevolentia *f*; (feeling) affectus, impetus, motus; sensus *m*

affectionate *adj* amans, benevolus, pius; blandus
■ ~**ly** *adv* amanter; pie, blande

affinity *n* affinitas; cognatio, proximitas *f*

affirm *vt* affirmo, assevero, testificor ①

affirmation *n* affirmatio *f*; asseveratio *nt*

affix *vt* affigo ③

afflict *vt* torqueo ②; vexo, crucio ①

affliction *n* miseria *f*; res adversae *fpl*

affluence *n* abundantia, copia *f*; (wealth) divitiae *fpl*

affluent *adj* abundans, affluens; (rich) dives

afford *vt* praebeo ②; (yield) reddo ③, fero *ir*, fundo ③; (supply) sufficio ③; (buy) emo ③

affront¹ *vt* irrito ①; contumelia afficio ③

affront² *n* contumelia, iniuria *f*

afloat *vi*:
□ **be** ~ navigo ①, navi vehor ③

afoot *adv*:
□ **be** ~ parari ①

afraid *adj* timidus, pavidus
□ **be** ~ (**of**) timeo ②; (much) pertimesco; expavesco ③
□ **make** ~ terreo ②; territo ①
□ **not** ~ impavidus, intrepidus

afresh *adv* de integro, ab integro, iterum, denuo

after *prep* post + *acc*; a, de, e, ex + *abl*; (following immediately upon) sub; (of degree *or* succession) iuxta; secundum; (in imitation of) ad *all* + *acc*
□ **one** ~ **another** alius ex alio
■ ~ *adv* (afterwards) exinde, postea, posterius; post
□ ~ **all** tamen; saltem
□ **a little** ~ paulo post
□ **the day** ~ postridie
■ ~ *conj* (when) postquam, posteaquam

after-ages *n* posteritas *f*

afternoon *n* post meridiem *nt*
■ ~ *adj* postmeridianus, pomeridianus

afterthought *n* posterior cogitatio *f*

afterwards *adv* post; postea; deinde, deinceps, dehinc

again *adv* iterum, denuo, rursum, rursus; (likewise, in turn) invicem, mutuo, vicissim; contra; (besides) praeterea

□ **over** ~ ab integro
□ ~ **and** ~ iterum atque iterum

against *prep* (opposite to) contra; adversus; (denoting attack) in; (by, at) ad, ante *all* + *acc*
□ **be** ~ adversor, oppugno ①
□ **fight** ~ pugno cum

age *n* aetas *f*; (century) saeculum; (time in general) tempus *nt*; (old ~) senectus *f*
□ **under** ~ impubis
□ **of the same** ~ aequaevus

aged *adj* aetate provectus; senilis; (of a certain age) natus + *acc of* annus
□ ~ **five** natus annos quinque

agent *n* actor *m*; auctor; (assistant) satelles *m/f*; administer *m*

aggrandize *vt* amplifico ①; attollo ③; augeo ②

aggrandizement *n* amplificatio *f*; incrementum *nt*

aggravate *vt* augeo ②; exaggero ①

aggravation *n* exaggeratio *f*

aggression *n* incursio *f*

aggressive *adj* arma (ultro) inferens; (pugnacious) pugnax

aggrieved *adj*:
□ **feel** ~ aegre fero *ir*

aghast *adj* attonitus, consternatus

agile *adj* agilis; pernix

agility *n* agilitas; pernicitas *f*

agitate *vt* agito ①; commoveo ②; perturbo ①
■ ~**d** *adj* tumultuosus; turbulentus; (anxious) sollicitus

agitation *n* agitatio; commotio; iactatio *f*; *fig* tumultus *m*; trepidatio *f*

agitator *n* concitator; turbator (populi *or* vulgi) *m*

ago *adv* abhinc
□ **long** ~ iamdudum
□ **how long** ~**?** quamdudum
□ **some time** ~ pridem

agog *adv* (astonished) attonitus

agonizing *adj* crucians

agony *n* dolor; cruciatus *m*

agree *vi* (be in agreement) congruo ③; concordo ①; concino ③; consentio ④; (make a bargain) paciscor ③; (be agreeable) placeo ②; (assent) annuo ③; assentior ④
□ **it is** ~**d** constat ①

agreeable *adj* gratus, acceptus; amabilis
□ **very** ~ pergratus

agreeably *adv* grate, iucunde; suaviter

agreement *n* consensus *m*; (covenant) pactum *nt*; stipulatio *f*; conventum *nt*; (bargain) condicio *f*; (harmonious arrangement) concinnitas *f*; fig (harmony) consensio *f*

agricultural *adj* rusticus

agriculture *n* agri cultura *f*; res rustica *f*

aground *adv*:
□ **run ~** in terram appello; (be stranded) eicior ③
□ **be ~** (touch bottom) sido ③

ah *int* ah! eia! vah! vae!

ahead *adv* ante
□ **get ~ of** praetereo *ir*

aid[1] *n* auxilium; subsidium *nt*
□ **with the ~ of** opera

aid[2] *vt* adiuto, iuvo ① + *acc*; succurro ③ + *dat*; subvenio ④ + *dat*

aide-de-camp *n* optio *m*

ailment *n* malum *nt*; morbus *m*; aegritudo, aegrotatio *f*

aim[1] *n* propositum *nt*

aim[2] *vt* intendo; dirigo, tendo ③; fig (~ at) affecto; specto ①; expeto ③; molior ④

air[1] *n* aer *m*, aura *f*; (sky) caelum *nt*; fig habitus; gestus *m*; (appearance) species *f*; (tune) numeri *mpl*, modus *m*
□ **in the open ~** sub divo

air[2] *vt* sicco ①
□ **~ opinions** profero *ir*

airy *adj* aerius; apertus, patens, ventosus; fig levis

aisle *n* ala *f*

ajar *adj* (of doors) semiapertus; semiadapertus

akin *adj* cognatus; propinquus; fig finitimus, cognatus

alacrity *n* alacritas *f*; studium *nt*

alarm[1] *n* (signal in war) classicum *nt*; (sudden fear) trepidatio *f*; tumultus *m*

alarm[2] *vt* terreo ②; consterno ③; territo ①
□ **be ~ed** perturbor ①

alarming *adj* terribilis

alas *int* eheu! heu, hei mihi misero! (alas for the conquered!) vae victis!

alcove *n* (corner) angulus *m*

alder *n* alnus *f*

alert *adj* alacer, promptus, vigil

alertness *n* alacritas *f*

alien *adj & n* peregrinus; alienigena *m*

alienate *vt* alieno; abalieno ①; fig averto ③

alienation *n* abalienatio; alienatio; (estrangement) disiunctio, alienatio *f*

alight[1] *vi* descendo ③; (from a horse) desilio ④; (of birds) insido ③

alight[2] *adj* ardens

alike *adj* aequus, par, similis
■ **~** *adv* pariter, similiter

alive *adj* vivus; fig vividus, alacer
□ **be ~** vivo ③; supersum *ir*

all[1] *adj* omnis, cunctus; universus; (whole) totus; (every one individually) unusquisque
□ **by ~ means** quoquomodo
□ **on ~ sides** ubique, passim, undique
□ **~ this while** usque adhuc
□ **~ the better** tanto melius
□ **~ the more** eo plus
□ **it is ~ over with** actum est de + *abl*
□ **it is ~ one to me** nihil mea interest

all[2] *n* omnia *ntpl*
□ **at ~** omnino
□ **not at ~** nihil (nullus *etc.*) admodum
□ **in ~** in summa

allay *vt* lenio ④; mitigo ①; (quench) restinguo ③; sedo ①

allegation *n* affirmatio *f*

allege *vt* arguo ③; affirmo ①; (bring forward) affero *ir*

allegiance *n* fides *f*

alleviate *vt* levo, allevo, sublevo ①

alleviation *n* levamen *nt*

alley *n* (narrow street) angiportus *m*; ambulatio *f*

alliance *n* (by blood) consanguinitas *f*; (by marriage) affinitas *f*; (of states) foedus *nt*; (mutual connection) societas *f*

allied *adj* cognatus; propinquus; (of states) foederatus, socius

all-mighty *adj* omnipotens

allot *vt* distribuo ③; assigno ①; tribuo ③; do ①

allotment *n* assignatio, portio; pars *f*

allow *vt* concedo, permitto ③; (permit) patior, sino ③
□ **~ of** admitto ③; (confess) fateor, confiteor ②
□ **~ for** indulgeo ② + *dat*
□ **I am ~ed** licet + *dat*

allowable *adj* licitus, concessus

allowance *n* (daily ration of food) cibarium *nt*
□ **make ∼s for** indulgeo ② + *dat*

alloy[1] *n* mixtura *f*

alloy[2] *vt* misceo ②; vitio ③; adultero ①

all-powerful *adj* omnipotens

allude *vi* (∼ to) attingo ③; designo, denoto; specto ①

allure *vt* allicio ③; allecto ①

allurement *n* illecebra *f*; fig blandimentum *nt*; blanditiae *fpl*

alluring *adj* blandus
■ **∼ly** *adv* blande

allusion *n* significatio *f*

allusive *adj* obliquus
■ **∼ly** *adv* oblique

ally[1] *n* socius *m*

ally[2] *vt* socio ①

almighty *adj* omnipotens

almond *n* amygdala *f*; amygdalum *nt*

almost *adv* fere, paene, prope; tantum non
□ **it ∼ happens that** paulum abest ut, hand multum abest ut

alms *n* stips *f*

aloft *adv* sublime

alone *adj* solus; unus; solitarius
■ **∼** *adv* solum; tantum
□ **leave ∼** desero ③
□ **let ∼** omitto, mitto ③

along *prep* secundum, praeter + *acc*
□ **∼ with** cum + *abl*

aloof *adv* procul
□ **stand ∼** discedo ③; removeo (me) ②; non attingo ③

aloud *adv* clara voce, clare

alpine *adj* Alpinus

already *adv* iam

also *adv* etiam; item, quoque, necnon; (moreover) praeterea, porro, insuper

altar *n* ara *f*; altaria *ntpl*

alter *vt* muto, commuto, vario, novo ①; verto ③
■ **∼** *vi* mutor, commutor ① *etc.*

alterable *adj* mutabilis, commutabilis

alteration *n* mutatio; commutatio *f*

altercation *n* altercatio *f*, iurgium *nt*

alternate[1] *adj* alternus

alternate[2] *vt&i* alterno, vario ①

alternately *adv* in vicem, per vices; alternis

alternation *n* vicissitudo *f*; vices *fpl*

alternative *n* (condition) condicio *f*; (refuge) refugium *nt*
□ **I have no ∼** nihil mihi reliqui est
■ **∼** *adj* alternus

although *conj* etsi, tametsi, quamquam, quamvis, licet

altitude *n* altitudo, sublimitas *f*

altogether *adv* omnino; prorsus; plane, penitus

always *adv* semper; in aeternum

am *vi* sum *ir* ► **be**

amalgamate *vt* misceo ②
■ **∼** *vi* coeo *ir*

amalgamation *n* mixtura *f*; (combination) coitus *m*

amaranth *n* amarantus *m*

amass *vt* coacervo, cumulo ①

amateur *adj* (unskilful) rudis, imperitus

amaze *vt* obstupefacio ③

amazed *adj* attonitus, stupefactus
□ **be ∼** stupeo ②; obstupesco ③

amazement *n* stupor *m*

amazing *adj* mirus, mirabilis, mirandus
■ **∼ly** *adv* mirabiliter, admirabiliter

ambassador *n* legatus *m*

amber *n* sucinum, electrum *nt*
■ **∼** *adj* sucineus

ambiguity *n* ambiguitas *f*, ambages *fpl*

ambiguous *adj* ambiguus, dubius, anceps
■ **∼ly** *adv* ambigue

ambition *n* ambitio *f*

ambitious *adj* laudis *or* gloriae cupidus; ambitiosus
■ **∼ly** *adv* ambitiose

amble *vi* tolutim incedo ③

amblingly *adv* tolutim

ambrosia *n* ambrosia *f*

ambrosial *adj* ambrosius

ambush *n* insidiae *fpl*
□ **lie in ∼** insidior ①

ameliorate *vt* meliorem *or* melius facio *ir*
■ **∼** *vi* melior *or* melius fio ③

amenable *adj* oboediens, docilis

amend *vt* emendo ①; corrigo ③
■ **∼** *vi* proficio ③

amendment *n* correctio, emendatio *f*

amends *n*:
- □ **make** ~ expio ⟨1⟩; satisfacio, luo ⟨3⟩; compenso ⟨1⟩

amenity *n* amoenitas *f*

amiability *n* lenitas, humanitas, suavitas *f*

amiable *adj* amabilis, suavis, lenis, humanus

amiably *adv* amabiliter, suaviter, leniter, humaniter

amicable *adj* pacatus; benevolus; benignus

amicably *adv* pacate; amice, benevole

amid *prep* (also **amidst**) inter + *acc*

amiss *adv* perperam, prave, male; secus

ammunition *n* arma *ntpl*; apparatus bellicus *m*

amnesty *n* impunitas, venia, oblivio *f*

amok *adv*:
- □ **run** ~ furo ⟨3⟩

among *prep* (also **amongst**) inter; apud; ad *all* + *acc*
- □ **from** ~st e, ex + *abl*

amorous *adj* amatorius; amore captus

amount[1] *n* summa *f*

amount[2] *vi*:
- □ **it** ~s **to the same thing** idem est, par est

amphitheatre *n* amphitheatrum *nt*

ample *adj* amplus; copiosus; largus; (enough) satis

amplification *n* amplificatio *f*

amplify *vt* dilato; amplifico ⟨1⟩

amply *adv* ample, abunde, satis

amputate *vt* amputo; seco ⟨1⟩

amputation *n* amputatio; sectio *f*

amuse *vt* oblecto, delecto ⟨1⟩
- □ ~ **oneself** ludo ⟨3⟩; mihi placeo ⟨2⟩

amusement *n* delectatio, oblectatio *f*; delectamentum, oblectamentum *nt*; (game) ludus *m*

amusing *adj* festivus; (funny) iocosus

analyse *vt* enodo, explico ⟨1⟩

anarchical *adj* fig turbulentus

anarchist *n* civis seditiosus et turbulentus *m*

anarchy *n* licentia *f*

ancestor *n* avus, proavus, atavus; auctor *m*
- ■ ~s *pl* maiores; priores *mpl*

ancestral *adj* avitus, proavitus

ancestry *n* stirps *f*; genus *nt*;
- ▶ **ancestors**

anchor[1] *n* ancora *f*
- □ **weigh** ~ ancoram tollo *or* solvo ⟨3⟩
- □ **cast** ~ ancoram iacio ⟨3⟩
- □ **ride at** ~ in ancoris consisto ⟨3⟩

anchor[2] *vt&i* ancoras iacio ⟨3⟩; (of ships) sto ⟨1⟩

anchorage *n* statio *f*

ancient *adj* antiquus, vetus, vetustus; priscus; (former) pristinus
- □ **from** ~ **times** antiquitus
- □ **the** ~s (fore-fathers, ancestors) veteres, priores *mpl*; (authors) antiqui *mpl*; (abstractly) antiquitas *f*

and *conj* et, ac, atque; -que; necnon

anecdote *n* fabella; narratiuncula *f*

anew *adv* denuo; ab integro

anger[1] *n* ira, iracundia, bilis *f*; furor *m*

anger[2] *vt* irrito, exacerbo ⟨1⟩; commoveo ⟨2⟩

angle *n* angulus *m*

angler *n* piscator *m*

angrily *adv* iracunde, irate

angry *adj* iratus, iracundus
- □ **be** ~ irascor ⟨3⟩; suscenseo ⟨2⟩; stomachor ⟨1⟩
- □ **make** ~ irrito, exacerbo ⟨1⟩

anguish *n* angor, dolor *m*

anguished *adj* animo fractus

angular *adj* angularis; (full of angles) angulosus

animal *n* animal *nt*; (wild beast) fera *f*; (beast) pecus *f*

animate[1] *vt* (give life to) animo; fig hortor; excito ⟨1⟩; erigo ⟨3⟩

animate[2] *adj* (living) animans; (of nature) vividus

animated *adj* (lively) vividus, alacer

animation *n* alacritas *f*; ardor; spiritus *m*

animosity *n* (grudge) simultas, acerbitas, malevolentia *f*; odium *nt*

ankle *n* (**ankle-bone**) talus *m*

annals *n* annales, fasti *mpl*

annex *vt* annecto, adiungo, suppono ⟨3⟩; (seize) rapio ⟨3⟩

annihilate *vt* deleo ⟨2⟩; exstinguo, everto ⟨3⟩

annihilation *n* exstinctio; internecio *f*; (ruin) excidium *nt*

a

anniversary *adj* anniversarius; annuus
■ ∼ *n* festus dies anniversarius *m*

annotate *vt* annoto, commentor ①

annotation *n* annotatio; nota *f*

announce *vt* nuntio; (report) renuntio ①; (laws) promulgo ①

announcement *n* nuntiatio; renuntiatio *f*; (news) nuntius *m*

annoy *vt* incommodo ①; male habeo ②; (vex) irrito ①
□ **be** ∼**ed** stomachor ①; offensus sum

annoyance *n* molestia *f*; (anger) ira *f*

annoying *adj* molestus, incommodus

annual *adj* anniversarius, annuus
■ ∼**ly** *adv* quotannis

annul *vt* abrogo ①; rescindo, tollo ③

annulment *n* abolitio, abrogatio *f*

anoint *vt* ungo, inungo, perungo ③

anointer *n* unctor *m*

anointing *n* unctio *f*

anon *adv* statim, illico; mox

anonymous *adj*:
■ ∼**ly** *adv* sine nomine

another *adj* alius
□ ∼**'s** alienus
□ **one** ∼ alius alium, inter nos (vos, se)

answer[1] *vt* respondeo ②; (in writing) rescribo ③; (correspond to) respondeo ②
□ ∼ **for** rationem reddo ③; praesto ①

answer[2] *n* responsio *f*, responsum *nt*; (of an oracle) sors *f*; (solution of a problem) explicatio *f*

answerable *adj* (responsible) reus; obnoxius
□ **be** ∼ praesto ①
□ **make** ∼ obligo ①

answering *adj* congruens; (echoing) resonus

ant *n* formica *f*

antagonism *n* adversitas *f*; (dislike) inimicitia *f*

antagonist *n* adversarius *m*; adversatrix *f*; aemulus, hostis, inimicus *m*

antechamber *n* vestibulum *nt*

antelope *n* dorcas *f*

anthem *n* canticum *nt*

anticipate *vt* anticipo ①; praesumo ③; (forestall) praevenio ④

anticipation *n* anticipatio; praesumptio *f*

antidote *n* antidotum *nt*; antidotus *f*; remedium *nt*

antipathy *n* odium, fastidium *nt*

antiquarian *n* (also **antiquary**) antiquarius, rerum antiquarum studiosus; rerum antiquarum peritus *m*

antiquated *adj* obsoletus

antique[1] *adj* antiquus

antique[2] *n* opus antiqui artificis; monumentum antiquitatis *nt*

antiquity *n* antiquitas; vetustas *f*

antler *n* ramus *m*

anvil *n* incus *f*

anxiety *n* anxietas; sollicitudo, trepidatio *f*

anxious *adj* anxius; sollicitus; trepidus
□ **be** ∼ **(to)** laboro (ut *or* ne) ①; anxius sum de aliqua re

anxiously *adv* anxie; sollicite; trepide

any *pn* quivis, quilibet; (*after negative*) ullus; (*after* si, nisi, num, ne) quis; (interrogatively) ecquis; (all) omnis
□ ∼ **longer** diutius
□ ∼ **more** amplius
□ **at** ∼ **time** unquam

anybody *pn* quivis, quilibet; (*after negative*) quisquam; (*after* si, nisi, num, ne) quis; (interrogatively) ecquis; (all) omnis

anyhow *adv* quoquomodo

anything *pn* quicquam, quidpiam, quodvis; (*after* si, nisi, num, ne) quid

anywhere *adv* ubilibet, alicubi, ubivis
□ **if** ∼ sicubi

apace *adv* celeriter; cito, propere

apart *adv* seorsum, separatim
□ ∼ **from** praeter, extra + *acc*
□ **stand** ∼ disto ①
□ **set** ∼ sepono ③

apartment *n* conclave *nt*

apathetic *adj* lentus; socors

apathy *n* stupor *m*; ignavia, socordia, lentitudo *f*

ape *n* simius *m*; simia *f*
■ ∼ *vt* imitor ①

aperture *n* apertura *f*; foramen *nt*

apex *n* cacumen *nt*; apex *m*

aphorism *n* sententia *f*

apiece *adv* singuli (*pl*); quisque

apologize *vt* excuso ①; defendo, veniam peto ③

apology *n* excusatio; defensio; (written treatise) apologia *f*
□ **make an ~ for** excuso ①

appal *vt* exterreo ②; percello ③

appalling *adj* horrendus

apparatus *n* apparatus *m*

apparel *n* vestis *f*, vestitus *m*

apparent *adj* manifestus; (feigned) simulatus, fictus
□ **be ~** appareo, videor ②

apparently *adv* (plainly) aperte, manifeste; (pretendedly) per speciem
□ **he is ~ dead** mortuus esse videtur

apparition *n* spectrum, simulacrum *nt*

appeal¹ *vi* appello; provoco; obsecro ①

appeal² *n* (law) appellatio; provocatio; (entreaty) obsecratio *f*

appealing *adj* (pleading) supplex; (charming) lepidus

appear *vi* appareo, compareo ②; me ostendo ③; (seem) videor ②; (arise) exorior ④; surgo ③; (before a court) me sisto ③
□ **it ~s** patet, liquet ②

appearance *n* (becoming visible) aspectus *m*; (outward show) species *f*; (vision) spectrum *nt*; (arrival) adventus *m*
□ **first ~** exortus *m*
□ **to all ~s he has been killed** occisus esse videtur

appease *vt* placo, mitigo, expio; (hunger) sedo ①

append *vt* addo ③

appendage *n* appendix; accessio; appendicula *f*

appertain *vt* (to) pertineo ad; attineo ad ② + *acc*

appetite *n* appetitus *m*; cupiditas *f*
□ **have an ~** esurio ④

applaud *vt* applaudo ③; laudo ①; plaudo ③

applause *n* plausus, applausus *m*; laus *f*

apple *n* malum, pomum *nt*; (of the eye) pupula, pupilla *f*

apple-tree *n* malus *f*

appliance *n* (instrument) instrumentum *nt*

applicable *adj* commodus, conveniens
□ **not be ~** alienum esse *ir*

applicant *n* petitor *m*

application *n* (use) usus *m*; usurpatio *f*; (zeal) studium *nt*, sedulitas, diligentia, cura *f*

apply *vt* adhibeo; admoveo ②; appono ③; apto, accommodo ①
■ **~** *vi* pertineo ②; (~ to someone for something) aggredior ③

appoint *vt* creo ①; facio ③; designo, destino ①; constituo ③

appointment *n* (office) munus *nt*; (order) mandatum; (rendezvous) constitutum *nt*

apportion *vt* divido, distribuo ③

apposite *adj* aptus, idoneus; appositus
■ **~ly** *adv* apte; apposite

appraisal *n* aestimatio *f*

appraise *vt* aestimo ①

appreciable *adj* qui aestimari potest

appreciate *vt* aestimo ①; (value highly) magni facio ③

appreciation *n* aestimatio; (praise) laus *f*

apprehend *vt* comprehendo, apprehendo; percipio ③; (fear) timeo ②; (suspect) suspicor ①; (seize) capio; (take unawares) intercipio; (arrest) comprehendo ③

apprehension *n* (fear) timor *m*; (suspicion) suspicio; (seizing) comprehensio *f*; (understanding) ingenium *nt*, intelligentia *f*

apprehensive *adj* timidus

apprentice *n* discipulus; tiro *m*

apprenticeship *n* tirocinium *nt*

approach *vt&i* appropinquo ① + *dat*; accedo ③; adeo *ir*; (be imminent) immineo ②; insto ①

approachable *adj* patens; fig affabilis, facilis

approbation *n* approbatio, laus *f*

appropriate¹ *vt* mihi arrogo ①; mihi assero ③; vindico ①; assumo ③

appropriate² *adj* proprius; congruens
■ **~ly** *adv* apte, congruenter

appropriateness *n* convenientia *f*

approval *n* approbatio *f*

approve *vt* approbo, probo, laudo ①

approximate *adj* propinquus

approximately *adv* fere, prope

April *n* Aprilis *m*

apron *n* subligaculum *nt*

a

apt *adj* aptus, idoneus; (inclined, prone) pronus, propensus, proclivis

aptitude *n* habilitas *f*; ingenium *nt*

aptly *adv* apte, apposite

aptness *n* convenientia, congruentia; (tendency, propensity) proclivitas *f*

aquatic *adj* aquatilis; aquaticus

aqueduct *n* aquae ductus, aquarum ductus *m*

Arab *n* Arabius *m*

arable *adj* arabilis
■ ~ **land** *n* arvum, novale *nt*; novalis *f*

arbiter *n* arbiter; dominus *m*

arbitrarily *adv* ad arbitrium; ad libidinem

arbitrary *adj* imperiosus; superbus

arbitrate *vt&i* discepto, diiudico ①

arbitration *n* arbitrium *nt*

arbitrator *n* arbiter; (private) disceptator *m*

arbour *n* umbraculum *nt*

arbute *n* (tree) arbutus *f*; (fruit) arbutum *nt*
■ ~-**berry** *n* arbutum *nt*

arc *n* arcus *m*

arcade *n* porticus *f*

arch¹ *n* arcus, fornix *m*

arch² *vt* arcuo ①

archaeology *n* scientia antiquitatis *f*

archaic *adj* obsoletus

arched *adj* curvus

archer *n* sagittarius *m*

archery *n* ars sagittandi *f*

archetype *n* archetypum, exemplum *nt*

architect *n* architectus *m*; artifex *m*

architectural *adj* architectonicus

architecture *n* architectura *f*

archives *n* tabulae *fpl*; tabularium *nt*

archway *n* porticus *f*

arctic *adj* arcticus; Arctous

ardent *adj* ardens, fervidus
■ ~**ly** *adv* ardenter

ardour *n* ardor, fervor *m*

arduous *adj* (difficult) arduus; difficilis
■ ~**ly** *adv* difficulter

area *n* area; superficies *f*

arena *n* arena *f*

argonaut *n* argonauta *m*

argue *vt&i* disputo, discepto ①; dissero ③; (prove) arguo, evinco ③; probo ①

argument *n* disceptatio, disputatio *f*; (subject) argumentum *nt*

argumentative *adj* (fond of dispute) litigiosus

arid *adj* aridus, siccus

aridity *n* ariditas, siccitas *f*

aright *adv* recte, bene

arise *vi* surgo ③; orior ④; (be born from) nascor ③

aristocracy *n* optimates, nobiles *mpl*

aristocrat *n* optimas, patricius *m*

aristocratic *adj* patricius
■ ~**ally** *adv* more patricio

arithmetic *n* arithmetica *ntpl*

arithmetical *adj* arithmeticus

arm¹ *n* bracchium *nt*; lacertus *m*

arm² *n* (weapon) telum *nt*; ▶ **arms**

arm³ *vt* armo ①
■ ~ *vi* armor ①; arma capio ③; bellum paro ①

armament *n* armatura *f*; apparatus bellicus *m*

armed *adj* armatus

armistice *n* indutiae *fpl*

armour *n* armatura *f*; armatus *m*; arma *ntpl*
■ ~-**bearer** *n* armiger *m*

armoury *n* armamentarium *nt*

arms *n* arma; fig bellum *nt*
□ **lay down** ~ ab armis discedo; arma dedo ③
□ **take (up)** ~ sumo arma
□ **be under** ~ in armis esse

army *n* exercitus *m*; (in battle array) acies *f*; (on the march) agmen *nt*; (forces) copiae *fpl*

aroma *n* odor *m*

aromatic *adj* fragrans

around *adv & prep* circum, circa + *acc*
□ **all** ~ undique

arouse *vt* suscito, excito, concito ①; (produce) cieo, moveo ②; conflo ①; (encourage) erigo ③
□ ~ **oneself** expergiscor ③

arraign *vt* accuso ①

arraignment *n* accusatio *f*

arrange *vt* instruo, struo, (battle) instituo ③; ordino ①; dispono ③; colloco ①; (make a plan) constituo ③

arrangement *n* collocatio, compositio; dispositio; (of battle) ordinatio *f*; (plan) consilium *nt*

array[1] *n* (of battle) acies *f*; (clothing) vestitus *m*; (arrangement, order) ordo *m*; dispositio, compositio *f*

array[2] *vt* vestio ④; adorno ①; compono, instruo ③

arrears *n* reliqua *ntpl*; residuae *fpl*

arrest[1] *n* comprehensio *f*

arrest[2] *vt* comprehendo ③; (detain) detineo ②; (stop) sisto ③

arrival *n* adventus *m*

arrive *vi* advenio, pervenio ④; (as a ship) advehor, appellor ③

arrogance *n* arrogantia; superbia, insolentia *f*

arrogant *adj* arrogans; superbus; insolens
■ ~**ly** *adv* arroganter; insolenter

arrow *n* sagitta, arundo *f*; telum *nt*

arsenal *n* armamentarium *nt*; navalia *ntpl*

arson *n* incendium *nt*

art *n* ars *f*; (cunning) artificium *nt*; (skill) sollertia *f*
□ **fine** ~**s** artes elegantes *or* ingenuae *fpl*
□ **black** ~ magice *f*

artery *n* arteria; vena *f*

artful *adj* callidus, subtilis; subdolus
■ ~**ly** *adv* callide, subtiliter, subdole

artfulness *n* artificium *nt*; calliditas *f*

arthritic *adj* arthriticus

article *n* (item) res; (part of treaty) condicio; pactio; (for sale) merx *f*

articulate[1] *adj* distinctus; dilucidus

articulate[2] *vt* articulo, enuntio ①

artifice *n* artificium *nt*; ars *f*; dolus *m*; fraus *f*

artificer *n* artifex *m*; opifex *m/f*

artificial *adj* artificiosus; facticius
■ ~**ly** *adv* arte

artillery *n* tormenta *ntpl*

artisan *n* faber *m*; artifex *m*; opifex *m/f*

artist *n* artifex *m*

artistic *adj* artificiosus
■ ~**ally** *adv* artificiose; affabre

artless *adj* incomptus; incompositus; ingenuus, simplex
■ ~**ly** *adv* incompte; ingenue

artlessness *n* simplicitas *f*

as *adv & conj* (of time) dum, cum; (of manner) ut; quam; ita ut; sicut; velut
□ ~**far** ~ quoad, quantum; usque ad + *acc*

□ ~ **for** de + *abl*
□ ~ **if** quasi, perinde ac si; ita ut si
□ ~ **it were** ceu, tanquam, velut
□ ~ **long** ~ quamdiu
□ ~ **many** ~ quotquot, quotcunque
□ ~ **much** tantum
□ ~ **often** ~ quotiens
□ ~ **soon** ~ cum primum, simul atque
□ ~ **yet** adhuc
□ **not** ~ **yet** nondum

ascend *vt&i* ascendo, conscendo, scando ③

ascension *n* ascensio *f*; ascensus *m*

ascent *n* ascensio *f*; ascensus *m*; acclivitas *f*

ascertain *vt* comperio, pro certo scio ④; cognosco ③

ascribe *vt* imputo ①; ascribo, tribuo ③

ash *n* (tree) fraxinus *f*; (cinders) cinis *m*;
▶ **ashes**

ashamed *adj* pudibundus
□ **be** ~ erubesco ③
□ **I am** ~ **of** me pudet ② + *gen or infin*

ashen *adj* (of the tree) fraxineus; (pale) pallidus

ashes *n* cinis *m*; favilla *f*

ashore *adv* in terram, ad litus
□ **be cast** ~ eicior ③
□ **go** ~ egredior ③
□ **put** ~ expono ③

Asian *adj* Asiaticus, Asius

aside *adv* seorsum, oblique
□ **call** ~ sevoco ①
□ **lay** *or* **set** ~ sepono ③

asinine *adj* asininus

ask *vt* (for) rogo ①, posco, peto, quaero ③; (a question) interrogo ①

askance *adv*:
□ **look** ~ torva tueor ②

askew *adv* in obliquum

aslant *adv* oblique, in obliquum

asleep *adj* dormiens
□ **be** ~ dormio ④
□ **fall** ~ obdormio ④
□ **lull** ~ sopio, consopio ④

aspect *n* (what is seen) aspectus; prospectus; (face) vultus *m*, facies *f*

asperity *n* acerbitas *f*

asphalt *n* bitumen *nt*

aspiration *n* (desire) affectatio *f*; (longing) votum *nt*

aspire *vt* (~ to) affecto, aspiro ①; peto, annitor ③

aspiring *adj* appetens + *gen*

ass *n* asinus *m*, asina *f*; (wild ~) onager
■ ~**-driver** *n* asinarius *m*

assail *vt* aggredior ③; oppugno ①;
invehor ③

assassin *n* sicarius *m*

assassinate *vt* insidiis interficio ③

assassination *n* caedes *f*

assault¹ *n* impetus *m*; oppugnatio;
(violence) vis *f*; ▶ **attack**

assault² *vt* adorior ④; oppugno ①;
manus infero *ir*

assemblage *n* congregatio; (multitude)
multitudo *f*

assemble *vt* congrego, convoco ①;
contraho ③
■ ~ *vi* convenio ④

assembly *n* coetus, conventus *m*;
concilium *nt*; (in politics) comitia *ntpl*;
contio *f*; (small) conventiculum *nt*; (of
people standing round) corona *f*

assembly-room *n* curia *f*

assent¹ *vi* assentior ④; annuo ③

assent² *n* assensus *m*

assert *vt* affirmo, assevero ①; (vindicate)
defendo ③; tueor ②

assertion *n* affirmatio, asseveratio;
sententia *f*

assess *vt* (tax) censeo ②; (value)
aestimo ①

assessment *n* census *m*; aestimatio
f; (tax) vectigal; tributum *nt*

assessor *n* (judge) assessor; (of taxes)
censor *m*

assets *n* bona *ntpl*

assiduity *n* assiduitas, diligentia *f*

assiduous *adj* assiduus, sedulus
■ ~**ly** *adv* assidue, sedulo

assign *vt* attribuo ③; delego, assigno ①;
(determine) statuo, constituo ③

assignation *n* constitutum *nt*

assignment *n* assignatio; attributio *f*

assimilate *vt* assimulo; (make equal)
aequo ①; (digest) concoquo ③

assimilation *n* assimilatio *f*

assist *vt* iuvo, adiuvo; auxilior ①;
succurro ③, subvenio ④ *both + dat*

assistance *n* auxilium *nt*, opis (*gen
sing*) *f*

assistant *n* adiutor *m*, adiutrix *f*,
administer, auxiliator, advocatus *m*

associate¹ *vt* consocio ①; adscisco;
(impute) ascribo ③
■ ~ *vi* (~ with) versor cum ① + *abl*

associate² *adj* socius

associate³ *n* socius *m*; consors *m/f*;
particeps *m/f*

association *n* societas; communitas;
consociatio; congregatio *f*; (corporation)
collegium *nt*

assuage *vt* allevo, levo ①; lenio ④

assume *vt* induo; assumo ③; (claim)
arrogo ①; (pretend) simulo ①; (take for
granted) pono ③

assumption *n* (act of taking for granted)
sumptio *f*

assurance *n* fiducia; (confidence)
audacia, (presumptuousness) impudentia
f; (pledge) pignus *nt*

assure *vt* confirmo, affirmo ①;
promitto ③; (encourage) adhortor ①
□ **be ~d** confido ③

assuredly *adv* profecto, certe

astern *adv* in puppi; a puppi

asthma *n* dyspnoea *f*, asthma *nt*

asthmatic *adj* asthmaticus

astonish *vt* obstupefacio ③
□ **be ~ed** miror ①; obstupesco ③

astonishing *adj* mirabilis, mirandus
■ ~**ly** *adv* admirabiliter

astonishment *n* admiratio *f*;
stupor *m*

astound *vt* stupefacio, obstupefacio ③

astray *adj*:
□ **go ~** erro ①
□ **lead ~** via recta abduco,
transversum ago ③

astringent *adj* astrictorius

astrologer *n* astrologus;
mathematicus *m*

astrological *adj* Chaldaicus

astrology *n* astrologia; mathematica *f*

astronomer *n* astrologus;
astronomus *m*

astronomical *adj* astronomicus

astronomy *n* astrologia; astronomia *f*

astute *adj* callidus, astutus, sagax
■ ~**ly** *adv* callide, astute, sagaciter

astuteness *n* calliditas, sagacitas *f*

asunder *adv* seorsum, separatim; (in
two) dis…
□ **cut ~** disseco ①
□ **pull ~** distraho ③

asylum *n* asylum *nt*

at *prep* ad, apud; (during) inter *all* + *acc*; in + *abl*; (of time) *use* *abl*; (of price) *use* *abl*

athirst *adv* sitiens

athlete *n* athleta *m*

athletic *adj* athleticus

atmosphere *n* aer *m*; caelum; inane *nt*

atom *n* atomus *f*; corpus individuum, corpus insecabile *nt*; fig mica, particula *f*
□ **not an ∼ of** nihil omnino + *gen*

atone *vt* pio; expio ①; solvo, luo ③

atonement *n* piaculum *nt*; expiatio; compensatio, satisfactio *f*

atrocious *adj* nefarius, nefandus; (monstrous) immanis; (of crimes) dirus; atrox

atrocity *n* atrocitas *f*; nefas, facinus *nt*

attach *vt* annecto, adiungo ③; applico ①
□ **be ∼ed (to)** haereo, adhaereo ②; (be fond of) amo ①

attachment *n* (affection) amor *m*, caritas *f*

attack[1] *n* (onset) impetus *m*; oppugnatio *f*; incursus *m*; fig (of a disease) tentatio *f*

attack[2] *vt* (the enemy) aggredior, irruo ③; (a town) oppugno; fig provoco ①; lacesso ③; (verbally) invehor ③; (of diseases) corripio, invado ③; tento ①

attacker *n* oppugnator; provocator *m*

attain *vt* adipiscor, consequor ③; pervenio ④ ad + *acc*

attainable *adj* impetrabilis

attainment *n* comparatio, impetratio *f*

attempt[1] *n* conatum; inceptum, ausum, periculum *nt*
□ **a first ∼** tirocinium *nt*

attempt[2] *vt* conor ①; nitor ③; molior ④; audeo ②; tento ①

attend *vt* (accompany) comitor ①; (escort) deduco ③; (be present) intersum, (be present at) adsum *ir* + *dat*
□ **∼ to** curo, procuro ①; servio ④; (comply with) obtempero; invigilo ①; (pay attention) animum adverto ③

attendance *n* (service) obsequium; officium, ministerium *nt*; (care) cura, diligentia *f*; (retinue) comitatus *m*; (presence) praesentia *f*

attendant *n* comes; assectator, assecla, apparitor; famulus *m*; famula *f*
■ **∼s** *pl* comitatus *m*

attention *n* animus attentus *m*; intentio; sedulitas *f*; cultus *m*; observantia *f*
□ **pay ∼ to** observo ①; operam do ①; colo ③; studeo ②

attentive *adj* attentus; sedulus; officiosus
■ **∼ly** *adv* attente, intento animo; sedulo; officiose

attest *vt* testor, testificor ①

attire[1] *n* ornatus; vestitus *m*

attire[2] *vt* adorno ①; vestio ④

attitude *n* (appearance) habitus; status *m*; (opinion) sententia *f*

attorney *n* cognitor, causidicus, advocatus *m*

attract *vt* traho, attraho; allicio ③

attraction *n* illecebra *f*; ▶ **charm**

attractive *adj* lepidus, blandus

attractiveness *n* lepos *m*

attribute[1] *vt* tribuo, attribuo, ascribo ③; (falsely) affingo ③; imputo ①

attribute[2] *n* (characteristic) proprium *nt*

attrition *n* attritus *m*

attune *vt* modulor ①

auburn *adj* flavus; aureus

auction *n* auctio *f*
□ **sell by ∼** auctionor ①; sub hasta vendo ③

auctioneer *n* praeco *m*

audacious *adj* audax; confidens
■ **∼ly** *adv* audacter; confidenter

audacity *n* confidentia, audacia *f*

audible *adj* quod audiri potest

audibly *adv* clara voce, ut omnes exaudire possint

audience *n* (admittance) aditus *m*; (conversation) colloquium *nt*; (hearers) auditores *mpl*; (bystanders) corona *f*

audit *vt* rationes inspicio ③

auditor *n* (hearer) auditor *m*

auditorium *n* auditorium *nt*

auger *n* terebra *f*

augment *vt* augeo ②; amplio ①
■ **∼** *vi* (be augmented) augeor ②; cresco, accresco ③

augmentation *n* incrementum *nt*

augur[1] *n* augur *m/f*; hariolus, haruspex *m*

augur[2] *vi&t* auguror; vaticinor, hariolor ①

augury *n* augurium, auspicium *nt*; auguratio *f*

august[1] *adj* augustus; magnificus

August[2] *n* Sextilis, Augustus *m*

aunt *n* (on the father's side) amita; (on the mother's side) matertera *f*

auspices *n* auspicium *nt*
□ **under your ~** te auspice

auspicious *adj* faustus; secundus, prosperus; auspicatus
■ **~ly** *adv* auspicato; feliciter; prospere

austere *adj* austerus, severus

austerity *n* austeritas, severitas *f*

authentic *adj* certus; verus; fide dignus

authentically *adv* certo auctore; cum auctoritate

authenticate *vt* recognosco ③; firmo, confirmo ①

authentication *n* auctoritas; confirmatio *f*

authenticity *n* auctoritas; fides *f*

author *n* auctor; scriptor; (inventor) conditor, inventor; (beginner) princeps *m*; (of a crime) caput (sceleris) *nt*

authoritative *adj* auctoritate firmatus; (imperious) imperiosus

authority *n* auctoritas; potestas; (leave) licentia *f*; (power) ius; imperium *nt*; (office or official) magistratus *m*

authorization *n* confirmatio, licentia *f*

authorize *vt* potestatem *or* copiam do ①; (excuse) excuso; (approve) probo ①

autobiography *n* res gestae *fpl*

autocrat *n* dominus *m*

autograph *n* chirographum *nt*

autumn *n* autumnus *m*

autumnal *adj* autumnalis

auxiliary *adj* auxiliaris, auxiliarius
■ **~** *n* adiutor *m*
□ **auxiliaries** *npl* mil auxilia *ntpl*

avail[1] *vi*:
□ **~ oneself of** utor ③ + *abl*

avail[2] *n*:
□ **be of no ~** usui non esse

available *adj* utilis; efficax; (at hand) praesto *indecl*

avalanche *n* nivis casus *m*

avarice *n* avaritia, parsimonia, sordes *f*

avaricious *adj* avarus, sordidus
■ **~ly** *adv* avare, sordide

avenge *vt* vindico ①; ulciscor ③

avenger *n* ultor *m*, ultrix *f*; vindex *m/f*

avenging *adj* ultrix, vindex

avenue *n* aditus, introitus; (of trees) xystus *m*

average[1] *n* medium inter maximum et minimum *nt*; aequa distributio *f*
□ **on ~** peraeque; (about) circiter

average[2] *adj* medius inter maximum minimumque

averse *adj* alienus; aversus, abhorrens
□ **be ~ to** abhorreo ② + *dat*

aversion *n* odium, fastidium *nt*
□ **~ to** taedium *nt* + *gen*

avert *vt* amoveo ②; averto, depello ③; (beg off) deprecor ①

aviary *n* aviarium *nt*

avid *adj* avidus

avidity *n* aviditas *f*

avoid *vt* fugio ③; vito, devito ①; (turn aside, decline) declino, detrecto ①

avoidable *adj* evitabilis, qui effugi potest

avoidance *n* vitatio; declinatio *f*; (flight from) fuga *f* + *gen*

avow *vt* profiteor, confiteor ②

avowal *n* professio, confessio *f*

avowedly *adv* ex professo, aperte

await *vt* exspecto ①

awake[1] *adj* vigil, vigilans; (sleepless) exsomnis
□ **be ~** vigilo ①

awake[2] *vt* (also **awaken**) excito, suscito ①; expergefacio ③
■ **~** *vi* expergiscor ③

award[1] *n* sententia *f*; iudicium, arbitrium *nt*

award[2] *vt* adiudico ①; addico, tribuo ③; assigno ①

aware *adj* (of) gnarus, conscius + *gen*; sciens
□ **not ~ of** ignarus, nescius + *gen*
□ **be ~ (of)** sentio, scio ④

awareness *n* scientia *f*

away *adv* procul
□ **~!** abi! apage!
□ **be ~** absum *ir*

□ **go** ∼ abeo *ir*
□ **take** ∼ aufero *ir*; tollo ③

awe *n* reverentia *f*; (fear) metus, terror *m*, formido *f*
□ **stand in** ∼ metuo ③; timeo ②

awestruck *adj* pavefactus

awful *adj* (awe-inspiring) verendus; (dreadful) formidolosus, terribilis, dirus
■ ∼**ly** *adv* formidolose

awhile *adv* (briefly) paulisper

awkward *adj* ineptus; rusticus, rudis, inscitus; (things) incommodus
■ ∼**ly** *adv* inepte; rustice; inscite

awkwardness *n* imperitia, rusticitas *f*; (inconvenience) incommoditas *f*

awning *n* velarium, velum *nt*

awry *adj* obliquus
■ ∼ *adv* oblique; perverse; prave, perperam

axe *n* securis, ascia; (battle-axe) bipennis; (pick-axe) dolabra *f*

axis *n* axis *m*

axle *n* axis *m*

azure *adj* caeruleus

Bb

baa *vi* (like a sheep) balo ①

babble¹ *n* garrulitas *f*

babble² *vi* blatero ①; garrio ④

babbling *adj* garrulus, loquax

baby *n* infans, parvulus *m*

babyhood *n* infantia *f*

babyish *adj* puerilis

Bacchanalia *n* Bacchanalia *ntpl*

bacchanalian *adj* bacchanalis

Bacchante *n* Baccha *f*

Bacchic *adj* Bacchicus

bachelor *n* caelebs *m*

back¹ *n* tergum, dorsum *nt*
□ **wound in the** ∼ aversum vulnero ①
□ **turn one's** ∼ tergum verto ③

back² *adv* retro; retrorsum; re...

back³ *vt* (support) faveo ② + *dat*; (help) adiuvo ①
□ ∼ **water** navem remis inhibeo ②
■ ∼ *vi* me recipio ③
□ ∼ **out of** evado ③

backbite *vt* maledico + *dat*, dente carpo ③

backbiter *n* maledicus, obtrectator *m*

backbiting *n* obtrectatio *f*

backbone *n* spina *f*

back door *n* posticum ostium *m*

backer *n* adiutor *m*

background *n* scaena *f*; fig recessus *m*
■ ∼ *vt* (keep in the background) abscondo ③

backing *adj* (help) auxilium; (political) suffragium *nt*

backward *adj* (slow) piger, tardus, segnis; (averse to) alienus; (lying on the back) supinus
□ **be** ∼ (delay) cunctor ①

backwardness *n* tarditas; pigritia *f*

backwards *adv* (also **backward**) retro; retrorsum

bacon *n* lardum *nt*

bad *adj* malus, pravus, nequam; improbus; (ill) aeger; (unfortunate) malus, tristis
□ ∼ **weather** tempestas adversa *f*

badge *n* insigne, signum, indicium *nt*

badger *n* meles, melis *f*

badly *adv* male, prave, nequiter; improbe

badness *n* nequitia; improbitas *f*

baffle *vt* decipio, fallo, eludo ③

bag *n* saccus; crumena *f*; (of leather) uter *m*; (of netting) reticulum *nt*

baggage *n* sarcinae *fpl*; impedimenta *ntpl*

bail¹ *n* vadimonium *nt*; (surety) vas; (for debt) praes *m*

bail² *vt* (give ∼ for) spondeo ②; fidepromitto ③; (accept ∼ for) vador ①

bailiff *n* (of a farm) vilicus; (of a court of justice) apparitor *m*

bailiwick *n* iurisdictio *f*

bait¹ *n* esca *f*; fig incitamentum *nt*

bait² *vt* inesco ①; (tease) lacesso ③

bake *vt* torreo ②; coquo ③; igne obduro ①

baker *n* pistor *m*
■ ~'s shop *n* pistrina *f*; pistrinum *nt*

bakery *n* pistrina *f*

balance¹ *n* (scales) libra, statera, trutina *f*; (equipoise) aequipondium *nt*; (in book-keeping) reliquum *nt*
□ **lose one's** ~ labor ③

balance² *vt* libro ①, pendo ③; (weigh one thing against another) penso, compenso ①; (accounts) dispungo ③

balcony *n* maeniana *ntpl*

bald *adj* calvus, glaber; fig ieiunus, aridus

balderdash *n* farrago *f*

baldness *n* calvitium *nt*

baldric *n* cingulum *nt*, balteus *m*

bale *n* sarcina *f*, fascis *m*

baleful *adj* funestus; perniciosus, exitialis, noxius

balk *vt* (frustrate) frustror ①; eludo, decipio, fallo ③

ball *n* globus, globulus *m*; (to play with) pila *f*

ballad *n* nenia *f*; carmen triviale *nt*

ballast *n* saburra *f*

ballet *n* pantomimus *m*; embolium *nt*

ballet-dancer *n* pantomimus *m*; pantomima *f*

ballot¹ *n* (token used in voting) tabella *f*; (voting) suffragium *nt*

ballot² *vi* tabella *or* tabellis suffragor ①

ballot-box *n* cista *f*

balm *n* balsamum; fig solatium *nt*

balustrade *n* (rails enclosing a place) cancelli *mpl*

ban¹ *n* interdictio *f*

ban² *vt* interdico ③

banal *adj* ieiunus

band¹ *n* (chain) vinculum; (headband) redimiculum *nt*; (troop) caterva *f*; (chorus) grex *m*; fig catena, copula *f*; vinculum *nt*

band² *vt* socio, consocio ①
■ ~ *vi* (league together) coniuro ①

bandage¹ *n* fascia *f*

bandage² *vt* deligo ①

bandit *n* latro *m*

bandy-legged *adj* loripes, valgus

bane *n* venenum *nt*; pestis; pernicies *f*

baneful *adj* pestifer; perniciosus; funestus; exitialis

bang¹ *vt&i* crepo ①; (hit) ferio ④

bang² *n* crepitus, sonitus *m*; (blow) plaga *f*; (shock) percussus *m*

banish *vt* in exilium mitto, pello ③; relego ①; fig pono ③

banishment *n* (act) eiectio; relegatio *f*; (state) exilium *nt*; fuga *f*

bank *n* (hillock) tumulus *m*; (of a river) ripa *f*; (for money) argentaria taberna *f*

banker *n* argentarius, mensarius, trapezita *m*

bankrupt *n* decoctor *m*
□ **be** *or* **go** ~ rationes conturbare ①; decoquo ③

bankruptcy *n* novae tabulae *fpl*

banner *n* vexillum *nt*

banquet¹ *n* convivium *nt*; epulae, dapes *fpl*

banquet² *vi* convivor; epulor ①
■ ~ *vt* convivio excipio ③

banqueter *n* epulo, conviva *m*

banqueting *n* epulatio *f*

banter¹ *n* iocus *m*; cavillatio *f*

banter² *vt* cavillor ①; derideo ②

banteringly *adj* per ludibrium

bar¹ *n* vectis; (of a door) obex *m*; repagulum *nt*; pessulus *m*; fig impedimentum *nt*; (ingot) later *m*; (in a court of justice) cancelli *mpl*; claustra *ntpl*; (barristers) advocati *mpl*; iudiciale *nt*

bar² *vt* (a door, etc.) obsero ①; (shut out) excludo ③; (prevent) prohibeo ②; veto ①

barb *n* (hook) uncus; hamus *m*

barbarian *adj* & *n* barbarus *m*

barbaric *adj* barbaricus

barbarity *n* barbaries; feritas, truculentia *f*

barbarous *adj* barbarus; ferus; immanis; saevus, truculentus; (uncultivated) rudis, barbarus
■ ~**ly** *adv* barbare; saeve

barbed *adj* hamatus

barber *n* tonsor *m*, tonstrix *f*
□ ~'s shop tonstrina *f*

barbican *n* turris; specula *f*

bard *n* vates *m/f*

bare¹ *adj* (unclothed) nudus; (mere) merus; (of style) pressus; (plain) manifestus; (empty) nudus, vacuus

bare² *vt* nudo, denudo ①; aperio ④

barefaced *adj* impudens; audax

barefoot *adj* (also **barefooted**) nudo pede, nudis pedibus; discalceatus

bareheaded *adj* nudo capite

barely *adv* vix, aegre

bargain¹ *n* pactio *f*, pactum *nt*

bargain² *vi* stipulor ①; paciscor ③

barge *n* navicula, linter *f*

bargeman *n* portitor *m*

bark¹ *n* (of trees) cortex *m/f*; (inner bark) liber *m*

bark² *n* (of dogs) latratus *m*

bark³ *vi* (sound) latro ①
□ ∼ **at** also fig allatro ①

barking *n* latratus *m*

barley *n* hordeum *nt*

barmaid *n* ministra cauponae *f*

barn *n* granarium, horreum *nt*

barque *n* navicula, ratis, linter *f*

barracks *n* castra (stativa) *ntpl*

barrel *n* (cask) cadus *m*, dolium *nt*; orca *f*; (cylinder) cylindrus *m*

barren *adj* sterilis; infecundus

barrenness *n* sterilitas, infecunditas *f*

barricade¹ *n* agger *m*; vallum *nt*

barricade² *vt* obstruo ③

barrier *n* cancelli *mpl*; sacpta *ntpl*; (in the circus) carcer *m*; claustra *ntpl*; fig impedimentum *nt*

barrister *n* advocatus, causidicus *m*

barrow *n* (vehicle) ferculum *nt*; (mound) tumulus *m*

barter¹ *n* permutatio *f*; commercium *nt*

barter² *vt&i* muto, commuto, permuto ①; paciscor ③

base¹ *adj* humilis, ignobilis, obscurus; inferior; infamis, vilis, turpis; foedus
■ ∼**ly** *adv* abiecte; turpiter

base² *n* basis *f*; fundus *m*; fundamentum *nt*

baseless *adj* vanus, inanis; falsus

baseness *n* humilitas; turpitudo; nequitia *f*

bashful *adj* pudens; pudicus, pudibundus, modestus; verecundus
■ ∼**ly** *adv* timide; modeste, verecunde; pudenter

bashfulness *n* pudor; rubor *m*; verecundia, modestia *f*

basin *n* (for washing the hands) pelvis *f*, trulleus *m*; (tub) labrum *nt*; (lake) lacus *m*; (dock) navalia *ntpl*

basis *n* fundamentum *nt*; (cause) causa *f*

bask *vi* apricor ①

basket *n* corbis *f*; canistrum; qualum *nt*; calathus *m*; (large basket) cophinus *m*

bass *n* (sound) sonus gravis *m*

bastard *n* nothus, spurius *m*; fig fictus, falsus
■ ∼ *adj* spurius

baste *vt* perfundo, conspergo ③

bastion *n* propugnaculum, castellum *nt*

bat¹ *n* (animal) vespertilio *m*

bat² *n* (club) clava *f*, fustis *m*

batch *n* (troop) turma *f*; (of things) numerus *m*
■ **in** ∼**es** *adv* turmatim

bath *n* balneum *nt*; lavatio *f*; (tub) alveus *m*, labrum *nt*

bathe *vt* lavo; (steep) macero ①; (sprinkle) perfundo ③
■ ∼ *vi* lavor ①

bathing *n* lavatio *f*

bath-keeper *n* balneator *m*

battalion *n* cohors *f*; (army in battle-array) acies *f*

batter *vt* verbero, pulso ①; percutio, obtundo, diruo ③; ferio ④

battering-ram *n* aries *m*

battery *n* (mound for artillery) agger *m*; (artillery) tormenta *ntpl*; (assault) vis *f*

battle¹ *n* proelium *nt*, pugna *f*

battle² *vi* proelior, pugno ①; (with someone) contendo ③

battle-array *n* acies *f*

battle-axe *n* bipennis *f*

battlefield *n* acies *f*, campus *m*

battlement *n* pinna *f*

bauble *n* tricae, nugae *fpl*

bawd *n* lena *f*; leno *m*

bawdy *adj* impudicus, immodestus

bawl *vi* clamito, vociferor ①

bawling *n* vociferatio *f*; clamor *m*

bay¹ *n* (of the sea) sinus *m*

bay² *n* (tree) laurus, laurea *f*

bazaar *n* forum *nt*

be *vi* sum, esse, fui *ir*; (exist) existo ③
- ☐ **how are you?** quid agis?
- ☐ ∼ **against** adversor ①; abhorreo ②
- ☐ ∼ **amongst** *or* **between** intersum
- ☐ ∼ **away** absum
- ☐ ∼ **for (one)** faveo ② + *dat*; cum aliquo sto ①
- ☐ ∼ **in** insum
- ☐ **so ∼ it** ita fiat, esto!
- ☐ **let ∼** mitto ③
- ☐ ∼ **present** adsum
- ☐ ∼ **without** careo ② + *abl*

beach *n* litus *nt*; (coast) ora *f*

beacon *n* specula *f*; (lighthouse) pharus *m*; (fire) ignis *m*

bead *n* globus, globulus *m*

beak *n* rostrum *nt*; (of ships) rostra *ntpl*

beaked *adj* rostratus

beaker *n* poculum, carchesium *nt*

beam¹ *n* (wooden) tignum *nt*, trabs *f*; (of ships) transtrum *nt*; (of a balance) scapus; (light) radius *m*

beam² *vi* radio ①; refulgeo, niteo ②

beaming *adj* nitens, lucidus

bear¹ *vt* fero *ir*; fig patior; gero ③; subeo ④; sustineo ②; tolero ①; (of children) pario ③; (bring forth) fero, effero *ir*; fundo, profundo ③
- ☐ ∼ **away** *or* **off** aufero *ir*
- ☐ ∼ **out** effero *ir*; praesto ①
- ☐ ∼ **witness** testor ①
- ☐ ∼ **with** indulgeo ② + *dat*

bear² *n* ursus *m*, ursa *f*; (constellation) septentriones *mpl*

bearable *adj* tolerandus, tolerabilis

beard *n* barba; (of corn) arista *f*

bearded *adj* barbatus; intonsus

beardless *adj* imberbis

bearer *n* (porter) baiulus; (of litters) lecticarius; (of corpses) vispillo *m*

bearing *n* (physical) gestus *m*
- ☐ **it has a ∼ on** pertinet ad + *acc*

beast *n* belua; bestia *f*; (cattle) pecus *nt*
- ☐ **wild ∼** fera *f*
- ☐ ∼ **of burden** iumentum *nt*

beat *vt* verbero; (knock) pulso ①; caedo ③; (conquer) vinco; (bruise) tero ③; (excel) supero ①
- ☐ ∼ **back** *or* **off** repello ③
- ■ ∼ *vi* (of the heart) palpito ①

beaten *adj* victus; (of a path, *etc.*) tritus

beating *n* verberatio *f*; (blow) ictus *m*; verbera *ntpl*; (of time in music) percussio *f*; (of the heart) palpitatio *f*

beautiful *adj* pulcher; (of form) formosus

beautifully *adv* pulchre

beautify *vt* decoro, orno ①; excolo ③

beauty *n* pulcritudo; forma; (grace, *etc.*) Venus *f*

beaver *n* castor, fiber *m*; (cheek-piece of a helmet) buccula *f*

becalm *vt* paco, sedo ①
- ☐ ∼**ed** vento destitutus

because *conj* quia, quod; quoniam
- ☐ ∼ **of** ob, propter + *acc*

beckon *vi* nuto ①; annuo, innuo ③

become *vi* fio *ir*

becoming *adj* decorus; decens; conveniens

bed *n* lectus, torus *m*; cubile *nt*; (in a garden) areola *f*; (of a river) alveus *m*

bedaub *vt* lino, perunguo ③; inquino, conspurco ①

bedclothes *n* stragulum *nt*; vestis *f*

bedding *n* stragulum *nt*; vestis *f*

bedeck *vt* decoro, orno, exorno ①; excolo ③

bedew *vt* irroro, umecto ①; perfundo ③

bed-fellow *n* socius *m* or socia *f* tori

bedpost *n* fulcrum *nt*

bedridden *adj* lecto affixus

bedroom *n* cubiculum *nt*

bedstead *n* sponda *f*

bedtime *n* hora somni *f*

bee *n* apis *f*
- ■ ∼ **hive** *n* alveus *m*; apiarium, alvearium *nt*
- ■ ∼**-keeper** *n* apiarius *m*

beech *n* fagus *f*

beechen *adj* faginus, fagineus, fageus

beef *n* bubula (caro) *f*

beer *n* cervisia *f*

beet *n* beta *f*

beetle *n* scarabaeus *m*

befall *vi* contingo, accido ③; evenio ④

befit *vt* convenio ④
- ☐ **it ∼s** par est, convenit ④; decet ② *all* + *dat*

befitting *adj* decens; conveniens, idoneus

before¹ *prep* ante + *acc*; prae, pro; (in the presence of) coram + *abl*; apud + *acc*
- ■ ∼ *adv* ante; antea prius
- ☐ ∼ **now** antehac
- ☐ **long ∼** iamdudum

□ **a little** ~ paulo ante
■ ~ *conj* antequam, priusquam
before² *adj* prior
beforehand *adv* ante, antea, prius; prae...
befriend *vt* sublevo, adiuvo ①, faveo ② + *dat*
beg *vt&i* peto, posco ③; oro, precor, obsecro, flagito, rogo ①; (be a beggar) mendico ①
beget *vt* gigno ③; procreo, creo, genero ①
beggar¹ *n* mendicus *m*, mendica *f*
beggar² *vt* ad inopiam redigo ③
beggarly *adj* mendicus; vilis, abiectus; (wretched) exilis
beggary *n* mendicitas, egestas, paupertas *f*
begin *vt&i* initium facio ③; incoho ①; ordior ④; coepi, incipio ③; (arise) exorior ④
beginner *n* (originator) auctor; fig (novice) tiro *m*
beginning *n* inceptio *f*; initium; principium, exordium *nt*; origo *f*
begrudge *vt* invideo + *acc of thing and dat of person*
beguile *vt* fraudo, frustror ①; fallo ③; circumvenio ④
behalf *n*:
□ **on** ~ **of** pro + *abl*, propter + *acc*, causa + *gen*
behave *vi&t*:
□ ~ **oneself** (conduct oneself) me gero; (~ towards) utor ③ + *abl*
behaviour *n* mores *mpl*; (actions) facta *ntpl*
□ **good** ~ urbanitas *f*
□ **bad** ~ rusticitas *f*
behead *vt* decollo ①; securi percutio ③
behind *adv* pone, a tergo, post; (remaining) reliquus
□ **be left** ~ relinquor ③
■ ~ *prep* post + *acc*
behold¹ *vt* conspicio ③; obtueor ②; specto ①; cerno ③; aspicio ③
behold² *int* ecce! en! aspice!
beholden *adj* obnoxius
□ **be** ~ obligor ①; gratiam debeo ②
being *n* natura; (essence) essentia *f*; (person) homo *m*
□ **supreme** ~ numen *nt*
belabour *vt* verbero, pulso ①
belated *adj* serus

belch¹ *vi* ructo; eructo ①
belch² *n* ructus *m*
beleaguer *vt* obsideo ②
belief *n* fides, opinio, persuasio, religio *f*; (teaching) doctrina *f*
believe *vt* credo ③; (trust to) confido ③; (think) existimo, opinor, arbitror, puto ①
□ ~ **in the gods** deos esse credo ③
belittle *vt* rodo ③
bell *n* tintinnabulum *nt*
bellow *vi* rugio, mugio ④
bellowing *n* mugitus *m*
bellows *n* (a pair of ~) follis *m*
belly *n* venter *m*; abdomen *nt*; alvus *f*; stomachus, uterus *m*
belong *vi* (~ to) pertineo ad ② + *acc*
belongings *n* bona *ntpl*
beloved *adj* delectus, carus; amatus
below *prep* infra; subter + *acc*
■ ~ *adv* infra; deorsum, subter
□ **from** ~ ab inferiore parte
belt *n* cingulum *nt*; zona *f*; (sword-belt) balteus *m*
bemoan *vt* ingemo ③; deploro ①; defleo ②
bench *n* scamnum, sedile; (of the senate) subsellium *nt*; (court of justice) subsellia *ntpl*
bend¹ *vt* flecto ③; curvo, inclino ①; fig domo ①
□ ~ **down** deflecto ③
■ ~ *vi* flector ③; curvor ① *etc.*
bend² *n* sinus, flexus *m*, curvamen *nt*; fig inclinatio *f*
beneath *prep* & *adv* ▷ **below**
□ **it is** ~ **me to** ... me indignum est
benefaction *n* largitio *f*; beneficium *nt*
benefactor *n* patronus *m*
benefactress *n* patrona *f*
beneficent *adj* beneficus, benignus, liberalis
beneficial *adj* utilis, commodus; salutaris
■ ~**ly** *adv* utiliter
benefit¹ *n* beneficium *nt*, gratia *f*
benefit² *vt* iuvo ①; prosum *ir* + *dat*
■ ~ *vi* lucror ①
benevolence *n* benevolentia; largitio *f*
benevolent *adj* benevolus; benignus
■ ~**ly** *adv* benevole, benigne

benign *adj* benignus

bent[1] *adj* curvus, flexus; (backwards) recurvus; (forwards) pronus; (inwards) camur; (winding) sinuosus

bent[2] *n* fig (inclination) ingenium *nt*; animus *m*; voluntas *f*

bequeath *vt* lego ①; relinquo ③

bequest *n* legatum *nt*

bereave *vt* (of) orbo, spolio, privo ①

bereavement *n* orbitas; spoliatio; (loneliness) solitudo *f*

bereft *adj* (∼ of) orbus (ab) + *abl*

berry *n* baca *f*; acinus *m*

berth *n* (of ship) statio *f*; (sleeping-place) cubiculum *nt*; (place, office) munus *nt*

beseech *vt* obsecro, imploro, supplico, obtestor ①

beset *vt* circumdo ①; obsideo; circumsideo; urgeo ②; vexo ①

beside *prep* (in addition to) ad, (outside) extra, (near) iuxta, (except) praeter (along) secundum *all* + *acc*
□ **be ∼ oneself** deliro ①

besides *prep* (in addition to) ad, (outside) extra, (except) praeter *all* + *acc*
■ ∼ *adv* porro, praeterea, praeterquam; insuper

besiege *vt* circumsedeo, obsideo ②

besieger *n* obsessor *m*

best[1] *adj* optimus, praestantissimus
■ ∼ **of all** *adv* optime, potissimum
□ **to the ∼ of one's ability** pro viribus

best[2] *adv* optime

bestir *vi*:
□ ∼ **oneself** expergiscor; (make an effort) incumbo ③

bestow *vt* tribuo ③, confero *ir*; dono ①; largior ④

bet[1] *n* pignus *nt*; sponsio *f*; ▶ **wager**

bet[2] *vt* pignore contendo ③

betoken *vt* indico ①; portendo ③

betray *vt* trado, prodo ③, (leave in the lurch) desum *ir* + *dat*; fig (reveal one's presence) oleo ② + *acc*; (show) profero *ir*; (give proof of) arguo ③

betrayal *n* proditio *f*

betrayer *n* proditor *m*

betroth *vt* spondeo, despondeo ②

betrothal *n* sponsalia *ntpl*

betrothed *adj* & *n* sponsus *m*, sponsa *f*

better[1] *adj* melior, potior, praestantior; superior
□ **get the ∼ (of)** supero ①; vinco ③; praevaleo ②
□ **it is ∼** praestat ①

better[2] *adv* melius, potius; rectius; satius
□ **get ∼** (in health) convalesco ③

better[3] *vt* emendo ①; corrigo ③

between *prep* inter + *acc*, in medio + *gen*

beverage *n* potio *f*, potus *m*

bewail *vt* deploro ①; ingemo, queror ③; lamentor ①; defleo ②

beware *vi&t* caveo, praecaveo ②
□ ∼! cave, cavete

bewilder *vt* perturbo ①; confundo ③

bewilderment *n* perturbatio *f*

bewitch *vt* fascino ①; (charm) demulceo ②; capio ③

beyond *prep* ultra, supra; praeter; (across) trans *all* + *acc*
■ ∼ *adv* supra, ultra; ulterius

bias[1] *n* inclinatio *f*; momentum *nt*; impetus *m*

bias[2] *vt* inclino ①

bibulous *adj* bibulus, vinosus

bicker *vi* altercor, rixor ①

bickering *n* altercatio, rixa *f*; iurgium *nt*

bid[1] *vt* iubeo ②; impero + *dat*, mando; (invite) invito, rogo, (money for wares) licitor ①; liceor ②
□ ∼ **goodbye** valedico ③

bid[2] *n* licitatio *f*

bidding *n* iussum, mandatum *nt*; (at the ∼ of) iussu + *gen*; (auction) licitatio *f*

bide *vi* (one's time) exspecto ①

bier *n* feretrum *nt*, sandapila *f*

big *adj* ingens, immanis, vastus, grandis; (in bulk) crassus; fig potens; (with pride) tumidus
□ **talk ∼** ampullor ①

bigamist *n* bimaritus *m*; bigamus *m*

bigoted *adj* superstitiosus; (obstinate) pervicax

bigotry *n* superstitio *f*; (obstinacy) pervicacia *f*

bile *n* bilis *f*

bilge-water *n* sentina *f*

bilious *adj* biliosus

bill *n* (of a bird) rostrum *nt*; (in writing) libellus *m*; (law proposed) rogatio; lex *f*; plebiscitum *nt*; (account) syngrapha *f*

billet *vt* milites per hospitia dispono ③

bill-hook *n* falx, falcula *f*

billow *n* fluctus *m*

billowy *adj* fluctuosus, undabundus

bin *n* (in a wine-cellar) loculus *m*

bind *vt* ligo ①; necto, stringo ③; vincio ④; fig astringo ③; (by oath, law) obligo ①; devincio ④
    ▫ ∼ **down** deligo ①
    ▫ ∼ **over** obligo; vador ①
    ▫ ∼ **together** colligo ①
    ▫ ∼ **up** ligo; alligo; colligo ①; substringo ③; (be bound up in) fig contineor ②

binding[1] *adj* obligatorius

binding[2] *n* religatio *f*; (wrapper) involucrum *nt*

biographer *n* vitae rerumque gestarum alicuius scriptor *m*

biography *n* vitae descriptio *f*

birch *n* betulla *f*

bird *n* avis, volucris, ales *f*; (bird of omen) praepes *f*; oscen *m*

birdcage *n* cavea *f*

birdcatcher *n* auceps *m*

birdcatching *n* aucupium *nt*

birdlime *n* viscum *nt*

birth *n* partus; ortus *m*; (race) stirps *f*, genus *nt*, natales *mpl*
    ▫ **give** ∼ pario ③

birthday *n* dies natalis *m*

birthplace *n* solum natale *or* genitale *nt*

birthright *n* ius ex genere ortum *nt*

bit *n* (for a horse) frenum; (little piece) frustum *nt*, offa, offula *f*

bitch *n* canis *f*

bite[1] *n* morsus *m*

bite[2] *vt* mordeo ②; (as pepper, etc.) uro ③

biting *adj* mordax; fig asper

bitter *adj* amarus; acerbus; asper; gravis; infensus
    ■ ∼**ly** *adv* amare; acerbe, aspere; graviter; infense

bitterness *n* amaritudo; acerbitas; asperitas, gravitas *f*

bitumen *n* bitumen *nt*

bivouac[1] *n* excubiae *fpl*

bivouac[2] *vi* excubo ①

black[1] *adj* niger; ater; fig (gloomy) tristis; scelestus, improbus
    ▫ ∼ **and blue** lividus
    ▫ ∼ **eye** sugillatio *f*

black[2] *n* nigrum *nt*
    ▫ **dressed in** ∼ pullatus

blackberry *n* morum *nt*
    ■ ∼**-bush** *n* rubus *m*

blackbird *n* merula *f*

blacken *vt* also fig nigro; denigro ①

blacking *n* atramentum *nt*

blackish *adj* subniger

blackness *n* nigritia, nigrities, nigritudo *f*

Black Sea *n* Pontus *m*

blacksmith *n* ferrarius faber *m*

bladder *n* vesica *f*

blade *n* lamina *f*; (of grass, etc.) caulis *m*; herba *f*; culmus *m*; (of an oar) palma, palmula *f*

blame[1] *vt* reprehendo ③; culpo, vitupero ①

blame[2] *n* reprehensio; culpa *f*

blameless *adj* integer, innoxius; innocens, innocuus; irreprehensus
    ■ ∼**ly** *adv* integre, innocenter

blamelessness *n* integritas; innocentia *f*

blanch *vi* expallesco ③, palleo ②; pallesco ③

bland *adj* blandus

blandishment *n* blanditiae *fpl*, blandimentum; (charm) lenocinium *nt*

blank[1] *adj* (empty) vacuus; (unwritten on) purus
    ▫ **look** ∼ confundor ③

blank[2] *n* inane *nt*; res vana *f*

blanket *n* stragulum *nt*; lodix *m*

blare[1] *vi* clango ③

blare[2] *n* sonus, strepitus *m*

blast *n* (of wind) flatus *m*; flamen *nt*; flabra *ntpl*; (blight) sideratio, rubigo *f*; (sound) clangor *m*

blaze[1] *n* flamma *f*; fulgor *m*; incendium *nt*

blaze[2] *vi* flagro ①; ardeo ②; ardesco ③

bleach *vt* candefacio ③
    ■ ∼ *vi* albesco ③

bleak *adj* algidus, frigidus; immitis

bleakness *n* algor *m*; frigus *nt*

blear-eyed *adj* lippus
    ▫ **be** ∼ lippio ④

bleat *vi* (as a sheep) balo ①

bleating *n* balatus *m*

bleed *vi* (of blood) fluo ③; (emit blood) sanguinem effundo ③

bleeding[1] *adj* (of wounds) crudus

bleeding[2] *n* (flowing of blood) sanguinis profluvium *nt*

blemish *n* (flaw) vitium *nt*, labes, macula *f*

blend *vt* misceo, immisceo, commisceo ②

bless *vt* benedico ③; (consecrate) consecro ①; (with good success) bene verto ③; prospero, aspiro, secundo ①

blessed *adj* beatus; pius; (fortunate) felix, fortunatus

blessing *n* benedictio; (good wish) fausta precatio *f*; (benefit) beneficium, bonum, munus *nt*

blight[1] *n* lues; (of corn, *etc.*) robigo, uredo; sideratio *f*

blight[2] *vt* uro ③; (ruin) deleo ②; (frustrate) frustror ①; fallo ③

blind[1] *adj* caecus

blind[2] *n* (screen of cloth) velum *nt*; fig praetextum *nt*

blind[3] *vt* caeco, occaeco ①; (deceive) fallo ③

blindness *n* caecitas *f*; tenebrae *fpl*

blink *vi* conniveo ②; nicto ①

bliss *n* beatitudo *f*

blissful *adj* beatus
 ■ ∼ly *adv* beate

blister[1] *n* pustula *f*

blister[2] *vt&i* pustulo ①

bloated *adj* sufflatus; inflatus, tumefactus, tumidus; (immense) immanis

block[1] *n* (lump) massa *f*

block[2] *vt* impedio ④
 □ ∼ **up** obstruo, intercludo ③

blockade[1] *n* obsidium *nt*; obsidio *f*

blockade[2] *n vt* obsideo ②

blockage *n* impedimentum *nt*

blockhead *n* caudex *m*

blood *n* sanguis *m*; (gore) cruor *m*; fig (slaughter) caedes; (lineage) natura *f*, genus *nt*

bloodless *adj* exsanguis; (without bloodshed) incruentus

blood-red *adj* cruentus; sanguineus, sanguinolentus

bloodshed *n* caedes *f*

bloodshot *adj* cruore suffusus

bloodstained *adj* cruentus, cruentatus, sanguinolentus

bloodthirsty *adj* sanguinarius; sanguineus; cruentus

blood-vessel *n* arteria, vena *f*

bloody *adj* sanguineus; sanguinolentus; sanguinarius; cruentus

bloom[1] *n* also fig flos *m*; robur *nt*

bloom[2] *vi* also fig floreo, vigeo ②

blooming *adj* florens; floridus; nitidus

blossom *n & vi* ▸ **bloom**

blot[1] *n* macula, litura; fig labes *f*, dedecus *nt*

blot[2] *vt* maculo ①
 □ ∼ **out** deleo ②; exstinguo ③; (erase) oblittero ①

blow[1] *n* (stroke) plaga *f*, ictus *m*; (with the fist) colaphus *m*; plaga *f*; vulnus *nt*
 □ **it came to ∼s** res ad pugnam venit

blow[2] *vi* flo; (breathe) spiro ①; (musical instruments) cano ③; (pant) anhelo ①
 ■ ∼ *vt* flo, afflo; (a wind instrument) inflo ①; (blow the nose) emungo ③
 □ ∼ **out** exstinguo ③

blue *adj* caeruleus, caerulus; (dark blue) cyaneus
 ■ ∼ *n* caeruleum *nt*

bluff *adj* (unsophisticated) rusticus; (steep) declivis; (windy) ventosus; (hearty) vehemens

bluish *adj* lividus, livens

blunder[1] *n* mendum, erratum *nt*; error *m*

blunder[2] *vi* offendo ③; erro ①

blunt[1] *adj* hebes; obtusus; retusus; fig inurbanus, rusticus; (plain) planus
 ■ ∼ly *adv* plane, libere

blunt[2] *vt* hebeto ①; obtundo, retundo ③

blur *vt* maculo ①; (darken) obscuro ①

blurt *vt*:
 □ ∼ **out** divulgo, vulgo ①

blush[1] *vi* erubesco, rubesco ③; rubeo ②

blush[2] *n* rubor *m*

blushing *adj*:
 ■ ∼ly *adv* rubens, erubescens

boar *n* aper; verres *m*

board[1] *n* (plank) tabula; (table) mensa *f*; (food, *etc.*) victus; (playing-table) abacus,

alveus lusorius *m*; (council) collegium; consilium *nt*
□ **on** ～ in nave

board² *vt* (cover with boards) contabulo ①

board³ *vt* (a ship) navem conscendo ③

boarder *n* convictor; hospes *m*

boast¹ *vi* iacto, glorior ①

boast² *n* iactantia, iactatio, gloriatio, vanitas *f*

boaster *n* iactator *m*

boastful *adj* gloriosus, vaniloquus

boasting *adj* gloriosus, vaniloquus

boat *n* linter, scapha, navicula, cumba *f*

boat-hook *n* contus *m*

boatman *n* nauta *m*; (ferryman) portitor *m*

bode *vt* portendo ③; praesagio ④; praemonstro ①

bodiless *adj* incorporalis; sine corpore

bodily *adj* corporeus; corporalis
■ ～ *adv* corporaliter

body *n* corpus; (corpse) cadaver *nt*; (trunk) truncus; mil numerus *m*, vis *f*; (collection of people) societas; multitudo *f*; collegium *nt*

bodyguard *n* stipatores, satellites *mpl*; cohors praetoria *f*

bog *n* palus *f*

boggy *adj* paludosus, palustris

boil¹ *vi* ferveo ②; effervesco ③; aestuo, exaestuo ①
■ ～ *vt* fervefacio; coquo ③

boil² *n* (pustule) furunculus *m*; ulcus *nt*

boisterous *adj* procellosus; violentus; turbidus

bold *adj* audax; fortis; impavidus; intrepidus; (free) liber; (rash) temerarius; (impudent) insolens; procax
■ ～ly *adv* audacter; libere; insolenter; fortiter

boldness *n* audacia; fidentia; (of speech) libertas; impudentia; (rashness) temeritas *f*

bolster¹ *n* pulvinus *m*; (of a bed) cervical *nt*

bolster² *vt* (up) fulcio ④

bolt¹ *n* (of a door) pessulus *m*; claustrum *nt*; obex *m*; (dart) iaculum, pilum; (of thunder) fulmen *nt*; (rivet) clavus *m*

bolt² *vt* obsero ①; occludo ③

bombard *vt* tormentis verbero ①

bombastic *adj* inflatus, tumidus

bond *n* vinculum *nt*; nodus *m*; copula; catena; (imprisonment) custodia *f*; (obligation) necessitas, necessitudo *f*; (legal document) syngrapha *f*

bondage *n* servitus *f*, servitium *nt*; captivitas *f*

bondsman *n* servus; addictus *m*; verna *m/f*

bone¹ *n* os *nt*; (of fish) spina *f*

bone² *vt* exosso ①

boneless *adj* exos

bonfire *n* ignes festi *mpl*

bonnet *n* mitra *f*

bony *adj* osseus; (thin) macer

booby *n* stultus *m*

book *n* liber, libellus *m*; volumen *nt*; codex *m*

bookcase *n* foruli *mpl*

bookish *adj* libris deditus

bookseller *n* bibliopola, librarius *m*
□ ～'s **shop** taberna (libraria) *f*

bookshelf *n* pluteus *m*

bookworm *n*:
□ **be a** ～ fig libris helluor ①

boom¹ *n* (of a ship) longurius *m*; (noise) stridor *m*

boom² *vi* resono ①

boon *n* bonum, donum *nt*; gratia *f*

boor *n* rusticus *m*

boorish *adj* agrestis, rusticus
■ ～ly *adv* rustice

boorishness *n* rusticitas *f*

boot *n* calceus *m*; caliga *f*

booth *n* taberna *f*, tabernaculum *nt*

booty *n* praeda *f*; spolia *ntpl*; (stripped from a foe) exuviae *fpl*

border¹ *n* (edge) margo *m/f*; (of dress) limbus *m*; (boundary) finis, terminus *m*; confinium *nt*

border² *vi* tango, attingo ③; circumiaceo ②
■ ～ *vt* praetexo ③

bordering *adj* affinis, finitimus

bore¹ *vt* terebro, perforo; cavo ①; fig fatigo ①

bore² *n* (hole) foramen *nt*; (tool) terebra *f*; fig (tedious person) importunus, molestus, odiosus *m*

boredom *n* taedium *nt*

boring *adj* molestus

b

born *adj* natus; genitus
  □ **be** ~ nascor, gignor ③; fig orior ④
  □ **a** ~ **soldier** aptus militiae

borough *n* municipium *nt*

borrow *vt* mutuor ①; mutuum sumo ③;
  fig imitor ①

borrowed *adj* mutuatus, mutuus;
  alienus

bosom *n* (breast) pectus *nt*, sinus *m*;
  gremium *nt*
  □ ~ **friend** amicus coniunctissimus

Bosphorus *n* Bosphorus *m*

boss *n* (of a shield) umbo *m*

botanist *n* herbarius *m*

botany *n* herbarum scientia *f*

botch *vt* fig male gero ③

both¹ *adj* (taken together) ambo; (pair)
  geminus; duo; (taken individually)
  uterque
  □ ~ **ways** bifariam

both² *conj*:
  □ ~ ... **and** et ... et, cum ... tum; -que ...
  -que

bother¹ *vt* vexo ①

bother² *n* vexatio, sollicitudo, cura *f*

bottle¹ *n* ampulla; (with handles) lagena *f*

bottle² *vt* in ampullas infundo ③

bottom¹ *n* fundus *m*; (of a ship) carina *f*;
  (dregs) faex *f*; (of a mountain) radix *f*; (depth of
  a thing) profundum *nt*
  □ **at** ~ ad imum (imam) ...
  □ **go to the** ~ subsido, resido ③; (sink)
  mergor ③
  □ **from top to** ~ funditus, penitus
  □ **get to the** ~ **of** scrutor ①

bottom² *adj* imus, infimus

bottomless *adj* fundo carens,
  immensus; profundus

bough *n* ramus *m*, bracchium *nt*

bounce *vi* resilio ④; resulto ①

bound¹ *n* finis, terminus, limes *m*;
  meta *f*; (leap) saltus *m*

bound² *vt* finio, definio ④; termino ①;
  (delimit) circumscribo ③
  ■ ~ *vi* (leap) salio, exsilio ④

boundary *n* finis, terminus, limes *m*;
  confinium *nt*

boundless *adj* infinitus; immensus

boundlessness *n* infinitas;
  immensitas *f*

bounteous *adj* benignus, largus,
  munificus
  ■ ~**ly** *adv* benigne, large, munifice

bountiful *adj* benignus, largus,
  munificus
  ■ ~**ly** *adv* benigne, large, munifice

bounty *n* largitas; benignitas,
  munificentia *f*; praemium, munus *nt*

bouquet *n* fasciculus (florum) *m*; (of
  wine) flos *m*

bovine *adj* bubulus

bow¹ *vt* flecto ③; inclino ①; (one's head)
  demitto ③; fig submitto ③
  ■ ~ *vi* flector ③; (yield) cedo ③

bow² *n* arcus *m*

bow³ *n* (of a ship) prora *f*

bowels *n* intestina, viscera *ntpl*; fig
  misericordia *f*

bowl *n* cratera; patera, phiala *f*; (shallow
  bowl) pelvis *f*

bow-legged *adj* valgus

bowman *n* sagittarius *m*

bowstring *n* nervus *m*

box¹ *n* arca; cista *f*; loculus *m*; capsa *f*;
  (for letters, *etc.*) scrinium *nt*; (for ointments,
  etc.) pyxis *f*
  □ ~ **on the ear** alapa *f*

box² *n* (tree) buxus *f*

box³ *vi* pugnis certo ①

boxer *n* pugil *m*

boxing-match *n* pugilatio *f*

boy *n* puer; (little ~) puerulus *m*

boyhood *n* pueritia; aetas puerilis *f*

boyish *adj* puerilis
  ■ ~**ly** *adv* pueriliter

brace¹ *n* (strap) fascia *f*; copula *f*; (couple)
  par *nt*

brace² *vi* (~ oneself) contendo ③

bracelet *n* armilla *f*, bracchiale *nt*

brag *vi* iacto ①

braggart¹ *n* iactator *m*

braggart² *adj* gloriosus

braid¹ *n* limbus *m*; (of hair) cincinnus *m*

braid² *vt* plecto, texo, praetexo ③

brain *n* cerebrum; (sense) cor *nt*;
  (understanding) mens *f*

bramble *n* (blackberry-bush) rubus *m*;
  (thicket) rubetum *nt*; (thorny bush) sentis,
  vepris *m*

bran *n* furfur *nt*

branch *n* (of a tree) ramus *m*; bracchium *nt*;
  (of a river) cornu *nt*; (of a pedigree) stemma
  nt; fig pars *f*

branching *adj* ramosus; (wide-spreading)
  patulus

brand *n* (mark) nota *f*; (torch) torris *m*; fax, taeda *f*

branding-iron *n* cauter *m*; cauterium *nt*

brandish *vt* vibro, libro, corusco ①

brand-new *adj* recentissimus

brass¹ *n* orichalcum, aes *nt*

brass² *adj* aenus, aereus, aeneus, aeratus

brat *n* infans *m/f*

brave¹ *adj* fortis; strenuus; animosus ■ ~**ly** *adv* fortiter; animose

brave² *vt* provoco ①; lacesso ③

bravery *n* fortitudo; virtus; magnanimitas *f*; (finery) splendor *m*

bravo *int* eu! euge!

brawl¹ *vi* rixor, iurgo ①

brawl² *n* rixa *f*; iurgium *nt*

brawler *n* rixator; rabula *m*

brawny *adj* lacertosus, torosus

bray¹ *vi* (of asses) rudo ③; (cry out) vociferor ①

bray² *n* (noise) strepitus *m*

brazen *adj* (of brass) aenus, aeneus, aereus, aeratus
□ ~-**faced** impudens

brazier *n* aerarius *m*; (coal-pan) foculus *m*

breach *n* ruptura; ruina; (of a treaty) violatio *f*; (falling out) discidium *nt*; discordia *f*
□ ~ **of law** lex violata *f*
□ **commit** ~ **of duty** officium neglego ③

bread *n* panis; fig victus *m*

bread-basket *n* panarium *nt*

bread-making *n* panificium *nt*

breadth *n* latitudo *f*

break¹ *vt* frango; rumpo ③; fig violo ①
■ ~ *vi* frangor; (cease) desino ③
□ ~ **apart** diffringo, dirumpo ③
□ ~ **down** demolior ④; destruo ③
□ ~ **forth** erumpo ③
□ ~ **in** (tame) domo ①; subigo ③
□ ~ **into** irrumpo; invado ③
□ ~ **loose** eluctor ①
□ ~ **off** *vt* abrumpo; (friendship) dirumpo; (a conference) dirimo; (a conversation) interrumpo ③; *vi* praefringor
□ ~ **open** effringo ③
□ ~ **out** erumpo; (a calamity, *etc.*) prorumpo ③; (a war) exorior ④
□ ~ **through** perrumpo ③

□ ~ **up** frango, effringo, dissolvo; (an army, assembly) dimitto; (ground) fodio ③
□ ~ **with** dissideo ②

break² *n* intermissio *f*; intervallum; (of day) diluculum *nt*

breakable *adj* fragilis

breakage *n* fractura *f*

breaker *n* (wave) fluctus *m*

breakfast¹ *n* prandium, ientaculum *nt*

breakfast² *vi* prandeo ②; iento ①

break-up *n* dissolutio *f*

breakwater *n* moles, pila *f*

breast *n* pectus *nt*; (of a woman) mamma, papilla *f*; (full of milk) uber *nt*; fig praecordia *ntpl*, pectus, cor *nt*

breastplate *n* lorica *f*; thorax *m*

breath *n* halitus, spiritus, flatus *m*; anima; (of air) aura *f*
□ **take** ~ respiro ①

breathe *vt* duco ③; (pant) anhelo; (whisper) susurro ①
□ ~ **out** exspiro; (the life) exhalo ①
■ ~ *vi* spiro, respiro ①

breathing *n* respiratio *f*

breathing-hole *n* spiraculum, spiramen, spiramentum *nt*

breathless *adj* exanimis, exanimus; exanimatus; (panting) anhelus

bred *adj*:
□ **well** ~ humanus, urbanus

breeches *n* bracae *fpl*

breed¹ *vt* pario, gigno ③; genero, creo ①; (cause) produco ③; (engender) procreo ①; (horses, *etc.*) pasco ③; alo ③; nutrio ④; (bring up) educo ①; alo ③

breed² *n* genus *nt*

breeding *n* fetura; (education) educatio *f*
□ **good** ~ humanitas, urbanitas *f*

breeze *n* aura *f*

breezy *adj* ventosus

brevity *n* brevitas *f*

brew *vt* coquo ③; fig concito, conflo ①
■ ~ *vi* excitor, concitor ①
□ **be** ~**ing** immineo ②

briar *n* ▶ **bramble**

bribe¹ *n* pretium *nt*, merces, pecunia *f*

bribe² *vt* corrumpo ③

bribery *n* corruptio, corruptela, largitio *f*; ambitus *m*

brick *n* later *m*

bricklayer n caementarius m

brickmaker n laterarius m

brickwork n latericium nt

bridal adj nuptialis
□ ∼ **song** n epithalamium nt
□ ∼-**chamber** n thalamus m

bride n sponsa; nupta, nympha f

bridegroom n sponsus; novus maritus m

bridesmaid n pronuba f

bridge¹ n pons m; (of instrument or nose) iugum nt

bridge² vt:
□ ∼ **over** flumen ponte iungo ③

bridle¹ n also fig frenum nt; habena f

bridle² vt freno; fig infreno, refreno ①; coerceo ②

brief adj brevis, concisus

briefly adv breviter, brevi; paucis (verbis)

briefness n brevitas f

brier n ▷ bramble

brigade n (of infantry) legio; (of cavalry) turma f

brigadier n tribunus militum m

brigand n latro, latrunculus m

bright adj clarus; lucidus, splendidus; nitidus; candidus; (flashing) fulgidus; (smart, clever) argutus, sollers; (cloudless) serenus

brighten vt polio ④
■ ∼ vi lucesco; splendesco; claresco ③; (gladden) hilaro, exhilaro ①

brightly adv lucide, clare, splendide, nitide

brightness n splendor; nitor; fulgor m; (of the sun) lumen nt; fig hilaritas f; (of intellect) sollertia f

brilliance n splendor m; fig (of style) lumen nt

brilliant adj splendidus; nitens; nitidus; fig luculentus; praeclarus; (clever) ingeniosus
□ **be** ∼ splendeo, niteo ②

brim n ora f, margo m/f, labrum nt

brimstone n sulfur, sulpur nt

brine n muria f, salsamentum; (sea) salum nt

bring vt fero, affero, infero ir; gero, duco ③; porto ①; (by carriage, etc.) adveho ③
□ ∼ **about** efficio ③
□ ∼ **back** refero ir, reduco ③; reporto; fig revoco ①; (by force) redigo ③

□ ∼ **before** defero ir; produco ③
□ ∼ **down** defero ir; deduco; (by force) deicio ③
□ ∼ **forth** prodo; depromo; pario ③; (yield) fero, effero ir
□ ∼ **forward** profero, effero ir; ago ③
□ ∼ **in(to)** infero ir; inveho; induco; (as income) reddo ③
□ ∼ **off** praesto ①; (carry through) perficio ③
□ ∼ **on** affero ir; adduco; fig obicio ③
□ ∼ **out** effero ir; produco ③; excio ④
□ ∼ **over** perduco, traduco; fig perduco, traho ③; concilio ①
□ ∼ **to** adduco; appello ③; fig persuadeo ②
□ ∼ **together** confero ir; (assemble, etc.) contraho ③; fig concilio ①
□ ∼ **up** subduco ③; (children) educo ①; (vomit) evomo ③

brink n margo m/f

briny adj salsus; subsalsus

brisk adj alacer, agilis, vividus; laetus; impiger, acer
■ ∼**ly** adv alacriter, acriter, impigre

briskness n alacritas f, vigor m

bristle¹ n saeta f

bristle² vi horreo ②; horresco ③

bristly adj saetiger, saetosus; hirsutus

Britain n Britannia f

British adj Britannicus

brittle adj fragilis, caducus

brittleness n fragilitas f

broach vt (a cask) (dolium) relino ③

broad adj latus, largus, amplus; fig manifestus, apertus

broadly adv late

broadness n amplitudo, latitudo f

broken adj fractus; intermissus; dirutus; (off) abruptus; (open) effractus; (in pieces) contusus; (up) dismissus; violatus; (of the heart) vulneratus

broken-hearted adj abiectus, spe deiectus, afflictus

broker n (money-changer) nummularius m

bronze¹ n aes nt

bronze² adj aenus, aeneus, aereus, aeratus

brooch n fibula f

brood¹ n proles; progenies; suboles; (of chickens) pullities f

brood² vi (as a hen) incubo ①; fig (∼ upon) foveo ②; agito ①

b

brook¹ *n* amniculus, rivulus *m*

brook² *vt* fero *ir*, patior ③; tolero ①

broom *n* scopae *fpl*

broomstick *n* scoparum manubrium *nt*

broth *n* ius *nt*

brothel *n* lupanar, lustrum *nt*

brother *n* frater, germanus *m*
■ ∼**-in-law** *n* levir, sororis maritus *m*

brotherhood *n* germanitas; fraternitas *f*; fig sodalicium, collegium *nt*

brotherly *adj* fraternus

brow *n* supercilium *nt*; frons *f*

browbeat *vt* terreo ②; deprimo ③

brown *adj* fulvus, fuscus, pullus, spadix
■ ∼ *n* fulvus color *m*

brownish *adj* subniger, suffuscus

browse *vt* (graze on) carpo, depasco ③; tondeo ②

bruise¹ *vt* contundo ③; sugillo ①; infringo ③

bruise² *n* contusio; sugillatio *f*

brush¹ *n* scopula *f*; (painter's ∼) penicillus *m*; (bushy tail) muscarium *nt*; (fray, skirmish) concursatio *f*

brush² *vt* verro ③; tergeo; detergeo
□ ∼ **away** amoveo ②
□ ∼ **up** orno ①; reficio ③

brushwood *n* sarmenta, virgulta, ramalia *ntpl*

brusque *adj* praeceps

brutal *adj* ferus; immanis; inhumanus; saevus; furiosus
■ ∼**ly** *adv* inhumane; saeve

brutality *n* feritas, ferocitas, saevitia; immanitas *f*

brute *n* bestia, pecus *f*

brutish *adj* ferus; fatuus, stupidus

bubble¹ *n* bulla *f*

bubble² *vi* bullio ④; (gush up) scateo ②

buccaneer *n* pirata, praedo *m*

bucket *n* hama, situla *f*

buckle¹ *n* fibula *f*

buckle² *vt* fibula necto ③

buckler *n* parma *f*, ▶ **shield**

bucolic *adj* bucolicus, pastoralis, pastorius, rusticus, agrestis

bud¹ *n* gemma *f*, germen *nt*; (of a flower) calyx; (in grafting) oculus *m*

bud² *vi* gemmo, germino ①

budge *vi* me moveo ②; cedo, loco cedo ③

buff *adj* luteus

buffet¹ *n* (blow) alapa *f*, colaphus *m*

buffet² *vt* (strike) ferio ④

buffoon *n* scurra; sannio, balatro *m*
□ **play the** ∼ scurror ①

buffoonery *n* scurrilitas *f*; lascivia *f*; iocus *m*

bug *n* cimex *m*

bugle *n* bucina *f*; cornu *nt*

build *vt* aedifico ①; struo, construo, exstruo, condo ③; fabrico ①; (upon) inaedifico ①; fig (rely on) nitor ③ + *abl*

builder *n* aedificator; conditor, structor; fig auctor, fabricator *m*

building *n* (act) aedificatio, exstructio *f*; (structure) aedificium *nt*

bulb *n* bulbus *m*

bulge *vi* tumeo, turgeo ②; procurro ③
□ ∼ **out** tumesco ③

bulk *n* amplitudo; moles *f*

bulky *adj* crassus; ingens; gravis; onerosus

bull *n* taurus, bos *m*; (edict) edictum *nt*

bulldog *n* canis molossus *m*

bullet *n* glans *f*

bullock *n* taurus castratus; iuvencus *m*

bully¹ *n* salaco, rixator *m*

bully² *vt* insulto ①; lacesso ③

bulrush *n* scirpus; iuncus *m*

bulwark *n* agger *m*; propugnaculum *nt*; moenia, munimenta *ntpl*; fig praesidium, propugnaculum *nt*

bump¹ *n* (swelling) tuber *nt*; (thump) plaga *f*

bump² *vt* (into) offendo ③; pulso ①

bumpkin *n* rusticus *m*

bun *n* libum, crustulum *nt*; placenta *f*

bunch *n* (bundle) fasciculus
□ ∼ **of grapes** racemus *m*

bundle¹ *n* fascis, fasciculus *m*; (pack) sarcina *f*; (of rods) fasces *mpl*

bundle² *vt* colligo ①

bungle *vt* rem inscite gero, inscite ago ③
■ ∼ *vi* erro ①

bungler *n* homo rudis; imperitus *m*

buoy *vt* (up) attollo ③; sustineo ②; sustento ①; fulcio ④

buoyancy *n* levitas; fig hilaritas *f*

buoyant *adj* levis; fig hilaris

bur *n* lappa *f*

burden[1] *n* onus *nt*; fascis *m*; sarcina *f*

burden[2] *vt* onero, gravo ①; opprimo ③
□ **beast of** ∼ iumentum *nt*

burdensone *adj* onerosus, gravis, molestus, iniquus

burglar *n* fur *m*

burglary *n* effractura *f*

burial *n* (act of burying) sepultura *f*; funus *nt*; exsequiae *fpl*

burial-place *n* locus sepulturae *m*; sepulcrum *nt*

burly *adj* corpulentus, robustus, lacertosus

burn *vt* uro ③; cremo ①; (set on fire) incendo ③
■ ∼ *vi* flagro ①; ardeo ②; (with love, *etc.*) ardeo ②; flagro ①; caleo ②; calesco ③
□ ∼ **down** deuro ③
□ **be** ∼**t down** deflagro ①
□ ∼ **out** *vt* exuro; *vi* exstinguor ③
□ ∼ **up** concremo ①

burning[1] *n* ustio, adustio; deflagratio *f*, incendium *nt*

burning[2] *adj* ardens; fig fervens

burnish *vt* polio, expolio ④; levigo ①

burrow[1] *n* cuniculus *m*; cubile *nt*

burrow[2] *vi* (dig down) defodio ③

burst[1] *vt* rumpo, dirumpo; (with a noise) displodo ③
□ ∼ **forth** erumpo, prorumpo ③
□ ∼ **into tears** in lacrimas effundor ③
□ ∼ **open** effringo ③; dirumpor ③; dissilio ④

burst[2] *n* (noise) fragor *m*

bury *vt* sepelio ④; humo ①; (hide, *etc.*) abdo, condo; (put into the ground) infodio, defodio ③

bush *n* frutex, dumus, sentis, vepres *m*

bushy *adj* dumosus; fruticosus; (of hair) hirsutus, horridus

busily *adv* industrie, sedulo

business *n* negotium *nt*; (calling, trade) ars; (matter) res; (employment) occupatio *f*; studium; (duty) officium; (work) opus *nt*

bust *n* statua, effigies *f*

bustle[1] *n* festinatio *f*; tumulus *m*

bustle[2] *vi* (hurry) festino ①; (run to and fro) discurro ③

bustling *adj* operosus

busy *adj* occupatus; negotiosus; (industrious) strenuus, industrius, navus; (meddling) curiosus, molestus; (active, laborious) operosus

busybody *n* ardelio *m*

but *conj* sed, ast, at; autem; ceterum; vero, verum
□ ∼ **for** absque + *abl*; (except) praeter, nisi; (only) modo, solum, tantum
□ ∼ **if** sin, sin autem; quod si
□ ∼ **if not** sin aliter, sin minus
□ ∼ **yet** nihilominus, veruntamen
□ **I cannot** ∼ non possum facere quin + *subj*

butcher[1] *n* lanius; fig carnifex *m*
■ ∼**'s shop** *n* macellum *nt*

butcher[2] *vt* caedo ③; trucido ①

butchery *n* caedes, trucidatio *f*

butler *n* promus *m*

butt[1] *n* (mark) meta *f*; (cask) dolium *nt*; fig (laughing-stock) ludibrium *nt*

butt[2] *vi* arieto ①
■ ∼**ing** *adj* petulcus

butter *n* butyrum *nt*

butterfly *n* papilio *m*

buttock *n* clunis *m/f*; natis *f*

buttress *vt* fulcio, suffulcio ④

buxom *adj* alacer, hilaris, laetus, lascivus, procax; (fat) pinguis

buy *vt* emo ③; mercor ①
□ ∼ **back** *or* **off** redimo ③
□ ∼ **up** emercor ①; coemo ③

buyer *n* emptor *m*

buying *n* emptio, mercatura *f*

buzz[1] *vi* murmuro, susurro ①; (in the ear) insusurro ①

buzz[2] *n* bombus *m*, murmur *nt*; susurrus *m*

buzzard *n* buteo *m*

by *prep* (of place) ad, apud; sub; (along) secundum, praeter; (near) propter, iuxta; (of time) sub; (denoting the instrument *or* cause) per; (in oaths) per *all* + *acc*; (of the agent, *e.g.* 'by a soldier') a, ab + *abl*
□ ∼ **oneself** solus, solum
□ ∼ **and** ∼ mox, brevi, postmodo
□ **go** ∼ praetereo *ir*

bygone *adj* praeteritus; priscus

by-law *n* praescriptum *nt*

bystander *n* arbiter *m*
■ ∼**s** *pl* circumstantes *mpl*

byword *n* proverbium *nt*; fig fabula *f*
□ **be a** ∼ ludibrio sum

Cc

cabbage n brassica f, caulis m; crambe f

cabin n (hut) tugurium nt; (small room) cellula f

cabinet n conclave; (piece of furniture) scrinium, armarium nt, cistula f; (government) summum principis consilium nt

cable n ancorale nt, rudens m

cackle¹ vi strepo ③; clango ③; (of hens) gracillo ①; fig garrio ④

cackle² n strepitus, clangor m; fig gerrae fpl

cadaverous adj cadaverosus; (thin) macer

cadet n tiro m

cage¹ n cavea f, avarium nt; (prison) carcer m; (for large animals) saeptum nt

cage² vt includo ③

cajole vt adulor ①; illicio ③; blandior ④

cajolery n blanditiae fpl; adulatio f

cake¹ n placenta f, libum nt; (doughy mass) massa f

cake² vi concresco ③

calamitous adj calamitosus; lacrimosus; funestus; gravis; infelix
■ ~ly adv calamitose, infeliciter

calamity n calamitas; clades f; malum nt; res adversa f

calculate vt&i computo, supputo; aestimo, existimo ①

calculated adj aptus, ad rem accommodatus; (intentional) meditatus

calculation n computatio, ratio f, calculus m; fig ratiocinatio f

calculator n abacus m

calendar n kalendarium nt, fasti mpl; (diary) ephemeris f

calf¹ n (animal) vitulus m

calf² n (of the leg) sura f

calibre n fig ingenium nt, indoles f

call¹ vt voco ①; (name) appello, nomino ①
□ ~ **aside** sevoco ①
□ ~ **away** avoco ①; fig devoco ①
□ ~ **back** revoco ①
□ ~ **down** devoco ①
□ ~ **for** postulo; flagito ①

□ ~ **forth** evoco, provoco ①; fig excieo ②; elicio ③
□ ~ **in** introvoco ①; (money) cogo ③
□ ~ **off** avoco, revoco ①
□ ~ **on** inclamo ①; cieo ②; appello ①; (visit) viso ③; saluto ①
□ ~ **out** evoco ①; exclamo ①
□ ~ **to** advoco ①
□ ~ **to mind** recordor ①
□ ~ **to witness** testor ①
□ ~ **together** convoco ①
□ ~ **up** excito; suscito ①; elicio ③

call² n (summons) vocatio; (sound of the voice) vox f; (shout) clamor m; (short visit) salutatio f

caller n salutator m

calling n (summoning) vocatio f; (profession) studium nt; ars f; (bent) impetus m (rank, position) condicio f
□ ~ **in** (of money) coactio f
□ ~ **together** convocatio f
□ ~ **upon** invocatio f

callous adj callosus; fig (insensible) durus
□ **become** ~ occallesco; obduresco ③

callousness n duritia f

calm¹ adj tranquillus, placidus, sedatus, placatus, quietus, serenus

calm² n tranquillitas, quies f; (a calm sea) tranquillum nt

calm³ vt paco, placo, sedo ①; mulceo ②; tranquillo ①

calmly adv placide, sedate, tranquille

calmness n tranquillitas; serenitas, quies f
□ **bear with** ~ aequo animo fero ir

calumny n maledictum nt, criminatio f, calumnia f

camel n camelus m

camp¹ n castra ntpl
□ **winter** ~ hiberna; stativa ntpl
□ **summer** ~ aestiva ntpl

camp² vi castra pono ③

campaign¹ n expeditio f; (service) militia f; stipendium; (war) bellum nt
□ **one's first** ~ tirocinium nt

campaign² vi expeditioni intersum ir, milito ①

camp-follower n lixa m

can¹ n hirnea, hirnula f

can² *vi* possum *ir*; queo *ir*
  □ **I ∼not** nequeo *ir*; nescio ④

canal *n* fossa *f*; canalis *m*

cancel *vt* deleo ②; rescindo ③; abrogo
  ①; tollo ③

cancer *n* (disease, and sign of the zodiac)
  cancer *m*

candelabrum *n* candelabrum *nt*

candid *adj* candidus; apertus;
  sincerus
  ■ **∼ly** *adv* candide; sincere; sine
  fraude

candidate *n* candidatus *m*

candidateship *n* petitio *f*

candle *n* candela *f*

candlelight *n* lucerna *f*
  □ **study by ∼** lucubro ①

candlestick *n* candelabrum *nt*

candour *n* candor *m*, sinceritas *f*

cane¹ *n* canna, arundo *f*; baculus,
  calamus *m*; (rod for striking) ferula *f*

cane² *vt* ferula ferio ④

canine *adj* caninus

canister *n* pyxis *f*

canker *n* (of plants) robigo *f*; fig lues *f*;
  pestis *f*

cannibal *n* anthropophagus *m*

canoe *n* linter *f*

canopy *n* vela; (curtain) aulaea *ntpl*

cantankerous *adj* difficilis, morosus

canteen *n* caupona *f*

canter¹ *vi* curro ③; volo ①
  ■ **∼ing** *adj* quadrupedans

canter² *n* cursus incitatus *m*

canvas *n* (for sails) linteum *nt*; carbasus
  f; (for painters) textile *nt*

canvass *vt* ambio; circumeo *ir*;
  prenso ①; (be a candidate) peto ③

canvassing *n* ambitio, petitio *f*;
  (unlawful) ambitus *m*

cap *n* pilleus, galerus *m*; mitra *f*

capability *n* facultas *f*

capable *adj* capax; idoneus, potens

capacious *adj* capax; amplus

capaciousness *n* capacitas;
  amplitudo *f*, spatium *nt*

capacity *n* (measure) mensura *f*; modus
  m; (intelligence) ingenium *nt*; facultas *f*

cape *n* (headland) promonturium;
  (garment) umerale *nt*; lacerna *f*

caper¹ *n* saltus *m*, exsultatio *f*

caper² *vi* tripudio, exsulto ①

capital¹ *adj* (of crimes) capitalis; fig
  (outstanding) insignis, eximius

capital² *n* (chief city) caput; (money) caput
  nt, sors *f*

Capitol *n* Capitolium *nt*

capitulate *vi* arma trado, me dedo ③

capitulation *n* deditio *f*

caprice *n* libido; inconstantia *f*

capricious *adj* levis, inconstans;
  mobilis; ventosus
  □ **∼ly** ex libidine; inconstanter

capsize *vi* everto ③

captain *n* (of infantry) centurio; (of cavalry)
  praefectus; (of a merchantship)
  navicularius, magister *m*; (general) dux,
  imperator *m*

captivate *vt* mulceo ②; capto ①; capio,
  allicio ③

captive *n* captivus *m*
  ■ **∼** *adj* captivus

captivity *n* captivitas *f*; (confinement)
  custodia *f*; (chains) vincula *ntpl*

captor *n* expugnator *m*

capture¹ *n* captura; expugnatio *f*

capture² *vt* capio, excipio ③; expugno
  ①

carbuncle *n* (tumour) carbunculus,
  furunculus; (precious stone) carbunculus
  m

carcass *n* cadaver *nt*

card *vt* (wool) pecto, carpo ③; carmino ①

carder *n* carminator *m*

cardinal *adj* (chief) praecipuus

care¹ *n* cura, sollicitudo; (heed) cautio;
  (diligence) diligentia; (anxiety) anxietas;
  (protection, guardianship) tutela; (management)
  procuratio; curatio; custodia *f*
  □ **take ∼** caveo ②
  □ **take ∼ of** curo ①

care² *vi* curo ①
  ■ **∼ for** *vt* provideo ②, invigilo ① + *dat*
  □ **I don't ∼** non mihi curae est

career *n* curriculum *nt*; cursus,
  decursus *m*; (life) vita *f*

carefree *adj* hilarus, hilaris

careful *adj* (diligent) diligens; attentus;
  (cautious) cautus, providus; (of things)
  accuratus
  ■ **∼ly** *adv* caute; diligenter; accurate,
  exquisite
  □ **be ∼!** cave, cavete

carefulness *n* cura; (diligence)
  diligentia; (caution) cautio *f*

careless *adj* securus; neglegens; imprudens
■ ∼**ly** *adv* neglegenter; secure; incuriose

carelessness *n* incuria; neglegentia; imprudentia; securitas *f*

caress[1] *n* blanditiae *fpl*; complexus *m*

caress[2] *vt* blandior ④; foveo, permulceo ②; osculor ①

cargo *n* onus *nt*

carnage *n* caedes, strages, trucidatio *f*

carnival *n* saturnalia *ntpl*; festum *nt*

carnivorous *adj* carnivorus

carouse *vt&i* comissor, poto; perbacchor ①

carp *vt* (∼ at) carpo, rodo ③; vellico ①; mordeo ②

carpenter *n* faber tignarius *m*

carpentry *n* ars fabrilis, opera fabrilis *f*

carpet *n* tapete *nt*; stragulum *nt*

carping *n* cavillatio *f*

carriage *n* (act of carrying) vectura *f*; (vehicle) vehiculum *nt*; raeda *f*; currus *m*; carpentum *nt*; fig habitus, gestus, incessus *m*

carrion *n* cadaver *nt*, caro morticina *f*

carrot *n* pastinaca *f*

carry *vt* porto ①; fero *ir*; gero ③; gesto ①; (by carriage) veho; (lead) duco, conduco ③
□ ∼ **away** aufero *ir*; aveho; fig rapio ③
□ ∼ **along** perduco; ago ③
□ ∼ **back** refero *ir*; reveho ③
□ ∼ **in** importo ①; inveho ③
□ ∼ **off** aufero *ir*; rapio; abstraho ③
□ ∼ **on** (continue) permaneo ② in + *abl*, perduco ③; fig exerceo ②; gero ③
□ ∼ **out** effero *ir*; exporto ①; eveho; fig exsequor ③
□ ∼ **round** circumfero *ir*
□ ∼ **together** comporto ①; confero *ir*
□ ∼ **through** perfero *ir*; fig exsequor ③

cart *n* carrus *m*, plaustrum, vehiculum *nt*
□ put the ∼ **before the horse** fig praeposteris consiliis uti ③

cart-horse *n* caballus *m*; iumentum *nt*

cartilage *n* cartilago *f*

cartwright *n* faber carpentarius *m*

carve *vt* sculpo, exsculpo ③; caelo ①; incido ③; (meat) seco ①

carver *n* (artist) caelator; (of meat) carptor, scissor *m*

carving *n* caelatura *f*
□ ∼**-knife** *n* cultellus *m*

cascade *n* aquae lapsus *or* deiectus *m*

case *n* (sheath) involucrum *nt*, theca; vagina; (matter) res; (in law) causa; (condition, state, *etc.*) condicio *f*, status *m*, quaestio *f*; (event) eventus *m*
□ **it is often the** ∼ saepe accidit
□ **nothing to do with the** ∼ nihil ad rem

cash *n* pecunia numerata; (deposit) praesens pecunia *f*

cash-book *n* codex *m*

cask *n* cadus *m*; dolium *nt*; amphora *f*

casket *n* arca, arcula; pyxis, cista, cistula *f*

cast[1] *vt* (throw) iacio; conicio; mitto ③; iaculor, iacto ①; (metal) fundo ③
□ ∼ **away** *or* **aside** abicio, reicio ③
□ ∼ **down** deicio; fig affligo ③
□ ∼ **off** (the skin) exuo ③; fig amoveo ②; pono ③; repudio ①
□ ∼ **out** eicio, expello ③

cast[2] *n* (throw and distance) iactus; missus *m*; (pattern) imago *f*

castanet *n* crotalum *nt*

castaway *n* (shipwrecked) naufragus *m*

castigate *vt* castigo ①

castigation *n* castigatio *f*

casting *n* (of metals) fusura *f*; (throwing) iactatus, iactus *m*
□ ∼**-net** *n* iaculum, rete iaculum *nt*

castle *n* castellum *nt*; turris, arx *f*

castrate *vt* castro, exseco ①; excido ③

castration *n* castratio, castratura *f*

casual *adj* fortuitus
■ ∼**ly** *adv* fortuito; temere; (by the way) obiter

casualty *n* casus *m*

cat *n* feles *f*

catacombs *n* puticuli *mpl*

catalogue *n* index *m*; tabula *f*

catapult *n* catapulta *f*

cataract *n* cataracta, catarracta *f*, catarractes *m*; (disease of the eye) glaucoma *nt*

catarrh *n* gravedo *f*

catastrophe *n* exitus, eventus *m*; (ruin) pernicies *f*; exitium *nt*

catastrophic *adj* damnosus, exitialis

catch[1] *vt* capio ③; capto ①; (by surprise) deprehendo; (understand) intellego ③;

comprehendo ③; (in a net) illaqueo; (with bait) inesco ①; (fire) concipio; (a disease) contraho ③
□ ~ **up** excipio ③

catch² *n* (prize) captura *f*; (of locks, *etc.*) ansa *f*

catching *adj* contagiosus

category *n* categoria *f*; (class) genus *nt*

cater *vi* obsonor; cibos suppedito ①

caterer *n* obsonator *m*

caterpillar *n* eruca *f*

cattle *n* boves *mpl*

cattle-market *n* forum boarium *nt*

cauldron *n* aenum *nt*, lebes *m*; cortina *f*

cauliflower *n* brassica *f*

cause¹ *n* causa *f*; (source) fons *m*; origo *f*; (matter) res; (reason) ratio; (action at law) actio, lis *f*

cause² *vt* facio, efficio ③; creo ①; excito ①; moveo ②; (induce) suadeo ②; adduco ③

causeway *n* agger viae *m*

caustic *adj* causticus; fig mordax, acerbus

caution¹ *n* cautio; cura; prudentia; (warning) monitio *f*

caution² *vt* moneo, admoneo ②

cautious *adj* cautus, consideratus; circumspectus; providus, prudens
■ ~**ly** *adv* caute; pedetemptim, pedetemtim

cavalcade *n* pompa equestris *f*

cavalier *n* eques *m*

cavalry *n* equitatus *m*, equites *mpl*, copiae equestres *fpl*

cave *n* specus *m/f/nt*, antrum *nt*; caverna, spelunca *f*

cavern *n* spelunca, caverna *f*, antrum *nt*; specus *m/f/nt*

cavernous *adj* cavus

caw *vi* crocio ④; crocito ①

cease *vt* desino; omitto; intermitto ③
■ ~ *vi* + *inf* mitto, desino; desisto; omitto ③; cesso ①; (come to an end) desino, desisto ③; cesso ①

ceaseless *adj* perpetuus; assiduus
■ ~**ly** *adv* perpetuo; assidue; usque; continenter

cedar¹ *n* cedrus *f*

cedar² *adj* cedreus

cede *vt* cedo, dedo ③
■ ~ *vi* cedo, decedo ③

ceiling *n* lacunar, laquear *nt*

celebrate *vt* celebro, laudo ①; (solemnize) ago ③; agito, celebro ①

celebrated *adj* celeber; nobilis; clarus, praeclarus, illustris, notus

celebration *n* celebratio *f*

celebrity *n* fama, celebritas *f*

celery *n* apium *nt*

celestial *adj* caelestis; divinus
■ ~ *n* caeles *m*; caelicola *m/f*

cell *n* cella *f*

cellar *n* cella *f*, cellarium *nt*

cement¹ *n* ferrumen, caementum *nt*

cement² *vt* conglutino; ferrumino ①; fig (confirm) firmo, confirmo ①

cemetery *n* sepulcretum *nt*

cenotaph *n* tumulus inanis *m*; cenotaphium *nt*

censer *n* turibulum *nt*

censor *n* censor; (one who blames) reprehensor, castigator *m*

censorious *adj* austerus, severus

censorship *n* censura *f*

censure¹ *n* vituperatio, censura, reprehensio *f*

censure² *vt* animadverto, reprehendo ③; vitupero, improbo ①

census *n* census *m*

centaur *n* centaurus *m*

centenary *adj* centenarius
■ ~ *n* centenarius numerus; centesimus annus *m*

centipede *n* centipeda *f*

central *adj* medius
■ ~**ly** *adv* in medio

centralize *vt* in unum contraho ③

centre *n* centrum *nt*; medius locus *m*; (the centre of the line) media acies *f*

centurion *n* centurio *m*

century *n* (political division, subdivision of a legion) centuria *f*; (number of years) saeculum *nt*

ceremonial *adj* sollemnis
■ ~**ly** *adv* rite; sollemniter

ceremonious *adj* sollemnis
■ ~ *adv* sollemniter

ceremony *n* caerimonia *f*; sollemne, officium *nt*; ritus; (pomp) apparatus *m*

certain *adj* certus; compertus
□ **a** ~ quidam
□ **for** ~ certe, pro certo
□ **it is** ~ constat ①

■ ~**ly** *adv* certe, certo; profecto; vero, sane

certainty *n* certum *nt*, veritas, fides *f*

certify *vt* confirmo, affirmo ①

cessation *n* cessatio; intermissio *f*; (end) finis *m/f*

cesspool *n* cloaca *f*

chafe *vt&i* (with the hand) frico ①; (make sore) attero ③; (vex) vexo ①

chaff *n* palea *f*; acus *nt*

chaffinch *n* fringilla *f*

chagrin *n* vexatio *f*

chain[1] *n* catena *f*; vinculum *nt*; (ornament) torques *m/f*; fig series *f*; (of mountains) iugum *nt*

chain[2] *vt* catenis constringo; catenas alicui inicio ③

chair *n* sella; cathedra, sedes *f*; sedile *nt*; (sedan) lectica *f*

chairman *n* (of a club, *etc.*) praeses *m*

chalice *n* calix *m*

chalk[1] *n* creta *f*

chalk[2] *vt* creta noto ①; creta illino ③ ◻ ~ **out** designo ①

chalky *adj* (chalk-like) cretaceus; (full of chalk) cretosus

challenge[1] *n* provocatio; (law) reiectio *f*

challenge[2] *vt* provoco ①; lacesso; (law) reicio ③

chamber *n* cubiculum, conclave *nt*; (bedroom) thalamus *m*

chambermaid *n* ancilla *f*

champ *vt&i* mando ③; mordeo ②

champion *n* propugnator; defensor *m*; vindex *m/f*

chance[1] *n* (accident) casus *m*; fors, fortuna, fig alea; (probability) spes *f*; (opportunity) occasio *f* ◻ **by** ~ casu, fortuito, forte

chance[2] *adj* fortuitus; inexpectatus

change[1] *vt* muto, commuto; novo, vario; (one's place) demigro ①; (money) permuto ■ ~ *vi* mutor, vario ①

change[2] *n* mutatio; commutatio; vicissitudo *f*; vices *fpl*; (variety) varietas *f*; (small money) nummuli *mpl*

changeable *adj* mutabilis; inconstans; levis; (of colour) versicolor

changeableness *n* mutabilitas; mobilitas, inconstantia, levitas, volubilitas *f*

changeless *adj* immutabilis, immutatus

channel *n* canalis; (of rivers) alveus *m*; (arm of the sea) fretum *nt*; fig cursus *m*; via *f*

chant[1] *n* cantus *m*

chant[2] *vt&i* canto ①

chaos *n* chaos *nt*; fig confusio *f*

chaotic *adj* confusus; indigestus

chapel *n* sacellum, sacrarium *nt*

chaplet *n* sertum *nt*; corona *f*

chapter *n* caput *nt*

char *vt* amburo ③

character *n* mores *mpl*; indoles *f*; ingenium *nt*; habitus *m*; natura; proprietas *f*

characteristic[1] *adj* proprius + *gen* ■ ~**ally** *adv* ex more (tuo, suo, *etc.*)

characteristic[2] *n* proprium *nt*

characterize *vt* describo ③

charcoal *n* carbo *m*

charge[1] *vt* accuso ①; arguo ③; criminor ①; (attack) adorior ④; aggredior ③; (burden) onero; (command) impero ①; (entrust) committo, credo ③; mando ①; (exact), exigo ③ ■ ~ *vi* irruo, invado ③

charge[2] *n* accusatio *f*; crimen *nt*; (attack) impetus, incursus *m*; (command) mandatum *nt*; (trust) cura, custodia *f*; (office) munus *nt*; (cost) impensa *f*, sumptus *m*

charger *n* (war-horse) equus bellator, sonipes, quadrupedans *m*

chariot *n* currus *m*, curriculum *nt*; (for war) essedum *nt*

charioteer *n* auriga *m*

charitable *adj* benignus, beneficus; fig mitis

charitably *adv* benigne; indulgenter, in meliorem partem

charity *n* (love) caritas; (alms) stips *f*; (goodwill) benevolentia *f*; (indulgence) indulgentia, venia *f*

charlatan *n* pharmacopola circumforaneus; fig ostentator, iactator *m*

charm[1] *n* (incantation) cantus *m*; carmen *nt*; cantio *f*; incantamentum *nt*; fig illecebra; gratia *f*; (physical charms) venustas *f*; veneres *fpl*; (amulet) amuletum *nt*

charm[2] *vt* incanto, fascino, canto ①; (delight) capio ③; delecto ①

charming *adj* venustus, amoenus, lepidus, blandus

charnel-house *n* ossuarium *nt*

chart *n* tabula *f*

charter[1] *n* (privilege) licentia *f*

charter[2] *vt* conduco ③

charwoman *n* operaria *f*

chase[1] *vt* persequor ③; venor, sector ①; (drive) pello, ago ③; agito ①

chase[2] *n* (hunting) venatio *f*; venatus *m*

chasm *n* hiatus *m*; specus *m/f/nt*

chaste *adj* castus, pudicus; purus

chasten *vt* castigo ①

chastise *vt* castigo ①

chastisement *n* castigatio; animadversio *f*

chastity *n* pudicitia, castitas *f*; (modesty) pudor *m*

chat[1] *vi* fabulor ①; garrio ④

chat[2] *n* sermo *m*
□ **have a** ∼ fabulor ①; garrio ④

chattel *n* bona *ntpl*; res *f*

chatter[1] *vi* nugor ①; garrio, effutio ④; (of the teeth) crepito ①

chatter[2] *n* strepitus *m*; (idle talk) garrulitas *f*; nugae *fpl*; (of the teeth) crepitus *m*

chatterbox *n* lingulaca *f*

chattering *adj* garrulus

chatty *adj* garrulus

cheap *adj* vilis

cheaply *adv* bene, vili

cheapness *n* vilitas *f*

cheat[1] *vt* decipio, fallo, eludo ③; fraudo ①

cheat[2] *n* (act) fraus, ars *f*, dolus *m*; (person) fraudator *m*

check[1] *vt* (restrain) cohibeo, inhibeo ②; reprimo ③; (stop) retardo, tardo ①; (bridle) refreno ①; (accounts) dispungo ③; (verify) confirmo, probo ①

check[2] *n* (hindrance) impedimentum *nt*; (disadvantage) detrimentum *nt*; (delay) mora *f*; (verification) probatio *f*

cheek *n* gena, bucca *f*
■ ∼-**bone** *n* mala, maxilla *f*

cheeky *adj* impudens

cheer[1] *vt* (gladden) hilaro, exhilaro ①; (encourage) hortor, adhortor ①; (comfort) solor ①; (applaud) plaudo ③

cheer[2] *n* (shout) clamor, plausus *m*; (cheerfulness) hilaritas *f*
□ **be of good** ∼ bono animo esse

cheerful *adj* hilaris, alacer, laetus
■ ∼**ly** *adv* hilare, laete; (willingly) libenter

cheerfulness *n* alacritas, hilaritas *f*

cheering *n* acclamatio *f*, plausus *m*

cheery *adj* ▶ **cheerful**

cheese *n* caseus *m*

chemist *n* pharmacopola *m*

chequered *adj* tessellatus, distinctus; varius

cherish *vt* (nourish) alo ③; (treat tenderly) foveo ②; fig colo ③

cherry *n* cerasus *f*; cerasum *nt*
■ ∼-**tree** *n* cerasus *f*

chess *n* ludus latruncularius
■ ∼**board** *n* tabula latruncularia
■ ∼**man** *n* latrunculus, calculus *m*

chest *n* (breast) pectus *nt*; (box) cista, arca, capsa *f*; (for clothes) vestiarium *nt*; (cabinet) scrinium *nt*

chestnut *n* castanea *f*
■ ∼-**tree** *n* castanea *f*

chew *vt* mando ③; manduco ①; (the cud) rumino ①; fig meditor ①

chicken *n* pullus (gallinaceus) *m*

chick-pea *n* cicer *nt*

chicory *n* cichorium *nt*; intubus *m*

chide *vt&i* obiurgo, vitupero ①; reprehendo ③; (sharply) corripio ③

chiding *n* obiurgatio, reprehensio *f*

chief[1] *adj* primus; praecipuus, summus, supremus
■ ∼**ly** *adv* praecipue, imprimis

chief[2] *n* princeps, procer, dux, auctor *m*, caput *nt*

chieftain *n* dux, ductor *m*

chilblain *n* pernio *m*

child *n* infans *m/f*; puer, filius *m*; puella, filia *f*; (children) liberi *mpl*
□ **bear a** ∼ parturio ④
□ **with** ∼ gravida

child-bed *n* puerperium *nt*
□ **woman in** ∼-**bed** puerpera *f*

childbirth *n* partus *m*; Lucinae labores *mpl*

childhood *n* infantia; pueritia *f*
□ **from** ∼ a puero *or* pueris; a parvo

childish *adj* puerilis, infans
■ ∼**ly** *adv* pueriliter

childishness *n* puerilitas *f*

childless *adj* orbus

childlike *adj* puerilis

chill[1] *n* frigus *nt*; algor *m*; horror *m*; (fever) febris *f*

chill[2] *vt* refrigero ①

chilly *adj* alsiosus; frigidulus

chime[1] *n* (harmony) concentus *m*

chime[2] *vi* (of bells) cano ③
 □ ∼ **in** succino ③

chimera *n* chimaera *f*

chimney *n* caminus *m*

chin *n* mentum *nt*

china *n* murrha *f*, murrhina *ntpl*

chine *n* tergum *nt*, spina *f*

chink *n* rima, fissura *f*; (sound) tinnitus *m*

chip[1] *n* segmen *nt*, assula *f*; (for lighting fire) fomes *m*; (fragment) fragmentum, fragmen *nt*

chip[2] *vt* dolo, dedolo ①

chirp[1] *vi* (also **chirrup**) (of birds) pipio ①; pipilo ①; (of crickets) strideo ②

chirp[2] *n* (also **chirrup**) pipatus *m*

chisel[1] *n* scalprum, caelum *nt*

chisel[2] *vt* scalpo ③

chit-chat *n* garrulitas *f*; nugae *fpl*

chivalrous *adj* magnanimus, nobilis

chivalry *n* virtus *f*, magnanimitas *f*

choice[1] *n* delectus *m*; electio; (power of choosing) optio; (diversity) varietas *f*

choice[2] *adj* electus, exquisitus, praestans, eximius

choir *n* chorus *m*

choke *vt* suffoco; strangulo ①; fauces elido ③; fig praecludo ③
 ■ ∼ *vi* suffocor; strangulor ①

choler *n* ira, bilis *f*

cholera *n* cholera *f*

choose *vt* eligo, deligo, lego ③; opto ①
 ■ ∼ *vi* (prefer) malo; (be willing) volo *ir*

chop[1] *vt* abscido ③; trunco ①
 □ ∼ **off** detrunco ①; abscido ③
 □ ∼ **up** concido ③

chop[2] *n* (of meat) ofella *f*

chord *n* (string) chorda *f*, nervus *m*

chore *n* officium, munus, eris *nt*

chorus *n* chorus *m*; concentus *m*

Christ *n* Christus *m*

Christian *adj* Christianus

chronicle[1] *n* annales, fasti *mpl*

chronicle[2] *vt* in annales refero ③

chronicler *n* annalium scriptor *m*

chronology *n* aetatum ordo *m*; ratio temporum *f*

chrysalis *n* chrysallis *f*

chubby *adj* bucculentus

chuckle *vi* cachinno ①

chum *n* contubernalis *m*

chunk *n* (of food) frustum *nt*

churchyard *n* caemeterium, sepulcretum *nt*

churl *n* homo rusticus, homo illiberalis *m*

churlish *adj* inhumanus; agrestis
 ■ ∼**ly** *adv* inhumaniter

churlishness *n* inhumanitas, rusticitas *f*

cinder *n* cinis *m*; favilla *f*

cinnamon *n* cinnamum *nt*

circle[1] *n* circulus, orbis; (whirling motion) gyrus *m*; (of people) corona *f*; (social meeting) circulus *m*

circle[2] *vt* circumdo ①; cingo ③
 ■ ∼ *vi* (move round) circumvolvor ③

circuit *n* circuitus; ambitus *m*; circumscriptio *f*; (of judges) conventus *m*
 □ **make a** ∼ circumire ④

circuitous *adj* devius

circular *adj* orbiculatus, rotundus

circulate *vt* spargo ③, differo *ir*
 ■ ∼ *vi* circulor ①

circulation *n* circumactus *m*
 □ **come into** ∼ in usum venio ④

circumcise *vt* circumcido ③

circumcision *n* circumcisio *f*

circumference *n* peripheria *f*, circulus, orbis *m*

circumlocution *n* circumlocutio *f*; ambages *fpl*

circumnavigate *vt* circumvehor ③

circumstance *n* res *f*; tempus *nt*; condicio *f*; status *m*
 □ **under these** ∼**s** cum res ita se habeant

circus *n* circus *m*

cistern *n* cisterna *f*; puteus *m*

citadel *n* arx *f*

citation *n* vocatio, prolatio *f*

cite *vt* (law) cito, evoco ①; (quote) profero *ir*

citizen *n* civis *m/f*; (townsman) oppidanus *m*

citizenship *n* civitas *f*

city¹ *n* urbs *f*

city² *adj* urbanus; urbicus

civic *adj* civilis, civicus

civil *adj* civilis; (polite) comis, urbanus
■ ~**ly** *adv* comiter, urbane

civilian *n* (non-military person) togatus *m*

civility *n* urbanitas *f*

civilization *n* cultus *m*

civilize *vt* excolo ③; expolio, emollio ④

clad *adj* vestitus, indutus, amictus

claim¹ *vt* postulo; flagito ①; exposco, exigo ③; (demand for oneself) vindico ①

claim² *n* vindicatio; postulatio *f*; postulatum *nt*
☐ **legal** ~ vindiciae *fpl*

claimant *n* petitor *m*

clamber *vi* scando, conscendo ③

clammy *adj* lentus, viscidus

clamour *n* clamor, tumultus *m*

clamp *n* confibula *f*

clan *n* gens *f*

clandestine *adj* clandestinus, furtivus

clang¹ *n* clangor *m*

clang² *vi* clango; strepo ③

clap¹ *vi* (hands) plaudo ③

clap² *n* (blow) ictus; (noise) crepitus; (of thunder) fragor; (with the hands) plausus *m*

clarify *vt* deliquo, defaeco ①

clarity *n* claritas *f*

clash¹ *n* crepitus *m*; concursus *m*; (opposition) repugnantia *f*

clash² *vi* crepito ①; concurro ③; fig configo ③; repugno ①

clasp¹ *n* fibula *f*; (embrace) amplexus *m*

clasp² *vt* fibulo ①; (embrace) amplector; (grasp) comprehendo ③

class¹ *n* classis *f*; ordo *m*; genus *nt*; (of pupils) classis *f*

class² *vt* in classes distribuo ③; (value) aestimo ①

classification *n* distributio *f*

classify *vt* in classes distribuo ③

clatter¹ *vi* crepo, crepito ①

clatter² *n* strepitus, crepitus *m*

claw¹ *n* unguis *m*; ungula *f*; (of a crab) bracchium *nt*

claw² *vt* (scratch) scalpo ③; lacero ①
☐ ~ **away** *or* **off** diripio ③

clay *n* argilla; creta *f*; lutum *nt*

clean¹ *adj* mundus, purus; nitidus

clean² *vt* mundo, purgo ①; (sweep) verro ③; (by wiping, brushing *or* rubbing) tergeo, detergeo ②; (by washing) abluo ③

cleanness *n* munditia *f*; nitor *m*; fig innocentia *f*

cleanse *vt* purgo, depurgo, expurgo, purifico ①

cleansing *n* purgatio *f*

clear¹ *adj* (bright) lucidus, clarus; (of fluids) limpidus; (transparent) liquidus; (clean) purus; (fair) serenus; (of voice) candidus; (manifest) conspicuus, manifestus; (of space) apertus, patens; (of style) lucidus; fig (in the head) sagax
☐ ~ **of** (free from) solutus, liber
☐ **keep** ~ **of** caveo ②

clear² *vt* purgo ①; (acquit) absolvo ③; (a doubt) explano; (from) libero; (land, forests) extrico; (exculpate) purgo (de aliqua re) ①
☐ ~ **away** detergeo; amoveo ②; (a debt) solvo ③
☐ ~ **out** emundo ①
☐ ~ **up** *vt* enodo; explano, illustro; *vi* (of the weather) sereno ①

clearly *adv* clare; (of sounds) liquide; fig dilucide; plane; aperte, haud dubie, manifesto

clearness *n* claritas; (of sky) serenitas *f*; fig candor *m*

cleft *n* rima, fissura *f*

clemency *n* clementia, mansuetudo, indulgentia *f*

clement *adj* clemens, mitis

clench *vt* contraho, astringo ③

clerk *n* (scholar) doctus; (accountant) actuarius; scriba *m*

clever *adj* sollers; dexter; ingeniosus; (knowing) scitus; (quick) versutus; (sly, cunning) callidus, astutus

cleverly *adv* sollerter, perite; ingeniose; scite; astute; callide

cleverness *n* dexteritas, sollertia, astutia, calliditas *f*

click *vi* crepito ①

client *n* cliens *m*; (one who consults another) consultor *m*

clientele *n* clientela *f*

cliff *n* (sharp rock) cautes, rupes *f*, scopulus; (hill) collis *m*

climate *n* regio *f*; aer *m*; caelum *nt*
☐ **a mild** ~ temperies *f*

climb *vt&i* ascendo, conscendo, scando, enitor, evado ③

clinch *vt* (an argument) astringo ③

cling *vi* adhaereo, haereo ②; amplector ③; (remain) maneo ②

clinging *adj* lentus, tenax, sequax

clink¹ *vi* tinnio ④

clink² *n* tinnitus *m*

clip *vt* tondeo ②; circumcido, praecido ③; amputo ①

clipper *n* (ship) celox *f*

clipping *n* tonsura *f*

clique *n* factio *f*

cloak¹ *n* pallium, sagum *nt*; lacerna, laena, chlamys *f*; amictus *m*

cloak² *vt* pallio vestio ④; fig dissimulo ①; praetendo, tego ③

clock *n* horologium *nt*

clod *n* glaeba *f*

clog¹ *n* (heavy shoes) sculponeae *fpl*; fig impedimentum *nt*; mora *f*

clog² *vt* impedio, praepedio ④; onero ①

close¹ *vt* claudo ③; operio ④; (end) finio ④; termino ①
□ ∼ **in** includo ③
■ ∼ *vi* (come together) coeo *ir*; (end) terminor ①
□ ∼ **up** praecludo, occludo ③

close² *adj* (thick) densus; (narrow) angustus; artus; (near to) contiguus; fig taciturnus, tectus
□ ∼ **by** vicinus, propinquus
□ ∼ **together** confertus, continuus

close³ *adv* dense; (near) prope, proxime
■ ∼ **to** prope + *acc*

close⁴ *n* (end) finis *m/f*; (∼ of a speech) peroratio *f*
□ **bring to a** ∼ finio ④; termino ①
□ **draw to a** ∼ terminor ①

closeness *n* (nearness) proximitas *f*

closet *n* cella *f*, conclave; (for clothes) vestiarium *nt*

clot *vi* concresco ③

cloth *n* pannus *m*; (linen) linteum; (for horses) stragulum *nt*

clothe *vt* vestio, amicio ④; induo ③; velo ①

clothes *n* vestis *f*; vestitus *m*, vestimenta *ntpl*

clothing *n* vestitus *m*, vestimenta *ntpl*

cloud *n* nubes, nebula *f*; nubila *ntpl*

cloudless *adj* serenus, sudus

cloudy *adj* nubilus; (of liquids) turbidus
□ **grow** ∼ nubilo ①

cloven *adj* bisulcus, bifidus

clover *n* trifolium *nt*

clown *n* (buffoon) scurra *m*

club *n* (cudgel) clava *f*; fustis *m*; (of people) sodalicium *nt*; sodalitas *f*; circulus *m*

cluck *vi* singultio ④

clue *n* glomus *nt*; (trace, mark) indicium *nt*

clump *n* massa *f*; globus *m*
□ ∼ **of bushes** dumentum *nt*

clumsily *adv* crasse; rustice; inscite, ineleganter, male

clumsiness *n* rusticitas *f*

clumsy *adj* inhabilis; inelegans; inscitus; rusticus, agrestis

cluster¹ *n* (of grapes, *etc.*) racemus; (of flowers) corymbus *m*

cluster² *vi* congregor, conglobor ①

clutch¹ *vt* arripio ③

clutch² *n*:
□ **in one's** ∼**es** in sua potestate

coach *n* currus *m*, raeda *f*; pilentum, petoritum *nt*

coachman *n* raedarius *m*, auriga *m/f*

coagulate *vi* concresco ③

coal *n* carbo *m*; (burning) pruna *f*

coalesce *vi* coalesco ③; fig coeo *ir*

coalition *n* societas *f*

coalmine *n* fodina *f*

coarse *adj* crassus; fig incultus; rudis, rusticus, infacetus, illiberalis
■ ∼**ly** *adv* crasse; infacete

coarseness *n* crassitudo; rusticitas *f*

coast *n* ora *f*, litus *nt*

coastal *adj* maritimus

coat¹ *n* vestis; tunica *f*
□ ∼ **of arms** insignia *ntpl*
□ ∼ **of mail** lorica; (skin) pellis *f*; corium *nt*; tegumentum *nt*

coat² *vt* illino, induco ③

coax *vt* mulceo ②; blandior ④; (persuade) adduco ③

coaxing¹ *n* blandimenta *ntpl*; blanditiae *fpl*

coaxing² *adj* blandus

cobble *vt* resarcio ④

cobbler *n* sutor, veteramentarius *m*

cobweb *n* aranea tela, aranea *f*; aranea texta *ntpl*

cock *n* gallus *m*

cockle *n* (shell-fish) chema *f*

cockroach *n* blatta *f*

cocoon *n* globulus *m*

code n leges fpl

coerce vt coerceo ②; refreno ①; cogo ③

coercion n coercitio f; (force) vis f; (necessity) necessitas f

coffin n arca f; loculus m

cog n (of a wheel) dens m

cogent adj gravis, efficax
■ ~**ly** adv efficaciter, graviter

cogitate vi meditor, reputo ①

cogitation n reputatio f

cohabitation n concubitus m

cohere vi cohaereo ②; fig consentio ④; concordo ①

coherence n contextus m; (order) ordo m

coherent adj contextus, continens; (clear) clarus

cohesive adj tenax, lentus

cohort n cohors f

coil¹ n spira f; volumen, glomus nt

coil² vt&i glomero; glomeror ①; (wind) volvo, volvor ③

coin¹ n nummus m; (collectively) pecunia f; (small ~) nummulus m

coin² vt (money) cudo ③; ferio ④; fig (invent) fingo ③

coinage n res nummaria; (coined money) pecunia publice signata, moneta; (invention) fictio f

coincide vi congruo ③; convenio ④

coincidence n concursio fortuitorum f; (agreement) consensus m

colander n colum nt

cold¹ adj frigidus, gelidus
□ **be** ~ frigeo, algeo ②
□ **become** ~ frigesco ③

cold² n frigus nt, algor m; (illness) gravedo f
□ **catch** ~ perfrigesco, algesco ③

coldly adv fig frigide, gelide, lente

coldness n frigus nt; algor m; fig lentitudo f

collapse¹ vi collabor; concido, corruo ③

collapse² n lapsus, casus m; labes, ruina f

collar n (of a garment) collare nt; (ornament) torques m/f; monile nt; (for horses) helcium nt; (for dogs) mellum nt

colleague n collega m; consors m/f

collect vt lego, colligo ③, confero ir; (an army) comparo, convoco ①; (gather) cogo

③; comporto ①; (money) exigo ③; (heap up) coacervo ①
□ ~ **oneself** se or animum colligere
■ ~vi convenio ③, coeo ir; congregor ①

collection n collectio; conquisitio; (of money) collatio f

college n collegium nt; academia f

collide vi confligo, concurro ③

colliery n fodina f

collision n conflictio f; concursus m

colloquial adj communis (sermo) m

collusion n collusio; praevaricatio f

colonist n colonus m

colonize vt coloniam deduco ③ in +acc

colonnade n porticus f, xystus m

colony n colonia f

colossal adj (of statues) colossicus, colosseus; (huge) ingens, immanis

colossus n colossus m

colour¹ n color m, pigmentum nt; (ensign) vexillum, signum nt

colour² vt coloro ①; (dye) tingo, inficio, imbuo ③
■ ~ vi erubesco ③

coloured adj coloratus

colouring n color; fig ornatus m

colt n equuleus, pullus equinus m

column n columna f

comb¹ n pecten m

comb² vt pecto ③

combat¹ n pugna f, proelium; certamen nt

combat² vt&i pugno, proelior ①; certo, dimico ①; contendo ③; (oppose) repugno, adversor ① both + dat

combatant n miles, pugnator, proeliator m

combination n coniunctio, iunctura f; concursus m

combine vt coniungo ③; misceo ②
■ ~ vi coeo ④

combustion n crematio, deflagratio f

come¹ vi venio ④; (arrive) pervenio ④ ad + acc; (happen) fieri ir
□ ~ **about** evenio ④, accido ③
□ ~ **after** sequor ③
□ ~ **again** revenio ④
□ ~ **along** procedo ③
□ ~ **away** abscedo ③; abeo ir
□ ~ **back** revenio ④; redeo ir
□ ~ **before** praevenio ④
□ ~ **by** praetereo ir; (get) acquiro ③

□ ~ **down** descendo ③; (fall down) decido ③

□ ~ **forth** exeo *ir*; egredior ③; fig exorior ④

□ ~ **forward** procedo ③

□ ~ **in(to)** introeo *ir*, intro ①

□ ~ **in!** intra, intrate

□ ~ **near** appropinquo ①; accedo ③

□ ~ **of** originem traho de *or* e *both* + *abl*

□ ~ **off** recedo; fig discedo ③; (of hair, *etc.*) cado ③

□ ~ **on** procedo, pergo ③

□ ~ **on!** agite!

□ ~ **out** (be published) edor, emittor ③; (become known) evulgor ①; ▶ ~ **forth** *and* ~ **off**

□ ~ **round** circumagor; fig adducor ③; (recover one's senses) me recipio ③

□ ~ **to** advenio ad; pervenio ④ ad + *acc*

□ ~ **to pass** evenio ④; fio *ir*

□ ~ **together** convenio ④, coeo *ir*

□ ~ **up** subvenio ④; (spring up) provenio ④; (surprise) deprehendo ③

come[2] *int* age! eia!

comedian *n* comoedus; comicus *m*

comedy *n* comoedia *f*; soccus *m*

comely *adj* decens, pulcher, venustus

comet *n* cometes *m*, stella crinita *f*

comfort[1] *vt* consolor, solor ①

comfort[2] *n* solacium, solamen *nt*, consolatio *f*

comfortable *adj* (commodious) commodus

comfortably *adv* commode

comforter *n* consolator *m*

comic *adj* (also **comical**) comicus; ridiculus

comically *adv* comice; ridicule

coming[1] *n* adventus *m*

coming[2] *adj* venturus, futurus

command[1] *vt* impero ①, praecipio ③ *both* + *dat*; iubeo ②

command[2] *n* mandatum, praeceptum, imperium *nt*; (order) iussus *m*; iussum *nt*; (office, place) praefectura *f*, imperium *nt*

commander *n* dux, praefectus, imperator *m*

commandment *n* ▶ **command**[2]

commemorate *vt* celebro ①

commemoration *n* celebratio *f*

commence *vt&i* incipio ③; incoho ①; ordior ④; coepi ③

commencement *n* initium, principium *nt*

commend *vt* (commit) commendo ①; committo ③; (approve) approbo, laudo, probo ①

commendable *adj* commendabilis, probabilis, laudabilis

commendably *adv* laudabiliter

commendation *n* commendatio, laus *f*

comment[1] *vt&i* commentor, interpretor ①; (remark) animadverto ③

comment[2] *n* (criticism) animadversio *f*

commentary *n* commentarius *m*, commentarium *nt*

commentator *n* interpres *m/f*

commerce *n* commercium *nt*; mercatus *m*; mercatura *f*

commiserate *v*:
■ ~ **with** *vt* miseror, commiseror ①; miseresco ③ + *gen*

commiseration *n* miseratio *f*

commission[1] *n* mandatum *nt*; (in the army) tribunatus *m*
□ **a** ~ **of two** duumviri *mpl*

commission[2] *vt* delego ①

commit *vt* (give) do ①; (trust) committo ③; (be guilty of) patro, perpetro ①; admitto ③; (imprison) in custodiam do ①
□ ~ **oneself** se dedere ③

committee *n* delecti
□ ~ **of ten** decemviri *mpl*

commodity *n* res venalis, merx *f*

common[1] *adj* communis; publicus; (ordinary, *etc.*) vulgaris; (well known) pervulgatus; fig tritus; mediocris; (social status) plebeius

common[2]:
□ **in** ~ in medium, in commune; communiter; promiscue

commoner *n* plebeius *m*

commonly *adv* vulgo, fere, plerumque

commonplace *n* locus communis *m*
■ ~ *adj* (hackneyed) vulgaris, pervulgatus, tritus
■ ~-**book** *n* commentarius *m*

commonwealth *n* respublica, civitas *f*

commotion *n* agitatio *f*; tumultus, motus, concursus *m*

communicate *vt* impertio ④; communico ①

communication *n* communicatio *f*; commercium; colloquium *nt*; (message) nuntius *m*
□ **cut off** ∼**s** omnes aditus intercludo ③

communicative *adj* affabilis, apertus

community *n* communitas; (partnership) societas; (state) civitas, respublica *f*

compact¹ *adj* densus, spissus; solidus; (of style) pressus
■ ∼**ly** *adv* dense, spisse; presse

compact² *n* pactum *nt*; conventio *f*; foedus *nt*

companion *n* socius, sodalis; comes; (as soldier) contubernalis; (in games and gambling) collusor *m*
□ **boon** ∼ compotor *m*

companionship *n* sodalitas *f*; contubernium *nt*

company *n* societas, sodalitas; (of soldiers) cohors *f*, manipulus *m*; (at table) convivium *nt*; (troop) caterva; turba, manus *f*; (corporation) collegium *nt*

comparable *adj* comparabilis

comparative *adj* comparativus

comparatively *adv*: *use the comparative, e.g.*
□ ∼ **slow** tardior

compare *vt* comparo, aequo ①; confero *ir*

comparison *n* comparatio, collatio *f*
■ **in** ∼ **with** *prep* prae + *abl*

compartment *n* loculus *m*, cella *f*

compass *n* (circuit) ambitus, circuitus *m*; (limits) fines *mpl*; (pair of compasses) circinus *m*

compassion *n* misericordia, miseratio *f*

compassionate *adj* misericors
■ ∼**ly** *adv* misericorditer

compatibility *n* congruentia; (conformity) convenientia *f*

compatible *adj* congruus, conveniens

compatriot *n* civis *m/f*; popularis *m*

compel *vt* cogo, compello ③

compensate *vt* (for) penso, compenso ①

compensation *n* compensatio *f*

compete *vi* contendo ③; certo ①

competence *n* (also **competency**) facultas *f*

competent *adj* capax; (suitable) congruens, idoneus; (of authorities) locuples
■ ∼**ly** *adv* idonee, satis

competition *n* contentio, aemulatio *f*, certamen *nt*

competitive *adj* aemulus

competitor *n* aemulus, rivalis *m*

compilation *n* collectio *f*; excerpta *ntpl*

compile *vt* colligo, conscribo, compono ③

complacency *n* delectatio *f*

complacent *adj* (contented) contentus; (smug) qui sibi placet

complacently *adv* aequo animo

complain *vt* (of) queror, conqueror ③; ploro ①
■ ∼ *vi* gemo ③; lamentor ①

complaining *adj* querulus

complaint *n* querela, querimonia *f*; (charge) crimen *nt*; lamentatio *f*; (disease) morbus *m*

complaisant *adj* officiosus, comis, facilis, humanus

complement *n* complementum, supplementum *nt*

complete¹ *adj* plenus; integer; perfectus
■ ∼**ly** *adv* plane, prorsus

complete² *vt* compleo; suppleo; expleo ②; (accomplish) perficio ③

completeness *n* integritas; perfectio *f*

completion *n* (accomplishment) perfectio *f*

complex *adj* multiplex

complexion *n* (of the skin) color *m*

complexity *n* ambages *fpl*; difficultas *f*

compliance *n* obtemperatio *f*, obsequium *nt*

compliant *adj* officiosus; facilis

complicate *vt* impedio ④; confundo ③; turbo ①

complicated *adj* nodosus, difficilis, perplexus

complication *n* nodus *m*; ambages *fpl*; difficultas *f*

complicity *n* conscientia *f*

compliment¹ *n* verba honorifica *ntpl*; blanditiae *fpl*
□ **pay one's** ∼**s (to)** saluto ①

compliment² *vt* laudo ①

complimentary *adj* honorificus; blandus

comply *vi* (with) concedo + *dat*; cedo ③; pareo ②; (humour) morigeror; (me) accommodo ①; (accept) accipio ③

component *n* pars *f*, elementa *ntpl*

compose *vt* compono; (arrange) digero, dispono ③; (calm) sedo ①
□ ∼ **oneself** tranquillor ①

composed *adj* quietus, tranquillus
■ ∼**ly** *adv* quiete, aequo animo

composer *n* scriptor *m*

composition *n* compositio; confectio *f*; (book) liber *m*

compost *n* stercus *nt*

composure *n* tranquillitas *f*, animus aequus *m*

compound¹ *vt* compono ③; misceo ②

compound² *adj* compositus; concretus

comprehend *vt* (embrace) contineo ②, complector; (understand) capio, percipio, comprehendo, intellego ③

comprehensible *adj* comprehensibilis

comprehension *n* intellectus *m*, intelligentia, comprehensio *f*

comprehensive *adj* amplus

compress *vt* comprimo, astringo ③, coarto ①

compression *n* compressio *f*

comprise *vt* contineo, cohibeo ②; comprehendo, complector ③

compromise¹ *n* compromissum *nt*; (agreement) pactum *nt*

compromise² *vt* compromitto; (bring into disrepute) in invidiam adduco ③
■ ∼ *vi* paciscor ③

compulsion *n* vis, necessitas *f*

compulsorily *adv* vi, per vim

compulsory *adj* necessarius

computer *n* calculator *m*

comrade *n* sodalis, socius; (military) contubernalis *m*

concave *adj* cavus; concavus

conceal *vt* celo, occulto ①; abdo, condo, occulo ③; (dissemble) dissimulo ①

concealment *n* occultatio; dissimulatio *f*

concede *vt* concedo, permitto ③; do ①

conceit *n* (fancy) opinio; (pride) arrogantia, superbia *f*
□ **witty** ∼ lepos *m*

conceited *adj* arrogans, superbus, tumidus

conceivable *adj* comprehensibilis

conceive *vt* concipio; (comprehend) percipio, intellego ③; (imagine) fingo ③

concentrate *vt* in unum locum contraho ③
■ ∼ *vi* fig animum intendo (in aliquid) ③

concentration *n* in unum locum contractio, fig animi intentio *f*

concept *n* imago, notio, opinio *f*

conception *n* (in the womb) conceptus *m*; (idea) imago, species, notio *f*

concern¹ *n* (affair) res *f*, negotium *nt*; cura *f*; (importance) momentum *nt*; (anxiety, trouble) sollicitudo *f*

concern² *vt* pertineo ②
□ **it** ∼**s** interest, refert *ir*
□ **be** ∼**ed** occupor ①; particeps sum; (be anxious) sollicitus sum *ir*
□ **it does not** ∼ **me** non mihi curae est

concerning *prep* (about) de + *abl*; (as to) quod ad + *acc*

concession *n* concessio *f*; (thing) concessum *nt*; (allowance) venia *f*

conch *n* concha *f*

conciliate *vt* concilio ①

conciliation *n* conciliatio *f*

conciliatory *adj* pacificus; pacificatorius

concise *adj* brevis, concisus; (style) pressus
■ ∼**ly** *adv* breviter, concise

conciseness *n* brevitas *f*

conclude *vt&i* concludo ③; finio ④; (end) perficio; (settle) statuo ③; (infer) concludo ③

conclusion *n* (end) conclusio *f*; finis *m*/ *f*; (of a speech) peroratio *f*; epilogus *m*; (inference) conclusio *f*

conclusive *adj* (of arguments) certus

concoct *vt* concoquo ③; (contrive) excogito, machinor ①

concord *n* concordia; conspiratio *f*; consensus *m*; mus concentus *m*

concourse *n* concursus; conventus *m*; frequentia *f*

concrete *adj* concretus

concubinage *n* concubinatus *m*

concubine *n* concubina *f*

concur *vi* convenio; (agree) consentio ④

concurrence *n* concursus, consensus *m*

concurrently *adv* una, simul

concussion *n* concussio *f*

condemn *vt* damno, condemno; (blame) vitupero ①

condemnation *n* damnatio, condemnatio *f*

condemnatory *adj* damnatorius

condensation *n* densatio, spissatio *f*

condense *vt* denso, condenso, spisso ①; fig coarto ①

condescend *vi* dignor ①; descendo, me summitto ③

condescending *adj* comis, facilis, officiosus
■ ~ly *adv* comiter, officiose

condescension *n* obsequium *nt*; comitas *f*

condiment *n* condimentum *nt*

condition *n* condicio *f*, status *m*; (of agreement) pactum *nt*, lex *f*; (rank) ordo *m*

condolence *n* consolatio *f*

condone *vt* condono, veniam do ①; ignosco ③ *all + dat*

conduct¹ *n* vita, ratio *f*; mores *mpl*; (management) administratio, cura *f*; (deeds) facta *ntpl*

conduct² *vt* adduco; deduco; perduco ③; administro ①; (direct) dirigo ③; (preside over) praesum *ir + dat*

conduit *n* canalis *m*, aquaeductus *m*

cone *n* conus *m*

confectioner *n* crustularius, pistor dulciarius *m*

confectionery *n* cuppedia *ntpl*

confederacy *n* (alliance) foedus *nt*; societas *f*

confederation *n* foedus *nt*; societas *f*

confer *vt* (bestow) confero *ir*; (compare) comparo ①
□ ~ **with** colloquor ③; convenio ④

conference *n* colloquium *nt*; congressus *m*

confess *vt* fateor, confiteor ②

confession *n* confessio *f*

confidant *n* familiaris *m/f*

confide *vt* confido, committo; credo ③
□ ~ **in** (trust) confido, fido ③ *both + dat*

confidence *n* fides; fiducia; confidentia; (boldness) audacia *f*; (self-confidence) sui fiducia *f*
□ **in** ~ (secretly) clam

confident *adj* confidens; securus; (bold) audax
■ ~ly *adv* confidenter

confidential *adj* (secret) arcanus

confine *vt* claudo, includo ③; coerceo, cohibeo ②; circumscribo ③; termino ①

confinement *n* inclusio; (imprisonment) custodia *f*; carcer *m*; (childbirth) puerperium *nt*

confirm *vt* confirmo; firmo; (prove) comprobo ①; (ratify) sancio ④

confirmation *n* confirmatio *f*

confirmed *adj* inveteratus

confiscate *vt* proscribo ③; publico, confisco ①

confiscation *n* publicatio, confiscatio, proscriptio *f*

conflagration *n* incendium *nt*

conflict¹ *n* contentio; controversia *f*; certamen *nt*; pugna *f*

conflict² *vi* contendo ③; (struggle) luctor ①; (be at variance) discrepo ①

conflicting *adj* contrarius, adversus

conform *vi* (comply with) obtempero ① *+ dat*

conformity *n* convenientia, congruentia *f*
□ **in** ~ **with** secundum *+ acc*

confound *vt* confundo ③; permisceo ②; perturbo ①; (destroy) deleo ②; perimo ③

confront *vt* (match) committo ③
■ ~ *vi* (meet) congredior ③ cum *+ abl*

confuse *vt* confundo ③; perturbo ①

confused *adj* confusus, perplexus; indistinctus; pudibundus

confusion *n* confusio; perturbatio *f*; tumultus; pudor *m*

confute *vt* confuto, refuto ①; refello, redarguo ③

congeal *vt* congelo, glacio ①
■ ~ *vi* consisto, concresco ③

congenial *adj* (pleasant) gratus, consentaneus; (amicably shared) concors

congestion *n* congestus *m*

congratulate *vt* gratulor, grator ① *both + dat*

congratulation *n* gratulatio *f*

congratulatory *adj* gratulatorius

congregate *vi* congregor, conglobor ①; convenio ④

congregation *n* contio *f*; coetus *m*; auditores *mpl*

conifer *n* arbor conifera *f*

conjectural *adj* opinabilis, coniecturalis
■ ~**ly** *adv* ex coniectura

conjecture¹ *n* coniectura *f*

conjecture² *vt* coniecto ①; conicio ③

conjugal *adj* coniugalis; coniugialis

conjunction *n* coniunctio *f*; concursus *m*

conjure *vt* (entreat) obtestor ①
■ ~ *vi* praestigiis utor ③

conjurer *n* magus; (juggler) praestigiator *m*

conjuring *n* (juggling) praestigiae *fpl*

connect *vt* connecto ③; copulo ①; (in a series) sero ③

connected *adj* coniunctus; continuus
□ **be** ~ cohaereo ②

connection *n* coniunctio *f*; contextus *m*; (relation) affinitas; cognatio *f*
□ **have a** ~ **with** pertineo ② ad + *acc*

connive *vi* coniveo, indulgeo ②

connoisseur *adj* homo doctus, peritus, intellegens, elegans

connubial *adj* coniugalis

conquer *vt* vinco ③; supero; domo ①; (gain) capio ③; potior ④

conqueror *n* victor; domitor *m*, victrix *f*

conquest *n* victoria *f*; (what is gained) partum *nt*

conscience *n* conscientia *f*

conscientious *adj* religiosus; sanctus; (hard-working) diligens

conscientiousness *n* aequi reverentia, religio, fides *f*; (application) diligentia *f*

conscious *adj* conscius
■ ~**ly** *adv* use *adj* sciens, prudens

consciousness *n* conscientia *f*; (feeling) sensus *m*
□ **lose** ~ concido ③; exanimor ①

conscript *n* tiro *m*

conscription *n* (of soldiers) delectus *m*

consecrate *vt* sacro, consecro; dedico ①

consecration *n* consecratio; dedicatio *f*

consecutive *adj* continuus
■ ~**ly** *adv* per ordinem; continenter; deinceps

consent¹ *vi* assentior, consentio ④

consent² *n* consensus *m*, consensio *f*
□ **without my** ~ me invito

consequence *n* consequentia, consecutio; (logical) conclusio *f*; (issue) exitus *m*; (importance) momentum *nt*

consequent *adj* consequens, consectarius
■ ~**ly** *adv* ergo, igitur, proinde

conservation *n* conservatio *f*

conservative *adj* (moderate) mediocris
□ **a** ~ **in politics** optimatium fautor *m*

conserve *vt* conservo, servo ①

consider *vt* considero, contemplor ①; intueor, contueor ②; (turn over in the mind) volvo ③; verso, voluto, reputo ①; (regard) aestimo; (reckon) numero ①

considerable *adj* aliquantus; (of size) amplus

considerably *adv* aliquantum; multum, maxime

considerate *adj* consideratus, prudens; (kind) humanus
■ ~**ly** *adv* considerate; (kindly) humaniter

consideration *n* consideratio; contemplatio; prudentia *f*; (regard) respectus *m*; (kindness) humanitas *f*
□ **take into** ~ rationem habeo ② + *gen*
□ **without** ~ inconsulte

considering *prep* (having regard to) pro + *abl*
□ ~ **that** utpote; (since) quoniam, quando

consign *vt* confido ③; assigno ①; trado ③

consist *vi*:
□ ~ **of** consto ①; consisto ③; (be) sum *ir*

consistency *n* convenientia; constantia *f*; (hardness) firmitas *f*; (thickness) densitas *f*

consistent *adj* constans; congruens; consentaneus
■ ~**ly** *adv* constanter; congruenter

consolable *adj* consolabilis

consolation *n* consolatio *f*; solamen, solacium *nt*

console *vt* solor, consolor ①

consolidate *vt* consolido, firmo ①; stabilio ④

consort *vi*:
  □ ~ **with** vivo cum + *abl*; familiariter utor ③ + *abl*

conspicuous *adj* conspicuus; insignis; manifestus
  ■ ~**ly** *adv* manifesto

conspiracy *n* coniuratio, conspiratio *f*

conspirator *n* coniuratus, conspiratus *m*

conspire *vi* coniuro, conspiro ①

constancy *n* constantia, firmitas; perseverantia *f*

constant *adj* constans, firmus; perpetuus; assiduus; fidelis; fidus
  ■ ~**ly** *adv* constanter, fideliter; perpetuo, assidue

constellation *n* sidus, astrum *nt*

consternation *n* consternatio, trepidatio *f*, pavor *m*

constitute *vt* constituo, facio ③, creo ①; (be) sum *ir*

constitution *n* (of the body, *etc.*) habitus *m*, constitutio *f*; (political) civitas *f*; fig condicio, natura *f*

constitutional *adj* legitimus, e republica; natura insitus

constrain *vt* cogo, compello ③

constraint *n* vis, coercitio, necessitas *f*

constrict *vt* constringo ③

construct *vt* construo, struo, exstruo ③; aedifico ①

construction *n* constructio, aedificatio; figura, forma *f*; (meaning, sense) sensus *m*
  □ **put a bad** ~ **on** in malam partem accipio ③

consul *n* consul *m*

consular *adj* consularis

consulate *n* consulatus *m*

consulship *n* consulatus *m*

consult *vt&i* consulo ③; consulto; delibero ①
  □ ~ **a person's interests** consulo ③ + *dat*

consultation *n* consultatio; deliberatio *f*

consume *vt* (destroy, use up) consumo, absumo, conficio; (squander) effundo ③; dissipo ①; (eat) edo *ir*

consumer *n* consumptor *m*

consumption *n* consumptio; (disease) tabes; phthisis *f*

contact *n* contactus *m*

contagion *n* contagium *nt*

contagious *adj* pestilens, pestifer, contagiosus

contain *vt* contineo, habeo ②; comprehendo ③
  □ ~ **oneself** se tenere ②

container *n* arca *f*

contaminate *vt* inquino ①; polluo, inficio ③; foedo, violo ①

contamination *n* contagium *nt*

contemn *vt* temno, contemno, sperno, despicio ③; fastidio ④

contemplate *vt&i* contemplor ①; intueor, contueor ②

contemplation *n* contemplatio, meditatio *f*

contemplative *adj* contemplativus

contemporary¹ *adj* aequalis, contemporaneus

contemporary² *n* aequalis, aequaevus *m*

contempt *n* contemptio *f*, contemptus *m*; fastidium *nt*

contemptible *adj* contemnendus; abiectus; sordidus

contemptuous *adj* fastidiosus, superbus
  ■ ~**ly** *adv* fastidiose, contemptim

contend *vi* contendo ③; pugno, certo ①; (struggle) luctor ①; (dispute) verbis certo ①; (maintain) confirmo, affirmo ①
  □ ~ **against** repugno, adversor ① *both* + *dat*

contending *adj* adversus; rivalis

content¹ *adj* contentus

content² *vt* satisfacio ③; placeo ② *both* + *dat*

content³ *n* aequus animus *m*

contented *adj* ▶ **content** *adj*

contentedly *adv* aequo animo, placide

contention *n* contentio, lis *f*; certamen *nt*

contentious *adj* litigiosus; pugnax

contentment *n* ▶ **content** *n*

contents *n* quod inest; (of a book) argumentum *nt*

contest¹ *vt&i* (oppose) repugno ① + *dat*

contest² *n* certatio, contentio; controversia; lis *f*; certamen *nt*

context *n* contextus *m*

continent[1] *adj* abstinens, continens; castus, pudicus
∎ ~**ly** *adv* temperanter

continent[2] *n* continens *f*

continental *adj* continentem incolens; in continenti positus, ad continentem pertinens

contingency *n* casus, eventus *m*

contingent[1] *adj* (accidental) fortuitus
□ **it is** ~ **on** pendit ex + *abl*

contingent[2] *n* numerus *m*

continual *adj* continuus; perpetuus; assiduus; perennis
∎ ~**ly** *adv* continenter; perpetuo; semper; assidue

continuation *n* continuatio; series *f*

continue *vt* persevero ①; in + *abl*; (prolong) produco ③
∎ ~ *vi* maneo, remaneo ②; duro ①; persisto ③; (go on) pergo ③

continuity *n* continuitas; perpetuitas *f*

continuous *adj* continens; continuus; perpetuus
∎ ~**ly** *adv* continenter, perpetuo

contort *vt* distorqueo ②

contortion *n* distortio *f*

contour *n* lineamenta *ntpl*

contraband[1] *adj* illicitus, vetitus

contraband[2] *n* merces vetitae *fpl*

contract[1] *vt* (compress) contraho, astringo ③; (a disease, *etc*.) contraho ③
□ ~ **for** loco ①; (undertake by contract) redimo ③
∎ ~ *vi* (make an arrangement by bargaining) paciscor ③; (shrink) contrahor ③

contract[2] *n* (bargain) locatio *f*; pactum *nt*

contraction *n* contractio *f*; compendium *nt*

contractor *n* (of work) susceptor, redemptor, conductor *m*

contradict *vt* contradico, obloquor ③; adversor ① *all* + *dat*

contradiction *n* contradictio; (of things) repugnantia *f*

contradictory *adj* contrarius, repugnans

contrary[1] *adj* (opposite) contrarius; diversus; adversus; repugnans

contrary[2] *adv* & *prep*:
□ ~ **to** contra; praeter *both* + *acc*

contrary[3] *n* contrarium *nt*, contraria pars *f*
□ **on the** ~ contra, e contrario; immo

contrast[1] *n* diversitas; varietas; dissimilitudo *f*

contrast[2] *vt* comparo ①; confero *ir*
∎ ~ *vi* discrepo ①

contravene *vt* violo ①; frango ③

contribute *vt* confero *ir*; (give) do ①

contribution *n* collatio; (of money) collecta *f*; (gift) donum *nt*

contrivance *n* inventio, machinatio *f*; (thing contrived) inventum *nt*; machina *f*

contrive *vt* (invent) fingo ③; excogito ①; invenio ④; machinor ①
□ ~ **to** efficio ③ ut + *subj*

control[1] *n* (power) potestas, dicio *f*; (check) coercitio *f*; (command) imperium, regimen *nt*; (management) administratio *f*
□ **self-**~ moderatio *f*

control[2] *vt* (check) reprimo ③; (restrain) coerceo ②; (be at the head of) praesum *ir* + *dat*; (manage) administro, moderor ①; (rule) rego ③

controversial *adj* controversus

controversy *n* controversia *f*; concertatio; (debate) disceptatio; (disagreement) dissensio *f*

contumely *n* contumelia *f*, probrum, opprobrium *nt*

contusion *n* contusio *f*, contusum *nt*

convalesce *vi* convalesco ③

convalescent *adj* convalescens

convene *vt* convoco ①

convenience *n* commoditas *f*; commodum *nt*; utilitas *f*

convenient *adj* commodus, idoneus, opportunus
∎ ~**ly** *adv* commode; opportune

convention *n* conventus *m*; (agreement) pactum, conventum *nt*; (custom) mos *m*

conventional *adj* usitatus, translaticius

converge *vi* vergo ③

conversant *adj* peritus, exercitatus

conversation *n* colloquium *nt*, sermo *m*

converse *vi* colloquor ③

conversion *n* conversio *f*

convert *vt* converto ③; commuto ①; reduco, transfero ③

convex *adj* convexus

convexity *n* convexitas *f*

convey *vt* veho ③, asporto, deporto ①; adveho ③; porto, vecto; (transfer) abalieno; fig significo ①

conveyance *n* (act) advectio, vectura *f*; (vehicle) vehiculum *nt*; (law) abalienatio *f*

convict[1] *vt* convinco ③; (detect) comperio ④; (by sentence) condemno ①

convict[2] *n* convictus, ad poenam damnatus *m*

conviction *n* (condemnation) damnatio; (belief) persuasio *f*

convince *vt* suadeo, persuadeo ② + *dat*

convincing *adj* gravis
  ■ ∼**ly** *adv* graviter

convivial *adj* hilaris, laetus

convoke *vt* convoco ①

convoy *n* (escort) praesidium *nt*

convulse *vt* concutio, convello ③

convulsed *adj* convulsus

convulsion *n* convulsio *f*, spasmus *m*

cook[1] *n* coquus *m*, coqua *f*

cook[2] *vt&i* coquo ③

cookery *n* ars coquinaria *f*

cooking *n* coctura *f*
  ■ ∼ *adj* coquinarius

cool[1] *adj* frigidus; frigidulus; (shady) opacus; fig sedatus; immotus; impavidus; (indifferent) lentus; (impudent) impudens

cool[2] *n* ▶ **coolness**

cool[3] *vt&i* refrigero; refrigeror ①; fig frigesco, defervesco, languesco ③

coolly *adv* frigide; fig sedate; aequo animo; lente; impudenter

coolness *n* frigus *nt*; (pleasant ∼) refrigeratio *f*; (shadiness) opacum *nt*; fig lentitudo; cautela *f*; aequus animus *m*

coop[1] *n* (for hens) cavea *f*

coop[2] *vt*:
  □ ∼ **up** includo ③

cooperate *vi* una ago ③; adiuvo, cooperor ①

cooperation *n* auxilium, adiumentum *nt*, cooperatio *f*

coot *n* fulica *f*

cope *vi*:
  □ ∼ **with** certo ①, contendo ③ cum + *abl*

copious *adj* copiosus, abundans, uber
  ■ ∼**ly** *adv* abundanter, copiose

copper[1] *n* aes; cyprium *nt*

copper[2] *adj* aeneus, aenus, cypreus

copper-smith *n* faber aerarius *m*

coppice *n* (also **copse**) dumetum, fruticetum *nt*

copulate *vi* coeo *ir*

copulation *n* concubitus *m*

copy[1] *n* exemplar, exemplum *nt*; imitatio; imago *f*

copy[2] *vt&i* transcribo ③; imitor ①; (follow) sequor ③

coral *n* corallium *nt*

cord *n* funis *m*

cordial *adj* benignus; sincerus
  ■ ∼**ly** *adv* ex animo; benigne; sincere

cordiality *n* animus benignus *m*; comitas *f*

cordon *n* corona *f*

core *n* (of fruit) vulva *f*

cork[1] *n* (tree) suber *nt*; (bark) cortex *m/f*

cork[2] *adj* subereus

cork[3] *vt* (seal up a container) obturo ①

corn *n* frumentum *nt*; (cereals) fruges *fpl*; annona *f*; (on the toes) callus *m*

corner *n* angulus *m*; (lurking-place) latebra *f*, recessus *m*; (of a street) compitum *nt*

cornfield *n* seges *f*, arvum *nt*
  ■ ∼**s** *pl* sata *ntpl*

corn-merchant *n* frumentarius *m*

cornucopia *n* cornu copiae *nt*

coronet *n* diadema *nt*

corporal[1] *n* decurio *m*

corporal[2] *adj* corporeus, corporalis

corporation *n* societas *f*, sodalicium *nt*

corporeal *adj* corporeus, corporalis

corps *n* legio *f*

corpse *n* cadaver *nt*

corpulent *adj* corpulentus, pinguis, obesus

correct[1] *adj* emendatus; rectus; accuratus; elegans
  ■ ∼**ly** *adv* emendate; recte; accurate; eleganter

correct[2] *vt* corrigo ③; emendo ①; fig animadverto ③; castigo ①

correction *n* correctio, emendatio; fig animadversio; castigatio *f*

correspond *vi* congruo ③; respondeo ②

correspondence n congruentia; (letters) epistulae fpl

correspondent n scriptor m

corresponding adj par + dat

corridor n andron m

corroborate vt confirmo ①

corrode vt erodo; peredo ③

corroding adj mordax

corrosion n rosio f

corrosive adj mordax

corrupt¹ vt corrumpo ③; depravo ① ■ ~ vi putresco ③

corrupt² adj corruptus, putridus; fig pravus; impurus; venalis

corruptible adj corruptibilis; venalis

corruption n corruptio; putredo f; fig depravatio, pravitas; (by money) corruptela f

corselet n lorica f; thorax m

cortège n pompa f

cosmetic n medicamen nt

cosmopolitan adj cosmicus

cost¹ n (price) pretium nt; (expense) impensa f

cost² vt&i consto, sto ①

costliness n caritas f

costly adj pretiosus, carus, sumptuosus

costume n vestitus m

cosy adj commodus

cot n (bed) lectulus m

cottage n casa f, tugurium nt

couch n cubile; pulvinar nt; lectus, torus m

cough¹ n tussis f □ **have a bad** ~ male tussio ④

cough² vi tussio ④

council n concilium, consilium nt, senatus m

councillor n consiliarius m

counsel¹ n (advice) consilium nt; (person) advocatus m

counsel² vt consulo ③; moneo ②

counsellor n consiliarius, consiliator; advocatus m

count¹ vt&i numero ①; censeo; (consider, deem) habeo ②; existimo ①; duco ③ □ ~ **on** confido ③ + dat

count² n (calculation) computatio f

countenance n (face, look) facies f, vultus, aspectus; (encouragement) favor m

counter¹ n (of a shop) mensa f; (for games) calculus m

counter² adv contra □ **run** ~ **to** adversor, repugno ① + dat

counteract vt obsisto ③ + dat

counterbalance vt exaequo, penso, compenso ①

counterfeit¹ vt imitor; adultero; simulo ①

counterfeit² adj ficticius; simulatus; falsus, fictus; adulterinus

counterfeiter n imitator; falsarius m

countermand vt renuntio ①

countless adj innumerabilis, innumerus, infinitus

country n (as opposed to the town) rus nt; regio; terra f; loca ntpl □ **native** ~ solum natale nt; patria f

country-house n villa f

countryman n rusticus m

countryside n rus nt

couple¹ n par nt

couple² vt copulo ①; connecto, coniungo ③

courage n animus m, virtus, audacia, fortitudo f

courageous adj animosus, ferox; audax; fortis ■ ~**ly** adv ferociter; audacter; fortiter

courier n cursor; nuntius; (letter-carrier) tabellarius m

course n (running) cursus; (of water) ductus m; (means) ratio f ■ **of** ~ adv profecto, sane

court¹ n (palace) regia domus, aula f; (retinue) comitatus m; (in law) forum, tribunal nt; iudices mpl

court² vt (cultivate friendship of) colo ③; ambio, blandior ④; observo ①; (of a suitor) peto ③

courteous adj comis, humanus, benignus; affabilis ■ ~**ly** adv comiter, humaniter, benigne, affabiliter

courtesan n meretrix f

courtesy n comitas, affabilitas, urbanitas f

courtier n aulicus, purpuratus m

court martial n iudicium castrense nt

courtship n amor m

courtyard n area f, atrium nt

cousin n consobrinus m; consobrina f; patruelis m/f

cove n (small bay) sinus m

covenant n pactum nt; conventio f

cover¹ vt tego ③; operio ④; celo ①; instruo ③; fig (protect) protego ③

cover² n tegmen; (lid) operculum; (wrapper) involucrum; (shelter) praesidium nt; (for game) operimentum nt; lustra ntpl; fig praetextus m

covering n (act) obductio f; (cover) tegmen, velamen; (wrapper) involucrum; (lid) operculum; (of a bed) stragulum nt

coverlet n stragulum nt

covert adj tectus; occultus; (indirect) obliquus
  ■ ~**ly** adv tecte, occulte; oblique

covet vt concupisco, cupio, appeto ③

covetous adj avidus, avarus, appetens, cupidus
  ■ ~**ly** adv avide, avare; appetenter

covetousness n avaritia, aviditas, cupiditas f

cow n vacca, bos f

coward n ignavus, timidus m

cowardice n ignavia; timiditas f

cowardly adj ignavus, timidus

cower vi subsido ③

cowherd n bubulcus, armentarius m

cowshed n bubile nt

coy adj modestus; timidus; verecundus
  ■ ~**ly** adv verecunde, timide

coyness n modestia; timiditas f

cozen vt fallo ③; ludificor ①

crab n cancer m

crabbed adj morosus; (sour) acerbus

crack¹ vt findo; frango ③; (a whip) flagello insono ①
  ■ ~ vi dehisco, displodor ③; dissilio ④

crack² n fissura, rima f; (noise) crepitus m

cracked adj (of walls, etc.) rimosus

crackle vi crepito ①

cradle n cunae fpl; fig cunabula, incunabula ntpl

craft n (cunning) astutia f; astus m; (calling, trade) ars f; (ship) navicula, linter f

craftily adv astute, callide

craftiness n astutia, calliditas; (skill) sollertia f

craftsman n artifex m

crafty adj astutus, callidus; (deceitful) subdolus, fallax, dolosus

crag n scopulus m

craggy adj scopulosus; (rough) asper

cram vt farcio ④
  □ ~ **together** constipo ①

cramp n (disease) spasmus m; (tool) uncus m

crane n (bird) grus m/f; (machine) tolleno f

cranny n rima, fissura f

crash¹ n fragor, strepitus m

crash² vi strepo ③; sono, fragorem do ①

crass adj crassus

crate n corbis f

crater n (of a volcano) crater m

crave vt (beg) rogo, imploro, efflagito ①, posco, expeto ③; (desire) cupio ④

craven adj ignavus, timidus

craving n desiderium nt; appetitus m; sitis, fames f

crawl vi repo, serpo ③; repto ①

craziness n imbecillitas, vesania, insania f, furor m

crazy adj imbecillus, insanus, vesanus

creak¹ vi strideo ②; crepito ①

creak² n stridor, crepitus m

creaking adj stridulus

cream n flos lactis m; fig (the pick of) flos m; robur nt

crease¹ n ruga f

crease² vt corrugo, rugo, replico ①

create vt creo ①; pario, gigno ③; fig formo ①; fingo ③; invenio ④; (appoint) creo ①

creation n (act) creatio f; (origin) origo f; (whole world) mundus m; fig (work of art) opus nt, ars f

creative adj creatrix; effectrix

creator n creator, procreator; fig fabricator; auctor m

creature n res creata f; animal nt

credence n (belief) fides f
  □ **give** ~ **to** credo ③ + dat

credentials n auctoritates, litterae fpl

credibility n fides, probabilitas f

credible adj credibilis

credibly adv credibiliter

credit¹ n (authority) auctoritas; (belief, faith) fides; (reputation) fama, existimatio; (praise) laus f; (financial) fides f

credit² *vt* credo; (financial) acceptum refero *ir* + *dat*

creditable *adj* honorificus, honestus

creditor *n* creditor *m*

credulity *n* credulitas *f*

credulous *adj* credulus

creed *n* fides, doctrina, opinio *f*

creek *n* aestuarium *nt*

creep *vi* repo, serpo ③; repto ①

crescent-shaped *adj* lunatus; (of the moon) crescens

crest *n* (of animals) crista; (of a horse) iuba; (of a helmet) crista *f*; (heraldic) insigne *nt*; (of a hill) apex *m*

crested *adj* cristatus

crestfallen *adj* demissus, deiectus

crevice *n* rima, rimula *f*

crew *n* grex *m*, turba, multitudo *f*; (of a ship) remiges, nautae *mpl*

cricket *n* (insect) gryllus *m*, cicada *f*

crime *n* crimen, delictum, maleficium; facinus; (shameful deed) flagitium, scelus *nt*

criminal¹ *n* nocens *m*

criminal² *adj* scelestus, sceleratus, nefarius; (of a charge) capitalis

crimson *n* coccum *nt*
■ ~ *adj* coccineus, coccinus

cringe *vt* adulor ①

cripple¹ *n* claudus *m*

cripple² *vt* claudum facio ③; fig debilito ①; accido ③

crippled *adj* claudus, mancus

crisis *n* discrimen, momentum *nt*

crisp *adj* crispus; (brittle) fragilis

criterion *n* signum, insigne; indicium *nt*

critic *n* existimator; iudex; criticus, censor *m*

critical *adj* criticus; (censorious) mordax

criticism *n* ars critica *f*; iudicium *nt*; censura, reprehensio *f*

criticize *vt* iudico, examino ①; carpo, reprehendo ③

croak¹ *vi* (as frogs) coaxo ①; (as ravens) crocio ④

croak² *n* crocitus *m*

crockery *n* fictilia *ntpl*

crocodile *n* crocodilus *m*

crocus *n* crocus *m*, crocum *nt*

crone *n* anicula, vetula *f*

crook *n* (of shepherds) pedum *nt*
□ **by hook or by** ~ quocumque modo

crooked *adj* curvatus, curvus, incurvus, flexus; fig (dishonest) pravus; dolosus
■ ~**ly** *adv* torte; prave

crookedness *n* curvatura *f*, curvamen *nt*; fig (dishonesty) pravitas *f*

crop¹ *n* (of corn) messis *f*; (yield) reditus *m*

crop² *vt* abscido ③, decurto ①; tondeo ②; (browse) carpo, depasco ③; tondeo ②

cross¹ *n* crux; fig molestia *f*; cruciatus *m*; infortunium *nt*

cross² *adj* (ill-tempered) morosus
■ ~**ly** *adv* morose

cross³ *vt* (pass over) transeo *ir*; (send across) transmitto, traicio ③; fig (thwart) frustror ①
□ ~ **one's mind** subeo *ir*; succurro ③
□ ~ **over** transcendo, traicio, transgredior ③

crossbar *n* repagulum *nt*

crossbow *n* arcuballista *f*

crossbowman *n* arcuballistarius *m*

cross-examination *n* interrogatio, percontatio *f*

cross-examine *vt* percontor ①

crossing *n* transitus; traiectus *m*; (of roads) bivium; (of three or four roads) trivium, quadrivium *nt*

crossness *n* morositas *f*

cross-question *vt* percontor ①

crossroads *n* trames *m*

crouch *vi* me demitto, subsido ③; (hide) delitesco ③

crow¹ *n* (bird) cornix *f*; (voice of the cock) cantus *m*; gallicinium *nt*

crow² *vi* (of cocks) cano ③; canto; fig (boast) iacto ①

crowbar *n* (lever) vectis *m*

crowd¹ *n* turba; frequentia, caterva, multitudo *f*; concursus *m*

crowd² *vt* arto, stipo ①; premo ③
■ ~ *vi* (around) circumfundor ③; (together) convolo, congregor ①; concurro, confluo ③

crowded *adj* condensus, confertus; frequens; celeber

crowing *n* (of the cock) gallicinium *nt*, cantus *m*

crown¹ *n* corona *f*, diadema *nt*; (top) vertex *m*; (completion) cumulus *m*; fig (royal power) regnum *nt*

crown² *vt* corono ①; (with a garland, *etc.*) cingo ③; (add finishing touch to) cumulo ①
□ **be ~ed with success** felicem exitum habeo ②

crucial *adj* maximi momenti (= of the greatest importance)

crucifixion *n* summum supplicium *nt*

crucify *vt* cruci suffigo ③

crude *adj* crudus; fig rudis; incultus
■ **~ly** *adv* imperfecte, inculte

cruel *adj* crudelis, atrox, saevus; immanis; barbarus, durus, ferus
■ **~ly** *adv* crudeliter, saeve; dure; atrociter

cruelty *n* crudelitas; atrocitas, saevitia *f*

cruise¹ *vi* pervagor, circumvector ①

cruise² *n* navigatio *f*

crumb *n* (of bread) mica *f*; frustum *nt*

crumble *vt* frio ①; comminuo, contero ③
■ ~ *vi* frior ①; collabor, corruo ③

crumple *vt* rugo, corrugo ①

crunch *vi* dentibus frango, morsu divello ③

crush *vt* contundo, contero; (press) premo, comprimo ③; elido; fig opprimo; affligo ③; (weaken) debilito ①

crust *n* crusta *f*

crusty *adj* crustosus; fig morosus

crutch *n* baculum *nt*; (support) fulcrum *nt*

cry¹ *vt&i* clamo, exclamo, conclamo; (weep) lacrimo ①; fleo ②
□ ~ **against** obiurgo ①
□ ~ **out** exclamo, vociferor ①

cry² *n* clamor *m*, vox, exclamatio *f*; (of infants) vagitus; (weeping) ploratus *m*

crying *n* fletus, ploratus *m*

crypt *n* crypta *f*

cryptic *adj* ambiguus

crystal¹ *n* crystallum *nt*

crystal² *adj* crystallinus, vitreus; pellucidus

cub *n* catulus *m*

cube *n* cubus *m*

cubic *adj* cubicus

cubit *n* cubitum *nt*, ulna *f*

cuckoo *n* coccyx, cuculus *m*

cucumber *n* cucumis *m*

cud *vi*:
□ **chew the ~** rumino ①

cuddle *vt* amplector ③

cudgel¹ *n* fustis *m*, baculum *nt*

cudgel² *vt* fustibus verbero ①

cue *n* (hint) nutus *m*; (watchword) signum *nt*; tessera *f*

cuff *n* (blow) colaphus *m*; alapa *f*

cuirass *n* lorica *f*; thorax; cataphracta *m*

culinary *adj* culinarius; coquinarius

cull *vt* carpo, lego, decerpo ③

culminate *vi* ad summum fastigium pervenio ④

culmination *n* fastigium *nt*

culpable *adj* culpandus; nocens

culprit *n* (person accused) reus *m*, rea *f*; (guilty person) nocens, noxius *m*

cult *n* cultus *m*

cultivate *vt* colo ③; (develop) formo ①; fingo, excolo ③; (train) exerceo; (show attentions to) foveo ②; observo ①

cultivation *n* cultura *f*, cultus *m*

culture *n* cultura *f*, cultus *m*; (of the mind) humanitas *f*

cumbersome *adj* iniquus, gravis, incommodus, onerosus

cunning¹ *n* peritia; astutia, calliditas, ars *f*

cunning² *adj* doctus, peritus; sollers; (in a pejorative sense) astutus, vafer

cunningly *adv* docte, perite, sollerter; astute, vafre, dolose

cup *n* poculum *nt*, calix *m*; (beaker) patera *f*

cup-bearer *n* pocillator *m*

cupboard *n* armarium *nt*

Cupid *n* Cupido, Amor *m*

cupidity *n* cupiditas *f*

cur *n* canis *m/f*

curable *adj* medicabilis, sanabilis

curative *adj* medicabilis

curator *n* curator; custos *m*

curb¹ *n* frenum *nt*; fig coercitio *f*

curb² *vt* freno, refreno ①; compesco, comprimo ③; coerceo ②

curdle *vt* cogo ③; coagulo ①
■ ~ *vi* coeo ir; concresco ③

cure¹ *n* (of wounds) sanatio *f*; (remedy) remedium *nt*, medicina *f*

cure² *vt* (heal) sano ①, medeor ②; (preserve) salio ④

curiosity *n* curiositas; audiendi *or* spectandi studium *nt*; (object) res rara, raritas *f*

curious *adj* (inquisitive) curiosus; (wondrously made) elaboratus; rarus; mirus
  ■ ~**ly** *adv* curiose; mirabiliter; arte

curl[1] *vt* (hair) crispo [1]; torqueo [2]
  ■ ~ *vi* crispor [1]

curl[2] *n* (natural) cirrus; (artificial) cincinnus *m*; (curve) flexus *m*

curling-iron *n* calamister *m*, ferrum *nt*

curly *adj* crispus

currency *n* (money) moneta *f*; nummi *mpl*; (use) usus *m*

current[1] *adj* vulgaris, usitatus
  □ **be** ~ valeo [2]
  ■ ~**ly** *adv* vulgo

current[2] *n* (of a river) flumen *nt*; (of the sea) aestus; (of air) afflatus *m*; aura *f*

curry *vt*:
  □ ~ **favour with** morem gero [3] + *dat*

curse[1] *n* exsecratio *f*, maledictum *nt*

curse[2] *vt* exsecror, detestor [1]; devoveo [2]

cursed *adj* exsecrabilis

cursory *adj* brevis, properatus

curt *adj* brevis, abruptus
  ■ ~**ly** *adv* breviter

curtail *vt* decurto, mutilo [1]; praecido [3]; fig coarto [1]; minuo [3]

curtain *n* velum; (in a theatre) aulaeum *nt*; (for beds, *etc*.) plagula *f*; (mosquito net) conopium *nt*

curtness *n* brevitas *f*

curve[1] *n* curvamen *nt*, flexus; sinus *m*; (thing curved) curvatura *f*

curve[2] *vt* curvo, incurvo, sinuo [1]; flecto [3]

curved *adj* curvus, incurvus, recurvus; curvatus; sinuosus; (as sickle) falcatus

cushion *n* pulvinar *nt*, pulvinus *m*, culcita *f*

custody *n* custodia, tutela *f*; (imprisonment) carcer *m*

custom *n* (use) usus, mos *m*, consuetudo *f*; (fashion) institutum, praescriptum *nt*; (rite) ritus *m*
  □ ~**s duty** portorium, vectigal *nt*

customary *adj* usitatus, consuetus, translaticius

customer *n* emptor *m*

custom-house *n* telonium *nt*
  ■ ~**s-officer** *n* portitor *m*

cut[1] *vt* seco [1]; (fell) caedo; (mow) succido, meto [3]
  □ ~ **apart** intercido [3]; disseco [1]
  □ ~ **away** recido, abscindo [3]; amputo [1]
  □ ~ **down** caedo; (kill) occido [3]
  □ ~ **to pieces** concido [3]
  □ ~ **off** praecido; abscindo [3]; (amputate) amputo [1]; (the head) detrunco [1]; (intercept) intercludo [3]; prohibeo [2]; fig (destroy, *etc*.) exstinguo, perimo, adimo [3]
  □ ~ **open** incido [3]
  □ ~ **out** exseco [1]; (out of a rock, *etc*.) excido [3]
  □ ~ **short** intercido [3]; (abridge) praecido [3]; fig (interrupt) intermitto [3]
  □ ~ **through** disseco [1]; (e.g. the enemy) perrumpo [3]
  □ ~ **up** minutatim concido [3]

cut[2] *n* incisura *f*; (slice) segmentum; (wound) vulnus *nt*, plaga *f*; (a short cut) via compendiaria *f*

cutlery *n* ferramenta *ntpl*

cutpurse *n* saccularius, sector zonarius *m*

cut-throat *n* sector collorum, sicarius *m*

cutting[1] *adj* (sharp) acutus; fig mordax

cutting[2] *n* (act) sectio; (of a plant) propago, talea *f*

cuttle-fish *n* loligo, sepia *f*

cycle *n* orbis *m*

cylinder *n* cylindrus *m*

cylindrical *adj* cylindratus

cymbal *n* cymbalum *nt*

cynic *adj* & *n* cynicus *m*

cynical *adj* mordax, difficilis, severus
  ■ ~**ly** *adv* cynice, mordaciter, severe

cypress *n* cupressus, cyparissus *f*

Dd

dab *vt* illino ③

dabble *vi* (in) strictim attingo ③

daffodil *n* narcissus *m*

dagger *n* pugio *m*, sica *f*

daily *adj* diurnus; quotidianus
■ ~ *adv* cotidie, in dies

daintiness *n* fastidium *nt*

dainty *adj* (of people) fastidiosus; elegans; (of things) delicatus; exquisitus, mollis

daisy *n* bellis *f*

dale *n* vallis, convallis *f*

dalliance *n* blanditiae *fpl*

dam¹ *n* (mole) moles, pila *f*, agger *m*; (barrier) obex *m*

dam² *vt* coerceo ②; obstruo ③; oppilo ①

damage¹ *n* damnum, incommodum; (loss) detrimentum *nt*; (injury) iniuria, noxa *f*

damage² *vt* (hurt) laedo ③; (impair) obsum ir

damn *vt* (condemn) damno, condemno ①

damnation *n* damnatio *f*

damp¹ *adj* umidus, udus

damp² *n* umor *m*

damp³ *vt* (also **dampen**) umecto ①; fig infringo; restinguo ③

dampness *n* uligo *f*; umor *m*

damsel *n* puella, virgo *f*

dance¹ *n* saltatus *m*, saltatio *f*; chorus *m*; chorea *f*

dance² *vi* salto ①

dancer *n* saltator *m*

dancing *n* saltatio *f*, saltatus *m*

dancing-girl *n* saltatrix *f*

dandruff *n* furfur *m*; porrigo *f*

danger *n* periculum, discrimen *nt*

dangerous *adj* periculosus, gravis
■ ~ly *adv* periculose; graviter

dangle *vi* pendeo, dependeo ②; fluctuo ①

dangling *adj* pendulus

dank *adj* umidus, uvidus, udus

dappled *adj* variatus, varius

dare *vi* audeo ②
■ ~ *vt* provoco ①

daring *adj* audens; ferox; audax; animosus
■ ~ly *adv* audenter, audacter, animose

dark¹ *adj* obscurus, fuscus; opacus; niger; caecus; tenebrosus; caliginosus; (of mourning-dress) pullus; fig obscurus, ambiguus, dubius, anceps; (gloomy) atrox
■ ~ly *adv* obscure; fig per ambages

dark² *n* tenebrae *fpl*; obscurum *nt*; nox *f*

darken *vt* obscuro; (of colours) infusco; fig occaeco ①

darkness *n* obscuritas, caligo *f*; (shadiness) opacitas *f*; tenebrae *fpl*; color fuscus *m*

darling *n* deliciae *fpl*; amores *mpl*; corculum *nt*
■ ~ *adj* suavis, mellitus; amatus

darn *vt* resarcio ④

darnel *n* lolium *nt*

dart¹ *n* iaculum, spiculum, missile *nt*; hasta, lancea *f*

dart² *vi* provolo ①; me inicio ③

dash¹ *vt* (against) allido, illido; offendo ③; (frustrate) frustror ①; (confound) confundo ③
□ ~ **to pieces** discutio ③
□ ~ **out** *vt* elido ③; *vi* ruo ③
■ ~ *vi* (rush) ruo ③

dash² *n* (onset) impetus *m*

dashing *adj* acer, alacer; splendidus

date¹ *n* (of time) dies *m/f*; tempus *nt*; (fruit) balanus *f*; palma *f*
□ **out of** ~ obsoletus, desuetus

date² *vt* (establish age) diem ascribo ③
■ ~ *vi* (from) incipio, originem traho ③

daub¹ *vt* oblino, illino ③

daub² *n* litura *f*

daughter *n* filia *f*

daughter-in-law *n* nurus *f*

daunt *vt* pavefacio ③; terreo, perterreo ②

dauntless *adj* impavidus, intrepidus

dawdle *vi* (loiter) moror, cesso ①

dawn[1] *vi* illucesco, dilucesco ③; fig eluceo ②
 □ ∼ **upon** fig subeo *ir*; succurro ③ *both + dat*

dawn[2] *n* aurora, prima lux *f*, diluculum *nt*

day[1] *n* dies *m/f*; lux *f*, sol *m*; tempus *nt*
 □ **the** ∼ **before** pridie
 □ **the** ∼ **after** postridie

day[2] *adj* diurnus

daybreak *n* lux prima *f*

daylight *n* lux *f*, dies *m*

daytime *n* tempus diurnum *nt*

daze *vt* obstupefacio ③

dazzle *vt* praestringo ③; fig capio ③

dazzling *adj* fulgidus, splendidus

dead[1] *adj* mortuus; vita defunctus; (lifeless, senseless) exanimis; fig torpidus; (dull) segnis

dead[2] *n* manes *mpl*; (of night) intempesta (nox) *f*

deaden *vt* hebeto ①; obtundo ③; (weaken) debilito, enervo ①; (lessen) imminuo ③

deadly *adj* mortifer, letalis; fig capitalis, implacabilis

deadness *n* torpor; stupor *m*, inertia; (dullness) insulsitas *f*

deaf *adj* surdus

deafen *vt* exsurdo ①; obtundo ③

deafness *n* surditas *f*

deal[1] *n* (quantity) numerus *m*; vis, copia *f*; (business) negotium *nt*
 □ **a great** ∼ multum

deal[2] *vt* distribuo ③; (handle) tracto ①
 □ ∼ **in** (sell) vendo
 □ ∼ **with** utor ③ + *abl*
 ■ ∼ *vi* mercor, negotior ①

dealer *n* mercator, negotiatior *m*

dealing *n* (trade) negotiatio, mercatura *f*, commercium *nt*; usus *m*; (doing) factum *nt*; (treatment) tractatio *f*

dear *adj* (costly) carus, pretiosus; (beloved) dilectus, carus
 ■ ∼**ly** *adv* care; valde

dearness *n* caritas *f*

dearth *n* inopia, penuria; fames *f*

death *n* mors *f*; letum *nt*; interitus, obitus *m*
 □ **violent** ∼ nex *f*; funus *nt*

deathbed *n*:
 □ **on one's** ∼ moriens

debar *vt* excludo ③; prohibeo, arceo ②

debase *vt* depravo; adultero; vitio ①; corrumpo ③; fig dedecoro ①

debatable *adj* disputabilis, controversiosus, dubius

debate[1] *vt* disputo, discepto ①; dissero ③
 ■ ∼ *vi* cogito, meditor ①

debate[2] *n* controversia, disceptatio *f*; (friendly) colloquium *nt*

debauch *vt* stupro; vitio ①; corrumpo ③

debauchery *n* libido, luxuria *f*, stuprum *nt*

debit[1] *n* expensum *nt*

debit[2] *vt* expensam pecuniam alicui fero *ir*

debris *n* ruina *f*

debt *n* (of money) debitum, aes alienum; fig debitum *nt*

debtor *n* also fig debitor *m*

decade *n* decennium *nt*

decay[1] *vi* (of buildings) dilabor, labor; (of flowers) defloresco; (rot) putresco; (waste away) tabesco ③; fig deficio ③; declino ①

decay[2] *n* tabes, caries; fig defectio; deminutio *f*

deceased *adj* mortuus, defunctus

deceit *n* fraus, fallacia *f*, dolus *m*

deceitful *adj* fallax; dolosus; fraudulentus; falsus
 ■ ∼**ly** *adv* fallaciter; fraudulenter; dolose; per fallacias

deceive *vt* decipio, fallo ③; (cheat) fraudo ①; circumduco ③; circumvenio ④
 ■ ∼ *vi* fig mentior ④

deceiver *n* fraudator *m*

December *n* December *m*

decency *n* decorum *nt*; pudor *m*

decent *adj* decens; decorus; pudicus; honestus
 ■ ∼**ly** *adv* decore, decenter, honeste

deception *n* fraudatio, fraus, fallacia *f*

deceptive *adj* fallax, vanus

decide *vt&i* discepto, diiudico ①; decerno; constituo ③

decided *adj* firmus, constans; (of things) certus
 ■ ∼**ly** *adv* certe

decimate *vt* decimo; fig depopulor ①

decipher *vt* explico ①

decision *n* sententia *f*, arbitrium, iudicium *nt*

decisive *adj* decretorius, haud
dubius, certus
■ **~ly** *adv* haud dubie

deck *n* pons *m*; transtra *ntpl*

declaim *vt&i* declamo, declamito ⓵;
invehor ③ (in) + *acc*

declamation *n* declamatio *f*

declaration *n* professio; (of war)
denuntiatio *f*; (speech) oratio *f*; (opinion)
sententia *f*

declare *vt* declaro ⓵; aperio ④;
profiteor ②; (war) denuntio; (as a judge)
iudico ⓵
■ **~** *vi* affirmo ⓵

decline¹ *vt* (recoil from) detrecto; (refuse)
recuso ⓵
■ **~** *vi* (slope) vergo ③; inclino ⓵; (decay)
deficio, minuor ③; (abate) laxo ⓵

decline² *n* defectio; (wasting away) tabes *f*

decompose *vt* dissolvo ③
■ **~** *vi* dissolvor, putresco ③

decomposition *n* dissolutio; (decay)
tabes *f*

decorate *vt* orno, exorno, decoro ⓵

decoration *n* (act) ornatio, exornatio
f; ornatus *m*; (ornament) ornamentum *nt*

decorator *n* exornator *m*

decorous *adj* decorus
■ **~ly** *adv* decore

decorum *n* decorum, quod decet *nt*

decoy¹ *vt* inesco ⓵; fig allicio, illicio,
pellicio ③

decoy² *n* illecebra *f*, illicium *nt*; (bird)
allector *m*

decrease¹ *vt* minuo, imminuo,
deminuo ③
■ **~** *vi* decresco, minuor ③; minor fio *ir*

decrease² *n* deminutio, imminutio *f*

decree¹ *n* decretum, edictum *nt*;
(judgment) sententia *f*

decree² *vt* statuo; decerno, edico ③

decrepit *adj* decrepitus, debilis,
enervatus

decry *vt* detrecto, obtrecto ⓵

dedicate *vt* dedico; consecro ⓵;
voveo ②

dedication *n* dedicatio; consecratio;
(of a book) nuncupatio *f*

deduce *vt* (infer) concludo ③

deduct *vt* detraho, subtraho, deduco ③

deduction *n* deductio *f*; (in logic)
conclusio *f*

deed *n* factum; facinus *nt*; res gestae
fpl; (law) syngrapha *f*, instrumentum *nt*

deem *vt* iudico, puto, existimo ⓵;
duco ③

deep¹ *adj* altus, profundus; (of sounds)
gravis; (of colours) satur

deep² *n* profundum; (sea) mare *nt*

deepen *vt* excavo ⓵; defodio,
deprimo ③
■ **~** *vi* altior fio *ir*; (night, *etc.*) densor ⓵

deeply *adv* alte, profunde; (inwardly)
penitus; fig graviter, valde

deepness *n* ▶ **depth**

deer *n* cervus *m*; cerva *f*

deface *vt* deformo, turpo ⓵

defamation *n* obtrectatio *f*

defamatory *adj* probrosus

defame *vt* diffamo, calumnior,
obtrecto ⓵

default *vi* (fail) deficio ③
□ **let a legal case go by ~** ad
vadimonium non venio ④

defeat¹ *n* clades, calamitas; (frustration)
frustratio *f*

defeat² *vt* (baffle) frustror ⓵; (conquer)
vinco ③; supero ⓵

defect¹ *n* vitium, mendum *nt*; menda
f; (want) defectus *m*

defect² *vi* deficio ③

defection *n* defectio *f*

defective *adj* mancus, vitiosus;
imperfectus

defence *n* (act) defensio; (excuse)
excusatio; (means of) tutela *f*; tutamen *nt*
□ **~s** munimentum *nt*

defenceless *adj* inermis;
defensoribus nudatus

defend *vt* defendo ③; (at law) patrocinor
⓵ + *dat*

defendant *n* reus *m*, rea *f*
□ **the ~** iste

defender *n* defensor; patronus *m*

defensible *adj* qui defendi potest;
excusabilis

defer *vt* differo, profero *ir*, produco ③
□ **~ to** obsequor ③ + *dat*

deference *n* observantia; reverentia *f*

defiance *n* provocatio *f*
□ **in ~ of** contra + *acc*

defiant *adj* ferox

deficiency *n* defectio *f*, defectus *m*;
pars relicta; (want) lacuna *f*

deficient *adj* mancus; (deficient in) inops + *gen*
 □ **be** ∼ **in** deficio ③; careo ② + *abl*

deficit *n* lacuna *f*

defile¹ *vt* contamino, inquino, maculo, commaculo; fig foedo; incesto, violo ①

defile² *n* fauces, angustiae *fpl*; saltus *m*

define *vt* circumscribo ③; termino ①; definio ④

definite *adj* certus, status, definitus
 ∎ ∼**ly** *adv* definite, certe

definition *n* definitio *f*

definitive *adj* definitivus, decretorius

deflect *vt&i* deflecto ③; declino ①

deform *vt* deformo ①

deformed *adj* deformis; deformatus; distortus

deformity *n* deformitas; pravitas *f*

defraud *vt* fraudo, defraudo ①

deft *adj* habilis

defunct *adj* vita defunctus, defunctus, mortuus

defy *vt* (challenge) provoco ①; (spurn) contemno ③

degenerate¹ *vi* degenero ①

degenerate² *adj* degener

degradation *n* ignominia; deiectio *f*

degrade *vt* deicio ③; loco moveo ②; fig ignominia afficio ③

degree *n* gradus, ordo *m*
 □ **in the highest** ∼ summe
 □ **by** ∼**s** paulatim, sensim, pedetentim, gradatim

deification *n* apotheosis, consecratio *f*

deify *vt* divum habeo ②; in numero deorum colloco ①

deign *vi* dignor ①; non aspernor ③, non gravor ①; sustineo ②

deity *n* numen *nt*; deus *m*; dea *f*

dejected *adj* demissus, tristis

dejection *n* animi demissio *f*; animus afflictus *m*

delay¹ *n* mora, cunctatio; dilatio, retardatio *f*

delay² *vt* detineo ②; tardo; retardo; (keep back) remoror ①
 ∎ ∼ *vi* cunctor; moror, cesso ①

delectable *adj* amoenus

delegate¹ *n* legatus *m*

delegate² *vt* (depute) delego; (commit) commendo ①

delegation *n* delegatio *f*

deliberate¹ *adj* deliberatus, consideratus, cautus, prudens; lentus
 ∎ ∼**ly** *adv* deliberate, cogitate; lente; consulto

deliberate² *vi* consulto, delibero, considero, reputo, verso, voluto ①; volvo ③

deliberation *n* deliberatio *f*

delicacy *n* subilitas, tenuitas; elegantia *f*; cuppediae *fpl*; (weakness) infirmitas *f*

delicate *adj* delicatus; mollis, tener; exquisitus; elegans; fastidiosus; (of texture) subtilis; (in taste) suavis; (weak) infirmus
 ∎ ∼**ly** *adv* delicate; exquisite; subtiliter; molliter

delicious *adj* delicatus, suavis; exquisitus

delight¹ *n* delectatio *f*; deliciae *fpl*; gaudium *nt*; voluptas *f*

delight² *vt* delecto ①
 ∎ ∼ *vi* gaudeo ②; laetor ①

delightful *adj* suavis, iucundus, amoenus
 ∎ ∼**ly** *adv* iucunde, suaviter

delinquency *n* delictum *nt*

delinquent *n* nocens *m*

delirious *adj* non sui compos, mente alienatus

delirium *n* mentis alienatio *f*; delirium *nt*

deliver *vt* do ①; (hand over) trado ③; (free) libero ①; (surrender) prodo ③; (a speech) habeo ②; (sentence) dico (ius) ③; (an opinion) promo ③; (a message) perfero *ir*; (of childbirth) parienti adsum *ir*; (∼ up) cedo ③

deliverance *n* liberatio *f*

deliverer *n* liberator, conservator *m*; vindex *m/f*

delivery *n* liberatio; (of goods) traditio; (utterance) pronuntiatio *f*; (child-birth) partus *m*

delude *vt* decipio, deludo ③; derideo ②

deluge¹ *n* diluvies, inundatio *f*, diluvium *nt*

deluge² *vt* inundo ①

delusion *n* error *m*; fraus *f*

delve *vt* ▸ **dig**

demand¹ *vt* postulo, flagito ①; posco, deposco, peto ③

demand² *n* postulatio, petitio *f*
 □ **be in** ∼ a multis expetor ③

d

demarcation *n* designatio *f*; (boundary) confinium *nt*

demean *vi*:
□ ∼ **oneself** (condescend to) descendo ③ ad + *acc*

demeanour *n* mores *mpl*; (deportment) gestus *m*

democracy *n* civitas popularis *f*; liber populus *m*

democrat *n* plebicola, homo popularis *m*

democratic *adj* popularis
■ ∼**ally** *adv* populi voluntate, per populum

demolish *vt* demolior ④; everto, disicio ③

demolition *n* demolitio, eversio *f*

demon *n* daemon *m*

demonstrable *adj* demonstrabilis, manifestus

demonstrate *vt* demonstro, firmo ①; convinco ③

demonstration *n* demonstratio *f*

demur¹ *vi* haesito, dubito ①
□ ∼ **to** nego, repudio ①

demur² *n* mora; (objection) exceptio *f*

demure *adj* modestus, gravis, severus
■ ∼**ly** *adv* modeste

demurral *n* mora; (objection) exceptio *f*

den *n* (cave) specus *m/f/nt*; (of beasts) latibulum *nt*; spelunca, latebra *f*; lustra *ntpl*

denial *n* negatio; infitiatio; (refusal) repudiatio; repulsa *f*

denote *vt* significo ①

denounce *vt* (accuse) accuso; (blame) culpo ①

dense *adj* densus, spissus, confertus
■ ∼**ly** *adv* dense; crebro

density *n* densitas *f*

dent¹ *n* (mark) nota *f*

dent² *vt* (mark) noto ①

dentist *n* dentium medicus *m*

denude *vt* denudo, nudo ①; detego ③; (rob) spolio ①

denunciation *n* denuntiatio; accusatio *f*

deny *vt* nego, infitior; (refuse) nego, recuso, denego ①; renuo, abnuo ③

depart *vi* abeo; exeo *ir*; (leave) discedo ③; (move) demigro ①; (set out) proficiscor ③

department *n* (area of responsibility) provincia *f*; cura *f*; munus *nt*; (branch) genus *nt*

departure *n* abitus, discessus *m*, profectio; (deviation) digressio *f*

depend *vi* (on) pendeo ②+ab *or* ex +*abl*; (trust) confido, fido + *dat*

dependable *adj* fidus

dependant *n* cliens *m/f*; assecla *m*

dependence *n* servitus; (reliance) fiducia; fides *f*; (poverty) inopia *f*

dependent *adj* subiectus; (poor) inops

depict *vt* pingo, depingo; effingo; describo; exprimo ③

deplorable *adj* miserabilis, flebilis, lugendus, plorabilis, calamitosus

deploy *vt* explico ①

depopulate *vt* desolo, vasto ①

deportment *n* gestus, habitus *m*

depose *vt* abrogo ①; amoveo ②

deposit¹ *vt* depono ③; (commit) commendo ①

deposit² *n* depositum; (pledge) pignus *nt*; (first instalment) arrabo *m*

deposition *n* (evidence) testimonium *nt*

depraved *adj* corruptus

depravity *n* pravitas *f*

deprecate *vt* deprecor ①

deprecation *n* deprecatio *f*

depredation *n* praedatio, spoliatio *f*; latrocinium *nt*

depress *vt* deprimo; fig infringo; affligo ③

depressed *adj* (downcast) afflictus; (flat) planus; (hollow) cavus

depressing *adj* tristis

depression *n* fig animi demissio *f*; animus afflictus *m*

deprivation *n* (act) privatio; spoliatio; (state) orbitas; inopia *f*

deprive *vt* privo; spolio; orbo ①; (take away) adimo, eripio ③

deprived *adj* expers, exsors

depth *n* altitudo *f*; profundum *nt*; (sea) pontus; (bottom) fundus *m*

deputation *n* legati; (spokesmen) oratores *mpl*

depute *vt* lego, mando ①

deputy *n* legatus; vicarius *m*

deranged *adj* (mentally) mente captus, delirus

derangement *n* (of mind) mens alienata, mentis alienatio *f*

derelict *adj* derelictus

deride *vt* rideo, derideo, irrideo ②

derision *n* risus, derisus *m*; irrisio *f*

derisive *adj* acerbus

derivation *n* derivatio; etymologia *f*

derive *vt* duco, deduco ③
 ■ ~ *vi* proficiscor ③; orior ④

derogatory *adj* inhonestus, turpis

descend *vt&i* descendo; (fall suddenly) delabor ③
 ▢ **be ~ed from** orior ④ ab + *abl*; originem traho ③ ab + *abl*

descendant *n* progenies, proles, stirps *f*

descent *n* descensus *m*; descensio; (slope) declivitas *f*; fig lapsus *m*; (origin) origo *f*; genus *nt*

describe *vt* describo; depingo ③; narro ①

description *n* descriptio; narratio *f*

desecrate *vt* profano, violo ①; polluo ③

desecration *n* violatio *f*

desert[1] *n* (wilderness) desertum *nt*, vastitas, solitudo *f*

desert[2] *n* meritum *nt*

desert[3] *vt* desero, relinquo, destituo ③
 ■ ~ *vi* transfugio, signa relinquo ③

deserter *n* desertor; transfuga *m*

desertion *n* derelictio; (betrayal) proditio *f*

deserve *vt&i* mereo, mereor ②; dignus sum *ir*

deservedly *adv* merito, iure

deserving *adj* dignus; bonus, optimus, probus

design[1] *vt* describo ③; fig machinor, excogito ①; molior ④; (destine) destino ①

design[2] *n* (drawing) descriptio *f*; fig (purpose) consilium, propositum *nt*

designate *vt* designo; nomino ①

designation *n* designatio *f*; (name) nomen *nt*

designer *n* inventor; fabricator; machinator *m*

designing *adj* callidus, subdolus

desirable *adj* optabilis, expetendus

desire[1] *vt* desidero, opto ①; expeto, cupio ③

desire[2] *n* desiderium *nt*; cupido *f*; appetitus *m*; appetitio *f*

desirous *adj* cupidus, appetens

desist *vi* desisto; absisto; (cease) desino ③

desk *n* scrinium; pulpitum *nt*

desolate *adj* solus, desertus, vastus, desolatus; fig (of persons) afflictus

desolation *n* vastitas; solitudo *f*; (bereavement) orbitas *f*

despair[1] *n* desperatio *f*

despair[2] *vi* despero (de aliqua re) ①

despairingly *adv* desperanter

despatch *vt* mitto; dimitto ③; (finish) absolvo; exsequor; (settle) transigo; conficio; (kill) interficio ③

desperate *adj* (without hope) exspes, desperatus; (dangerous) periculosus
 ■ ~**ly** *adv* ita ut spes amittatur
 ▢ **be ~ly in love** perdite amo ①

desperation *n* desperatio *f*

despicable *adj* aspernandus, vilis

despicably *adv* turpiter

despise *vt* despicio, sperno, temno, contemno ③; aspernor ①

despite *conj* (even if) etiamsi

despoil *vt* ▶ **spoil** *vt*

despondency *n* animi demissio *f*

despondent *adj* demissus

despot *n* dominus; tyrannus *m*

despotic *adj* imperiosus, superbus, tyrannicus
 ■ ~**ally** *adv* tyrannice

despotism *n* dominatio, regia potestas *f*

dessert *n* secunda mensa *f*; bellaria *ntpl*

destination *n* (purpose) destinatio *f*; propositum *nt*; (goal) meta *f*

destine *vt* destino; (mark out) designo ①

destiny *n* fatum *nt*; sors *f*

destitute *adj* egens, egenus, inops; destitutus, expers; viduus

destitution *n* inopia; egestas *f*; mendicitas *f*

destroy *vt* destruo, perdo, everto, tollo, consumo ③; aboleo, deleo ②; vasto ①
 ▢ **be ~ed** intereo, pereo *ir*

destruction *n* eversio *f*; exitium *nt*; clades *f*

destructive *adj* exitialis, perniciosus; calamitosus

detach *vt* seiungo; solvo, secerno ③

detached *adj* seiunctus

detachment *n* separatio; (of troops) manus *f*; (fairness) aequitas *f*

detail[1] *vt* enumero ①; singillatim dico ③

detail[2] *n* singulae res *fpl*; singula *ntpl*

detain *vt* retineo ②; retardo ①

detect *vt* comperio ④; deprendo ③

detection *n* deprehensio *f*; indicium *nt*

detective *n* inquisitor *m*

detention *n* mora *f*

deter *vt* deterreo, absterreo ②; averto ③

deteriorate *vi* deterior fio *ir*, in peius mutor ①

deterioration *n* depravatio, corruptio *f*

determination *n* definitio *f*; arbitrium, iudicium *nt*; mens, voluntas *f*; (purpose) consilium *nt*; (resoluteness) constantia *f*

determine *vt* determino ①; definio ④; statuo, constituo, decerno ③; diiudico ①
□ **I am ∼d** certum est mihi

detest *vt* abominor, detestor ①; odi, perodi ③

detestable *adj* detestabilis, foedus, odiosus

detestation *n* odium *nt*; detestatio *f*

dethrone *vt* regno expello ③

detract *vt* detraho, imminuo ③; (slander) detrecto, obtrecto ①

detraction *n* obtrectatio *f*

detriment *n* detrimentum, damnum *nt*

detrimental *adj* damnosus, iniuriosus, iniquus

devastate *vt* vasto, populor, depopulor ①; fig percello ③

devastation *n* (act) vastatio, populatio; (state) vastitas *f*

develop *vt* evolvo ③; explico ①; fig excolo ③
■ ∼ *vi* cresco ③

development *n* explicatio *f*; (issue) exitus *m*

deviate *vi* aberro ①; digredior ③

deviation *n* aberratio; declinatio; digressio *f*; fig error *m*

device *n* (emblem) insigne *nt*; (motto) inscriptio *f*; (contrivance) artificium *nt*; machina *f*

devious *adj* devius; vagus; erraticus
□ ∼ **course** ambages *fpl*

devise *vt* fingo ③; excogito ①; concoquo ③; molior ④; machinor ①
□ ∼ **a plan** consilium capio ③

devoid *adj* inanis, vacuus; liber; expers

devote *vt* devoveo ②; consecro, dico ①; (set apart) sepono ③
□ ∼ **oneself to** studeo ②; incumbo ③ *both + dat*

devoted *adj* studiosus; (loving) pius

devotedly *adv* studiose, summo studio

devotion *n* devotio *f*; (affection) pietas *f*; (zeal) studium *nt*; diligentia *f*

devour *vt* voro, devoro ①; haurio ④; consumo ③

devout *adj* pius, devotus
■ ∼**ly** *adv* pie, religiose, sancte

dew *n* ros *m*

dewy *adj* roscidus, roridus, rorulentus

dexterity *n* calliditas, sollertia *f*

dexterous *adj* (also **dextrous**) callidus, sollers, sciens, habilis
■ ∼**ly** *adv* callide, scienter, sollerter

diabolical *adj* diabolicus

diagnosis *n* (examination) exploratio *f*; (judgment) sententia *f*

diagonal *adj* diagonalis
■ ∼ *n* diagonalis linea *f*
■ ∼**ly** *adv* in quincuncem, in transversum

diagram *n* forma; forma geometrica *f*

dial *n* solarium *nt*

dialect *n* dialectos *f*; sermo *m*

dialogue *n* sermo *m*; colloquium *nt*; (written discussion) dialogus *m*

diameter *n* diametros, dimetiens *f*

diamond *n* adamas *m*

diaphragm *n* praecordia *ntpl*

diarrhoea *n* profluvium *nt*

diary *n* diarium *nt*; ephemeris *f*

dice *npl* tali *mpl*; tesserae *fpl*; (the game) alea *f*

dictate *vt* dicto ①; praescribo ③; (command) impero ① + *dat*

dictation *n* dictatum *nt*; (command) imperium, praescriptum *nt*

dictator *n* dictator *m*

dictatorial *adj* dictatorius; arrogans; imperiosus

dictatorship *n* dictatura *f*

diction *n* dictio *f*

dictionary *n* lexicon *nt*; thesaurus *m*

die[1] *n* (for gaming) talus *m*
□ **the ~ is cast** alea iacta est

die[2] *vi* morior; fig exstinguor; (decay) labor ③; pereo, intereo *ir*; (fade) cado ③

diet *n* (food) victus *m*; med diaeta *f*

differ *vi* differo ③; discrepo, disto ①; (in opinion, *etc.*) dissentio ④; dissideo ②

difference *n* differentia; diversitas; varietas *f*; discrimen *nt*; (of opinion) discrepantia; dissensio *f*

different *adj* diversus; alius; dispar; (unlike) dissimilis; (various) diversus, varius
■ **~ly** *adv* aliter; diverse; secus

difficult *adj* difficilis; arduus

difficulty *n* difficultas *f*; (dilemma, need) angustiae *fpl*
□ **with ~** aegre

diffident *adj* diffidens; verecundus; timidus; modestus

dig *vt&i* fodio ③
□ **~ up** eruo, effodio ③

digest *vt* (food) concoquo ③; (*also* fig)

digestion *n* (of food) concoctio *f*; (stomach) stomachus *m*

digit *n* (finger) digitus; (number) numerus *m*

dignified *adj* gravis

dignify *vt* honesto, honoro, orno ①

dignity *n* dignitas, gravitas *f*, honor *m*

digress *vi* digredior ③; aberro ①

digression *n* digressio *f*

dike *n* ▶ **dyke**

dilapidated *adj* ruinosus, prolapsus

dilapidation *n* ruina *f*

dilate *vt&i* dilato; dilator ①

dilatory *adj* cunctabundus, lentus, tardus

dilemma *n* dilemma *nt*; fig (difficulty) angustiae *fpl*

diligence *n* diligentia, sedulitas *f*

diligent *adj* diligens, sedulus
■ **~ly** *adv* diligenter, sedulo

dilute *vt* diluo ③; misceo ②; tempero ①

dilution *n* temperatio, mixtura *f*

dim *adj* hebes; obscurus
□ **be ~** hebeo ②
□ **become ~** hebesco ③

dimension *n* dimensio, mensura *f*

diminish *vt* minuo, imminuo, deminuo ③; (reduce) extenuo ①
■ **~** *vi* minuor ③; extenuor ①

diminution *n* imminutio, deminutio *f*

dimly *adv* obscure

dimness *n* hebetatio; obscuritas; caligo *f*

din *n* strepitus, sonitus, fragor *m*
□ **make a ~** strepo ③

dine *vi* ceno ①; prandeo ②

dingy *adj* fuscus, squalidus, sordidus, subniger

dining-room *n* cenatio *f*

dinner *n* cena *f*

dinner-party *n* convivium *nt*

dint *n*:
□ **by ~ of** per + *acc*

dip[1] *vt* immergo; tingo ③
■ **~** *vi* mergor; tingor; (sink) premor, vergo ③; declino ①

dip[2] *n* declivitas *f*

diploma *n* diploma *nt*

diplomacy *n* ars, astutia *f*

diplomat *n* (ambassador) legatus *m*

dire *adj* dirus, terribilis

direct[1] *adj* rectus, directus
■ **~ly** *adv* directe, recta (via); (immediately) statim, confestim

direct[2] *vt* dirigo; (turn) flecto, verto; (address) inscribo ③; (order) iubeo ②; (rule) guberno; (manage) curo, procuro ①

direction *n* (act) directio *f*; (way) iter *nt*, via; (quarter) regio; (ruling) gubernatio; (management) administratio *f*; (order) praeceptum *nt*
□ **in both ~s** utroque

director *n* rector; magister; praeses, praefectus; gubernator; (manager) curator *m*

dirge *n* nenia *f*, carmen funebre *nt*

dirt *n* sordes *f*; caenum, lutum *nt*; limus *m*

dirtiness *n* spurcitia; fig obscenitas *f*

dirty[1] *adj* spurcus, sordidus, immundus, lutulentus, caenosus; (unwashed) illotus; fig obscenus

d

dirty² *vt* foedo, spurco, maculo, commaculo ①

disability *n* impotentia *f*

disable *vt* debilito; enervo ①

disabled *adj* debilis; mancus

disadvantage *n* incommodum, detrimentum, damnum *nt*; (inequality) iniquitas *f*

disadvantageous *adj* incommodus; iniquus

disaffected *adj* alienatus; aversus; seditiosus

disaffection *n* alienatus animus *m*; seditio *f*

disagree *vi* discrepo ①; dissideo ②; dissentio ④

disagreeable *adj* iniucundus; ingratus; molestus; insuavis; gravis; (of people) difficilis, morosus

disagreement *n* dissensio, discordia *f*

disappear *vi* vanesco; evanesco; dilabor ③

disappearance *n* exitus *m*

disappoint *vt* fallo ③; frustror, fraudo ①

disappointment *n* frustratio *f*; (inconvenience) incommodum *nt*

disapprobation *n* improbatio, reprehensio *f*

disapproval *n* improbatio, reprehensio *f*

disapprove *vt* reprehendo ③; improbo ①

disarm *vt* exarmo ①; armis exuo ③; fig mitigo ①

disaster *n* calamitas, clades *f*; incommodum *nt*

disastrous *adj* calamitosus, funestus; pestifer
■ ~**ly** *adv* calamitose; pestifere

disband *vt* dimitto ③; missum facio ③

disbelief *n* diffidentia; incredulitas *f*

disbelieve *vt* fidem non habeo ②; non credo ③

disc *n* discus *m*; orbis (solis, lunae) *m*

discard *vt* repudio ①; reicio, excutio ③

discern *vt* discerno, distinguo ③

discerning *adj* perspicax, acutus

discernment *n* perspicientia *f*; (faculty) prudentia *f*; acumen *nt*

discharge¹ *vt&i* (unload) exonero ①; (dismiss) dimitto ③; (of rivers) effundo ③;

(perform) fungor, perfungor ③; (pay) solvo ③; (shoot, let fly) mitto, immitto; (acquit) absolvo ③

discharge² *n* (unloading) exoneratio; (dismissal) missio; (acquittal) absolutio; (payment) solutio *f*; (matter poured out) profluvium, effluvium *nt*

disciple *n* discipulus *m*; discipula *f*; fig sectator *m*

discipline¹ *n* disciplina *f*

discipline² *vt* instituo; assuefacio ③

disclaim *vt* infitior ①; diffiteor ②; nego ①; (let go) remitto, dimitto ③

disclaimer *n* negatio, infitiatio *f*

disclose *vt* patefacio, pando, detego ③; aperio ④; enuntio, vulgo ①

disclosure *n* indicium *nt*

discolour *vt* decoloro ①

discomfort *n* incommoda *ntpl*; molestiae *fpl*; vexatio *f*

disconcert *vt* conturbo, perturbo ①; (frustrate) frustror ①

disconnect *vt* disiungo, seiungo ③

disconsolate *adj* afflictus, tristis
■ ~**ly** *adv* insolabiliter; triste

discontent *n* animus parum contentus *m*; (anger) ira *f*; (hatred) odium *nt*

discontented *adj* parum contentus; (disagreeable) morosus

discontinue *vt&i* intermitto; desino, desisto ③

discord *n* discordia *f*

discordant *adj* discors; discrepans; dissonus; absonus

discount *vt* deduco; (disregard) neglego ③

discourage *vt* deterreo ②; examino ①; (dissuade) dissuadeo ②
□ **be ~d** animum demitto ③

discouragement *n* animi demissio *f*; (dissuasion) dissuasio *f*

discouraging *adj* adversus, incommodus

discourse *n* sermo *m*; colloquium *nt*; (written) libellus *m*

discourteous *adj* inurbanus; inhumanus
■ ~**ly** *adv* inurbane; inhumaniter

discourtesy *n* inhumanitas *f*

discover *vt* comperio ④; (search out) exploro, investigo ①

discoverer *n* inventor; repertor *m*; inventrix, repertrix *f*; (searcher) investigator *m*

discovery *n* inventio; (searching out) investigatio *f*; (thing found out) inventum *nt*; (making known) patefactio *f*

discreet *adj* cautus, prudens
■ ∼**ly** *adv* caute, prudenter

discrepancy *n* discrepantia *f*

discretion *n* prudentia, circumspectio *f*
□ **at the** ∼ **of** arbitrio + *gen*, ad arbitrium + *gen*

discriminate *vt* diiudico ①; distinguo ③

discriminating *adj* proprius; (intelligent) acutus, perspicax, sagax

discrimination *n* (distinguishing) distinctio *f*; (discernment) iudicium; (distinction) discrimen *nt*

discuss *vt* disputo ①; dissero, ago ③

discussion *n* disputatio, disceptatio, controversia *f*

disdain¹ *vt* dedignor ①, aspernor; despicio, sperno, contemno ③; fastidio ④

disdain² *n* contemptus *m*; fastidium *nt*; superbia *f*

disdainful *adj* fastidiosus, superbus
■ ∼**ly** *adv* fastidiose, contemptim, superbe

disease *n* morbus *m*, malum *nt*; (plague) pestilentia, pestis, lues *f*

diseased *adj* aegrotus, aeger

disembark *vt&i* e navi (navibus) expono; e navi egredior (in terram) ③

disembowel *vt* eviscero ①

disengage *vt* solvo, exsolvo ③; avoco ①

disentangle *vt* extrico, explico ①; expedio ④

disfavour *n* invidia *f*

disfigure *vt* deformo, turpo, mutilo ①

disfigurement *n* deformatio; deformitas, foeditas *f*; (blemish) vitium *nt*; labes *f*

disgorge *vt* revomo, evomo ③

disgrace¹ *n* (shame) infamia; ignominia *f*; dedecus *nt*; (disfavour) offensa, invidia *f*

disgrace² *vt* dedecoro, dehonesto ①

disgraceful *adj* turpis, inhonestus, ignominiosus
■ ∼**ly** *adv* turpiter, inhoneste, ignominiose

disguise¹ *n* (mask) persona *f*; fig dissimulatio *f*; (false appearance) species *f*; (pretence) praetextum *nt*

disguise² *vt* vestem muto; fig celo; dissimulo ①

disgust¹ *n* (loathing) fastidium, taedium, odium *nt*

disgust² *vt* fastidium moveo ②
□ **be** ∼**ed** piget (me rei) ②; aegre fero *ir*

disgusting *adj* foedus; fig odiosus

dish¹ *n* catinus *m*; (flat ∼) patina; (a large dish) lanx *f*; (course) mensa *f*, ferculum *nt*

dish² *vt*:
□ ∼ **up** appono ③

dishearten *vt* animum frango ③; exanimo ①
□ **be** ∼**ed** animum demitto ③

dishevelled *adj* passus, effusus, irreligatus

dishonest *adj* improbus, malus, perfidus, fradulentus
■ ∼**ly** *adv* improbe, dolo malo, fraude ac dolo

dishonesty *n* improbitas, fraus *f*; dolus malus *m*

dishonour¹ *n* infamia *f*; dedecus *nt*; ignominia *f*

dishonour² *vt* dehonesto; dedecoro ①

dishonourable *adj* inhonestus, turpis

disinherit *vt* exheredo ①

disinterested *adj* aequus, integer

disjointed *adj* intermissus

dislike¹ *vt* aversor, non amo ①
■ **I** ∼ **it** res mihi non placet ②; res mihi displicet ②

dislike² *n* aversatio *f*; odium, fastidium *nt*

dislocate *vt* luxo ①

dislocation *n* luxatura *f*

dislodge *vt* deturbo ①; depello ③

disloyal *adj* infidelis, perfidus, perfidiosus

disloyalty *n* infidelitas, perfidia *f*

dismal *adj* tristis, miser; maestus; (dreadful) dirus
■ ∼**ly** *adv* misere, maeste

dismantle *vt* diruo ③

dismay¹ *n* consternatio, perturbatio *f*; pavor *m*

dismay² *vt* perterrefacio ③; territo, consterno, perturbo ①

dismiss *vt* dimitto ③; demoveo ②

dismissal *n* missio, demissio *f*

dismount *vi* ex equo desilio ④

disobedience *n* contumacia *f*

disobedient *adj* non oboediens; contumax
■ ~ly *adv* contra (alicuius) iussum

disobey *vi* non pareo ② *or* non oboedio ④ + *dat*; neglego ③; detrecto ①

disorder *n* confusio *f*; (disturbance of the peace) tumultus *m*; (illness) aegrotatio; (of mind) perturbatio (animi) *f*

disorderly *adj* inordinatus, turbatus; turbidus; incompositus; tumultuosus

disorganization *n* dissolutio *f*

disorganized *adj* dissolutus

disown *vt* diffiteor ②; infitior ①

disparage *vt* obtrecto, detrecto ①

disparagement *n* obtrectratio *f*

disparity *n* inaequalitas, diversitas *f*

dispatch *vt* ▸ **despatch**

dispel *vt* dispello, depello, solvo ③

dispense *vt* distribuo ③
□ ~ with careo + *abl* ②

dispenser *n* dispensator *m*

disperse *vt* spargo, dispergo ③; dissipo ①; (put to flight) fundo ③; fugo ①
■ ~ *vi* dilabor; diffugio ③

dispersion *n* dissipatio *f*

dispirited *adj* abiectus, animo fractus

displace *vt* summoveo ②; (a person) loco moveo ②

display[1] *n* (show) ostentus *m*; fig iactatio, ostentatio *f*

display[2] *vt* (expose) expono; (spread) expando ③; fig iacto, ostento ①; (exercise) praesto ①; exhibeo ②

displease *vt* displiceo ② + *dat*

displeasure *n* offensa; offensio; (grudge) ira *f*

disposable *adj* in promptu

disposal *n* arbitrium *nt*
■ at the ~ of *prep* penes + *acc*

dispose *vt* dispono ③; ordino ①; (induce) adduco ③
□ ~ of (sell) vendo ③; (get rid of) tollo ③

disposed *adj* inclinatus ad + *acc*; propensus (ad); pronus (ad)
□ well-~ aequus
□ ill-~ malevolus, iniquus

disposition *n* (arrangement) dispositio; (nature) natura, indoles *f*; ingenium *nt*; mens *f*; animus *m*

disproof *n* refutatio *f*

disproportionate *adj* inaequalis, impar
■ ~ly *adv* inaequaliter, impariter

disprove *vt* confuto, refuto ①; refello, redarguo ③

disputable *adj* disputabilis; (doubtful) dubius, ambiguus

dispute[1] *n* disputatio, disceptatio, contentio; controversia *f*; (quarrel) rixa *f*; iurgium *nt*

dispute[2] *vt&i* disputo ①; contendo ③
□ it is ~d ambigitur; non constat

disqualification *n* impedimentum *nt*

disqualify *vt* impedimento esse + *dat*

disquiet *n* sollicitudo, inquies *f*

disregard[1] *n* incuria, neglegentia *f*; contemptus *m*

disregard[2] *vt* neglego; parvi facio ③

disreputable *adj* infamis

disrepute *n* infamia *f*

disrespect *n* neglegentia, irreverentia *f*

disrespectful *adj* irreverens
■ ~ly *adv* irreverenter

disrupt *vt* disturbo ①

disruption *n* diruptio *f*; fig discidium *nt*

dissatisfaction *n* taedium, fastidium *nt*; indignatio *f*

dissatisfied *adj* male (parum) contentus

dissect *vt* disseco ①; incido ③

dissection *n* sectio, incisio, anatomia *f*

dissemble *vt&i* dissimulo ①

dissembler *n* dissimulator *m*

dissension *n* dissensio *f*; dissidium *nt*

dissent[1] *vi* dissentio ④; dissideo ②

dissent[2] *n* dissensio *f*

dissident *adj* & *n* rebellis

dissimilar *adj* dissimilis, dispar

dissimilarity *n* dissimilitudo *f*

dissimulation *n* dissimulatio *f*

dissipate *vt&i* dissipo; dissipor ①

dissipated *adj* perditus, dissolutus

dissipation *n* dissipatio *f*

dissolute *adj* dissolutus, corruptus, immoderatus

dissoluteness *n* mores dissoluti *mpl*

dissolution *n* dissolutio; mors *f*

dissolve *vt* dissolvo; (melt) liquefacio ③; liquo ①; (break up) dirimo ③
■ ~ *vi* liquesco ③; (break up) dissolvor ③

dissonant *adj* dissonus, absonus

dissuade *vt* dissuadeo ② + *dat*; abduco ③

distaff *n* colus *f*

distance *n* distantia *f*; intervallum, (space) spatium *nt*; (remoteness) longinquitas *f*
□ **at a** ~ procul, longe

distant *adj* distans, disiunctus, longinquus, remotus, amotus
□ **be** ~ absum *ir*

distaste *n* fastidium *nt*

distasteful *adj* odiosus, molestus, gravis

distend *vt* distendo ③

distended *adj* tumidus, tumefactus

distil *vt&i* stillo, destillo; exsudo ①

distinct *adj* (different) diversus, alius; (clear) clarus; distinctus
■ ~**ly** *adv* clare, distincte

distinction *n* distinctio *f*; (difference) differentia *f*; discrimen *nt*

distinctive *adj* proprius

distinguish *vt&i* distinguo, discerno ③
□ ~ **oneself** eniteo ②; praecello ③

distinguishable *adj* qui secerni *or* internosci potest

distinguished *adj* insignis; clarus, praeclarus, celeber, notus, eximius

distort *vt* distorqueo; detorqueo ②; depravo ①

distortion *n* distortio, depravatio *f*

distract *vt* distraho ③; (divert) avoco ①

distracted *adj* amens, demens, mente alienatus, vesanus, vecors

distress¹ *n* dolor *m*; miseria, tristitia *f*; angustiae *fpl*; (poverty) inopia *f*

distress² *vt* affligo, ango ③

distressing *adj* molestus, gravis

distribute *vt* distribuo, divido ③; dispertio ④

distribution *n* distributio *f*

district *n* regio *f*

distrust¹ *n* diffidentia *f*

distrust² *vt* diffido ③ + *dat*

distrustful *adj* diffidens, suspicax, suspiciosus
■ ~**ly** *adv* diffidenter

disturb *vt* perturbo; sollicito, inquieto ①; (break up) dirimo ③

disturbance *n* perturbatio; confusio *f*; tumultus *m*; seditio *f*

disuse *n* desuetudo *f*

ditch *n* fossa *f*

dive¹ *vi* mergor ③

dive² *n* (den of vice) lustrum *nt*

diverge *vi* deflecto ③; declino ①

divergence *n* declinatio; fig discrepantia *f*

divergent *adj* diversus; (contrary) contrarius

diverse *adj* alius, varius, diversus

diversification *n* variatio *f*; vices *fpl*

diversify *vt* vario ①; distinguo ③

diversion *n* (turning aside) derivatio; fig oblectatio *f*; oblectamentum *nt*

diversity *n* diversitas, varietas *f*

divert *vt* diverto ③; fig oblecto ①; (distract) avoco ①

divide *vt* divido ③; partior ④; distribuo ③
■ ~ *vi* discedo; (gape open) dehisco ③

divination *n* divinatio, vaticinatio *f*

divine *adj* divinus; caelestis

divinity *n* divinitas *f*; numen *nt*; (god) deus *m*

divisible *adj* dividuus, divisibilis

division *n* divisio, distributio, partitio; (part) pars *f*; fig (dissent) seditio, discordia *f*; dissidium *nt*

divorce¹ *n* divortium, discidium *nt*

divorce² *vt* repudio ①; dimitto ③

divulge *vt* vulgo, divulgo ①; palam facio ③, in medium profero *ir*

dizziness *n* vertigo *f*

dizzy *adj* vertiginosus; (precipitous) praeceps

do *vt* ago, facio, efficio ③
□ ~ **away with** tollo, perdo ③
□ ~ **for** conficio ③
□ ~ **up** (bind) constringo ③
□ ~ **without** egeo, careo ② *both* + *abl*
■ ~ *vi* (be suitable) convenio ④

d

docile *adj* docilis; tractabilis

dock¹ *n* navale *nt*

dock² *vt* (ships) subduco ③; (curtail) curto ①

dockyard *n* navalia *ntpl*

doctor *n* (physician) medicus *m*

doctrine *n* doctrina *f*

document *n* litterae *fpl*

dodge *vt* eludo ③

doe *n* cerva *f*

dog¹ *n* canis *m/f*

dog² *vt* indago ①

dogged *adj* pervicax
■ ∼ly *adv* pervicaciter

doggedness *n* pervicacia *f*

doggerel *n* versus inculti *mpl*

dogma *n* dogma, placitum, praeceptum *nt*

dogmatic *adj* imperiosus

doing *n* factum, facinus *nt*

dole¹ *vt*:
□ ∼ **out** metior ④

dole² *n* donatio *f*; congiarium *nt*; diurnus victus *m*

doll *n* pupa *f*

dolphin *n* delphinus, delphin *m*

dolt *n* caudex, stipes *m*

domestic *adj* domesticus, familiaris; intestinus; (private) privatus

domesticate *vt* (tame) mansuefacio ③

domicile *n* domicilium *nt*; domus *f*

dominant *adj* praevalens

dominate *vt&i* dominor ① in + *acc*, praevaleo ②, supero ①

domination *n* dominatio *f*

domineer *vi* dominor ①; imperito ①

domineering *adj* arrogans, imperiosus

dominion *n* imperium *nt*; potestas *f*; dicio *f*; regnum *nt*

donate *vt* dono ①

donation *n* donum, munus *nt*; stips *f*

donkey *n* asinus, asellus *m*

donor *n* donator, dator *m*; donatrix *f*

doom¹ *n* fatum, exitium *nt*

doom² *vt* damno, condemno ①
□ ∼ **to** destino ① + *dat*

door *n* ianua, foris *f*; ostium *nt*
□ **folding** ∼ valvae *fpl*

doorkeeper *n* ianitor *m*; ianitrix *f*; custos *m/f*

door-post *n* postis *m*

doorway *n* ianua *f*; ostium *nt*

dormant *adj* (lying idle) reses; (hidden) latens

dormitory *n* cubiculum, dormitorium *nt*

dormouse *n* glis *m*

dot *n* punctum *nt*

dotage *n* deliratio *f*; (old age) senium *nt*; senectus *f*

dotard *n* senex delirus *m*

dote *vt* (on) depereo *ir*; deamo ①

double¹ *adj* duplex; (of pairs) geminus; (as much again) duplus

double² *n* duplum *nt*

double³ *vt* duplico ①

double-dealer *n* homo duplex *m*

double-dealing *n* fraus, fallacia *f*; dolus *m*

doubly *adv* dupliciter; bis

doubt¹ *n* dubitatio *f*; scrupulus *m*
□ **there is no** ∼ **that** non est dubium quin

doubt² *vt* dubito, suspicor ①; (distrust) diffido ③ + *dat*
■ ∼ *vi* haesito, dubito ①

doubtful *adj* (of people) dubius; (of things) incertus; ambiguus; anceps
■ ∼ly *adv* (of people) dubie; (of things) ambigue

doubtless *adv* sine dubio, haud dubie

dove *n* columbus *m*; columba *f*

dove-coloured *adj* columbinus

dovecot *n* columbarium *nt*

down¹ *adv* deorsum; (on the ground) humi

down² *prep*:
□ ∼ **from** de + *abl*
□ ∼ **to** usque ad + *acc*
□ **up and** ∼ sursum deorsum

down³ *adj* declivis; (sad) tristis

downcast *adj* (of the eyes *or* head) deiectus, demissus; fig afflictus

downfall *n* occasus *m*; ruina *f*; exitium *nt*

downhill *adj* declivis

downstream *adv* secundo flumine

downward *adj* declivis; pronus

downwards *adv* deorsum

dowry *n* dos *f*

doze *vi* dormito ①

dozen *n* duodecim; *adj* duodeni

drab *adj* cinereus; pullus

draft¹ *vt* (levy) conscribo, scribo ③

draft² *n* (first copy) exemplar *nt*

drag *vt* traho ③
■ ∼ *vi* (on the ground) trahor ③

dragon *n* draco; anguis, serpens *m*

drain¹ *n* cloaca; fossa *f*

drain² *vt* sicco ①; (drink) exhaurio ④; ebibo ③; epoto, exsicco ①

drake *n* anas *m*

drama *n* drama *nt*; fabula *f*

dramatic *adj* dramaticus, scaenicus
■ ∼**ally** *adv* scaenice

dramatist *n* poeta scaenicus *m*

dramatize *vt* fabulam ad scaenam compono ③

drape *vt* induo ③; amicio ④; velo ①

drapery *n* (cloth) vestis *f*

draught *n* (of drink) haustus *m*; (of air) aura *f*

draughty *adj* ventosus

draw *vt* (pull) traho; duco ③; (a picture, *etc.*) delineo ①; describo ③; (the sword) stringo, destringo; (teeth) extraho ③; (water) haurio ④; (attract) illicio ③
□ ∼ **aside** abduco, seduco ③
□ ∼ **away** averto, distraho ③
□ ∼ **back** *vt* retraho; *vi* pedem refero, cedo; fig recedo ③
□ ∼ **near** *vi* appropinquo; insto ①
□ ∼ **off** *vt* detraho; abduco; (wine) promo; *vi* cedo ③
□ ∼ **out** extraho; (sword, *etc.*) educo; (prolong) extendo ③; fig elicio ③
□ ∼ **together** contraho ③
□ ∼ **up** subduco; scribo; (troops) instruo, constituo ③

drawback *n* impedimentum; detrimentum; incommodum *nt*; mora *f*; retardatio *f*

drawing *n* (art) pictura linearis; (picture) tabula, imago *f*

drawing-room *n* exedra *f*

dread¹ *n* terror, pavor *m*; formido *f*

dread² *vt* timeo ②; metuo, expavesco ③; formido ①

dreadful *adj* terribilis, horribilis; dirus; (violent) atrox
■ ∼**ly** *adv* foede, atrociter

dream¹ *n* somnium *nt*; quies *f*

dream² *vt&i* somnio; fig dormito ①

dreamer *n* somniator *m*

dreamy *adj* somniculosus

dreary *adj* vastus, solus, incultus; horridus; tristis

dregs *n* faex; sentina *f*

drench *vt* madefacio ③; irrigo ①

dress¹ *n* (clothing) habitus, vestitus *m*; vestis *f*; ornatus *m*

dress² *vt* vestio ④; induo ③; orno, exorno; (wounds) curo ①
■ ∼ *vi* (I get dressed) me vestio ④

dressing *n* ornatus *m*; (of food) coctura; (wounds, *etc.*) curatio *f*; (poultice) fomentum *nt*

dribble *vi* stillo ①

drift¹ *n* (meaning) propositum *nt*; (purpose) consilium; (of sand) cumulus *m*; (of snow) vis *f*

drift² *vi* feror *ir*; fluito ①

drill¹ *vt* terebro, perforo ①; (troops) exerceo ②; (discipline) instituo ③

drill² *n* terebra; (of troops) exercitatio *f*

drink¹ *vt&i* bibo ③; poto ①
□ ∼ **in** absorbeo ②; bibo ③
□ ∼ **up** ebibo ③; haurio ④; epoto ①
□ ∼ **to** propino ① + *dat*

drink² *n* potus *m*; potio *f*

drinkable *adj* potabilis

drinker *n* potor, potator *m*

drinking *n* (act) potatio; (drunkenness) ebrietas *f*
■ ∼**-bout** *n* compotatio *f*

drip¹ *vi* stillo; roro, mano ①

drip² *n* stillicidium *nt*

drive *vt* ago; pello; impello; (force) compello, cogo ③; (horses, carriages) ago ③
■ ∼ *vi* (in a carriage) vehor ③; (be carried along) deferor *ir*
□ ∼ **along** ▶ ∼ **on**
□ ∼ **away** abigo; depello ③; fugo ①
□ ∼ **back** repello ③
□ ∼ **in(to)** (a nail, *etc.*) infigo; (sheep, *etc.*) cogo; fig compello ③
□ ∼ **off** *vt* abigo; *vi* avehor ③
□ ∼ **on** impello ③
□ ∼ **out** expello ③
□ ∼ **past** praetervehor ③

drivel *n* fig ineptiae *fpl*

driver *n* agitator; agaso *m*; (of carriages) auriga *m/f*

drizzle¹ *vi* roro, irroro ①

drizzle² *n* pluvia *f*

droll *adj* facetus, iocosus; ridiculus

drone[1] *n* fucus; (person) deses; (noise) bombus *m*

drone[2] *vi* murmuro, susurro ①

droop *vi* langueo ②; marcesco; tabesco ③
■ ~ *vt* demitto ③

drop[1] *n* gutta, stilla *f*; (a little bit) paululum *nt*
□ ~ **by** ~ guttatim, stillatim

drop[2] *vt* (pour) stillo ①; (let slip) omitto ③; (pour out) effundo; (dismiss) dimitto ③
■ ~ *vi* stillo ①; (fall *or* glide down) delabor ③; (decrease) deminuor ③

dross *n* scoria; spurcitia *f*; (dropsy) aqua intercus *f*; fig quisquiliae *fpl*; faex *f*

drought *n* siccitas, ariditas *f*

drover *n* pecuarius, armentarius *m*

drown *vt* immergo, demergo; fig opprimo ③
□ **his voice was ~ed by shouts** vox prae clamoribus audiri non potuit

drowsily *adv* somniculose

drowsiness *n* somni cupiditas *f*

drowsy *adj* somniculosus

drudge[1] *vi* me exerceo ②; laboro ①

drudge[2] *n* (a slave) mediastinus; fig homo clitellarius *m*

drudgery *n* opera servilis *f*

drug[1] *n* medicamentum, medicamen *nt*; medicina *f*

drug[2] *vt* medico ①

Druids *npl* Druidae *mpl*

drum *n* tympanum *nt*

drummer *n* tympanista *m*

drunk *adj* ebrius, potus

drunkard *n* use adj temulentus, ebriosus, vinolentus *m*

drunken *adj* ▶ **drunk**

drunkenness *n* ebrietas, temulentia *f*

dry[1] *adj* aridus, siccus; (thirsty) siticulosus; fig ieiunus; insulsus

dry[2] *vt* sicco, desicco ①; arefacio ③; (in the sun) insolo ①
■ ~ *vi* aresco ③

dryness *n* ariditas, siccitas *f*

dual *adj* duplex

dub *vt* (name) nomino ①

dubious *adj* dubius
■ ~**ly** *adv* dubie

duck[1] *n* anas *f*

duck[2] *vt* mergo, submergo, demergo ③
■ ~ *vi* (head) caput demitto ③

duckling *n* anaticula *f*

dudgeon *n* ira, indignatio *f*

due[1] *adj* debitus; iustus; meritus; idoneus, aptus

due[2] *n* debitum; ius; (tax) vectigal *nt*

duel *n* singulare certamen *nt*

duet *n* bicinium *nt*

dull[1] *adj* hebes; obtunsus; surdus; (cloudy) caliginosus; nebulosus; fig tardus; languidus; tristis; segnis; insulsus; stupidus

dull[2] *vt* hebeto ①; obtundo; stupefacio ③

duly *adv* rite; recte

dumb *adj* mutus
□ **be ~** obmutesco ③

dumbfound *vt* obstupefacio ③

dunce *n* homo stupidus, stipes *m*

dung *n* stercus *nt*; fimus *m*

dungeon *n* carcer *m*; ergastulum *nt*

dunghill *n* sterculinium, fimetum *nt*

dupe[1] *n* homo credulus *m*; victima *f*

dupe[2] *vt* decipio ③; ludifico ①; fallo ③

duplicate[1] *adj* duplex

duplicate[2] *n* exemplum, exemplar, apographum *nt*

duplicity *n* fraus; fallacia *f*

durable *adj* stabilis; durabilis; solidus; constans

duration *n* spatium (temporis) *nt*; diuturnitas *f*

during *prep* per; inter *both* + *acc*

dusk *n* crepusculum *nt*

dusky *adj* obscurus, tenebrosus; fuscus

dust[1] *n* pulvis *m*; (of filing *or* sawing) scobis *f*

dust[2] *vt* detergeo ②

duster *n* peniculus *m*

dustman *n* scoparius *m*

dusty *adj* pulverulentus, pulvereus

dutiful *adj* pius; officiosus, oboediens, obsequens
■ ~**ly** *adv* pie; officiose; oboedienter

duty *n* officium; munus; (tax) vectigal *nt*; mil statio *f*

dwarf[1] *n* nanus, pumilio *m*

dwarf² *vt* (diminish) imminuo ③; (overtop) superemineo ②

dwell *vi* habito ①; incolo ③; fig (upon) commoror ①

dwelling-place *n* domicilium *nt*; sedes, domus, habitatio *f*

dwindle *vi* decresco, imminuor ③

dye¹ *vt* tingo, inficio, imbuo ③; coloro ①

dye² *n* tinctura *f*; color *m*

dying *adj* moriens, moribundus; (last) extremus, ultimus

dyke *n* (ditch) fossa *f*; (dam, mound) agger *m*

dynasty *n* imperium *nt*; domus regnatrix *f*

dysentery *n* dysenteria *f*

Ee

each *adj* (every) quisque; (every one) unusquisque
  □ ~ **other** alter alterum
  □ ~ **of two** uterque
  □ **one** ~ singuli

eager *adj* acer, studiosus, cupidus, avidus; (fierce) ferox; (earnest) vehemens
  ■ ~**ly** *adv* acriter; avide, cupide

eagerness *n* aviditas, cupiditas; fig alacritas *f*; impetus *m*; studium *nt*

eagle *n* (bird, also legionary standard) aquila *f*

ear *n* auris; (of corn) spica *f*; (hearing) aures *fpl*

ear-ache *n* aurium dolor *m*

earliness *n* maturitas *f*

early¹ *adj* (in the morning) matutinus; (of early date) antiquus; (beginning) novus; (forward) maturus, praematurus, praecox

early² *adv* (in the morning) mane; (untimely) mature; (too ~) praemature; (quickly, soon) cito

earn *vt* lucror ①; mereo ②; consequor, quaero ③

earnest¹ *adv* intentus; impensus; vehemens; ardens; (important) gravis; (serious) serius
  ■ ~**ly** *adv* acriter; impense, intente

earnest² *adv*:
  □ **in** ~ serio; bona fide

earnings *n* stipendium *nt*

earring *n* inaures *fpl*

earshot *n* unde quis exaudiri potest

earth *n* (land) terra, tellus *f*; (world) orbis *m*; (of a fox) specus *m/f/nt*; (ground) solum *nt*; humus *f*

earthenware *n* fictilia *ntpl*

earthly *adj* terrenus; terrestris; humanus

earthquake *n* terrae motus *m*

earth-work *n* agger *m*

earthy *adj* terrosus; fig terrenus

ease¹ *n* otium *nt*; quies, requies *f*; fig (grace) lepor *m*; facilitas; (pleasure) voluptas *f*
  □ **with** ~ facile

ease² *vt* levo, exonero, laxo ①

easily *adv* facile

east¹ *adj* orientalis

east² *n* oriens; ortus *m*

easterly *adj* (also **eastern**) orientalis; ad orientem vergens

eastwards *adv* ad orientem versus

east wind *n* Eurus *m*

easy *adj* facilis; solutus; expeditus; (at leisure) otiosus; quietus; (graceful) lepidus; (of temper) facilis

eat *vt&i* edo, comedo *ir*, vescor; fig rodo ③
  □ ~ **away** peredo *ir*; fig corrodo ③
  □ ~ **up** comedo ③; voro, devoro ①

eatable *adj* esculentus, edulis

eating *n* esus *m*
  ■ ~**-house** *n* popina *f*

eaves *n* suggrunda *ntpl*

eavesdrop *vi* subausculto ①

eavesdropper *n* auceps *m*

ebb¹ *n* recessus *m*

ebb² *vi* recedo; fig decresco ③

echo¹ *n* imago, echo; resonantia *f*

echo² *vt* repercutio ③; resono ①
■ ~ *vi* resulto ①; (resound, be loud) sono, resono, persono ①

eclipse¹ *n* defectus *m*; defectio *f*

eclipse² *vt* obscuro, obumbro ①
□ **be ~d** deficio ③

economical *adj* oeconomicus; (sparing) parcus
■ ~**ly** *adv* parce

economize *vt&i* (with) parco ③ + *dat*

economy *n* oeconomia; (stinginess) parsimonia *f*

ecstasy *n* ecstasis, insania *f*; furor *m*

ecstatic *adj* furibundus, lymphatus

eddy¹ *n* vortex *m*

eddy² *vi* circumferor *ir*

edge *n* (brink) margo *m/f*; (of a knife, *etc.*) acies; (of a forest, *etc.*) ora *f*; (lip) labrum *nt*

edible *adj* esculentus, edulis

edict *n* edictum, decretum *nt*

edit *vt* edo ③

edition *n* editio *f*

educate *vt* educo ①; erudio ④

education *n* educatio; eruditio; disciplina *f*

educational *adj* scholasticus

eel *n* anguilla *f*

eerie¹ *n* nidus *m*

eerie² *adj* lugubris

effect *n* vis *f*; effectus *m*
□ **in ~** re vera; etenim
□ **take ~** bene succedere ③; efficax sum *ir*

effective *adj* efficax; potens
■ ~**ly** *adv* efficaciter

effects *npl* bona *ntpl*

effectual *adj* efficax, valens, potens

effeminacy *n* mollitia *f*

effeminate *adj* effeminatus, mollis, muliebris

efficacious *adj* efficax
■ ~**ly** *adv* efficaciter

efficacy *n* efficacitas, vis *f*

efficiency *n* efficacitas, vis *f*

efficient *adj* efficiens; efficax
■ ~**ly** *adv* efficaciter

effigy *n* imago, effigies *f*

effort *n* conatus, nisus, impetus, labor *m*
□ **make an ~** nitor ③, molior ④

effrontery *n* audacia, impudentia *f*

egg¹ *n* ovum *nt*
□ **lay ~s** ova pario ③

egg² *vt* (on) impello, incendo ③; excito ①

eggshell *n* ovi putamen *nt*; ovi testa *f*

egotism *n* sui iactantia *f*

eight *adj* octo
□ ~ **times** octies

eighteen *adj* duodeviginti

eighteenth *adj* duodevicesimus

eighth *adj* octavus
■ ~ *n* octava pars *f*

eight hundred *adj* octingenti

eightieth *adj* octogesimus

eighty *adj* octoginta

either¹ *pn* alteruter; uter; alter; (whichever of two) utervis, uterlibet
□ **not ~** neuter

either² *conj*:
□ ~ **... or** aut ... aut; vel ... vel; -ve ... -ve

eject *vt* eicio; expello ③

ejection *n* eiectio *f*

eke *vt*:
□ ~ **out** suppleo ②; (livelihood) colligo ③

elaborate¹ *vt* elaboro, evigilo ①

elaborate² *adj* elaboratus; accuratus
■ ~**ly** *adv* accurate

elapse *vi* praetereo *ir*; labor ③

elastic *adj* (pliant) lentus

elasticity *n* lentitia *f*

elate *vt* inflo ①; effero *ir*
□ **be ~d** intumesco ③

elation *n* superbia *f*; animus elatus *m*

elbow *n* cubitum *nt*; ulna *f*

elbow-room *n* fig spatium *nt*

elder *adj* maior natu; (in date) prior

elderly *adj* aetate provectior

eldest *adj* maximus natu; antiquissimus

elect *vt* eligo ③; creo ①

election *n* electio *f*, delectus *m*; (political) comitia *ntpl*

electioneering *n* petitio, ambitio, prensatio *f*
■ ~ *adj* candidatorius

elegance *n* elegantia *f*; nitor *m*

elegant *adj* elegans; nitidus; lautus; concinnus
■ ~**ly** *adv* eleganter, nitide, laute

elegy *n* elegia *f*; elegi *mpl*

element *n* elementum *nt*
■ ~**s** *pl* principia rerum; fig rudimenta *ntpl*

elementary *adj* simplex, puerilis, primus

elephant *n* elephantus, elephas *m*

elevate *vt* levo ①; effero *ir*, attollo ③; fig inflo ①

elevation *n* elatio; (loftiness) altitudo *f*; (rising ground) locus superior *m*

eleven *adj* undecim
□ ~ **times** undecies

eleventh *adj* undecimus

elicit *vt* elicio ③; evoco ①

eligible *adj* dignus

eliminate *vt* amoveo ②

elm *n* ulmus *f*

elocution *n* elocutio *f*

elongate *vt* produco ③

elope *vi* (domo) clam fugio, aufugio ③

elopement *n* fuga clandestina *f*

eloquence *n* eloquentia, facundia *f*; eloquium *nt*

eloquent *adj* eloquens, disertus, facundus
■ ~**ly** *adv* diserte, eloquenter

else¹ *adj* alius
□ **no one** ~ nemo alius; nemo alter

else² *adv* praeterea; (otherwise) aliter; (if not) si non, si minus

elsewhere *adv* (at another place) alibi; (to another place) aliquo

elucidate *vt* illustro, explico ①

elucidation *n* explicatio *f*

elude *vt* eludo, effugio ③; frustror ①; evito ①

elusive *adj* fallax, fugax

emaciated *adj* macer, macilentus

emaciation *n* macies; tabes *f*

emanate *vi* emano ①; orior ④

emancipate *vt* emancipo ①; manumitto ③; fig libero ①

emancipation *n* (of a slave) manumissio; (of a son) emancipatio; fig liberatio *f*

embalm *vt* condio ④, pollingo ③

embankment *n* agger *m*; moles *f*

embark *vt* (goods, troops) in navem impono ③
■ ~ *vi* in navem conscendo ③

embarkation *n* (in navem) conscensio *f*

embarrass *vt* (hinder) impedio ④; (entangle) implico; fig perturbo ①

embarrassment *n* implicatio *f*; angustiae *fpl*; scrupulus *m*; perturbatio *f*; (hindrance) impedimentum *nt*; mora *f*

embassy *n* legatio *f*; legati *mpl*

embellish *vt* orno, exorno ①

embellishment *n* ornamentum, decus, insigne *nt*

embers *n* cinis *m/f*; (live coals) favilla *f*

embezzle *vt* averto ③

embezzlement *n* peculatus *m*

embezzler *n* interceptor, peculator *m*

embitter *vt* exacerbo ①

emblem *n* signum *nt*; imago *f*; (example) exemplum *nt*

embolden *vt* animo, confirmo ①

emboss *vt* caelo ①

embrace¹ *vt* complector ③; (contain) contineo ②; amplector ③

embrace² *n* amplexus, complexus *m*

embroider *vt* acu pingo ③

embroidery *n* (art) ars plumaria *f*

embroil *vt* confundo ③; permisceo ②; fig implico ①; impedio ④; (match, set to fight) committo ③

embryo *n* semen *nt*

emerald *n* smaragdus *m*

emerge *vi* emergo; (arise) exsisto ③

emergency *n* (accident) casus *m*; (crisis) discrimen *nt*; necessitas *f*

emigrant *n* colonus *m*

emigrate *vi* migro ①

emigration *n* migratio (in alias terras) *f*

eminence *n* praestantia *f*

eminent *adj* eminens; egregius, eximius, insignis, praestans
■ ~**ly** *adv* eximie, insigniter

emit *vt* emitto ③; (breathe out) exhalo ①

emolument *n* lucrum, emolumentum *nt*; quaestus *m*

emotion *n* animi motus, affectus *m*; commotio; perturbatio *f*

emperor *n* imperator, princeps *m*

emphasis *n* vis *f*; pondus *nt*

emphasize *vt* vehementer dico ③

emphatic *adj* gravis
■ ~**ally** *adv* graviter

empire *n* imperium, regnum *nt*

employ *vt* adhibeo; exerceo ②; occupo ①; (use) utor ③ + *abl*; usurpo ①

employer *n* conductor; dominus *m*

employment *n* occupatio *f*; (business) negotium, studium *nt*

empower *vt* potestatem (alicui) facio ③; copiam (alicui) do ①

empress *n* imperatrix *f*

emptiness *n* inanitas; fig vanitas *f*

empty¹ *adj* vacuus, inanis; fig vanus

empty² *vt* vacuo ①; vacuefacio ③; exinanio ④; (drink up) haurio, exhaurio ④

emulate *vt* aemulor; imitor ①

emulation *n* aemulatio *f*

enable *vt* facultatem (alicui) facio ③

enact *vt* decerno ③; sancio ④

enactment *n* sanctio; (law) lex *f*; decretum *nt*

enamoured *adj*:
□ **be ∼** amo, deamo ①

encampment *n* castra *ntpl*

enchant *vt* fascino ①; fig capio ③; delecto ①

enchanted *adj* cantatus, incantatus

enchanting *adj* venustus, suavissimus, pulcherrimus

enchantment *n* incantamentum *nt*; fig illecebrae *fpl*; (magic) carmen *nt*

enchantress *n* maga; cantatrix *f*; (beloved one) amata *f*

encircle *vt* circumplector; cingo ③; circumdo ①

enclose *vt* saepio ④; includo; (encircle) cingo ③; circumdo ①

enclosure *n* saeptum *nt*

encounter¹ *n* (meeting) congressus *m*; (fight) certamen *nt*; pugna *f*

encounter² *vt&i* congredior ③ cum + *abl*; obviam eo *ir*, incurro ③ *both* + *dat*

encourage *vt* hortor, cohortor, animo, confirmo ①

encouragement *n* hortatus *m*; cohortatio, confirmatio *f*

encroach *vi* usurpo ①; praesumo ③

encroachment *n* usurpatio *f*

encumber *vt* onero ①; impedio ④; (weigh down) praegravo ①

encumbrance *n* impedimentum; onus *nt*; (trouble) molestia *f*

end¹ *n* finis *m/f*; terminus; exitus *m*; (aim, design) propositum *nt*; (death) mors *f*; obitus *m*

end² *vt* finio ④; termino ①; concludo ③
■ **∼** *vi* (cease) desino ③; finior ④

endanger *vt* periclitor ①; in periculum deduco ③

endearing *adj* carus

endearment *n* blanditiae *fpl*; blandimenta *ntpl*

endeavour¹ *vi* tempto, conor ①; nitor, enitor ③; contendo ③

endeavour² *n* conatus, nisus *m*; conamen *nt*

ending *n* exitus *m*

endless *adj* infinitus; perpetuus; aeternus; sempiternus
■ **∼ly** *adv* sine fine, perpetuo; in aeternum

endorse *vt* confirmo ①

endorsement *n* confirmatio *f*

endow *vt* doto ①; instruo ③; orno ①
□ **∼ed with** praeditus + *abl*

endowment *n* dos *f*

endurable *adj* tolerabilis

endurance *n* patientia; (stability) stabilitas *f*

endure *vt* tolero ①; patior, perpetior ③; fero *ir*; sustineo ②
■ **∼** *vi* duro ①; permaneo ②

enemy *n* hostis, inimicus *m*

energetic *adj* strenuus; alacer, acer
■ **∼ally** *adv* strenue; acriter

energy *n* vis; alacritas; vehementia *f*; impetus *m*

enervate *vt* enervo; debilito ①

enfeeble *vt* debilito, infirmo, labefacto ①

enforce *vt* (compel) cogo ③; (put in execution) exerceo ②

enfranchise *vt* libero ①; manumitto ③; civitatem do ①

engage *vt* (hire) conduco ③; (involve, entangle) implico ①; (occupy) occupo ①
■ **∼** *vi* (in battle) confligo ③; (promise) spondeo ②; (undertake) suscipio ③

engaged *adj* (to marry) sponsus

engagement *n* (agreement) stipulatio *f*; pactum *nt*; (occupation) occupatio *f*; (battle) proelium *nt*; (betrothal) pactio nuptialis *f*; (promise) fides *f*

engine *n* machina; machinatio *f*

engineer *n* machinator; architectus *m*

England *n* Anglia *f*

English *adj* Anglicus, Britannicus¯

Englishman *n* Anglus *m*

engrave *vt* scalpo, sculpo; incido ③; caelo ①

engraver *n* scalptor, sculptor *m*

engraving *n* (art) scalptura, sculptura *f*

engrossed *adj* (∼ in) deditus + *dat*

engulf *vt* devoro, ingurgito ①

enhance *vt* augeo ②; amplifico, orno ①; (raise) accendo ③

enigma *n* aenigma *nt*; ambages *fpl*

enigmatic *adj* aenigmaticus, ambiguus
■ ∼**ally** *adv* ambigue

enjoin *vt* iubeo ②; iniungo, praecipio ③ *both* + *dat*

enjoy *vt* fruor ③ + *abl*; percipio ③; (rejoice in) gaudeo in + *abl*; (possess) possideo ②
□ ∼ **oneself** me oblecto ①

enjoyable *adj* gratus

enjoyment *n* fructus *m*; gaudium *nt*; possessio *f*; oblectatio; voluptates *fpl*

enlarge *vt* amplifico; dilato ①
■ ∼ *vi* amplificor, dilator ①
□ ∼ **upon** (a subject) uberius dico de + *abl* ③

enlargement *n* amplificatio *f*; (increase) auctus *m*

enlighten *vt* erudio ④; doceo ②

enlightened *adj* (cultivated) cultus

enlightenment *n* eruditio *f*; (culture) humanitas *f*

enlist *vt* conscribo ③; (win over) concilio ①
■ ∼ *vi* sacramentum dico ③

enliven *vt* animo; incito; exhilaro ①

enmity *n* inimicitia *f*; odium *nt*

enormity *n* immanitas; fig atrocitas *f*

enormous *adj* ingens, enormis, immensus; vastus, immanis
■ ∼**ly** *adv* admodum, multum, mire

enough *adv* satis, sat, affatim
□ ∼ **of this** sed haec hactenus

enquire *vt&i* ▶ **inquire**

enrage *vt* irrito; exaspero ①

enraged *adj* iratus, furens

enrich *vt* locupleto, dito ①

enrol *vt* inscribo ③
■ ∼ *vi* (enlist) sacramentum dico ③

ensign *n* (flag) vexillum; (mark) insigne *nt*; (officer) signifer *m*

enslave *vt* subigo, in servitutem redigo ③

enslavement *n* servitus *f*; servitium *nt*

ensnare *vt* illaqueo ①; irretio ④; fig illicio, capio ③

ensue *vi* sequor, insequor ③

ensuing *adj* sequens, insequens, posterus, proximus

ensure *vt* (guarantee) praesto ①; (see to it that) curo ① ut + *subj*

entail *vt* affero *ir*

entangle *vt* implico, illaqueo ①; irretio; impedio ④

enter *vt&i* intro ①; ineo *ir*; ingredior ③
□ ∼ **in a book** refero *ir*
□ ∼ **on** *or* **upon** (undertake) incipio, suscipio ③

enterprise *n* (undertaking) inceptum; ausum *nt*; (boldness) audacia *f*

enterprising *adj* audax, strenuus, acer

entertain *vt* (a guest) accipio, excipio ③; (an opinion) habeo ②; (amuse) oblecto ①

entertainment *n* (by a host) hospitium; (feast) convivium *nt*; (amusement) oblectatio, delectatio *f*

enthral *vt* mancipo ①; servum facio ③; fig capio ③

enthusiasm *n* fervor *m*; alacritas *f*

enthusiast *n* fanaticus *m*

enthusiastic *adj* fervidus, fanaticus
■ ∼**ally** *adv* fanatice

entice *vt* allicio ③; allecto ①

enticement *n* allectatio; illecebra *f*

enticing *adj* blandus

entire *adj* integer, totus
■ ∼**ly** *adv* omnino; penitus, prorsus

entitle *vt* (name) appello, nomino ①; inscribo (titulum) ③; (give a right) potestatem ① do + *dat*

entrails *n* viscera *ntpl*

entrance[1] *n* aditus; introitus *m*; (beginning) principium *nt*

entrance[2] *vt* rapio, capio ③

entrance-hall *n* vestibulum *nt*

entreat *vt* obsecro; oro; deprecor, obtestor ①; (beg) peto ③

entreaty *n* obsecratio *f*; preces *fpl*

entrust *vt* committo, credo ③; mando, commendo ①

entry *n* (act of entering) introitus *m*; (in a book) nomen *nt*

entwine *vt* implico; circumplico ①; necto ③

enumerate *vt* enumero ①; recenseo ②

envelop *vt* involvo ③; amicio ④

envelope *n* involucrum *nt*

enviable *adj* dignus cui invideatur, fortunatus

envious *adj* invidus, invidiosus

envoy *n* nuntius, legatus *m*

envy[1] *n* invidia; malignitas *f*; livor *m*

envy[2] *vt* invideo ② + *dat*

ephemeral *adj* brevis; caducus

epic *adj* epicus
   □ ∼ **poem** epos *nt*

epidemic[1] *n* lues, pestilentia *f*

epidemic[2] *adj* epidemus

epigram *n* epigramma *nt*

epilepsy *n* morbus comitialis, morbus caducus *m*; epilepsia *f*

epileptic *adj* epilepticus

epilogue *n* epilogus *m*

episode *n* embolium *nt*; (affair) res *f*

epistle *n* epistula *f*; litterae *fpl*

epitaph *n* epitaphium; carmen *nt*

epitome *n* epitome *f*; breviarium *nt*

epoch *n* saeculum *nt*; aetas *f*; tempus *nt*

equal[1] *adj* aequalis, aequus, par
   ■ ∼**ly** *adv* aeque; aequaliter; pariter

equal[2] *n* par *m*/*f*

equal[3] *vt* aequo, adaequo, aequiparo ①; assequor ③

equality *n* aequalitas *f*; aequum *nt*

equalize *vt* aequo, adaequo, exaequo ①

equanimity *n* aequus animus *m*

equestrian *adj* equestris
   ■ ∼ *n* eques *m*

equilibrium *n* aequilibrium *nt*

equinoctial *adj* aequinoctialis

equinox *n* aequinoctium *nt*

equip *vt* armo; exorno ①; instruo ③

equipment *n* armamenta *ntpl*; armatura *f*

equitable *adj* aequus, iustus

equivalent *adj* tantusdem; par

era *n* tempus *nt*; aetas *f*; saeculum *nt*

eradicate *vt* eradico, exstirpo ①; tollo ③

eradication *n* exstirpatio *f*; excidium *nt*

erase *vt* erado ③; deleo ②

erect[1] *adj* erectus, arrectus

erect[2] *vt* (raise) erigo, educo; (build up) exstruo; fig statuo, (found) condo ③

erection *n* exstructio; aedificatio *f*

erode *vt* erodo ③

erotic *adj* amatorius

err *vi* erro, aberro; fig pecco ①; delinquo ③

errand *n* mandatum *nt*

erratic *adj* erraticus; fig inconstans

erroneous *adj* falsus, vanus
   ■ ∼**ly** *adv* falso

error *n* (fault) delictum, peccatum, erratum *nt*; (mistake) fraus *f*, error *m*

erudite *adj* eruditus, doctus

erudition *n* eruditio *f*

eruption *n* (of a volcano) eruptio; (of the skin) scabies *f*

escapade *n* ausum *nt*

escape[1] *vt&i* evado, effugio, elabor ③; (secretly) subterfugio ③; (with difficulty) eluctor ①

escape[2] *n* fuga *f*; effugium *nt*

escort[1] *n* comitatus *m*; (protection) praesidium *nt*; custodia *f*

escort[2] *vt* comitor ①; deduco ③; prosequor ③

especial *adj* ▶ **special**

especially *adv* ▶ **specially**

espy *vt* conspicor ①; aspicio ③; video ②
   ■ ∼ *vi* speculor ①

essay *n* (treatise) libellus, tractatus *m*

essence *n* essentia; natura, vis *f*

essential *adj* proprius, necessarius
   ■ ∼**ly** *adv* natura, necessario

establish *vt* statuo; constituo ③; firmo, confirmo ①; stabilio ④

estate *n* fundus, ager *m*; (means, wealth) bona *ntpl*; divitiae *fpl*; (class, in politics) ordo *m*; dignitas *f*

esteem[1] *vt* aestimo, puto ①; habeo ②; (judge) existimo ①; (respect) magni facio ③

esteem[2] *n* aestimatio *f*; honor *m*; reverentia *f*

estimate[1] *vt* aestimo ①; (assess) censeo ②

estimate² *n* (valuation) aestimatio *f*; pretium; iudicium *nt*

estimation *n* aestimatio; opinio *f*

estrangement *n* alienatio *f*; discidium *nt*

estuary *n* aestuarium *nt*

eternal *adj* aeternus, sempiternus, immortalis
■ ~**ly** *adv* in aeternum, semper

eternity *n* aeternitas; immortalitas *f*

ethereal *adj* aethereus

eulogistic *adj* panegyricus, laudativus

eulogize *vt* collaudo ①

eulogy *n* laus, laudatio *f*; panegyricus *m*

eunuch *n* eunuchus *m*

evacuate *vt* vacuo ①; vacuefacio ③; (leave) relinquo ③

evacuation *n* (departure) excessus *m*

evade *vt* subterfugio, eludo ③

evaporate *vi* evaporor ①; evanesco ③
■ ~ *vt* evaporo, exhalo ①

evaporation *n* evaporatio, exhalatio *f*

evasion *n* effugium *nt*; fuga; tergiversatio *f*

evasive *adj* vafer; subdolus; ambiguus
■ ~**ly** *adv* vafre; subdole; ambigue

eve *n* vesper *m*; (of a feast) vigiliae *fpl*

even¹ *adj* aequalis, aequus; (level) planus; (of numbers) par

even² *adv* etiam, quoque; (with superlatives) vel
□ **not** ~ ne … quidem
□ ~ **as** perinde ac si, quemadmodum
□ ~ **if** etiamsi

evening¹ *n* vesper *m*

evening² *adj* vespertinus

Evening-star *n* Vesper, Hesperus *m*

evenly *adv* aequaliter, aequabiliter

event *n* eventus, exitus, casus *m*

eventful *adj* (remarkable) memorabilis

eventually *adv* denique, aliquando, tandem

ever *adv* unquam; aliquando; semper
□ **for** ~ in aeternum
□ **who**~ quicumque

evergreen *adj* semper viridis

everlasting *adj* sempiternus

every *adj* quisque; omnis
□ ~ **day** cotidie, in dies

everybody *pn* quisque; unusquisque; nemo non; omnes; quivis; quilibet

everyday *adj* cotidianus; usitatus

everything *n* omnia *ntpl*; quidvis; quidlibet

everywhere *adv* ubique, ubivis, undique

evict *vt* expello ③, deturbo ①

eviction *n* (law) expulsio ④

evidence *n* (proof) argumentum; (in law) testimonium *nt*; (witness) testis *m/f*; (information) indicium *nt*

evident *adj* apertus, manifestus, clarus, liquidus
□ **it is** ~ apparet, liquet ②
■ ~**ly** *adv* aperte, manifesto, liquide

evil *adj* malus, pravus, improbus
■ ~ *n* malum, incommodum *nt*

evince *vt* praesto ①

evoke *vt* evoco ①; elicio ③

evolve *vt* evolvo ③

ewe *n* ovis femina *f*

exact¹ *adj* (attentive to detail) diligens, subtilis; (of things) exactus
■ ~**ly** *adv* exacte, ad unguem

exact² *vt* exigo ③

exaggerate *vt* exaggero, aggravo ①; augeo ②

exaggeration *n* amplificatio *f*; immoderatio *f*

exalted *adj* celsus, altus, sublimis

examination *n* investigatio; inspectio; (of witnesses) interrogatio *f*

examine *vt* investigo; exploro ①; inspicio ③; (witnesses) interrogo ①

example *n* exemplum, exemplar, documentum *nt*
□ **for** ~ verbi gratia

exasperate *vt* exaspero, exacerbo, irrito ①

exasperation *n* ira *f*; animus iratus *m*

excavate *vt* excavo ①; effodio ③

excavation *n* excavatio *f*

exceed *vt* excedo ③; supero ①

exceedingly *adv* valde, egregie, magnopere; vehementer

excel *vt* praesto ① + *dat*; supero ①
■ ~ *vi* excello ③

excellence *n* excellentia, praestantia *f*

excellent *adj* excellens, praestans, egregius, eximius

e

except[1] *vt* excipio, eximo ③

except[2] *prep* extra, praeter + *acc*;
(unless) nisi
□ ~ **that** nisi quod, nisi si

exception *n* exceptio *f*
□ **take** ~ **to** reprehendo ③; culpo ①
□ **with the** ~ **of Cicero** Cicerone
excepto

exceptional *adj* rarus
■ ~**ly** *adv* raro; (outstandingly) eximie;
(contrary to custom) praeter solitum

excess *n* exsuperantia, immoderatio;
(licence) intemperantia, licentia *f*
□ **to** ~ nimis

excessive *adj* nimius; immodicus;
immoderatus
■ ~**ly** *adv* nimis; immodice;
immoderate

exchange[1] *n* (barter) mutatio,
permutatio *f*; (of money) collybus *m*

exchange[2] *vt* muto, permuto ①

excitable *adj* irritabilis; fervidus

excite *vt* excito, incito, stimulo ①;
(inflame) incendo ③; (thrill) agito ①;
commoveo ②; (produce) cieo, moveo ②;
conflo ③

excited *adj* agitatus

excitement *n* commotio;
perturbatio *f*

exclaim *vt* exclamo; (several voices)
conclamo ①

exclamation *n* vox; exclamatio; (of
several people) conclamatio *f*

exclude *vt* excludo ③; arceo; prohibeo;
removeo ②

exclusion *n* exclusio *f*

exclusive *adj* (one's own) proprius;
(especial) praecipuus
■ ~**ly** *adv* (only) solum

excrement *n* excrementum, stercus
nt; proluvies *f*

excruciating *adj* acerbissimus

excursion *n* excursio, incursio; fig
digressio *f*

excusable *adj* excusabilis

excuse[1] *vt* excuso; (exculpate) purgo ①;
(pardon) ignosco ③ + *dat*; condono ①

excuse[2] *n* excusatio *f*; causa *f*; (pretence)
praetextum *nt*

execute *vt* (fulfil, perform) exsequor,
persequor, perficio, perago ③; (as
punishment) securi ferio ④

execution *n* (performance) exsecutio *f*;
(punishment) supplicium *nt*; (death) mors *f*
□ **place of** ~ furca *f*

executioner *n* carnifex *m*

exemplary *adj* egregius, eximius,
excellens

exemplify *vt* (give example of) exemplum
do ① + *gen*

exempt[1] *vt* eximo ③; immunitatem
do ①

exempt[2] *adj* immunis

exemption *n* vacatio, immunitas *f*

exercise[1] *n* exercitatio *f*; (of soldiers)
exercitium *nt*; (task) pensum *nt*

exercise[2] *vt* exerceo ②; (an office)
fungor ③ + *abl*; (trouble) vexo ①
■ ~ *vi* exerceor ②

exert *vt* exhibeo, exerceo ②
□ ~ **oneself** contendo, nitor ③

exertion *n* contentio *f*; nisus *m*

exhalation *n* exhalatio *f*; vapor *m*

exhale *vt* exhalo, exspiro ①; spargo,
emitto ③

exhaust *vt* exhaurio ④; conficio ③;
debilito, infirmo ①

exhausted *adj* fessus, defessus,
confectus, languidus

exhaustion *n* languor *m*; lassitudo,
defectio (virium) *f*

exhibit *vt* exhibeo ②; expono, propono
③, profero *ir*, ostendo ③; (qualities)
praesto ①

exhibition *n* prolatio *f*; (show)
spectaculum *nt*

exhilarate *vt* exhilaro ①

exhilaration *n* hilaritas *f*

exhort *vt* hortor ①

exhortation *n* hortatio *f*

exile[1] *n* (banishment) exsilium, exilium
nt; fuga *f*; (person banished) exsul, exul,
extorris *m/f*

exile[2] *vt* relego ①; in exilium pello ③

exist *vi* sum *ir*, exsisto; vivo ③

existence *n* vita *f*

existing *adj* qui nunc est

exit *n* exitus *m*; effugium *nt*

exonerate *vt* culpa libero, excuso ①

exorbitant *adj* nimius, immodicus

exotic *adj* externus, peregrinus

expand *vt* expando; extendo ③;
dilato ①; augeo ②

■ ~ *vi* expandor, extendor, cresco ③; dilator ①

expanse *n* spatium *nt*

expect *vt&i* exspecto; spero ①

expectant *adj* suspensus

expectation *n* exspectatio; spes *f*

expediency *n* utilitas *f*

expedient¹ *adj* utilis, commodus, salutaris
□ **it is** ~ expedit

expedient² *n* modus *m*; ratio *f*

expedite *vt* maturo ①

expedition *n* mil expeditio *f*

expel *vt* expello, eicio ③

expend *vt* expendo, impendo; consumo ③

expenditure *n* sumptus *m*; impensa *f*

expense *n* impensa *f*; sumptus *m*

expensive *adj* sumptuosus, pretiosus, carus
■ ~ly *adv* sumptuose, pretiose, care

expensiveness *n* caritas *f*; magnum pretium *nt*

experience¹ *n* experientia; peritia *f*; usus *m*

experience² *vt* experior ④; utor + *abl*, cognosco ③

experienced *adj* peritus, experiens; callidus

experiment¹ *n* experimentum, periculum *nt*

experiment² *vt* experimentum facio ③

experimental *adj* usu comparatus
■ ~ly *adv* usu, experimentis

expert¹ *n* artifex *m*

expert² *adj* callidus, sciens
■ ~ly *adv* callide, scienter

expertise *n* ars, calliditas, sollertia *f*

expiate *vt* expio ①; luo ③

expiration *n* exspiratio *f*; finis *m/f*; exitus *m*

expire *vi* (die) exspiro ①; (terminate) exeo *ir*

explain *vt* explano, explico ①; expono ③

explanation *n* explanatio, explicatio *f*

explicit *adj* explicatus; apertus
■ ~ly *adv* aperte, plane, nominatim

explode *vt* (blow up) displodo; fig explodo, reicio ③
■ ~ *vi* displodor ③

exploit¹ *vt* (positively) utor ③ + *abl*; (negatively) abutor ③ + *abl*

exploit² *n* res gesta *f*; facinus *nt*

exploration *n* indagatio, investigatio *f*

explore *vt* exploro; perscrutor; vestigo, indago ①

explorer *n* explorator *m*

explosion *n* crepitus, fragor *m*

export¹ *vt* eveho ③; exporto ①

export² *n* exportatio *f*

expose *vt* expono, retego ③; nudo ①
□ ~ **to** obicio ③; obiecto ①

exposition *n* explicatio, expositio; interpretatio *f*

exposure *n* expositio *f*; (disclosure) indicium *nt*; (cold) frigus *nt*

expound *vt* expono ③; interpretor ①

express¹ *vt* exprimo, loquor, dico ③; significo ①

express² *adj* clarus; certus; expressus
■ ~ly *adv* expresse, nominatim

expression *n* (word) vox; (maxim, epigram) sententia *f*; fig (of the face) vultus *m*

expressive *adj* significans; fig (of) index; (speaking) loquax; (clear) argutus
■ ~ly *adv* significanter

expulsion *n* exactio *f*

expurgate *vt* expurgo ①

exquisite *adj* conquisitus; exquisitus; elegans, subtilis, eximius
■ ~ly *adv* exquisite, eximie, eleganter

exquisiteness *n* elegantia; subtilitas *f*

extant *adj* superstes
■ **be** ~ *vi* exsto ①

extemporary *adj* extemporalis

extempore *adv* subito; ex tempore

extemporize *vt* ex tempore dico ③

extend *vt* extendo; produco ③; propago ①
■ ~ *vi* extendo; porrigor ③

extension *n* extensio; propagatio; (of boundaries, *etc.*) prolatio *f*; (space) spatium *nt*

extensive *adj* late patens, amplus, diffusus
■ ~ly *adv* late

extent *n* spatium *nt*; (of a country) tractus *m*; fines *mpl*; (range) circuitus *m*; (amount) vis *f*

exterior[1] *adj* externus, exterior

exterior[2] *n* species, facies, forma *f*

exterminate *vt* exstirpo, extermino ①; deleo ②; tollo, exstinguo ③

extermination *n* exstirpatio *f*

external *adj* externus; extraneus
■ ∼**ly** *adv* extrinsecus

extinct *adj* exstinctus; obsoletus
□ **become** ∼ exstinguor, obsolesco ③

extinction *n* extinctio *f*; interitus *m*

extinguish *vt* exstinguo ③

extol *vt* laudibus effero *ir*; laudo ①

extort *vt* extorqueo ②; exprimo ③

extortion *n* (pecuniae) repetundae *fpl*

extra[1] *adj* praecipuus

extra[2] *adv* insuper, praeterea
■ ∼ *n* supplementum *nt*

extract[1] *vt* extraho ③

extract[2] *n* (juice) sucus *m*; (literary) excerptum; (epitome) compendium *nt*

extraction *n* (birth) stirps; origo *f*; genus *nt*

extraordinarily *adj* extra modum; praeter solitum

extraordinary *adj* extraordinarius, insolitus, mirabilis

extravagance *n* intemperantia, effusio; luxuria *f*

extravagant *adj* immodicus, nimius; profusus; effusus; luxuriosus; (dissolute) perditus
■ ∼**ly** *adv* immodice; effuse; prodige; nimis

extreme[1] *adj* extremus; ultimus; summus; *fig* ingens
■ ∼**ly** *adv* summe

extreme[2] *n* extremum, summum *nt*

extremity *n* extremitas *f*; extremum *nt*; (distress) miseria *f*; (danger) discrimen, periculum *nt*; (difficulty) angustiae *fpl*

extricate *vt* expedio ④; extraho ③; libero ①

exuberance *n* luxuria, redundantia; ubertas *f*

exuberant *adj* luxuriosus; redundans

exude *vt&i* exsudo ①

exult *vi* exsulto, ovo ①; gestio ④

exultant *adj* laetus, ovans

exultation *n* laetitia *f*; gaudium *nt*

eye[1] *n* oculus, ocellus *m*; lumen *nt*; (of a needle) foramen *nt*; (sight) acies *f*

eye[2] *vt* aspicio ③; intueor ②; contemplor ①

eyeball *n* pupula *f*

eyebrow *n* supercilium *nt*

eyelid *n* palpebra *f*

eyesight *n* acies oculi *f*

eyesore *n* res odiosa *f*

eyewitness *n* arbiter *m*; testis *m/f*; spectator *m*

Ff

fable *n* fabula *f*

fabric *n* (woven material), textile, textum *nt*

fabricate *vt* fabrico ①; struo ③

fabrication *n* (construction) fabricatio *f*; *fig* mendacium *nt*

face[1] *n* facies *f*; os *nt*; vultus; *fig* conspectus *m*; (boldness) audacia, impudentia *f*; (appearance) species *f*
□ ∼ **to** ∼ coram

face[2] *vt* aspicio ③; intueor ②; (of position) specto ad + *acc* ①; (meet) obeo *ir* + *dat*; (cover in part) praetexo ③

facetious *adj* facetus, lepidus
■ ∼**ly** *adv* facete, lepide

facetiousness *n* facetiae *fpl*; lepos *m*

facilitate *vt* facilius reddo ③

facility *n* facilitas *f*; (opportunity) copia, facultas *f*

facing[1] *prep* adversus, ante *both* + *acc*

facing[2] *adj* contrarius, adversus

facsimile *n* imago scripturae *f*

fact *n* factum *nt*; res *f*
□ **in** ∼ re ipsa; re vera, enim

faction *n* (party) factio *f*

factor *n* (agent) procurator *m*; (element) pars *f*

factory *n* officina *f*

faculty *n* facultas; vis *f*; ingenium *nt*

fade *vt* marcesco, defloresco ③; langueo ②; (decay) deficio ③; (become pale) albesco ③

faggot *n* fascis *m*; sarmenta *ntpl*

fail¹ *vt* (disappoint) deficio, desero ③
  ■ ~ *vi* (break down) succumbo ③; (of duty) delinquo ③; (become bankrupt) decoquo ③; (be unsuccessful) cado ③; male cedo ③

fail² *n*:
  □ **without** ~ certo

failing *n* (deficiency) defectus *m*; (fault) culpa *f*; delictum *nt*

failure *n* defectio *f*; defectus *m*; (fault) culpa *f*; delictum *nt*

faint¹ *n* exanimatio *f*

faint² *adj* (weary) defessus; (dropping) languidus; (of sight, smell, *etc.*) hebes; (of sound) surdus; (unenthusiastic) frigidus; (timid) demissus
  ■ ~**ly** *adv* languide; timide

faint³ *vi* (swoon) collabor ③

faintness *n* defectio *f*; languor *m*

fair *adj* (of complexion) candidus; (beautiful) formosus, pulcher; (of weather) serenus, sudus; (of winds) secundus, idoneus; (of hair) flavus; *fig* aequus; mediocris; modicus
  ■ ~ **play** *n* aequitas *f*

fairly *adv* iuste; (moderately) mediocriter

fairness *n* (beauty) forma, pulchritudo *f*; (justice) aequitas *f*; candor animi *m*

faith *n* (trust) fides, (confidence) fiducia, (religion) religio *f*

faithful *adj* fidelis; fidus
  ■ ~**ly** *adv* fideliter, fide

faithfulness *adj* fides, fidelitas, integritas *f*

faithless *adj* infidus, infidelis, perfidus; perfidiosus

fake *adj* falsus

falcon *n* falco *m*

fall¹ *vi* cado; concido; (die) occido; (decrease) decresco; (violently and completely) corruo ③
  □ ~ **apart** dilabor ③
  □ ~ **away** deficio ③
  □ ~ **back** recido; relabor ③; (retreat) pedem refero *ir*; *fig* recurro ③
  □ ~ **down** decido; (completely) concido ③
  □ ~ **forwards** procido; procumbo; prolabor ③

  □ ~ **in(to)** incido ③
  □ ~ **in with** (meet) incido ③; (find) invenio ④; (agree) assentior ④
  □ ~ **in love with** adamo ①
  □ ~ **off** decido ③
  □ ~ **on** ▶ ~ **upon**
  □ ~ **out** excido; (happen) contingo, accido ③; evenio ④; (with someone) dissideo ②
  □ ~ **short of** non contingo ③
  □ ~ **sick** in morbum incido ③
  □ ~ **under** succumbo ③; (be classed) pertineo ② ad + *acc*; (be subjected to) patior ③
  □ ~ **upon** accido; incido; (assail) invado, ingruo, incurro ③; occupo ①
  □ **let** ~ demitto; (out of the hand) emitto ③

fall² *n* casus; lapsus *m*; (ruin) ruina *f*; labes *f*; (of ground, *etc.*) libramentum *nt*; (waterfall) cataracta; (diminution) deminutio *f*; (autumn) autumnus *m*; (death) mors *f*

fallacious *adj* fallax, fictus, falsus
  ■ ~**ly** *adv* fallaciter, ficte, falso

fallible *adj* errori obnoxius

fallow *adj* (of land) inaratus; (never having been ploughed) novalis
  □ ~ **land** *n* novalis *m*; novale *nt*

false *adj* falsus; fictus; (counterfeit) adulterinus
  ■ ~**ly** *adv* falso, perperam, ficte

falsehood *n* (untrue story) commentum; (lie) mendacium *nt*

falseness *n* perfidia *f*; dolus *m*

falsification *n* adulteratio, corruptio *f*

falsify *vt* suppono, corrumpo ③; depravo, (documents) vitio ①; interlino ③

falter *vi* haereo ②; haesito, labo; (reel, totter) titubo ①

fame *n* fama; laus, gloria *f*; nomen, decus *nt*; (famousness) claritas; celebritas *f*

familiar *adj* familiaris; solitus; notus; intimus
  ■ ~**ly** *adv* familiariter

familiarity *n* familiaritas; necessitudo, notitia; (in bad sense) licentia *f*

familiarize *vt* assuefacio ③

family *n* familia; domus *f*; genus *nt*; cognatio *f*; (clan) gens *f*

famine *n* fames *f*; *fig* inopia *f*

famished *adj* famelicus; fame enectus

famous *adj* clarus, praeclarus, notus, celeber, inclutus
  ■ ~**ly** *adv* praeclare; insigniter

f

fan¹ *n* flabellum *nt*; (for winnowing) vannus *f*

fan² *vt* ventilo ①; (fire) accendo ③; fig excito, conflo ①

fanatical *adj & n* fanaticus
■ ∼**ally** *adv* fanatice

fanciful *adj* vanis imaginibus deditus; (capricious) inconstans, levis; libidinosus

fancy¹ *n* opinio, imaginatio; *f* (mind) animus *m*; (caprice) libido *f*; (dream) somnium *nt*; (liking, inclination) voluntas *f*

fancy² *vt&i* imaginor; somnio; (like) amo ①

fang *n* dens; (claw) unguis *m*

fantastic *adj* (unreal) vanus; (absurd) absurdus

fantasy *n* phantasia *f*

far¹ *adj* longinquus, remotus

far² *adv* procul, longe
□ ∼ **off** procul
□ **by** ∼ multo
□ **from** ∼ procul + *abl*
□ **how** ∼ quousque?
□ **as** ∼ **as** quantum; quatenus
□ **so** ∼ hactenus
□ ∼ **be it from me** longe absit
□ ∼ **and near** longe lateque

farce *n* mimus *m*

farcical *adj* mimicus
■ ∼**ly** *adv* mimice

fare¹ *n* (food) cibus, victus *m*; (money) vectura *f*; naulum *nt*

fare² *vi* ago ③; habeo (me) ②; cedo ③

farewell *int & n* vale! salve!
□ **bid** ∼ valere *or* salvere iubeo ②; valedico + *dat* ③

far-fetched *adj* quaesitus; longe petitus

farm¹ *n* fundus, agellus *m*; praedium *nt*

farm² *vt* (till) aro ①; colo ③

farmer *n* agricola; colonus *m*

farmhouse *n* villa *f*

farming *n* agricultura *f*; res rusticae *fpl*

farther *adj* ulterior
■ ∼ *adv* longius, ulterius

farthest *adj* ultimus, extremus

fascinate *vt* fascino ①; fig capio ③

fascination *n* fascinatio *f*; illecebrae *fpl*; gratia *f*

fashion¹ *n* (form) figura, forma *f*; (manner) mos, modus; ritus *m*; (custom) consuetudo *f*; usus *m*; (sophistication) urbanitas *f*

fashion² *vt* (shape) formo, informo, fabrico ①; effingo ③

fashionable *adj* elegans; concinnus
□ **be** ∼ in usu sum *ir*, valeo ②

fashionably *adv* ad morem; eleganter

fast¹ *adj* (firm) firmus, stabilis; (tight) astrictus; (swift) celer; (shut) occlusus

fast² *adv* (unflinchingly) firmiter; (quickly) celeriter

fast³ *vi* cibo abstineo ②; ieiuno ①

fast⁴ *n* ieiunium *nt*

fasten *vt* astringo, affigo ③; fig infero *ir* ③; (down) defigo; (to) annecto; impingo ③; (together) colligo ①; configo ③

fastening *n* vinculum *nt*

fastidious *adj* fastidiosus; delicatus; elegans; morosus

fat¹ *adj* pinguis, obesus; opimus

fat² *n* adeps *m/f*; pingue *nt*; arvina *f*; (suet) sebum *nt*; (of a pig) lardum *nt*; (in general) pinguitudo *f*

fatal *adj* mortifer, letifer; exitialis; funebris; funestus
■ ∼**ly** *adv* fataliter; fato

fate *n* Fatum *nt*; sors *f*
■ **the Fates** *pl* Parcae *fpl*; (fortune) fortuna *f*; (chance) casus *m*

fated *adj* fatalis
□ **ill-**∼ infaustus

father *n* pater, genitor, parens *m*
□ ∼ **of a family** paterfamilias *m*

fatherhood *n* paternitas *f*

father-in-law *n* socer *m*

fatherless *adj* orbus

fatherly *adj* paternus, patrius

fathom *n* ulna *f*

fatigue *n* fatigatio, defatigatio, lassitudo *f*

fatness *n* pinguitudo, sagina *f*

fatten *vt* sagino ①; farcio ④

fattening *n* saginatio; (cramming of fowls) fartura *f*

fatty *adj* pinguis

fatuous *adj* stultus, fatuus

fault *n* delictum, mendum, vitium *nt*; (responsibility) culpa *f*; (mistake) error *m*; (blemish) menda, labes, macula *f*
□ **at** ∼ in culpa
□ **find** ∼ **with** vitupero ①; carpo ③

faultless *adj* perfectus; integer

faulty *adj* vitiosus; mendosus

favour[1] *n* favor *m*; gratia; (goodwill) benevolentia *f*; beneficium *nt*; (present) munus *nt*
□ **do a** ∼ gratificor ① + *dat*

favour[2] *vt* faveo ② + *dat*; secundo ①

favourable *adj* prosperus, felix, faustus; commodus, idoneus; benignus; (of the gods) propitius, aequus, secundus

favourably *adv* prospere, feliciter, fauste; benigne, opportune

favourite *adj* dilectus, gratus; (popular) gratiosus
■ ∼ *n* (darling, etc.) deliciae *fpl*

favouritism *n* gratia *f*; studium *nt*

fawn[1] *n* hinnuleus *m*

fawn[2] *vi* (on, upon) adulor ①

fawning *adj* adulatorius, blandus

fax *n* imago scripturae *f*

fear[1] *n* timor, metus *m*; formido *f*

fear[2] *vt&i* timeo, paveo ②; metuo ③; formido ①; (reverentially) vereor ②

fearful *adj* timidus, pavidus; (terrible) dirus; formidolosus
■ ∼**ly** *adv* timide, formidolose

fearfulness *n* timiditas *f*

fearless *adj* impavidus, intrepidus
■ ∼**ly** *adv* impavide

fearlessness *n* audacia, audentia *f*

feasible *adj* quod fieri potest

feast[1] *n* (holiday) dies festus *m*; sollemne *nt*; (banquet) convivium *nt*; epulae, dapes *fpl*

feast[2] *vi* epulor, convivor ①
□ ∼ **one's eyes on** oculos pasco ③

feat *n* facinus; factum *nt*; res gesta *f*

feather *n* (big or wing ∼) penna; (small, downy) pluma *f*

feathered *adj* pennatus; plumosus, penniger

feature *n* lineamentum *nt*; vultus *m*; os *nt*; fig (part) pars *f*

February *n* Februarius *m*

federal *adj* foederatus

federation *n* societas *f*

fee *n* (pay) merces *f*; praemium, pretium *nt*

feeble *adj* infirmus, debilis, languidus
□ **grow** ∼ languesco ③

feebleness *n* infirmitas, debilitas *f*; languor *m*

feebly *adv* infirme; languide

feed *vt* (animals) pasco; (nourish) alo ③; (support) sustento ①
■ ∼ *vi* pascor; vescor ③

feel[1] *vt&i* (touch) tango ③; (handle) tracto ①; (perceive) sentio ④; concipio, percipio ③; (be moved, affected) moveor, commoveor ③
□ **how do you** ∼? quid agis?
□ ∼ **for** doleo cum + *abl*, misereor ② + *gen*

feel[2] *n* tactus *m*

feeler *n* (of an insect) crinis *m*; fig tentamen *n*

feeling *n* (touch) tactus; (sensibility in general) sensus; (emotion) affectus *m*; (judgement) iudicium *nt*

feign *vt&i* fingo, comminiscor ③; (pretend) dissimulo, simulo ①; (lie) mentior ④

feint *n* simulatio; (in fencing) captatio *f*

fell *vt* (trees) caedo; (knock down) sterno, prosterno, everto ③

fellow *n* (companion) socius; (in office) collega; (any individual) homo; (equal) par *m*

fellow-citizen *n* civis *m/f*

fellow-countryman *n* civis *m/f*

fellow-creature *n* homo *m*

fellow-feeling *n* (pity) misericordia *f*

fellow-servant *n* conservus *m*; conserva *f*

fellowship *n* societas, communitas *f*; sodalicium *nt*

fellow-traveller *n* convector; socius itineris *m*

felt *n* coactilia *ntpl*

female[1] *n* femina, mulier *f*

female[2] *adj* femineus, muliebris

feminine *adj* femineus, muliebris; femininus

fence[1] *n* (barrier) saepes *f*; saeptum *nt*

fence[2] *vt* (barricade) saepio ④; defendo ③
■ ∼ *vi* (spar with swords) battuo ③

fencer *n* gladii peritus, gladiator, lanista *m*

fencing *n* ars gladii *f*

fend *vi*:
□ ∼ **for oneself** suis opibus nitor ③

fennel *n* faeniculum *nt*

ferment[1] *n* fermentum *nt*; fig aestus *m*

ferment[2] *vt&i* fermento; fermentor ①

fern *n* filix *f*

ferocious *adj* ferus, truculentus, saevus, atrox
■ ~**ly** *adv* truculente, saeve, atrociter

ferociousness *n* saevitia, feritas, atrocitas *f*

ferocity *n* saevitia, feritas, atrocitas *f*

ferret¹ *n* viverra *f*

ferret² *vt*:
□ ~ **out** rimor, expiscor ①

ferry *vt* traicio, transveho ③

ferry-boat *n* scapha, cumba *f*

ferryman *n* portitor *m*

fertile *adj* fertilis, fecundus, ferax, uber

fertility *n* fertilitas, ubertas *f*

fertilize *vt* fecundo ①

fervent *adj* ardens, fervidus; vehemens
■ ~**ly** *adv* ardenter; vehementer

fervour *n* ardor, fervor, impetus *m*

fester *vi* suppuro, ulceror ①

festival *n* dies festus *m*; sollemne *nt*

festive *adj* festus, festivus

festivity *adj* sollemnia *ntpl*; (gaiety) festivitas *f*

festoon *n* sertum *nt*
■ ~ *vt* corono, adorno ①

fetch *vt* adduco ③, affero *ir*; arcesso, peto ③
□ ~ **back** reduco ③
□ ~ **down** deveho ③
□ ~ **in** importo ①
□ ~ **out** depromo; (cause to appear) elicio ③

fetter¹ *vt* (alicui) compedes impingo ③; colligo ①; vincio ④; fig impedio ④; illaqueo ①

fetter² *n* compes, pedica *f*

feud *n* lis, simultas; inimicitia *f*; odium *nt*

fever *n* febris *f*

feverish *adj* febriculosus; fig ardens

few *adj* pauci, perpauci; aliquot *indecl*
□ **in a** ~ **words** paucis, breviter

fib *n* mendaciolum, mendaciunculum *nt*

fibre *n* fibra *f*; filum *nt*

fickle *adj* inconstans, mobilis; instabilis; levis

fickleness *n* inconstantia; mutabilitas; mobilitas, levitas *f*

fiction *n* fictio *f*; commentum *nt*; fabula *f*

fictitious *adj* fictus, commenticius; (simulated), simulatus
■ ~**ly** *adv* ficte

fiddle *n* fides *f*

fidelity *n* fidelitas; constantia, fides *f*

fidget *vi* cursito ①

fidgety *adj* inquietus

field *n* campus, ager *m*; arvum, rus *nt*; (~ of grass) pratum; (battle) proelium *nt*; fig (scope) area *f*

field-mouse *n* mus agrestis *m*

fiend *n* Erinys *f*

fierce *adj* atrox; saevus; vehemens
■ ~**ly** *adv* atrociter; saeve; ferociter; vehementer

fierceness *n* atrocitas; saevitia; ferocitas; ferocia; vehementia *f*

fiery *adj* igneus; fig ardens, fervidus, iracundus

fifteen *adj* quindecim

fifteenth *adj* quintus decimus

fifth¹ *adj* quintus

fifth² *n* quinta pars *f*

fifthly *adj* quintum, quinto

fiftieth *adj* quinquagesimus

fifty *adj* quinquaginta

fig *n* (fruit and tree) ficus *f*

fight¹ *n* pugna *f*; proelium *nt*; (struggle) contentio *f*

fight² *vt&i* pugno; dimico ①; contendo ③; (in battle) proelior; (with sword) digladior; (hand to hand) comminus pugno ①
□ ~ **against** repugno ①

fighter *n* pugnator, proeliator *m*

figurative *adj* translatus
■ ~**ly** *adv* per translationem, tropice

figure *n* figura; forma; (shape) imago *f*; (appearance) species *f*; (of speech) tropus *m*; (number) numerus *m*

figured *adj* sigillatus; (chased) caelatus

filament *n* fibrae *fpl*; filum *nt*

filch *vt* surripio ③; suffuror ①

file¹ *n* (tool) lima *f*; (for or of papers) scapus; (line, string, row) ordo *m*; series *f*
□ **the rank and** ~ milites gregarii *mpl*

file² *vt* (rub smooth) limo ①

filial *adj* pius

filings *n* scobis *f*

fill¹ *vt* compleo; impleo, expleo; (supply) suppleo ②
□ ~ **out** impleo ②

□ ~ **up** expleo; (completely) compleo ②; (heap) cumulo ①

fill² *n* satietas *f*
□ **have one's ~ of** satior ① + *abl*

filter¹ *n* colum *nt*

filter² *vt&i* percolo; percolor ①

filth *n* sordes, colluvies, illuvies *f*;
▶ **dirt**

filthiness *n* foeditas *f*; squalor *m*; fig obscenitas *f*

filthy *adj* sordidus, foedus, spurcus; fig obscenus

fin *n* pinna *f*

final *adj* ultimus, extremus, postremus
■ ~**ly** *adv* postremo; denique

finance *n* res familiaris *f*, fiscus, aerarii reditus *m*

financial *adj* aerarius

finch *n* fringilla *f*

find *vt* invenio, reperio ④; (hit upon) offendo ③; (catch in the act) deprehendo ③
□ ~ **out** comperio ④; (discover) rescisco; nosco, cognosco ③; (guess) coniecto ①

fine¹ *adj* (of texture) subtilis; (thin) tenuis; (of gold) purus; (handsome) bellus; elegans; (excellent) optimus, (ironically) bonus, egregius, praeclarus
■ ~**ly** *adv* subtiliter; tenuiter; fig pulchre; egregie

fine² *n* mul(c)ta *f*

fine³ *vt* mul(c)to ①

fineness *n* subtilitas; tenuitas; fig pulchritudo; elegantia, praestantia *f*

finery *n* ornatus, cultus *m*; lautitia *f*

finger¹ *n* digitus *m*

finger² *vt* tango ③; tracto ①

finish¹ *vt* conficio, perficio ③; (put an end to) termino ①; finio ④
□ ~ **off** consummo ①; ultimam manum operi impono ③
■ ~ *vi* finio ④

finish² *n* (end) finis *m/f*

finishing-touch *n* ultima manus *f*

finite *adj* caducus, moriturus

fir¹ *n* (**fir-tree**) abies, pinus *f*

fir² *adj* (of fir) abiegnus, pineus

fire¹ *n* ignis *m*; (conflagration) incendium *nt*; fig fervor, ardor, impetus *m*
□ **catch** ~ ignem concipio ③
□ **set** ~ **to** incendo ③
□ **on** ~ incensus, inflammatus

fire² *vt* (weapons) mitto, dirigo ③

firebrand *n* torris *m*

fire-engine *n* sipho *m*

firemen *n* excubiae vigilesque adversus incendia *mpl*

fireplace *n* caminus; focus *m*

fireproof *adj* ignibus impervius

fireside *n* focus *m*

firewood *n* lignum *nt*

firm¹ *adj* firmus; solidus; (of purpose) tenax
□ **be** ~ (endure) persevero, persto ①

firm² *n* (company) societas *f*

firmly *adv* firme, firmiter; solide; (of purpose) tenaciter

firmness *n* firmitas; constantia *f*

first¹ *adj* primus; princeps

first² *adv* primum
□ **at** ~ primo
□ ~ **of all** imprimis

fiscal *adj* fiscalis

fish¹ *n* piscis *m*

fish² *vt&i* piscor; fig expiscor ①

fish-bone *n* spina piscis *f*

fisherman *n* piscator *m*

fish-hook *n* hamus *m*

fishing *n* piscatus *m*; piscatio *f*

fishing-boat *n* piscatoria navis *f*

fishing-line *n* linum *nt*

fishing-net *n* funda *f*; iaculum, everriculum *nt*

fishing-rod *n* arundo *f*; calamus *m*

fishmonger *n* cetarius, piscarius *m*

fish-pond *n* piscina *f*; vivarium *nt*

fishy *adj* piscosus, pisculentus; fig suspectus

fissure *n* rima, fissura *f*

fist *n* pugnus *m*

fit¹ *n* (of a disease) accessio *f*; (whim) libido *f*
□ **epileptic** ~ morbus caducus *m*
■ **by** ~**s and starts** *adv* carptim

fit² *adj* aptus, idoneus; conveniens; opportunus; habilis; (becoming) decens; (ready) paratus; (healthy) sanus

fit³ *vt* accommodo, apto; (apply) applico ①; (furnish) instruo ③; orno ①
□ ~ **out** instruo ③; orno, adorno ①; suppedito ①
■ ~ *vi* (of dress) sedeo ②; fig convenio ④

fitful *adj* mobilis, mutabilis, inconstans

fitness *n* convenientia; (healthiness) valetudo *f*

fitting *adj* decens; ▶ **fit** *adj*

five *adj* quinque
  □ ~ **times** quinquies

fix *vt* (attach) figo ③; (the eyes, *etc.*) intendo ③; (establish) stabilio ④; (on, upon) eligo ③; (appoint) statuo, constituo ③; (repair) reficio ③
  ■ ~ *vi* (be fixed, stick) inhaereo ②

fixed *adj* fixus, firmus; certus; (intent upon) intentus
  ■ ~**ly** *adv* firmiter, constanter

flabby *adj* flaccidus, flaccus; fluidus; (drooping) marcidus

flaccid *adj* flaccidus

flag[1] *n* (banner) vexillum; insigne *nt*

flag[2] *vi* languesco; refrigesco, remittor ③; laxor ①

flagon *n* lagena *f*

flagrant *adj* immanis, insignis; atrox, nefarius; (open) apertus

flagship *n* navis praetoria *f*

flake *n* floccus *m*; frustum *nt*; squama *f*
  □ **snow** ~**s** nives *fpl*

flaky *adj* squameus

flame[1] *n* flamma *f*; ardor *m*

flame[2] *vi* flammo, flagro ①
  □ ~ **up** fig exardesco ③

flamingo *n* (bird) phoenicopterus *m*

flank *n* (of an animal) ilia *ntpl*; (of an army) latus *nt*

flap[1] *n* lacinia *f*

flap[2] *vt&i* (wings) alis plaudo ③; (hang loosely) fluito ①; dependeo ②

flare *vi* flagro ①; fulgeo ②

flash[1] *n* fulgor *m*; (of lightning) fulmen *nt*

flash[2] *vi* fulgeo, splendeo ②; corusco ①

flask *n* ampulla, laguncula *f*

flat *adj* (even, level) planus; (not mountainous) campester; (lying on the face) pronus; (sheer) merus; (insipid, of drinks) vapidus; fig frigidus; insulsus; ieiunus

flatness *n* planities; (evenness) aequalitas; (of a discourse, *etc.*) ieiunitas; (of drinks) vappa *f*

flatten *vt* complano, aequo ①

flatter *vt* adulor, assentor ①; blandior ④

flatterer *n* adulator, assentator *m*

flattering *adj* adulans, blandus, adulatorius

flattery *n* adulatio, assentatio *f*; blanditiae *fpl*

flaunt *vt* obicio ③; ostento ①

flautist *n* tibicen *m*

flavour[1] *n* sapor *m*

flavour[2] *vt* condio ④

flavouring *n* condimentum *nt*

flaw *n* (defect) vitium *nt*; menda, macula, labes *f*; (chink) rima *f*

flawless *adj* sine mendo, perfectus, integer

flax *n* linum *nt*

flaxen *adj* lineus; (of colour) flavus

flay *vt* pellem detraho ③

flea *n* pulex *m*

fleck[1] *n* macula *f*

fleck[2] *vt* maculo ①

flee *vt&i* fugio ③
  □ ~ **away** aufugio ③
  □ ~ **to** confugio ③
  □ ~**from** effugio ③

fleece[1] *n* vellus *nt*

fleece[2] *vt* (shear) tondeo ②; fig spolio; privo; expilo ①

fleecy *adj* laniger

fleet *n* classis *f*

fleeting *adj* fugax; fluxus; lubricus; caducus

flesh *n* caro *f*; viscera *ntpl*; fig (body) corpus *nt*; (sensuality) libido *f*

fleshy *adj* (abounding in flesh) carnosus

flexibility *n* mollitia, facilitas *f*

flexible *adj* flexibilis, flexilis, mollis, lentus; fig exorabilis

flicker *vi* (flutter) volito; (flash) corusco ①

flight *n* fuga *f*; (escape) effugium *nt*; (of birds) volatus *m*; (of stairs) scala *f*
  □ **put to** ~ in fugam impello ③; fugo ①; fundo ③
  □ **take (to)** ~ aufugio ③

flimsiness *n* tenuitas, exilitas *f*

flimsy *adj* tenuis, praetenuis; fig frivolus

flinch *vi* abhorreo ②

fling *vt* iacio, mitto ③
  □ ~ **away** abicio ③
  □ ~ **down** deicio ③
  □ ~ **off** reicio ③

flint *n* silex *m/f*

flippancy *n* levitas, protervitas *f*

flippant *adj* levis, protervus, petulans
  ■ ~**ly** *adv* proterve, petulanter

flirt *vi* ludo ③

flirtation *n* lusus *m*

flit *vi* volito, circumvolito ①

float *vi* fluito, nato, innato; fluctuor ①; pendeo ②; (hang loosely) volito ①
■ ~ *vt* (launch) deduco ③

flock¹ *n* (of sheep, birds, *etc.*) grex *m*

flock² *vi* (together) coeo *ir*, convenio ④, congregor; convolo ①

flog *vt* verbero ①; caedo ③

flogging *n* verberatio *f*; verbera *ntpl*

flood *n* (inundation) diluvies *f*; (stream) flumen *nt*; (tide) aestus *m*; fig flumen *nt*

floor¹ *n* solum *nt*; (paved ~) pavimentum *nt*; (of a barn) area; (storey) contignatio *f*; tabulatum *nt*

floor² *vt* pavimentum struo ③; (with planks) contabulo ①; (throw down) sterno ③; (silence) confuto ①

flooring *n* contabulatio *f*; ▶ **floor** *n*

floral *adj* florens

florid *adj* (of complexion) rubicundus; fig (of style) floridus

flounder *vi* voluto, titubo ①

flour *n* farina *f*

flourish¹ *vi* floreo; vireo ②

flourish² *n* ornamentum *nt*; (of style) calamistri, flosculi *mpl*; (of a trumpet) cantus *m*

flourishing *adj* florens

floury *adj* farinulentus

flout *vt* derideo ②; repudio ①

flow¹ *vi* fluo ③, feror *ir*; mano ①; (of the tide) affluo, accedo ③

flow² *n* fluxus *m*; (gliding motion) lapsus; (of the tide) accessus *m*; (stream) flumen *nt*; (course) cursus *m*

flower¹ *n* flos, flosculus *m*; fig (the best) flos *m*

flower² *vi* floreo ②; floresco ③

flower-bed *n* area *f*

flowery *adj* floreus; floridus; florifer

fluctuate *vt* fluctuo; fluito, iactor ①

fluctuation *n* fluctuatio; fig mutatio *f*

flue *n* cuniculus fornacis *m*

fluency *n* volubilitas linguae; copia verborum *f*

fluent *adj* volubilis; profluens; (eloquent) disertus; facundus
■ ~**ly** *adv* volubiliter

fluid¹ *adj* fluidus, liquidus

fluid² *n* liquor, umor, latex *m*

flurry *n* perturbatio *f*; tumultus *m*

flush¹ *n* (sudden attack) impetus *m*; (abundance) copia *f*; (blush) rubor *m*

flush² *vi* erubesco ③

fluster *vt* perturbo; inquieto ①; sollicito ①

flute *n* tibia *f*

flutter *vt* agito, perturbo, sollicito ①
■ ~ *vi* (of birds) volito; (with alarm) trepido ①

fly¹ *n* musca *f*

fly² *vi* volo, volito ①; (flee) fugio ③
    □ ~ **off** avolo ①
    □ ~ **open** dissilio ④
    □ ~ **out** provolo ①
    □ ~ **up** subvolo ①

flying *adj* volatilis; volucer; ales

foal *n* (of the horse) equuleus *m*

foam¹ *n* spuma *f*

foam² *vi* spumo ①

foamy *adj* spumans; spumeus, spumosus, spumifer

fodder *n* pabulum *nt*

foe *n* hostis, inimicus *m*

fog *n* caligo, nebula *f*

foggy *adj* caliginosus, nebulosus

foible *n* vitium *nt*; error *m*

foil¹ *n* (for fencing) rudis *f*; (leaf of metal) lamina; (very thin) brattea *f*; (contrast) exemplum contrarii *nt*

foil² *vt* frustror ①; repello ③
    □ **be** ~**ed** spe deicior ③

fold¹ *n* sinus *m*; (wrinkling) ruga *f*; (for cattle) stabulum; (for sheep) ovile *nt*

fold² *vt* plico, complico ①

folding-doors *n* valvae *fpl*

foliage *n* frons, coma *f*; folia *ntpl*

folk *n* homines *mpl*

follow *vi* sequor, insequor, consequor ③; (close) insto, sector, assector ①; (on) persequor; (out) exsequor, prosequor; (up) subsequor ③

follower *n* sectator, assectator; fig discipulus *m*

following *adj* sequens, insequens; posterus, proximus; (uninterruptedly) continuus
    □ **on the** ~ **day** postridie

folly *n* stultitia; insipientia; (madness) dementia *f*

foment *vt* foveo ②; (disorder, *etc.*) stimulo ①; cieo ②

fond *adj* amans; deditus; cupidus; (indulgent) indulgens; (foolishly infatuated) demens
□ **be ∼ of** amo ①
■ **∼ly** *adv* amanter, peramanter

fondle *vt* permulceo, foveo ②

fondness *n* amor *m*; indulgentia; caritas *f*

food *n* (for cattle, *etc.*) pabulum; (any nourishing substance) alimentum *nt*; (for people) cibus *m*; esca *f*

fool¹ *n* stultus, insipiens; (idiot) fatuus; (in a play) sannio *m*
□ **make a ∼ of** ludificor (aliquem) ①
□ **play the ∼** ineptio ④; nugor ①

fool² *vt* ludificor ①; ludo, illudo ③
□ **∼ around** ineptio ④; nugor ①

foolery *n* ineptiae, nugae *fpl*

foolhardiness *n* temeritas *f*

foolhardy *adj* temerarius

foolish *adj* stultus, fatuus, ineptus, stolidus
■ **∼ly** *adv* stulte, inepte

foot *n* pes *m*; (of a mountain) radix *f*; (of a pillar, *etc.*) basis *f*
□ **on ∼** pedester
□ **to the ∼ of** sub + *acc*

football *n* pila *f*

footing *adj* (condition) status *m*; condicio *f*

footpath *n* semita *f*; callis, trames *m*

footprint *n* vestigium *nt*

foot-soldier *n* pedes *m*

footstep *n* vestigium *nt*

footstool *n* scabellum *nt*

for¹ *prep* (on behalf of) pro + *abl*; (for the sake of) causa + *gen*; (because of) ob, propter + *acc*; (after negatives) prae + *abl*
□ **∼ some time** aliquandiu
□ **food ∼ a day** cibus unius diei

for² *conj* nam, enim

forage *vt&i* pabulor; frumentor ①; fig rimor ①

forager *n* pabulator; frumentator *m*

foraging *n* pabulatio; frumentatio *f*

foray *n* incursio, populatio *f*

forbear *vi* abstineo ②; (leave off) desisto ③

forbearance *n* patientia; indulgentia *f*

forbid *vt* veto ①; prohibeo ②; interdico ③

forbidding *adj* insuavis, odiosus; (ugly) deformis; (frightful) immanis

force¹ *n* vis; (law) manus *f*; mil copiae *fpl*; (weight) momentum, pondus *nt*; (strength) vires *fpl*; robur *nt*
□ **in ∼** valens, validus

force² *vt* cogo; (a door, a wall, *etc.*) perrumpo; (drive away) expello ③
□ **∼ down** detrudo ③
□ **∼ in** (a nail, *etc.*) infigo ③
□ **∼ out** extorqueo ②; depello ③
□ **∼ open** rumpo ③

forced *adj* (unnatural) arcessitus, quaesitus
□ **∼ march** magnum *or* maximum iter *nt*

forceful *adj* validus

forcible *adj* per vim factus; (violent) vehemens; (compulsory) coactus

forcibly *adv* per vim, vi; violenter

ford¹ *n* vadum *nt*

ford² *vt* vado transeo *ir*

forearm¹ *n* bracchium *nt*

forearm² *vt* praemunio ④

forebode *vt* portendo ③; praesagio ④; (forewarn) moneo ②

foreboding *n* portentum, praesagium *nt*; (prophetic feeling) praesensio *f*

forecast¹ *vt* praevideo ②; prospicio ③; auguror ①

forecast² *n* providentia *f*; augurium *nt*

forefather *n* atavus *m*
■ **∼s** *pl* maiores *mpl*

forefinger *n* digitus index *m*

foregoing *adj* prior, proximus

forehead *n* frons *f*

foreign *adj* externus, alienus, peregrinus

foreigner *n* peregrinus, externus; (stranger) advena *m*

foreknowledge *n* providentia *f*

foreland *n* promontorium *nt*; lingua *f*

forelock *n* cirrus *m*

foremost *adj* primus; princeps, praecipuus

forensic *adj* forensis

forerunner *n* praenuntius, antecursor *m*

foresee *vt* praevideo ②; prospicio ③

foresight *n* providentia, prospicientia, prudentia; (precaution) provisio *f*

forest *n* silva *f*; nemus *nt*; saltus *m*
■ ∼ *adj* silvestris, nemorensis

forestall *vt* anticipo ①; praecipio ③

foretaste *n* gustus *m*

foretell *vt* praedico ③; vaticinor ①

forethought *n* providentia,
prospicientia *f*

forever *adv* in aeternum, in
perpetuum

forewarn *vt* praemoneo; moneo ②

forfeit[1] *n* mul(c)ta, poena *f*

forfeit[2] *vt* mul(c)tor ①; (lose) amitto ③

forfeiture *n* (loss) amissio; (of goods)
publicatio *f*

forge[1] *vt* (metal, *etc.*) cudo, procudo ③;
fabricor ①; (devise) fingo; (counterfeit)
corrumpo ③; (a document) interlino ③
□ ∼ **ahead** progredior ③

forge[2] *n* fornax *f*

forger *n* fabricator; (of writings)
falsarius *m*

forgery *n* (of documents) subiectio *f*;
(forged document) litterae falsae *fpl*

forget *vt* obliviscor + *gen*; (unlearn)
dedisco ③

forgetful *adj* obliviosus, immemor

forgetfulness *n* oblivio *f*; oblivium
nt

forgive *vt* condono ①; ignosco ③ + *dat*

forgiveness *n* venia *f*

forgiving *adj* ignoscens; clemens

forgo *vt* renuntio ①; dimitto ③; (abstain
from) abstineo ② ab + *abl*; (lose) amitto ③

fork[1] *n* furca *f*; (of roads) bivium, trivium,
quadrivium *nt*

fork[2] *vi* scindor ③

forked *adj* bifurcus, bicornis

forlorn *adj* solus, desertus, miser

form[1] *n* forma, figura *f*; (bench)
scamnum *nt*; (rite) ritus *m*; (class in a
school) classis *f*

form[2] *vt* formo ①; fingo; (produce) efficio
③; (constitute) sum *ir*

formal *adj* formalis; fig frigidus; (stiff)
rigidus, durus

formality *n* ritus *m*

formation *n* conformatio; forma,
figura *f*

former *adj* prior, priscus, pristinus;
(immediately preceding) superior
■ ∼**ly** *adv* antea, prius, antehac; olim;
quondam

formidable *adj* formidabilis,
formidolosus, metuendus

formless *adj* informis; fig rudis

formula *n* formula *f*; exemplar *nt*

forsake *vt* desero, derelinquo,
relinquo, destituo ③

fort *n* castellum *nt*; arx *f*

forth *adv* foras; (of time) inde
□ **and so** ∼ et cetera

forthcoming *adj* promptus; in
promptu

forthwith *adv* extemplo, protinus,
statim, continuo

fortieth *adj* quadragesimus

fortification *n* munitio *f*; munimen,
munimentum *nt*

fortify *vt* munio, circummunio ④

fortitude *n* fortitudo, virtus *f*

fortnight *n* semestrium *nt*; dies
quatuordecim *mpl*

fortress *n* arx *f*; castellum *nt*

fortuitous *adj* fortuitus
■ ∼**ly** *adv* fortuito

fortunate *adj* fortunatus, felix,
prosperus
■ ∼**ly** *adv* fortunate, prospere,
feliciter

fortune *n* fortuna, fors, sors *f*; casus *m*
□ **good** ∼ fortuna *f*; (wealth) divitiae,
opes *fpl*
□ **tell** ∼**s** hariolor ①

fortune-teller *n* hariolus *m*; hariola *f*

forty *adj* quadraginta

forum *n* forum *nt*

forward[1] *adv* (also **forwards**) porro,
prorsus, prorsum

forward[2] *adj* (early, soon ripe) praecox;
(bold) audax; (saucy) protervus

forward[3] *vt* (despatch) mitto ③; (promote)
promoveo ②; consulo ③ + *dat*

foster *vt* foveo ②; nutrio ④; alo ③

foster-child *n* alumnus *m*; alumna *f*

foster-father *n* nutricius, nutritor *m*

foster-mother *n* nutrix, altrix,
educatrix *f*

foul[1] *adj* (dirty) foedus, lutulentus,
squalidus; (of language) obscenus; (of
weather, stormy) turbidus; fig turpis

foul[2] *vt* foedo, inquino ①

foul-mouthed *adj* maledicus

foulness *n* foeditas,*f*; (dirt) squalor *m*; (of a crime) atrocitas; fig turpitudo; obscenitas *f*

found *vt* fundo ①; condo, constituo, construo ③

foundation *n* fundamentum, fundamen *nt*; substructio, sedes *f*

founder¹ *n* fundator, conditor; auctor *m*

founder² *vi* (of ships) submergor, deprimor ③

foundling *n* expositicius *m*

fountain *n* fons *m*

four *adj* quattuor
  □ ~ **times** quater
  □ **on all** ~**s** repens

fourfold *adj* quadruplex, quadruplus

four-footed *adj* quadrupes

fourteen *adj* quattuordecim

fourteenth *adj* quartus decimus

fourth *adj* quartus
  ■ ~**ly** *adv* quarto

fowl *n* avis, volucris *f*
  □ **domestic** ~ gallina *f*

fox *n* vulpes, vulpecula *f*; fig homo astutus *m*

fraction *n* pars exigua *f*; fragmentum, fragmen *nt*

fractious *adj* difficilis, morosus

fractiousness *n* morositas *f*

fracture¹ *n* fractura *f*

fracture² *vt* frango ③

fragile *adj* fragilis; fig caducus

fragility *n* fragilitas *f*

fragment *n* fragmentum, fragmen *nt*

fragrance *n* odor *m*

fragrant *adj* suave olens, odorus; odorifer

frail *adj* fragilis; caducus; infirmus

frailty *n* fragilitas; infirmitas *f*

frame¹ *n* compages; (of body) figura; (of a window, *etc.*) forma; (of a bed) sponda *f*; (edge) margo *m/f*; fig habitus animi *m*

frame² *vt* (shape) formo; (build) fabrico ①; (join together) compingo ③; (contrive) molior ④

framework *n* compages *f*

franchise *n* ius suffragii *nt*

frank *adj* candidus, liber, ingenuus, sincerus, simplex
  ■ ~**ly** *adv* candide, libere, ingenue, sincere, simpliciter

frankness *n* libertas *f*; candor *m*; ingenuitas; simplicitas; sinceritas *f*

frantic *adj* fanaticus, furens, insanus, amens
  ■ ~**ally** *adv* insane

fraternal *adj* fraternus
  ■ ~**ly** *adv* fraterne

fraternity *n* (association) sodalitas *f*

fraternize *vi* amice convenio ④

fratricide *n* (murderer) fratricida *m*; (murder) fraternum parricidium *nt*

fraud *n* fraus, fallacia *f*; dolus *m*

fraudulent *adj* fraudulentus, dolosus
  ■ ~**ly** *adv* fraudulenter, dolo malo

fray¹ *n* rixa, pugna *f*; certamen *nt*

fray² *vi* (wear away) atteror ③

freak *n* (monster) monstrum, portentum *nt*

freckled *adj* lentiginosus

freckles *n* lentigo *f*

free¹ *adj* liber; (from business) otiosus; (not bound by) solutus; (of space) vacuus; (immune) immunis; (gratuitous) gratuitus; (impudent) procax; fig candidus, sincerus
  □ ~ **from** expers + *gen*, vacuus + *abl*

free² *vt* libero ①; (a slave) manumitto ③

freebooter *n* praedo, latro; (at sea) pirata *m*

freeborn *adj* ingenuus

freedman *n* libertus, libertinus *m*

freedom *n* libertas; immunitas; (from) vacuitas *f*; (franchise) civitas *f*

freedwoman *n* liberta, libertina *f*

freely *adv* libere; (of one's own accord) sponte; (liberally) large; copiose; liberaliter, munifice; (far and wide) late; (for nothing) gratis

freeman *n* liber *m*

free-will *n* voluntas *f*; liberum arbitrium *nt*

freeze *vt* congelo, gelo, glacio ①
  ■ ~ *vi* consisto, rigesco ③
  □ **it is freezing** gelat

freight *n* onus *nt*

frenzied *adj* furens, lymphatus

frenzy *n* furor *m*; insania *f*

frequency *n* crebritas; frequentia *f*

frequent¹ *adj* creber; frequens
  ■ ~**ly** *adv* crebro; frequenter, saepe

frequent² *vt* frequento, celebro ①

fresco¹ *n* tectorium *nt*

fresco²:
□ **al** ~ sub divo, foris

fresh *adj* (new) recens, novus; (cool) frigidulus; (lusty) vigens; (not tired) integer; (green) viridis; (not salt) dulcis

freshen *vt* recreo ①
■ ~ *vi* increbresco ③

freshly *adv* recenter

freshness *n* (newness) novitas *f*; (vigour) vigor *m*

fret *vi* (grieve) doleo ②; crucior ①; aegre fero *ir*

fretful *adj* morosus; difficilis

fretfulness *n* morositas *f*

fretwork *n* caelatum opus *nt*

friction *n* frictio *f*; tritus, attritus *m*

friend *n* amicus *m*; amica *f*; familiaris *m/f*; necessarius *m*; sodalis *m*

friendless *adj* amicorum inops, desertus

friendliness *n* benevolentia; comitas, affabilitas *f*

friendly *adj* benevolus; comis; amicus

friendship *n* amicitia, sodalitas, necessitudo, familiaritas *f*

frieze *n* (in architecture) zoophorus *m*

frigate *n* navis longa *f*

fright *n* pavor, terror, metus *m*; formido *f*

frighten *vt* terreo, perterreo ②
□ ~ **away** absterreo ②

frightful *adj* terribilis, terrificus; dirus
■ ~**ly** *adv* terribilem in modum

frigid *adj* frigidus
■ ~**ly** *adv* frigide

frigidity *n* frigiditas *f*

frill *n* segmentum *nt*

frilly *adj* segmentatus

fringe *n* fimbriae *fpl*; limbus *m*

frisk *vi* lascivio; salio, exsilio ④; luxurio ①

frisky *adj* lascivus, procax, protervus

fritter *vt*:
□ ~ **away** contero; comminuo ③; fig dissipo ①

frivolity *n* levitas, inconstantia *f*

frivolous *adj* levis; frivolus, futilis
■ ~**ly** *adv* nugatorie, tenuiter

fro *adv*:
□ **to and** ~ huc illuc; ultro citroque

frock *n* palla, stola *f*

frog *n* rana *f*

frolic¹ *n* lascivia *f*; (play, prank) ludus *m*

frolic² *vi* exsulto ①; lascivio ④

from *prep* a, ab, de, ex *all + abl*; (owing to) propter + *acc*
□ ~ **above** desuper
□ ~ **day to day** de die in diem
□ ~ **time to time** continuo

front¹ *n* frons, prior pars *f*; mil primum agmen *nt*

front² *adj* prior, primus; mil primoris
□ **in** ~ ex adverso

frontage *n* frons *f*

frontier *n* finis, terminus *m*

frost *n* gelu *nt*; (hoar-frost) pruina *f*

frostbitten *adj* frigore adustus

frosty *adj* gelidus, glacialis; fig (of manner) frigidus

froth¹ *n* spuma *f*; fig (empty words) vaniloquentia *f*

froth² *vi* spumo ①

frothy *adj* spumeus, spumosus; fig tumidus

frown¹ *n* contractio frontis *f*; vultus severus *m*

frown² *vi* frontem contraho ③; fig (~ upon) aversor ①

frozen *adj* conglaciatus, gelatus, gelu rigens, concretus

frugal *adj* abstinens, parcus, frugalis
■ ~**ly** *adv* frugaliter, parce

frugality *n* parsimonia; frugalitas *f*

fruit *n* fructus *m*; fruges *fpl*; fig (gain) lucrum *nt*; (result) fructus *m*

fruitful *adj* fecundus, fertilis; ferax, uber
■ ~**ly** *adv* fecunde, feraciter

fruitfulness *n* fecunditas, fertilitas, ubertas *f*

fruition *n* fructus *m*

fruitless *adj* irritus
■ ~**ly** *adv* frustra; re infecta

fruit-tree *n* pomum *nt*

frustrate *vt* frustror ①; (baffle) decipio, fallo ③; (break up) dirimo ③

frustration *n* frustratio *f*

fry *vt* frigo ③

frying-pan *n* sartago *f*

fuck *vt* futuo ③

fuel *n* fomes *m*; ligna *ntpl*; nutrimen *nt*

fugitive¹ *adj* fugitivus; fugax

fugitive² *n* profugus *m*; profuga *f*

fulfil *vt* expleo ②; exsequor ③

fulfilment *n* exsecutio, perfectio *f*; (result) exitus *m*

full *adj* plenus; (filled up) expletus; (entire) integer; solidus; (satiated) satur; (of dress) fusus
■ **(in)** ∼ *adv* ▶ **fully**

full-grown *adj* adultus

full moon *n* plenilunium *nt*

fully *adv* plene; copiose; omnino, prorsus

fume¹ *n* vapor, halitus *m*

fume² *vt&i* exhalo ①; fig irascor ③

fumigate *vt* fumigo ①; suffio ④

fumigation *n* suffitus *m*; suffitio *f*

fun *n* iocus, ludus *m*; ludibrium *nt*

function *n* munus, officium *nt*

functional *adj* utilis

fund *n* pecunia *f*; opes *fpl*; fig copia *f*

fundamental *adj* primus, simplex, necessarius, stabilis
■ ∼**ly** *adv* (by nature) natura; (essentially) necessario; (altogether) penitus, omnino

funeral¹ *n* funus *nt*; exsequiae *fpl*

funeral² *adj* funebris, funereus
□ ∼ **rites** iusta funebria *ntpl*
■ ∼ **pyre** *n* rogus *m*; pyra *f*

fungus *n* fungus *m*

funnel *n* infundibulum *nt*

funny *adj* ridiculus, festivus

fur *n* villi *mpl*; pellis *f*

furious *adj* (frenzied) furialis, furiosus, furens; (angry) iratus

furl *vt* contraho, lego ③

furnace *n* fornax *f*

furnish *vt* ministro, suppedito; orno, exorno ①; instruo ③

furniture *n* supellex *f*; apparatus *m*

furrow¹ *n* sulcus *m*; (groove) stria *f*

furrow² *vt* sulco; aro ①

furry *adj* pellicius

further¹ *adv* ultra, longius, ulterius
■ ∼ *adj* ulterior

further² *vt* promoveo ②; proveho, consulo ③ + *dat*; (aid) adiuvo ①

furthermore *adv* porro, insuper

furthest *adj* extremus, ultimus

furtive *adj* furtivus
■ ∼**ly** *adv* clam, furtim, furtive

fury *n* furor *m*; ira, rabies *f*

fuse *vt* fundo, liquefacio ③; conflo ①

fusion *n* fusura *f*

fuss *n* tumultus *m*; turba *f*

fussy *adj* curiosus

futile *adj* futilis, frivolus, vanus

futility *n* futilitas *f*

future¹ *adj* futurus

future² *n* futura *ntpl*; posterum tempus *nt*
□ **in** *or* **for the** ∼ in posterum

Gg

gabble *vi* blatero ①; garrio ④

gable *n* fastigium *nt*

gadfly *n* tabanus, oestrus, asilus *m*

gag¹ *n* oris obturamentum *nt*

gag² *vt* os obturo, praeligo ①; obstruo ③

gaiety *n* festivitas, hilaritas *f*; nitor, splendor *m*

gain¹ *vt* lucror ①; consequor, acquiro ③; (get possession of) potior ④

gain² *n* lucrum, emolumentum *nt*; quaestus *m*

gainful *adj* lucrosus

gait *n* incessus, ingressus *m*

galaxy *n* via lactea *f*

gale *n* ventus *m*; aura, tempestas, procella *f*

gall *n* bilis *f*; fel *nt*

gallant *adj* nitidus, elegans; urbanus; (brave) fortis

gallantry *n* virtus *f*; (politeness) urbanitas, elegantia *f*

galleon *n* navis oneraria *f*

gallery *n* porticus *f*; (open) peristylium *nt*; (top seats) summa cavea *f*

galley *n* navis longa, biremis, triremis *f*

gallop[1] *n* cursus citatus *m*

gallop[2] *vi* citato equo contendo ③; (of the horse) quadrupedo ①

gallows *n* patibulum *nt*

gamble *vi* alea ludo ③
  □ ∼ **away** ludo amitto ③

gambler *n* aleator; lusor *m*

gambling *n* alea *f*

gambling-house *n* aleatorium *nt*

gambling-table *n* alveus *m*

gambol *vi* lascivio ④; ludo ③; exsulto ①

game *n* ludus; (act of playing) lusus *m*; (in hunting) ferae *fpl*
  □ ∼ **of chance** alea *f*
  □ **make** ∼ **of** ludificor ①

gamekeeper *n* saltuarius *m*

gaming *n* ▶ **gambling**

gander *n* anser *m*

gang *n* grex *m*; (troop) caterva *f*; sodalicium *nt*

gangrene *n* gangraena *f*

gangway *n* (in a ship) forus, aditus *m*

gaol *n* etc. ▶ **jail** etc.

gap *n* rima, fissura; lacuna *f*; hiatus *m*

gape *vi* hio ①; dehisco ③; (with mouth open) oscito ①; fig stupeo ②
  □ ∼ **at** inhio ①

gaping *adj* hians, hiulcus; fig stupidus

garb *n* vestitus *m*

garbage *n* quisquiliae *fpl*

garden *n* hortus *m*

gardener *n* hortulanus *m*
  □ **market-**∼ holitor *m*

gardening *n* hortorum cultus *m*

gargle *vi* gargarizo ①

garland *n* sertum *nt*; corona *f*

garlic *n* allium *nt*

garment *n* vestimentum *nt*; vestitus *m*

garnish[1] *vt* decoro, orno ①; (season) condio ④

garnish[2] *n* ornamentum *nt*

garotte *vt* laqueo strangulo ①

garret *n* cenaculum *nt*

garrison[1] *n* praesidium *nt*

garrison[2] *vt* praesidium colloco ①

garrulous *adj* garrulus, loquax

gash[1] *n* vulnus *nt*; plaga *f*

gash[2] *vt* seco, vulnero ①

gasp[1] *n* anhelitus *m*

gasp[2] *vi* anhelo ①

gate *n* ianua *f*; ostium *nt*; fores *fpl*; (of a town) porta *f*

gateway *n* porta *f*

gather *vt* (assemble) congrego ①; (bring together) colligo; (of fruits) decerpo, lego; (pluck) carpo; (in logic) concludo ③; (suspect) suspicor ①
  ■ ∼ *vi* (assemble) convenio ④
  □ ∼ **round** *vi* convolo ①; confluo ③
  □ ∼ **up** colligo; (pick up) sublego ③

gathering *n* collectio *f*; (assembling) congregatio *f*; (assembly) coetus *m*

gaudiness *n* ornatus, nitor *m*; lautitia *f*

gaudy *adj* lautus, splendidus, speciosus

gauge[1] *vt* metior ④

gauge[2] *n* modulus *m*

gaunt *adj* macer

gay *adj* laetus, hilaris; floridus; splendidus

gaze[1] *n* conspectus; (fixed look) obtutus *m*

gaze[2] *vi* intueor ②; specto, contemplor ①

gear *n* instrumenta *ntpl*; arma *ntpl*; supellex *f*

gem *n* gemma; baca *f*

gender *n* genus *nt*

general[1] *adj* generalis; vulgaris, publicus, universus
  □ **in** ∼ in universum; (for the most part) plerumque

general[2] *n* dux, imperator *m*

generally *adv* generatim; universe; (commonly) plerumque, vulgo

generalship *n* ductus *m*; (skill of a commander) ars imperatoria *nt*

generate *vt* genero, procreo ①; gigno ③

generation *n* generatio *f*; (lineage) genus *nt*; (period of time) saeculum *nt*

generosity *n* liberalitas, generositas *f*; munificentia *f*

generous *adj* generosus; liberalis; munificus; magnanimus
  ■ ∼**ly** *adv* liberaliter, munifice

genial *adj* genialis, hilaris

geniality *n* geniale ingenium *nt*

genitals *n* genitalia *ntpl*

genius *n* ingenium *nt*; (nature) indoles *f*; (person) vir ingeniosus *m*

genteel *adj* elegans, urbanus

g

gentle *adj* (mild) lenis, mitis, clemens; (gradual) mollis

gentleman *n* homo nobilis; fig vir honestus; (well-bred man) homo liberalis *m*

gentleness *n* lenitas, clementia *f*

gently *adv* leniter; clementer; placide; (gradually) sensim; paulatim; pedetemptim

genuine *adj* sincerus; purus; verus; germanus
■ ∼**ly** *adv* sincere, vere

genus *n* genus *nt*

geography *n* geographia *f*

geometrical *adj* geometricus

geometry *n* geometria *f*

germ *n* germen *nt*

germinate *vi* germino, pullulo ①

germination *n* germinatio *f*; germinatus *m*

gesticulate *vi* gestum ago ③

gesticulation *n* gestus *m*

gesture *n* gestus, motus *m*

get *vt* adipiscor, consequor, acquiro ③; (by entreaty) impetro ①
■ ∼ *vi* (become) fio *ir*
□ ∼ **away** aufugio ③
□ ∼ **back** *vt* (receive) recupero ①; *vi* (return) reverto ③
□ ∼ **the better of** fig supero ①; praevaleo ②
□ ∼ **down** *vi* descendo ③
□ ∼ **hold of** prehendo ③; occupo ①
□ ∼ **off** *vi* aufugio; dimittor; absolvor ③
□ ∼ **on** (succeed) bene cedo, succedo ③
□ ∼ **out** *vi* exeo *ir*; (e curru) descendo ③
□ ∼ **over** *vt* traicio, transgredior ③; supero ①
□ ∼ **something done** curo ① aliquid faciendum
□ ∼ **rid of** amoveo ②; tollo ③
□ ∼ **through** pervenio ④; fig perago, perficio ③
□ ∼ **together** *vt* colligo, cogo ③; *vi* congrego ①
□ ∼ **up** surgo ③

ghastly *adj* (sallow) luridus; (pale) pallidus, pallens; (horrid, shocking) foedus

ghost *n* (phantom) larva *f*; (of a dead person) umbra *f*; manes *mpl*

ghostly *adj* (unsubstantial) inanis

giant[1] *n* gigas *m*

giant[2] *adj* praegrandis

gibberish *n* inanis strepitus *m*

gibbet *n* furca *f*; patibulum *nt*

gibe[1] *n* (sneer) sanna *f*; (mockery) ludibrium *nt*

gibe[2] *vt* illudo ③

giddiness *n* vertigo *f*; fig levitas, inconstantia *f*

giddy *adj* vertiginosus; fig levis, inconstans

gift *n* donum; beneficium, munus *nt*; (talent) dos *f*

gifted *adj* (endowed) praeditus; fig ingeniosus

gigantic *adj* praegrandis, ingens

giggle *vi* cachinno ①

gild *vt* inauro ①

ginger *n* zingiberi *nt*

giraffe *n* camelopardalis *f*

girdle *n* cingulum *nt*; balteus *m*; (of women) zona *f*

girl *n* puella, virgo *f*

girlhood *n* puellaris aetas *f*

girlish *adj* puellaris; virginalis; virgineus

girth *n* fascia; (of a horse) cingula *f*; (circuit) ambitus *m*

gist *n* (main point) summa *f*

give *vt* do, dono ①; confero *ir*; praebeo ②; (deliver) trado ③
□ ∼ **away** dono ①
□ ∼ **back** reddo ③
□ ∼ **in** *vi* (yield) cedo ③
□ ∼ **out** edo; emitto ③; nuntio ①; distribuo ③; *vi* (fail) deficio
□ ∼ **up** *vt* trado; (betray) prodo; (abandon) dimitto ③; *vi* (surrender) me dedo ③
□ ∼ **way** pedem refero *ir*; (yield) cedo; (comply with) obsequor ③ + *dat*

glad *adj* laetus, contentus; hilaris, libens
□ **be** ∼ gaudeo ②; laetor ①

gladden *vt* laetifico, hilaro, exhilaro ①

glade *n* nemus *nt*; saltus *m*

gladiator *n* gladiator *m*

gladly *adv* laete; libenter

gladness *n* gaudium *nt*; laetitia *f*

glamour *n* pulchritudo *f*

glance[1] *n* aspectus, obtutus *m*

glance[2] *vi* aspicio
□ ∼ **at** stringo, perstringo ③

gland *n* glandula *f*

glare[1] *n* fulgor, ardor *m*; (fierce look) oculi torvi *mpl*

glare[2] *vi* (of light) fulgeo, ardeo [2]; (of expression) torvis oculis aspicio [3]

glaring *adj* fulgens; fig manifestus

glass[1] *n* vitrum; (mirror) speculum *nt*; (for drinking) calix *m*; (glassware) vitrea *ntpl*

glass[2] *adj* vitreus

gleam[1] *n* fulgor, splendor *m*; iubar *nt*; fig aura *f*

gleam[2] *vi* corusco, mico [1]; fulgeo [2]

gleaming *adj* coruscus, renidens

glee *n* laetitia *f*; gaudium *nt*

gleeful *adj* laetus

glib *adj* volubilis
■ ~**ly** *adv* volubiliter

glide *vi* labor, prolabor [3]

glimmer[1] *n* lux dubia *f*; crepusculum *nt*; ▶**gleam**

glimmer[2] *vi* subluceo [2]

glimpse *n* aspectus *m*
□ **have a ~ of** dispicio [3]

glisten *vi* luceo, fulgeo [2]; radio [1]

glitter[1] *n* fulgor *m*

glitter[2] *vi* fulgeo [2]; radio, mico, corusco [1]

gloat *vi* (over) oculos pasco [3]

globe *n* globus; fig orbis terrae *or* terrarum *m*

globule *n* globulus *m*; pilula *f*

gloom *n* tenebrae *fpl*; caligo; fig tristitia *f*

gloominess *n* ▶**gloom**

gloomy *adj* tenebrosus, nubilus; fig maestus, tristis

glorify *vt* celebro, glorifico [1]

glorious *adj* gloriosus, illustris; splendidus; eximius

glory[1] *n* gloria; laus, fama *f*

glory[2] *vi* glorior [1]; superbio [4]

gloss *n* (lustre) nitor *m*

glossy *adj* nitidus; expolitus; levis

glove *n* digitabulum *nt*

glow[1] *n* ardor, fervor, calor *m*

glow[2] *vi* candeo, caleo [2]; excandesco [3]

glowing *adj* candens, fervens; fig fervidus

glow-worm *n* cicindela, lampyris *f*

glue[1] *n* gluten, glutinum *nt*

glue[2] *vt* glutino, conglutino [1]

glum *adj* tristis, deiectus

glut[1] *n* satietas *f*

glut[2] *vt* satio, saturo [1]; (feast) pasco [3]

glutton *n* helluo, homo gulosus *m*

gluttonous *adj* gulosus, edax

gluttony *n* gula *f*

gnarled *adj* nodosus

gnash *vt* frendeo, infrendeo [2]; dentibus strido [3]

gnat *n* culex *m*

gnaw *vt&i* rodo [3]

go *vi* eo *ir*; proficiscor, incedo [3]; cedo [3]; fig (become) fio *ir*
□ ~ **around** circumeo *ir*; fig aggredior [3]
□ ~ **abroad** peregre abeo *ir*
□ ~ **after** sequor [3]
□ ~ **astray** aberro, vagor [1]
□ ~ **away** abeo *ir*
□ ~ **back** revertor [3]
□ ~ **before** praeeo *ir*; antecedo [3]
□ ~ **beyond** egredior; fig excedo [3]
□ ~ **by** praetereo *ir*; fig (adhere to) sto [1] + *abl*
□ ~ **down** descendo; (of the sun) occido [3]
□ ~ **for** peto [3]
□ ~ **forth** exeo *ir*
□ ~ **in(to)** ineo *ir*, ingredior [3], intro [1]
□ ~ **off** abeo *ir*
□ ~ **on** pergo [3]; (happen) fio *ir*; (succeed, thrive) succedo [3]
□ ~ **out** exeo *ir*; fig (of fire) extinguor [3]
□ ~ **over** transgredior; fig (a subject) percurro [3]
□ ~ **round** circumeo (locum) *ir*
□ ~ **through** transeo; obeo *ir*, pertendo [3]; (endure) patior [3]
□ ~ **to** adeo *ir*; accedo [3]
□ ~ **towards** peto [3]
□ ~ **under** subeo *ir*
□ ~ **up** ascendo [3]
□ **let ~** dimitto; (let fall) omitto [3]
□ ~ **without** careo, egeo [2] *both* + *abl*

goad[1] *n* pertica *f*; stimulus *m*

goad[2] *vt* instigo; fig stimulo [1]

goal *n* (in the Roman circus) meta, calx *f*; fig finis *m/f*

goat *n* caper *m*
□ **she-~** capra *f*

gobble *vi* voro, devoro [1]; exsorbeo [2]

go-between *n* internuntius *m*; internuntia *f*; conciliator *m*; conciliatrix *f*

goblet *n* poculum *nt*; scyphus *m*; ▶**cup**

god *n* deus *m*; divus *m*; numen *nt*

goddess *n* dea, diva *f*

g

godly *adj* pius, sanctus

gold *n* aurum *nt*
■ ~ *adj* aureus

golden *adj* aureus; (yellow) flavus

goldfinch *n* carduelis *f*

goldfish *n* hippurus *m*

gold-mine *n* aurifodina *f*

goldsmith *n* aurifex *m*

good¹ *adj* bonus; (effective) efficax;
salutaris; utilis; (kind-hearted) benevolus
□ ~ **for nothing** nequam
□ **do** ~ **to** prosum *ir* + *dat*
□ **make** ~ compenso ①; restituo ③;
sano ①

good² *n* (profit) commodum, lucrum *nt*;
salus; utilitas *f*; (in abstract sense)
bonum *nt*

good³ *int* bene! euge!

goodbye *int* vale, valete

good-humoured *adj* facilis

good-natured *adj* comis, benignus,
facilis

goodness *n* bonitas; probitas;
benignitas *f*

goods *n* bona *ntpl*; res *f*

goodwill *n* benevolentia; gratia *f*

goose *n* anser *m*

gore¹ *n* cruor *m*; sanies *f*

gore² *vt* cornu ferio ④

gorge¹ *n* fauces; angustiae *fpl*

gorge² *vi* devoro, ingurgito ①

gorgeous *adj* nitidus, lautus,
splendidus; magnificus

gorse *n* ulex *m*

gory *adj* cruentus, cruentatus,
sanguineus, sanguinolentus

gossip¹ *n* (idle talk) nugae, gerrae *fpl*;
(person) homo garrulus *m*; mulier
loquax *f*

gossip² *vi* garrio ④

gouge *vt* evello, eruo ③

gout *n* morbus articularis *m*; (in the feet)
podagra *f*

govern *vt* impero, imperito ① *both*
+ *dat*; rego ③; (check) coerceo ②;
moderor ①

governess *n* magistra *f*

government *n* gubernatio (civitatis);
administratio *f*; imperium, regnum
nt; provincia *f*

governor *n* gubernator; praefectus;
dominus *m*

gown *n* (woman's garment) stola; (of a Roman
citizen) toga *f*

grab *vt* corripio ③

grace *n* gratia; (elegance, *etc.*) venustas *f*;
veneres *fpl*; decor, lepos *m*; (pardon)
venia *f*
■ **Graces** *pl* Gratiae *fpl*

graceful *adj* elegans; lepidus,
venustus
■ ~**ly** *adv* venuste; eleganter, lepide

gracious *adj* benignus; clemens,
humanus; (propitious) aequus, propitius
■ ~**ly** *adv* benigne; humane

graciousness *n* benignitas,
humanitas, clementia *f*

grade *n* gradus, ordo *m*

gradient *n* clivus *m*

gradual *adj* per gradus
■ ~**ly** *adv* gradatim, pedetemptim,
paulatim

graft¹ *n* (of plants) insitum *nt*; surculus *m*

graft² *vt* insero ③

grain *n* granum *nt*; fig particula *f*

grammar *n* grammatica *f*

grammatical *adj* grammaticus

granary *n* horreum, granarium *nt*

grand *adj* grandis, magnificus;
praeclarus, splendidus

grandchild *n* nepos *m*; neptis *f*

granddaughter *n* neptis *f*

grandeur *n* magnificentia; granditas;
sublimitas; maiestas *f*; splendor *m*

grandfather *n* avus *m*

grandmother *n* avia *f*

grandson *n* nepos *m*

grant¹ *vt* concedo, permitto ③;
(acknowledge) fateor ②; do ①; praebeo ②

grant² *n* concessio *f*

grape *n* acinus *m*; uva *f*
□ **bunch of** ~**s** racemus *m*

graphic *adj* expressus
■ ~**ally** *adv* expresse

grapple *vi* luctor ①

grasp¹ *vt* prehendo, corripio ③; affecto
①; (understand) teneo ②
□ ~ **at** capto ①; fig appeto ③

grasp² *n* complexus *m*; (power) potestas;
(hand) manus *f*

grasping *adj* avidus, cupidus; avarus

grass *n* gramen *nt*; herba *f*

grasshopper *n* grillus *m*

grassy *adj* graminosus, gramineus, herbosus, herbidus

grate¹ *n* clathri, cancelli *mpl*

grate² *vt* (grind) tero, contero ③
■ ~ *vi* strideo ②

grateful *adj* gratus, iucundus
■ ~ly *adv* grate; (thankfully) grato animo

gratification *n* expletio; gratificatio; (pleasure, delight) voluptas; oblectatio *f*

gratify *vt* (indulge) indulgeo ②; gratificor ① *both* + *dat*

gratifying *adj* gratus

grating *n* clathri, cancelli *mpl*; (sound) stridor *m*

gratitude *n* gratia *f*; gratus animus *m*

gratuitous *adj* gratuitus

gratuity *n* stips *f*; munus, praemium *nt*

grave¹ *adj* gravis, serius; (stern) severus
■ ~ly *adv* graviter; severe

grave² *n* sepulcrum, bustum *nt*; tumulus *m*

gravel *n* glarea *f*; sabulo *m*

gravestone *n* monumentum *nt*

gravity *n* gravitas *f*; pondus *nt*; (personal) severitas; dignitas; tristitia *f*

graze¹ *vt* (pasture) pascor; (touch lightly) stringo, perstringo ③; (scrape) rado ③

graze² *n* vulnus *nt*

grease¹ *vt* ungo, perungo, illino ③

grease² *n* unguen, pingue *nt*; arvina *f*; (for wheels) axungia *f*

greasy *adj* pinguis; unctus; (dirty) squalidus

great *adj* magnus; ingens; amplus, grandis; (powerful) potens
□ so ~ tantus
□ as ~ as tantus, quantus

great-grandfather *n* proavus *m*

great-hearted *adj* magnanimus

greatly *adv* magnopere, valde

greatness *n* magnitudo *f*

greaves *n* ocreae *fpl*

Greece *n* Graecia *f*

greed *n* aviditas; voracitas *f*

greedily *adv* avide, cupide

greediness *n* aviditas; voracitas *f*

greedy *adj* avidus, avarus, cupidus; vorax

Greek *adj* & *n* Graecus *m*

green¹ *adj* viridis; virens; prasinus; fig recens; (unripe) crudus, immaturus
□ **become** ~ viresco ③

green² *n* color viridis; (lawn) locus *or* campus herbidus *m*
□ ~s holera *ntpl*

greengrocer *n* holerum venditor *m*

greenish *adj* subviridis

greenness *n* color viridis *m*; (in abstract sense) viriditas *f*; fig immaturitas *f*

greet *vt* saluto ①; salutem dico ③ + *dat*

greeting *n* salutatio, salus *f*

gregarious *adj* gregalis

grey *adj* cinereus; (blue-grey) glaucus; (with age) canus
□ **become** ~ canesco ③

grey-headed *adj* canus

greyish *adj* canescens

greyness *n* canities *f*

grief *n* dolor, maeror; luctus *m*; aegritudo; molestia, tristitia *f*

grievance *n* querimonia, querela, iniuria *f*; malum *nt*

grieve *vt* dolore afficio (aliquem) ③; excrucio, sollicito ①
■ ~ *vi* doleo, lugeo ②

grievous *adj* gravis, durus, atrox, acerbus

griffin *n* gryps *m*

grill *vt* torreo ②

grim *adj* torvus; trux, truculentus, horridus
■ ~ly *adv* horride

grimace *n* vultus distortus *m*; oris depravatio *f*

grime *n* squalor *m*; ▸ dirt

grimy *adj* squalidus

grin¹ *vi* ringor ③; (laugh) rideo ②

grin² *n* rictus *m*

grind *vt* (corn) molo ③; (in a mortar) contundo ③; (on a whetstone) exacuo ③; (the teeth) dentibus frendeo ③

grindstone *n* cos *f*

grip¹ *n* manus *f*

grip² *vt* comprehendo ③

grisly *adj* horrendus, horridus

gristle *n* cartilago *f*

gristly *adj* cartilagineus, cartilaginosus

grit *n* glarea *f*; arena *f*, sabulo *m*

gritty *adj* arenosus, sabulosus

groan¹ *vi* gemo, ingemo ③

groan² *n* gemitus *m*

grocer *n* condimentarius *m*

groin *n* inguen *nt*

groom¹ *n* agaso, equiso *m*

groom² *vt* (equum) curo ①
■ ~ *n* (bridegroom) sponsus *m*

groove *n* canalis *m*; stria *f*

grope *vi* praetento ①

gross *adj* (fat) crassus, densus; pinguis; (coarse) rusticus, incultus; (dreadful) atrox; (whole) totus
■ ~**ly** *adv* graviter; crasse; turpiter

grotesque *adj* absurdus, ridiculus

ground *n* solum *nt*; terra; humus *f*; (place) locus *m*; fig causa *f*
□ **on the** ~ humi
□ **gain** ~ proficio ③
□ **lose** ~ recedo ③
□ ~**s** (sediment) faex *f*

groundless *adj* vanus, falsus; fictus

groundwork *n* subtructio *f*; fig fundamentum *nt*

group¹ *n* corona, turba *f*; globus, circulus *m*

group² *vt* dispono ③
■ ~ *vi* circulor ①

grouse *n* lagopus, tetrao *m*

grove *n* lucus, saltus *m*; nemus *nt*

grovel *vi* provolvor ③; fig servio ④

grovelling *adj* humilis, supplex, servilis

grow *vi* cresco ③; (increase) augeor ②; adolesco ③; (become) fio *ir*
■ ~ *vt* (cultivate) sero ③; (a beard, *etc.*) promitto ③
□ ~ **out of** fig orior ④; nascor ③; (grow up) adolesco ③

grower *n* cultor *m*

growl¹ *n* fremitus *m*

growl² *vi* fremo ③; mussito, murmuro ①

grown-up *adj* adultus; puber

growth *n* incrementum *nt*; auctus
□ **full** ~ maturitas *f*

grub *n* vermiculus *m*

grudge¹ *n* odium *nt*; simultas *f*
□ **hold a** ~ **against** succenseo ② + *dat*

grudge² *vt* invideo ②

grudgingly *adv* invite, gravate

gruff *adj* asper, taetricus, torvus
■ ~**ly** *adv* aspere

grumble *vi* murmuro, mussito ①; queror ③

grunt¹ *vi* grunnio ④

grunt² *n* grunnitus *m*

guarantee¹ *n* fides, satisdatio *f*

guarantee² *vt* satisdo, praesto ①; (promise) spondeo ②

guard¹ *n* custodia; tutela *f*; (military) praesidium *nt*; (person) custos *m/f*
□ **be on one's** ~ caveo ②

guard² *vt* custodio ④; defendo, protego ③; munio ④; (against) caveo ②

guarded *adj* cautus, circumspectus

guardian *n* custos; praeses *m/f*; defensor; (of orphans) tutor; curator *m*

guess¹ *vt&i* conicio ③; divino, suspicor ①; (solve) solvo ③

guess² *n* coniectura *f*

guest *n* hospes; (stranger) advena; (at a feast) conviva *m/f*

guidance *n* ductus *m*; cura, curatio, administratio *f*

guide¹ *n* dux *m/f*; ductor *m*

guide² *vt* duco ③; (rule) guberno ①; rego ③

guidebook *n* itinerarium *nt*

guild *n* collegium *nt*

guile *n* dolus, astus *m*; astutia *f*

guilt *n* culpa, noxa *f*; crimen, peccatum *nt*

guiltless *adj* innocens, insons, innocuus

guilty *adj* sons, nocens, noxius + *abl or gen*; sceleratus

guise *n* (manner) modus; mos *m*; (appearance) species *f*

guitar *n* cithara *f*

gulf *n* sinus *m*; (abyss) vorago *f*

gullet *n* gula *f*; fauces *fpl*

gullibility *n* credulitas *f*

gullible *adj* credulus

gum¹ *n* (of the mouth) gingiva *f*; (adhesive) cummi *nt*, cummis *f*

gum² *vt* glutino ①

gush *vi* (out) effluo, profluo ③; prosilio ④; scateo ②

gust *n* flatus *m*; flamen *nt*

gusty *adj* procellosus

gut¹ *n* intestinum *nt*
□ ~**s** viscera *ntpl*

gut² *vt* exentero ①; fig exinanio ④

gutter *n* canalis *m*; (of streets) colliciae *fpl*

gymnasium *n* gymnasium *nt*; palaestra *f*

gymnastic *adj* gymnicus, gymnasticus

gymnastics *n* palaestrica *f*

gyrate *vi* volvor ③

gyration *n* gyrus *m*

Hh

habit *n* (custom) consuetudo *f*; mos *m*; (dress) vestitus *m*; (state) habitus *m*

habitable *adj* habitabilis
□ **not** ∼ inhabitabilis

habitation *n* habitatio, domus *f*

habitual *adj* inveteratus, assuetus, consuetus, solitus
■ ∼**ly** *adv* de (ex) more

hack *vt* concido ③; mutilo ①

hackneyed *adj* tritus; pervulgatus

haemorrhage *n* haemorrhagia *f*

hag *n* anus *f*

haggard *adj* macer, exsanguis

haggle *vt* cavillor; (bargain) licitor ①

hail¹ *n* grando *f*

hail² *vt* (salute) saluto ①
■ ∼ *vi* grandino ①

hail³ *int* salve! ave!

hailstone *n* grando *f*

hair *n* capillus, crinis *m*, caesaries, coma *f*; (single) pilus *m*; (of animals) villus *m*
□ **grey** ∼ canities *f*

hairdresser *n* capitis et capilli concinnator *m*; ornatrix *f*

hairy *adj* pilosus; crinitus; comatus; (shaggy) hirsutus

halcyon *n* alcedo, alcyon *f*

half *adj* dimidius
■ ∼ *n* dimidia pars *f*; dimidium *nt*

half-dead *adj* semianimis

half-eaten *adj* semiesus

half-hearted *adj* piger

half-yearly *adj* semestris

hall *n* atrium; (entrance-∼) vestibulum; (for business) conciliabulum *nt*; (of the senate) curia *f*

hallucination *n* alucinatio *f*; error *m*; somnium *nt*

halt¹ *vi* consisto ③; fig haesito ①

halt² *n* pausa, mora *f*

halve *vt* ex aequo divido ③

hammer¹ *n* malleus *m*

hammer² *vt* cudo ③

hamper¹ *n* qualus *m*; fiscina *f*

hamper² *vt* impedio ④; implico, retardo ①

hand¹ *n* manus, palma *f*; (handwriting) chirographum *nt*; (of a dial) gnomon *m*
□ **at** ∼ ad manum; prae manibus; praesto
□ **by** ∼ manu
□ ∼ **in** ∼ iunctis manibus
□ ∼ **to** ∼ comminus
□ **in** ∼ (of money) prae manu
□ **on the other** ∼ altera parte
□ **on the right** ∼ ad dextram

hand² *vt* trado ③
□ ∼ **out** distribuo ③
□ ∼ **over** trado ③
□ ∼ **round** circumfero ③

handcuffs *npl* manicae *fpl*

handful *n* manipulus, pugillus *m*

handicap *n* impedimentum *nt*

handicraft *n* ars *f*; artificium *nt*

handiwork *n* opus *nt*; opera *f*

handkerchief *n* sudarium *nt*

handle¹ *vt* tracto ①

handle² *n* manubrium *nt*; ansa *f*; (of a sword) capulus *m*

handsome *adj* pulcher, formosus; honestus; elegans, bellus

handwriting *n* manus *f*; (manuscript) chirographum *nt*

handy *adj* (useful) utilis

hang *vt* suspendo
■ ∼ *vi* pendeo, dependeo ②
□ **let** ∼ demitto ③
□ ∼ **back** haesito ①
□ ∼ **over** immineo ② + *dat*

hanger-on n asseclā; fig parasitus m

hangman n carnifex m

hanker vi desidero ①; expeto ③

haphazard adj fortuitus

happen vi accido ③; evenio ④; contingo ③; fio ir

happiness n vita beata; (good fortune) felicitas f

happy adj felix, fortunatus, faustus; beatus

harangue[1] n contio f

harangue[2] vt&i contionor ①

harass vt fatigo; vexo; inquieto ①; lacesso ③

harbinger n praenuntius, antecursor m

harbour[1] n portus m; fig refugium, perfugium nt

harbour[2] vt excipio ③; (feelings, etc.) habeo ②; afficior ③ + abl

hard adj durus; fig (difficult) arduus; (severe) acer, rigidus; (hard-hearted) crudelis

harden vt duro; induro ①
  ■ ~ vi duresco; obduresco ③

hard-hearted adj durus, ferreus, inhumanus, crudelis

hard-heartedness n crudelitas f; ingenium durum nt

hardihood n audacia f

hardiness n robur m

hardly adv (with difficulty, scarcely) vix; aegre

hardness n duritia f

hardship n aerumna; difficultas f; labor m; dura ntpl

hardware n ferramenta ntpl

hardy adj durus; robustus

hare n lepus m

harem n gynaeceum nt

harm[1] n damnum nt; iniuria; fraus; noxa; calamitas f

harm[2] vt laedo ③; noceo ② + dat

harmful adj noxius, perniciosus

harmless adj (things) innocuus; innoxius; (person) innocens

harmonious adj concors, consonus; canorus; fig concors, consentiens

harmonize vt compono ③
  ■ ~ vi concino ③; fig consentio ④

harmony n harmonia f; concentus m; fig concordia f

harness[1] n ornatus m

harness[2] vt adiungo, iungo, subiungo ③; (saddle) insterno ③

harp n lyra f

harpist n psaltes m; psaltria f

harpoon[1] n iaculum nt

harpoon[2] vt iaculor ①, transfigo ③

harridan n anus, vetula f

harrow[1] n rastrum nt

harrow[2] vt occo ①; fig crucio, excrucio ①

harsh adj asper; (in sound) discors, stridulus; (hoarse) raucus; (in taste) acer; fig gravis; severus, durus
  ■ ~ly adv aspere; graviter, acerbe, duriter

harshness n asperitas; acerbitas; saevitia; severitas f

harvest[1] n messis f

harvest[2] vt meto ③

harvester n messor m

hash n:
  □ **make a ~ of** male gero ③ + acc

haste n celeritas; festinatio, properatio f
  □ **in ~** propere; properanter
  □ **make ~** propero, festino ①

hasten vt accelero, propero; (hurry on) praecipito ①
  ■ ~ vi propero, festino ①

hastily adv propere; raptim

hastiness n celeritas f

hasty adj properus; praeceps; fig iracundus

hat n pilleus, galerus, petasus m

hatchet n ascia, securis, bipennis f

hate[1] vt odi, perodi ③; destestor ①

hate[2] n ▶ **hatred**

hateful adj odiosus, invisus; inamabilis

hatred n odium nt; invidia, simultas, inimicitia f

haughtiness n superbia; arrogantia f; fastidium nt

haughty adj superbus; arrogans; fastidiosus

haul vt traho, subduco ③

haunt[1] vt frequento ①; fig (of spirits) adsum ir

haunt[2] n latebra f; lustra ntpl

have *vt* habeo; possideo, teneo ②
□ ~ **on** gero ③
□ **I would ~ you know** velim scias

haven *n* portus *m*; fig salus *f*

havoc *n* strages, caedes *f*

hawk *n* accipiter *m*

hay *n* faenum *nt*

hazard *n* periculum, discrimen *nt*;
(chance) alea *f*

hazardous *adj* periculosus; anceps

haze *n* nebula *f*; vapor *m*

hazel[1] *n* (tree) corylus *f*

hazel[2] *adj* colurnus; (of colour) spadix,
flavus

hazy *adj* nebulosus, caliginosus; fig
(doubtful) dubius, ambiguus

he *pn* hic, is, ille

head[1] *n* caput *nt*; vertex *m*; also fig (mental
faculty) ingenium *nt*; (chief) princeps *m/f*;
(top) culmen, cacumen *nt*

head[2] *adj* princeps, summus

head[3] *vt* dux sum *ir* + *gen*; praesum *ir* +
dat
□ ~ **for** peto ③

headache *n* capitis dolor *m*

headband *n* vitta *f*

heading *n* titulus *m*

headland *n* promontorium *nt*

headlong *adj* praeceps; temerarius

headquarters *n* praetorium *nt*

headstrong *adj* pervicax, contumax;
▶ **stubborn**

heal *vt* sano ①; medeor ②
■ ~ *vi* sanesco; (wounds) coalesco ③;
coeo *ir*

healing[1] *adj* salutaris, saluber

healing[2] *n* sanatio *f*

health *n* sanitas, valetudo, salus *f*

healthful *adj* salutaris, saluber

healthiness *n* firma valetudo; (of place
or things) salubritas *f*

healthy *n* sanus; integer; (places or things)
saluber

heap[1] *n* acervus, cumulus *m*;
congeries *f*

heap[2] *vt* acervo, coacervo, accumulo ①

hear *vt&i* audio; exaudio ④; ausculto ①;
(find out) certior fio *ir*

hearing *n* (act) auditio *f*; (sense)
auditus *m*

hearsay *n* fama *f*; rumor *m*

hearse *n* feretrum *nt*

heart *n* cor *nt*; fig (feeling) pectus *nt*;
(courage) animus *m*
□ **have the ~ to** sustineo, audeo ②

heartbreaking *adj* miserabilis

heartbroken *adj* angoribus
confectus, afflictus

hearten *vt* confirmo ①

hearth *n* focus *m*

heartily *adv* sincere; effuse; valde;
vere; ex animo

heartless *adj* ferreus, crudelis,
inhumanus
■ ~**ly** *adv* inhumane, crudeliter

heartlessness *n* inhumanitas,
saevitia *f*

heat[1] *n* calor, ardor; fervor, aestus *m*

heat[2] *vt* calefacio, incendo ③
■ ~ *vi* calesco ③

heating *n* calefactio *f*

heave *vt* attollo ③; levo ①; (sighs, *etc.*)
traho, duco ③
■ ~ *vi* tumeo ②; fluctuo ①

heaven *n* caelum *nt*; fig di, superi *mpl*

heavenly *adj* caelestis, divinus

heaviness *n* gravitas; (slowness)
tarditas; (dullness) stultitia *f*; (drowsiness)
sopor *m*

heavy *adj* gravis; onerosus,
ponderosus

hedge *n* saepes *f*; saeptum *nt*

hedgehog *n* erinaceus, ericius *m*

heed *n*:
□ **pay ~ to** curo ①
□ **take ~** caveo, praecaveo ②

heedless *adj* incautus; temerarius

heel *n* calx *f*

heifer *n* iuvenca *f*

height *n* altitudo; (tallness) proceritas *f*;
(top) culmen *nt*; (hill) clivus, collis,
tumulus *m*

heighten *vt* altius effero *ir*; fig
amplifico; exaggero ①

heinous *adj* atrox; nefarius; foedus

heir *n* (also **heiress**) heres *m/f*

heirloom *n* res hereditaria *f*

hell *n* Tartarus *m*

hellish *adj* infernus, nefarius

hello *int* salve, salvete; ave, avete

helm *n* gubernaculum *nt*; calvus *m*

helmet *n* cassis, galea *f*

helmsman *n* gubernator, rector
navis *m*

help[1] *n* auxilium *nt*; opem *f acc sing*

help[2] *vt* iuvo, adiuvo ①; succurro ③; subvenio ④ *both* + *dat*; auxilior, sublevo ①

helper *n* adiutor, auxiliator *m*

helpful *adj* utilis

helpless *adj* inops

helplessness *n* inopia *f*

hem[1] *n* ora *f*; limbus *m*

hem[2] *vt* praetexo; *fig* cingo ③
□ ∼ **in** circumsideo ②

hemisphere *n* hemisphaerium *nt*

hemlock *n* cicuta *f*

hen *n* gallina *f*

hence *adv* hinc

henceforth *adv* posthac; dehinc, in posterum

henhouse *n* gallinarium *nt*

henpecked *adj fig* uxorius

her[1] *pn* eam

her[2] *adj* suus; eius

herald[1] *n* caduceator; (crier) praeco *m*

herald[2] *vt* nuntio ①

herb *n* herba *f*

herd[1] *n* grex *m*; *fig* (in contempt) vulgus *m*

herd[2] *vi* congregor ①

herdsman *n* pastor; armentarius; bubulcus *m*

here *adv* hic; (hither) huc
□ ∼ **and there** raro

hereditary *adj* hereditarius

heritage *n* hereditas *f*

hero *n* heros, vir fortis; (in a play) qui primas partes agit *m*

heroic *adj* heroicus
■ ∼**ally** *adv* fortiter

heroine *n* heroina; virago; (of a play) quae primas partes agit *f*

heroism *n* virtus, fortitudo *f*

heron *n* ardea *f*

herring *n* harenga *f*

hers *pn* eius, illius

herself *pn* ipsa; (reflexive) se

hesitant *adj* haesitans
■ ∼**ly** *adv* cunctanter

hesitate *vi* dubito, haesito, cunctor, cesso ①

hesitation *n* dubitatio; haesitatio *f*

hew *vt* dolo ①; caedo ③; seco ①

hey *int* ohe!

hiccough[1] *n* (also **hiccup**) singultus *m*

hiccough[2] *vi* (also **hiccup**) singulto ①

hide[1] *n* pellis *f*; corium *nt*

hide[2] *vt* abdo, condo, occulo, abscondo ③; celo ①; (dissemble) dissimulo ①
■ ∼ *vi* lateo ②

hideous *adj* foedus, turpis, deformis

hiding *n* (beating) verberatio *f*

hiding-place *n* latebra *f*; latibulum *nt*

hierarchy *n* sacerdotium, collegium *nt*; (ranking) ordo *m*

high *adj* altus, excelsus; sublimis; (tall) procerus; (of price) pretiosus; carus; *fig* magnus; amplus
■ ∼ *adv* alte; sublime; valde; vehementer
□ **aim** ∼ magnas res appeto ③

highland *n* regio aspera *or* montuosa *f*

highly *adv* (much) valde, multum; (value) magni, permagni

high priest *n* summus sacerdos, pontifex maximus *m*

high-spirited *adj* generosus, animosus

highway *n* via *f*

highwayman *n* latro, grassator *m*

hike *vi* ambulo ①

hilarious *adj* hilaris, festivus

hill *n* collis; tumulus; (slope) clivus *m*

hilly *adj* montuosus, clivosus

hilt *n* (of a sword) capulus *m*

him *pn* eum, hunc, illum
□ **of** ∼ eius, huius; illius; de illo

himself *pn* ipse; (reflexive) se

hind *adj* posterior, aversus

hinder *vt* impedio ④; obsto ① + *dat*; retardo ①; (prevent) prohibeo ②

hindrance *n* impedimentum *nt*

hinge *n* cardo *m*

hint[1] *n* indicium *nt*; nutus *m*; significatio *f*

hint[2] *vt&i* innuo, suggero ③; summoneo ②
□ ∼ **at** perstringo ③

hip *n* coxa, coxendix *f*

hippopotamus *n* hippopotamus *m*

hire[1] *n* merces *f*; stipendium *nt*

hire[2] *vt* conduco ③; loco ①

hired *adj* conductus, conducticius; mercenarius

his *adj & pn* eius, huius; illius, ipsius
  □ ∼ **own** suus, proprius

hiss¹ *vt&i* sibilo ①; strideo ②

hiss² *n* sibilus; stridor *m*

historian *n* historicus *m*

historic *adj* historicus
  ■ ∼**ally** *adv* historice

history *n* historia, memoria rerum
gestarum *f*; res *f*; (narrative) narratio *f*

hit *vt* ferio ④; percutio ③
  □ ∼ **upon** (discover) invenio, reperio ④

hitch *n* impedimentum *nt*; mora *f*

hither *adv* huc
  □ ∼ **and thither** huc illuc

hitherto *adv* adhuc

hive *n* alvus *f*; alvearium *nt*

hoard¹ *n* acervus *m*

hoard² *vt* coacervo ①

hoarder *n* accumulator *m*

hoar-frost *n* pruina *f*

hoarse *adj* raucus
  □ **get** ∼ irraucesco ③
  ■ ∼**ly** *adv* rauca voce

hoarseness *n* raucitas *f*

hoax¹ *n* ludificatio *f*; fraus *f*; dolus *m*

hoax² *vt* ludificor ①

hobble *vi* claudico ①

hobby *n* studium *nt*; cura *f*

hoe¹ *n* sarculum, pastinum *nt*

hoe² *vt* sarculo ①; pastino ①; (weeds)
pecto ③

hog *n* sus, porcus *m*

hoist *vt* sublevo ①; tollo ③

hold¹ *vt* teneo; possideo, habeo ②;
(contain) capio ③
  ■ ∼ *vi* permaneo ②; (think) existimo ①;
censeo ②
  □ ∼ **back** *vt* retineo ②; *vi* cunctor ①
  □ ∼ **forth** *vi* contionem habeo ②
  □ ∼ **in** inhibeo, cohibeo ②
  □ ∼ **off** abstineo ②
  □ ∼ **out** porrigo, extendo ③; (offer)
praebeo ②; fig ostendo ③; (endure) duro ①;
(persevere) obduro, persevero ①
  □ ∼ **together** contineo ②
  □ ∼ **up** (lift up) attollo ③; sustineo ②;
(delay) moror ①
  □ ∼ **with** consentio ④

hold² *n* manus; custodia *f*; (influence)
momentum *nt*; potestas *f*; (of a ship)
alveus *m*

holder *n* possessor *m*; colonus *m*;
(handle) manubrium *nt*

hole *n* foramen *nt*; rima *f*; fig latebra *f*;
(of mice, *etc.*) cavum *nt*

holiday *n* dies festus *m*
  ■ ∼**s** *pl* feriae *fpl*

holiness *n* sanctitas, religio, pietas *f*

hollow¹ *adj* cavus; concavus; fig vanus

hollow² *n* caverna *f*; cavum *nt*;
(depression) lacuna *f*

hollow³ *vt* cavo, excavo ①

hollowness *n* fig vanitas *f*

holm-oak *n* ilex *f*

holy *adj* sanctus; sacer, religiosus;
(dutiful) pius

homage *n* obsequium *nt*; cultus *m*;
observantia *f*
  □ **pay** ∼ **to** colo ③; observo ①

home¹ *n* domicilium *nt*; domus *f*
  □ **at** ∼ domi

home² *adj* domesticus
  ■ ∼ *adv* (homewards) domum

home-bred *adj* domesticus,
vernaculus

homeless *adj* tecto carens, profugus

homely *adj* (unsophisticated) simplex;
rudis; incompositus; rusticus

home-made *adj* domesticus,
vernaculus

homesick *n* suorum desiderium *nt*

homeward *adv* domum

homicide *n* (person) homicida *m*; (deed)
homicidium *nt*

honest *adj* probus; sincerus; integer,
verus
  ■ ∼**ly** *adv* probe, sincere, integre,
vere

honesty *n* probitas, sinceritas,
integritas *f*

honey *n* mel *nt*

honeycomb *n* favus *m*

honorary *adj* honorarius

honour¹ *n* honos *m*; fama, laus, gloria;
honestas, fides *f*; (high position) dignitas *f*

honour² *vt* honoro; celebro ①; (hold in ∼)
in honore habeo ②; (pay homage to) colo ③;
observo ①

honourable *adj* honestus;
honorificus; bonus

hood *n* cucullus *m*; palliolum *nt*

hoodwink *vt* ludificor ①

hoof *n* ungula *f*

hook¹ *n* hamus; uncus *m*

hook² *vt* inunco ①; fig capio ③

hooked *adj* hamatus; (crooked) curvatus, aduncus, curvus, recurvus

hoop *n* circulus *m*

hoot *vt&i* gemo, queror ③; acclamo ①; explodo ③

hop *vi* salio ④; subsulto ①

hope[1] *n* spes *f*

hope[2] *vt* spero ①
 □ **~ for** exspecto ①

hopeful *adj* bonae spei
 ■ **~ly** *adv* cum magna spe

hopeless *adj* exspes; desperatus
 ■ **~ly** *adv* sine spe, desperanter

horde *n* turba *f*; ▶ **crowd**

horizon *n* orbis finiens *m*

horizontal *adj* libratus
 ■ **~ly** *adv* ad libram

horn *n* cornu *nt*; (to blow on) bucina *f*; cornu *nt*

hornet *n* crabro *m*

horoscope *n* horoscopus *m*; genesis *f*

horrible *adj* horribilis, foedus, nefarius

horrid *adj* horridus, horrens, immanis

horrific *adj* horrificus, terribilis

horrify *vt* horrifico ①; terreo, exterreo ②

horror *n* horror, pavor *m*; (hatred) odium *nt*

horse *n* equus *m*; equitatus *m*

horseback *n*:
 □ **on ~** equo, ex equo
 □ **ride on ~** equito ①

horseman *n* eques *m*

horse-race *n* curriculum equorum *nt*; certatio equestris *f*

horseshoe *n* solea *f*

horticulture *n* hortorum cultus *m*

hose *n* (pipe) tubulus *m*

hospitable *adj* hospitalis, liberalis, munificus

hospital *n* valetudinarium *nt*

hospitality *n* hospitium *nt*; hospitalitas; liberalitas *f*

host *n* (of guests) hospes *m*; (at an inn) caupo *m*; (crowd) multitudo *f*; (army) exercitus *m*

hostage *n* obses *m*/*f*

hostess *n* hospita; (at an inn) caupona *f*

hostile *adj* hostilis, hosticus, inimicus, infestus

hostility *n* inimicitia *f*
 □ **hostilities** (war) bellum *nt*

hot *adj* calidus; fervens, candens; fervidus; (of spices) acer; (furious) furens, iratus; (keen) vehemens, acer
 □ **grow ~** excandesco ③

hotchpotch *n* farrago *f*; miscellanea *ntpl*

hotel *n* hospitium *nt*; caupona *f*; deversorium *nt*

hotly *adv* acriter, ardenter, vehementer

hound *n* catulus *m*; canis *m*/*f*

hour *n* hora *f*
 □ **half an ~** semihora *f*
 □ **three-quarters of an ~** dodrans horae *m*

hourglass *n* horarium *nt*

hourly *adj & adv* in singulas horas; in horas, singulis horis

house[1] *n* domus, sedes *f*; tectum; domicilium *nt*; fig familia; domus, gens *f*; (in politics) (senatorum, *etc.*) ordo *m*; (meeting place of senate) curia *f*

house[2] *vt* domo excipio; (store) condo ③

household[1] *n* domus, familia *f*

household[2] *adj* domesticus, familiaris

householder *n* paterfamilias *m*

household-god *n* Lar *m*
 □ **~s** Penates *mpl*

housekeeper *n* promus; dispensator *m*; (female) dispensatrix *f*

housekeeping *n* cura rei familiaris *f*

housewife *n* materfamilias *f*

hovel *n* tugurium *nt*; casa *f*

hover *vi* pendeo ②; volito ①; libror ①; (over) immineo ②

how[1] *adv* quomodo; ut; (to what degree) quam
 □ **~ many** quot, quam multi
 □ **~ often** quoties
 □ **~ much** quantum

how[2] *adv* ut! quam!

however *adv* -cumque, quamvis, utcumque; quantumvis
 ■ **~** *conj* nihilominus, tamen

howl[1] *vi* ululo ①

howl[2] *n* ululatus *m*

hubbub *n* tumultus *m*; turba *f*

hue *n* color *m*
 □ **~ and cry** conclamatio *f*

huff *n* ira *f*

hug[1] *n* complexus, amplexus *m*

hug[2] *vt* complector, amplector ③

huge *adj* ingens; vastus; immanis
■ ~**ly** *adv* immaniter, egregie

hull *n* (of a ship) alveus *m*

hum[1] *vi* susurro; murmuro ①

hum[2] *n* bombus *m*; fremitus *m*;
murmur *nt*; susurrus *m*

human[1] *adj* humanus; mortalis

human[2] *n*:
□ ~ **being** homo *m*

humane *adj* humanus, misericors
■ ~**ly** *adv* humaniter; misericorditer

humanity *n* (humaneness) humanitas;
misericordia *f*; (mankind) homines,
mortales *mpl*

humble[1] *adj* humilis; summissus,
supplex; (mean) obscurus

humble[2] *vt* infringo, deprimo ③
□ ~ **myself** me demitto ③

humbly *adv* humiliter, summisse

humid *adj* umidus

humidity *n* umor *m*

humiliate *vt* humilio ①; deprimo ③

humiliation *n* humiliatio *f*; dedecus
nt; ignominia, turpitudo *f*

humility *n* animus summissus *m*;
modestia *f*

humorous *adj* facetus; lepidus;
ridiculus

humour[1] *n* (frame of mind) ingenium *nt*;
(whim) libido *f*; (liveliness) festivitas *f*;
lepos *m*; facetiae *fpl*

humour[2] *vt* obsequor, morem gero ③;
indulgeo ② *all* + *dat*

hump *n* gibber, gibbus *m*

humpbacked *adj* gibber

hundred *adj* centum
□ ~ **times** centiens
■ ~ *n* centuria *f*

hundredth *adj* centesimus

hunger[1] *n* fames *f*; ieiunium *nt*

hunger[2] *vi* esurio ④; fig cupio ③

hungrily *adv* voraciter

hungry *adj* esuriens; ieiunus; fig
avidus, vorax

hunt[1] *vi* venor ①
■ ~ **for** *vt* peto, quaero ③

hunt[2] *n* venatio *f*; venatus *m*

hunter *n* venator; (hunting horse) equus
venaticus *m*

hunting *n* venatio *f*; venatus *m*

hunting-spear *n* venabulum *nt*

huntress *n* venatrix *f*

huntsman *n* venator *m*

hurdle *n* crates *f*

hurl *vt* iacio, proicio ③; iacto ①;
iaculor ①

hurly-burly *n* tumultus *m*

hurrah *int* (also **hurray**) euge!

hurricane *n* procella, tempestas *f*;
turbo *m*

hurriedly *adv* raptim; festinanter

hurry[1] *vi* festino, propero, praecipito ①;
curro ③
■ ~ *vt* urgeo ②; festino, propero,
praecipito ①
□ ~ **along** *vi* curro ③
□ ~ **away** *vi* propero ①; aufugio ③

hurry[2] *n* festinatio, properatio *f*
□ **in a** ~ festinanter

hurt[1] *vt* noceo ② + *dat*; laedo ③; fig
offendo ③
■ ~ *vi* doleo ②

hurt[2] *n* vulnus; damnum *nt*; iniuria *f*

hurtful *adj* noxius, perniciosus; (cruel)
crudelis

husband *n* maritus, vir, coniunx *m*

hush[1] *int* st! tace, tacete

hush[2] *vt* paco ①; comprimo ③
■ ~ *vi* taceo ②
□ ~ **up** fig celo ①

husk *n* folliculus *m*; siliqua *f*; (of corn)
gluma *f*

husky *adj* (of voice) surraucus

hustle *vt* proturbo ①

hut *n* tugurium *nt*; casa *f*

hutch *n* cavea *f*; mapalia *ntpl*

hyacinth *n* hyacinthus *m*

hydraulic *adj* hydraulicus

hyena *n* hyaena *f*

hygiene *n* munditia *f*

hygienic *adj* mundus

hymn *n* hymnus *m*

hypochondria *n* atra bilis *f*

hypocrisy *n* simulatio, dissimulatio;
pietas ficta *f*

hypocrite *n* simulator, dissimulator;
hypocrita *m*

hypocritical *adj* simulatus, fictus

hypothesis *n* (guess) coniectura;
(opinion) sententia *f*

hysteria *n* animi concitatio *f*

Ii

I *pn* ego
  □ ~ **myself** egomet, ipse ego

ice *n* glacies *f*; gelu *nt*

icicle *n* stiria *f*

icy *adj* glacialis; gelidus

idea *n* species, forma; imago; notitia; notio; (opinion) opinio, sententia; (suspicion) suspicio; (guess) coniectura *f*

ideal[1] *adj* perfectus; mente conceptus

ideal[2] *n* exemplar (perfectum) *nt*

identical *adj* idem; unus atque idem

identify *vt* agnosco ③
  □ ~ **with** sto ① cum + *abl*

idiocy *n* fatuitas, stultitia *f*

idiomatic *adj* proprius linguae; vernaculus

idiosyncrasy *n* proprium *nt*

idiot *n* fatuus; stupidus, stultus; excors *m*

idiotic *adj* fatuus

idle *adj* (at leisure) otiosus, vacuus; (of people) ignavus, piger, segnis, desidiosus, iners

idleness *n* otium *nt*; ignavia, segnitia, desidia *f*

idly *adv* otiose; segniter; fig frustra, incassum

idol *n* idolum, simulacrum *nt*; fig deliciae *fpl*

idolize *vt* (be desperately in love with) depereo *ir* + *acc*

if *conj* si
  □ **as** ~ quasi, tamquam
  □ **but** ~ sin, quod si
  □ **even** ~ etiamsi
  □ ~ **only** dummodo; (would that) utinam
  □ ~ **not** ni, nisi, si non; si minus

ignite *vt* accendo
  ■ ~ *vi* exardesco, excandesco ③

ignominious *adj* contumeliosus, ignominiosus, turpis

ignorance *n* ignoratio, ignorantia, inscitia *f*

ignorant *adj* (unaware) inscius, ignarus, nescius; (unlearned) indoctus, inscitus
  □ **be** ~ **of** ignoro ①; nescio ④

ignore *vt* praetereo *ir*

ill[1] *adj* malus; (in health) aegrotus
  □ **be** ~ aegroto ①
  □ **fall** ~ in morbum incido ③

ill[2] *n* malum *nt*
  □ **take it** ~ aegre fero *ir*

ill-advised *adj* inconsideratus, inconsultus, temerarius

ill-bred *adj* agrestis, inurbanus

ill-disposed *adj* malevolus, malignus

illegal *adj* quod contra leges fit; illicitus
  ■ ~**ly** *adv* contra leges; illicite

illegible *adj* quod legi non potest

illegimacy *n* (of birth) ortus infamia *f*

illegitimate *adj* (of birth) haud legitimus; spurius; nothus; (wrong) vitiosus

ill health *n* (infirma) valetudo *f*

illicit *adj* illicitus
  ■ ~**ly** *adv* illicite

illiterate *adj* illitteratus

ill-natured *adj* malevolus, malignus

illness *n* morbus *m*; aegrotatio *f*

illogical *adj* vitiosus

ill-omened *adj* dirus, infaustus

ill-temper *n* iracundia, morositas *f*

ill-tempered *adj* iracundus, acerbus, stomachosus; difficilis

ill-treat *vt* lacesso ③

illuminate *vt* illustro; illumino ①

illumination *n* lux *f*; lumen *nt*; festi ignes *mpl*

illusion *n* error *m*

illusory *adj* fallax

illustrate *vt* illustro; fig explano ①; patefacio ③

illustration *n* illustratio *f*; fig exemplum *nt*

illustrious *adj* clarus, illustris, praeclarus, inclutus, insignis

ill will *n* malevolentia, malitia, malignitas *f*

image *n* simulacrum *nt*; (likeness, portrait) effigies, imago *f*; (form) species, forma *f*

imaginary *adj* (unreal) imaginarius, fictus, falsus

imagination *n* cogitatio; imaginatio *f*; (dream) somnium *nt*

imaginative *adj* ingeniosus

imagine *vt* imaginor ⒈; fingo ⒊; (think) existimo, arbitror ⒈; (guess) conicio ⒊; (dream) somnio ⒈

imbecile *n* fatuus *m*

imbecility *n* imbecillitas animi *f*

imitate *vt* imitor, assimulo ⒈

imitation *n* imitatio *f*; imitamentum *nt*

immaculate *adj* castus, integer, inviolatus

immaterial *adj* simplex, incorporalis; (unimportant) levis

immature *adj* immaturus

immaturity *n* immaturitas *f*

immeasurable *adj* immensus, infinitus

immediate *adj* praesens
  ■ ~**ly** *adv* confestim, extemplo, protinus; continuo

immemorial *adj*:
  □ **from time** ~ ex omni memoria aetatum

immense *adj* ingens, immensus, enormis
  ■ ~**ly** *adv* immensum, multum

immensity *n* immensitas; vastitas *f*

immerse *vt* mergo, demergo, immergo ⒊

immersion *n* immersio *f*

immigrant *n* advena *m/f*

imminent *adj* instans, praesens

immobile *adj* immobilis

immobility *n* immobilitas *f*

immoderate *adj* immodicus, nimius, immoderatus

immoral *adj* corruptus, pravus, improbus

immorality *n* improbitas morum *f*

immortal *adj* immortalis; aeternus

immortality *n* immortalitas *f*

immortalize *vt* aeterno ⒈; immortalem reddo ⒊

immovable *adj* immobilis; immotus

immune *adj* immunis

immunity *n* immunitas *f*

impact *n* impetus *m*

impair *vt* laedo; imminuo; attero ⒊; debilito ⒈

impart *vt* impertio ⒋; communico ⒈

impartial *adj* aequus
  ■ ~**ly** *adv* sine ira et studio

impartiality *n* aequitas, aequabilitas *f*

impassable *adj* insuperabilis, invius, impervius

impassioned *adj* vehemens, ardens

impatience *n* impatientia *f*

impatient *adj* impatiens; iracundus
  ■ ~**ly** *adv* impatienter

impeach *vt* accuso ⒈

impede *vt* impedio ⒋; retardo ⒈

impediment *n* impedimentum *nt*; mora *f*; (in speech) haesitatio *f*

impel *vt* impello ⒊; excito, stimulo ⒈; cieo ⒉

impending *adj* praesens

impenetrable *adj* impenetrabilis, impervius; fig occultus

imperceptible *adj* qui sensu percipi non potest

imperceptibly *adv* (little by little) sensim; (step by step) pedetentim; obscure

imperfect *adj* imperfectus, mancus; (faulty) mendosus; vitiosus

imperfection *n* defectus *m*; vitium *nt*

imperial *adj* imperatorius; imperialis

imperious *adj* imperiosus; superbus; arrogans

imperishable *adj* perennis; fig immortalis

impersonate *vt* partes (alicuius) sustineo ⒉

impersonation *n* partes (actoris) *fpl*

impertinence *n* insolentia *f*

impertinent *adj* insolens; (things) ineptus, absurdus
  ■ ~**ly** *adv* insolenter

impervious *adj* impervius; (inexorable) inexorabilis

impetuous *adj* vehemens, fervidus
  ■ ~**ly** *adv* vehementer

impetus *n* vis *f*; impetus, impulsus *m*

impious *adj* impius; scelestus, sceleratus; nefandus, nefarius
  ■ ~**ly** *adv* impie; sceleste, scelerate; nefarie

implacable *adj* implacabilis, inexorabilis

implant *vt* ingigno; insero ③

implement *n* instrumentum *nt*; arma *ntpl*

implicate *vt* implico ①
□ **be ∼d** particeps sum *ir*

implicit *adj* tacitus
■ **∼ly** *adv* tacite

implore *vt* imploro, obsecro, supplico, obtestor ①

imply *vt* significo ①
□ **be implied** subsum *ir*

impolite *adj* inurbanus
■ **∼ly** *adv* inurbane

impoliteness *n* rusticitas, importunitas *f*

import¹ *vt* importo ①; inveho ③; (mean) significo ①

import² *n* (meaning) significatio; (of goods) invectio *f*

importance *n* momentum, pondus *nt*; gravitas *f*

important *adj* magni momenti, gravis

importer *n* qui merces peregrinas invehit

impose *vt* (a task) iniungo, impono ③
□ **∼ upon** (deceive) fraudo ①

impossibility *n* impossibilitas *f*

impossible *adj* impossibilis

impostor *n* fraudator, praestigiator *m*; planus *m*

impotent *adj* infirmus, impotens

impound *vt* confisco ①; (animals) includo ③

impoverish *vt* pauperem reddo ③; fig vitio ①

impracticable *adj* qui fieri non potest

impregnable *adj* inexpugnabilis

impress *vt* (stamp, imprint) imprimo ③; (mark) signo ①; fig inculco ①; (move) moveo ②

impression *n* (stamping) impressio *f*; (track, footstep) vestigium *nt*; (of a book) editio *f*; fig animi motus *m*; (effect) momentum *nt*

impressive *adj* gravis

imprint¹ *n* (mark) vestigium *nt*

imprint² *vt* imprimo ③

imprison *vt* includo, in vincula conicio ③

imprisonment *n* captivitas, custodia *f*

improbable *adj* haud verisimilis

impromptu *adj* ex tempore dictus

improper *adj* indecorus; indignus

impropriety *n* improprietas *f*; indecorum *nt*

improve *vt* emendo ①; excolo, corrigo ③
■ **∼** *vi* melior fio *ir*, proficio ③

improvement *n* cultura *f*; (progress) profectus *m*

improvise *vt* ex tempore dico *or* compono ③

impudence *n* impudentia, procacitas, protervitas *f*

impudent *adj* impudens; procax, protervus
■ **∼ly** *adv* impudenter; procaciter, proterve

impulse *n* impulsus, impetus *m*

impulsive *adj* vehemens, ardens, temerarius

impunity *n*:
□ **with ∼** impune

impure *adj* (of morals) impurus; incestus; impudicus

impurity *n* impuritas *f*

impute *vt* (ascribe) attribuo ③; do ①; verto ③; (as a fault) imputo ①

in *prep* in + *abl*; (in the works of) apud + *acc*

inability *n* infirmitas; (lack of means) inopia *f*

inaccessible *adj* inaccessus, difficilis aditu

inaccuracy *n* neglegentia *f*; error *m*

inaccurate *adj* parum accuratus, minime exactus; falsus

inactive *adj* iners, ignavus, otiosus

inactivity *n* inertia, socordia; cessatio *f*

inadequate *adj* impar; mancus
■ **∼ly** *adv* haud satis

inadvertent *adj* imprudens
■ **∼ly** *adv* imprudenter

inane *adj* ineptus

inanimate *adj* inanimus

inanity *n* ineptiae *fpl*

inapplicable *adj*:
□ **be ∼** non pertineo ② ad + *acc*

inappropriate *adj* haud idoneus, parum aptus

inarticulate *adj* indistinctus, confusus

inattention *n* animus parum attentus *m*; neglegentia, incuria *f*

inattentive *adj* haud *or* parum attentus; neglegens
■ ∼**ly** *adv* animo parum attento; neglegenter

inaudible *adj* quod audiri nequit

inaugurate *vt* inauguro ①

inauguration *n* inauguratio, consecratio *f*

inauspicious *adj* infaustus; infelix, funestus

inborn *adj* ingenitus, innatus, insitus

inbred *adj* ingenitus, innatus, insitus

incalculable *adj* qui aestimari nequit; fig immensus; incredibilis

incapable *adj* inhabilis, imperitus

incapacitate *vt* noceo ② + *dat*; laedo ③

incense¹ *n* tus *nt*

incense² *vt* exaspero ①; incendo ③

incentive *n* incitamentum *nt*; stimulus *m*

incessant *adj* continuus, assiduus, perpetuus
■ ∼**ly** *adv* assidue; perpetuo

incest *n* incestum *nt*; incestus *m*

incestuous *adj* incestus

inch *n* uncia *f*
□ ∼ **by** ∼ unciatim; fig paulatim, sensim

incident *n* (event) eventus *m*; res *f*; casus *m*

incidental *adj* fortuitus
■ ∼**ly** *adv* fortuito

incision *n* incisura *f*; incisus *m*

incisive *adj* acer, acerbus

incite *vt* incito, stimulo ①; impello ③

incitement *n* incitamentum *nt*; incitatio *f*; stimulus *m*

inclination *n* (tilt) inclinatio; (slope) acclivitas; fig voluntas, inclinatio *f*

incline¹ *vt* inclino ①; fig adduco ③; inclino ①
■ ∼ *vi* propendeo ②; inclino ①

incline² *n* acclivitas *f*

inclined *adj* proclivis; propensus

include *vt* includo, comprehendo ③

incognito *adv* dissimulato nomine

incoherent *adj* confusus

income *n* reditus; fructus *m*

incomparable *adj* incomparabilis, unicus

incompatibility *n* repugnantia *f*

incompatible *adj* discors, repugnans, contrarius

incompetence *n* inscitia, imperitia *f*

incompetent *adj* inhabilis; inscitus, imperitus

incomplete *adj* imperfectus, incohatus; mancus

incomprehensible *adj* qui comprehendi non potest

inconceivable *adj* qui cogitari *or* mente percipi non potest

inconclusive *adj* levis; infirmus

incongruous *adj* inconveniens, male congruens
■ ∼**ly** *adv* parum apte

inconsiderate *adj* inconsideratus

inconsistency *n* inconstantia, mutabilitas; repugnantia *f*

inconsistent *adj* inconstans; contrarius, absonus
■ ∼**ly** *adv* inconstanter

inconsolable *adj* inconsolabilis

inconspicuous *adj* obscurus

inconstant *adj* inconstans, levis, mutabilis, mobilis

incontrovertible *adj* certus

inconvenience¹ *n* incommodum *nt*

inconvenience² *vt* incommodo ①

inconvenient *adj* incommodus; molestus
■ ∼**ly** *adv* incommode

incorporate *vt* adiungo ③; admisceo ②

incorrect *adj* mendosus, falsus

incorrigible *adj* insanabilis

increase¹ *vt* augeo ②; amplifico ①
■ ∼ *vi* augeor ②; cresco; ingravesco ③

increase² *n* incrementum *nt*; auctus *m*

incredible *adj* incredibilis

incredibly *adv* incredibiliter; incredibile quantum; ultra fidem

incredulity *n* incredulitas *f*

incredulous *adj* incredulus

incriminate *vt* accuso ①

incubate *vi* incubo ①

incubation *n* incubatio *f*; incubitus *m*

inculcate *vt* inculco ①

incur *vt* incurro ③ in + *acc*; mereor ②

incurable *adj* insanabilis, immedicabilis

i

indebted *adj* obaeratus
□ **I am ∼ to you for this** hoc tibi debeo ②

indecency *n* indecorum *nt*; indignitas *f*

indecent *adj* indecens, indecorus
■ ∼**ly** *adv* indecenter, indecore

indecision *n* haesitatio, dubitatio *f*

indecisive *adj* dubius, incertus, anceps, ambiguus

indeed *adv* (it is true) re vera, profecto
□ ∼**?** itane?
□ **very good** ∼ vel optimum

indefinite *adj* incertus; anceps, obscurus

indelible *adj* indelebilis

indemnity *n* indemnitas *f*
□ **act of** ∼ impunitas *f*

indentation *n* incisura *f*

independence *n* libertas *f*

independent *adj* sui potens; liber; fig sui iuris
■ ∼**ly** *adv* libere; suis legibus; (each by itself) singillatim

indescribable *adj* inenarrabilis, infandus

index *n* (of a book) index *m*; fig indicium *nt*

indicate *vt* indico; significo ①

indication *n* signum, indicium *nt*

indict *vt* accuso ①; defero *ir*

indictment *n* (accusation) accusatio *f*

indifference *n* (neutrality) aequus animus *m*; (carelessness) neglegentia *f*; (contempt) contemptus *m*

indifferent *adj* aequus, medius; remissus, neglegens, frigidus

indigent *adj* egens, inops

indigestion *n* cruditas *f*

indignant *adj* indignans, indignabundus, iratus
■ ∼**ly** *adv* indignanter

indignation *n* indignatio; ira *f*

indirect *adj* obliquus
■ ∼**ly** *adv* oblique
□ **touch on** ∼**ly** perstringo ③

indiscreet *adj* inconsultus

indiscretion *n* imprudentia *f*

indiscriminate *adj* promiscuus
■ ∼**ly** *adv* promiscue

indispensable *adj* necessarius

indisposed *adj* (in health) minus valens

indisposition *adj* (illness) aegrotatio, commotiuncula *f*

indisputable *adj* certus; haud dubius

indisputably *adv* haud dubie

indistinct *adj* indistinctus, obscurus

individual[1] *adj* individuus, proprius
■ ∼**ly** *adv* singillatim

individual[2] *n* homo *m*

indolence *n* inertia, desidia, ignavia, socordia *f*

indolent *adj* iners, ignavus, deses, socors, segnis

indomitable *adj* indomitus, invictus

indoor *adj* domesticus, umbratilis

indoors *adv* domi

indubitable *adj* indubitabilis, haud dubius, certus

indubitably *adv* haud dubie

induce *vt* adduco, impello ③; persuadeo ② + *dat*; incito ①

inducement *n* incitamentum *nt*; causa *f*; stimulus *m*

indulge *vt* (in) indulgeo ② + *dat*

indulgence *n* indulgentia; (pardon) venia; (kindness) clementia *f*

indulgent *adj* indulgens, facilis, clemens
■ ∼**ly** *adv* indulgenter, clementer

industrious *adj* industrius; diligens; sedulus; strenuus
■ ∼**ly** *adv* industrie, diligenter, sedulo, strenue

industry *n* industria; sedulitas; diligentia *f*; studium *nt*; (manufacturing) officina *f*

inebriated *adj* ebrius

ineffective *adj* inefficax, inutilis

ineffectual *adj* inefficax, inutilis

inefficiency *n* inutilitas *f*

inefficient *adj* inefficax; inhabilis; inutilis

inelegant *adj* inelegans; inconcinnus

inept *adj* ineptus

inequality *n* inaequalitas *f*

inert *adj* iners, segnis

inertia *n* inertia *f*

inevitable *adj* ▶ **unavoidable**

inexcusable *adj* inexcusabilis

inexhaustible *adj* inexhaustus

inexorable *adj* inexorabilis, durus, implacabilis

inexpensive *adj* vilis

inexperience *n* imperitia, inscitia *f*

inexperienced *adj* imperitus; inexpertus inscitus; rudis

inexplicable *adj* inexplicabilis, inenodabilis

inexpressible *adj* inenarrabilis, infandus

infallible *adj* qui errare non potest; certus, haud dubius

infallibly *adv* haud dubie

infamous *adj* infamis; turpis, inhonestus, foedus, ignominiosus

infamy *n* infamia, ignominia *f*; opprobrium, probrum *nt*

infancy *n* infantia, aetas iniens *f*

infant *n* infans *m/f*

infantile *adj* infantilis, puerilis

infantry *n* peditatus *m*; pedestres copiae *fpl*

infatuated *adj*:
□ **be ~ with** depereo ④

infect *vt* inficio ③; contamino ①

infection *n* contagium *nt*; contagio *f*; contactus *m*

infectious *adj* contagiosus

infer *vt* conicio ③, infero *ir*, colligo ③

inference *n* coniectura, conclusio *f*

inferior[1] *adj* inferior, deterior, minor

inferior[2] *n* impar *m/f*

infernal *adj* infernus

infertile *adj* sterilis

infertility *n* sterilitas *f*

infidelity *n* infidelitas *f*

infinite *adj* infinitus; immensus
■ **~ly** *adv* infinite; infinito

infinity *n* infinitas, infinitio *f*

infirm *adj* infirmus, debilis, imbecillus

infirmity *n* infirmitas, imbecillitas, debilitas *f*

inflame *vt* inflammo ①; incendo ③

inflammation *n* inflammatio *f*

inflammatory *adj* turbulentus, seditiosus

inflate *vt also fig* inflo ①
□ **be ~d** tumeo ②

inflexibility *n* rigor *m*

inflexible *adj* rigidus; *fig* obstinatus

inflict *vt* infligo; impono ③; irrogo ①

influence[1] *n* momentum, pondus *nt*; auctoritas, gratia *f*; (prompting) impulsus *m*

influence[2] *vt* moveo ②; impello ③; valeo ②

influential *adj* (auctoritate) gravis, potens

inform *vt* (teach) doceo ②; instruo; (give information) certiorem facio; (against) defero *ir*

informal *adj* privatus

informant *n* (messenger) nuntius *m*

information *n* (news) nuntius *m*; (knowledge) scientia *f*

informer *n* delator *m*

infringe *vt* violo ①

infringement *n* violatio *f*

infuriate *vt* effero *ir*, exaspero ①

ingenious *adj* sollers; subtilis; ingeniosus

ingenuity *n* ingenium *nt*

ingot *n* later *m*

ingrained *adj* insitus, inveteratus

ingratiate *vi* (oneself) gratiam ineo *ir* apud (aliquem) ④; gratiam (mihi) concilio ①

ingratitude *n* animus ingratus *m*; beneficii oblivio *f*

ingredient *n* pars *f*

inhabit *vt* colo, incolo ③; habito ①

inhabitant *n* incola *m/f*; habitator, colonus *m*

inhale *vt* duco ③; haurio ④

inherent *adj* inhaerens, proprius

inherit *vt* hereditate accipio ③

inheritance *n* hereditas *f*; patrimonium *nt*

inhibit *vt* coerceo ②

inhospitable *adj* inhospitalis, inhospitus

inhuman *adj* inhumanus; crudelis
■ **~ly** *adv* inhumane; crudeliter

inhumanity *n* inhumanitas; crudelitas *f*

inimitable *adj* inimitabilis

initial *adj* primus
■ **~** *n* prima verbi littera *f*

initiate *vt* initio ①

initiation *n* initiatio *f*; initiamenta *ntpl*

initiative *n*:
□ **take the ~** initium capio ③

inject *vt* infundo, immitto ③

injection *n* (act) infusio *f*; infusus *m*

injure *vt* noceo ② + *dat*; laedo; offendo ③

injury *n* iniuria *f*; damnum, detrimentum *nt*

injustice *n* iniustitia; iniquitas; iniuria *f*

ink *n* atramentum *nt*

inkling *n* (hint) rumusculus *m*; (suspicion) suspicio *f*

inlet *n* (of the sea) aestuarium *nt*

inmate *n* incola, inquilinus *m*

inmost *adj* intimus, imus
□ ~ **recesses** penetralia *ntpl*

inn *n* caupona, taberna *f*; deversorium, hospitium *nt*

innate *adj* innatus; insitus; ingenitus

inner *adj* interior

innermost *adj* intimus; imus

innkeeper *n* caupo *m*

innocence *n* innocentia; integritas; castitas *f*

innocent *adj* innocuus; innocens; insons; (chaste) castus
■ ~**ly** *adv* innocue; innocenter; caste

innocuous *adj* innocuus

innovation *n* res novae *fpl*

innumerable *adj* innumerabilis, innumerus

inoffensive *adj* innocens, innoxius

inopportune *adj* intempestivus

inordinate *adj* immoderatus
■ ~**ly** *adv* immoderate

inquest *n* inquisitio *f*

inquire *vt&i* quaero, inquiro ③; investigo ①

inquiry *n* inquisitio *f*

inquisitive *adj* curiosus
■ ~**ly** *adv* curiose

inroad *n* incursio, irruptio *f*
□ **make** ~**s into** incurro ③ in + *acc*

insane *adj* insanus; vecors; amens; demens

insanity *n* insania, dementia, amentia, vecordia *f*

insatiable *adj* insatiabilis, inexplebilis, inexpletus

inscribe *vt* inscribo; insculpo; incido ③

inscription *n* inscriptio *f*; titulus *m*; carmen *nt*

insect *n* insectum *nt*

insecure *adj* intutus, periculosus; infestus, lubricus

insecurity *n* periculum *nt*

inseparable *adj* inseparabilis

insert *vt* insero; ascribo, interpono ③

inside¹ *n* interior pars *f*; interiora *ntpl*

inside² *adj* interior

inside³ *adv* intrinsecus; intra, intro, intus

inside⁴ *prep* intra + *acc*

insidious *adj* insidiosus; subdolus
■ ~**ly** *adv* insidiose; subdole

insight *n* prudentia, cognitio *f*

insignificant *adj* exiguus; nullius momenti; levis

insincere *adj* insincerus, simulatus; fallax; dolosus

insincerity *n* fallacia; simulatio *f*

insinuate *vt*:
□ ~ **oneself into** irrepo ③; (hint) significo ①

insinuation *n* insinuatio *f*; (suspicion) suspicio *f*
□ **make** ~**s against** oblique perstringo ③

insipid *adj* insulsus; fig hebes; frigidus

insist *vi* insto ①; urgeo ②; exigo ③
□ ~ **on** flagito ①

insolence *n* insolentia, arrogantia, superbia *f*

insolent *adj* insolens, arrogans, superbus
■ ~**ly** *adv* insolenter; impudenter; superbe

inspect *vt* inspicio, introspicio ③

inspection *n* inspectio; cura *f*

inspector *n* curator; praefectus *m*

inspiration *n* (divine) afflatus *m*; numen *nt*; instinctus *m*

inspire *vt* inspiro ①; inicio ③; (kindle) incendo ③; excito ①

instability *n* instabilitas, inconstantia *f*

install *vt* inauguro ①; constituo ③

instalment *n* (payment in part) pensio, portio *f*

instance *n* exemplum *nt*
□ **for** ~ exempli gratia

instant¹ *adj* (immediate) praesens
■ ~**ly** *adv* (at once) statim

instant² *n* momentum, punctum temporis *nt*
□ **this ~** statim, actutum

instantaneous *adj* qui momento temporis fit
■ **~ly** *adv* continuo; statim

instead *adv*:
□ **~ of** loco, vice *both* + *gen*; pro + *abl*

instigate *vt* instigo, stimulo, incito ①; cieo ②

instigation *n* incitatio *f*; stimulus *m*

instil *vt* instillo ①

instinct *n* natura *f*

instinctive *adj* naturalis
■ **~ly** *adv* naturaliter

institution *n* (thing instituted) institutum *nt*

instruct *vt* (teach) doceo ②; instruo, instituo ③; erudio ④; (order, command) mando ①

instruction *n* institutio, disciplina *f*; (order, commission) mandatum *nt*

instructor *n* praeceptor, magister *m*; magistra *f*

instrument *n* instrumentum *nt*

instrumental *adj* aptus, utilis

insubordinate *adj* seditiosus

insubordination *n* seditio *f*; tumultus *m*

insufferable *adj* intolerandus, intolerabilis

insufficiency *n* inopia, egestas *f*

insufficient *adj* non *or* parum sufficiens, impar
■ **~ly** *adv* haud satis

insulate *vt* insulo ①

insult¹ *n* opprobrium, probrum, convicium *nt*; contumelia *f*

insult² *vt* maledico ③ + *dat*

insulting *adj* contumeliosus

insurmountable *adj* inexsuperabilis, insuperabilis

insurrection *n* rebellio, seditio *f*; tumultus *m*

intact *adj* integer; incolumis

integral *adj* necessarius

integrity *n* integritas, probitas; sinceritas, innocentia *f*

intellect *n* intellectus *m*; intellegentia, mens *f*

intelligence *n* ingenium *nt*; (cleverness) sollertia *f*; (news) nuntius *m*

intelligent *adj* intellegens; sollers
■ **~ly** *adv* intellegenter

intelligible *adj* intellegibilis

intend *vt* destino ①; (resolve) constituo, decerno ③

intense *adj* acer, vehemens; (excessive) nimius
■ **~ly** *adv* acriter; vehementer; (extremely) valde, magnopere

intensity *n* vehementia, vis *f*; (of winter, etc.) asperitas *f*

intent¹ *adj* intentus, attentus
■ **~ly** *adv* intente

intent² *n* consilium, propositum *nt*; (meaning) significatio *f*

intention *n* consilium, propositum *nt*

intentionally *adv* de industria, consilio, consulto

intercede *vi* intercedo ③; deprecor ①

intercept *vt* intercipio, intercludo; deprehendo ③

interchange¹ *vt* permuto, commuto ①

interchange² *n* permutatio; vicissitudo *f*

intercourse *n* (sexual) coitus, concubitus *m*

interest¹ *vt* teneo ②; capio ③; delecto ①

interest² *n* (advantage) emolumentum *nt*; utilitas *f*; (for money) faenus *nt*, usura *f*; (concern) studium *nt*

interesting *adj* (appealing) iucundus

interfere *vi* intercedo ③; intervenio ④; (hinder) obsto ① + *dat*

interference *n* intercessio *f*; interventus *m*

interim *n* intervallum *nt*
□ **in the ~** interim

interior¹ *adj* interior, internus

interior² *n* pars interior *f*

interjection *n* interiectio *f*

interlude *n* (entr'acte) embolium *nt*

intermarriage *n* conubium *nt*

intermediate *adj* medius

interminable *adj* infinitus

intermingle *vt* intermisceo, immisceo ②

intermission *n* intermissio; cessatio, remissio *f*

intermittent *adj* rarus

internal *adj* intestinus, domesticus
■ **~ly** *adv* intus

international *adj*:
  ■ ~ **law** *n* ius gentium *nt*

interpret *vt* interpretor ①; (figure out) conicio ③

interpretation *n* interpretatio, coniectio *f*

interpreter *n* interpres *m/f*

interrogate *vt* interrogo, percontor ①

interrogation *n* interrogatio, percontatio *f*

interrupt *vt* interrumpo, intermitto ③; interpello ①

interruption *n* interruptio; interpellatio *f*

intersect *vt* interseco ①

intersection *n* decussatio *f*

intersperse *vt* intermisceo, immisceo ②

interval *n* intervallum, spatium *nt*

intervene *vi* (be between) interiaceo ②; (come between) intercedo ③; (hinder) intervenio ④ + *dat*

intervening *adj* medius

intervention *n* interventus, interiectus *m*

interview¹ *n* colloquium *nt*; congressus *m*

interview² *vt* convenio ④

interweave *vt* intertexo; intexo ③

intestines *npl* intestina; viscera *ntpl*

intimacy *n* familiaritas, consuetudo *f*

intimate *adj* familiaris, intimus
  ■ ~**ly** *adv* familiariter, intime

intimidate *vt* metum inicio ③; minor ① + *dat*; terreo ②

intimidation *n* minae *fpl*

into *prep* in + *acc*

intolerable *adj* intolerabilis, intolerandus

intolerance *n* intolerantia, impatientia *f*

intolerant *adj* intolerans, impatiens

intoxicate *vt* ebrium reddo ③

intoxication *n* ebrietas *f*

intrepid *adj* intrepidus, impavidus

intricacy *n* ambages *fpl*

intricate *adj* contortus, perplexus
  ■ ~**ly** *adv* contorte; perplexe

intrigue *n* consilium clandestinum *nt*; fraus, ars *f*; (amour) amores *mpl*

intrinsic *adj* internus; innatus
  ■ ~**ally** *adv* intrinsecus

introduce *vt* introduco; (institute) instituo ③

introduction *n* inductio; (to a person) introductio; (preface) praefatio *f*; exordium, prooemium *nt*

introductory *adj* introductorius

intrude *vt&i* immitto, me immitto ③; molestus sum *ir*

intrusion *n* importunitas; usurpatio *f*

intrusive *adj* molestus

inundate *vt* inundo ①

inundation *n* inundatio *f*; diluvium *nt*

inure *vt* assuefacio ③

invade *vt* invado, irrumpo ③, bellum infero *ir*

invader *n* invasor *m*

invalid¹ *adj* infirmus, vitiosus, nugatorius, irritus

invalid² *n* aeger, aegrotus, valetudinarius *m*

invalidate *vt* irritum reddo; rescindo ③

invaluable *adj* inaestimabilis

invariable *adj* constans, immutabilis, immobilis

invariably *adv* immutabiliter; semper

invasion *n* incursio, irruptio *f*

invective *n* convicium *nt*

inveigle *vt* illicio, pellicio ③

invent *vt* invenio, reperio ④; (contrive) excogito ①; fingo ③

invention *n* (act) inventio *f*; (thing invented) inventum *nt*; (lie, *etc.*) commentum *nt*

inventive *adj* habilis, ingeniosus

inventor *n* inventor, repertor *m*

inventress *n* inventrix *f*

inverse *adj* inversus, conversus

inversion *n* inversio, conversio *f*

invert *vt* inverto ③

invest *vt* do, mando; (money) colloco ①; pono ③; (besiege) obsideo ②

investigate *vt* investigo, indago, scrutor ①; inquiro, cognosco ③

investigation *n* investigatio, inquisitio *f*

investment *n* (of money) pecunia in faenore posita

inveterate *adj* inveteratus

invidious *adj* invidus, malignus, invidiosus
■ ∼**ly** *adv* invidiose; maligne

invigorate *vt* corroboro, confirmo ①

invincible *adj* invictus; insuperabilis

invisible *adj* invisibilis

invitation *n* invitatio *f*

invite *vt* invito, voco ①

inviting *adj* gratus, blandus, suavis

invocation *n* obtestatio *f*

invoke *vt* invoco, imploro, obtestor ①

involuntary *adj* invitus, coactus

involve *vt* (contain) contineo ②; (entangle) implico ①; (imply) habeo ②

involved *adj* (intricate) perplexus

invulnerable *adj* invulnerabilis

inward *adj* interior

inwardly *adv* intus, intrinsecus, introrsus

inwards *adv* intus, intrinsecus, introrsus

irascible *adj* iracundus

irate *adj* iratus

iris *n* (plant) iris *f*

irksome *adj* molestus, odiosus

iron[1] *n* ferrum *nt*
■ ∼**s** *pl* vincula *ntpl*

iron[2] *adj* ferreus; fig durus

ironic *adj* (also **ironical**) deridens
■ ∼**ally** *adv* ironice

ironmonger *n* negotiator ferrarius *m*

irony *n* ironia, dissimulatio *f*

irrational *adj* rationis expers, irrationalis

irreconcilable *adj* implacabilis; (incompatible) repugnans

irrefutable *adj* qui confutari non potest

irregular *adj* (disorderly) tumultuarius; (spasmodic) rarus, infrequens; (uneven) iniquus

irrelevant *adj* non pertinens, alienus

irreligious *adj* impius, irreligiosus, religionis neglegens

irreparable *adj* irreparabilis; irrevocabilis

irresistible *adj* invictus; cui nullo modo resisti potest

irresolute *adj* incertus animi; dubius; parum firmus
■ ∼**ly** *adv* dubitanter

irresolution *n* dubitatio *f*; animus parum firmus *m*

irresponsible *adj* levis

irreverent *adj* irreverens, parum reverens

irrevocable *adj* irrevocabilis

irrigate *vt* rigo, irrigo ①

irrigation *n* irrigatio, inductio aquae *f*

irritability *n* iracundia *f*

irritable *adj* irritabilis, stomachosus, iracundus

irritate *vt* irrito; inflammo ①

irritation *n* irritatio *f*; stomachus *m*; ira *f*

island *n* insula *f*

isolate *vt* seiungo, secerno ③

isolation *n* solitudo *f*

issue[1] *n* (outlet) egressus *m*; (result) eventus, exitus *m*; (end) finis *m*/*f*; (matter) res *f*; (offspring) liberi *mpl*; (of money) erogatio *f*; (profit) reditus *m*

issue[2] *vt* (publish) edo; (post up) propono ③; (money) erogo ①
■ ∼ *vi* emano ①; egredior ③; (end) evenio ④

isthmus *n* isthmus *m*

it *pn* id, hoc

Italy *n* Italia *f*

itch[1] *n* scabies, prurigo *f*

itch[2] *vi* prurio ④

itchy *adj* scabrosus

item *n* res *f*

itinerary *n* itinerarium *nt*

itself *pn* ipsum

ivory[1] *n* ebur *nt*

ivory[2] *adj* eburneus; eburnus

ivy *n* hedera *f*

Jj

jackal *n* canis aureus *m*

jackdaw *n* monedula *f*

jade *n* (horse) caballus *m*; fig (woman) importuna mulier *f*

jaded *adj* defessus

jagged *adj* dentatus, serratus

jail¹ *n* carcer *m*

jail² *vt* in carcerem conicio ③

jailer *n* custos *m*

jam¹ *n* conditae baccae *fpl*

jam² *vt* comprimo ③

jangle *vi* (make a jangling sound) tinnio ④; tintinno ①

January *n* Ianuarius *m*

jar¹ *n* (pitcher, bottle, cask) olla; amphora *f*; urceus *m*

jar² *vi* discrepo, discordo ①

jargon *n* confusae voces *fpl*; barbarus sermo *m*

jarring *adj* dissonus, discors

jasper *n* iaspis *f*

jaundice *n* morbus regius, icterus *m*

jaundiced *adj* ictericus; fig morosus; invidiosus

jaunt *n* excursio *f*

javelin *n* pilum, iaculum; telum, veru *nt*

jaw *n* mala; maxilla *f*; fig fauces *fpl*

jawbone *n* maxilla *f*

jay *n* corvus glandarius *m*

jealous *adj* invidus; aemulus; invidiosus

jealousy *n* invidia; aemulatio *f*; livor *m*

jeer¹ *vi* derideo, irrideo ②

jeer² *n* risus; irrisus *m*

jelly *n* cylon, quilon *nt*

jellyfish *n* pulmo, halipleumon *m*

jeopardize *vt* in periculum adduco ③

jeopardy *n* periculum, discrimen *nt*

jerk¹ *n* impetus, subitus motus *m*

jerk² *vt* subito moveo ②

jest¹ *n* iocus, lusus *m*; facetiae *fpl*
  □ **in ~** ioco, iocose

jest² *vi* iocor ①; ludo ③

jester *n* ioculator; (buffoon) scurra *m*

jet *n* (spout of water) scatebra *f*; (mineral) gagates *m*

jet-black *adj* nigerrimus

jetty *n* moles, pila *f*

Jew *n* Iudaeus *m*

jewel *n* gemma *f*

jewelled *adj* gemmeus, gemmifer

jeweller *n* gemmarius *m*

jewellery *n* gemmae *fpl*

jig *n* saltatio *f*

jilt *vt* fallo ③

jingle *vi* tinnio ④

jingling *n* tinnitus *m*

job *n* negotiolum *nt*; res lucrosa *f*

jockey *n* agaso *m*

jocular *adj* iocularis, iocosus, facetus
  ■ **~ly** *adv* ioculariter, facete, iocose

jocularity *n* facetiae *fpl*, animus iocosus *m*

jog *vt* concutio, quatio ③

join *vt* iungo, coniungo ③; (border on) contingo
  ■ **~** *vi* adiungor ③; cohaereo ②
  □ **~ battle** *vi* confligo, manum consero ③; congredior ③ cum + *abl*
  □ **~ in** (take part in) particeps *or* socius sum *ir* + *gen*

joiner *n* lignarius *m*

joint *n* commissura *f*; articulus *m*; vertebra; iunctura *f*

jointly *adv* coniuncte, coniunctim, una, communiter

joist *n* tignum transversarium *nt*

joke¹ *n* iocus *m*; sales *mpl*; facetiae *fpl*

joke² *vt&i* (at) iocor ①; ludo ③; irrideo ②

joker *n* ioculator *m*

jollity *n* festivitas, hilaritas *f*

jolly *adj* festivus, hilaris

jolt¹ *vt* concutio ③; iacto, quasso ①
  ■ **~** *vi* concutior ③; iactor, quassor ①

jolt² *n* iactatio *f*

jostle *vt* pulso, deturbo ①

journal *n* ephemeris *f*; diarium *nt*; (newspaper) acta diurna *ntpl*

journey *n* iter *nt*; profectio *f*; via *f*

Jove *n* Iupiter *m*

jovial *adj* hilaris, festivus

joviality *n* hilaritas, festivitas *f*

joy *n* gaudium *nt*; laetitia *f*

joyful *adj* laetus, hilaris
■ ~**ly** *adv* laete, hilare; libenter

joyous *adj* laetus, hilaris
■ ~**ly** *adv* laete, hilare; libenter

jubilant *adj* laetitia exsultans; ovans

jubilation *n* triumphus *m*; gaudium *nt*

Judaism *n* Iudaismus *m*

judge[1] *n* iudex; quaesitor, arbiter; (critic) existimator, censor *m*; (umpire) arbiter *m*

judge[2] *vt&i* iudico; existimo 1; censeo 2; (value) aestimo 1

judgment *n* sententia *f*; arbitrium; fig (opinion, faculty of judging) iudicium *nt*

judicial *adj* iudicialis

judicious *adj* sapiens, prudens
■ ~**ly** *adv* sapienter, prudenter

jug *n* urceus *m*

juggle *vi* praestigias ago 3

juggler *n* praestigiator; pilarius *m*

juggling *n* praestigiae *fpl*

juice *n* sucus *m*

juicy *adj* sucosus

July *n* Quintilis *m*

jumble[1] *vt* confundo 3; permisceo 2

jumble[2] *n* confusio, congeries, strages *f*

jump[1] *vi* salio, exsilio 4; exsulto 1

jump[2] *n* saltus *m*

junction *n* coniunctio, iunctura *f*

June *n* Iunius *m*

jungle *n* locus virgultis obsitus *m*

junior *adj & n* iunior, minor

jurisdiction *n* iurisdictio *f*

juror *n* iudex *m*

jury *n* iudices *mpl*

just[1] *adj* iustus; meritus; aequus

just[2] *adv* (a moment ago) modo; (only) modo; (only just) vix
□ ~ **so** haud secus

justice *n* iustitia, aequitas *f*

justifiable *adj* excusandus

justifiably *adv* iure; cum causa, excusate

justification *n* excusatio, purgatio *f*

justify *vt* purgo; excuso 1

justly *adv* iuste; iure; merito

jut *vi* (out) promineo 2; procurro 3

juvenile *adj* iuvenilis, puerilis

j

k

Kk

Kalends *n* Kalendae *fpl*

keel *n* carina *f*

keen *adj* acer; alacer; sagax; (sharp) acutus
■ ~**ly** *adv* acute, acriter; sagaciter

keenness *n* sagacitas, subtilitas *f*

keen-sighted *adj* perspicax

keep[1] *vt* teneo; habeo 2; (preserve) servo, conservo 1; (guard) custodio 4; (store) recondo; (support, sustain) alo 3; (animals) pasco 3; (a holiday) celebro 1; ago 3; (reserve) reservo 1; (one's word, law, etc.) servo 1
■ ~ *vi* maneo 2; duro 1
□ ~ **away** *vt* arceo, prohibeo; *vi* abstineo 2

□ ~ **back** retineo, cohibeo 2; (conceal) celo 1
□ ~ **company** comitor 1
□ ~ **down** comprimo 3
□ ~ **from** *vt* prohibeo 2; *vi* abstineo 2
□ ~ **in** includo 3
□ ~ **off** ▸ ~ **away**
□ ~ **on** *vi* persevero 1
□ ~ **out** *vt* excludo 3
□ ~ **up** (maintain) *vt* tueor 2; sustineo 2; *vi* subsequor 3

keep[2] *n* (citadel) arx *f*; (food) cibus *m*

keeper *n* custos *m/f*

keeping *n* tutela; custodia; cura *f*

keepsake *n* pignus *nt*

keg *n* cadus *m*; testa *f*

kennel *n* cubile *nt*; stabulum *nt*

kernel *n* (of a fruit) nucleus *m*

kettle *n* lebes *m*; aenum *nt*

key *n* clavis *f*; (key position controlling access) claustra *ntpl*; fig cardo *m*

kick[1] *vi* calcitro ①; calce ferio ④

kick[2] *n* calcitratus *m*

kid *n* (young goat) haedus *m*

kidnap *vt* surripio ③

kidnapper *n* plagiarius *m*

kidneys *n* renes *mpl*

kill *vt* interficio, caedo, occido, interimo, perimo ③; neco ①

killer *n* interfector *m*

kiln *n* fornax *f*

kin *n* consanguinitas *f*; genus *nt*;
▶ **relation**

kind[1] *n* genus *nt*; modus *m*; species *f*
□ **of what** ∼ qualis, cuiusmodi
□ **of such a** ∼ talis, eiusmodi

kind[2] *adj* amicus; benignus; benevolus; comis; humanus; suavis

kind-hearted *adj* benignus

kindle *vt* accendo ③; fig inflammo ①
■ ∼ *vi* exardesco ③

kindly *adj* ▶ **kind**
■ ∼ *adv* amice; benigne; humane; comiter

kindness *n* benignitas; humanitas *f*; (kind act) beneficium *nt*

king *n* rex *m*

kingdom *n* regnum *nt*

kingfisher *n* alcedo *f*

kinsman *n* necessarius, cognatus, consanguineus *m*

kiss[1] *n* suavium, osculum, basium *nt*

kiss[2] *vt* suavior, osculor, basio ①

kit *n* impedimenta *ntpl*

kitchen *n* culina *f*

kite *n* (bird) milvus *m*

kitten *n* catulus felinus *m*

knack *n* ars, sollertia *f*

knapsack *n* sarcina *f*

knavish *adj* scelestus, nefarius

knead *vt* depso, subigo ③

knee *n* genu *nt*

kneecap *n* patella *f*

kneel *vi* in genua procumbo, genibus nitor ③

knife *n* culter, cultellus *m*

knight *n* eques *m*

knighthood *n* equestris dignitas *f*

knit *vt*:
□ ∼ **the brow** supercilium (frontem) contraho ③

knob *n* tuber *nt*; nodus *m*; (of a door) bulla *f*

knock[1] *vt&i* pulso ①; ferio ④; tundo ③
□ ∼ **against** (one's head, etc.) offendo ③
□ ∼ **at** (a door), pulso ①; ferio ④
□ ∼ **down** deicio, sterno ③; fig (at an auction) addico (bona alicui) ③
□ ∼ **over** deturbo ①
□ ∼ **up** (awake) suscito ①

knock[2] *n* pulsatio *f*

knock-kneed *adj* varus

knoll *n* tumulus *m*

knot[1] *n* nodus *m*; geniculum *nt*; fig (of people) circulus *m*; fig difficultas *f*

knot[2] *vt* nodo ①

knotty *adj* nodosus; fig spinosus, difficilis

know *vt* scio ④; (learn, become acquainted with) cognosco ③; (be acquainted with) nosco ③
□ ∼ **how to** scio ④ + *infin*
□ ∼ **not** ignoro ①
□ ∼ **again** recognosco ③

knowing *adj* sciens, prudens; (cunning) astutus
■ ∼**ly** *adv* scienter; prudenter; (cunningly) astute

knowledge *n* scientia, cognitio; (skill) peritia; (learning) eruditio *f*; (understanding) intellectus *m*

knowledgeable *adj* sciens

known *adj* notus
□ **be** ∼ enotesco ③
□ **it is** ∼ constat
□ **become** ∼ emano ①
□ **make** ∼ palam facio ③; divulgo ①
□ **well** ∼ (famous) celeber

knuckle *n* condylus, articulus *m*
■ ∼**-bones** *pl* (game) tali *mpl*

k

Ll

label¹ *n* titulus *m*

label² *vt* titulum affigo ③

laborious *adj* laboriosus; (difficult) operosus
■ ~**ly** *adv* laboriose; operose; multo labore

labour¹ *n* labor *m*; (manual) opera *f*; (work) opus *nt*; (of childbirth) partus *m*

labour² *vt&i* laboro, operor ①; (struggle, etc.) contendo ③

labourer *n* operarius *m*; opifex *m/f*

labyrinth *n* labyrinthus *m*

lace *vt* (edge) praetexo ③; (tie) necto, astringo ③

lacerate *vt* lacero, lanio ①

laceration *n* laceratio *f*

lack¹ *vt* egeo, careo ② + *abl*

lack² *n* inopia, egestas *f*

laconic *adj* Laconicus, brevis

lad *n* puer, adulescens *m*

ladder *n* scala *f*

laden *adj* onustus, oneratus

ladle *n* ligula, spatha, trulla *f*; coclear *nt*

lady *n* domina; matrona, era *f*

lag *vi* cesso, cunctor, moror ①

lagoon *n* lacuna *f*

lair *n* cubile; latibulum, lustrum *nt*

lake *n* lacus *m*; stagnum *nt*

lamb *n* agnus *m*; agna *f*

lame¹ *adj* claudus, debilis; fig inconcinnus, ineptus

lame² *vt* mutilo; debilito ①

lament¹ *vt&i* lamentor; deploro ①; fleo ②

lament² *n* ▶ **lamentation**

lamentable *adj* miserandus; lamentabilis; luctuosus, flebilis, miser

lamentation *n* lamentatio *f*; lamenta *ntpl*; (act) ploratus, fletus *m*

lamp *n* lucerna, lampas *f*; lychnus *m*

lance *n* lancea, hasta *f*

land¹ *n* (soil) terra, tellus; (country) regio *f*; (estate) fundus *m*; praedium *nt*; (field) ager *m*

land² *vt* in terram expono ③
■ ~ *vi* egredior ③

land-forces *npl* copiae terrestres *fpl*

landing *n* (on shore) egressus *m*

landlord *n* (innkeeper) caupo; (owner of land) dominus *m*

landmark *n* limes *m*

landscape *n* forma et situs agri; (picture) topia *f*

landslide *n* lapsus terrae *m*

lane *n* angiportus *m*

language *n* lingua, oratio *f*; sermo *m*; verba *ntpl*

languid *adj* languidus

languish *vi* langueo ②; languesco ③

lank *adj* (also **lanky**) macer

lantern *n* lanterna *f*

lap¹ *n* sinus *m*; gremium *nt*; (of a racecourse) spatium *nt*

lap² *vt* (lick) lambo ③

lap-dog *n* catellus *m*

lapse¹ *n* lapsus *m*; fig (error) erratum, peccatum *nt*

lapse² *vi* labor ③; (come to an end) exeo ④; (err) pecco ①

lard *n* laridum, lardum *nt*

larder *n* carnarium *nt*; cella *f*

large *adj* magnus, amplus, grandis, largus

largess *n* largitio *f*; donativum *nt*

lark *n* alauda *f*

lascivious *adj* salax; lascivus, petulans
■ ~**ly** *adv* lascive; petulanter

lasciviousness *n* salacitas, lascivia; petulantia *f*

lash¹ *n* (stroke) verber *nt*; (whip) scutica *f*; flagellum *nt*

lash² *vt* (whip) verbero, flagello; (fasten) alligo; fig castigo ①

last¹ *adj* postremus, ultimus; summus, extremus, (most recent) novissimus
□ ~ **but one** paenultimus
□ **at** ~ demum, tandem; denique, postremo

last² *adv* postremum; novissime

last[3] *vi* duro, perduro ①; maneo ②

lasting *adj* mansurus; perennis; stabilis

lastly *adv* postremo, denique

latch *n* obex *m/f*; pessulus *m*

late *adj* serus; tardus; (new) recens; (dead) mortuus
■ ∼ *adv* sero
□ **it grows** ∼ vesperascit

lately *adv* nuper, modo

latent *adj* latens, latitans, occultus

later *adj* posterus

lateral *adj* lateralis

lathe *n* tornus *m*

lather *n* spuma *f*

Latin *adj & n* Latinus; (language) lingua Latina *f*

latitude *n* latitudo; (liberty) licenta *f*

latter *adj* posterior
□ **the** ∼ hic
■ ∼**ly** *adv* nuperrime

lattice *n* cancelli, clathri *mpl*

laudable *adj* laudabilis, laude dignus

laudatory *adj* laudativus

laugh[1] *vi* rideo ②
□ ∼ **at** derideo, irrideo ②

laugh[2] *n* risus *m*

laughable *adj* ridiculus

laughing-stock *n* ludibrium *nt*

laughter *n* risus *m*

launch *vt* deduco ③; (hurl) iaculor ①; contorqueo ②

laurel[1] *n* (tree) laurus *f*; laurea *f*

laurel[2] *adj* laureus

laurelled *adj* laureatus, laurifer, lauriger

lava *n* torrens igneus *m*, liquefacta massa *f*

lavatory *n* latrina *f*

lavish[1] *adj* prodigus; profusus
■ ∼**ly** *adv* profuse, prodige

lavish[2] *vt* prodigo, profundo, effundo ③

law *n* lex *f*; (right) ius *nt*; (rule) norma *f*; (court of justice) iurisdictio *f*
□ ∼**suit** lis *f*
□ **international** ∼ ius gentium *nt*

lawful *adj* legitimus; iustus; licitus
■ ∼**ly** *adv* legitime; lege

lawless *adj* exlex; illicitus; inconcessus
■ ∼**ly** *adv* contra leges

lawlessness *n* licentia *f*

lawn *n* (of grass) pratum *nt*; (fine linen) carbasus, sindon *f*

lawsuit *n* lis, causa *f*

lawyer *n* iurisconsultus; causidicus, advocatus *m*

lax *adj* remissus; fig neglegens

laxity *n* (also **laxness**) remissio, neglegentia *f*

lay *vt* pono; (eggs) pario; (spread) spargo, expando ③
□ ∼ **aside** amoveo ②; repono ③
□ ∼ **by** repono, recondo, sepono ③
□ ∼ **claim to** vindico ①
□ ∼ **down** depono; (state) statuo ③
□ ∼ **on** impono ③; fig imputo ①
□ ∼ **out** expono; (money) expendo ③
□ ∼ **waste** vasto ①

laziness *n* segnities, pigritia; desidia *f*

lazy *adj* iners, ignavus, piger, segnis, desidiosus

lead[1] *n* plumbum *nt*

lead[2] *vt* duco ③; praeeo *ir*; (pass, spend) ago, dego ③; (manage) moderor ①
□ ∼ **away** abduco ③
□ ∼ **off** diverto; adduco ③
□ ∼ **on** (induce) conduco ③

leaden *adj* plumbeus

leader *n* dux *m/f*; ductor; fig auctor *m*

leadership *n* ductus *m*

leading *adj* princeps; primarius

leaf *n* folium *nt*; (of paper) pagina; (of metal) brattea *f*

leafless *adj* fronde nudatus

leafy *adj* frondosus, frondeus, frondifer

league *n* (confederacy) foedus *nt*; societas *f*
□ **be in** ∼ **with** consocio ① cum + *abl*

leak[1] *n* rima *f*; hiatus *m*

leak[2] *vi* perfluo; humorem transmitto ③

leaky *adj* rimosus

lean[1] *adj* macer; exilis, gracilis

lean[2] *vt* inclino, acclino ①
■ ∼ *vi* inclino ①
□ ∼ **on** *vi* innitor ③ + *dat*
□ ∼ **(over)** *vi* incumbo ③ ad + *acc*

leap *vi* salio ④; fig exsulto ①
□ ∼ **across** transilio ④

leap year *n* bisextilis annus *m*

learn *vt&i* disco; cognosco ③; (hear) audio ④
□ ∼ **by heart** edisco, perdisco ③

learned *adj* eruditus, doctus

learner *n* discipulus *m*

learning *n* doctrina, humanitas *f*; litterae *fpl*; (knowledge) eruditio *f*

lease¹ *n* conductio, locatio *f*

lease² *vt* conduco ③; loco; (out) eloco ①

leash *n* (thong) lorum *nt*; (rein) habena, (leash) copula *f*

least *adj* minimus
- ■ ~ *adv* minime
- □ **at** ~ saltem
- □ **not in the** ~ ne minimum quidem

leather¹ *n* corium *nt*; (tanned) aluta *f*

leather² *adj* scorteus

leave¹ *vt* linquo, relinquo, desero ③; (entrust) mando ①; trado ③; (bequeath) relinquo ③; lego ①; (depart from) exeo *ir* ex + *abl*, discedo ③ ex + *abl*, relinquo ③
- □ ~ **behind** relinquo ③
- □ ~ **off** *vi* desino; *vt* fig depono; (through interruption) intermitto ③
- □ ~ **out** omitto ③; praetereo *ir*

leave² *n* permissio, licentia, copia, potestas *f*; (of absence) commeatus *m*

lecherous *adj* libidinosus, salax

lecture¹ *n* schola, acroasis *f*; praelectio *f*

lecture² *vt* praelego ③; (reprove) obiurgo ①; corripio ③

lecturer *n* praelector *m*

ledge *n* dorsum *nt*; ora *f*

ledger *n* codex *m*

leech *n* sanguisuga, hirudo *f*

leek *n* porrum, allium *nt*

leer *vi* limis oculis intueor ③

left *adj* sinister, laevus
- ■ ~ *n* manus sinistra *f*
- □ **on the** ~ a sinistra
- □ **to the** ~ ad sinistram, sinistrorsum

leg *n* tibia *f*; crus *nt*; (of a table, *etc.*) pes *m*

legacy *n* legatum *nt*

legal *adj* legalis, legitimus; iudicialis
- ■ ~**ly** *adv* legitime; legibus

legalize *vt* legibus confirmo ①

legate *n* legatus *m*

legation *n* legatio *f*

legend *n* fabula *f*

legendary *adj* fabulosus

legible *adj* qui legi potest

legion *n* legio *f*

legionary *n* (soldier) legionarius *m*

legislate *vt* legem fero *ir*

legislation *n* legum datio *f*

legislator *n* legum lator *m*

legitimate *adj* legitimus; licitus; fig sincerus, verus

leisure *n* otium *nt*
- □ **at** ~ otiosus; vacuus

lemon *n* citrum *nt*

lend *vt* pecuniam mutuam do; commodo; (at interest) faeneror ①; fig praebeo ②

lender *n* qui pecuniam mutuam dat *m*

length *n* longitudo; (of time) longinquitas; (tallness) proceritas *f*
- □ **at** ~ tandem, demum

lengthen *vt* extendo, protraho; fig produco ③

lengthy *adj* longus; prolixus

leniency *n* lenitas, clementia, mansuetudo, indulgentia *f*; (pardon) venia *f*

lenient *adj* mitis, lenis, clemens; mansuetus

lentil *n* lens *f*

leopard *n* leopardus *m*

leprosy *n* leprae *fpl*

less *adj* minor
- ■ ~ *adv* minus

lessen *vt* minuo, imminuo
- ■ ~ *vi* decresco, minuor ③

lesson *n* schola *f*

lest *conj* ne + *subj*

let *vt* permitto ③ + *dat*; sino; patior ③; (lease) loco ①
- □ ~ **alone** omitto ③
- □ ~ **down** demitto ③
- □ ~ **in** admitto ③
- □ ~ **out** emitto ③; (hire) eloco ①
- □ ~ **pass** omitto ③; praetereo *ir*

lethal *adj* letalis

lethargic *adj* languidus

lethargy *n* languor; veternus *m*

letter *n* (of alphabet) littera *f*; (communication) epistula *f*; litterae *fpl*
- ■ ~**s** *pl* (learning) litterae *fpl*

lettering *n* titulus *m*

lettuce *n* lactuca *f*

level¹ *adj* planus, aequus

level² *n* planities *f*

level³ *vt* aequo, coaequo, complano ①

lever *n* vectis *m*

levity *n* levitas; iocatio *f*

levy¹ *n* delectus *m*

levy[2] *vt* (troops) conscribo ③; (money) exigo ③

lewd *adj* incestus, impudicus; libidinosus

liability *n* (obstacle) impedimentum *nt*

liable *adj* obnoxius
□ **~ to** obnoxius + *dat*

liaison *n* amicitia *f*

liar *n* mendax *m/f*

libel[1] *n* libellus famosus *m*

libel[2] *vt* diffamo ①

libellous *adj* probrosus; famosus

liberal *adj* liberalis, munificus; fig ingenuus
■ **~ly** *adv* liberaliter, munifice; ingenue

liberality *n* liberalitas, munificentia *f*

liberate *vt* libero ①; (in law) manumitto ③

liberation *n* liberatio *f*

liberator *n* liberator *m*

liberty *n* libertas; licentia *f*
□ **at ~** liber

librarian *n* bibliothecae praefectus *m*

library *n* bibliotheca *f*

licence *n* licentia; (lack of restraint) licentia, intemperantia *f*; venia *f*

licentious *adj* dissolutus, impudicus, lascivus; incestus
■ **~ly** *adv* inceste, lascive

licentiousness *n* mores dissoluti *mpl*; licentia, lascivia, intemperantia *f*

lick *vt* lambo ③; (daintily) ligurrio ④

lictor *n* lictor *m*

lid *n* operculum; operimentum *nt*

lie[1] *n* mendacium *nt*
□ **tell a ~** mentior ④

lie[2] *vi* (tell falsehoods) mentior ④

lie[3] *vi* iaceo ②; (in bed, *etc.*) cubo ①; (be situated) situs sum *ir*
□ **~ down** decumbo ③
□ **~ in wait** insidior ①
□ **~ on** incubo ①; incumbo ③ *both* + *dat*

lieu *n*:
□ **in ~ of** loco + *gen*

life *n* vita; anima *f*; spiritus *m*; fig vigor *m*; alacritas *f*

lifeless *adj* inanimus; exanimis; fig exsanguis, frigidus

lifetime *n* aetas *f*; aevum *nt*

lift *vt* tollo, attollo, erigo ③; levo, sublevo ①

ligament *n* ligamentum, ligamen *nt*

light[1] *n* lux *f*; lumen *nt*; (lamp) lucerna *f*
□ **bring to ~** in lucem profero *ir*

light[2] *adj* (bright, *etc.*) lucidus, fulgens; (in weight) levis; (of colours) candidus, dilutus; (easy) facilis; (nimble) agilis; pernix; (inconstant) instabilis

light[3] *vt* accendo ③
■ **~** *vi* exardesco ③
□ **~ up** illumino ①

lighten *vt* (illumine) illumino, illustro ①; (a weight) allevo; exonero ①

light-hearted *adj* hilaris, laetus, alacer

lighthouse *n* pharus *f*

lightly *adv* leviter; perniciter; fig neglegenter; temere

lightness *n* levitas; (quickness) agilitas, pernicitas *f*

lightning *n* fulmen *nt*

like[1] *adj* similis; assimilis, consimilis *all* + *gen*; (equal) par, aequus *all* + *dat*
■ **~** *adv* tamquam, velut; (in ~ manner) pariter, similiter

like[2] *vt&i* (approve) comprobo ①; (be fond of) amo ①
□ **would you ~?** velis?

likelihood *n* verisimilitudo *f*

likely *adj* probabilis, verisimilis
■ **~** *adv* probabiliter

liken *vt* assimulo, comparo ①; confero *ir*

likeness *n* similitudo; (portrait) imago, effigies *f*

likewise *adv* pariter, similiter

liking *n* approbatio *f*; favor *m*; (fancy) libido *f*

lily *n* lilium *nt*

limb *n* membrum *nt*; artus *m*

lime[1] *n* calx *f*
□ **bird-~** viscum *nt*; (tree) tilla *f*

lime[2] *vt* visco illino ③

limestone *n* calx *f*; lapis calcarius *m*

limit[1] *n* limes, terminus *m*; finis *m/f*; modus *m*

limit[2] *vt* termino ①; finio ④; circumscribo ③

limitation *n* exceptio *f*

limited *adj* circumscriptus

limitless *adj* infinitus

limp[1] *vi* claudico ①

limp[2] *n* claudicatio *f*

limp³ *adj* flaccidus, lentus

line¹ *n* (drawn) linea *f*; (row) series *f*; ordo *m*; (lineage) stirps, progenies *f*; genus *nt*; (cord) funiculus *m*; (in poetry) versus *m*; (entrenchment) vallum *nt*; (fishing-) linea *f*

line² *vt* (up) in ordinem instruo ③

lineage *n* stirps *f*; genus *nt*

linear *adj* linearis

linen¹ *n* linteum *nt*; carbasus *f*; (fine) sindon *f*

linen² *adj* linteus, lineus, carbaseus

linger *vi* cunctor, cesso, moror ①

lingering *adj* cunctabundus; tardus

linguist *n* linguarum peritus *m*

link¹ *n* (of a chain) anulus *m*; (bond) vinculum *nt*

link² *vt* connecto ③

lintel *n* limen superum *nt*

lion *n* leo *m*

lioness *n* leaena, lea *f*

lip *n* labrum, labellum *nt*; fig os *nt*; (edge) ora *f*

liquefy *vt* liquefacio ③
■ ~ *vi* liquefio ③

liquid¹ *adj* liquidus; (transparent) pellucidus

liquid² *n* liquidum *nt*; liquor *m*

liquor *n* umor, liquor *m*

lisp¹ *n* os blaesum *nt*

lisp² *vi* balbutio ④

list *n* index *m*

listen *vi* ausculto ①; audio ④

listener *n* auscultator, auditor *m*

listless *adj* remissus, neglegens, languidus

listlessness *n* inertia, socordia *f*; languor *m*

literal *adj* accuratus
■ ~ly *adv* ad litteram, ad verbum

literary *adj* ad litteras pertinens

literature *n* litterae *fpl*

litigant *n* litigator *m*

litigation *n* lis *f*

litter *n* (of straw, *etc.*) substramen, substramentum, stramentum *nt*; (vehicle) lectica *f*; (brood) partus *m*

little¹ *adj* parvus, exiguus
□ **a** ~ paulum
■ ~ *adv* parum

little² *n* paulum, exiguum; (somewhat) aliquantulum; nonnihil *n*
□ ~ **by** ~ paulatim

live¹ *vi* vivo, dego ③; spiro ①; vitam ago ③; (reside) habito ①; (on) vescor ③

live² *adj* vivus; vivens

livelihood *n* (trade) ars *f*; (means of maintenance) victus *m*

liveliness *n* vigor *nt*

lively *adj* vivus, vividus, alacer; vegetus

liver *n* iecur *nt*

livid *adj* (of colour) lividus, livens; fig (angry) iratus

living¹ *adj* vivus, vivens, spirans

living² *n* (way of life, food) victus *m*

lizard *n* lacertus *m*; lacerta *f*

load¹ *n* onus *nt*; sarcina *f*; (quantity) vehis *f*

load² *vt* onero ①

loaf *n* panis *m*

loan *n* mutua pecunia *f*

loathe *vt* fastidio ④; aspernor ①; odi, perodi ③

loathing *n* fastidium, taedium *nt*; satietas *f*

loathsome *adj* foedus; odiosus

lobby *n* vestibulum *nt*

lobster *n* locusta *f*; cammarus *m*

local *adj* loci, locorum *both gen*; (neighbouring) vicinus

locality *n* locus *m*

locate *vt* (place) loco ①; (find) invenio ④

location *n* locus *m*

lock¹ *n* sera *f*; claustrum *nt*; (of hair, wool, *etc.*) cirrus; floccus *m*

lock² *vt&i* (a door) obsero ①
□ ~ **in** includo ③
□ ~ **out** excludo ③
□ ~ **up** occludo ③

locker *n* loculamentum *nt*; capsa *f*

locksmith *n* claustrarius artifex *m*

locust *n* locusta *f*

lodge¹ *vi* habito ①; (stick fast in) haereo ② in + *abl*

lodge² *n* casa, cella *f*

lodger *n* inquilinus *m*

lodging *n* (stay) commoratio *f*; (room) cubiculum; (inn) deversorium *nt*

loft *n* cella *f*; tabulatum, cenaculum *nt*

lofty *adj* altus; celsus, excelsus; sublimis; fig superbus, elatus, arrogans

log *n* lignum *nt*; stipes; (trunk) truncus *m*

loggerhead *n*:
□ **be at** ∼**s** rixor ① cum + *abl*

logic *n* logica, dialectica *f*

logical *adj* logicus, dialecticus
■ ∼**ly** *adv* dialectice

loiter *vi* cesso, cunctor; moror ①

loll *vi* dependo ③; langueo ②
□ ∼ **on** innitor ③ + *dat*

lone *adj* solus; solitarius

loneliness *n* solitudo *f*

lonely *adj* solus; solitarius; (of places) desolatus; avius

long¹ *adj* longus; (of time) diuturnus; diutinus; (lengthened) productus

long² *adv* diu
□ ∼ **after** multo post
□ ∼ **ago** iamdudum
□ ∼ **before** multo ante

long³ *vi* aveo ②; (for) desidero ①; cupio ③

longevity *n* longaevitas *f*

longing *n* desiderium *nt*; appetitus *m*; cupido *f*

longitude *n* longitudo *f*

long-suffering *adj* patiens

look¹ *vi* video ②; aspicio, conspicio ③; specto ①; (seem) videor ② ▶ **seem**
□ ∼ **around** circumspicio ③
□ ∼ **after** fig curo ①
□ ∼ **at** intueor ②
□ ∼ **back** respicio ③
□ ∼ **down on** despicio ③
□ ∼ **for** (seek) quaero ③
□ ∼ **forward** prospicio ③; exspecto ①
□ ∼ **in** inspicio, introspicio ③; (examine) perscrutor ①
□ ∼ **on** intueor ②
□ ∼ **out** prospicio ③; (for) quaero ③
□ ∼ **out!** cave! cavete!
□ ∼ **round** circumspicio; respicio ③
□ ∼ **through** per … aspicio; fig perspicio ③
□ ∼ **to** fig curo ①
□ ∼ **up** suspicio ③
□ ∼ **upon** fig (value) habeo ②; aestimo ①
□ ∼ **up to** fig veneror ①

look² *n* aspectus, vultus *m*; os *nt*; facies *f*; (glance) obtutus *m*

look³ *int* ecce! en! aspice!

looking-glass *n* speculum *nt*

lookout *n* (**lookout post**) specula *f*

loom¹ *n* tela *f*

loom² *vi* appareo, obscure videor ②

loop *n* laqueus *m*

loophole *n* fig effugium *nt*

loose¹ *adj* laxus; solutus; neglegens; dissolutus

loose² *vt* solvo, resolvo ③; laxo, relaxo ①

loosen *vt* solvo, resolvo ③; laxo, relaxo ①; *vi* solvor ③

loot *n* praeda *f*

looter *n* raptor *m*

loquacious *adj* loquax, garrulus

lord *n* dominus *m*

lordly *adj* superbus, imperiosus

lordship *n* imperium *nt*

lore *n* doctrina; eruditio *f*; (rites) ritus *mpl*

lose *vt* amitto, perdo ③; (be deprived of) privor ① + *abl*; (be defeated) vincor ③
□ ∼ **one's way** aberro ①
□ **be lost** pereo *ir*

loss *n* (act) amissio, iactura *f*; damnum, detrimentum *nt*; mil clades *f*

lot *n* pars, portio; (chance) sors *f*; casus *m*
□ **by** ∼ sorte
□ ∼ **of** multus

lotion *n* medicamen *nt*

lottery *n* sortitio *f*

loud *adj* clarus, sonorus
■ ∼**ly** *adv* clare, magna voce

loudness *n* claritas *f*

lounge¹ *vi* cesso, otior ①

lounge² *n* lectulus *m*

louse *n* pedis, pediculus *m*

lout *n* homo agrestis, rusticus *m*

loutish *adj* agrestis, rusticus

love¹ *n* amor, ardor *m*; flamma *f*; (desire) desiderium *nt*; (dearness) caritas *f*
■ **in** ∼ *adj* amans

love² *vt* amo ①; diligo ③

love-letter *n* nota blanda *f*

loveliness *n* venustas; forma, pulchritudo *f*

lovely *adj* formosus pulcher; venustus

love-potion *n* philtrum *nt*

lover *n* amator, amans; (devotee) studiosus *m*

lovingly *adv* amanter, blande

low¹ *adj* humilis; (of price) vilis; (of birth) obscurus; (of the voice) summissus; fig turpis; (downcast) abiectus

low² *adv* humiliter; summissa voce

low³ *vi* mugio ④

lower¹ *vt* (let down) demitto; (humiliate) abicio; (the price) imminuo ③; (the voice) submitto ③

lower² *adj* inferior

lowermost *adj* infimus, imus

lowing *n* mugitus *m*

lowliness *n* humilitas *f*; fig animus demissus *m*

lowly *adj* humilis, obscurus

loyal *adj* fidelis
  ■ ~**ly** *adv* fideliter

loyalty *n* fides, fidelitas *f*

lucid *adj* lucidus; (transparent) pellucidus

luck *n* fortuna *f*; successus *m*
  □ **bad** ~ res adversae *fpl*
  □ **good** ~ res secundae *fpl*

luckily *adj* feliciter; fauste, prospere, fortunate

lucky *adj* felix, faustus, prosperus, fortunatus

lucrative *adj* quaestuosus, lucrosus

ludicrous *adj* ridiculus, iocularis

lug *vt* traho ③

luggage *n* sarcinae *fpl*; impedimenta *ntpl*; onus *nt*

lukewarm *adj* egelidus, tepidus; fig frigidus

lull¹ *vt* sopio ④; fig demulceo ②

lull² *n* quies *f*

luminous *adj* illustris, lucidus

lump *n* glaeba; massa; (heap) congeries *f*

lumpy *adj* glaebosus

lunacy *n* alienatio mentis *f*; amentia, dementia *f*

lunar *adj* lunaris

lunatic *adj* insanus, demens
  ■ ~ *n* homo insanus *m*

lunch¹ *n* (also **luncheon**) merenda *f*; prandium *nt*

lunch² *vi* prandeo ②

lung *n* pulmo *m*

lunge *n* ictus *m*; plaga *f*

lurch¹ *n*:
  □ **leave in the** ~ desero, destituo ③

lurch² *vi* titubo ①

lure¹ *n* illecebra, (bait) esca *f*

lure² *vt* allicio, pellicio ③

lurk *vi* lateo ②; latito ①

luscious *adj* suavis, praedulcis

lust¹ *n* libido, cupido, cupiditas *f*; appetitus *m*

lust² *vt* (for) concupisco ③

lustful *adj* libidinosus, salax, lascivus

lustre *n* also fig splendor *m*

lusty *adj* robustus, vegetus

luxuriant *adj* luxuriosus; sumptuosus; fig luxurians

luxurious *adj* luxuriosus; sumptuosus; fig luxurians

luxury *n* luxus *m*; luxuria *f*

lying *adj* mendax; fallax; vanus

lynx *n* lynx *m/f*
  ■ ~-**eyed** *adj* lynceus

lyre *n* cithara; lyra *f*

lyric *adj* (also **lyrical**) lyricus

Mm

mace *n* sceptrum *nt*

machination *n* dolus *m*; (trick) machina; ars *f*

machine *n* machina *f*; machinamentum *nt*

machinery *n* machinamentum *nt*; machinatio *f*

mackerel *n* scomber *m*

mad *adj* insanus, vesanus, demens, amens

madam *n* domina, era *f*

madden *vt* mentem alieno; fig furio ①; ad insaniam adigo ③

maddening *adj* fig furiosus; (troublesome) molestus

madly *adv* insane, dementer; furiose

madman *n* homo furiosus; fig demens *m*

madness *n* insania; rabies; amentia, dementia *f*; furor *m*

maggot *n* vermiculus, termes *m*

magic *adj* magicus
■ ∼ *n* magica ars *f*; veneficium *nt*

magician *n* magus, veneficus *m*; (conjurer) praestigiator *m*

magistracy *n* magistratus *m*

magistrate *n* magistratus *m*

magnanimity *n* magnanimitas, magnitudo animi *f*

magnanimous *adj* magnanimus
■ ∼**ly** *adv* pro magnitudine animi

magnet *n* magnes *m*

magnetic *adj* magnes

magnificence *n* magnificentia *f*; splendor *m*

magnificent *adj* magnificus, splendidus
■ ∼**ly** *adv* magnifice; splendide

magnify *vt* amplifico ①

magnitude *n* magnitudo *f*

magpie *n* corvus pica *f*

maid *n* (female servant) ancilla, famula *f*

maiden[1] *adj* virginalis
■ ∼ **speech** *n* prima oratio *f*

maiden[2] *n* virgo *f*

maidenhood *n* virginitas *f*

mail *n* (letter-carrier) tabellarius *m*; (coat) lorica *f*; thorax *m*

maim *vt* mutilo; trunco ①

main[1] *adj* praecipuus, primus, maximus
■ ∼**ly** *adv* praecipue, maxime; praesertim

main[2] *n* (sea) mare *nt*

mainland *n* terra continens *f*

maintain *vt&i* affirmo ①; (defend) tueor, sustineo ②; (keep) nutrio ④; sustento ①; alo ③; (keep in good condition) conservo ①

maintenance *n* (support) defensio *f*; (means of living) alimentum *nt*; victus *m*

maize *n* zea *f*

majestic *adj* augustus; sublimis; imperatorius

majesty *n* maiestas; dignitas, sublimitas *f*

majority *n* pars maior *f*; plures *m/fpl*

make *vt* facio ③; (elect) creo ①; (form, fabricate) conficio; fingo ③; (render) reddo ③
□ ∼ **for** peto ③
□ ∼ **good** resarcio ④
□ ∼ **much of** magni facio ③
□ ∼ **up** (compensate) resarcio ④; (resolve) decerno ③; (numerically) expleo ②; (invent) fingo ③

maker *n* fabricator *m*; auctor *m/f*

makeshift *adj* subitarius

maladministration *n* administratio mala *f*

male[1] *adj* mas; masculinus, masculus, virilis

male[2] *n* mas, masculus *m*

malefactor *n* maleficus *m*

malevolence *n* malevolentia, malignitas, invidia *f*

malevolent *adj* malevolus, malignus

malice *n* malevolentia, malitia *f*

malicious *adj* malevolus, malitiosus
■ ∼**ly** *adv* malevolo animo, malitiose

malign[1] *adj* malevolus

malign[2] *vt* obtrecto ①

malignant *adj* malevolus

malleable *adj* ductilis, mollis

mallet *n* malleus *m*

malpractice *n* male facta, delicta *ntpl*; maleficium *nt*

maltreat *vt* vexo ①; laedo ③

maltreatment *n* iniuria *f*

mammal *n* animal *nt*

man[1] *n* (human being) homo; (as opposed to woman) vir; mas *m*
□ **a** ∼ (some one) aliquis
□ ∼ **of war** navis longa *f*

man[2] *vt* (a ship) compleo ②

manacle[1] *n* manicae *fpl*; compes *f*

manacle[2] *vt* manicas (alicui) inicio ③

manage *vt* administro; curo, tracto ①; gero ③
■ ∼ *vi* (cope) rem prospere gero ③

manageable *adj* tractabilis

management *n* administratio; cura, procuratio *f*

manager *n* curator; (steward) procurator, vilicus *m*

mandate *n* mandatum *nt*

mandatory *adj* necessarius

mane *n* iuba *f*

mange *n* scabies *f*

mangle¹ *vt* lacero, lanio, dilanio ①
mangle² *n* prelum *nt*
mangy *adj* scaber
manhood *n* pubertas; virilitas; fortitudo *f*
mania *n* fig insania, amentia *f*
maniac *n* homo furiosus *m*
manifest¹ *adj* manifestus, clarus, apertus, evidens
  ■ ~**ly** *adv* manifeste, aperte; evidenter
manifest² *vt* declaro ①; ostendo ③; praebeo ②
manifestation *n* patefactio *f*
manifesto *n* edictum *nt*
manifold *adj* multiplex; varius
maniple *n* manipulus *m*
manipulate *vt* (manibus) tracto ①
manipulation *n* tractatio *f*
mankind *n* genus humanum *nt*; homines *mpl*
manliness *n* virtus, fortitudo *f*
manly *adj* virilis; strenuus; fortis
manner *n* modus *m*; ratio, consuetudo *f*
  □ ~**s** mores *mpl*
  □ **good** ~**s** urbanitas *f*
  □ **bad** ~**s** rusticitas *f*
mannerism *n* mala affectatio *f*
manoeuvre¹ *n* mil decursus *m*; fig artificium *nt*
manoeuvre² *vi* mil decurro ③; (plot) machinor ①
mansion *n* domus, sedes *f*
manslaughter *n* homicidium *nt*
manual *adj* manualis
  ■ ~ **labour** *n* opera *f*
manufacture¹ *n* fabrica *f*; opificium *nt*
manufacture² *vt* fabricor ①; fabrefacio ③
manufacturer *n* fabricator *m*, opifex *m/f*
manumission *n* manumissio *f*
manumit *vt* manumitto ③
manure¹ *n* stercus *nt*; fimus *m*
manure² *vi* stercero ①
manuscript *n* codex *m*
many *adj* multi; plerique; complures
  □ **as** ~ **as** quot … tot
  □ **how** ~ quot

  □ **so** ~ tot
  □ ~ **ways** multifarie
map¹ *n* tabula geographica *f*
map² *vt* (out) designo ①
maple¹ *n* acer *nt*
maple² *adj* acernus
mar *vt* foedo, vitio ①; corrumpo ③
marauder *n* praedator *m*
marauding *n* praedatio *f*
marble *n* marmor *nt*
  ■ **of** ~ *adj* marmoreus
March¹ *n* (month) Martius *m*
march² *n* iter *nt*; (step) gradus *m*
march³ *vi* iter facio, incedo, gradior, proficiscor ③
  ■ ~ *vt* exercitum duco ③
  □ ~ **in** ingredior ③
  □ ~ **off** recedo ③
mare *n* equa *f*
margin *n* margo *m/f*
marginal *adj* in margine positus, margini ascriptus
marine *adj* marinus, maritimus
mariner *n* nauta *m*
marital *adj* conubialis
maritime *adj* maritimus
marjoram *n* amaracum, origanum *nt*
mark¹ *n* nota *f*; signum; (brand) stigma; (impression) vestigium *nt*; (to shoot at) scopus *m*; (of a stripe) vibex; (of a wound) cicatrix *f*; fig indicium *nt*
mark² *vt* noto, signo ①; (observe) animadverto ③; (with a pencil, *etc*.) designo ①
  □ ~ **out** metor ①; metior ④
market *n* (place) forum *nt*; mercatus *m*
market-day *n* nundinae *fpl*
marketing *n* emptio, mercatura *f*
market-place *n* forum *nt*
marksman *n* iaculator *m*
marriage¹ *n* conubium, coniugium, matrimonium *nt*; nuptiae *fpl*
marriage² *adj* nuptialis, coniugalis, conubialis
marriageable *adj* nubilis, adultus
married *adj* (of a woman) nupta; (of a man) maritus
marrow *n* (of bones) medulla *f*
marry *vt* (of a priest) conubio iungo; (as the man) uxorem duco; (as the woman) viro nubo ③

marsh *n* palus *f*

marshal *vt* dispono ③

marshy *adj* paluster, paludosus

martial *adj* bellicosus, ferox; militaris, bellicus
■ **court** ~ *n* castrense iudicium *nt*

martyr *n* martyr *m/f*

marvel *n* res mira *f*; mirum *nt*; miraculum *nt*

marvellous *adj* mirus, mirabilis
■ ~**ly** *adv* mire; mirabiliter

masculine *adj* masculus; mas; virilis

mask[1] *n* persona, larva *f*; fig praetextum *nt*

mask[2] *vt* personam induo ③; fig dissimulo ①

mason *n* lapicida, structor *m*

masonry *n* saxa *ntpl*

mass *n* moles, massa; immensa copia *f*; ingens pondus *nt*; (of people) multitudo, turba *f*

massacre *n* caedes, trucidatio *f*
■ ~ *vt* trucido ①

massive *adj* solidus

mast *n* (of a ship) malus *m*

master[1] *n* dominus, erus; (teacher) magister, praeceptor *m*; fig potens, compos *m/f* + *gen*; (expert) peritus *m* + *gen*

master[2] *vt* supero ①; vinco ③; dominor ①; (learn) perdisco ③

masterly *adj* (of an artist) artificiosus

masterpiece *n* opus palmare *nt*

master-stroke *n* artificium singulare *nt*

mastery *n* dominatus *m*; imperium *nt*; (skill) peritia *f*

mat *n* matta, teges *f*; stragulum *nt*

match[1] *n* (marriage) nuptiae *fpl*; (contest) certamen *nt*; (an equal) par, compar *m/f*

match[2] *vt* compono ③; adaequo, exaequo
■ ~ *vi* (be suitable) quadro ①

matchless *adj* incomparabilis, eximius, singularis

matchmaker *n* conciliator nuptiarum *m*; conciliatrix nuptiarum *f*

mate[1] *n* socius, collega *m*; coniunx *m/f*

mate[2] *vi* (of animals) coniungor ③

material[1] *adj* corporeus; fig (important) magni momenti

material[2] *n* materia *f*; (cloth) textile *nt*
■ ~**s** *pl* res necessariae *fpl*

maternal *adj* maternus

maternity *n* condicio matris *f*

mathematical *adj* mathematicus

mathematician *n* mathematicus *m*

mathematics *n* mathematica *f*

matricide *n* (murder) matricidium *nt*; (murderer) matricida *m/f*

matrimonial *adj* coniugalis, conubialis, nuptialis

matted *adj* concretus

matter[1] *n* (substance) materia; (affair, business, *etc.*) res *f*; negotium; (purulent) pus *nt*; sanies *f*
□ **no** ~ nihil interest

matter[2] *vi impers*
□ **it does not** ~ nihil interest, nihil refert

matting *n* tegetes *fpl*

mattress *n* culcita *f*

mature *adj* maturus; tempestivus
■ ~ *vt&i* maturo ①

maturity *n* maturitas; aetas matura *f*

maul *vt* mulco ①

mausoleum *n* mausoleum *nt*

mawkish *adj* (of taste) putidus; fastidiosus
■ ~**ly** *adv* putide, fastidiose

maxim *n* praeceptum *nt*; sententia *f*

May[1] *n* (month) Maius *m*

may[2] *vi* possum; licet

maybe *adv* forsitan, forsan; forte, fortasse

mayor *n* praefectus urbanus *m*

maze *n* labyrinthus *m*; ambages *fpl*

me *prep* me
□ **to** ~ mihi

meadow *n* pratum *nt*

meagre *adj* macer; fig aridus; ieiunus; exilis

meal *n* (flour) farina *f*; (food) cibus *m*; (dinner, *etc.*) epulae *fpl*

mealtime *n* cibi hora *f*

mean[1] *adj* (middle) medius; (moderate) mediocris; (low) humilis; (miserly) avarus; (unkind) malignus; fig sordidus; vilis
□ **in the** ~**time** interea

mean[2] *n* medium *nt*; (manner) modus *m*; ratio *f*

□ **by all** ∼s quam maxime
□ **by no** ∼s nullo modo

mean[3] *vt&i* volo; mihi volo *ir*; cogito; significo ①

meander[1] *n* cursus; flexus *m*

meander[2] *vi* labor ③; sinuor ①

meaning *n* significatio *f*; animus, sensus *m*

meanness *n* humilitas; fig avaritia; ignobilitas *f*

means *n* (method) modus *m*, ratio *f*

meanwhile *adv* interea, interim

measurable *adj* quem metiri potes, mensurabilis

measure[1] *n* mensura *f*; (of land, liquids) modus *m*
■ ∼s *pl* consilium *nt*
□ **in some** ∼ aliquatenus

measure[2] *vt* metior ④; metor ①
□ ∼ **out** admetior ④

measurement *n* mensura *f*

meat *n* caro *f*

mechanic *n* opifex *m/f*, faber *m*

mechanical *adj* mechanicus
■ ∼ly *adv* mechanica quadam arte

mechanics *n* mechanica ars; machinalis scientia *f*

mechanism *n* machinatio; mechanica ratio *f*

medal *n* nomisma *nt*

meddle *vi* (with) me immisceo ②; intervenio ④

mediate *vi* intercedo ③

mediation *n* intercessio *f*

mediator *n* intercessor, conciliator *m*

medical *adj* medicus, medicinalis

medicinal *adj* medicus; salutaris

medicine *n* (science) medicina *f*; (remedy) medicamentum, medicamen *nt*

mediocre *adj* mediocris, modicus

mediocrity *n* mediocritas *f*

meditate *vi* meditor, cogito ①

meditation *n* meditatio, cogitatio *f*

meditative *adj* cogitabundus

Mediterranean *n* mare mediterraneum *or* internum *or* medium *nt*

medium[1] *n* (middle) medium *nt*; (mode, method) modus *m*, ratio *f*; (agent) conciliator *m*

medium[2] *adj* mediocris

medley *n* farrago *f*

meek *adj* mitis; fig summissus, humilis
■ ∼ly *adv* summisse

meekness *n* animus summissus *m*

meet *vt* obvenio ④; occurro ③; obviam eo *ir all + dat*; congredior ③ cum + *abl*
□ ∼ **with** offendo ③; (bad) subeo *ir*; patior ③; (good) nanciscor ③

meeting *n* congressio *f*; congressus *m*; (assembly) conventus *m*

melancholy[1] *n* tristitia, maestitia *f*

melancholy[2] *adj* melancholicus, maestus, tristis

mellow[1] *adj* maturus, mitis

mellow[2] *vi* maturesco ③

melodious *adj* canorus, numerosus

melody *n* melos *nt*; modulatio *f*; numerus *m*

melt *vt* liquefacio, solvo, dissolvo ③
■ ∼ *vi* liquefio *ir*, liquesco ③

membrane *n* membrana *f*

memento *n* monumentum *nt*

memoir *n* commentarius *m*

memorable *adj* memorabilis, notabilis, memoria dignus

memorial *n* monumentum *nt*

memory *n* memoria *f*

menace *n & vt* ▶ **threat, threaten**

menagerie *n* vivarium *nt*

mend *vt* emendo ①; corrigo ③; reparo ①; (clothes) sarcio ④
■ ∼ *vi* melior fio *ir*

menial *adj* servilis; sordidus

mental *adj* mentis, animi *gen sing*; mente conceptus, internus
■ ∼ly *adv* mente, animo

mention[1] *n* commemoratio, mentio *f*

mention[2] *vt* commemoro ①; mentionem facio + *gen* ③
□ **not to** ∼ silentio praetereo *ir*

mercenary[1] *adj* mercenarius, venalis

mercenary[2] *n* miles conductus *m*

merchandise *n* merx; (trade) mercatura *f*

merchant *n* mercator, negotiator *m*

merciful *adj* misericors, clemens

merciless *adj* immisericors, inclemens; immitis, durus

mercury *n* (metal) argentum vivum *nt*

mercy *n* misericordia, clementia, indulgentia *f*
□ **at the ~ of** in manu + *gen*

mere *adj* merus
■ **~ly** *adv* tantummodo, solummodo, nihil nisi

merge *vt* confundo ③; misceo ②
■ **~** *vi* commisceor ② cum + *abl*

merit¹ *n* meritum *nt*; virtus *f*

merit² *vt* mereo, demereor, promereo ②

merry *adj* hilaris, festivus

merrymaking *n* festivitas *f*

mesh *n* (of a net) macula *f*

mesmerize *vt* consopio ④

mess¹ *n* mil (place for eating) contubernium *nt*; (dirt) squalor *m*; fig (confusion) turba *f*

mess² *vi* (about) ludo ③

message *n* nuntius *m*

messenger *n* nuntius; (letter-carrier) tabellarius *m*

metal *n* metallum *nt*

metallic *adj* metallicus

metamorphose *vt* transformo, transfiguro ①

metamorphosis *n* transfiguratio *f*

metaphor *n* translatio *f*

metaphorical *adj* translaticius
■ **~ly** *adv* per translationem

meteor *n* fax caelestis *f*

method *n* ratio, via *f*

methodical *adj* dispositus, ratione et via factus
■ **~ly** *adv* ratione et via; disposite

meticulous *adj* curiosus, diligens

metre *n* metrum *nt*; numerus *m*; versus *m*

metrical *adj* metricus

mettle *n* vigor, animus *m*; (courage) virtus, fortitudo; magnanimitas *f*

mid *adj* medius

midday *n* meridies *m*; meridianum tempus *nt*
■ **of ~** *adj* meridianus

middle¹ *adj* medius

middle² *n* medium *nt*; (waist) medium corpus *nt*

middling *adj* mediocris; modicus

midnight *n* media nox *f*

midst *n* medium *nt*
□ **in the ~ of** inter + *acc*

midsummer *n* media aestas, summa aestas *f*

midway *n* media via *f*

midwife *n* obstetrix *f*

midwinter *n* media hiems *f*

mien *n* vultus *m*; os *nt*; species *f*

might¹ *n* vis, potestas, potentia *f*
□ **with all one's ~** summa ope

might² *vi in subordinate clauses often expressed by subj verb and/or subj of* possum (*expressing or possibility*) *or* licet (*permission*)

mighty *adj* potens, pollens, validus; magnus

migrate *vi* migro, transmigro ①; abeo *ir*

migration *n* migratio, peregrinatio *f*

mild *adj* mitis, lenis; placidus; clemens; mansuetus
■ **~ly** *adv* leniter, clementer, placide, mansuete

mildew *adj* (mould) mucor, situs *m*

mildness *n* clementia, lenitas, mansuetudo *f*

mile *n* mille passus *mpl*

milestone *n* miliarium *nt*

militant *adj* pugnax

military *adj* militaris
■ **~** *n* milites *mpl*

milk¹ *n* lac *nt*

milk² *vt* mulgeo ②

milky *adj* lacteus, lactans
■ **~ way** *n* orbis lacteus *m*; via lactea *f*

mill *n* mola *f*; pistrinum *nt*

miller *n* molitor *m*

millet *n* milium *nt*

million *n* decies centena milia *f*

millionaire *n* homo praedives *m*

millstone *n* mola *f*; molaris *m*

mime *n* (play and player) mimus *m*

mimic¹ *n* mimus *m*

mimic² *vt* imitor ①

mimicry *n* imitatio *f*

mince *vt* concido ③

mind¹ *n* animus *m*; mens *f*; ingenium *nt*; sensus *m*; (desire) desiderium *nt*; voluntas, cupido *f*; (recollection) memoria *f*

mind² *vt* (look after) curo ①; (regard) respicio ③; (consider) animadverto ③; considero ①
□ **I don't ~** nihil moror ①

mindful *adj* attentus, diligens; memor

mine¹ *n* fodina *f*; metallum *nt*; mil cuniculus *m*

mine² *vt&i* effodio ③; mil cuniculos ago ③

mine³ *adj* meus

miner *n* (of metals) metallicus *m*

mineral *n* metallum *nt*
■ ~ *adj* metallicus

mingle *vt* misceo, commisceo ②; confundo ③
■ ~ *vi* commisceor ②

minimum *n* minimum *nt*

minion *n* satelles *m*

minister *n* minister; (of state) rerum publicarum administer *m*

minor *n* pupillus *m*; pupilla *f*

minority *n* minor pars *f*; (under age) pupillaris aetas *f*

minstrel *n* fidicen *m*

mint¹ *n* moneta *f*

mint² *n* (plant) menta *f*

mint³ *vt* cudo ③; signo ①

minute¹ *n* punctum temporis *nt*

minute² *adj* minutus, exiguus

miracle *n* miraculum *nt*

miraculous *adj* prodigiosus, mirabilis
■ ~ly *adv* divinitus

mirror *n* speculum *nt*

mirth *n* hilaritas; laetitia; festivitas *f*

misadventure *n* infortunium *nt*

misapprehension *n* falsa conceptio *f*; error *m*

misbehave *vi* indecore se gerere ③

misbehaviour *n* morum pravitas *f*

miscalculate *vt* erro ①; fallor ③

miscalculation *n* error *m*

miscarriage *n* (in childbirth) abortus; fig malus successus *m*

miscarry *vi* parum succedo ③

miscellaneous *adj* promiscuus, miscellaneus

miscellany *n* coniectanea, miscellanea *ntpl*

mischief *n* (harm, loss) incommodum, damnum; (injury, wrong) maleficium, malum *nt*; (nuisance) pestis *f*

mischievous *adj* maleficus; noxius, funestus

misconception *n* falsa opinio *f*

misconduct *n* delictum, peccatum *nt*

misconstrue *vt* male *or* perverse interpretor ①

misdeed *n* delictum, peccatum *nt*; scelus *nt*

misdemeanour *n* vitium *nt*

miser *n* avarus *m*

miserable *adj* miser, miserabilis, miserandus, aerumnosus

miserly *adj* avarus

misery *n* miseria *f*; aerumnae *fpl*; angor *m*

misfortune *n* adversa fortuna, calamitas *f*; infortunium, incommodum *nt*

misgivings *n*:
□ **have ~** parum confido, diffido ③

misguided *adj* demens

mishap *n* incommodum *nt*

misinterpret *vt* male interpretor ①

misinterpretation *n* falsa interpretatio *f*

misjudge *vt* male iudico ①

mislay *vt* amitto ③

mislead *vt* decipio, fallo ③

mismanage *vt* male gero ③

misnomer *n* falsum nomen *nt*

misplace *vt* alieno loco pono ③

misrepresent *vt* perverse interpretor; calumnior ①; detorqueo ②

miss¹ *n* error *m*; (loss) damnum *nt*; (failure) malus successus *m*

miss² *vt&i* (pass over) omitto ③; (one's aim) non attingo ③; (be disappointed) de spe decido ③; (not find) reperire non possum *ir*; (feel the loss of) desidero ①; careo ② + *abl*

misshapen *adj* deformis, pravus

missile *n* telum, missile *nt*

mission *n* legatio; missio *f*; (instructions) mandatum *nt*

mist *n* nebula; caligo *f*

mistake¹ *n* erratum, mendum, vitium *nt*; error *m*

mistake² *vt* male interpretor ①

mistaken *adj* falsus
□ **be ~** erro ①

mistletoe *n* viscum *nt*

mistress *n* domina, era; (sweetheart) amica; (teacher) magistra *f*

mistrust¹ *n* diffidentia, suspicio *f*

mistrust² *vi* diffido ③; suspicor ①

mistrustful *adj* diffidens

misty *adj* nebulosus, caliginosus; fig obscurus

misunderstand *vt* perperam intellego ③

misunderstanding *n* error *m*; (disagreement) offensa, offensio *f*

misuse¹ *vt* abutor ③ + *abl*

misuse² *n* abusus *m*; (ill-treatment) iniuria *f*

mitigate *vt* mitigo, levo ①; lenio ④; remitto ③; extenuo ①

mitre *n* mitra *f*

mix *vt* misceo, commisceo, permisceo ②
□ ∼ **up** admisceo ②
□ ∼ **with** (socially) me immisceo ②

mixed *adj* mixtus, promiscuus, confusus

mixture *n* (act and result) mixtura *f*; (hotchpotch) farrago *f*

moan¹ *vi* gemo, ingemisco ③

moan² *n* gemitus *m*

moat *n* fossa *f*

mob *n* turba *f*; vulgus *nt*

mobile *adj* mobilis, expeditus

mobility *n* mobilitas *f*

mock¹ *vt&i* ludo ③; ludificor ①; irrideo ②

mock² *adj* fictus, fucatus, simulatus

mockery *n* irrisio *f*; irrisus *m*

mode *n* modus *m*; ratio *f*; (fashion) usus *m*

model¹ *n* exemplar, exemplum *nt*

model² *vt* formo; delineo ①

moderate¹ *adj* moderatus; mediocris; modicus
■ ∼**ly** *adv* moderate; modice; mediocriter

moderate² *vt* moderor, tempero ①; (restrain) coerceo ②

moderation *n* moderatio; temperantia, modestia *f*

modern *adj* recens; hodiernus

modest *adj* (moderate) mediocris, modicus; (not proud) verecundus; modestus
■ ∼**ly** *adv* modeste, verecunde, mediocriter

modesty *n* pudor *m*; modestia, pudicitia, verecundia *f*

modification *n* immutatio *f*

modify *vt* immuto ①

moist *adj* umidus, uvidus, udus, madidus

moisten *vt* umecto, irroro, rigo ①

moisture *n* umor *m*; uligo *f*

molar *n* molaris *m*

mole *n* (massive structure, pile) moles, pila *f*; (earthwork) agger *m*; (on the body) naevus *m*; (animal) talpa *m/f*

molest *vt* vexo, sollicito ①

molten *adj* fusus, fusilis; liquidus

moment *n* (of time) punctum temporis; (importance) momentum, pondus *nt*; (opportunity) occasio *f*
□ **in a** ∼ statim
□ **of great** ∼ magni ponderis
□ **this** ∼ ad tempus

momentarily *adv* subito

momentary *adj* brevis, brevissimus, subitus

momentous *adj* magni momenti

momentum *n* impetus *m*

monarch *n* rex *m*, princeps *m/f*

monarchy *n* regnum *nt*

Monday *n* dies lunae *m*

money *n* pecunia *f*; argentum *nt*; nummus *m*

moneylender *n* faenerator *m*

monitor *n* admonitor *m*

monkey *n* simius *m*; simia *f*

monologue *n* soliloquium *nt*

monopolize *vi* monopolium exerceo ②; fig solus habeo ②

monopoly *n* monopolium *nt*

monotonous *adj* fig continuus; nulla varietate delectans

monster *n* monstrum; portentum, prodigium *nt*

monstrous *adj* monstruosus, portentosus, prodigiosus

month *n* mensis *m*

monthly *adj* menstruus

monument *n* monumentum; (tomb) mausoleum *nt*

monumental *adj* monumentalis

mood *n* animi affectus, habitus *m*, voluntas *f*

moody *adj* morosus; tristis

moon *n* luna *f*

moonlight *n* lunae lumen *nt*
◻ **by** ∼ per lunam

moor¹ *n* loca patentia et ericis obsita *ntpl*

moor² *vt* (a ship) navem religo ①

mop¹ *n* peniculus *m*

mop² *vt* detergeo ②

mope *vi* tristis sum *ir*

moral *adj* moralis; qui ad mores pertinet; (virtuous) integer, honestus

morality *n* mores *mpl*; (virtue) virtus *f*; (duty) officium *nt*

morals *n* mores *mpl*; instituta *ntpl*

morbid *adj* morbidus, morbosus

more *adj* plus, maior
■ ∼ *adv* plus, magis; amplius; ultra
◻ ∼ **and** ∼ magis et magis
◻ ∼ **than enough** plus satis
◻ **nothing** ∼ nihil amplius

moreover *adv* praeterea, ultra

morning¹ *n* mane *nt indecl*; matutinum tempus *nt*
◻ **early** ∼ prima lux *f*
■ **good** ∼ *int* salve! (when parting) ave!

morning² *adj* matutinus

morose *adj* morosus, difficilis, serverus

morsel *n* offa *f*; frustum *nt*

mortal¹ *adj* mortalis; (deadly) mortifer, letifer, letalis; fig (of an enemy) infensissimus

mortal² *n* homo *m*
■ ∼**s** *pl* mortales *mpl*

mortality *n* mortalitas; mors; pestis *f*

mortar *n* mortarium *nt*

mortgage¹ *n* hypotheca *f*; pignus *nt*

mortgage² *vt* pignori oppono ③

mosaic¹ *n* tessellatum (opus) *nt*

mosaic² *adj* tessellatus

mosquito *n* culex *m*

moss *n* muscus *m*

mossy *adj* muscosus

most¹ *adj* plurimus, maximus, plerique

most² *adv* maxime, plurimum
■ ∼**ly** *adv* (usually) plerumque; vulgo

moth *n* blatta, tinea *f*

mother *n* mater; genetrix *f*

motherhood *n* condicio matris *f*

mother-in-law *n* socrus *f*

motherless *adj* matre orbus

motherly *adj* maternus

mother-of-pearl *n* concha Persica *f*

motion *n* motio *f*; motus *m*; (proposal) rogatio *f*

motionless *adj* immotus, immobilis, fixus

motivate *vt* incito ①

motive *n* causa, ratio *f*; incitamentum *nt*

motto *n* sententia *f*; praeceptum *nt*

mould¹ *n* (for casting) forma *f*; (mustiness) mucor, situs *m*

mould² *vt* formo ①; fingo; (knead) subigo ③

moulder *vi* putresco, dilabor ③

mouldy *adj* mucidus; situ corruptus
◻ **go** ∼ putresco ③

moult *vi* plumas exuo ③

mound *n* tumulus, agger *m*; moles *f*

mount *vt&i* scando, ascendo ③; supero ①; (rise) sublime feror ③; subvolo ①; (get on a horse) equum conscendo ③

mountain *n* mons *m*

mountaineer *n* homo montanus *m*

mountainous *adj* montuosus, montanus

mounted *adj* (on horseback) eques

mourn *vt&i* lugeo; maereo, doleo ②; lamentor ①

mourner *n* plorator; pullatus *m*

mournful *adj* luctuosus, lugubris; maestus; tristis, lamentabilis, flebilis
■ ∼**ly** *adv* maeste; flebiliter

mourning *n* luctus, maeror *m*; (clothes) vestis lugubris *f*
◻ **be in** ∼ lugeo ②
◻ **go into** ∼ vestitum muto ①

mouse *n* mus *m*

mouse-hole *n* cavum (muris) *nt*

mousetrap *n* muscipulum *nt*

mouth *n* os *nt*; rictus *m*; (of a bird) rostrum *nt*; (of a bottle) lura *f*; (of a river) ostium *nt*

mouthful *n* buccella *f*

mouthpiece *n* fig (speaker) interpres *m/f*; orator *m*

movable *adj* mobilis

move¹ *vt* moveo ②
■ ∼ *vi* moveor ②; feror *ir*; (change dwelling, etc.) migro ①
◻ ∼ **on** progredior ③

move² *n* motus *m*; fig artificium *nt*

m

movement n motus m
moving adj flebilis, miserabilis
  ■ ~**ly** adv flebiliter
mow vt meto ③
mower n faenisex m; messor m
much adj multus
  ■ ~ adv multum; (with comparative) multo
  □ **as** ~ **as** tantus … quantus; tantum
  … quantum
  □ **how** ~ quantus; quantum
  □ **so** ~ tantus; tantum
  □ **too** ~ nimius; adv nimis
  □ **very** ~ plurimus; plurimum
muck n stercus nt
mud n caenum, lutum nt; limus m
muddle¹ vt turbo; perturbo ①
muddle² n confusio, turba f
muddy adj lutosus, lutulentus;
  limosus, caenosus; (troubled) turbidus
muffle vt obvolvo ③
mug n poculum nt; ▶**cup**
muggy adj umidus
mulberry n morum nt
  ■ ~ **tree** n morus f
mule n mulus m; mula f
muleteer n mulio m
multiple adj multiplex
multiplication n multiplicatio f
multiply vt multiplico ①
  ■ ~ vi cresco ③; augeor ②
multitude n multitudo; turba, plebs f;
  vulgus nt
mumble vi murmuro, musso ①
munch vt manduco ①; mando ③
mundane adj mundanus
municipal adj municipalis
municipality adj municipium nt
munificence n munificentia,
  largitas f
murder¹ n caedes f; homicidium nt
murder² vt neco, trucido, obtrunco ①
murderer n homicida m/f; sicarius m
murderous adj sanguinarius,
  cruentus
murky adj caliginosus, tenebrosus,
  obscurus
murmur¹ n murmur nt; susurrus m;
  fremitus m; (complaint) questus m;
  querela f
murmur² vt&i murmuro, musso,
  mussito, susurro ①; fremo ③; (complain)
  queror ③

muscle n musculus; lacertus;
  torus m
muscular adj musculosus;
  lacertosus; robustus, torosus
Muse¹ n Musa f
muse² vi cogito, meditor ①
museum n museum nt
mushroom n fungus; boletus m;
  agaricum nt
music n (art) musica f; (of instruments and
  voices) cantus; concentus m
musical adj musicus; (tuneful) canorus
musician n musicus m
muslin n sindon f
mussel n (shell-fish) mytilus m;
  conchylium nt
must vi necesse est
  □ **I** ~ debeo ②; oportet ② me + infin
mustard n sinapi nt; sinapis f
muster¹ vt colligo ①; fig (up) colligo ③
  ■ ~ vi convenio ④
muster² n:
  □ **pass** ~ approbor ①
musty adj mucidus
mute adj mutus, tacitus
  ■ ~**ly** adv tacite, silenter
mutilate vt mutilo, trunco ①
mutilation n mutilatio, detruncatio f
mutineer n seditiosus; homo
  turbulentus m
mutinous adj seditiosus, turbulentus
mutiny¹ n seditio f; tumultus m
mutiny² vi tumultuor ①
mutter¹ vt&i murmuro, musso,
  mussito ①
mutter² n murmur nt; murmuratio f
mutton n ovilla (caro) f
mutual adj mutuus
  ■ ~**ly** adv mutuo, invicem
muzzle¹ n capistrum nt
muzzle² vt capistro ①, constringo ③
my pn meus
  □ ~ **own** proprius
myriad n decem milia ntpl; (countless
  number) sescenti adj
myrtle¹ n myrtus f
myrtle² adj myrteus
myself pn ipse, ego
  □ **I** ~ egomet

m

mysterious *adj* arcanus; occultus; mysticus
■ ∼**ly** *adv* occulte
mystery *n* mysterium, arcanum *nt*; fig res occultissima *f*
mystical *adj* mysticus

mystify *vt* ludificor ①; fallo ③
myth *n* fabula *f*
mythical *adj* fabulosus
mythological *adj* mythologicus
mythology *n* mythologia *f*

Nn

nab *vt* prehendo ③
nag¹ *vt* sollicito ①
nag² (horse) caballus *m*
Naiad *n* Naias *f*
nail¹ *n* unguis; (of metal) clavus *m*
nail² *vt* clavum pango *or* defigo ③
naive *adj* ingenuus, simplex
naivety *n* ingenuitas, simplicitas *f*
naked *adj* nudus, apertus; (of a sword) strictus
nakedness *n* nuditas *f*
name¹ *n* nomen, vocabulum *nt*; appellatio; fig (reputation) fama; celebritas *f*
□ **by** ∼ nominatim
name² *vt* nomino, appello, nuncupo ①; (mention) mentionem facio ③
nameless *adj* sine nomine, nominis expers
namely *adv* scilicet, videlicet
namesake *n* cognominis, eodem nomine dictus *m*
nap *n* somnus brevis *m*; (of cloth) villus *m*
□ **take a** ∼ obdormisco ③; (at noon) meridior ①
nape *n*:
□ ∼ **of the neck** cervix *f*
napkin *n* (serviette) mappa *f*; (little towel) mantele *nt*
narcotic *adj* somnificus, somnifer
■ ∼ *n* medicamentum somnificum *nt*
narrate *vt* narro, enarro ①
narration *n* narratio; expositio *f*
narrative *n* narratio; expositio *f*
narrator *n* narrator *m*
narrow¹ *adj* angustus; artus
■ ∼**ly** *adv* (with difficulty) aegre
narrow² *vt* coarto ①; contraho ③

narrow-minded *adj* animi angusti *or* parvi
narrowness *n* angustiae *fpl*
nastiness *n* foeditas; obscenitas *f*
nasty *adj* (foul) foedus; obscenus; (ill-natured) malignus
nation *n* gens, natio *f*; (as political body) populus *m*
national *adj* popularis
nationality *n* totum populi corpus *nt*
native¹ *adj* nativus, vernaculus
native² *n* indigena *m*
native land *n* patria *f*
natural *adj* naturalis; nativus, innatus; proprius; fig sincerus; simplex
■ ∼**ly** *adv* naturaliter; (unaffectedly) simpliciter; (of its own accord) sponte; (of course) plane
naturalist *n* rerum naturalium investigator *m*
naturalization *n* civitatis donatio *f*
naturalize *vt* aliquem civitate dono ①
nature *n* natura *f*; (natural disposition) indoles *f*, ingenium *nt*; (peculiarity) proprietas *f*; (universe) mundus *m*
naughtiness *n* malitia, petulantia *f*
naughty *adj* improbus, malus
nausea *n* (seasickness, feeling sick) nausea *f*; (squeamishness) fastidium *nt*
nauseate *vt* fastidium pario ③; satio ①
nautical *adj* nauticus
naval *adj* navalis, maritimus
navel *n* umbilicus *m*
navigable *adj* navigabilis
navigate *vt* guberno ①
■ ∼ *vi* navigo ①
navigation *n* navigatio *f*

m
n

navigator *n* nauta, navigator *m*

navy *n* classis *f*; copiae navales *fpl*

near[1] *adj* propinquus, vicinus; (of relationship) proximus

near[2] *adv* prope; iuxta; proxime
■ ~ *prep* ad, apud, prope, iuxta *all* + *acc*
□ ~ **at hand** propinquus, in promptu
□ **far and** ~ longe lateque

near[3] *vt* appropinquo ① + *dat*

nearby *adj* propinquus, vicinus

nearly *adv* prope; fere; ferme; (almost) paene

nearness *adj* propinquitas; vicinia; (of relationship) propinquitas *f*

neat *adj* mundus; lautus; lepidus; nitidus; concinnus, elegans

neatness *n* munditia; concinnitas *f*

necessaries *npl* (of life) necessitates *fpl*; necessaria *ntpl*

necessarily *adv* necessario

necessary *adj* necessarius
□ **it is** ~ necesse est

necessitate *vt* cogo ③

necessity *n* necessitas; (want) egestas, necessitudo; (indispensable thing) res omnino necessaria *f*

neck *n* collum *nt*; cervix *f*; (of a bottle) collum *nt*

necklace *n* monile *nt*; (as ornament) torques *m/f*

nectar *n* nectar *nt*

need[1] *n* (necessity) opus *nt*, necessitas; (want) egestas, penuria *f*

need[2] *vt* (require) requiro ③; egeo ② + *abl*
■ ~ *vi* (must) debeo ②

needle *n* acus *f*

needless *adj* minime necessarius, supervacaneus
■ ~**ly** *adv* sine causa

needlework *n* opus acu factum *nt*

needy *adj* egens, indigens, egenus, inops

negative[1] *adj* negativus

negative[2] *n* negatio; repulsa *f*
□ **answer in the** ~ nego ①

neglect[1] *vt* neglego; desero, praetermitto ③

neglect[2] *n* neglegentia, incuria *f*; neglectus *m*

neglectful *adj* neglegens

negligence *n* neglegentia; incuria *f*

negligent *adj* neglegens, indiligens, remissus; incuriosus
■ ~**ly** *adv* neglegenter, incuriose

negligible *adj* minimi momenti

negotiable *adj* mercabilis

negotiate *vt* ago, gero ③
■ ~ *vi* negotior ①

negotiation *n* actio *f*

negotiator *n* conciliator; (spokesman) orator *m*

neigh[1] *vi* hinnio ④

neigh[2] *n* hinnitus *m*

neighbour *n* vicinus, finitimus, propinquus *m*

neighbourhood *n* vicinitas; vicinia; proximitas; propinquitas *f*

neighbouring *adj* vicinus; finitimus; propinquus

neither *adj* & *pn* neuter
■ ~ *conj* nec, neque
□ ~ ... **nor** nec ... nec

nephew *n* fratris *or* sororis filius *m*; nepos *m*

nerve *n* nervus *m*; fig fortitudo *f*

nervous *adj* nervosus; (fearful) timidus, trepidus, anxius
■ ~**ly** *adv* nervose; (fearfully) trepide, timide, anxie

nervousness *n* anxietas *f*; timor *m*

nest *n* nidus *m*

nestle *vi* recubo ①

net *n* (for hunting) rete *nt*; iaculum *nt*; plaga *f*; (for fishing) funda *f*

netting *n* opus reticulatum *nt*

nettle *n* urtica *f*

network *n* reticulum *nt*

neuter *adj* neuter

neutral *adj* medius; neuter, aequus

neutrality *n* aequitas *f*

neutralize *vt* aequo; compenso ①

never *adv* nunquam
□ ~**more** nunquam posthac

nevertheless *adv* nihilominus, tamen, attamen

new *adj* novus, novellus, recens; integer

newcomer *n* advena *m/f*; hospes *m*

newfangled *adj* novicius

newly *adv* nuper, modo; recenter

newness *n* novitas *f*

news *n* res novae *fpl*; (report) fama *f*; rumor, nuntius *m*

newspaper *n* acta diurna *ntpl*

next[1] *adj* proximus; (of time) insequens

next[2] *adv* proxime; iuxta; (of time) deinde

nib *n* (of a pen) acumen *nt*

nibble *vt* rodo, arrodo ③

nice *adj* (dainty) delicatus; (choice) exquisitus; (exact) accuratus; subtilis; (fine) bellus; (pleasant) iucundus; (amiable) suavis
■ ~**ly** *adv* delicate; exquisite; subtiliter; accurate; belle

niche *n* loculamentum *nt*

nick *n* (cut, notch) incisura *f*
□ **in the very ~ of time** in ipso articulo temporis

nickname *n* nomen probrosum *nt*

niece *n* fratris *or* sororis filia *f*

niggardly *adj* parcus, tenax; avarus

night *n* nox *f*
□ **by ~** nocte, noctu

nightfall *n*:
□ **at ~** sub noctem, primis tenebris

nightingale *n* luscinia, Philomela *f*

nightly *adj* nocturnus
■ ~ *adv* noctu, de nocte

nightmare *n* incubo *m*; suppressio *f*

night-watch *n* vigilia *f*; (person) vigil *m*

nimble *adj* pernix; agilis, mobilis

nimbleness *n* pernicitas, agilitas, mobilitas *f*

nimbly *adv* perniciter

nine *adj* novem *indecl*
□ ~ **times** novies

nineteen *adj* undeviginti *indecl*

nineteenth *adj* undevicesimus

ninetieth *adj* nonagesimus

ninety *adj* nonaginta *indecl*

ninth *adj* nonus

nip *vt* vellico ①; (of cold) uro ③
□ ~ **off** deseco ①

nipple *n* papilla *f*

no[1] *adj* nullus; nemo; nihil *indecl*
□ ~ **one** nemo

no[2] *adv* haud, non; minime

nobility *n* nobilitas *f*; nobiles *mpl*; fig magnanimitas *f*

noble[1] *adj* nobilis, fig generosus; magnanimus

noble[2] *n* (**nobleman**) vir nobilis *m*

nobly *adv* praeclare; generose

nobody *n* nemo

nocturnal *adj* nocturnus

nod *n* nutus *m*
■ ~ *vi* nuto ①; annuo, innuo ③; (be drowsy) dormito ①

noise *n* strepitus, stridor; fragor; sonus, sonitus; (of voices) clamor *m*
□ **make a ~** strepito, sono ①; fremo, strepo ③

noiseless *adj* tacitus; silens
■ ~**ly** *adv* tacite

noisily *adv* cum strepitu

noisy *adj* tumultuosus

nomad *n* vagus *m*

nominal *adj* nominalis
■ ~**ly** *adv* nomine, verbo

nominate *vi* nomino, designo ①

nomination *n* nominatio, designatio; (of an heir) nuncupatio *f*

nonchalantly *adv* aequo animo

nondescript *adj* nulli certo generi ascriptus

none *adj* & *pn* nemo, nullus

nones *n* Nonae *fpl*

nonplus *vt* (checkmate) ad incitas redigo ③

nonsense *n* ineptiae, nugae *fpl*
□ **talk ~** absurde loquor ③; garrio ④
■ ~! *int* gerrae! fabulae! somnia!

nonsensical *adj* ineptus, absurdus

nook *n* angulus *m*; latebra *f*

noon *n* meridies *m*

noose *n* laqueus *m*

nor *conj* nec, neque; neve, neu

normal *adj* secundum normam

normally *adv* ut solet

north *n* septentrio *m*

northerly *adj* septentrionem spectans

northern *adj* septentrionalis, aquilonius, boreus

north pole *n* Arctos *f*

northward *adv* septentrionem versus

north wind *n* aquilo *m*; boreas *m*

nose *n* nasus *m*; nares *fpl*

nostril *n* naris *f*

not *adv* non; haud; minime; (in prohibitions) ne
□ ~ **at all** nullo modo
□ ~ **yet** nondum

n

notable *adj* notabilis, insignis

notably *adv* insignite, insigniter, notabiliter; (especially) praecipue, praesertim

notch[1] *n* incisura *f*

notch[2] *vt* incido ③

note[1] *n* (mark) nota *f*; signum, indicium *nt*; (writing) chirographum *nt*

note[2] *vt* (mark) noto; (in a book) annoto ①; ▶ **notice**

notebook *n* commentarius *m*; tabulae *fpl*

noted *adj* nobilis; insignis, notus; clarus, praeclarus, celeber

noteworthy *adj* notandus, notabilis

nothing *n* nihil *nt*
□ **for** ∼ gratis

notice[1] *n* (noticing) animadversio, observatio *f*; (proclamation) edictum *nt*
□ **public** ∼ proscriptio *f*; (placard) titulus *m*
□ **escape** ∼ lateo ②
□ **give** ∼ edico ③
□ **take no** ∼ **of** ignoro ①

notice[2] *vt* observo ①; animadverto ③

notification *n* denuntiatio, proscriptio *f*

notify *vt* significo, denuntio ①

notion *n* notio, notitia; opinio *f*

notoriety *n* notitia *f*

notorious *adj* (in a bad sense) famosus

noun *n* nomen *nt*

nourish *vt* nutrio ④; alo ③

nourishment *n* alimentum *nt*; cibus *m*

novel[1] *adj* novus

novel[2] *n* fabula *f*

novelist *n* fabulator *m*

novelty *n* novitas *f*

November *n* Novembris *m*

novice *n* tiro *m*; novicius *m*; novicia *f*

now *adv* nunc
□ ∼ **and then** nonnunquam

nowadays *adv* hodie, his temporibus

nowhere *adv* nusquam, nullo in loco

noxious *adj* nocens, noxius, perniciosus

nude *adj* nudus

nudge[1] *n* cubiti ictus *m*

nudge[2] *vt* fodico ①

nudity *n* nudatio *f*

nugget *n* massa *f*

nuisance *n* incommodum *nt*; molestia *f*

null *adj* (and void) irritus; nullus

numb[1] *adj* torpens, torpidus, hebes

numb[2] *vt* hebeto ①; obstupefacio ③

number[1] *n* numerus *m*; (of things) copia; vis; (of people) frequentia, multitudo *f*

number[2] *vt* numero, computo ①

numberless *adj* innumerus, innumerabilis

numbness *n* torpor; fig stupor *m*

numerous *adj* frequens, creber, multus

nuptial *adj* nuptialis, coniugalis, conubialis, coniugialis

nurse[1] *n* nutrix, altrix *f*

nurse[2] *vt* nutrio ④; fig foveo ②; (to the sick) ancillor ① + *dat*

nursery *n* (for children) cubiculum infantium *nt*; (of plants) seminarium *nt*

nurture *vt* educo ①; nutrio ④

nut *n* nux *f*

nutcracker *n* nucifrangibulum *nt*

nutrition *n* nutrimentum *nt*

nutritious *adj* (also **nutritive**) alibilis

nutshell *n* putamen *nt*
□ **in a** ∼ fig paucis verbis

nymph *n* nympha; (girl) puella *f*

Oo

oaf *n* stultus, hebes *m*

oak *n* quercus, aesculus, ilex *f*; robur *nt*

oar *n* remus *m*

oarsman *n* remex *m*

oat(s) *n* avena *f*

oath *n* iusiurandum *nt*; (of soldiers) sacramentum *nt*
  □ **take an ~** iuro ① (in verba)

obedience *n* oboedientia *f*; obsequium *nt*

obedient *adj* oboediens, obsequens
  ■ **~ly** *adv* oboedienter

obese *adj* obesus; ▶ **fat**

obesity *n* obesitas *f*

obey *vt* pareo ②, oboedio ④, obtempero ① *all + dat*

object¹ *n* obiectum *nt*; res *f*; (aim, design) consilium *nt*

object² *vt* (to) repugno + *dat*, improbo ①

objection *n* impedimentum *nt*; mora *f*
  □ **if you have no ~** si per te licet

objectionable *adj* improbabilis

objective *adj* medius

obligation *n* officium; beneficium *nt*

oblige *vt* cogo ③; obligo ①; devincio ④; (by kindness) bene de aliquo mereor ②
  □ **be ~d to** debeo ② + *infin*

obliging *adj* officiosus, comis, blandus; benignus, beneficus
  ■ **~ly** *adv* comiter; benigne; officiose

oblique *adj* obliquus
  ■ **~ly** *adv* oblique

obliterate *vt* deleo ②; oblittero ①

oblivion *n* oblivio *f*; oblivium *nt*

oblivious *adj* obliviosus, immemor

oblong *adj* oblongus

obnoxious *adj* (hateful) invisus; (hurtful) noxius

obscene *adj* obscenus, spurcus, turpis

obscenity *n* obscenitas; turpitudo *f*

obscure¹ *adj* obscurus; fig perplexus; (intricate, puzzling) difficilis; (of style) intortus; (of people) ignobilis, ignotus

obscure² *vt* obscuro, obumbro ①

obscurity *n* obscuritas *f*; tenebrae *fpl*; fig ignobilitas, humilitas *f*

obsequious *adj* officiosus, morigerus
  ■ **~ly** *adv* cum nimia obsequentia; assentatorie

observance *n* observantia, obtemperatio *f*

observant *adj* attentus; oboediens

observation *n* observatio; animadversio *f*; (remark) dictum *nt*

observe *vt* observo ①; animadverto ③; (utter) dico ③; (spy out) speculor ①; (obey) pareo ②, obtempero ① *both + dat*

observer *n* spectator *m*

obsolete *adj* obsoletus

obstacle *n* impedimentum *nt*; mora *f*

obstinacy *n* obstinatio, pertinacia, pervicacia, contumacia *f*

obstinate *adj* obstinatus, pertinax, pervicax, contumax
  ■ **~ly** *adv* obstinate; pervicaciter, contumaciter, pertinaciter

obstruct *vt* obstruo ③; (hinder) impedio ④

obstruction *n* obstructio *f*; impedimentum *nt*

obtain *vt* paro ①; consequor, quaero, nanciscor; adipiscor ③; (by entreaty) impetro ①

obtainable *adj* impetrabilis

obtrusive *adj* molestus; importunus

obtuse *adj* obtusus; hebes

obvious *adj* apertus, perspicuus, manifestus
  ■ **~ly** *adv* aperte, manifesto

occasion *n* occasio, causa *f*

occasional *adj* rarus, infrequens
  ■ **~ly** *adv* per occasionem, occasione oblata

occult *adj* occultus, arcanus

occupant *n* possessor *m*

occupation *n* (including military) possessio *f*; (employment) quaestus *m*; (business) studium, negotium *nt*

occupier *n* possessor *m*

occupy *vt* occupo ①; (possess) teneo ②; (inhabit) habito ①; (detain) detineo ②

occur *vi* occido, contingo ③; evenio; obvenio; fig in mentem venio ④

occurrence *n* casus, eventus *m*; res *f*

ocean *n* oceanus *m*

octagon *n* octagonon *nt*

octagonal *adj* octagonos

October *n* October *m*

odd *adj* (of number) impar; (strange) insolitus, inusitatus
  ■ ~**ly** *adv* inusitate

oddity *n* res inusitata *f*; monstrum *nt*

odds *n* discordia, dissensio, contentio *f*; (difference) discrimen *nt*
  □ **be at** ~ **with someone** ab aliquo dissideo ②

odious *adj* odiosus, invisus; (disgusting) foedus
  ■ ~**ly** *adv* odiose

odorous *adj* odoratus

odour *n* odor *m*

of *prep use genitive case*

off¹ *prep* (out of) extra + *acc*; (from, of) de, ex + *abl*

off² *adv* procul, longe
  □ **be well** ~ bene me habeo ②

offal *n* quisquiliae *fpl*

offence *n* (fault) offensa, culpa *f*; (insult) iniuria, contumelia *f*; (displeasure) offensio *f*

offend *vt* (insult, *etc.*) offendo; laedo ③; (against) violo ①
  ■ ~ *vi* (transgress) pecco ①

offender *n* reus *m*

offensive *adj* iniuriosus; (things) odiosus; foedus

offer¹ *vt* offero *ir*; do ①; praebeo ②; (at an auction) licitor ①

offer² *n* oblatio; (proposal) condicio *f*

offering *n* oblatio *f*; donum *nt*; (of a sacrifice) immolatio *f*

office *n* (duty) officium, munus; (room) tabularium *nt*

officer *n* magistratus *m*; (in the army) praefectus, tribunus militaris *m*

official¹ *adj* publicus; (holding an official position) magistratui praepositus

official² *n* minister; accensus, lictor *m*

officiate *vi* officium praesto ①; (in religious ceremonies) rem divinam facio ③; (for another) alterius vice fungor ③

officious *adj* molestus

offspring *n* proles, progenies, stirps, suboles *f*

often *adv* saepe
  □ **very** ~ persaepe, saepenumero

ogle *vt* limis oculis intueor ②

ogre *n* larva *f*

oh *int* oh! ah! ohe!

oil *n* oleum *nt*; olivum *nt*

oily *adj* (like oil) oleaceus; oleosus

ointment *n* unguentum, unguen; (as medicament) collyrium *nt*

old *adj* (in age) aetate provectus, senex; (ancient) vetus, vetustus; (out of use) obsoletus; (worn) exesus, tritus; (of former days) antiquus, priscus, pristinus
  □ ~ **man** *n* senex *m*
  □ ~ **woman** *n* anus *f*
  □ ~ **age** *n* senectus *f*
  □ **of** ~ olim, quondam
  □ ~**er** senior; vetustior
  □ ~**est** natu maximus
  □ **grow** ~ senesco ③

old-fashioned *adj* priscus, antiquus

oldness *n* antiquitas, vetustas *f*

oligarchy *n* paucorum potestas *f*

olive *n* olea, oliva *f*

Olympic *adj* Olympicus
  □ **the** ~ **games** Olympia *ntpl*

omen *n* omen, auspicium, augurium, ostentum *nt*

ominous *adj* infaustus, infelix
  ■ ~**ly** *adv* malis ominibus

omission *n* praetermissio *f*

omit *vt* praetermitto, omitto; (temporarily) intermitto ③

on¹ *prep* in, super *both* + *abl*; (near) ad + *acc*; (depending, hanging on) de; (immediately, after) e, ex *all* + *abl*
  □ ~ **his side** cum illo

on² *adv* porro; (continually) usque
  □ **and so** ~ et cetera
  □ **go** ~ procedo, pergo ③

once *adv* (one time) semel; (formerly) olim, quondam; aliquando
  □ **at** ~ illico, statim; (at the same time) simul, uno tempore
  □ ~ **(and) for all** semel

one *adj* unus; (a certain person *or* thing) quidam
  □ ~ **another** alius alium
  □ ~ **after another** alternus; *adv* invicem
  □ ~ **by** ~ singillatim
  □ **it is all** ~ perinde est
  □ ~ **or the other** alteruter

O

onerous *adj* gravis, praegravis, onerosus

oneself *pn* ipse; (with reflexive verbs) se

one-sided *adj* inaequalis, iniquus

onion *n* caepa *f*

only[1] *adj* unicus; unus, solus

only[2] *adv* solum, tantum, dumtaxat; (except) non nisi

onset *n* impetus, incursus *m*; incursio *f*

onslaught *n* impetus, incursus *m*; incursio *f*

onwards *adv* porro; protinus

ooze *vi* mano, emano; stillo, destillo ①

opal *n* opalus *m*

opaque *adj* densus, opacus

open[1] *vt* aperio ④; patefacio, pando ③; (uncover) retego ③; (a letter) resigno ①; (begin) ordior ④
■ ~ *vi* patesco ③; (gape open) dehisco ③

open[2] *adj* (not shut) apertus, patens; (visible) in conspectu positus; (evident) manifestus; (sincere) candidus, ingenuus; (public) communis, publicus
□ **in the** ~ **air** sub divo

opening *n* (act of making accessible) apertio *f*; (aperture) foramen *nt*; (air-hole) spiramentum *nt*

openly *adv* aperte; manifesto; (publicly) palam; *fig* libere, simpliciter

operate *vt&i* operor ①; ago ③; (cut open) seco ①; (have force) vim habeo ②

operation *n* effectus *m*; (surgical) sectio *f*; (business) negotium *nt*

operative *adj* efficax; potens

opinion *n* opinio, sententia; censura; mens *f*; iudicium *nt*; animus *m*; (esteem) existimatio *f*
□ **in my** ~ mea sententia

opponent *n* adversarius *m*

opportune *adj* opportunus, idoneus, commodus

opportunity *n* occasio; opportunitas, facultas, copia *f*

oppose *vt* oppono, obicio ③
■ ~ *vi* (resist) repugno, adversor, obsto ①; resisto ③ *all* + *dat*

opposed *adj* adversus; adversarius; contrarius

opposite[1] *adj* adversus, contrarius, diversus

opposite[2] *n* contrarium *nt*

opposite[3] *adv* & *prep*:
□ ~ **to** contra + *acc*, ex adverso

opposition *n* oppositio; repugnantia; discrepantia *f*; (obstacle) impedimentum *nt*

oppress *vt* affligo ③; vexo; gravo, onero ①

oppression *n* gravatio; iniuria; vexatio *f*

oppressive *adj* gravis; acerbus, molestus, iniquus

oppressor *n* tyrannus *m*

opt *vt* (for) opto ①

optical *adj* oculorum *gen pl*

option *n* optio *f*

optional *adj* cuius rei optio est

opulence *n* opulentia *f*

opulent *adj* opulens, opulentus, dives
■ ~**ly** *adv* opulenter

or *conj* vel; aut; (interrogatively) an
□ **either** … ~ vel … vel, aut … aut, -ve … -ve
□ **whether** … ~ sive … sive, seu … seu

oracle *n* oraculum, responsum *nt*; sors *f*

oral *adj* verbo traditus; praesens
■ ~**ly** *adv*

orange *adj* luteus

oration *n* oratio; (before the people or to the army) contio *f*

orator *n* orator *m*

oratory *n* oratoria ars, rhetorica; (eloquence) eloquentia *f*

orbit *n* orbis *m*; orbita *f*; (in astronomy) ambitus *m*

orchard *n* pomarium *nt*

orchestra *n* (body of musical performers) symphoniaci *mpl*

orchid *n* orchis *f*

ordain *vt* ordino ①; iubeo ②; instituo ③

ordeal *n* *fig* discrimen *nt*

order[1] *n* ordo *m*; (rank) ordo *m*; (row) series *f*; (command) praeceptum, mandatum, decretum *nt*; (custom) mos *m*; consuetudo *f*; (instruction) rescriptum; (decree) edictum *nt* (association) societas *f*
□ **in** ~ ordine, ex ordine
□ **out of** ~ (out of turn) extra ordinem

order[2] *vt* (put in order) dispono ③; ordino ①; (give orders to) impero ① + *dat*; iubeo ②

orderly[1] *adj* compositus, ordinatus; (of people) oboediens; (quiet, sober) modestus, temperatus

orderly[2] *n* mil tesserarius *m*

ordinarily *adv* usitate, fere, plerumque, vulgo

ordinary *adj* usitatus, solitus, vulgaris

ordination *n* ordinatio *f*

ore *n* metallum *nt*

organ *n* (musical instrument) organum *nt*; (of the body) membrum *nt*

organism *n* compages, natura *f*

organist *n* organicus *m*

organization *n* ordinatio; temperatio *f*

organize *vt* ordino [1]; constituo, dispono [3]; formo [1]

orgies *n* orgia *ntpl*

orgy *n* (revelry) comissatio *f*

oriental *adj* orientalis

origin *n* origo *f*; principium *nt*; ortus *m*

original[1] *adj* primitivus; pristinus; principalis
 ■ ~ly *adv* ab origine; primum

original[2] *n* archetypum, exemplar; (writing) autographum *nt*

originality *n* proprietas quaedam ingenii *f*

originate *vi* orior [4]; proficiscor [3]

ornament[1] *n* ornamentum *nt*; ornatus *m*; decus *nt*

ornament[2] *vt* orno, decoro [1]

ornamental *adj* qui ornamento *or* decori est

ornate *adj* ornatus; pictus

orphan *adj & n* orbus

orthodox *adj* orthodoxus

oscillate *vi* fluctuo [1]

oscillation *n* fluctuatio *f*

osier *n* vimen *nt*; salix *f*

ostensible *adj* simulatus, fictus

ostensibly *adv* specie, per speciem

ostentation *n* ostentatio; iactatio *f*

ostentatious *adj* ambitiosus; gloriosus; vanus
 ■ ~ly *adv* ambitiose, gloriose, iactanter

ostracism *n* testarum suffragia *ntpl*

ostrich *n* struthiocamelus *m*

other *adj* (another) alius; alter
 □ **the** ~s ceteri, reliqui

otherwise *adv* alio modo, aliter; (if not) si non, si minus; (besides) insuper

otter *n* lutra *f*

ought *vi* debeo, oportet [2]

our *pn* (and **ours**) noster; (of ~ country) nostras

ourselves *pn* nosmet, nosmet ipsi

oust *vt* eicio [3]

out[1] *adv* (out of doors) foris; (to outside) foras
 □ **get** ~! apage!

out[2] *prep*:
 □ ~ **of** e, ex + *abl*; (on account of) propter; (~side, beyond) extra *both* + *acc*
 □ ~ **of the way** devius

outbreak *n* eruptio; fig (revolt) seditio *f*

outcast *n* exsul, extorris, profugus *m*

outcome *n* eventus *m*

outcry *n* clamor *m*; acclamatio *f*

outdo *vt* supero [1]

outer *adj* exterior

outfit *n* apparatus *m*

outflank *vt* circumeo *ir*

outgrow *vt* fig dedisco [3]

outlandish *adj* externus; barbarus

outlast *vt* durando supero [1]

outlaw[1] *n* proscriptus *m*

outlaw[2] *vt* aqua et igni interdico + *dat*, proscribo [3]

outlay *n* sumptus *m*; impensa *f*

outlet *n* exitus, egressus *m*

outline *n* forma rudis *f*

outlive *vt* supervivo [3]; supersum *ir*; supero [1]; superstes sum *ir*

outlook *n* prospectus *m*

outlying *adj* (distant) remotus

outnumber *vt* numero supero [1]

outpost *n* statio *f*

outrage[1] *n* iniuria *f*; (outrageous deed) flagitium *nt*

outrage[2] *vt* iniuria afficio [3]; laedo [3]

outrageous *adj* iniuriosus; atrox; (exaggerated) immodicus; immanis; immoderatus

outright *adv* (completely) prorsus

outrun *vt* praecurro [3]; cursu supero [1]

outset *n* principium, initium *nt*

outside[1] *n* pars exterior; superficies; (appearance) species *f*

outside[2] *adj* exterus

outside[3] *adv* foris, extrinsecus

outside[4] *prep* extra + *acc*

outskirts *n* (of towns) suburbium *nt*

outspoken *adj* candidus

outstanding *adj* prominens; (excellent) egregius; (of debts) solvendus

outstretch *vt* expando, extendo ③

outstrip *vt* cursu supero ①; praeverto ③

outvote *vt* suffragiis supero ①

outward *adj* externus, exterus
■ ∼ *adv* foras

outwardly *adv* extrinsecus, extra

outwards *adv* in exteriorem partem; extra

outweigh *vt* praepondero ①

outwit *vt* deludo ③; circumvenio ④

oval *adj* ovatus

ovation *n* ovatio *f*

oven *n* furnus *m*

over *prep* super; supra, trans *all* + *acc*
■ ∼ *adv* super; supra
□ ∼ **and** ∼ **again** iterum ac saepius
□ **all** ∼ per totum
□ ∼ **and above** insuper

overawe *vt* metu coerceo ②

overbalance *vt* praepondero ①

overbearing *adj* insolens, superbus

overcast *adj* nubilus, tristis

overcharge *vi* (in price) plus aequo exigo ③

overcoat *n* lacerna, paenula *f*; pallium *nt*

overcome *vt* supero ①; vinco ③

overdo *vt* nimis studeo ② + *dat*; nimis incumbo ③ in + *acc*

overdue *adj* iamdudum solvendus

overflow *vi* exundo, redundo, restagno ①; superfluo ③
■ ∼ *vt* inundo ①

overgrown *adj* obductus, obsitus

overhang *vi* impendeo, immineo ② *both* + *dat*

overhead *adv* desuper; supra, superne

overhear *vt* subausculto ①

overjoyed *adj* ovans, exsultans

overlap *vt* excedo ③

overload *vt* nimio pondere onero ①

overlook *vt* (not notice) praetermitto; (have view of) prospecto ①

overpower *vt* opprimo ③; supero, exsupero ①

overrate *vt* nimis aestimo ①

override *vt* (cancel) rescindo ③

overripe *adj* praematurus

overrule *vt* (check) coerceo ②; (cancel) rescindo ③

overrun[1] *vt* (devastate) vasto ①

overrun[2] *adj* obsitus

oversee *vt* curo ①; inspicio ③

overshadow *vt* obumbro, opaco; fig obscuro ①

oversight *n* (carelessness) incuria; neglegentia *f*; error *m*; (guardianship) cura, custodia *f*

overt *adj* manifestus, apertus
■ ∼**ly** *adv* manifesto, aperte

overtake *vt* assequor, excipio ③; supervenio ④

overthrow *vt* subverto, everto, proruo; (the enemy) devinco, prosterno; fig opprimo ③

overture *n* (proposal) condicio *f*; (beginning) exordium *nt*

overturn *vt* everto, subverto ③

overvalue *vt* nimis aestimo ①

overwhelm *vt* obruo; opprimo ③

owe *vt* debeo ②

owing *prep* (to) propter, ob + *acc*
□ **be** ∼ **(to)** per (aliquem) stat ① ut + *subj*

owl *n* bubo *m*; strix, noctua, ulula *f*

own[1] *adj* proprius, peculiaris
□ **one's** ∼ suus, proprius

own[2] *vt* possideo, teneo, habeo; (acknowledge) confiteor ②; (claim) vindico ①

owner *n* dominus, possessor, erus *m*

ownership *n* dominium *nt*

ox *n* bos, iuvencus *m*

oyster *n* ostrea *f*

Pp

pace[1] *n* gressus; incessus; passus *m*

pace[2] *vi* incedo ③; spatior ①
■ ~ *vt* passibus emetior ④

pacific *adj* pacificus; tranquillus; placidus, pacifer

pacify *vt* placo, sedo, paco, pacifico ①; lenio ④

pack[1] *n* (bundle) sarcina *f*; fasciculus *m*; (crowd) grex *m*; turba *f*

pack[2] *vt* (cram) stipo, suffarcino ①; (bring together) colligo ③

package *n* sarcina *f*; fasciculus *m*

packet *n* fasciculus *m*

pact *n* foedus *nt*

pad *n* (cushion) pulvinus *m*

paddle *n* remus *m*

paddock *n* saeptum *nt*

padlock *n* sera *f*

page *n* (of a book) pagina *f*

pageant *n* spectaculum *nt*; pompa; fig species *f*

pageantry *n* species atque pompa *f*

pail *n* hama, situla *f*

pain *n* dolor; angor, cruciatus *m*

painful *adj* gravis, aeger; (laborious) operosus

painless *adj* sine dolore, doloris expers

pains *n* cura *f*; studium *nt*
□ **take** ~ operam do ①

painstaking *adj* operosus

paint[1] *vt* (colour) (colore) induco; pingo, depingo ③; (the face) fuco ①
■ ~ *vi* (as artist) pingo ③

paint[2] *n* pigmentum *nt*

paintbrush *n* penicilus *m*

painter *n* (artist) pictor *m*

painting *n* (art) pictura; (picture) tabula, pictura *f*

pair[1] *n* (couple) par *nt*

pair[2] *vt* iungo, coniungo ③; copulo ①

palace *n* regia (domus) *f*; palatium *nt*

palatable *adj* sapidus; iucundus

palate *n* palatum *nt*

pale *adj* pallidus; exsanguis
□ **be** ~ palleo ②
□ **grow** ~ pallesco ③

paleness *n* pallor *m*

pall[1] *n* pallium *nt*

pall[2] *vi* nil sapio ③

palm[1] *n* (of the hand) palma *f*; (tree) palma *f*

palm[2] *vt*:
□ ~ **off** vendito ①

palpitate *vi* palpito ①

palpitation *n* palpitatio *f*

paltry *adj* vilis; (trifling) minutus, exiguus

pamper *vt* indulgeo ② + *dat*

pamphlet *n* libellus *m*

pan *n* (vessel) patina *f*

panacea *n* panacea *f*; panchrestum medicamentum *nt*

pander *n* leno *m*
■ ~ **to** *vi* lenocinor ①; indulgeo ② + *dat*

panegyric *n* laudatio *f*; panegyricus *m*

panel *n* (of a door) tympanum *nt*; (list of names) index *m*; album *nt*

pang *n* dolor, angor *m*

panic *n* terror, pavor, metus *m*; formido *f*

panic-stricken *adj* (also **panic-struck**) pavidus, exterritus

panorama *n* prospectus *m*

pant *vi* palpito; trepido; anhelo ①

panther *n* panthera *f*

panting[1] *adj* anhelus

panting[2] *n* anhelitus *m*

pantry *n* cella penaria *f*; promptuarium *nt*

paper *n* (for writing on) charta *f*; (newspaper) acta diurna *ntpl*
■ ~**s** *pl* scripta *ntpl*; litterae *fpl*

parable *n* parabola *f*

parade[1] *n* mil decursus; locus exercendi; (display) apparatus *m*; pompa, ostentatio *f*

parade[2] *vt* mil instruo ③; fig ostento ①
■ ~ *vi* (march ceremonially) decurro ③

paradise *n* Elysii campi *mpl*

paradox *n* quod contra opinionem omnium est

paradoxical *adj* praeter opinionem accidens

paragon *n* specimen, exemplum *nt*

paragraph *n* caput *nt*

parallel[1] *adj* parallelos; fig consimilis

parallel[2] *n* parallelos *m*; (comparison) collatio, comparatio *f*

parallel[3] *vt* exaequo; (compare) comparo [1]; (be equal) par sum *ir*

paralyse *vt* debilito, enervo [1]

paralysis *n* paralysis; fig torpedo *f*; torpor *m*

paralytic *n* paralyticus *m*

paramount *adj* supremus; summus

parapet *n* pluteus *m*

paraphernalia *n* apparatus *m*

paraphrase[1] *n* paraphrasis *f*

paraphrase[2] *vt* liberius interpretor [1]

parasite *n* parasitus, assecla *m*

parasitic *adj* parasiticus

parasol *n* umbella *f*; umbraculum *nt*

parcel *n* pars *f*; (bundle) fasciculus *m*

parch *vt* arefacio [3]; torreo [2]

parched *adj* torridus

parchment *n* membrana *f*

pardon[1] *n* venia *f*

pardon[2] *vt* ignosco [3]; condono [1] *both* + *dat*

pardonable *adj* condonandus

parent *n* parens *m/f*

parentage *n* genus *nt*; prosapia, origo *f*

parental *adj* paternus; maternus

parenthesis *n* interpositio, interclusio *f*

park *n* (for game) vivarium; (for pleasure) viridarium *nt*; horti *mpl*

parley[1] *n* colloquium *nt*

parley[2] *vi* colloquor [3]

parrot *n* psittacus *m*

parry *vt* averto, defendo [3]; propulso [1]

parsimonious *adj* parcus, sordidus

parsimony *n* parsimonia *f*

part[1] *n* pars, portio; (in a play) persona *f*, partes *fpl*; (duty) officium *nt*; (of a town) regio *f*
  □ **in** ~ partim

part[2] *vt* separo [1]; divido [3]
  ■ ~ *vi* (go away) discedo [3]; digredior [3], abeo *ir*; (gape open) dehisco, fatisco [3]
  □ ~ **with** dimitto [3]

partial *adj* per partes; (biased) iniquus
  □ ~ **to** cupidus + *gen*
  ■ ~**ly** *adv* partim

partiality *n* gratia; iniquitas *f*

participant *n* particeps *m/f*

participate *vi* particeps sum *or* fio *ir*

participation *n* participium *nt*; societas *f*

particle *n* particula *f*

particoloured *adj* versicolor; varius

particular[1] *adj* proprius; peculiaris; singularis; (fastidious) fastidiosus; (especial) praecipuus
  ■ ~**ly** *adv* particulatim; singillatim; (especially) praesertim, praecipue

particular[2] *n* singula *ntpl*

parting *n* divisio *f*; (from) discessus *m*

partisan *n* fautor, homo factiosus *m*

partition *n* partitio *f*; (enclosure) saeptum *nt*; (of rooms) paries *m*

partly *adv* partim; nonnulla ex parte, in parte

partner *n* socius *m*; socia *f*; particeps, consors *m/f*

partnership *n* societas, consociatio, consortio *f*

partridge *n* perdix *m/f*

party *n* factio; secta *f*; partes *fpl*; (detachment) manus *f*

pass[1] *vt* (go) eo *ir*; vado, cedo [3]; (go by) praeterco; (cross) transeo *ir*; (a law, *etc.*) fero *ir*; (approve) approbo [1]
  ■ ~ *vi* praetereo *ir*; praetervehor [3]; (of time) praetereo *ir*; (from one to another) migro [1]; (for) habeor [2]; (hand over) trado [3]
  □ ~ **away** transeo *ir*; (die) pereo *ir*; labor, effluo [3]; (cease) cesso [1]
  □ ~ **by** praetereo *ir*
  □ ~ **over** traicio, transgredior [3]; fig praetereo *ir*
  □ ~ **round** circumfero, trado [3]
  □ **let** ~ praetermitto, dimitto [3]

pass[2] *n* fauces, angustiae *fpl*; saltus *m*; (ticket) tessera *f*

passable *adj* (of a way) pervius; fig mediocris, tolerabilis

passage *n* (action) transitus *m*; transitio *f*; transmissio, traiectio; (thoroughfare) transitio pervia *f*; (of a book) locus *m*

p

passenger *n* viator; (by water) vector *m*

passing *adj* transiens; praeteriens; fig brevis, caducus

passion *n* cupiditas *f*; fervor *m*; impetus, animi motus *m*; (anger) ira *f*; (for) studium *nt*; (love) amor *m*

passionate *adj* fervidus, ardens, vehemens; iracundus
■ ~**ly** *adv* ardenter; iracunde, vehementer

passive *adj* patibilis; passivus
■ ~**ly** *adv* passive

passport *n* syngraphus *m*

password *n* tessera *f*

past[1] *adj* praeteritus; (immediately preceding) proximus, superior

past[2] *n* praeteritum tempus *nt*; actum tempus *nt*

past[2] *prep* praeter; (beyond) ultra *both* + *acc*

paste[1] *n* gluten *nt*

paste[2] *vt* glutino ①

pastime *n* oblectamentum *nt*; ludus *m*

pastoral *adj* pastoralis; pastorius

pastry *n* crustum *nt*, bellaria *ntpl*; crustula *ntpl*

pasture *n* pabulum *nt*

pat *n* plaga levis *f*

patch[1] *n* pannus *m*

patch[2] *vt* sarcio, resarcio ④; assuo ③

patent[1] *adj* apertus, manifestus
■ ~**ly** plane

patent[2] *n* diploma *nt*

paternal *adj* paternus, patrius

paternity *n* paternitas *f*

path *n* semita *f*; trames, callis *m*; fig (course) via *f*

pathetic *adj* patheticus
■ ~**ally** *adv* pathetice

pathway *n* semita *f*; callis *m*

patience *n* patientia *f*; tolerantia

patient[1] *adj* patiens; tolerans
■ ~**ly** *adv* patienter; aequo animo

patient[2] *n* aegrotus *m*; aegrota *f*

patrician *adj & n* patricius

patrimony *n* patrimonium *nt*; hereditas *f*

patriot *n* amans patriae *m*; bonus civis *m*

patriotic *adj* amans patriae; bonus, pius

patriotism *n* amor patriae *m*; pietas *f*

patrol *n* vigil *m*; excubiae *fpl*
■ ~ *vi* excubias ago ③

patron *n* patronus *m*

patronage *n* patrocinium, praesidium *nt*

patronize *vt* faveo, studeo ② + *dat*; (be present at) adsum *ir* + *dat*

patter[1] *n* crepitus *m*

patter[2] *vi* crepo, crepito ①

pattern *n* (sample) exemplar, exemplum; (model) specimen *nt*

paunch *n* venter *m*

pauper *n* pauper, egens, inops *m/f*

pause[1] *n* pausa, mora; intermissio *f*; intervallum *nt*

pause[2] *vi* intermitto, quiesco ③

pave *vt* (viam saxo) sterno ③

pavement *n* pavimentum *nt*; stratura *f*

pavilion *n* tentorium *nt*

paw[1] *n* ungula *f*; pes *m*

paw[2] *vt* pedibus pulso (terram) ①

pawn[1] *n* pignus *nt*; (in chess) latrunculus *m*

pawn[2] *vt* pignero; oppignero, obligo ①

pawnbroker *n* pignerator *m*

pay[1] *n* mil stipendium *nt*; (wages, hire) merces *f*; (profit) quaestus, fructus *m*

pay[2] *vt* (pecuniam debitam) solvo ③; (stipendium) numero ①; fig persolvo ③
■ ~ *vi* pendo ③; (be profitable) prosum *ir*, proficio ③
□ ~ **for** (hire) conduco ③; (buy) emo ③; fig (suffer) poenas do ①
□ ~ **off** dissolvo ③

payable *adj* solvendus

pay-day *n* dies stipendii solvendi *m*

payment *n* (act) solutio *f*; (sum of money) pensio *f*

pea *n* pisum, cicer *nt*

peace *n* pax; quies *f*; otium *nt*; (of mind) tranquillitas animi *f*

peaceable *adj* pacis amans; placabilis; (of things) pacatus; placidus, quietus

peaceably *adv* pacate; cum (bona) pace

peaceful *adj* pacis amans; placabilis; (of things) pacatus; placidus, quietus
■ ~**ly** *adv* pacate; cum (bona) pace

peacefulness *n* tranquillitas *f*

peacemaker *n* pacificator *m*

peach *n* malum Persicum *nt*

peacock *n* pavo *m*

peak *n* (of a mountain) cacumen, culmen *nt*; apex, vertex *m*

peal¹ *n* (of thunder) fragor; (of bells) concentus *m*

peal² *vi* sono, resono ①

pear *n* pirum *nt*
■ ~-**tree** *n* pirus *f*

pearl *n* margarita, baca, gemma *f*

pearly *adj* gemmeus, gemmans

peasant *n* rusticus, agrestis, agricola *m*

pebble *n* lapillus, calculus *m*

peck *vt* rostro impeto ③; mordeo ②

peculiar *adj* (one's own) proprius; peculiaris; (unusual) praecipuus, singularis
■ ~**ly** *adv* praesertim, imprimis; praecipue

pedantic *adj* litterarum ostentator, putidus; professorius
■ ~**ally** *adv* putide

pedantry *n* scholasticorum ineptiae *fpl*; eruditio insulsa *f*

pedestal *n* stylobates *m*; spira *f*

pedestrian *adj* pedester; pedibus *abl*
■ ~ *n* pedes *m*

pedigree *n* stemma *nt*

pedlar *n* institor *m*

peel¹ *n* cutis, tunica *f*; cortex *m*

peel² *vt* decortico, desquamo ①

peep¹ *n* (look) contuitus *m*

peep² *vi* per rimam speculor ①

peer *n* (equal) par

peer at *vt* (scrutinize) rimor ①

peevish *adj* stomachosus, morosus, difficilis
■ ~**ly** *adv* stomachose, morose

peg *n* paxillus *m*

pelican *n* pelicanus, onocrotalus *m*

pellet *n* globulus *m*; pilula *f*

pell-mell *adv* effuse, sine ordine, promiscue

pelt¹ *n* pellis *f*

pelt² *vt* peto ③; lapido; (beat) verbero ①

pen¹ *n* (to write with) calamus, stylus *m*; (for sheep) ovile *nt*

pen² *vt* scribo, compono ③; (shut in) includo ③

penal *adj* poenalis

penalty *n* poena; mul(c)ta *f*; supplicium *nt*

penance *n* satisfactio *f*; (atonement) piaculum *nt*; (punishment) poena *f*

pencil *n* graphis *f*; peniculus, penicillus *m*

pending *adj* instans; (law) sub iudice

pendulum *n* libramentum *nt*

penetrate *vt* penetro ①

penetration *n* acies mentis; sagacitas *f*

peninsula *n* paeninsula *f*

penitence *n* paenitentia *f*

penitent *adj* paenitens

penknife *n* scalprum *nt*

pennant *n* vexillum *nt*

penniless *adj* omnium rerum egens, inops

penny *n* as, nummus, denarius *m*

pension *n* merces annua *f*; annuum beneficium *nt*

pensive *adj* cogitabundus

penultimate *adj* paenultimus

people *n* populus *m*; homines *mpl*; (nation) natio *f*
□ ~ **say** dicunt
□ **common** ~ vulgus *nt*; plebs *f*

pepper *n* piper *nt*

perceive *vt* sentio ④; percipio ③; video ②; intellego ③

percentage *n* rata portio *f*

perception *n* perceptio, animadversio *f*

perch¹ *n* (for birds) sedile (avium) *nt*; (fish) perca *f*

perch² *vi* insido + *dat*; assido ③ in + *abl*

perennial *adj* perennis

perfect¹ *adj* perfectus; absolutus; (intact) plenus, integer
■ ~**ly** *adv* perfecte; absolute; (entirely) plane

perfect² *vt* perficio, absolvo ③

perfection *n* perfectio; absolutio, summa *f*

perforate *vt* perforo, terebro ①

perforation *n* (hole) foramen *nt*

perform *vt* perficio; exsequor; fungor + *abl*; (bring to pass) efficio; (accomplish) perago ③

performance *n* exsecutio; actio *f*; (work) opus *nt*

performer *n* effector; (player) actor, histrio *m*

perfume[1] *n* odor *m*

perfume[2] *vt* suffio ④

perhaps *adv* fortasse, forte, forsitan

peril *n* periculum, discrimen *nt*

perilous *adj* periculosus
■ ∼**ly** *adv* periculose

period *n* tempus *nt*; aetas *f*

periodical *adj* periodicus
■ ∼**ally** *adv* temporibus certis

perish *vi* pereo, intereo *ir*; exstinguor, cado ③

perishable *adj* fragilis, caducus, infirmus

perjure *vi* (oneself) peiero, periuro ①

perjury *n* periurium *nt*
□ **commit** ∼ peiero, periuro ①

permanent *adj* diuturnus, mansurus, perpetuus
■ ∼**ly** *adv* perpetuo

permeate *vt* penetro, pervagor, pererro ①

permission *n* permissio, venia *f*
□ **with your** ∼ pace tua, tua bona venia

permit *vt* sino, permitto, concedo ③
□ **it is** ∼**ted** licet ②

pernicious *adj* perniciosus; noxius
■ ∼**ly** *adv* perniciose

perpendicular *adj* directus

perpetrate *vt* perficio; facio, committo, admitto ③; perpetro ①

perpetual *adj* sempiternus; perpetuus; perennis; continuus
■ ∼**ly** *adv* perpetuo, semper, usque, continenter

perplex *vt* (confound) turbo ①; confundo ③

perplexity *n* perturbatio; anxietas *f*

persecute *vt* insector; vexo ①

persecution *n* insectatio; vexatio *f*

perseverance *n* perseverantia, constantia, assiduitas *f*

persevere *vi* persevero, persto ①

persevering *adj* constans; tenax (propositi); assiduus

persist *vi* persto, persevero ①

persistence *n* permansio (in aliqua re) *f*

persistent *adj* pertinax

person *n* homo *m*
□ **any** ∼ quilibet, quivis
□ **in** ∼ ipse (ego, ille, *etc.*)

personage *n* homo notus *m*

personal *adj* privatus
■ ∼**ly** *adv* per se; ipse

perspiration *n* sudor *m*

perspire *vi* sudo ①; sudorem emitto ③

persuade *vt* suadeo, persuadeo ②
+ *dat*

persuasion *n* persuasio; fides; opinio *f*

persuasive *adj* suasorius
■ ∼**ly** *adv* apte ad persuadendum

pert *adj* procax

pertinent *adj* appositus (ad rem), aptus, idoneus

perturb *vt* turbo, perturbo ①

peruse *vt* lego, perlego ③

pervade *vt* perfundo ③; permano ①; pervagor ①

perverse *adj* perversus, pravus

perversion *n* depravatio *f*

perversity *n* perversitas, pravitas *f*

pervert *vt* depravo ①; perverto, corrumpo ③

pest *n* pestis, pernicies *f*

pester *vt* infesto, sollicito, vexo ①

pet[1] *n* (little favourite) corculum *nt*; deliciae *fpl*

pet[2] *adj* dilectus, carus

pet[3] *vt* ▶ **caress, fondle**

petal *n* floris folium *nt*

petition *n* preces *fpl*; libellus *m*; petitio *f*

petrify *vt* in lapidem converto ③; fig obstupefacio ③

petty *adj* minutus, angustus; (trifling) parvus

phantom *n* phantasma *nt*; vana species *f*; spectrum *nt*

phase *n* vices *fpl*

pheasant *n* phasiana; avis phasiana *f*

phenomenal *adj* singularis

phenomenon *n* res nova *f*; ostentum *nt*

philanthropic *adj* benignus, humanus

philanthropist *n* generi humano amicus *m*

philanthropy *n* benignitas, humanitas *f*

philosopher *n* philosophus; sapiens *m*

philosophical *adj* philosophicus
■ ~**ly** *adv* philosophice; fig aequo animo

philosophize *vi* philosophor ①

philosophy *n* philosophia; sapientia; (theory) ratio *f*

phoenix *n* phoenix *m*

phrase¹ *n* locutio *f*

phrase² *vt* loquor ③

physical *adj* corporis *gen*; physicus
■ ~**ly** *adv* natura *abl*; physice

physician *n* medicus *m*

physics *n* physica *ntpl*

physique *n* corpus *nt*

pick¹ *vt* (pluck) carpo, decerpo ③; lego; (choose) eligo
  □ ~ **off** avello ③
  □ ~ **out** eligo ③
  □ ~ **up** tollo; colligo ③
  □ ~ **holes in** carpo, rodo ③

pick² *n* (tool) dolabra *f*; (choicest part) flos *m*, robur *nt*

pickaxe *n* dolabra *f*

picket *n* mil statio *f*

pickpocket *vt&i* manticulor ①

picture¹ *n* tabula, tabella; effigies; fig descriptio *f*

picture² *vt* depingo ③; (imagine) fingo ③

picture-gallery *n* pinacotheca *f*

picturesque *adj* venustus, pulcher, amoenus

pie *n* (pastry) crustum *nt*

piece *n* (part) frustum *nt*; pars, portio *f*; (fragment) fragmentum *nt*; (coin) nummus *m*
  □ **tear to** ~**s** dilanio, lacero ①

pier *n* pila; (massive structure) moles *f*; agger *m*

pierce *vt* perforo, terebro ①; (with a sword, *etc.*) transfigo, perfodio, transadigo; fig (with grief) (aliquem) dolore afficio ③

piercing *adj* penetrabilis; (of sounds) acutissimus; fig sagax
  ■ ~**ly** *adv* acute

piety *n* pietas *f*

pig *n* porcus, sus *m*

pigeon *n* columba *f*; columbus *m*

pigeon-hole *n* loculamentum *nt*

pigheaded *adj* obstinatus

pigment *n* pigmentum *nt*

pigsty *n* hara *f*

pike *n* (spear) hasta, lancea *f*; (fish) lucius, lupus *m*

pile¹ *n* (heap) acervus, cumulus *m*; congeries *f*; (of firewood) rogus *m*; (nap of cloth) villus *m*

pile² *vt* (up) coacervo, cumulo, aggero, accumulo ①; exstruo, congero ③

pilfer *vt* surripio ③; suffuror ①

pilfering *n* direptio *f*

pilgrim *n* peregrinator *m*

pilgrimage *n* peregrinatio *f*

pill *n* pilula *f*

pillage¹ *n* (act) vastatio, direptio; (booty) praeda *f*; spolium *nt*

pillage² *vt* populor, praedor, vasto, spolio ①; diripio ③

pillar *n* (support, prop) columna; pila *f*

pillow *n* pulvinus *m*; cervical *nt*

pilot¹ *n* gubernator, rector *m*

pilot² *vt* guberno ①; rego ③

pimp *n* leno *m*

pimple *n* pustula, pusula *f*

pin¹ *n* acus; acicula *f*; (nail, peg) clavus *m*

pin² *vt* acu figo; affigo ③

pincers *n* forceps *f*

pinch¹ *vt* vellico ①; (as cold) uro, aduro ③; (hurt) laedo ③

pinch² *n* vellicatio *f*
  □ **feel the** ~ urgeor ②, premor ③

pine¹ *n* pinus *f*

pine² *vi* (away) tabesco ③; marcesco, conficior ③

pink *adj* (of colour) roseus

pinnacle *n* fastigium *nt*

pint *n* (measure) sextarius *m*

pioneer *n* mil cunicularius; explorator viae; fig praecursor *m*

pious *adj* pius; (pure) sanctus
  ■ ~**ly** *adv* pie, sancte

pip *n* (of fruit) semen *nt*; nucleus *m*; (of grapes) acinus *m*

pipe *n* (tube) tubus *m*; (mus) fistula *f*; tibia, arundo *f*; calamus *m*

piper *n* fistulator, tibicen *m*

piquant *adj* fig salsus, facetus; acutus

pique *n* offensio *f*; offensa *f*; odium *nt*

piracy *n* piratica *f*

pirate *n* praedo maritimus, pirata *m*

pit *n* fossa, fovea, scrobis *f*; puteus *m*;
(abyss, gulf) barathrum *nt*; (in theatre) cavea
f; (quarry) fodina *f*

pitch¹ *n* pix *f*

pitch² (highest point) summum fastigium
nt

pitch³ mus sonus *m*

pitch⁴ *vt* (a tent, the camp) pono ③; (fling)
conicio ③
■ ~ *vi* fluctuo ①

pitch-black *adj* (also **pitch-dark**)
fuscus, niger; obscurus, caliginosus

pitcher *n* urceus *m*

pitchfork *n* furca *f*

pith *n* medulla *f*

pithy *adj* medulla abundans; nervosus;
fig sententiosus

pitiable *adj* miserabilis; flebilis,
lamentabilis; afflictus

pitiful *adj* misericors; (pitiable)
miserabilis; (contemptible, mean) abiectus
■ ~**ly** *adv* misericorditer;
miserabiliter; abiecte

pitiless *adj* immisericors; durus,
▶ **cruel**

pity¹ *n* misericordia, miseratio *f*

pity² *vt&i* miseret (me alicuius),
misereor ②; miseror ①; miseresco ③ *all*
+ *gen*

pivot *n* cardo *m*

placard *n* edictum *nt*

place¹ *n* locus *m*; (office) munus *nt*
□ **in the first** ~ fig primum, primo

place² *vt* pono ③; loco, colloco ①

placid *adj* placidus, tranquillus;
quietus
■ ~**ly** *adv* placide, tranquille, quiete

plague¹ *n* pestilentia; fig pestis *f*

plague² *vt* vexo, crucio ①

plain¹ *n* campus *m*; planities *f*;
aequor *nt*

plain² *adj* (smooth) planus; (not ornamented)
inornatus; (distinct) clarus; (simple)
simplex; (evident) apertus, manifestus;
sincerus

plainly *adv* distincte, clare, plane;
simpliciter; (evidently) manifeste, aperte,
perspicue

plaintiff *n* petitor *m*; accusator *m*

plaintive *adj* flebilis; querulus
■ ~**ly** *adv* flebiliter

plait *vt* implico ①; intexo ③

plan¹ *n* (project) consilium, propositum
nt; (of ground) forma, designatio *f*

plan² *vt* (scheme) excogito ①; (draw)
designo ①

plane¹ *n* (tool) runcina *f*; (level surface)
superficies *f*

plane² *vt* runcino ①

planet *n* planeta *m*; stella erratica *f*

plane-tree *n* platanus *f*

plank *n* axis *m*; tabula *f*

plant¹ *n* herba, planta *f*

plant² *vt* planto ①; sero ③

plantation *n* plantarium *nt*

plaque *n* tabula *f*

plaster¹ *n* tectorium; gypsum; med
emplastrum *nt*

plaster² *vt* trullisso, gypso ①; induco;
illino ③

plasterer *n* tector *m*

plate *n* (thin sheet of metal) lamina, brattea
f; (silver for table) vasa argentea *ntpl*; (dish)
patella *f*

plated *adj* bratteatus

platform *n* suggestus *m*; suggestum *nt*

plaudit *n* plausus, clamor *m*

plausible *adj* probabilis; speciosus

play¹ *n* (act of playing) ludus; lusus *m*;
(movement) motus *m*; (scope) area *f*; locus
m; (at a theatre) fabula, comoedia,
tragoedia *f*
□ **fair** ~ aequitas *f*

play² *vt&i* ludo ③; (frolic, etc.) lascivio ④;
luxurio ①; (on musical instruments) cano ③;
(gamble) aleam exerceo ②; (as actor) partes
ago ③

player *n* (on the stage) histrio, actor; (on an
instrument) fidicen, tibicen, citharista *m*;
(of a game) lusor *m*

playful *adj* lascivus, iocosus,
ludibundus
■ ~**ly** *adv* iocose

plaything *n* (rattle) crepundia *ntpl*; (doll)
pupa *f*

plea *n* (excuse) excusatio, causa *f*

plead *vt&i* causas ago; (for one) aliquem
defendo; (against) contra aliquem
causam dico ③; (in excuse) excuso ①

pleasant *adj* amoenus, iucundus,
gratus; urbanus, lepidus

please *vt&i* (give pleasure) placeo ② + *dat*;
delecto ①
□ **as you** ~ ut vobis libet

pleased *adj* laetus, felix

pleasing *adj* gratus; lepidus; iucundus

pleasure *n* voluptas; iucunditas *f*; deliciae *fpl*; (caprice) libido *f*; (will) arbitrium *nt*

plebeian *adj & n* plebeius; vulgaris

pledge¹ *n* pignus *nt*; (surety) vas, praes *m*; (proof) testimonium *nt*

pledge² *vt* pignero 1; spondeo 2; promitto 3

plentiful *adj* largus, affluens, uber, copiosus, abundans
■ ~**ly** *adv* large, abunde, copiose, ubertim

plenty *n* copia, abundantia, ubertas *f*

pliable *adj* flexibilis; lentus, mollis; flexilis; tractabilis; mansuetus

pliant *adj* flexibilis; lentus, mollis; flexilis; tractabilis; mansuetus

plight *n* condicio *f*; status *m*

plot¹ *n* (conspiracy) coniuratio *f*; (of land) agellus *m*; (surveying) designatio *f*; fig (of a play, *etc.*) argumentum *nt*

plot² *vi* coniuro 1
■ ~ *vt* molior 4; excogito 1

plotter *n* ▶ **conspirator**

plough¹ *n* aratrum *nt*

plough² *vt* aro 1

ploughman *n* arator *m*

pluck¹ *n* (courage) animus *nt*

pluck² *vt* (pull) vello 3; vellico 1; (gather) carpo, decerpo; (off) avello; deripio; (out) evello, eripio 3
□ ~ **up** (courage) colligo 3

plug¹ *n* obturamentum *nt*

plug² *vt* obturo 1

plum *n* prunum *nt*
■ ~ **tree** *n* prunus *f*

plumage *n* plumae, pennae *fpl*

plumber *n* (worker in lead) plumbarius *m*

plumb-line *n* perpendiculum *nt*; linea *f*

plume *n* penna, pluma; (crest) crista *f*

plummet *n* perpendiculum *nt*; linea *f*

plump *adj* nitidus, obesus; corpulentus

plumpness *n* obesitas *f*; nitor *m*

plunder¹ *n* (booty) praeda *f*; spolium *nt*; (act of plundering) rapina, direptio *f*; (stolen goods) furta *ntpl*

plunder² *vt* praedor 1; diripio 3; spolio, vasto, populor 1

plunge *vt* mergo, summergo; (a sword) condo, subdo 3 in + *abl*
■ ~ *vi* immergor; fig me mergo 3 in …

plural *adj* pluralis

ply *vt* exerceo 2

pocket *n* (pouch) marsupium *nt*; crumena *f*

pocket-money *n* peculium *nt*

pod *n* siliqua *f*

poem *n* poema, carmen *nt*

poet *n* poeta, vates *m*

poetess *n* poetria *f*

poetic *adj* (also **poetical**) poeticus
■ ~**ally** *adv* poetice

poetry *n* (art) poetice; (poems) poesis *f*; carmen *nt*

point¹ *n* punctum; (pointed end) acumen *nt*; (of swords, *etc.*) mucro *m*; (of a spear) cuspis *f*; fig quaestio *f*; casus *m*; res *f*; argumentum *nt*
□ ~ **of view** iudicium *nt*
□ **main** *or* **chief** ~ caput *nt*

point² *vt* (aim) intendo 3
□ ~ **at** monstro 1
□ ~ **out** monstro 1

pointed *adj* praeacutus; acutus; fig salsus; (stinging) aculeatus
■ ~**ly** *adv* acriter, acute; plane, aperte

pointer *n* index *m/f*

pointless *adj* fig insulus, frigidus

poise *n* (equilibrium) aequipondium *nt*; fig (sophistication) urbanitas *f*

poised *adj* libratus

poison¹ *n* venenum, virus *nt*

poison² *vt* (a thing) veneno; (a person) veneno neco; fig vitio 1

poisoner *n* veneficus *m*; venefica *f*

poisoning *n* veneficium *nt*

poisonous *adj* venenatus; veneficus; venenifer

poke *vt* (alicui) latus fodico 1; (touch) tango 3; (move) moveo 2

poker *n* rutabulum *nt*

polar *adj* arctous

pole *n* (staff) asser *m*; pertica *f*; contus *m*; (of the earth) polus, axis *m*

police *n* securitatis urbanae cura *or* custodia *f*

policeman *n* vigil, lictor *m*

policy *n* reipublicae administratio; (craft) astutia, calliditas *f*; (stratagem) ars *f*; dolus *m*; (in good sense) consilium *nt*

p

polish[1] *vt* polio; expolio ④; limo, levo ①

polish[2] *n* nitor, levor *m*; fig lima *f*

polite *adj* comis, urbanus; affabilis, humanus

politely *adv* comiter, humane

politeness *n* urbanitas, comitas, humanitas *f*

politic *adj* prudens

political *adj* publicus, civilis
■ ∼**ly** *adv* quod ad rempublicam attinet

politician *n* vir rerum publicarum peritus *m*

politics *n* res publica *f*

poll *n* (voting) suffragium *nt*

pollen *n* pollen *nt*

polling-booth *n* saeptum, ovile *nt*

poll tax *n* exactio capitum *f*

pollute *vt* inquino, contamino, maculo, commaculo, foedo ①; polluo ③

pollution *n* colluvio; impuritas, macula, labes *f*

polygon *n* polygonum *nt*

polygonal *adj* polygonius, multangulus

pomp *n* pompa *f*; splendor, apparatus *m*

pompous *adj* magniloquus; fig inflatus

pond *n* stagnum *nt*; lacus *m*

ponder *vt&i* considero, pensito, meditor ①; perpendo ③

pony *n* mannulus *m*

pool *n* lacuna *f*; stagnum *nt*

poop *n* puppis *f*

poor *adj* pauper; egenus, inops; (of soil) macer; fig tenuis; mediocris; miser

poorly *adj* aeger

poplar *n* populus *f*

poppy *n* papaver *nt*

populace *n* vulgus *nt*; plebs *f*

popular *adj* popularis; gratiosus; (common) vulgaris
■ ∼**ly** *adv* populariter, vulgo

popularity *n* favor populi *m*; studium populi *nt*; gratia *f*

population *n* incolae urbis, civitatis, *etc. m/fpl*

populous *adj* populo frequens, celeber

porcelain *n* murra *f*; murrina *ntpl*

porch *n* vestibulum *nt*; porticus *f*

porcupine *n* hystrix *f*

pore *vi* (over) incumbo ③ + *dat*

pork *n* porcina, suilla *f*

porous *adj* rarus

porpoise *n* porculus marinus *m*

porridge *n* puls *f*

port *n* portus *m*

portable *adj* qui (facile) portari potest

portcullis *n* cataracta *m*

portend *vt* praesagio ④; auguror ①; portendo ③; praemonstro, significo ①

portent *n* ostentum, portentum, prodigium *nt*

porter *n* ianitor, ostiarius, custos; (carrier) baiulus *m*

portfolio *n* scrinium *nt*

portico *n* porticus *f*

portion *n* pars; portio *f*

portly *adj* obesus

portrait *n* imago, effigies *f*

portray *vt* pingo ③; delineo ①; fig depingo, describo ③

pose *n* status *m*; (pretence) simulatio *f*

position *n* situs, positus; fig status *m*; condicio *f*

positive *adj* certus; fig confidens; pervicax
■ ∼**ly** *adv* praecise; confidenter; pervicaciter

possess *vt* possideo, teneo, habeo ②; (of feelings) occupo ①; invado ③; (induce) animum induco ③

possession *n* (occupancy) possessio *f*; (goods) bona *ntpl*
□ **in the** ∼ **of** penes + *acc*

possessor *n* possessor, dominus *m*

possibility *n* possibilitas *f*; (opportunity) facultas, copia, potestas *f*

possible *adj* possibilis
□ **as (quickly) as** ∼ quam celerrime

possibly *adv* (perhaps) fortasse

post[1] *n* (stake) sudis *f*; stipes, palus *m*; (doorpost) postis *m*; (letter-carriers) tabellarii *mpl*; (station) statio, sedes *f*, locus *m*; (office) munus *nt*

post[2] *vt* (put up) colloco ①; pono; constituo ③; (a letter) tabellario litteras do ①

poster *n* tabula *f*

posterior *adj* posterior

posterity *n* posteri; minores *mpl*

posthumous *adj* postumus

postman *n* tabellarius *m*

postpone *vt* differo, profero *ir*; prorogo ①

posture *n* status, habitus, gestus *m*

posy *n* ▶ bouquet

pot *n* olla *f*; aenum, vas *nt*

potent *adj* potens

potion *n* potio *f*

potter *n* figulus *m*

pottery *n* (trade) figlina *f*; (ware) figlinum *nt*; fictilia *ntpl*; (workshop) figlina *f*

pouch *n* pera *f*; sacculus *m*

poultice *n* malagma, fomentum, cataplasma *nt*

poultry *n* aves cohortales *fpl*

pounce[1] *n* (swoop) impetus *m*

pounce[2] *vi* involo ①; insilio ④

pound[1] *n* (weight and money) libra *f*; (for cattle) saeptum *nt*

pound[2] *vt* (crush) contundo, contero; (cattle) includo ③

pour *vt&i* fundo; fundor ③
  □ ∼ **down** (of rain) ruo; fig ingruo ③
  □ ∼ **out** *vt* effundo, profundo ③; *vi* effundor ③

poverty *n* paupertas, pauperies, inopia, penuria, egestas *f*

powder[1] *n* pulvis *m*

powder[2] *vt* pulvere conspergo ③; (reduce to powder) in pulverem redigo ③

power *n* vis; potestas *f*; (authority) ius; imperium *nt*; mil copiae *fpl*; fig (of mind) dos animi *f*
  □ **in (one's)** ∼ penes + *acc*

powerful *adj* validus, praevalidus; potens; (effectual) efficax
  ■ ∼**ly** *adv* potenter; efficaciter

powerless *adj* invalidus; infirmus, imbecillus; impotens; (vain) irritus; inefficax
  □ **be** ∼ **to** non possum *ir*, nequeo ④

practicable *adj* quod fieri potest

practical *adj* (opposite to theoretical) activus; (taught by experience) usu doctus
  ■ ∼**ly** *adv* ex usu; (almost) paene

practice *n* usus *m*; exercitatio; experientia; (custom) consuetudo *f*

practise *vt&i* exerceo ②; tracto ①; (do habitually) factito ①

praetor *n* praetor *m*

praetorian *adj* praetorius

praetorship *n* praetura *f*

praise[1] *n* laus, laudatio; *f*; praeconium *nt*

praise[2] *vt* laudo, collaudo, praedico ①; effero ③

praiseworthy *adj* laudabilis, laudandus

prance *vi* exsulto ①

prank *n* ludus *m*; fraus *f*

prattle[1] *n* garrulitas *f*

prattle[2] *vi* garrio ④; blatero ①

prawn *n* squilla *f*

pray *vt* precor, exoro, supplico, flagito ①; oro ①
  □ ∼ **for** intercedo ③ pro + *abl*; (for a thing) peto, posco ③
  □ ∼ **to** adoro; supplico ①

prayer *n* preces *fpl*; precatio *f*

preach *vt&i* praedico ①

preamble *n* exordium, prooemium *nt*

precarious *adj* incertus, precarius
  ■ ∼**ly** *adv* precario

precaution *n* cautio, provisio *f*

precede *vt* antecedo, praegredior, praecurro ③; anteeo, praeeo *ir*

precedence *n* ius praecedendi *nt*; principatus *m*

precedent *n* exemplum *nt*

preceding *adj* praecedens, antecedens

precept *n* praeceptum *nt*

precinct *n* termini, limites *mpl*

precious *adj* pretiosus, carus; dilectus

precipice *n* locus praeceps *m*; praeruptum *nt*

precipitate[1] *vt&i* praecipito ①; (hurry) accelero, festino, maturo ①

precipitate[2] *adj* praeceps; fig inconsultus

precipitous *adj* praeceps, praeruptus, declivis

precise *adj* certus, definitus; (very) ipse; fig (exact) accuratus, exactus; (of manner) rigidus
  ■ ∼**ly** *adv* accurate

precision *n* accuratio *f*

preclude *vt* praecludo ③; arceo, prohibeo ②

precocious *adj* praecox; festinatus, praematurus

preconception *n* praeiudicata opinio *f*

p

precursor *n* praenuntius, praecursor *m*

predatory *adj* praedatorius; rapax

predecessor *n* decessor, antecessor *m*

predestination *n* praedestinatio *f*

predestine *vt* praedestino ①

predicament *n* praedicamentum *nt*; (difficulty) angustiae *fpl*

predict *vt* praedico ③; auguror, vaticinor ①

prediction *n* praedictio *f*; praedictum; vaticinium *nt*; vaticinatio *f*

predominant *adj* praepollens
  □ **be ~** praevaleo ②

predominate *vi* praevaleo ②

pre-eminence *n* excellentia, praestantia *f*; (supreme rule) principatus *m*

pre-eminent *adj* insignis, praestans, praecipuus, praeclarus
  ■ **~ly** *adv* praestanter, praecipue

preface *n* praefatio *f*; exordium, prooemium *nt*

prefer *vt* praefero *ir*, praepono ③, antefero *ir*; antepono ③; (like better) malo *ir*

preferable *adj* potior, praestantior
  □ **it is ~** praestat

preferably *adv* potius

preference *n*:
  □ **give ~** (to) antepono ③

pregnancy *n* graviditas; praegnatio *f*

pregnant *adj* gravida, praegnans, gravis

prejudge *vt* praeiudico ①

prejudice[1] *n* opinio praeiudicata *f*; detrimentum *nt*

prejudice[2] *vt* in suspicionem adduco ③; (injure) laedo ③
  □ **be ~d against** suspicor ①

prejudicial *adj* noxius

preliminary[1] *n* prooemium *nt*; prolusio *f*

preliminary[2] *adj* primus

prelude *n* prooemium *nt*; fig prolusio *f*

premature *adj* praematurus; fig praeproperus

premeditation *n* praemeditatio *f*

premises *n* (house) domus *f*; (estate) fundus *m*; villa *f*; praedium *nt*

premiss *n* praemissa *f*; praemissa *ntpl*

premium *n* praemium *nt*

premonition *n* praesagium *nt*

preoccupation *n* praeoccupatio *f*

preoccupy *vt* praeoccupo ①

preparation *n* praeparatio *f*; paratus, apparatus *m*

prepare *vt* paro, comparo, praeparo ①; (furnish) orno, adorno; (study) meditor ①
  ■ **~** *vi* comparo ①; me accingo ③

prepared *adj* paratus

preposterous *adj* praeposterus; perversus; absurdus
  ■ **~ly** *adv* perverse, absurde

prerogative *n* praerogativa *f*; privilegium *nt*

presage[1] *n* praesagium; augurium, omen, portentum *nt*

presage[2] *vt&i* portendo ③; significo ①; praesagio ④; praedico ③; vaticinor ①

prescribe *vt* praecipio; praescribo; propono ③

prescription *n* praescriptum *nt*; (custom) usus *m*

presence *n* praesentia *f*
  □ **in my ~** me praesente
  □ **in the ~ of** coram + *abl*

present[1] *adj* praesens; hic
  □ **for the ~** in praesens
  □ **be ~** adsum *ir*

present[2] *n* donum, munus *nt*

present[3] *vt* offero *ir*; dono, do ①; largior ④; introduco; (law) sisto ③; fig (~ itself) obvenio ④

presentation *n* donatio *f*

presentiment *n* praesagium *nt*
  □ **have a ~ of** praesentio ④

presently *adv* (soon) mox; (immediately) illico, statim

preservation *n* conservatio *f*

preserve *vt* servo, conservo ①; tueor ②; (fruits) condio ④

preside *vi* (over) praesideo ②; praesum *ir both* + *dat*

presidency *n* praefectura *f*

president *n* praeses, praefectus *m*

press[1] *n* (for wine, oil, clothes, *etc.*) prelum *nt*; (of people) turba *f*

press[2] *vt* premo; comprimo ③; fig urgeo ②; insto, flagito ①; (force to serve) vi comparo ①
  □ **~ on** *or* **upon** insto ①, insisto ③ *both* + *dat*

pressing *adj* instans

pressure *n* pressura *f*; fig angor *m*; aerumna *f*

prestige *n* gloria *f*

presume *vt&i* (be conceited) arrogo, (hope) spero ①; (suppose) conicio ③; (dare) audeo ②

presumption *n* arrogantia; (conjecture) suspicio *f*; (opinion) sententia *f*

presumptuous *adj* arrogans; audax, temerarius
 ■ ∼ly *adv* arroganter, audacter

pretence *n* simulatio *f*; ▶ **pretext**

pretend *vt&i* simulo, dissimulo ①

pretension *n* (claim) postulatio; (display) ostentatio *f*

pretext *n* species *f*; praetextum *nt*
 □ **under the ∼ of** specie + *gen*

prettiness *n* elegantia, venustas *f*

pretty *adj* bellus; lepidus; venustus
 □ ∼ **well** mediocriter

prevail *vi* praevaleo, polleo; persuadeo ②; (become current) increbresco ③
 □ ∼ **upon** impetro ① ab + *abl*

prevalent *adj* vulgatus
 □ **be ∼** increbresco ③

prevaricate *vi* tergiversor, praevaricor ①

prevarication *n* praevaricatio, tergiversatio *f*

prevent *vt* praevenio ④; praeverto ③; (stop) impedio ④; prohibeo ②

prevention *n* prohibitio *f*

previous *adj* antecedens, prior
 ■ ∼ly *adv* antea, antehac, prius

prey[1] *n* praeda *f*
 □ **beast of ∼** animal rapax *nt*, fera *f*

prey[2] *vi* (on, upon) praedor ①; rapio ③; fig vexo ①

price *n* pretium *nt*
 □ **at what ∼?** quanti?

priceless *adj* inaestimabilis

prick[1] *n* punctus *m*; (goad) stimulus *m*

prick[2] *vt* pungo ③; fig stimulo ①
 □ ∼ **up** (aures) arrigo ③

prickle *n* aculeus *m*; spina *f*

prickly *adj* spinosus

pride[1] *n* superbia *f*; fastidium *nt*; fastus *m*

pride[2] *vt* (oneself on) iacto ①; superbio ④ + *abl*

priest *n* sacerdos, antistes, vates *m*

priestess *n* sacerdos, antistita, vates *f*

priesthood *n* (office) sacerdotium *nt*; (collectively) sacerdotes *mpl*

prim *adj* rigidus

primarily *adv* praecipue

primary *adj* principalis; praecipuus

prime[1] *n* (of life) florens aetas *f*; fig flos *m*; robur *nt*

prime[2] *adj* egregius, optimus

primeval *adj* primigenius, primaevus; priscus

primitive *adj* principalis, primitivus; (simple) simplex

prince *n* rex, princeps, regulus; (king's son) regis filius *m*

princess *n* regina; regia puella; regis filia *f*

principal[1] *adj* principalis, praecipuus; maximus, potissimus
 ■ ∼ly *adv* maxime, praecipue; potissimum, praesertim

principal[2] *n* caput *nt*; praeses, praefectus *m*

principle *n* principium *nt*; origo *f*; (in philosophy) ratio *f*; (precept) praeceptum *nt*; (maxim) institutum *nt*

print[1] *vt* imprimo ③

print[2] *n* (mark) nota *f*; vestigium *nt*

prior *adj* prior

prise *vt*:
 □ ∼ **open** vecti refringo ③

prison *n* carcer *m*; custodia *f*

prisoner *n* (of war) captivus; (law) reus *m*; rea *f*

privacy *n* solitudo *f*; secretum *nt*

private *adj* privatus; (domestic) domesticus
 ■ ∼ly *adv* privatim, secreto; clam

privation *n* privatio; (need) inopia *f*

privilege *n* privilegium, beneficium *nt*; immunitas *f*

prize[1] *n* (reward) praemium *nt*; (victory) palma *f*

prize[2] *vt* (value) aestimo ①; (highly) magni facio ③

probability *n* similitudo veri, probabilitas *f*

probable *adj* verisimilis, probabilis

probably *adv* probabiliter

probation *n* probatio *f*

probe[1] *n* specillum *nt*

probe[2] *vt* specillo tento ①

P

problem n (problems) problemata ntpl; quaestio f

problematical adj incertus, dubius

procedure n ratio agendi f, ordo m; forma f; (proceedings) acta, facta ntpl

proceed vi progredior; procedo, incedo; (continue) pergo ③; (advance) proficio ③; (arise, spring from) orior ④; proficiscor ③

proceeding n facinus, factum nt
□ ~s acta, facta ntpl
□ **legal** ~s actio f; controversia iudiciaria f

proceeds n reditus, proventus m

process n processus m; (method) ratio f; (law) lis, actio f

procession n pompa f

proclaim vt promulgo, pronuntio ①; edico, propono ③

proclamation n pronuntiatio, promulgatio f; edictum nt

proconsul n proconsul m; pro consule

proconsular adj proconsularis

proconsulship n proconsulatus m

procrastinate vt differo ir
■ ~ vi cunctor, moror ①

procrastination n tarditas, procrastinatio, cunctatio f

procure vt (get) acquiro, adipiscor, consequor ③; comparo ①

prod vt pungo ③

prodigal adj prodigus; profusus, effusus

prodigious adj (monstrous) prodigiosus; (great) immanis; ingens
■ ~ly adv prodigiose; valde

prodigy n prodigium, monstrum; portentum; fig miraculum nt

produce[1] vi (bring forward) produco ③, profero ir; (bring forth) pario ③; (yield) fero, effero, profero ir; (cause) facio ③; creo ①; cieo, moveo ②

produce[2] n fructus m

product n (of earth) fructus m; fruges fpl; (of work) opus nt

production n prolatio; (manufacture) fabricatio f

productive adj ferax, fertilis, fecundus; fig efficiens

profane[1] adj profanus; fig impius

profane[2] vt violo, profano ①

profanity n impietas f; nefas nt

profess vt profiteor ②

profession n (avowal; calling, trade) professio f; (business, trade) ars f

professional adj ad professionem pertinens

professor n (literary) professor m

proffer vt offero ir, propono ③

proficiency n ars, peritia f

proficient adj peritus

profile n facies obliqua f; (as portrait) catagrapha ntpl

profit[1] n emolumentum; lucrum nt; reditus, fructus, quaestus m

profit[2] vt prosum ir + dat
■ ~ vi proficio ③; (get advantage) lucror ①; fructum percipio ③

profitable adj fructuosus, quaestuosus; lucrosus; utilis
□ **be** ~ prosum ir

profligate adj perditus, flagitiosus, nequam indecl

profound adj (deep) altus; fig subtilis; abstrusus
■ ~ly adv penitus; subtiliter, abscondite

profundity n altitudo, subtilitas f

profuse adj effusus, profusus
■ ~ly adv effuse, profuse

profusion n effusio, profusio, ubertas; abundantia f

programme n libellus m

progress[1] n iter nt; progressus, processus m

progress[2] vi progredior, fig proficio ③

progression n progressus m

progressively adv (gradually) paulatim, sensim, gradatim

prohibit vt veto ①; interdico ③; prohibeo ②

prohibition n interdictum nt

project[1] n propositum, consilium nt

project[2] vt molior ④
■ ~ vi consilium capio ③; (jut out) promineo, emineo ②

projectile n missile nt

projecting adj prominens; proiectus

projection n proiectum nt; proiectura f

proletariat n plebs f; vulgus nt

prolific adj fecundus, ferax, fertilis

prologue n prologus m

prolong vt produco ③; prorogo ①; extendo, traho ③

prominence *n* eminentia *f*

prominent *adj* eminens; conspicuus

promiscuous *adj* promiscuus; mixtus
■ ∼**ly** *adv* promiscue, sine ullo discrimine

promise¹ *n* promissum *nt*; (act) promissio, fides *f*

promise² *vt&i* promitto ③; polliceor, spondeo ②

promising *adj* bona *or* summa spe

promote *vt* augeo ②; tollo ③, effero *ir*, proveho ③; (serve) consulo + *dat* ③

promotion *n* amplior gradus *m*; dignitas *f*

prompt¹ *adj* promptus, paratus; (speedy) maturus
■ ∼**ly** *adv* prompte; (speedily) mature

prompt² *vt* subicio ③; (incite, *etc.*) impello ③

prone *adj* pronus; propensus; proclivis

prong *n* dens *m*

pronounce *vt* pronuntio; (articulate syllables) enuntio ①; loquor ③

pronouncement *n* iudicium *nt*; sententia *f*

pronunciation *n* pronuntiatio *f*

proof *n* documentum, argumentum; indicium; signum; specimen *nt*; ratio demonstrandi *or* probandi *f*; (trial) experimentum *nt*

prop¹ *n* fulcrum; fig columen *nt*

prop² *vt* (up) fulcio ④; adminiculor ①

propagate *vt* propago; (spread) dissemino ①

propagation *n* propagatio *f*

propel *vt* impello; propello ③

propensity *n* proclivitas *f*

proper *adj* proprius; (suitable) aptus; (becoming) decorus
■ ∼**ly** *adv* proprie; apte; decore

property *n* fortuna *f*; bona *ntpl*; (characteristic) proprium *nt*

prophecy *n* praedictum *nt*; vaticinatio; (power) praedictio, divinatio *f*

prophesy *vt&i* vaticinor, divino, auguror ①; praedico ③

prophet *n* vates *m/f*; fatidicus, propheta *m*

prophetess *n* vates *f*

prophetic *adj* fatidicus; (of inward feeling) praesagus

propitious *adj* propitius; faustus, felix, secundus
■ ∼**ly** *adv* fauste, feliciter

proportion *n* ratio, proportio; symmetria *f*
◻ **in** ∼ pro portione

proposal *n* condicio *f*; (plan) consilium *nt*

propose *vt* condicionem offero *ir*; (intend) cogito ①; (marriage) condicionem quaero ③; (a toast) propino ①; (a law) fero *ir*; promulgo ①

proposition *n* condicio; (bill) rogatio *f*; (advice) consilium *nt*; (logic) propositio *f*

propound *vt* propono ③, profero *ir*

proprietor *n* dominus, erus *m*

propriety *n* decorum *nt*; convenientia *f*

propulsion *n* impulsus *m*

prosaic *adj* pedester, solutae orationi proprior; fig aridus, ieiunus

proscribe *vt* proscribo ③

proscription *n* proscriptio *f*

prose *n* oratio soluta, prosa *f*; pedester sermo *m*

prosecute *vt* exsequor, persequor ③; insto ① + *dat*; persevero ① in + *abl*; (accuse) reum facio ③

prosecution *n* exsecutio; (law) accusatio *f*

prospect *n* prospectus, despictus *m*; (hope, expectation) spes, exspectatio *f*

prospective *adj* futurus

prospectus *n* titulus *m*, index *m/f*

prosper *vi* prospera fortuna utor ③; successus prosperos habeo ②; bene cedo, cedo ③

prosperity *n* res secundae *fpl*; prospera fortuna, prosperitas *f*

prosperous *adj* secundus, prosperus; florens
■ ∼**ly** *adv* prospere; bene

prostitute *n* scortum *nt*; meretrix *f*

prostitution *n* meretricium *nt*

prostrate *adj* prostratus, proiectus; fig afflictus, fractus
◻ **fall** ∼ me (ad pedes alicuius) proicio; procumbo ③

prostration *n* animus fractus *m*

protect *vt* tueor ②; protego; defendo ③; servo ①; custodio ④

protection *n* tutela, custodia *f*; praesidium, tutamen *nt*

p

protector *n* patronus, defensor, propugnator *m*

protest[1] *n* acclamatio; intercessio; interpellatio *f*

protest[2] *vi&t* obtestor, acclamo, interpello ①; (against) aegre fero *ir*, intercedo (*vi*); (profess) profiteor ③

prototype *n* exemplar *nt*

protract *vt* traho, protraho ③, differo *ir*, produco ③

protrude *vi* promineo, emineo ②

protuberance *n* tuber *nt*; tumor, gibbus *m*

proud *adj* superbus, arrogans; magnificus
□ **be** ~ superbio, fastidio ④
■ ~**ly** *adv* superbe; arroganter; (of things) magnifice

prove *vt* probo ①; evinco, arguo ③; (try) experior ④; (as false) refello ③; (show) monstro, demonstro; (make good) praesto ①
■ ~ *vi* (become) fio *ir*; (turn out to be) evado ③

proverb *n* proverbium *nt*

proverbial *adj* proverbialis

provide *vt* paro, comparo ①; (supply) praebeo ②; suppedito ①
■ ~ *vi* (against) provideo ne + *subj*, praecaveo ②; (for) provideo (alicui) ②; (with) instruo ③ + *acc and dat*

provided *conj*:
□ ~ **that** dummodo, dum, modo

providence *n* providentia, diligentia, cura; (divine) providentia *f*

provident *adj* providus; cautus

province *n* provincia; regio *f*; fig provincia *f*; munus *nt*

provincial *adj* provincialis; fig rusticus

provision *n* praeparatio *f*; apparatus *m*; copia *f*
□ ~**s** (food) alimentum *nt*; victus *m*; penus *m/f*; (for an army) commeatus *m*; cibaria *ntpl*; (for a journey) viaticum *nt*

provisional *adj* temporarius
■ ~**ly** *adv* ad tempus

proviso *n* exceptio, cautio, condicio *f*

provocation *n* provocatio *f*; (wrong) iniuria *f*

provoke *vt* lacesso ③, provoco, irrito, stimulo ①

prow *n* prora *f*

prowess *n* virtus *f*

prowl *vi* praedor; (roam about) vagor ①
□ ~ **round** obambulo, oberro ①

prowler *n* praedator *m*

proximity *n* propinquitas, proximitas *f*

proxy *n* vicarius *m*
□ **by** ~ vice, vicem *both* + *gen*

prudence *n* prudentia; circumspectio *f*

prudent *adj* cautus, prudens, consideratus
■ ~**ly** *adv* caute; considerate

prune[1] *n* prunum *nt*

prune[2] *vt* (trees) decacumino, amputo, puto ①; fig reseco ①; recido ③

pruning-knife *n* falx *f*

pry *vi* scrutor, perscrutor, exploro ①

prying *adj* curiosus

pseudo *adj* fictus, simulatus

puberty *n* pubertas, pubes *f*

public[1] *adj* publicus; communis; (known) pervulgatus
■ ~**ly** *adv* in publico; palam, aperte

public[2] *n* homines *mpl*; fig vulgus *nt*; multitudo *f*

publican *n* (farmer of taxes) publicanus; (innkeeper) caupo *m*

publication *n* promulgatio; (of a book) editio *f*; (published book) liber *m*

publicity *n* celebritas *f*; fig lux *f*

publish *vt* (make known) vulgo; divulgo ①; patefacio ③; (a book) edo ③

publisher *n* bibliopola, librarius *m*

publishing *n* (of a work) editio *f*

puddle *n* lacuna *f*

puerile *adj* puerilis

puff[1] *n* (of wind) flatus *m*

puff[2] *vt* inflo, sufflo ①
■ ~ *vi* (pant) anhelo ①
□ ~ **up** inflo ①
□ **be** ~**d up** intumesco ③

puffy *adj* sufflatus; tumens; turgidus; inflatus

pugnacious *adj* pugnax

pull[1] *vt* vello ③; vellico ①; (drag) traho ③
■ ~ *vi* vires adhibeo ②; annitor ③
□ ~ **away** avello ③
□ ~ **apart** diripio ③
□ ~ **back** revello, retraho ③
□ ~ **down** (houses, *etc.*) demolior ④; destruo; (violently) everto ③
□ ~ **off** avello; detraho ③

□ ~ **out** extraho, evello, eximo ③
□ ~ **up** extraho; eripio, eruo ③

pull² n (act) tractus; (effort) nisus m

pulley n trochlea f

pulp n (flesh) caro, pulpa f

pulpit n rostra ntpl; suggestus m; tribunal nt

pulsate vi vibro ①

pulsation n pulsus m

pulse n (venarum) pulsus m

pulverize vt pulvero ①

pumice n pumex m

pump¹ n antlia f

pump² vt haurio ④; fig (question) exploro ①

pumpkin n pepo, melopepo m; cucurbita f

pun n lusus verborum, iocus m

punch¹ n (blow) pugnus, ictus m; (tool) terebra f

punch² vt (perforate) terebro ①; (strike) pugno percutio ③

punctilious adj scrupulosus, religiosus

punctual adj promptus, accuratus, ad tempus veniens or rediens
■ ~**ly** adv ad tempus, accurate

punctuate vt interpungo ③

punctuation n (act) interpunctio f; (break between sentences) interpunctum nt

puncture n (act) punctio f; (hole) punctum nt

pungent adj (to the senses) acutus; fig mordax; aculeatus

Punic adj Punicus

punish vt punio ④; castigo ①; animadverto ③; vindico ①
□ **be ~ed** poenas do ①

punishment n (act) castigatio; poena f; supplicium nt

punt n (small boat) ratis f

puny adj pusillus, exiguus

pup n catulus m

pupil n discipulus m; discipula f; (of the eye) pupilla, pupula f

puppet n pupa f

puppy n catulus m

purchase¹ n (act) emptio; (merchandise) merx f

purchase² vt emo ③; (procure) comparo ①

purchaser n emptor; mercator m

pure adj mundus; purus; (unmixed) merus; fig purus; (chaste) castus; (of character) integer

purge¹ vt purgo, mundo ①

purge² n purgatio f

purification n purgatio; purificatio; expiatio; lustratio f; lustrum nt

purify vt purifico, purgo; lustro, expio ①

purity n munditia; fig castitas; integritas f

purple¹ n purpura f; ostrum, conchylium nt; mureux m
□ **dressed in ~** purpuratus

purple² adj purpureus

purpose¹ n propositum, consilium nt; animus m; (end, aim) finis m/f; (wish) mens, voluntas f
□ **on ~** de industria; consulto; consilio
□ **to the ~** ad rem …
□ **to no ~** frustra

purpose² vi propono, statuo, constituo, decerno ③

purposely adv consulto, consilio, de industria

purr¹ vi murmuro, susurro ①

purr² n murmur nt; susurrus m

purse¹ n crumena; (money-belt) zona f

purse² vt (up) corrugo ①; contraho ③

pursue vt sequor, insequor, insequor; fig insisto + dat; utor ③ + abl

pursuit n insectatio f; (occupation) studium nt

pus n pus nt; sanies f

push¹ vt trudo, pello ③; urgeo ②
□ ~ **forward** protrudo, propello ③
□ ~ **in** intrudo ③
□ ~ **on** impello ③; urgeo ②; vi contendo ③; (hasten) festino ①

push² n pulsus, impetus, impulsus, fig conatus m; (energy) strenuitas f

put vt pono ③; loco, colloco ①; (a question) quaero; (again) repono; (aside) sepono ③
□ ~ **away** sepono ③; amoveo ②; (in safety) recondo; (send away) dimitto ③
□ ~ **back** repono ③
□ ~ **by** (place in safety) condo ③
□ ~ **down** depono; (lower, let down) demitto; (suppress, abolish) supprimo; tollo; (in writing) scribo ③; (in an account) fero ir
□ ~ **forward** (promote) promoveo ②; (excuses, etc.) profero ir; (as a candidate) produco ③

p

□ ∼ **in** impono; (forcibly) immitto; interpono ③

□ ∼ **off** (deter) repello ③; (disconcert) perturbo ①; (distract) distraho ③; (postpone) differo; profero *ir*

□ ∼ **on** impono; (dress, clothes) induo; (add) addo ③

□ ∼ **out** expello, eicio; (fire, light) exstinguo; (stretch out) extendo; fig (disconcert, *etc.*) confundo ③; perturbo ①; (dislocate) extorqueo ②

□ ∼ **together** compono ③, confero *ir*

□ ∼ **up** erigo; arrigo ③; (for sale) propono; (as a candidate) peto ③; (at auctions) auctionor ①; (with) fero *ir*

□ ∼ **upon** superimpono, superpono;

addo ③ *all* + *acc and dat*; (impose upon) verba (alicui) do ①

putrefy *vi* putresco ③, putrefio *ir*

putrid *adj* puter, putridus

puzzle[1] *n* quaestio abstrusa *or* obscura; fig difficultas *f*; nodus *m*

puzzle[2] *vt* confundo ③; perturbo ①
■ ∼ *vi* haereo ②

puzzling *adj* perplexus, obscurus

pygmy *n* nanus, pumilio *m*

pyramid *n* pyramis *f*

pyre *n* rogus *m*; bustum *nt*; pyra *f*

Qq

quadrangular *adj* quadriangulus

quadruped *n* quadrupes *m/f*

quadruple[1] *adj* quadruplex; quadruplus

quadruple[2] *n* quadruplum *nt*

quadruple[3] *vt* quadruplico ①

quaestor *n* quaestor *m*

quaestorship *n* quaestura *f*

quagmire *n* palus, lacuna *f*

quail[1] *n* coturnix *f*

quail[2] *vi* despondeo ②; paveo ②

quaint *adj* mirus, insolitus; (strange, odd) rarus
■ ∼**ly** *adv* mire

quake *vi* tremo ③

qualification *n* (endowment) indoles; (condition) condicio *f*; status *m*

qualified *adj* aptus, idoneus; capax, dignus; (moderate) mediocris

qualify *vt* aptum reddo; instruo ③; (limit, restrict, *etc.*) tempero; extenuo ①

quality *n* qualitas; natura *f*; fig dos, (degree) ordo, gradus *m*

qualm *n* (of conscience) religio *f*

quandary *n* angustiae *f*

quantity *n* quantitas; magnitudo *f*; numerus *m*; vis, copia *f*

quarrel[1] *n* iurgium *nt*; altercatio; rixa, simultas *f*

quarrel[2] *vi* iurgo; altercor; rixor ①

quarrelsome *adj* iurgiosus, rixosus, pugnax

quarry *n* (stone-quarry) lapicidinae, lautumiae *fpl*; (prey) praeda *f*

quarter[1] *n* quarta pars *f*; quadrans *m*; (side, direction, district) regio *f*
■ ∼**s** *pl* (dwelling) tectum *nt*; habitatio *f*; (temporary abode) hospitium, deverticulum *nt*; mil castra
□ **winter** ∼**s** hiberna *ntpl*
□ **at close** ∼**s** comminus

quarter[2] *vt* in quattor partes divido ③; (soldiers, *etc.*) colloco ①; dispono ③; (receive in one's house) hospitium praebeo ②

quarterly *adj* (for three months) trimestris; (by the quarter) tertio quoque mense
■ ∼ *adv* tertio quoque mense

quash *vt* (law) rescindo ③; aboleo ②; abrogo ①

queen *n* regina *f*

queer *adj* (strange) ineptus, insulsus, ridiculus

quell *vt* opprimo, restinguo ③; sedo; domo ①

quench *vt* exstinguo, restinguo ③; (thirst) (sitim) sedo ①, restinguo ③

querulous *adj* querulus; queribundus

query *n* quaestio; interrogatio; dubitatio *f*

quest *n* investigatio *f*

question[1] *n* interrogatio; (doubt) dubitatio *f*; (disputed point) quaestio *f*; controversia; fig (matter) res, causa *f*
  □ **call into** ~ dubito ①
  □ **without** ~ non dubium est, haud dubie

question[2] *vt&i* interrogo; dubito; (examine) in ius voco; (investigate) scrutor ①

questionable *adj* dubius, incertus

quibble[1] *n* captio; cavillatio *f*

quibble[2] *vi* captiose dico ③; cavillor ①

quick *adj* (nimble, swift) agilis, celer; pernix; (keen, sharp) acer, acutus; fig (of mind; clever) sollers
  □ **be** ~ (go fast) propero; maturo ①

quicken *vt* (enliven) animo; (hasten) celero, propero; maturo; (rouse) excito, instigo ①

quickly *adv* (also **quick**) cito; velociter; propere; (hastily) festinanter

quickness *n* (nimbleness) agilitas; (liveliness) vivacitas; fig sagacitas *f*; acumen (ingenii) *nt*

quicksand *n* syrtis *f*

quick-witted *adj* sollers

quiet[1] *adj* quietus, tranquillus; placidus; (silent) tacitus; silens, mutus

be *or* **keep** ~ quiesco ③; (be silent) sileo; taceo ②; conticesco ③

quiet[2] *n* quies, tranquillitas *f*; (silence) silentium *nt*; (peace) pax *f*

quiet[3] *vt* (also **quieten**) tranquillo; paco, sedo ①

quietly *adv* quiete, tranquille; sedate; tacite

quietness *n* quies, requies *f*; pax *f*; silentium *nt*

quill *n* penna *f*; calamus *m*; (of porcupines) spina *f*

quilt *n* stragulum *nt*

quit *vt* (leave) relinquo, desero ③
  ■ ~ *vi* discedo ③; migro ①

quite *adv* (completely) omnino, penitus, prorsus; valde; (fairly) satis
  □ ~ **so** ita est

quiver[1] *vi* tremo, contremisco ③; trepido ①

quiver[2] *n* pharetra *f*; corytus *m*

quota *n* rata pars, portio *f*

quotation *n* (passage quoted) locus allatus *m*

quote *vt* affero, profero *ir*; cito ①

Rr

rabbit *n* cuniculus *m*

rabble *n* plebecula, faex populi *f*; vulgus *nt*; (crowd) turba *f*; grex *m*

rabid *adj* rabidus, rabiosus

rabies *n* rabies *f*

race[1] *n* genus *nt*; stirps; prosapia; proles; (nation) gens *f*; (running) cursus *m*; (contest) certamen *nt*

race[2] *vi* cursu contendo ③

racecourse *n* stadium, spatium *nt*; hippodromus *m*

racehorse *n* celes *m*

racing *n* cursus *m*; certamen *nt*

rack[1] *n* (for punishment) eculeus *m*; tormentum *nt*; (for holding fodder) falisca *f*

rack[2] *vt* (torture) torqueo ②; (one's brain) cum animo reputo ①

racket *n* (noise, stir) strepitus, tumultus *m*

racy *adj* salsus

radiance *n* fulgor, splendor *m*

radiant *adj* radians, nitidus, clarus, fulgidus, splendidus

radiate *vi* radio ①; fulgeo, niteo ②
  ■ ~ *vt* spargo ③

radiation *n* radiatio *f*

radically *adv* radicitus; penitus

radish *n* raphanus *f*

radius *n* radius *m*

raft *n* ratis *f*

rafter *n* canterius *m*; trabs *f*; tignum *nt*

rag *n* pannus; *m*; (ragged clothes) pannuli *mpl*; dilabidae vestes *fpl*

rage[1] *n* furor *m*; rabies *f*; ira *f*

rage[2] *vi* furo ③; saevio ④; (as the sea) aestuo ①

q

r

ragged *adj* (in tatters) lacer; (wearing such clothes) pannosus

raging *adj* furens, furiosus; furibundus, rabidus

raid¹ *n* incursio, irruptio *f*

raid² *vt* invado ③

rail *n* (fence) saepimentum *nt*; (baluster) cancelli *mpl*

railing *n* (fence) saepimentum *nt*

rain¹ *n* pluvia *f*; imber *m*

rain² *vi*:
□ **it is ~ing** pluit

rainbow *n* arcus pluvius, arcus *m*

rainwater *n* aqua caelestis *f*; aquae pluviae *fpl*

rainy *adj* pluvius, pluvialis; pluviosus

raise *vt* attollo ③; elevo ①; (erect) erigo ③; (build) exstruo, extruo ③; (money) cogo ③; (an army) exercitum contraho ③; (a siege) solvo ③; (increase) augeo ②; (up) sublevo ①

raisins *n* uva passa *f*

rake¹ *n* rastrum *nt*, irpex *m*

rake² *vt* rado; (together) corrado ③; fig
□ ~ **up** colligo ③

rally *vt* (troops) reduco; (recover) recolligo ③
■ ~ *vi* ex fuga convenio ④

ram¹ *n* aries *m*
□ **battering** ~ *n* aries *m*

ram² *vi* (ram down) festuco ①; pavio ④; (stuff) infercio ④

ramble¹ *n* vagatio, ambulatio *f*

ramble² *vi* vagor, erro, ambulo ①

rambler *n* ambulator *m*

rambling *adj* vagus

rampage *vi* saevio ④

rampart *n* vallum, propugnaculum *nt*; agger *m*

rancid *adj* rancidus

rancorous *adj* infensus, infestus; invidus; malignus

rancour *n* simultas *f*; odium *nt*

random *adj* fortuitus
□ **at ~** temere

range¹ *n* series *f*; ordo *m*; (class) genus *nt*; (of mountains) iugum *nt*; (tract) tractus *m*; (reach) teli iactus *m*; (great size) magnitudo *f*

range² *vt* (wander through) pervagor, lustro ①

rank¹ *n* series *f*; ordo; gradus *m*; dignitas *f*

rank² *vt* colloco; ordino ①
■ ~ *vi* collocor, numeror ①

rank³ *adj* luxurians; immodicus; (of smell) fetidus; rancidus

ransack *vt* diripio ③; (search) exquiro ③

ransom *n* redemptio *f*; pretium *nt*

rant *vi* superbe loquor ③; bacchor ①

rap¹ *n* (slap) alapa *f*; (blow) ictus *m*; (with the knuckles) talitrum *nt*; (at the door) pulsatio *f*

rap² *vt&i* pulso ①; ferio ④

rapacious *adj* rapax; avidus

rapacity *n* rapacitas; aviditas *f*

rape¹ *n* raptus *m*; vitium virginis, stuprum *nt*

rape² *vt* constupro, violo ①

rapid *adj* rapidus, celer; velox, citus
■ ~ly *adv* rapide; cito; velociter, celeriter

rapidity *n* rapiditas; velocitas *f*

rapist *n* stuprator, violator *m*

rapture *n* animus exsultans (laetitia); furor *m*

rapturous *adj* (of things) mirificus; iucundus; (of persons) laetitia elatus

rare *adj* rarus; inusitatus; (infrequent) infrequens; mirus; fig eximius, singularis
■ ~ly *adv* raro

rarity *n* raritas; paucitas; (thing) res rara *or* singularis *f*

rascal *n* homo nequam, scelestus *m*

rash¹ *adj* praeceps, temerarius; inconsultus
■ ~ly *adv* temere; inconsulte

rash² *n* formicatio *f*

rashness *n* temeritas, imprudentia *f*

rat *n* mus *m*

rate¹ *n* (price) pretium; (of interest) faenus *nt*; (speed) celeritas *f* (tax) census *m*; (manner) modus *m*

rate² *vt* aestimo ①; (tax) censeo ②

rather *adv* potius; libentius; (slightly, somewhat) aliquantum, paulo, sub ...; *expressed also by the comparative of adjectives*
□ **I had ~** malo *ir*

ratification *n* confirmatio *f*

ratify *vt* ratum facio ③; confirmo ①; sancio ④

ratio *n* proportio *f*

ration *n* (portion) demensum *nt*; mil cibaria *ntpl*

rational *adj* rationis particeps; intellegens; sapiens
■ ~**ly** *adv* sapienter

rattle[1] *n* crepitus, strepitus; fragor *m*; (children's ~) crepitaculum *nt*; crepundia *ntpl*

rattle[2] *vt&i* crepito; crepo ①

ravage *vt* vasto, spolio, populor ①; diripio ③

rave *vi* furo ③; saevio ④; fig (be in a frenzy) bacchor ①

raven *n* corvus *m*

ravenous *adj* rapax, vorax; edax

ravine *n* angustiae, fauces *fpl*; saltus *m*

raving *adj* furiosus, furens, insanus, rabiosus, rabidus

ravish *vt* rapio ③; (a woman) constupro ①; (delight) delecto ①

ravisher *n* raptor; stuprator *m*

ravishing *adj* iucundus, suavis, mirificus

raw *adj* crudus, incoctus; (of wounds) crudus; (unripe) immaturus; (unwrought) rudis; (of weather) frigidus; fig rudis; imperitus

ray *n* (of the sun) radius *m*

raze *vt* (a town, *etc.*) solo aequo ①; everto ③

razor *n* novacula *f*

reach[1] *vt&i* attingo ③; (come up to) assequor ③; (approach) appropinquo ①; (hand) trado ③; (arrive at) pervenio ④ ad + *acc*; consequor; (stretch) extendor ③

reach[2] *n* tractus *m*; spatium *nt*; (of a missile) iactus; (capacity) captus *m*

read *vt&i* lego ③; verso; (aloud) recito ①

readable *adj* legibilis, lectu facilis

reader *n* lector; recitator *m*

readily *adv* (willingly) libenter; (easily) facile

readiness *n* facultas, facilitas *f*
□ **in** ~ in promptu

reading *n* lectio; recitatio; (interpretation) lectio *f*

ready *adj* paratus; promptus; expeditus; (willing) libens; (easy) facilis
□ ~ **money** *n* praesens pecunia *f*
□ **be** ~ praesto sum *ir*

real *adj* verus; certus; germanus
■ ~**ly** *adv* re vera; (surely) sane, certe

reality *n* res; veritas *f*; verum *nt*

realization *n* effectio *f*; effectus *m*; (of ideas) cognitio rerum *f*

realize *vt* (fulfil) efficio, ad exitum perduco; (convert into money) redigo; (understand) comprehendo ③

realm *n* regnum *nt*

reap *vt* meto ③; deseco ①; fig capio, percipio ③

reaper *n* messor *m*

reaping-hook *n* falx *f*

reappear *vi* rursus appareo ②; redeo ④; resurgo ③

rear[1] *vt* educo ①; alo ③
■ ~ *vi* (of horses) arrectum se tollere ③

rear[2] *n* tergum *nt*; mil novissimum agmen; extremum agmen *nt*

reason[1] *n* mens, intellegentia; (faculty) ratio; (motive) causa *f*; (understanding) consilium *nt*; (right) ius, aequum *nt*

reason[2] *vi* ratiocinor, disputo ①

reasonable *adj* (rational) rationalis, rationis particeps; (sane) sanus; (judicious) prudens; (just) iustus, aequus; (moderate) mediocris, modicus

reasonably *adv* merito; iure; iuste

reasoning *n* ratio; ratiocinatio; disceptatio *f*

reassemble *vt* recolligo ③

reassure *vt* confirmo ①

rebel[1] *adj & n* rebellis, seditiosus *m*

rebel[2] *vi* deficio, descisco ③; rebello ①; rebellionem facio ③

rebellion *n* rebellio, seditio, defectio *f*

rebellious *adj* rebellis, seditiosus; (disobedient) contumax

rebound *vi* resilio ④; resulto ①

rebuff[1] *n* repulsa *f*

rebuff[2] *vt* repello, reicio; sperno ③

rebuild *vt* reficio, restituo ③

rebuke[1] *vt* vitupero ①; reprehendo ③

rebuke[2] *n* vituperatio, reprehensio *f*

recall *vt* revoco ①; (to the mind) in memoriam redigo ③

recapitulate *vt* breviter repeto, summatim colligo ③

recapture *vt* recipio ③; recupero ①

recede *vi* recedo; refugio, discedo ③

receipt *n* (act) acceptio; (verbal release from an obligation) acceptilatio *f*; (money received) acceptum *nt*

receive *vt* accipio, recipio, excipio; (get) percipio ③

recent *adj* recens
■ ~**ly** *adv* nuper, modo

r

receptacle *n* receptaculum *nt*;
cisterna *f*

reception *n* aditus *m*; admissio *f*; (of a guest) hospitium *nt*

recess *n* (place) recessus, secessus *m*;
latebra *f*; (vacation) feriae *fpl*;
iustitium *nt*

recipe *n* praescriptum *nt*; compositio *f*

recipient *n* acceptor *m*

reciprocal *adj* mutuus
■ ∼**ly** *adv* mutuo; vicissim

reciprocate *vt* alterno ①

recital *n* narratio; enumeratio;
recitatio *f*

recitation *n* recitatio; lectio *f*

recite *vt* narro; recito ①

reciter *n* recitator *m*

reckless *adj* neglegens; (rash)
temerarius; imprudens
■ ∼**ly** *adv* temere

recklessness *n* neglegentia,
incuria; temeritas *f*

reckon *vt* numero; computo, aestimo
①; (consider, estimate) duco, pendo ③; (on)
confido ③ + *dat/abl*
□ ∼ **up** enumero ①

reckoning *n* numeratio; (account)
ratio *f*

reclaim *vt* reposco; repeto ③

recline *vi* recubo ①; recumbo ③; iaceo
②; (at table) accubo ①; accumbo ③

recognition *n* recognitio *f*
□ **in** ∼ **of** pro + *abl*

recognize *vt* agnosco; recognosco,
cognosco ③

recoil *vi* resilio ④, recido ③; (from)
recedo, refugio, discedo ③

recollect *vt* (remember) recordor ①;
reminiscor ③; memini ③

recollection *n* memoria; recordatio *f*

recommence *vt* itero, renovo ①;
repeto ③

recommend *vt* commendo ①

recommendation *n* commendatio *f*

recompense¹ *n* praemium *nt*;
merces, remuneratio *f*

recompense² *vt* remuneror;
(indemnify) compenso ①

reconcile *vt* reconcilio ①; in gratiam
restituo ③
□ **be** ∼**d to** aequo animo fero *ir*
□ **be** ∼**d** (in harmony) convenio ④

reconciliation *n* reconciliatio *f*;
reditus in gratiam *m*

reconnoitre *vt* exploro, speculor ①

reconsider *vt* recognosco ③;
retracto ①

record¹ *vt* memoro, commemoro,
narro ①

record² *n* mentio, narratio *f*;
monumentum *nt*; historia *f*
■ ∼**s** *pl* annales *mpl*

recount *vt* refero *ir*; memoro, narro,
enarro ①

recoup *vt* (regain) recipero ①

recourse *n*:
□ **have** ∼ **to** confugio, perfugio ③,
adeo *ir* ad + *acc*

recover *vt* (get back) recipero ①;
recipio ③
■ ∼ *vi* convalesco ③

recovery *n* reciperatio; (from illness)
recreatio, refectio *f*

recreation *n* animi remissio,
oblectatio *f*; (for children) lusus *m*

recrimination *n* mutua accusatio *f*

recruit¹ *vt* (troops) suppleo ②

recruit² *n* tiro *m*

recruitment *n* delectus *m*;
supplementum *nt*

rectangular *adj* orthogonius

rectify *vt* corrigo ③; emendo ①

recur *vi* recurro ③

recurrence *n* reditus *m*

recurrent *adj* recurrens

red *adj* ruber; (ruddy) rubicundus; (of hair)
rufus
□ **be** ∼ rubeo ②
□ **grow** ∼ rubesco, erubesco ③

redden *vt* rubefacio ③
■ ∼ *vi* rubesco; erubesco ③

reddish *adj* surrufus, surrubicundus,
rubicundulus

redeem *vt* redimo ③; libero; (a pledge)
repignero ①

red-hot *adj* candens

redness *n* rubor *m*

redouble *vt* gemino, ingemino ①

redress¹ *vt* emendo ①; corrigo ③;
medeor ②

redress² *n* (remedy) remedium *nt*

reduce *vt* reduco; redigo ad *or* in + *acc*;
(lessen) minuo ③

reduction *n* deminutio *f*

redundancy *n* redundantia *f*

redundant *adj* redundans, supervacaneus, superfluus

reed *n* arundo *f*; calamus *m*; canna *f*

reef *n* scopulus *m*; dorsum *nt*; cautes *f*

reel *vi* (stagger) vacillo, titubo ①

re-enter *vt* iterum intro ①

re-establish *vt* restituo, reficio ③

refectory *n* cenatio *f*

refer *vt* refero *ir*; remitto ③ ad + *acc*
■ ~ *vi* (allude to) perstringo, attingo ③; (regard) specto ①

referee *n* arbiter, disceptator *m*

reference *n* (respect) ratio *f*

refill *vt* repleo ②

refine *vt* purgo ①; excolo ③; expolio ④; (metals) excoquo ③

refined *adj* cultus, politus; elegans; urbanus; humanus

refinement *n* urbanitas, humanitas; elegantia *f*

reflect *vt* repercutio ③
■ ~ *vi* considero, meditor, reputo ①; revolvo ③

reflection *n* repercussus *m*; (thing reflected) imago; fig consideratio *f*

reform[1] *vt* reficio; (amend) corrigo ③; emendo ①
■ ~ *vi* me corrigo ③

reform[2] *n* correctio *f*

reformer *n* corrector, emendator *m*

refrain[1] *n* versus intercalaris *m*

refrain[2] *vi* abstineo ② ab + *abl*; parco ③ + *dat*

refresh *vt* (restore) recreo ①; reficio ③; (the memory) redintegro ①; (cool) refrigero ①

refreshing *adj* (cool) frigidus; (pleasant) iucundus

refreshment *n* refectio *f*; (food) cibus *m*

refuge *n* refugium, perfugium, asylum *nt*
□ **take ~** (in) confugio ③ in + *acc*

refugee *n* profugus *m*; exsul, exul *m/f*

refund *vt* reddo ③

refusal *n* recusatio; repudiatio; detrectatio; repulsa *f*

refuse[1] *vt* recuso, nego; repudio ①; renuo ③; denego, detrecto ①

refuse[2] *n* recrementum, purgamentum *nt*; faex *f*; quisquiliae *fpl*

refute *vt* refuto, confuto ①; refello, redarguo ③

regain *vt* recipio ③; recupero ①

regal *adj* regalis, regius, regificus
■ ~**ly** *adv* regie, regaliter, regifice

regard[1] *n* respectus *m*; ratio; (care, *etc*.) cura *f*

regard[2] *vt* respicio ③; intueor ②; (observe) observo; (concern) specto; (mind, care) curo; (esteem) aestimo ①; pendo ③; (respect) rationem habeo ②

regarding *prep* ▶ **concerning**

regardless *adj* neglegens, incuriosus; ▶ **heedless**
■ ~ *adv* nihilominus

regenerate *vt* regenero; fig redintegro, renovo, restauro ①

regime *n* (government) rerum administratio *f*

regiment *n* legio, caterva *f*

regimental *adj* legionarius

region *n* regio, plaga *f*; tractus *m*; (neighbourhood) vicinitas *f*

register[1] *n* tabulae *fpl*; index *m/f*

register[2] *vt* in tabulas refero *ir*

registrar *n* tabularius; ab actis; actuarius *m*

registration *n* perscriptio *f*

registry *n* tabularia *f*; tabularium *nt*

regret[1] *vt* (be sorry for) aegre fero *ir*; (bemoan) doleo; piget ②; (repent) paenitet ②; (miss) desidero ①

regret[2] *n* paenitentia *f*; dolor *m*; (feeling of loss) desiderium *nt*

regular *adj* (fixed) certus; (according to law) legitimus, iustus; (usual) usitatus
■ ~**ly** *adv* ordine; iuste, legitime; (at fixed times) certis temporibus

regularity *n* symmetria; constantia; (uniformity) aequabilitas *f*

regulate *vt* ordino ①; dispono; praescribo ③; administro ①

regulation *n* ordinatio; moderatio, temperatio *f*; (law) lex *f*; (rule) praescriptum *nt*

rehabilitate *vt* restituo ③

rehearsal *n* (recital) narratio, recitatio; (of a play, *etc*.) prolusio, exercitatio, meditatio *f*

rehearse *vt* recito ①; repeto ③; (practise) meditor ①; praeludo ③

r

reign[1] *n* regnum *nt*

reign[2] *vi* regno; dominor ①

reimburse *vt* rependo ③

rein[1] *n* habena *f*; frenum, lorum *nt*

rein[2] *vt* freno ①; fig cohibeo ②

reindeer *n* tarandrus *m*

reinforce *vt* suppleo ②; auxiliis confirmo ①

reinforcement *n* mil novae copiae *fpl*; subsidium *nt*

reinstate *vt* restituo ③

reiterate *vt* itero ①

reject *vt* reicio ③; repudio ①; repello; (scorn) sperno ③

rejection *n* reiectio, repudiatio, repulsa *f*

rejoice *vi* gaudeo ②; exsulto, laetor ①

rejoin *vt* (meet) convenio ④ cum + *abl*
■ ~ *vi* (answer) respondeo ②; resequor ③

rejoinder *n* responsum *nt*

rekindle *vi* refoveo ②; excito ①

relapse[1] *vi* recido, relabor ③

relapse[2] *n* morbus recidivus *m*

relate *vt* refero *ir*; memoro; narro ①

related *adj* (by blood) consanguineus; (by marriage) affinis; fig propinquus, cognatus; coniunctus

relation *n* narratio; (reference) ratio; (relationship) cognatio *f*; (person) cognatus *m*; cognata *f*

relationship *n* propinquitas; necessitudo; cognatio; (by blood) consanguinitas; (by marriage) affinitas; fig coniunctio *f*

relative[1] *adj* cognatus
■ ~ly *adv* pro ratione

relative[2] *n* cognatus *m*; cognata *f*;
▶ related

relax *vt* remitto ③; laxo, relaxo ①; resolvo ③
■ ~ *vi* relanguesco; (abate) remittor ③

relaxation *n* remissio; relaxatio *f*

relay *n* cursus publici *mpl*

release[1] *vt* libero ①; resolvo ③; laxo ①; (relieve) exonero, levo, relevo ①

release[2] *n* liberatio; absolutio; (discharge) missio *f*

relegate *vt* relego ①

relent *vi* mitesco ③; mitigor ①; lenior ④

relentless *adj* immisericors, inexorabilis, atrox, durus

relevant *adj* aptus, appositus

reliable *adj* fidus, certus

reliance *n* fiducia *f*; fides *f*

relic *n* reliquiae *fpl*; monumentum *nt*

relief *n* (comfort) solacium; (alleviation) levamentum; (help) auxilium *nt*; (remedy) medicina *f*; remedium *nt*; (in sculpture) caelatura *f*

relieve *vt* levo, allevo; mitigo ①; (aid) succurro ③; (succeed) subeo *ir both* + *dat*; (take over a duty) excipio ③

religion *n* religio, pietas *f*

religious *adj* religiosus; pius

relinquish *vt* relinquo ③; derelinquo, demitto, omitto, depono ③

relish[1] *n* (flavour) sapor *m*; (seasoning) condimentum; (fondness) studium *nt*

relish[2] *vt* (like) gusto ①; (enjoy) fruor ③ + *abl*

reluctance *n* aversatio *f*

reluctant *adj* invitus
■ ~ly *adv* invitus *adj*; aegre

rely *vi* (trust) confido ③ + *dat/abl*

remain *vi* (stay) maneo, permaneo ②; resto ①; (last) sto, duro ①, (be left over) supersum *ir*

remainder *n* reliquum *nt*

remaining *adj* reliquus

remains *npl* reliquiae *fpl*

remark[1] *vt* observo ①; animadverto ③

remark[2] *n* observatio, animadversio *f*; (something said) dictum *nt*

remarkable *adj* insignis, memorabilis, notabilis; mirus; egregius

remarkably *adv* insigniter; mire; egregie

remedial *adj* medicus, medicabilis

remedy[1] *n* remedium *nt*; medicina *f*

remedy[2] *vt* sano ①; medeor ②; corrigo ③

remember *vt* memini ③; recordor ①; reminiscor ③

remind *vt* commoneo ②; commonefacio ③

reminiscence *n* recordatio *f*

remiss *adj* neglegens; incuriosus

remission *n* remissio; venia *f*

remit *vt* (abate) remitto ③; (forgive) condono ①; (money) transmitto ③
■ ~ *vi* relaxor ①

remittance *n* remissio *f*

remnant *n* reliquum *nt*; reliquiae *fpl*

remonstrate *vt* obtestor, acclamo, interpello ①; aegre fero *ir*

remorse *n* angor conscientiae *m*; stimuli *mpl*

remorseless *adj* immisericors; durus; crudelis

remote *adj* remotus; amotus, ultimus; longinquus; disiunctus

removal *n* remotio; exportatio; (banishment) amandatio; relegatio; (changing one's dwelling) migratio *f*

remove *vt* amoveo ②; depello, tollo, detraho ③; amando ①

remunerate *vt* remuneror ①

remuneration *n* remuneratio *f*

render *vt* reddo; facio; (hand over) trado; (a town, *etc.*) dedo; (translate) verto ③

rendezvous *n* locus praescriptus (ad conveniendum); (meeting itself) conventus *m*

renegade *n* transfuga *m*

renew *vt* renovo; novo; redintegro ①

renewal *n* renovatio; integratio *f*

renounce *vt* missum facio; pono, depono ③; (deny) nego ①

renovate *vt* renovo, redintegro ①; (repair) reparo, instauro ①

renovation *n* renovatio *f*

renown *n* fama, gloria *f*; nomen *nt*

renowned *adj* insignis, celeber, clarus; praeclarus

rent[1] *n* reditus *m*; vectigal *nt*; merces, pensio *f*; (fissure) scissura, rima *f*

rent[2] *vt* (let out) loco ①; (hire) conduco ③

renunciation *n* abdicatio, repudiatio *f*

reopen *vt* iterum aperio ④; fig (a case) retrecto ①

reorganize *vt* restituo ③

repair[1] *vt* (buildings) reparo, instauro ①; (make good) reficio; restituo ③; (clothes) resarcio ④; (cure) sano ①; (make amends for) sarcio ④

repair[2] *n* refectio *f*

repairer *n* refector *m*

reparation *n* restitutio *f*; (amends) satisfactio *f*

repartee *n* salsum dictum *nt*

repay *vt* repono, retribuo ③; remuneror ①; (compensate) penso, compenso, repenso ①

repayment *n* solutio; remuneratio *f*

repeal[1] *vt* abrogo ①; rescindo, tollo ③

repeal[2] *n* abrogatio *f*

repeat *vt* itero ①; repeto ③

repeatedly *adv* iterum atque iterum, saepius

repel *vt* repello ③; fig aspernor ①

repent *vi* paenitet (me) ②

repentance *n* paenitentia *f*

repentant *adj* paenitens

repercussion *n* repercussio *f*

repetition *n* iteratio; repetitio *f*

replace *vt* repono; (restore) restituo; (substitute) substituo, suppono ③

replenish *vt* repleo, suppleo ②

reply[1] *n* responsum *nt*; responsio *f*

reply[2] *vt&i* respondeo ②; refero *ir*

report[1] *vt* fero *ir*; narro, nuntio ①; (state) propono ③

report[2] *n* (rumour) fama *f*; rumor *m*; (hearsay) auditio *f*; (noise) fragor, crepitus *m*; relatio; narratio *f*

repose[1] *vi* (rest) quiesco, requiesco ③

repose[2] *n* quies, requies *f*

represent *vt* repraesento ①; exprimo; propono ③; (act on behalf of) vicem impleo + *gen* ②; loco sum *ir* + *gen*

representation *n* (act) repraesentatio; (statement) editio; (likeness) imago *f*

representative *n* vicarius; procurator *m*

repress *vt* reprimo, comprimo ③; coerceo ②; (tame) domo ①

repression *n* refrenatio, coercitio *f*

reprieve[1] *n* dilatio (supplicii) *f*

reprieve[2] *vt* diem prorogo damnato

reprimand[1] *vt* reprehendo ③

reprimand[2] *n* reprehensio *f*

reprisal *n* talio; vindicta *f*

reproach *vt* obicio ③; exprobro; vitupero; accuso ①

reproachful *adj* obiurgatorius

reproduce *vt* refero *ir*

reproof *n* reprehensio, vituperatio, obiurgatio *f*

reprove *vt* obiurgo, vitupero ①; reprehendo ③

reptile *n* repens animal *nt*

republic *n* respublica, civitas popularis, libera civitas *f*

republican *adj* popularis

r

repudiate *vt* repudio ①; respuo, renuo, abnuo, sperno ③

repugnance *n* aversatio *f*; fastidium *nt*; fuga *f*

repugnant *adj* odiosus; alienus

repulse *vt* repello ③; propulso, fugo ①

repulsion *n* repulsus *m*; (dislike) odium *nt*

repulsive *adj* odiosus; foedus

reputable *adj* honestus, bonae famae

reputation *n* (also **repute**) fama, existimatio *f*; nomen *nt*

request[1] *n* preces *fpl*
□ **at the ~ of** rogatu + *gen*

request[2] *vt* rogo ①; peto ③; supplico, precor ①

require *vt* (demand) postulo ①, posco ③; (need) egeo ② + *abl*; desidero ①

requirements *n* necessaria *ntpl*

requisite *adj* necessarius

rescue[1] *vt* libero, recupero; (save) servo ①

rescue[2] *n* liberatio, recuperatio *f*

research *n* investigatio *f*

resemblance *n* similitudo *f*; instar *nt indecl*

resemble *vi* similis sum *ir*

resent *vt* aegre *or* graviter fero *ir*; indignor ①

resentful *adj* iracundus; indignans

resentment *n* indignatio *f*

reservation *n* retentio *f*

reserve[1] *vt* reservo ①; repono, condo, recondo ③; retineo ②

reserve[2] *n* (silence) taciturnitas *f*; mil subsidium *nt*

reserved *adj* (silent) taciturnus, tectus

reservoir *n* cisterna *f*; receptaculum *nt*; lacus *m*

reside *vi* habito, commoror ①

residence *n* habitatio; sedes *f*; domicilium *nt*; (sojourn) commoratio *f*

resident *n* habitator *m*

residue *n* residuum, reliquum *nt*

resign *vt* cedo, depono ③; abdico ①
□ **~ oneself to** aequo animo fero *ir*

resignation *n* (act) abdicatio; (surrendering (in law)) cessio *f*; fig aequus animus *m*

resin *n* resina *f*

resist *vi* resisto ③; obsto, adversor ① + *dat*

resistance *n* repugnantia; mil defensio *f*

resolute *adj* audax; constans; fortis; firmus
■ **~ly** *adv* constanter; fortiter; audacter; firme

resoluteness *n* constantia *f*; consilium *nt*

resolution *n* (plan) consilium *nt*; (of mind) constantia *f*; (courage) animus *m*; (of an assembly) decretum *nt*

resolve[1] *n* constantia *f*; consilium *nt*

resolve[2] *vt* decerno, statuo, constituo ③; (solve) solvo ③; resolvo, reduco, redigo ③

resonant *adj* resonus

resort[1] *vi* (have recourse to) confugio ③; convenio ④ *both* + ad + *acc*

resort[2] *n* (refuge) refugium, perfugium *nt*

resound *vi* resono, persono ①

resource *n* refugium, auxilium *nt*
□ **~s** opes *fpl*

resourceful *adj* callidus

respect[1] *vt* revereor ②; veneror; observo ①

respect[2] *n* (regard) respectus *m*; (reverence) reverentia, observantia *f*; (relation, reference) ratio *f*
□ **with ~ to** ad + *acc*, de + *abl*; (as regards) quod attinet ad + *acc*

respectability *n* honestas *f*

respectable *adj* honestus; (fairly good) tolerabilis

respectful *adj* observans; reverens
■ **~ly** *adv* cum summa observantia; reverenter

respecting *prep* ad + *acc*, de + *abl*, quod attinet ad + *acc*

respiration *n* respiratio *f*

respite *n* (delay) mora; cessatio; intermissio *f*

resplendent *adj* resplendens, clarus, nitidus
■ **~ly** *adv* clare, nitide

respond *vi* respondeo ②

response *n* responsum *nt*

responsible *adj* obnoxius; (trustworthy) fidus; (able to pay) locuples
□ **be ~ for** praesto ① + *dat*

r

rest[1] *n* quies; requies; pax *f*; (prop) fulcrum *nt*, statumen *nt*; (remainder) residuum, reliquum *nt*; (of people) reliqui, ceteri *mpl*

rest[2] *vi* quiesco, requiesco ③; (pause) cesso ①; (lean) nitor; (on) innitor ③ + *dat*
■ ∼ *vt* (lean) reclino ①

restaurant *n* caupona *f*

restive *adj* sternax, petulans

restless *adj* inquietus; turbidus, tumultuosus; (agitated) sollicitus
■ ∼ly *adv* turbulente

restoration *n* refectio; (recall) reductio *f*

restore *vt* restituo, reddo ③; restauro, reparo ①; (health, *etc.*) sano ①; (recall) reduco ③

restrain *vt* refreno ①; coerceo ②; (limit) circumscribo ③; contineo ②; (prevent) impedio ④; prohibeo ②

restraint *n* coercitio; moderatio *f*

restrict *vt* cohibeo ②; restringo, circumscribo ③

restriction *n* restrictio, limitatio *f*

result[1] *vi* orior, exorior ④; proficiscor ③; fio *ir*; (follow) consequor ③

result[2] *n* (effect) exitus, eventus *m*; (conclusion) summa *f*

resume *vt* resumo; repeto ③; redintegro ①

resuscitate *vt* resuscito, revoco ①

retain *vt* retineo ②; servo ①

retaliate *vi* ulciscor ③; par pro pari refero *ir*

retaliation *n* lex talionis; ultio *f*

retch *vi* nauseo ①

reticent *adj* taciturnus

retinue *n* comitatus *m*; pompa; turba clientium *f*

retire *vi* (go away) recedo, regredior, decedo ③; abeo *ir*

retirement *n* solitudo *f*; recessus *m*; (from office) abdicatio *f*

retort[1] *vt* regero, refero ③
■ ∼ *vi* respondeo ②

retort[2] *n* responsum *nt*

retrace *vt* repeto ③
□ ∼ one's steps revertor ③

retract *vt* retracto, recanto ①

retreat[1] *vi* recedo, refugio ③; pedem refero *ir*

retreat[2] *n* recessus *m*; refugium *nt*; latebrae *fpl*; lustrum *nt*; mil receptus *m*

retribution *n* poena, vindicta *f*; supplicium *nt*

retrieve *vt* (recover) recupero ①; (make good) sarcio ④; sano ①

return[1] *vt* (give back) restituo, reddo ③; (send back) remitto ③
■ ∼ *vi* (go back) redeo *ir*; revertor ③; (come back) revenio ④

return[2] *n* (coming back) reditus; regressus *m*; (giving back) restitutio; (repayment) remuneratio *f*; (income, profit, *etc.*) fructus, quaestus; reditus *m*

reunion *n* reconciliatio *f*

reunite *vt&i* reconcilio ①

reveal *vt* retego; recludo, patefacio, prodo ③; nudo; (unveil) revelo ①; (make known) evulgo, divulgo ①

revel *vi* debacchor, comissor ①

revelation *n* patefactio *f*

revelry *n* comissatio *f*; orgia *ntpl*

revenge[1] *vt* ulciscor ③

revenge[2] *n* ultio, vindicta *f*
□ take ∼ (on) vindico in + *acc* ①; poenas repeto ab + *abl* ③

revenger *n* ultor *m*; ultrix *f*; vindex *m/f*

revenue *n* reditus, fructus *m*; vectigal *nt*

reverberate *vt* repercutio ③; *vi* resono, persono ①

reverberation *n* repercussus *m*

revere *vt* revereor ②; veneror, observo ①; colo ③

reverence *n* reverentia, veneratio, observantia *f*

reverent *adj* reverens; pius
■ ∼ly *adv* venerabiliter, reverenter

reversal *n* rescissio, infirmatio *f*

reverse[1] *n* (change) conversio, commutatio (fortunae); (defeat) clades *f*; (contrary) contrarium *nt*; (of a medal) aversa pars *f*

reverse[2] *vt* inverto; (alter) converto; (annul) rescindo ③

revert *vi* revertor, recurro ③; redeo *ir*

review[1] *n* recensio *f*; recensus *m*; (critique) censura *f*

review[2] *vt* recenseo ②; lustro ①

reviewer *n* censor *m*

revise *vt* recenseo ②; retracto ①; relego, corrigo ③; fig limo ①

revision *n* correctio; (of a literary work) fig lima *f*

revisit *vt* reviso ③

revival *n* renovatio *f*

revive *vt* resuscito ①; (renew) renovo; (encourage) animo; (refresh) recreo; (recall) revoco ①
  ■ ∼ *vi* revivisco ③

revoke *vt* revoco ①; (a law) rescindo, tollo ③

revolt[1] *vt* offendo ③
  ■ ∼ *vi* rebello ①; descisco, secedo, deficio ③

revolt[2] *n* rebellio; defectio *f*

revolution *n* circuitus *m*; circumversio *f*; circumactus *m*; (change) commutatio *f*; (of planets) cursus, meatus *m*; (political) res novae *fpl*

revolutionary[1] *adj* seditiosus, novarum rerum cupidus

revolutionary[2] *n* rerum novarum molitor *m*

revolve *vt* volvo ③; voluto ①
  ■ ∼ *vi* circumvolvor, circumvertor, circumagor ③

revolving *adj* versatilis, versabundus

revulsion *n* taedium *nt*

reward[1] *vt* remuneror ①

reward[2] *n* praemium *nt*; merces *f*; fructus *m*

rewrite *vt* rescribo ③

rhetoric *n* rhetorice, oratoria *f*; rhetorica *ntpl*

rhetorical *adj* rhetoricus; oratorius

rheumatism *n* dolor artuum *m*

Rhine *n* Rhenus *m*

rhinoceros *n* rhinoceros *m*

rhododendron *n* rhododendron *nt*

Rhone *n* Rhodanus *m*

rhyme *n* versus *m*

rhythm *n* numerus, rhythmus *m*

rhythmic *adj* (also **rhythmical**) numerosus, rhythmicus

rib *n* costa *f*

ribald *adj* obscenus, spurcus, turpis

ribbon *n* taenia, vitta, fascia *f*; lemniscus *m*

rice *n* oryza *f*

rich *adj* dives, locuples, pecuniosus, opimus; abundans, copiosus; (of the soil, *etc.*) fertilis, uber

riches *n* divitiae, opes *fpl*

richness *n* opulentia, abundantia, copia; ubertas, fertilitas *f*

rickety *adj* instabilis

rid *vt* libero ①
  □ **get** ∼ **of** also fig amolior ④; amoveo, removeo ②; dimitto, depono ③

riddle[1] *n* aenigma *nt*; ambages *fpl*

riddle[2] *vt* (with wounds, *etc.*) confodio ③

ride[1] *vt* (a horse) equo vehor ③
  ■ ∼ *vi* equito ①
  □ ∼ **away** *or* **off** avehor ③
  □ ∼ **past** praetervehor ③

ride[2] *n* equitatio; vectatio, vectio *f*

rider *n* eques; vector *m*; (addition) adiectio *f*

ridge *n* iugum, dorsum; culmen *nt*

ridicule[1] *n* ludibrium *nt*; risus *m*

ridicule[2] *vt* rideo, irrideo ②

ridiculous *adj* ridiculus
  ■ ∼**ly** *adv* ridicule

riding *n* equitatio *f*

riding-school *n* hippodromos *m*

rife *adj* frequens, vulgatus
  □ **become** ∼ increbresco ③

riffraff *n* plebecula *f*; vulgus *nt*; faex populi *f*

rig *vt* adorno, armo ①; instruo ③

rigging *n* armamenta *ntpl*

right[1] *adj* rectus; (hand, side) dexter; fig verus; iustus; aequus; idoneus, aptus
  ■ ∼**ly** *adv* recte; iuste; iure; vere; rite
  □ **you are** ∼ vera dicis

right[2] *n* (hand) dextra *f*; (law) ius, aequum, fas *nt*; (permission, licence) licentia, venia *f*
  □ **on the** ∼ dextrorsus
  □ **I have a** ∼ **to** mihi licet + *infin*

righteous *adj* aequus, iustus; pius, sanctus

rightful *adj* legitimus, iustus
  ■ ∼**ly** *adv* legitime, iure, iuste

rigid *adj* rigidus

rigidity *n* rigor *m*

rigorous *adj* asper, severus, rigidus

rigour *n* asperitas, severitas *f*

rim *n* labrum *nt*; ora *f*; margo *m*/*f*

rind *n* crusta, cutis *f*; cortex, liber *m*

ring[1] *n* anulus; (hoop) circulus, orbis *m*; (of people) corona *f*; (ground for fighting) arena *f*; (sound) sonitus *m*; (of bells) tinnitus *m*

ring[2] *vi* tinnio ④; resono ①

ringleader *n* caput *nt*; dux, auctor *m*/*f*

r

ringlet *n* (of hair) cincinnus, cirrus *m*

rinse *vt* alluo, eluo ③

riot¹ *n* tumultus *m*

riot² *vi* tumultuor ①

rioter *n* seditiosus, turbulentus *m*

riotous *adj* seditiosus, tumultuosus, turbulentus

rip *vt* (unsew) dissuo; (tear) diffindo, divello ③

ripe *adj* maturus; tempestivus

ripen *vt* maturo ①
■ ~ *vi* maturesco ③

ripeness *n* maturitas *f*

ripple¹ *n* fluctus *m*; unda *f*

ripple² *vi* murmuro, lene sono ①

rise¹ *vi* orior, coorior ④; surgo, consurgo ③; (out of, from) exorior ④; (mount) ascendo ③; (as a bird) evolo ①; (up) assurgo ③; (increase) cresco ③; (of rebels) consurgo ③; rebello ①
□ ~ **again** resurgo; revivisco ③

rise² *n* (ascent) ascensus; (increase) augmentum *nt*; (of the sun) ortus *m*; (rising ground) tumulus *m*; (origin) origo *f*; fons *m*
□ **give** ~ **to** pario ③

rising¹ *adj* (sloping) acclivis; (about to be) futurus

rising² *n* (of the sun, *etc.*) ortus *m*; (insurrection) tumultus *m*; seditio *f*

risk¹ *vt* periclitor ①

risk² *n* periculum, discrimen *nt*

risky *adj* periculosus

rite *n* ritus *m*; solemne *nt*

ritual *adj* sollemnis
■ ~ *n* sollemne *nt*

rival¹ *n* rivalis, aemulus, competitor *m*

rival² *vt* aemulor ①

rivalry *n* aemulatio *f*; certamen *nt*; (in love) rivalitas *f*

river *n* flumen *nt*; amnis, rivus *m*
■ ~-**bed** *n* alveus *m*

rivet¹ *n* clavus *m*

rivet² *vt* fig clavo figo ③; fig teneo ②

road *n* via *f*; iter *nt*
□ **on the** ~ in itinere

roam *vi* ▶ ramble

roar¹ *vi* fremo, rudo ③, mugio ④; (of voices) vociferor ①

roar² *n* fremitus *m*; strepitus, mugitus, clamor *m*

roast *vt&i* torreo ②; (in a pan) frigo ③; asso ①; coquo ③

rob *vt* latrocinor; furor; praedor; spolio, despolio ①; diriplo ③; (deprive) privo, orbo ①

robber *n* latro, praedo, raptor, fur *m*

robbery *n* latrocinium *nt*; spoliatio, direptio, rapina *f*

robe *n* vestis, palla *f*

robust *adj* robustus, validus, lacertosus, firmus

rock¹ *n* rupes, cautes *f*; saxum *nt*; scopulus *m*

rock² *vt* moveo ②; agito ①
■ ~ *vi* vibro ①; moveor ②; agitor, fluctuo ①

rocky *adj* saxosus, saxeus, scopulosus

rod *n* virga; ferula *f*

roe *n* (of fishes) ova *ntpl*

rogue *n* nequam (homo), furcifer, mastigia *m*

role *n* persona *f*; partes *fpl*

roll¹ *vt* volvo ③; verso ①
■ ~ *vi* volvor ③

roll² *n* volumen *nt*; (coil) spira *f*; orbis *m*; (of names) index *m/f*; album *nt*

roller *n* (tool) cylindrus *m*

Roman *adj & n* Romanus; Quiris *m*

romance *n* (story) fabula, narratio ficta *f*; (love) amor *m*

romantic *adj* fabulosus, commenticius; (chivalrous) sublimis; (pleasing) gratus

romp¹ *n* lusus *m*

romp² *vi* exsulto ①; ludo ③; lascivio ④

roof¹ *n* tectum; fastigium; (of the mouth) palatum *nt*

roof² *vt* contego, intego ③

roofing *n* tegulae *fpl*

rook *n* corvus *m*

room *n* (space) spatium *nt*; locus *m*; (apartment) conclave, cubiculum, cenaculum *nt*

roomy *adj* laxus; spatiosus; amplus

roost *vi* insisto ③; insideo ②

root¹ *n* radix, stirps *f*; fig fons *m*; origo *f*
□ **by the** ~s radicitus
□ **take** ~ coalesco ③; inveterasco ③

root² *vi* radices ago ③
□ ~ **out** *or* **up** exstirpo, eradico ①

r

rope *n* funis *m*; rudens *m*

rose *n* rosa *f*

rosebud *n* calyx rosae *m*

rose-bush *n* rosa *m*

rostrum *n* rostra *ntpl*

rosy *adj* roseus

rot¹ *vi* putresco, putesco ③
  ■ ~ *vt* corrumpo, putrefacio ③

rot² *n* putor *m*; caries *f*

rotate *vi* volvor ③

rotation *n* ordo *m*

rote *n*:
  □ **by** ~ memoriter
  □ **learn by** ~ edisco, perdisco ③

rotten *adj* puter, putidus, putridus; cariosus

rough *adj* asper; (with hair, thorns) hirsutus; horridus; scabrous; scaber; (of weather) procellosus; fig agrestis, durus, incultus

roughen *vt* aspero ①

roughly *adv* aspere; duriter; horride; inculte; (approximately) fere, ferme

roughness *n* asperitas *f*; (of surface) scabies; fig (coarseness) rusticitas; (brutality) feritas *f*

roughshod *adj*:
  □ **ride** ~ **over** calco, proculco ①; obtero ③

round¹ *adj* rotundus; globosus; (as a circle) circularis; (rounded) teres

round² *n* orbis, circulus *m*
  □ **go the** ~**s** circumeo *ir*

round³ *vt* (make round) rotundo; torno ①; (go round) circumeo *ir*
  □ ~ **off** (end) concludo ③

round⁴ *adv & prep* circum, circa + *acc*
  □ ~ **about** undique

roundabout *adj* devius

rouse *vt* excito; stimulo; animo ①; cieo, moveo ②; (awaken) expergefacio ③

rout¹ *n* tumultus *m*; turba; (defeat) clades *f*; (flight) fuga *f*

rout² *vt* fugo, profligo ①; fundo ③

route *n* via *f*; iter *nt*

routine *n* mos, usus *m*; consuetudo *f*

row¹ *n* series *f*; ordo *m*; (quarrel) rixa *f*; (riot) turba *f*
  □ **in a** ~ deinceps

row² *vt&i* remigo ①; remis propello ③; (quarrel) rixor ①

rower *n* remex *m*

rowing *n* remigatio *f*; remigium *nt*

royal *adj* regalis, regius, regificus

royalty *n* maiestas regia; dignitas regia; regia potestas *f*

rub *vt&i* frico ①; tero ③
  □ ~ **against** attero ③
  □ ~ **off** detergeo ②
  □ ~ **out** deleo ②

rubbish *n* rudus *nt*; fig quisquiliae *fpl*; (nonsense) fabulae, gerrae *fpl*

ruby *n* carbunculus *m*

rudder *n* gubernaculum *nt*; clavus *m*

rude *adj* rudis, incultus; rusticus, inurbanus; (artless) incomptus, incompositus; inconditus; (insolent) insolens; (rude) asper; (unskilful) inexpertus, imperitus

rudeness *n* rusticitas; inhumanitas; insolentia *f*

rudiment *n* elementum, initium, rudimentum, principium *nt*

rudimentary *adj* rudis

rueful *adj* maestus, tristis

ruffian *n* homo perditus, sicarius, latro *m*

ruffle *vt* agito, turbo ①

rug *n* stragulum *nt*

rugged *adj* asper, inaequalis, confragosus; (precipitous) praeruptus

ruin¹ *n* pernicies *f*; exitium, excidium *nt*; ruina *f*
  ■ ~**s** *pl* ruinae *fpl*
  □ **in** ~ ruinosus

ruin² *vt* perdo; corrumpo ③; depravo, vitio ①

ruinous *adj* damnosus; exitiosus; exitialis, perniciosus, funestus

rule¹ *n* (for measuring) regula *f*; fig praeceptum *nt*; lex, norma, regula, formula *f*; (government) regimen *nt*

rule² *vt* (a line) duco ③; (govern) rego ③; praesum *ir* + *dat*
  ■ ~ *vi* dominor; impero ① + *dat*; (of a custom) obtineo ②

ruler *n* rector; regnator, gubernator, dominus, moderator *m*; (for drawing lines) regula *f*

ruling *adj* potens; regius; (chief, most powerful) potentissimus

rumble¹ *vi* murmuro; crepo ①

rumble² *n* murmur *nt*; crepitus, sonitus *m*

ruminate *vi* ruminor ①; fig meditor ①

r

rummage *vt* rimor, perscrutor ①

rumour *n* rumor *m*; fama *f*

rumple *vt* corrugo ①

run¹ *vi* curro; (flow) fluo; (of rivers) labor ③
□ ∼ **about** curso ①
□ ∼ **after** sequor ③; sector ①
□ ∼ **away** fugio, aufugio ③
□ ∼ **down** decurro; (as water) defluo ③; fig vitupero ①
□ ∼ **off** aufugio; (as water) defluo ③
□ ∼ **out** excurro ③; (of time) exeo *ir*
□ ∼ **over** *vt* (a person) obtero; fig percurro; (touch lightly) perstringo; *vi* (of fluids) superfluo ③
□ ∼ **through** also fig percurro; (with a sword) transfigo, traicio, transigo ③; (squander) dissipo ①
□ ∼ **together** concurro ③
□ ∼ **up** *vt* erigo, exstruo; *vi* accurro ③

run² *n* cursus *m*

runaway *n* fugitivus *m*; transfuga *m*

rung *n* gradus *f*

runner *n* cursor *m*

running *adj* (of water) perennis, iugis; (consecutive) continuus

rupture¹ *n* violatio, seditio; dissensio; med hernia *f*

rupture² *vt* violo ①; rumpo, abrumpo ③

rural *adj* rusticus; agrestis

rush¹ *n* iuncus, scirpus *m*; (hurry) festinatio *f*

rush² *vi* ruo ③, feror *ir*; praecipito ①; (on, forward) irruo, irrumpo, prorumpo, (out) erumpo ③; evolo ①

rust¹ *n* robigo; (of copper) aerugo; (of iron) ferrugo *f*

rust² *vi* robiginem contraho ③; fig torpeo ②

rustic *adj* rusticus; agrestis

rustle¹ *vi* crepito; murmuro; susurro ①

rustle² *n* stridor; susurrus *m*; murmur *nt*; crepitus *m*

rusty *adj* robiginosus, aeruginosus; (rust-coloured) ferrugineus

rut *n* (made by a wheel) orbita *f*

ruthless *adj* immisericors; immitis; immansuetus, crudelis, ferus, saevus

rye *n* secale *nt*

Ss

sack¹ *n* saccus *m*

sack² *vt* (pillage) vasto ①; diripio ③

sacking *n* spoliatio, vastatio *f*; (coarse cloth) calicium *nt*

sacred *adj* sacer; sanctus; sacrosanctus; religiosus

sacrifice¹ *n* (act) sacrificium *nt*; (victim) victima *f*; fig detrimentum, damnum *nt*

sacrifice² *vt* immolo, sacrifico, macto ①; fig posthabeo ②; (give up) devoveo ②; profundo ③

sacrilege *n* sacrilegium *nt*; impietas *f*

sacrilegious *adj* sacrilegus; impius

sad *adj* tristis, maestus, miser, miserabilis

sadden *vt* contristo ①

saddle¹ *n* ephippium, stratum *nt*

saddle² *vt* (equum) sterno; fig impono ③; onero ①

sadness *n* tristitia, maestitia, miseria *f*

safe *adj* tutus; (without hurt) incolumis; (sure) certus
□ ∼ **and sound** salvus

safeguard *n* praesidium *nt*; tutela *f*

safety *n* salus, incolumitas *f*

saffron¹ *n* crocus *m*

saffron² *adj* croceus

sail¹ *n* velum *nt*; carbasa, lintea *ntpl*; (excursion) navigatio *f*

sail² *vi* vela facio ③; navigo ①; (set out to sea) vela do ①; solvo ③
■ ∼ *vt* navigo ①

sailing *n* navigatio *f*; (of a ship) cursus *m*

sailor *n* nauta *m*

saint *n* vir sanctus *m*; femina sancta *f*

saintly *adv* sanctus, pius

sake *n*:
□ **for the** ∼ **of** gratia, causa + *gen*; pro + *abl*; (on account of) propter, ob + *acc*

salad *n* acetaria *ntpl*

r

s

salary n merces f; stipendium; salarium nt

sale n venditio f; (auction) auctio f
□ **for** ∼ venalis
□ **be on** ∼ veneo ir
□ **put up for** ∼ venalem propono ③

salesman n venditor m

salient adj prominens; (chief) praecipuus

saliva n saliva f; sputum nt

sallow adj pallidus, luridus

sally[1] n eruptio f

sally[2] vi mil erumpo, excurro ③

salmon n salmo m

salt[1] n sal m

salt[2] adj salsus

salt[3] vt salio, sale condio ④

salt-cellar n salinum m

salty adj salsus

salubrious adj salubris, salutaris

salutary adj salutaris, salubris; utilis

salute[1] n salus, salutatio f

salute[2] vt saluto ①

salvation n salus, salvatio f

same adj idem
□ **it is all the** ∼ **thing** nihil interest
□ **at the** ∼ **time** eodem tempore
□ **in the** ∼ **place** ibidem

sample n exemplum; exemplar; specimen nt

sanctify vt sanctifico; (consecrate) consecro ①

sanctimonious adj sanctitatem affectans

sanction[1] n auctoritas, confirmatio f

sanction[2] vt ratum facio ③; sancio ④; confirmo, firmo ①

sanctity n sanctitas; sanctimonia, religio f

sanctuary n asylum, adytum, sacrarium nt

sand n sabulo m; arena f

sandal n solea, crepida f

sandstone n tofus, tophus m

sandy n (full of sand) arenosus, sabulosus; arenaceus; (of colour) rufus

sane adj sanus, mentis compos

sanity n sanitas, mens sana f

sap n sucus m; lac nt

sapling n surculus m

sapphire n sapphirus f

sarcasm n dictum acerbum nt

sarcastic adj acerbus, mordax

sarcophagus n sarcophagus m

sardine n sarda f

sardonic adj acerbus

sash n cingulum nt

satchel n saccus, sacculus m; pera f; loculi mpl

sate vt satio, saturo ①

satellite n satelles m/f; (planet) stella minor or obnoxia f

satiate vt satio, saturo ①

satiety n satietas f; fastidium nt

satire n satura f

satirical adj satyricus, acerbus

satirist n scriptor (or poeta) satyricus

satirize vt derideo ②; perstringo ③

satisfaction n satisfactio f; fig oblectatio animi; voluptas f

satisfactory adj (suitable) commodus; (pleasant) gratus, iucundus

satisfy vt (please) satisfacio ③ + dat; (fill) satio, saturo ①; fig persuadeo ②; (one's expectations) respondeo ② both + dat; (be satisfied) contentus sum ir

saturate vt saturo ①; imbuo, madefacio ③

satyr n satyrus m

sauce n condimentum; ius nt

saucepan n cacabus m

saucer n patella f

saucy adj petulans, procax, protervus

saunter vi ambulo ①; incedo ③

sausage n farcimen, tomaculum nt

savage adj ferus; ferox, immansuetus; immanis; saevus; atrox; (furious) efferus; (uncivilized) ferus, incultus
■ ∼**ly** adv crudeliter; immaniter; atrociter; saeve

savagery n feritas; immanitas; saevitia f

save vt servo, conservo; (from danger) libero ①; periculo eripio; (spare) parco ③ + dat; (gain) lucror ①

savings n peculium nt

saviour n servator m

savour[1] n sapor, odor, nidor m

savour[2] vi sapio ③
■ ∼ vt fruor ③ + abl

savoury adj sapidus

saw[1] n (tool) serra f

saw² *vt&i* serra seco ⊡; serram duco ③
sawdust *n* scobis *f*
say *vt&i* dico, loquor, aio ③; fari *inf* ⊡
  □ **he ∼s** inquit
  □ **they ∼** dicunt, ferunt
  □ **that is to ∼** scilicet
saying *n* dictum *nt*
scab *n* (of a wound) crusta *f*
scabbard *n* vagina *f*
scaffold *n* tabulatum *nt*; catasta *f*
scaffolding *n* tabulatum *nt*
scald *vt* fervente aqua macero ⊡
scale¹ *n* (of a fish) squama; (of a balance) lanx *f*
  ■ **∼s** *pl* libra; trutina *f*; (degree) gradus *m*
scale² *vt* (walls) ascendo ③; scalas admoveo ② ad + *acc*
scaling-ladder *n* scalae *fpl*
scallop *n* (shell-fish) pecten *m*
scalp *n* calva *f*
scalpel *n* scalpellum, scalprum *nt*
scaly *adj* squamosus; squameus
scamper *vi* ruo ③; provolo ⊡
  □ **∼ away** aufugio, effugio ③
scan *vt* examino, exploro, lustro ⊡
scandal *n* ignominia, turpitudo *f*; opprobrium *nt*
scandalize *vt* offendo ③
scandalous *adj* ignominiosus, probrosus, turpis
scant *adj* (and **scanty**) angustus, exiguus, tenuis
scapegoat *n* caper emissarius *m*
scar¹ *n* cicatrix *f*
scar² *vt* noto ⊡
scarce *adj* rarus
  ■ **∼ly** *adv* vix, aegre
scarcity *n* paucitas; penuria, inopia *f*
scare *vt* terreo ②; territo, formido ⊡
scarecrow *n* terricula *ntpl*
scared *adj* territus
scarf *n* fascia *f*
scarlet¹ *n* (colour) color coccineus *m*
scarlet² *adj* coccineus
scatter *vt* spargo, dispergo ③; dissipo ⊡; (put to flight) fundo ③; fugo ⊡
  ■ **∼** *vi* dilabor ③
scene *n* scaena *f*; (spectacle) spectaculum *nt*; (place) locus; (landscape) prospectus *m*

scenery *n* (of nature) species regionis *f*
  □ **beautiful ∼** amoena loca *ntpl*; (of a theatre) scaena *f*
scenic *adj* scaenicus
scent¹ *n* (sense) odoratus; (fragrance) odor *m*; (of dogs) sagacitas *f*
scent² *vt* (perfume) odoro; (get wind of, scent out) odoror ⊡
scent-bottle *n* olfactorium *nt*
scented *adj* odoratus, odorifer, odorus, fragrans
sceptical *adj* (suspicious) suspicax
sceptre *n* sceptrum *nt*
schedule *n* libellus *m*
scheme¹ *n* consilium *nt*
scheme² *vt&i* molior ④; (plot) coniuro ⊡
scholar *n* discipulus *m*; discipula *f*; (learned man) homo doctus *m*
scholarship *n* litterae *fpl*; eruditio, humanitas *f*
school *n* also fig schola; secta *f*; ludus *m*
schoolboy *n* discipulus *m*
school-fellow *n* condiscipulus *m*; condiscipula *f*
schoolmaster *n* ludi magister, magister, praeceptor *m*
schoolmistress *n* magistra, praeceptrix *f*
sciatica *n* ischias *f*
science *n* scientia; doctrina; disciplina, ars; (theory) ratio *f*
scientific *adj* ad scientiam conformatus
  ■ **∼ly** *adv* ex disciplinae praeceptis
scissors *n* forfipes *fpl*
scoff *vi* (mock) irrideo, derideo ②; cavillor ⊡; (eat) comedo *ir*
scold *vt&i* obiurgo, increpo, increpito ⊡
scolding *n* obiurgatio *f*; iurgium *nt*
scoop¹ *n* trulla *f*
scoop² *vt* cavo, excavo ⊡
scope *n* finis *m*; propositum *nt*; fig campus *m*; area *f*; spatium *nt*
scorch *vt* uro, aduro ③; torreo ②
score¹ *n* nota; (bill) ratio *f*; (twenty) viginti
score² *vt* (mark) noto ⊡
  □ **∼ a point** superior sum *ir*
scorn¹ *vt* temno, contemno, sperno ③; aspernor ⊡; fastidio ④

S

scorn² *n* contemptio *f*; contemptus *m*; supercilium, fastidium *nt*

scornful *adj* fastidiosus
■ ~**ly** *adv* contemptim; fastidiose

scorpion *n* scorpio, scorpius *m*

scotch *vt* incido ③; vulnero ①

scot-free *adj* impunitus
■ ~ *adv* impune

scoundrel *n* nebulo, furcifer *m*

scour *vt* tergeo, detergeo ②; fig pervagor ①; percurro ③

scourge¹ *n* flagellum *nt*; fig pestis *f*

scourge² *vt* caedo ③; verbero ①

scout¹ *n* explorator, speculator, emissarius *m*

scout² *vt* speculor, exploro ①

scowl¹ *vi* frontem contraho ③

scowl² *n* frontis contractio *f*

scramble *vi* nitor, enitor ③

scrap *n* fragmentum, fragmen, frustum *nt*

scrape *vt&i* rado; (together) corrado ③

scraper *n* (tool) radula *f*; rallum *nt*

scratch¹ *vt* rado; scalpo ③; scabo ①; (inscribe) inscribo ③
□ ~ **out** erado ③

scratch² *n* vulnus *nt*

scream¹ *vi* strideo ②; vociferor ①; (of a child) vagio ④

scream² *n* stridor *m*; vociferatio *f*; (of an infant) vagitus *m*

screech¹ *vi* strideo ②; vociferor ①; (of a child) vagio ④

screech² *n* stridor *m*; vociferatio *f*; (of an infant) vagitus *m*

screen¹ *n* umbraculum *nt*; (protection) praesidium *nt*; defensio *f*

screen² *vt* occulo, protego, defendo ③

scribe *n* scriba, amanuensis, librarius *m*

scroll *n* volumen *nt*

scrub¹ *vt* frico ①; tergeo ③

scrub² *n* (brushwood) virgulta *ntpl*

scruple¹ *n* scrupulus *m*; religio, dubitatio *f*

scruple² *vi* dubito ①

scrupulous *adj* religiosus, scrupulosus
■ ~**ly** *adv* religiose; scrupulose

scrutinize *vt* scrutor, perscrutor ①

scrutiny *n* scrutatio, perscrutatio *f*

scuffle¹ *n* rixa; turba *f*

scuffle² *vi* rixor ①

sculptor *n* sculptor, scalptor *m*; artifex *m*; caelator *m*

sculpture¹ *n* (art) sculptura; scalptura *f*; (work) opus (marmoreum, *etc.*) *nt*

sculpture² *vt* sculpo, scalpo ③; caelo ①

scum *n* spuma; (of metals) scoria; fig sentina *f*

scurrilous *adj* scurrilis, probrosus

scurvy *n* scrofula *f*

scuttle *vt* navis fundum perforo ①

scythe *n* falx *f*

sea *n* mare, aequor, marmor *nt*; pontus *m*

seacoast *n* ora *f*; litus *nt*

seafaring *adj* maritimus

seagull *n* larus *m*; gavia *f*

seahorse *n* hippocampus *m*

seal¹ *n* signum *nt*; (animal) phoca *f*

seal² *vt* signo, consigno, obsigno ①; fig sancio ④

sealing-wax *n* cera *f*

seam *n* sutura; commissura *f*

seaman *n* nauta *m*

seamanship *n* navigandi peritia *f*

search¹ *vt&i* scrutor, perscrutor ①; (into) inquiro ③; investigo ①

search² *n* scrutatio; investigatio; inquisitio *f*

seasick *adj* nauseabundus
□ **be** ~ nauseo ①

seasickness *n* nausea *f*

seaside *n* ora *f*

season¹ *n* tempus (anni) *nt*; (right moment) opportunitas *f*

season² *vt* condio ④; fig assuefacio ③; duro, exercito ①

seasonable *adj* tempestivus, opportunus

seasoned *adj* exercitatus

seasoning *n* (act) conditio *f*; (the seasoning itself) condimentum *nt*

seat¹ *n* sedes; sella *f*; sedile, subsellium *nt*; (dwelling-place) domicilium *nt*; (place) locus *m*; (dwelling) sedes *f*

seat² *vt* sede loco ①; (oneself) consideo ③

sea-urchin *n* echinus *m*

seaweed *n* alga *f*; fucus *m*

seaworthy *adj* navigandi capax

secluded *adj* solitarius; remotus

seclusion *n* solitudo *f*; secessus *m*; locus remotus *m*

second[1] *adj* secundus; alter
□ **for the ~ time** iterum

second[2] *n* (person) adiutor *m*; (of time) punctum temporis *nt*

secondary *adj* secundarius; inferior

secondly *adv* deinde, tum

secrecy *n* secretum *nt*; taciturnitas *f*; (keeping secret) silentium *nt*

secret[1] *adj* arcanus; secretus; occultus; furtivus; clandestinus
□ **in ~** clam
□ **keep ~** celo [1]
■ **~ly** *adv* clam; occulte, furtim

secret[2] *n* secretum, arcanum *nt*; res arcana *f*

secretary *n* scriba; amanuensis *m*

secrete *vt* celo, occulto [1]; abdo [3]
□ **~ oneself** lateo [2]; delitesco [3]

sect *n* secta, schola *f*

section *n* pars; (geometry) sectio *f*

sector *n* sector *m*

secular *adj* saecularis; (worldly) profanus

secure[1] *adj* securus; tutus
■ **~ly** *adv* tuto, secure

secure[2] *vt* confirmo [1]; munio [4]; a periculo defendo [3]; in custodiam trado [3]; (bring about, get) pario [3]; paro [1]

security *n* salus; incolumitas; (pledge) satisdatio *f*; pignus *nt*; (person) vas, sponsor, praes *m*

sedan-chair *n* lectica *f*

sedate *adj* gravis, sedatus

sedentary *adj* sedentarius, sellularius

sediment *n* faex *f*

sedition *n* seditio, rebellio *f*; tumultus *m*

seditious *adj* seditiosus, turbulentus

seduce *vt* corrumpo [3]; depravo [1]; decipio [3]

seducer *n* corruptor *m*

seduction *n* illecebra; corruptela *f*

seductive *adj* blandus

see *vt&i* video [2]; specto [1]; cerno, conspicio, aspicio [3]; (take precautions) caveo, video [2]; (understand) intellego [3]
□ **go to ~** viso [3]
□ **~ to** curo [1]

seed *n* semen *nt*

seedling *n* planta *f*

seeing *conj*:
□ **~ that** quandoquidem, quoniam

seek *vt&i* quaero, peto, expeto, sequor [3]; (endeavour) conor; (strive to attain) affecto, consector [1]

seem *vi* videor [2]

seeming *adj* speciosus
■ **~ly** *adv* in speciem, ut videtur

seemly *adj* decorus, decens

seer *n* vates, fatidicus, augur, propheta *m*

seethe *vi* ferveo [2]; aestuo [1]; (with rage) furo [3]

segment *n* segmentum *nt*

segregate *vt* segrego [1]

seize *vt* prehendo, comprehendo; arripio [3]; (take possession) occupo [1]; (attack) invado; incesso; fig afficio [3]

seizure *n* comprehensio; occupatio *f*

seldom *adv* raro

select[1] *vt* seligo, eligo, deligo [3]

select[2] *adj* exquisitus

selection *n* selectio, electio *f*; delectus *m*

self *pn* ipse, se, sese
□ **by one's ~** solus

self-confidence *n* sui fiducia *f*

self-conscious *adj* verecundus

self-control *n* temperantia *f*

selfish *adj* nimis se amans

selfishness *n* amor sui *m*

self-possessed *adj* placidus, tranquillus, imperturbatus

self-willed *adj* obstinatus, contumax

sell *vt* vendo [3]
■ **~** *vi* veneo *ir*

seller *n* venditor *m*

semblance *n* similitudo, species *f*

semicircle *n* semicirculus *m*

semicircular *adj* semicirculus, semicirculatus

senate *n* senatus *m*; curia *f*

senate-house *n* curia *f*

senator *n* senator *m*

senatorial *adj* senatorius

send *vt* mitto [3]; (on public business) lego [1]; (away) dimitto [3]
□ **~ for** accerso [3]

senile *adj* senilis

senior *adj* natu maior

S

seniority *n* aetatis privilegium *nt*

sensation *n* sensus *m*; (astonishment) stupor *m*; (subject of talk) fabula *f*

sense *n* (faculty) sensus *m*; (intellect) mens; (opinion) opinio, sententia *f*; (meaning) significatio *f*

senseless *adj* nihil sentiens; (lifeless) exanimis; fig mentis expers; absurdus

sensible *adj* sensilis; sensu praeditus, sensibilis; fig sapiens

sensitive *adj* mollis
   □ ~ **to** impatiens + *gen*

sensual *adj* voluptarius; libidinosus

sentence¹ *n* iudicium *nt*; (set of words) sententia *f*

sentence² *vt* damno, condemno ①

sentiment *n* sententia, opinio *f*; sensus *m*

sentimental *adj* animi mollioris *gen*; (in contempt) flebilis

sentinel *n* excubitor, vigil *m*; excubiae *fpl*

sentry *n* excubitor, vigil *m*; excubiae *fpl*
   ■ ~-**box** *n* specula *f*

separate¹ *vt* separo ①; disiungo, seiungo, secerno ③
   ■ ~ *vi* separor ①; disiungor ③; (go different ways) digredior ③

separate² *adj* separatus; disiunctus

separation *n* separatio; disiunctio *f*; (going different ways) digressus *m*

September *n* September *m*

sequel *n* exitus, eventus *m*

sequence *n* ordo *m*; series *f*

serene *adj* serenus; tranquillus

serenity *n* serenitas; tranquillitas *f*

series *n* series *f*

serious *adj* gravis, serius, severus
   ■ ~**ly** *adv* graviter; serio; severe

seriousness *n* gravitas *f*; serium *nt*; severitas *f*

sermon *n* oratio, contio *f*

serpent *n* serpens, anguis *m/f*; coluber, draco *m*

servant *n* minister; famulus *m*; ministra, ancilla *f*; famula *f*

serve *vt&i* servio ④ + *dat*; (for wages) stipendia mereo *or* mereor ②; (be useful) prosum *ir*; (be sufficient) sufficio ③ *both* + *dat*
   □ ~ **up** offero *ir*

service *n* servitium; (kindness) officium *nt*; (advantage) utilitas *f*; mil militia *f*

serviceable *adj* utilis; commodus
   □ **be** ~ prosum *ir* + *dat*

servile *adj* servilis, humilis

servility *n* humilitas *f*; animus abiectus *m*

session *n* sessio *f*; consessus, conventus *m*

set¹ *vt* pono, sisto ③; loco, colloco ①; (prescribe) praescribo ③; (an example) do ①; (enclose) includo ③; (on fire) accendo ③
   ■ ~ *vi* (of sun) occido ③
   □ ~ **about** incipio ③
   □ ~ **apart** *or* **aside** sepono; fig rescindo ③
   □ ~ **down** (in writing) noto ①; perscribo
   □ ~ **forth** *vt* expono; propono ③, profero *ir*; *vi* proficiscor ③
   □ ~ **in** insero ③
   □ ~ **off** *vt* (adorn) adorno; illustro ①; *vi* abeo ④; proficiscor ③
   □ ~ **on** (incite) instigo ①; (attack) invado ③
   □ ~ **out** *vi* discedo, proficiscor ③
   □ ~ **up** erigo; exstruo; statuo; (institute) instituo, constituo ③

set² *adj* (well-ordered) compositus

settee *n* lectulus *m*

setting *n* collocatio *f*; (of the sun) occasus *m*

settle *vt* statuo, constituo; (a quarrel) dirimo ③; (adjust) compono; (an account) solvo ③
   ■ ~ *vi* (reside) consido; (sink) subsido ③

settlement *n* constitutio; (dowry) dos *f*; (agreement) pactum *nt*; (colony) colonia *f*

settler *n* colonus *m*

seven *adj* septem
   □ ~ **times** septies

seven hundred *adj* septingenti

seventeen *adj* septendecim, decem et septem

seventeenth *adj* septimus decimus

seventh *adj* septimus

seventieth *adj* septuagesimus

seventy *adj* septuaginta

sever *vt* separo ①; dissolvo ③; dissocio ①; disiungo ③

several *adj* plures, complures; diversus, varius

severe *adj* severus; gravis; durus
   ■ ~**ly** *adv* severe, graviter

severity *n* severitas; gravitas; inclementia *f*

sew *vt&i* suo, consuo ③

sewer *n* cloaca *f*

sewing *n* sutura *f*

sex *n* sexus *m*

sexual *adj* sexualis; naturalis

shabby *adj* pannosus; sordidus

shackles *n* vincula *ntpl*; pedica, compes *f*

shade[1] *n* umbra *f*; (parasol) umbraculum *nt*; fig (difference) discrimen *nt*

shade[2] *vt* opaco; obscuro; obumbro; adumbro [1]

shadow *n* umbra *f*

shadowy *adj* umbrosus, opacus; fig tenuis, inanis, vanus

shady *adj* opacus, umbrosus

shaft *n* sagitta *f*; (of a spear) hastile *nt*; (in a mine) puteus *m*; (of a column) scapus *m*

shaggy *adj* hirsutus, hirtus, villosus

shake *vt* quatio, concutio [3]; quasso [1]; (the head) nuto [1]; (undermine) labefacio [3]; labefacto [1]
■ ~ *vi* concutior; (with fear) tremo [3]; (totter) vacillo, nuto [1]

shallow *adj* vadosus; fig levis

shallows *n* vada *ntpl*

sham[1] *adj* fictus, simulatus; fallax

sham[2] *n* fallacia *f*; dolus *m*; simulatio, species *f*

sham[3] *vt* simulo [1]; fingo [3]

shame[1] *n* pudor *m*; (disgrace) dedecus; opprobrium *nt*; ignominia *f*

shame[2] *vt* ruborem incutio [3] + *dat*

shamefaced *adj* pudens, pudibundus, verecundus

shameful *adj* turpis, probrosus
■ ~ly *adv* turpiter; probrose

shameless *adj* impudens
■ ~ly *adv* impudenter

shape[1] *n* forma, figura; species, facies *f*

shape[2] *vt* formo, figuro [1]; fingo [3]

shapeless *adj* informis; deformis, indigestus, rudis

shapely *adj* formosus

share[1] *n* pars, portio *f*

share[2] *vt* partior [4]; (with another) communico [1] cum + *abl*
■ ~ *vi* particeps sum *ir*; in partem venio [4]

sharer *n* particeps *m/f*; socius *m*; socia *f*; consors *m/f*

shark *n* (fish) pristis *f*; fig (person) fraudator *m*

sharp *adj* acutus; acer; (bitter) acerbus; (tart) acidus; fig mordax; argutus; subtilis
■ ~ly *adv* acute; (keenly) acriter; (bitterly) acerbe; (cleverly) subtiliter

sharpen *vt* acuo, exacuo [3]

sharpness *n* (of edge) acies; (sourness) acerbitas; fig subtilitas, perspicacitas *f*; acumen *nt*

sharp-sighted *adj* perspicax

shatter *vt* quasso [1]; frango, confringo; elido [3]

shave *vt* rado [3]; tondeo [2]
□ ~ **off** abrado [3]

shaving *n* ramentum *nt*; scobis *f*

shawl *n* amiculum *nt*

she *pn* haec, illa, ea

sheaf *n* manipulus, fascis *m*; merges *f*

shear *vt* tondeo [2]; fig spolio, nudo [1]

shears *n* forfex *f*

sheath *n* vagina *f*; (wrapper) involucrum *nt*

sheathe *vt* (in vaginam) recondo [3]

shed[1] *vt* fundo, effundo, profundo, spargo [3]; (blood) (one's own) do [1]; (another's) haurio [4]; (tears) effundo, profundo [3]

shed[2] *n* tugurium *nt*

sheep *n* ovis, pecus, bidens *f*

sheepish *adj* timidus, modestus

sheepskin *n* pellis ovilla, mastruca *f*

sheer *adj* merus; purus; (precipitous) praeceps

sheet *n* linteum *nt*; (of metal) lamina *f*

shelf *n* pluteus *m*; tabula *f*

shell *n* concha; crusta, testa *f*; (husk) folliculus *m*; (of nuts, etc.) putamen *nt*

shellfish *n* concha *f*

shelter[1] *n* tegmen; fig refugium, perfugium; (asylum) receptaculum *nt*

shelter[2] *vt* tego; protego; defendo [3]

shepherd *n* pastor, upilio, pecorum custos *m*

shield[1] *n* scutum *nt*; clipeus *m*

shield[2] *vt* tego, protego, defendo [3]

shift[1] *vt* muto [1]; amoveo [2]
■ ~ *vi* (as the wind) verto [3]; (shuffle) tergiversor [1]

shift[2] *n* (expedient) ratio *f*; modus *m*; (remedy) remedium *nt*; (trick) dolus *m*; ars *f*

S

shin *n* (**shin-bone**) tibia *f*

shine *vi* luceo, fulgeo, niteo, splendeo
② ; corusco, mico ①
□ ∼ **forth** eluceo; eniteo ② ;
exsplendesco ③
□ ∼ **on** affulgeo ② + *dat*

shingle *n* glarea *f*; scandula *f*

shining *adj* lucidus, fulgidus, nitidus

shiny *adj* nitidus

ship¹ *n* navis *f*; navigium *nt*

ship² *vt* in navem (*or* naves) impono;
accipio ③

shipbuilder *n* naupegus *m*

ship owner *n* navicularius *m*

shipping *n* navigia *ntpl*

shipwreck *n* naufragium *nt*; fig ruina
f; interitus *m*

shipwrecked *adj* naufragus
□ **be** ∼ naufragium facio ③

shipyard *n* navale *nt*, navalia *ntpl*

shirk *vt* detrecto ①

shirt *n* indusium *nt*; tunica *f*

shiver¹ *vi* contremisco, horresco ③ ;
horreo ②

shiver² *n* (shudder) horror *m*
□ **cold** ∼ frigus *nt*

shoal *n* (of fishes, *etc.*) caterva *f*; grex *m*;
(shallow) brevia, vada *ntpl*

shock¹ *n* concussio *f*; impetus,
concursus *m*; fig (of feeling) offensio; (blow)
plaga *f*

shock² *vt* percutio, percello; fig
offendo ③

shocking *adj* foedus; atrox

shoe¹ *n* calceus *m*; caliga; (slipper) solea
f; soccus *m*; (for horses) solea *f*

shoe² *vt* calceos induo ③ ; (a horse) soleas
apto ① + *dat*

shoemaker *n* sutor *m*

shoot¹ *vt* (telum) mitto; conicio ③ ;
iaculor ①; (a person) figo, transfigo ③
■ ∼ *vi* (of plants) germino ①; (of pains)
vermino ①

shoot² *n* (of plants) surculus *m*; propago
f; germen *nt*

shooting star *n* fax (caelestis), stella *f*

shop *n* taberna, officina *f*

shopkeeper *n* tabernarius *m*

shore *n* litus *nt*; ora *f*

short *adj* brevis; (little) exiguus
□ **in** ∼ breviter, denique
□ **be** ∼ **of** egeo ② + *abl*

shortcoming *n* defectus *m*; (fault)
delictum, vitium *nt*; (failure) inopia *f*

shorten *vt* coarto ①; contraho ③
■ ∼ *vi* contrahor; minuor ③

shorthand *n* notae breviores *fpl*

short-lived *adj* brevis

shortly *adv* (of time) brevi; mox
□ ∼ **after** haud multum post

shortness *n* brevitas; exiguitas *f*; (of
breath) anhelitus *m*

short-sighted *adj* myops; fig
improvidus

short-sightedness *n* myopia; fig
minima imprudentia *f*

shot *n* ictus *m*; (reach, range) iactus;
(marksman) iaculator *m*; (bullet) glans *f*;
tormentum *nt*

shoulder *n* umerus *m*

shoulder-blade *n* scapulae *fpl*

shout¹ *n* clamor *m*; acclamatio, vox *f*

shout² *vt&i* clamo; acclamo; vociferor
①

shove *vt* trudo ③ ; pulso ①

shovel *n* pala *f*; batillum; (for the fire)
rutabulum *nt*

show¹ *vt* monstro, declaro; indico ①;
ostendo ③ ; (display) exhibeo; (teach) doceo
② ; (prove) confirmo ①; (qualities) praebeo ②
□ ∼ **off** ostento, vendito ①

show² *n* (appearance) species; (display)
ostentatio; (pretence) simulatio; (parade)
pompa *f*; (spectacle) spectaculum *nt*

shower¹ *n* imber, nimbus *m*; fig vis,
multitudo *f*

shower² *vt* superfundo, effundo; fig
ingero ③

showery *adj* pluviosus, nimbosus,
pluvius, pluvialis

showy *adj* speciosus

shred *n* segmentum *nt*

shrewd *adj* acutus, astutus, callidus;
sagax; prudens
■ ∼ **ly** *adv* acute, callide; sagaciter;
astute, prudenter

shrewdness *n* calliditas; astutia;
sagacitas *f*; acumen *nt*; prudentia *f*

shriek¹ *vi* ululo, eiulo ①

shriek² *n* eiulatio *f*; ululatus *m*

shrill *adj* acutus, peracutus, stridulus

shrimp *n* squilla *f*

shrine *n* (for holy things) sacrarium,
sacellum, adytum *nt*; cella *f*

S

shrink *vt* contraho ③
■ ∼ *vi* contrahor; (withdraw) refugio ③;
(from) abhorreo ②; detrecto ①

shrivel *vt* corrugo ①; torreo ②
■ ∼ *vi* corrugor ①; torreor ②

shroud[1] *n* (of ships) rudentes *mpl*; (of
corpse) linteum (mortuorum) *nt*

shroud[2] *vt* involvo; obduco ③

shrub *n* frutex *m*; arbuscula *f*

shrubbery *n* fruticetum *nt*

shrug[1] *n* umerorum allevatio *f*

shrug[2] *vi* umeros allevo ①

shudder[1] *n* horror, tremor *m*

shudder[2] *vi* horreo ②; horresco ③

shuffle *vt* misceo ②
■ ∼ *vi* tergiversor ①

shun *vt* vito, devito, evito, declino,
detrecto ①; fugio ③

shut *vt* claudo, occludo ③; (out) excludo
③; (up) concludo ③

shutter *n* claustrum *nt*

shuttle *n* radius *m*

shy *adj* timidus; pudibundus;
verecundus

shyness *n* timiditas; verecundia *f*

Sibyl *n* Sibylla *f*

sick *adj* aeger, aegrotus
□ **be** ∼ aegroto ①; (of, with) taedet (me
rei) ②, fastidio ④

sicken *vt* fastidium moveo ② + *gen*;
satio ①
■ ∼ *vi* in morbum incido ③

sickle *n* falx *f*
■ ∼-**shaped** *adj* falcatus

sickly *adj* infirmus; (pale) pallidus

sickness *n* aegrotatio, aegritudo *f*;
morbus *m*

side[1] *n* latus *nt*; (part, quarter) pars; regio;
(edge) ora *f*; (of a hill) clivus *m*; (party in a
contest) partes *fpl*

side[2] *adj* lateralis

side[3] *vi* (with) partes sequor ③ + *gen*; ab
aliquo sto ①

sideboard *n* abacus *m*

sideways *adv* in obliquum, oblique

sidle *vi* obliquo incessu progredior ③

siege *n* oppugnatio, obsessio,
obsidio *f*

siesta *n* meridiatio *f*
□ **take a** ∼ meridior ①

sieve *n* cribrum *nt*

sift *vt* cribro ①; cerno ③; fig exploro,
scrutor ①

sigh[1] *n* suspirium *nt*

sigh[2] *vi* suspiro ①; (for) desidero,
suspiro ①

sight *n* (sense) visus; (act of seeing)
aspectus, conspectus *m*; (of the eye) acies
(oculi *or* oculorum) *f*; (show)
spectaculum *nt*; (appearance) species *f*;
visum *nt*
□ **in** ∼ in conspectu,
□ **out of** ∼ e conspectu

sign[1] *n* signum, indicium *nt*; (mark) nota
f; (of a shop, *etc.*) insigne; fig portentum,
omen; augurium *nt*

sign[2] *vt&i* subscribo; annuo ③; signum
do ①

signal[1] *n* signum; mil classicum *nt*

signal[2] *vt* signum do ①

signature *n* nomen *nt*; subscriptio *f*

signet-ring *n* anulus *m*; signum *nt*

significance *n* (meaning) significatio *f*;
sensus *m*; fig vis *f*; momentum *nt*

significant *adj* significans; fig magni
momenti *gen*

signify *vt&i* significo ①; valeo ②;
portendo ③

silence[1] *n* silentium *nt*; taciturnitas *f*
■ ∼! *int* tace! tacete!

silence[2] *vt* silentium facio ③; (confute)
refuto ①; (allay) sedo ①; compesco ③

silent *adj* tacitus, silens
■ ∼**ly** *adv* (cum) silentio, tacite

silk[1] *n* sericum *nt*; bombyx *m/f*

silk[2] *adj* (also **silken**) sericus,
bombycinus

sill *n* limen inferum *nt*

silliness *n* stultitia, fatuitas,
insulsitas, insipientia *f*

silly *adj* stultus, fatuus, ineptus,
insipiens, insulsus

silver[1] *n* argentum *nt*

silver[2] *adj* (also **silvery**) argenteus; (of
hair) canus

silversmith *n* faber argentarius *m*

similar *adj* similis
■ ∼**ly** *adv* similiter

similarity *n* similitudo; vicinitas;
proximitas *f*

simile *n* similitudo *f*

simmer *vt* fervefacio ③
■ ∼ *vi* aestuo ①; ferveo ②

S

simple *adj* simplex; rudis; fig (silly) ineptus; ingenuus

simpleton *n* stultus, fatuus, ineptus *m*

simplicity *n* simplicitas *f*

simplify *vt* simpliciorem reddo ③

simply *adv* simpliciter; (merely) solum, modo, tantummodo

simulate *vt* simulo ①

simulation *n* simulatio *f*

simultaneous *adj* eodem tempore
■ ~**ly** *adv* simul, una

sin[1] *n* peccatum; delictum, flagitium, nefas, vitium *nt*

sin[2] *vt* pecco ①; delinquo ③

since[1] *prep* post + *acc*
■ ~ *conj* cum, ex quo; (seeing that) cum; quando; quoniam

since[2] *adv* abhinc
□ **long** ~ iamdudum

sincere *adj* sincerus, candidus; simplex, verus
■ ~**ly** *adv* sincere, vere

sincerity *n* sinceritas, simplicitas *f*; candor *m*

sinew *n* nervus; lacertus *m*

sinful *adj* impius, pravus; flagitiosus, sceleratus

sing *vt&i* cano ③; canto ①

singe *vt* aduro, amburo ③

singer *n* cantor *m*

singing *n* cantus *m*; carmen *nt*

single[1] *adj* solus, unicus, unus

single[2] *vt* (out) eligo ③

singly *adv* singillatim

singular *adj* unicus, singularis; (exceptional) peculiaris; egregius, eximius

sinister *adj* mali ominis *gen*; malevolus, iniquus

sink *vi* (fall to the ground) consido, subsido; (into ruins) collabor; (of a ship) deprimor, summergor ③
■ ~ *vt* deprimo; demergo, summergo; (a well) demitto ③

sinner *n* peccans *m/f*

sinuous *adj* sinuosus

sip[1] *vt* sorbillo, degusto, libo, delibo ①

sip[2] *n* sorbitio *f*

siphon *n* sipho *m*

sir *n* (knight) eques *m*
■ ~! *int* (title of respect in address) bone vir! vir clarissime!

Siren *n* Siren *f*

sister *n* soror *f*

sisterhood *n* societas *f*; collegium *nt*

sister-in-law *n* glos *f*

sisterly *adj* sororius

sit *vi* sedeo; (at) assideo ②; (down) consido ③; (on) insideo ② + *dat*

site *n* situs; positus *m*; (space) area *f*

sitting *n* (act and session) sessio *f*

situated *adj* situs, positus

situation *n* situs, positus *m*; fig condicio *f*; status *m*

six *adj* sex
□ ~ **times** sexies

six hundred *adj* sescenti

sixteen *adj* sedecim

sixteenth *adj* sextus decimus

sixth *adj* sextus

sixtieth *adj* sexagesimus

sixty *adj* sexaginta

size *n* magnitudo; moles; mensura; forma *f*

skeleton *n* sceletus *m*; (bones) ossa *ntpl*
□ ~ **key** clavis adulterina *f*

sketch[1] *n* adumbratio *f*

sketch[2] *vt* adumbro; delineo ①; fig describo ③

skewer *n* veru *nt*

skilful *adj* dexter, expertus, peritus; sollers, ingeniosus
■ ~**ly** *adv* perite, sollerter, ingeniose

skilfulness *n* ars, sollertia, calliditas, peritia *f*

skill *n* ars, sollertia, calliditas, peritia *f*

skilled *adj* dexter, expertus, peritus; sollers, ingeniosus

skim *vt* despumo ①; fig percurro, stringo; perstringo, attingo ③; (fly over) volo ① per + *acc*; perlabor, verro ③

skin[1] *n* (of people) cutis; (of animals) pellis *f*; (prepared) corium *nt*; (membrane) membrana; (of vegetables) cutis, membrana, tunica *f*

skin[2] *vt* pellem detraho ③ + *gen*

skinny *adj* rugosus; macilentus; macer

skip[1] *vi* salio, exsilio ④; exsulto ①; lascivio
□ ~ **over** transilio ④; (leave out) omitto ③

skip[2] *n* saltus *m*

skirmish[1] *n* leve proelium *nt*

skirmish[2] *vi* velitor ①

skirt[1] *n* (dress) vestis *f*

skirt[2] *vt* lego ③

skull *n* calvaria, calva *f*

sky *n* caelum *nt*; aether *m*

skylark *n* alauda *f*

slab *n* quadra *f*

slack *adj* remissus, laxus; fig piger, neglegens

slacken *vt* remitto ③; laxo, relaxo ①; minuo ③
  ■ ~ *vi* minuor, remittor ③; laxor, relaxor ①

slag *n* scoria *f*

slake *vt* exstinguo ③; sedo ①; depello ③

slander[1] *vt* calumnior, detrecto ①

slander[2] *n* calumnia; obtrectatio *f*

slanderous *adj* maledicus

slanting *adj* obliquus

slap[1] *n* alapa *f*

slap[2] *vt* alapam do ①

slash[1] *n* (cut) incisura *f*; (blow) ictus *m*; (wound) vulnus *nt*

slash[2] *vt* concido, incido ③

slaughter[1] *n* caedes, trucidatio *f*

slaughter[2] *vt* macto, trucido, neco, iugulo ①

slaughterhouse *n* macellum *nt*

slave[1] *n* servus *m*; serva *f*; verna *m*/*f*; mancipium *nt*; famulus *m*; famula *f*

slave[2] *vi* fig sudo ①

slavery *n* servitus *f*; servitium *nt*

slave-trade *n* venalicium *nt*

slave-trader *n* venalicius *m*

slavish *adj* servilis; humilis

slay *vt* interficio, caedo, perimo, interimo, occido ③; trucido, obtrunco ①

sledge *n* traha, trahea *f*

sleek *adj* levis, politus; nitidus

sleep[1] *n* somnus; sopor *m*; quies *f*

sleep[2] *vi* dormio ④; quiesco ③
  □ ~ **off** edormio ④

sleepiness *n* somnolentia *f*; sopor *m*

sleepless *adj* insomnis; exsomnis, vigil, vigilax; pervigil

sleeplessness *n* insomnia; vigilantia *f*

sleepy *adj* somniculosus; fig iners

sleet *n* nivosa grando *f*

sleeve *n* manica *f*
  □ **laugh up one's** ~ furtim rideo ②

sleight *n* (of hand) praestigiae *fpl*

slender *adj* gracilis; tenuis; (sparing) parcus

slenderness *n* gracilitas; tenuitas *f*

slice[1] *n* segmentum, frustum *nt*; offula; (tool) spatha *f*

slice[2] *vt* seco ①

slide[1] *vi* labor ③

slide[2] *n* lapsus *m*

slight[1] *adj* levis; exiguus, tenuis, parvus
  ■ ~**ly** *adv* leviter; paulum, paulo

slight[2] *n* neglegentia; repulsa, iniuria *f*; contemptus *m*

slight[3] *vt* neglego; contemno, despicio ③

slim *adj* gracilis; ▸ **slender**

slime *n* pituita *f*; (mud) limus *m*

slimy *adj* limosus, mucosus

sling[1] *n* funda; (for the arm) fascia, mitella *f*

sling[2] *vt* e funda iaculor ①; (hang) suspendo ③

slink *vi* (away) furtim me subduco ③; (in) irrepo ③

slip[1] *vi* labor ③
  □ ~ **away** elabor, clanculum me subtraho ③
  □ ~ **out** excido ③

slip[2] *n* lapsus *m*; fig peccatum *nt*; culpa *f*; error *m*

slipper *n* solea, crepida *f*

slippery *adj* lubricus; fig (deceitful) subdolus; (dangerous) periculosus

slipshod *adj* neglegens

slit[1] *n* incisura, rima *f*

slit[2] *vt* incido ③

slope[1] *n* acclivitas, declivitas *f*; clivus *m*

slope[2] *vi* proclinor ①; demittor ③
  ■ ~ *vt* demitto ③

sloping *adj* acclivis; declivis; pronus

sloppy *adj* lutulentus, sordidus

sloth *n* ignavia, pigritia, inertia; socordia *f*

slothful *adj* iners, piger, segnis; ignavus, socors
  ■ ~**ly** *adv* pigre, ignave, segniter

S

slow *adj* tardus, lentus; piger; (gentle) lenis
■ ~**ly** *adv* tarde; lente; pigre; sensim

slug *n* limax *m/f*

sluggish *adj* piger, ignavus

sluice *n* obiectaculum *nt*; catarracta *f*

slumber¹ *n* somnus, sopor *m*

slumber² *vi* obdormisco ③; dormito ①; dormio ④

slur¹ *vt* (smear) inquino ①

slur² *n* macula, labes *f*

slut *n* mulier neglegens *f*

sly *adj* astutus, vafer, callidus
□ **on the** ~ clam, clanculum
■ ~**ly** *adv* callide, vafre

smack¹ *n* (relish) sapor *m*; (slap) alapa *f*; (ship) lenunculus *m*

smack² *vt* (taste) gusto ①; (strike) ferio ④
■ ~ **of** *vi* sapio ③ + *acc*

small *adj* parvus, exiguus, tenuis; brevis; pusillus; (insignificant) levis

smallness *n* exiguitas, tenuitas; parvitas; gracilitas; brevitas *f*

smart *adj* (clever) acutus, sollers, callidus; (energetic) alacer; (elegant) lautus, nitidus; (elegantly) nitide, laute

smartness *n* sollertia *f*; acumen *nt*; alacritas; (elegance) lautitia *f*, nitor *m*

smash¹ *n* ruina *f*

smash² *vt* confringo ③

smattering *n* (a small quantity) aliquantum *nt*

smear *vt* lino, illino, oblino, ungo ③

smell¹ *vt* olfacio ③; odoror ①
■ ~ *vi* oleo; redoleo ②; fragro ①

smell² *n* (sense) odoratus *m*; (odour) odor *m*

smelly *adj* olidus, graveolens

smile¹ *vi* subrideo, renideo ②; (at) arrideo ②

smile² *n* risus *m*

smiling *adj* renidens, subridens

smith *n* faber *m*

smithy *n* fabrica; officina *f*

smoke¹ *vt* fumigo, suffumigo; (dry by smoke) infumo ①
■ ~ *vi* fumo; vaporo ①

smoke² *n* fumus, vapor *m*

smoky *adj* fumeus, fumidus, fumosus; fumificus; (blackened by smoke) decolor fuligine

smooth¹ *adj* levis; glaber; (slippery) lubricus; (polished) teres; (calm) placidus; lenis; fig blandus
■ ~**ly** *adv* leniter, placide; fig blande

smooth² *vt* levigo ①; polio ④; (with the plane) runcino; fig complano ①

smother *vt* suffoco ①; opprimo ③; (conceal) celo ①

smoulder *vi* fumo ①

smudge¹ *n* sordes *f*

smudge² *vt* inquino ①

smug *adj* sibi placens

smuggle *vt* furtim importo, sine portorio importo ①

smut *n* (soot) fuligo *f*

snack *n* pars, portio; gustatio *f*

snail *n* coclea *f*; limax *m/f*

snake *n* anguis *m/f*; serpens *f*; vipera *f*; ▶ **serpent**

snap¹ *vt&i* (one's fingers or a whip) concrepo ①; (break) frango ③
■ ~ *vi* dissilio ④
□ ~ **at** mordicus arripio ③; fig hianti ore capto ①

snap² *n* crepitus *m*

snare¹ *n* laqueus *m*; pedica *f*; fig insidiae *fpl*

snare² *vt* illaqueo, implico ①; irretio ④

snarl¹ *vi* (as a dog) ringor ③; hirrio ④

snarl² *n* hirritus *m*

snatch *vt* rapio, corripio ③; (away) eripio; surripio, avello ③

sneak *vi* repo, serpo ③; latito ①
□ ~ **off** me subtraho ③

sneer¹ *vi* irrideo, derideo ②

sneer² *n* irrisio *f*; irrisus *m*

sneeze¹ *vi* sternuo ③

sneeze² *n* sternumentum, sternutamentum *nt*

sniff *vi* naribus capto ①; haurio ④

snip *vt* amputo ①; (off) decerpo, praecido ③

snob *n* homo novus et arrogans, divitum cultor *m*

snobbish *adj* fastidiosus

snore¹ *vi* sterto ③

snore² *n* rhonchus *m*

snort¹ *vi* fremo ③

snort² *n* fremitus (equorum) *m*

snout *n* rostrum *nt*

snow¹ *n* nix *f*

s

snow² *vi impers*:
□ **it is ∼ing** ningit ③

snowy *adj* niveus, nivalis; (full of snow) nivosus

snub¹ *vt* repello ③

snub² *n* repulsa *f*

snub-nosed *adj* simus, resimus

so¹ *adv* sic, ita; tam; adeo
□ **and ∼** itaque
□ **∼ far** eatenus
□ **∼ great** tantus
□ **∼ many** tot
□ **∼ much** tantum; tam
□ **so-so** mediocriter
□ **∼ that** ita ut

so² *conj* (therefore) ergo, igitur

soak *vt* macero ①; madefacio, imbuo, tingo ③
■ **∼** *vi* (be soaked) madeo ②; madesco, madefio ③
□ **∼ through** percolor ①

soap *n* sapo *m*

soar *vi* in sublime feror *ir*; (of birds) subvolo ①

sob¹ *n* singultus *m*

sob² *vi* singulto ①

sober *adj* sobrius; fig moderatus

sobriety *n* sobrietas *f*

sociable *adj* sociabilis, socialis; facilis, affabilis, comis

social *adj* socialis; communis; civilis

society *n* societas *f*; (fraternity) sodalicium, collegium *nt*

sock *n* pedale *nt*; udo *m*

socket *n* cavum *nt*

sod *n* (clod) caespes *m*

sofa *n* lectulus, grabatus *m*

soft *adj* mollis, tener; (gentle) lenis; clemens; mitis; (not loud) mollis; fig delicatus; effeminatus
■ **∼ly** *adv* molliter; leniter; clementer

soften *vt* mollio ④; mitigo ①; fig lenio ④; placo, levo ①
■ **∼** *vi* mollesco; (fruits) mitesco; fig mansuesco, mitesco ③

softness *n* mollitia; teneritas; lenitas; (effeminacy) mollitia *f*

soil¹ *n* solum *nt*; terra *f*

soil² *vt* inquino, contamino, maculo ①

solace *n* solacium, lenimen, levamen, levamentum *nt*

solar *adj* solaris; solis (genitive)

solder¹ *vt* ferrumino ①

solder² *n* ferrumen *nt*

soldier *n* miles *m*

sole¹ *adj* solitarius, unus, unicus, solus
■ **∼ly** *adv* solum, modo, tantum

sole² *n* (of the foot) planta; (of a shoe) solea *f*

solecism *n* soloecismus *m*

solemn *adj* sollemnis; severus; gravis; serius
■ **∼ly** *adv* sollemniter, graviter, severe, serio

solemnity *n* sollemne, festum *nt*; sollemnitas *f*

solicit *vt* rogo; flagito; (tempt) sollicito ①

solicitor *n* iuris consultus, causidicus; advocatus *m*

solid¹ *adj* solidus; densus; fig verus; firmus

solid² *n* corpus solidum *nt*

solitary *adj* solitarius; (of places) desertus, solus

solitude *n* solitudo *f*; locus solus *m*

soluble *adj* solubilis

solution *n* dilutum *nt*; fig solutio, explicatio *f*

solve *vt* solvo ③; explico ①

sombre *adj* (severe) tristis

some *adj* aliqui, nescio qui; nonnullus; quidam
□ **∼ ... others** alii ... alii

somebody *n* nescio quis, aliquis

somehow *adv* nescio quo modo

something *n* aliquid *nt*

sometime *adv* aliquando; quandoque
□ **∼ or other** aliquo tempore

sometimes *adv* quandoque, interdum; nonnunquam; (when repeated) modo ... modo

somewhat *adv* paullulum

somewhere *adv* alicubi

son *n* filius, natus *m*
■ **∼-in-law** *n* gener *m*

song *n* cantus *m*; carmen *nt*; (tune) melos *nt*

soon *adv* brevi, postmodo, mox
□ **∼ after** paulo post
□ **as ∼ as** simulatque, simulac
□ **as ∼ as possible** quam primum

sooner *adv* (earlier) citius, temperius, prius ... quam; (rather) libentius; potius
□ **no ∼ said than done** dicto citius

soot *n* fuligo *f*

S

soothe *vt* mulceo, permulceo ②; mitigo, levo ①; delenio ④

soothsayer *n* hariolus, sortilegus *m*; fatidicus, haruspex *m*; augur, vates *m/f*

sooty *adj* fuliginosus

sop *n* offa, offula *f*

sophisticated *adj* lepidus

soporific *adj* soporus, soporifer, somnifer

sorcerer *n* magus, veneficus *m*

sorceress *n* maga, saga, venefica *f*

sorcery *n* fascinatio *f*; veneficium *nt*; magice *f*

sordid *adj* sordidus, turpis, foedus

sore[1] *adj* tener
■ ~**ly** *adv* graviter, vehementer

sore[2] *n* ulcus *nt*

sorrow *n* dolor, maeror, luctus, angor *m*; anxietas *f*

sorrowful *adj* luctuosus, tristis, miser, maestus

sorry *adj*:
□ **I am** ~ aegre fero *ir*; paenitet ② me (alicuius rei)
□ **feel** ~ **for** misereor ② + *gen*

sort[1] *n* (kind) genus *nt*; species *f*; (manner) modus, mos *m*; (quality, of things) nota *f*

sort[2] *vt* ordino ①; dispono, digero ③

sortie *n* eruptio, excursio *f*; excursus *m*

soul *n* anima *f*; (person) homo *m*

sound[1] *adj* (healthy) validus, sanus; (strong) robustus; (entire) integer; (in mind) mentis compos; (true, genuine) verus; (valid) ratus; (of sleep) profundus; altus

sound[2] *n* sonus, sonitus *m*; vox *f*; (of a trumpet) clangor; (noise) strepitus *m*

sound[3] *vt* (a trumpet) cano ③; (try) tento, sollicito ①
■ ~ *vi* sono, persono ①; strepo ③

soup *n* ius *nt*

sour *adj* acidus, acerbus; amarus; fig morosus

source *n* fons *m*; fig origo *f*; principium *nt*

sourness *n* acor *m*; acerbitas; fig morositas *f*

south *n* meridies, auster *m*

southern *adj* australis, meridianus

southwards *adv* in meridiem, meridiem versus

south wind *n* Auster, Notus *m*

sovereign[1] *n* princeps *m/f*, rex, regnator *m*

sovereign[2] *adj* supremus

sovereignty *n* imperium *nt*; dominatio *f*; principatus *m*

sow[1] *n* sus; porca *f*

sow[2] *vt* sero ③; semino ①

space *n* spatium *nt*; area *f*; (of time) intervallum *nt*

spacious *adj* spatiosus, amplus

spade *n* (implement) ligo *m*; pala *f*

Spain *n* Hispania *f*

span *n* (width of the palm) palmus *m*

Spanish *adj* Hispanicus, Hispaniensis

spar[1] *n* (beam) trabs *f*

spar[2] *vi* dimico; fig digladior ①

spare[1] *vt&i* parco ③ + *dat*; parce utor ③ + *abl*

spare[2] *adj* parcus; exilis

sparing *adj* parcus

spark *n* scintilla *f*; igniculus *m*

sparkle *vi* scintillo, corusco, radio, mico ①

sparkling *adj* nitidus, coruscus

sparrow *n* passer *m*

Sparta *n* Sparta, Lacedaemon *f*

Spartan *adj* Laconicus, Spartanus, Lacedaemonius

spasm *n* spasmos *m*

spasmodic *adj* spasticus; fig rarus
■ ~**ally** *adv* raro

spatter *vt* inquino ①; aspergo ③; fig calumnior ①

spatula *n* spatha *f*

spawn[1] *n* ova (piscium) *ntpl*

spawn[2] *vi* ova gigno ③

speak *vi&t* loquor ③; for ①; dico ③
□ ~ **of** dico ③ de + *abl*; (mention) memoro ①
□ ~ **out** eloquor, proloquor ③
□ ~ **to** alloquor ③

speaker *n* orator *m*

spear[1] *n* hasta, lancea *f*; telum, pilum, iaculum *nt*

spear[2] *vt* transfigo ③

special *adj* peculiaris, specialis; praecipuus
■ ~**ly** *adv* specialiter, praecipue, peculiariter, praesertim

speciality *n* proprietas *f*; quod peculiare est

species n species f; genus nt

specific adj specialis; (definite) certus
■ ~**ally** adv specialiter

specify vt enumero ①; describo ③

specimen n exemplum,
documentum, specimen nt

speck n macula f

speckled adj maculosus

spectacle n spectaculum nt;
species f; aspectus m

spectator n spectator m; spectatrix f

spectre n simulacrum, umbra,
visum nt

speculate vt&i meditor ①;
coniecturam facio ③

speculation n contemplatio f

speech n lingua, loquela f; sermo m;
contio, oratio f

speechless adj mutus, elinguis; fig
obstupefactus

speed[1] n celeritas; festinatio f;
impetus m

speed[2] vt propero, festino, adiuvo,
prospero ①
■ ~ vi (hasten) propero, festino ①

speedy adj citus, properus

spell[1] n (charm) incantamentum,
cantamen, carmen nt; cantus m

spell[2] vt&i ordino ① syllabas
litterarum

spelling n orthographia f

spend vt impendo; consumo; (time) ago,
dego, consumo, contero; (exhaust)
effundo ③; (squander) dissipo ①

spendthrift n nepos, prodigus m

spew vt&i vomo ③

sphere n sphaera f; globus m; fig
provincia, area f

spherical adj sphaericus, sphaeralis,
globosus

sphinx n sphinx f

spice[1] n aroma nt; odores mpl

spice[2] vt condio ④

spicy adj aromaticus, conditus,
fragrans, odorus, odorifer

spider n aranea f
□ ~**'s web** araneum nt; casses fpl

spike n clavus m; (point) cuspis; (of corn)
spica f

spiky adj acutus, spinosus

spill vt effundo ③

spin vt neo ②; (draw out) duco, protraho ③;
(as a top) verso ①
■ ~ vi (be turned round) versor ①;
circumferor ir

spinal adj dorsualis

spindle n fusus; (of a wheel) axis m

spine n (vertebrae, thorn) spina f

spinster n innupta f

spiral[1] adj spirae formam habens

spiral[2] n spira f

spire n spira; (tower) turris f

spirit n spiritus m; anima f; fig
ingenium nt; vigor m; (ghost)
simulacrum nt; umbra, imago f; (god)
deus m

spirited adj animosus; alacer

spiritual adj animi, mentis both gen;
incorporalis; ecclesiasticus

spit[1] n veru nt; (of land) lingua f;
▶ **spittle**

spit[2] vt&i (from the mouth) spuo ③;
exscreo ①

spite[1] n livor m; invidia, malevolentia
f; odium nt
■ **in ~ of** use ablative absolute with
perfect participle passive of contemno

spite[2] vt vexo ①

spiteful adj lividus, malevolus,
invidus

spittle n sputum nt; saliva f

splash vt aspergo, respergo ③

splendid adj splendidus; nitidus;
lautus, sumptuosus; magnificus
■ ~**ly** adv splendide; magnifice; laute,
nitide, sumptuose

splendour n splendor, nitor m; fig
magnificentia; lautitia f

splint n (in medicine) ferula f

splinter[1] n assula f

splinter[2] vt confringo ③
■ ~ vi dissilio ④

split[1] vt&i findo; findor ③

split[2] n fissura, rima f

split[3] adj fissilis

spoil[1] n spolium nt; praeda f; exuviae
fpl

spoil[2] vt spolio; praedor; vasto ①;
diripio ③; (mar, etc.) corrumpo; (ruin)
perdo ③; depravo, vitio ①

spoke n radius m

spokesman n orator m

sponge[1] n spongia f

S

sponge² *vt* spongia detergeo ②

spongy *adj* spongiosus

sponsor *n* sponsor, vas, praes *m*

spontaneously *adv* sua sponte, ultro

spool *n* fusus *m*

spoon *n* coclear *nt*

spoonful *n* coclear *nt*

sport¹ *n* ludus, lusus *m*; (hunting) venatio; (mockery) irrisio *f*
◻ **in ~** per iocum

sport² *vi* ludo ③; lascivio ④

sportive *adj* iocosus, ludicer

sportsman *n* athleta *m*

spot¹ *n* macula; (mark) nota; (stain) labes *f*; (place) locus *m*

spot² *vt* (stain) inquino, maculo, commaculo; (speckle) maculis noto ①

spotless *adj* expers maculis; fig purus; integer
■ **~ly** *adv* sine labe

spotted *adj* maculosus, maculis distinctus

spouse *n* coniunx *m/f*; maritus *m*; uxor *f*

spout¹ *n* canalis; (of water) torrens *m*

spout² *vt* eiaculor (in altum); (speeches) declamo ①
■ **~** *vi* prosilio ④; emico ①

sprain¹ *vt* intorqueo ②; convello ③; luxo ①

sprain² *n* luxatura *f*

sprawl *vi* humi prostratus iaceo ②

spray¹ *n* aspergo, spuma *f*; (branch) ramus *m*; virga *f*

spray² *vt* spargo ③

spread *vt* pando, tendo, expando, distendo, extendo; diffundo ③; (make known) divulgo ①
■ **~** *vi* pandor, tendor, distendor, extendor, expandor, diffundor ③; (become known) divulgor; (of a disease, *etc.*) evagor ①; glisco ③

sprig *n* ramulus *m*; virga *f*

sprightly *adj* alacer; hilaris

spring¹ *n* (season) ver *nt*; (leap) saltus *m*; (of water) fons *m*

spring² *adj* vernus

spring³ *vi* (grow from) orior ④; enascor ③; (as rivers, *etc.*) scateo ②; effluo ③; (leap) salio, exsilio ④
◻ **~ a leak** rimas ago ③

springtime *n* vernum tempus *nt*

sprinkle *vt* spargo, aspergo, respergo ③; roro, irroro ①

sprout¹ *n* surculus *m*; germen *nt*
■ **~s** *pl* cauliculi *mpl*

sprout² *vi* pullulo, germino ①

spruce *adj* lautus, nitidus, comptus

spur¹ *n* calcar; fig incitamentum, irritamen, irritamentum *nt*

spur² *vt* equum calcaribus concito ①; equo calcaria subdo ③; fig incito, excito ①

spurious *adj* subditus, suppositus, falsus

spurn *vt* aspernor, repudio ①; sperno ③; proculco ①

spurt *vi* (as liquids) exsilio ④

spy¹ *n* explorator; speculator; emissarius *m*

spy² *vt&i* exploro; speculor ①

squabble¹ *vi* rixor ①

squabble² *n* iurgium *nt*; rixa *f*

squad *n* manipulus *m*

squadron *n* (of cavalry) turma, ala; (of ships) classis *f*

squalid *adj* squalidus, spurcus, sordidus, turpis

squall *n* vociferatio *f*; (sudden storm) procella *f*

squalor *n* squalor, situs *m*; sordes *fpl*; illuvies *f*

squander *vi* dissipo ①; profundo ③

square¹ *adj* quadratus; fig honestus, probus

square² *n* quadratum *nt*; quadra; (tool) norma *f*; mil agmen quadratum *nt*

squash *vt* contero, confringo ③

squat *vi* succumbo, recumbo, subsido ③

squeak *vi* strideo ②

squeamish *adj* fastidiosus

squeeze *vt* comprimo, premo ③; (out) exprimo ③

squint *vi* limis oculis intueor ②

squinting *adj* strabus, limis oculis

squirrel *n* sciurus *m*

squirt *vt* próicio ③
■ **~** *vi* emico ①; exsilio ④

stab¹ *n* vulnus *nt*; ictus *m*; plaga *f*

stab² *vt* fodio ③; perforo ①; perfodio, transfigo ③

stability *n* stabilitas *f*

S

stable[1] *adj* stabilis, solidus

stable[2] *n* stabulum *nt*
- ∼**-boy** *n* stabularius *m*

stack[1] *n* acervus *m*; strues *f*

stack[2] *vt* coacervo ①

stadium *n* (running-track) stadium *nt*

staff *n* baculum *nt*; fustis; (baton) scipio *m*; (officers) legati *mpl*; fig (support) subsidium, fulcimentum *nt*

stag *n* cervus *m*

stage *n* proscaenium; pulpitum; suggestum; theatrum *nt*; fig (field of action) campus *m*; area *f*; (on a journey) iter *nt*

stagger *vi* vacillo, titubo ①
- ∼ *vt* obstupefacio ③

stagnant *adj* stagnans; torpens; piger; iners

stagnate *vi* stagno ①; fig refrigesco ③

stagnation *n* torpor *m*

staid *adj* gravis, severus

stain[1] *n* macula, labes; fig infamia, nota *f*

stain[2] *vt* maculo, commaculo, contamino ①; (dye) tingo, inficio, imbuo ③

stainless *adj* immaculatus, purus; fig integer

stair *n* gradus *m*; scala *f*

staircase *n* scalae *fpl*

stake[1] *n* palus, stipes, vallus *m*; sudis *f*; (wager) depositum *nt*
- □ **be at** ∼ in discrimine sum *ir*

stake[2] *vt* depono ③; pignero, oppignero ①

stale *adj* vetus; obsoletus; tritus

stalk[1] *n* caulis; (of corn) culmus *m*

stalk[2] *vi* incedo, ingredior ③; spatior ①; (in hunting) venor ①

stall *n* stabulum; (seat) subsellium *nt*

stallion *n* (equus) admissarius *m*

stammer[1] *n* haesitatio linguae *f*

stammer[2] *vt&i* balbutio ④; lingua haesito ①

stamp[1] *n* (mark) nota *f*; signum *nt*; (with the foot) vestigium *nt*; (kind) genus *nt*

stamp[2] *vt* imprimo ③; noto ①; (money) cudo ③; (with the feet) supplodo ③; pulso ①
- □ ∼ **out** deleo ②

stand[1] *n* locus *m*; statio; mora *f*; (platform) suggestus *m*; (counter) mensa *f*
- □ **make a** ∼ subsisto ③

stand[2] *vi* sto ①; consisto ③; (remain) maneo ②; (endure) tolero ①; sustineo ②; (against) resisto ③ + *dat*; (aloof) absto ①; (by) asto ①; assisto ③ *both* + *dat*; fig persto ①; (out) exsto ①; promineo ②; (still) consisto, subsisto ③

standard *n* signum, vexillum *nt*; (pattern of practice or behaviour) norma; (yardstick) mensura *f*
- ∼**-bearer** *n* vexillarius, signifer *m*

standing *n* status, ordo *m*; condicio *f*

standstill *n*:
- □ **be at a** ∼ consisto ③; haereo ②

star *n* stella *f*; sidus, astrum; fig lumen *nt*

stare[1] *n* obtutus *m*

stare[2] *vt&i* inhio ①; stupeo ②
- □ ∼ **(at)** intueor ②; haereo ② defixus in aliquo

stark *adj* rigidus

starling *n* sturnus *m*

starry *adj* sidereus, stellans, stellatus, stellifer

start[1] *vi* (in agitation) trepido ①; subsilio ④; contremisco ③; (begin) ordior ④; incipio ③; (set out) proficiscor ③
- ∼ *vt* (game) excito ①; (set on foot) instituo ③; (put in motion) commoveo ②; (begin) incipio ③

start[2] *n* subita trepidatio *f*; tremor *m*; (departing) profectio *f*; (leap) saltus *m*; (beginning) initium, principium *nt*

starting-place *n* (at the races) carceres *mpl*; claustra *ntpl*

startle *vt* territo ①; terreo ②

starvation *n* fames, inedia *f*

starve *vt* fame interficio ③
- ∼ *vi* fame enecor ①

state[1] *n* status; locus *m*; (political) civitas, respublica *f*; (pomp) magnificentia; fig condicio *f*

state[2] *vt* narro; declaro, indico ①; perscribo ③

stately *adj* superbus; splendidus, lautus, augustus

statement *n* affirmatio *f*; testimonium, indicium *nt*

statesman *n* peritus qui in republica versatur *m*

station[1] *n* statio *f*; locus *m*

station[2] *vt* loco ①; dispono ③

stationary *adj* stabilis, loco fixus, immotus

stationer *n* chartarius *m*
  □ ~'s **shop** taberna chartaria *f*

stationery *n* charta *f*; res chartariae *fpl*

statue *n* statua, imago, effigies *f*; signum, simulacrum *nt*

stature *n* statura *f*; habitus *m*

status *n* status *m*

statute *n* statutum; decretum *nt*; lex *f*

staunch[1] *adj* firmus, fidus, constans

staunch[2] *vt* sisto ③; cohibeo ②

stay[1] *vi* maneo ②; commoror; (loiter) cunctor ①
  ■ ~ *vt* detineo ②; sisto ③; (curb) coerceo ②

stay[2] *n* (sojourn) commoratio, mansio; (delay) mora *f*; (prop) fulcrum *nt*; fig subsidium, columen *nt*

steadfast *adj* stabilis, firmus, constans
  ■ ~**ly** *adv* constanter, firmiter

steadiness *n* firmitas, stabilitas, constantia *f*

steady *adj* firmus, stabilis; constans; fig (serious) gravis

steal *vt* furor ①; (away) surripio ③
  ■ ~ *vi* repo, serpo ③; insinuo ①

stealth *n* (act) furtum *nt*
  □ **by** ~ furtim, clam

stealthy *adj* furtivus

steam[1] *n* (aquae) vapor *m*

steam[2] *vt&i* vaporo; fumo ①

steel *n* chalybs *m*; fig ferrum *nt*

steep[1] *adj* praeceps, arduus, praeruptus

steep[2] *vt* madefacio ③; macero ①; imbuo, tingo ③

steeple *n* turris *f*

steeply *adv* in praeceps

steepness *n* acclivitas, declivitas *f*

steer *vt&i* guberno, moderor ①; dirigo, rego ③

stem[1] *n* (of a plant) stirps *f*

stem[2] *vt* obsisto, obnitor *both* + *dat*; reprimo ③

stench *n* fetor, odor *m*

step[1] *n* passus, gradus, gressus *m*
  ■ ~ **by** ~ *adv* gradatim, sensim, pedetentim

step[2] *vi* gradior ③

stepbrother *n* (of father's side) vitrici filius; (of mother's side) novercae filius *m*

stepdaughter *n* privigna *f*

stepfather *n* vitricus *m*

stepmother *n* noverca *f*

stepson *n* privignus *m*

sterile *adj* sterilis, infecundus

sterility *n* sterilitas *f*

stern[1] *adj* durus, severus; torvus

stern[2] *n* puppis (navis) *f*

stethoscope *n* stethoscopium *nt*

steward *n* administrator, procurator; vilicus *m*

stick[1] *n* baculus, scipio, fustis *m*; baculum *nt*

stick[2] *vt* affigo ③
  ■ ~ *vi* haereo; adhaereo ②
  □ ~ **out** promineo ②

sticky *adj* lentus, tenax

stiff *adj* rigidus; fig severus; frigidus

stiffen *vt* rigidum facio ③
  ■ ~ *vi* rigesco, derigesco ③

stiffness *n* rigor *m*; fig pertinacia *f*; rigor *m*

stifle *vt* suffoco; strangulo ①; fig opprimo ③

stigma *n* nota, ignominia *f*

still[1] *adj* quietus, immotus, tacitus

still[2] *adv* nihilominus; (yet) adhuc; (however) tamen, attamen; (even now) etiam nunc; (always) semper

stillness *n* silentium *nt*; quies *f*

stilts *npl* grallae *fpl*

stimulant *n* irritamentum, irritamen *nt*; stimulus *m*

stimulate *vt* stimulo, exstimulo, excito ①

stimulus *n* ▶ **stimulant**

sting[1] *n* (of insects and plants) aculeus *m*; spiculum *nt*; (wound) ictus, morsus *m*; fig (of conscience) angor conscientiae *m*

sting[2] *vt* pungo ③; mordeo ②; (as nettles) uro ③; fig excrucio ①

stingy *adj* sordidus, parcus

stink[1] *vi* feteo, male oleo ②

stink[2] *n* fetor *m*

stint *vt* moderor ①; coerceo ②; circumscribo, parco ③ + *dat*

stipulate *vt* paciscor ③; stipulor ①

stipulation *n* stipulatio; condicio *f*; pactum *nt*

stir[1] *n* tumultus, motus *m*; turba *f*

stir² vt (arouse) excito ①; (move) moveo ②
■ ~ vi me moveo ②

stitch vt suo ③

stoat n mustela f

stock¹ n (of a tree) caudex, truncus,
stipes m; (handle) lignum nt; (race) genus
nt; (of goods) copia, vis f; (cattle) pecus nt;
stirps f; (of cattle) res pecuaria f

stock² vt instruo ③; orno, suppedito ①

stockade n vallum nt

stock-still adj immotus, immobilis

stoic adj (also **stoical**) stoicus; fig
patiens

stoicism n Stoica disciplina f; fig
patientia

stolen adj furtivus; clandestinus
□ ~ **goods** furta ntpl

stomach n stomachus, venter,
ventriculus; (appetite) appetitus m
■ ~ vt (put up with) fero ③; tolero ①

stone¹ n lapis m; saxum nt; med
calculus; (gem) gemma f; (of fruit)
nucleus m
□ **leave no ~ unturned** nihil reliqui
facio ③

stone² vt lapido ①

stone³ adj lapideus, saxeus

stony adj (full of stones) lapidosus; saxeus,
saxosus

stool n scabellum, scamnum nt; sella f

stoop vi proclino ①; fig me summitto ③

stop¹ vt prohibeo ②; sisto ③; moror,
tardo, retardo ①
■ ~ vi subsisto; (cease) desisto; desino,
omitto ③; (remain) maneo ②; (sojourn)
commoror ①
□ ~ **up** obturo ①; intercludo ③

stop² n (delay) mora f; impedimentum
nt; pausa f; (end) finis m/f

stoppage n obstructio f

stopper n obturamentum nt

store¹ n copia f; apparatus; (provisions)
commeatus m

store² vt coacervo ①; condo; (with)
instruo ③

storehouse n cella f; promptuarium;
(granary) horreum nt

storey n (of a house) tabulatum nt

stork n ciconia f

storm¹ n procella, tempestas; mil
expugnatio f

storm² vt expugno ①
■ ~ vi saevio, desaevio ④

stormy adj turbidus; procellosus; fig
tumultuosus

story n (tale) narratio; fabula; (history)
historia f; (lie) mendacium nt

storyteller n narrator; (liar) mendax m

stout adj robustus; firmus; validus; (fat)
pinguis; (brave) fortis

stove n fornax f; caminus m

stow vt condo, recondo, repono ③

straddle vi varico ①

straggle vi palor, vagor ①

straggler n vagus; erro m

straight adj rectus, directus
■ ~ adv (directly) recte, recta
□ ~ **away** statim, confestim,
protinus

straighten vt rectum facio ③;
corrigo ③

straightforward adj simplex,
apertus, directus, sincerus

strain¹ vt (stretch) contendo ③; (a joint)
luxo ①; (filter) percolo ①; (press out)
exprimo ③
■ ~ vi percolor ①; enitor ③

strain² n contentio; vis; (nervorum)
intentio f; (effort) conamen nt; nisus m

strainer n colum nt

strait n fretum nt; fig difficultas f;
angustiae fpl

strand n (shore) litus nt; (thread) filum nt

strange adj peregrinus; fig inusitatus;
rarus; novus; mirus; mirificus

stranger n advena m/f; hospes;
peregrinus m

strangle vt strangulo, suffoco ①

strangulation n strangulatio,
suffocatio f; strangulatus m

strap n lorum nt; struppus m;
amentum nt

strapping adj robustus

stratagem n insidiae fpl; fig dolus m

strategy n ars imperatoria f

straw¹ n stramentum, stramen nt;
stipula f

straw² adj stramineus

strawberry n fragum nt

stray¹ vi erro, aberro, palor, vagor ①

stray² adj vagus; (sporadic) rarus

streak¹ n linea, virga f

streak² vt (mark) distinguo ③

streaky adj virgatus

S

stream[1] *n* flumen *nt*; amnis *m*

stream[2] *vi* fluo, curro, effundor ③; mano ①

street *n* via; (with houses) platea *f*; vicus *m*

strength *n* robur *nt*; firmitas; (power) potentia, potestas *f*; vires *fpl*

strengthen *vt* roboro, confirmo ①; munio ④

strenuous *adj* strenuus; fortis; acer
■ ~**ly** *adv* strenue, fortiter, acriter

stress *n* (anxiety) angor *m*; (chief point) summa *f*; caput *nt*; (emphasis) vis *f*; pondus *nt*

stretch[1] *vt* tendo; produco, extendo; distendo ③
■ ~ *vi* extendo; producor; distendor; (of country) patesco ③
□ ~ **out** porrigo ③; (oneself) pandiculor ①

stretch[2] *n* (effort) intentio, contentio *f*; (expanse) spatium *nt*; tractus *m*

stretcher *n* lecticula *f*

strew *vt* spargo, conspergo, sterno, insterno ③

stricken *adj* vulneratus, afflictus

strict *adj* (precise) accuratus, exactus; (severe) rigidus, severus
■ ~**ly** *adv* accurate; rigide; severe

strictness *n* severitas *f*; rigor *m*

stride[1] *vi* varico ①

stride[2] *n* gradus *m*; passus *m*
□ **make** ~**s** fig proficio ③

strife *n* iurgium *nt*; lis; pugna; discordia, rixa *f*

strike *vt* ferio ④; pulso ①; percutio ③; (cudgel) verbero ①; (stamp) cudo ③; (the mind) subeo *ir*; succurro ③ + *dat*
□ **be struck** fig commoveor ②

string[1] *n* linea *f*; filum *nt*; (for a bow; sinew) nervus *m*; (for musical instruments) chorda; fig series *f*

string[2] *vt* persero ③

stringent *adj* severus

strip[1] *vt* (off) spolio; nudo; denudo ①; (clothes) exuo ③; (the rind, *etc.*) decortico ①

strip[2] *n* particula, lacinia *f*; (of paper) schida *f*

stripe *n* (mark of a blow) vibex *f*; (blow) ictus *m*; verbera *ntpl*; (for garments) virga *f*
■ **purple** ~ *n* clavus *m*

striped *adj* virgatus

strive *vi* nitor, enitor ③; molior ④; conor ①; contendo ③; (after, for) annitor ③; sector ①; (against) obnitor ③ + *dat*

stroke[1] *n* ictus *m*; plaga *f*; (of an oar) pulsus *m*

stroke[2] *vt* mulceo, permulceo ②

stroll[1] *vi* (about) perambulo, obambulo, spatior ①

stroll[2] *n* ambulatio *f*

strong *adj* robustus; fortis; firmus, valens; (powerful) potens, validus; fig vehemens; gravis
■ ~**ly** *adv* robuste; valide; firme; fortiter; vehementer; graviter

stronghold *n* arx *f*; castellum *nt*

structure *n* (construction) structura *f*; (building) aedificium *nt*

struggle[1] *vi* contendo ③; certo, luctor ①; nitor, obnitor ③; (fight) pugno ①

struggle[2] *n* certamen *nt*; pugna; luctatio *f*; luctamen *nt*

strut *vi* spatior ①

stubble *n* stipula *f*; culmus *m*

stubborn *adj* obstinatus, pervicax, contumax
■ ~**ly** *adv* pervicaciter, obstinate, contumaciter

stubbornness *n* pervicacia, contumacia *f*

stud *n* bulla *f*; clavus *m*

student *n* litterarum studiosus *m*

studious *adj* diligens, industrius, navus

study *n* studium; (room) umbraculum *nt*; bibliotheca *f*
■ ~ *vt&i* studeo ② + *dat*, exploro; meditor ①

stuff[1] *n* (material) materia *f*; (furniture, *etc.*) supellex *f*; (cloth) pannus *m*; (things) res *fpl*; (woven ~) textile *nt*

stuff[2] *vt* farcio ④; sagino ①; (fill) expleo, repleo ②

stuffing *n* (in cookery) fartum; (for chairs, *etc.*) tomentum *nt*

stumble[1] *vi* offendo ③; (falter) haesito ①; (upon) incido ③ in + *acc*

stumble[2] *n* offensio *f*

stumbling-block *n* offensio *f*

stump *n* truncus, caudex, stipes *m*

stun *vt* obstupefacio, obtundo, stupefacio ③; perturbo ①; sopio ④

stunt *vt* (hinder growth) incrementum (alicuius, *etc.*) impedio ④

stupefy *vt* obstupefacio ③; terreo ②; perturbo; hebeto ①; sopio ④

stupid *adj* stupidus, fatuus, stultus
■ ∼**ly** *adv* stulte

stupidity *n* stupiditas, fatuitas, stultitia *f*

stupor *n* stupor; torpor *m*

sturdiness *n* firmitas *f*; robur *nt*

sturdy *adj* robustus, validus, firmus

stutter *vi* balbutio ④

sty *n* hara *f*

style *n* sermo; modus *m*; genus *nt*

stylish *adj* nitidus, lautus

suave *adj* blandus

suavity *n* suavitas, dulcedo *f*; blanditia *f*

subdue *vt* subicio, subigo, vinco ③; domo ①

subject[1] *adj* subiectus; (liable to) obnoxius + *dat*

subject[2] *n* (member of population) subditus; civis *m*; (theme) materia *f*; argumentum *nt*

subject[3] *vt* subicio, subigo ③

subjection *n* servitus; patientia *f*

subjugate *vt* subigo ③; domo ①

sublime *adj* altus, celsus; fig excelsus, sublimis

submerge *vt&i* summergo ③; inundo ①

submersion *n* summersio *f*

submission *n* obsequium *nt*

submissive *adj* submissus; supplex
■ ∼**ly** *adv* summisse, suppliciter

submit *vt* summitto, subicio
■ ∼ *vi* (condescend) descendo ③; (endure) subeo *ir*; (yield) cedo ③

subordinate[1] *vt* posthabeo ②

subordinate[2] *adj & n* inferior *m*

subscribe *vt* subscribo ③; subsigno ①; assentior ④; (give money) pecuniam do ①

subscriber *n* subscriptor *m*

subscription *n* (act) subscriptio, collecta *f*

subsequent *adj* sequens, posterior
■ ∼**ly** *adv* deinde, postea

subservient *adj* summissus

subside *vi* sido, consido, resido, subsido ③

subsidiary *adj* subsidiarius

subsidize *vt* pecunias suppedito ①

subsidy *n* collatio *f*; subsidium *nt*

subsistence *n* victus *m*; vita *f*

substance *n* substantia; materia, res *f*; (wealth) opes *fpl*

substantial *adj* solidus, firmus; (real) verus; (chief) praecipuus; (rich) opulentus
■ ∼**ly** *adv* solide; (truly) vere; (by nature) natura

substantiate *vt* confirmo ①; ratum facio ③

substitute[1] *n* vicarius *m*

substitute[2] *vt* substituo, suppono ③

substitution *n* substitutio *f*

subterfuge *n* tergiversatio *f*; effugium *nt*; praetextus *m*

subtle *adj* subtilis; acutus, vafer

subtlety *n* subtilitas; tenuitas, astutia *f*; acumen *nt*

subtract *vt* subtraho, adimo, aufero ③

suburb *n* suburbium *nt*

suburban *adj* suburbanus

subversion *n* excidium *nt*

subvert *vt* everto, subverto ③

succeed *vi* succedo, sequor ③; fig succedo ③; prospere evenio ④
□ ∼ **to** (take over) excipio ③

success *n* bonus *or* felix exitus, successus *m*

successful *adj* fortunatus, prosperus, faustus, felix
■ ∼**ly** *adv* fortunate, prospere, fauste, feliciter

succession *n* series, successio *f*

successive *adj* continuus
■ ∼**ly** *adv* in ordine; continenter; deinceps

successor *n* successor *m*

succinct *adj* succinctus; brevis, concisus
■ ∼**ly** *adv* succincte, brevi

succulent *adj* sucosus, suculentus

succumb *vi* succumbo, cado ③

such *adj* talis; eius modi
■ ∼ *adv* sic, adeo, tam
□ ∼ **as** qualis

suck *vt* sugo ③; (in, up) sorbeo ②; exsugo ③
■ ∼ *vi* ubera duco ③

suckle *vt* ubera do, do mammam ①
both + *dat*

suction *n* suctus *m*

S

sudden *adj* subitus, repentinus, inexspectatus; inopinatus, inopinus, necopinus
■ ~**ly** *adv* subito, repente

sue *vt* in ius voco ①
■ ~ *vi* oro, precor, flagito ①; posco, peto ③

suet *n* sebum *nt*; adeps *m/f*

suffer *vt* patior ③, fero *ir*; tolero ①; sustineo ②
■ ~ *vi* laboro ①

suffering *n* perpessio, toleratio *f*; (labours) labores *mpl*

suffice *vi* sufficio ③; satis sum *ir*

sufficiency *n* satias *f*

sufficient *adj* sufficiens
■ ~**ly** *adv* satis, affatim

suffocate *vt* suffoco ①

suffocation *n* suffocatio *f*

suffrage *n* suffragium *nt*

sugar *n* saccharon *nt*

suggest *vt* subicio, suggero ③; moneo ②

suggestion *n* admonitio *f*

suicide *n* mors voluntaria *f*
□ **commit** ~ mihi mortem conscisco ③

suit[1] *n* (lawsuit) lis, causa *f*; (of clothes) vestimenta *ntpl*, synthesis *f*

suit[2] *vt* accommodo, apto ①
■ ~ *vi* convenio ④; congruo ③ *both* + *dat*

suitable *adj* aptus, idoneus, opportunus, congruus

suite *n* (of rooms) series *f*

suitor *n* (suppliant) supplex *m/f*; (wooer) procus *m*

sulky *adv* morosus

sullen *adj* taetricus; morosus

sullenness *n* morositas *f*

sulphur *n* sulpur *nt*

sultry *adj* aestuosus, torridus, fervidus

sum[1] *n* (total) summa; (money) pecunia *f*; fig caput *nt*

sum[2] *vt* (up) consummo ①; fig breviter repeto ③

summary[1] *n* epitome *f*; summarium *nt*

summary[2] *adj* brevis

summer *n* aestas *f*
■ ~**-house** *n* umbraculum *nt*
■ **of** ~ *adj* aestivus

summit *n* culmen, cacumen *nt*; apex, vertex *m*; fastigium *nt*

summon *vt* cito; (challenge) provoco ①; (send for) accio ④; accesso ③; (up) excito ①; (animum) erigo ③

summons *n* accitus *m*; evocatio *f*

sumptuous *adj* sumptuosus; magnificus, lautus

sun[1] *n* sol *m*

sun[2] *vt* insolo ①

sunburnt *adj* adustus

sundial *n* solarium *nt*

sundry *adj* diversus, varius

sunny *adj* apricus

sunrise *n* solis ortus *m*

sunset *n* solis occasus *m*

sunshine *n* sol *m*; apricitas *f*

superb *adj* magnificus, speciosus, splendidus

supercilious *adj* arrogans, superbus, fastidiosus
■ ~**ly** *adv* superbe, arroganter, fastidiose

superficial *adj* levis, indoctus
■ ~**ly** *adv* leviter

superfluous *adj* supervacaneus; superfluus; supervacuus

superintend *vt* praesum *ir* + *dat*; administro ①

superintendent *n* praefectus; curator *m*

superior[1] *adj* superior, melior

superior[2] *n* praepositus *m*

superiority *n* praestantia *f*

superlative *adj* eximius

supersede *vt* aboleo ②; in locum (alicuius) succedo ③

superstition *n* superstitio *f*

superstitious *adj* superstitiosus
■ ~**ly** *adv* superstitiose

supervise *vt* curo, procuro ①

supervision *n* cura, curatio *f*

supervisor *n* curator *m*

supper *n* cena *f*

supplant *vt* supplanto ①; per dolum deicio, praeverto ③

supple *adj* flexibilis, flexilis; mollis

supplement *n* supplementum *nt*; appendix *f*

suppleness *n* mollitia *f*

suppliant *n* supplex *m/f*

s

supplicate *vt* supplico, obsecro ①

supplication *n* obsecratio *f*; preces *fpl*

supply¹ *n* supplementum *nt*; copia, vis *f*; (supplies) commeatus *m*

supply² *vt* suppleo; praebeo ②; suppedito ①

support¹ *n* (prop) fulcrum *nt*; fig subsidium *nt*; (favour) gratia *f*; favor *m*

support² *vt* sustineo ②; (prop) fulcio ④; (maintain) alo ③; (aid) adiuvo ①; (favour) faveo ② + *dat*

supporter *n* adiutor; fautor *m*

suppose *vt* (imagine) opinor, puto ①; credo ③; reor ②; arbitror ①

supposition *n* opinio, coniectura *f*

suppress *vt* supprimo, comprimo ③; aboleo, coerceo ②

suppurate *vi* suppuro ①

supremacy *n* principatus *m*; imperium *nt*

supreme *adj* supremus, summus
■ **~ly** *adv* prae omnibus aliis, summe

sure *adj* certus; (reliable) fidus; (safe) tutus

surely *adv* certe; tuto; firme; profecto; (in questions) nonne
□ **~ not?** num

surf *n* fluctus *m*; unda *f*

surface *n* superficies *f*; aequor *nt*

surfeit *n* satietas *f*; taedium, fastidium *nt*

surge¹ *n* fluctus, aestus *m*

surge² *vi* tumesco ③; aestuo ①

surgeon *n* chirurgus *m*

surgery *n* chirurgia *f*

surgical *adj* chirurgicus

surly *adj* morosus, difficilis

surmise¹ *n* coniectura *f*

surmise² *vt* coniecto ①; conicio ③; suspicor ①

surmount *vt* supero ①; vinco ③

surname *n* cognomen *nt*

surpass *vt* supero ①; excedo, excello ③

surplus *n* reliquum, residuum *nt*

surprise¹ *n* admiratio *f*; (sudden attack) repens adventus hostium *m*

surprise² *vt* deprehendo ③

surprising *adj* mirus, mirabilis; inexpectatus; inopinatus
■ **~ly** *adv* mirandum in modum

surrender¹ *n* mil deditio; (law) cessio *f*

surrender² *vt* cedo; dedo; trado ③
■ **~** *vi* me dedo ③

surreptitious *adj* furtivus, clandestinus
□ **~ly** clam, furtim

surround *vt* circumdo; circumsto ①; cingo ③; circumvallo ①

survey¹ *n* (act) inspectio; contemplatio; (measuring) mensura *f*

survey² *vt* inspicio ③; contemplor ①; (measure land) permetior ④

surveyor *n* mensor, metator, decempedator *m*

survive *vi* superstes sum, supersum *ir*; supero ①

survivor *n* superstes *m/f*

susceptible *adj* mollis; (capable) capax

suspect *vt* suspicor ①

suspend *vt* suspendo ③; fig intermitto ③; differo *ir*; abrogo ①

suspense *n* dubitatio *f*
□ **in ~** incertus, dubius

suspicion *n* suspicio *f*

suspicious *adj* suspicax; suspiciosus; (suspected) suspectus; suspiciosus

sustain *vt* (prop) sustineo ②; sustento ①; fulcio ④; (bear, *etc.*) tolero ①; fero *ir*; (defend) defendo ③; (strengthen) corroboro ①

sustenance *n* victus *m*

swallow¹ *n* hirundo *f*

swallow² *vt* glutio ④; voro; devoro ①; haurio ④

swamp¹ *n* palus *f*

swamp² *vt* demergo ③; inundo ①

swampy *adj* paludosus, palustris, uliginosus

swan *n* cycnus *m*; olor *m*

swarm¹ *n* (of bees) examen *nt*; fig turba *f*

swarm² *vi* examino ①; confluo ③

swarthy *adj* fuscus, subniger

sway¹ *n* dicio *f*; imperium *nt*; (motion) aestus *m*

sway² *vt* rego ③
■ **~** *vi* aestuo, titubo ①

swear *vi* iuro; (curse) exsecror ①

sweat¹ *n* sudor *m*

sweat² *vi* sudo ①

sweep¹ *n* ambitus; iactus *m*

sweep² *vt* (brush, *etc.*) verro ③; purgo ①; (pass quickly over) percurro; verro ③

S

sweet *adj* dulcis, suavis; blandus; iucundus

sweeten *vt* dulcem facio *or* reddo ③; fig lenio ④; mulceo ②

sweetheart *n* deliciae *fpl*; amica *f*

sweetness *n* dulcedo; suavitas *f*

swell¹ *vt* inflo ①; tumefacio ③
■ ~ *vi* tumeo, turgeo ②; intumesco ③

swell² *n* aestus *m*

swelling *n* tumor *m*

swerve *vi* aberro, vagor; declino ①

swift *adj* celer, velox, rapidus, citus
■ ~**ly** *adv* celeriter, velociter, cito

swiftness *n* celeritas, velocitas *f*

swill *vt* haurio ④; ingurgito ①

swim *vi* nato, no; fluito ①; madeo ②

swimmer *n* natator *m*

swimming *n* natatio *f*

swindle *vt* fraudo ①; circumvenio ④

swindler *n* fraudator *m*

swing¹ *n* oscillatio *f*; impetus *m*

swing² *vt* huc illuc iacto, vibro ①
■ ~ *vi* fluito ①; pendeo ②; huc illuc iactor ①

swivel *n* verticula *f*

swoop *n* impulsus, impetus *m*

sword *n* ensis, gladius *m*; ferrum *nt*

sycamore *n* sycamorus *f*

sycophant *n* sycophanta, adulator *m*

syllable *n* syllaba *f*

symbol *n* signum, symbolum *nt*

symmetrical *adj* symmetrus, concinnus

symmetry *n* symmetria, concinnitas *f*

sympathetic *adj* (gentle) lenis, mitis, humanus
■ ~**ally** *adv* humane

sympathize *vi* (pity) misereor ② + *gen*

sympathy *n* (agreement) consensus *m*; (fellow-feeling) sympathia *f*

symphony *n* symphonia *f*; concentus *m*

symptom *n* signum, indicium *nt*

synagogue *n* synagoga *f*

synonym *n* vocabulum idem declarans, synonymum *nt*

synonymous *adj* idem declarans

syntax *n* syntaxis *f*; constructio verborum *f*

synthesis *n* synthesis *f*

syringe *n* sipho *m*

system *n* systema *nt*; ratio, disciplina *f*

systematic *adj* ad certam disciplinam redactus, ordinatus

systematically *adv* ordinate

Tt

table *n* mensa *f*; (register) index *m*

tablecloth *n* mantele *nt*

tablet *n* tabula, tabella, tessera *f*

tacit *adj* tacitus
■ ~**ly** *adv* tacite

taciturn *adj* taciturnus

taciturnity *n* taciturnitas *f*

tack¹ *n* clavulus *m*

tack² *vt* assuo; affigo ③

tackle¹ *vt* tracto ①

tackle² *n* armamenta, arma *ntpl*

tact *n* dexteritas; prudentia *f*

tactful *adj* dexter

tactics *n* ars militaris, ratio *f*

tactless *adj* ineptus, insulsus, molestus

tadpole *n* ranunculus *m*; ranula *f*

tag *n* ligula *f*

tail *n* cauda *f*; (of a comet) crinis *m*

tailor *n* vestitor *m*

taint¹ *vt* inficio ③; contamino ①; polluo; fig corrumpo ③

taint² *n* contagio *f*; vitium *nt*; contactus *m*

take *vt* capio; sumo; accipio, recipio; rapio ③; (consider, *etc.*) interpretor ①; accipio ③
■ ~ *vi* (be successful) efficax sum *ir*; bene succedo; (fire) accendor ③
□ ~ **after** similis sum *ir* + *gen*

☐ ~ **away** adimo ③; aufero *ir*, tollo ③

☐ ~ **back** recipio ③

☐ ~ **down** demo ③

☐ ~ **for** habeo ②; puto ①

☐ ~ **in** percipio, intellego ③; fig decipio ③

☐ ~ **off** exuo, demo ③; fig imitor ①

☐ ~ **up** sumo ③

tale *n* narratio; fabula *f*

☐ ~-**bearer** famigerator *m*; delator *m*

talent *n* fig ingenium *nt*; facultas *f*

talented *adj* ingeniosus

talk[1] *n* sermo *m*; colloquium *nt*; (idle ~) fabulae *fpl*; (rumour) rumor *m*; fama *f*

talk[2] *vi* loquor, colloquor ③; confabulor ①

talkative *adj* loquax, garrulus

tall *adj* altus, celsus, procerus

tallness *n* proceritas; altitudo *f*

tally[1] *n* tessera *f*

tally[2] *vi* (agree) convenio ④

talon *n* unguis *m*; ungula *f*

tambourine *n* tympanum *nt*

tame[1] *adj* cicur; mansuefactus, mansuetus; fig frigidus, insulsus

tame[2] *vt* perdomo, domo ①; mansuefacio, subigo ③

tangible *adj* tractilis

tangle *vt* ▶ **entangle**

tangled *adj* irreligatus, incomptus

tank *n* cisterna; piscina *f*; lacus *m*

tankard *n* cantharus *m*

tantalize *vt* crucio ①

tantamount *adj* tantusdem, par

tap[1] *n* (blow) ictus *m*; (pipe) fistula *f*

tap[2] *vt* leviter pulso ①; (wine, *etc.*) relino ③

tape *n* taenia *f*

taper[1] *n* cereus *m*; funale *nt*

taper[2] *vt&i* fastigo; fastigor ①

tapestry *n* aulaeum, tapete *nt*

tapeworm *n* taenia *f*

tar[1] *n* pix *f*

tar[2] *vt* pice oblino ③

tardy *adj* tardus, lentus

target *n* parma *f*; (mark to aim at) scopus *m*

tarnish *vt* infusco; hebeto; fig obscuro ①

■ ~ *vi* hebesco ③

tart[1] *n* scriblita *f*; crustulum *nt*; (girl) scortillum *nt*

tart[2] *adj* acidus; acerbus; fig mordax

■ ~**ly** *adv* acerbe; mordaciter

task *n* pensum, opus *nt*; labor *m*

tassel *n* cirrus *m*

taste[1] *n* (sense) gustatus; (flavour) gustus, sapor *m*; fig iudicium; palatum *nt*

taste[2] *vt* gusto, degusto ①

■ ~ *vi* sapio ③

tasteful *adj* elegans

■ ~**ly** *adv* fig eleganter

tasteless *adj* insulsus; inelegans

■ ~**ly** *adv* ineleganter, insulse

tasty *adj* sapidus, conditus

tatters *n* panni *mpl*

taunt[1] *n* convicium *nt*; contumelia *f*

taunt[2] *vt* exprobro ①

tavern *n* taberna, caupona *f*

tawdry *adj* speciosus

tawny *adj* fuscus, fulvus, ravus, flavus

tax[1] *n* vectigal; tributum, stipendium *nt*

tax[2] *vt* (financially) vectigal impono ③

taxable *adj* vectigali solvendo obnoxius

tax-collector *n* exactor *m*

teach *vt* doceo, perdoceo ②; instruo ③; erudio ④

teacher *n* magister, praeceptor *m*

teaching *n* doctrina, eruditio *f*

team *n* protelum *nt*; iugales *mpl*

tear[1] *n* lacrima; fig gutta *f*; (rent) scissura *f*

tear[2] *vt* scindo ③; (in pieces) lacero, dilacero, lanio, dilanio ①

■ ~ *vi* ▶ **rush**

tear[3] *n* scissura *f*

tease *vt* vexo, crucio ①

technical *adj* artificialis; (word) arti proprium (verbum)

tedious *adj* tardus, lentus; longus; diuturnus, molestus

■ ~**ly** *adv* tarde; moleste

tedium *n* taedium *nt*; molestia *f*

teem *vi* scateo ②; redundo; abundo ①

teeming *adj* gravidus; fig frequens

tell *vt* (say) dico ③; (relate) narro ①; (inform) aliquem certiorem facio ③; (order) iubeo ③

temper[1] *vt* tempero ①; diluo ③; commisceo ②; (mitigate) mitigo ①; remitto ③

temper[2] *n* temperatio *f*; animus *m*; ingenium *nt*; (anger) iracundia *f*

temperament *n* temperamentum *nt*

temperate *adj* temperatus; sobrius; abstinens
 ■ ~**ly** *adv* temperanter, sobrie

temperature *n* temperatura, temperies *f*

temple *n* templum, fanum *nt*; aedes *f*; (of the head) tempora *ntpl*

temporary *adj* temporarius, ad tempus

tempt *vt* tento, sollicito ⟨1⟩; allicio ⟨3⟩

temptation *n* sollicitatio; illecebra *f*

tempter *n* tentator *m*

tempting *adj* illecebrosus

ten *adj* decem
 □ ~ **times** decies

tenacious *adj* tenax
 ■ ~**ly** *adv* tenaciter

tenacity *n* tenacitas *f*

tenant *n* conductor; inquilinus *m*

tend *vt* curo ⟨1⟩
 ■ ~ *vi* tendo ⟨3⟩; specto ⟨1⟩

tendency *n* inclinatio *f*
 □ **having a ~ to** proclivis ad + *acc*

tender¹ *adj* tener, mollis; fig misericors
 ■ ~**ly** *adv* tenere; molliter; misericorditer

tender² *vt* offero *ir*

tenderness *n* teneritas, mollitia; misericordia, bonitas *f*

tendon *n* nervus *m*

tendril *n* (of a vine) pampinus *m/f*; (of climbing plants) clavicula *f*

tenement *n* insula *f*

tenet *n* dogma, institutum *nt*; doctrina *f*

tense *adj* tensus, rigidus

tension *n* intentio *f*

tent *n* tentorium, tabernaculum *nt*
 □ **general's ~** praetorium *nt*

tenterhook *n*:
 ■ **on ~s** *adj* suspensus

tenth *adj* decimus
 ■ ~ *n* decima pars *f*

tenure *n* possessio *f*

tepid *adj* tepidus

term¹ *n* (word) verbum *nt*; (limit) terminus *m*; (period) spatium *nt*; (condition) condicio, lex *f*

term² *vt* dico ⟨3⟩; appello, voco ⟨1⟩

terminate *vt* termino ⟨1⟩; finio ⟨4⟩; concludo ⟨3⟩
 ■ ~ *vi* terminor ⟨1⟩; finem habeo ⟨2⟩

termination *n* terminatio *f*; finis *m/f*; exitus *m*

terrace *n* solarium *nt*

terrible *adj* terribilis, horribilis, dirus

terribly *adv* horrendum in modum

terrific *adj* terrificus, terribilis, formidabilis

terrify *vt* terreo, perterreo ⟨2⟩; territo ⟨1⟩

territory *n* regio; terra *f*; fines *mpl*; (around a town) territorium *nt*

terror *n* terror, metus, pavor *m*; formido *f*

terse *adj* (neat, polished) tersus; brevis; pressus

test¹ *n* (trial) tentamentum, tentamen, periculum *nt*

test² *vt* tento, exploro ⟨1⟩; experior ⟨4⟩; periclitor ⟨1⟩

testify *vt* testificor, testor ⟨1⟩

testimonial *n* litterae testimoniales *fpl*

testimony *n* testimonium, indicium *nt*

testy *adj* stomachosus, morosus

tetanus *n* tetanus *m*

tether¹ *n* retinaculum *nt*

tether² *vt* religo ⟨1⟩

text *n* verba scriptoris *ntpl*; contextus *m*

textile *adj* textilis

texture *n* textum *nt*; textura *f*

than *conj* quam

thank *vt* gratias ago ⟨3⟩ + *dat*
 □ ~ **you** tibi gratias ago

thankful *adj* gratus

thankless *adj* ingratus

thanks *n* gratia *f*; grates *fpl*

that¹ *adj* & *pn* ille, is, iste; (who, which) qui

that² *conj* ut; (after verbs of fearing) ne

thatch¹ *n* stramentum *nt*

thatch² *vt* stramento tego ⟨3⟩

thaw *vt* solvo, dissolvo, liquefacio ⟨3⟩
 ■ ~ *vi* regelo ⟨1⟩; solvor, liquesco ⟨3⟩

theatre *n* theatrum *nt*; scaena, cavea *f*

theatrical *adj* theatralis; scaenicus

theft *n* furtum *nt*

their *adj* (and **theirs** *pn*) suus; eorum, earum; illorum, illarum

theme *n* argumentum *nt*; materies *f*

themselves *pn* se, sese
□ **they** ~ lli ipsi, illae ipsae
□ **of** ~ sui

then *adv* (at that time) tum, tunc; (after that) deinde, inde; (therefore) igitur
□ **now and** ~ nonnunquam, interdum, aliquando

theologian *n* theologus *m*

theology *n* theologia *f*

theorem *n* theorema *nt*

theoretical *adj* theoreticus

theory *n* theoria, ratio, ars *f*

there *adv* ibi, illic; (thither) illo, illac, illuc
□ ~**abouts** circiter
□ ~**after** exinde
□ ~**by** inde
□ ~**fore** igitur, idcirco; propterea
□ ~**upon** exinde; deinde; tum

thesis *n* thesis *f*; propositum *nt*

they *pn* ii, eae; illi, illae

thick *adj* densus, spissus; (gross) crassus; (fat) pinguis; (muddy) turbidus, lutosus; (crowded) frequens; creber

thicken *vt* denso; condenso; spisso ①
■ ~ *vi* densor ①; spissor ③

thicket *n* dumetum *nt*; virgulta *ntpl*

thickness *n* densitas; crassitudo *f*

thief *n* fur *m*

thieve *vt* furor ①

thigh *n* femur *nt*

thin¹ *adj* tenuis; angustus; rarus; (lean) macer

thin² *vt* tenuo, attenuo, extenuo ①

thing *n* res *f*; (affair) negotium *nt*
■ ~**s** *pl* bona *ntpl*

think *vt&i* cogito ①; (imagine, believe, etc.) puto ①; credo ③; opinor ①; reor ②; arbitror ①

thinker *n* philosophus *m*

thinness *n* tenuitas; raritas *f*

third *adj* tertius
■ ~ *n* tertia pars *f*
■ ~**ly** *adv* tertio

thirst *n* sitis *f*

thirsty *adj* sitiens; aridus, siccus; bibulus
□ **be** ~ sitio ④

thirteen *adj* tredecim

thirteenth *adj* tertius decimus

thirtieth *adj* tricesimus

thirty *adj* triginta

this *adj & pn* hic

thistle *n* carduus *m*

thong *n* lorum, amentum *nt*

thorn *n* spina *f*; aculeus *m*

thorny *adj* spinosus; spineus; fig difficilis

thorough *adj* germanus, perfectus; accuratus
■ ~**ly** *adv* penitus, plane, prorsus, funditus

thoroughfare *n* pervium *nt*; via pervia *f*

though *conj* etsi, etiamsi, quamvis, quamquam, licet

thought *n* (thinking, idea, opinion) cogitatio, sententia, mens *f*

thoughtful *adj* cogitabundus; providus; humanus

thoughtless *adj* incuriosus, neglegens, inconsultus
■ ~**ly** *adv* temere

thousand *adj* mille
□ **a** ~ **times** millies

thousandth *adj* millesimus

thrash *vt* tero, tundo ③; fig verbero ①

thread *n* filum *nt*; linea *f*; fig tenor *m*

threadbare *adj* tritus, detritus

threat *n* minae *fpl*

threaten *vt* minor ①
■ ~ *vi* impendeo, immineo ② *all + dat*

three *adj* tres
□ ~ **times** ter

threefold *adj* triplex, triplus

thresh *vt* tero, tundo ③
□ ~**ing-floor** area *f*

threshold *n* limen *nt*

thrift *n* frugalitas, parsimonia *f*

thrifty *adj* parcus, frugalior

thrill¹ *vt* percello
■ ~ *vi* percellor ③

thrill² *n* (excitement) animi concitatio *f*

thrilling *adj* periculosus

thrive *vi* vireo, floreo; valeo ②

thriving *adj* prosperus

throat *n* iugulum, guttur *nt*; gula *f*

throb¹ *vi* palpito ①

throb² *n* palpitatio *f*; pulsus *m*

throne *n* solium *nt*; fig regia dignitas *f*; (kingdom) regnum *nt*

t

throng[1] *n* multitudo, turba, frequentia *f*

throng[2] *vt&i* premo; circumfundor; confluo ③

throttle *vt* strangulo ①

through *prep* per, propter, ob *all* + *acc*

throughout *adv* penitus, prorsus

throw[1] *vt* iacio, conicio; mitto ③; iaculor, iacto ①; (away) abicio; (down) deicio, sterno, everto ③; (oneself) me praecipito ①; (open) patefacio; (off) excutio; deicio; (clothes) exuo; (out) eicio; (together) conicio; (up) egero ③

throw[2] *n* iactus *m*; iaculatio *f*

thrush *n* turdus *m*

thrust[1] *vt* trudo, impello; (with a sword) perfodio ③
  □ ∼ **out** extrudo ③

thrust[2] *n* ictus; impetus *m*; petitio *f*

thumb[1] *n* pollex *m*

thumb[2] *vt* (a book) pollice verso ①

thump[1] *vt* contundo ③

thump[2] *n* ictus *m*; percussio *f*

thunder[1] *n* tonitrus; fragor *m*

thunder[2] *vt&i* tono, intono ①

thunderbolt *n* fulmen *nt*

thunderstruck *adj* attonitus; obstupefactus

thus *adv* ita, sic
  □ **and** ∼ itaque

thwart *vt* obsto + *dat*; frustror ①

thyme *n* thymum *nt*

tiara *n* tiara *f*; tiaras *m*

ticket *n* tessera *f*; titulus *m*

tickle *vt&i* titillo ①

ticklish *adj* difficilis, periculosus, lubricus

tide *n* aestus, fig cursus *m*

tidings *n* rumor *m*; (message) nuntius *m*; (news) novum *nt*

tidy *adj* mundus

tie[1] *vt* ligo, alligo; nodo ①; vincio ④

tie[2] *n* vinculum *nt*; nodus *m*; coniunctio, necessitas *f*

tier *n* ordo, gradus *m*

tiger *n* tigris *m/f*

tight *adj* artus, astrictus
  ■ ∼**ly** *adv* arte, stricte

tighten *vt* stringo, astringo ③

tightness *n* soliditas, firmitas *f*

tile[1] *n* tegula, imbrex *f*

tile[2] *vt* tegulis tego ③

till[1] *adv & prep* usque ad + *acc*

till[2] *conj* dum, donec

tiller *n* (helm) gubernaculum *nt*; clavus *m*

tilt[1] *n* (inclination) inclinatio *f*; (rush) impetus *m*

tilt[2] *vt* proclino ①

timber *n* materia *f*; lignum *nt*; tignum *nt*; trabs *f*

time *n* tempus *nt*; dies *m*; (age, *etc.*) aetas *f*; aevum *nt*; (century) saeculum *nt*; (leisure) otium *nt*; (opportunity) occasio *f*; (hour) hora *f*
  □ **at this** ∼ in praesenti
  □ **at any** ∼ unquam
  □ **if at any** ∼ siquando
  □ **at a** ∼ una
  □ **all the** ∼ continuo

timely *adj* tempestivus, opportunus

timid *adj* timidus, anxius

timidity *n* timiditas *f*

tin *n* stannum, plumbum album *nt*

tinge *vt* tingo, imbuo, inficio ③

tinkle[1] *n* tinnitus *m*

tinkle[2] *vi* tinnio ④; crepito ①

tint[1] *vt* tingo ③

tint[2] *n* color *m*

tiny *adj* parvulus, exiguus

tip[1] *n* (top) cacumen; acumen *nt*; apex *m*

tip[2] *vt* (attach to end of) praefigo; (incline) inverto ③

tipsy *adj* ebrius, temulentus, vinosus

tiptoe *adv*:
  □ **on** ∼ in digitos erectus

tire *vt* fatigo, lasso
  ■ ∼ *vi* defatigor ①

tired *adj* fessus, defessus, lassus

tiresome *adj* laboriosus; molestus; operosus

tissue *n* textum *nt*

titbit *n* cuppedia *ntpl*

title *n* titulus *m*; inscriptio *f*; (label) index *m/f*; (name, *etc.*) appellatio, dignitas *f*

titter *vi* subrideo ②

to[1] *prep* ad + *acc*; (in comparison with) prae + *abl*; (until) usque ad + *acc*
  □ ∼ **and fro** huc illuc

to[2] *conj* (in order to) ut

toad *n* bufo *m*

toadstool *n* fungus *m*

toast[1] *n* (health drunk) propinatio *f*

toast[2] *vt* torreo ②; (in drinking) propino ①

today *adv* hodie

toe *n* digitus *m*

together *adv* simul, una; coniunctim

toil[1] *n* labor *m*; opera *f*; sudor *m*

toil[2] *vi* laboro ①

toilet *n* cultus, ornatus *m*; (lavatory) latrina *f*

token *n* signum, pignus *nt*

tolerable *adj* tolerabilis; mediocris

tolerance *n* tolerantia, toleratio, indulgentia *f*

tolerant *adj* tolerans, patiens, indulgens

tolerate *vt* tolero ①; patior ③, fero *ir*

toleration *n* toleratio; indulgentia *f*

toll *n* vectigal, tributum *nt*

tomb *n* sepulcrum, bustum *nt*; tumulus *m*

tomorrow *n* crastinus dies *m*
 ■ ~ *adv* cras
 □ **the day after** ~ perendie

tone *n* sonus *m*; fig color *m*; vox *f*

tongs *n* forceps *f*

tongue *n* lingua *f*

tonight *adv* hac nocte

too *adv* nimis, nimium; (also) etiam, insuper

tool *n* instrumentum; (of iron) ferramentum *nt*; fig minister *m*

tooth *n* also fig dens *m*

toothache *n* dolor dentium *m*

toothless *adj* edentulus

top[1] *n* cacumen, culmen *nt*; apex *m*; (of a house) fastigium *nt*; (toy) trochus, turbo *m*

top[2] *adj* summus; (the top of the mountain) summus mons

topic *n* res *f*; argumentum *nt*; quaestio *f*

topical *adj* hodiernus

topmost *adj* summus

topsy-turvy *adv* sursum deorsum

torch *n* fax, taeda *f*; funale *nt*

torment[1] *vt* crucio, excrucio ①; torqueo ②

torment[2] *n* cruciatus *m*; tormentum *nt*

torrent *n* also fig torrens *m*

tortoise *n* testudo *f*
 ■ ~-**shell** *n* testudo *f*

torture[1] *n* tormentum *nt*; cruciatus *m*

torture[2] *vt* also fig torqueo ②

torturer *n* tortor *m*

toss[1] *vt* iacto; agito, verso ①
 ■ ~ *vi* iactor ①; aestuo ①

toss[2] *n* iactus *m*; iactatio *f*

total[1] *adj* totus, universus
 ■ ~**ly** *adv* omnino, prorsus

total[2] *n* summa *f*

totter *vi* vacillo, titubo, labo ①

touch[1] *vt* tango, attingo ③; fig moveo ②; afficio ③

touch[2] *n* tactus, contactus *m*; fig commotio *f*
 □ **finishing** ~ fig manus extrema *f*

touchy *adj* offensioni pronior, stomachosus

tough *adj* tenax, lentus; durus; fig difficilis; (stout) strenuus

toughness *n* tenacitas *f*; lentor *m*; duritia; fig difficultas; (courage) fortitudo *f*

tour *n* circuitus *m*; peregrinatio *f*; iter *nt*

tourist *n* viator, peregrinator *m*

tournament *n* decursio equestris *f*; ludus equester *m*

tow *vt* (a ship) navem remulco trahere ③
 ■ ~-**rope** *n* remulcum *nt*

towards *prep* (also **toward**) adversus, ad, (of people) erga; contra, in; (of time) sub *all* + *acc*

towel *n* mantele, sudarium *nt*

tower[1] *n* turris, arx *f*; castellum *nt*

tower[2] *vi* emineo, superemineo ②

town *n* urbs *f*; oppidum, municipium *nt*
 □ ~ **hall** curia *f*

toy *n* crepundia *ntpl*

trace[1] *n* vestigium; indicium; signum; *nt*; (for horse) helcium *nt*

trace[2] *vt* delineo; (down) indago ①

track[1] *n* vestigium *nt*; (path) semita *f*

track[2] *vt* vestigo, investigo ①

tract *n* tractus *m*; regio *f*; (small treatise) tractatus *m*

trade[1] *n* mercatura *f*; commercium, negotium *nt*; (calling) ars *f*; quaestus *m*

trade² *vi* mercaturas facio ③; negotior, mercor ①

trader *n* mercator *m*

tradesman *n* negotiator; caupo *m*

tradition *n* fama *f*

traditional *adj* ab maioribus traditus; translaticius

traffic¹ *n* (trade) commercium *nt*; mercatura *f*

traffic² *vi* negotior, mercor ①

tragedy *n* tragoedia *f*; cothurnus *m*

tragic *adj* tragicus
■ ~**ally** *adv* tragice

trail¹ *vi* traho, verro ③

trail² *n* vestigium *nt*; ductus *m*

train¹ *n* series *f*; ordo *m*; (of a robe) peniculamentum *nt*; (retinue) comitatus *m*

train² *vt* educo ①; instruo; fig assuefacio ③

trainer *n* exercitor *m*

training *n* disciplina; exercitatio *f*

traitor *n* proditor *m*

traitorous *adj* perfidus; perfidiosus
■ ~**ly** *adv* perfide, perfidiose

tramp *n* homo vagus *m*

trample *vi* (on, upon) conculco ①; opprimo, obtero ③

trance *n* animus a corpore abstractus *m*

tranquil *adj* tranquillus, placidus, aequus

tranquillity *n* tranquillitas, quies *f*; tranquillus animus *m*

transact *vt* transigo, gero, ago, perficio, fungor ③

transaction *n* negotium *nt*; res *f*

transcribe *vt* transcribo, exscribo ③

transcription *n* transcriptio *f*

transfer¹ *vt* transfero *ir*; transmitto ③

transfer² *n* translatio *f*

transform *vt* transformo, transfiguro ①; verto ③

transformation *n* mutatio *f*

transgress *vt* violo ①; contra leges facio ③

transient *adj* (fleeting) fragilis, fluxus, caducus

transition *n* transitus *m*

transitory *adj* ▸ transient

translate *vt* verto, transfero ③

translation *n* translatio *f*; liber translatus *m*

translator *n* interpres *m/f*

transmission *n* transmissio *f*

transmit *vt* transmitto ③

transparency *n* perspicuitas *f*

transparent *adj* pellucidus, perspicuus, translucidus
□ **be ~** pelluceo, transluceo ②

transpire *vi* evenio ④; fio *ir*

transplant *vt* transfero *ir*

transport¹ *vt* transporto ①; transveho, transmitto ③; fig delecto ①

transport² *n* transvectio *f*; (ship) navigium vectorium *nt*; fig elatio *f*

transpose *vt* transpono ③

transposition *n* traiectio *f*

transverse *adj* transversus

trap¹ *n* laqueus *m*; tendicula, pedica *f*; fig insidiae *fpl*

trap² *vt* irretio ④

trash *n* scruta *ntpl*; nugae, res vilissimae *fpl*

travel¹ *vi* iter facio ③; peregrinor ①

travel² *n* iter *nt*; (abroad) peregrinatio *f*

traveller *n* viator, peregrinator *m*

tray *n* repositorium *nt*

treacherous *adj* perfidus; perfidiosus; dolosus
■ ~**ly** *adv* perfide, perfidiose

treachery *n* perfidia *f*

tread¹ *vt* calco, conculco ①
■ ~ *vi* incedo ③

tread² *n* gradus, incessus *m*

treason *n* perduellio, proditio *f*

treasure¹ *n* thesaurus *m*; gaza *f*; opes *fpl*

treasure² *vt* (value) magni aestimo ①

treasurer *n* aerarii praefectus *m*

treasury *n* fiscus *m*; aerarium; (building) thesaurus *m*

treat *vt* (handle) tracto ①; (use) utor ③ + *abl*; (entertain) convivio (aliquem) accipio ③

treatise *n* libellus *m*

treatment *n* tractatio; cura, curatio *f*

treaty *n* foedus; pactum *nt*

treble¹ *adj* triplex, triplus

treble² *vt* triplico ①

tree *n* arbor *f*

tremble *vi* tremo, contremisco ③;
trepido ①

trembling *n* trepidatio *f*; tremor *m*

tremendous *adj* formidolosus,
ingens, immanis

trench *n* fossa *f*; vallum *nt*; agger *m*

trespass *vi*:
□ ~ **on** ingredior ③

trial *n* tentatio *f*; (law) iudicium *nt*;
(attempt) conatus *m*; periculum *nt*

triangle *n* triangulum *nt*

triangular *adj* triangulus, triquetrus

tribe *n* tribus, natio *f*

tribunal *n* tribunal; (court) iudicium *nt*

tribune *n* tribunus *m*

tributary *n* amnis in alium influens *m*

tribute *n* tributum; vectigal *nt*; fig
□ **pay ~ to** laudo ①

trice *n*:
□ **in a ~** momento temporis *f*

trick[1] *n* dolus *m*; artificium *nt*; fraus *f*

trick[2] *vt* dolis illudo ③; circumvenio ④

trickery *n* fraus *f*; dolus *m*; ars *f*

trickle *vi* stillo, mano ①

trident *n* tridens *m*

trifle *n* res parvi momenti *f*;
nugae *fpl*

trifling *adj* levis, exiguus, parvi
momenti, frivolus

trim[1] *adj* nitidus, comptus, bellus

trim[2] *vt* (prune) puto ①; tondeo ②

trinket *n* gemma *f*

trip[1] *n* (stumble) pedis offensio *f*; (journey)
iter *nt*

trip[2] *vt* supplanto ①
■ ~ *vi* pedem offendo ③; fig erro ①

triple[1] *adj* triplex, triplus

triple[2] *vt* triplico ①

tripod *n* tripus *m*; cortina *f*

trireme *n* (navis) triremis *f*

trite *adj* tritus; pervulgatus

triumph[1] *n* triumphus *m*; ovatio; fig
victoria; exsultatio *f*

triumph[2] *vi* triumpho, ovo ①

triumphant *adj* triumphans, victor

triumvirate *n* triumviratus *m*

trivial *adj* levis

triviality *n* levitas *f*; nugae, ineptiae
fpl

troop *n* turma, caterva *f*; grex; globus
m; manus *f*
■ ~**s** *pl* copiae *fpl*

trophy *n* tropaeum *nt*

tropical *adj* tropicus

trot[1] *n* gradus *m*

trot[2] *vi* tolutim eo *ir*

trouble[1] *n* (nuisance) molestia *f*;
incommodum; (business) negotium *nt*;
labor; (grief) dolor *m*; aerumna *f*

trouble[2] *vt* turbo; vexo ①; ango ③

troublesome *adj* molestus;
operosus; difficilis

trough *n* alveus *m*

trousers *n* feminalia *ntpl*; bracae *fpl*

trowel *n* trulla *f*

truant *adj* otiosus; vagus

truce *n* indutiae *fpl*

truck *n* carrus *m*

true *adj* verus; sincerus; germanus;
rectus

truly *adv* vere; sincere; profecto

trump *vi* (up) conflo ①; confingo ③;
machinor ①

trumpet[1] *n* tuba, bucina *f*; lituus *m*;
cornu *nt*

trumpet[2] *vt* fig praedico, vendito,
celebro ①

trumpeter *n* tubicen *m*

trundle *vt* volvo
■ ~ *vi* volvor ③

trunk *n* truncus *m*; (of an elephant)
proboscis; (chest) cista *f*

trust[1] *n* fiducia *f*; fides *f*

trust[2] *vt* fido; confido; credo ③ *all* + *dat
of person*; (entrust) commendo ①;
permitto ③

trustworthy *adj* ▶ **trusty**

trusty *adj* fidus, fidelis; constans

truth *n* veritas; fides *f*; verum *nt*

truthful *adj* verax
■ ~**ly** *adv* veraciter

try[1] *n* conatus *m*

try[2] *vt* tento, probo, periclitor ①;
experior ④; (law) cognosco ③; in ius
voco ①
■ ~ *vi* conor ①; nitor ③; tento ①;
molior ④

tub *n* labrum *nt*; lacus *m*

tube *n* tubulus, tubus *m*

tubular *adj* tubulatus

t

tuck *vt* succingo ③

tuft *n* (of hair) cirrus *m*

tug *vt&i* traho; nitor ③

tuition *n* disciplina *f*

tumble *vi* corruo, labor, collabor, cado; volvor ③

tumour *n* tumor, tuber *m*

tumult *n* tumultus *m*; turba *f*

tumultuous *adj* tumultuosus, turbulentus

tune *n* numeri, moduli *mpl*
 ■ **in ~** *adj* consonus
 ■ **out of ~** *adj* dissonus

tuneful *adj* canorus

tunic *n* tunica *f*

tunnel *n* canalis *m*; cuniculum *nt*

turbid *adj* turbidus; (muddy) caenosus

turbulence *n* tumultus *m*; seditio *f*; animus turbulentus *m*

turbulent *adj* turbulentus

turf *n* caespes *m*; herba *f*

turgid *adj* turgidus, tumidus; inflatus

turmoil *n* turba, perturbatio *f*; tumultus *m*

turn¹ *n* (circuit) circuitus *m*; (bend) flexus *m*; (turning round) conversio *f*; circumactus *m*; (change, course) vicissitudo; (inclination) inclinatio *f*
 □ **good ~** officium, beneficium *nt*
 □ **by ~s** alternis, in vicem; vicissim

turn² *vt* (bend) flecto, verto; (~ round) volvo, circumago ③; (change) muto ①; converto ③; (on the lathe) torno ①
 ■ **~** *vi* convertor; flector; volvor ③; torqueor ②; mutor ①; (become) fio *ir*; evado ③
 □ **~ aside** deflecto ③; detorqueo ②
 □ **~ away** *vt&i* averto ③
 □ **~ back** *vt* reflecto ③; recurvo ①; *vi* reverto ③; redeo ④
 □ **~ down** inverto ③, (reject) reicio ③
 □ **~ off** *vt* averto ③; derivo ①; *vi* deflecto ③
 □ **~ out** *vt* eicio ③; *vi* evenio ④; evado; contingo ③
 □ **~ over** everto ③; (a page) verso ①; (cede) transfero *ir*

 □ **~ round** *vt* circumago ③; contorqueo ②; *vi* versor ①; circumagor ③
 □ **~ up** recurvo ①; (come into view) appareo ②

turning-point *n* cardo *m*; momentum, discrimen *nt*

turnip *n* rapum *nt*

turret *n* turricula *f*

turtle *n* testudo *f*

turtle-dove *n* turtur *m*

tusk *n* dens *m*

tutor¹ *n* educator; praeceptor, paedagogus; grammaticus *m*

tutor² *vt* doceo ②

tweezers *n* volsella *f*

twelfth *adj* duodecimus
 □ **for the ~ time** duodecimo

twelve *adj* duodecim
 □ **~ times** duodecies

twentieth *adj* vicesimus

twenty *adj* viginti

twice *adv* bis

twig *n* surculus *m*; virga *f*

twilight *n* (evening) crepusculum; (dawn) diluculum *nt*

twin *adj & n* geminus, gemellus

twine *vt* circumvolvo ③; circumplico ①; contorqueo ②
 ■ **~** *vi* circumvolvor, circumplector ③

twinge *n* dolor *m*

twinkle *vi* mico, corusco ①

twirl *vt* verso ①; circumago ③
 ■ **~** *vi* versor ①

twist *vt* torqueo ②; flecto ③
 ■ **~** *vi* torqueor ②; flector ③

two *adj* duo

twofold *adj* duplex, duplus

type *n* exemplar, exemplum *nt*; forma *f*

typical *adj* typicus

tyrannical *adj* tyrannicus

tyranny *n* tyrannis, dominatio *f*

tyrant *n* tyrannus *m*

Uu

udder *n* uber *nt*; mamma *f*

ugliness *n* deformitas, foeditas *f*

ugly *adj* deformis, foedus, turpis

ulcer *n* ulcus *nt*

ulterior *adj* ulterior

ultimate *adj* ultimus
■ ∼**ly** *adv* denique, tandem

umpire *n* arbiter, disceptator *m*

unable *adj* invalidus
■ **be** ∼ *vi* non possum, nequeo *ir*

unacceptable *adj* ingratus, odiosus

unaccompanied *adj* incomitatus, solus

unaccountable *adj* inexplicabilis, inenodabilis

unaccountably *adv* praeter opinionem; sine causa

unaccustomed *adj* insolitus, insuetus, inexpertus

unadorned *adj* inornatus; incomptus; simplex

unadulterated *adj* merus, sincerus

unaided *adj* non adiutus, solus

unanimity *n* unanimitas, consensio *f*; consensus *m*

unanimous *adj* unanimus, concors
■ ∼**ly** *adv* consensu omnium, omnium sententiis

unapproachable *adj* inaccessus

unarmed *adj* inermis, inermus

unassailable *adj* inexpugnabilis

unassuming *adj* modestus, moderatus; demissus

unattainable *adj* arduus, qui consequi non potest

unattempted *adj* intentatus, inexpertus; inausus

unattended *adj* incomitatus

unauthorized *adj* inconcessus

unavailing *adj* inutilis, inanis

unavoidable *adj* inevitabilis

unaware *adj* inscius, nescius, ignarus

unawares *adv* (de) improviso, inopinato

unbearable *adj* intolerabilis

unbecoming *adj* indecorus, indecens, indignus, inhonestus

unbelievable *adj* incredibilis

unbending *adj* inflexibilis, rigidus

unbiased *adj* incorruptus; integer; sine ira et studio

unblemished *adj* purus, integer, intactus

unborn *adj* nondum natus

unbreakable *adj* infragilis

unbroken *adj* irruptus; integer

unburden *vt* exonero 🗓

unburied *adj* inhumatus, insepultus

uncanny *adj* inscitus

uncared *adj* (∼ for) neglectus

unceasing *adj* perpetuus, assiduus
■ ∼**ly** *adv* perpetuo, continenter

uncertain *adj* incertus, dubius; ambiguus, anceps

uncertainty *n* quod incertum est; dubitatio *f*

unchangeable *adj* immutabilis; constans

unchanged *adj* immutatus, perpetuus

unchanging *adj* immutatus, perpetuus

uncharitable *adj* immisericors, iniquus, inhumanus

uncivilized *adj* incultus, barbarus

uncle *n* (on the father's side) patruus; (on the mother's side) avunculus *m*

uncombed *adj* impexus, incomptus

uncomfortable *adj* incommodus, molestus, gravis, anxius

uncommon *adj* rarus, insolitus; enormis; insignis; singularis
■ ∼**ly** *adv* raro; praeter solitum, plus solito

unconcerned *adj* neglegens; incuriosus; securus

unconditional *adj* simplex

unconscious *adj* (unaware) inscius; nescius
■ ∼**ly** *adv* nesciens

uncontrollable *adj* impotens, effrenatus

u

uncouth *adj* barbarus, impolitus, rudis; vastus

uncover *vt* detego, recludo, retego ③; revelo ①

undaunted *adj* impavidus, intrepidus

undecided *adj* incertus, dubius, sine exitu; par; integer

undeniable *adj* quod negari non potest

under *prep* sub, subter; infra *all* + *acc*; (in number) minor + *abl*

undercurrent *n* torrens subterfluens *m*

underdone *adj* minus percoctus, subcrudus

underestimate *vt* minoris aestimo ①

undergo *vi&t* subeo *ir*; patior ③; tolero ①; fero *ir*

underground *adj* subterraneus

undergrowth *n* virgulta *ntpl*

underhand *adj* clandestinus
■ in an ∼ manner *adv* clam

underline *vt* subnoto ①

underling *n* administer *m*; assecla, satelles *m/f*

undermine *vt* suffodio ③; fig supplanto, labefacto ①

underneath *adv* subter, infra + *acc*

understand *vt&i* intellego; sapio ③; scio; (hear) audio ④

understanding¹ *adj* peritus; sapiens, prudens; (sympathetic) humanus

understanding² *n* mens *f*; intellectus *m*; intellegentia *f*

undertake *vt&i* suscipio; incipio; aggredior ③; conor ①

undertaker *n* (of funerals) libitinarius *m*

undertaking *n* ausum, inceptum; propositum *nt*

undervalue *vt* parvi facio ③; parvi aestimo ①

underworld *n* Tartarus *m*

undeserved *adj* immeritus; indignus; iniustus
■ ∼ly *adv* immerito, indigne

undisciplined *adj* rudis, inexercitatus

undisputed *adj* indubitabilis, certus

undisturbed *adj* imperturbatus; immotus

undivided *adj* indivisus

undo *vt* solvo, dissolvo; resolvo; dissuo; irritum facio; (ruin) perdo ③

undone *adj* infectus; imperfectus; perditus

undoubted *adj* indubitatus; certus
■ ∼ly *adv* haud dubie

undress *vt* vestem exuo; (another) vestem detraho (alicui) ③

undue *adj* indebitus; iniquus

undulate *vi* undo, fluctuo; vibro ①

unduly *adv* iniuste, plus iusto

undying *adj* immortalis; sempiternus

unearth *vt* recludo; detego ③

unearthly *adj* humano maior; terribilis

uneasy *adj* anxius

unemployed *adj* otiosus

unencumbered *adj* liber, expeditus

unenviable *adj* haud invidiosus

unequal *adj* inaequalis, dispar, impar
■ ∼ly *adv* inaequaliter, impariter

unerring *adj* certus

uneven *adj* inaequalis; iniquus; (of ground) asper

unexpected *adj* inexpectatus, insperatus, improvisus, inopinatus, inopinus
■ ∼ly *adv* (ex) improviso

unfailing *adj* certus

unfair *adj* iniquus
■ ∼ly *adv* inique

unfaithful *adj* infidus, perfidus
■ ∼ly *adv* perfide

unfamiliar *adj* peregrinus; ignarus; ignotus

unfasten *vt* laxo ①; solvo, resolvo ③

unfathomable *adj* profundus

unfavourable *adj* sinister; adversus

unfeeling *adj* durus, inhumanus, crudelis
■ ∼ly *adv* dure, crudeliter, inhumane

unfinished *adj* imperfectus

unfit *adj* inhabilis, incommodus, inutilis; (not physically fit) impiger

unfold *vt* explico ①; aperio ④; pando ③
■ ∼ *vi* dehisco ③

unforeseen *adj* inexpectatus, insperatus

unforgiving *adj* inexorabilis

unfortunate *adj* infelix; infortunatus
■ ∼ly *adv* infeliciter

unfounded *adj* vanus; sine causa

unfriendly *adj* parum amicus

unfulfilled *adj* infectus, imperfectus

unfurl *vt* expando, solvo, (vela) facio ③

ungainly *adj* inhabilis, rusticus

ungovernable *adj* impotens, effrenatus

ungrateful *adj* ingratus

unguarded *adj* incustoditus; fig inconsultus

unhappiness *n* miseria, tristitia *f*

unhappy *adj* infelix, infortunatus, miser

unharmed *adj* incolumis, integer

unhealthiness *n* infirmitas; pestilentia, gravitas *f*

unhealthy *adj* ad aegrotandum proclivis; morbosus; (things) insalubris

unholy *adj* impius; profanus

unhoped *adj* (∼ for) insperatus

unhurt *adj* inviolatus, illaesus

unicorn *n* monoceros *m*

uniform[1] *adj* uniformis, sibi constans

uniform[2] *n* ornatus, habitus *m*

uniformity *n* uniformitas *f*

unimaginable *adj* qui animo fingi non potest

unimportant *adj* levis, parvus

uninhabitable *adj* inhabitabilis, non habitabilis

uninhabited *adj* cultoribus inanis; desertus

uninjured *adj* incolumis, illaesus

unintelligent *adj* crassus

unintelligible *adj* obscurus

unintentional *adj* haud meditatus

uninterrupted *adj* continuus, perpetuus, inoffensus

uninvited *adj* invocatus

union *n* (act) coniunctio; (alliance) consociatio; consensio; societas *f*; (marriage) matrimonium *nt*

unique *adj* unicus, singularis

unison *n* concentus *m*

unite *vt* consocio ①; coniungo ■ ∼ *vi* coalesco ③; coniuro ①

unity *n* (oneness) unitas; fig concordia *f*

universal *adj* universus ■ ∼**ly** *adv* universe; (everywhere) undique, ubique

universe *n* mundus *m*

university *n* academia *f*

unjust *adj* iniustus, iniquus ■ ∼**ly** iniuste, inique

unkempt *adj* incomptus

unkind *adj* inhumanus, parum officiosus ■ ∼**ly** *adv* inhumane

unkindness *n* inhumanitas *f*

unknown *adj* ignotus, incognitus

unlawful *adj* illicitus; inconcessus ■ ∼**ly** *adv* contra leges

unless *conj* nisi, ni, nisi si

unlike *adj* dissimilis, dispar, diversus

unlikely *adj* non verisimilis

unlimited *adj* infinitus, immensus

unload *vt* exonero ①

unlock *vt* recludo ③; resero ①

unluckily *adv* infeliciter

unlucky *adj* infelix, infaustus

unman *vt* (castrate) castro; fig enervo ①

unmanageable *adv* intractabilis; contumax

unmarried *adj* caelebs, innuptus, innubus

unmask *vt* detego ③; nudo ①

unmerciful *adj* immisericors

unmindful *adj* immemor; incuriosus; securus

unmistakable *adj* certus

unmixed *adj* merus, sincerus

unmoved *adj* also fig immotus

unnatural *adj* crudelis, monstruosus, immanis; (preternatural) praeter naturam

unnecessary *adj* haud necessarius

unnerve *vt* debilito, infirmo, enervo ①

unnoticed *adj* praetermissus

unobserved *adj* inobservatus

unoccupied *adj* otiosus, vacuus; (of land) apertus

unpack *vt* expedio ④; eximo ③

unpaid *adj* (of debt) qui adhuc debetur; gratuitus

unpalatable *adj* molestus

unparalleled *adj* unicus; eximius

unpardonable *adj* non ignoscendus

unpatriotic *adj* patriae non amans

unpleasant *adj* iniucundus; incommodus; molestus ■ ∼**ly** *adv* iniucunde; incommode

unpleasing *adj* ingratus

unpopular *adj* populo ingratus, invidiosus

unpopularity *n* invidia *f*; odium *nt*

unprecedented *adj* novus, inauditus, unicus

unpremeditated *adj* subitus, non elaboratus

unprepared *adj* imparatus

unprincipled *adj* corruptis moribus *abl*, improbus

unproductive *adj* infecundus, infructuosus

unprofitable *adj* inutilis, vanus

unprotected *adj* indefensus

unpunished *adj* impunitus

unqualified *adj* haud idoneus, inhabilis; merus

unquestionable *adj* certus

unravel *vt* extrico, enodo ①; expedio ④

unreasonable *adj* contra rationem, rationis expers, absurdus; iniquus

unrelenting *adj* implacabilis, inexorabilis

unreliable *adj* infidus

unremitting *adj* continuus, perpetuus, assiduus

unrepentant *adj* impaenitens

unrequited *adj* non mutuus, sine mercede

unreserved *adj* apertus, candidus
■ ~**ly** *adv* aperte, libere, candide

unrest *n* tumultus *m*

unripe *adj* immaturus, crudus

unrivalled *adj* singularis

unroll *vt* evolvo ③; explico ①; pando ③; expedio ④

unruffled *adj* tranquillus, immotus

unruly *adj* effrenatus; turbulentus; petulans

unsafe *adj* intutus; periculosus

unsatisfactory *adj* non idoneus; improbabilis

unsavoury *adj* insulsus, foedus

unscathed *adj* salvus

unseal *vt* resigno ①; aperio ④

unseemly *adj* indecorus, indecens

unseen *adj* invisus; invisitatus; inobservatus

unselfish *adj* suae utilitatis immemor

unselfishness *n* suarum utilitatum neglegentia *f*

unsettled *adj* dubius, instabilis, inconstans, inquietus

unshaven *adj* intonsus

unsheath *vt* e vagina educo; (gladium) destringo ③

unsightly *adj* deformis; turpis, foedus

unsociable *adj* insociabilis

unsolicited *adj* ultro oblatus

unsophisticated *adj* simplex, sincerus, incorruptus

unsought *adj* non quaesitus

unspeakable *adj* ineffabilis, infandus, inenarrabilis

unstable *adj* instabilis; fluxus; incertus

unsteadily *adv* infirme, instabiliter

unsteadiness *n* instabilitas; infirmitas; levitas, inconstantia *f*

unsteady *adj* instabilis; infirmus; tremulus; vagus, levis

unsuccessful *adj* improsper; infaustus; infelix; (vain) irritus, vanus
■ ~**ly** *adv* infeliciter, improspere; (in vain) frustra, re infecta

unsuitable *adj* incongruens, inhabilis, incommodus

unsuspecting *adj* minime suspicax

untamed *adj* indomitus, ferus

untidy *adj* immundus

untie *vt* solvo, resolvo ③; laxo ①

until *conj* dum; quoad; donec
■ ~ *prep* ad, in; usque ad *all + acc*

untimely *adj* immaturus; importunus; intempestivus

untold *adj* indictus; immemoratus; (vast) vastus

untouched *adj* intactus; integer; immotus

untoward *adj* adversus, contumax

untrained *adj* inexercitatus

untrodden *adj* non tritus; avius

untroubled *adj* placidus; aequus; securus, imperturbatus

untrue *adj* falsus, mendax

untruth *n* mendacium *nt*

unused *adj* inusitatus; novus, non tritus

unusual *adj* inusitatus, insuetus; insolitus, novus, rarus
■ ~**ly** *adv* praeter solitum, raro

unvarnished *adj* non fucatus; fig sincerus, nudus

u

unveil *vt* velamen detraho; fig patefacio ③

unwarlike *adj* imbellis

unwary *adj* imprudens, incautus, inconsultus, temerarius

unwelcome *adj* non acceptus, ingratus, iniucundus

unwell *adj* aeger, invalidus, infirmus

unwieldy *adj* inhabilis, pinguis

unwilling *adj* invitus; coactus
■ ∼**ly** *adv* invite, non libenter

unwind *vt* revolvo, retexo ③

unwise *adj* imprudens; inconsultus; stultus
■ ∼**ly** *adv* stulte; imprudenter, inconsulte

unwitting *adj* inscius

unwonted *adj* insolitus, insuetus, inusitatus

unworthy *adj* indignus; immeritus

unwrap *vi* explico ①; evolvo ③

unwritten *adj* non scriptus, inscriptus

unyielding *adj* obstinatus

unyoke *vt* abiungo, disiungo ③

up *adv & prep* sursum
□ ∼ **to** tenus; (of time) usque ad *both* + *acc*
□ ∼ **and down** sursum deorsum; huc illuc

uphill *adv* adverso colle *abl*

uphold *vt* sustineo ②; sustento ①; tueor ②

upland *adj* editus, montanus

upon *prep* super, supra; (of time) e, ex; (on) in *all* + *abl*

upper *adj* superus; superior
□ ∼**most** summus

upright *adj* erectus; rectus; fig honestus; integer

uprising *n* tumultus *m*

uproar *n* tumultus *m*; turba *f*

uproot *vt* radicitus tollo, eruo ③

upset[1] *adj* sollicitatus, perculsus

upset[2] *vt* everto, subverto; sterno ③

upshot *n* exitus, eventus *m*

upside *n*:
□ ∼ **down** sursum deorsum
■ **turn** ∼ **down** *vt* misceo ②; confundo ③

upstart *n* homo novus, terrae filius *m*

upstream *adv* in adversum flumen, adverso flumine

upwards *adv* sursum; sublime; superne; (of number) plus

urban *adj* urbanus

urge[1] *n* incitamentum *nt*

urge[2] *vt* urgeo ②; impello ③; insto ①; suadeo ② *both* + *dat*; (on) stimulo ①

urgent *adj* instans; vehemens; gravis
■ ∼**ly** *adv* vehementer

urine *n* urina *f*

urn *n* urna; (water-pot) hydria *f*

usage *n* mos *m*; consuetudo *f*; usus *m*

use[1] *n* usus *m*; utilitas *f*; commodum *nt*; consuetudo *f*; (interest) faenus *nt*
□ **be of** ∼ valeo ②; prosum *ir* + *dat*

use[2] *vt* utor ③ + *abl*; adhibeo ②; in usum verto ③; (treat) tracto ①
□ ∼ **up** consumo ③

used *vi*:
□ **be** ∼ **to** soleo ②; consuesco ③

useful *adj* utilis; aptus, commodus; salutaris
■ ∼**ly** *adv* utiliter; apte, commode

usefulness *n* utilitas; commoditas *f*

useless *adj* inutilis; inhabilis; irritus, vanus
■ ∼**ly** *adv* inutiliter, nequicquam, frustra

uselessness *n* inutilitas *f*

usher[1] *vi* praeeo *ir*; introduco ③

usher[2] *n* apparitor *m*

usual *adj* usitatus, solitus, consuetus; cottidianus
□ ∼**ly** usitate; vulgo; plerumque, fere

usurp *vt* usurpo; vindico (mihi) ①; assumo ③

usurper *n* usurpator *m*

utensils *npl* utensilia; vasa *ntpl*; supellex *f*

utility *n* utilitas, commoditas *f*

utmost *adj* extremus; ultimus, summus
□ **do one's** ∼ summis viribus contendo ③

utter[1] *adj* (total) totus
■ ∼**ly** *adv* omnino, penitus; funditus

utter[2] *vt* eloquor, dico, mitto, fundo ③, profero *ir*; pronuntio ①

utterance *n* elocutio; pronuntiatio *f*; dictum *nt*; vox *f*

Vv

vacancy *n* (emptiness) inanitas *f*; inane *nt*; (place) locus *m*

vacant *adj* vacuus, inanis; fig mentis vacuus

vacate *vt* vacuefacio; (leave) relinquo ③

vacation *n* (law) iustitium *nt*; (holidays) feriae *fpl*

vacillate *vi* vacillo, fluctuo ①

vacuum *n* inane, vacuum *nt*

vagabond *n* homo vagus, erro *m*

vagrant *n* homo vagus, erro *m*

vague *adj* dubius; ambiguus; incertus

vain *adj* (pointless) vanus; futtilis; inanis, irritus; (proud) superbus, arrogans; (boastful) gloriosus
■ **in ∼, ∼ly** *adv* frustra; nequicquam, incassum

valet *n* cubicularius, famulus *m*

valiant *adj* fortis; audax, animosus
■ **∼ly** *adv* fortiter; audacter, animose

valid *adj* validus; legitimus, ratus

validity *n* firmitas; auctoritas *f*

valley *n* vallis, convallis *f*

valour *n* fortitudo, virtus *f*; animus *m*

valuable *adj* pretiosus; carus

valuation *n* aestimatio *f*

value[1] *n* pretium *nt*; aestimatio *f*

value[2] *vt* aestimo ①; pendo ③
□ **∼ highly** magni aestimo ①

valueless *adj* vilis, parvi pretii

valve *n* valvae *fpl*

vanguard *n* primum agmen *nt*

vanish *vi* vanesco, diffugio, evanesco ③; abeo, pereo *ir*

vanity *n* (pointlessness) vanitas; levitas *f*; nugae *fpl*; (boastfulness) iactatio, ostentatio *f*

vapour *n* vapor *m*; exhalatio *f*; halitus *m*

variable *adj* mutabilis; varius; levis, inconstans

variance *n* discordia; discrepantia, dissensio, simultas *f*
■ **be at ∼** *vi* discrepo ①; dissideo ②

variation *n* varietas; variatio; vicissitudo *f*

varied *adj* varius, diversus

variety *n* varietas; diversitas; multitudo *f*

various *adj* varius, diversus
■ **∼ly** *adv* varie, diverse

varnish[1] *n* atramentum *nt*; fig fucus *m*

varnish[2] *vt* coloro ①

vary *vt* vario ①; distinguo ③
■ **∼** *vi* vario ①

vase *n* amphora *f*; urceus *m*; vas *nt*

vast *adj* vastus; ingens, immensus
■ **∼ly** *adv* vaste; valde; multum

vastness *n* immensitas *f*

vat *n* cupa *f*; dolium *nt*

vault[1] *n* fornix *m*; camera *f*; (underground) hypogeum *nt*; (leap) saltus *m*

vault[2] *vt* (cover with a vault) concamero ①; (leap over) transilio ④

vaunt *vt* iacto ①; glorior ①, vendo ③; ostento ①

veal *n* vitulina *f*

veer *vi* vertor, vergo ③

vegetable *n* holus *nt*

vegetation *n* herba *f*

vehemence *n* vehementia, vis *f*; fervor, impetus *m*

vehement *adj* vehemens, violentus; fervidus; acer
■ **∼ly** *adv* vehementer; acriter

vehicle *n* vehiculum *nt*

veil[1] *n* velamen; flammeolum *nt*; amictus; fig praetextus *m*; simulacrum *nt*; species *f*

veil[2] *vt* velo ①; tego ③

vein *n* vena *f*

velocity *n* velocitas, celeritas *f*

veneer *n* ligni brattea *f*; fig species *f*

venerable *adj* venerabilis, reverendus

venerate *vt* veneror, adoro ①; colo ③

veneration *n* veneratio, adoratio *f*; cultus *m*

venereal *adj* venereus

vengeance *n* ultio; vindicta, poena *f*
□ **take ∼** ulciscor ③
□ **with a ∼** valde

venison _n_ caro ferina _f_

venom _n_ venenum, virus _nt_

venomous _adj_ venenosus, virulentus

vent[1] _n_ spiramentum _nt_; exitus _m_; foramen _nt_
◻ **give ∼ to** (utter) fundo, promo ③; (exercise) exerceo ②

vent[2] _vt_ aperio ④; per foramen emitto ③
◻ **∼ one's anger on** stomachum in aliquem effundo ③

ventilate _vt_ ventilo ①; fig in medium profero _ir_

ventilation _n_ ventilatio; fig prolatio _f_

venture[1] _n_ discrimen, periculum _nt_; (hazard) alea _f_; (deed of daring) ausum _nt_

venture[2] _vt_ periclitor ①
■ **∼** _vi_ (dare) audeo ②

verandah _n_ subdiale _nt_

verb _n_ verbum _nt_

verbatim _adv_ ad verbum

verbose _adj_ verbosus
■ **∼ly** _adv_ verbose

verbosity _n_ loquacitas _f_

verdant _adj_ viridis, virens; florens

verdict _n_ (of a jury) iudicium _nt_; sententia _f_

verge[1] _n_ (border) confinium _nt_; margo _m/f_; ora _f_; (limit) limes _m_
◻ **on the ∼ of** use _future participle_

verge[2] _vi_ vergo ③

verification _n_ affirmatio _f_

verify _vt_ ratum facio ③; confirmo ①

vermin _n_ bestiolae molestae _fpl_

vernacular _adj_ vernaculus

vernal _adj_ vernus

versatile _adj_ versatilis; versabilis; agilis; varius

versatility _n_ agilitas _f_

verse _n_ versus _m_; carmen _nt_

versed _adj_ peritus, exercitatus

version _n_ translatio _f_

vertebra _n_ vertebra _f_

vertex _n_ vertex _m_

vertical _adj_ rectus, directus
■ **∼ly** _adv_ ad lineam; recta linea

vertigo _n_ vertigo _f_

very _adj_ verus
■ **∼** _adv_ valde, admodum; multum

vessel _n_ vas; (ship) navigium _nt_

vest _n_ vestimentum _nt_; tunica _f_; (of a charioteer) pannus _m_

vestal _n_ (virgo) vestalis _f_

vestige _n_ vestigium; indicium _nt_

veteran[1] _adj_ veteranus

veteran[2] _n_ veteranus miles _m_

veterinary _adj_ veterinarius

veto[1] _n_ intercessio _f_

veto[2] _vt_ veto ①

vex _vt_ vexo, inquieto ①

vexation _n_ vexatio; offensio _f_; stomachus, dolor _m_

vibrate _vi_ vibro ①; tremo ③

vibration _n_ vibratus, motus, tremor _m_

vicarious _adj_ vicarius

vice _n_ vitium _nt_; turpitudo _f_; (instrument) forceps _m_

vicinity _n_ vicinitas, vicinia _f_

vicious _adj_ vitiosus; perditus; turpis

victim _n_ victima, hostia _f_

victimize _vt_ fig noceo ② + _dat_; laedo ①

victor _n_ victor _m_; victrix _f_

victorious _adj_ superior; victor _m_, victrix _f_
■ **∼ly** _adv_ victoris instar

victory _n_ victoria _f_; triumphus _m_; palma _f_

victuals _npl_ cibaria _ntpl_; victus; mil commeatus _m_

vie _vi_ (with) aemulor ①; contendo ③; certo ① _both_ + _dat or_ cum + _abl_

view[1] _n_ (act) aspectus, conspectus _m_; oculi _mpl_; species _f_; spectaculum _nt_; (prospect) prospectus _m_; fig (opinion) sententia; opinio _f_
◻ **have in ∼** cogito ①

view[2] _vt_ viso, inviso, conspicio; inspicio ③; contemplor; investigo; lustro ①; (regard, feel) sentio ④

vigil _n_ vigilia, pervigilatio _f_; pervigilium _nt_

vigilance _n_ vigilantia, cura _f_

vigilant _adj_ vigil, vigilans
■ **∼ly** _adv_ vigilanter

vigorous _adj_ vigens, validus, acer, fortis, strenuus
■ **∼ly** _adv_ strenue; acriter; fortiter

vigour _n_ vigor _m_; robur _nt_; impetus _m_

vile _adj_ vilis, abiectus; (wicked) perditus, flagitiosus; foedus

villa _n_ villa _f_

village _n_ vicus, pagus _m_

v

villager *n* vicanus, paganus, rusticus *m*

villain *n* scelus *nt*; scelestus *m*; nequam *m indecl*

villainous *adj* sceleratus, scelestus, nefarius

villainy *n* improbitas, nequitia *f*; scelus *nt*

vindicate *vt* vindico ①; assero ③; (justify) purgo ①; (defend) defendo ③

vindication *n* defensio *f*

vindictive *adj* ultionis cupidus, acerbus

vine *n* vitis *f*

vinegar *n* acetum *nt*

vineyard *n* vinea *f*; vinetum *nt*

vintage *n* vindemia *f*

violate *vt* violo ①; rumpo, frango ③

violation *n* violatio *f*

violence *n* violentia; vis *f*; (energy) impetus *m*; (cruelty) saevitia *f*

violent *adj* violentus; furiosus; vehemens
■ ~**ly** *adv* violenter, vehementer

violet *n* (flower) viola; (colour) viola *f*

viper *n* vipera *f*

virgin[1] *n* virgo *f*; puella *f*

virgin[2] *adj* virginalis, virgineus

virginity *n* virginitas *f*

virile *adj* virilis, masculus

virility *n* virilitas *f*

virtual *adj* insitus, innatus

virtue *n* virtus; probitas; fortitudo; (efficacy) vis, virtus *f*

virtuous *adj* virtute praeditus; probus; integer
■ ~**ly** *adv* cum virtute; integre

virulence *n* acerbitas, gravitas *f*

virulent *adj* virulentus; acerbus, gravis

virus *n* virus *nt*

viscous *adj* viscosus, lentus

visibility *n* visibilitas *f*

visible *adj* aspectabilis, conspicuus; manifestus

visibly *adv* fig aperte, manifesto

vision *n* (faculty of sight) visus *m*; fig visio *f*; visum; somnium *nt*

visit[1] *n* aditus *m*; salutatio *f*

visit[2] *vt* viso ③; visito ①; adeo *ir*

visitor *n* salutator *m*; salutatrix *f*

visor *n* (cheek-piece of helmet) buccula *f*

vital *adj* vitalis; fig necessarius

vitality *n* vitalitas *f*; vigor *m*

vivacious *adj* vivax; vividus, alacer

vivacity *n* vivacitas; alacritas *f*

vivid *adj* vividus; (plain) manifestus
■ ~**ly** *adv* vivide; (plainly) manifesto

vocabulary *n* vocabulorum index *m*

vocal *adj* vocalis; canorus
■ ~**ly** *adv* voce, ore

vocation *n* officium, munus *nt*

vociferous *adj* clamosus

vogue *n* mos *m*; fama, aestimatio *f*
□ **be in** ~ invalesco ③

voice *n* vox *f*; sonus *m*; (vote) suffragium *nt*

void[1] *adj* vacuus, inanis; fig sterilis; invalidus, irritus, cassus
□ **be** ~ vaco ①

void[2] *n* vacuum, inane *nt*

void[3] *vt* vacuefacio ③; vacuo ①; fig irritum facio, rescindo ③

volatile *adj* volatilis; fig levis, volaticus, inconstans

volcano *n* mons igneus *m*

volley *n* nubes *f*

voluble *adj* volubilis, loquax, garrulus

volume *n* volumen *nt*; tomus *m*; (size) magnitudo *f*

voluntarily *adv* sponte, libenter

voluntary *adj* voluntarius

volunteer[1] *n* miles voluntarius *m*

volunteer[2] *vi* me offero *ir*; audeo ②

voluptuous *adj* voluptarius, voluptuosus

vomit[1] *vt&i* vomo, evomo ③; eructo ①

vomit[2] *n* vomitus *m*

voracious *adj* vorax, edax
■ ~**ly** *adv* voraciter

voracity *n* voracitas, edacitas, gula *f*

vortex *n* vertex, turbo, gurges *m*

vote[1] *n* suffragium *nt*; fig (judgment) sententia *f*

vote[2] *vt* censeo ②
■ ~ *vi* suffragium fero *ir*

voter *n* suffragator *m*

voting-tablet *n* tabella *f*

votive *adj* votivus
□ ~ **tablet** tabella *f*

vouch *vt&i* testificor, testor, affirmo ①

voucher *n* (ticket) tessera *f*
vow¹ *n* votum *nt*
vow² *vt* voveo, devoveo ②; spondeo ②; (promise) promitto ③
vowel *n* vocalis *f*
voyage¹ *n* navigatio *f*
voyage² *vi* navigo ①
voyager *n* navigator *m*

vulgar *adj* vulgaris, plebeius; inurbanus; rusticus
■ **~ly** *adv* vulgo; rustice

vulgarity *n* mores vulgi *mpl*; rusticitas *f*

vulnerable *adj* quod vulnerari potest

vulture *n* vultur, vulturius *m*

Ww

wad *n* fasciculus *m*
waddle *vi* anatis in modum incedo ③
wade *vi* per vada eo *ir*
waft *vt* deduco ③, defero, fero *ir*; traicio ③
wag *vt* agito, vibro ①; (the tail) moveo ②
wager¹ *n* sponsio *f*; pignus *nt*
wager² *vt&i* spondeo ②; sponsione provoco ①; pignore contendo ③
wages *n* merces *f*; stipendium *nt*
wagon *n* carrus *m*; plaustrum *nt*
waif *n* erro *m*
wail *vt&i* ploro ①; plango ③; fleo ②
wailing *n* ploratus, planctus *m*
waist *n* medium corpus *nt*
waistcoat *n* subucula *f*
wait¹ *vi* (stay) maneo ②; (for) exspecto ①; (on) inservio ④ + *dat*
wait² *n* (delay) mora *f*
waiter *n* minister, pedisequus *m*
waive *vt* decedo de + *abl*, remitto ③
wake *vt* exsuscito, excito ①; expergefacio ③
■ **~** *vi* expergiscor ③
wakeful *adj* exsomnis, insomnis, vigil, vigilans
waken *vt* ▶ wake
walk¹ *n* (act) ambulatio *f*; (place) ambulacrum *nt*; ambulatio *f*; (manner of walking) incessus *m*
walk² *vi* incedo ③; ambulo ①; gradior ③
walker *n* ambulans; pedes *m*
walking *n* ambulatio *f*
□ **~ stick** baculum *nt*

wall *n* paries; (of a town, *etc.*) murus *m*; mil moenia *ntpl*
wallet *n* pera; mantica *f*; saccus *m*
wallow *vi* volutor ①
walnut *n* iuglans, nux iuglans *f*
wan *adj* pallidus, exsanguis
wand *n* virga *f*; caduceus *m*
wander *vi* vagor, erro, palor; (about) pervagor; (over) pererro ①
wandering¹ *adj* errabundus; vagus; erraticus
wandering² *n* erratio *f*; error *m*
wane *vi* decresco; minuor; tabesco ③
want¹ *n* egestas, inopia, penuria, defectio *f*
want² *vt* (lack) careo, egeo, indigeo ② *all* + *abl*; desidero ①; (wish) volo ③; opto ①; cupio ③
■ **~** *vi* deficio ③; desum, absum *ir*
wanting *adj*:
□ **be ~** deficio ③, desum *ir*
wanton *adj* petulans, procax; libidinosus; lascivus; protervus
war *n* bellum *nt*; Mars *m*; arma *ntpl*
warble *vi* cano ③; fritinnio ④
ward¹ *n* (minor) pupillus *m*; pupilla *f*
ward² *vt* (off) arceo ②; averto ③; prohibeo ②
warden *n* custos *m/f*
warder *n* excubitor *m*; vigil; custos *m/f*
wardrobe *n* arca vestiaria *f*; vestiarium *nt*; (clothes) vestimenta *ntpl*
warehouse *n* mercium receptaculum *nt*; cella *f*
wares *n* merces *fpl*
warfare *n* bellum *nt*; res militaris *f*

warily *adv* caute, circumspecte

wariness *n* cautio, circumspectio *f*

warlike *adj* militaris, bellicosus, bellicus, pugnax

warm¹ *adj* calidus; tepidus; fig acer; iracundus

warm² *vt* tepefacio, calefacio ③; foveo ②

warmth *n* calor, tepor *m*

warn *vt* moneo; praemoneo ②

warning *n* monitio *f*; monitum *nt*; monitus *m*; fig exemplum *nt*

warp *vt* perverto ③
■ ~ *vi* (as wood) curvor ①; fig pervertor ③

warrant¹ *n* cautio; auctoritas, fides; licentia, facultas *f*; mandatum *nt*

warrant² *vt* (securum) praesto ①; promitto ③; sancio ④; copiam do ① + *dat*; (excuse) excuso ①

warranty *n* satisdatio *f*

warrior *n* miles *m*; homo militaris, bellator *m*

wart *n* verruca *f*

wary *adj* cautus, providus; prudens, circumspectus

wash¹ *vt* lavo ①; abluo ③
■ ~ *vi* lavor ①; perluor ③

wash² *n* lavatio *f*; (colour) fucus *m*

washing *n* lavatio; lotura *f*

washtub *n* alveus *m*; labrum *nt*

wasp *n* vespa *f*

waste¹ *n* (laying waste) vastatio *f*; (loss) detrimentum; (financial) dispendium *nt*; (refuse) ramenta *ntpl*

waste² *vt* (lay waste) vasto ①; (spend) prodigo, profundo, consumo, absumo ③
■ ~ **away** *vi* tabesco ③

wasteful *adj* profusus, prodigus

wasteland *n* solitudo *f*; deserta *ntpl* (desert)

watch¹ *n* (guard) vigilia *f*; excubiae *fpl*; (clock) horologium *nt*

watch² *vt* custodio ④; observo ①
■ ~ *vi* vigilo ①

watchful *adj* vigilans; vigil, vigilax

watchman *n* vigil, excubitor, custos *m*

watch-tower *n* specula *f*

watchword *n* tessera *f*; signum *nt*

water¹ *n* aqua *f*; latex *m*; lympha *f*; (urine) urina *f*

water² *vt* rigo, irrigo ①; aqua misceo ②

watercress *n* nasturcium *nt*

waterfall *n* aqua desiliens *f*; cataracta *f*

water-mill *n* mola aquaria *f*

waterproof *adj* impervius

waterworks *n* aquarum ductus, aquaeductus *m*

watery *adj* aquaticus; aquosus; (in appearance) aquatilis

wave¹ *n* unda *f*; fluctus *m*

wave² *vi* fluctuo, undo, fluito ①
■ ~ *vt* moveo ②, agito ①

waver *vi* fluctuo; (vacillate) labo; fig dubito ①

wavering *adj* dubius, incertus

wavy *adj* undans; undosus; (curling) crispus

wax¹ *n* cera *f*

wax² *vt* cero, incero ①

wax³ *vi* (grow) cresco ③; augeor ②

waxy *adj* cerosus

way *n* via *f*; iter *nt*; fig (manner, *etc.*) ratio *f*; modus; (custom) mos; (course) cursus *m*

wayfarer *n* viator *m*

waylay *vt* insidior ① + *dat*

wayward *adj* libidinosus; inconstans; levis; mutabilis

we *pn* nos
□ ~ **ourselves** nosmet ipsi

weak *adj* infirmus, debilis, enervatus, imbecillus, invalidus

weaken *vt* infirmo, debilito, enervo; (things) extenuo ①

weakness *n* infirmitas, debilitas; imbecillitas *f*; (failing) vitium *nt*

wealth *n* divitiae, opes *fpl*; opulentia; abundantia *f*

wealthy *adj* opulentus, dives; locuples; abundans

wean *vt* infantem ab ubere depello ③; fig dedoceo ②

weapon *n* telum *nt*; arma *ntpl*

wear *vt* (on the body) gero ③; gesto ①
■ ~ *vi* duro ①; (be worn out) atteror ③
□ ~ **out** tero, exedo, consumo ③

weariness *n* lassitudo, fatigatio *f*; languor *m*

weary¹ *adj* lassus, fessus, defessus, fatigatus; languidus; operosus

weary[2] *vt* lasso, fatigo, defatigo ①; conficio ③
  ■ ∼ *vi* defatigor ①

weasel *n* mustela *f*

weather *n* caelum *nt*; tempestas *f*

weather-beaten *adj* adustus, tempestate iactatus

weave *vt* texo; necto ③

weaver *n* textor *m*

web *n* textura *f*; textum *nt*
  □ **spider's** ∼ aranea *f*

web-footed *adj* palmipes

wedding *n* nuptiae *fpl*

wedding-day *n* dies nuptiarum *m*

wedge[1] *n* cuneus *m*

wedge[2] *vt* cuneo ①

wedge-shaped *adj* cuneatus

wedlock *n* matrimonium *nt*

weed[1] *n* herba inutilis *or* noxia *f*

weed[2] *vt* runco, erunco ①; sarrio ④

week *n* hebdomas, septimana *f*

weekly *adj* hebdomadalis

weep *vi* fleo ②; lacrimo ①; (for) deploro ①

weeping *n* ploratus, fletus *m*; lacrimae *fpl*

weigh *vt* pendo ③; pondero; penso; fig meditor ①; (down) gravo, degravo ①; opprimo ③

weight *n* pondus *nt*; (heaviness) gravitas *f*; (burden) onus *nt*; fig momentum, pondus *nt*

weighty *adj* ponderosus, onerosus, (heavy, important) gravis

welcome[1] *adj* gratus, acceptus
  □ ∼! salve!

welcome[2] *n* gratulatio, salutatio *f*

welcome[3] *vt* salvere iubeo ②; excipio ③

weld *vt* ferrumino, conferrumino ①

welfare *n* salus; utilitas, prosperitas *f*; bonum *nt*

well[1] *n* puteus, fons *m*

well[2] *adj* sanus, validus; integer
  □ **be** ∼ valeo ②
  ■ ∼ *adv* bene; recte; scite, scienter; praeclare
  □ **very** ∼ optime

well-being *n* salus *f*

well-born *adj* nobilis, nobili genere ortus

well-bred *adj* liberaliter educatus; comis

well-known *adj* pervulgatus; notus; celeber, nobilis

well-wisher *n* benevolus, amicus *m*

west *n* occidens, occasus
  ■ ∼ **wind** *n* Favonius, Zephyrus *m*

westerly *adj* occidentalis, occiduus

western *adj* occidentalis, occiduus

westward(s) *adv* in occasum, occasum versus

wet[1] *adj* umidus, uvidus, madidus, udus

wet[2] *vt* madefacio ③; rigo, umecto ①

wetness *n* umor *m*

whale *n* balaena *f*; cetus *m*

what *pn* quid, quidnam, ecquid
  ■ ∼ *adj* qualis, quantus; qui

whatever *adj & pn* quodcumque, quicquid

whatsoever *adj & pn* quodcumque, quicquid

wheat *n* triticum *nt*

wheedle *vt* blandior, delenio ④; adulor ①

wheel *n* rota *f*; (lathe) tornus *m*
  ■ ∼ *vt&i* circumago(r) ③, roto(r) ①; converto(r) ③

wheelbarrow *n* pabo *m*

wheeze *vi* anhelo ①

when *adv & conj* cum, ubi; ut, postquam; interrog quando?

whence *adv* unde

whenever *rel adv* quandocunque, quoties, quotiescunque

where *adv* interrog ubi? qua? rel qua, ubi
  □ ∼**as** quoniam, quandoquidem, cum; quo
  □ ∼**upon** quo facto

wherever *rel adv* quacunque, ubicumque

whet *vt* acuo; exacuo ③

whether *conj*:
  □ ∼ … **or** seu, sive; utrum … an, -ne … an

whey *n* serum *nt*

which *adj* interrog quis, qui?; uter? rel qui
  □ ∼**ever** quicunque, quisquis

whiff *n* halitus *m*

while[1] *n* tempus, spatium *nt*; mora *f*
  □ **in a little** ∼ mox, brevi, postmodo
  □ **for a** ∼ paullulum

while[2] *conj* dum, quoad; donec

whilst *conj* ▶ **while**[2]

W

whim n libido f

whimper vi vagio [4]

whimsical adj ridiculus, absurdus

whine[1] vi vagio [4]; queror [3]

whine[2] n vagitus m; querela f

whip[1] n flagellum nt; scutica f

whip[2] vt flagello, verbero [1]

whipping n verberatio f

whirl[1] n vertex, turbo m; (of a spindle) verticillus m; vertigo f

whirl[2] vt torqueo, intorqueo [2]; roto [1] ■ ~ vi rotor [1]; torqueor [2]

whirlpool n vertex, gurges m

whirlwind n turbo, typhon m

whisk[1] n scopula f

whisk[2] vt verro [3] ■ ~ vi circumagor [3]

whisper[1] n susurrus m; murmur nt

whisper[2] vt&i insusurro; susurro, murmuro [1]

whistle[1] vi sibilo [1]

whistle[2] n (pipe) fistula f; (sound) sibilus m; sibila ntpl; stridor m

white[1] adj albus, candidus; (of hair) canus

white[2] n album nt; candor m

whiten vt dealbo [1]; candefacio [3] ■ ~ vi albesco; candesco; canesco [3]

whiteness n albitudo f; candor m; (of hair) canities f

whitewash vt dealbo [1]

whither rel & adv quo; quorsum □ ~soever quocunque

whitish adj albidus, subalbus

who pn interrog quis? quae? quid? rel qui □ ~ever quicumque; quisquis

whole[1] adj totus, omnis, cunctus; integer; plenus, solidus; (safe) salvus

whole[2] n summa f; omnia ntpl □ on the ~ plerumque

wholesome n salubris, salutaris

wholly adv omnino, prorsus

whoop[1] n ululatus, clamor m

whoop[2] vi clamo, vociferor [1]

whore n meretrix f; scortum nt

whose rel pn cuius

why adv cur; quare? quamobrem?

wick n ellychnium nt

wicked adj impius, nefarius, flagitiosus; malus, scelestus, sceleratus

wickedness n nequitia, impietas f; scelus, flagitium nt

wicker n vimen nt ■ of ~ adj vimineus

wide adj latus, amplus; spatiosus □ far and ~ late, passim, undique ■ ~ly adv late, spatiose

widen vt&i dilato(r); laxo(r) [1]; extendor [3]; promoveor [2]

widespread adj longe lateque diffusus, pervulgatus

widow n vidua f

widowed adj viduatus, viduus

widower n viduus vir m

width n latitudo; amplitudo; laxitas f

wield vt tracto; guberno [1]; gero [3]; exerceo [2]

wife n coniunx; uxor, marita f

wig n capillamentum, caliendrum nt

wild adj ferus, silvestris; (of places) vastus; immanis; fig incultus; saevus; insanus

wilderness n locus desertus m; vastitas, solitudo f

wile n fraus f; dolus m; ars f

wilful adj pervicax, obstinatus ■ ~ly adv pervicaciter; (deliberately) de industria

will[1] n voluntas; libido; auctoritas f; arbitrium nt; (purpose) propositum; (last ~) testamentum nt

will[2] vt volo ir, iubeo [2] □ leave by ~ lego [1]; relinquo [3]

willing adj libens, facilis, promptus ■ ~ly adv libenter; prompte

willow n salix f

wily adj vafer, astutus, callidus, dolosus, subdolus

win vt&i lucror [1]; lucrifacio [3]; (obtain) potior [4] + abl; consequor, adipiscor [3]; fig expugno [1]; (the battle, etc.) victoriam adipiscor [3]; supero [1]; vinco [3]

wince vi abhorreo [2]

winch n sucula f

wind[1] n ventus m; aura f; flatus m; flabra ntpl

wind[2] vt circumvolvo; circumverto [3]; glomero [1]; torqueo [2] ■ ~ vi sinuor, glomero [1]; circumvolvor [3] □ ~ up fig concludo [3]

windfall n fig lucrum insperatum nt

winding adj flexuosus, sinuosus

windmill n mola f

window n fenestra f; specularia ntpl

windpipe n arteria f

windy adj ventosus

wine n vinum, merum nt
 □ ∼ **cellar** apotheca f

wing n ala f; pennae fpl; fig cornu; latus nt

winged adj alatus; aliger, penniger, pennatus

wink[1] n nictus m

wink[2] vi nicto ①; coniveo ②
 □ ∼ **at** ignosco, praetermitto ③

winner n victor; superior m

winter[1] n hiems, bruma f

winter[2] vt&i hiemo, hiberno ①

wintry adj hiemalis, hibernus

wipe vt tergeo, detergeo ②; (the nose) emungo ③; (dry) sicco ①; (out) deleo ②

wire n filum metallicum nt

wisdom n sapientia, prudentia f

wise adj sapiens, prudens
 ■ ∼**ly** adv sapienter; prudenter

wish[1] n optatio f; optatum; desiderium nt; voluntas f

wish[2] vt&i opto ①; cupio ③, volo ir; (long for) desidero ①

wisp n fasciculus, manipulus m

wistful adj desiderii plenus

wit n (intelligence) ingenium nt; (humour) facetiae fpl; sal, lepos m; (person) vir acerrimo ingenio m

witch n saga, venefica, maga f

witchcraft n ars magica f; veneficium nt

with prep cum + abl; apud, penes both + acc; in + abl

withdraw vt seduco ③; avoco ①
 ■ ∼ vi recedo ③

wither vt torreo ②; sicco ①; uro, aduro ③
 ■ ∼ vi marceo ②; aresco, languesco ③

withhold vt detineo, retineo; cohibeo ②

within adv intus, intro
 ■ ∼ prep in + abl, intra + acc
 □ ∼ **a few days** paucis diebus

without prep sine, absque + abl

withstand vt obsisto, resisto ③ + dat

witness[1] n testis m/f; arbiter m; testimonium nt
 ■ **call to** ∼ vt testor, obtestor

witness[2] vt&i testificor, testor ①

witticism n dictum nt; sales mpl

wittingly adv scienter; cogitate

witty adj argutus, lepidus; salsus; facetus; dicax

wizard n magus, veneficus m

wizened adj retorridus

woad n vitrum nt

wobble vi titubo ①

woe n dolor, luctus m; calamitas f

woeful adj tristis, luctuosus, miser; maestus

wolf n lupus m; (she-∼) lupa f

woman n femina, mulier f

womanly adj muliebris

womb n uterus, venter m; alvus f

wonder[1] n miraculum; (astonishment) miratio f; stupor m

wonder[2] vi admiror; miror ①; stupeo ②; (would like to know) scire velim ir

wonderful adj mirabilis, mirus, mirificus, admirandus

wood n lignum nt; (timber) materies f; (forest) silva f

wooded adj silvosus; saltuosus

wooden adj ligneus

woodland n silvae fpl; nemora ntpl

wood-nymph n Dryas, Hamadryas f

woodpecker n picus m

woodworm n teredo, tinea f

woody adj silvosus; silvestris; saltuosus

wool n lana f

woollen adj laneus

woolly adj (of wool) laneus; (as sheep, etc.) lanatus, laniger

word[1] n verbum; vocabulum; nomen; dictum nt

word[2] vt verbis exprimo, describo ③

wordy adj verbosus

work[1] n opera f; opus; (task) pensum nt; (trouble) labor m

work[2] vi laboro, operor ①
 ■ ∼ vt (handle) tracto ①; (ply) exerceo ②; (fashion) fabrico ①; (on) persuadeo ② + dat

work-basket n calathus m

worker n operarius m; opifex m/f

w

working *adj* operans
  □ ~ **day** negotiosus dies *m*

workman *n* opifex, artifex, faber, operarius *m*

workmanship *n* opus *nt*; ars *f*

workshop *n* officina, fabrica *f*

world *n* mundus, orbis, orbis terrarum *m*
  □ **the next** ~ vita futura *f*
  □ **where in the** ~ ubi gentium

worldly *adj* terrenus, humanus; saecularis, profanus

worm[1] *n* vermis, vermiculus *m*

worm[2] *vt* fig (~ out) extorqueo ②; expiscor ①

worried *adj* anxius

worry[1] *n* anxietas, sollicitudo, vexatio *f*

worry[2] *vt* dilacero; fig vexo, excrucio ①

worse *adj* peior, deterior
  ■ ~ *adv* peius
  □ **make** ~ corrumpo ③; depravo ①; exaspero ①
  □ **get** ~ ingravesco ③

worsen *vi* ingravesco ③

worship[1] *n* reverentia; adoratio *f*; cultus *m*

worship[2] *vt* veneror, adoro ①; colo ③

worst *adj* pessimus; extremus, ultimus
  ■ ~ *adv* pessime

worth[1] *n* pretium *nt*; dignitas *f*; (excellence) virtus *f*

worth[2] *adj* dignus
  □ **be** ~ valeo ②
  □ **it is** ~**while** operae pretium est

worthiness *n* meritum *nt*; dignitas *f*

worthless *adj* vilis, levis; inutilis; nequam *indecl*

worthlessness *n* levitas *f*; inane *nt*

worthy *adj* dignus, condignus

wound[1] *n* vulnus *nt*; plaga *f*

wound[2] *vt* vulnero, saucio ①; fig offendo, laedo ③

wounded *adj* saucius

wrangle[1] *n* rixa, altercatio *f*; iurgium *nt*

wrangle[2] *vi* rixor, altercor ①

wrap *vt* involvo, obvolvo ③; velo ①

wrapper *n* involucrum; tegmen *nt*

wrath *n* ira; iracundia *f*; furor *m*

wreath *n* (of flowers) sertum *nt*; corona *f*

wreathe *vt* torqueo ②; convolvo; necto ③

wreck[1] *n* (shipwreck) naufragium; fig damnum *nt*; ruina *f*

wreck[2] *vt* frango ③

wrecked *adj* (shipwrecked) naufragus; fig fractus

wrench *vt* detorqueo, contorqueo ②; luxo ①

wrestle *vi* luctor ①

wrestler *n* luctator *m*

wrestling *n* luctamen *nt*; luctatio *f*

wrestling-school *n* palaestra *f*

wretch *n* miser, perditus *m*, nequam *m indecl*

wretched *adj* miser, miserabilis, infelix, malus, vilis

wriggle *vi* torqueor ②

wring *vt* torqueo ②

wrinkle[1] *n* ruga *f*

wrinkle[2] *vt* rugo, corrugo ①; (the brow) (frontem) contraho ③

wrinkled *adj* rugosus

wrist *n* carpus *m*

write *vt&i* scribo; perscribo; (a literary work) compono ③

writer *n* (author) auctor *m*

writhe *vi* torqueor ②

writing *n* (act) scriptio *f*; scriptum *nt*; scriptura; (hand) manus *f*; chirographum *nt*; (document) tabulae *fpl*

writing-desk *n* scrinium *nt*

wrong[1] *adj* pravus, perversus; vitiosus; fig falsus; iniustus, iniquus
  ■ ~**ly** *adv* falso; male, prave, perperam
  □ **be** ~ erro ①; fallor ③

wrong[2] *n* nefas *nt indecl*; iniuria *f*

wrong[3] *vt* laedo ③; violo ①; iniuriam infero *ir*

wrongful *adj* iniustus, iniuriosus

wry *adj* distortus, obliquus; curvus

Yy

yacht *n* celox *f*

yard *n* (court) area; (for poultry) cohors; (measure) ulna *f*

yarn *n* filum *nt*; lana *f*; linum *nt*; fig fabula, narratio *f*

yawn¹ *vi* oscito; fig hio ①; (gape open) hisco, dehisco ③

yawn² *n* oscitatio *f*

year *n* annus *m*

yearly *adj* annuus, anniversarius

yearn *vi* desidero ①; requiro; cupio ③

yearning *n* desiderium *nt*

yeast *n* fermentum *nt*

yell¹ *vi* ululo, clamo ①

yell² *n* ululatus, clamor *m*

yellow *adj* flavus, luteus, croceus

yellowish *adj* sufflavus, fulvus, gilvus

yelp *vi* gannio ④

yes *adv* ita, ita est; recte; immo; sane, certe

yesterday *adv* heri
  □ **of ~** hesternus *m*

yet *conj* nihilominus, quamquam; tamen; (of time) adhuc
  □ **even ~** etiam nunc
  □ **not ~** nondum

yew *n* taxus *f*

yield¹ *n* fructus *m*

yield² *vt* (bring forth) fero *ir*, pario ③; praebeo ②; (give up) cedo, concedo ③
  ■ **~** *vi* cedo ③; manus do ①

yielding *adj* obsequiosus; fig mollis; lucrum afferens

yoke¹ *n* iugum *nt*; fig servitus *f*

yoke² *vt* iugum impono, iungo, coniungo ③

yolk *n* luteum *nt*; vitellus *m*

you *pn* (singular) tu; (plural) vos
  □ **~ yourself** tu ipse

young¹ *adj* parvus, infans; fig novus

young² *n* adulescens, puer *m*; (offspring) progenies *f*; genus *nt*; fetus *m*; proles *f*

younger *adj* iunior, minor

youngster *n* adulescentulus *m*

your *prep* tuus; vester

yourself *pn* tu ipse, tute
  □ **yourselves** vos ipsi

youth *n* (age) adulescentia; iuventus, iuventa, iuventas; (collectively) iuventus *f*; (young man) adulescens, iuvenis *m*

youthful *adj* iuvenilis; puerilis

Zz

zeal *n* studium *nt*; fervor *m*; alacritas *f*

zealous *adj* studiosus; alacer, acer, ardens

zero *n* nihil *nt*

zest *n* sapor, gustus; fig gustatus; impetus *m*; studium *nt*

zigzag¹ *n* anfractus *m*

zigzag² *adj* obliquus

zodiac *n* zodiacus, signifer orbis *m*

zone *n* (region of the earth) zona *f*

zoology *n* descriptio animantium *f*

Historical and Mythological Names

A. = **Aulus**

Achaeī, **ōrum** the ruling nation among the Greeks in Homeric times

Achillēs, **is** son of Peleus and of Thetis

Ācis, **idis** son of Faunus loved by Galatea

Actaeōn, **onis** a huntsman torn to pieces by his own dogs for having seen Diana bathing

Adōnis, **is** & **idis** son of Cinyras, king of Cyprus, beloved by Venus; beautiful young man

Aegēus, **ī** father of Theseus

Aemilius Paullus, Lūcius victor over Perseus, king of Macedon, at Pydna in 168 BC

Aenēās, **ae** son of Anchises and Venus

Aeolus, **ī** god of the winds

Agamemnōn, **onis** king of Mycenae, commander-in-chief of the Greek forces at Troy

Agathoclēs, **is** (361–289 BC) king of Sicily, celebrated for his victory over the Carthaginians to win Sicily

Agricola, **ae**: **Cn. Iūlius** ~ (40–93 AD) governor of Britain for seven years (77–84 AD)

Aiāx, **ācis** one of two Greek heroes in the Trojan War, **Aiāx Telamōnius** and **Aiāx** son of Oileus, known together as the **Aiācēs**

Alexander, **drī**, Alexander (the Great) (356–23 BC), king of Macedon (336–23 BC)

Alcīdēs, **ae** Hercules (*lit.* descendant of Alceus)

Alcmaeōn, **ōnis** son of Amphiaraüs, who killed his mother Eriphyle

Alcyonē, **ēs** wife of Ceÿx; she was changed into a kingfisher

Amāta, **ae** in Virgil's *Aeneid*, the wife of Latinus and mother of Lavinia

Amphitrītē, **ēs** wife of Neptune, goddess of the sea

Anchīsēs, **ae** father of Aeneas

Andromacha, **ae** (also **Andromachē**, **ēs**) wife of Hector

Andromeda, **ae** daughter of Cepheus and Cassiope; rescued by Perseus from a sea-monster

Anna, **ae** in Virgil's *Aeneid*, sister of Dido

Antōnius, Mārcus (Mark Antony) (83–30 BC) the lover of Cleopatra, defeated by Octavius Caesar at Actium in 31 BC

Anūbis, **is** & **idis** Egyptian dog-headed god

Apellēs, **is** renowned Greek painter

Apollō, **inis** god of the sun, prophecy, music and poetry, archery and medicine, son of Jupiter and Leto

Arachnē, **ēs** a Lydian woman who challenged Athena to a contest of weaving and was turned into a spider

Archimēdēs, **is** mathematician and mechanical inventor at Syracuse in the 3rd century BC

Argō *f.* ship in which the Greek heroes under Jason sailed to Colchis to obtain the golden fleece

Argonautae, **ārum** *m. pl.* the heroes who sailed in the *Argo*

Argus, **ī** the hundred-eyed keeper of Io

Ariadnē, **ēs** daughter of Minos, king of Crete

Ascanius, **iī** son of Aeneas; founder of Alba Longa

Atalanta, **ae** (1) daughter of Iasias; took part in the hunt of the Calydonian boar; (2) daughter of Schoeneus; very swift of foot; engaged in a race with Hippomenes and was defeated by a ruse

Athēna, **ae**, patron goddess of Athens, war-goddess and goddess of spinning and weaving.

Atlās, **antis** a giant who supported the heavens on his shoulders

Atreus, **ī** king of Mycenae, father of Agamemnon and Menelaüs

Augustus *see* OCTAVIUS; after Octavian the title was held by all emperors

Bacchus, **ī** god of wine, son of Jupiter and Semele

Bellerophōn, **ontis** slayer of the Chimaera; rode the winged horse Pegasus

Bellōna, **ae** goddess of war

Bona Dea a goddess worshipped by Roman women as goddess of Fertility and Chastity on 1st May

Boreās, **ae** the north wind

Boudicca, **ae** *f.* British leader (from East Anglia) of the famous, though doomed, revolt against the occupying Romans in 61 AD

Brūtus, M. Iūnius (85–42 BC) one of the assassins of Julius Caesar, defeated at and taking his own life at Philippi in 42 BC

C. = **Gaius**

Cācus, ī a giant, son of Vulcan, slain by Hercules

Cadmus, ī legendary founder of Thebes

Caesar, **aris** a Roman family name, borne by all the Roman emperors until Hadrian and thereafter by both the emperor and his heir; **C. Iūlius Caesar** (100–44 BC), one of the great military men of the ancient world, who became dictator and was assassinated on the Ides (15th) of March, 44 BC

Calypsō, **ūs** f. a nymph, daughter of Oceanus, ruling over the island Ogygia

Camēnae, **ārum** Roman goddesses identified with the Muses

Camilla, **ae** in Virgil's *Aeneid*, a maiden-warrior of the Volsci, an Italian tribe

Cassandra, **ae** prophetess, daughter of Priam and Hecuba

Cassius, **C. Longīnus** one of the assassins of Julius Caesar, defeated at and taking his own life at Philippi in 42 BC

Castor, **oris** twin-brother of Pollux, son of Tyndareus

Catilīna, **ae**: **L. Sergius** ~ supposedly a conspirator against the Roman state when Cicero was consul (63 BC), killed on the battlefield near Pistoria in 62 BC

Catō, **ōnis**: (1) **M. Porcius** ~ (234–149 BC) the censor, author of the phrase **dēlenda est Carthāgō** ('Carthage must be destroyed'); (2) **M. Porcius** ~ **Uticēnsis** an opponent of Caesar; committed suicide at Utica when his cause was defeated, 49 BC

Centaurī, **ōrum** m. pl. a wild race of Thessaly, half-man, half-horse

Cephalus, ī husband of Procris, beloved by Eos (Dawn); he accidentally killed his wife

Cerberus, ī three-headed dog, guarding the entrance to Hell

Charōn, **ōnis** ferryman of the Lower World

Chimaera, **ae** f. a fire-breathing monster with the head of a lion, body of a she-goat, and tail of a snake

Chīrō(n), **ōnis** a Centaur who tutored Aesculapius, Hercules and Achilles

Cicerō, **ōnis**: **M. Tullius** ~ (106–43 BC) one of the greatest politicians, writers and lawyers of the ancient world

Cincinnātus, ī Roman dictator (485 BC)

Circē, **ēs** & **ae** a famous sorceress

Cleopātra, **ae** queen of Egypt, daughter of Ptolemy Auletes; loved by Mark Antony

Clīō, **ūs** f. the Muse of History

Clōthō, (acc. **ō**), f. one of the Fates (who span the thread of life)

Clytaemnēstra, **ae** wife of Agamemnon

Cn. = **Gnaeus**

Coriolānus surname of C. Marcius, who took Corioli; became an enemy of his countrymen, the Romans

Crassus, **M. Licinius**, a member (with Julius Caesar and Pompey) of the First Triumvirate; killed by the Parthians near Carrhae in 53 BC

Creūsa, **-ae** in Virgil's *Aeneid*, daughter of the Trojan king Priam and his wife Hecuba, and mother of Ascanius

Croesus, ī king of Lydia; a (proverbially) rich man

Cupīdō, **inis** the love god Cupid, son of Venus

Cybelē, **ēs** the great Phrygian mother goddess

Cyclōps, **ōpos** Cyclops; **Cyclōpes**, **um** m. pl. one-eyed giants, workmen in Vulcan's smithy

Cytherēa, **ae** f. Venus

D. = **Decimus**

Daedalus, ī legendary Athenian craftsman and inventor, creator of the labyrinth and father of Icarus

Danaē, **ēs** mother of Perseus

Daphnē, **ēs** daughter of the river god Peneus, loved by Apollo

Dardanus, ī ancestor of the Trojan dynasty

Decius Mūs consul 340 BC; devoted himself to death to save his country

Dēiphobus, ī a son of Priam who married Helen after the death of Paris

Deucaliōn, **ōnis** king of Phthia in Thessaly, son of Prometheus; with his wife Pyrrha was the only mortal saved from the flood

Diāna, **ae** goddess of hunting, sister of Apollo

Dīdō, **ōnis** foundress of Carthage

Dīs, **Dītis** Pluto

Drancēs, **ae** m. in Virgil's *Aeneid*, the Italian chief who taunts the Rutulian king Turnus

Dryades, **um** f. pl. wood-nymphs

Echidna, **ae** f. Lernaean hydra, killed by Hercules

Ēlectra, **ae** daughter of Agamemnon and Clytemnestra

Endymiōn, **ōnis** a beautiful youth, beloved by Diana

Epēus, ī constructor of the Wooden Horse at Troy

Epicūrus, ī Greek philosopher, originator of the Epicurean philosophy

Eratō f. one of the Muses, associated by Ovid with love poetry

Erebus, ī god of darkness; the Lower World

Eurōpa, ae (also **Eurōpē**, ēs) daughter of Agenor, king of Phoenicia; carried off by Jupiter in the form of a bull

Eurydicē, ēs wife of Orpheus

Euterpē, ēs f. a Muse, later associated with the reed-pipe

Evander, drī emigrated from Arcadia to Italy 60 years before the Trojan War

Fabius Maximus Verrūcōsus, Quīntus (died 203 BC) the Roman dictator whose famous policy of attrition rather than direct confrontation with Hannibal earned him the name **Cūnctātor** ('Delayer')

Faunī, ōrum m. pl. Fauns

Feretrius, iī an epithet of Jupiter as worshipped on the Capitol at Rome

Flōra, ae goddess of the flowers and spring

Fōrtūna, ae the Goddess Fortune

Galatēa, ae a sea-nymph, loved by Acis

Ganymēdēs, is Jupiter's cupbearer

Gēryōn, onis a mythical three-bodied monster who lived in Erythea, an island in the far west; his oxen were carried off by Hercules

Gigantes, um the Giants

Gorgō(n), onis the snake-haired daughter of Phorcus, Medusa, and her two sisters were called the Gorgons

Gracchus, ī. (1) **C. Semprōnius** ~ a radical tribune of the people and younger brother of Tiberius, killed in 121 BC; (2) **Ti. Semprōnius** ~ a radical tribune of the people and older brother of Gaius, killed in 133 BC

Grādīvus, ī a title of Mars

Hamilcar, aris father of Hannibal

Hannibal, alis Punic surname; the great Carthaginian general during the Second Punic War, son of Hamilcar

Hannō, ōnis Punic surname, opponent of Hannibal

Harpyae, ārum f. pl. mythical rapacious monsters, half-bird, half-woman

Hasdrubal, alis (1) brother of Hannibal; (2) son-in-law of Hamilcar

Hēbē, ēs goddess of youth, cupbearer to the gods

Hecatē, ēs goddess of the Lower World, worshipped as goddess of spells and enchantments

Hector, oris son of Priam and Hecuba

Helena, ae (also **Helenē**, ēs) (1) daughter of Jupiter and Leda, wife of Menelaüs; (2) mother of Constantine the Great

Helenus, ī after the fall of Troy, husband of Hector's widow Andromache and king of Chaonia, a part of Epirus

Hellē, ēs f. daughter of Athamas, king of Boeotia, who was drowned in the narrow sea (Hellespont) called after her

Herculēs, is & (e)ī son of Jupiter and Alcmene, a demigod and divine hero

Hesperides, um f. pl. daughters of Erebus and the Night; they lived in an island garden beyond Mt Atlas and guarded the golden apples which Juno received on her wedding

Hesperus, ī son of Atlas, or of Cephalus, and Aurora; planet Venus as evening-star

Hōrae, ārum f. pl. the Hours, goddesses of the seasons

Hyacinthus, ī beautiful youth beloved by Apollo, and accidentally killed by him

Hȳdra, ae f. seven-headed serpent, killed by Hercules

Hylās, ae beautiful youth who accompanied Hercules on the Argonautic expedition

Hyperiōn, ōnis son of a Titan and the Earth; the Sun

Iacchus, ī Bacchus

Iāsōn, onis son of Aeson, king of Thessaly, Grecian hero

Īcarus, ī son of Daedalus; tried to fly from Crete and fell into the sea

Īlia, ae Rhea Silvia, mother of Romulus and Remus

Īō daughter of Inachus; beloved of Zeus, turned into a cow and pursued by Argus

Īphigenīa, ae daughter of Agamemnon and Clytemnestra

Iris, idis & is daughter of Thaumus and Electra, messenger of the gods and goddess of the rainbow

Īsis, idis & is Egyptian goddess, wife of Osiris

Itys, yos son of Tereus and Procne; made into a stew and served up to his father

Iūlius see CAESAR

Iūlus, ī son of Aeneas, also called Ascanius

Iūnō, **ōnis** goddess and wife of Jupiter

Iuppiter, **Iovis** Jupiter, the chief Roman god

K. = **Kaesō**

L. = **Lūcius**

Lāocoōn, **oontis** a Trojan priest of Neptune

Lāodamīa wife of Protesilaus

Lāomedōn, **ontis** father of Priam, king of Troy, killed by Hercules

Latīnus, **ī** king of the Laurentians

Lātōna, **ae** mother of Apollo and Diana

Lausus, **ī** in Virgil's *Aeneid*, the son of the monstrous Mezentius

Lāvīnia, **ae** daughter of Latinus, wife of Aeneas

Lēander, **drī** the lover of Hero

Lēda, **ae** (also **Lēdē**, **ēs**) wife of Tyndareus, mother of Clytemnestra, Helen, Castor and Pollux

Līber, **erī** Bacchus

Lībera, **ae** Proserpine

Libitīna, **ae** goddess of funerals

Līvia Drūsilla (58 BC–29 AD) wife of the first Roman emperor Augustus and mother, by her first husband, of the second, Tiberius

Lūcifer, **erī** *m.* planet Venus as morning-star

Lūcīna, **ae** goddess of childbirth

Lucrētia, **ae** *f.* the rape victim of the son of the Etruscan king Tarquinius Superbus; she committed suicide and thus proved the catalyst for the expulsion of the Tarquins

Lūna, **ae** the goddess of the Moon

Lupercālia, **ium** *nt. pl.* festival of the god Lupercus on 15th February

Lycāōn, **onis** son of Pelasgus and king of Arcadia, who was transformed into a wolf

M. = **Mārcus**; **M'.** = **Mānius**

Maecēnās, **Gaius** (died 8 BC) a friend of Augustus and a great patron of the arts

Maeonidēs, **ae** Homer

Māia, **ae** mother of Mercury by Jupiter

Mam. = **Māmercus**

Marius name of a Roman gens; **C.** ~ conquered Jugurtha; crushed the Cimbri and Teutons; consul in 107 BC and six times subsequently

Mārs, **tis** (also **Māvors**, **ortis**) the god of war

Mausōlus, **ī** king of Caria, died 353 BC; his tomb was a costly monument called the Mausoleum

Māvors, **ortis** *see* MARS

Maximus, Q. Fabius *see* FABIUS

Mēdēa, **ae** daughter of Aeëtes, king of Colchis; deserted by Jason, killed her own children

Medūsa, **ae** one of the three Gorgons; anyone who looked at her head, even after it had been cut off, was turned to stone

Meleager, **grī** son of Oeneus and Althaea, who took part in the Calydonian boar hunt; his survival depended on the continuing existence of a fire brand

Melpomenē, **ēs** *f.* one of the Muses, later associated with tragedy

Memnōn, **onis** son of Tithonus and Aurora, king of the Ethiopians

Menelāus, **ī** brother of Agamemnon

Mentor, **ōris** faithful friend of Ulysses

Mercurius, **iī** son of Jupiter and Maia, the messenger of the gods; the god of eloquence and of merchants and thieves

Mēzentius, **iī** in Virgil's *Aeneid*, a brutal tyrant of Caerē in Etruria

Midās, **ae** king of Phrygia; all he touched was turned into gold

Minerva, **ae** daughter of Zeus, goddess of wisdom, of the arts, of handicraft and women's works

Mīnōs, **ōis** son of Zeus and Europa, king of Crete

Mīnōtaurus, **ī** *m.* monster with the head of a bull in the Labyrinth of Crete

Mīsēnus, **ī** in Virgil's *Aeneid*, the Trojan trumpeter who roused the jealousy of the sea-god Triton and was drowned

Mnēmosynē, **ēs** *f.* Memory, the mother of the Muses

Morpheus, (*acc.* **ea**) god of dreams

Mūsa, **ae** *f.* Muse, one of the nine patron goddesses of the arts

Narcissus, **ī** son of Cephissus, enamoured of his own beauty and turned into a flower named after him

Nemesis, **eōs** goddess of retribution

Neoptolemus, **ī** (also called **Pyrrhus**) son of Achilles and Deidamia, the brutal killer of the Trojan king Priam

Neptūnus, **ī** the god of the sea

Nēreus, **ei** & **eos** a sea-god, son of Oceanus and Tethys

Nessus, ī *m*. a Centaur, killed by Hercules

Nestor, oris king of Pylos, one of the oldest of the Greek heroes at Troy

Nīsus, ī homosexual athlete in Virgil's *Aeneid*, partner of Euryalus, both of whom were killed in a sortie from the Trojan camp in Italy

Numitor, ōris king of Alba, father of Ilia, grandfather of Romulus and Remus

Octāvius a Roman family name; **C. Iūlius Caesar Octāviānus** (often also **Octāvius**) (63 BC–14 AD) great-nephew of Julius Caesar; victorious at Actium (31 BC); given the title **Augustus**; ruled as first Roman emperor

Olympia, ōrum *nt. pl.* the Olympic games at Olympia

Ops, Opis goddess of plenty, wife of Saturn

Orestēs, is son of Agamemnon killed his mother Clytemnestra

Ōrīōn, ōnis son of Hyrieus, a hunter; the constellation of Orion

Orpheus, eī & **eos** legendary musician, son of Oeagrus and Calliope, husband of Eurydice

Osīris, is Egyptian god, husband of Isis

P. = **Pūblius**

Palēs, is *f*. or *m*. tutelary goddess of flocks and herds

Palinūrus, ī the pilot of Aeneas

Palladium, ī *n*. statue of Pallas in the citadel of Troy; captured by Ulysses and Diomedes

Pallas, adis & ados Minerva, Athena

Pān, **Pānos** son of Mercury, the god of woods and shepherds, half-man, half-goat

Parca, ae *f*. one of the Fates; **Parcae**, ārum *pl.* the Fates, three sisters

Paris, idis a son of Priam and Hecuba; carried off Helen, wife of Menelaüs

Pāsiphaē, ēs daughter of Helios, wife of Minos, and sister of Circe

Patroclus, ī friend of Achilles, slain by Hector

Pēgasus, ī a winged horse, sprung from the blood of the slain Medusa; with the aid of Pegasus, Bellerophon slew the Chimaera

Pēleus, eī & **eos** king of a part of Thessaly, husband of Thetis, father of Achilles

Pēnelopē, ēs (also **Pēnelopa**, ae) *f*. wife of Ulysses, king of Ithaca; famed for her fidelity

Pēnēus, ī *m*. god of a river flowing through the vale of Tempe in Thessaly

Pentheus, eī & **eos** king of Thebes, grandson of Cadmus; opposed the worship of Bacchus and was torn to pieces by his mother

Perseus, eī & **eos** son of Jupiter and Danaë, killer of Medusa, husband of Andromeda

Phaedra, ae daughter of Minos, and second wife of Theseus; fell in love with Hippolytus

Phaëthōn, ontis son of Helios and Clymene; tried to drive the chariot of the sun

Philomēla, ae daughter of Pandion, sister of Procne; turned into a nightingale

Phoebus, ī Apollo

Pīcus, ī the Italian god of agriculture, changed into a woodpecker

Plēiades, um the seven daughters of Atlas and Pleione

Plūtō(n), ōnis the god of the Underworld

Pollūx, ūcis son of Tyndareus and Leda, brother of Castor

Polyphēmus, ī a Cyclops; son of Neptune

Polyxena, ae daughter of Priam; sacrificed to Achilles after the Trojan War

Pōmōna, ae the goddess of fruits

Portūnus, ī tutelary god of harbours

Priamus, ī king of Troy, son of Laomedon

Priāpus, ī *m*. a god of procreation

Procnē, ēs daughter of Pandion, wife of Tereus; she was turned into a swallow

Procrustēs, ae highwayman in Attica, slain by Theseus; had a bed which all his victims were made to fit

Promētheus, eī & **eos** son of Iapetus and Clymene; stole fire from heaven and gave it to mortals

Proserpina, ae daughter of Ceres, wife of Pluto

Prōtesilāus, ī husband of Laodamia; the first of the Greek expedition to land at Troy and the first to be killed

Psychē, ēs the mistress and eventually the wife of Cupid

Pygmaliōn, ōnis king of Cyprus; fell in love with a statue he had made himself; Venus then brought it to life

Pyladēs, is son of king Strophius, bosom-friend of Orestes

Pyramus, ī the lover of Thisbe

Pyrrhus, ī *see* NEOPTOLEMUS

Pythōn, ōnis *m*. a serpent slain by Apollo near Delphi

Q. = **Quīntus**

Remus, ī brother of Romulus

Rhadamanthus, ī son of Jupiter, brother of Minos, judge in the Lower World

Rhēa Silvia daughter of Numitor, mother of Romulus and Remus

Rōmulus, ī founder and first king of Rome

S. (also **Sex.**) = **Sextus**

Sāturnia, ae Juno

Sāturnus, ī father of Jupiter, originally a mythical king of Latium

Satyrī, ōrum Satyrs; companions of Bacchus

Scīpiō, ōnis: **P. Cornēlius ~** the conqueror of Hannibal at Zama in 202 BC, for which he received the cognomen **Āfricānus**

Scylla, ae f. a sea-monster; lived on the Italian side of the Straits of Messina, opposite Charybdis

Semelē, ēs daughter of Cadmus, mother of Bacchus, by Jupiter

Ser. = **Servius**

Serāpis, is & idis m. an Egyptian god

Sibylla, ae one of a class of prophetic females variously located

Sīlēnus, ī tutor of Bacchus, elderly, drunken, and bestial in character

Silvānus, ī m. god of the woods

Sp. = **Spurius**

Spartacus, ī a Thracian gladiator, leader of the gladiators in their war against Rome; killed 71 BC

Sulla, ae: **L. Cornēlius ~** (c.138–79 BC) dictator of Rome and legislator

Sȳrīnx, ingis f. a nymph changed into the reed from which Pan made his pipes

T. = **Titus**

Tantalus, ī son of Jupiter, father of Pelops and Niobe; divulged the secrets of the gods; was punished in the Underworld by a raging thirst which he could not quench

Tarpeia, ae Roman maiden, who treacherously opened the citadel to the Sabines

Tarquinius Superbus the last king of Rome

Tēreus, eī & eos king of Thrace, husband of Procne, and father of Itys; cut out the tongue of his wife's sister Philomela; Procne, in revenge, killed Itys and served him up to her husband in a stew

Terpsichorē, ēs f. a Muse, in later times associated with lyric poetry (dance)

Tēthys, yos a sea-goddess, wife of Oceanus

Thalēa (also **Thalīa**), ae f. the Muse of comedy or light verse

Themis, is goddess of justice and order

Thēseus, eī & eos king of Athens, son of Aegeus

Thespis, is a pioneer of Greek tragedy

Thetis, idis & idos a sea-nymph, daughter of Nereus, wife of Peleus, and mother of Achilles

Thisbē, ēs maiden of Babylon, loved by Pyramus

Ti. (also **Tib.**) = **Tiberius**

Tīresiās, ae a blind prophet of Thebes

Tīsiphonē, ēs f. a Fury

Tītān, ānos one of the Titans, a race of gods descended from Heaven and Earth, who preceded the Olympians; the sun-god

Tīthōnus, ī son of Laomedon, husband of Aurora

Tityos, ī a giant punished in the Underworld for attempting, on Juno's orders, to rape Latona

Trītōn, ōnis m. one of a kind of supernatural marine beings, represented as blowing conches and attending on Neptune

Trītōnis, idis & idos Minerva, Athena

Turnus, ī king of the Rutuli, killed by Aeneas

Tyndaris, idis Helen, daughter of Tyndareus

Typhōeus, eos a giant, struck with lightning by Jupiter, and buried under Etna

Ulixēs, is & eī Ulysses, king of Ithaca, one of the Greek heroes at Troy, also known as Odysseus

Ūrania, ae f. the Muse of Astronomy

Venus, eris f. the goddess of Love

Verrēs, is governor of Sicily, 73–71 BC; denounced by Cicero for his rapacity

Vertumnus, ī god of the seasons

Vesta, ae daughter of Saturn and Rhea, goddess of the hearth-fire and of domestic life

Vulcānus, ī (also **Volcānus**, ī) lame son of Juno, god of fire

Zephyrus, ī the west wind

Geographical Names

Acadēmīa, **ae** a gymnasium near Athens in which Plato taught

Achelōus, ī *m.* the largest river in Greece, rises in Mt Pindus and flows into the Ionian Sea

Acherōn, **ontis** *m.* river in the Underworld

Achīvus, **a**, **um** *adj.* Achaean, Grecian

Actium, ī *nt.* promontory and town in Epirus; celebrated for the victory of Augustus over Anthony in 31 BC

Aegyptius, **a**, **um** *adj.* Egyptian

Aegyptus, ī *f.* Egypt

Aetna, **ae** (also **Aetnē**, **ēs**) *f.* Mt Etna, a volcano in Sicily

Āfrī, **ōrum** *m. pl.* Africans

Āfrica, **ae** *f.* Africa, Libya

Alba (Longa), **ae** *f.* mother city of Rome (between the Alban Lake and Mons Albanus)

Albānī, **ōrum** *m. pl.* inhabitants of Alba Longa

Alexandrīa, **ae** *f.* city on the north coast of Egypt, founded by Alexander the Great

Alpēs, **ium** *f. pl.* the Alps

Alpīnus, **a**, **um** *adj.* of the Alps

Āpennīnus, ī *m.* the Apennine mountains

Āpūlia, **ae** *f.* region of south-east Italy

Arabia, **ae** *f.* Arabia

Arabicus, Arabus, **a**, **um** *adj.* Arabian

Argīlētum, ī *nt.* quarter of the city of Rome which contained many booksellers' and cobblers' shops

Argīvus, **a**, **um** *adj.* of Argos; Greek

Asia, **ae** *f.* (1) Asia; (2) the Roman province of Asia Minor

Ātella, **ae** *f.* an Oscan town of Campania, the home of a particular kind of farce

Athēnae, **ārum** *f. pl.* Athens

Athēniēnsis, **e** *adj.* Athenian

Atlās, **antis** *m.* mountain range in the north-west of Africa

Attica, **ae** *f.* city state of Greece, the capital of which was Athens

Atticus, **a**, **um** *adj.* Attic, Athenian

Aulis, **idis** *f.* seaport town in Boeotia from which the Greek fleet sailed for Troy

Ausonia, **ae** *f.* Italy

Aventīnus, ī *m.* the Aventine (one of the seven hills of Rome); ∼, **a**, **um** *adj.* relating to the Aventine

Avernus (lacus), ī *m.* Lago d'Averno, a lake near Naples that gave off mephitic vapours, considered to be the entrance to the Underworld

Belgae, **ārum** *m. pl.* the Belgians

Belgicus, **a**, **um** *adj.* Belgian, Belgic

Bēnācus, ī *m.* Lago di Garda, a lake of northern Italy

Bīthynia, **ae** *f.* district of Asia Minor between the Propontis and the Black Sea

Bīthȳnicus, Bīthȳnus, **a**, **um** *adj.* Bithynian

Boeōtia, **ae** *f.* district of Greece, the capital of which was Thebes

Bosp(h)orus, ī *m.*: (1) ∼ **Thrācius** the strait between the sea of Marmora and the Black Sea; (2) ∼ **Cimmerius** the strait between the sea of Azof and the Black Sea

Britannia, **ae** *f.* Britain

Britannicus, Britannus, **a**, **um** *adj.* British

Brundisium, **iī** *nt.* Brindisi, a seaport of Calabria

Byzantium, **iī** *nt.* Istanbul

Caecubum, ī *nt.* marshy district in southern Latium (producing the most excellent kind of Roman wine)

Calabria, **ae** *f.* a district of south-east Italy

Calēdonia, **ae** *f.* northern part of Britain

Campānia, **ae** *f.* a district of Italy south of Latium

Cannae, **ārum** *f. pl.* village in Apulia; the scene of the defeat of the Romans by Hannibal in 216 BC

Cantium, **iī** *nt.* Kent

Cappadocia, **ae** *f.* province of Asia Minor, between Silicia and Pontus

Cāria, **ae** *f.* country in the south-west of Asia Minor

Carthāgō, **inis** *f.* Carthage; ∼ **Nova** the modern Cartagena on the south-east coast of Spain

Castalia, **ae** *f.* fountain on Mt Parnassus at Delphi sacred to Apollo and the Muses

Castalius, **a**, **um** *adj*. Castalian

Caucasus, **ī** *m*. chain of mountains between the Black and Caspian Seas

Caÿstros, **ī** *m*. river in Lydia noted for its swans

Celtae, **ārum** *m*. *pl*. the Celts

Celticus, **a**, **um** *adj*. Celtic

Charybdis, **is** *f*. dangerous whirlpool between Italy and Sicily opposite to Scylla

Chersonēsus (also **Cherronēsus**), **ī** *f*. Chersonese; (1) Thracian, Gallipoli peninsula; (2) Tauric, between the Black Sea and the Sea of Azof.

Cilices, **um** *m*. *pl*. Cilicians

Cilicia, **ae** *f*. province in the south-east of Asia Minor

Cōcÿtus, **ī** *m*. river in the Underworld

Colchis, **idis** *f*. country in Asia, east of the Black Sea

Colch(ic)us, **a**, **um** *adj*. of Colchis

Corinthi(ac)us, **a**, **um** *adj*. Corinthian

Corinthus, **ī** *f*. a city of Greece, on the Corinthian isthmus

Crēs, **ētis** *m*. Cretan

Crēta, **ae** *f*. Crete

Cūmae, **ārum** *f*. *pl*. city on the coast of Campania

Cynthius, **a**, **um** *adj*. relating to Cynthus

Cynthus, **ī** *m*. mountain of Delos

Cyprius, **a**, **um** *adj*. of Cyprus

Cyprus, **ī** *f*. island in the Mediterranean Sea south of Cilicia

Dācī, **orum** *m*. *pl*. the Dacians

Dācia, **ae** *f*. country of the Dacians on the north of the Danube

Danaī, **ōrum** *m*. *pl*. the Greeks

Dānuvius, **ii** *m*. Danube

Dēlius, **a**, **um** *adj*. of Delos

Dēlos, **ī** *f*. the smallest of the Cyclades, famous for the worship of Apollo

Delphī, **ōrum** *m*. *pl*. Delphi (in Phocis), containing a famous oracle of Apollo; ∼ inhabitants of Delphi

Delphicus, **a**, **um** *adj*. of Delphi

Dēva, **ae** *f*. Chester

Dīa, **ae** *f*. Naxos

Dictaeus, **a**, **um** *adj*. of Dicte

Dictē, **ēs** *f*. mountain in Crete

Dōdōna, **ae** *f*. town in Epirus with a famed oracle of Jupiter

Eborācum, **ī** *nt*. town in Britain, the modern York

Ēlysium, **ii** *nt*. the abode of the blessed in the Underworld

Ēlysius, **a**, **um** *adj*. Elysian

Ēmathia, **ae** *f*. district of Macedonia

Ēpīrōticus, **a**, **um** *adj*. of Epirus

Ēpīrus (also **Ēpiros**), **ī** *f*. country in the north-west of Greece

Erebus, **ī** *m*. the Underworld; the god of darkness

Eryx, **ycis** *m*. mountain in Sicily on which stood a temple of Venus

Esquiliae, **ārum** *f*. *pl*. the Esquiline (one of the seven hills of Rome)

Esquilīnus, **a**, **um** *adj*. of the Esquiline hill

Etrūria, **ae** *f*. country on the west coast of central Italy

Etruscus, **a**, **um** *adj*. Etrurian

Eurōpa, **ae** *f*. (the continent of) Europe

Euxīnus Pontus *m*. Black Sea

Gādēs, **ium** *f*. *pl*. Cadiz

Galatia, **ae** *f*. country of the Galatians; a district of Asia Minor

Gallī, **ōrum** *m*. *pl*. the Gauls

Gallia, **ae** *f*. Gaul

Gallic(ān)us, **a**, **um** *adj*. Gallic

Germānī, **ōrum** *m*. *pl*. the Germans

Germānia, **ae** *f*. Germany

Germān(ic)us, **a**, **um** *adj*. German

Glēvum, **ī** *n*. Gloucester

Graecī, **ōrum** *m*. *pl*. Greeks

Graecia, **ae** *f*. Greece

Graecus, **a**, **um** *adj*. Greek

Graiī, **ōrum** *m*. *pl*. Greeks

Hadria, **ae** *m*. Adriatic Sea

Helicōn, **ōnis** *m*. mountain in Boeotia (sacred to Apollo and the Muses)

Hellēspontus, **ī** *m*. the Dardanelles

Helvētiī, **ōrum** *m*. *pl*. a Gallic people, in modern Switzerland

Helvēti(c)us, **a**, **um** *adj*. Swiss

Hibēria, **ae** *f*. Spain

Hibēricus, **a**, **um** *adj*. Spanish

Hibernia, **ae** *f*. Ireland

Hierosolyma, ōrum *nt. pl.* Jerusalem

Hippocrēnē, ēs *f.* a spring on Mt Helicon, made by Pegasus with a blow of his hoof

Hispānī, ōrum *m. pl.* the Spaniards

Hispānia, ae *f.* Spain

Hispāniēnsis, e, **Hispān(ic)us**, a, um *adj.* Spanish

Hymettus (also **Hymettos**), ī *m.* mountain near Athens, famous for its honey and marble

Īda, ae (also **Īdē**, ēs) *f.* (1) mountain in Crete; (2) mountain range near Troy

Īlium (also **Īlion**), iī *nt.*, **Īlios**, ī *f.* Troy

Īlius, a, um *adj.* of Troy, Trojan

Ind(ic)us, a, um *adj.* Indian

Iōnium mare part of the Mediterranean between Italy and Greece

Ister, trī *m.* (lower part of the) Danube

Italia, ae *f.* Italy

Italicus, Italius, Italus, a, um *adj.* Italian

Ithaca, ae *f.* island in the Ionian Sea, the kingdom of Ulysses

Iūdaea, ae *f.* Judaea, the country of the Jews

Iūdaeus, iūdaicus, a, um *adj.* Jewish

Lacedaemonius, a, um *adj.* Spartan

Latium, iī *n.* a district of Italy in which Rome was situated

Latius, Latīnus, a, um *adj.* Latin

Lāvīnium, iī *n.* a city of Latium

Lerna, ae (also **Lernē**, ēs) *f.* a forest and marsh near Argos, the haunt of the Hydra

Lēthē, ēs *f.* river of the Underworld which conferred oblivion on those who drank from it

Libya, ae (also **Libyē**, ēs) *f.* Lybia; North Africa

Lybicus, a, um *adj.* Lybian

Londinium, iī *nt.* London

Lupercal, ālis *nt.* grotto on the Palatine Hill, sacred to the god Lupercus

Lutētia, ae *f.* the modern Paris

Lycēum, ī *nt.* a gymnasium near Athens where Aristotle taught

Lycia, ae *f.* a country in the south of Asia Minor

Lycius, a, um *adj.* Lycian

Lȳdia, ae *f.* a country in western Asia Minor, the capital of which was Sardis

Macedones, um *m. pl.* the Macedonians

Macedonia, ae *f.* country of the Macedonians, a large district in the north of Greece

Macedoni(c)us, a, um *adj.* Macedonian

Massicus, ī *m.* Monte Massico, a mountain of Campania celebrated for its wine

Massilia, ae *f.* Marseilles

Maurī, ōrum *m. pl.* the Moors

Maurītānia, ae *f.* country of the Moors, Morocco

Mēdī, ōrum *m. pl.* the Medes

Mēdia, ae *f.* country of the Medes, situated between Armenia, Parthia, Hyrcania, and Assyria

Mēdicus, a, um *adj.* of the Medes

Mediolānum, ī *nt.* Milan, a town of North Italy

Melita, ae (also **Melitē**, ēs) *f.* Malta, island in the Mediterranean

Mesopotamia, ae *f.* a country of Asia, between the Euphrates and Tigris

Mīlēsius, a, um *adj.* of Miletus

Mīlētus, ī *m.* city in Asia Minor

Mona, ae *f.* (1) Isle of Man; (2) Isle of Anglesey

Mycēnae, ārum *f. pl.*, **Mycēnē**, ēs *f. sg.* a city in Argolis, the city of Agamemnon

Myrmidones, um *m. pl.* a people of Thessaly, ruled by Achilles

Neāpolis, is *f.* Naples, a city of Campania

Neāpolītānus, a, um *a.* Neapolitan

Nīlus, ī *m.* the Nile

Nōricum, ī *nt.* a country between the Danube and the Alps, west of Pannonia

Nōricus, a, um *adj.* of Noricum

Numidae, ārum *m. pl.* a people of northern Africa

Numidia, ae *f.* country of the Numidians

Numidicus, a, um *adj.* Numidian

Olympia, ae *f.* the grove and shrine of Olympian Zeus in Elis where the Olympian games were held

Olympi(a)cus, a, um *adj.* Olympian, Olympic

Olympus, ī *m.* (1) a mountain on the boundary of Macedonia and Thessaly, dwelling of the gods; (2) a mountain in Mysia

Ōstia, ae *f.*, **Ōstia**, ōrum *nt. pl.* a seaport

town in Latium, at the mouth of the Tiber

Padus, ī *m*. the Po

Palātium, iī *nt*. the Palatine, one of the seven hills of Rome

Pannonia, ae *f*. a country between the Danube and the Alps, east of Noricum

Paphlagonia, ae *f*. a province of Asia Minor on the Black Sea

Parnās(s)os (also **Parnās(s)us**), ī *m*. a mountain in Phocis sacred to Apollo and to the Muses

Paros, ī *f*. one of the Cyclades, noted for its marble

Parthī, ōrum *m*. *pl*. a Scythian people, the Parthians

Parthia, ae *f*. country of the Parthians

Parth(ic)us, a, um *adj*. Parthian

Patavīnus, a, um *adj*. of Padua

Patavium, iī *nt*. Padua

Pelasgī, ōrum *m*. *pl*. the oldest inhabitants of Greece; the Greeks

Pelion, iī *nt*. a mountain in eastern Thessaly

Pēnēus, ī *m*. river of Thessaly, flowing through the valley of Tempe

Pergamum, ī *nt*., **Pergamos**, ī *f*., **Pergama**, ōrum *nt*. *pl*. the citadel of Troy; Troy

Persae, ārum *m*. *pl*. the Persians

Persis, idis *f*. Persia

Persicus, a, um *adj*. Persian

Pharsālos (also **Pharsālus**), ī *f*. a town in Thessaly, noted for the defeat of Pompey by Caesar, 48 BC

Pharus (also **Pharos**), ī *f*. an island near Alexandria, famous for its lighthouse

Philippī, ōrum *m*. *pl*. a city in Macedonia

Phlegethōn, ontis *m*. a river in the Underworld

Phoenissa, ae *f*. a Phoenician woman

Phryges, um *m*. *pl*. Phrygians; Trojans

Phrygia, ae *f*. Phrygia; Troy

Phrygius, a, um, **Phryx**, ygis *adj*. Phrygian; Trojan

Pīeria, ae *f*. (1) a district of Macedonia, famous for the worship of the Muses; (2) a district of Syria

Pīraeus, ī *m*. the port at Athens

Pīrēnē, ēs *f*. a fountain in the citadel of Corinth

Pīsa, ae *f*. *sg*., **Pīsae**, ārum *f*. *pl*. a city of

Elis, near which the Olympic games were held

Poenī, ōrum *m*. *pl*. the Carthaginians

Pompeiī, ōrum *m*. *pl*. a maritime city in the south of Campania, near Vesuvius

Ponticus, a, um *adj*. of the Pontus

Pontus, ī *m*. (1) the Black Sea; (2) north-eastern province of Asia Minor

Propontis, idos & idis *f*. the Sea of Marmara

Pūnicus, a, um *adj*. Punic, Carthaginian

Pȳrēnaeus, a, um *adj*. of the Pyrenees

Pȳthō(n), ōnis *f*. old name of Delphi

Rhēnus, ī *m*. the Rhine

Rhodanus, ī *m*. the Rhone

Rhodos (also **Rhodus**), ī *f*. Rhodes; town of the same name on the island of Rhodes

Rōma, ae *f*. Rome

Rōmānus, a, um *a*. Roman

Rubicō(n), ōnis *m*. a small boundary-stream between Italy and Cisalpine Gaul; the crossing of the Rubicon by Caesar, 49 BC, was the prelude to civil war

Rutulī, ōrum *m*. *pl*. a people of Latium, whose capital was Ardea

Sabell(ic)us, a, um *adj*. Sabine

Sabīnī, ōrum *m*. *pl*. the Sabines, an ancient Italian people

Samnium, iī *nt*. a country of central Italy, inhabited by the Samnites

Samnīs, ītis *adj*. Samnite

Samnīticus, a, um *adj*. of the Samnites

Scamander, drī *m*. a river near Troy

Scylla, ae *f*. a rock between Italy and Sicily, opposite Charybdis

Scythae, ārum *m*. *pl*. the Scythians, people dwelling north and east of the Black Sea

Scythia, ae *f*. country inhabited by the Scythians

Scythicus, a, um *adj*. Scythian

Sēricus, a, um *adj*. Chinese; made of silk

Siculī, ōrum *m*. *pl*. Sicilians

Siculus, a, um *adj*. Sicilian

Sīdōn, ōnis & ōnos *f*. a Phoenician city, the mother-city of Tyre

Sīdōni(c)us, a, um *adj*. of or relating to Sidon

Simoīs, entis *m*. a river in Troas, which runs into the Scamander

Sirmiō, ōnis *m*. peninsula of Lake Garda

Sparta, ae *f*. the capital of Laconia, in the Peloponnese

Spartānus, Sparticus, a, um *adj*. Spartan

Stygius, a, um *adj*. of or belonging to the Styx

Stymphālus, ī *m*., **Stymphālum**, ī *nt*. a district in Arcadia, with a town and lake of the same name; here lived the man-eating birds killed by Hercules

Styx, gis *f*. the principal river of the underworld

Sybaris, is *f*. a town of Lucania on the Gulf of Tarentum, proverbial for its luxury

Symplēgades, um *f. pl*. two floating islands at the entrance of the Euxine

Syrācūsae, ārum *f. pl*. Syracuse, the ancient capital of Sicily

Syrācūsānus, Syrācūsius, a, um *adj*. Syracusan

Syria, ae *f*. Syria

Syrius, Syrus, Syriacus, Syriscus, a, um *adj*. Syrian

Syrtēs, ium *f. pl*. two very dangerous sandy flats on the north coast of Africa

Tamesis, is *m* the Thames

Tempē *nt. indecl*. a valley in Thessaly, through which ran the River Peneus

Thēbae, ārum *f. pl*. (1) a city in upper Egypt; (2) the capital of Boeotia

Thēbānus, a, um *adj*. Theban

Thessalia, ae *f*. Thessaly, a district in the north of Greece

Thessal(ic)us, a, um *adj*. Thessalian, Thessalic

Thrāc(i)a, ae (also **Thrācē**, ēs) *f*. Thrace,

a district of North Greece

Thrācius, a, um *adj*. Thracian

Thrāx, ācis *f*. a Thracian

Thūle, ēs *f*. an island in the far north, usually in references to Iceland or Scandinavia

Tiberis, is *m*. a river of Latium, on which Rome stood, the Tiber

Tomis, is *f*., **Tomī**, ōrum *m. pl*. a town of Moesia, on the Black Sea, to which Ovid was banished; modern Costanţa

Trīnacria, ae *f*. Sicily

Trīnacrius, a, um *adj*. Sicilian

Trōas, adis & ados *f*. a Trojan woman; the region about Troy, the Troad

Trōi(c)us, Trōiānus, a, um *a*, Trojan

Trōia, ae *f*. Troy, city of Asia Minor

Trōiugena, ae *adj*. Trojan

Trōs, Trōis *m*. a Trojan

Tyrr(h)ēnia, ae *f*. Etruria

Tyrr(h)ēnus, a, um *adj*. Etrurian, Tuscan

Umber, bra, brum *adj*. Umbrian

Umbrī, ōrum *m. pl*. the people of Umbria

Umbria, ae *f*. country of the Umbri, a district of Italy on the Adriatic, north of Picenum

Vāticānus (mōns, collis), ī *m*. the Vatican (one of the seven hills of Rome)

Venetī, ōrum *m. pl*. a people in the north-east of Italy; a people in the north-west of Gaul

Vesuvius, iī *m*. a volcano in Campania

Vīminālis collis *m*. the Viminal (one of the seven hills of Rome)

Volscī, ōrum *m. pl*. a people to the south of Latium

Volscus, a, um *adj*. of the Volsci

The Latin Writers

APULEIUS—Lucius Apuleius (*fl.* 155 AD). Born at Madaura in Africa and educated at Carthage—where he later settled—, Athens, and Rome, he is famous for his *Metamorphoses* or *Golden Ass* (written in 160), a Latin novel in eleven books, the last of which reveals its philosophico-religious purpose.

AUGUSTINE—Aurelius Augustinus, St Augustine of Hippo (350–430 AD). Born in Roman Africa at Thagaste (Souk Ahras in Algeria), he was a passionate exponent of Christianity. The author of some ninety-three books as well as letters and sermons, he is best known for his *Confessions* (*c.*397–400) and *The City of God* (413–26).

AURELIUS—Marcus Aurelius (121–80 AD). Roman emperor from 161–80. His major literary achievement is his *Meditations*, a collection of Stoic aphorisms and reflections written in Greek over the last ten years of his reign while he was on campaign.

CAESAR—Gaius Iulius Caesar (100–44 BC). One of the great figures of the ancient world, both as a general and a statesman, he wrote his *Commentaries*, seven books on his campaign in Gaul and Britain (58–2 BC) and three on the Civil War between himself and Pompey (49–8 BC). Cicero remarked that only a fool would try to improve on his accounts (*Brutus* 262).

CATO—Marcus Porcius Cato ('The Elder') (234–149 BC). The only surviving work of this famously severe Roman statesman and moralist is *De Re Rustica* (*On Farming*).

CATULLUS—Gaius Valerius Catullus (*c.*84–*c.*54 BC). Born in Verona, he wrote poetry on a number of themes but is most famous for his passionate love poems addressed to 'Lesbia', who may have been a historical person, if so, probably the notorious aristocrat Clodia.

CICERO—Marcus Tullius Cicero (106–43 BC). Born at Arpinum some 70 miles south-east of Rome, this celebrated Roman orator and statesman was a prolific writer on many themes. Among his 58 surviving speeches are the six against Verres (*In Verrem*), the four against Catiline (*In Catilinam*), the sixteen *Philippics* against Mark Antony, and the speech in defence of Milo (*Pro Milone*). Two works on oratory are *On the Orator* (*De Oratore*) and *Brutus*. We have more than 800 letters (including the collections *To his Friends* (*Ad Familiares*) and *To Atticus* (*Ad Atticum*)). Among his philosophical works are the epistemological *Academics* (*Academica*), the political *On the Republic* (*De Republica*), *On the Laws* (*De Legibus*), the theological *On the Nature of the Gods* (*De Natura Deorum*), and the ethical *On Ends* (*De Finibus*), *Tusculan Disputations* (*Tusculanae Disputationes*), *On Old Age* (*De Senectute*), and *On Duties* (*De Officiis*). The *Treatise on Rhetoric addressed to Herennius* (*Rhetorica ad Herennium*) has been ascribed to Cicero but is not in fact by him.

CLAUDIAN—Claudius Claudianus (died *c.*404 AD). Born in Alexandria in Egypt, and thus a native Greek-speaker, he turned to composing in Latin and became the last great Latin poet in the classical tradition. *The Rape of Persephone*, a poem in four books of which 1,100 lines survive, is today thought to be his finest work.

COLUMELLA—Lucius Iunius Moderatus Columella (*fl.* 60 AD). Columella, who came from Gades (Cadiz) in Spain, composed a twelve-book treatise called *On Farming* (*De Re Rustica*) in about 60–65 AD. This is written in prose except for book 10 which is in hexameters.

ENNIUS—Quintus Ennius (239–169 BC). Born at Rudiae in Calabria in South Italy, Ennius was a leading writer of Roman tragedy. His principal work was the *Annals* (*Annales*), a history of Rome from earliest times to his own in eighteen books of hexameter verse. Fewer than 600 lines of this survive. He reputedly wrote his own epitaph: 'Let no one honour me with tears or attend my funeral with weeping. Why? I fly, still living, through the mouths of men.'

ERASMUS—Desiderius Erasmus (1466–1536 AD). Erasmus was a Dutch scholar and theologian who was Professor of Divinity at Cambridge from 1511–13. A fine writer of Latin—the language in which he wrote his *Praise of Folly* (*Moriae Encomium*)—, he launched modern biblical scholarship with his Greek New Testament.

FLORUS—Lucius Annaeus Florus (*fl.* 30–104 AD). Florus wrote the Latin history known as the *Epitome of all the Wars during Seven Hundred Years*, a two-book summary of Roman history up to the age of Augustus designed as a panegyric of the Roman people.

GELLIUS—Aulus Gellius (*c.*130–*c.*180 AD). Gellius wrote *Attic Nights* (*Noctes Atticae*) in twenty books, which has survived almost complete. A random collection of brief essays dealing with such topics as philosophy, history, law, grammar, and literary and textual criticism, it is especially valuable for the preservation of many passages from early Latin literature. It includes a number of good stories, that of Androclus and the lion among them.

HORACE—Quintus Horatius Flaccus (65–8 BC). Born the son of a freedman in Venusia (Venosa) in Apulia in South Italy, he later became part of the circle of Maecenas, the famous patron of the arts, and rubbed shoulders with the most powerful politicians and the leading poets of his day. His published works, all of which survive, consist of the *Epodes* and *Satires* (published in 30 BC), the *Epistles* (*Epistulae*), which end with the *Art of Poetry* (*Ars Poetica*), and his major achievement, the *Odes* (*Carmina*) (published in 23 and 13 BC).

JEROME—Eusebius Hieronymus, St Jerome (*c.*347–420 AD). Born in a Christian family at Strido near Aquileia in north Italy, he was the translator and editor of the version of the Bible which we call the *Vulgate* (i.e. the 'common text').

JUSTINIAN—Flavius Petrus Sabbatius Iustinianus (*c.*482–565 AD). Justinian, the Roman emperor at Constantinople from 527–65 AD, rationalized and codified the Roman legal system. A team of codifiers assisted him to produce *The Complete Civil Law* which included the *Institutes*. Their greatest debt was to Ulpian (Domitius Ulpianus, died 223 AD), one of the last of the leading Roman jurists, who wrote nearly 280 books.

JUVENAL—Decimus Iunius Iuvenalis (*c.*55–*c.*130 AD). Little is known about this celebrated satirical poet, who was born at Aquinum in Latium. His sixteen *Satires* were published in five books.

LABERIUS—Decimus Laberius (*c.*105–43 BC). This Roman knight was a distinguished writer of mimes (licentious farces).

LIVIUS ANDRONICUS—Lucius Livius Andronicus (*c.*284–204 BC). This Greek-speaking prisoner of war from Tarentum in south Italy translated Homer's *Odyssey* into Latin (only 46 lines survive) and produced the first drama in Rome in 240. He is the father of Roman literature.

LIVY—Titus Livius (59 BC–17 AD). Born in Patavum (Padua) in north-east Italy, he became the friend of the emperor Augustus. His history of Rome from its foundation to 9 BC was in 142 books. Only 1–10 (dealing with 753–293 BC), 21–45 (dealing with 219–167) and a fragment of 91 survive.

LUCAN—Marcus Annaeus Lucanus (39–65 AD). Born at Corduba (Cordoba) in Spain, he was educated at Rome. After joining a conspiracy against the emperor Nero, he was forced to commit suicide. His incomplete poem (ten books), the *Civil War* (*Bellum Civile*) deals with the war between Caesar and Pompey. Also known as *Pharsalia* after Caesar's victory over Pompey at Pharsalus in 48 BC, it espouses the republican cause, a bold stance under Nero.

LUCILIUS—Gaius Lucilius (*c.*180–102 BC). This wealthy knight from Suessa Aurunca in Latium wrote 30 books of *Satires*, of which some 1,300 lines survive. He was the creator of the purely Roman form of satire.

LUCRETIUS—Titus Lucretius Carus (*c.*99–*c.*55 BC). Lucretius' great philosophical poem *On Nature* (*De Rerum Natura*) communicates the teachings of the Greek philosopher Epicurus who was himself following in the footsteps of Democritus. This didactic work aims to free men from a sense of guilt and the fear of death.

MANILIUS—Marcus Manilius (*fl.* at the start of the first century AD). His apparently unfinished hexameter poem in five books entitled *Astronomica*, which sees design and 'heavenly reason' in the universe (*cf.* Lucretius), breaks off abruptly in the fifth book.

MARTIAL—Marcus Valerius Martialis (*c.*40–103/4 AD). Born in Bilbilis in Spain, he came to Rome in 64 and retired to Bilbilis in 98 BC. The twelve books of his satirical epigrams appeared between 86 and 101. Pliny speaks of him as 'talented, subtle, penetrating, witty, and sincere'.

NEPOS—Cornelius Nepos (*c.*100–*c.*25 BC). A native of Cisalpine Gaul, he is remembered for his *Lives of Famous Men* (*De Viris Illustribus*), of which only one book out of at least sixteen survives. These lives are eulogizing and moralizing biographical sketches rather than historical biographies.

OVID—Publius Ovidius Naso (43 BC–17 AD). Born at Sulmo in the Apennines about ninety miles east of Rome, he was educated at Rome and based there until in 8 AD he was somehow involved in an imperial scandal and banished by the emperor Augustus to Tomis (Costantza) on the Black Sea where he died. A prolific poet, he wrote *Loves* (*Amores*), *Heroines* (*Heroides*), *The Technique of Love* (*Ars Amatoria*), and *How to Fall out of Love* (*Remedia Amoris*, 1 AD). Decidedly more politically correct are *Calendar Days* (*Fasti*) and *Metamorphoses*, both begun in 2 AD, the latter proving to be his masterpiece. Other works include the two great poems of his exile, *Sad Poems* (*Tristia*) and *Letters from the Black Sea* (*Epistulae ex Ponto*). The cheerful immorality of much of his verse belies the fact that, alone of the Augustan poets, he was a respectable married man.

PERSIUS—Aulus Persius Flaccus (34–62 AD). Born in an equestrian family at Volaterrae in Etruria, he fell under the influence of the Stoics at Rome. He wrote one book of six *Satires*, modelled on Lucilius and Horace.

PETRONIUS ARBITER—(died 66 AD). Petronius pursued a successful political career and was admitted by the emperor Nero to his inner circle of intimates. He committed suicide

The Latin Writers

after becoming involved in a conspiracy against the emperor. His vast picaresque novel, *Satyrica*, was in twenty or twenty-four books, of which only parts of books 14, 15, and 16 survive. The principal episode of the surviving fragments is the dinner-party flung by one of the most vivid characters in ancient literature, the *nouveau riche* Trimalchio.

PHAEDRUS—Gaius Iulius Phaedrus (*c.*15 BC–*c.*50 AD). A Thracian slave who became a freedman in the household of Augustus in Rome, he wrote a collection in verse of fables (*Fabulae Aesopiae*) in five books comprising some hundred stories. Serious or satirical in intent, they are based on the beast-stories of Aesop and other sources in the Aesopian tradition.

PLAUTUS—Titus Maccius Plautus (*c.*250–184 BC). Born at Sarsina in Umbria, he was the writer of up to 130 comedies, twenty of which survive. The plays are all adapted from Greek originals.

PLINY—Gaius Plinius Caecilius Secundus (61/62–*c.*113 AD), nephew and adopted son of Gaius Plinius Secundus (23/4–79 AD), writer of the vast *Natural History* (*Historia Naturalis*) in 37 books. Pliny the Younger had a highly successful political career which culminated in his admirable service as governor of Bithynia. His fame is due to his ten books of *Letters* (*Epistulae*). He delivered his speech in praise of the emperor Trajan (*Panegyricus*) when he became consul in 100 AD.

PROPERTIUS—Sextus Propertius (*c.*50 BC–after 16 BC). Born at Asisium (Assisi) in Umbria, he was educated at Rome and became part of the circle of Maecenas, the great Augustan patron of the arts. He left four books of elegies, mainly love poems. His work is remarkable for its hypnotic intensity.

PUBLILIUS SYRUS—(first century BC). Brought to Rome, perhaps from Antioch, as a slave, he gained his freedom. He wrote a collection of moral maxims (*Sententiae*) for schools.

QUINTILIAN—Marcus Fabius Quintilianus—born *c.*35 AD. Born at Calagurris in Spain, Quintilian was a celebrated teacher of rhetoric at Rome. His most famous work is his *Education of an Orator* (*Institutio Oratoria*), published in twelve books in about 95 AD.

SALLUST—Gaius Sallustius Crispus (86–35 BC). Born at Amiternum in the Sabine country north-east of Rome, he had a high-profile, if chequered political career. After being unsuccessfully prosecuted for extortion after his governorship of Numidia in 46 BC, he withdrew from public life and wrote the historical monographs, *The War with Catiline* (*Bellum Catilinae*), *The War with Jugurtha* (*Bellum Iugurthinum*), and the *Histories* of the years 78–67 BC. Of the *Histories* only fragments survive.

SENECA—Lucius Annaeus Seneca (*c.*4 BC–65 AD), son of the rhetoric teacher of the same name (born *c.*55 BC), whose *Debates* (*Controversiae*) and *Speeches of Advice* (*Suasoriae*) survive in part. Seneca the Younger became the tutor of the emperor Nero, but fell out of favour and was forced to commit suicide after being implicated in a conspiracy against the emperor. His profound Stoic beliefs sat ill with his fabulous wealth, since Stoicism places no value on worldly goods. Among other works, he wrote ten dialogues (*Dialogi*), including *Concerning Anger* (*De Ira*) and a collection of 124 *Letters to Lucilius* divided into twenty books. His most important poetical works are his nine tragedies adapted from Greek originals.

SILIUS ITALICUS—Tiberius Catius Asconius Silius Italicus (*c.*26–101 AD). Born at Patavium (Padua), Silius pursued a successful political career. He wrote the longest surviving Latin poem *The War with Carthage* (*Punica*), an epic in seventeen books on the Second Punic War (218–201 BC).

STATIUS—Publius Papinius Statius (*c.*45–*c.*96 AD). Statius was born at Naples, the son of a schoolmaster. His major work is the *Thebaid*, an epic in twelve books about the quarrel between Oedipus' sons Eteocles and Polyneices. The debt to Virgil's *Aeneid* is strong.

SUETONIUS—Gaius Suetonius Tranquillus (born *c.*69 AD). He became a secretary at the imperial palace and thus had access to the imperial archives, but he was dismissed by Hadrian in 121/2 apparently for some indiscretion involving the emperor's wife. His surviving works include the *Lives of the Caesars* (*De Vita Caesarum*), biographies of the first twelve emperors including Julius Caesar, and part of *On Famous Men* (*De Viris Illustribus*).

TACITUS—Publius (or Gaius) Cornelius Tacitus (born 56 or 57 AD, died after 117). Possibly born in Narbonese Gaul, Tacitus had a successful political career. His historical writings include his monograph about his father-in-law, *Agricola*, and his major works, his *Histories* (covering the years 69–96 AD) and *Annals* (covering the years 14–68 AD). Much of these works is lost. Edward Gibbon, author of *The Decline and Fall of the Roman Empire*, thought more highly of Tacitus than of any other ancient historian.

TERENCE—Publius Terentius Afer (died 159 BC?). An ex-slave from Carthage, Terence wrote six comedies adapted from the Greek.

TERTULLIAN—Florens Quintus Septimius Tertullianus (*c.*160–225 AD). Born in Carthage and brought up as a pagan, Tertullian was converted to Christianity before 197. He was the father of Latin theology. Among his works is his *Speech for the Defence* (*Apologeticum*) in which he aims to secure protection for Christians.

TIBULLUS—Albius Tibullus (*c*.55–19 BC). A friend of Horace and Ovid, Tibullus wrote two books of elegies. His favoured themes are love and country life.

VARRO—Marcus Terentius Varro (116–27 BC). Born at Reate in Sabine territory, Varro was Rome's outstanding antiquarian and philologist. We know the titles of 55 of his works but only two of them survive in more than fragmentary form. These are Books 5–10 of *On the Latin Language* (*De Lingua Latina*), dedicated to Cicero, and the three books of *On Farming* (*De Re Rustica*).

VEGETIUS—Flavius Vegetius Renatus—a military writer under the emperor Theodosius (379–95 AD). His *Military Epitome* (*Epitoma Rei Militaris*) in four books is the sole account of Roman military practice which has survived intact.

VELLEIUS PATERCULUS (*c*.19 BC–after 30 BC). From Campania in south Italy, he wrote two books of *Roman Histories* which cover the period from Romulus to 30 AD. Part of Book 1 is missing.

VIRGIL—Publius Vergilius Maro (70–19 BC). Born at Mantua in Cisalpine Gaul, Virgil was educated at Cremona, Milan and Rome. He became part of the circle of Maecenas, the great Augustan patron, and a friend and supporter of Augustus. His pastoral poems, the *Eclogues*, were perhaps published in 37 BC, the *Georgics*, his four-book didactic poem on farming, in 29 BC, and his great twelve-book epic, the *Aeneid*, posthumously. He was buried near Naples. Dante regarded Virgil as *il nostro maggior poeta* ('our greatest poet').

VITRUVIUS—Vitruvius Pollio (*fl*. 50 BC). Vitruvius was an engineer and architect of the first century BC. His treatise in ten books *On Architecture* (*De Architectura*) is dedicated to the emperor Augustus.

VULGATE—*see* JEROME.

Some Key Dates in Roman History

BC

753	foundation of Rome (traditional date).
510/9	expulsion of Tarquins, the royal family of Rome, and establishment of Roman republic under two consuls.
496	battle of Lake Regillus, in which the Romans defeated the Latins.
494	secession of the plebeians, and creation of the tribunes of the people.
451/0	publication of the Twelve Tablets, the Roman law code.
396	territory of the Etruscan city of Veii annexed by Rome.
390	Gauls capture Rome, but are defeated by Camillus.
367	consulship opened to plebeians.
366	L. Sextius becomes first plebeian consul.
340–338	Rome fights and defeats the Latins; dismantling of the Latin League.
321	disaster of Caudine Forks in war with Samnites.
312	Appian Way begun.
295	Rome defeats combined force of Samnites and Gauls at Sentinum.
c.287	the *lex Hortensia* makes decisions of the plebeians binding on the entire population.
280–275	war with King Pyrrhus of Epirus, won by Rome.
264–241	First Punic War (war with Carthage), won by Rome; Rome creates large fleet and gains Sicily as its first province.
218–202	Second Punic War; Rome defeated by the Carthaginian Hannibal at the Trebia (218), Lake Trasimene (217), and Cannae (216). Scipio defeats Hannibal at Zama in Africa in 202.
197	Rome defeats Philip V of Macedon at Cynoscephalae in Thessaly.
196	Greece becomes part of Roman empire.
190	Rome defeats Antiochus III of Syria at the battle of Magnesia.
168	Rome defeats Perseus of Macedon at the battle of Pydna.
149	Third Punic War begins.
146	Rome destroys Carthage and Corinth.

133	Numantia in Spain reduced. Agrarian bill of Tiberius Gracchus. Province of Asia added to Roman empire.
132	Tiberius Gracchus clubbed to death.
123–2	tribunates of Gaius Gracchus, who was killed in 122.
112–105	war with Jugurtha; victory of Rome under Gaius Marius who reforms Roman army.
101	Marius defeats German tribes (Cimbri and Teutones).
91	murder of tribune Marcus Livius Drusus.
90–89	Social War (Rome against her Italian allies), won by Rome, which soon gave citizenship to the allied communities.
88	Sulla marches on Rome and carries out a coup.
87–4	Sulla wins war against Mithridates VI, king of Pontus.
82	Sulla captures Rome and becomes dictator; massacres and proscriptions.
81	Sulla ceases to be dictator.
74–63	renewed war with Mithridates; successes of Lucullus and Pompey.
63	consulship of Cicero; conspiracy of Catiline.
60	the First Triumvirate between Caesar, Pompey and Crassus.
58–51	Caesar's Gallic Wars; he invades Britain in 55 and 54.
53	defeat and death of Crassus at Carrhae in Parthia.
52	Pompey sole consul.
49	Caesar crosses river Rubicon; outbreak of civil war.
48	Caesar defeats Pompey at the Battle of Pharsalus in Greece; Pompey murdered in Egypt.
44	appointment of Caesar as perpetual dictator; assassination of Caesar on the Ides (15th) of March.
43	the Second Triumvirate between Antony, Octavian and Lepidus; proscriptions; murder of Cicero.
42	Antony and Octavian defeat the assassins of Caesar at Philippi in Macedonia.

| 31 | Octavian defeats Antony and the Egyptian queen Cleopatra at Actium in north-west Greece. Octavian has supreme power. |
| 27 | constitutional arrangement made by which Octavian is named Augustus and in effect becomes the first Roman emperor. |

AD

9	disaster of Varus in Germany.
14	Augustus dies. Tiberius succeeds.
31	fall of Tiberius' favourite, Sejanus.
37	Tiberius dies. Gaius (Caligula) succeeds.
41	Caligula assassinated. Claudius succeeds.
43	Aulus Plautius invades Britain.
54	Claudius dies. Nero succeeds.
61	revolt of Boudicca in Britain, put down by Suetonius Paulinus.
64	Great fire at Rome.
68	revolt of Vindex. Nero kills himself. Galba succeeds.
69	Year of Four Emperors: Galba, Otho, Vitellius and Vespasian.
70	Jerusalem captured by Vespasian's son Titus.
79	Vespasian dies. Titus succeeds. Eruption of Vesuvius.
81	Titus dies. His younger brother Domitian succeeds.
96	Domitian assassinated. Nerva succeeds.
98	Nerva dies. Trajan succeeds.
117	Trajan dies. Hadrian succeeds.
122	Hadrian's Wall built in Britain between Solway and Tyne.
212	citizenship given to all free men in the Roman empire.
312	Constantine wins Battle of Milvian Bridge under the sign of the Cross and gains Rome.
325	Council of Nicaea makes Christianity the religion of the Roman empire.
330	Constantine founds Constantinople (now Istanbul) in the east.
410	sack of Rome by Alaric the Visigoth.
476	end of Roman empire in the west.
1453	conquest of Constantinople by the Turks and end of eastern Roman Empire.

Late and Medieval Latin

After the fall of the Roman empire, the Latin language continued to change and evolve as it had always done. While the literary language of the classical golden and silver age authors remained a model for the written language, the spoken varieties of the language (so-called 'vulgar Latin', from *vulgus* 'people'), which had constantly changed throughout the imperial and republican periods and earlier, began to diverge both from one another and from any resemblance they had once borne to that literary norm. This linguistic fragmentation was the birth of the Romance languages, many (but not all) of which survive to the present day: Italian, French, Portuguese, Spanish, Catalan, Occitan, Romanian, Sardinian, Romansh, Dalmatian etc.

At the same time as these languages were developing, the Latin language itself continued to be used, particularly in literary, religious, legal and educational contexts. Though sometimes this Latin (learnt no longer as a native tongue but as a second language) met the norms of classical usage, it often differed markedly as a result of the influence of speakers' everyday vernacular language. This state of affairs persisted for many centuries, and indeed Latin remains a prestigious language in many countries even today, being still used in a very small number of official contexts.

Given, among other things, the diversity of other languages spoken by Latin users in the medieval period, it is impossible to describe all the variation to be found in late Latin and medieval Latin texts, which may show different features according to region or period. Nonetheless, there are some general principles which should enable someone who knows the classical language to make reasonable sense of a post-classical text:

1 The pervasive influence of the Christian church is strongly felt in many late and medieval Latin texts, with whole phrases often being borrowed or adapted from the Vulgate Bible (the 'official' Latin translation of the Bible made by St. Jerome in the 4th century AD) and from the Latin liturgy. In practical terms this means that words used in classical Latin may acquire a new meaning associated with their use in the religious vocabulary. For example, classical Latin *ōrātiō* and *ōrāre* meant 'speech' and 'deliver an oration', while in Christian usage they came to mean 'prayer' and 'pray'. We have given a selection of the more common such 'changes' in the main text of the dictionary, marked clearly as **LM**.

2 Both within the religious language and outside, there was a need for new vocabulary to denote new inventions and concepts in science, philosophy, law, politics, and the arts. While Cicero himself had striven to create a philosophical vocabulary for Latin, the medieval period saw many authors expanding the fields of human knowledge and coining new 'Latin' words to express this. In the realm of technical terminology, some existing classical words also acquired additional meanings; we have marked both new words and new meanings of existing words as **LM**.

3 There was a good deal of 'morphological flexibility': words which had belonged to one declension or conjugation in the classical language could come to belong to a class with different endings. Thus, many deponent verbs acquired/became active forms, and appropriate regular first conjugation verbs superseded or were substituted for many third conjugation verbs (frequently formed using the stem of the supine, e.g. *cantō, cantāre* for *canō, canere, cecinī, cantum*). Some nouns

changed gender and/or declension. For example, neuter plural nouns in -*a* were commonly reanalysed as being collective feminine singular nouns and inflected accordingly (e.g. *folia, -ae* replacing *folia, -ōrum*), while fourth declension nouns were often declined as second declension.

4 Verbs and prepositions that had governed one case in classical Latin sometimes came to govern complements in a different case in the later language: for example, *misereor* (+ gen. in classical Latin) is commonly found with the dative/ablative in phrases like *miserēre nōbīs* (but contrast the opening of Psalm 51 *miserēre meī*). Some meanings expressed by case forms on their own in classical Latin acquired alternative prepositional constructions: the genitive could, for example, commonly be replaced by *dē* with the noun in the ablative (or sometimes in the accusative); the ablative of 'time at which' could be replaced by *in* + abl. Some prepositions indeed acquire additional meanings they had not had in the classical language, and the classical distinctions between static and motion meanings of, for example, *in* + abl. and *in* + acc. are often blurred.

5 Constructions which had demanded the subjunctive in classical Latin are occasionally found with indicative verbs and vice versa; the infinitive is also common in a wider range of usage, particularly to express purpose.

6 In the classical language the usual way to express indirect statement had been to use an infinitive with its subject in the accusative case; this construction was widely replaced by *quod* or *quia* (classical 'because') with a finite indicative (sometime subjunctive) verb.

7 The spelling of words, whether they were etymologically classical or not, was often seriously affected by the speakers' pronunciation of the language, which was very often heavily influenced by their native tongue and somewhat at variance with the 'classical' pronunciation. The most common substitutions and alterations are the following:

$$ae \sim e \sim oe \qquad ti \sim ci \sim zi \qquad d \sim t$$
$$y \sim i \sim e \qquad c \sim ch \sim h$$
$$o \sim u \qquad p \sim ph \sim f$$
$$v \sim f \sim b$$

h is often omitted. Consonantal *i* is often written *j*.

A modern reader who comes across an unfamilar word in a medieval text may well find it in this dictionary simply by substituting appropriate classical spellings for these.

8 The effects of changes and variation in pronunciation were particularly strong in the system of vowels in late and medieval Latin. Readers should be aware that it is often difficult or impossible to identify the quantities of the vowels in new coinages in the later periods, nor is it always relevant to do so. In this dictionary, we have for the sake of consistency intentionally not indicated **any** quantities (even of endings) on words which are marked as **LM** only.

9 The expense of writing materials and scribal time was such that abbreviations for words and phrases were widespread. The diversity of these makes it impossible to provide a list here but the correct expansion of such abbreviations can often be 'guessed' from the context. A few general principles may, nonetheless, be useful. Abbreviations typically begin with the initial letter (sometimes syllable) of the abbreviated word and often end with the final syllable or inflexional ending, omitting what one might expect to find between them. The symbol 'x', as well as representing Latin *x*, may sometimes be a Greek chi (standing for 'ch') especially in abbreviating *Christ-* (e.g. *Xti* for *Christi*); at the ends of words, the 'x' symbol was also a short way of writing *-us*. The tilde over a vowel (e.g. ũ) is an abbreviation for an omitted following 'n' or 'm'. The abbreviation '*e u o u a e*' was frequently used in manuscripts of liturgical music to stand beneath notes sung to the common phrase [*in saecula*] *saeculorum, amen.*

For further reference, readers may like to consult either A. Souter, *A Glossary of Later Latin to 600AD* (Oxford, 1949) or R.E. Latham, *Revised Medieval Latin Word-List from British and Irish Sources* (London, 1965). On the late Latin language in general, V. Väänänen, *Introduction au latin vulgaire* 3rd ed. (Paris, 1963) and J. Herman, *Vulgar Latin* (Pennsylvania, 2000) are indispensable; on medieval Latin language, a useful starting point is K. Sidwell, *Reading Medieval Latin* (Cambridge, 1995).

RICHARD ASHDOWNE
New College, Oxford

THE EASTERN ROMAN WORLD

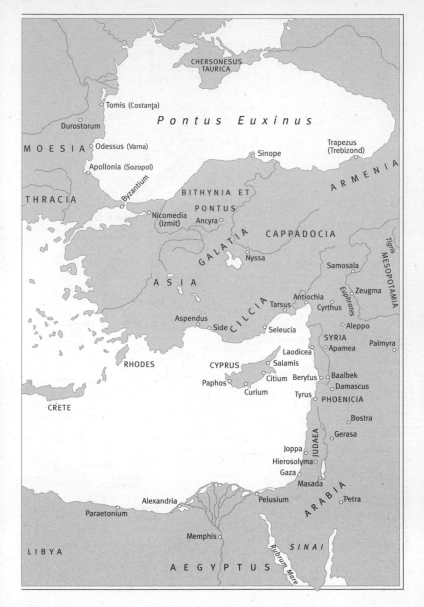

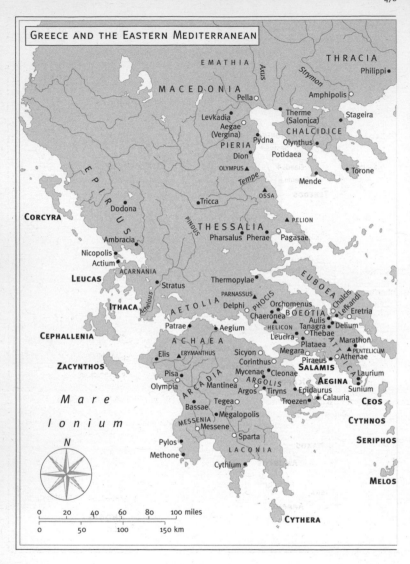

GREECE AND THE EASTERN MEDITERRANEAN

EMATHIA

THRACIA

Philippi

Axius

Strymon

MACEDONIA

Pella

Amphipolis

Therme
(Salonica)

Stageira

Levkadia
Aegae
(Vergina)

Pydna

CHALCIDICE

PIERIA

Olynthus

Dion

Potidaea

OLYMPUS ▲

Tempe

Mende

Torone

CORCYRA

E P I R U S

Dodona

Tricca

OSSA ▲

▲ PELION

THESSALIA

PINDUS

Pharsalus Pherae

Pagasae

Ambracia

Nicopolis
Actium

ACARNANIA

Stratus

Thermopylae

EUBOEA

LEUCAS

Achelous

AETOLIA

PARNASSUS ▲

Delphi PHOCIS

Orchomenus

Chalcis

Lefkandi

ITHACA

Chaeronea

BOEOTIA

Aulis

Eretria

Patrae

Aegium

HELICON ▲

Leuctra

Tanagra

Thebae

Delium

CEPHALLENIA

ACHAEA

Megara

Plataea

Marathon

Elis

ERYMANTHUS ▲

Sicyon

PENTELICUM ▲

ZACYNTHOS

Corinthus

Piraeus

Athenae

Pisa

Mycenae

Cleonae

SALAMIS

Laurium

Olympia

ARCADIA

Mantinea

ARGOLIS

Argos

Tiryns

AEGINA

Sunium

Mare

Tegea

Epidaurus

Troezen

Calauria

CEOS

Ionium

Bassae

Megalopolis

CYTHNOS

N

MESSENIA

Messene

SERIPHOS

Pylos

Sparta

Methone

LACONIA

Cythium

MELOS

0 20 40 60 80 100 miles

0 50 100 150 km

CYTHERA

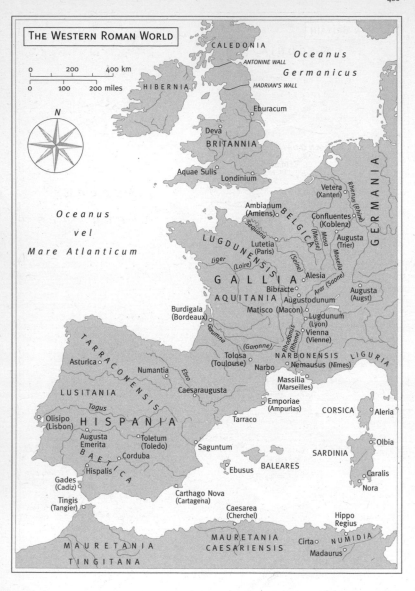

THE WESTERN ROMAN WORLD

0   200   400 km
0   100   200 miles

N

CALEDONIA

Oceanus

ANTONINE WALL

Germanicus

HADRIAN'S WALL

HIBERNIA

Eburacum

Deva

BRITANNIA

Aquae Sulis

Londinium

Oceanus

vel

Mare Atlanticum

Vetera
(Xanten)

Rhenus (Rhine)

Ambianum
(Amiens)

BELGICA

Confluentes
(Koblenz)

Sequana

Augusta
(Trier)

Mosa (Meuse)

LUGDUNENSIS

Lutetia
(Paris)

Liger (Loire)

(Seine)

GERMANIA

Mosella

GALLIA

Alesia

AQUITANIA

Bibracte

Augustodunum

Augusta
(Augst)

Arar (Saône)

Burdigala
(Bordeaux)

Matisco (Macon)

Lugdunum
(Lyon)

Garumna

Vienna
(Vienne)

Asturica

TARRACONENSIS

Numantia

Ebro

Tolosa
(Toulouse)

(Garonne)

Rhodanus (Rhône)

NARBONENSIS

Narbo

Nemausus (Nimes)

LIGURIA

LUSITANIA

Caesaraugusta

Massilia
(Marseilles)

Tagus

HISPANIA

Olisipo
(Lisbon)

Augusta
Emerita

Toletum
(Toledo)

Corduba

BAETICA

Hispalis

Tarraco

Saguntum

Emporiae
(Ampurias)

CORSICA

Aleria

SARDINIA

Olbia

Ebusus

BALEARES

Caralis

Gades
(Cadiz)

Nora

Tingis
(Tangier)

Carthago Nova
(Cartagena)

Caesarea
(Cherchel)

Hippo
Regius

MAURETANIA
TINGITANA

MAURETANIA
CAESARIENSIS

Cirta

NUMIDIA

Madaurus

ROMAN BRITAIN

CALEDONIA

Inchtuthil

PICTI

Bodotria (Forth)

ANTONINE WALL
(Built 139–42)

Clota (Clyde)

DUMNONII

VOTADINI

Trimontium
(Newstead)

SELGOVAE

HADRIAN'S
WALL
(Built 122–6)

Corstopitum
(Corbridge)

NOVANTAE

(Bowness)

(Wallsend)

Oceanus

Germanicus

Cataractorium
(Catterick)

PARISI

Eburacum
(York)

Mona
(I. of Man)

DERE STREET

BRIGANTES

ERMINE STREET

Mona
(Anglesey)

Deva
(Chester)

CORNOVII

Lindum
(Lincoln)

CORITANI

ORDOVICES

Viriconium
(Wroxeter)

WAY

Venonae
(High Cross)

ICENI

Sabrina (Severn)

WATLING STREET

Lactodorum
(Towcester)

CATUVELLAUNI

TRINOVANTES

Glevum
(Gloucester)

FOSSE

STREET

Camulodunum
(Colchester)

SILURES

Isca Silurum
(Caerleon)

AKEMAN STREET

Verulamium
(St Albans)

Corinium
(Cirencester)

Tamesis (Thames)

Londinium (London)

Rutupiae
(Richborough)

ATREBATES

Aquae Sulis
(Bath)

BELGAE

Venta Belgarum
(Winchester)

STANE STREET

Durovernum
(Canterbury)

CANTIACI

Dubris
(Dover)

DUROTRIGES

DUMNONII

Tamarus (Tamar)

Isca Dumnoniorum
(Exeter)

Durnovaria
(Dorchester)

Vectis
(I. of Wight)

Noviomagus Regensium
or Regnum (Chichester)

Portus Adurni (Porchester)

Fretum Britannicum

0   20   40   60   80   100 miles

0   40   80   120   160 km

N